Yearbook of European Football 1994–95

BRUCE SMITH

Copyright © Bruce Smith 1994

First published in 1994
by HEADLINE BOOK PUBLISHING

10 9 8 7 6 5 4 3 2 1

All rights reserved. No part of this publication may be reproduced, stored in a retrieval system, or transmitted, in any form or by any means without the prior written permission of the publisher, nor be otherwise circulated in any form of binding or cover other than that in which it is published and without a similar condition being imposed on the subsequent purchaser.

A CIP catalogue record for this book is available from the British Library

ISBN 0-7472-7835-0

Designed and produced by Book Production Consultants Plc,
25–27 High Street, Chesterton, Cambridge CB4 1ND

Printed and bound in Great Britain by
Butler & Tanner Ltd., Frome

HEADLINE BOOK PUBLISHING
A division of Hodder Headline PLC
338 Euston Road
London NW1 3BH

Photos: Empics, Neil Jensen, Hill Agencies, Photo World, Bruce Smith.

Contents

Editorial	5
Your Map to Europe	7
European Diary	10
European Football Championship 1996	25
European & World Footballer of the Year	29
Team of the Year 1993–94	33
One to Watch	36
Record Breaker	40
European Cups: Format and Rankings	41
UEFA Champions' League Draw 1994–95	44
Cup-Winners' Cup Draw 1994–95	45
UEFA Cup Draw 1994–95	46

THE 1994 WORLD CUP

Qualifying Group 1	48
Qualifying Group 2	52
Qualifying Group 3	58
Qualifying Group 4	62
World Cup colour plates section	
Qualifying Group 5	65
Qualifying Group 6	68
Qualifiers and Scorers	71
World Cup Finals: Group Matches	73
Group A	73
Group B	77
Group C	80
Group D	84
Group E	87
Group F	91
Second Round	95
Quarter-Finals	101
Semi-Finals	105
Play-off	108
World Cup Final	109

EUROPEAN CUPS 1993–94

General Introduction	114
Champions' Cup Preliminary Round	115
Champions' Cup First Round	117
Champions' Cup Second Round	123
UEFA Champions' League	127
Champions' Cup Semi-Finals	141
Champions' Cup Final	144
Cup-Winners' Cup Preliminary Round	147
Cup-Winners' Cup First Round	150
Cup-Winners' Cup Second Round	154
Cup-Winners' Cup Quarter-Finals	157
Cup-Winners' Cup Semi-Finals	160
Cup-Winners' Cup Final	163
UEFA Cup First Round	167
UEFA Cup Second Round	173
UEFA Cup Third Round	177
UEFA Cup Quarter-Finals	181
UEFA Cup Semi-Finals	184
UEFA Cup Final	186
World Club Championship 1993	189
European Super Cup	191

AROUND THE LEAGUES

Albania	194
Austria	196
Belgium	199
Bulgaria	203
Croatia	206
Cyprus	208
Czech Republic	210
Denmark	212
England	216
Estonia	224
Faeroe Islands	226
Finland	227
France	230
Germany	237
Greece	244
Holland	247
Hungary	254
Iceland	256
Israel	258
Italy	261
Latvia	270
Lithuania	272
Luxembourg	274
Malta	276
Moldova	278
Northern Ireland	280
Norway	283

Poland	286
Portugal	288
Republic of Ireland	292
Romania	295
Russia	299
Scotland	301
Slovakia	307
Slovenia	309
Spain	311
Sweden	317
Switzerland	321
Turkey	325
Ukraine	328
Wales	330
Minor Countries	
Armenia/Azerbaijan	332
Belarus	333
FYR Macedonia/Georgia	334
Liechtenstein	335
San Marino	336
Yugoslavia	337

EUROPEAN INTERNATIONALS AND FINALS 1993–94

Full Internationals 1993–94	340
World Cup Finals 1930–94	351
Colour plates section	
European Championship Finals 1960–92	353
Champions' Cup Finals 1956–94	354
Cup-Winners' Cup Finals 1961–94	357
Fairs Cup/UEFA Cup Finals 1958–94	360
World Club Championship 1960–93	365
European Super Cup Finals 1973–93	369

CLUBS IN EUROPE 1994–95

UEFA Champions' League	375
Cup-Winners' Cup	381
UEFA Cup	390

FIXTURES 1994–95

Belgium	408
Cyprus	408
England	409
Finland	409
France	410
Germany	410
Holland	411
Italy	411
Northern Ireland	412
Portugal	412
Republic of Ireland	413
Scotland	413
Spain	414
Diary of Events 1994–95	415

Editorial

It was a fabulous World Cup. Having managed to watch every single game of the tournament I was left with a nice after-taste, and the event was a much needed pick-me-up after the unsavoury events of Italia '90. However, while matches such as Switzerland v Romania, Brazil v Holland, Germany v South Korea and Bulgaria v Germany will linger long in the memory, it is more likely that the events surrounding the last stage of games will linger even longer.

The semi-finals and final were a disappointing anti-climax – but then the realists always knew they would be, for two reasons. Firstly, there was simply too much at stake for all concerned and secondly, for the four semi-finalists it was a couple of matches too many, in unbearable heat, and in an intolerably short period of time at the end of a long, hard season. But what do you do to change this?

In the first instance there isn't anything you can do – cup semis and finals the world over are always tense affairs. More forgiving venues might have helped. The Giants Stadium would have been a more fitting stage for football's premier final, rather than the American choice of the Rosebowl. Equally the semis might have been better played in the East in Foxboro and Soldier Field – thus saving two of the semi-finalists another tiring six-hour flight. Playing games in mid-day heat we always knew was going to be energy sapping so there's no 'wise after the event' cleverness here. Catering for European television needs was one reason of many given – but frankly I would much rather have gone to bed early and got up mid morning to watch matches rather than find myself dozing off at 11.30pm kick-offs. And 11.30pm BST was an hour earlier than the rest of Europe.

Bruce Smith.

In the second instance there is plenty that can be done just by reducing the number of games played. This doesn't necessarily mean reducing the number of teams in the event – just the number of games. If only the Group winners qualified for the next round we could have virtually done away with the second round in USA94. Or perhaps we should take a leaf out of the San Marino book and start the knock-out phase immediately, but with a team eliminated only when they have lost two games, maybe modifying that rule slightly so that a draw counts as a defeat! That would promote attacking football. Certainly a reorganisation is essential for the next event in France in 1998, when the finalists will increase from 24 to 32. Perhaps also if qualification for future World Cups took into account more fully a country's performance in recent World Cups, all matches would retain a degree of significance. By reducing the number of matches, players also have more time to recover between games and get over injuries and knocks.

Penalty shoot-outs also dominated the headlines. Why oh why does anyone want to get rid of these? They are wonderful! They are hugely entertaining and create immediate interest even among those who may not be glued to the box watching the whole game. I for one don't subscribe to the view that they should be dispensed with. Penalties are part and parcel of the game and if two teams cannot separate themselves after 120 minutes of play then why should we make life any easier for them? To say that it puts unfair pressure on the player whose miss costs his team dear is trite. For the sort of money even average players can command nowadays I for one would be more than happy to live with that particular 'pressure'.

One way to reduce the amount of time played in these competitions is to dispense with extra time altogether. If it is to continue I am totally against the introduction of sudden death during the additional period. Can anyone honestly believe that the prospect of the first goal being decisive would make a team attack during extra time? Think again – we are more likely to see more defence and more penalty shoot-outs. There are those who think that games should be played on until someone scores – I can't imagine the local police, TV and all the major services that are part of the infrastructure of the game putting up with that particular gem even if the licensing authorities agreed to it.

The game is all about goals so let's ensure plenty of them by dispensing with the men employed to stop them – the goalkeepers. Use an extra outfield player if so desired but encourage shots on goal. We may end up with a final score of

10-8 after extra time but isn't that more desirable? It would also limit the number of penalty shoot-outs quite drastically.

The World Cup was also about referees. There were more yellow cards issued than at Italia 90 but we also had more goals. It was also the World Cup in which players were to be sent off if they tackled from behind. What a red herring that proved to be. Having to go off the pitch for treatment was an unqualified success – nearly. This must be persisted with and perhaps altered slightly so that a player who has gone off for treatment must remain off for a minimum of two minutes. This could be controlled by the fourth official and would go some way to ensuring that players get up even quicker, knowing that they could not instantly return once they had left.

The so-called change in the interpretation of the offside law produced another point of contention. But really the law has been misinterpreted for so long by referees anyway. The law states that a player is offside if he is trying to gain advantage. How can a player be trying to gain an advantage if the opposing back four rush out? Surely it is the defending team who are seeking to gain the advantage here. Or am I being naive?

The three European club competitions offered an interesting contrast in styles and staging. Full marks to the Danish authorities for the way in which they handled the Cup-Winners' Cup final in Copenhagen. Full marks to both the Arsenal and Parma supporters who mingled together for three or four days without incident in what was the first meeting in competition between an English and an Italian club since the Heysel Stadium disaster. I wonder how much of this also was down to the low profile taken by the police. Probably the first time any supporters noticed them was when they turned up to the excellent Parken Stadium, and then they were greeted with smiles and politeness. All power to UEFA for giving the event to the Danish – the first in what should be a long line.

One country should definitely not be on the agenda for future finals – Greece. The Champions' Cup final was a marvellous affair, albeit rather one-sided. The quality of the stadium in Athens was excellent but the infrastructure around it simply wasn't there. Many supporters didn't even get to the ground, and many who did were faced with intolerable delays in getting back from whence they came. Add the problems created by having a full blown civil war a few hundred miles north and you had a sure recipe for disaster.

All is not lost though – UEFA have admitted the problem and we can expect to see our major events limited to a few countries that have both the stadia and the communications network to handle them. That should be good news for England, Denmark, Germany, Italy and Spain. Perhaps also a final venue should not be announced until the finalists are known, so that a logical choice can be made.

Fair Play to the Fans Now

UEFA have done a splendid job of promoting their Fair Play campaign to teams and for the most part it has been largely successful. Now, however, UEFA must set about a policy of fair play towards the supporters. How can the finals of premier events be staged when the teams participating in them are deprived of their best players because of suspension often caused by an overzealous referee? With the hard-line booking attitude from USA94 likely to prevail Euro-wide this and coming seasons, it is likely to become an even bigger talking point.

Both Franco Baresi (Milan) and Ian Wright (Arsenal) missed finals by picking up silly second cautions. That two of the best players from these sides missed the big night cannot be right. There are equally citeable cases down through history of great players missing great events, thus robbing the viewing public – who have often forked out a small fortune to do so – of the chance to see them.

UEFA should allow players in such positions to produce a fixed appeal which frees them from missing the final, perhaps at the expense of an extra match suspension thereafter. The question arises of red cards, and unless a player is dismissed for violent conduct I cannot see why the same argument is not applied. Was it really acceptable that Costacurta missed Milan's Champions' Cup win as well as the World Cup final?

Come on UEFA, Fair Play!

Acknowledgements

Many words of thanks to all those who have helped in one way or another towards the completion of this edition of the Yearbook. Particular thanks go to Phil Heady and John Kelly who researched a great deal of material for me. The club histories are largely the work of Phil, and the Diary and several of the country reviews were provided by John. Thanks also to David Prole and World Soccer. The following also contributed information and material for inclusion: Graham Turner, Arthur Rotmil, Neil Jensen, Susan Fakes, Marco Zunino, Valery Karpoushkin, Valeriu Rogzenco, J. Gagan, Jorge Perek Arias, Dan Cristea, Darren Beech, Anil Ramsewak, Louis Micallef, Esko Hahtinen, Geir Thorsteinsson, Marios Leflaritis, Lanbros Adamou, Tony Sheehan. Many thanks also to Salvatorre Cuccu at UEFA and all the various Press Officers and national FAs who have supplied information.

Prize for the best national publication goes to Finland for their excellent handbook 'Jalkapallokirja 1994'. Having scoured it from cover to cover I must now confess to being a convert and a supporter of FC Santa Claus from Rovaniemi, who play in the regional north division of Division Two!

Your Map to Europe

Six months of my life have gone into the making of this book. It attempts to provide a record of the football year which was the 1993–94 season. I refrain from saying 'complete record' because there are still a number of gaps to be plugged as the UEFA membership expands to include nations which will take time to find their footballing feet, let alone talk to the European press at large. But given time the gaps will be plugged to provide even greater depth to what is possibly already the most comprehensive written history of a season that provided much joy and entertainment.

The next two pages contain a simple map of Europe, or more correctly a map to show the members of UEFA. If, like me, you were unaware exactly where Moldova was, you'll now know it is sandwiched between Romania and Ukraine. But there are a number of other details you'll need to be aware of and in effect this page is a brief key to what follows, which is expanded upon at the relevant points within the text.

Club Naming Conventions

The increased coverage of football within Europe has meant that we have become more familiar with the local usage of teams' names. Wherever possible the current common-place name of a side is used. This is, of course, a subjective decision on my behalf, but hopefully one that will allow you to locate and follow the progress of a particular team through this book and the European season. No doubt this will throw up areas of contention among readers. I'm open to persuasion for future editions!

European Cups Review

For each round of the three club competitions a brief summary is provided. This includes a summary of the round in terms of games played in the form of P, HW, D, AW, HG, AG, TG where H stands for Home and A stands for Away, HW Home Wins, AG Away Goals. TG stands for Total Goals scored in the round. Thus a summary such as:

P	HW	D	AW	HG	AG	TG
20	10	5	5	35	15	50

shows that out of 20 games played, ten were home wins, five were draws, 5 were away wins, there were 35 home goals scored and 15 away goals scored.

A summary as to how the ties were won – straight aggregate, on away goals and on penalties – is also provided along with details relating to the biggest wins.

The Club Section

This is a complete alphabetical listing of all clubs accepted for entry into all three European competitions. A more detailed explanation can be found at the start of this section.

Country by Country

This section is a guide to all UEFA members and provides association details and final league tables. This is supplemented with 5-year winners' guides to domestic league and cup competitions along with the country's international record for the year and the complete record in the European Championship, World Cup qualifying rounds and World Cup finals. For most nations a results grid is also provided with the few gaps being due to the late nature of the league's climax.

Abbreviations

A standard three letter system is used for abbreviating country names. As a general rule of thumb this follows the traditional Olympic system.

Alb	Albania	Lat	Latvia
Aus	Austria	Lie	Liechtenstein
Bel	Belgium	Lit	Lithuania
Bls	Belarus	Lux	Luxembourg
Bos	Bosnia-Hercegovina	Mac	Macedonia
Bul	Bulgaria	Mal	Malta
Cro	Croatia	Mol	Moldavia
Cyp	Cyprus	NIr	Northern Ireland
Cze	Czech Republic	Nor	Norway
Den	Denmark	Pol	Poland
Eng	England	Por	Portugal
Est	Estonia	Rom	Romania
Fae	Faeroe Islands	Rus	Russia
Fin	Finland	Smr	San Marino
Fra	France	Sco	Scotland
Geo	Georgia	Svk	Slovakia
Ger	Germany	Slo	Slovenia
Gre	Greece	Esp	Spain
Hol	Holland	Swe	Sweden
Hun	Hungary	Swi	Switzerland
Ice	Iceland	Tur	Turkey
Irl	Rep. of Ireland	Ukr	Ukraine
Isr	Israel	Wal	Wales
Ita	Italy		

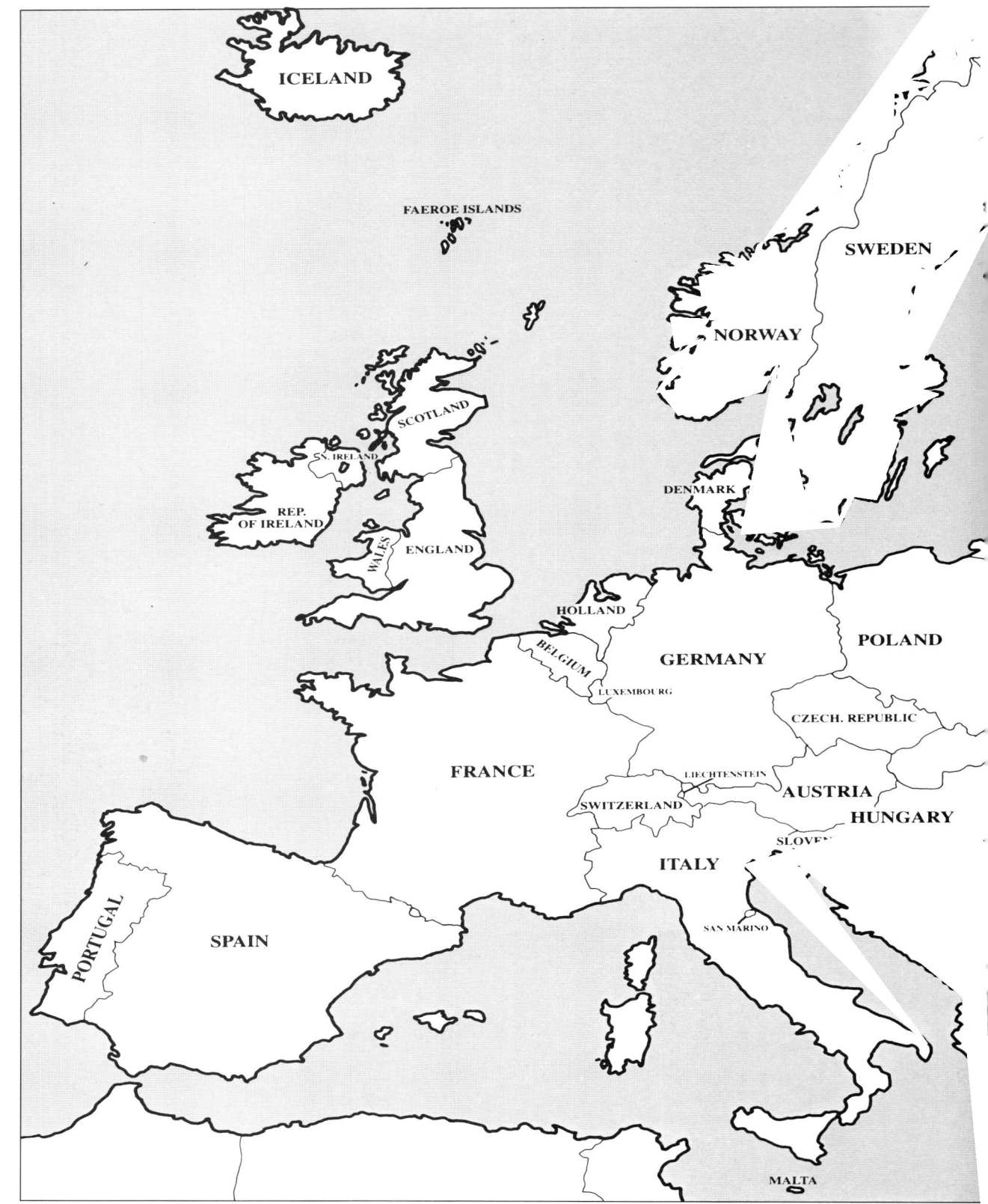

European Diary

August 1993

1. The annual Makita tournament final is held in London at White Hart Lane. Chelsea thrash home side Tottenham 4-0, while Ajax beat Lazio 2-0 for third place. Werder Bremen beat Bayer Leverkusen 7-6 on penalties after a 2-2 draw to take the German Super Cup.
2. UEFA announce that a record number of 149 clubs (compared with 136 for the previous season) have entered the three main European club competitions.
3. The world's most expensive footballer, Milan forward Gianluigi Lentini, suffers a fractured eye socket and severe bruising when his Porsche crashes in the early hours of the morning.
4. Milan have their two-match home ban cut to one game by the Italian authorities. The ban followed crowd trouble during the Sampdoria v Milan league fixture. At the same hearing Sampdoria's own one-match ban is lifted and a £40,000 fine imposed in its place.
5. Roma club Lazio pay £2m for the signature of Juventus' Pierluigi Casiraghi.
6. The Bundesliga season opens in Germany, with pride of place going to Eintracht Frankfurt who win 4-0 at Borussia Monchengladbach. Andy Brehme, Kaiserslautern's veteran defender, has surgery on an Achilles tendon and is sidelined for at least one month. The Polish FA suspend Roman Zup, the Legia Warsaw defender, for a year after he failed a drug test following his side's 2-1 win over Widzew Lodz in May.
7. At Wembley Manchester United win the FA Charity Shield 5-4 on penalties after a 1-1 draw with Arsenal. Colombian striker Adolfo Valencia scores twice on his debut for Bayern Munich as they beat newly promoted Freiburg 3-1 in their opening Bundesliga fixture. Scottish champions Rangers start their league season with a 2-1 win at Hearts despite a massive injury list. Nantes go top in France after a 3-0 win at Toulouse.
8. German champions Werder open their campaign with a 5-1 demolition of VfB Stuttgart. Further east cash-stricken Dynamo Kiev open their Ukraine season with a 2-1 win over Karparty Lvov. Disgraced French champions Marseille are held at home 1-1 by Le Havre on the opening day of the season. Anderlecht win 4-2 at Waregem in front of just 2,000 as the season gets under way in Belgium. In pre-season tournaments Barcelona beat Milan 3-0 in the final of the Ciudad de Oviedo and FC Porto win their own tournament, beating Cruzeiro 2-1 in Oporto.
11. Sweden lose 2-1 at home to Switzerland in a friendly international. Herr scores the winner 17 minutes from time. Ostenstad hits a hat-trick in 13 minutes as Norway thrash the Faeroe Islands 7-0 in Toftir in a friendly international. In Portugal Benfica beat FC Porto 1-0 in the first leg of the Super Cup.
12. Xavier Gravelaine is dropped from the French World Cup squad to face Sweden. The FFF announce that those implicated in the Marseille scandal will attend hearings on 27 and 28 August. Roma's Argentine striker Claudio Caniggia has his one-year ban from Italian soccer for failing a drugs test on cocaine confirmed by FIFA.
13. The Belgian FA are presented with the 1992 FIFA Fair Play prize. Chelsea sign Danish defender Jakob Kjeldbjerg for £400,000 from Silkeborg. Milan forward Gianluigi Lentini leaves hospital 11 days after his car crash and hopes to be back in the first team by October. FIFA release their national league table based on results and various other factors. Germany are ranked number one, with Italy second and – surprisingly – Switzerland third!
14. The English league season gets under way and last season's runners-up, Aston Villa, have an impressive 4-1 win at QPR. Meanwhile double cup winners Arsenal crash 0-3 at home to Coventry. The coach of Italian club Perugia, Ilario Castagner, is attacked by hooligans after a pre-season training session and ordered to rest for a week. In La Coruna Barcelona beat Sao Paulo 1-0 to win the Trofeo Teresa Herrera tournament. The host side beat Lazio for third place. Ajax open their league campaign with a 3-0 win over RKC.

Colombian striker Adolfo Valencia scored twice on his debut for Bayern Munich, 7 August 1993.

15 English champions Manchester United get off to a winning start to their defence of the title with a 2-0 win at Norwich City. A goal by Alen Boksic three minutes from time gives Marseille a 1-0 win over Paris Saint-Germain.
16 After nearly three years in the international wilderness Danish football star Michael Laudrup makes his peace with manager Richard Moller Nielsen and hopes for an international recall. Tenerife loan Argentine midfielder Pizzi to Valencia for one year. Arsenal win the North London derby 1-0 at Tottenham.
17 Milan beat Real Madrid in a friendly in the Stadio Meazza.
18 The first legs of the Champions' Cup and Cup-Winners' Cup preliminary round get under way. In Tbilisi, 60,000 pack the Dynamo stadium to see the home side beat Linfield 2-1 while Croatia Zagreb win 5-0 in Toftir in the Champions' Cup. In the Cup-Winners' Cup Maccabi Haifa win 1-0 in Dudelange. In Spain Rayo Vallecano buy former Mexico and Real Madrid veteran Hugo Sanchez from America of Mexico City. Meanwhile Sevilla borrow Spanish defender Soler from Barcelona for a year and Tenerife complete the signing of Peruvian Percy Olivares.
19 Santander sign Spartak Moscow midfielder Dimitri Popov. A knee injury forces Burgos' Romanian international Gavrila Balint to retire.
20 Cameroon international Cyril Makanaky signs for Maccabi Tel Aviv after a spell in Spain. FIFA World Under-17 Championships get under way in Japan.
21 Milan beat Torino 1-0 with a goal after just four minutes by Simone to lift the Italian Super Cup. The game is played in Washington!
22 In the World European Group 6 Martin Dahlin scores a last-minute equaliser as Sweden salvage a 1-1 draw with France in Stockholm. FC Porto and Benfica play out an exciting 3-3 draw in front of 60,000 on the opening day of the Portuguese season.
23 Manchester United win 2-1 at last season's runners-up, Aston Villa.
24 Second Division Carl Zeiss Jena win 1-0 at Borussia Dortmund in the German Cup. Barcelona captain Jose Ramon Alexanco retires.
25 Michael Laudrup makes his international comeback for Denmark as the European champions beat Lithuania 4-0 in a World Cup Qualifying game. Austria have an easy 3-0 win over Finland in Vienna. In the second round of the German Cup VfB Stuttgart have two players sent off as they crash 2-6 at home to Kaiserslautern after extra time.
26 Peter Reid is sacked as player-manager of Manchester City.
27 On the south coast of France Monaco and Marseille play out a 0-0 draw.
28 In Germany Eintracht Frankfurt go top of the Bundesliga after thrashing Nurnberg 5-1 – Anthony Yeboah scores twice. Portuguese champions FC Porto lose 1-0 away to Maritimo. Scottish champions Rangers also lose, 2-1 at home to Kilmarnock. Paris Saint-Germain beat Caen 2-0 amid fighting between rival hooligans.
29 Milan win 1-0 away at Lecce on the opening day of the season while Ruud Gullit and David Platt score on their league debuts as Sampdoria win 2-1 at Napoli. Ajax stay top in Holland with a one-goal victory over Vitesse. In Portugal a 10-man Estoril hold Benfica 1-1.
30 Stuart Pearce of relegated Nottingham Forest is recalled to the England squad as captain after recovering from an injury that sidelined him for much of the previous season. Cagliari coach Gigi Radice is sacked.
31 Iceland lose 0-1 in Reykjavik to the USA. Balzers make history when they become the first ever side from Liechtenstein to win a round of a European competition, beating Albania's Albpetrol 3-1 on aggregate in the Cup-Winners' Cup. German champions Werder Bremen continue their indifferent start to the season, being thrashed 5-1 at home by newly promoted MSV Duisburg. FIFA warn France that they risk being thrown out of the World Cup unless they make progress in the Marseille affair.

September 1993

1 Real Madrid lose 10-9 on penalties to Internazionale after a 2-2 draw in the Santiago Bernabeu Trophy. Marseille record a 3-1 win over St Etienne. Swiss striker Stephane Chapuisat scores a hat-trick as Borussia Dortmund beat Dynamo Dresden 4-0 in the Bundesliga.
2 Havnar Boltfelag become the first team from the Faeroe Islands to progress to the second round of a European competition when awarded a walk-over because RAF Jelgava fail to appear for a game in the Cup-Winners' Cup.
3 Georgia's Dynamo Tbilisi are expelled from the Champions' Cup for trying to bribe the referee in their tie with Northern Ireland's Linfield.
4 Eintracht Frankfurt win 3-1 at Schalke 04 to stay two points clear at the top of the Bundesliga.
5 Ajax beat PSV Eindhoven 2-0 in Holland's first 'Match of the Season'. Juventus lose 2-1 to Roma as Roberto Baggio and Gianluca Vialli both miss penalties. Romario scores a hat-trick on his debut for Barcelona against Real Sociedad.
6 Marseille are banned from defending their Champions' Cup title by UEFA. Club president Bernard Tapie threatens legal action against the French Federation, League and UEFA. USA midfielder John Harkes moves from Sheffield Wednesday to ambitious Derby County for £800,000.
7 The French Federation begin looking for Marseille's replacements in this season's Champions' Cup. Paris Saint-Germain, Monaco and Bordeaux say they do not want the 'honour'. Hungarian goalkeeper Gabor Zsiboras dies in hospital after collapsing in training six days ago with a brain haemorrhage.
8 A major night of World Cup actions brings wins for England (3-0 v Poland), Northern Ireland (2-0 v Latvia), Denmark (1-0 v Albania), the Republic of Ireland (2-0 v Lithuania), Romania (4-0 v Faeroe Islands), Iceland (1-0 v Luxembourg), Russia (3-1 v Hungary) and France

(2-0 v Finland). UEFA accept the French Federation's nomination of Monaco to replace Marseille in the Champions' Cup, with Auxerre stepping up to take Monaco's place in the UEFA Cup.

9 Marseille are granted an injunction by a Bern court which orders UEFA to reinstate Marseille in the Champions' Cup. FIFA react by ordering a crisis summit with UEFA and the FFF. Albert Roosens, the so-called 'Father of Belgian football' dies aged 77. Roosens was secretary of the Belgian FA from 1951 to 1988.

10 Bernard Tapie withdraws his legal action apparently having been warned by the FFF that France risked losing the right to host the World Cup in 1998.

11 Dispirited Marseille are held to a 0-0 draw at bottom club Toulouse. Promoted Freiburg knock Bundesliga leaders Eintracht Frankfurt out of the Cup in the third round, 5-2 after extra-time. Koln lose 5-4 on penalties to Bayern Munich's amateur team after a 0-0 draw.

12 Torino and Milan are the joint leaders in Italy after victories over Udinese and Atalanta respectively. In Spain, Real Madrid lose 3-1 at home to Valladolid, a source of embarrassment as it was their first League game at the refurbished Bernabeu.

13 Scotland coach Andy Roxburgh resigns, but agrees to stay on as a technical director.

14 Diego Maradona's proposed transfer to Argentina's Newell's Old Boys is blocked by his club Sevilla, who cite his failure to fulfil his contract last season as the nub of the problem.

15 In the Champions' Cup first round first-leg ties there are shock defeats for Feyenoord (1-0 to IA Akranes of Iceland) and Barcelona (3-1 to Dynamo Kiev). Marseille begin their debt-clearing sell-out by transferring midfielder Jean-Marc Ferreri to Martigues.

16 FC Porto, still without a League win, threaten coach Tomislav Ivic with the sack if the team do not win their next game against Sporting Braga.

17 Hadjuk Split beat Ajax 1-0 in the Cup-Winners' Cup in a match switched to Ljubljana because of the continuing violence in Croatia. Liverpool trade Mike Marsh and David Burrows to West Ham in exchange for defender Julian Dicks.

18 Everton win the Mersey derby, beating Liverpool 2-0. Marseille beat old rivals Bordeaux 3-1. Eintracht Frankfurt scrape a 2-2 draw with Bayer Leverkusen to stay on top of the Bundesliga.

19 Faustino Asprilla scores a hat-trick in Parma's 3-0 win over Torino. Benfica record their first League win of the season, beating Farense 4-1. Israel are granted provisional membership of UEFA, Azerbaijan and Moldova are given associate membership. Nurnberg goalkeeper Andy Kopke is voted German Footballer of the Year.

20 Real Madrid's under-fire coach Benito Floro is given the dreaded vote of confidence by the club's board of directors. Slovakia's DAC Dunajska Streda sell goalkeeper Miroslav Mentel to Japan's Urawa Red Diamonds.

21 Tomislav Ivic breathes again as FC Porto beat Sporting Braga 2-0, their first win of the season. The Spanish Federation rules against Sevilla and permits Diego Maradona's move to Newell's Old Boys to proceed.

22 More bad news for Marseille as they are stripped of their French League title by the FFF. General secretary Jean-Pierre Bernes and midfielder Jean-Jacques Eydelie are banned for life. In World Cup action Norway beat Poland, Holland thrash San Marino 7-0, Spain thump Albania 5-1 and Italy beat Estonia 3-0.

23 Paris Saint-Germain beat Auxerre 4-0, George Weah scoring twice.

24 More trouble for Marseille as their home game with Metz is abandoned three minutes from time when fans invade the pitch. Marseille were 3-0 down and had Basile Boli and Fabien Barthez dismissed. Dinamo Bucharest have a 1-1 draw with Progresul turned into a 3-0 defeat by the FA as punishment for unruly behaviour among the coaching staff.

25 Bayern Munich and Borussia Dortmund draw 0-0 in Germany. FC Porto are jeered off the pitch after a drab 0-0 home draw with Pacos Ferreira.

26 Feyenoord maintain their 100 per cent record in Holland with a 1-0 win over Go Ahead Eagles. Another disaster for Real Madrid as they lose 1-0 at home to Real Oviedo.

27 FIFA ban Marseille from taking part in the Toyota Cup World Club Championship and the European Super Cup, their places being taken by Milan. Andrzej Strejlau resigns as Poland manager. Assistants Leslaw Cmikiewicz and Joszef Mlynarczyk are appointed caretakers for the rest of the season.

28 Udinese dismiss former Italy national coach Azeglio Vicini after three successive defeats. Adriano Fedele takes over. Maccabi Haifa become the first Israeli club to reach the second round of a European competition when they beat Moscow Torpedo 3-2 on aggregate.

29 In the first round of the Champions' Cup, Barcelona hit back to beat Dynamo Kiev but Rangers lose to a last-minute goal by Levski Sofia. Borussia Monchengladbach are ordered to replay a Cup tie against Karlsruhe (because visiting goalkeeper Oliver Kahn was concussed by a chestnut thrown from the crowd) and fined £4,000.

30 Marseille's Stade Velodrome is closed for one game as punishment for the crowd trouble at the home match with Metz.

October 1993

1 Eintracht Frankfurt's Uwe Bein announces his retirement from international football.

2 Alan Shearer returns from a serious knee injury with two goals in Blackburn's 3-1 win over Swindon. The Madrid derby ends goalless, but Real have Rafael Martin Vazquez sent off.

3 Ruud Gullit scores twice in Sampdoria's 4-1 win at Atalanta which takes them to within a point of leaders Milan.

4 Tomas Brolin and Johnny Ekstrom refuse selection for Sweden's vital World Cup qualifier with Finland.
5 Germany lose 2-0 to an Imports XI in a charity match in Augsburg. Stephane Chapuisat scores both the goals.
6 Rapid Bucharest sack coach Marcel Puscas following their UEFA Cup exit to Internazionale.
7 Liam Brady quits as manager of Celtic, and assistant Joe Jordan takes over as caretaker.
8 Joe Jordan resigns as caretaker manager of Celtic after just one day. 300 angry Lazio fans invade the club's training ground following the 2-0 defeat by third division Avellino in an Italian Cup tie.
9 Eintracht Frankfurt set a best-ever start to the season record with 20 points from 11 games following their 2-1 win over Leipzig. In Bulgaria Yantra are expelled from the top division and fined £5,000 for trying to fix a game against Beroe Stara Zagora.
10 With a busy week of World Cup qualifiers ahead, most of Europe's major leagues take the weekend off to prepare.
11 Johan Cruyff brands Dutch coach Dick Advocaat's teams as 'a joke'. 'When I watch Holland play my toes curl up,' he added.
12 Greece beat Luxembourg 3-1 in a World Cup qualifier. Schalke 04 sack coach Helmut Schulte and replace him with Jorg Berger.
13 In the World Cup qualifiers Norway go through with a 3-1 win over Poland, Sweden join them thanks to France's shock 3-2 home defeat by Israel and Holland beat England 2-0 amid controversy in Rotterdam. Marseille sell Alen Boksic to Lazio for £8m to ease the club's financial crisis.
14 Sampdoria president Paolo Mantovani dies aged 63 following heart trouble. Spartak Moscow retain their Russian title with four matches to go after a 1-1 draw with Okean Nakhodka.
15 Belgium's Lierse buy Norway striker Jahn Ivar Jakobsen from Germany's MSV Duisburg. Eintracht Frankfurt suffer their first defeat of the season, 1-0 away to Duisburg.
16 Paris Saint-Germain beat Metz 1-0 to go clear at the top as Marseille's match at Montpellier is postponed because of a waterlogged pitch. Sporting Lisbon drop their first points of the season in a 0-0 draw at Gil Vicente. Barcelona's unbeaten record goes as they lose 1-0 to Deportivo La Coruna.
17 Gunter Eichberg quits as president of bottom club Schalke 04. Parma's Faustino Asprilla is sent off in a 0-0 draw with Cremonese. Milan goalkeeper Sebastiano Rossi concedes his first League goal of the season when Foggia's Igor Kolyvanov beats him in a 1-1 draw.
18 RSC Anderlecht receive a boost when international striker Marc Degryse reports that he will be fit for the Champions' League – if they qualify.
19 Norwich City score an impressive 2-1 victory in Munich over Bayern in the UEFA Cup second round.
20 Manchester United scrape a 3-3 home draw with Turkey's Galatasaray in the second round of the Champions' Cup.
21 Atletico Madrid dismiss coach Jair Pereira after just seven games in charge. Ramon Heredia returns as caretaker.
22 Hungarian referee Sandor Puhl is named to take charge of the World Cup play-off between Argentina and Australia. Denmark's Peter Mikkelsen will handle the return leg.
23 Manchester United go nine points clear after a 1-0 win at Everton. Paris Saint-Germain stay top in France by beating Cannes 1-0.
24 Ally McCoist returns from injury with a late winner for Rangers in the League Cup Final against Hibernian.
25 Standard Liege sack coach Arie Haan following a 10-0 aggregate defeat by Arsenal in the Cup-Winners' Cup. Rapid Bucharest appoint Viorel Hizo as new coach.
26 Celtic appoint former player Lou Macari as coach in succession to Liam Brady.
27 In the World Cup qualifiers, Turkey beat Poland 2-1, RCS beat Cyprus 3-0, Hungary beat Luxembourg 1-0 and Israel draw 1-1 with Austria.
28 FIFA rule that the World Cup qualifier between Northern Ireland and the Republic of Ireland should go ahead in Belfast despite the threat of sectarian violence in the province.
29 Universitatea Craiova's veteran goalkeeper Silviu Lung retires after 25 years in the game.
30 Adolfo Valencia scores twice as Bayern Munich thrash Kaiserslautern 4-0. Benfica go top in Portugal after beating Salgueiros 4-1 as Sporting lose 2-1 at Boavista. Atletico Madrid recover from 3-0 down to beat Barcelona 4-3 despite having midfielder Pirri sent off.
31 Ruud Gullit takes revenge on Milan by scoring the winner for Sampdoria in a 3-2 victory over his old club. Roberto Baggio of Juventus and Ruben Sosa of Inter both score hat-tricks, against Genoa and Parma respectively.

November 1993

1 Oldham buy Norway international defender Tore Pedersen from Brann Bergen for £500,000. The English FA announce the stadia to be used for the 1996 European Championship finals: Wembley, Villa Park (Aston Villa), Old Trafford (Manchester United), Hillsborough (Sheffield Wednesday), Elland Road (Leeds United), St James' Park (Newcastle United), the City Ground (Nottingham Forest) and Anfield (Liverpool).
2 Cercle Bruges sack coach Henk Hoewaart and replace him with Trabzonspor's Belgian manager Georges Leekens. Nottingham Forest buy Norway international Lars Bohinen for £450,000 from Lillestrom.
3 Manchester United are knocked out of the Champions' Cup on away goals by Turkey's Galatasaray after a 3-3 aggregate draw. Tottenham are fined a record £25,000 by the FA for poaching manager Ossie Ardiles from West Bromwich Albion. Uli Stielike quits as coach of Neuchatel Xamax and Don Givens replaces him.

4 Blackburn buy England goalkeeper Tim Flowers from Southampton for £2.4m. Borussia Monchengladbach sell Danish midfielder Johnny Molby to Mechelen of Belgium. Half of Albania's Under-21 side 'stay' in Italy after a friendly against a regional league side.

5 Cannes sell former East German striker Rainer Ernst to FC Zurich. Fiorentina president Mario Cecchi Gori dies, aged 72. The UEFA Champions' League draw is made.

6 France's match of the day produces a 1-1 draw between Monaco and leaders Paris Saint-Germain. Bayern Munich lose 2-0 to Nurnberg while Eintracht beat Borussia Dortmund 2-0. In Sweden, Martin Dahlin is voted Footballer of the Year.

7 Eric Cantona scores twice as United beat City 3-2 in the Manchester derby. Milan win the San Siro derby, beating Inter 2-1. Parma beat Juventus 2-0 to stay joint top of Serie A.

8 Marseille attempt to borrow Polish striker Wojciech Kowalczyk from Legia Warsaw, having failed to get Inter's Darko Pancev.

9 Nurnburg sack coach Willi Entemann despite the recent 2-0 win over Bayern, who lose 2-1 to Dynamo Dresden in a DFB Cup tie.

10 Norway lose 2-1 to Turkey in a World Cup qualifier while Israel go down 3-1 at home to Finland. Marseille, desperate for cash, sell Marcel Desailly to Milan and Paulo Futre to Reggiana. Lecce sack coach Nedo Sonetti; Parma buy Argentinian international Nestor Sensini from Udinese, who in turn buy Polish defender Dariusz Adamczuk from Dundee. Atletico Madrid appoint Emilio Cruz as team boss in succession to Ramon Heredia.

11 Valencia lose 3-0 at home to Real Madrid. Eric Cantona is banned for four European club matches for being sent off at the end of Manchester United's game with Galatasaray in Turkey.

12 Champions Werder Bremen suffer a surprise 1-0 defeat at home to Dresden.

13 Aston Villa goalkeeper Mark Bosnich is ruled out of Australia's World Cup play-off with Argentina by a hip injury.

14 Most domestic European leagues are inactive because of the up-coming World Cup qualifiers. Peter Schmeichel rejects a £6,000-a-week contract from Manchester United because he wants more money.

15 Valencia dismiss Dutch coach Guus Hiddink and replace him with Francisco Real as caretaker.

16 Moroccan veteran Aziz Bouderbala joins Switzerland's St Gallen until the end of the season.

17 In the World Cup qualifiers, Italy, Switzerland, Holland, Spain, the Republic of Ireland, Romania, Belgium, Bulgaria and Argentina all secure their places in the finals. Lothar Matthaus earns a record 104th cap as Germany beat Brazil 2-1 in Koln in a friendly.

18 Marseille sign Brazilian striker Anderson 'Sonny' Da Silva from Servette of Geneva.

19 Bundesliga leaders Eintracht surprisingly lose 3-0 at home to Koln. Turkey's Genclerbirligi sign Donald Khuse from South Africa's Kaizer Chiefs.

20 Barcelona crash 1-0 at home to newly-promoted Lleida. Marseille lose 3-0 to Auxerre.

21 Milan beat Napoli 2-1 with a last-minute goal to keep pace with Parma. Real Madrid beat Celta Vigo 2-1 to join a six-way tie for first place in Spain.

22 Dutch coach Leo Beenhakker is appointed coach of Saudi Arabia. Turkey's Bursaspor sack Danish coach Sepp Piontek.

23 Graham Taylor resigns as England manager in the wake of his team's failure to qualify for the World Cup finals.

24 The UEFA Champions' League opens with two 0-0 draws and two victories – for Monaco, 4-1 against Spartak Moscow, and FC Porto, 3-2 against Werder Bremen.

25 Gerald Houllier resigns as manager of France in the wake of their World Cup failure against Bulgaria.

26 Sunderland dismiss former England defender Terry Butcher as manager.

27 Paris Saint-Germain beat St Etienne 1-0 to extend their lead to four points following Bordeaux's 1-0 defeat at Lens.

28 Sonny Da Silva scores on his debut for Marseille as they beat Martigues 3-0 away. In Italy, Milan and Parma battle out a dull 0-0 draw.

29 Controversial Jean Fournet-Fayard resigns as president of the French Federation. Senior vice-president Jacques Georges steps up as interim president.

30 Barilla, the food and pasta group, end their 13-year sponsorship of AS Roma. Sporting Lisbon beat Estoril 2-0 to regain joint first place with Benfica in Portugal.

December 1993

1 Milan beat FC Porto in an advanced Champions' League match. Sampdoria beat AS Roma 2-1 in a third round Italian Cup tie despite Ruud Gullit missing a penalty. Bernd Schuster is sent off as Bayer Leverkusen crash out of the DFB Cup to Dynamo Dresden.

2 UEFA unveil plans for an expanded Champions' League and a 100-club UEFA Cup.

3 Roland Nilsson announces that he will quit Sheffield Wednesday to return to Sweden at the end of the season. Steaua Bucharest sack striker Ion Vladoiu after he breaks Sportul defender Nicolae Vochin's nose.

4 Eintracht Frankfurt lose 1-0 to Werder Bremen, allowing Bayer Leverkusen to regain the lead. Barcelona are held 2-2 at home by struggling Logrones.

5 Hugo Sanchez becomes the all-time second highest scorer in Spain after his goal against Zaragoza for Rayo Vallecano lifts his total to 228 – one more than Alfredo Di Stefano (Real Madrid), but still 23 short of Telmo Zarra (Athletic Bilbao).

6 A row brews in Russia when national coach Pavel Sadyrin accuses former boss Anatoli Byshovets of masterminding a letter signed by 14 rebel national team players demanding Sadyrin's resignation.

7 The French Parliament votes to lift Bernard Tapie's immunity from prosecution.

8 Werder Bremen recover from 3-0 down to beat Anderlecht 5-3 in an amazing Champions' League tie. UEFA Cup-holders Juventus lose 2-1 to Tenerife, but go through to the quarter-finals 4-2 on aggregate.

9 Anderlecht pay Beveren £700,000 for Nigerian defender Chidi Nwanu, needed as cover for long-term injury victim Michel De Wolf. Stuttgart coach Christoph Daum announces that he will succeed Gordon Milne at Turkey's Besiktas.

10 Bobby Robson is fired as coach of Sporting Lisbon after they are knocked out of the UEFA Cup by Austria Salzburg. National team boss Carlos Queiros takes over. Ajax release Danish defender John Hansen to OB Odense after three injury-wrecked years in Amsterdam.

11 Paris Saint-Germain go six points clear in France after a 2-0 win over Strasbourg. Bayer Leverkusen are held 1-1 by Wattenscheid in the last round of matches before Germany's winter break, but still retain the leadership of the Bundesliga.

12 Milan lose 3-2 to Sao Paolo in the World Club Cup in Tokyo. Parma take advantage of Milan's absence by winning 4-0 at Cagliari to go clear at the top on goal difference.

13 Sporting Lisbon beat Beira-Mar 1-0 in Carlos Queiros' first match in charge. Besiktas officially welcome Christoph Daum as new coach. Dynamo Kiev sack coach Mikhail Fomenko and replace him with Iosif Sabo.

14 Bayer Leverkusen's Bernd Schuster is banned for six weeks after being sent off in a Cup game with Dynamo Dresden. Atletico Madrid take Ivory Coast skipper Serge-Alain Maguy on trial.

15 Argentina beat Germany 2-1 in Miami in a World Cup draw special. Sporting Lisbon's Russian striker Sergei Cherbakov breaks his back in a car crash and is told he will never play again. Valencia appoint Hector Nunez as coach in succession to Guus Hiddink.

16 Metz re-sign midfielder Dragoljub Brnovic. The 30-year-old former Yugoslav international had been without a club since Metz released him in 1992.

17 Sweden are invited to take part in the Joe Robbie Cup against the US, Colombia and Bolivia in Miami in February.

18 Germany beat the USA 3-0 in a World Cup draw curtain-raiser. Roberto Baggio is named FIFA's World Footballer of the Year. The Dutch Federation announce that negotiations with Johan Cruyff have broken down and that Dick Advocaat will take charge of their World Cup bid.

19 The World Cup draw takes place in Las Vegas without Pele.

20 Italian Federation chief Antonio Matarrese is asked, by the Argentinian FA, to appeal to FIFA for a reduction in Claudio Caniggia's 13-month ban for drugs violations.

Serge Maguy (Atletico Madrid) in action for the Ivory Coast.

22 Mexico hold Germany to a goalless draw in Mexico City. Bolivia lose 3-1 to a Basque XI in San Sebastian.

23 Leeds United and Manchester City conclude a £1.25m swap deal in which David White moves to Elland Road with David Rocastle making the trip in the opposite direction.

25 Bruce Smith has a rare day off.

26 Roberto Baggio wins *France Football*'s 'European Footballer of the Year' award.

27 Franz Beckenbauer takes over from Erich Ribbeck as Bayern Munich coach.

28 Feyenoord's technical director Wim Jansen quits to help fellow Dutchman Leo Beenhakker prepare the Saudi Arabian team for the World Cup finals.

29 Galatasaray sign Swedish World Cup defender Roger Ljung from Admira Wacker. Barcelona's Romario and Ronald Koeman lead a string of top internationals who agree to play in a benefit match for Sporting Lisbon's crippled Sergei Cherbakov.

30 Four players are sent off as FC Porto draw 1-1 with local rivals Boavista.

31 Jean-Pierre Papin confirms that he will leave Milan at the end of his contract, hinting that he would welcome a return to Marseille. Ukraine's bottom club, Metallug Zaporizhja, are implicated in a match-fixing scandal.

January 1994

1. Rayo Vallecano draw 0-0 with Spanish league leaders Deportivo La Coruna in the only major competitive match outside the UK.
2. Milan have Jean-Pierre Papin sent off, but still win 1-0 at Reggiana. Barcelona lose 2-0 to Gijon.
3. Nurnberg appoint Rainer Zobel as coach in succession to Dieter Renner.
4. Monaco coach Arsene Wenger says he favours reducing teams to 10 men each to put the excitement back into football.
5. FC Porto move into second place – behind Benfica – with a 4-1 home win over Uniao Madeira.
6. Karlsruhe goalkeeper Oliver Kahn agrees to join Bayern Munich at the season's end for £1.8m – a German record for a keeper.
7. More than 3,000 Bayern Munich fans turn out to see Franz Beckenbauer lead his first training session as coach.
8. Romario scores a hat-trick as Barcelona thrash Real Madrid 5-0. Real's Alfonso is carried off with torn knee ligaments – ruling him out of the rest of the season.
9. Sampdoria's Roberto Mancini scores twice to complete a century of Italian League goals as Sampdoria beat Napoli 4-1. AEK Athens beat Apollon 3-1 to maintain their six-point lead in Greece.
10. Dimitar Penev calls up 12 foreign-based players for Bulgaria's pre-World Cup warm-up matches, among them Ipswich's Bontcho Guentchev.
11. Southampton manager Ian Branfoot quits.
12. Milan beat Parma 1-0 in the first leg of the European Super Cup.
13. Real Madrid beat neighbours Atletico 3-2 away to reach the quarter-finals of the Spanish Cup.
14. Paris Saint-Germain and Marseille draw 1-1 at the Parc des Princes. UEFA announce that they are admitting FYR Macedonia into the qualifying rounds of the 1996 European Championship.
15. Norway lose 2-1 to the USA in Tempe, Arizona.
16. Milan are held 0-0 by Genoa but stay three points clear in Serie A. Deportivo La Coruna continue at the top in Spain after winning 3-1 in Valencia.
17. Hamburg's Valdas Ivanauskas is voted Footballer of the Year for the third successive season in Lithuania. Emilio Cruz quits as coach to Atletico Madrid two months and one week after succeeding Jair Pereira. Chief scout Jose Luis Romero takes over as caretaker.
18. Bayern coach Franz Beckenbauer says that Monaco's Arsene Wenger has been given until 31 March to accept or decline an offer to take over in Munich next season. Milan confirm that Marco Van Basten will start his latest training comeback with Ajax in his native Holland.
19. Tunisia draw 2-2 with Holland, Spain are held 2-2 by Portugal. More trouble for Marseille as the French League asks the Swiss Federation for further information concerning the terms under which Servette loaned Brazilian striker Anderson da Silva to Marseille.

Matt Busby, manager of Manchester United, seen with the European Champions' Cup in 1968, passed away in 1994.

20. Former Manchester United manager Sir Matt Busby dies aged 84. Oleg Protasov, former Soviet Union striker, quits Olympiakos to sign for J League club Gamba Osaka.
21. Luka Peruzovic quits as coach of Belgium's bottom club RC Genk after only 10 games. Assistant Pierre Denier and former player Norbert Beuls take over.
22. The draw for the 1996 European Championship qualifiers is made in Manchester. The USA and Switzerland draw 1-1 in Fullerton, California. Marseille need penalties to beat third division Brive in the French Cup.
23. Milan beat Piacenza 2-0 to open up a four-point lead in Italy. Real Madrid coach Benito Floro blames the Bernabeu pitch after a 0-0 draw at home to Osasuna. UEFA's executive committee decides to award three points for a victory in the qualifying stages of the 1996 European Championship.
24. Nurnberg president Gerhard Voack resigns after death threats which followed the departure of coach Willi Entenmann. Atalanta goalkeeper Fabrizio Ferron is released from hospital after undergoing heart massage on the pitch the previous day following a collision with Reggiana striker Michele Padovano.

25 Torino reach the Italian Cup semi-finals. Tomislav Ivic quits as coach to FC Porto to take up an appointment to the FIFA technical department.
26 Liverpool sell Israeli striker Ronny Rosenthal to Tottenham for £250,000. Parma thrash Foggia 6-1 to reach the semi-finals of the Italian Cup 9-1 on aggregate. Bobby Robson, sacked just before Christmas by Sporting Lisbon, is appointed new coach of champions FC Porto in succession to Tomislav Ivic.
27 Darko Pancev joins VfB Leipzig on loan from Internazionale. Sporting buy Brazilian defender Lula (Luis Bras) from World Club champions Sao Paolo.
28 Terry Venables is appointed England manager, John Toshack of Real Sociedad is appointed part-time Wales manager (with ex-boss Mike Smith as man-on-the-spot) and Jimmy Nicholl is appointed caretaker of Northern Ireland. Graeme Souness quits as manager of Liverpool, three days after the shock home defeat by Bristol City in the FA Cup third round replay.
29 The USA draw 1-1 with Russia in Seattle. Paris Saint-Germain maintain their four-point lead in the French League by winning 2-0 at Caen.
30 Manchester United maintain their progress towards a unique English treble by winning 2-0 at Norwich in the FA Cup. Benfica crash 2-1 to Belenenses in the Portuguese Cup while Porto win 2-0 at Salgueiros.
31 Roy Evans, former reserve team coach, is appointed manager of Liverpool. Benfica's Russian defender Vasili Kulkov escapes with minor injuries from an early-morning car crash in Lisbon but the driver of the car is seriously injured. Italian dairy products group Parmalat sign up as sponsors of Moscow Dynamo, the company's sixth club contract after Parma, Videoton, Boca Juniors, Penarol and Palmeiras.

John Toshack didn't last long as the Welsh national team manager – just one match and 47 days.

February 1994

1 Real Madrid have three players sent off and crash 3-0 at home in their Cup quarter-final return against Tenerife. Madrid lose 5-1 on aggregate.
2 Parma win 2-0 after extra time in the Stadio Meazza to defeat Milan 2-1 on aggregate in the European Super Cup. The Dunhill Cup opens in Kuala Lumpur with a 3-3 draw between Denmark and Norway. Russia beat Mexico 4-1 in Oakland.
3 Marseille defender Jocelyn Angloma is suspended for four games after his double sending-off in successive weeks. Swiss international left-back Regis Rothenbuhler, of Servette, says he is quitting soccer at 23 because he has become a 'football zombie'.
4 Norway beat Japan 3-2 in the Dunhill Cup.
5 Real Madrid defeat Spanish league-leaders Deportivo La Coruna 2-0. Lazio loan Germany forward Thomas Doll to Eintracht Frankfurt.
6 Internazionale sack coach Osvaldo Bagnoli after losing 2-1 at home to Lazio. Benfica take a major step towards regaining the Portuguese league title when they beat FC Porto 2-0. Porto finish with 10 men after Fernando Couto is sent off for elbowing Mozer in the face. In Spain, Barcelona complete a gloomy week of their own by losing 3-2 at home to Bilbao.
7 FIFA general secretary and refereeing adviser Paolo Casarin tells a Lisbon symposium that World Cup officials will be instructed to crack down on the illegal tackle from behind and give advantage over offside doubt to attackers rather than defenders.
8 Feyenoord reject Newcastle United's offer of £700,000 for World Cup defender Ulrich Van Gobbel. Sampdoria beat holders Parma 2-1 in Genoa in an Italian Cup semi-final first leg.
9 Spain draw 1-1 in Tenerife with Poland. Ancona of Serie B beat Torino 1-0 in an Italian Cup semi-final first leg.
10 Denmark beat the USA 4-2 on penalties in the Carlsberg Cup semi-final in Hong Kong. Romania lose 5-4 on penalties after drawing 1-1 with a Hong Kong League XI.

11 Belgian league leaders and champions Anderlecht lose 1-0 to Mechelen. Werder Bremen general manager Willi Lemke admits that he worked as a double agent for the KGB between 1970 and 1974!

12 Slovenia win the *Rothmans* spring tournament in Malta, defeating their hosts 1-0 in the last match. Club Bruges beat Lierse 1-0 to pull level at the top in Belgium with Anderlecht. Bayern Munich's first league appearance under Franz Beckenbauer ends in a 3-1 defeat at home to Stuttgart.

13 Denmark win the Carlsberg tournament in Hong Kong, beating the Hong Kong League XI 2-0 in the final. In Italy, Signori scores a hat-trick as Lazio thrash Cagliari 4-0. In Spain, Barcelona crash 6-3 to Real Zaragoza, their worst defeat in 32 years!

14 China beat a Germany XI 2-0.

15 Belenenses crash 2-0 to second division Lourosa in the quarter-finals of the Portuguese Cup. FC Porto reach the semi-finals with a 6-0 defeat of Desportivo Aves.

16 Three World Cup finalists suffer warm-up set-backs as Italy lose 1-0 to France in Naples, Belgium go down 1-0 to Malta and South Korea lose 2-1 to fellow-finalists Romania. Bryan Hamilton is appointed new manager of Northern Ireland, winning the vote from favourite Jimmy Nicholl.

17 Valencia's Bulgarian forward Luboslav Penev begins a prospective five-month course of chemotherapy treatment in Barcelona for a malignant tumour discovered by tests carried out after he was hit in the groin by a medicine ball.

18 Italy beat Japan 3-2 in a youth international friendly in Tokyo.

19 Bayern Munich win 3-1 at VfB Leipzig, their first victory under Franz Beckenbauer. MSV Duisburg are the surprise new leaders in Germany. Real Madrid beat Atletico 1-0 in the capital derby. Barcelona thrash Osasuna 8-1 with a Romario hat-trick.

20 Sweden win the Robbie Cup in Miami on goals after beating the USA 3-1.

21 Allan Simonsen, former Denmark forward, is appointed new coach of the Faeroe Islands' national team in succession to Pall Gudlaugsson.

22 Johan Cruyff is shown the red card for dissent and Andoni Zubizarreta the red card for handling outside his penalty area but Barcelona still win 3-1 at Valladolid.

23 Turkey lose 4-1 to the Czech Republic in Istanbul while Israel beat Georgia 2-0 in Tel Aviv. Cercle Bruges' Croat-born striker Josip Weber completes all stages of his citizenship application and is now formally available to play for Belgium. Sampdoria reach the Italian Cup Final, beating Parma 3-1 on aggregate.

24 Finland draw 0-0 with Morocco in Casablanca. Second division Ancona reach the Italian Cup Final.

25 Marseille president Bernard Tapie is questioned for four hours by investigating judge Bernard Beffy over the Valenciennes match scandal.

26 Bayern Munich thrash leaders MSV Duisburg 4-0 in Germany. Barcelona beat Spanish League leaders Deportivo La Coruna 3-0.

Luboslav Penev needed surgery for cancer.

27 Milan goalkeeper Sebastiano Rossi extends his unbeaten record to 929 minutes before he is beaten by a goal from Igor Kolivanov in Milan's 2-1 win over Foggia. Aston Villa beat Tranmere in a penalty shoot-out in the Coca-Cola (League) Cup semi-final second leg. Jose Luis Romero hands Atletico Madrid president Jesus Gil his resignation as coach before the match against Real Sociedad in San Sebastian.

28 Vitesse of Holland beat Saudi Arabia 4-3 in Jeddah.

March 1994

1 In European competitions Benfica scramble a 1-1 draw at home to Bayer Leverkusen in the Cup-Winners' Cup, Juventus lose 1-0 away to fellow Italians Cagliari in the UEFA Cup, but Inter surprisingly win 3-1 in Dortmund.

2 Monaco beat Galatasaray 3-0 to overtake Barcelona at the top of the Champions League Group A; Barcelona concede a 2-0 lead in Moscow where Spartak fight back to draw. In Group B, Milan stay top by defeating Werder Bremen 2-1 and Bobby Robson's European debut with FC Porto ends in a 1-0 defeat by Anderlecht in Brussels.

3 Real Madrid's Estadio Bernabeu is shut for one match by the sporting disciplinary committee because a linesman was struck on the back by an apple after Madrid's 3-0 home defeat by Tenerife in the Spanish Cup quarter-final second leg.

4 FIFA confirm that a goalkeeper can additionally be substituted at the World Cup finals in case of injury; that referees will be instructed to crack down on violent play including, in particular, the tackle from behind; and that the International Board will study ways and means of streamlining the offside law.

5 English leaders Manchester United lose at home for the first time in 16 months, by 1-0 to Chelsea; Norway's Jan Aage Fjortoft scores his ninth goal in seven games as Swindon draw 1-1 with West Ham.

6 Anderlecht hold on for a 0-0 draw away to pursuers Club Bruges in Belgium. French league leaders Paris Saint-Germain are held 2-2 at home by struggling Martigues. Ajax hit back from 2-0 down at home at half-time to beat Cambuur 3-2 in Holland. Milan stay six points clear by winning 1-0 away to Juventus in Italy; the Parma *v* Reggiana match is abandoned at half-time after referee Pierluigi Parietti pulls a muscle. Moscow Spartak open the Russian season with a 2-1 win away to Dynamo Stavropol. Barcelona move to within three points of leaders Deportivo La Coruna.

7 Real Madrid dismiss coach Benito Floro and appoint former Spain midfielder Vicente Del Bosque as caretaker to the end of the season.

8 Rot-Weiss Essen beat fellow second division side Tennis Borussia Berlin 2-0 in a German Cup semi-final tie.

9 England beat Denmark 1-0 to celebrate Terry Venables's debut as national coach. Switzerland win 2-1 in Hungary and Norway win 3-1 in Wales. Werder Bremen beat Dynamo Dresden 2-0 in their German Cup semi-final. Real Zaragoza beat Real Betis 3-1 (and 4-1 on aggregate) after extra time in the second leg of their Spanish Cup semi-final.

10 Uruguayan Hector Nunez quits Valencia, the third coach to go this season after Guus Hiddink and Francisco Leal. Hiddink's former right-hand man, Jose Manuel Rielo, is named caretaker.

11 Koln agree to sign Wolfgang Rolff from Karlsruhe and Reinhard Stumpf from Turkey's Galatasaray at the end of the season.

12 German league leaders Bayern Munich extend their winning run to four games with a 3-1 victory at Wattenscheid. Benfica thrash Famalicao 8-0 in Portugal. Romario scores three goals and Hristo Stoichkov two as Barcelona defeat Atletico Madrid 5-3. Norway defender Tore Pedersen is ruled out of the World Cup finals after wrecking knee ligaments in Oldham's 1-0 defeat of Bolton in the FA Cup quarter-finals; Denmark goalkeeper Peter Schmeichel is sent off for deliberate handball as Manchester United beat Charlton 3-1 in the day's other FA Cup quarter-final.

13 AEK Athens beat Iraklis 1-0 to extend their lead over Panathinaikos, Aris Salonica and Olympiakos to seven points. Milan move eight points clear in Italy by defeating second-place Sampdoria. Four players are sent off, two apiece, as Sporting Lisbon draw 0-0 with Uniao Madeira in Portugal. Deportivo La Coruna miss a penalty and slip back in the Spanish title race by drawing 0-0 in Osasuna, which leaves them only two points ahead of Barcelona.

14 Arsenal are cleared by the FA Premiership to revert to 1-11 numbering in an experiment until the end of the season.

15 Israel beat Ukraine 1-0. Arsenal, Benfica and Paris Saint-Germain qualify for the semi-finals of the Cup-Winners' Cup; Cagliari and SV Casino Salzburg reach the last four of the UEFA Cup. German Cup finalists Rot-Weiss Essen are sentenced to the loss of their professional licence at the season's end and mandatory relegation to the amateur league as punishment for trying to hide the size of their debts. Panathinaikos of Greece sack coach Ivica Osim and appoint Argentinian Juan Ramon Rocha, a former Panathinaikos midfielder, as caretaker to the end of the season.

16 Barcelona thrash Moscow Spartak 5-1 in the Champions League Group A while Milan stay top in Group B after a 1-1 draw away to Werder Bremen. Eric Gerets says he will quit as coach of Belgium's FC Liege at the end of this season. Panathinaikos, revived after the dismissal of coach Ivica Osim, beat Iraklis in the Greek Cup semi-final. Champions and league leaders AEK beat Aris 2-1 in the other tie. John Toshack quits as Wales manager after one match and 47 days in the job.

17 Borussia Dortmund win 2-1 away to Internazionale in the UEFA Cup but Inter take the quarter-final 4-2 on aggregate.

18 The draw for the Cup-Winners' Cup semi-finals matches Paris Saint-Germain against Arsenal and Benfica against title-holders Parma. In the UEFA Cup, SV Casino Salzburg are drawn against Karlsruhe; the other tie is an all-Italian matter between Cagliari and Internazionale.

19 Eric Cantona is sent off for stamping on rival forward John Moncur as Manchester United are held 2-2 by bottom club Swindon Town. Marseille beat Monaco on penalties in the third round of the French Cup. Eintracht Frankfurt keep the pressure on Bayern, by winning 4-0 at Dynamo Dresden.

20 Juventus thrash Parma 4-0 with a hat-trick from injured Baggio's deputy, Alessandro Del Piero. Atletico Madrid dismiss coach Iselin Ovejero after a 4-0 home defeat by Real Zaragoza.

21 Iceland beat Japan 2-1 in Utsunomiya. Former Bordeaux president Claude Bez is sentenced to a two-year jail term for fraud, with one year suspended. A local court also fines him £200,000 after he is found guilty of embezzling £1million from a contract to build a new club training centre. Britta Steilmann, 28, is elected president of Wattenscheid, the first woman on the board of a Bundesliga club. Atletico Madrid appoint their sixth coach of the season, former Argentinian goalkeeper Jorge D'Alessandro replacing Iselin Ovejero, dismissed in the wake of the 4-0 home defeat by Real Zaragoza.

22 France beat Chile 3-1 in Lyon. FC Liege announce they are facing bankruptcy with debts of £2.5m.

23 Germany beat Italy 2-1; a weakened Irish Republic are held 0-0 by Russia in Dublin; Morocco win 2-1 in Luxembourg; Greece are held 0-0 at home by Poland; the continent's oldest duel, between Austria and Hungary, ends

1-1 with three players sent off; Holland win 1-0 in Scotland.
24 Arsenal sell Sweden winger Anders Limpar to Everton for £1.6m. UEFA select Athens as venue for the Champions' Cup Final and Copenhagen for the Cup-Winners' Cup Final.
25 Ottavio Bianchi quits as general manager-cum-coach of Napoli amid speculation that he is top target for Internazionale.
26 Swede Martin Dahlin scores his first hat-trick in Germany as Borussia Monchengladbach beat VfB Leipzig 6-1.
27 Aston Villa beat Manchester United 3-1 in the Coca-Cola (League) Cup Final. Bayern Munich win 2-1 away to Hamburg to go two points clear of Eintracht Frankfurt in Germany. Ajax stay top in Holland despite losing 2-1 away to second-placed Feyenoord.
28 Internazionale appoint Ottavio Bianchi (late of Napoli) as coach for 1994-95 season and announce the impending departures of internationals Toto Schillaci (to Jubilo Iwata of Japan), Walter Zenga, Riccardo Ferri and Giuseppe Bergomi.
29 In European competitions Cup-Winners' Cup holders Parma lose 2-1 to Benfica in a semi-final first leg; Paris Saint-Germain are held 1-1 at home by Arsenal. In the UEFA Cup, SV Casino Salzburg are held 0-0 at home by Karlsruhe.
30 Barcelona, Monaco, Milan and FC Porto qualify for the semi-finals of the Champions' League. Cagliari beat Inter 3-2 in their all-Italian UEFA Cup semi-final first leg.
31 Coach Hans Westerhof, sacked by PSV in Holland, returns to Groningen. UEFA's executive confirms a proposal from its club competitions committee that from next season UEFA Cup matches be played only on Tuesday, Champions' League ties only on Wednesdays and Cup-Winners' Cup ties only on Thursdays.

April 1994

1 The Swedish FA names Helsingborg, Vasteras, Karlstad, Gavle and the Rasunda stadium in Stockholm as proposed venues for the 1995 Women's World Cup.
2 Blackburn Rovers narrow Manchester United's Premiership lead to three points by defeating the leaders 2-0 at Ewood Park. Paris Saint-Germain extend their unbeaten run in the French league to a record 27 matches with a 2-1 home win over Cannes. Real Madrid fade from the Spanish title race after a 3-2 defeat at bottom club Celta.
3 Two more goals in Spain for Bebeto as league leaders Deportivo La Coruna thrash Oviedo 5-2.
4 Bob Petrovic, a Serbian businessman and former Red Star Belgrade player, spends £600,000 buying all the shares in the Marbella second division team from Mayor (and Atletico Madrid president) Jesus Gil.
5 Belgium's Standard Liege decide not to renew the contract of coach Rene Vandereycken, who took over in mid-season from Arie Haan. French league leaders Paris Saint-Germain go down 3-0 to Nantes, their first defeat in 28 matches.
6 Italy embarrassingly lose 2-1 in a training match against fourth division Pontedera, Hungary lose 1-0 at home to Slovenia. Austria's Rapid Vienna formally file for bankruptcy, some £1.2m in debt, but may stay in existence if they can find a major sponsor by the start of next season. The FA pull England out of the friendly with Germany, scheduled for Berlin on Hitler's birthday, 20 April. Guido Buchwald, VfB Stuttgart's World Cup veteran, agrees to transfer to Urawa Red Diamonds of Japan after the World Cup finals.
7 Paul Gascoigne breaks his right leg in two places tackling Lazio youth player Alessandro Nesta in a training game.
8 Internazionale ease their relegation fears by beating Lecce 4-1. Sporting Lisbon agree the sale of midfielder Paulo Sousa to Juventus for £5m plus Julio Cesar in part exchange.
9 Bayern Munich take a decisive step towards the German title by defeating challengers Eintracht Frankfurt 2-1.
10 Milan draw 0-0 away to Torino to move within one point of the first Italian League hat-trick since Torino in the 1940s. Deportivo La Coruna edge three points clear at the top in Spain by winning 1-0 at Racing Santander.
11 AS Roma general manager Luciano Moggi offers to resign after being pipped by Juventus to the signing of Sporting Lisbon midfielder Paulo Sousa.
12 Arsenal reach the Cup-Winners' Cup Final, while SV Casino Salzburg reach the UEFA Cup, where they will face Internazionale. In Switzerland Bob Houghton is appointed new coach of FC Zurich.
13 The sixth and final Champions' League match day ends with Barcelona and Milan topping the groups and scheduled to face FC Porto and Monaco respectively in the semi-finals. Parma reach the Cup-Winners' Cup Final for the second successive season. Poland beat Saudi Arabia 1-0 in front of only 200 in Cannes. Milan agree the end-of-season sale of French striker Jean-Pierre Papin to Bayern Munich for £2.1m. Papin's two-year deal will be worth £500,000 a year, half his salary with Milan.
14 Kaiserslautern bring new life to the championship race by defeating Bayern Munich 4-0 and cutting the gap between them to two points. Christian Ziege, Bayern's left-back, suffers a knee injury which rules him out of the World Cup finals. Real Madrid formally announce that Jorge Valdano will take over as coach at the season's end.
15 Bulgaria draw 1-1 in Oman. Russia's bottom club, Lada Togliatti, just promoted, sack coach Alexander Irkhin and replace him with Alexander Kochetkov. Bob Petrovic, new owner of second division Marbella, appoints former England midfielder Peter Reid to the coaching staff. Torino are cleared, by UEFA's control and disciplinary commission, of charges of trying to sweeten referees during their 1991-92 UEFA Cup run.

Giovanni Trapattoni (second from left), seen here with Kit Rummenigge, President Scherer and Uli Hoeness announcing his 'transfer' to Bayern Munich.

16 Moldova hold the USA 1-1 in Jacksonville. AEK secure a third successive Greek league title by winning 2-1 away to Kalamaria. Brazilian striker Romario is carried off with an ankle injury in Barcelona's 3-1 win over Valencia.

17 Paris Saint-Germain extend their lead over Marseille to six points. Ajax beat FC Twente 6-0 despite the second-half expulsion of Danny Blind. Milan clinch their third consecutive Italian title, collecting the vital point from a 2-2 draw at home to Udinese. Juventus thrash Lazio 6-1 with a hat-trick from Gianluca Vialli.

18 Charleroi coach Robert Waseige signs a two-year contract to succeed Rene Vandereycken at end of season.

19 Juventus coach Giovanni Trapattoni confirms that he has reached an agreement in principle to take over at Bayern Munich in the summer. Officials of Tenerife and Real Madrid approach an agreement for the transfer of Argentine midfielder Fernando Redondo for £2m plus striker Jean Esnaider and the receipts of three friendly matches.

20 The Republic of Ireland win 1-0 in Holland. Panathinaikos beat AEK 4-3 on penalties after the Greek Cup Final ends in a 3-3 draw. Sampdoria win the Italian Cup, defeating Ancona 6-1 in the second leg of the Final after a 0-0 draw in the first game. Real Zaragoza beat Celta 5-4 on penalties after a 0-0 draw in the Spanish Cup Final.

21 Zambia are announced as replacements for Tunisia as World Cup warm-up opponents for Belgium in Brussels on 4 June.

22 The French Federation cracks down on Marseille in a definitive judgement on the scandal over the match-fixing allegations concerning last season's match against Valenciennes. President Bernard Tapie and former general-secretary Jean-Pierre Bernes are banned *sine die*; the three players involved, Christophe Robert, Jorge Burruchaga and Jean-Jacques Eydelie, are suspended for two years each. The federation postpones Marseille's weekend cup-tie against Montpellier for fear of crowd trouble following the punishments.

23 Iceland beat the USA 2-1. Bayern Munich appear to step closer to German league victory but their 2-1 victory over struggling Nurnberg is a subject of controversy because the opening goal, by Thomas Helmer, comes from a shot which rolls wide of goal. Spanish league leaders Deportivo La Coruna drop an important point when they are held goalless away to relegation-threatened Lleida.

24 Blackburn slip further back in the English Premiership race, held 1-1 by Queens Park Rangers. Barcelona win 4-0 away to Celta to move within two points of Deportivo.

25 Marseille's French Cup quarter-final with Montpellier, postponed from the weekend, is rescheduled for 4 May. Bayern Munich stage the coaching coup of the year as Juventus boss Giovanni Trapattoni, one of Europe's most successful trainers, agrees to join the German league leaders during the summer, to take over from Franz Beckenbauer.

26 SV Casino Salzburg lose 1-0 'at home' in Vienna to Internazionale in the first leg of the UEFA Cup Final. Former World Cup midfielder Leo Clijsters is appointed new coach to Gent in succession to Walter Meeuws, while Georges Leekens is named to succeed Standard-bound Robert Waseige as coach to Charleroi at the season's end. Bayern Munich and Nurnberg are ordered to replay their league match in which video evidence showed that Bayern's opening goal had not crossed the goal-line. Romanian midfielder Danut Lupu signs a two-year contract with Rapid Bucharest after returning from Greece where he spent 10 months in prison for theft after spells with Panathinaikos, Korinthos and OFI Crete.

27 In World Cup warm-ups, Greece beat Saudi Arabia 5-1 and Germany win 2-0 in the UAE. Milan and Barcelona qualify for the Champions' Cup Final, beating Monaco and FC Porto respectively by 3-0 apiece. UEFA rule that Marseille should be allowed back into European competition next season (whether in the Cup-Winners' Cup or UEFA Cup) despite their relegation punishment for last season's bribery scandal. Steaua Bucharest win 5-2 away to Dacia Unirea Braila on the last day of the Romanian league season to finish 13 points clear of runners-up Universitatea Craiova.

28 Bulgaria can only manage a 2-2 with Kuwait. UEFA's Congress in Vienna re-elects Lennart Johansson of Sweden as president; admits former provisional members Israel, Moldova, Azerbaijan and FYR Macedonia as full members (lifting the total membership to 49); but delays a decision on the reintegration of Yugoslavia.

29 RSC Anderlecht agree terms to buy veteran defender or midfielder Georges Grun back from Parma.

30 Paris Saint-Germain make sure of the French title with two rounds of matches to go, defeating Toulouse 1-0.

May 1994

1 Milan rest all their top players and lose their last league match 1-0 at home to Reggiana, who thus escape relegation. Barcelona thrash Sporting Gijon 4-0 to narrow the gap behind Deportivo La Coruna to one point at the top of the Spanish league.

2 Manchester United become English champions as pursuers Blackburn Rovers lose at Coventry. Dutch midfielder Erwin Koeman becomes the latest player ruled out of the World Cup after tearing a groin muscle in training with PSV.

3 Bayern Munich thrash Nurnberg 5-0 in the replay of the controversial 'no goal' league match. Sporting Lisbon's title bid hits a double set-back: they lose 2-0 away to FC Porto and have three players sent off.

4 Arsenal beat holders Parma 1-0 in the Cup-Winners' Cup Final in Copenhagen.

5 Sweden beat a weakened Nigeria 3-1 in Stockholm. Former Everton manager Howard Kendall is appointed coach to Greek club Xanthi for next season.

6 Milan midfielder Stefano Eranio tears his left Achilles tendon and is ruled out of both the Champions' Cup Final against Barcelona and the World Cup finals. Ruud Gullit agrees details of his transfer back to Milan from Sampdoria. Cagliari sign Uruguayan coach Oscar Washington Tabarez.

7 The USA beat Estonia 4-0. The English Premiership ends in relegation-zone drama as Oldham and Sheffield United join Swindon in going down while Everton hit back from 2-0 down to beat Wimbledon 3-2 and stay up. Nantes and Bordeaux secure UEFA Cup qualification in France. Bayern Munich beat Schalke 2-0 on the last day in Germany to win their first title in four years. Barcelona win 1-0 away to Real Madrid.

8 Ajax lose to Willem II by 2-1 on the last day of their latest Dutch championship-winning season. Deportivo La Coruna win 2-0 away to Logrones to keep one point clear of Barcelona in Spain with one game to go.

9 Greece crash 3-0 at home in Athens to Cameroon, who include Roger Milla for the full 90 minutes. Ruud Gullit signs his new one-year contract, worth £700,000, with Milan.

10 Claudio Caniggia makes his return to action after his 13-month dope-test ban. Caniggia helps his Italian club, AS Roma, beat his original club River Plate 3-1 in a tournament in Buenos Aires, scoring Roma's second goal and creating the third.

11 Internazionale win the UEFA Cup, beating SV Casino Salzburg 1-0 (2-0 on aggregate) in the second leg in Milan. Samsunspor of Turkey beat Ioannina of Greece 2-0 (5-0 on agg) in the second leg of the Balkan Cup Final. Montpellier (2-0 winners at Lens) and Auxerre (1-0 winners at home to Nantes) win the French Cup semi-finals to earn places in the Final. Eintracht Frankfurt buy World Cup goalkeeper Andy Kopke from relegated Nurnberg. Servette win their first league title in nine years when they beat Young Boys 4-1, finishing one point clear of Grasshoppers.

12 Feyenoord beat second division NEC 2-1 in the Dutch Cup Final. Milan sign Italy midfielder Giovanni Stroppa from Foggia and sell Brazilian forward Elber (who had been on loan to new Swiss champions Servette) to German club VfB Stuttgart. Rangers forward Duncan Ferguson is banned for 12 matches for butting Raith's John McStay in a league game on April 16. IFK Norrkoping beat Helsingborg 4-3 in extra time in the Swedish Cup Final.

13 Greece and Bolivia draw 0-0 in Athens. Former Scotland midfielder Jim Bett joins Iceland's KR as player-coach. UEFA call up English referee Philip Don to take charge of the Champions' Cup Final after death threats to the scheduled Dutch official, John Blankenstein.

14 Manchester United become English football's fourth double-winners of the century when they beat Chelsea 4-0 in the FA Cup Final. Auxerre win their first major trophy, beating Montpellier 3-0 in the French Cup Final. Werder Bremen beat Rot-Weiss Essen 3-1 in the German Cup Final. Barcelona overtake Deportivo La Coruna on goal aggregate to win the Spanish league title in the last round of the season. Deportivo's Djukic misses what would have been a decisive last-minute penalty in their 0-0 draw home to Valencia while Barcelona hit back from 1-0 and 2-1 down to beat Sevilla 5-2. Benfica regain control of the Portuguese title race after thrashing neighbours Sporting Lisbon 6-3 with a hat-trick from Joao Vieira Pinto.

15 Armenia lose 1-0 to the USA. Grasshoppers beat Schaffhausen 4-0 in the Swiss Cup Final. Galatasaray win the Turkish league title on the last day, for the second year in succession.

16 New champions Paris Saint-Germain dismiss coach Artur Jorge and appoint Cannes boss Luis Fernandez, a former Paris Saint-Germain player. Jupp Heynckes returns from Atletic Bilbao to take over Eintracht Frankfurt.

17 England thrash Greece 5-0 at Wembley while Poland lose 4-3 at home to Austria. Maccabi Tel Aviv and Hapoel Tel Aviv both win their Israeli Cup semi-finals in penalty shoot-outs.

18 Milan rout Barcelona 4-0 in the Champions' Cup Final in Athens.

19 Dutch World Cup defender Stan Valckx signs a new contract with Sporting Lisbon.

20 Real Madrid formally confirm that Fernando Redondo is joining them from Tenerife for £2.5m.

21 Dundee United beat Rangers 1-0 in the Scottish Cup Final.

22 Germany's Ulf Kirsten may miss the World Cup finals after tearing a muscle during a training game at the Germans' HQ at Malente. Juventus reserves beat Cameroon 4-1 in a friendly in Turin!

23 Estonia lose 2-1 at home to Wales for whom Neville Southall wins a national record 74th cap, overtaking Peter Nicholas' record.

24 The Republic of Ireland beat Bolivia 1-0 in Dublin. Liverpool buy Danish Under-21 goalkeeper Michael Stensgaard from Hvidovre for £300,000. Olympiakos sign Yugoslav Footballer of the Year Ilija Ivic from Red Star Belgrade. Turkish champions Galatasaray dismiss German coach Reiner Hollmann after just one–successful–season.

25 Romania beat Nigeria 2-0; the Czech Republic beat Lithuania 5-3 and Ukraine beat Belarus 3-1. Australian champions Adelaide City sell Australia striker Carl Veart to Sheffield United for £400,000. The Italian league votes to adopt three points for a win in Serie A and Serie B next season. Benfica secure a record 30th league title, beating Gil Vicente 3-0 away and making certain of the championship with two games remaining.

26 Sweden lose 1-0 to Denmark in Copenhagen while France beat Australia 1-0 in the Kirin Cup in Japan. Mechelen agree the sale of Belgian World Cup goalkeeper Michel Preud'homme to newly-crowned Portuguese champions Benfica.

27 Holland beat Scotland 3-1 in Utrecht; Italy beat Finland 2-0 in Parma; and Switzerland defeat Liechtenstein 2-0 in Basel. In France Saint-Etienne dismiss Jacques Santini. VfB Stuttgart sell Swiss striker Adrian Knup to Karlsruhe.

28 The USA draw 1-1 with Greece. SV Casino Salzburg extend their lead in Austria to three points after winning 3-1 away to Vorwarts Steyr. Legia Warsaw beat Warta Poznan 3-2 and, despite their three-point penalty for match-fixing last season, go top of the table in Poland with four games to go.

29 World Cup holders Germany suffer a shock 2-0 home defeat by the Republic of Ireland. Russia end their home-based warm-up programme with a 2-1 win over Slovakia. France win the Kirin Cup in Japan, beating their hosts 4-1 in the final match of the event. Anderlecht sell Belgium striker Luc Nilis to PSV.

30 Blackburn Rovers central defender David May signs a four-year contract with champions Manchester United. Ruud Gullit quits Holland's World Cup squad, infuriating his team-mates and aggravating the crisis for coach Dick Advocaat by saying he will not explain until after the finals.

31 Argentina beat Israel 3-0 in Tel Aviv with two goals from Batistuta and one from Caniggia, his first since returning from suspension.

June 1994

1 Holland thrash Hungary 7-1; Norway beat Denmark 2-1; Romania and Slovenia draw 0-0; Macedonia beat Estonia 2-0. In Spain Compostela win promotion to first division, beating Rayo Vallecano in a play-off. Rayo are relegated.

2 Finland lose 1-2 at home to Spain; Hooligans run riot as Germany win 5-1 in Austria. Troubled Valencia announce that Brazil boss Carlos Alberto Parreira will take over as coach after the World Cup Finals.

3 Italy beat Switzerland 1-0 while Bulgaria are held to a 0-0 draw by Ukraine; Latvia beat Malta 2-0 in Riga. Bulgarian FA president Valentine Mihov resigns over World Cup bonuses for players. UEFA impose fine of £70,000 on Milan for misbehaviour of their fans during Champions' League matches. Yugoslav FA announce that they cannot comply with UEFA security and entry guarantees, and do not enter clubs in European club competitions.

4 Croatia hold Argentina to a goalless draw; Belgium thrash Zambia 9-0 – Josip Weber scores five goals on his debut. Northern Ireland lose 2-0 to Colombia. Avenir Beggen win the Luxembourg championship.

5 The Czech Republic beat the Republic of Ireland 3-1 in Dublin. VAC FC Samsung win the Hungarian championship. FC Porto and Sporting Lisbon draw 0-0 in the Portuguese Cup Final.

6 Nicola Berti signs a new contract with Internazionale. Michael Laudrup of Barcelona agrees a two-year contract with Real Madrid.

7 England win the Under-21 tournament, beating Portugal 2-0 in the final in Toulon. Newly promoted Nottingham Forest agree terms with Dutch player Bryan Roy.

8 Germany beat Canada 2-0 bus lose Mario Basler, who breaks a leg; Belgium beat Hungary 3-1. SV Casino Salzburg win the Austrian championship. In Genoa, Carlos Aguilera is sentenced to jail for two years on charges involving a prostitution ring.

10 Spain beat Canada 2-0. FC Porto win the Portuguese cup, beating Sporting Lisbon 2-1 in the Final replay.

11 Italy scrape a 1-0 win over Costa Rica in New Haven; Switzerland draw 0-0 with Bolivia but Northern Ireland fall 0-3 to Mexico.

12 Holland beat Canada 3-0; Sweden and Romania draw 1-1 in the last of the World Cup warm-up matches.

17 World Cup 1994 begins. Group C: Germany beat Bolivia 1-0 in Chicago, with Klinsmann scoring the opening goal. Kohler is the first player booked at the finals. Spain draw 2-2 with South Korea having led 2-0. Defender Nadal is sent off after 25 minutes.

18 Group A: Switzerland draw 1-1 with the USA; Romania beat Colombia 3-1. Group E: The Republic of Ireland beat Italy 1-0.

19 Group B: Sweden twice come from behind to draw 2-2 with Cameroon. Russia lose 0-2 to Brazil. Group E: Norway beat Mexico 1-0. Group F: Belgium beat Morocco 1-0.

20 Group F: Dutch player John de Wolf tears a muscle in training and may be out of the World Cup. Holland come from behind to beat Saudi Arabia 2-1.

21 Group A: Switzerland beat Romania 4-1 – their first win in the finals for 40 years – and ensure qualification for next stage. Romania's Vladoiu is sent off only four minutes after going on as a substitute. Group D: Bulgaria fall 0-3 to Nigeria and Greece are thrashed 0-4 by Argentina. Group C: Spain and Germany draw 1-1.

22 Group A: Vladoiu is banned for three games by UEFA and sent home by the Romanian management.

23 Group E: Italy beat Norway 1-0, having had 10 men for 69 minutes, after Pagliuca becomes the first goalkeeper ever to be sent off in the finals.

24 Group B: Dahlin scores twice as Sweden beat Russia 3-1. Russia's Gorlukovich is sent off after 49 minutes. Group E: The Republic of Ireland lose 1-2 to Mexico. Substitute Aldridge scores the late goal for Ireland, after he and manager Jack Charlton are involved in a touch-line fracas with a UEFA official. Italy's Baresi undergoes arthroscopic surgery on a knee cartilage.

25 Group E: UEFA ban Charlton from the touchline for one game and impose fines on him, Aldridge and the Irish FA. Group F: Belgium score a significant 1-0 win over Holland to qualify for the second phase.

26 Group A: Petrescu's goal gives Romania a 1-0 win over the USA to finish top of the group. Switzerland crash 0-2 to Colombia but finish second. Group C: Bulgaria record their first ever win at the finals, beating Greece 4-0 in their 18th game. Greece return home after a 0-2 defeat by Nigeria.

27 Group C: Germany squeeze past South Korea 3-2 after being 3-0 ahead. Spain record their first win, 3-1 over Bolivia.

28 Group B: Sweden draw 1-1 with Brazil to qualify for the second phase. Salenko creates a finals record by scoring five goals in the 6-1 thrashing of Cameroon, but it's not enough to see the Russians through to the next phase. Group C: Germany's Effenberg is sent home in disgrace by manager Berti Vogts after making rude gestures to fans. Group E: The Republic of Ireland and Norway draw 0-0, and Italy and Mexico draw 1-1. Mexico, the Republic and Italy qualify for the next round, but Norway go home despite having four points. One more goal would have put them top of the group instead of bottom.

29 Group F: Holland beat Morocco 2-1 to qualify for the next round. Belgium are sensationally beaten by Saudi Arabia 1-0.

30 Group D: Bulgaria qualify for the second stage with a surprise 2-0 win over Argentina, shocked by Diego Maradona's expulsion from the competition, for drugs abuse, a few hours earlier.

July 1994

2 The second round of the World Cup starts. Germany beat Belgium 3-2, and Spain defeat Switzerland 3-0.

3 Sweden ease past Saudi Arabia 3-1 and Romania create a sensation by knocking out Argentina 3-2.

4 A mistake by goalkeeper Bonner seals Holland's 2-0 defeat of the Republic of Ireland.

5 A last-minute goal by Italy's Roberto Baggio forces extra time against Nigeria. Baggio adds a second in extra time as Italy win 2-1. Mexico and Bulgaria draw 1-1 but Bulgaria qualify by winning penalty shoot-out. Bulgaria's win means that seven of the eight quarter-finalists are from Europe.

9 The quarter-finals of the World Cup start. Another late goal by Roberto Baggio enables Italy to beat Spain 2-1. Holland come from two goals down to draw level with Brazil but a late goal puts the Brazilians through 3-2.

10 Bulgaria beat Germany 2-1 with two goals in three minutes late in the game. Romania and Sweden draw 2-2, but Sweden go through on penalties despite having Schwarz sent off.

13 In the first semi-final Roberto Baggio scores twice to give Italy a 2-1 win over the Bulgarians. A late goal by Romario is enough for Brazil to beat ten-man Sweden in the other semi-final after Thern is dismissed.

16 Sweden win the third-place play-off match, beating Bulgaria 4-0.

17 Brazil win the World Cup. The 0-0 draw is the first goalless World Cup Final, followed by the first penalty shoot-out, and Roberto Baggio misses the last, decisive, kick.

20 In Geneva the draw for the Champions' League is made along with the preliminary rounds of all three club competitions.

European Football Championship 1996

Dignitaries and footballing stars past and present gathered in January for the draw for the 1996 European Championships. The stage for the event was both a curious and rather embarrassing one all around – although when the day arrived it proved to be a most poignant one. The Granada Television studios in Manchester may well be suited to house the world's longest-running soap opera but not the draw for one of the world's major sporting events. Even the overflow area for those who could not be accommodated in the studio's Tours theatre did not suffice. And while national team managers mingled shoulder to shoulder, the host nation remained managerless, although the surrounding Sherlock Holmes scenery in the overflow area was a rather fitting backdrop to the endless speculation about the on-off appointment of Terry Venables as England manager. In the end the name picking was elementary but saddened by the death of Sir Matt Busby. After the draw was made the dignitaries were able to witness the emotionally human side of the English game as guests of the Football Association at Old Trafford, where Busby's beloved Manchester United played hosts to Everton. Many of those European officials who had been so critical of the English national game just days before were clearly moved by the lone Scots piper who led both sides into the eerie silence of a packed Old Trafford arena.

Prior to the draw the 47 teams seeking qualification to join hosts England had been split into six groups who were sorted on the basis on performances in the 1992 qualifying tournament and the 1994 World Cup. Interestingly, this led to nations such as Wales, Romania and the Ukraine (when were they in the two aforementioned competitions?) being accorded second seed status while the likes of World Cup qualifiers Belgium and Bulgaria could only gain spots in the group of third seeds. The top seeds offered no surprises. Despite the finals being doubled in size from the normal eight-team competition to 16, UEFA decreed that holders would continue not to qualify automatically for the finals – Denmark though were at least assured a spot among the top seeds.

There had been hope that the dramatic rise in new European nations would lead to some marginalising of them into a preliminary round of play-offs. This in the end did not materialise and once again it seems certain that a number of qualification places will be decided on goal-gluts or otherwise against the likes of the Faeroe Islands, Estonia and San Marino to name but three. There also must be concern at the inclusion of the likes of strife-torn Azerbaijan, Armenia, Croatia and Georgia, where military conflicts mean that some games are likely to be played at neutral venues, thereby imposing heavier burdens on already stretched financial tightropes. It also seems safe to bet that one or two of these countries will withdraw, adding further imbalance to teetering groups. Time will tell and when it does one hopes that the lessons are learned.

The draw provided eight qualifying groups and as always seems to happen at these events some pairings were reminiscent of recent World Cup qualifying groups. As the draw progressed the centre point became Group Four, with Slovenia, Estonia, Lithuania, Croatia and Ukraine forming the basis of the 'new-age' group. Italy were provided as the group's top seeded side and face an interesting test as well as travels – many local – into uncharted

Seeding

Top Seeds:	Germany, France, Russia, Holland, Denmark, Sweden, Italy, Republic of Ireland.
Second Seeds:	Norway, Romania, Switzerland, Portugal, Greece, Spain, Wales, Ukraine.
Third Seeds:	Bulgaria, Belgium, Scotland, Northern Ireland, Poland, Hungary, Czech Republic, Croatia.
Fourth Seeds:	Iceland, Austria, Finland, Lithuania, Israel, FYR Macedonia, Belarus, Georgia.
Fifth Seeds:	Turkey, Latvia, Albania, Cyprus, Malta, Faeroe Islands, Estonia, Slovakia.
Sixth Seeds:	Luxembourg, San Marino, Liechtenstein, Slovenia, Moldova, Armenia, Azerbaijan.

The Draw

Group One:	France, Romania, Poland, Israel, Slovakia, Azerbaijan.
Group Two:	Denmark, Spain, Belgium, FYR Macedonia, Croatia, Armenia.
Group Three:	Sweden, Switzerland, Hungary, Iceland, Turkey.
Group Four:	Italy, Ukraine, Croatia, Lithuania, Estonia, Slovenia.
Group Five:	Holland, Norway, Czech Republic, Belarus, Malta, Luxembourg.
Group Six:	Republic of Ireland, Portugal, Northern Ireland, Austria, Latvia, Liechtenstein.
Group Seven:	Germany, Wales, Bulgaria, Georgia, Albania, Moldova.
Group Eight:	Russia, Greece, Scotland, Finland, Faeroe Islands, San Marino.

ABOVE: *The draw for the 1996 European Championships unfolds in Manchester.*

RIGHT: *Jimmy Quinn scored twice for Northern Ireland against Liechtenstein.*

territory. Certainly the new political entities will not provide an easy passage. Croatia – conflicts permitting – could well be a surprise package with the likes of Boksic, Boban and Prosinecki just three of 16 internationals playing overseas. The Croats recorded a 2-0 win in Spain soon after the draw.

In Group One France were paired with Israel, whose astonishing win in the Parc des Princes did so much damage to French World Cup qualification hopes. Holders Denmark were again paired with Spain, who qualified for USA94 at their expense following a single-goal win in Seville in the final group game. In Group Five Holland and Norway found a World Cup double-take as did Russia and Greece in Group Eight. But as these sides filled their qualification spots in their respective World Cup qualifying groups they will probably not be too unhappy. The two Ireland associations asked to be seeded apart, were denied, and almost inevitably found that they would be renewing their wits on the field and providing headaches for the security forces off of it. Tense encounters all round.

Practically the draw produced eight groups – seven of which contained six teams and one – Group Three – with five. Each group comprises one team from each seed ranking, except Group Three which does not have a sixth-seeded team.

After the event Lennart Johansson, the UEFA president, cited why the European Championship was to be played in England, 'We felt it was time to bring the event back to the motherland.' The 31 games to be played in the refurbished stadiums of Wembley, Manchester United, Leeds United, Nottingham Forest, Newcastle United, Liverpool and Aston Villa expect attendances in the order of 1.4 million, generating a profit of some £5m for the Football Association under Glen Kirton, the director of Euro '96.

EUROPEAN FOOTBALL CHAMPIONSHIP 1996

The Fixtures

England will stage a 16-team European Championship tournament in which the hosts qualify automatically. The eight Group winners along with the six best runners-up from the six-team groups also qualify. The final place goes to a two-legged play-off between the remaining runner-up from the six-team groups, ie, the one with the worst record, and the runner-up in the five-team group – Group Three.

Group One

4/9/94	Israel v Poland
7/9/94	Slovakia v France
7/9/94	Romania v Azerbaijan
8/10/94	France v Romania
12/10/94	Israel v Slovakia
12/10/94	Poland v Azerbaijan
12/11/94	Romania v Slovakia
16/11/94	Poland v France
16/11/94	Azerbaijan v Israel
14/12/94	Azerbaijan v France
14/12/94	Israel v Romania
29/3/95	Romania v Poland
29/3/95	Israel v France
29/3/95	Slovakia v Azerbaijan
25/4/95	Poland v Israel
26/4/95	France v Slovakia
26/4/95	Azerbaijan v Romania
7/6/95	Poland v Slovakia
7/6/95	Romania v Israel
16/8/95	France v Poland
16/8/95	Azerbaijan v Slovakia
6/9/95	France v Azerbaijan
6/9/95	Slovakia v Israel
6/9/95	Poland v Romania
11/10/95	Romania v France
11/10/95	Israel v Azerbaijan
11/10/95	Slovakia v Poland
15/11/95	Slovakia v Romania
15/11/95	Azerbaijan v Poland
15/11/95	France v Israel

Group Two

7/9/94	Cyprus v Spain
7/9/94	FYR Macedonia v Denmark
7/9/94	Belgium v Armenia
8/10/94	Armenia v Cyprus
12/10/94	Denmark v Belgium
12/10/94	FYR Macedonia v Spain
16/11/94	Belgium v FYR Macedonia
16/11/94	Spain v Denmark
16/11/94	Cyprus v Armenia
17/12/94	Belgium v Spain
17/12/94	FYR Macedonia v Cyprus
29/3/95	Spain v Belgium
29/3/95	Cyprus v Denmark
26/4/95	Armenia v Spain
26/4/95	Belgium v Cyprus
26/4/95	Denmark v FYR Macedonia
10/5/95	Armenia v FYR Macedonia
7/6/95	Denmark v Cyprus
10/5/95	Armenia v FYR Macedonia
7/6/95	FYR Macedonia v Belgium
7/6/95	Spain v Armenia
16/8/95	Armenia v Denmark
6/9/95	Belgium v Denmark
6/9/95	Spain v Cyprus
6/9/95	FYR Macedonia v Armenia
7/10/95	Armenia v Belgium
11/10/95	Denmark v Spain
11/10/95	Cyprus v FYR Macedonia
15/11/95	Spain v FYR Macedonia
15/11/95	Cyprus v Belgium
15/11/95	Denmark v Armenia

Group Three

7/9/94	Iceland v Sweden
7/9/94	Hungary v Turkey
12/10/94	Turkey v Iceland
12/10/94	Switzerland v Sweden
16/11/94	Switzerland v Iceland
16/11/94	Sweden v Hungary
14/12/94	Turkey v Switzerland
29/3/95	Turkey v Sweden
29/3/95	Hungary v Switzerland
26/4/95	Hungary v Sweden
26/4/95	Switzerland v Turkey
1/6/95	Sweden v Iceland
11/6/95	Iceland v Hungary
16/8/95	Iceland v Switzerland
6/9/95	Sweden v Switzerland
6/9/95	Turkey v Hungary
11/10/95	Switzerland v Hungary
11/10/95	Iceland v Turkey
11/11/95	Hungary v Iceland
15/11/95	Sweden v Turkey

Group Four

4/9/94	Estonia v Croatia
7/9/94	Slovenia v Italy
7/9/94	Ukraine v Lithuania
8/10/94	Estonia v Italy
9/10/94	Croatia v Lithuania
12/10/94	Ukraine v Slovenia
13/11/94	Ukraine v Estonia
16/11/94	Slovenia v Lithuania
16/11/94	Italy v Croatia
25/3/95	Italy v Estonia
25/3/95	Croatia v Ukraine
29/3/95	Slovenia v Estonia
29/3/95	Ukraine v Italy
29/3/95	Lithuania v Croatia
26/4/95	Lithuania v Italy
26/4/95	Croatia v Slovenia
26/4/95	Estonia v Ukraine
7/6/95	Lithuania v Slovenia
11/6/95	Estonia v Slovenia
11/6/95	Ukraine v Croatia
16/8/95	Estonia v Lithuania
3/9/95	Croatia v Estonia
6/9/95	Italy v Slovenia
6/9/95	Lithuania v Ukraine
8/10/95	Croatia v Italy
11/10/95	Slovenia v Ukraine
11/10/95	Lithuania v Estonia
11/11/95	Italy v Ukraine
15/11/95	Slovenia v Croatia
15/11/95	Italy v Lithuania

Group Five

6/9/94	Czech Republic v Malta
7/9/94	Luxembourg v Holland
7/9/94	Norway v Belarus
12/10/94	Malta v Czech Republic
12/10/94	Belarus v Luxembourg
12/10/94	Norway v Holland
16/11/94	Belarus v Norway
16/11/94	Holland v Czech Republic
14/12/94	Malta v Norway
14/12/94	Holland v Luxembourg
22/2/95	Malta v Luxembourg
29/3/95	Czech Republic v Belarus
29/3/95	Luxembourg v Norway
29/3/95	Holland v Malta
26/4/95	Belarus v Malta
26/4/95	Czech Republic v Holland
26/4/95	Norway v Luxembourg
7/6/95	Belarus v Holland
7/6/95	Luxembourg v Czech Republic
7/6/95	Norway v Malta
16/8/95	Norway v Czech Republic
6/9/95	Czech Republic v Norway
6/9/95	Luxembourg v Malta
6/9/95	Holland v Belarus
7/10/95	Belarus v Czech Republic
8/10/95	Malta v Holland
11/10/95	Luxembourg v Belarus
12/11/95	Malta v Belarus
15/11/95	Czech Republic v Luxembourg
15/11/95	Holland v Norway

Group Six

20/4/94	Northern Ireland v Liechtenstein
7/9/94	Liechtenstein v Austria
7/9/94	Northern Ireland v Portugal
7/9/94	Latvia v Rep. of Ireland
9/10/94	Latvia v Portugal
12/10/94	Austria v Northern Ireland
12/10/94	Rep. of Ireland v Liechtenstein
13/11/94	Portugal v Austria
15/11/94	Liechtenstein v Latvia
16/11/94	Northern Ireland v Rep. of Ireland
18/12/94	Portugal v Liechtenstein
29/3/95	Rep. of Ireland v Northern Ireland
29/3/95	Austria v Latvia
26/4/95	Rep. of Ireland v Portugal
26/4/95	Latvia v Northern Ireland
26/4/95	Austria v Liechtenstein
3/6/95	Portugal v Latvia
4/6/95	Liechtenstein v Rep. of Ireland

The Fixtures – continued

7/6/95	Northern Ireland v Latvia	29/3/95	Bulgaria v Wales	16/11/94	Greece v San Marino
11/6/95	Rep. of Ireland v Austria	29/3/95	Albania v Moldova	16/11/94	Finland v Faeroe Islands
15/8/95	Liechtenstein v Portugal	26/4/95	Germany v Wales	14/12/94	Finland v San Marino
16/8/95	Latvia v Austria	26/4/95	Moldova v Bulgaria	18/12/94	Greece v Scotland
3/9/95	Portugal v Northern Ireland	26/4/95	Georgia v Albania	29/3/95	Russia v Scotland
6/9/95	Austria v Rep. of Ireland	7/6/95	Bulgaria v Germany	29/3/95	San Marino v Finland
6/9/95	Latvia v Liechtenstein	7/6/95	Wales v Georgia	26/4/95	San Marino v Scotland
11/10/95	Rep. of Ireland v Latvia	7/6/95	Moldova v Albania	26/4/95	Greece v Russia
11/10/95	Austria v Portugal	6/9/95	Germany v Georgia	26/4/95	Faeroe Islands v Finland
11/10/95	Liechtenstein v Northern Ireland	6/9/95	Wales v Moldova	6/5/95	Russia v Faeroe Islands
15/11/95	Portugal v Rep. of Ireland	6/9/95	Albania v Bulgaria	25/5/95	Faeroe Islands v San Marino
15/11/95	Northern Ireland v Austria	7/10/95	Bulgaria v Albania	7/6/95	Faeroe Islands v Scotland
Group Seven		8/10/95	Germany v Moldova	7/6/95	San Marino v Russia
7/9/94	Wales v Albania	11/10/95	Wales v Germany	11/6/95	Finland v Greece
7/9/94	Georgia v Moldova	11/10/95	Georgia v Bulgaria	16/8/95	Scotland v Greece
12/10/94	Moldova v Wales	15/11/95	Germany v Bulgaria	16/8/95	Finland v Russia
12/10/94	Bulgaria v Georgia	15/11/95	Albania v Wales	6/9/95	Scotland v Finland
16/11/94	Albania v Georgia	15/11/95	Moldova v Georgia	6/9/95	Faeroe Islands v Russia
16/11/94	Georgia v Wales	**Group Eight**		6/9/95	San Marino v Greece
16/11/94	Bulgaria v Moldova	7/9/94	Finland v Scotland	11/10/95	Russia v Greece
14/12/94	Wales v Bulgaria	7/9/94	Faeroe Islands v Greece	11/10/95	Scotland v Faeroe Islands
14/12/94	Moldova v Germany	12/10/94	Scotland v Faeroe Islands	15/11/95	Scotland v San Marino
14/12/94	Albania v Georgia	12/10/94	Greece v Finland	15/11/95	Russia v Finland
18/12/94	Germany v Albania	12/10/94	Russia v San Marino	15/11/95	Greece v Faeroe Islands
29/3/95	Georgia v Germany	16/11/94	Scotland v Russia		

GROUP SIX

20 April   *Belfast*   *Att: 7,000*
N.IRELAND 4   (Quinn 5, 33; Lomas 23; Dowie 48)
LIECHTENSTEIN 1   (Hasler 84)

N.Ireland: Wright, Fleming, Taggart, Donaghy, Worthington, Magilton, Wilson, Lomas (O'Neill 80), Hughes, Quinn, Dowie
Liechtenstein: Oehry, Stocker (Hasler 68), C.Frick, Moser, Ospelt, Ritter, Quaderer, Zech, Telser, Matt (Hanselmann 64), M.Frick
Ref: Luinge (Hol)

The march towards the 1996 European Championships got off to an almost premature start at Windsor Park as Northern Ireland secured three points with relative ease against the amateurs of Liechtenstein. The Principality were taking part in their first ever competitive match, having played just a smattering of friendlies since they joined UEFA in 1974. They sneaked a consolation goal near the end of the game through Daniel Hasler and they celebrated it as if it was the championship winner itself. In truth Northern Ireland should have reached double figures as the ball whizzed past Oehry's goal and rattled the three lengths of wood around him on at least three occasions. One such effort cruelly denied Mal Donaghy his first international goal in his 89th appearance.

Reading striker Jimmy Quinn opened the scoring after five minutes, stabbing home Iain Dowie's knockdown from Jim Magilton's cross. It was the perfect start and should have opened the gates but Liechtenstein held out, until the 25th minute. Then Magilton's free-kick cannoned off the wall, Kevin Wilson's follow-up header bounced off the bar and Stephen Lomas was on hand to hook the ball into the net over his right shoulder. Quinn scored his second just after the half hour with a venomous right-footed drive to bring him just three goals short of Colin Clarke's all-time scoring record for Northern Ireland.

As they did in the first half, the Irish had a perfect start to the second when Dowie scored three minutes after the restart. But as much as they dominated, Ireland failed to increase their lead and after Mario Frick's curled shot mid-way through the second half had been comfortably saved, Hasler fired home from 10 yards after a rare corner.

European & World Footballer of the Year

If ever a vote was a foregone conclusion then surely the various polls for the *France Football* European Footballer of the Year and the FIFA World Footballer of the Year for 1993 were a dead cert. The only questions to be answered were just how many of the votes cast would Roberto Baggio take and who would finish second? The votes that placed Baggio in top spot in both polls were emphatic but the runners-up spot was not so clear cut. Dennis Bergkamp took second place in the European award – perhaps surprisingly given his rather ineffectual form since his move to Internazionale, where he has been eclipsed by the effervescent Ruben Sosa, who didn't warrant a single vote in either poll. The Dutchman finished third in the FIFA poll with Barcelona-based Brazilian Romario taking second spot. The discrepancies between the results of the two polls did not stop there, which illustrates further just how opinionated a game football is.

All of the ten places awarded in the FIFA World Player awards went to players currently with European clubs and six were European. Eric Cantona finished third in the European list while not figuring in the FIFA top ten. His Manchester United team mate, Danish goalkeeper Peter Schmeichel, finished fourth in the FIFA list but only equal 12th in the European award. Perhaps embarrassingly, the controversial Ronald Koeman took eighth spot in the FIFA World list. FIFA have taken pains in recent years to promote their Fair Play Awards – and it was Koeman who was involved in perhaps the season's most controversial incident when he blatantly fouled David Platt in Rotterdam in Holland's World Cup qualifying encounter with England. The Barcelona defender did not figure anywhere in the *France Football* voting.

PROFILE: Roberto Baggio (Juventus and Italy)

For so many who make it to the very top their drive and ambition come from a divine love of the game that is instilled at an early age. It is not perhaps surprising then that Roberto Baggio recalls his finest ever performance coming at the tender age of eight, when he scored six times for his local town side in a 7-0 thrashing of Leva. That local side was the place of his birth – Caldogno, a small town in the north of Italy near Vicenza – on 18 February 1967. He was sixth in a line of eight children, and his footballing exploits soon caught the attention of Lanerossi Vicenza for whom he signed and made his debut in the 1982–83 season, playing a single game in their Serie C campaign.

France Football, Footballer of the Year 1993 – How the Votes were Cast

1	Roberto Baggio	Juventus	142
2	Dennis Bergkamp	Internazionale	83
3	Eric Cantona	Manchester United	34
4	Alen Boksic	Lazio	29
5	Michael Laudrup	Barcelona	27
6	Franco Baresi	Milan	24
7	Paolo Maldini	Milan	19
8	Emil Kostadinov	FC Porto	11
9	Stephane Chapuisat	Borussia Dortmund	9
	Ryan Giggs	Manchester United	9
11	Andreas Moller	Juventus	7
12	Ruud Gullit	Milan/Sampdoria	6
	Peter Schmeichel	Manchester United	6
	Hristo Stoichkov	Barcelona	6
15	Basile Boli	Marseille	5
	Rune Bratseth	Werder Bremen	5
17	Enzo Scifo	Torino/Monaco	4
18	Andreas Herzog	Werder Bremen	3
	Ronald Koeman	Barcelona	3
	Jaari Litmanen	Ajax	3
21	Dino Baggio	Juventus	2
	Sergei Kiryakov	Karlsruhe SC	2
	Franck Sauzee	Marseille/Atalanta	2
	Giuseppe Signori	Lazio	2
26	Tomas Brolin	Parma	1
	Martin Dahlin	Borussia Monchengladbach	1
	George Grun	Parma	1
	Stelios Manolas	AEK Athens	1
	Paul McGrath	Aston Villa	1

FIFA World Footballer of the Year 1993

1	Roberto Baggio	Juventus	152
2	Romario	Barcelona	84
3	Dennis Bergkamp	Internazionale	58
4	Peter Schmeichel	Manchester United	29
5	Hristo Stoichkov	Barcelona	22
6	Faustino Asprilla	Parma	21
7	Bebeto	Deportivo La Coruna	16
8	Ronald Koeman	Barcelona	15
9	Anthony Yeboah	Eintracht Frankfurt	13
10	Rai	Paris Saint-Germain	12

Roberto Baggio Player File

Nationality:	Italian
Birthdate:	18 February 1967
Birthplace:	Caldogno
Height:	1.74 m
Weight:	72 kg
Club:	Juventus
Previous Clubs:	LR Vicenza, Fiorentina
Serie A Debut:	21 September 1986, Fiorentina v Sampdoria (2-0)
International Debut:	16 November 1988, Italy v Holland (1-0) in Rome
Honours:	World Cup Finalist 1994, UEFA Cup Winner 1992–93, Italian Cup Finalist 1991–92 (both Juventus), UEFA Cup Finalist 1989–90 (Fiorentina)

OPPOSITE: *Roberto Baggio – European and World Footballer of the Year.*

Within three seasons Baggio had established himself as a regular in the Vicenza line-up, scoring 12 goals in 29 games in his last full season. But at the end of this period – 5 May 1985 to be precise – he suffered an injury to his cruciate ligament in his right knee after scoring against Rimini on the Adriatic coast. A devastating injury to one so young and promising, it was treated philosophically by the quickly maturing patient. Surgery repaired the ligament and a long lay-off let the wound heal and Baggio returned to action a more accomplished and thoughtful player. 'It made me appreciate what I had,' he says in recollection.

As with any national league system, scouts in the lower divisions were already aware of Baggio's potential and his performances earned him a lucrative move to Fiorentina for the start of the 1985–86 season. By the end of it he had logged five appearances for the first team in the Italian Cup and established himself as a firm favourite with Fiorentina President Piercesare Baretti, who declared that he would one day be the best player in Europe. A prophecy that sadly Baretti would not see him realise.

Baggio was to experience further injury problems, though. After making his Serie A debut against Sampdoria in September 1986 he was forced out of action for three months with further knee problems. As the season drew to a close he had figured in the top league five times and made his mark on the score sheet – something he would do with increasing regularity in later seasons – scoring at Napoli in a 1-1 draw. His exploits for Fiorentina soon drew him international recognition and in November 1988 he made his debut for the Azzurri in a 1-0 win over the Dutch. By the end of that 1988–89 season he had two more caps and scored in a 1-1 draw with Uruguay.

During his five years at Fiorentina he made 94 appearances in Serie A, scoring 39 goals, and established himself as a firm favourite with the fans. His self-confessed love affair with them was put under severe pressure when Baggio signed for Juventus – the team Fiorentina fans love to hate – immediately before the start of Italia 90, an event where Baggio would make his arrival on the world scene. It was a double blow for the Artemio Franchi faithful who had seen their side lose the 1990 UEFA Cup final 3-1 on aggregate to Juventus, with Baggio playing in both legs.

The move proved to be a big burden for the rising star – a record transfer fee of £7.5m hanging round his neck and the remorse he felt in deserting his followers – who rioted at the news of his departure. Never was this more evident than when, six months after his move to Turin, Juve travelled to Fiorentina for a Serie A fixture and an event that has already become a part of Scudetto folklore.

The home side took an early lead, but Juve were awarded a penalty when Baggio was tripped inside the penalty area. Baggio

Baggio – Season by Season

Season	Club	Serie	League Apps	League Goals	Cup Apps	Cup Goals	Europe	Europe Apps	Europe Goals	National Apps	National Goals
1982–83	LR Vicenza	C	1	–	–	–					
1983–84	LR Vicenza	C	6	1	4	–					
1984–85	LR Vicenza	C	29	12	5	2					
1985–86	Fiorentina	A	0	5	–	–					
1986–87	Fiorentina	A	5	1	4	1	UEFA:	1	–		
1987–88	Fiorentina	A	27	6	7	3					
1988–89	Fiorentina	A	30	15	10	9				3	1
1989–90	Fiorentina	A	32	17	2	1	UEFA:	11	1	10	4
1990–91	Juventus	A	33	14	5	3	CWC:	8	9	3	2
1991–92	Juventus	A	32	18	9	3				6	5
1992–93	Juventus	A	27	21	8	1	UEFA:	9	6	8	4
1993–94 *	Juventus	A	16	9	2	2	UEFA:	6	3	3	2
Total	Serie C		36	13	9	2					
Total	Fiorentina		94	44	23	14					
Total	Juventus		108	62	23	9					
Total	Serie A		202	101	46	23					
	Totals		238	114	55	25		35	20	33	18

* to date of award

– the normal penalty taker – refused to take the spot kick and so Gigi de Agostini did. He missed, and moments later Baggio was substituted. As he made his way back to the bench he picked up a Fiorentina scarf that had been thrown down at him from the stands and wrapped it around his neck.

Baggio – like his supporters and the enraged Juve fans – needed time to come to terms with one another. But slowly they did and by the end of the first season he had scored 14 goals in 33 Serie A matches, his first coming in a 2-1 defeat at Parma in September of 1990.

'It's always difficult to settle with a new club and I found my situation particularly delicate,' he said then. But time heals and as he found his feet in Turin, his rapport with the Juve fans turned the corner when he began to provide a series of outstanding performances. During these years in Turin, Baggio lived in the shadows of more established world stars, including Michel Platini, and he found it difficult to establish himself in a particular role. Was he a centre forward, a creative inside forward or Platini's playmaker – the player that Juve so desperately sought? Platini himself regarded the maturing Baggio as 'A number nine and a half'. Now – four seasons on – he has licence to roam and this has brought the very best out of him and his team mates.

Baggio himself sees the 1992–93 season as the year that he really arrived and speaks about it with the enthusiasm he mirrors on the field of play. '1992–93 was such a positive year for me in so many ways. I won the UEFA Cup and qualified for USA94 with the national team. I also scored 35 goals, which in Italy is a lot!'

Since joining Juve he has scored at least one hat-trick per season – no mean feat in Italian football. Many of those goals were spectacular – curled or driven in from all extremities of the area. Now captain of Juve he averages a goal every other game and as January 1994 arrived was just one of three current players who have scored over 100 goals in Serie A – all by the ripe old age of 27!

He was a losing UEFA Cup finalist to Juventus in 1990, but almost single-handedly regained the prize for Juve in 1993. In the semi final against Paris Saint-Germain he turned the tide with two goals in the home leg – one a last-minute winner before getting the all important away strike to take them through. In the final, against a vibrant Borussia Dortmund side who had taken a second-minute lead, he was in devastating form and orchestrated a goal for his namesake Dino before helping himself to two to virtually assure Juve of the cup.

Looking back on an already glittering career Baggio recalls his goal against Czechoslovakia for Italy in the 1990 World Cup as his most memorable to date. 'For me, it was just great,' he said. An established and integral part of the national team qualification

Footballer of The Year – Roll of Honour 1956–93 (From *France Football*)

Year	Player	Team	Country	Votes
1956	Stanley Matthews	Blackpool	Eng	47
1957	Alfredo Di Stefano	Real Madrid	Spa	72
1958	Raymond Kopa	Real Madrid	Fra	71
1959	Alfredo Di Stefano	Real Madrid	Spa	80
1960	Luis Suarez	Barcelona	Spa	54
1961	Omar Sivori	Juventus	Ita	46
1962	Josef Masopust	Dukla Prague	Cze	65
1963	Lev Yashin	Dinamo Moscow	USSR	73
1964	Denis Law	Man. United	Sco	61
1965	Eusebio	Benfica	Por	–
1966	Bobby Charlton	Man. United	Eng	81
1967	Florian Albert	Ferencvaros	Hun	68
1968	George Best	Man. United	NIr	61
1969	Gianni Rivera	Milan	Ita	83
1970	Gerd Muller	Bayern Munich	W. Ger	77
1971	Johan Cruyff	Ajax	Hol	116
1972	Franz Beckenbauer	Bayern Munich	W. Ger	81
1973	Johan Cruyff	Barcelona	Hol	96
1974	Johan Cruyff	Barcelona	Hol	116
1975	Oleg Blokhin	Dynamo Kiev	USSR	122
1976	Franz Beckenbauer	Bayern Munich	W. Ger	91
1977	Allan Simonsen	Borussia MG	Den	74
1978	Kevin Keegan	SV Hamburg	Eng	87
1979	Kevin Keegan	SV Hamburg	Eng	118
1980	KH Rummenigge	Bayern Munich	W. Ger	122
1981	KH Rummenigge	Bayern Munich	W. Ger	106
1982	Paolo Rossi	Juventus	Ita	115
1983	Michel Platini	Juventus	Fra	110
1984	Michel Platini	Juventus	Fra	128
1985	Michel Platini	Juventus	Fra	127
1986	Igor Belanov	Dynamo Kiev	USSR	84
1987	Ruud Gullit	Milan	Hol	106
1988	Marco Van Basten	Milan	Hol	129
1989	Marco Van Basten	Milan	Hol	119
1990	Lothar Matthaus	Internazionale	W. Ger	137
1991	Jean-Pierre Papin	Marseille	Fra	141
1992	Marco Van Basten	Milan	Hol	98
1993	Roberto Baggio	Juventus	Ita	142

for USA94 was completed with Baggio contributing 18 goals in his 33 appearances for the Azzurri.

A practising Buddhist for six years, he has a love for the cinema, lists hunting as one of his favourite hobbies and likes the music of the Eagles. Baggio says that his faith gives him 'great energy' above all else and allows him to 'elevate his vital state' and generally to live life in a better way. His chanting in the peace of his own home is also echoed by his now devoted followers in the stands of the Stadia Delle Alpi.

Team of the Year 1993–94

PROFILE: Bulgaria

The Bulgarian national side win hands down in the vote for the Team of the Year for 1993–94. Their astonishing progression to the semi-finals of the World Cup made what was probably the biggest impact on European football in the past two years and ranks alongside the performance of Denmark in winning the 1992 European Championships.

Bulgaria only qualified by the skin of their teeth. Emil Kostadinov's dramatic last-minute winner in Paris last November squeezed Dimitar Penev's team past the French and on the trans-Atlantic haul. Their pre-tournament preparations could hardly have set the faithful at home alight with encouragement as they drew matches with Oman and Kuwait, needing a late equaliser and an own goal to rescue them in both. But succeeding in competition in any arena is about peaking at the right time – it's not how you start, but how you finish. While Bulgaria didn't win the World Cup their achievement in reaching the semi-finals was, to my mind, a greater achievement than reaching the final and even winning it. That was expected of both Brazil and Italy.

Consider the facts. Before the tournament started Bulgaria had not won one of their previous 16 games in five World Cup Finals. Indeed they had managed just six draws and suffered ten defeats, conceding more than three times as many goals as they had scored. Football and winners at football are based on tradition. Thus Brazil won, Italy reached the final – both sides making record appearances at that point. Tradition for Bulgaria was not to win, and to break with history is a monumental achievement.

That wasn't all. Internal strife and a precarious financial crisis within the national game meant what amounted to second-class accommodation at a first-class tournament, which would have done little to encourage the team. Indeed by qualifying for the World Cup Finals the squad had increased the cash burden on the Bulgarian Football Union, but in the end will probably provide a regeneration of the game within the stadia of Sofia, Plovdiv, Bourgas, Varna and Blagoevgrad.

Tradition in the Bulgarian sense seemed to be going with history when Nigeria fired a three-goal salvo in the first Group D game in Dallas. Few heads turned, apart from noticing the power of the new emerging nation. Few had realised that the real emerging nation was about to do just that. Emerge! Greece followed their horrendous warm-up series of matches with a 4-0 thrashing by the Argentines, and were in no frame of mind to take on Bulgarians needing nothing less than victory.

Now, too, Hristo Stoichkov was about to announce his arrival on the world stage. Already a multi-millionaire with a string of

Bulgarian manager Dimitar Penev.

businesses in his native Sofia, Stoichkov had made his fortune in Barcelona. The Iberian peninsula was indeed a pre-finals training ground for a number of Bulgarians making their impact slowly in Spain and Portugal. But it was an early penalty conversion by Stoichkov, playing with an unrelenting passion throughout the tournament, that fuelled the spark that brought the country's first win – and by a margin of four goals as the Greeks were totally outclassed.

Suddenly the so-called quality players started to play and

Bulgaria's World Cup Finals Record

1962 – Chile
Bulgaria	v	Argentina	0-1
Bulgaria	v	Hungary	1-6
Bulgaria	v	England	0-0

1966 – England
Bulgaria	v	Brazil	0-2
Bulgaria	v	Portugal	0-3
Bulgaria	v	Hungary	1-3

1970 – Mexico
Bulgaria	v	Peru	2-3
Bulgaria	v	West Germany	2-5
Bulgaria	v	Morocco	1-1

1974 – West Germany
Bulgaria	v	Sweden	0-0
Bulgaria	v	Uruguay	1-1
Bulgaria	v	Holland	1-4

1986 – Mexico
Bulgaria	v	Italy	1-1
Bulgaria	v	South Korea	1-1
Bulgaria	v	Argentina	0-2
Bulgaria	v	Mexico	0-2

1994 – USA
Bulgaria	v	Nigeria	0-3
Bulgaria	v	Greece	4-0
Bulgaria	v	Argentina	2-0
Bulgaria	v	Mexico	1-1 *3-1 on pens*
Bulgaria	v	Germany	2-1
Bulgaria	v	Italy	1-2
Bulgaria	v	Sweden	0-4

deliver quality. Good technical players started to find the vision for threaded passes that cut angles of delight through defences. And players of potential started to do what so many fail to do in the modern game – realise their potential. Iordan Lechkov – a competent player in the German colours of Hamburg – turned into one of the stars of the tournament and his diving header that sent the World Champions home ensured that he will be well remembered around the Bundesliga grounds in the coming season. Goalkeeper Borislav Mikhailov produced vital saves that produced talk of his ability and not of his big-money hair transplant. And completing the spine of the side was defender Trifon Ivanov, who timed tackles to perfection and had a great ability to play intelligent passes out of defence while under the greatest of pressure. The one disappointment throughout this was Emil Kostadinov, who might have made a big difference if the spark had lit his particular fire.

The defeat of Argentina in the last group match finally opened eyes. Stoichkov again opened a door that was firmly bolted by Borimov in the final moments. What had looked like a traditionally quick return for Bulgaria had be turned around into second-phase qualification, despite having to play nearly half the match with ten men.

Mexico, in Mexico in 1986, had ended Bulgaria's last appearance in the World Cup Finals. Ironically they were the opposition at the start of the knock-out phase. Stoichkov again set the game alight, Bulgaria held on with great resolve after a quick equaliser for the South Americans, and with Lechkov's penalty-kick won the shoot-out.

Faced with a match against the World Cup holders, few gave Bulgaria much chance. Most observers expected the Eastern Europeans to bow out gracefully as Germany moved towards what would have been their sixth final appearance in eight events. Matthaus' penalty at the start of the second half looked to have put the motion into gear but suddenly, as the Germans eased off and allowed the Bulgarians to do what they are good at – play – there was inner belief as a few efforts troubled Illgner. Then an incredible free-kick from Stoichkov – who else? – was followed by Lechkov's diving header and the impossible dream was becoming highly possible.

That it failed at the penultimate stage, to an average Italian side, was down to a combination of Baggio magic and the big occasion perhaps being just too much for the Bulgars to cope with. Tradition perhaps got the better of them. Even so, a penalty just before the interval, by you know who, reduced the deficit and in less forgiving heat another story might, and I expect probably would, have unfolded.

'This is the best Bulgarian side in history,' claimed Stoichkov before the encounter with the Germans. Of that there can be little doubt, and it has largely been due to the movement of better players to the Western scene since the fall of the Berlin Wall. That fall had led to other barriers being breached, the most important being the one of inferiority. The best Bulgarian players can now play alongside the best in Europe and hone their skills further.

All this seems a very long way from the dark days of Bulgarian football when, in 1985, the likes of Stoichkov and Mikhailov were banned for life, with four others, by the Bulgarian Football Union after a brawl in the cup final between Levski Spartak and CSKA Sofia. When it became apparent that they had effectively removed the heart of the national side and that there were no starlets waiting in the wings, the ban was lifted. That debt has now been fully repaid.

The squares and streets of Sofia and other Bulgarian cities were throbbing with supporters who have waited long and hoped hard for success in the international arena. After the quarter-final defeat of Germany, President Zhelyv Zhelev addressed the nation, and when the team arrived home to a tumultuous welcome the squad were awarded the Stara Planina, the highest honour possible for a citizen of the country.

But there will inevitably be a price to pay and one that the ruling Communist Party and BFU must work together on. With all of this success it seems likely that more players will move abroad – only nine of the 22-man World Cup squad were home-based players – but that should be the spur for more talent to

![Bulgaria celebrate victory over Germany.]

Bulgaria celebrate victory over Germany.

come through the ranks and tread the paths now being carved out by the current team. The large levy imposed by the Government on foreign transfers must be handed back into the game to ensure this happens.

Now that Bulgaria have arrived they face their toughest test, as they strive to create that much-needed winning tradition. In a European Championship qualifying group that also contains, ironically, Germany, they need to heed a lesson from Denmark and realise that success in one competition doesn't automatically guarantee it in another. The question left answered, though, was posed by Stoichkov, when asked if he thought that the Bulgarians had played like gods. 'No,' he answered, 'But perhaps God was a Bulgarian?'

One to Watch

PROFILE: Jurgen Klinsmann

You either hate him or you hate him. Indeed there can't be a player anywhere in Europe who is more likely to infuriate opposing fans than Jurgen Klinsmann. But there can be no doubting that the 30-year-old striker is a player of the highest quality and could be a real snip for his new employers at Tottenham Hotspur at £2m despite approaching his playing twilight years. The move from Monaco will provide him with the biggest challenge of his career as he lines up as the jewel in what has basically been a poor side in recent years. But the arrival of Klinsmann and Romanian Ilie Dumitrescu and the return from injury of England international Teddy Sheringham should ensure that the North London club have one of the most potent attacks in Europe.

Talk of feigning injury brings a wry smile to the face of Klinsmann, the former Stuttgart, Internazionale and Monaco player – 'I never dive, I always go straight for goal,' he insists. It is a view that Milan defender Alessandro Costacurta for one will not share. Klinsmann's death throes saw to it that the Costacurta was dismissed from the pitch in the Champions' Cup semi-final and forced to miss Milan's Final victory. Replays of the event can only lead one to be sceptical about Klinsmann's claims. Ironic then that Klinsmann gave referees his personal backing during the World Cup Finals and supported their hard-line stand saying; 'I am glad to see that officials have been ordered to caution players who feign injury. It is good for the game.'

But while there are doubts about his integrity, there can be none regarding his goal-scoring ability and touch on the ball. A willingness to stay on his feet during Germany's five games in America brought him five goals and a cluster of near misses as he produced some of the finest of his 65 games in a German shirt.

His relaxed demeanour off the field of play may well be responsible for his incisiveness on it. After the 1990 World Cup Finals he threatened to retire and go back-packing around North America to experience his other great love – the environment. He is a keen ecologist and a supporter of the Green Party, and now spends much of his spare time helping children in strife-torn regions such as Sarajevo and Uganda. Born in Geislingen, the son of a pretzel baker, Klinsmann claims that he is not motivated by money but with a reported £15,000 per week salary that's easy to say.

Klinsmann the player had started his career with Stuttgart before making a high-profile move to Internazionale in 1989 for £1.3m. A year later he won a World Cup medal and added a UEFA Cup medal the following year. Two years on the French Riviera with Monaco failed to bring him any more honours, although his goals did help the French club reach that fateful Champions' Cup semi-final.

Klinsmann says he chose Tottenham because of the challenge of playing in the Premiership and there could be no greater challenge as the season started with Spurs facing deduction of six vital points for financial irregularities. His scoring prowess should ensure the White Hart Lane faithful their future in the top flight, while the very mention of the name Klinsmann is sure to bring howls of derision from supporters around the rest of the country.

OPPOSITE: *No looking back for Jurgen Klinsmann – a star being reborn at Tottenham Hotspur.*

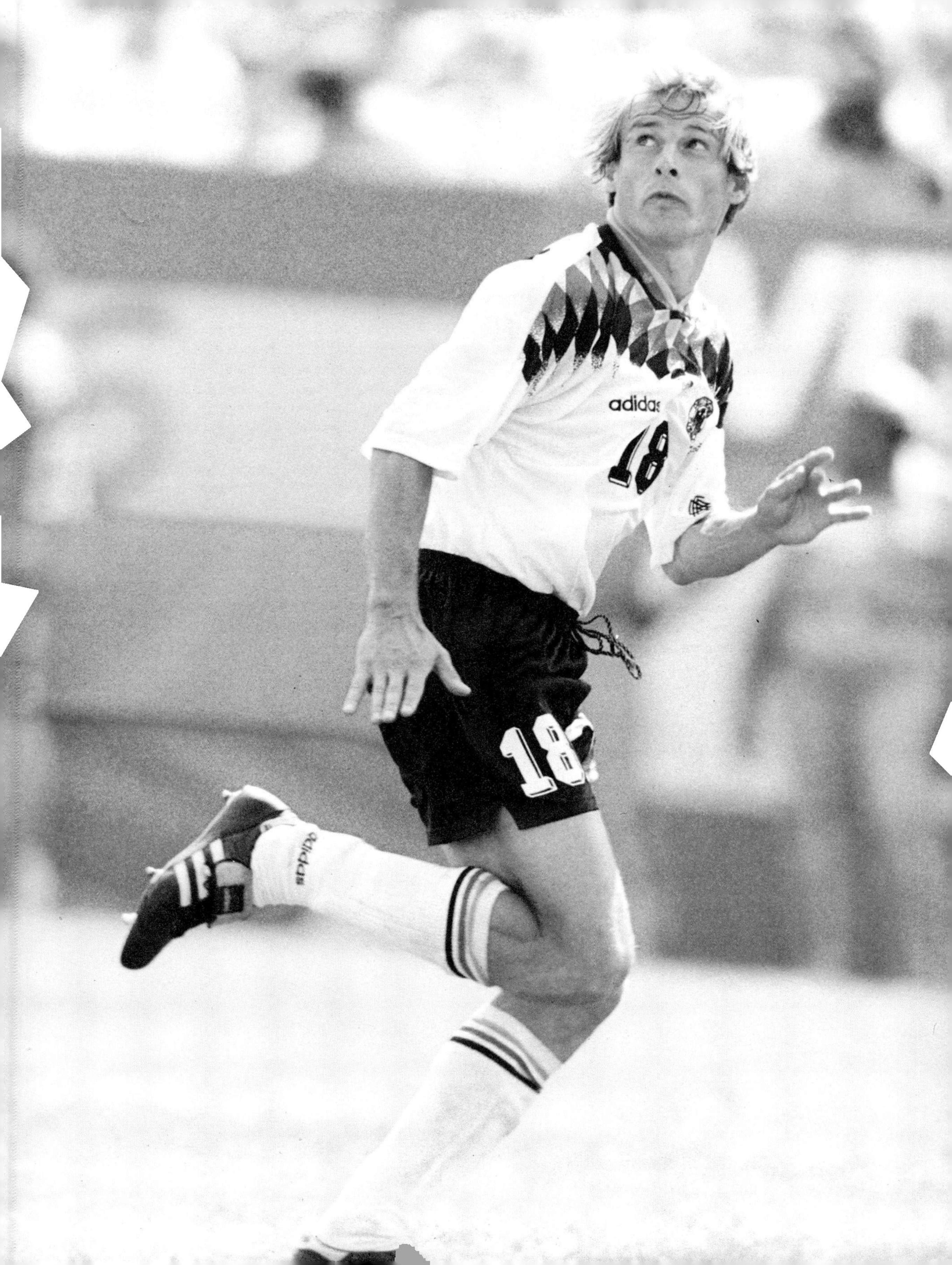
adidas
18
18
adidas

One to Watch

PROFILE: Rashidi Yekini

A lasting memory of the 1994 World Cup Finals will be of Rashidi Yekini celebrating his opening goal for Nigeria in the 3-0 defeat of Bulgaria – standing in the back of the goal with his fists clenched tight, showing just how much pleasure the goal gave him and his countrymen.

Scoring goals is a happy knack that Yekini has always had, and his avalanche of them during the African Cup of Nations and World Cup qualifiers inevitably led to his being crowned the African Footballer of the Year. Yekini, now 29, thus joins an elite roll of honour that includes a number of players now based in Europe, such as Paris Saint-Germain's Liberian George Weah and former Marseille striker Abedi Pele of Ghana. Such prominence has earned Yekini a well-paid job in the port of Piraeus with his new club, Olympiakos.

Yekini had already earned his reputation within Nigeria and neighbouring borders long before he moved to be part of the European scene. Nigeria's top side, Shooting Stars, were one of three leading African clubs to feature in Yekini's list of employers. But his career nearly went disastrously wrong as a move to Abiola Babes finished a year later, when the club folded. His talents had not been forgotten and he was snapped up by Africa Sport of the Ivory Coast. That move ultimately led to a transfer to Portuguese side Vitoria Setubal three seasons later, aided by Africa Sport's president Simplice Zinsou. The new surroundings and new language didn't help in a dramatic first season, with Vitoria relegated as the Portuguese first division was reduced in size. But despite these setbacks the Nigerian had already made his mark by scoring 13 goals in 24 appearances. After finishing fifth in the Division of Honour in 1991–92, Yekini's goals helped his club bounce back into the top flight by virtue of finishing third in 1992–93.

Goals continued to flow and two against Sporting Lisbon opened his season's account, to which he added a further 19 to make him the league's top scorer. Those goals helped Vitoria recover some lost pride, lifting them to sixth position and only just missing out on a UEFA Cup placing. Added to this, eight goals for Nigeria helped them brush aside the opposition to qualify for the World Cup Finals and provide another stage for the striker known as The Kaduna Bull on which to perform.

His contract with Vitoria expired in June, and Greece's most popular club, Olympiakos, eventually won his signature before the start of the World Cup, as they continue to put financial restrictions and huge debts to one side in an effort to break the dominance of AEK Athens. If they succeed then you can be sure that Yekini's goals will be a major factor.

Rashidi Yekini only knows one way to goal!

One to Watch

PROFILE: Julio Salinas

When you average just about a goal a game you'd expect to be one of the first names on your manager's team-sheet. But for Julio Salinas that hasn't been the case. Indeed at some points in his career it has seemed as if Salinas has had more international caps than Barcelona appearances to his credit. Now all that is about to change, as the 32-year-old Salinas swaps the south coast of Spain for the north-west in a transfer to Deportivo La Coruna.

His predicament is pretty exceptional, especially as he is one of national manager Javier Clemente's first choices when it comes to naming a squad. Clemente is not known for his like of attacking players, wishing to flood the midfield and get players into the box late on. Nevertheless Salinas made his own impression on Group C at the World Cup Finals. Despite being born a Basque, Salinas did not find it difficult to gain acceptance in Catalonia, where he has been used by Barcelona coach Johan Cruyff largely as replacement cover for Brazilian Romario and Bulgarian Hristo Stoichkov: two important reasons why Salinas was unable to make a regular breakthrough into the Barca team.

Salinas was 20 when he joined the junior side of Atletic Bilbao, and he scored 17 goals in his first season in the regional third division. Those exploits earned him two outings in the first team the following season, as Bilbao surged to the first of two back-to-back Spanish title triumphs. How ironic that a decade later Salinas would again find himself playing minor roles in another championship-winning side.

After he finished league top scorer the then national manager, Miguel Munoz, awarded him his first cap, against the USSR in February 1986. Salinas opened the scoring in the 2-0 win and subsequently found himself lining up alongside Emilio Butragueno for the 1986 World Cup Finals.

Despite the clamour for his signature, Salinas played out his contract with Atletic Bilbao but in 1987 he moved to Atletico Madrid. Fifteen goals later he found that the capital was only a temporary stop-over en route to the Nou Camp. The partnership with Gary Lineker didn't work too well, and when the England striker left for Tottenham, Salinas believed his chance had arrived. But since then Cruyff has always managed to have a better striking partnership to limit chances for Salinas during his six years at the club. Ironically those six years have proved to be the most successful in Barcelona's history, with a hat-trick of league championships and a long-awaited victory in the Champions' Cup.

Julio Salinas, playing one of his last games for Spain as a Barcelona player, holds off the challenge of Park Jung Bae of South Korea.

Eventually Barcelona decided that Salinas could move on, and curiously it is a move that has every chance of back-firing. Come May 1995 his former employers may be regretting letting him go. Barcelona have managed to sneak the title away from Real Madrid (twice) and Deportivo on the last day of the season in each of the past three years. The addition of Salinas to the squad who finished third and then second may be just the impetus that Deportivo need to go one better in the coming season.

Record Breaker

PROFILE: Oleg Salenko

Six games, six goals – not a bad start to any international career. But those simple statistics hide the fact that their deliverer, Oleg Salenko, also made his mark in the record books by scoring five of them in that sixth international appearance for Russia, and in doing so set a World Cup Finals record for the most goals scored by any one player in a single game.

Yet Salenko had not made the starting line-up for the World Cup opener with Brazil in Group B – indeed he was only included in the squad due to the refusal of several star players to travel to the finals under coach Pavel Sadyrin. Salenko, a Ukrainian based in Spain, had opted to play for Russia on the break-up of the Soviet Union, managed to get off the bench early in the second half but couldn't make any difference to the score as Russia went down 0-2. After the game a stormy exchange of words between Sadyrin and Yuran, the player Salenko replaced, meant that Salenko stayed in the starting line-up for the second group match against Sweden. The Valencia player repaid the selection by converting a fourth-minute penalty, but once again the Russians crumbled and Salenko found himself on the losing side.

The final group match, against Cameroon, left Russia needing a win and a substantial number of goals to have any chance of making the second round. Thanks to Salenko they achieved the win and the goals but unfortunately not the qualification. Salenko's first goal came in the 16th minute with a shot under the advancing keeper, Songo'o. He added another two before the interval to complete a hat-trick, first taking advantage of woeful marking after a quick free-kick to walk the ball into the net, and then from the penalty spot. Salenko continued where he left off in the second half with goals in the 72nd and 75th minutes – a shot and a lob displaying the player's full repertoire of skills – which might have included a sixth had his header been better directed shortly thereafter.

Salenko had no idea of his achievement – the first he learned of it was from the PA announcer in the Stanford Stadium who, satisfying the Americans' thirst for statistics, announced it to a cheering stadium as the fateful 75th-minute goal flew past a bemused Songo'o.

Salenko, now 24, starts the 1994–95 season with a new club and the expectations of him will be greater than before. He signed for Valencia as the finals were due to start, having scored 16 goals for perennial relegation candidates Logrones – no mean achievement. Valencia, Deportivo La Coruna and Atletico Madrid battled it out for the player's signature, with Valencia finally agreeing to pay £1.3m for his services. Logrones were no doubt kicking themselves after his five-goal salvo, and equally the player may have wished he had waited until after the Finals to secure an even better deal for himself. But the Rioja-based Logrones made a handsome profit on the £400,000 they paid Dynamo Kiev for his signature.

Russian record breaker Oleg Salenko.

Salenko's only memory of a hat-trick before the one he scored in the first half against Cameroon was of another 6-1 win – this time in the Soviet Cup final of 1990, when Dynamo Kiev thrashed Lokomotiv Moscow. Ironically, it was Yuran who had also limited Salenko's chances in the Kiev side to that point, at a time when Salenko might have been playing for Tottenham in the English first division under Terry Venables had the British Home Office not rejected Spurs' application for a work permit. So Salenko, who had won two Ukrainian caps, headed south to Logrones, where he was among the lowest soccer wage earners in the country. Now he will find himself alongside the top earners and the Valencia fans will be hoping that he can maintain his scoring form and breathe much-needed life into the club, who topped the Spanish league for the early part of the season but fell away in dramatic fashion.

28 June – World Cup Group B
Stanford Stadium, San Francisco

CAMEROON	1	RUSSIA	6
Milla 47		Salenko 16, 41, 45pen, 72, 75	
		Radchenko 81	

Att: 74,914

European Cups Format and Rankings

The possibility of a European Super League took a step nearer reality during the past season with the restructuring of the Champions' Cup. The financial rewards that have allowed clubs like Barcelona and Milan to make nearly £3m from last season's UEFA Champions' League games alone have been a major influence in the decision. The top clubs have been calling for a guarantee of more games to ensure their income from the competition. While the normal knock-out competition offers excitement it has become a risky environment for many clubs who, like Milan for example, have invested huge sums of money in players to ensure success. But of course, players and teams can have off-days and off-days can happen on European nights.

Thus for 1994–95 the Champions' Cup entrant list is limited to the top 24 countries' champion clubs. The top eight sides, including the holders, gain automatic entry into the UEFA Champions' League. The remaining 16 sides are drawn against one another for a knock-out preliminary round to determine the last eight to qualify for the Champions' League. The 16 clubs form four leagues of four teams to play each other home and away. At the end of these games the top two sides in each league move into a knock-out phase with two-legged quarter- and semi-finals to produce the two finalists.

The 24 'elite' clubs are decided by a ranking list. This is determined by awarding each country's champion club a 'coefficient' which determines positions in the ranking list. Coefficients have been used in this way in past seasons but there are slight changes to the way they are calculated from 1994–95. Two points are awarded for each win and one point for a draw. In addition bonus points are awarded for teams reaching the quarter-finals, semi-finals and final. Note that results from preliminary round matches are not taken into account. Up until last season, teams reaching the UEFA Champions' League were awarded two bonus points; however from this season this has been reduced to a single bonus point. The points are calculated over a five-year period which is taken up to the start of the preceding season. Thus for the 1994–95 season the five seasons in question run from 1989–90 to 1993–94. Obviously this system falls flat on its face if a club make their debut in Europe. Therefore, each country's coefficient is also calculated, the two numbers compared and the highest value taken as the club coefficient.

The ranking list for the Champions' Cup is shown here. The teams in places 1 to 24 are the sides that take part in the Champions' Cup. The teams ranked 1-8 qualify directly for the league stage. Teams ranked 9 to 16 are drawn against those teams ranked 17 to 24. These form the Champions' Cup preliminary round. This means that from 1994–95 there will be 77 matches played: 16 qualifying matches, 48 group matches, eight quarter-finals, four semi-finals and a final.

For the teams who fail to make the cut for the Champions' Cup, the UEFA Cup has been expanded and teams ranked 25 and lower compete here. These teams play in the preliminary round on the basis of their position in the UEFA Cup seeding list. The final ranking list numbering from 1 to 91 is compiled from the coefficients of the total field, ie, those who qualify for the UEFA Cup as a matter of course, and those who qualify as domestic champions. The best 37 clubs qualify directly for the first round, leaving the remaining 54 teams to play out a new preliminary round. For this draw, these teams are allocated to groups based on geographical criteria.

The Cup-Winners' Cup remains virtually unchanged. The best 20 clubs from the ranked list of 44 qualify for the first round, with the top 16 sides being seeded. The remaining 24 clubs play out the preliminary round and the 12 winners progress to the first round.

The day before the draw for the 1994–95 competitions UEFA's Club Competitions' Committee met and made a number of revisions to their original decisions as far as the calculations of the coefficients were concerned. It was decided that the coefficient of an association that had not been represented at least three times, and by three different clubs, in the previous five seasons would be zero. This change was made to ensure that the overall standard of domestic football would be reflected within a country and not the results of just one or two dominant clubs. The various ranking lists given below are based on the original calculations released in July. In practical terms there is only one change in that Luxembourg's Avenir Beggen were promoted into the Champions' Cup at the expense of Slovan Bratislava who were included in the UEFA Cup draw.

UEFA Champions' League Ranking List

1	Milan	Ita	24	Silkeborg	Den
2	Ajax	Hol	25	Avenir Beggen	Lux
3	Manchester United	Eng	26	Rosenborg	Nor
4	Bayern Munich	Ger	27	Levski Sofia	Bul
5	Barcelona	Esp	28	Dinamo Minsk	Bls
6	Benfica	Por	29	Apollon	Cyp
7	Spartak Moscow	Rus	30	IA Akranes	Ice
8	RSC Anderlecht	Bel	31	Linfield	Nir
9	Paris Saint-Germain	Fra	32	FC Jazz	Fin
10	Rangers	Sco	33	SK Teuta	Alb
11	Legia Warsaw	Pol	34	Olympia Ljubljana	Slo
12	AS Casino Salzburg	Aut	35	Skonto Riga	Lat
13	IFK Gothenburg	Swe	36	Shamrock Rovers	Ire
14	Dynamo Kiev	Ukr	37	Hibernians	Mal
15	Steaua Bucharest	Rom	38	Bangor City	Wal
16	Galatasaray	Tur	39	Ararat Yerevan	Arm
17	Sparta Prague	Cze	40	Turan Tauz	Aze
18	Hajduk Split	Cro	41	GI Gotu	Far
19	AEK Athens	Gre	42	Dynamo Tbilisi	Geo
20	Maccabi Haifa	Isr	43	FC Romar	Lit
21	Slovan Bratislava	Svk	44	Vardar Skopje	Mac
22	Servette	Swi	45	Zimbru	Mol
23	Vac FC Samsung	Hun	46	Skonto Riga	Est

UEFA Cup Ranking List

1	Juventus	Ita			
2	Marseille	Fra	36	FC Tirol Innsbruck	Aus
3	Parma	Ita	37	Dinamo Bucharest	Rom
4	Lazio	Ita	38	Aberdeen	Sco
5	Napoli	Ita	39	Motherwell	Sco
6	Internazionale	Ita	40	Inter Bratislava	Svk
7	Real Madrid	Esp	41	AIK Stockholm	Swe
8	Borussia Dortmund	Ger	42	FC Copenhagen	Den
9	FC Nantes	Fra	43	Fenerbahce	Tur
10	Bordeaux	Fra	44	Aris Salonika	Gre
11	AS Cannes	Fra	45	FC Aarau	Sui
12	Bayer Leverkusen	Ger	46	Univ. Craiova	Rom
13	Kaiserslautern	Ger	47	Rapid Bucharest	Rom
14	Eintracht Frankfurt	Ger	48	Shaktor Donetsk	Ukr
15	Deportivo La Coruna	Esp	49	CSKA Sofia	Bul
16	Athletic Bilbao	Esp	50	Gornik Zabrze	Pol
17	Blackburn Rovers	Eng	51	GKS Katowice	Pol
18	Aston Villa	Eng	52	Trelleborgs	Swe
19	Newcastle United	Eng	53	OB	Den
20	Sporting Lisbon	Por	54	Slavia Prague	Cze
21	Boavista	Por	55	Kispest Honved	Hun
22	Maritimo	Por	56	Shumen	Bul
23	Trabzonspor	Tur	57	Bekescsaba	Hun
24	Seraing	Bel	58	Hapoel Beersheba	Isr
25	Charleroi	Bel	59	Lillestrom SK	Nor
26	Royal Antwerp	Bel	60	MyPa	Fin
27	Admira Wacker	Aut	61	Inter Cardiff	Wal
28	Rotor Volograd	Rus	62	Anorthosis	Cyp
29	Dynamo Moscow	Rus	63	FH	Ice
30	Tekstilchik	Rus	64	Mura Murska	Slo
31	FC Sion	Swi	65	Portadown	Nir
32	Olympiakos	Gre	66	Cork City	Irl
33	Vitesse	Hol	67	Valletta	Mal
34	PSV	Hol	68	CS Grevenmacher	Lux
35	FC Twente	Hol	69	HB	Far

Cup-Winners' Cup Ranking List

1	Sampdoria	Ita	23	Ferencvaros	Hun
2	Arsenal	Eng	24	Maribor Branik	Slo
3	Werder Bremen	Ger	25	Pirin	Bul
4	AJ Auxerre	Fra	26	Maccabi Tel Aviv	Isr
5	FC Porto	Por	27	Bodo/Glimt	Nor
6	Real Zaragoza	Esp	28	Fandok	Bls
7	Chelsea	Eng	29	HJK Helsinki	Fin
8	Club Bruges	Bel	30	Omonia Nicosia	Cyp
9	CSKA Moscow	Rus	31	IBK	Ice
10	Brondby IF	Den	32	FC Tirana	Alb
11	Feyenoord	Hol	33	Bangor	Nir
12	FK Austria	Aut	34	Floriana	Mal
13	Dundee United	Sco	35	Zhalgiris Vilnius	Lit
14	Panathinaikos	Gre	36	Sligo Rovers	Irl
15	Tatran Presov	Svk	37	F91 Dudelange	Lux
16	Croatia Zagreb	Cro	38	Barry Town	Wal
17	Besiktas	Tur	39	Viktoria Zizkov	Cze
18	Grasshopper Club	Swi	40	B71 Sandoyar	Far
19	Gloria Bistrita	Rom	41	FC Schaan	Lie
20	Chernomorets Odessa	Ukr	42	Tiligul Tiraspol	Mol
21	LKS Lodz	Pol	43	Norma Tallinn	Est
22	IFK Norrkoping	Swe	44	Olimpija Riga	Lat

EUROPEAN CUPS: FORMAT AND RANKINGS   43

Qualifiers by Country

Country	Champions' Cup	Cup-Winners' Cup	UEFA Cup
Albania		SK Tirana	SK Teuta
Armenia			Ararat Erevan
Austria	SV Casino Salzburg	FK Austria	Admira Wacker, FC Tirol-Innsbruck
Azerbaijan			Turan Tauz
Belarus		FC Fandok	Dinamo Minsk
Belgium	RSC Anderlecht	Club Bruges	Seraing, Royal Antwerp, Charleroi
Bulgaria		Pirin Blagoevgrad	Levski Sofia, CSKA Sofia, Shumen
Croatia	Hajduk Split	Croatia Zagreb	
Cyprus		Omonia Nicosia	Apollon, Anorthosis
Czech Republic	Sparta Prague	Viktoria Zizkov	Slavia Prague
Denmark	Silkeborg	Brondby IF	FC Copenhagen, OB
England	Manchester United	Arsenal, Chelsea	Blackburn Rovers, Newcastle United, Aston Villa
Estonia		Norma Tallinin	Flora Tallinin
Faeroe Islands		B71 Sandoyar	GI Gota, HB
Finland		HJK Helsinki	FC Jazz, MyPa
France	Paris Saint-Germain	AJ Auxerre	Marseille, Bordeaux, FC Nantes, AS Cannes
FYR Macedonia			Vardar Skopje
Georgia			Dynamo Tbilisi
Germany	Bayern Munich	Werder Bremen	Kaiserslautern, Bayer Leverkusen, Borussia Dortmund, Eintracht Frankfurt
Greece	AEK Athens	Panathinaikos	Olympiakos, Aris Salonika
Holland	Ajax	Feyenoord	PSV, Vitesse, FC Twente
Hungary	Vac FC Samsung	Ferencvaros	Bekescsaba, Kispest Honved
Iceland		IBK	IA Akranes, FH
Israel	Maccabi Haifa	Maccabi Tel Aviv	Hapoel Beersheba
Italy	Milan	Sampdoria	Juventus, Parma, Lazio, Napoli, Internazionale
Latvia		Olimpija Riga	Skonto Riga
Liechtenstein		FC Schaan	
Lithuania		Zhalgiris Vilnius	FC Romar
Luxembourg	Avenir Beggen	F91 Dudelange	CS Grevenmacher
Malta		Floriana	Hibernians, Valletta
Moldova		Tiligul Tiraspol	Zimbru
Northern Ireland		Bangor	Linfield, Portadown
Norway		Bodo/Glimt	Rosenborg, Lillestrom SK
Poland	Legia Warsaw	LKS Lodz	Gornik Zabrze, GKS Katowice
Portugal	Benfica	FC Porto	Sporting Lisbon, Boavista, Maritimo
Republic of Ireland		Sligo Rovers	Shamrock Rovers, Cork City
Romania	Steaua Bucharest	Gloria Bistrita	Universitatea Craiova, Rapid Bucharest, Dinamo Bucharest
Russia	Spartak Moscow	CSKA Moscow	Rotor Volograd, Dynamo Moscow, Tekstilchik
San Marino			
Scotland	Rangers	Dundee United	Aberdeen, Motherwell
Slovakia		Tatran Presov	Slovan Bratislava, Inter Bratislava
Slovenia		Maribor Branik	Olijmpia Ljubljana, Mura Murska
Spain	Barcelona	Real Zaragoza	Deportivo La Coruna, Real Madrid, Athletic Bilbao
Sweden	IFK Gothenberg	IFK Norrkoping	Trellborgs, AIK Stockholm
Switzerland	Servette	Grasshopper Club	FC Sion, FC Aarau
Turkey	Galatasaray	Besiktas	Fenerbahce, Trabzonspor
Ukraine	Dynamo Kiev	Chernomorets Odessa	Shaktor Donetsk
Wales		Barry Town	Bangor City, Inter Cardiff

UEFA Champions' League Draw 1994-95

Designated match days for all ties are Wednesdays.

Preliminary Round
10 August and 24 August 1994

			1st leg	2nd leg	Agg.
AEK Athens (Gre)	v	Rangers (Sco)	2-0	1-0	3-0
Avenir Beggen (Lux)	v	Galatasaray (Tur)	1-5	0-4	1-9
Legia Warsaw (Pol)	v	Hajduk Split (Cro)	0-1	0-4	0-5
Maccabi Haifa (Isr)	v	SV Casino Salzburg (Aus)	1-2	1-3	2-5
Paris Saint-Germain (Fra)	v	VAC FC Samsung (Hun)	3-0	2-1	5-1
Silkeborg (Den)	v	Dynamo Kiev (Ukr)	0-0	1-3	1-3
Sparta Prague (Cze)	v	IFK Gothenburg (Swe)	1-0	0-2	1-2
Steaua Bucharest (Rom)	v	Servette (Swi)	4-1	1-1	5-2

Group A
14/09/94
| Galatasaray | v | Barcelona |
| Manchester United | v | IFK Gothenburg |

28/09/94
| Galatasaray | v | Manchester United |
| IFK Gothenburg | v | Barcelona |

19/10/94
| IFK Gothenburg | v | Galatasaray |
| Manchester United | v | Barcelona |

02/11/94
| Galatasaray | v | IFK Gothenburg |
| Barcelona | v | Manchester United |

23/11/94
| IFK Gothenburg | v | Manchester United |
| Galatasaray | v | Barcelona |

07/12/94
| Manchester United | v | Galatasaray |
| Barcelona | v | IFK Gothenburg |

Group B
14/09/94
| Dynamo Kiev | v | Spartak Moscow |
| Paris Saint-Germain | v | Bayern Munich |

28/09/94
| Bayern Munich | v | Dynamo Kiev |
| Spartak Moscow | v | Paris Saint-Germain |

19/10/94
| Spartak Moscow | v | Bayern Munich |
| Dynamo Kiev | v | Paris Saint-Germain |

02/11/94
| Bayern Munich | v | Spartak Moscow |
| Paris Saint-Germain | v | Dynamo Kiev |

23/11/94
| Spartak Moscow | v | Dynamo Kiev |
| Bayern Munich | v | Paris Saint-Germain |

07/12/94
| Dynamo Kiev | v | Bayern Munich |
| Paris Saint-Germain | v | Spartak Moscow |

Group C
14/09/94
| Hajduk Split | v | Benfica |
| RSC Anderlecht | v | Steaua Bucharest |

28/09/94
| Steaua Bucharest | v | Hajduk Split |
| Benfica | v | RSC Anderlecht |

19/10/94
| Benfica | v | Steaua Bucharest |
| Hajduk Split | v | RSC Anderlecht |

02/11/94
| Steaua Bucharest | v | Benfica |
| RSC Anderlecht | v | Hajduk Split |

23/11/94
| Benfica | v | Hajduk Split |
| Steaua Bucharest | v | RSC Anderlecht |

07/12/94
| Hajduk Split | v | Steaua Bucharest |
| RSC Anderlecht | v | Benfica |

Group D
14/09/94
| SV Casino Salzburg | v | AEK Athens |
| Ajax | v | Milan |

28/09/94
| AEK Athens | v | Ajax |
| Milan | v | SV Casino Salzburg |

19/10/94
| SV Casino Salzburg | v | Ajax |
| AEK Athens | v | Milan |

02/11/94
| Ajax | v | SV Casino Salzburg |
| Milan | v | AEK Athens |

23/11/94
| Milan | v | Ajax |
| AEK Athens | v | SV Casino Salzburg |

07/12/94
| Ajax | v | AEK Athens/Rangers |
| SV Casino Salzburg | v | Milan |

Quarter-Finals
1 March and 15 March 1995
1. Group A Winner v Group B Runner-up
2. Group B Winner v Group A Runner-up
3. Group C Winner v Group D Runner-up
4. Group D Winner v Group C Runner-up

Semi-Finals
5 April and 19 April 1995
Winner Match 1 v Winner Match 2
Winner Match 3 v Winner Match 4
NB: A draw will be made to determine which side will play at home in the first leg

Final
24 May 1995
Venue to be announced

Cup-Winners' Cup Draw 1994–95

Designated match days for all ties are Thursdays with the exception of the Final.

Preliminary Round
11 August and 25 August 1995

B71 (Far)	v	HJK Helsinki (Fin)
Bangor (NIr)	v	Tatran Presov (Svk)
Barry Town (Wales)	v	Zhalgiris Vilnius (Lit)
Bodo/Glimt (Nor)	v	Olimpija Riga (Lat)
FC Fandok (Bls)	v	SK Tirana (Alb)
Ferencvaros (Hun)	v	F91 Dudelange (Lux)
Floriana (Mal)	v	Sligo Rovers (Rep)
IBK (Ice)	v	Maccabi Tel Aviv (Isr)
Norma Tallinin (Est)	v	Maribor Branik (Slo)
Pirin (Bul)	v	FC Schaan (Lie)
Tiligul Tiraspol (Mol)	v	Omonia Nicosia (Cyp)
Viktoria Zizkov (Cze)	v	IFK Norrkoping (Swe)

First Round
Draw: 26 August 1994
Matches: 15 September and 29 September 1994

Second Round
Draw: 30 September 1994
Matches: 20 October and 3 November 1994

Quarter-Finals
Draw: 4 November 1994
Matches: 2 March and 16 March 1995

Semi-Finals
Draw: 17 March 1995
Matches: 6 April and 20 April 1995

Final
10 May 1995
Venue to be announced

UEFA Cup Draw 1994–95

Designated match days for all ties are Tuesdays with the exception of the Final.

Preliminary Round
9 August and 23 August 1995

Anorthosis (Cyp)	v	Shumen (Bul)
Ararat Erevan (Arm)	v	CSKA Sofia (Bul)
Aris Salonika (Gre)	v	Hapoel Beersheba (Isr)
Bangor City (Wal)	v	IA Akranes (Ice)
Dinamo Minsk (Bls)	v	Hibernians (Mal)
Dynamo Tiblisi (Ukr)	v	Universitatea Craiova (Rom)
FC Aarau (Swi)	v	Mura Murska (Slo)
FC Copenhagen (Den)	v	FC Jazz (Fin)
Fenerbahce (Tur)	v	Turan Tauz (Aze)
FH (Ice)	v	Linfield (NIr)
GI Gotu (Far)	v	Trelleborgs (Swe)
Gornik Zabrze (Pol)	v	Shamrock Rovers (Ire)
Inter Cardiff (Wales)	v	GKS Katowice (Pol)
Kispest Honved (Hun)	v	Zimbru (Mol)
Lillestrom SK (Nor)	v	Shaktor Donetsk (Ukr)
Motherwell (Sco)	v	HB (Far)
MyPa (Fin)	v	Inter Bratislava (Svk)
OB (Den)	v	Flora Tallinin (Est)
Olimpija Ljubljana (Slov)	v	Levski Sofia (Bul)
Portadown (NIr)	v	Slovan Bratislava (Svk)
FC ROMAR (Lit)	v	AIK Stockholm (Swe)
Rosenborg (Nor)	v	CS Grevenmacher (Lux)
SK Teuta (Alb)	v	Apollon (Cyp)
Skonto Riga (Lat)	v	Aberdeen (Sco)
Slavia Prague (Cze)	v	Cork City (Rep)
Valletta (Mal)	v	Rapid Bucharest (Rom)
Vardar Skopje (Mac)	v	Bekescsaba (Hun)

First Round
Draw: 26 August 1994
Matches: 13 September and 17 September 1994

Second Round
Draw: 30 September 1994
Matches: 18 October and 1 November 1994

Third Round
Draw: 4 November 1994
Matches: 18 October and 1 November 1994

Quarter-Finals
Draw: 4 November 1994
Matches: 22 November and 6 December 1994

Semi-Finals
Draw: 17 March 1995
Matches: 4 April and 18 April 1995

Final
2 May and 17 May 1995
Order of venue to be decided.

The 1994 World Cup

QUALIFYING GROUPS

Qualifying Group 1	48
Qualifying Group 2	52
Qualifying Group 3	58
Qualifying Group 4	62
Qualifying Group 5	65
Qualifying Group 6	68
Qualifiers and Scorers	71

WORLD CUP FINALS: GROUP MATCHES

Group A	73
Group B	77
Group C	80
Group D	84
Group E	88
Group F	91
Second Round	95
Quarter-Finals	101
Semi-Finals	105
Play-off	108
World Cup Final	109

ROTHMANS PUBLICATIONS

Qualifying Groups

GROUP 1: Hodgson's choice as Italy and Swiss roll through

As the dust settled on the 1992–93 season Switzerland looked cast-iron certainties to reach their first World Cup Finals for 28 years. Two points ahead of second-placed Italy and four in front of third-placed Portugal, who had a game in hand, their fate was very clearly at their own feet. However, the Swiss still had to travel to Portugal and faced a potentially tough encounter with the Scots who had qualified for the previous five sets of finals, but for whom a sixth consecutive appearance looked improbable if not impossible. The fixture list for the qualification matches meant that Italy entertained the Portuguese in the very last round of matches, while Switzerland would be hosts to Estonia.

A winning start to the season was of vital importance to Portugal if they were to keep up the pressure on Italy. It was achieved early in September in Tallinin with a 2-0 win over Estonia, but only after the Baltic state had put up stubborn resistance. A goal from Rui Costa on the hour eased the Portuguese worries and Folha secured the points with 14 minutes of the match remaining. The win lifted them into second spot, in front of the Italians on goal difference.

5 September　　　　*Tallinin*　　　　*Att: 2,750*
ESTONIA　　0
PORTUGAL　　2　　(Rui Costa 60; Folha 76)
Estonia: Poom, R. Kallaste, Alonen, Hepner, Prins, T. Kallaste, Kristal (Vilderson 70), Bragin, Borisov, Reim, Klavan (Olumets 87)
Portugal: Vitor Baia, Abel Xavier, Oceano, Fernando Couto, Nogueira, Paulo Sousa, Rui Costa (Joao Pedro Pinto 74), Joao Vieira Pinto, Folha, Futre, Cadete (Esar Brito 70)

Three days later, the stage moved to Aberdeen's Pittodrie Stadium for the arrival of Switzerland, where a win for the visitors would almost ensure qualification bar a dramatic change in fortunes. For the Scots anything less than victory would mean being cast out into the World Cup wilderness. Indeed the situation was such that victories in their three remaining matches were vital – a do-or-die situation had developed from which there could be no return.

Leeds United skipper Gary McAllister was given the role of captaining Scotland for the first time – a big responsibility having represented his country at full international level only 22 times prior to the encounter. This was in stark contrast to his Swiss counterpart, the Sion defender Alain Geiger, who weighed in with 84 caps as the match got under way.

Scotland went into the game depleted by injuries and suspensions and with a 17-man squad that contained only two of the players who lost 3-1 in Switzerland the previous season. Scotland's luck did not hold, and the Swiss were fortunate to snatch a point. National coach Andy Roxburgh had sought an early goal – it nearly came within minutes of the start but Gordon Durie failed to take his chance. Switzerland, happy to play the game at a slower pace, prodded away at the home defence on the break and with 13 minutes of the game gone, Borussia Dortmund's Stephane Chapuisat sent Adrian Knup away on the right. Only intervention from David Robertson prevented a disastrous start for the Scots.

The game changed direction, though, five minutes into the second half. Robertson cleared from deep in his own half and the ball somehow ran through to the marauding John Collins, who beat Pascolo from the edge of the area. The goal brought more out of the Swiss, for whom a point at least was vital. It came in the 69th minute from the penalty spot after keeper Bryan Gunn upended Ciri Sforza, and Georges Bregy duly dispatched the ball into the net.

The 1-1 draw meant that the Scots were out of the running for either of the qualification spots and, while not mathematically guaranteeing the Swiss passage to the USA, they were all but there. For the Scots the game was the last in charge for Roxburgh, who relinquished his role to look for pastures greener, subsequently within UEFA.

8 September　　　　*Aberdeen*　　　　*Att: 24,000*
SCOTLAND　　1　　(Collins 50)
SWITZERLAND　　1　　(Bregy 69)
Scotland: Gunn, McKimmie, Irvine, Levein, Robertson, Nevin, Bowman (O'Donnell 75), McAllister, Collins, Booth (Jess 75), Durie
Switzerland: Pascolo, Quentin, Herr, Geiger, Rothenbuhler (Grassi 55), Ohrel, Bregy, Sforza, A. Sutter, Knup, Chapuisat
Ref: Quiniou (Fra)

Italy returned to the frame as September entered its final week. They followed in the footsteps of their main rivals for the second qualification place with a trip to Tallinin, where they went one better by beating Estonia 3-0. They had the advantage of a 20th minute lead when Roberto Baggio converted a spot kick. Mancini – on as a substitute for Lombardo – added a second early in the second half before Baggio notched his second of the game to make it safe.

22 September　　　　*Tallininn*　　　　*Att: 5,350*
ESTONIA　　0
ITALY　　3　　(R. Baggio 20 pen, 73; Mancini 59)
Estonia: Poom, R. Kallaste, Bragin, Prins, Alonen, T. Kallaste, Borisov, Ratnikov, Reim, Hepner, Klavan
Italy: Pagliuca, Benarrivo, Fortunato, Albertini, Costacurta, Baresi, Lombardo (Mancini 46), Manicone, Casiraghi, R. Baggio, Eranio
Ref: Damgaard (Den)

With Italy now just a point behind Switzerland but two ahead of Portugal, albeit having played a game more, the Swiss visit to Oporto in mid-October assumed the importance it always looked like having as the season commenced. Nothing short of victory was required by the Portuguese while a point would make Switzerland's qualification a mathematical certainty. Meanwhile, a couple of thousand kilometres to the east, Italy were looking to keep up the pressure with a win over the demoralised Scots.

The game in Oporto was played before a full house and the points were secured for the home side when Joao Vieira Pinto struck after only eight minutes.

Scotland approached their game in Italy with an interim manager in the form of Craig Brown, whose first decision was to relieve Celtic playmaker Paul McStay of the captaincy and then to leave him out of the side for the first match under his reign. It was the first time McStay had ever been dropped in his career. To add insult to injury the Stade Olimpico's scoreboard operator confused by the event introduced him on the bench as P. McCart!

For Italy this was a game that they desperately needed to win and they came into it with the confidence of only one defeat against the Scots in their previous five encounters and that 28 years before – but it had been a World Cup qualifier!

While Brown was looking for new talent to take advantage of any edginess the Italians might be feeling, his counterpart Arrigo Sacchi was hit with the blow of losing a number of key players including Maldini, Signori, Lentini and Dino Baggio. However, despite a nagging knee injury, Roberto Baggio was to play. As he said before the game 'If this was an ordinary match I wouldn't be playing, but it's so important that I don't have a choice.'

With the pressure of a win on them, what the Azzurri needed was an early goal to calm the nerves. And they achieved it with three minutes of the game gone when Donadoni caught Bryan Gunn cold with a snap effort at the near post. Roberto Baggio had done the hard work when he held the ball up on the edge of the area before delivering it perfectly into the path of the oncoming Donadoni. It was a disaster for Gunn, who later took full blame for the first two Italian goals.

Casiraghi looked to have made the game relatively safe for the 61,178 in Rome with a goal on 16 minutes. Again Roberto Baggio was instrumental in producing the approach work of a connoisseur. A succession of passes through the middle of the field culminated in an inch-perfect pass from the Juventus star that split the Scots defence for Casiraghi to meet on the turn.

However, within two minutes the home nerves were again on edge. Jess, lying deep behind the front line, struck a shot that Pagliuca failed to hold and Gallacher was on hand to snap up the rebound and lob over the failing keeper. But for dreadful luck the Scots should have completed their comeback but Gordon Durie's goalbound effort was accidentally blocked on the line by team-mate Gallacher. Gary McAllister had an outstanding game for the visitors but he could do nothing to reverse matters once Stefan Eranio had struck a thunderous 22-yard drive into the Scottish net after some more meticulous crafting from Roberto

Estonia's Martin Reim (left) leaves Malta's Martin Gregory in his wake.

Baggio. As the final seconds approached there were loud appeals for a penalty when Baggio fell dramatically inside the area after a tackle by Boyd but the Romanian referee Craciunescu waved away the appeal.

The Italians secured two more vital points but, despite the scoreline, it was a far from impressive display by the Italians which was helped by the Scots' decision not to man-mark Roberto Baggio, who was in turn instrumental in all three of the Italian goals.

Portugal's victory over Switzerland left the group wide open. Italy, thanks to their win over Scotland, took over as group leaders with Switzerland relegated to second spot. However, Portugal knew they would go into second place if they won their game in hand at home to the whipping boys from Estonia. With Italy due to meet Portugal in the final decisive game, Switzerland were guaranteed qualification provided they beat Estonia in Zurich, a task that wouldn't prove difficult against a side who had scored only one goal and conceded 20 in the group to that point.

If Italy had the luxury of an early goal against the Scots then the Portuguese also did against the Estonians, when Futre scored inside 120 seconds of the start. In front of a packed Stadium of Light, Oceano made it two from the penalty spot. Any thoughts

Portugal's Cadete (rear) and Caughi of Malta challenge for the ball during their World Cup qualifying encounter. Both sides failed to make the finals.

of a rout were dispelled as the visitors put on a stubborn display to limit the Portuguese to just a third goal from Rui Aguas four minutes from the final whistle.

13 October   *Oporto*   Att: 47,500
PORTUGAL 1 (Joao Vieira Pinto 8)
SWITZERLAND 0
Portugal: Vitor Baia, Joao Pedro Pinto, Peixe, Semedo (Paneira 81), Costa, Sousa, Oceano, Rui Costa, Joao Vieira Pinto, Futre, Cadete (Nogueira 55)
Switzerland: Pascolo, Hottiger, Quentin, Herr, Geiger, Bregy (Rueda 89), A. Sutter, Ohrel, Knup (Grassi 81), Sforza, Chapuisat
Ref: Krug (Ger)

13 October   *Rome*   Att: 61,178
ITALY 3 (Donadoni 3; Casiraghi 16; Eranio 80)
SCOTLAND 1 (Gallacher 18)
Italy: Pagliuca, Mussi (Lanna 68), Benarrivo, D. Baggio, Costacurta, Baresi, Eranio, Donadoni, Casiraghi, R. Baggio, Stroppa (Zola 90)
Scotland: Gunn, McKimmie, Boyd, McLaren, Irvine, Bowman (McStay 70), Durie, McCall, Jess (Durrant 46), McAllister, Gallacher
Ref: Craciunescu (Rom)

10 November   *Lisbon*   Att: 107,000
PORTUGAL 3 (Futre 2; Oceano 37 pen; Rui Aguas 86)
ESTONIA 0
Portugal: Vitor Baia, Joao Pedro Pinto, Oceano, Fernando Couto, Nogueira (Folha 75), Paulo Sousa, Rui Barros, Rui Costa (Vitor Paneira 60), Joao Vieira Pinto, Rui Aguas, Futre
Estonia: Poom, R Kallaste, Prins, Kaljend, Hepner, Ratnikov, Bragin, Borisov, Klavan (Linnumae 70), Rajala (Pustov 46), Reim
Ref: Blareau (Bel)

The final round of games would decide who qualified for USA94. On paper Switzerland looked certain to record a comfortable win over Estonia. That meant that the match in Milan between Italy and Portugal was the key. Italy simply needed a draw to qualify. Despite an identical goal difference with second-placed Portugal, they led the group by virtue of having scored more goals. A win for Portugal was essential unless Switzerland failed to beat Estonia, in which case a draw would send both Italy and Portugal Stateside.

By half-time in the group matches, Portugal knew that nothing less than a win would suffice. Switzerland led Estonia 3-0 and were full value for their advantage, using the power of Adrian Knup in the air and the educated feet of Stephane Chapuisat to produce goals from Knup, Bregy and Ohrel right at the interval whistle. The sell-out crowd were already celebrating their qualification in the Hardturm Stadium.

Things were much more tense in the Giuseppe Meazza Stadium, with the match scoreless but with the Azzurri being roared on by 80,000 fanatical supporters. Chapuisat scored just after the hour to ensure the Swiss roll and secure a 4-0 win for Roy Hodgson's side. In Milan the game entered the 83rd minute with a goalless draw fully on the cards. But given the spate of late away goals in recent vital group matches, nothing could be left to chance. There was a suspicion of offside as the two Baggios combined. Endless television replays showed that the pass from Roberto took a deflection off a desperate Portuguese defender. Dino was waved onside and he scored the only goal of the game to secure the Italians two points and their air tickets. Fernando Couto was given his marching orders with three minutes remaining to kill off any real chances the Portuguese had of turning the game around.

Almost unnoticed the Scottish won 2-0 in Valletta in a match which signalled the start of a new managerial reign. Craig Brown had been offered the national job before the game in Malta and gleefully accepted the position. Looking to the future the manager saw one of his debutants score after a quarter of an hour's play when Dundee United's Billy McKinlay unleashed a 25-yard volley past Maltese keeper David Cluett. Colin Hendry, the Blackburn defender, added a second 16 minutes from time to secure the win which did nothing more than confirm the Scots' fourth position in the final group table.

Malta and Estonia presented no surprises and it was just a matter of who would be vying for the wooden spoon. Estonia failed to win a single point at home, indeed they failed also to score a single goal at home. They achieved both away, the point coming in a 0-0 draw in Malta and the goal in a 3-1 defeat by Scotland.

Group 1 – Final Table

	P	W	D	L	F	A	Pts
ITALY	10	7	2	1	22	7	16
SWITZERLAND	10	6	3	1	23	6	15
Portugal	10	6	2	2	18	5	14
Scotland	10	4	3	3	14	13	11
Malta	10	1	1	8	3	23	3
Estonia	10	0	1	9	1	27	1

Group 1 – Results

	Estonia	Italy	Malta	Portugal	Scotland	Switzerland
Estonia	—	0-3	0-1	0-2	0-3	0-6
Italy	2-0	—	6-1	1-0	3-1	2-2
Malta	0-0	1-2	—	0-1	0-2	0-2
Portugal	3-0	1-3	4-0	—	5-0	1-0
Scotland	3-1	0-0	3-0	0-0	—	1-1
Switzerland	4-0	1-0	3-0	1-1	3-1	—

Switzerland moved on to their participation in a major finals for the first time since 1966 when they were eliminated from the first round and from a group that contained West Germany, Spain and Argentina. Their manager, Roy Hodgson, ensured that at least one Englishman would be at the finals in a participatory role!

17 November *Zurich* *Att: 20,000*
SWITZERLAND 4 (Knup 32; Bregy 34; Ohrel 45; Chapuisat 61)
ESTONIA 0
Switzerland: Pascolo, Hottiger, Herr, Geiger, Quentin (Turkyilmaz 67), Ohrel (Rueda 46), Bregy, Bickel, A. Sutter, Knup, Chapuisat
Estonia: Poom, Hepner, Kaljend, Prins, R. Kallaste, Reim, Borisov, Olumets, Bragin, Klavan (Pustov 78), Rajala (Linnumae 47)
Ref: Petrovic (Yug)

November 17 *Milan* *Att: 80,000*
ITALY 1 (D. Baggio 83)
PORTUGAL 0
Italy: Pagliuca, Benarrivo, Maldini, Stroppa (Albertini 61), Costacurta, Baresi, Donadoni, D. Baggio, Casiraghi, R. Baggio, Signori (Mancini 76)
Portugal: Vitor Baia, Joao Pedro Pinto (Rui Aguas 76), Veloso, Vitor Paneira, Jorge Costa, Fernando Couto, Paulo Sousa, Rui Barros, Joao Vieira Pinto, Futre, Rui Costa (Domingos 68)
* Fernando Couto sent off in the 87th minute.
Ref: Wojcik (Pol)

Group 1 – Scorers

6	Chapuisat	Switzerland
5	Baggio R.	Italy
	Knup	Switzerland
4	Bregy	Switzerland
3	Baggio D.	Italy
	Cadete	Portugal
	Mancini	Italy
	McCoist	Scotland
	Nevin	Scotland
	Ohrel	Switzerland
	Signori	Italy
2	Casiraghi	Italy
	Collins	Scotland
	Eranio	Italy
	Futre	Portugal
	Gallacher	Scotland
	Joao Vieira Pinto	Portugal
	Rui Aguas	Portugal
	Rui Barros	Portugal
	Rui Costa	Portugal
	Sforza	Switzerland
1	Bickel	Switzerland
	Booth	Scotland
	Bragin	Estonia
	Busuttil	Malta
	Donadoni	Italy
	Fernando Couto	Portugal
	Folha	Portugal
	Gregory	Malta
	Hendry	Scotland
	Hottiger	Switzerland
	Laferla	Malta
	Maldini	Italy
	McClair	Scotland
	McKinlay	Scotland
	Nogueira	Portugal
	Oceano	Portugal
	Semedo	Portugal
	Turkyilmaz	Switzerland
	Vialli	Italy
	Vierchowod	Italy

17 November *Valletta* *Att: 7,000*
MALTA 0
SCOTLAND 2 (McKinlay 15; Hendry 74)
Malta: Cluett, S. Vella, Buhagiar (Saliba 45), Galea, Brincat, Buttigieg, Busuttil, Spiteri, Suda (Scerri 74), Laferla, Gregory
Scotland: Leighton, McLaren, McKinnon, Durrant (Boyd 74), Hendry, Irvine, Ferguson, McKinlay (Booth 45), Nevin, McAllister, Gallacher
Ref: Vassilakis (Gre)

GROUP 2: Norway the surprise package as Dutch trip up English

Group 2 had turned out to be far from the safe cruising zone that many had thought it would be, transporting Holland and England to the USA with ease. As with any game of football the odd swell along the way was anticipated but, come November, the group had been won by one of the smaller nations of Europe who were on the crest of qualification. In short an emerging nation had taken all by surprise and emerged! Norway qualified on merit and were boosted by the confidence of a well-arranged fixture schedule that allowed them to run up a good tally of points and goals by the time the tickets were on sale for the final rounds of fixtures in the latter part of 1993.

As the season got underway the Norwegians were three points clear at the top of the group table and had the assurance that a win in one of their remaining three games would probably be enough to win qualification. For England and Holland the waters were decidedly cloudy. It was neck and neck all the way, becoming increasingly likely that their penultimate game against each other would go a long way to deciding their destiny. But still there was Poland, just a point behind the jostling twosome and with two games in hand. With games left against Norway, England and Holland it was possible, but not probable, that they could muscle their way into the second qualification spot. Once again Turkey flattered to deceive and San Marino were there to boost the opposition strikers' confidence – surely there was no other sensible reason for their participation in this theatre?

First up were England for the visit of Poland to the Twin Towers. Following a humiliating 2-0 defeat in Oslo earlier in June, they knew that at least five points from their final three games would pretty much ensure qualification, so a win was essential. The much-maligned England manager, Graham Taylor, confessed that he had not enjoyed his summer – if any English supporter had – 'I've had a lousy, miserable summer and I've been waiting for this game to start since I walked out of the dressing room in Norway,' he said.

Out of the starting line-up went Des Walker, the first time he had felt the axe in his 55-game international career. Given his performance against the Dutch at Wembley and the Norwegians in Oslo, when he was responsible for at least a goal in each game, it was hardly surprising. David Seaman was also back in favour after Walker's Sheffield Wednesday team-mate, Chris Woods, was also shunted out of the Number 1 shirt and on to the bench following a series of unconvincing displays for both club and country.

If the English camp was rocking then so was the Polish one. They looked to be robbed of key players, either through injury or by curious selection choices by coach Andrzej Strejlau. The starting line-up at Wembley included only four of the brilliant Olympic squad that had played to such high acclaim in Barcelona just 13 months earlier. Strejlau's relationship with Koln's highly rated Andrzej Rudy did little to quell the storm in the Polish camp, where not only the fans but also the players wanted him included. It was a situation that Taylor will have been familiar with in relation to the mercurial Paul Gascoigne.

England overcame the Poles with an emphatic display which was as resounding as the 3-0 scoreline suggests. Indeed, the team were given a standing ovation as they left the field at the end of a memorable evening. For Poland it was their first defeat in Group 2 and would not help to heal the rifts that were developing within.

The tone of the evening had been set inside the first minute when Lee Sharpe's centre from the left fell at the feet of Gascoigne whose shot hit – rather than being saved by – Polish goalkeeper Jaroslaw Bako. Ian Wright went close two minutes later and then with the clock showing five minutes, David Platt, deposed as captain by the return of Nottingham Forest's Stuart Pearce, delivered a quite magnificent 50-yard pass that carved the visitors' defence in half. The ball fell perfectly between Czachowski and Adamczuk for Les Ferdinand. Instinctively the Queens Park Rangers striker controlled the ball and hit the net from eight yards out.

Poland nearly found their way back into the game shortly after when Jan Furtok, the sole survivor from the 1986 World Cup Finals in Mexico, got free on the left following a slip by Rob Jones. The 31-year-old Eintracht Frankfurt player looked to be clear through before Jones scythed him down. The card came out, but luckily for the Liverpool player it was only yellow in colour.

England increased their lead four minutes into the second half. A free-kick by Jones was nodded on by Ferdinand and Gascoigne's close control allowed him to beat Brzeczek before driving home from nine yards for his sixth goal in 28 internationals. England continued to go forward and Pearce made it 3-0 in the 53rd minute. Sharpe touched a free kick to Gascoigne who simply teed the ball up for Pearce, and Bako was beaten hands down from 25 yards.

8 September   *Wembley*   *Att: 71,220*
ENGLAND 3 (Ferdinand 5; Gascoigne 49; Pearce 53)
POLAND 0
England: Seaman, Jones, Adams, Pallister, Pearce, Platt, Ince, Gascoigne, Sharpe, Ferdinand, I.Wright
Poland: Bako, Adamczuk (Bak 78), Lesiak, Kozminski, Czachowski, Brzeczek, Warzycha, Swierczewski, Kosecki, Lesniak, Furtok (Ziober 45)
Ref: Van den Wijingaert (Bel)

England moved into second place but the three goals also boosted their goal difference – an area that looked like being ever decisive.

As September neared a conclusion the Dutch travelled to San Marino. Or rather they travelled to Bologna where the principality now had to stage their home games. A win was never in doubt – just how many goals would the Dutch score? The answer was seven but it might have been 15. Manager Dick Advocaat – never afraid to choose a side to suit a particular job – handed an orange shirt to just about every striker available to him and it paid off. The Dutch line-up started with seven of the

11 who had drawn 2-2 at Wembley earlier in the year and two changes from the side that shared goalless points with Norway in Rotterdam. Out went Van Gobbel and Blinker, in came Roy and Kieft. Holland lined up with a five-man attack comprising Overmars, Bosman, Kieft, Roy and Bergkamp.

Both goalkeepers would have busy roles to play. Pierluigi Benedettini, a bus driver by day, and collector of goals conceded by night for San Marino, and at the other end Ed de Goey preoccupied in keeping warm.

It took just thirty seconds for Jonny Bosman to score from Ronald Koeman's cross and the lambs looked to be lining up in preparation. However, the San Marino reargard held fast for a further 23 minutes until Wim Jonk hit a long-range effort past Benedettini and repeated the feat two minutes before the interval to make it 3-0. Ronald De Boer went on at the break and within six minutes had shown Jonk that he too can also score from distance. That goal evened out the difference in the goals between England and Holland. Any more would be insurance for the Dutch. Bosman made it 5-0 after 66 minutes and he completed his hat-trick ten minutes later after Bergkamp had provided the cross. In between Bosman's goals San Marino had been reduced in numbers when Marco Mazza was sent off for a none-too-healthy tackle on Ronald De Boer. Koeman completed the scoring from the spot 11 minutes from time to give the Dutch a 7-0 win and, perhaps more importantly, a three-goal advantage over England.

22 September   *Bologna*   *Att: 3,340*
SAN MARINO   0
HOLLAND   7   (Bosman 1, 66, 76; Jonk 21, 43; R. De Boer 51; Koeman 79 pen)

San Marino: Benedettini, Gennari, Valentini, Canti, Gobbi, I. Toccaceli, Bonini, M. Mazza, P. Della Valle, Bacchiocchi (Gualtieri 55), P. Mazza
*Mazza sent off in the 70th minute
Holland: De Goey, R. Koeman, F. De Boer, Wouters, Rijkaard, Jonk, Overmars, Bergkamp, Bosman, Kieft (R. De Boer 46), Roy
Ref: Agius (Malta)

As the goals were raining in in Bologna, Egil Olsen's Norwegians were seeking just one to give them a win over the Poles in Oslo that would virtually seal their qualification to USA 94. It eventually came in a bad-tempered game when Jostein Flo, the Sheffield United striker, put the ball away ten minutes into the second period. Up until then the Poles had acquitted themselves well and were unfortunate not to be ahead before Flo pounced. Certainly the home woodwork had come to the rescue when a goal had looked certain. But two minutes after Flo's goal the Poles looked like they might get a lifeline when Thorstvedt, the Tottenham goalkeeper affectionately known as Erik the Viking, produced a professional foul and received his marching orders. Substitute keeper Grodas went on for the luckless Ingebrigtsen and took over between the uprights.

That should have been the signal for the Poles to step up their play, which they did briefly, but only for a further two minutes after which the teams were levelled when Roman Szewczyk was also dismissed. Norway held on amid a few frayed tempers and at the end of the game, their last home World Cup qualification fixture completed, they produced a prolonged lap of honour. Only comprehensive thrashings in their final two games – away to the Poles and Turks – would deny them their place in the 1994 finals.

22 September   *Oslo*   *Att: 21,968*
NORWAY   1   (Flo 55)
POLAND   0

Norway: Thorstvedt, Berg, T. Pedersen, Bratseth, Bjornebye (Nilsen 46), Halle, Bohinen, Rekdal, Ingebrigtsen (Grodas 57), Flo, Fjortoft
*Thorstvedt sent off in the 57th minute
Poland: Bako, Szewczyk, Wegrzyn, Bak, Kozminski, Swierczewski, Rudy, R. Warzycha (Brzeczek 84), Ziobar, Kosecki, Lesniak
*Szewczyk sent off in the 59th minute
Ref: Pairetto (Ita)

It was 13 October but not a Friday, although it might well have been as England prepared for their match against the Dutch in Rotterdam. The mathematics of the situation had produced thousands of words on both sides of the North Sea. The certainties were that a win for England would put them through barring defeat in San Marino. A win for Holland would put them through barring a collapse in their final game in Poland. A draw would reduce the final decision as to who qualified to goal difference, with the English to travel to San Marino as favourites to claw back the three extra the Dutch had in the bank and then score more than the Dutch might get in Poznan.

The tension was heightened in the English camp by Taylor's inability to handle the press. No doubt there was tension in the Dutch camp where rumours were rife that their long-lost son Johan Cruyff would return to take the helm should the boat be pushed out to the USA. That also added fuel to the fire speculating that the estranged Ruud Gullit would also return to produce a Dutch equivalent of the Dream Machine. If there was tension it was hardly noticed.

With no Gascoigne, the gangly frame of Carlton Palmer was selected in midfield while Lee Sharpe was added to give much needed width as both sides set about their tasks. England had never lost to the Dutch in Holland – but then it had been 24 years since they had last played a full international there. Within the first seven minutes the Dutch had carved out three scoring chances and the ease with which Overmars cruised past Dorigo was worrying for the visitors.

It proved to be an evening of ultimate frustration for England, Dorigo and Merson both hitting a post. Merson was particularly unlucky when his vicious free-kick left De Goey stranded only to rattle the upright. Had the Arsenal striker's finishing matched his approach work he might already have given England the lead when he cut inside from the left wing to drive a yard wide. His club captain Tony Adams saw his low shot booted off the line by Koeman and Dorigo's 30-yard drive fared no better than Merson's curling free-kick.

But England were lucky too, especially five minutes from the interval when Rijkaard made a late run through the defence, controlling Ronald De Boer's telling cross from the left with a

Holland's Frank Rijkaard 'scores' against England. Unfortunately for the Ajax player his goal was disallowed for an offside that never was.

single touch before volleying beyond Seaman. As he did so an offside flag was raised and England escaped thanks to the linesman's wrong decision.

Palmer, who had been giving the ball away with annoying regularity, was replaced by Andy Sinton to play wide on the right when the real need was for reinforcements in midfield. This was never more evident than when Bergkamp was allowed to run unchallenged from the halfway line to the edge of the England penalty area before producing a shot low to the corner that Seaman pushed away for a corner – just.

Then a free-kick at each end, just outside the penalty areas, in the space of five minutes changed the course of the game and provided as much debate as did Maradona's Hand of God. A long cross-field pass by substitute Sinton left David Platt edging in front of Ronald Koeman and into the Dutch penalty area for a highly likely opening goal. Koeman pulled and pushed Platt, who went sprawling. For a moment it looked as though the German referee Karl-Josef Assenmacher had given a penalty. Instead the ball was placed inches outside the Dutch area and, with a rueful Koeman awaiting his marching orders for a blatant professional foul, Assenmacher decided on a yellow card, much to the chagrin of the English players.

As the hour mark ticked past Wouters was fouled on the edge of the area and a free-kick was awarded. Koeman blasted the ball into a fast-advancing England wall and referee Assenmacher ordered it to be taken again. At the second attempt, with Seaman clearly anticipating the blast, Koeman flighted the ball into the top left-hand corner of the goal out of reach of the goalkeeper's flailing arms.

Six minutes later the Dutch added a second when once again Bergkamp was allowed to run from deep after an English attack had broken down. Unchallenged he advanced nearer Seaman's penalty area before unleashing a low drive that whistled in by the post to put the Dutch firmly into the driving seat against a dispirited England side.

The debates carried on long after the game, the mainstay of arguments being that, had Koeman been dismissed for his foul on Platt, he would not have been available to score from a similarly placed free-kick. Koeman when questioned was typically forthright – but then he could afford to be – 'The foul was outside the area but I expected the red card.'

The German referee, who came in for criticism for his performance of the game including some from the Dutch, was quick to defend his actions. 'I felt I refereed the game objectively,' Assenmacher said. 'Three or four officials from FIFA told me that afterwards,' he added. Within two weeks of the game he had been dropped by FIFA from their international list.

The debates continued but could not overshadow the fact that, on the night, and on other nights in the group, England were simply not good enough. The Dutch fans celebrated their victory in style knowing that they only needed to avoid defeat against Poland in their last match to make USA94.

13 October   *Rotterdam*   *Att: 48,000*
HOLLAND   **2**   (R. Koeman 61; Bergkamp 67)
ENGLAND   **0**
Holland: De Goey, De Wolf, F. De Boer, R. Koeman, Wouters, Overmars (Winter 76), Rijkaard, R. De Boer (Van Gobbel 89), Bergkamp, Roy
England: Seaman, Parker, Dorigo, Palmer (Sinton 46), Adams, Pallister, Platt, Merson (I. Wright 76), Shearer, Sharpe, Ince
Ref: Assenmacher (Ger)

Meanwhile, three second-half goals in Poznan secured Norway's position as group winners. Two goals in as many minutes just after the hour totally demoralised a shabby-looking Polish side when first Flo and then Fjortoft scored. Substitute Johnsen added a third a minute from time and the only thing that had looked certain in a topsy-turvy group became so. The Norwegians were there playing their own brand of football – quite often the long ball, but quite often a quick, decisive passing game that was a delight to watch. Don't believe anything else you may be told.

13 October   *Poznan*   *Att: 15,000*
POLAND   **0**
NORWAY   **3**   (Flo 61; Fjortoft 63; Johnsen 89)
Poland: Bako, Bak, Kozminski, Waldoch (Czachowski 80), Wegrzyn, R. Warzycha, Swierczewski, K. Warzycha, Ziober, Kosecki (Brazeczek 26), Lesniak
Norway: Grodas, Halle (J. Jakobsen 80), T. Pedersen, Bratseth, Bjornebye, Flo, Mykland, Berg, Rekdal, Bohinen, Fjortoft (R. Johnsen 70)
Ref: Khrondl (Cze)

Two weeks later, in Istanbul, Turkey beat Poland in an almost meaningless fixture. Kowalczyk gave the Poles a 17th-minute lead but then Sukur and later Bulent replied and Turkey achieved their second win of the tournament.

27 October   *Istanbul*   *Att: 8,000*
TURKEY   **2**   (Sukur 53; Bulent 67)
POLAND   **1**   (Kowalczyk 17)
Turkey: Engin, Recep, Bulent, Gokhan, Emre, Tugay, Abdullah Ercan (Mehmet Ozdilek 86), Sukur, Hakan, Oguz, Orhan (Ertugrul 80)
Poland: Matysek, Lewandovski, Michalski, Kruszankin, Waldock, Jalocha, Leszek Pisz, Adamczuk, Staniek, Kowalczyk (Ziober 60), Juskowaik
Ref: Wieser (Aus)

With goalkeeper Thorstvedt winning his 80th cap and their qualification for the World Cup sewn up, Norway travelled to Turkey full of confidence. Turkey had other ideas and inflicted on Norway their first defeat in the group. The Turks got off to a great start inside five minutes when Ertugrul struck. He did so again just over 20 minutes later to leave the group winners floundering. Norway struggled to get back into a game that had little meaning for them but although Bohinen pulled a goal back early in the second half they never looked like winning.

10 November   *Istanbul*   *Att: 15,000*
TURKEY   **2**   (Ertugrul 5, 26)
NORWAY   **1**   (Bohinen 49)
Turkey: Hayrettin, Gokhan, Ogun (Emre 46), Bulent, Yusuf, Suat (Mehmet 80), Tugay, Abdullah, Oguz, Ertugrul, Orhan
Norway: Thorstvedt, Berg, Bjornebye, Bratseth, Halle, T. Pedersen, Bohinen, J.I. Jacobsen (Fjortoft 70), Johnsen, Mykland (Leonhardsen 59), Kjetil Rekdal
Ref: Khusainov (Rus)

November 17 and judgement day had arrived – but who would be the terminator? The mathematics were once again forced down the throats at breakfast time and repeated *ad nauseam* in countless previews through the day. Poland had to beat the Dutch and provided England won by at least seven clear goals World Cup Willy could be dusted off. Anything else and the Oranje would qualify – and they started as firm favourites to do so.

In Poznan the home support had lost interest in a national side whose manager had openly announced his lack of intent. Most of the 19,000 crowd had made the journey across Germany from Holland. This was in stark contrast to England's game in Bologna, where the visiting supporters numbered just hundreds in the 2,378 crowd.

Within moments of the kick-off the roar in the Renato Dall'Ara stadium was probably heard all the way back across the Alps in Poznan as a scenario unfolded that had never really been contemplated when Gualtieri made an indelible mark on English footballing history and pushed electronic match timing to hundredths of seconds. The San Marino player was put clear by Nicola Bacchiocchi's pass and, although Pearce intercepted

Group 2 – Final Table

	P	W	D	L	F	A	Pts
NORWAY	10	7	2	1	25	5	16
HOLLAND	10	6	3	1	29	9	15
England	10	5	3	2	26	9	13
Poland	10	3	2	5	10	15	8
Turkey	10	3	1	6	11	19	7
San Marino	10	0	1	9	2	46	1

Group 2 – Results

	England	Holland	Norway	Poland	Turkey	San Marino
England	—	2-2	1-1	3-0	4-0	6-0
Holland	2-0	—	0-0	2-2	3-1	6-0
Norway	2-0	2-1	—	1-0	3-1	10-0
Poland	1-1	1-3	0-3	—	1-0	1-0
Turkey	0-2	1-3	2-1	2-1	—	4-1
San Marino	1-7	0-7	0-2	0-3	0-0	—

Group 2 – Scorers

Goals	Player	Country
7	Platt	England
6	Van Vossen	Holland
5	Bergkamp	Holland
	Rekdal	Norway
	Wright	England
4	Gascoigne	England
3	Bosman	Holland
	De Boer R.	Holland
	Ferdinand	England
	Feyyaz	Turkey
	Flo	Norway
	Halle	Norway
	Lesniak	Poland
	Sorloth	Norway
2	Bohinen	Norway
	De Wolf	Holland
	Ertugrul	Turkey
	Fjortoft	Norway
	Hakan	Turkey
	Ince	England
	Jakobsen	Norway
	Jonk	Holland
	Koeman R.	Holland
	Kowalczyk	Poland
	Nilsen	Norway
	Pearce	England
	Witschge Ro.	Holland
1	Adamczuk	Poland
	Bacchiocchi	San Marino
	Barnes	England
	Bulent	Turkey
	Furtok	Poland
	Gualtieri	San Marino
	Gullit	Holland
	Hami	Turkey
	Johnsen	Norway
	Kozminski	Poland
	Leonhardsen	Norway
	Mykland	Norway
	Orhan	Turkey
	Overmars	Holland
	Palmer	England
	Shearer	England
	Sukur	Turkey
	Van den Brom	Holland
	Waldock	Poland
	Warzycha K.	Poland
	Own goals	

the ball, his back-pass was so woefully underhit that the forward was presented with a chance that he could not refuse: San Marino 1 England 0.

England now had to score eight and trust that the Dutch would falter in Poznan. The bleak became bleaker. A ponderous England set about their recovery against a San Marino side who – for the first time in their international career – had a lead to defend, and they proceeded to do so with relish.

By the tenth minute of the synchronised games, Bergkamp had fired the Dutch into a lead. Jan Wouters lobbed the ball with some panache over a static Polish defence and as Bergkamp lost his marker he hit the most perfect of volleys into the bottom left-hand corner of Matysek's net. For English supporters it was the ultimate nightmare, for the Dutch supporters it was their wildest dreams come true.

But there was hope of a Polish revival within two minutes when Koeman lost the ball and it broke loose just outside the Dutch area. Lesniak pounced and hit a fierce drive into the roof of De Goey's net. All square in Poznan, but in Bologna England were still finding it tough. Finally, after 21 minutes, Ince seized the initiative in typical style when he collected a loose ball and drove home his first international goal with a shot from outside the area. Ian Wright scored the first of his four goals of the evening just over the half-hour and Les Ferdinand got onto the score sheet a couple of minutes before half-time to give the scoreboard a degree of respectability.

Wright notched his second a minute into the second half and England were on their way to the eight goals they required. All that was now needed was for the Poles to have an attack of national pride to edge ahead of the Dutch. After Lesniak's equaliser they found some self-belief and for a 20-minute period they took the game to the Dutch but didn't have the wherewithal to capitalise on their approach play. After an erratic opening half hour the Dutch calmed down and in the second half were more consistent in their passing and holding of the ball. In the

San Marino's overworked goalkeeper fists the ball away from the head of England's Gary Pallister.

56th minute Roy set up Bergkamp to score with a half-volley from six yards out. After that it was simply a matter of how many they would score to add fuel to their voracious fans' celebrations. In the end it was just the one, two minutes from time, when Ronald De Boer struck – and the Dutch were through regardless.

Back in Bologna England had continued to search for their eight goals – just in case. Ince produced his second of the evening and Wright completed his quartet at the final whistle.

The result in Poznan was not even important now as the English side had failed to achieve what had been asked of them. The final indictment of the evening arrived when San Marino's manager, Giorgi Leoni, was interviewed. He was clearly unimpressed with the opposition. 'Holland's football is calmer, more controlled and more technical than England's. England's play is faster but you can see what they are going to do,' he said.

Without doubt English football had sunk to its lowest point. Perhaps it was fitting that the 2,378 attendance was the lowest ever to watch a full England international.

17 November   *Poznan*   *Att: 19,000*
POLAND   **1**   (Lesniak 12)
HOLLAND   **3**   (Bergkamp 10, 56; R. De Boer 88)
Poland: Matysek, Jalocha (Czerwiec 78), Michalski, Kruszankin, Waldoch, Kozminski, R. Warzycha (Cebula 65), Lewandowski, Adamczuk, Lesniak, Kowalczyk
Holland: De Goey, Van Gobbel, R. Koeman, F. De Boer, E. Koeman, Wouters, Winter, R. De Boer, Overmars, Bergkamp, Roy
Ref: Sundell (Swe)

17 November   *Bologna*   *Att: 2,378*
SAN MARINO   **1**   (Gualtieri 9 sec)
ENGLAND   **7**   (Ince 21, 73; Wright 32, 46, 78, 90; Ferdinand 43)
San Marino: Benedettini, Valentini (Gobbi 47), Gennari, Zanotti, Canti, Guerra, Manzaroli, Della Valle, Bacchiocchi (P. Mazza 62), Bonini, Gualtieri
England: Seaman, Dixon, Pearce, Ripley, Walker, Pallister, Platt, Wright, Ferdinand, Sinton, Ince
Ref: Nazri (Malay)

GROUP 3: Last-gasp Republic join Spain

Group 3 always looked as though it was going to be one of the more interesting qualification groups, and so it proved. The Republic of Ireland, who have never been short of gifted players, were continuing to consolidate their position as a major international force while Spain, with their world-class club sides, have always offered potential but never quite delivered the goods. Denmark, of course, were reigning European champions and were seeking to show that that particular upset was not a flash in the pan. It seemed at the outset of the group games that it would be a case of any two from three. The results of games between these three and possibly the odd intervention of Northern Ireland would go a long way to sorting it out, as well as who scored the most goals against Albania and the two Baltic states which made up the group.

As the new season dawned a feature of the group table was the sheer meanness of the defences of the leading trio. Just five goals conceded between the three in 26 games. However, the Republic and Spain were netting at a healthy rate, while the Danes had managed just nine in eight games. How costly would that be?

As if to prove a point the Danes gave their goals-for tally a much needed infusion with four against the Lithuanians as August drew to a close. Lars Olsen and Pingel provided a two-goal cushion at the interval with Brian Laudrup adding a third in the second half before Skarbalius put through his own goal to complete the rout.

25 August   *Copenhagen*   *Att: 40,282*
DENMARK 4   (L. Olsen 13; Pingel 44; B. Laudrup 64; own goal 71)
LITHUANIA 0
Denmark: Schmeichel, L. Olsen, Rieper, Kjeldbjerg, Friis-Hansen, J. Jensen (Hough 81), Vilfort, Steen Nielsen, M. Laudrup, B. Laudrup, Pingel
Lithuania: Stauce, Ziukas, Mazeikis, Baltasnikas, Tereskinas, Skarbalius, Baranauskas, Olshanskis, Stumbrys (Apanavicius 57), Kirilovas (Urbonas 69), Sleyks
Ref: Bergman (Ice)

Pingel was again on the score sheet when he notched the only goal of a tight game in Tirana as the Danes secured the points from the Albanians two weeks later. On the same evening both the Irish sides were also in action. In Belfast a goal in each half gave the North a 2-0 win over Latvia. The first came from striker Jimmy Quinn following a corner and the second from Philip Gray. In Dublin first-half goals for John Aldridge and Alan Kernaghan gave the Republic victory by the same score over Lithuania.

The result set a record for the Republic in that they achieved their first ever sequence of four straight wins. The game had threatened to provide them with a landslide victory after an embarrassingly one-sided first half, but the Lithuanians responded well following the interval and often had the better of the play. They would not have been flattered had they taken the chances they had to level the scores. The visitors had been depleted of many of their foreign players before the game because of a problem with insurance cover for them but those less likely to be regulars were eager to please.

It took just four minutes for Aldridge to turn in Steve Staunton's low drive. In doing so he claimed the distinction of scoring the 100th goal in the 71st match of manager Jack Charlton's reign. Aldridge's 13th goal for his country was supplemented by Kernaghan's first, when he headed in Irwin's cross.

The Lithuanians should have equalised in the 51st minute when Virginijus Baltusnikas found himself clear, only to shoot well wide. Vidotas Slekys clipped the outside of a post and it needed two excellent saves by Bonner to deny the Lithuanians.

8 September   *Belfast*   *Att: 6,400*
N. IRELAND 2   (J. Quinn 35; Gray 80)
LATVIA 0
N Ireland: Wright, Fleming, Worthington, Taggart, Donaghy, Magilton, Wilson, Quinn, Hughes, Dowie, Gray
Latvia: Karavayev, Troitski, Alexeienko, Ivanov, Gnedouys, Popkov, Sharando, Shevlakov, Babichev, Linards, Yeliseyev
Ref: Pinto Correia (Por)

8 September   *Tirana*   *Att: 8,000*
ALBANIA 0
DENMARK 1   (Pingel 63)
Albania: Strakosha, Bano, Shulku, Vata, Kacaj, Kushta, Lekbello, Millo, Demollari, Sortuzi (Zalla 46), Zmijani
Denmark: Schmeichel, Olsen, Kjeldbjerg, Rieper, Friis-Hansen (Larsen 61), Steen Nielsen, Jensen (Hogh 51), Vilfort, B. Laudrup, M. Laudrup, Pingel
Ref: Leizou (Cyp)

8 September   *Dublin*   *Att: 30,000*
REP. IRELAND 2   (Aldridge 4; Kernaghan 25)
LITHUANIA 0
Rep. Ireland: Bonner, Irwin, Moran, Kernaghan, Phelan, Houghton, Keane, Townsend (Whelan 67), Staunton, Aldridge, Quinn (Cascarino 74)
Lithuania: Stauce, Ziukas, Baltusnikas, Kalvaitis, Tereskinas, Apasavicius, Baranauskas, Skarbalius (Staliunas 84), Stumbrys, Kirilovas (Maciulevicius 68), Slekys
Ref: Petersen (Den)

Wins for the Republic and Denmark on 8 September had pushed the Spanish into third place, three points behind the Danes, when they travelled to Tirana for their next game. Anything other than a win was probably never likely for the Spaniards, but it was still absolutely essential given that their next game was in Dublin against the Republic. The win was achieved comprehensively enough, 5-1, with Salinas helping himself to a hat-trick. The Albanians did add an air of respectability to the score five minutes before half-time when Kushta struck, but the destination of the two points was never in doubt.

Clash of the Irish: Gerry Taggart of the North (left) and John Aldridge of the Republic.

After the game the Spanish Football Federation announced that they were preparing to submit a report to FIFA regarding an alleged offer they had received to fix the game.

22 September	Tirana	Att: 8,000
ALBANIA	1	(Kushta 40)
SPAIN	5	(Salinas 4, 30, 58; Toni 18, Caminero 67)

Albania: Strakosha, Abazi, Dashi, Vata, Kacaj, Shulku, Millo, Fortuzi, Kepa (Dalipi 79), Kushta, Shehu
Spain: Zubizarreta, Francisco Camarasa, Alkorta, Nadal, Toni, Goikoetxea, Hierro, Guerrero (Guardiola 55), Caminero, Salinas, Alfonso (Quique Estebaranz 72)
Ref: Harrel (Fra)

Two points separated the top three sides with 10 rounds of matches gone. Of the remaining four games to be played two would involve the trio as they vied for qualification, with Northern Ireland the fourth nation involved. The Republic were clearly in the driving seat as the first two games took place. On a sunny October afternoon at Landsdowne Road, the Republic knew that a win would make them certainties for USA94 and the whole of the Republic was clearly gearing up for the Mother of all Celebrations. In the end it turned into a wake as the Irish – unbeaten at home in major competition since Charlton had taken over seven years earlier – found themselves three goals behind against an experimental Spanish side, and all inside the opening half hour.

The Irish could offer no real excuses. Injuries to Aldridge and Townsend had meant a reshuffle with Whelan coming into midfield alongside McGrath, and Moran and Kernaghan at the centre of the defence. The lanky frame of Niall Quinn was left alone to forage up front. Spain's side was made up of players who were for the most part internationally ignorant and weighted with defenders. But it was the one real player with experience who did the damage – the Barcelona striker Julio Salinas.

From the kick-off the Republic started well with Keane and McGrath looking like the class players they are, but with their first attack, after three minutes, the Spanish sent warning signals to the crowd of 33,000. A cross from the left wing reached an unmarked Goikoetxea but his volley flew wide. Camarasa nearly made his mark shortly after when his 40 yard free-kick sped past the home defence but also past the upright.

Group 3 – Final Table

	P	W	D	L	F	A	Pts
SPAIN	12	8	3	1	27	4	19
REP. IRELAND	12	7	4	1	19	6	18
Denmark	12	7	4	1	15	2	18
N. Ireland	12	5	3	4	14	13	13
Lithuania	12	2	3	7	8	21	7
Latvia	12	0	5	7	4	21	5
Albania	12	1	2	9	6	26	4

Group 3 – Results

	Albania	Denmark	Latvia	Lithuania	N. Ireland	Rep. Ireland	Spain
Albania	—	0-1	1-1	1-0	1-2	1-2	1-5
Denmark	4-0	—	2-0	4-0	1-0	0-0	1-0
Latvia	0-0	0-0	—	1-2	1-2	0-2	0-0
Lithuania	3-1	0-0	1-1	—	0-1	0-1	0-2
N. Ireland	3-0	0-1	2-0	2-2	—	1-1	0-0
Rep. Ireland	2-0	1-1	4-0	2-0	3-0	—	1-3
Spain	3-0	1-0	5-0	5-0	3-1	0-0	—

Group 3 – Scorers

Goals	Player	Country
7	Salinas	Spain
6	Aldridge	Rep. Ireland
4	Pingel	Denmark
3	Beguristain	Spain
	Hierro	Spain
	Linards	Latvia
	Magilton	N. Ireland
	Staunton	Rep. Ireland
	Wilson K.	N. Ireland
2	Bakero	Spain
	Caminero	Spain
	Fridrikas	Lithuania
	Guerrero	Spain
	Kushta	Albania
	Laudrup B.	Denmark
	McGrath	Rep. Ireland
	Michel	Spain
	Quinn J.	N. Ireland
	Quinn N.	Rep. Ireland
	Taggart	N. Ireland
	Vilfort	Denmark
1	Abazi	Albania
	Aldana	Spain
	Alexeyenko	Latvia
	Alfonso	Spain
	Baltusnikas	Lithuania
	Baranauskas	Lithuania
	Cascarino	Rep. Ireland
	Christiansen	Spain
	Clarke	N. Ireland
	Cristobal	Spain
	Demollari	Albania
	Dowie	N. Ireland
	Gray	N. Ireland
	Guardiola	Spain
	Jensen	Denmark
	Kepa	Albania
	Kernaghan	Rep. Ireland
	Larsen	Denmark
	McDonald	N. Ireland
	McLoughlin	Rep. Ireland
	Moller	Denmark
	Narbekovas	Lithuania
	Olsen L.	Denmark
	Own Goal	Denmark
	Poderis	Lithuania
	Povlsen	Denmark
	Raklli	Albania
	Sheedy	Rep. Ireland
	Sheridan	Rep. Ireland
	Strudal	Denmark
	Sukristovas	Lithuania
	Tereskinas	Lithuania
	Toni	Spain
	Townsend	Rep. Ireland

Then with 11 minutes gone Spain won a throw-in on the right. It came long and Salinas back-headed to the awaiting boot of Caminero, whose volley into the roof of the net was a peach. Three minutes later goal-provider became goal-scorer, as Salinas outmanoeuvred Kernaghan, the only defender in retreat, and turned near the by-line to bulge the net with a low shot from a tight angle.

Irish eyes were starting to weep, although there were nearly tears of joy when Irwin's free-kick was met perfectly by Kernaghan, but the Manchester City player's header crashed against the bar and to safety.

By now Spain were well in control and keeping possession well and they sealed the Irish fate on 26 minutes when Sheridan, on for the injured Moran, sliced the ball into Salinas' path to set up a one-on-one situation which the striker won with ease to put the visitors three up.

The Republic continued to try to get back into a game that was now being dominated by the confident Spanish. But a siesta in the visitors' concentration produced a flicker of hope for the Republic. Halfway through the second half some close passing on the periphery of the Spanish area ended when Houghton laid a pass to Sheridan, who buried it into the back of the net – 3-1. The sun came back out and the crowd came to life. However, Spain again took control and the match again drifted away from the home side to its inevitable conclusion.

In Copenhagen things appeared to be going only slightly better for the home side. The Northern Irish nearly made a dramatic start, slicing through the Danish defence with some excellent approach work which gave Michael Hughes possession on the left. The Strasbourg player kept his cross-cum-shot low only to see it smothered on the line by Peter Schmeichel – this inside the first 60 seconds of play. Northern Ireland saw several other good opportunities go begging thanks to either wayward finishing or goalkeeper intervention.

The Danes should have had a penalty in the 58th minute when McDonald up-ended Brian Laudrup but their appeals were waved away by the Belarus referee. Northern Ireland had the ball in the net after 70 minutes when substitute Jimmy Quinn beat Schmeichel with a glancing header, but he had fouled Vilfort en route to doing so and a free-kick was the correct outcome. The game looked as though it were heading for a draw until, with nine minutes remaining, Brian Laudrup beat Wright, after the keeper had saved Povlsen's angled drive.

13 October   *Dublin*   *Att: 33,000*
REP. IRELAND   **1**   (Sheridan 72)
SPAIN   **3**   (Caminero 11; Salinas 14, 26)
Rep. Ireland: Bonner, Irwin, Phelan, Moran (Sheridan 22), Kernaghan, Keane, McGrath, Houghton, Quinn, Whelan, Staunton (Cascarino 45)
Spain: Zubizarreta, Ferrer, Voro, Nadal, Giner, Hierro, Goikoetxea, Camarasa, Salinas (Guardiola 68), Caminero (Bakero 31), Luis Enrique
Ref: Baldas (Ita)

13 October   *Copenhagen*   *Att: 40,000*
DENMARK   **1**   (B. Laudrup 81)
N. IRELAND   **0**
Denmark: Schmeichel, Vilfort, Rieper, Olsen, Kjeldbjerg, Steen Nielsen, Jensen, Pingel (H. Larsen 87), Povlsen, B. Laudrup, M. Laudrup
N. Ireland: Wright, Fleming, McDonald, Taggart, Worthington, Wilson (Black 85), Donaghy, Magilton, Hughes, Dowie (Quinn 61), P. Gray
Ref: Zhuk (Bls)

And so to the final two games, and what games they looked to be. With Spain at home to Denmark, the Republic knew that a win over their bitter rivals from the north would see them qualify. Denmark, a point clear at the top of the group, could afford to draw in Spain, while the Spanish had to win to be sure. The Danes though had conceded only a single goal in their previous 11 games and that coming 15 minutes from time in a 1-1 draw with the Republic.

In Seville the Danes should have been given a perfect boost when veteran goalkeeper Andoni Zubizarreta received his marching orders after just ten minutes of play for a professional foul. The Danes laboured heavily against the 10-man Spanish for whom substitute goalkeeper Santiago Canizares performed well. Goalless at the interval, Spain scored a priceless goal on 63 minutes when Fernando Hierro headed home from a right-wing centre. The goal was not without controversy and Jose-Maria Bakero admitted afterwards that he had backed into Schmeichel to prevent him from getting to the cross.

In Belfast things looked to be going the home side's way as well in what was Billy Bingham's 117th and last match in charge of Northern Ireland. With the Republic largely on top and having to take the game to Northern Ireland, Iain Dowie crossed and Jimmy Quinn unleashed a volley which lashed into the net. Trailing by a goal in a game they had to win to be sure of qualification, the Republic still had 17 minutes left to sort the situation out. They needed just five of those to get back at level pegging. Alan McLoughlin, who had been on the field for only eight minutes, let go an opportunist shot to make it 1-1.

Tommy Wright, the North's goalkeeper, continued to make a series of fine saves, the best of them at the feet of Ray Houghton, and the final whistle went. A 1-1 draw and utter confusion around Landsdowne Road. The Spanish win put them at the top of the group, Denmark and the Republic had identical goal differences of 13 but the Republic snatched second spot by virtue of having scored more goals. The news broke and so did pandemonium.

17 November   *Belfast*   *Att: 10,200*
N. IRELAND   **1**   (J. Quinn 73)
REP. IRELAND   **1**   (McLoughlin 78)
N. Ireland: Wright, Fleming, Worthington, Taggart, McDonald, Donaghy, Wilson (Black 82), Magilton, Quinn, Gray (Dowie 72), Hughes
Rep. Ireland: Bonner, Irwin, Phelan, McGrath, Keane, Townsend, Houghton (McLoughlin 70), Quinn, Aldridge (Cascarino 81), McGoldrick
Ref: Cakar (Tur)

17 November   *Sevilla*   *Att: 40,000*
SPAIN   **1**   (Hierro 63)
DENMARK   **0**
Spain: Zubizarreta, Ferrer, Giner, Alkorta, Camarasa (Canizares 10), Nadal, Hierro, Goikoetxea, Salinas (Quique Narvaez 52), Bakero, Luis Enrique
* *Zubizarreta sent off after 10 minutes.*
Denmark: Schmeichel, Steen Nielsen (Kjeldbjerg 46), Rieper, John Jensen, Friis-Hansen, Vilfort, L. Olsen, H. Larsen, M. Laudrup, Povlsen (Christensen 71), B. Laudrup
Ref: Nikakis (Gre)

GROUP 4: Comfortable passage for Romania and Belgium

With seven wins from eight games, Belgium had every right to look forward to the remaining stages of their qualifying campaign. Only a 2-0 defeat in Cardiff early in 1993 had blotted their record and they sat top of the pile, five points clear of the other three contenders as the 1993–94 season dawned albeit having played a game more. But, as history has proved so many times, points in the bag are more use than games in hand. With that in mind Belgium, under the guidance of Paul Van Himst, were favourites to go forward to the final stages.

With Cyprus and the Faeroes there to make up the numbers, the second qualifying place looked to be a straight fight between Romania, the RCS and Wales. In the first group game of the new season the latter two were brought together in Cardiff. What had looked to be a night of promise for Wales turned into one of disappointment when the Representation of Czech and Slovak Republics stole a point at the Arms Park. A win was vital for both sides as Romania had won 4-0 in Toftir earlier in the day, Raducioiu helping himself to all four of the goals after the Faeroe Islanders had limited the visitors to a single first-half strike.

The RCS opened the scoring after 16 minutes when a mistake by Mark Hughes let in Pavel Kuka. Neville Southall came out of his goal and the Slavia Prague player rammed the ball home off the goalkeeper's body despite the close attentions of Eric Young. It was only the second goal the Welsh had conceded in their eight internationals at the Arms Park and they set about restoring the equilibrium in a positive fashion. The equaliser came in the 21st minute when David Phillips produced a superb cross from the right that Ryan Giggs stretched a leg to, and diverted, past Petr Kouba.

Giggs was instrumental in Wales taking the lead ten minutes before the break. Ivan Hasek fouled Dean Saunders and from the free kick taken by Phillips, Giggs won the ball in the air and set it on to Rush, who stumbled but still beat Kouba from ten yards.

On the hour Vaclav Jezek, the RCS manager, brought on Tomas Skuhravy for Latal. A run across the edge of the area by the Genoa player resulted in a foul by Young and from the resultant free kick Dubovsky, the £2.5 million Real Madrid forward, fired home from 25 yards.

8 September		Cardiff	Att: 37,558
WALES	**2**	(Giggs 21; Rush 35)	
RCS	**2**	(Kuka 16; Dubovsky 67)	

Ian Rush of Wales (right) is just beaten to the ball by Romania's Miodrag Belodedici.

QUALIFYING GROUPS

Wales: Southall, Phillips, Bowen, Aizlewood, Young, Symons, Horne, Saunders, Rush, Hughes, Giggs
RCS: Kouba, Latal (Skuhravy 60), Suchoparek, Hasek, Kadlec, Nemecek, Hapal, Novotny, Kuka, Dubovsky, Moravcik
Ref: Ansuategui Roca (Spa)

8 September *Toftir* *Att: 2,724*
FAEROE ISLANDS 0
ROMANIA 4 (Raducioiu 23, 58, 60, 76)
Faeroes: Knudsen, Jakobsen, Johannesen, Kurt Morkore, Justinussen, Allan Morkore (Nolsoe 78), Jarnskor, Dam, Hansen, Reynheim, Hansen (Pall a Reynatugvu 76)
Romania: Prunea, Petrescu (Craioveanu 76), Selimesi, Prodan, Lupescu, Popescu, Munteanu, Sabau, Raducioiu, Hagi, Vladoiu (Panduru 68)
Ref: Zhuk (Bls)

Romania's win over the Faeroes had consolidated their second place behind Belgium, while the draw in Cardiff had opened up a small gap between them and the RCS and Wales. At least a point from their encounter with Belgium, if not a victory, in Bucharest in their next game was therefore of the utmost importance if they were to keep their advantage over the other two contenders.

As it turned out Romania beat the group leaders. Milan's Raducioiu broke the deadlock with a 67th minute penalty and Ilie Dumitrescu made it 2-0 five minutes from time before Enzo Scifo hit back for Belgium from the spot with only two minutes remaining.

Elsewhere on the evening of 13 October Wales were entertaining Cyprus in Cardiff. The flow of the game for the first half was predominantly towards Petrides but his goal remained intact as the sides turned around. In the second half little changed and Terry Yorath's side became ever more anxious. As the Welsh eagerness increased so did that of the Cypriots and shortly after a Mark Hughes header had cannoned off the bar, Costa was sent off for a second bookable offence. As Wales tried to press home their attacking and numerical advantage they continued to go close – Speed and Rush in particular. The breakthrough came with ten minutes remaining, thanks to Saunders. With nine minutes remaining Constantinou also received his marching orders and Rush secured a second goal four minutes from time against the nine remaining.

13 October *Bucharest* *Att: 38,000*
ROMANIA 2 (Raducioiu 67 pen; Dumitrescu 85)
BELGIUM 1 (Scifo 88 pen)
Romania: Prunea, Petrescu, Prodan, Belodedici, Lupescu, Popescu, Munteanu, Sabau (Selimesi 27), Raducioiu, Hagi (Vladoiu 88) Dumitrescu
Belgium: Preud'homme, Medved, Grun, Albert, Smidts, Borkelmans (Oliveira 70), F. Van Der Elst, Boffin, Staelens, Scifo, Wilmots (Czerniatynski 78)
Ref: Puhl (Hun)

13 October *Cardiff* *Att: 30,825*
WALES 2 (Saunders 70; Rush 86)
CYPRUS 0
Wales: Southall, Phillips, Symons (Goss 70), Aizlewood, Young, Horne, Speed, Saunders, Rush, Hughes, Giggs
Cyprus: Petrides, Costa, Pittas (Xiourouppas 78), Constantinou, Christofi, Yiangoudakis (Panayi 78)D. Ioannou, Larkou, Sotiriou, Papavassilou, M. Charalambous.
*Costa sent off in the 50th minute. Constantinou sent off in the 80th minute
Ref: Don (Eng)

The RCS kept up their momentum when they encountered the Cypriots in Kosice later in the month. An early goal by Dubovsky was followed by Hapal's strike to give the Representation side a 2-0 advantage at half time. As if to prove that the sendings-off in Cyprus were not flukes, Kleanthous after 65 minutes and Larkou on 88 minutes received their red cards. In between Skuhravy had netted a third for the RCS to seal a 3-0 win.

27 October *Kosice* *Att: 16,602*
RCS 3 (Dubovsky 10; Hapal 22; Skuhravy 76)
CYPRUS 0
RCS: Ladislav Molnar, Hasek, Smicer (Timko 73), Suchoparek, Kadlec, Nemecek, Hapal, Dubovsky, Kuka (Postulka 80), Skuhravy, Moravcik
Cyprus: Petrides, Costas Constantinou, George Constantinou, Kleanthous, Panayiu, Andreou (Kalotheu) 69, Larkou, Hatzilukas, Stiru, Papavassiliou, Xiuruppas (Stefani 62)
*Kleanthous sent off in the 65th minute. Larkou sent off in the 88th minute
Ref: Spassov (Bul)

Wales, without the suspended Mark Hughes and Mark Aizlewood, who received their second cautions in the game against Cyprus, went into their game in Cardiff – Terry Yorath's 100th as player and manager – knowing that they needed to win by at least two clear goals to ensure qualification. A victory would suffice if the injury-hit Belgians earned the point they needed against the RCS in the other group game, being played in Brussels. The RCS needed to win to ensure qualification, not being reliant on results elsewhere. With the Romanians needing a point from the Welsh, the final two group games had all the elements of a sudden death cup tie.

The Romanians – riding high since Anghel Iordanescu took over in the close season – included nine overseas players in the side to face the Welsh in front of 40,000 fervent supporters. Romania had beaten Wales 5-1 in the reverse fixture 17 months earlier and they repeated their victory as the home side were unable to match the technical superiority.

The Romanians took the lead in the 32nd minute when Belodedici passed to Gheorghe Hagi – now playing his weekly football for Brescia in Italy's Serie B – who unleashed a shot which crossed the line after the normally reliable Southall allowed the ball to sneak through his arms. The Romanians led at the interval but there was hope for the home side as Saunders equalised just after the hour, when he side-footed home Speed's header across the goal.

Group 4 – Final Table

	P	W	D	L	F	A	Pts
ROMANIA	10	7	1	2	29	12	15
BELGIUM	10	7	1	2	16	5	15
RCS	10	4	5	1	21	9	13
Wales	10	5	2	3	19	12	12
Cyprus	10	2	1	7	8	18	5
Faeroe Islands	10	0	0	10	1	38	0

Group 4 – Results

	Belgium	Cyprus	Faeroe Islands	RCS	Romania	Wales
Belgium	—	1-0	3-0	0-0	1-0	2-0
Cyprus	0-3	—	3-1	1-1	1-4	0-1
Faeroe Islands	0-3	0-2	—	0-3	0-4	0-3
RCS	1-2	3-0	4-0	—	5-2	1-1
Romania	2-1	2-1	7-0	1-1	—	5-1
Wales	2-0	2-0	6-0	2-2	1-2	—

Group 4 – Scorers

Goals	Player	Country
10	Raducioiu	Romania
8	Rush	Wales
6	Dubovsky	RCS
5	Hagi	Romania
	Wilmots	Belgium
4	Balint	Romania
	Dumitrescu	Romania
	Saunders	Wales
	Scifo	Belgium
	Sotriou	Cyprus
3	Kuka	RCS
2	Albert	Belgium
	Giggs	Wales
	Hughes	Wales
	Latal	RCS
	Lupescu	Romania
	Nemecek	RCS
	Postulka	RCS
1	Arge	Faeroe Islands
	Blackmore	Wales
	Bowen	Wales
	Czerniatynski	Belgium
	Degryse	Belgium
	Hanganu	Romania
	Hapal	RCS
	Hasek	RCS
	Ioannou Yiannos	Cyprus
	Kadlec	RCS
	Lacatus	Romania
	Moravcik	RCS
	Own Goal	Belgium
	Pana C.	Romania
	Papavassiliou	Cyprus
	Pittas	Cyprus
	Popescu	Romania
	Skuhravy	RCS
	Smidts	Belgium
	Staelens	Belgium
	Vrabec	RCS
	Xiourouppas	Cyprus
	Young	Wales

With the news that Belgium and the RCS were drawing, the home side having been reduced to ten men after Phillipe Albert was sent off for a foul on the edge of his area, a win would have been enough to see Wales through. And within two minutes of Saunders' equaliser they had the perfect opportunity to take the lead.

Gary Speed was upended by Dan Petrescu and referee Kurt Rothlisberger awarded the penalty. Ian Rush, Wales' normal penalty-taker clearly did not relish the tension of the moment and so Paul Bodin – three times taker and three times successful for his country – stepped up to the hot spot. But the defender, whose penalty for Swindon at Wembley a year earlier had taken his side into the Premiership, fired the ball against the bar.

Welsh heads dropped further in despair seven minutes from time when Raducioiu stole a late winning goal. The win, coupled with the Belgians' 0-0 draw against the RCS, meant that Romania topped the group and qualified with the Belgians. But the Welsh defeat meant that the World Cup finals had been deprived of the chance of seeing Ryan Giggs. Things were perhaps put into perspective at the end of the game when a rocket, fired from one side of the stadium, hit and tragically killed a fan on the other side of the Arms Park.

17 November   *Brussels*   *Att: 21,000*
BELGIUM 0
RCS 0
Belgium: De Wilde, Medved, De Wolf, Smidts, Albert, Staelens, Van der Est, Versavel, Scifo, Oliveira (Boffin 52), Nilis (Czerniatynski 79)
**Albert sent off in the 50th minute*
RCS: Kouba, Novotny, Kadlec, Suchoparek (Timko 80), Hasek, Dubovsky, Nemecek, Hapal (Latal 73), Moravcik, Skuhravy, Kuka
Ref: Krug (Ger)

17 November   *Cardiff*   *Att: 40,000*
WALES 1 (Saunders 61)
ROMANIA 2 (Hagi 32; Raducioiu 83)
Wales: Southall, Phillips, Bodin (Malcolm Allen 71), Melville, Young, Symons (Goss 53), Horne, Saunders, Rush, Speed, Giggs
Romania: Prunea, Petrescu, Prodan, Belodedici, Lupescu, Popescu, Selimesi (Munteanu 74), Sabau, Raducioiu, Hagi, Dumitrescu (Mihali 89)
Ref: Rothlisberger (Swi)

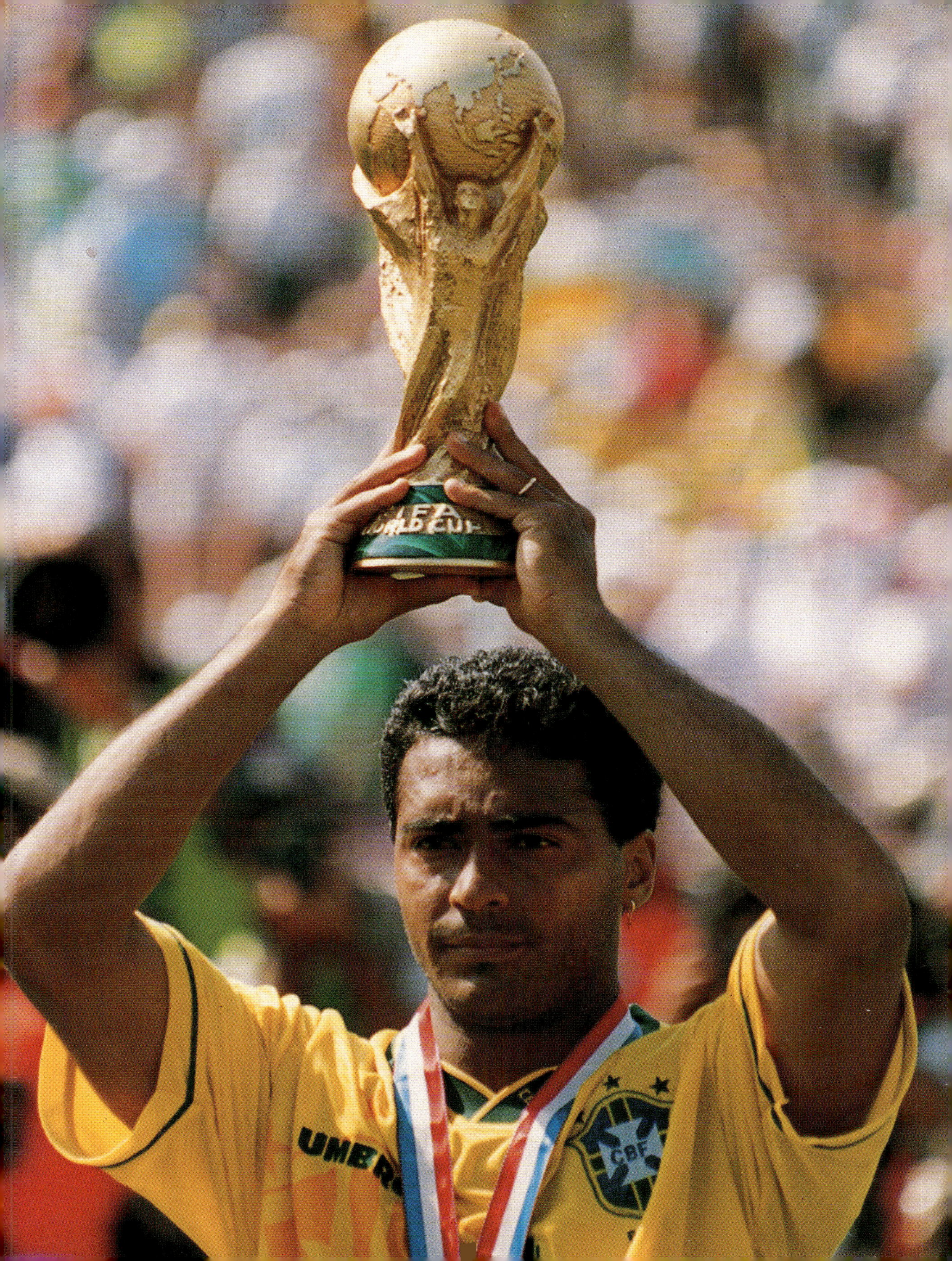
CBF

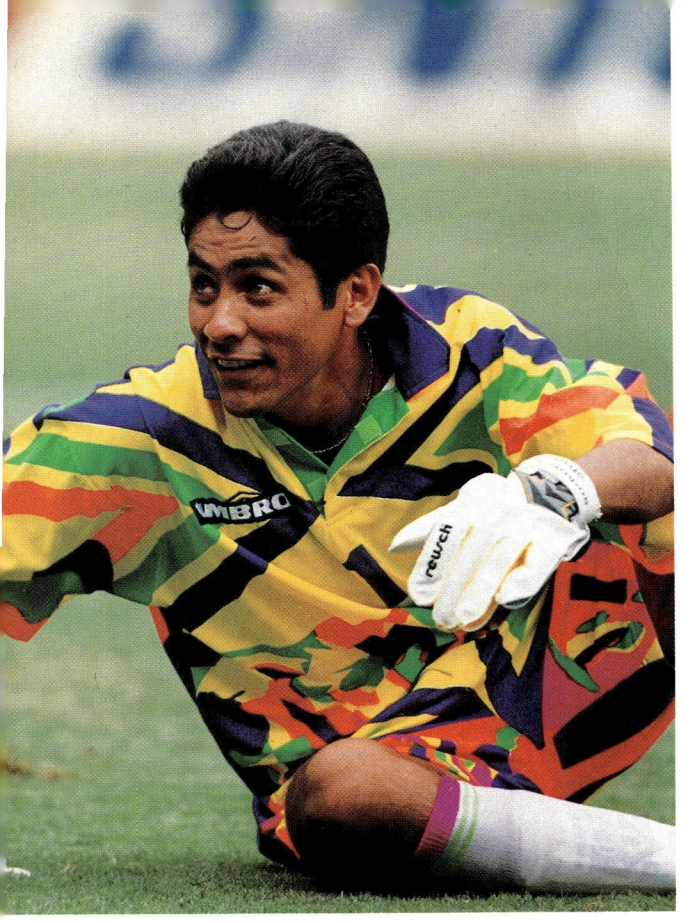

PREVIOUS PAGE: *He said it would be his World Cup. Here's the picture to prove it. Romario of Brazil and Barcelona.*

LEFT: *Jorge Campos – Mexico's colourful goalkeeper-cum-forward.*

FACING PAGE TOP: *Argentine Fernando Redondo fends off the challenge of Nikolos Machlas of Greece.*

FACING PAGE BOTTOM: *Ilie Dumitrescu of Romania gets away from Dominique Herr of Switzerland.*

OVERLEAF, TOP LEFT: *What's a World Cup without Brazilian fans? Oh for such sights on the terraces of Finland, Iceland, Estonia...*

OVERLEAF, BOTTOM LEFT: *John Aldridge scores against Mexico for the Republic of Ireland, after coming on as a substitute in their group match.*

OVERLEAF, RIGHT: *Belgium's Marc Degryse tries to fly past Ronald Koeman in the Benelux derby encounter of Group F.*

BELOW: *Brazil captain (at the start) and Paris Saint-Germain player Rai is challenged by Dmitri Kuznetsov of Russia.*

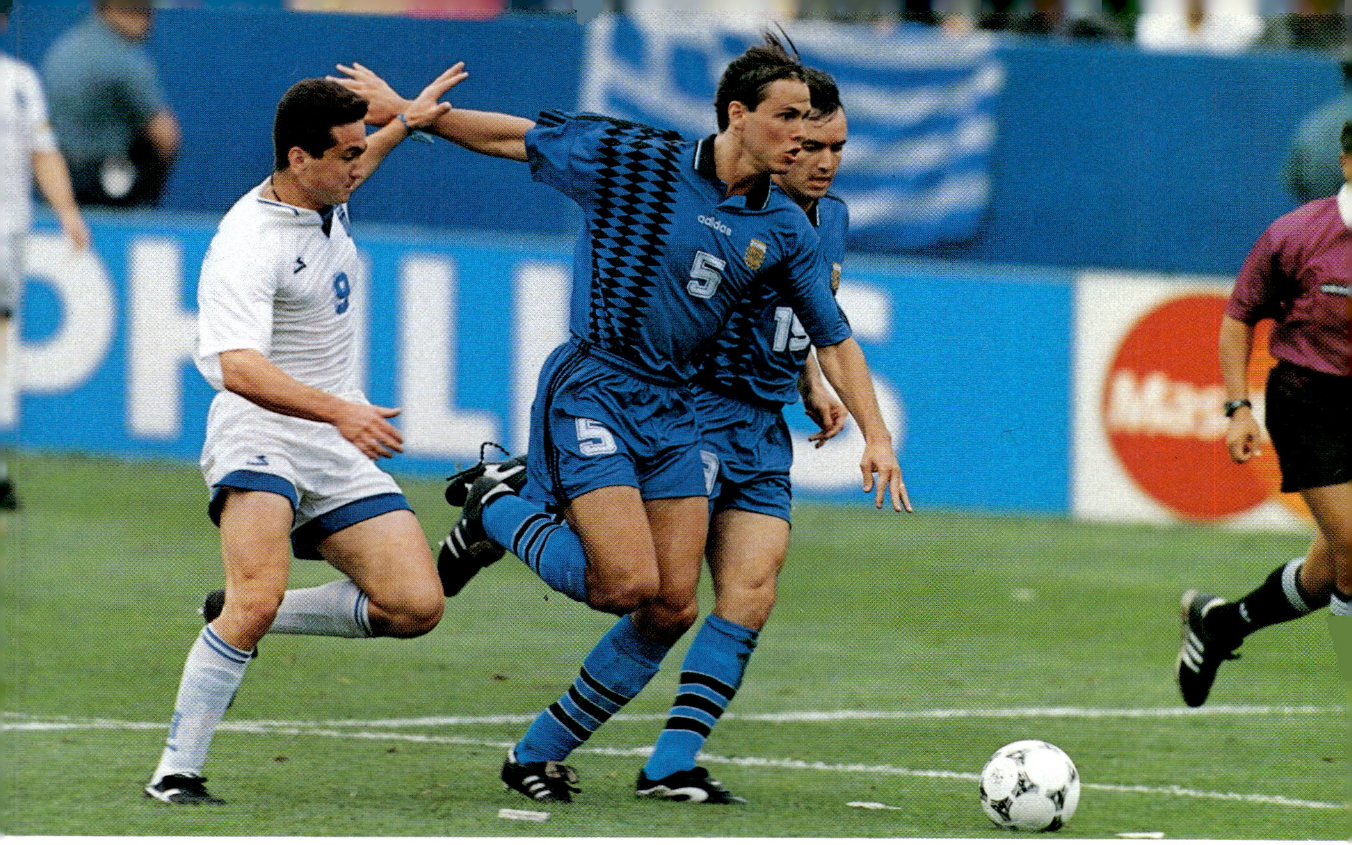

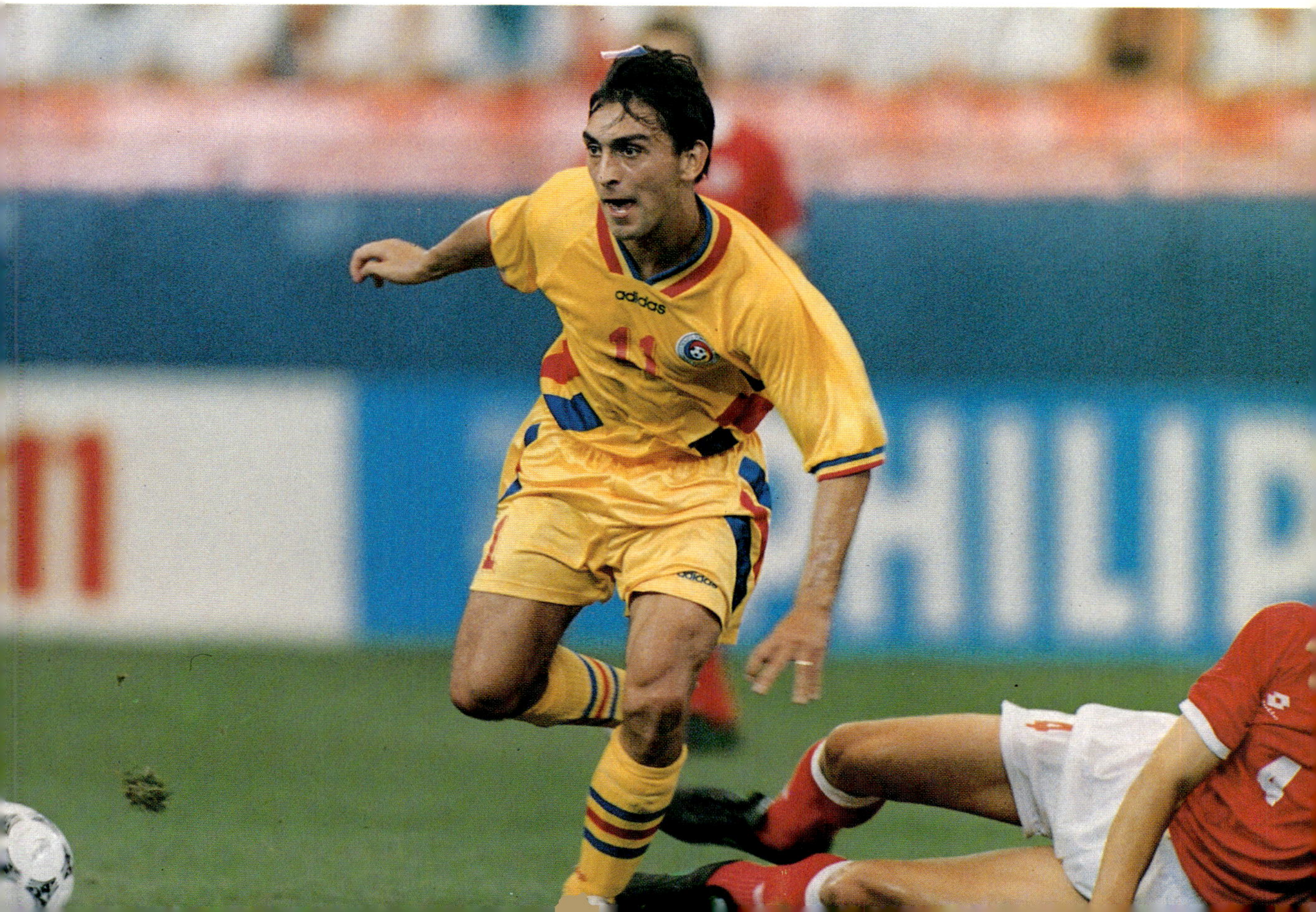

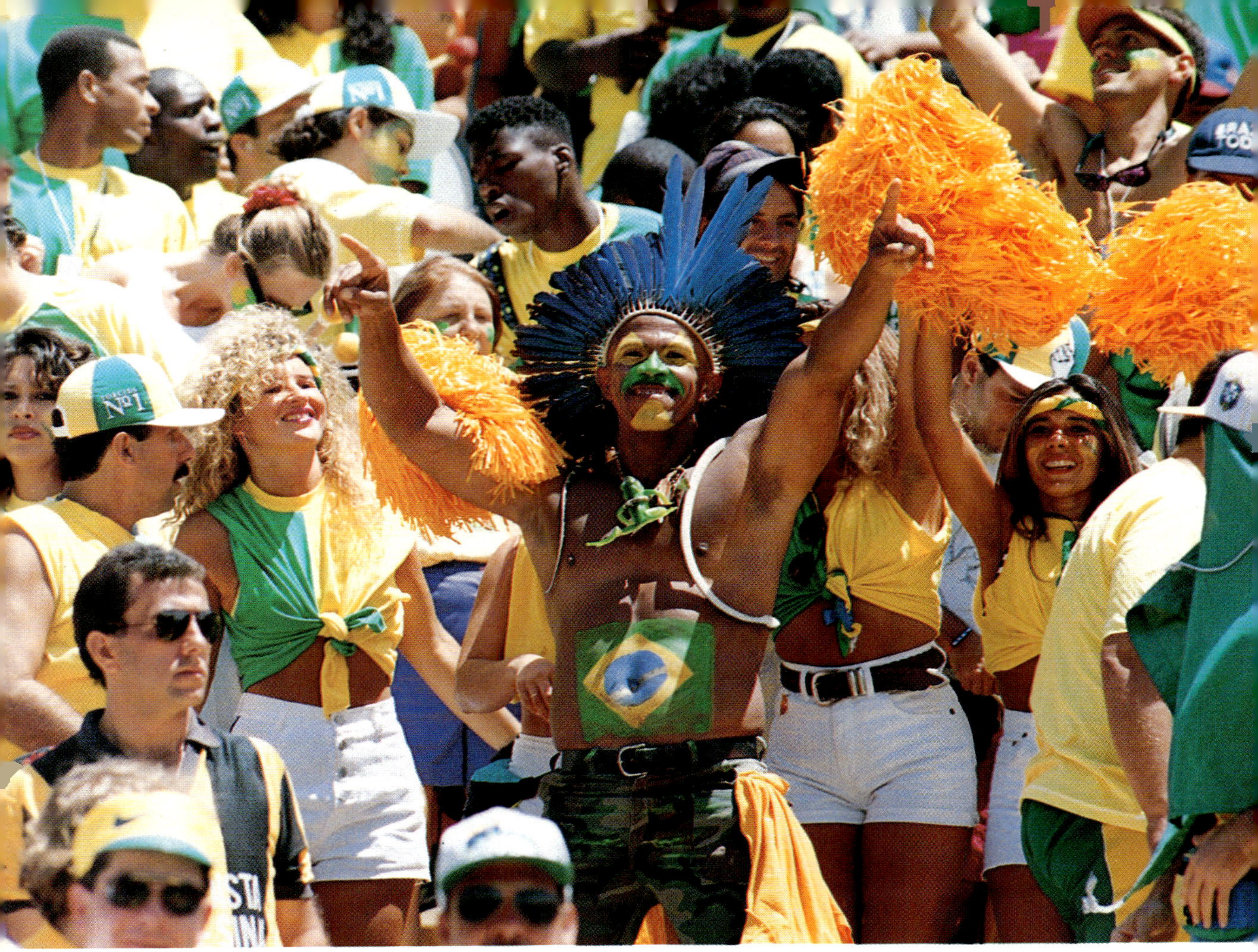

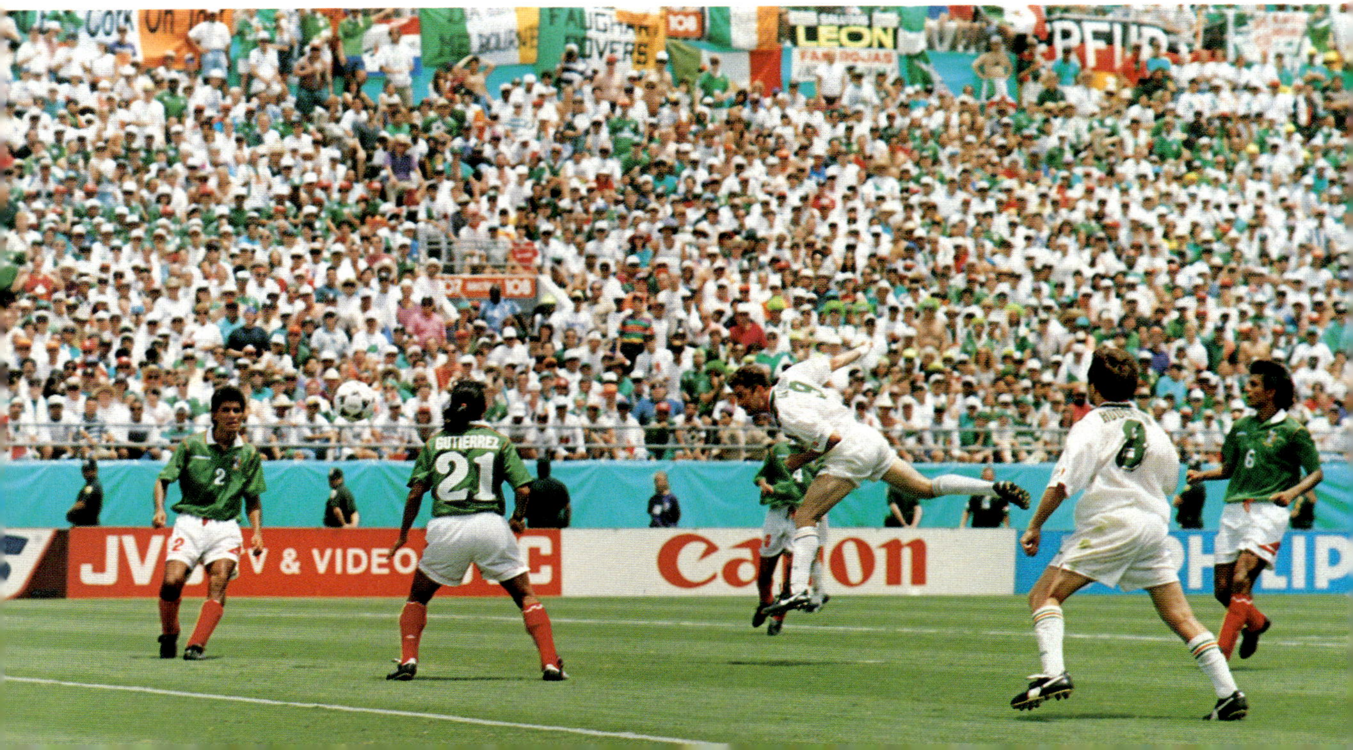
LEON
GUTIERREZ
21
Canon

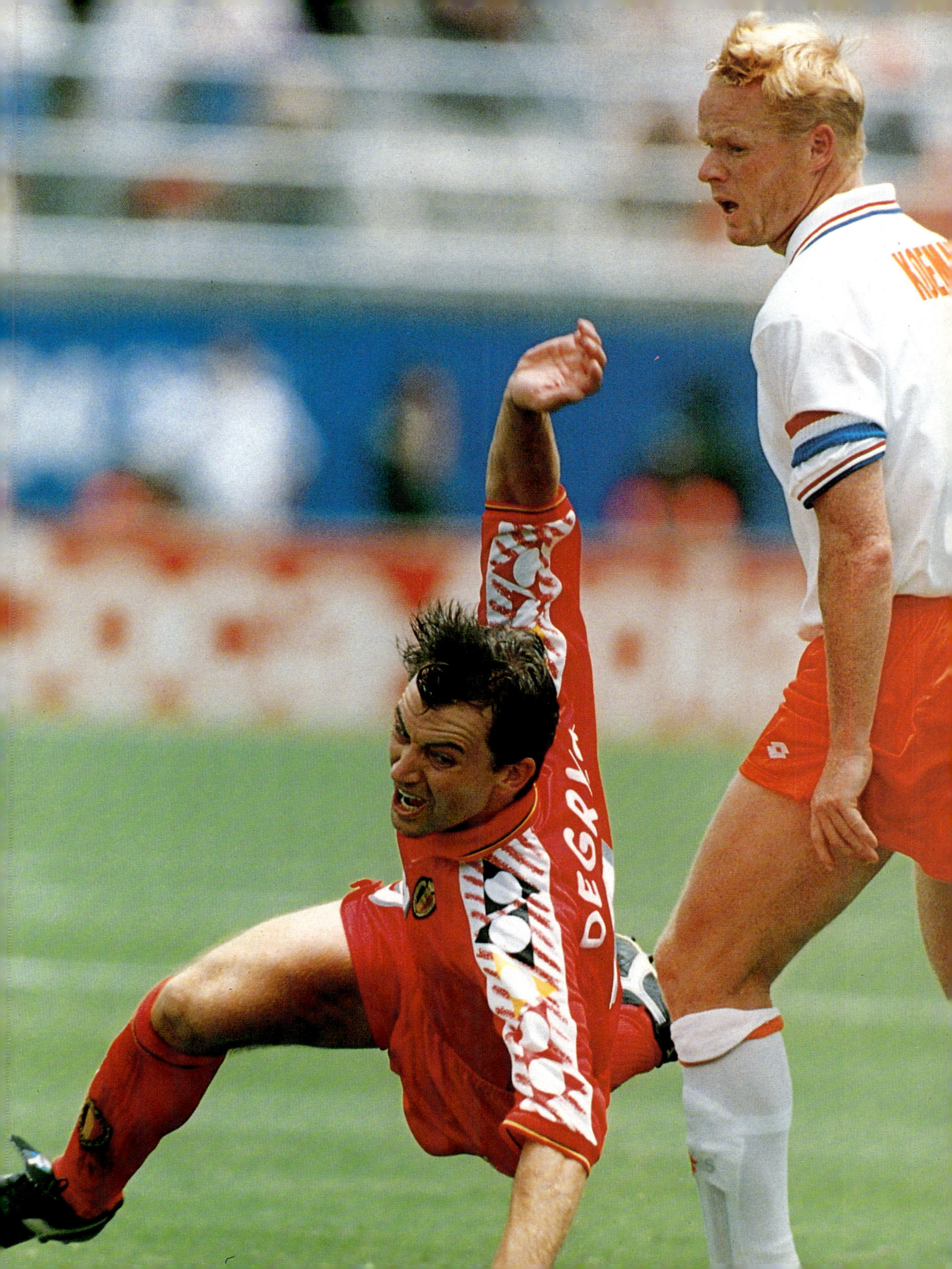

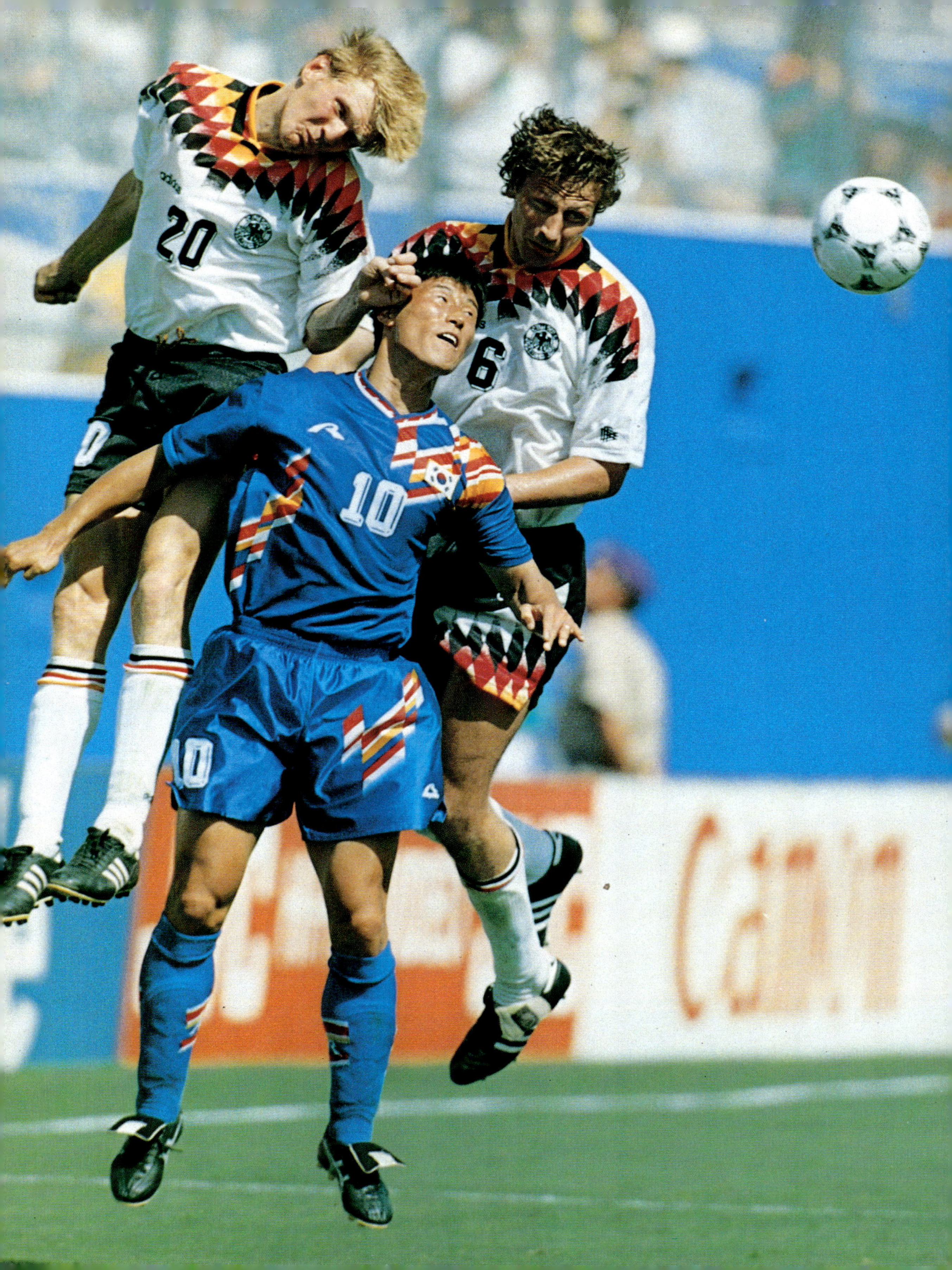
20
10
6

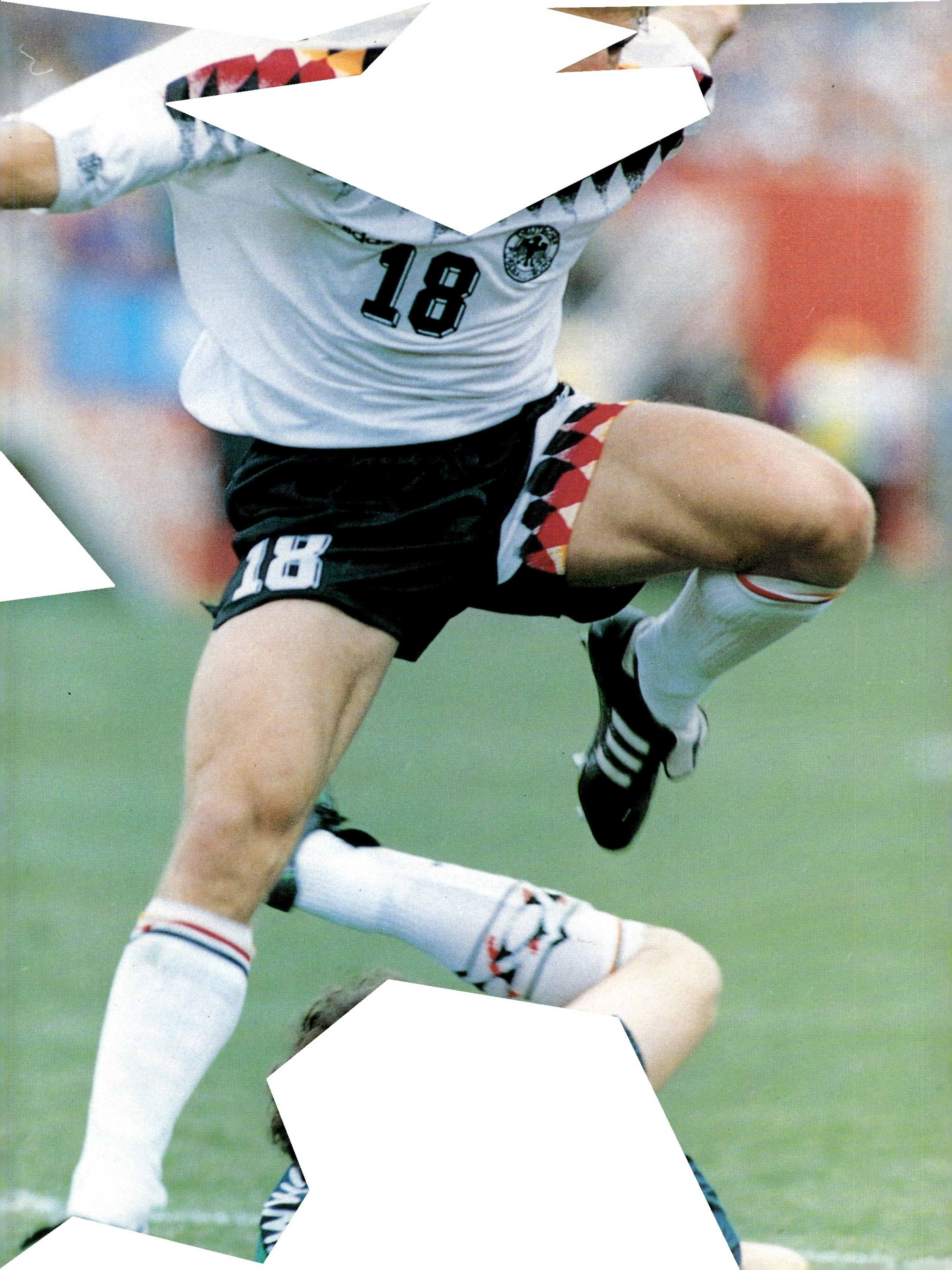
18
18

PREVIOUS PAGES, LEFT: *Stefan Effenberg (Germany), Ko Jeong-woon (South Korea), Guido Buchwald (Germany).*

PREVIOUS PAGES, RIGHT: *Michel Preud'homme was outstanding for Belgium. Here he foils Jurgen Klinsmann but couldn't stop the German striker from finding the target during Germany's 3-2 win in the second round.*

ABOVE: *Gabriel Batistuta of Argentina gets the full attention of Trifon Ivanov of Bulgaria.*

RIGHT: *The hero in '90, the villain in '94. The Republic's Packy Bonner points the way home.*

FACING PAGE: *Tomas Brolin – Sweden's powerhouse gets the right side of Fahad Bishi of Saudi Arabia.*

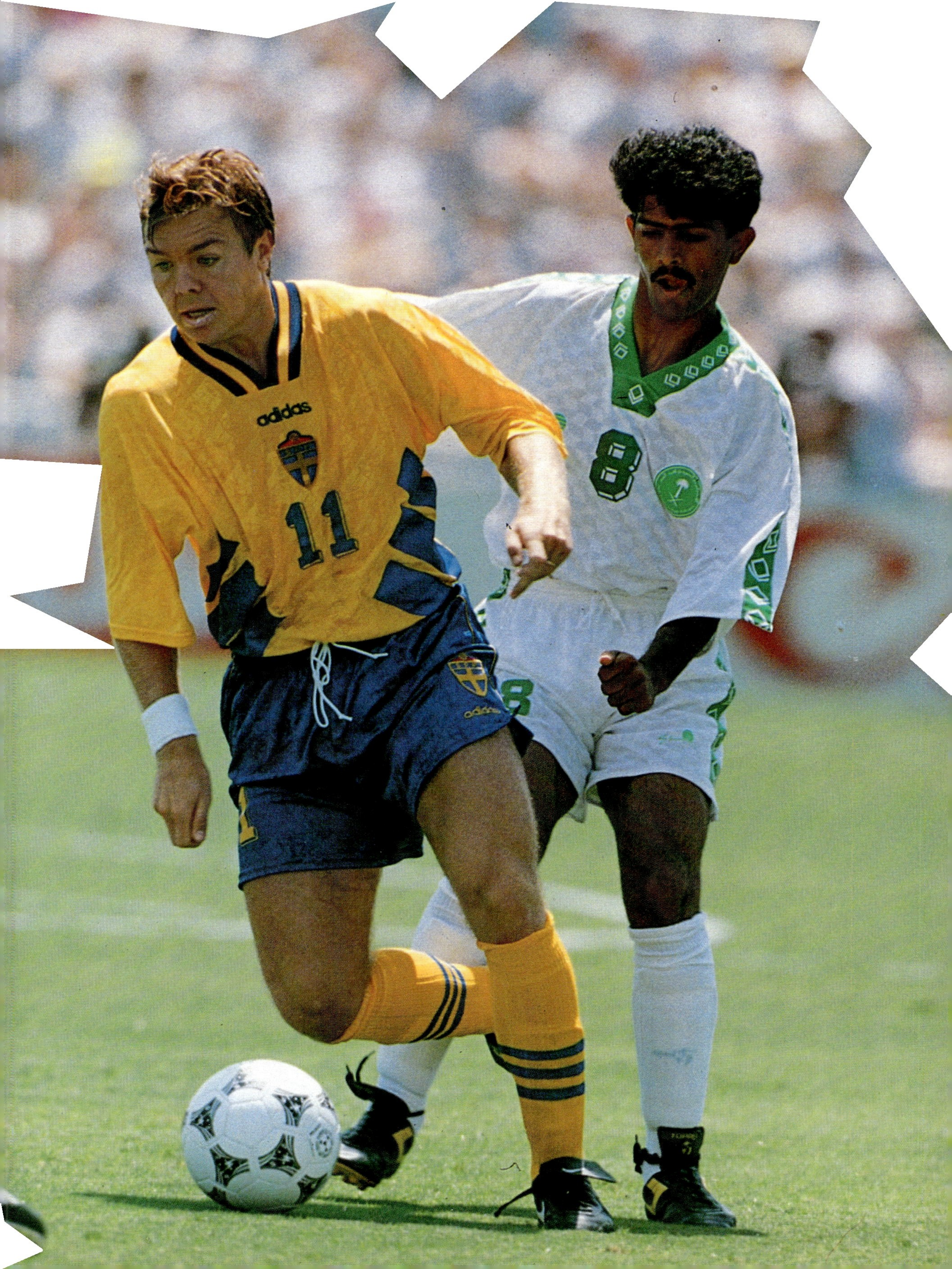
adidas
11
8

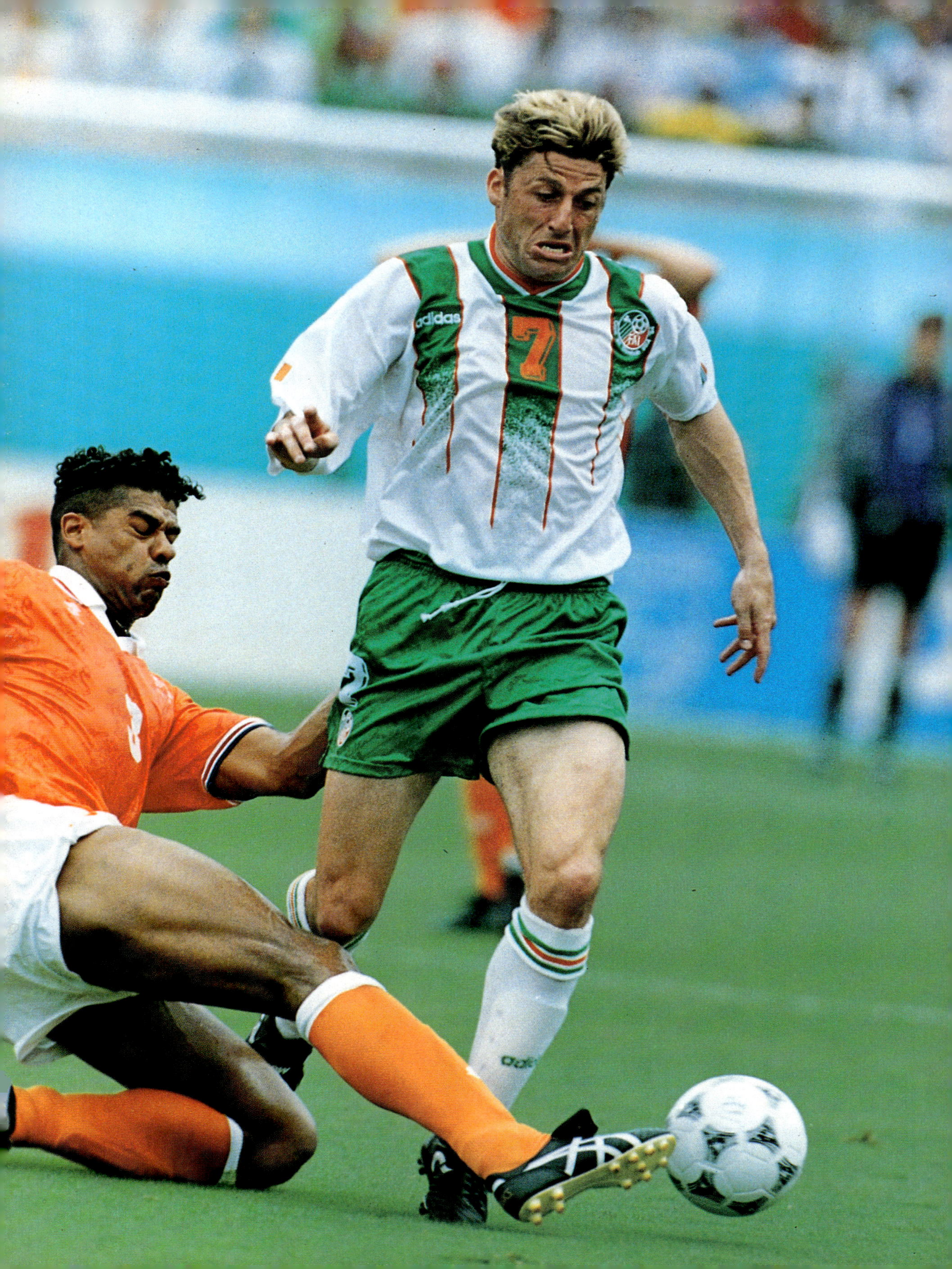
adidas

LEFT: *Roberto Baggio definitely liked Sundays. In this case Sunday Oliseh of Nigeria.*

FACING PAGE: *Frank Rijkaard just toes the ball out of the path of Andy Townsend during the Holland v Republic encounter.*

BELOW: *Paolo Maldini – perhaps the most consistent defender in the world – can't quite find a way out of the onion bag.*

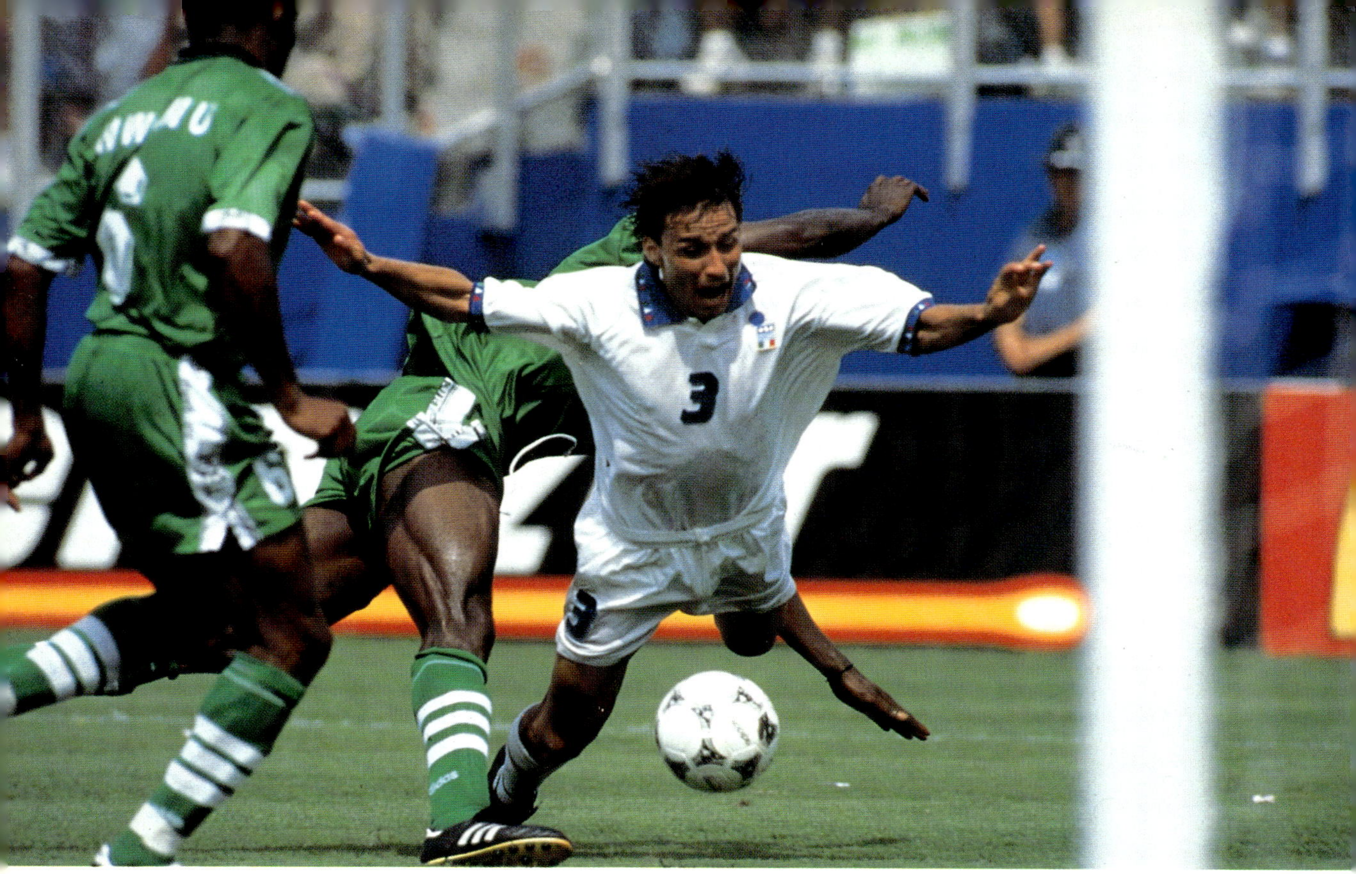

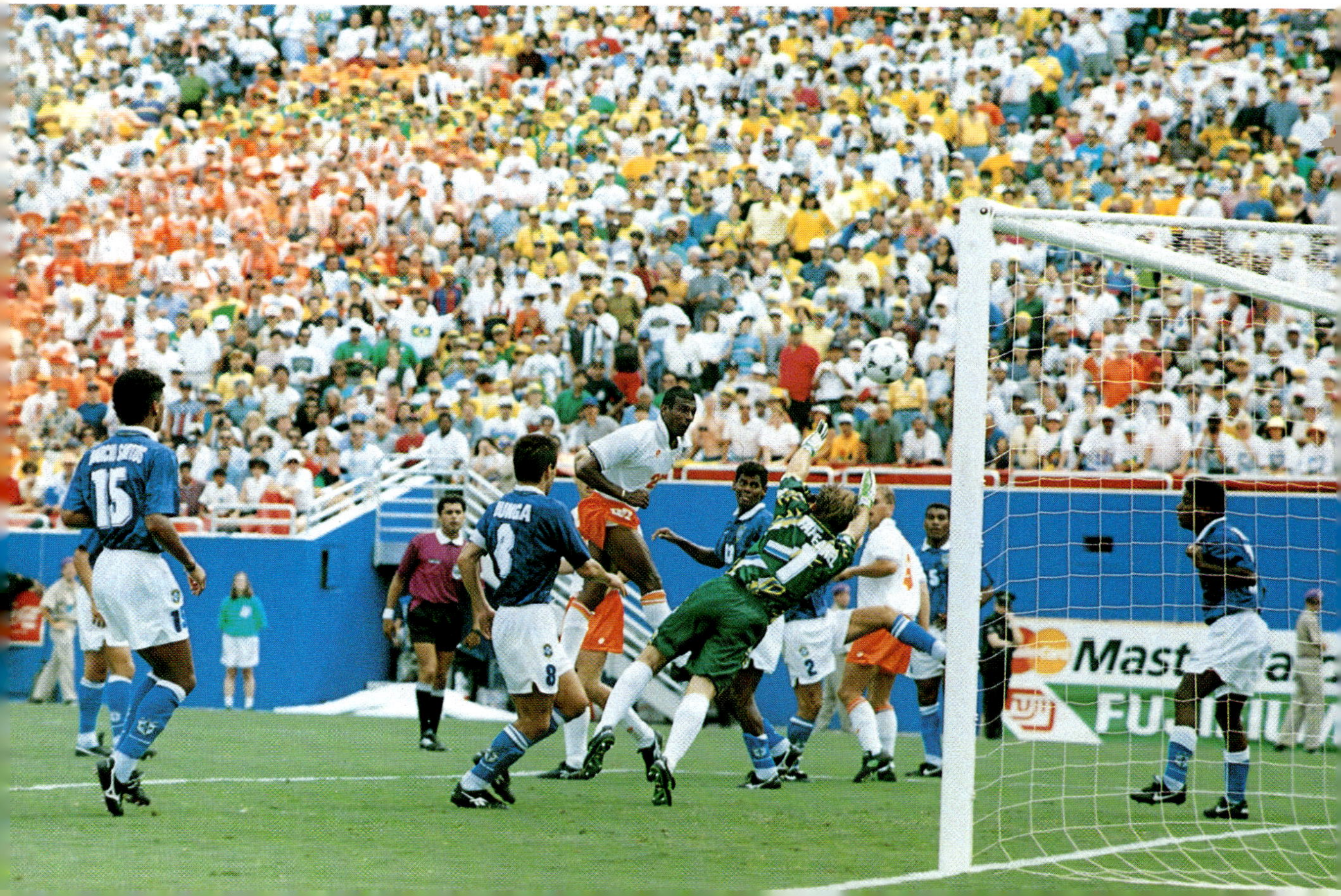

RIGHT: *The Bulgarians turned on the heat for a few sides but knew how to cool off when they had to.*

FACING PAGE TOP: *He didn't start the World Cup Finals but he played a significant part in ensuring Italy reached the final. Here Parma full-back Antonio Benarrivo is pulled down in the penalty area in the game against Nigeria. Roberto Baggio converted the match-winning penalty.*

FACING PAGE BOTTOM: *Aron Winter heads the Dutch equaliser against Brazil to make it 2-2.*

BELOW: *Gheorghe Hagi of Romania threads another precision pass as Fernando Caceres of Argentina looks on.*

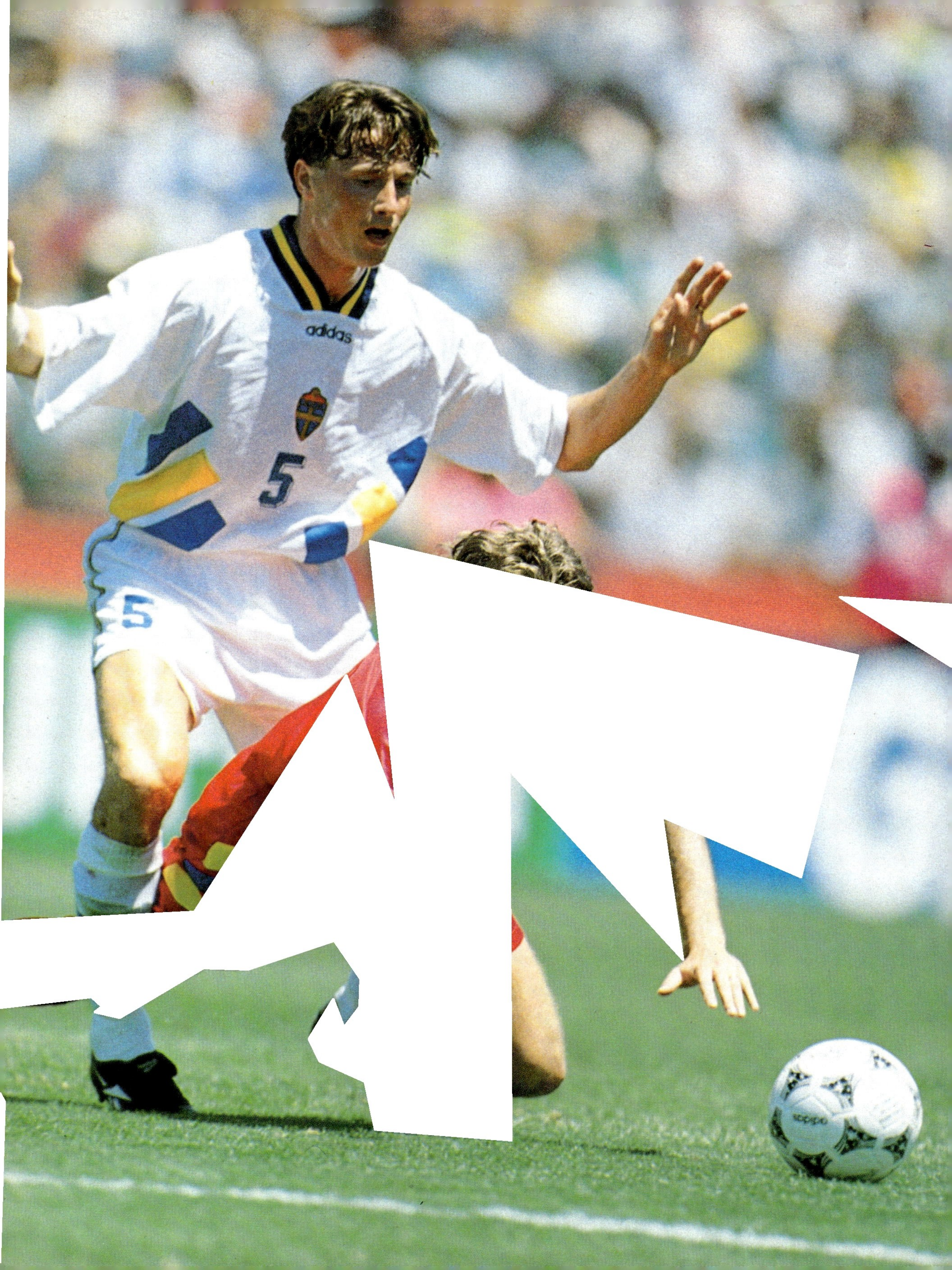
adidas
5

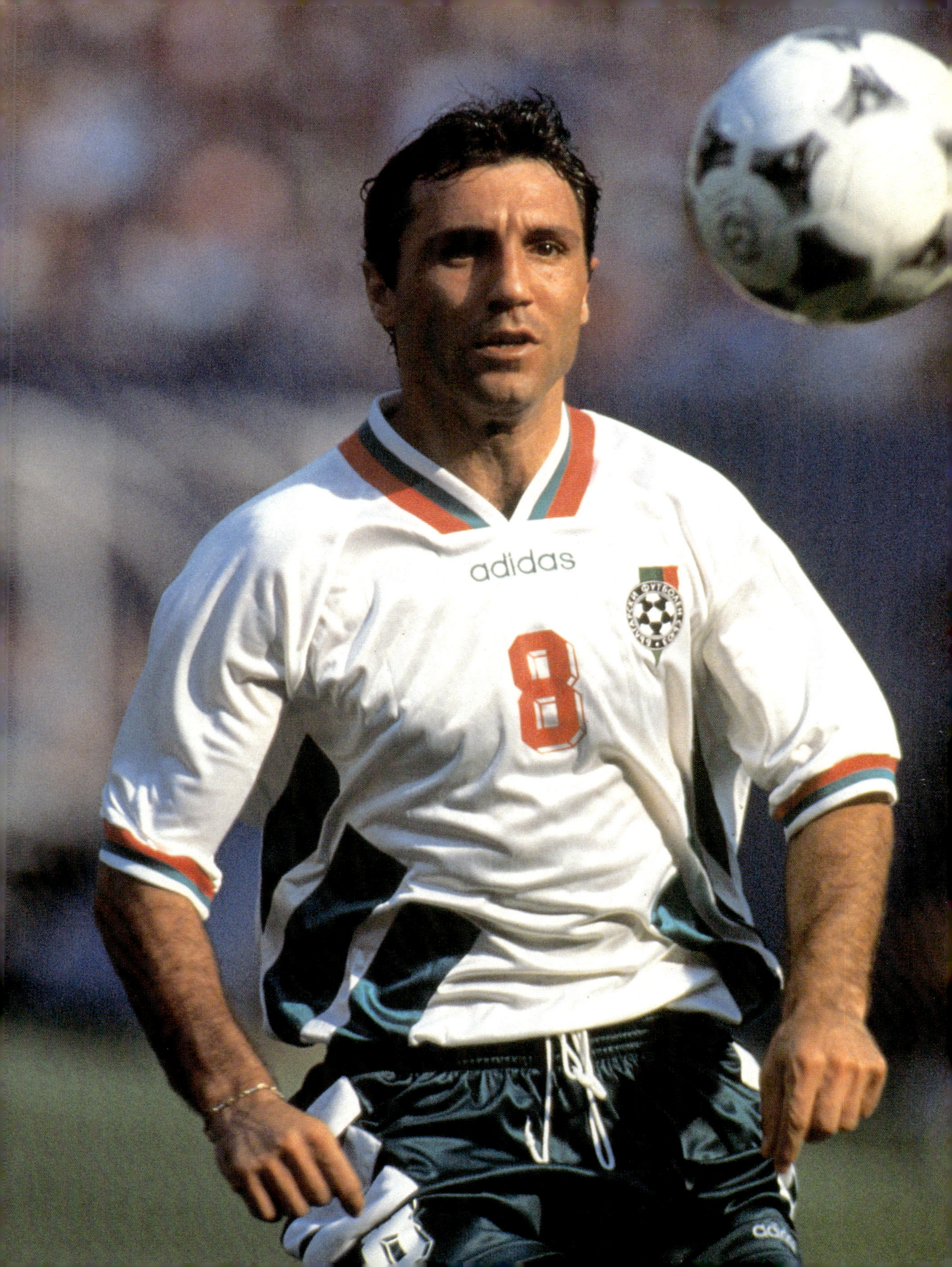
adidas
8

PREVIOUS PAGES, LEFT: *Sweden's Roger Ljung flattens Florin Raducioiu of Romania.*

PREVIOUS PAGES, RIGHT: *Hristo Stoichkov of Bulgaria.*

ABOVE: *The party and the ball are over. Roberto Baggio has missed. Brazil are World Champions.*

QUALIFYING GROUPS **65**

GROUP 5: *Greece lightning*

When FIFA announced the suspension of Yugoslavia from all international competition, Group 5 pretty much decided itself. Russia and Greece – the latter never previously to have graced the World Cup finals – had secured the two qualification spots before the 1993–94 season began. A matter of pride would determine who would finish top. Hungary were never really in contention once they lost their opening match to Iceland in a group of just five teams – not one of them a seeded nation. For the Greek national side the pre-season training included an invitation to a cocktail party in their honour by Prime Minister Constantine Mitsotakis.

The group's season got under way at the end of the first week in September when a second-half goal by Ingolfsson gave Iceland the win and points over Luxembourg. In Budapest on the same evening Russia moved two points ahead over Greece with a 3-1 win over Hungary. Hungary manager Jozsef Verebes had taken much criticism in his decision to disregard foreign-based players for this match, a policy which resulted in the recall of the

LEFT: *Marc Birsens of Luxembourg in action during his country's 3-1 home defeat by Greece.*

BELOW: *Greek skipper at the age of 36 – Tassos Mitropoulos.*

Group 5 – Final Table

	P	W	D	L	F	A	Pts
GREECE	8	6	2	0	10	2	14
RUSSIA	8	5	2	1	15	4	12
Iceland	8	3	2	3	7	6	8
Hungary	8	2	1	5	6	11	5
Luxembourg	8	0	1	7	2	17	1

Group 5 – Results

	Greece	Hungary	Iceland	Luxembourg	Russia
Greece	—	0-0	1-0	2-0	1-0
Hungary	0-1	—	1-2	1-0	1-3
Iceland	0-1	2-0	—	1-0	1-1
Luxembourg	1-3	0-3	1-1	—	0-4
Russia	1-1	3-0	1-0	2-0	—

Group 5 – Scorers

4	Kiryakov	Russia
3	Kovacs K.	Hungary
	Yuran	Russia
2	Detari	Hungary
	Gudjohnsen	Iceland
	Mitropoulos	Greece
	Sverrisson	Iceland
1	Apostolakis	Greece
	Birgison	Luxembourg
	Borodyuk	Russia
	Dimitriadis	Greece
	Dobrovolsky	Russia
	Fanelli	Luxembourg
	Ingolfsson	Iceland
	Kalitzakis	Greece
	Kanchelskis	Russia
	Kolyvanov	Russia
	Kulkov	Russia
	Machlas	Greece
	Maglas	Greece
	Magnusson	Iceland
	Orlygsson	Iceland
	Own Goal	Hungary
	Piatnitski	Russia
	Radchenko	Russia
	Saravakos	Greece
	Shalimov	Russia
	Sofianopoulos	Greece
	Tsalouhidis	Greece

MTV goalkeeper, 35-year-old Gabor Zsiboras. A week before the match, in a training game, Zsiboras was taken ill. He subsequently fell into a coma from which he never recovered, and he died on the day before the game.

Piatnitski gave the Russians an early lead that was wiped out when Nikiforov put through his own goal. The game remained level until the second half when Kiriakov scored. Borodyuk made it three a minute from time, but not before Lajos Detari had wasted the chance to level the scores from the penalty spot.

8 September *Reykjavik* Att: 3,969
ICELAND 1 (Ingolfsson 61)
LUXEMBOURG 0
Iceland: B. Kristinsson, Birgisson, Bergsson, K. Jonsson, O. Thordarsson, S. Jonsson, R. Kristinsson, Ingolfsson, A. Gudjohnsen, T. Gudjohnsson, Gunnlaugsson
Luxembourg: Koch, Bossi, Birsens, Petry, Wolf, Holtz, Hellers, Saibene, Malget (Cardoni 80), Langers (Morocutti 58), Groff
Ref: Nemus Napoleon Djurhuus (Fae)

8 September *Budapest* Att: 8,000
HUNGARY 1 (own goal 20)
RUSSIA 3 (Piatnitski 14; Kiryakov 53; Borodyuk 89)
Hungary: Vegh, Banfi, Puglits, Kuttor, Bordas, J. Kovacs (Albert 64), Detari, Lipcsei (Halmai 69), Vincze, Csetoei, Klausz
Russia: Kharin, Nikiforov, Gorlukovich, A. Ivanov, Kanchelskis, Piatnitski (Dobrovolski 71), Shalimov, Onopko, Kolivanov, Yuran (Borodyuk 56), Kiryakov
Ref: Constantin (Rom)

Greece travelled to the Duchy in the second week of October, where Luxembourg limited them to a single goal by Maglas at the interval. Goals by Apostolakis and Saravakos in the first part of the second period allowed the Greeks to take their foot off the pedal before Fanelli scored a consolation goal near the end for the home side. Two weeks later Hungary secured their second win in the group games with a single goal advantage over Luxembourg. Ferencvaros' midfield player Lajos Detari scored after 20 minutes.

12 October *Luxembourg* Att: 3,000
LUXEMBOURG 1 (Fanelli 82)
GREECE 3 (Maglas 31; Apostolakis 63; Saravakos 72)
Luxembourg: Koch, Petry, Wolf, Strasser, Holts, Cardoni (Malget 46), Birsens, Groff, Morocutti (Fanelli 76), Langers, Ferron
Greece: Minou, Nobilias, Manolas, Kalitzakis, Apostolakis, Tsalouhidis, Mitropoulos (Alexandris 72), Miotlias, Dimitriadis (Marangos 46), Tsiantakis, Maglas

27 October *Budapest* Att: 1,500
HUNGARY 1 (Detari 20)
LUXEMBOURG 0
Hungary: Vegh, Banfi, Mracsko, Kuttor, Bordas, Csertoei, Detari, Lipscei, Fule (Orosz 46), Klausz, Vincze (Puglits 40)

Martin Dahlin of Sweden fires home from close range during the 3-2 win over Finland.

Luxembourg: Koch, Bossi, Petry, Wolf, Birsens, Fanelli (Morocutti 70), Hellers, Strasser, Saibene, Groff (Malget 75), Langers
Ref: Ogun Sarvan (Tur)

Russia travelled to Athens for the final game of the group knowing that they only needed to draw to consolidate their position at the top of the group table. The teams had drawn the match in Moscow 1-1 and this latest encounter in front of a noisy crowd of 60,000 proved to be equally tight. Greece, who needed to win to top the group, did so with the only goal of the game scored when 20-year-old Nikos Machlas powered home a header in the 68th minute. Alketas Panagoulias' side had completed their qualifying matches undefeated and conceded just two goals.

After the game, Russian coach Pavel Sadyrin voiced his displeasure with the performance of several of his players, in particular his foreign-based stars. The players responded by criticising the coach's style and methods. The arguments would continue.

17 November   *Athens*   *Att: 60,000*
GREECE   **1**   (Machlas 68)
RUSSIA   **0**
Greece: Minou, Apostolakis, Karataides, Manolas, Ioannides, Tsalouhides, Saravakos (Alexandris 75), Nioplias, Machlas, Mitropoulos (Marangos 33), Tsiantakis
Russia: Cherchesov, Kulkov, Onopko, Khlestov, Nikiforov, Dobrovolsky, Popov (Mostovoi 80), Kolyvanov, Yuran (Salenko 46), Salenko, Kiryakov
Ref: Diramba (Gab)

GROUP 6: French stunned by Bulgarians' frog-leap

Group 6 had developed into a three-way race between Sweden, France and Bulgaria with the first two favourites by virtue of a point and game in hand. France, who were sitting behind Sweden on goal difference, were particularly keen to do well in the 1994 event, having missed out on the 1990 finals but having been confirmed as hosts for the 1998 tournament. Bulgaria had it all to do having lost two of their seven games but with the prospect of matches against both Sweden and France to come. Clearly though, they would be reliant on one or both of the other two slipping up along the way while they had to win their remaining three games to keep the pressure on.

Bulgaria were helped in that the first game of the group matches for the new season saw the Swedes entertain the French in Stockholm in the last week of August. The French produced an impressive performance and deservedly went ahead 13 minutes from time when the Atalanta midfielder Franck Sauzee found the top corner of the net with a shot from outside the area. Thomas Ravelli, Sweden's goalkeeper, had already been called on to make a series of fine saves. In the fifth minute he denied Jean-Pierre Papin, he turned away a goal-bound effort from Eric Cantona in the 24th minute, and continued to deny the Manchester United striker in the second half.

However, with the win and two points looking likely, a defensive lapse at the death cost the French victory. Martin Dahlin ran onto a through-pass which caught the visitors' defence square, before flicking the ball over the sprawling figure of Bernard Lama.

Three days later in Vienna, Austria completed their double over Finland with a comprehensive 3-0 victory. First-half goals from Kuhbauer and Pfeifenberger gave them a comfortable lead that they added to in the dying seconds of the match when Herzog scored with a penalty.

22 August	Stockholm	Att: 30,530
SWEDEN	1	(Dahlin 89)
FRANCE	1	(Sauzee 77)

Sweden: Ravelli, R. Nilsson, Eriksson, P. Andersson, Ljung, Ingesson, Zetteberg (Rehn 70), Thern, Landberg (Limpar 81), Dahlin, Brolin
France: Lama, Desailly, Roche, Blanc, Lizarazu, Deschamps, Le Guen, Pedros (Vahirua 81), Sauzee, Papin, Cantona
Ref: Schmidhuber (Ger)

25 August	Vienna	Att: 21,000
AUSTRIA	3	(Kuhbauer 28; Pfeifenberger 41; Herzog 89 pen)
FINLAND	0	

Austria: Wohlfahrt, Kogler, Streiter, Pfeffer, Feiersinger (Flogel 82), Artner, P. Stoger, Herzog, Kuhbauer (Baur 83), A. Ogris, Pfeifenberger
Finland: Jakonen, Kinnunen, Kanerva, Heikkinen, Petaja, Suominen, Lindberg (Ruhanen 68), Hjelm, Rajamaki, Litmanen (Gronholm 76), Paatelainen
Ref: Listkiewicz (Pol)

Bulgaria got their group season under way with a 1-1 draw with rivals Sweden in Sofia. Stoichkov put the home side into the lead with a 21st-minute penalty, but Sweden were level within five minutes as Martin Dahlin earned his country a draw for the second successive match. The draw left Bulgaria needing to win their final two games to have a chance of qualification.

In Tampere on the same September evening France moved to the top of the group table with a 2-0 win over Finland. The Finns held off the French onslaught until two minutes into the second half when Blanc struck. Papin made the game safe eight minutes later from the penalty spot.

8 September	Sofia	Att: 36,000
BULGARIA	1	(Stoichkov 21 pen)
SWEDEN	1	(Dahlin 26)

Bulgaria: Ananiev, Kranenliev, T. Ivanov, Tsvetanov, Rakov, Yankov, E. Kostadinov (I. Yordanov 77) Stoichkov, Alexandrov (Donkov 54), Lechkov, Balukov
Sweden: Ravelli, J. Nilsson, Eriksson, Andersson, Ljung, Schwarz, Limpar, Ingesson, Thern, Dahlin (Rehn 85), Brolin (Ekstrom 70)
Ref: Wojciech (Pol)

8 September	Tampere	Att: 7,500
FINLAND	0	
FRANCE	2	(Blanc 47; Papin 55 pen)

Finland: Jakonen, Kinnunen, Kanerva, Petaja, Eriksson, Suominen (Paavola 75), Lindberg, Litmanen, Hjelm, Rajamaki (Ruhanen 77), Paatelainen
France: Lama, Blanc, Desailly, Roche, Petit, Deschamps (Guerin 86), Sauzee, Le Guen, Martins (Pedros 71), Papin, Cantona
Ref: Lodge (Eng)

October 13 proved to be a very interesting evening in the development of the group and produced the surprise of the group results when Israel – out of it at the bottom of the table – conjured up a last-minute winner in Paris to throw the group wide open at the top. As expected the Bulgarians had a comfortable win over Austria in Sofia. Off to the perfect start inside six minutes when Panev gave them the lead, Stoichkov added a 32nd-minute penalty before the turn round. In the second half Austria pulled themselves back into the game when Herzog netted, but Penev and Lechkov ensured the points in the latter stages of the game.

In Stockholm Sweden went into their game against neighbours Finland with manager Tommy Svensson having to make a number of changes as more established stars such as Tomas Brolin and Johnny Ekstrom dropped out, while injuries and suspensions denied him the services of at least four other squad regulars. Finland shocked their hosts by taking the lead through Suominen on 14 minutes. But two goals by Martin Dahlin and one by debutant Henrik Larsson before the interval gave the Swedes a 3-1 advantage. In the second half Ajax striker Jari Litmanen reduced the deficit but Sweden held on to win.

In Paris it was hell for Houllier. Israel had taken a 21st-minute lead when Harazi pounced but two goals in ten minutes by Sauzee and Ginola left the French leading at the interval. That's the way it stayed until the final seven minutes when Ronny Rosenthal started to tie the French in knots and orchestrate some neat, precise one-touch football down the left flank. First to benefit was Berkovich who levelled the scores and then, as the game entered its final minute, Rosenthal did the business again to present Atar with an incredible winner.

To say the French were stunned by events in the final seven minutes would be an understatement. Before the game a draw would have placed them in the finals bar a catastrophe. Now they had to ensure at least a point in their final game against the born-again Bulgarians. For Bulgaria, the task was simple – a win in Paris would see them through to USA94 at the expense of the French!

As October drew to a conclusion Austria travelled to Tel Aviv to secure a draw with Israel. Rosenthal – the scourge of the French – fired the home side into the lead after just three minutes but Reinmayr hit the equaliser 12 minutes later, and that's the way the score remained.

13 October   *Stockholm*   *Att: 30,200*
SWEDEN 3 (Dahlin 27, 44; Larson 40)
FINLAND 2 (Suominen 14; Litmanen 60)
Sweden: Ravelli, R. Nilsson, Eriksson, Ljung, Karmark, Ingesson (Landberg 8), Zetterberg, Schwarz, Limpar, Dahlin, Henrik Larsson (Martinsson 80)
Finland: Jakonen, Kinnunen, Kanerva, Heikkinen, Eriksson (Jarvinen 46), Souminen, Lindberg, Aaltonen, Petaja, Litmanen, Hjelm
Ref: Cakar (Tur)

13 October   *Sofia*   *Att: 22,500*
BULGARIA 4 (Penev 6, 75; Stoichkov 32 pen; Lechkov 89)
AUSTRIA 1 (Herzog 51)
Bulgaria: Mikhailov, Kremenliev, Hubchev, Tsvetanov, Ivanov, Yankov (Todorov 79), Kostadinov (Borimirov 60), Stoichkov, Penev, Lechkov, Balakov
Austria: Wohlfahrt, Streiter, Kogler, Pfeffer, Schottel, Baur, A. Ogris, Artner, Polster, Herzog, Stoeger
Ref: Nicchi (Ita)

13 October   *Paris*   *Att: 32,741*
FRANCE 2 (Sauzee 29; Ginola 39)
ISRAEL 3 (R. Harazi 21; Berkovich 83; Atar 90)
France: Lama, Blanc, Desailly, Petit, Roche (Lizarazu 24), Le Guen, Deschamps, Sauzee, Ginola (Dkjorkaeff 85), Papin, Cantona
Israel: Ginsburg, Halfon (Schwartz 89), A. Harazi, Klinger, Shelach, Glam, Hazan, Atar, Nimny (Berkovich 64), R. Harazi, Rosenthal
Ref: Snoddy (Nlr)

27 October   *Tel Aviv*   *Att: 23,500*
ISRAEL 1 (Rosenthal 3)
AUSTRIA 1 (Reinmayr 15)
Israel: Ginsburg, Halfon, Klinger, A. Garazi, Glam, Hazan, Levy, Berkovich (Schwartz 78), Atar (Ohana 65), R. Harazi, Rosenthal
Austria: Wohlfahrt, Streiter, Kogler, Pfeffer, Winkelhofer, Stroger, Artner, Reinmayr, Feiersinger, A. Ogris, Polster (Pfeifenberger 65)
Ref: Vagner (Hun)

Eyes down as Eric Cantona of France (left) and Bulgaria's Zlato Yankov go head-to-head in not-so-gay Paris.

Austria were involved in another 1-1 draw two weeks later – the result being more significant for the visiting Swedes, as it secured their passage to the finals in front of 25,000. Both goals came within a minute of one another. Mild gave the Swedes a 68th-minute advantage before Herzog struck back for Austria almost immediately. On the same night Finland had a creditable win in Tel Aviv. Heikkinen gave the visitors the lead early in the second half and Hjelm added two more later on, before Harazi scored a consolation goal in the 89th minute.

10 November   *Vienna*   *Att: 25,000*
AUSTRIA 1 (Herzog 69)
SWEDEN 1 (Mild 68)
Austria: Wohlfahrt, Feiersinger, Lainer, Winkelhofer, Kogler, Reinmayr, Pacult (Westerthaler 71), Artner, Polster, Herzog, Stoeger
Sweden: Ravelli, R. Nilsson, P. Andersson, Kamark, Ljung, Schwarz, Mild, Landberg (Alexandersson 75), Zetterberg, Jan Jansson, Larsson (Lilienberg 73)
Ref: Diaz Vega (Esp)

Group 6 – Final Table

	P	W	D	L	F	A	Pts
SWEDEN	10	6	3	1	19	8	15
BULGARIA	10	6	2	2	19	10	14
France	10	6	1	3	17	10	13
Austria	10	3	2	5	15	16	8
Finland	10	2	1	7	9	18	5
Israel	10	1	3	6	10	27	5

Group 6 – Results

	Austria	Bulgaria	Finland	France	Israel	Sweden
Austria	—	3-1	3-0	0-1	5-2	1-1
Bulgaria	4-1	—	2-0	2-0	2-2	1-1
Finland	3-1	0-3	—	0-2	0-0	0-1
France	2-0	1-2	2-1	—	2-3	2-1
Israel	1-1	0-2	1-3	0-4	—	1-3
Sweden	1-0	2-0	3-2	1-1	5-0	—

10 November *Tel Aviv* Att: 15,000
ISRAEL 1 (Harazi 89)
FINLAND 3 (Heikkinen 54; Hjelm 74, 85)
Israel: Ginsburg, A. Harazi, Klinger, Shelach, Glam, Hazan, Levy, Nimny, Rosenthal, R. Harazi, Ohana
Finland: Jakonen, Kinnunen, Heikkinen, Petaja, Hyrylainen, Suominen, Litmanen, Lindberg, Helm, Aaltonen, Paavola
Ref: Roduit (Swi)

With Sweden already assured of their qualification, attention focused on Paris a week later where France entertained the Bulgarians needing to avoid defeat. They looked to have things very much under control when Eric Cantona gave them the lead in the 31st minute but within five minutes FC Porto's Emil Kostadinov had headed an equaliser. Then with just 10 seconds of play remaining Hristo Stoichkov sent a perfect pass to Kostadinov roaming on the right. He hit a thunderous drive which struck the underside of the crossbar before bouncing over Lama's line to produce the sort of end that only football can deliver. France had lost both their final games, both in Paris and both to goals in the final minute of play. Bulgaria had achieved what had looked highly unlikely as August dawned – qualification for the United States.

17 November *Paris* Att: 48,000
FRANCE 1 (Cantona 31)
BULGARIA 2 (Kostadinov 36, 90)
France: Lama, Blanc, Petit, Desailly, Le Guen, Roche, Deschamps, Sauzee (Guerin 81), Pedros, Papin (Ginola 69), Cantona
Bulgaria: Mihailov, Hubchev, Tsvetanov (Borimirov 82), Kremenliev, Ivanov, Lechkov (Alexandrov 82), Balakov, Yankov, Stoichkov, Kostadinov, Penev
Ref: Mottram (Sco)

Group 6 – Scorers

7	Dahlin	Sweden
6	Cantona	France
5	Herzog	Austria
	Stoichkov	Bulgaria
4	Kostadinov	Bulgaria
	Papin	France
3	Blanc	France
	Brolin	Sweden
	Harazi R.	Israel
	Hjelm	Finland
	Penev	Bulgaria
2	Balakov	Bulgaria
	Ingesson	Sweden
	Kuhbauer	Austria
	Pfeifenberger	Austria
	Polster	Austria
	Rosenthal	Israel
	Sauzee	France
	Sirakov	Bulgaria
	Zohar	Israel
1	Atar	Israel
	Banin	Israel
	Berkovich	Israel
	Eriksson	Sweden
	Ginola	France
	Heikkinen	Finland
	Ivanov	Bulgaria
	Jarvinen	Finland
	Kuhbauer	Austria
	Landberg	Sweden
	Larsson H.	Sweden
	Lechkov	Bulgaria
	Limpar	Sweden
	Litanen	Finland
	Mild	Sweden
	Ogris	Austria
	Paatelainen	Finland
	Pettersson	Sweden
	Rajamaki	Finland
	Reinmayr	Austria
	Roche	France
	Stoger	Austria
	Suominen	Finland
	Yankov	Bulgaria
	Zetterberg	Sweden
	Zisser	Austria

Qualifiers and Scorers

THE QUALIFIERS

Automatic	USA (Hosts)
	Germany (Holders)
Europe	Belgium
	Bulgaria
	Greece
	Holland
	Italy
	Norway
	Republic of Ireland
	Romania
	Russia
	Spain
	Sweden
	Switzerland
Africa	Cameroon
	Morocco
	Nigeria
South America	Bolivia
	Brazil
	Colombia
Concacaf	Mexico
Oceania – Asia	Saudi Arabia
	South Korea
Play-Offs	Argentina

EUROPE

There was a total of 39 entries to the European qualifying competition. Yugoslavia were excluded automatically because of UN sanctions and Germany qualified automatically as holders of the World Cup. The draw was arranged into six groups with the top two teams in each group qualifying for the final stages in the USA. See the group editorials for details of final tables.

Overall Top Scorers in European Qualifying Rounds

10	Raducioiu	Romania
8	Rush	Wales
7	Dahlin	Sweden
7	Platt	England
7	Salinas	Spain
6	Aldridge	Rep. Ireland
6	Cantona	France
6	Chapuisat	Switzerland
6	Dubovsky	RCS
6	Van Vossen	Holland
5	Baggio R.	Italy
5	Bergkamp	Holland
5	Hagi	Romania
5	Herzog	Austria
5	Knup	Switzerland
5	Rekdal	Norway
5	Stoichkov	Bulgaria
5	Wilmots	Belgium
5	Wright	England
4	Balint	Romania
4	Bregy	Switzerland
4	Dumitrescu	Romania
4	Gascoigne	England
4	Kiryakov	Russia
4	Kostadinov	Bulgaria
4	Papin	France
4	Pingel	Denmark
4	Saunders	Wales
4	Scifo	Belgium
4	Sotriou	Cyprus

AFRICA

Only 37 out of the 48 member states entered the qualifying competition. In several groups some games that would not affect the final qualifiers from each group were not played. Qualification was in two stages of round robin matches. The first round consisted of nine groups, with the winners only of each qualified for the second round. The second round consisted of three groups – the winners of each of these groups going on to the Finals in the USA.

Second Round

GROUP A FINAL TABLE

	P	W	D	L	F	A	Pts
NIGERIA	4	2	1	1	10	5	5
Ivory Coast	4	2	1	1	5	6	5
Algeria	4	0	2	2	3	7	2

GROUP B FINAL TABLE

	P	W	D	L	F	A	Pts
MOROCCO	4	3	0	1	6	3	6
Zambia	4	2	1	1	6	2	5
Senegal	4	0	1	3	1	8	1

GROUP C FINAL TABLE

	P	W	D	L	F	A	Pts
CAMEROON	4	3	0	1	7	3	6
Zimbabwe	4	2	0	2	3	6	4
Guinea	4	1	0	3	4	5	2

World Cup Draw: Eusebio, Tony Meola, Milla, Charlton, Platini, Van Basten and Sepp Blatter.

SOUTH AMERICA

Out of South America's 10 members, only nine were invited to take part in the qualifying tournament as Chile had previously been suspended from competition. The winners and runner-up of Group B qualifed for the Finals. The winners of Group A qualifed for the Finals with the runner-up in Group A meeting the winners of the Concacaf/Ocean play-off in a final play off for a place in the World Cup Finals.

GROUP A FINAL TABLE

	P	W	D	L	F	A	Pts
COLOMBIA	6	4	2	0	13	2	10
Argentina	6	3	1	2	7	9	7
Paraguay	6	1	4	1	6	7	6
Peru	6	0	1	5	4	12	1

GROUP B FINAL TABLE

	P	W	D	L	F	A	Pts
BRAZIL	8	5	2	1	20	4	12
BOLIVIA	8	5	1	2	22	11	11
Uruguay	8	4	2	2	10	7	10
Ecuador	8	1	3	4	7	7	5
Venezuela	8	1	0	7	4	34	2

CONCACAF

Twenty-two of Concacaf's 27 members entered the qualifying competition. Prior to competition Cuba withdrew. The entries where whittled down to eight teams following a series of pre-preliminary, preliminary, first and second round stages. This left a final group of four teams the winner of which qualified for the World Cup Finals. The runner-up from this group played the runner-up in the Oceania group to decide who would play the runner-up of South America Group A to decide a further qualifier for the Finals.

FINAL ROUND FINAL TABLE

	P	W	D	L	F	A	Pts
MEXICO	6	5	0	1	17	5	10
Canada	6	3	1	2	10	10	7
El Salvador	6	2	0	4	6	11	4
Honduras	6	1	1	4	7	14	3

OCEANIA

Seven out of the eight Oceania members took part in the qualifying competition – Western Samoa withdrawing. Divided into two groups, the winners of which played home & away to determine who would meet in a play-off with the runner-up from the Concacaf group. The winners of that match would then meet the South America Group A runners-up for a place in the Finals.

GROUP 1 – FINAL TABLE

	P	W	D	L	F	A	Pts
Australia	4	4	0	0	13	2	8
Tahiti	4	1	1	2	5	8	3
Solomon Islands	4	0	1	3	5	13	1

GROUP 2 – FINAL TABLE

	P	W	D	L	F	A	Pts
New Zealand	4	3	1	0	15	1	7
Fiji	4	2	1	1	6	3	5
Vanuatu	4	0	0	4	1	18	0

ASIA

Twenty-six of the 36 member states took part in the qualifying competitions. Divided into six first round groups – the winners of each qualifying for a final round of six teams from which the top two qualified for the World Cup Finals.

FINAL ROUND – FINAL TABLE

	P	W	D	L	F	A	Pts
SAUDI ARABIA	5	2	3	0	8	6	7
SOUTH KOREA	5	2	2	1	9	4	6
Japan	5	2	2	1	7	4	6
Iraq	5	1	3	1	9	9	5
Iran	5	2	0	3	8	11	4
North Korea	5	1	0	4	5	12	2

PLAY-OFFS

Argentina were the final qualifiers following the four team knock-out play-off series of games.

	1st leg	2nd leg	Agg.
Oceania Play-off			
New Zealand v Australia	0-1	0-3	0-4
Concacaf v Oceania			
Canada v Australia	2-1	1-2	3-3 1-4 aps
Concacaf/Oceania v South America			
Australia v ARGENTINA	1-1	0-1	1-2

World Cup Finals Group Matches

GROUP A

ROUND 1

The Pontiac Silverdome in Detroit hosted the first World Cup final match to be played indoors. Grass cultivated in California, conditioned in the surrounds of the stadium and laid on top of the astroturf provided the setting for the USA to start their inaugural match as hosts. In the history of the World Cup no host nation had ever failed to qualify for the second stage and given the status of their opponents in the first game – Switzerland – the match represented, many thought, America's best chance to get three points on the board before the might of Colombia and Romania was brought to bear.

Before the game a draw looked a likely result. USA had failed to win in the World Cup finals since 1950, while the Swiss could offer little better, their last victory at this stage of the competition coming in 1954. And at the end of an energy-sapping 90 minutes both sides knew that they would have to wait a few days more at the very least to record that long-awaited win, having played out a disappointing 1-1 draw.

While the game offered little to shout about it did sparkle briefly with two superbly-executed free-kicks shortly before the interval. First blood went to Switzerland when, six minutes from half-time, Alain Sutter was brought down on the edge of the penalty area. Georges Bregy, the 36-year-old midfield player from Young Boys, stepped up and curled the ball into the corner of Tony Meola's goal. The Swiss deserved the goal not least because they had controlled the game and in Bregy and Sutter had players who looked like they might produced a telling moment. They had.

But the USA responded positively. Well inside the final minute of the first half John Harkes was halted illegally and from 30 yards Eric Wynalda curled the ball over the Swiss wall with great pace and into the very top corner of Pascolo's goal.

Borussia Dortmund's Stephane Chapuisat flattered to deceive during the game and the introduction of Roy Wegerle for the USA briefly added more direction to their play. Chances were limited but Thomas Dooley and Tab Ramos wasted excellent opportunities and Christophe Ohrel sliced the ball wide of an open goal.

Stephane Chapuisat (centre right) of Switzerland scores the second goal in the 4-1 defeat of Romania.

Ilie Dumitrescu of Romania attacks the American defence.

Later in the day attention switched to Pasadena's Rose Bowl, where Colombia faced Romania. The South American side, following their 5-0 win over Argentina in Buenos Aires during the qualifying competition, were being touted as potential World Champions. Romania – the great pretenders who for years have had sides littered with outstanding players but always seem to fail to gel as a team – had one of the youngest squads in the tournament, and rumours of bickering and personal squabbles coming from their camp were hardly the best preparation for a traditionally volatile side. However, by the end of the evening the spotlight was on them and none more so than Gheorghe Hagi, who had spent the season languishing in Italy's Serie B with Brescia. He turned in a superb personal performance, creating two goals, scoring an outrageous third and being denied another by an excellent save.

The game had started with the Colombians in total control, playing their typical short-passing game pivoting around skipper Carlos Valderrama but too often over-elaborating in the final third. But after soaking up constant pressure for the opening quarter of an hour Anghel Iordanescu's side produced a fabulous goal straight out of the counter-attack manual. Hagi played carrier and then provider, sweeping the ball left into the path of Florin Raducioiu's intelligent run. The Milan player cut back into the area and curled the ball past Oscar Cordoba. No less than five Colombian defenders watched Raducioiu's movement and shot and it wasn't the last time the South American defence was left wanting.

Bogdan Stelea, the Rapid Bucharest goalkeeper, was in inspired form and he produced a series of saves worthy of the stage, none more so than a point-blank block from Freddy Rincon's first-time effort that bordered on the incredible. How important that proved to be, because almost immediately Hagi received the ball out wide on the left-hand touchline, looked up, and flighted the ball over Cordoba and into the far side of his goal. The Romanian looked to have directed a cross not a shot but it's doubtful he would admit to it at that moment, especially given the fact that only the fingertips of the Colombian keeper had kept out Hagi's chip from centre field, à la Pele, minutes earlier.

Colombia got themselves back into the game just before the interval when Aldolfo Valencia headed home Wilson Perez's left-wing corner at the near post after Andres Escobar had got the slightest of touches. The second half was a mirror image of the first but without the goal and with Stelea equal to all that was directed at him. Then in the dying embers of the game, Hagi found Raducioiu on the right, Cordoba was caught in no man's land and Raducioiu swerved the ball into the net to complete a magnificent 3-1 win, a fitting finale to an outstanding game of skill and drama.

ROUND 2

With the Colombians still to play, Roy Hodgson's Switzerland side took to the indoor field of the Silverdome knowing that three points were vital to ease the pressure on them and move it on to the South Americans, who played the USA later in the day. With goals required, Englishman Hodgson brought back Adrian Knup – the Stuttgart striker – into attack. There had been talk of a rift between Hodgson and Knup, who did not play in the opening game against the USA because he was not regarded as match fit by the Swiss manager. Knup was to repay Hodgson in the best way possible.

Having obliterated the Colombians, the Romanians were unchanged and a win would guarantee them a place in the second round. The early exchanges looked as though they might achieve it as a string of corners delivered with tantalising effect by Hagi produced two glorious chances that were wasted by Popescu. But Sutter's powerful running and sheer enthusiasm, despite playing with a broken toe, gradually turned the tide. Having had the ball in the net only to be ruled offside the new Bayern Munich player scored with a glorious 20-yarder curled past Stelea from the edge of the area.

Romania's reply was almost immediate and it came from Hagi, released by Petrescu to unleash a 25-yard shot that dipped past Pascolo and into the net by his left-hand post. The sides remained level in score and performance until the interval, but after the break the Swiss carried the match to their opponents in splendid style and with great fervour. They deservedly took the lead seven minutes after the restart when the ball broke to Chapuisat, who stabbed it into the net from 12 yards after it had ricocheted around the penalty spot.

The Swiss were now quite simply rampant in what was turning into one of the games of the tournament and 14 minutes later Ciriaco Sforza burst through the Romanian defence on the right-hand side before squaring to Knup, who had the simplest of tap-ins. Another attack brought a free-kick on the left. Bregy delivered it perfectly to the edge of the goal area and Knup

Florin Raducioiu (left) of Romania tussles with Switzerland's Ciriaco Sforza.

climbed to get the faintest of deflections with his head and score a goal typical of the Stuttgart player.

Iordanescu looked to change things and sent on Ioan Vladoiu for the final 20 minutes. His contribution lasted exactly four minutes when an outrageous tackle on Ohrel rightly earned him his marching orders – and instant dismissal from the squad by Iordanescu. In the final few minutes, Raducioiu had a couple of chances to reduce the deficit but Pascolo was equal to both his efforts.

Switzerland's emphatic win took them to the top of the group table with four points, leaving Romania behind them with three points and turning a worried eye to Pasadena where the USA took to the field with Colombia for a do or die encounter. A win for both sides was important and for the Colombians essential. Packed to capacity the game was shown live on network television and produced a further shock as the USA won 2-1, and more emphatically than the scoreline suggests.

Harkes split the Colombian defence with an excellent ball behind the flat back four and in trying to intercept it Andres Escobar directed it into his own net with tragic consequences, as the world was later to learn. In the second half Alexi Lalas had a superb strike ruled out for an offside that never was, but then Ernest Stewart, the Willem II player, raced on to a deft through-ball and directed it past Cordoba, who was not for the first time caught in no man's land. The goal oozed quality from an eight-man build-up that started near the USA's left corner flag. Colombia – so disappointing – started to make some progress in the final stages of the game and Meola was finally beaten in injury time by substitute Adolfo Valencia.

ROUND 3

The final round of games was staged on the California coast. In the Rose Bowl a capacity crowd had gathered to see if, in the wake of their captivating defeat of the Colombians, the USA could gain the point that would ensure them qualification for the second phase. Their opponents – Romania – couldn't afford a defeat that might allow the Colombians to send them to the bottom of the table, should they run up the convincing win they needed over the Swiss to see if they could get into the second phase as a best third-placed team. For Romania, Switzerland and the USA a win would guarantee top spot qualification. All very intriguing.

Iordanescu made no fewer than seven changes to the side that had collapsed against the Swiss, including recalling Florin Prunea for Stelea in goal. The USA kept the side that had served them so well and with four wins on the trot in the Rose Bowl, and undefeated for seven games, there was call for optimism. They failed to cope with Hagi, though, as the little Romanian had another inspired game, his left foot producing nutmegs and passes of quality.

Even so it was the Americans who might have taken the lead during the first quarter of an hour, which produced their best spell of the game, when Harkes hit the foot of Prunea's post after Balboa's corner was only half cleared. Then, as Romania started to take the initiative, captain Petrescu scored what proved to be the only goal of the game, and a goal that will haunt Meola. Tibor Selymes found space to work the ball down the right and linked with Petrescu, who burst inside the area and fired an angled shot past Meola, caught out by leaving his near post fatally unguarded. After the goal the Romanians, with Hagi

Group A Matches

18 June	Silverdome, Detroit	Att: 77,557

UNITED STATES 1 (Wynalda 44)
SWITZERLAND 1 (Bregy 39)
United States: Meola, Caligiuri, Lalas, Balboa, Kooiman, Ramos, Harkes, Dooley, Sorber, Wynalda (Wegerle 57), Stewart (Jones 81)
Switzerland: Pascolo, Herr, Geiger, Hottiger, Quentin, Ohrel, Bregy, Bickel (Subiat 72), Sutter, Sforza (Wyss 76), Chapuisat
Ref: Lamolina (Argentina)
Yellow Cards: USA (1) – Harkes; Switzerland (2) – Herr, Subiat

18 June	Rose Bowl, Pasadena	Att: 91,856

COLOMBIA 1 (Valencia 43)
ROMANIA 3 (Raducioiu 16, 89; Hagi 34)
Colombia: Cordoba, Herrera, Perea, Escobar, Perez, Alvarez, Gomez, Valderrama, Rincon, Asprilla, Valencia
Romania: Stelea, Petrescu, Prodan, Milhali, Belodedici, Munteanu, Popescu, Lupescu, Dumitrescu (Selymes 65), Hagi, Raducioiu (Papura 89)
Ref: Al Sharif (Syria)
Yellow Cards: Colombia (3) – Herrera, Valderrama, Alvarez; Romania (1) – Raducioiu

22 June	Silverdome, Detroit	Att: 61,428

ROMANIA 1 (Hagi 35)
SWITZERLAND 4 (Sutter 16; Chapuisat 52; Knup 65, 72)
Romania: Stelea, Petrescu, Prodan, Milhali, Belodedici, Munteanu, Popescu, Lupescu (Panduru 86), Dumitrescu (Vladoiu 70), Hagi, Raducioiu
Switzerland: Pascolo, Herr, Hottiger, Quentin, Geiger, Bregy, Sutter (Bickel 70), Ohrel (Sylvestre 81), Knup, Sforza, Chapuisat
Ref: Jouini (Tun)
Yellow Cards: Romania (4) – Milhali, Lupescu, Belodedici, Vladoiu.
Red Card: Romania – Vladoiu (74)

22 June	Rose Bowl, Pasadena	Att: 93,194

UNITED STATES 2 (Escobar own goal 33; Stewart 51)
COLOMBIA 1 (Valencia 89)
United States: Meola, Balboa, Lalas, Clavijo, Harkes, Caligiuri, Dooley, Sorber, Ramos, Stewart (Jones 67), Wynalda (Wegerle 61)
Colombia: Cordoba, Herrera, Perea, Escobar, Perez, Alvarez, Gaviria, Rincon, Valderrama, De Avila (Valenciano 46), Asprilla (Valencia 46)
Ref: Baldas (Ita)
Yellow Cards: USA (1) – Lalas; Colombia (1) – De Avila

27 June	Rose Bowl, Pasadena	Att: 93,869

UNITED STATES 0
ROMANIA 1 (Petrescu 17)
United States: Meola, Balboa, Lalas, Clavijo, Harkes, Caligiuri, Dooley, Sorber (Wegerle 74), Ramos (Jones 63), Stewart, Wynalda
Romania: Prunea, Petrescu, Prodan, Belodedici (Mihali 88), Popescu, Selymes, Lupescu, Munteanu, Hagi, Raducioiu (Gilca 83), Dumitrescu
Ref: van der Ende (Holland)
Yellow Cards: USA (2) – Harkes, Clavijo; Romania (2) – Raduciou, Petrescu

27 June	Stanford Stadium, San Francisco	Att: 83,769

SWITZERLAND 0
COLOMBIA 2 (Gaviria 45; Lozano 90)
Switzerland: Pascolo, Herr, Hottiger, Quentin, Geiger, Bregy, Sutter (Grassi 82), Ohrel, Knup (Subiat 70), Sforza, Chapuisat
Colombia: Cordoba, Escobar, Herrera, Mendoza, Perez, Gaviria (Lazano 79), Valderrama, Alvarez, Rincon, Valencia (De Avila 64), Asprilla
Ref: Mikkelsen (Denmark)
Yellow Cards: Switzerland (2) – Knup, Bregy; Colombia (3) – Gaviria, Valderrama, Alvarez

---

the focal point of everything, simply played keepball and made the Americans run in the searing 120-degree heat.

Only in the final 15 minutes did the USA start to threaten the Romanian goal but Prunea was on hand to save comfortably from Harkes and Wynalda. The three points for the Romanians ensured them of six points and qualification; the USA would need to wait and see.

Up the coast in San Francisco Switzerland knew they could finish top of the group with seven points out of a possible nine if they won. For Colombia nothing more than an emphatic win would do, and then they needed to rely on the USA beating Romania. As it transpired Colombia got the win they required but it couldn't prevent them from becoming the first team to be knocked out of the competition's final stages.

The goals that left Switzerland to sweat were scored at the very end of each half. Pascolo spoiled what had been an impressive display in the Swiss goal when he failed to hold Gaviria's diving header from Valderrama's free-kick. The ball slipped out of his hands and over the line. Almost immediately the half-time whistle went and the Colombians were able to return to their dressing room much happier than the Swiss, who had been in a defensive mood for the first half. Up until that slip, Pascolo had looked unbeatable, especially in denying Valencia and Rincon.

Despite trailing the Swiss still kept it tight at the back as the South Americans started to produce the free-flowing football that many thought could take them all the way. As it was, the way was going to be home, as Asprilla twice got free only to waste the chances. In the final seconds Lozano made sure of the points with a shot from inside the area, but it was academic. The result ensured that Romania finished top of the group with Switzerland edging out the USA for second spot on goal difference. The USA finished third, a point ahead of the crestfallen Colombians, and they would need to wait to see if they made the second phase.

Final Table

	P	W	D	L	F	A	Pts
Romania	3	2	0	1	5	5	6
Switzerland	3	1	1	1	5	4	4
United States	3	1	1	1	3	3	4
Colombia	3	1	0	2	4	5	3

Group B

ROUND 1

Sweden's preparations and lead-up to their opening encounter with Cameroon had been one of the quietest of all the European nations. The spotlight had fallen on their African opponents and in particular the return of 42-year-old Roger Milla to the world stage. The indomitable Lions had faced two years of turmoil and strife from within as disorganisation and the financial burdens their new-found status had accorded them had taken their toll.

The game itself – despite producing four goals – was best remembered for just how forgettable it was. Sweden started brightly, scored and then retreated into a shell of complacency that they never really broke out of. Martin Dahlin was a lone striker up front and seemed ill at ease with a role where he lacked adequate support. The Swedes had as much reason to thank the Cameroon keeper Joseph-Antoine Bell as the scorer, Roger Ljung. Napoli's Jonas Thern delivered a free-kick from the left into the far side of the goal area. Bell came and Bell went, the ball continued and Ljung headed into the wide open spaces of the Cameroon goal. Faced with a fight the Africans came good and drew level after the first of two costly errors by Patrik Andersson. The defender 'cleared' straight at Omam-Biyik and the player who had damaged Argentina's reputation four years earlier fed Embe, who made a meal of his celebrations.

Andersson was again at fault when Cameroon took the lead in the second half. A 40-yard pass found Omam-Biyik, whose turn left the defender for dead as he flicked the ball past Ravelli from 12 yards. Somehow though Sweden salvaged a draw when Bell totally missed substitute Henrik Larsson's 30-yard drive that hit the bar and rebounded to Dahlin, who scored from six yards.

Russia had come to the World Cup Finals under a cloud that had meant so many of their class players – the 'Refuseniks' – were not with them. The likes of Andrei Kanchelskis, Igor Shalimov and Aleksei Mikhailichenko were among the absentees who refused to play under coach Pavel Sadyrin. Not an ideal situation to face the highly fancied Brazilians. This was further compounded by the non-availability of captain Viktor Onopko, suspended for their first encounter having been dismissed in their last qualifying game in Greece. Ricardo Gomes of Paris Saint-Germain had been forced to withdraw from the Brazilian squad and return to France suffering muscle problems, and his place went to another French-based player, Bordeaux's Marcio Santos.

The game was a repeat of their encounter in an opening group match in the 1982 World Cup in Spain which Brazil won. On a day when temperatures in Palo Alto had dropped to more humane levels the Brazilians turned on the samba and played a desperately disappointing Russian outfit off the park. The team in turmoil had hardly a kick of real note and looked disjointed and in disarray. Indeed had Chelsea goalkeeper Kharin not been in fine form the score would have been much more emphatic than the final 2-0.

In a different world Romario found himself once again under the close attentions of Vladislav Ternavski. Months earlier the Spartak player had put the shackles on the Barcelona striker in a

Martin Dahlin of Sweden scored three vital goals in the Group B games.

Champions' League encounter. This time the tables were turned as Romario might and probably should have had a hat-trick. He did open the scoring after 20 minutes and for all the free-flowing play the opener came from a corner. Bebeto delivered in perfectly and Romario wrong-footed Ternavski to stab the ball home from eight yards. Rai – the younger brother of Socrates, who had starred in the '82 and '86 finals – controlled the midfield with relative ease. His pass sent Romario free and after Nikiforov's challenge had failed, Ternavski bundled the Brazilian over for the first penalty kick of the tournament. Rai stroked the ball home to complete a victory that might have been doubled had Bebeto been more alert.

ROUND 2

The pairing of Brazil and Cameroon was eagerly awaited. A win would ensure a place in the second round for the South Americans and condemn the Africans – who had to win – to an early departure date. Brazil used the encounter to show they had developed a ruthless streak against opponents who had threatened

Dmitri Radchenko of Russia.

a self-imposed boycott over their wages, unpaid for two months. The money didn't arrive, the players stayed, and Brazil scored three without reply.

Romario – almost inevitably – opened the scoring before half-time when the workmanlike Dunga used the outside of a foot to feed the Barca player, whose pace took him past Mbouh-Mbouh to slide the ball under the advancing Bell. In the start of the second half a sending-off was needed for the Brazilians to be able to make their advantage on the ball tell. Indeed the 63rd and 65th minutes marked a calamitous period for the fading Africans. The 17-year-old Rigobert Bahanang Song lunged at Bebeto and was shown the red card by the Mexican referee, and within two minutes – despite the introduction of the legendary Milla, the oldest player to appear in the World Cup Finals – Marcio Santos dived to head home Jorginho's cross. Brazil played keep-ball and added a third goal when Bebeto was on hand to slide the ball home from a tight angle after Bell's brave dive to deny Romario his second goal.

Not surprisingly, after their emphatic defeat by Brazil, Russian coach Sadyrin made five changes for their match against Sweden. The new formation seemed to be working early on as the side started brightly, forced the Scandinavians back, and took the lead after four minutes thanks to Oleg Salenko's penalty conversion – the Valencia player's first goal in a Russian shirt. For the second time in two games the Swedes found themselves having to come from behind and they got the break they needed six minutes from the interval, when Brolin equalised from the other spot after a foul by Gorlukovich on Dahlin.

Early in the second half the Swedes found themselves with a numerical advantage when Dahlin's marker, Gorlukovich, received his second yellow card of the game. So Russia were down to ten men and facing an uphill task. Dahlin gained most from the reorganisation and started to turn the Russian defence. As the game entered its final ten minutes the Monchengladbach player produced two fine diving headers in as many minutes to score and secure the three points and certain qualification for the Swedes. Not so for the Russians.

With Brazil and Sweden certain of a place in the second round much of the tension had been removed from their encounter indoors at the Pontiac Silverdome. Both coaches resisted the temptation to rest players, although Sweden were forced to make a change due to the suspension of Dahlin, who had picked up a second yellow card against Russia. Henrik Larsson took his place. With everyone waiting for the Brazilians to turn on the style it was the Scandinavians who had the capacity crowd revelling at their skill and continued improvement. Midway through the half the Swedes took the lead with a stunning goal. Brolin, using his considerable body strength, held off Dunga and delivered a perfectly flighted ball to Kennett Andersson coming in from the left. He ignored the challenge of Mauro Silva, took the ball on his chest and then curled in a shot with a mixture of power and accuracy.

Brazil needed an early goal after the interval to take the initiative. They got it in under two minutes as the Swedish defence – still not up to speed from their break – allowed Romario space to turn, run and toe-poke the ball past Ravelli. The goal instilled new life in the Brazilians who, like Sweden, had chances to win but the score remained 1-1 to ensure both sides qualified for the second phase at the end of a most watchable match.

Meanwhile the remaining game in the group brought together two sides who seemed to have had the heart driven out of them. Cameroon still had not been paid the money they were owed and Bell – under threat of the axe for performance and political reasons – packed his bags and departed of his own accord. So Cameroon began the match with reserve Songo'o, who would not want to remember the evening. Russia not only needed a win but one of emphatic proportions to stand a chance of a third place qualifying position. What transpired was one of the most bizarre games of World Cup history as Oleg Salenko created a tournament scoring record of five goals in a 6-1 win that breathed some life into their challenge.

Salenko's tally was all the more remarkable given that he had only just scored his first international goal for Russia, in the previous game against the Swedes, and had been drafted into the squad only because of the strife that had occurred during qualification. The first goal arrived after 16 minutes with a shot under the advancing Cameroon keeper and two more came in the last five minutes of the half, Salenko first taking advantage of woeful marking after a quick free-kick and then adding a third from the penalty spot.

Cameroon got back into the game with a goal from substitute

Group B Matches

19 June Rose Bowl, Pasadena *Att: 83,959*
CAMEROON 2 (Embe 30; Oman-Biyick 47)
SWEDEN 2 (Ljung 9; Dahlin 75)
Cameroon: Bell, Tataw, Song Bahanang, Kalla, Agbo, Libih, Mbouh-Mbouh, Foe, Omam-Biyik, Embe (Mouyeme 80), Mfde (Maboang Kessack 87)
Sweden: Ravelli, R. Nilsson, Bjorklund, P. Andersson, Ljung, Thern, Schwarz, Blomqvist (Larsson 60), Ingesson (K. Andersson 75), Dahlin, Brolin
Ref: Noriega (Peru)
Yellow Cards: Cameroon (1) – Mbouh-Mbouh; Sweden (1) – Dahlin

20 June Stanford Stadium, San Francisco *Att: 81,061*
BRAZIL 2 (Romario 20; Rai 52 pen)
RUSSIA 0
Brazil: Taffarel, Jorginho, Ricardo Rocha (Aldair 74), Marcio Santos, Leonardo, Mauro Silva, Dunga (Mazinho 84), Zinho, Rai, Bebeto, Romario
Russia: Kharin, Kuznetsov, Gorlukovich, Nikiforov, Ternavski, Khlestov, Karpin, Piatnitski, Tsymbalar, Radchenko (Boradiuk 77), Yuran (Salenko 55)
Ref: Lim Kee Chong (Mauritius)
Yellow Cards: Russia (3) – Nikiforov, Khlestov, Kuznetsov

24 June Stanford Stadium, San Francisco *Att: 83,401*
BRAZIL 3 (Romario 39; Santos 65; Bebeto 73)
CAMEROON 0
Brazil: Taffarel, Jorginho, Aldair, Marcio Santos, Leonardo, Mauro Silva, Dunga, Zinho (Paulo Sergio 76), Rai (Muller 81), Bebeto, Romario
Cameroon: Bell, Song Bahanang, Kalla, Tataw, Agbo, Libih, Mbouh-Mbouh, Omam-Biyik, Mfede (Maboang 71), Foe, Embe (Milla 64)
Ref: Brizio Carter (Mexico)
Yellow Cards: Brazil (1) – Mauro Silva; Cameroon (2) – Tataw, Kalla
Red Card: Cameroon – Song (63)

24 June Silverdome, Detroit *Att: 71,528*
RUSSIA 1 (Salenko 4 pen)
SWEDEN 3 (Brolin 39 pen; Dahlin 80, 82)
Russia: Kharin, Kuznetsov, Gorlukovich, Nikiforov, Onopko, Khlestov, Popov (Karpin 41), Mostovoi, Borodyuk (Galyamin 51), Radchenko, Salenko
Sweden: Ravelli, Nilsson, P. Andersson, Bjorklund (Erlingmark 89), Ljung, Schwarz, Ingesson, Thern, K. Andersson (Larsson 84), Dahlin, Brolin
Ref: Quiniou (France)
Yellow Cards: Russia (2) – Gorlukovich, Kharin; Sweden (3) – K. Andersson, Schwarz, Dahlin
Red Card: Russia – Gorlukovich.

28 June Silverdome, Detroit *Att: 74,914*
BRAZIL 1 (Romario 47)
SWEDEN 1 (K. Andersson 24)
Brazil: Taffarel, Jorginho, Leonardo, Marcio Santos, Aldair, Dunga, Mauro Silva, Rai (Paulo Sergio 83), Zinho (Mazinho 48), Bebeto, Romario
Sweden: Ravelli, Nilsson, Kaamark, P. Andersson, Ljung, Schwarz (Mild 75), Ingesson, Thern, Larsson (Blomqvist 65), Brolin, K. Andersson
Ref: Puhl (Hungary)
Yellow Cards: Brazil (1) – Aldair; Sweden (1) – Mild

28 June Stanford Stadium, San Francisco *Att: 74,914*
CAMEROON 1 (Milla 47)
RUSSIA 6 (Salenko 14, 41, 45 pen, 72, 75; Radchenko 81)
Cameroon: Songo'o, Tataw, Libih, Kalla, Ndip, Agdo, Mfede (Milla 46), Kana-Biyik, Foe, Embe (Tchami 48), Omam-Biyik
Russia: Cherchesov, Khlestov, Nikiforov, Onopko, Ternavski, Tetradze, Karpin, Salenko, Korneyev (Radchenko 65), Tsymbalar, Ledyakhov (Beschastnykh 79)
Ref: Al Sharif (Syria)
Yellow Cards: Cameroon (2) – Kana-Biyick, Songo'o; Russia (3) – Karpin, Khlestov, Nikiforov

Milla – 'Miller' on his shirt – and were desperately close to getting back on level terms through Omam-Biyik. However, Salenko ensured the safety of the points with goals in the 72nd and 75th minutes and he might have had a sixth had his header been better directed shortly afterwards. The Russians did score a sixth, though, from substitute Dmitri Radchenko eight minutes from time. Cameroon were out, Russia were still in with a shout and Salenko was in the history books!

Final Table

	P	W	D	L	F	A	Pts
Brazil	3	2	1	0	6	1	7
Sweden	3	1	2	0	6	4	5
Russia	3	1	0	2	7	6	3
Cameroon	3	0	1	2	3	11	1

Sergei Yuran of Russia, Marcio Santos of Brazil.

GROUP C

ROUND 1

A hiding to nothing was exactly what the holders were on to after the hullabaloo of the opening ceremony had died away, with the Germans lined up alongside the Bolivians for the respective national anthems. No great surprises in the German starting line-up which included seven of the side who had seen off Argentina to capture the trophy four years earlier. Thomas Hassler was winning his 50th cap. The Bolivians arrived at Soldier Field in Chicago already written off despite their qualifying round victory over Brazil.

Not since 1970, when England won their first game, had the holders gained victory in their opening defence. But, in the end, the World Cup got off to a predictable but promising start, Jurgen Klinsmann's simple winner coming after an hour of play in which the South American side gave their more illustrious rivals a thing or two to think about, none more so than Erwin Sanchez, whose 30-yard drive forced Bodo Illgner to dive full length and tip the ball around the post. Prior to that Karl-Heinz Riedle was presented with a first-class oppotunity from Andy Moller's cross but headed straight at Carlos Trucco.

Germany found it difficult to ruffle the feathers of Trucco – 'El Loco' – whose handling was immaculate throughout. However, a rush of blood to his feet rather than head presented Klinsmann with the opening goal of the tournament and probably the easiest he'll have to take. Matthaus – moving forward from his role as sweeper – hit a long ball seeking Sammer, who did well to avoid the South American move forward in an attempt to play him offside. It would be a little too kind to say that the

Borussia Dortmund player took the ball perfectly on his chest as he probably knew little about it. Nevertheless, the bandana-wearing Trucco, sensing the breach, rushed out of his area but slipped and the ball dropped perfectly for Klinsmann, who popped it into the empty net.

There were few other real opportunities; Cristaldo looked lively and might have done better when clear just after the interval but he blazed high and wide. Then 12 minutes from time the Bolivians looked to play their trump card with the introduction of Marco Etcheverry, sidelined for seven months with injury but still their most popular player. He needed just five minutes to become the first player of USA94 to receive the red card, for a silly swipe at Matthaus. Etcheverry later publicly apologised to Matthaus, the Bolivian players and the Bolivian people for his action that would keep him out of the forthcoming encounters with South Korea and Spain. Etcheverry's nickname is 'El Diablo' – The Devil.

The sending off was harsh, as were the five bookings handed out by referee Brizio in a match played in good spirit. But the referees were under strict instructions on the interpretation of the laws of the game and had the threat of banishment hanging over their heads if found wanting. For the record, Jurgen Kohler became the first player of the tournament to be booked, inside six minutes.

Later in the day – with the sun dipping behind the Cotton Bowl in Dallas – Spain took to the field seeking three points from a win over South Korea who, as the tournament opened, were regarded as 300-1 outsiders. The Spanish side fielded two of the players who had beaten South Korea 3-1 in Italia '90, but coach Javier Clemente was forced to make a change in goal, where Celta de Vigo's Jose Canizares replaced regular Andoni Zubizarreta, suspended following his sending off against Denmark in the qualifying stages. Clemente had stated before the game that Zubizarreta would return for the second game no matter how well Canizares played. However, by half-time he must have been rethinking as the stand-in produced a series of marvellous saves to keep the South Koreans at bay.

Spain had started in a confident manner, but the game turned in Korean favour when Ko Jeong-woon was bundled down from behind by Nadal, and referee Mikkelsen was flourishing his red card with only 25 minutes gone. The Spanish were down to 10 men with more than half the game to play. Half-time came as did substitute Josep Caminero, who made a big difference to the Spanish midfield, and he was instrumental in orchestrating a two-goal advantage for them within 10 minutes of the restart. His pass through the middle started the move that Salinas finished from four yards, and then after his two shots were blocked he produced a delightful hooked volley for Goikoetxea to head home his first international goal from eight yards. This after Choi In-young had produced two great blocks to deny Caminero. Two goals to the good, Clemente substituted the havoc-creating Salinas – a curious move at the time and one that proved their undoing. With 18 goals in 43 internationals the player who couldn't find a starting place in the Barcelona line-up all season was the main thrust of the Spanish attack. Going forward they had

Jurgen Klinsmann – love him or hate him, you can't ignore him – celebrates Germany's opening goal against Bolivia.

looked good and without him they lacked opportunity. In defence they looked poor without Nadal.

With six minutes remaining Korea were awarded a free-kick on the edge of the area and as the ball was rolled towards him Hong Myong-bo rifled in a shot that took a deflection past the luckless Canizares. Lifted by the goal, the Koreans bounced back with an amazing display of running and neat skill in stifling heat at the end of a draining game. And when sweeper Hong Myung-bo came forward again he laid the ball into the path of substitute Seo Jung-won, who raced into the area and found the inside of the net that several previous efforts had missed. A deserved equaliser for the South Koreans as the clock in the Cotton Bowl read 89 minutes 57 seconds.

ROUND 2

The pressure was clearly on the Spanish as their game with Germany started. A draw at the least was vital and a win ideal. With Nadal suspended for two games and heavily fined by FIFA, Clemente was forced to make at least one change. Hierro dropped back from midfield to fill the position as sweeper and Guardiola – a strange omission from the opening encounter – returned to midfield. Caminero kept his place at the expense of Guerrero. The

Luis Enrique was one of Spain's most consistent players.

Spanish coach also kept his pre-tournament promise to Zubizarreta and reinstated him instead of keeping Canizares.

While Germany knew a point would be a satisfactory result for them, they were also well aware that another three points would almost certainly secure pole position in the group, and that in turn would mean they would be able to remain in Chicago for their next match. Looking for a positive performance, Vogts brought in Moller for the out-of-form Riedle to link up with Klinsmann.

The encounter proved to be another highly entertaining match and after early German territorial advantage Spain started to control the mid ground, with Guardiola pulling the strings and Goikoetxea exposing Brehme's lack of pace on the right-hand side. Twice in two minutes Illgner had to produce excellent saves to deny powerful shots from both players. But the pressure told and on the quarter hour Spain took the lead. Goikoetxea took a short pass from Ferrer on his wing, looked up and from the touch line flighted what was assumed to be a cross into the goal area, beyond Illgner and into the net.

Moller should have equalised from the restart but he contrived to place his free diving header wide of an open goal. That seemed to frighten the Spanish, who embarked on a containing game and as the half came to a conclusion had allowed the Germans to get back into their stride. Within two minutes of the restart they were back in it numerically thanks to the irrepressible Klinsmann, when he beat Hierro to a looping cross from Hassler to direct a header down and then over an embarrassed Zubizarreta. That might have been the signal for both sides to sit back and aim for a draw, but both continued to create chances that might have secured all three points, Hierro and Klinsmann in particular wasting excellent openings.

Bolivia faced South Korea needing a win to keep them in the competition. South Korea, with a point in the bank, already knew that a win for them would give them a fighting chance of qualification before having to face the Germans, and after their display which included a host of near misses against Spain, goals from them seemed likely. However, the match had little to get excited about other than Cristaldo's dismissal seven minutes from full-time. The best chances fell the way of the South Koreans, especially towards the end, but the match ended with the first goalless draw of the '94 World Cup Finals.

ROUND 3

The final round of games came with the Germans sitting in reasonable safety and only an upset of nuclear proportions would enable the South Koreans to get the win that they would need to see them into the next set of games. For Spain a win against the Bolivians would be the best insurance.

By half-time in the Cotton Bowl the Germans had taken a three-goal lead, showing their usual streak of ruthless efficiency. Best of the bunch was the first, scored by an in-form Klinsmann. Taking a short pass to his feet from Hassler, and with his back to goal, he flicked the ball up with his right foot, spun and volleyed it home with his left. There was little In-young in the South Korean goal could do to stop Klinsmann's third goal of the tournament but he was definitely at fault for the next two. First Buchwald – reintroduced to the German midfield – stretched to fire a shot with the outside of his right boot. The goalkeeper left it and the ball bounced back off the far post for the grateful Riedle. Klinsmann added another when he controlled Hassler's free-kick and half-hit a volley straight at the keeper, who made a hash of the save. The ball slowly crossed the line for Germany's 150th World Cup goal.

Not surprisingly, South Korea started the second half with a change in goalkeeper, and Won-jae immediately made his mark with a couple of fine saves. Effenberg produced two stupid fouls in quick succession that earned him a booking and one-match suspension, as the South Koreans bounced back with a second-half display that will be long remembered in Dallas. After several wasted opportunities the attack-minded Koreans finally scored when Cho Jin-ho took a crossfield pass and fired home. Ten minutes later the captain, Hong Myong-bo, produced a spectacular shot from fully 25 yards that rocketed into Illgner's net. With the Germans visibly tiring and Matthaus off injured, only the brilliance of Illgner kept the Germans in the game. He dived full length on three occasions to turn away goal-bound efforts. The Germans, visibly shattered from the 100 degree plus heat, had little energy left to celebrate the final whistle but three points ensured they topped Group C and that

Group C Matches

17 June Soldier Field, Chicago *Att: 63,117*
GERMANY 1 (Klinsmann 60)
BOLIVIA 0
Germany: Illgner, Matthaus, Effenberg, Kohler, Berthold, Brehme, Sammer, Hassler (Strunz 83), Moller, Riedle (Basler 60), Klinsmann
Bolivia: Trucco, Sandy, Borja, Rimba, Quinteros, Soria, Melgar, Cristaldo, Sanchez, Baldivieso (Moreno 66), Ramallo (Etcheverry 79)
Ref: Arturo Brizio Carter (Mexico)
Yellow Cards: Germany (2) – Kohler, Moller ; Bolivia (3) – Sanchez, Baldivieso, Borja
Red Card: Bolivia – Etcheverry (82)

17 June Cotton Bowl, Dallas *Att: 56,247*
SPAIN 2 (Salinas 51, Goikoetxea 56)
SOUTH KOREA 2 (Hong Myong-bo 84, Soe Jung-won 90)
Spain: Canizares, Ferrer, Sergi, Nadal, Abelardo, Alkorta, Goikoetxea, Hierro, Guerrero (Caminero 46), Salinas (Felipe 62), Enrique
South Korea: In-young, Pan-keun, Jung-bae, Young-gin, Hong-gi , Jung-yoon (Seok-ju 73), Joo-sung (Jung-won 59), Jeong-woon, Young-il, Sun-hong, Myong-bo
Ref: Mikkelsen (Denmark)
Yellow Cards: Spain (2) – Enrique, Caminero; South Korea (2) – Joo-sung, Young-il
Red Card: Spain – Nadal (26)

21 June Soldier Field, Chicago *Att: 63,113*
GERMANY 1 (Klinsmann 47)
SPAIN 1 (Goikoetxea 14)
Germany: Illgner, Matthaus, Brehme, Berthold, Kohler, Effenberg, Sammer, Strunz , Hassler, Moller (Voller 61), Klinsmann
Spain: Zubizarreta, Ferrer, Abelardo, Hierro, Goikoetxea (Bakero 63), Guardiola (Camarasa 77), Sergi, Caminero, Alkorta, Salinas, Enrique
Ref: Filippi Cava (Uruguay)
Yellow Cards: Germany (1) – Effenberg; Spain (3) – Fernandez, Hierro, Salinas

23 June Foxboro Stadium, Boston *Att: 53,000*
BOLIVIA 0
SOUTH KOREA 0
Bolivia: Trucco, Rimba, Quinteros, Sandy, Cristaldo, Borja, Melgar, Soria, Sanchez, Baldivieso, Ramallo (Pena 67)
South Korea: In-young, Pan-keun, Myong-bo, Jung-bae, Hong-gi, Young-gin, Jung-yoon (Young-il 71), Joo-sung, Jeong-woon, Jung-won (Seok-ju 64), Sun-hong
Ref: Mottram (Scotland)
Yellow Cards: Bolivia (3) – Cristaldo, Rimba, Baldivieso. South Korea (3) – Jeong-woon, Hong-gi, Jung-bae
Red Card: Bolivia – Cristaldo (83)

27 June Cotton Bowl, Dallas *Att: 62,998*
GERMANY 3 (Klinsmann 12,36; Riedle 20)
SOUTH KOREA 2 (Hwang Sun Hong 52; Myong-bo 62)
Germany: Illgner, Effenberg (Helmer 75), Kohler, Matthaus (Moller 63), Berthold, Brehme, Hassler, Buchwald, Sammer, Klinsmann, Riedle
South Korea: In-young (Won-jae 45), Young-il , Myung- bo, Jung-bae, Hong-gi, Jeong-woon, Pan-keun, Young-gin (Jong-son 39), Joo-sung, Jin-ho (Jung-won 45), Sun-hong
Ref: Quiniou (France)
Yellow Cards: Germany (3) – Brehme, Klinsmann, Effenberg; South Korea (1) – Young-il

27 June Soldier Field, Chicago *Att: 63,089*
BOLIVIA 1 (Sanchez 66)
SPAIN 3 (Guardiola 19pen; Caminero 65,71)
Bolivia: Trucco, Pena, Borja, Rimba, Sandy, Soruco, Ramos (Moreno 46), Soria (Castillo 63), Sanchez, Ramallo, Melgar
Spain: Zubizarreta, Ferrer, Voro, Abelardo, Sergi, Goikoetxea, Guardiola (Bakero 68), Caminero, Felipe (Hierro 46), Salinas, Guerrero
Ref: Badillia (Costa Rica)
Yellow Cards: Spain (2) – Ferrer, Caminero

they would return to the relative cool of Chicago for their next match.

Clemente's team were under pressure to produce the goods against Bolivia in Chicago, where a win would guarantee second-round participation. With several players under threat of suspension the Spanish coach made a number of changes, which included the 'resting' of Hierro and Luis Enrique.

The first half was a disappointing affair and only the Spain bar stopped the Bolivians from taking a very early lead. Offering little up front, the Spanish did get their noses ahead with the award of a controversial penalty after Felipe was pushed. Guardiola converted the kick but only just. The second half was an improvement on the first and two goals by Caminero in the space of six minutes added a bit of sparkle to a dreary forward line. The first came from an acute angle and the second from close range after Ferrer's low cross.

There had been a few heart flutters. A minute after Caminero had made it 2-0, the best Bolivian player, Erwin Sanchez, scored when his long-range effort was deflected over Zubizarreta's left shoulder. It was Bolivia's first goal ever at this stage and they celebrated it accordingly! The Spanish had thoughts of South Korea but thanks to Caminero those worries lasted just five minutes more. With the news filtering in from Dallas, the Spanish knew that they had finished second in the group and that Switzerland would be their opponents in sudden death.

Final Table

	P	W	D	L	F	A	Pts
Germany	3	2	1	0	5	3	7
Spain	3	1	2	0	6	4	5
South Korea	3	0	1	2	1	4	1
Bolivia	3	0	0	3	1	4	0

Spain's Sergi leaps clear of German Thomas Strunz's tackle.

Group D

ROUND 1

Greece were the first country to qualify for the final stages of the World Cup – it also happened to be the first time ever they had gone this far, achieved with a strong surge that took them past the Russians to the top spot in a qualifying group without war-torn Yugoslavia. A fox by the name of Penelope had been decided upon as their mascot and in the preparatory games leading up to the finals they had produced some defensive performances that left their supporters crazy like a fox.

They faced an Argentinian side with several stars but one that, as the two previous World Cup Finals had shown, could be brilliant or blatant. Drug-abusing stars Maradona and Caniggia returned to the fold while Islas controversially got the nod in goal over Goycochea to earn his first cap after a wait of eight years. Ruggeri on the other hand set an Argentinian record by winning his 95th cap. Within three minutes of the starting whistle the Greek defence once more saw fit to bear another legendary gift as Batistuta swung a foot through the legs of Apostolakis to shove the ball past the keeper, Minou.

That the South Americans had to wait nearly 40 minutes for their next goal was more down to their indecision on whether to attack or defend than anything the Greeks could offer. With only Kofidis showing any guile in the middle of the park for Greece, Chamot went forward and played the ball short to Batistuta, who scored with a shot from just outside the area. Greece continued to look all at sea in the second half and on another day Caniggia would have netted three or four goals. But the spotlight turned inevitably to Maradona, who accepted Batistuta's cut inside before digging the ball out from under him and high into the net from 20 yards. In the final seconds Batistuta scored from the penalty spot after Apostolakis had handled just inside the area – to make it 4-0 and secure his first international hat-trick. Saravakos set a Greek record in winning his 77th cap but for the team it was a performance worthy of a sheep, not a fox.

Later that evening the group action switched from Boston to Dallas for an eagerly awaited encounter between Bulgaria and Nigeria. The Super Eagles were making their first appearance ever in the World Cup Finals and arrived in the USA as a centre of attraction. Having captured the African Nations Championship just a few months earlier they had earned a reputation of being a powerfully athletic side with a marvellous ability to attack. The Bulgarians also were not without flair, with the likes of Kostadinov and Stoichkov in their side. They had also run into a good vein of form, having pipped France for the final qualification spot. Indeed the Bulgarian starting line-up had only one change from the side who gained that memorable 3-2 victory in Paris, with Borimirov, the Levski Sofia player, coming in for the injured Penev.

But it was the lethal combination of Brazilian-like flair and European hardness that gave the Nigerians a comprehensive win to add credence to their pre-match claims that there were 'afraid of nobody'. They took the play to the out-manoeuvred Bulgarians and it was no real surprise when Yekini, African Footballer of the Year in 1993 and newly signed by Olympiakos of Athens, put Nigeria ahead after 20 minutes, sweeping in George's low cross from the right. Yekini's celebration at the back of the Bulgarian net was destined to be one of the moments of the World Cup.

Stoichkov thought he had produced a stunning equaliser shortly afterwards when he curled a 30-yard free-kick past goalkeeper Rufai only to have it disallowed because the status of the kick was indirect, as referee Badilla had clearly signalled. Hard luck for the Bulgarians, because Nigeria quickly increased their lead when Yekini supplied the cross for Amokachi to beat Yankov and round the keeper before slipping the ball into the net from an angle.

After Amunike headed home George's cross at the far post early in the second half, Nigeria lost what few shackles were on their play and began to play the ball around with great aplomb against a well-beaten Bulgarian outfit.

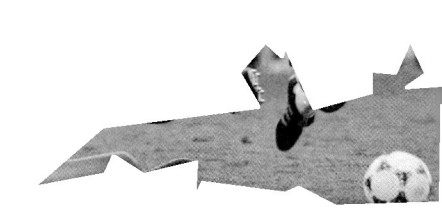

WORLD CUP FINALS: GROUP MATCHES

LEFT: *Emil Kostadinov of Bulgaria and Savvas Kofidis of Greece fight for the ball.*

ABOVE: *Iordan Lechkov of Bulgaria is tackled by Vaios Karagiannis of Greece.*

ROUND 2

With Nigeria having beaten European opposition quite convincingly and without having conceded a goal, the eyes of the world turned to the Foxboro Stadium for the second South America v Africa clash of the tournament. Once again it was the South Americans – in the form of an impressive Argentine side – who won the day, as once again Nigeria demonstrated naivety in defence.

Nigeria started boldly and took the lead after eight minutes when Siasia lobbed the ball over Islas from outside the area. Yekini almost made it 2-0 but Caniggia promptly equalised after Rufai had failed to hold Batistuta's powerful drive from Maradona's back-heeled free-kick. With the scores level Argentina took control and Caniggia was alive to the possibilities seven minutes later, when another free-kick was taken quickly by Maradona and laid into his path. With the Nigerian right-back off sightseeing, Caniggia curled the ball superbly past Rufai and into the far corner of the net. Both sides had further chances but after an electric first-half the second was a pale imitation and the final whistle signalled three points for Argentina and a place in the second phase. It also left Nigeria looking to the Bulgaria v Greece game to see what they had to do to join them.

With both Bulgaria and Greece having lost their opening games quite emphatically a win was absolutely vital for both if they were to have any chance of making the second phase, especially as they faced the vibrant Argentina and Nigerians in their final encounters. Alketas Panagoulias, the Greek coach, was very critical of the way his side had collapsed after Argentina had taken the lead in the opening group game. His anger was reflected in his team for this match – six changes, including the goalkeeper, where Atmatzides replaced Minou, for only his fourth cap.

Bulgaria, still seeking their first win in their sixth World Cup finals, finally got it at their 18th attempt but it needed a huge slice of good fortune to get the bandwagon rolling. Alexoudis went up for the ball in his own area and was pushed on to it by a Bulgarian forward only to see referee Bujsaim point to the spot for hand ball. There could hardly have been any intent but Stoichkov dispatched an excellent penalty with less than five minutes of play gone. Alexoudis had a mixed game; within two minutes of the penalty he was booked and despite being at the heart of the Greeks' play he was substituted in the second half.

Given the nature of their opening defeats and what was at stake, the quality of previous matches was always going to be difficult to maintain. However, the early goal forced the Greek players to take the game to their opponents, who were happy to defend in depth and there was little to trouble them. Both Stoichkov and Kostadinov – who had made their fortunes on the Iberian peninsular in the previous season – had little to offer and it was some surprise when Bulgaria took a two-goal advantage, but again it was from the

Group D Matches

21 June   Foxboro Stadium, Boston   *Att:* 53,644
ARGENTINA 4   (Batistuta 2,44,90 pen; Maradona 59)
GREECE 0
Argentina: Islas, Sensini, Caceres, Ruggeri, Chamot, Simeone, Redondo, Maradona (Ortega 83), Balbo (Mancuso 79), Caniggia, Batistuta
Greece: Minou, Manolas, Apostolakis, Kalitzakis, Kolitsidakis, Tsalouhides, Nioplias, Kofidis, Tsiantakis (Marangos 46), Saravakos, Machlas (Mitropoulos 59)
Ref: Angeles (USA)
Yellow Cards: Argentina (1) – Caceres; Greece (2) – Manolas, Tsalouhides

21 June   Cotton Bowl, Dallas   *Att:* 44,132
NIGERIA 3   (Yekini 21; Amokachi 43; Amunike 54)
BULGARIA 0
Nigeria: Rufai, Eguavoen, Iroha, Nwanu, Okechukwu, Siasia (Adepoju 68), Oliseh, George (Ezeugo 77), Amokachi, Amunike, Yekini
Bulgaria: Mihailov, Kremenliev, Ivanov, Tzvetanov, Hubchev, Balakov, Yankov, Lechkov (Sirakov 59), Borimirov (Yordanov 72), Stoichkov, Kostadinov
Ref: Badilla (Costa Rica)
Yellow Cards: Nigeria (1) – Amunike; Bulgaria (1) – Lechkov

25 June   Foxboro Stadium, Boston   *Att:* 54,453
ARGENTINA 2   (Caniggia 21, 28)
NIGERIA 1   (Siasia 8)
Argentina: Islas, Sensini (Diaz 87), Caceres, Ruggeri, Chamot, Simeone, Redondo, Maradona, Balbo (Mancuso 58), Caniggia, Batistuta
Nigeria: Rufai, Eguavoen, Emenalo, Okechukwu, Nwanu, Siasia (Adepoju 58), Amokachi, Oliseh (Okocha 87), Amunike, George, Yekini
Ref: Karlsson (Swe)
Yellow Cards: Argentina (1) – Caniggia; Nigeria (3) – Oliseh, Eguavoen, Emenalo

26 June   Soldier Field, Chicago   63,160
BULGARIA 4   (Stoichkov 5 pen, 56 pen; Lechkov 66; Borimov 90)
GREECE 0
Bulgaria: Mihailov, Kremenliev, Ivanov, Tzvetanov (Kiryakov 77), Hubchev, Yankov, Stoichkov, Balakov, Kostadinov (Borimirov 81) Lechkov, Sirakov
Greece: Atmatzides, Apostolakis, Karayannis, Karataidas, Nioplias, Marangos, Hatzidis (Mitropoulos 46), Kofidis, Machlas, Alexoudis (Dimitriadis 57), Kolitsidakis
Ref: Bujsaim (UAE)
Yellow Cards: Bulgaria (4) – Houbchev, Ivanov, Yankov, Borimirov; Greece (4) – Alexoudis, Hatzitis, Mitropoulos, Karayannis

30 June   Cotton Bowl, Dallas   *Att:* 63,998
ARGENTINA 0
BULGARIA 2   (Stoichkov 61; Sirakov 90)
Argentina: Islas, Diaz, Caceres, Ruggeri, Chamot, Balbo, Rodriguez (Bello 67), Redondo, Simeone, Caniggia (Ortega 25), Batistuta
Bulgaria: Mihailov, Kremenliev, Ivanov, Hubchev, Tzvetanov, Lechkov (Borimirov 75), Sirakov, Balakov, Yankov, Stoichkov, Kostadinov (Kiryakov 72)
Ref: Jouini (Tunisia)
Yellow Cards: Argentina (3) – Ruggeri, Rodriguez, Batistuta; Bulgaria (5) – Stoichkov, Yankov, Tzvetanov, Ivanov, Balakov
Red Card: Bulgaria – Tzvetanov (67)

30 June   Foxboro Stadium, Boston   *Att:* 53, 001
NIGERIA 2   (George 45, Amokachi 90)
GREECE 0
Nigeria: Rufai, Keshi, Okechukwu, Nwanu, Emenalo, Siasia, Amokachi, Oliseh, George (Adepoju 58), Yekini (Okocha 89), Amunike
Greece: Karkamanis, Kalizakis, Karayannis, Alexiou, Tsalouhides, Kofidis, Nioplias, Mitropoulos (Tsiantakis 72), Hatzitis, Alexandris, Machlas (Dimitriadis 80)
Ref: Mottram (Scotland)
Yellow Cards: Nigeria (2) – Oliseh, Keshi; Greece (2) – Mitropoulos, Kalizakis

---

penalty spot, after Atmatzides had held back Sirakov. Stoichkov dispatched the ball with simplicity once again. The Greeks had little chance to come back and Bulgaria used the opening spaces to add another two goals. In the 66th minute Lechkov – Bulgaria's best player – ran on to a fine pass from Yankov to slot the ball past the goalkeeper, and in injury time substitute Borimirov completed the misery from close range. That eliminated the Greeks from the competition and kept the Bulgarian hopes alive.

ROUND 3

Bulgaria met Argentina in their final game and faced elimination unless they secured at least a point. On the day before the game there seemed little chance of that given the nature of the Argentine play. But then FIFA announced that Maradona had failed a drug test after the Nigerian game and was out of the tournament in disgrace. Argentina's inspiration and play-maker was gone. Argentina knew a point would be good enough for them and for the first 45 minutes we looked to have a game where both sides were settling for that. The first half was one of the worst of this World Cup, but the second was a more sprightly affair and on the hour Stoichkov burst through the defence and turned a long ball from Kostadinov into the goal.

Six minutes later Bulgaria found themselves down to 10 men when Tzvetanov was sent off for his second bookable offence, but they reorganised themselves well enough to hold their lead. There was to be a further twist when Sirakov headed home a corner three minutes into stoppage time to make it a 2-0 win for Bulgaria that sent them above Argentina in the table – an amazing turnaround given a very poor performance against the Nigerians in the first round of games.

Panagoulias made another set of changes with Karkamanis, the third goalkeeper in the squad, brought in. The Greeks looked to have played their first 45 minutes without conceding a goal, but just as referee Mottram was about to blow his whistle, George put the Nigerians ahead.

With six minutes of stoppage time played at the end of the game, and the Nigerians still leading by one goal, the Bulgarians were heading the group, but then Amokachi got free and made it 2-0 to the Africans with the last kick of the game. That goal put the Nigerians at the head of the group on goal difference but Argentina and Bulgaria still made the second phase. Greece returned home having lost all three games and conceded 10 goals without scoring once.

Final Table

	P	W	D	L	F	A	Pts
Nigeria	3	2	0	1	6	2	6
Bulgaria	3	2	0	1	6	3	6
Argentina	3	2	0	1	6	3	6
Greece	3	0	0	3	0	10	0

RIGHT: *Fading faces – both Diego Maradona (Argentina) and Panagiotis Tsalouhidis of Greece (top) are about to leave the World Cup Finals, for different reasons.*

BELOW: *Dino Baggio (hidden) scores Italy's winning goal against Norway.*

Group E

ROUND 1

The opening game of Group E was to be a repeat of the Italia 90 quarter-final tie in which Italy ousted the Republic of Ireland by a single goal. The talk prior to the match though was not of revenge but of water. Not whether 'Saint Jack' the Irish manager could walk on it – his adopted countrymen knew that for a fact already – but of Charlton's concern for his players and FIFA's apparent reluctance to allow water breaks for players during the game that was to be played in near 100-degree temperatures in the Giants Stadium in New Jersey. The talk was also of whether the Irish could play their standard chasing game in such conditions, while the Italian coach Arrigo Sacchi was under pressure following a series of poor results and performances.

Charlton decided to go for the experience of Irwin and Houghton in place of the youthful inexperience of the impressive Gary Kelly and McAteer. Those decisions were vindicated as the Republic turned in a sparkling performance. Bonner in goal had little to do and when Dino Baggio started to find space in the second half to fire a few shots at the keeper he was more than equal to them.

By this time the Irish were well in control and Houghton had supported lone attacker Coyne well from deep. One such run in from the right allowed him to take advantage of Baresi's weak header out on his chest before turning to hit a dipping 20-yard left foot shot over Pagliuca. So shaken were the Italians by the goal – Baresi in particular looked in turmoil at trying to play in a flat back four – that the Irish might have doubled their advantage seven minutes later, but Townsend failed to control when clear in front of goal.

Italy introduced Massaro at the start of the second half and Dino Baggio, stepping out of the shadows of his namesake Roberto, looked to benefit the most. Babb and McGrath at the heart of the Irish defence had to be at their best and on several occasions produced tackles of the highest quality. Sheridan held his head when his shot from Keane's pass from the wing cannoned off the bar midway through the second half with Pagliuca well beaten. Time was eventually against the disappointing Italians and the Irish were dancing a jig of delight at the final whistle.

The next day the scene moved from New Jersey to the District of Columbia, where the Norwegians were taking their place in the final stages for the first time since 1938 and their direct fast play was offering an interesting contrast to the free passing style of the Mexicans. The South American side had a reputation for being poor travellers but had touched new heights the previous year in reaching the final of the Copa America, where they were unlucky to lose to the Argentinians.

In goal they had one of the most colourful players in the tournament in Jorge Campos of UNAM, who had featured as a forward in one of the qualifying games. The Mexican authorities needed to get special permission from FIFA to register him as a keeper and outfield player for the finals! Mexico also featured veteran Hugo Sanchez in their side, 36 years old and one of the few players to have represented all three senior Madrid clubs in the top flight. Norway coach Egil Olsen offered only one surprise in his starting line-up, preferring Nottingham Forest's Alf Inge Haaland at the heart of his defence.

As a spectacle the match was disappointing. Mexico started well but gradually the Norwegians grew in confidence and it looked only a matter of time until they scored, but there were no goals in the first period. The Vikings continued to press forward in the second half but as the game entered its final 15 minutes the Mexicans exploded into life and only two excellent saves at full-length by Thorstvedt denied first Luis Garcia and then Ambriz. As Mexico got the bit between their teeth, Norway got the decisive goal. A long pass was controlled by Fjortoft and despite his being fouled the ball ran on to substitute Rekdal, who found the far corner of the net from close range. Somehow, in the final minute, the ball stayed out after Ramirez shot and Alves's diving header from point-blank range hit the post, and then hit him on the back of the head and was cleared off the line by Henning Berg.

ROUND 2

Continued participation was at stake for the Italians as they went into their match against the cock-a-hoop Norwegians. Defeat would leave their ambitions hanging by slender threads and almost certainly signal the end of Arrigo Sacchi's term in charge. In the event he made three changes to the team who lost to the Irish. Casiraghi came into the attack with Signori moving out wide to the left at the expense of the injured Evani. Berti replaced Donadoni and Tassotti made way for Benarrivo at full-back. If Sacchi thought his pre-match shuffles had been a headache it was nothing compared to what the game itself was about to throw up.

No such problems for Norway though, as Egil Olsen brought in Rushfeldt for Jakobsen. The Norwegians started the match in a very defensive mode and it was obvious from an early point that they would be happy to settle for a point and hope to catch the Azzurri on the break. In the 22nd minute they did, and how. The Italian defence continued with their Milanese offside trap. However, for this game the original Milan back four had been dismantled with the introduction of Benarrivo and when Mykland pushed a short pass through for Leonhardsen to race on to, Benarrivo was not up with the other three defenders and the Rosenborg player was away on goal. Seeing the danger Pagliuca raced out of his penalty area and slid, feet first and arms raised, into Leonhardsen just as he curled his shot wide. German referee Krug had little option other than to send the goalkeeper off. In the reshuffle, Marchegiani – at £7m the world's most expensive hands – went on as a substitute for European and FIFA World Footballer of the Year Roberto Baggio. Sensation after sensation and the thinking behind the move seemed to be that Sacchi would sacrifice his 'luxury' player for the sake of his ten workers.

Norway had little to offer and dismally failed to take advantage of the situation. Italy also took time to readjust. Without Roberto Baggio the early balls through to Casiraghi that had looked like unhinging the Norwegian defence were no longer available and it needed a splendid display of front running by Signori to take Italy forward. The problems were compounded early in the second half when Baresi limped off with a knee injury that seemed sure to keep him out of the rest of the World Cup. For short periods the Italian were reduced to nine men as the heat and numerical disadvantage took their toll, but Norway still failed to take advantage. Then, as so often happens with ten men, Italy took control with a goal out of the blue. Signori flighted a free-kick that left the keeper in two minds and Dino Baggio powered in to produce a bullet header from seven yards that flashed into the goal.

Italy played out the final minutes with great bravery despite injuries to Maldini and Dino Baggio which made them little more than passengers. And while one can point to a performance par excellence from Italy it should not be forgotten that Norway should have been a goal ahead long before Dino Baggio scored. In a sense justice was not done by Pagliuca's dismissal, whatever your opinion of his sending off.

Much had been made of Ireland's victory over Italy and it would be tempting to say that they approached their next group game with Mexico with a wisp of overconfidence. Striker Coyne had recovered from the dehydration he suffered to ensure that he made the line-up in the midday heat of Orlando. Manager Charlton continued his altercations with FIFA and finally got the permission he was after, to be able to supply water bags to the players on the pitch. A win for Ireland would guarantee them a second-phase qualification – a draw would also give them an odds-on chance to move on. For Mexico though, having lost to Norway, a win was of the most vital importance. Not surprisingly they made changes from their original line-up; the most controversial was the axing of legendary striker Hugo Sanchez.

In temperatures touching 110 degrees the Irish made a bright start and went within a whisker of scoring after six minutes when Phelan's powerful run down the left ended in a penetrating cross that Coyne could only half reach and the ball went wide. Mexico gradually eased themselves back into the game but didn't provide Bonner in the Irish goal with too many problems. As the game moved towards its midway break the colourful Campos in the Mexican goal produced a save of outstanding quality to deny the sluggish Townsend, who met Coyne's cross with power.

But in the final minutes before half-time, the Mexicans imposed themselves on the game and just as the Irish looked like they would reach the safety of the dressing room on level terms, Mexico took the lead when Garcia struck a splendid right-foot shot from outside the area that dipped over the diving Bonner. The Irish failed to up the tempo in difficult conditions in the second half and – during a period of promising play – Mexico seized on Irwin's mistake to leave Garcia to hit another fine effort from the edge of the area to make it a fully deserved 2-0.

Substitutions saw the introduction of Jason McAteer and Tranmere's John Aldridge. But a mix-up on the touch-line left Ireland reduced to ten men for three and a half minutes as a situation of pure farce developed which meant that the FIFA touchline official – Mustafa Eahmy of Egypt – wouldn't let Aldridge take his place on the field for the now 'substituted' Coyne. The official proceeded to man-handle the incensed Aldridge and a none-too-happy Charlton as Aldridge's abusive

Roberto Donadoni on the ball for Italy. 'Stan' Staunton looks on as Terry Phelan lays down the tackle.

outburst was seen worldwide.

Thankfully, the nonsense didn't spill on to the pitch and with six minutes remaining the two substitutes combined and McAteer's centre was powerfully headed home by Aldridge to claw a goal back, but only after Bonner at the other end had made another fine save to deny the rampant Garcia his hat-trick. In the final minutes Campos produced a match-winning save to frustrate Townsend and leave the Group E table as tight as it could be, with everything depending on the final round of games.

The day after the Ireland *v* Norway match FIFA announced fines against the Irish FA, Charlton and Aldridge for their 'considerable misbehaviour'. Charlton's and the FA of Ireland's fine amounted to £10,000 while Aldridge was fined £1,500. More annoyingly for the Irish team, Charlton was banned from the touchline for their final encounter with Norway.

ROUND 3

The group had been known as the 'Group of Death' when it was first drawn and as the final round of games started that's exactly what it was, with four teams on three points and with only goals scored separating them. 'Group of Chess' might have been a more apt name as the two sets of 90 minutes finally came around.

With Mexico leading the table they faced an Italian side who had to win to be sure of the second phase. A draw could see them through as a third-placed qualifier but that would depend on the result in the other game. That was one of giant proportions and fittingly was played out in the Giants Stadium. Norway knew they had to win – a draw offered them nothing – yet they approached their game from the outset with safety in mind. It was no surprise when the half-time whistle went at 0-0 because their massed defence had allowed the Irish the ball almost exclusively but had denied them even one effort on goal. Second bookings, for Irwin and Phelan in the previous game meant that they missed the

Group E Matches

18 June Giants Stadium, New Jersey Att: 73,511
ITALY 0
REPUBLIC of IRELAND 1 (Houghton 11)
Italy: Pagliuca, Tassotti, Baresi, Costacurta, Maldini, Donadoni, D. Baggio, Albertini, Evani (Massaro 45), R. Baggio, Signori (Berti 83)
Ireland: Bonner, Irwin, Babb, McGrath, Phelan, Houghton (McAteer 67), Keane, Sheridan, Townsend, Staunton, Coyne (Aldridge 89)
Ref: van der Ende (Holland)
Yellow Cards: Ireland (3) – Phelan, Coyne, Irwin

19 June RFK Stadium, Washington DC Att: 52,359
NORWAY 1 (Rekdal 82)
MEXICO 0
Norway: Thorstvedt, Haaland, Berg, Bratseth, Bjornebye, Flo, Bohinen, Mykland (Rekdal 77), Leonhardsen, Jakobsen (Halle 45), Fjortoft
Mexico: Campos, Suarez, Perales, Gutierrez (Bernal 70), Ramirez, Valdez (Galindo 45), Ambriz, Del Olmo, Luis Garcia, Alves, Sanchez
Ref: Puhl (Hungary)
Yellow Cards: Norway (2) – Haaland, Leonhardsen; Mexico (1) – Suarez.

23 June Giants Stadium, New Jersey Att: 74,624
ITALY 1 (D. Baggio 68)
NORWAY 0
Italy: Pagliuca, Benarrivo, Baresi (Apolloni 48), Costacurta, Maldini, Berti, D. Baggio, Albertini, Casiraghi (Massaro 67), R. Baggio (Marchegiani 22), Signori
Norway: Thorstvedt, Haaland, Berg, Bratseth, Bjornebye, Flo, Bohinen, Mykland (Rekdal 80), Leonhardsen, Rushfeldt (Jakobsen 46), Fjortoft
Ref: Krug (Ger)
Yellow Cards: Italy (1) – Casiraghi; Norway (2) – Bjornebye, Haaland.
Red Card: Italy – Pagliuca (22)

24 June Citrus Bowl, Orlando Att: 61,219
REPUBLIC of IRELAND 1 (Aldridge 84)
MEXICO 2 (Luis Garcia 43, 66)
Ireland: Bonner, Irwin, Babb, McGrath, Phelan, Houghton, Keane, Sheridan, Townsend, Staunton (McAteer 67), Coyne (Aldridge 67)
Mexico: Campos, Suarez, Perales, Ambriz, Bernal, Del Olmo, Rodriguez (Gutierrez 80), Luis Garcia, Garcia Aspe, Hermosillo (Salvador 80), Alves
Ref: Rothlisberger (Switzerland)
Yellow Cards: Ireland (2) – Irwin, Phelan; Mexico (2) – Del Olmo, Campos.

28 June Giants Stadium, New Jersey Att: 76,322
NORWAY 0
REPUBLIC of IRELAND 0
Norway: Thorstvedt, Halle (Jakobsen 33), Berg, Bratseth, Bjornebye, Johnsen, Leonhardsen (Bohinen 67), Mykland, Sorloth, Rekdal, Flo
Ireland: Bonner, G. Kelly, Babb, McGrath, Staunton, McAteer, Houghton, Keane, Sheridan, Townsend (Whelan 74), Aldridge (D. Kelly 65)
Ref: Cadenas (Colombia)
Yellow Cards: Norway (2) – Sorloth, Johnsen; Ireland (3) – Keane, Houghton, G. Kelly

28 June RFK Stadium, Washington DC Att: 53,186
ITALY 1 (Massaro 48)
MEXICO 1 (Bernal 58)
Italy: Marchegiani, Benarrivo, Costacurta, Apolloni, Maldini, Berti, Albertini, D. Baggio (Donadoni 66), Signori, R. Baggio, Casiraghi (Massaro 48)
Mexico: Campos, Suarez, Perales, Ambriz, Del Olmo, Rodriguez, Bernal, Luis Garcia (Chavez 83), Garcia Aspe, Alves, Hermosillo
Ref: Lamolina (Argentina)
Yellow Cards: Italy (1) – Albertini; Mexico (3) – Del Olmo, Luis Garcia, Garcia Aspe

match but Gary Kelly and McAteer proved to be more than adequate replacements.

In Washington, the half-time score was the same but both Italy and Mexico had gone within a whisker of scoring, only to be denied by some excellent goalkeeping. If a game was going to produce a goal then it was in the RFK Stadium and it was taken elegantly by substitute Massaro, who controlled Albertini's intelligent pass on his chest before guiding it into the net past Campos. With defeat threatening elimination for the Mexicans they surged forward and Bernal drove home an equaliser from 20 yards ten minutes later. Back in New Jersey, Norway had adopted a more attack-minded approach for the second half and despite going close, efforts from Flo, Sorloth and Rekdal didn't trouble Bonner unduly. The space left by the Norwegians' more positive approach allowed Ireland extra scope going forward and Sheridan nearly won the game with a exquisite lob from Keane's pass that landed on top of Thorstvedt's net.

The final whistles sounded within a minute of each other at the two stadiums. Mexico's point ensured their qualification, perhaps surprisingly at the top of the group, while Ireland finished equal on points, goal difference and goals scored with Italy, but pipped them for second place on the strength of their win in the first game, and faced a trip back to Orlando for the second round. Four points meant that Italy would qualify but did little to ease the growing pressure on Sacchi and Roberto Baggio, who had had another anonymous game: four points were not enough for Norway to go through.

Final Table

	P	W	D	L	F	A	Pts
Mexico	3	1	1	1	3	3	4
Republic of Ireland	3	1	1	1	2	2	4
Italy	3	1	1	1	2	2	4
Norway	3	1	1	1	1	1	4

Group F

ROUND 1

Belgium arrived at the World Cup finals with the oldest squad on show – many with the experience of three previous World Cups to their advantage but that in itself led to speculation about the ability of ageing legs in high heat to stay the course. Indeed, in the days leading up to their opening game with Morocco, Lorenzo Staelens needed medical attention after suffering dizzy spells that were attributed to the conditions. There were doubts as to whether he would make the starting line-up. Marc Degryse was also a doubt but he recovered from a groin strain and lined up with Staelens in the midday sun of Orlando. As if to underline the high age of the Belgium side, Luc Nilis at 27 was the youngest player in their starting line-up. He formed a front line with Josip Weber, Croatian born but a newly naturalised Belgian, who scored five goals on his international debut against Zambia.

The Moroccans were not new to World Cup tradition – in 1970 they became the first African side to qualify for the Finals and the first side from that continent to progress into the second phase. Coach Abdellah Hajri had said before the game that his side were going to 'build a new Berlin Wall'. That statement proved to be a smokescreen as after a slow start the Africans proceeded to dominate the second half of an entertaining match.

By that point, though, Belgium were in front, Degryse arriving at the front of the goal area to flick Nilis's cross over the outstretched hands of Khalil Azmi. The Belgians' neat play didn't produce any further chances of real note while Morocco nearly got back into the game five minutes before the interval when Mohamed Chaouch, who plays for Nice, hit a shot from outside the area that dipped over Michel Preud'homme and thundered off the bar. As the second half progressed Morocco looked the more likely side to score even though chances went begging at the feet of both Nilis and Weber. Chaouch was denied once again by the woodwork midway through the half when his header was tipped on to the bar and with that Belgium secured three important points.

Dutch preparations leading up to their opening encounter with Saudi Arabia continued to be dogged with controversy. The withdrawal of Ruud Gullit just days before coach Dick Advocaat announced his squad continued to be big news in Holland, and the Dutch received a further blow on the morning of their opener when the burly Feyenoord defender John De Wolf tore a calf muscle in training. That ruled him out of the rest of the competition.

The news from the Saudi camp was that there was no news. A tight blanket of security meant there was little chance to mingle with the team who were now under their third coach since the previous October and were faced with their first ever appearance in the World Cup Finals. While the talk was of the number of goals that Holland might score, the Saudis set about their task with a vibrant vigour that nearly brought a sensational lead in the first 30 seconds.

That was just a prelude to the real thing when a foul by Jan Wouters led to a free-kick that was met perfectly by Amin, who did well to get in front of Ronald Koeman and beat Ed de Goey.

Erik Mykland of Norway has an overseer in Jason McAteer of the Republic.

The bolt from the blue did little to make the Oranje wake up and only some desperate defending and sometimes over-enthusiasm by the Saudi attackers kept the Dutch in the game. Ulrich van Gobbel in particular was having a nightmare in defence, often over exposed by the pace of Majed 'Mohammed' Abdullah – 116 goals in 166 appearances that had earned him the name of the 'Desert Pele'. When the Dutch did produce something of note, Al Deayea could match it with a save worthy of the occasion. Dennis Bergkamp's shot midway through the half, after being set up by Frank de Boer, was especially venomous and Al Deayea got down quickly at his near post.

With Rijkaard gradually moving more infield to support the Dutch midfield an equalising goal looked inevitable even if not deserved. And it came five minutes into the second half when Jonk hit a pacy shot from 25 yards that nestled in the corner of the net. The introduction of Taument for the lethargic Overmars did little to invigorate the Dutch early on but with four minutes remaining the heat finally got to the Saudi keeper. He went for a ball on the edge of the area he could never get, and Taument was able to head over his hands and into the unguarded net to steal the three points when none had looked likely.

ROUND 2

With unconvincing wins over Morocco and Saudi Arabia behind them, Belgium and Holland took to the midday heat of the Citrus Bowl in Orlando for what was the 117th game between the two countries but the first time they had ever met in the World Cup

Finals. The Dutch supporters packed the stadium that might have been better called the Orange Bowl for the day. Advocaat kept faith with the side who had finished the game against the Moroccans, with Taument getting the nod over Overmars on the right wing.

Coach Paul Van Himst included no fewer than nine players from just two clubs in his starting line-ups – six from RSC Anderlecht and three from Bruges. They started the better of the two sides and Weber's miss after just 40 seconds of play was a prelude of what was to follow in the next 89 minutes of an enthralling encounter. The first half ended goalless – and that in itself was amazing as chance after chance went begging. Preud'homme was in inspired form to stop two Koeman specials from free-kicks, and de Goey had to deal with an even heavier bombardment, in particular long-range blasts by Grun and more delicate shots from Degryse. Scifo had a goal disallowed for offside and when the goalkeepers couldn't reach shots the ball contrived to go narrowly wide.

The second half proved no different but the deadlock was finally broken in the 65th minute after a left-wing corner was flicked on, and Albert drove the ball home off a base of the post despite the presence of a defender. The Dutch tried hard to equalise and in the final ten minutes left only Wouters at the back. The Belgians should have added at least two in that final period as they countered quickly but Weber squandered inviting opportunities. Inside the last few minutes Roy's shot was cleared off the line and substitute Overmars saw his effort pushed on to the bar by the brilliant Preud'homme. The Belgians won all three points and ensured their continued participation in the competition. The Dutch – perhaps deserving a point – left the field knowing they had to get at least that against the Moroccans in their final match, maybe even more.

Much further north, in New Jersey, Saudi Arabia and Morocco were contesting the other Group F fixture in the Giants Stadium. It was a case of sudden death for the loser would need a convincing win in their final match to stand a chance of making the second phase. A winner was there in the form of Saudi Arabia and once again Morocco were left ruing their many wasted chances.

The Saudis made a flying start when Sami al-Jaber side-footed home a penalty after he had been fouled. But 20 minutes later Chaouch – who had wasted several good opportunities – had the easiest of tasks to score the equaliser from a couple of yards out after Ahmed Bahja had got in behind the defence.

Chaouch continued to be the danger man in the second half and he crafted a number of chances that were not accepted by his team-mates. When Faud Amin broke up a Moroccan attack on the half-way line he made 10 yards before hitting a swerving 35-yarder that had keeper Khalil Azmi floundering as it squeezed into the Moroccan net just before the interval. After the break the Africans laid siege to the Saudi goal but it remained intact. Owairan and the others could rarely launch an attack of their own, but somehow they held on for all three points and became only the second side from the Middle East to win a game at the Finals.

ROUND 3

Belgium went into their last game, against the Saudis needing a draw to finish top of the group. With several players having already received cautions, Van Himst 'rested' Grun, Weber and

The Dutchman cometh as Dennis Bergkamp pulls the ball back for the incoming Bryan Roy (hidden) to score against Morocco.

Lorenzo Staelens of Belgium.

Borkelmans, in case they received a second card and missed the second phase of games. But within five minutes of the start, Van Himst must have been re-thinking his pre-match planning as the Saudis stormed into the lead with a goal par excellence, a magical blend of individual skill, virtuosity and good fortune. A goal for the World Cup Hall of Fame.

There was no danger when Saeed Owairan received the ball around 20 yards inside his own half. Moving forward he progressed into and out of the centre circle and deep into the Belgium half, riding tackles and keeping the ball at his feet. A fortunate bobble allowed him to move into the penalty area and a cool head allowed him to slip the ball just far enough past Van Der Elst to allow him to reach it and fire his shot into the top corner of the net before Preud'homme could get there. The electrifying nature of the goal had the Belgian supporters applauding his artistry.

All of a sudden there was a very different game in prospect as Belgium attempted to gain control of the match, and Wilmots was guilty of bad misses in front of the Saudi goal. Nilis and Weber both appeared on the pitch but the confidence and energy started to drain from the side. Committed to attack, Saudi could break and both Falatah and Al Bishi could have made the final ten minutes a formality. Al Deayea was called on to make two fine saves in the dying period but the Saudis held on and the three points took them ahead of Belgium in the group table.

Whether Belgium would finish second or third depended on the result in the other group game between Holland and Morocco, being played simultaneously. The Dutch soon found themselves under pressure at the back that had been reorganised by coach Advocaat, who had omitted both Rijkaard and Ronald De Boer. Morocco had made six changes following their defeat by the Saudis but Holland continued to find it difficult to get through their midfield, which created several chances that might have embarrassed the Oranje. But with only three minutes of the half remaining Bergkamp was on hand to convert after Van Vossen had broken through on the left. It was Bergkamp's 20th goal in 34 outings.

Morocco equalised two minutes after half-time. Substitute Moustafa Hadji's first contribution was to deliver a driven centre in from the right for Hassan Nader to sidefoot home from a few yards and throw question marks, not for the first time, against the Dutch rearguard, especially Koeman, who was nowhere. With time running out and legs tiring, Roy was introduced and was on hand to score the winner from close range after Bergkamp had

Group F Matches

19 June   Citrus Bowl, Orlando   *Att: 60,790*
BELGIUM   **1**   (Degryse 10)
MOROCCO   **0**
Belgium: Preud'homme, Grun, Smidts, M. De Wolf, Boffin (Borkelmans 83), Staelens, Degryse, Scifo, Van Der Elst, Weber, Nilis (Emmers 53)
Morocco: Azmi (Alaoui 88), Nacer, Naybet, Tiiki, El Hadrioui, Azzouzi, El Hadaoui (Bahja 68), Hababi, Daoudi, Chaouch (Samadi 81), Hadji
Ref: Jose Torres Cadena (Colombia)
Yellow Cards: Belgium (2) – Grun, Weber; Morocco (3) – Naybet, Daoudi, Azzouzi

20 June   Stanford Stadium, San Francisco   *Att: 52,535*
SAUDI ARABIA   **1**   (Amin 18)
HOLLAND   **2**   (Jonk 50; Taument 86)
Saudi Arabia: Al Deayea, Al Dosari, Al Khilawi, Abdel-Jawaad, Madani, Amin, Al Bishi, al-Muwallid, Al Jibreen, Mohammed (Falatah 44), Owairan (Saleh 68)
Holland: De Goey, F. de Boer, R. Koeman, Van Gobbel, Jonk, Overmars (Taument 57), Wouters, Rijkaard, Roy (Van Vossen 81), R. de Boer, Bergkamp
Ref: Vega Diaz (Spain)
Yellow Cards: Saudi Arabia (3) – Dosari, Abdel-Jawaad, Amin; Holland (2) – Van Gobbel, F. de Boer

25 June   Citrus Bowl, Orlando   *Att: 61,219*
BELGIUM   **1**   (Albert 65)
HOLLAND   **0**
Belgium: Preud'homme, Emmers (Medved 78), M. De Wolf, Albert, Grun, Borkelmans (Smidts 61), Staelens, Van Der Elst, Scifo, Degryse, Weber
Holland: De Goey, Valckx, R. Koeman, Rijkaard, F. de Boer, Taument (Overmars 64), Jonk, Wouters, Roy, R. de Boer (Witschge 46), Bergkamp
Ref: Marsiglia (Brazil)
Yellow Cards: Belgium (1) – Borkelmans; Holland (5) – Wouters, Jonk, Witschge, Rijkaard, Bergkamp

25 June   Giants Stadium, New Jersey   *Att: 72,404*
MOROCCO   **1**   (Chaouch 27)
SAUDI ARABIA   **2**   (Al Jaber 7; Amin 45)
Morocco: Azmi, Nacer (Laghrissi 57), Tiiki, Naybet, El Hadrioui, El Khalej, Hababi (Hadji 72), Azzouzi, Chaouch, Daoudi, Bahja
Saudi Arabia: Al Deayea, Al Anadi (Zebermawi 30), Al Khilawi, Madani, Abdel-Jawaad, Amin, Al Bishi, Al Muwallid, Al Jibreen, Al Jaber (Al Ghashayan 80), Owairan
Ref: Don (England)
Yellow Cards: Morocco (2) – El Hadrioui, Laghrissi ; Saudi Arabia (3) – Al Jibreen, Al Muwallid, Amin

29 June   JFK Stadium, Washington DC   *Att: 52,959*
BELGIUM   **0**
SAUDI ARABIA   **1**   (Owairan 5)
Belgium: Preud'homme, Medved, M. De Wolf, Albert, Smidts, Scifo, Van Der Elst, Staelens, Boffin, Degryse (Nilis 23), Wilmots (Weber 53)
Saudi Arabia: Al Deayea, Sulaiman, Al Khilawi, Madani, Abdul-Jawad, Saleh, Al Bishi, Jabrin, Abduallah (Al Muallid 46), Owairan, Saeed Falatah
Ref: Krug (Germany)
Yellow Cards: Belgium (2) – Scifo, Smidts; Saudi Arabia (2) – Malani, Saeed Falatah

29 June   Citrus Bowl, Orlando   *Att: 60,578*
HOLLAND   **2**   (Bergkamp 43; Roy 77)
MOROCCO   **1**   (Nader 47)
Holland: De Goey, Valckx, R. Koeman, F. de Boer, Winter, Jonk, Witschge, Wouters, Overmars (Taument 56), Bergkamp, Van Vossen (Roy 67)
Morocco: Alaoui, Hababi , Nekrouz, Tiiki, El Hadrioui, Azzouzi (Daoudi 61), El Kahlej, Bouyboud (Hadji 46), Samadi, Nader, Bahja
Ref: Noriega (Peru)
Yellow Cards: Holland (1) – Wouters; Morocco (4) – El Khalej, Bouyboud, Hababi, Samadi

intelligently cut the ball back from the left-hand goal-line, having left two defenders in his wake.

Holland's win took them to the top of the final table by virtue of the fact that they had beaten Saudi Arabia in their first group match. The Saudis in turn finished above Belgium because they had scored more goals and the Moroccans finished bottom, pointless and wondering how, given their fine displays.

Final Table

	P	W	D	L	F	A	Pts
Holland	3	2	0	1	4	3	6
Saudi Arabia	3	2	0	1	4	3	6
Belgium	3	2	0	1	2	1	6
Morocco	3	0	0	3	2	5	0

Second Round

When the dust had settled on the matches in the group stage, the final tables presented a topsy-turvy picture. Most groups had offered a surprise or two with only Group C going according to international 'form' and Germany and Spain securing the top two spots. From a European point of view, of the 11 countries participating only three failed to make the second round of games, with Russia, Norway and Greece all ending their international seasons a week or two earlier than they would have hoped. Russia's 6-1 thrashing of Cameroon came just too late; Norway's lack of ambition gave them their just desserts, Greece failed abysmally and finished without a point and without a goal, by far the worst record at the competition. In Group A, though, Romania and Switzerland excelled and their 4-1 encounter was probably the most entertaining game of the first stage. Only a last-minute goal by Cameroon prevented Bulgaria from taking pole position in Group D, and Group E was as tight as everyone expected with only the more obtuse rules of placement separating the sides at the end. Russia's seven goals – six of them by Salenko – were the highest tally of any of the European sides.

The start of the knock-out stage was not without its problems. Germany sent home Effenberg for misbehaving – making gestures to the crowd following the match with Spain. Romania also dismissed Vladiou for indiscretions, not least his awful tackle on Switzerland's Ohrel that earned him his marching orders a few minutes after going on as a substitute.

Europe was guaranteed at least three countries in the quarter-final stages given the pairings of Germany v Belgium, Spain v Switzerland and Ireland v Holland. With one all-Americas tie (Brazil v USA) the other three European sides would face African (Nigeria v Italy) and South American opposition (Romania v Argentina and Mexico v Bulgaria). The second round of games began with all existing cautions erased, although suspensions earned in the first round were carried over into the knock-out phase.

The first game to get under way was between Germany and Belgium at Chicago's Soldier Field. German coach Vogts made a number of changes, the most notable of which was the recall of veteran Rudi Voller to partner Klinsmann in attack – a move that was to pay dividends. Belgium had not beaten Germany in six years before this encounter and they received a major blow before

Ilie Dumitrescu of Romania attempts to lob the ball over Luis Islas, the Argentine goalkeeper.

Demetrio Albertini (left) of Italy keeps close tabs on Nigeria's Daniel Amokachi.

the game when Degryse was ruled out with a groin strain. The 60,000-plus crowd witnessed a highly entertaining match that was just about settled inside the first 11 minutes.

Having hardly touched the ball in the opening five minutes as the Belgian players pushed the ball around between them, Germany gained possession and took the lead. Matthaus dispossessed Weber and knocked the ball forward to release Voller on the right of goal. The 34-year-old took the ball forward and as Preud'homme came diving at his feet, kept his composure to lift it over him and into the net for his 46th international goal.

Belgium exposed frailties in the German defence to snatch an equaliser two minutes later, when Scifo's free-kick was missed by all but Grun, who clipped the ball past Illgner from close range. Germany's response to that was emphatic and they restored their lead with a superb goal, Voller and Klinsmann exchanging passes to leave Klinsmann in space on the edge of the area to drill the ball into the far side of the net. Tempers flared briefly and after a flurry of bookings by the inconsistent Rothlisberger both keepers were kept busy and forced into fine saves. Germany restored their two-goal advantage near the interval, exploiting Preud'homme's reluctance to dominate his six-yard box at corners. When the ball was delivered by Hassler – who was the outstanding player of the night – Voller rose unchallenged to nod home.

The second half was as vibrant as the first and Preud'homme made excellent stops from Klinsmann, Voller and substitute Kuntz. As the half wore on Belgium went ever forward, but with 20 minutes remaining the game turned away from them. Weber controlled a through ball to get beyond Helmer and as he was about to fire home from 15 yards, Helmer took his legs away from behind. 'No foul' was the verdict of the Swiss referee, some 40 yards behind play. A goal at that point would have produced a finale fitting the match.

Czerniatynski went on with ten minutes to go, for his first international game in six years as Van Himst played his final card. It wasn't a trump, although Belgium did score a second in the final minute when their outstanding player, Albert, took the ball past two defenders before powering it past Illgner from eight yards. The Belgians nearly forced extra time, too. At a corner on the right, even Preud'homme went up, and Albert's header was only a foot wide. Despite the late revival Germany were worth their narrow win in a hugely entertaining game. The margin might have been more emphatic, given wasted chances, and once again the Germans announced that they were not letting go of their crown lightly.

Later that evening Spain and Switzerland faced one another in Washington. Spanish coach Clemente once again shuffled his pack, leaving out Salinas and playing Luis Enrique as a lone striker supported by midfield players running from deep. A curious move, but one that was to exploit the poor Swiss attempts to play a high, flat back four. Switzerland went into the game not having beaten Spain in their 17 previous meetings and received a major blow shortly before kick-off when Sutter – their star of the first phase and set to win his 50th cap – dropped out because of the nagging toe injury that had plagued him in earlier games.

The Swiss started the better side and with 15 minutes gone had wasted several chances. Then Chapuisat looked to be fouled on the edge of the area. With the Swiss players waiting for the free-kick Dutch referee Van Der Ende waved play on and Hierro raced through the square defence to steer the ball past Pascolo from 30 yards. After the protests died down the Swiss again set about their task with purpose, and only several fine saves by Zubizarreta kept his side ahead. As the half-time whistle sounded the Swiss could consider themselves unlucky to be behind.

Spain used the break to good effect and regrouped to present a more compact unit in the second half. With Sergi – in his first full season – alongside Bakero controlling play, Spain looked the side more likely to score and ten minutes into the second half they again exploited the Swiss offside trap. Ferrer raced away, Goikoetxea met with his low cross, but from eight yards drove it against a post. Needing to get back into the game, Roy Hodgson's side produced a period of concerted effort in which Zubizarreta produced one of the saves of the tournament to deny Knup a birthday goal.

The second goal was always going to be important and it was Spain who got it in the 74th minute, when Luis Enrique linked elegantly with Sergi to score. Three minutes from time Ferrer made another penetrating run and was pulled down in the area by Pascolo. Substitute Beguiristain wasted little time in scoring the penalty for a 3-0 win that was just a little flattering.

Roy Keane (left) of the Republic and Frank De Boer (Holland) fight for the ball.

The second day of the second round paired Sweden with surprise package Saudi Arabia in the mid-day heat of the Cotton Bowl. Saudi Arabia had taken exception to the fact that many regarded their conditioning to high temperatures as a major factor in their success, but interestingly Sweden had been the only side not to complain about the heat during their first-round games. Tommy Svensson's side had started slowly but looked increasingly impressive in the competition, and were boosted by the return of Dahlin after suspension.

In all three previous games the Saudis had taken an early lead which they defended while looking to hit on the break, and in the first five minutes constant pressure on the Swedish goal had created three good opportunities which went begging. Then the Scandinavians took the lead when Dahlin got free of his marker to head home Kennet Andersson's right-wing cross. The scorer should have doubled the lead midway through the half, but Al Deayea was quick off his mark to save the shot. Ravelli needed to be alert to save a couple of long-range efforts from Owairan, but his goal remain intact at the end of a disappointing half. The second period started in identical fashion – early pressure by the Saudis and a goal by the Swedes six minutes into it. Kennet Andersson battled for a through ball, won it and cut across the face of the area before unleashing a 20-yard shot that beat Al Deayea low to his left. Shortly afterwards a subdued Brolin came to life and nearly produced a marvellous goal for Dahlin, who lifted his shot over from 15 yards. Ravelli needed to be at his best to keep out a variety of shots as Al Jaber became the game's dominant player. Substitute Al Gheshayan was denied twice but with five minutes to go he cut in from the right and rifled the ball high into the net from a tight angle.

That might have produced a nervous final few minutes but Sweden restored their two-goal lead from the restart when Dahlin slipped the ball to Kennet Andersson, who took his time and shot in off the far post to secure a quarter-final berth for a third European side.

Attention then turned to the Rose Bowl for Romania v Argentina. The pre-match talk was inevitably dominated by Maradona but also by what was now being regarded as the best World Cup Finals since 1970. What transpired in Pasadena simply reinforced those views, and produced a match of outstanding quality. Both sides were deprived of top players – Argentina lost Caniggia through injury while Romania were without the suspended Raducioiu – and Dumitrescu stole the limelight in their absence. In a whirlwind opening period he scored twice and set up two gilt-edged chances that were wasted by Popescu. Hagi was at the centre of most things, but Munteanu eventually became the outstanding player on show.

Argentina could consider themselves unlucky, for they too played their part in their post-Maradona history. Prunea had to save at his near post to deny Batistuta early on, but when Romania went forward and were awarded a free-kick on the left, Dumitrescu curled the ball from near the touchline over Islas to put his side ahead against the run of play. Four minutes later Argentina were level when Batistuta was fouled by Prodan and sent Prunea the wrong way with his spot kick.

Romania regained their lead with the next attack when the bubbly Hagi slipped an exquisitely angled pass, perfectly weighted, for Dumitrescu to sidefoot home from eight yards. The thrills didn't subside and Islas produced two blocks from chances that Popescu should have put away. And so it continued, with the heat taking its toll and mistakes making chance after chance. Dumitrescu thought he had completed his hat-trick just before the interval but Caceres got back to clear the ball off the line.

The second half continued as the first had finished, albeit at a slower pace, and Romania made it 3-1 with their first attack of the period. This time Dumitrescu broke forward, after Basualdo had stumbled, before pushing the ball to Hagi, who fired it first time past Islas with his supposedly non-existent right foot. A mistake by Prunea ensured that the capacity crowd were treated to a nail-biting finish when he failed to hold Caceres' 40-yarder and Balbo raced in to whip the loose ball home. The final whistle signalled Romania's first appearance in the quarter-finals of the World Cup, and they celebrated accordingly: four qualifications out of four for European sides.

As the 218th Independence Day dawned in the USA, FIFA announced that they were sending home two referees for failing to reach the required standards in their second-round matches. Kurt Rothlisberger – widely tipped to be in charge of the Final was one – for not giving Belgium a penalty against Germany at a critical stage of the match. FIFA general secretary Sepp Blatter said: 'He admitted he made a mistake. He knows that's it for him.' Italian Pierluigi Pairetto also had been relieved of his duties for failing to meet the required standards in the Romania v Argentina encounter.

A fifth European side was certain to line up in the quarter-finals when Holland and the Republic of Ireland took to the Citrus Bowl in an overcast Orlando. A tight encounter had been anticipated, with pre-match talk of penalties being needed to separate the sides. Certainly it was equally tight in the form guide between the two, with both winning five and drawing two of the 12 encounters. The goals tally also told the same story, with 21 for each.

Coach Charlton recalled Coyne in preference to Aldridge in attack but the impressive Kelly kept his place in the starting line-up, at Irwin's expense. For the Dutch, Rijkaard returned to the midfield for the suspended Wouters and Winter started as a full-back. The Irish began brightly but after the Dutch had weathered the opening few minutes they took charge of the game. Advocaat – who had constantly changed his wide man – preferred Overmars in his starting line-up and the Ajax player was instrumental in the first of the Dutch goals. The normally reliable Phelan made a hash of a header, playing it to Overmars, who raced away before cutting the ball back for the predatory Bergkamp to pop it past Bonner from eight yards.

The Dutch often looked vulnerable at the back, but despite efforts by Staunton and Keane from the edge of the area the Irish had nobody with the guile to take advantage of neat but non-penetrative build-ups. Vulnerable at the back maybe, but quick on the break definitely, as Bergkamp motored on the right and the incoming Rijkaard was only just short of reaching the cross. The Irish success had been built on not giving away soft goals, and even after Phelan's indiscretion it was a surprise when Jonk's 25-yarder was fumbled by Bonner to give the Dutch a two-goal advantage.

The Republic faced an uphill task in the second half, and apart from a close-range header by Houghton that went way over, De Goey had little to trouble him. The introduction of McAteer lifted spirits and added some much-needed pace to the Irish attack, and he created shooting chances that were blazed over by Sheridan and Townsend. In the final ten minutes long passes aimed for substitute Cascarino failed to produce the spark of a goal, and had Dutch substitute Roy taken advantage of two glorious chances the eventual margin would have been greater. Paul McGrath cruelly had a fine goal disallowed in the last seconds, but the Dutch deserved their win.

Independence Day was a fitting date for the USA's arrival at the second stage, and as the nation enjoyed the holiday what more fitting opponents than Brazil? Even though the influential Harkes was suspended the USA produced an excellent rearguard action to keep the Brazilians, who had dropped skipper Rai, at bay and came within a whisker of taking the lead.

Leonardo was shown the red card moments before the interval for blatantly elbowing Ramos in the face. Romario wasted several opportunities, but despite the numerical disadvantage he found the energy to race through the tiring American defence to set up Bebeto with the winning goal 15 minutes from time. Clavijo was sent off late in the game for a second bookable offence and despite the heroics of Lalas, Brazil won by the narrowest of margins to book a quarter-final date with the Dutch. The Americans, though, had ensured that the tradition whereby no host team had ever failed to make the second phase was continued. Playing matches had been the key: this had been their 101st game since Italia '90!

The first match of the final day brought together two sides making headlines for different reasons – Nigeria and Italy. The Nigerians' powerful play had provided copious amounts of excitement while the Italians' poor form, not aided by a host of injuries to key players, had many predicting that an upset was on the cards. Those predictions looked spot on as Nigeria took the lead after 26 minutes when George's corner bounced off Maldini and into the path of Amunike, who lifted the ball over Marchegiani as the keeper rushed off his line. The goal was against the run of play and Italy might have established a two-goal lead by then had Roberto Baggio and Maldini had more luck with Signori's crosses.

Despite applying plenty of pressure there was no real

penetration and after the interval Dino Baggio went on for the disappointing Berti. Yellow cards became increasingly popular with Mexican referee Brizio and 14 minutes after going on as a substitute for Signori, Zola was shown the red card for simply stepping in front of Eguavoen to win the ball. Down to ten men, the Italians became increasing frantic, but Roberto Baggio gave them a lifeline when he side-footed home Mussi's pass in from the right wing in the final moments of the game. It was the European and World Footballer of the Year's first goal of a largely anonymous tournament, but not the last. In the first period of extra time Benarrivo was bundled over by Eguavoen and Baggio was able to convert the resultant penalty off the left-hand post. It was plain sailing for the relieved Italians after that, despite a late Nigerian storm.

The final match of the second round paired two nations not renowned for their World Cup endeavours. Bulgaria faced Mexico looking to become the seventh European side in the quarter-finals and thereby ensuring at least one European side in the Final itself. Despite having three defenders suspended, the Bulgarians took the game by the scruff of the neck and stormed into a seventh-minute lead when Stoichkov produced an explosive run on to Iordanov's weighted through ball and blasted it into the net. Bulgaria were inches away from taking a two-goal lead when Kostadinov fired a 30-yard free-kick on to the base of a post with Campos well beaten.

Bulgarian joy was turned into disbelief when Syrian referee Al Sharif awarded the South Americans a penalty for an innocuous challenge by Kremenliev on Alves. Garcia Aspe scored from the spot and Mexico had been handed a lifeline that brought them back into the game, which was then held up for nearly seven minutes when a goal stanchion was broken. Only in America could a substitute goal frame be produced – and the game got under way again with Mexico in the driving seat.

Al Sharif continued the second half in controversial style. Having handed out a series of yellow cards in the first half, he produced, almost inevitably, a red card for the luckless Kremenliev, who rightly wondered what he had done wrong. The referee continued to influence the game, which understandably died a death, and 12 minutes after the Bulgarian's dismissal Luis Garcia got his marching orders for a second bookable offence.

Rudi Voller scores for Germany against Belgium.

Second Round Matches

2 July Soldier Field, Chicago *Att: 60,246*
GERMANY 3 (Voller 5, 39; Klinsmann 10)
BELGIUM 2 (Grun 7; Albert 90)
Germany: Illgner, Berthold, Helmer, Matthaus (Brehme 45), Kohler, Wagner, Sammer, Hassler, Buchwald, Klinsmann (Kuntz 85), Voller
Belgium: Preud'homme, Emmers, Grun, M. De Wolf, Albert, Smidts (Boffin 63), Staelens, Van Der Elst, Scifo, Nilis, (Czerniatynski 77) Weber
Ref: Rothlisberger (Switzerland)
Yellow Cards: Germany (2) – Helmer, Wagner; Belgium (1) – Albert

2 July JFK Stadium, Washington DC *Att: 53,141*
SPAIN 3 (Hierro 15; Enrique 74; Beguiristain 87 pen)
SWITZERLAND 0
Spain: Zubizarreta, Ferrer, Abelardo, Camarasa, Hierro (Otero 76), Alkorta, Goikoetxea (Beguiristain 61), Nadal, Sergi, Bakero, Luis Enrique
Switzerland: Pascolo, Hottiger, Geiger, Quentin (Studer 58), Herr, Sforza, Ohrel (Subiat 73), Bregy, Bickel, Knup, Chapuisat
Ref: Van Der Ende (Holland)
Yellow Cards: Spain (4) – Goikoetxea, Ferrer, Camarasa, Otero; Switzerland (4) – Hottiger, Studer, Subiat, Pascolo

3 July Cotton Bowl, Dallas *Att: 60,277*
SAUDI ARABIA 1 (Al Gheshayan 86)
SWEDEN 3 (Dahlin 6; K. Andersson 51, 88)
Saudi Arabia: Al Deayea, Zebermawi, Madani, Al Khilawi, Abdel-Jawaad (Al Gheshayan 54), Amin, Al Bishi (Al Mulwallid 62), Owairan, Saleh, Al Jaber, Falatah
Sweden: Ravelli, R. Nilsson, P.Andersson, Bjorklund (Kaamark 54), Ljung, Brolin, Thern (Mild 69), Schwarz, Ingesson, Dahlin, K. Andersson
Ref: Marsiglia (Brazil)
Yellow Cards: Saudi Arabia (1) – Al Mulwallid; Sweden (2) – Ljung, Thern

3 July Rose Bowl, Pasadena *Att: 90,469*
ARGENTINA 2 (Batistuta 16 pen; Balbo 75)
ROMANIA 3 (Dumitrescu 11, 18; Hagi 56)
Argentina: Islas, Senseni (Bello 62), Caceres, Simeone, Ruggeri, Chamot, Redondo, Ortega, Basualdo, Balbo, Batistuta
Romania: Prunea, Belodedici, Petrescu, Mihali, Prodan, Selymes, Munteanu, Popescu, Lupescu, Hagi (Gilca 85), Dumitrescu (Papura 88)
Ref: Pairetto (Italy)
Yellow Cards: Argentina (4) – Ruggeri, Redondo, Chamot, Caceres; Romania (4) – Popescu, Hagi, Selymes, Dumitrescu

4 July Citrus Bowl, Orlando *Att: 61,335*
HOLLAND 2 (Bergkamp 11; Jonk 41)
REP. IRELAND 0
Holland: De Goey, Valckx, R. Koeman, F. de Boer, Winter, Jonk, Witschge (Numan 80), Rijkaard, Overmars, Bergkamp, Van Vossen (Roy 71)
Ireland: Bonner, G. Kelly, Babb, McGrath, Phelan, Houghton, Keane, Sheridan, Townsend, Staunton (McAteer 64), Coyne (Cascarino 75)
Ref: Mikkelsen (Denmark)
Yellow Cards: Holland (1) – R. Koeman

4 July Stanford Stadium, San Francisco *Att: 84,147*
BRAZIL 1 (Bebeto 74)
UNITED STATES 0
Brazil: Taffarel, Jorginho, Aldair, Leonardo, Marcio Santos, Mauro Silva, Dunga, Zinho (Cafu 69), Mazinho, Bebeto, Romario
United States: Meola, Dooley, Balboa, Caligiuri, Clavijo, Lalas, Ramos (Wynalda 46), Sorber, Perez (Wegerle 66), Stewart, Jones
Ref: Quiniou (France)
Yellow Cards: Brazil (2) – Jorginho, Mazinho; USA (4) – Dooley, Caligiuri, Ramos, Clavijo
Red Cards: Brazil – Leonardo (43); USA – Clavijo (85).

5 July Foxboro Stadium, nr Boston *Att: 54,367*
ITALY 2 (R. Baggio 89, 102 pen)
NIGERIA 1 (Amunike 26)
Italy: Marchegiani, Mussi, Costacurta, Maldini, Benarrivo, Berti (D. Baggio 46), Albertini, Donadoni, Signori (Zola 63), Massaro, R. Baggio
Nigeria: Rufai, Eguavoen, Nwanu, Okechukwu, Emenalo, Oliseh, Okocha, Amunike (Adepoju 35), George, Yekini, Amokachi
Ref: Brizio (Mexico)
Yellow Cards: Italy (5) – Massaro, Costacurta, Signori, D. Baggio, Maldini; Nigeria (4) – Emenalo, Adepoju, Oliseh, Nwanu
Red Card: Italy – Zola (76)

5 July Giants Stadium, New Jersey *Att: 71,030*
BULGARIA 1 (Stoichkov 7)
MEXICO 1 (Garcia Aspe 18 pen)
Bulgaria win 3-1 on penalties
Bulgaria: Mikhailov, Kremenliev, Houbchev, Borimirov, Kiryakov, Lechkov, Sirakov (Guentchev 103), Iordanov, Balakov, Kostadinov (Mihtarski 118), Stoichkov
Mexico: Campos, Suarez, Perales, Ambriz, Ramirez, Rodriguez, Bernal, Galindo, Garcia Aspe, Luis Garcia, Alves
Ref: Al Sharif (Syria)
Yellow Cards: Bulgaria (4) – Kremenliev, Sirakov, Iordanov, Kiryakov; Mexico (4) – Suarez, Luis Garcia, Ramirez, Garcia Aspe
Red Cards: Bulgaria – Kremenliev (49); Mexico – Luis Garcia (57)

What remained of the second half came and went with little real action, as did both periods of extra time, to produce the first penalty shoot-out of USA94. Amazingly Mexico missed their first three kicks, and after Balakov had missed his, Guentchev, the Ipswich Town player, and Borimov scored theirs to establish a 2-0 advantage after three kicks each. Suarez made it 2-1, but Lechkov won the game for the Bulgarians with one penalty to spare.

Quarter-Finals

From a pan-European perspective the line-up for the quarter-finals of the World Cup was a very healthy sight indeed, with seven of the eight countries coming from Europe. That made a bold statement for the state of play in the continent, especially given the perpetual overtures from the South American, African and Asian nations for more berths in major tournaments at UEFA country expense. While the talk of earlier rounds was predictably based around the romantic promise of Third World nations such as Nigeria, Cameroon and South Korea, plus Saudi Arabia, Europe had provided a couple of dark horses for the final straight in Romania and Bulgaria. Both had produced a consistently high standard of football that relied more on skill than power, but Hagi, Dumitrescu, Lechkov and Stoichkov were players who could explode and exploit a situation to the full. Of all the teams in the World Cup Finals, these were the two who could play football by putting the ball to feet with a plethora of angled passes and interchanges. The question was whether they had also the self belief to go all the way – they certainly had the ability. Now only Brazil, the lone South American representatives, could stop a European triumph.

The first encounter drew together the Latin quarter – Spain and Italy – for their 23rd meeting at international level. For the first time in the tournament, Spanish coach Clemente had a full squad available and as is his wont he produced a number of surprises in his starting line-up, from which he omitted Hierro and Salinas. Otero was preferred in defence, with Luis Enrique as a lone striker. Throughout the campaign Clemente was under constant pressure from the Spanish media about the lack of recognised attacking players in his squad, let alone his team, yet Spain went into the quarter-final stages as joint top scorers with nine goals.

While Spain's schedule had given them a full week to recover from their second-round tie with Switzerland, the Italians had had just three days to pull themselves together and make running repairs after their gruelling physical encounter with the Nigerians, that had included extra time and the handicap of having to play with ten men for an hour. Once again Sacchi shuffled his pack – Pagliuca returned to goal after his two-match suspension, which was hard on Marchegiani, who had looked accomplished, and Conte came in for only his second international appearance in place of the lacklustre Berti. Signori was unceremoniously dropped – the top scorer in Serie A for two seasons, but so far he had not managed one in USA94.

There was added spice to the encounter as both sides contained no fewer than six players from Barcelona and Madrid, who had contested the Champions' Cup Final a few weeks earlier. Indeed the early stages seemed to reflect that fact, with the Milanese players of the Azzurri making the play and generally controlling matters in the middle of the park. Spain were happy to play a waiting, counter-attacking game and the general view was

Iordan Lechkov (centre floor) scores the winning goal for Bulgaria against West Germany.

Holland's Rob Witschge (left) holds off the challenge of Brazil's Mazinho.

that, given their gruelling schedule, they would allow the Italians to wear themselves out and then take advantage of their greater rest period later in the game.

Even so it took nearly a quarter of an hour for the first real attempt on goal. Massaro produced an excellent run on the right before chipping the ball inside the area to Roberto Baggio, who might have done better with his shot, deflected off a defender to safety. But it was namesake Dino who opened the scoring when he unleashed a dipping shot from 25 yards that flew past Zubizarreta. Spain, trailing for the first time in the tournament, looked more urgent in the second half and when the ball was allowed to run across the front of the Italian area, Caminero – their best player on the night – was on hand to curl a shot with his right foot past Pagliuca, with the aid of a deflection off Benarrivo.

Both sides made substitutions. Spain brought on Hierro and Salinas – the powerhouse of their play – while Italy produced Signori and Berti. Spain were certainly in the ascendancy and for ever and a day Salinas will wonder how he failed to score when clean through seven minutes from time. In fairness to him it was probably the unorthodox goalkeeping of Pagliuca at that point which was the deciding factor. And then, just as he had done against Nigeria, up popped Roberto Baggio in the final moments. With most people wondering at the rationale behind Sacchi's changes, the two substitutes combined in decisive fashion. Berti's through ball was touched on by Signori, and Baggio found himself free on goal to take the ball around Zubizarreta and stroke it home from a tight angle, despite an attempted sliding clearance by Abelardo. It was a tight goal in a tight game, but the Italians were starting to play with the luck of World Champions. There was controversy in the final seconds when Tassotti elbowed Luis Enrique in the face to leave him with a bloody and broken nose – but it was missed by the officials, otherwise there might well have been a dramatic penalty and sending off with just seconds to go.

Later that evening attention turned from Foxboro to the Dallas Cotton Bowl for another eagerly awaited clash – this time between Holland and Brazil, where Romario found him up against Barcelona team-mate Ronald Koeman. Holland lined up without change from their second-phase game; the Brazilians brought in Branco for Leonardo, starting a four-match suspension for his indiscretion in the previous round.

The first half failed to produce the spectacle everyone had anticipated. Both sides seemed more content on not conceding goals than using their considerable talents to drive forward and produce them. The Dutch remained the more negative side, withdrawing Jonk into a central midfield role, keeping Van Vossen on the wing to limit the runs of Jorginho, and using a man-to-man marking system to stifle as much as possible. What chances there were generally came from free-kicks, with both Branco and Bergkamp shooting just over early on. The pattern of play took a change for the better in the final minute of the first half. Brazil drew the Dutch forward and Romario used his skills with a superb weaving run around two defenders before allowing Aldair a chance to finish which he squandered. That set the tone for a hugely entertaining second half that had skills, drama and five goals.

In the 51st minute a long pass from Mazinho sent Bebeto away down the left, and his well-timed cross found Romario in a good position to side-foot home, on the half-volley, his fourth goal of the tournament. But controversy raged ten minutes later when Brazil went two goals ahead. Romario was clearly in an offside position when the ball was played, but the linesman, supposedly following FIFA rulings, decided he was not interfering and allowed the play to run forward. Bebeto was also running forward and as the Dutch defence stood to look for the offside decision, he waltzed around De Goey to score and celebrate the birth of his child before the game.

The Oranje launched a breathtaking revival and two minutes later Bergkamp finished clinically at the near post to shock the South Americans, who had visibly relaxed. But that was nothing compared to the shock they had 14 minutes from time, when Winter beat Taffarel to Overmars' left-wing corner and headed home the equaliser. The Dutch were rampant and looked to be well in the driving seat but the game turned on another controversial decision. Branco clearly took a dive when two Dutch defenders went looking for the ball, then hit a magnificent free-kick past the seven-man wall and in off a post. It was a disappointing way for the Dutch to end their campaign, although in truth referee Badilla had an excellent game, as Puhl had done in the encounter earlier in the afternoon.

Day two of the quarter-finals produced another two fascinating ties. First up, the Germans and the Bulgarians. While

Romania's Georghe Hagi (left) and Sweden's Stefan Schwarz.

the rest of the teams in the competition had been based in up-market accommodation, the hard-up Bulgarian Football Union had been forced to opt for less extravagant settings. When several of the players had requested that they be rehoused in more fitting surroundings they were quickly dismissed. Nevertheless morale remained high. The team seemed to revel in their new-found status, and certainly the pressure was clearly on the holders.

The Bulgarian side included the three defenders who had been suspended before their second-round match with Mexico: Ivanov, Yankov and Tzvetanov, but Kremenliev was suspended following his sending off, despite protests from the Bulgarian authorities and the general uproar surrounding the unworthy nature of his red card.

German coach Vogts put Moller in for Sammer, who had not recovered from a leg injury, but the foot injury that was troubling Matthaus had cleared sufficiently to allow him to make his 21st appearance in the World Cup Finals. This matched the record already equalled in the finals by Diego Maradona, and shared by another German, Uwe Seeler, and a Pole, Wladyslaw Zmuda.

Before the game Stoichkov had declared that 'This is the best team in Bulgaria's history'. Few would have doubted him at the end of another sensational 90 minutes of World Cup football. A feverish first half had left nobody doubting that the Bulgarians could create an upset although you felt that they needed to believe it before it could happen. Two moments early on helped fuel those beliefs. First Illgner had to be at his best to save Stoichkov's shot and almost immediately, Stoichkov – for once demonstrating unheard-of unselfishness – pulled the ball back from the right side of the area and Balakov somehow contrived to push it against the base of a post with the goal at his mercy.

The Bulgarians continued to weave angled passes through the heart of the German midfield, but Klinsmann and Moller both served notice that the holders meant business. And they did the business two minutes into the second half. Lechkov – the best player on the field – found himself going for the ball with Klinsmann, and made sufficient contact for referee Torres to award a debatable penalty after the German had produced a combined Triple Toe Loop with Double Lutz. Skipper Matthaus stepped up and converted, seemingly without a worry.

Germany, having won nine of their previous ten quarter-final ties, nearly ensured maintenance of that high percentage rate when Voller scored after Moller's 25-yarder had cannoned off an upright. Had Moller's shot gone in then it's likely the score would have stood, but Voller had been in an offside position when Moller had taken his shot, and with such things matches and World Cups are won and lost.

Play moved to the other end and a free-kick was awarded on the right. Stoichkov – Bulgaria's richest footballer after four years with Barcelona – took aim and fired a shot up, over and down the wall into Illgner's net as the goalkeeper stood and watched. Stoichkov's celebrations were simple – he preferred to watch the replay on the giant video screen as his team-mates jigged in delight. The belief was now there, and two minutes later an astute dipping cross from the right by Yankov eluded the German defence and found Lechkov diving in front of an astonished Hassler to head the ball high into the net.

From pondering an equaliser the Germans were now facing defeat, with little more than ten minutes remaining. They huffed and puffed but the Bulgarian house held – the shock was complete and a semi-final with the Italians awaited. Once again this World Cup had shown that it was not about powerful teams but skilful players.

Matthaus was particularly disconsolate at the end; having equalled the record number of caps for an outfield player in the game he had been denied the chance to set a World Cup Finals appearance record. A chance that had been denied Maradona as well earlier in the competition.

The final match of the round was for the right to face Brazil in the semi-finals. Romania, like their Eastern bloc neighbours, had been capturing the attention with their skilful approach play, notably by Hagi. They faced Sweden largely unchanged but with Raducioiu back after suspension. The Swedes had suffered a big loss when skipper Thern had been ruled out through injury. His place went to Mild, his armband to Patrik Andersson.

The game failed dismally to live up to its billing and apart from a fourth-minute header by Dahlin that shook a post, the proceedings were dominated by the Fear Factor – a facet of football that thankfully had been missing from the World Cup up until this point. But a goal eventually came from what was the best-worked free-kick of the World Cup to date. Brolin stood at the side of the wall, Ingesson slipped the ball past it on the outside and Brolin peeled away before hitting a powerful shot past Prunea. With just 11 minutes of play remaining the match looked over, but Raducioiu took advantage of deflections to hit a last-minute equaliser to send the game forward to another 30 minutes. He was on hand five minutes into extra time to score again after a mix-up in defence. Then, when he was halted by Arsenal's new signing, Schwarz, English referee Don had no option but to show him his second yellow card. So Sweden were a man down and, more importantly, still down a goal.

But just as 11-man Romania seemed to be edging 10-man Sweden out of the competition there was another twist. With just four minutes of play left, Roland Nilsson crossed from the right and Kennet Andersson used his full six-foot frame to head the ball past Prunea, who never got anywhere near the cross. He held his head in his hands, his team-mates held their hands to their heads, and the Swedes had been handed a lifeline.

Now both sets of players were happy to play out the final seconds and settle for the second penalty shoot-out of the tournament. Sweden went first and missed when Mild blazed over the bar and the next six penalties were converted until Ravelli saved from Petrescu. Nilsson scored for Sweden. Dumitrescu scored for Romania. Substitute Larsson put the Swedes 5-4 in

Quarter Final Matches

9 July Foxboro Stadium, nr Boston *Att: 53,644*
ITALY 2 (D. Baggio 26, R. Baggio 87)
SPAIN 1 (Caminero 59)
Italy: Pagliuca, Tassotti, Costacurta, Maldini, Benarrivo, Conte (Berti 66), Albertini (Signori 46), D. Baggio, Donadoni, R.Baggio, Massaro
Spain: Zubizarreta, Ferrer, Fernandez, Otero, Alkorta, Nadal, Sergi (Salinas 61), Caminero, Luis Enrique, Goikoetxea, Bakero (Hierro 65)
Ref: Puhl (Hungary)
Yellow Cards: Spain (2) – Fernandez, Caminero

9 July Cotton Bowl, Dallas *Att: 63,998*
BRAZIL 3 (Romario 52, Bebeto 62, Branco 84)
HOLLAND 2 (Bergkamp 64, Winter 76)
Brazil: Taffarel, Jorginho, Aldair, Marcio Santos, Branco (Cafu 90), Mauro Silva, Dunga, Zinho, Mazinho (Rai 80), Bebeto, Romario
Holland: De Goey, Valckx, Rijkaard (R. De Boer 65), R. Koeman, Winter, Wouters, Jonk, Witschge, Overmars, Bergkamp, Van Vossen (Roy 54)
Ref: Badilla (Costa Rica)
Yellow Cards: Brazil (1) – Dunga; Holland (2) – Winter, Wouters

10 July Giants Stadium, New Jersey *Att: 71,416*
BULGARIA 2 (Stoichkov 76, Lechkov 78)
GERMANY 1 (Matthaus 48 pen)
Bulgaria: Mikhailov, Kiryakov, Houbchev, Ivanov, Tzvetanov, Iankov, Lechkov, Balakov, Kostadinov (Guentchev 90), Sirakov, Stoichkov (Iordanov 85)
Germany: Illgner, Matthaus, Kohler, Helmer, Berthold, Hassler (Brehme 83), Moller, Buchwald, Wagner (Strunz 59), Voller, Klinsmann
Ref: Torres (Colombia)
Yellow Cards: Bulgaria (3) – Ivanov, Stoichkov, Mikhailov; Germany (5) – Helmer, Wagner, Hassler, Klinsmann, Voller

10 July Stanford Stadium, San Francisco *Att: 81,715*
ROMANIA 2 (Raducioiu 88, 100)
SWEDEN 2 (Brolin 78, K. Andersson 114)
Sweden win 5-4 on penalties
Romania: Prunea, Petrescu, Prodan, Belodedici, Popescu, Selymes, Munteanu (Panduru 84), Hagi, Dumitrescu, Lupescu, Raducioiu
Sweden: Ravelli, R. Nilsson, P. Andersson, Bjorklund (Kaamark 83), Ljung, Schwarz, Ingesson, Dahlin (Larson 106), Brolin, Mild, K. Andersson
Ref: Don (England)
Yellow Cards: Romania (3) – Popescu, Prodan, Panduru; Sweden (2) – Ingesson, Schwarz
Red Card: Schwarz (101)

front, and finally Belodedici's kick was saved by the diving Ravelli. It was a fabulous way for the eccentric keeper to mark his 115th cap, equalling the Swedish record, but for the Romanians it was the second World Cup Finals in succession they had been knocked out on penalty kicks.

Semi-Finals

Once the line-up for the semi-finals had been decided the talk was largely of the achievement of the Bulgarians in reaching a position where they were just 90 minutes or so from a World Cup final. Not since 1962 had an Eastern European country reached the final, when Czechoslovakia lost 2-1 to Brazil. Many neutrals sided with Bulgaria, but it was hard to ignore the growing challenge of the Italians, and comparisons with their 1982 World Cup win in Spain were starting to take place. Then, Italy had started abysmally and only qualified for the second phase by the skin of their teeth. They had the luck, they had the determination and they had Paolo Rossi. The 1994 side had Roberto Baggio – playing like a lost boy for most of the games but being around at the vital moment to steal a goal or make a magic pass, and generally dig the Azzurri out of whatever hole they found themselves in.

Sacchi was close to being public enemy number one at home, but still the Italians moved on in the face of anything that could be thrown against them: dismissals, injuries, suspensions. Before the game with Bulgaria they were denied the services of Tassotti after FIFA had used video evidence to sort out the controversy that raged in the final moments of the quarter-final game. The result was an eight-match ban for Tassotti, who was found guilty of violent conduct when he broke Luis Enrique's nose. The Italians could have little cause for complaint, and it was a shame that they did not follow the lead of Germany and Romania and send their player home for his premeditated GBH. In terms of the semi-final it meant another reshuffle for Sacchi, who recalled Mussi, kept faith in Berti over Conte in midfield, and this time preferred Casiraghi in attack to Signori or Massaro. The Italians had not fielded the same team in consecutive fixtures during this World Cup, and their tally of five goals from six matches was a sorry statistic.

Not surprisingly the Bulgarian side remained unchanged from their quarter-final victory, but like the Italians they had a number of players facing a possible final suspension. In all 11 players had received one caution in this phase of the tournament, six Bulgarians, five Italians, and given that referees had been dishing out yellow and red plastic like confetti at a Chinese street party it seemed inevitable that heartbreak was around the corner for one or two players.

Robert Baggio was one of those who was not haunted by a booking and the so-called world's greatest player finally produced a ten-minute spell of magic to give some credence to that claim and put the Italians in command. In the 21st minute he received a throw-in on the left and in one movement lost his marker and, as the Bulgarian defence did an impersonation of the Red Sea, found more space than Moses to curl a shot from the edge of the area past Mikhailov. Five minutes later he ran from deep to beat the attempted offside trap as Albertini hit a through ball, and made it 2-0, firing across the face of goal and just inside the far post. Italy's goals tally had risen to seven, of which this particular Baggio had scored five.

Finally, Italy were flowing with an ease that their fans had not previously seen in the tournament, aided and abetted by a Bulgarian defence that was lamentable in its marking. Other than the efforts of Ivanov – an Addams Family lookalike and one of the best players on show – the match might have turned into a farce of goalcosmic proportions. Albertini hit a post and was denied almost instantly again when Mikhailov got his fingernails to a delicate lob. Casiraghi nearly broke his duck with a sharply taken effort.

With the Bulgarians being overwhelmed, they suddenly halved the deficit. The large gap that had separated defence from attack was finally bridged, and Sirakov produced a skilfully controlled run into the Italian area. A combination of Costacurta and Pagliuca saw to it that Sirakov was halted illegally, and Stoichkov stroked the penalty kick just slightly off-centre as Pagliuca dived away from it. The game suddenly became The Game as the Italians' second-half pace inevitably dropped and the

Trifon Ivanov (front) of Bulgaria and Pierluigi Casiraghi of Italy

Roberto Baggio scores what proved to be Italy's winning goal against Bulgaria.

Bulgarians found renewed sources of energy and inspiration in Stoichkov.

If Italy's selection problems were not numerous enough already they were given another when Costacurta was cautioned for a foul on Stoichkov. Close to tears like Paul Gascoigne four years previously, Costacurta knew that he would miss the final, having missed the Champions' Cup final through suspension a few weeks earlier. You could not help but feel for a man who was probably Italy's best player in the tournament to date.

What chance Bulgaria had all but withered away when Stoichkov left the field ten minutes from time limping with an injury. In truth Pagliuca had had little to worry him, but there was plenty to worry the Azzurri when, 19 minutes from the end, Roberto Baggio limped out of the proceedings holding a hamstring and with the look of a man who knew his World Cup might well be finished – even if his country's wasn't. The earlier departure of the other Baggio through injury meant a worrying few days for Sacchi – and the rest of the 'foot of Europe'.

Attention turned from the East coast to California's West coast where Brazil and Sweden took to the field in changed strips of blue and white. Sweden were the only side who had played and not been beaten by Brazil in these Finals. They had met two weeks earlier in the indoor setting of the Pontiac Silverdome in Detroit, and produced a 1-1 draw. In that game the Swedes surprised everyone by attacking from the off and only a lapse in concentration immediately after the half-time break had allowed the Brazilians back into the game. With that in mind, hopes were high for another exciting game.

This time around, though, Sweden opted for a safety-first approach and with the Brazilians unable to break them down to produce the goal that would open the game up, the result was a dull product. In fairness the Swedish side had been severely weakened. Captain and main play-maker Thern had recovered from injury but clearly was not ready for a return. Given the suspension of their other creator, Schwarz, the Swedes were left with little option but to include Thern and reorganise midfield.

Semi-Final Matches			
13 July	Giants Stadium, New Jersey		Att: 77,094
ITALY	2	(R. Baggio 21, 26)	
BULGARIA	1	(Stoichkov 44 pen)	

Italy: Pagliuca, Benarrivo, Costacurta, Maldini, Mussi, D. Baggio (Conte 56), Albertini, Berti, Donadoni, R. Baggio (Signori 71), Casiraghi
Bulgaria: Mihailov, Ivanov, Tzvetanov, Houbchev, Yankov, Stoichkov (Guentchev 79), Kiryakov, Balakov, Kostadinov (Iordanov 72), Lechkov, Sirakov
Ref: Quiniou (France)
Yellow Cards: Italy (2) – Costacurta, Albertini; Bulgaria (1) – Lechkov

13 July	Rose Bowl, Pasadena		Att: 84,569
BRAZIL	1	(Romario 80)	
SWEDEN	0		

Brazil: Taffarel, Jorginho, Aldair, Marcio Santos, Branco, Mauro Silva, Dunga, Zinho, Mazinho (Rai 46), Bebeto, Romario
Sweden: Ravelli, R.Nilsson, P.Andersson, Bjorklund, Ljung, Mild, Brolin, Thern, Ingesson, Dahlin (Rehn 68), K. Andersson
Ref: Torres Cadena (Colombia)
Yellow Cards: Brazil (1) – Zinho; Sweden (2) – Ljung, Brolin
Red Card: Thern (63)

Romario thought he had achieved the much-needed opening goal towards the end of the first half when he skipped through the defence and raced around Ravelli before pushing the ball towards the empty net. As he was preparing to wheel away in celebration, up popped Patrik Andersson to scoop the ball off of the line. Even then Brazil should have scored but Mazinho, intelligently following up, blasted a shot into the side netting from close range. Ljung picked up a silly booking after that, to deny him a place in the next match.

Ravelli, the Swedish goalkeeper, was making a record 116th appearance for his country and seemed determined to stop everything that was put in his direction, including a fabulous leap to fingertip Dunga's piledriver midway through the second half. Brazilian goalkeeper Taffarel had had only ten saves to make before the semi-final, and he didn't have to increase that count during the course of the game.

Parreira sent on deposed captain Rai for Mazinho in the second half. This added weight to the attack but also denied Romario and Bebeto the space they required to create and take chances. In the 63rd minute Thern produced a nasty foul on Branco and was immediately shown the red card by referee Cadena, a Colombian who had booked no fewer than 18 players in the three matches he had taken before this. The action did nothing for the game and the Swedes now looked to be settling

Kennet Andersson of Sweden couldn't find a way through the Brazilian defence.

for penalties. But they paid when Brazil scored in a most unlikely fashion. Jorginho finally found space on the right and crossed to the far post, where Romario scored. Nothing unusual about that other than the fact that the smallest player on the pitch, at 5'6", leapt in between two six-footers to head past Ravelli.

In the ten minutes or so that remained Sweden tried to push forward, but found it hard to change the pattern of play. Brazil ended the game on the attack, having set up a repeat of the 1970 final with Italy.

Play-off

After their disappointments in losing their respective semi-finals, Sweden and Bulgaria took to the Rose Bowl just three days later. There had been calls from both the Swedish coach and captain that the game should be dispensed with as nonsensical and that medals should be awarded to both teams, along the lines of the European Championships. The general consensus was that this was nothing more than another revenue stream for FIFA. The game did seem to be an irrelevance with the television networks in Europe, but certainly not with the Californian public, and an amazing crowd of 83,716 turned up to see a match that was never really a match.

Aided by some bizarre goalkeeping from Mikhailov – the man with the £25,000 hair transplant – Sweden stormed into a match-winning half-time lead from which the half-hearted Bulgars could never hope to recover. Stoichkov tried as hard as he could to get that elusive seventh goal that probably would make him the tournament's leading scorer, but bad luck and bad finishing denied him the title that he ultimately shared with the long-gone Russian, Salenko. Certainly there cannot have been a player more committed and more desperate to score in a game and few could have deserved it more – but the gods were not kind.

While blame could be apportioned to Mikhailov in some way for all of the goals, it should not take away from an attacking display by Sweden that left them as the top scorers of USA94 and onlookers wondering why they had not taken a similar approach against the Brazilians in their semi-final. Third place was fully deserved and dovetailed nicely with the third place they achieved in the 1992 European Championships.

The opening goal came as early as the eighth minute, when Brolin's header from Ingesson's cross squeezed in at the far post with Mikhailov long gone on a bushman's walk-about. Bulgaria were denied what looked a certain penalty in the 14th minute when Stoichkov was unceremoniously bundled to the ground, but UAE referee Bujsaim would have none of it. If looks could kill Stoichkov would have been guilty of murder. Two minutes later Ravelli produced a stunning save to deny Stoichkov's hooked shot and continue the frustrating trend of his afternoon.

On the half-hour, Brolin was fouled and took an instant free-kick that set Mild away on the right with space to fire past Mikhailov, whose poor positioning made the task much simpler than it should have been. Another cunning pass from Brolin sent Larsson – in for Dahlin – scampering away, leaving Ivanov on his backside and Mikhailov floundering, to roll the ball into an empty net. Two minutes later, with Sweden in total control, Schwarz waltzed his way down the left before firing in a cross that Kennet Andersson met perfectly to glance past the bewildered Mikhailov.

There were still six minutes left until the interval, which Sweden used to push the ball around in the increasingly intense heat. When the two sides emerged for the second half it was no surprise to see a new face in the Bulgarian goal, Nikolov coming on for his Finals debut. The second 45 minutes were much more evenly contested, as the Bulgarians looked to restore some pride. Stoichkov did everything but score and when one of the best opportunities presented itself to him the ball got under his feet and he scooped it at Ravelli with the goal gaping. Stoichkov lay sprawled on the turf with his head in his hands, which just about summed up his afternoon.

Third Place Play-off

16 July — Rose Bowl, Pasadena — Att: 83,716

SWEDEN 4 (Brolin 8, Mild 30, Larsson 37, K. Andersson 39)

BULGARIA 0

Sweden: Ravelli, R. Nilsson, P. Andersson, Bjorklund, Kaamark, Schwarz, Larsson (Limpar 79), Ingesson, Mild, Brolin, K. Andersson

Bulgaria: Mikhailov (Nikolov 46), Ivanov (Kremenliev 42), Tzvetanov, Houbchev, Yankov, Lechkov, Kiryakov, Balakov, Sirakov (Iordanov 46), Kostadinov, Stoichkov

Ref: Bujsaim (UAE)

Yellow Cards: Sweden (1) – K. Andersson; Bulgaria (1) – Yankov

Borislav Mikhailov and Zlatko Yankov of Bulgaria clear the ball away from Henrik Larsson of Sweden.

World Cup Final

The days leading up to the 15th World Cup Final were dominated by speculation regarding the fitness of the Baggios. Both Roberto and Dino were given only 50-50 chances after limping out of the semi-final with Bulgaria. The view of most observers was that they would start, but probably not finish. There was much speculation too about the centre back positions, with suspensions meaning that both Costacurta and Tassotti were not available for selection. Rumours suggested that Baresi would make a sensational return and so it transpired, when the 34-year-old skipper was announced alongside Maldini. Baresi would end the tournament, having started it in the Group games, just 23 days after arthroscopic surgery on his knee. The debate though was not whether the surgery would stand the test – players had returned within 10 days of such procedures – but if he had the match fitness required of such an occasion. What was never in doubt was that he had the experience, and that manifested itself throughout the game. That Sacchi had taken a big gamble there was no doubt, but then every game had been a gamble for him to that point. Both Baggios were announced in the starting 11 and this time Massaro was the preferred partner to Roberto.

For Brazil there were no such problems, and they named the side who had started the semi-final. Again there was no place for Rai, who had started as the Brazilian captain. For Dunga, who was

Paolo Maldini of Italy turns the ball away from Brazil's Romario.

Paying the penalty as Roberto Baggio fires the decisive kick over the bar.

finishing the competition as the Brazilian captain, it was a return to the venue where he had been on the losing side in the Olympic Games Final ten years before. Both countries were set to become the greatest footballing nation on Earth, as a record fourth win was there awaiting both sides, and while the media seemed preoccupied by this being a chance for Brazil to win their first World Cup for 24 years, most had forgotten that it was also a chance for revenge for which Italy had had to wait 24 years.

Hungarian Sandor Puhl had been named as the match referee and was an excellent choice, although the same could not be said of FIFA's selected linesmen, whose inexperience showed throughout the match. Their choice ultimately seemed to be a decision of politics rather than excellence.

All the pre-match hype proved to be overkill, as one of the most exciting World Cup tournaments produced one of the dullest games of the 52-match event. With so much at stake, neither side played with the freedom exhibited in the opening games. Brazil lacked any midfield player capable of providing a killing pass, while the Italians were clearly carrying injuries, although the remarkable Baresi showed no signs of his, or the predicted lack of match fitness, to turn in an accomplished display. Indeed it was the Brazilians who made the first change when Jorginho went off with an injury after 21 minutes, to be replaced by Cafu.

The first chance came after 12 minutes when the diminutive Romario placed a header right at the grateful Pagliuca. Almost immediately Baresi, who made several surging runs during the game, found Massaro, whose first-time shot with the outside of his right foot buried itself into Taffarel's midriff.

The best chance of the first half came in the 25th minute and fell to Brazil. Mussi fouled Zinho on the left and Branco's 30-yard drive was fumbled by Pagliuca, but Mazinho placed the loose ball wide of the left-hand post. Mussi limped off with a muscle injury after 35 minutes and was replaced by Apolloni, who lined up beside Baresi with the excellent Maldini moving to left-back. The reorganisation created teething problems and Apolloni was booked for up-ending Romario shortly afterwards.

In attack Robert Baggio offered little and lacked that turn of pace that had made him so deadly against Bulgaria; as such Massaro was largely left to his own devices and never received the midfield support he required. While Brazil's midfield and attack are often the talking point, their defence was one of the most underestimated of

Final

17 July	*Rose Bowl, Pasadena*	*Att: 94,194*

BRAZIL 0
ITALY 0

Brazil win 3-2 on penalties

Brazil: Taffarel, Jorginho (Cafu 21), Aldair, Marcio Santos, Branco, Mauro Silva, Dunga, Zinho (Cafu 109), Mazinho, Bebeto, Romario
Italy: Pagliuca, Benarrivo, Baresi, Maldini, Mussi (Apolloni 34), D. Baggio (Evani 101), Albertini, Berti, Donadoni, R. Baggio, Massaro
Ref: Sandor Puhl (Hungary)
Yellow Cards: Brazil (2) – Mazinho 4, Cafu 87; Italy (2) – Apolloni 41, Albertini 41

Red Cards

Total: 15 players
Average: 0.29 per game

Group Matches (8)
Vladoiu (Romania v Switzerland), Gorlukovich (Russia v Sweden), Song (Cameroon v Brazil), Etcheverry (Bolivia v Germany), Nadal (Spain v S Korea), Cristaldo (Bolivia v S Korea), Tzvetanov (Bulgaria v Argentina), Pagliuca (Italy v Norway).

Second Round (5)
Leonardo (Brazil v US), Clavijo (US v Brazil), Zola (Italy v Nigeria), L Garcia (Mexico v Bulgaria), Kremenliev (Bulgaria v Mexico).

Quarter-Finals (1)
Schwarz (Sweden v Romania).

Semi-Finals (1)
Thern (Sweden v Brazil).

Bookings: 227
Average: 4.36 per game

this World Cup, and in Marcio Santos and Mauro Silva they had possibly the two most consistent centre-backs.

Italy came more into the match as the second half progressed and only an excellent interception by Aldair denied Massaro an opportunity during a 10-minute spell in which the Italians looked like producing a goal. Brazil weathered the small storm, which hadn't produced any efforts of note, and then continued to look the more dangerous side. With 15 minutes remaining Pagliuca had the sort of luck that left you thinking Italy's name was already on the Cup. Mauro Silva hit a 30-yard drive which arrived at the right height for Pagliuca to stand and collect, but he made a hash of holding the ball and it bobbled out of his grasp, bounced on to a post and back into his arms. Pagliuca patted the post and blew out his cheeks in mock relief.

Extra time arrived, as for the first time in history the Final failed to produce a goal in 90 minutes. It produced none in the extra 30 minutes either although both sides made concerted efforts during the first 15 minutes. Brazil brought on Viola – the player the whole Brazilian media had been baying for since day one – to make a series of mazy dribbles that never had the appropriate termination. Romario and Bebeto both missed opportunities when scoring seemed easier, but it wasn't to be. And so the 1994 World Cup Final was to be decided on penalties. Baresi took the first for Italy and blazed the ball an incredible distance over Taffarel's bar. Marcio Santos had his shot saved by Pagliuca, and so both central defenders had missed and the game remained level. Albertini took three steps and placed his kick high into the left of the net, and then Romario drilled his to the other side of the goal and in off the post – 1-1. Evani, a surprise substitute late in the game, drove his into the middle of the goal, while Branco elected for finesse rather than the power of his free-kicks to put the ball low to the right – 2-2. Donadoni, whose miss had allowed Argentina to reach the final four years earlier, declined to take a penalty, so it was up to Massaro to take the fourth. Taffarel saved and when Dunga scored to the right, Brazil were one penalty away from crowning glory.

Attendances and Venues

Attendances
Total: 3,567,415
Average: 68,604
Highest: 94,194 – Brazil v Italy (Rose Bowl, Pasadena)
Lowest: 44,132 – Nigeria v Bulgaria (Cotton Bowl, Dallas)

By Venue

Venue	Total	Matches	Average
Rose Bowl, Pasadena	715,826	8	89,478
Giants Stadium, New Jersey	517,401	7	73,914
Stanford Stadium, nr San Francisco	489,006	6	81,501
Cotton Bowl, Dallas	414,078	7	59,154
Foxboro Stadium, nr Boston	322,109	6	53,684
Solder Field, Chicago	312,725	5	62,545
Citrus Bowl, Orlando	305,161	5	61,032
JFK Stadium, Washington DC	264,080	5	52,816
Pontiac Silverdome, Detroit	226,302	3	75,434

Roberto Baggio, who had defied the odds to last the full 120 minutes of play, was charged with the responsibility of Italy's fifth spot kick. Needing to score to keep hope alive, he followed Baresi in firing way over. Brazil were the World Champions.

Goals and Goal Scorers

Goals

Total:	141 goals in 52 matches
Average:	2.71 per match
Penalties:	15 – all scored
Top-scoring teams:	Sweden 15, Brazil 11.
Best defence:	Brazil 3, Italy 5.
Most goals conceded:	Cameroon 11, Greece 10.
Fewest goals scored:	Greece 0, Bolivia and Norway 1 each.
Fastest goal:	Batistuta – 2 minutes (Argentina v Greece)
Goalless draws:	3 – South Korea v Bolivia, Rep. of Ireland v Norway, Brazil v Italy (final).
Most goals in a game:	7 – Russia 6 Cameroon 1

Goal Scorers

6 O. Salenko (Russia), H. Stoichkov (Bulgaria).
5 J. Klinsmann (Germany), R. Baggio (Italy), Romario (Brazil), K. Andersson (Sweden).
4 G. Batistuta (Argentina), M. Dahlin (Sweden), F. V. Raducioiu (Romania), T. Brolin (Sweden).
3 Bebeto (Brazil), D. Bergkamp (Holland), J. Caminero (Spain), G. Hagi (Romania), L. Garcia (Mexico).
2 P. Albert (Belgium), Amin Anwar (Saudi Arabia), D. Amokachi (Nigeria), E. Amunike (Nigeria), D. Baggio (Italy), G. Bregy (Switzerland), C. Caniggia (Argentina), I. Dumitrescu (Romania), J. Goikoetxea (Spain), W. Jonk (Holland), Myong-bo (South Korea), A. Valencia (Colombia), R. Voller (Germany), Y. Lechkov (Bulgaria).
1 Aldridge (Rep. of Ireland), Andersson (Sweden), Balbo (Argentina), Beguiristain (Spain), Bernal (Mexico), Omam-Biyik (Cameroon), Borimirov (Bulgaria), Branco (Brazil), Brolin (Sweden), Chaouch (Morocco), Chapuisat (Switzerland), Degryse (Belgium), Embe (Cameroon), Enrique (Spain), Garcia (Mexico), Gaviria (Colombia), George (Nigeria), Grun (Belgium), Guardiola (Spain), Hierro (Spain), Houghton (Rep. of Ireland), Jung-won (South Korea), Knup (Switzerland), Larsen (Sweden), Ljung (Sweden), Lozano (Colombia), Maradona (Argentina), Massaro (Italy), Matthaus (Germany), Mild (Sweden), Milla (Cameroon), Nader (Morocco), Owairan (Saudi Arabia), Petrescu (Romania), Radchenko (Russia), Rai (Brazil), Rekdal (Norway), Riedle (Germany), Roy (Holland), Salinas (Spain), Sanchez (Bolivia), Santos (Brazil), Siasia (Nigeria), Sirakov (Bulgaria), Stewart (US), Sun-hong (South Korea), Sutter (Switzerland), Taument (Holland), Wynalda (US), Yekini (Nigeria), al-Gheshayan (Saudi Arabia), al-Jaber (Saudi Arabia).

Total:	81 players
Most in match:	5 – Oleg Salenko (Russia v Cameroon) – Record
Hat-tricks:	Salenko (Russia v Cameroon) Batistuta (Argentina v Greece)
Own goal:	Escobar (Colombia, for US)

General

Extra time:	Italy v Nigeria, Mexico v Bulgaria, Sweden v Romania, Brazil v Italy.
Record finals games played:	21 – Uwe Seeler, Wladislaw Zmuda, Diego Maradona, Lothar Matthaus.
Youngest player at finals:	Rigobert Song (Cameroon, born 1.7.76).
Oldest player at finals:	Roger Milla (Cameroon, 20.5.52).
Youngest team:	Saudi Arabia (24 years average age).
Oldest team:	Belgium (29 years average age).

European Cups 1993–94

General introduction	114

CHAMPIONS' CUP

Preliminary Round	115
First Round	117
Second Round	123
UEFA Champions' League – Group A	128
UEFA Champions' League – Group B	133
Semi-Finals	141
Final	144

CUP-WINNERS' CUP

Preliminary Round	147
First Round	150
Second Round	154
Quarter-Finals	157
Semi-Finals	160
Final	163

UEFA CUP

First Round	167
Second Round	173
Third Round	177
Quarter-Finals	181
Semi-Finals	184
Final	186

World Club Championship 1993	189
European Super Cup	191

ROTHMANS PUBLICATIONS

General introduction

As the draw for the 1993–94 club competitions approached there had been considerable speculation on the question of whether clubs from the new member associations of UEFA would be allowed to take part in the coming season's events. In the case of the UEFA Cup a decision earlier in the year (18 March 1993 to be precise) had already decided that the 1993–94 competition would remain at 64 clubs by virtue of the fact that clubs who are members of associations that have never been represented in the UEFA Cup in the past would not be able to take part in the competition in the forthcoming season. This decision was also applied to associations that were not represented in the 1992–93 UEFA Cup. Places as always were to be allocated according to the ranking list of national associations and the results of their member clubs in all competitions over the previous five seasons.

With Yugoslavia suspended from international competition by FIFA, the two places it had previously been allocated were assigned to Romania and Czechoslovakia under UEFA rules.

The draw for the three European club competitions for 1993–94 was held on 14 July in Geneva with a record entry of 149 clubs for all three events. Despite several new member associations not being granted entry, the draw still featured a number of newcomers. The Champions' Cup was to be contested by 42 clubs; the Cup-Winners' Cup by 43 and the UEFA Cup by 64.

The Champions' and Cup-Winners' Cups would see the return of Albanian clubs and feature the participation of clubs from Belarus and Croatia. The latter's Cup winners, Hajduk Split, were being accepted at the eleventh hour. In addition there were to be inaugural appearances of clubs from the Czech Republic, Moldavia and Slovakia.

The Champions' Cup would see an entrant from Wales for the first time, with clubs from Estonia, Latvia, Lithuania competing in the Champions' Cup (for the second time) and the Cup-Winners' Cup.

It was decided that the representatives from Armenia and Azerbaijan would not be allowed entry as they could not guarantee the security and ease of passage, given the relatively poor communications in each country, for potential visiting clubs. After providing such guarantees Georgian champions Dynamo Tbilisi were granted entry into the premier competition.

The UEFA Committee also accepted a proposal by the Club Competitions Committee that the two winners of the national cup competitions in Slovakia and the Czech Republic would be allowed to compete in the Cup-Winners' Cup. The associations from these two countries had combined to play in a single league for the 1992–93 season and the outcome of this was used to determine entrants into both the Champions' Cup and the UEFA Cup.

Prior to the draw for the Champions' and Cup-Winners' Cup a ranking list was drawn up to decide the 16 seeded clubs in each competition. These clubs were assigned a seeding status and were kept apart from the unseeded clubs during the draw. This seeding was applied for the first two rounds proper of both competitions.

For the UEFA Cup the arrangements for seeding were slightly more complex because of the greater number of entrants – 64 for the 1993–94 season. The draw was manipulated by creating eight groups of eight clubs and placing two seeded teams (1 to 16) and six other teams (17 to 64) in each group.

A touch of controversy added flavour to the supposedly set draw for the UEFA Cup. An error in the first list of coefficients published by UEFA meant that Bulgaria were allocated an extra UEFA Cup place. The error was spotted and corrected but not until after Bulgaria had announced its two entrants. After an appeal by the Bulgarian Football Association, UEFA decided that they should not be penalised for an error for which they were not responsible. This then meant that the standard 64-club field would be increased to 65 clubs. However, to add spice to an increasingly farcical situation, on the day before the draw UEFA were required to settle a dispute involving the Polish FA, which ultimately barred Legia Warsaw and LKS Lodz. This reduced the number of participants to 63, one fewer than required, which was awarded to Scotland and Heart of Midlothian.

Following press speculation UEFA made a statement concerning the inquiry into the alleged bribery charges involving the European Champions, Marseille. The statement was to the effect that the Club Competitions Committee had taken note of the allegations and if the allegations were proven and Marseille were disqualified then, provided this happened before 30 August, the French Federation would be allowed to name a replacement side.

Seeded Teams 1993–94

Champions' Cup

1	Milan	3.408
2	Marseille *	3.138
3	Barcelona	2.986
4	Manchester United	2.910
5	Werder Bremen	2.848
6	RSC Anderlecht	2.671
7	FC Porto	2.589
8	Spartak Moscow	2.536
9	Rangers	2.504
10	Steaua Bucharest	2.366
11	Feyenoord	2.325
12	Galatasaray	2.227
13	Sparta Prague	2.205
14	Lech Poznan	2.089
15	Austria FK	2.076
16	FC Copenhagen	2.053

* Marseille were eventually replaced by Monaco

Cup-Winners' Cup

1	Parma	3.196
2	Torino	3.060
3	Real Madrid	2.975
4	Benfica	2.771
5	Ajax	2.721
6	Standard Liege	2.599
7	Paris Saint-Germain	2.428
8	Bayer Leverkusen	2.366
9	Torpedo Moscow	2.360
10	FC Tirol Innsbruck	2.138
11	Arsenal	1.994
12	Panathinaikos	1.903
13	Aberdeen	1.895
14	Universitatea Craiova	1.806
15	CSKA Sofia	1.791
16	Besiktas	1.600

UEFA Cup

1	Juventus	3.410
2	Bayern Munich	2.999
3	Atletico Madrid	2.892
4	Internazionale	2.878
5	Borussia Dortmund	2.830
6	Aston Villa	2.744
7	AS Monaco *	2.660
8	Eintracht Frankfurt	2.616
9	Bordeaux	2.607
10	Sporting Lisbon	2.556
11	KV Mechelen	2.538
12	KSV Waregem	2.516
13	Admira Wacker	2.451
14	Vitesse	2.388
15	Royal Antwerp	2.313
16	Valencia	2.292

* AS Monaco transferred into Champions' Cup and replaced by AS Auxerre

Champions' Cup

Preliminary Round

The preliminary round of the Champions' Cup is hardly the place of scandals. It is here that the lesser sides of the competition fight it out for a chance to have a crack at the bigger, money-spinning seeded sides. However, if the simmering Marseille controversy wasn't enough to sour the start of UEFA's premier club event, the once proud Dynamo club of Tbilisi fell foul of fair play when they were found guilty of a bribery attempt in their preliminary round tie with Linfield.

The club from Northern Ireland had flown out to the Georgian capital in a plane chartered jointly with their neighbours from south of the border, Shelbourne, who had an encounter with nearby Karpaty of Lvov in the Cup-Winners' Cup. Linfield, who are more used to playing in front of hundreds rather than thousands, found a hostile reception awaiting them in the Dynamo stadium where 60,000 Georgians had gathered. Goals from Arveladze and Inalishvili looked to have given the home side the tie but a vital away goal scored by 25-year-old Ritchie Johnston gave the Irish side hope in the return.

Two weeks later some 5,000 Irishmen gathered at Windsor Park for the second leg looking to see if Linfield could become the first Irish team for nine seasons to progress in the Champions' Cup. Their dreams looked to be dashed a minute after the restart when Shota Arveladze struck for a vital away goal cancelling the one pouched by Linfield in Georgia. A goal 19 minutes from time by Garry Haylock – in his first season with the club following a move from Shelbourne – gave the home side brief hope but Tbilisi held on for a 3-2 aggregate win.

Linfield were out on aggregate but the referee was to change all that. The Turkish official's report prompted an official UEFA investigation and the Georgian club were found guilty of attempted bribery of the match officials who had been handed $5,000 by a sponsor of the club – Shalva (Badri) Ninua – prior to the game. The latter was subsequently banned for life by UEFA and Tbilisi were expelled from the competition and suspended from European club competitions for a further year. Linfield were immediately reinstated in their place and into the first round draw!

While about 65,000 saw the two encounters between Tbilisi and Linfield only slightly more than 2,000 saw the tie involving HJK Helsinki and Estonia's debutants, Norma Tallinn. Two goals inside a minute meant that the first leg in Finland ended all square and, with less than 10 minutes of the second leg remaining, Norma Tallinn looked to be making an overall winning start to their Champions' Cup exploits thanks to Borisov's away goal. But a disastrous own goal by Belokhovstov nine minutes from time gave HJK a 1-0 win and their ticket into the first round.

While controversy reigned in England and Wales among supporters as to the authenticity of a League of Wales minus Cardiff, Swansea and Wrexham, Cwmbran Town's first venture into Europe as the first Welsh representatives in the Champions' Cup got off to an impressive start at the Cwmbran Stadium. A capacity crowd of 8,000 saw them storm into a 3-0 lead inside the first half hour with two goals from Francis Ford after a fourth-minute penalty by left-back Simon King had given them a great start to their campaign. However, goals from New Yorker John Caulfield and Tony Buckley midway through the second half changed the tone of the tie for the second leg as Cork clawed their way back into a match that had looked lost. Cwmbran travelled to Cork vowing to restore their advantage, which they did when 36-year-old Phillip McNeil gave them a priceless lead after only seven minutes. Pat Morley levelled the scores on the night late in the second half and with just five minutes of the tie remaining Johnny Glynn pounced to level the aggregate scores at 4-4. Despite a late charge by the Welsh champions, Cork held on and progressed to the first round proper, courtesy of the away goals rule.

Cork City had a tough encounter with Cwmbran Town. Cormac Cotter (white shirt) was typical of the Irish players in showing gritty determination to turn the tie around.

Francis Ford the Cwmbran Town striker was a cut above the rest during the preliminary round – scoring two goals in as many minutes against Cork City.

The surprise Swiss champions, FC Aarau, found themselves trailing 2-0 in the first leg of their tie against Omonia of Nicosia. But a goal by Brazilian Edson Ratinho moments after Omonia had taken their 2-0 lead gave the Swiss side ample encouragement for the return leg. Their optimism was founded when an early goal by defender Arne Stiel levelled the aggregate scores. The Swiss champs made sure of their place in the next round when their international Heinz Heldmann scored seven minutes before the interval.

Floriana, guided by returning player-coach Mark Miller, broke new ground when they overcame the Lithuanians Ekranas Pnanevezys 2-0 on aggregate to record their first ever qualification since they started taking part in European competition. In fact it was only the fourth time that a Maltese side had advanced into another round in Europe overall. They did it thanks to a 1-0 win in Pnanevezys, followed by a similar result in Floriana with a goal from John Buttigieg on the hour – his second of the tie.

Norwegian champions Rosenborg all but secured their passage into the first round with a 2-0 away win over Avenir Beggen. The seven-times Norwegian champions got off to a great start with a goal by Bjorn Otto Bragstad after just nine minutes and when Karl-Petter Loken made it 2-0 early in the second half the tie was all but over. Nevertheless nearly 5,000 turned out for the second

Preliminary Round Results

Avenir Beggen	**Rosenborg BK** Bragstad (9), Loken (54)	0-2	789
Rosenborg BK Skammelsrud (70)	**Avenir Beggen**	1-0	4,481
Rosenborg BK win 3-0 on aggregate			
Cwmbran Town King (4 pen), Ford (25, 27)	**Cork City** Caulfield (62), Buckley (75)	3-2	8,000
Cork City Morley (74), Glynn (85)	**Cwmbran Town** McNeil (7)	2-1	4,000
Cork City win 4-4 on away goals rule			
Ekranas Pnanevezys	**Floriana** Buttigieg (42)	0-1	
Floriana Buttigieg (60)	**Ekranas Pnanevezys**	1-0	4,000
Floriana win 2-0 on aggregate			
HJK Helsinki Heinola (15)	**Norma Tallinn** Borisov (16)	1-1	2,000
Norma Tallinn	**HJK Helsinki** Belokhovstov (Own goal 81)	1-0	200
HJK Helsinki win 2-1 on aggregate			
Dynamo Tbilisi Arveladze (6), Inalishvili (56)	**Linfield** Johnston (66)	2-1	60,000
Linfield Haylock (71)	**Dynamo Tbilisi** Arveladze (46)	1-1	5,000
Dynamo Tbilisi win 3-2 on aggregate.			
Tie awarded to Linfield due to bribery attempt.			
Omonia Nicosia Shilikashvili (15, 61)	**FC Aarau** Ratinho (62)	2-1	5,000
FC Aarau Stiel (6), Heldmann (38)	**Omonia Nicosia**	2-0	4,000
FC Aarau win 3-2 on aggregate			
Partizan Tirana	**IA Akranes**	0-0	8,000
IA Akranes Hognason (70), Gudjohnsson (74, 81)	**Partizan Tirana**	3-0	1,200
IA Akranes win 3-0 on aggregate			
Skonto Riga	**Olimpija Ljubljana** Milinovic (16)	0-1	3,000
Olimpija Ljubljana	**Skonto Riga** Proitski (68)	0-1	1,000
1-1 on aggregate after extra time.			
Skonto Riga win 11-10 on penalties			
Tofta B68	**Croatia Zagreb** Cvitanovic (15), Leshak (32), Vlaovic (44), Turkovic (84), Adzic (89)	0-5	1,000
Croatia Zagreb Zivkovic (17), Vlaovic (53, 84, 88, 88, 89)	**Tofta B68**	6-0	8,000
Croatia Zagreb win 11-0 on aggregate			
Zimbru Chisinau Revda (83)	**Beitar Jerusalem** Harazi (10)	1-1	10,000
Beitar Jerusalem R. Harazi (5), Greshnayev (72 pen)	**Zimbru Chisinau**	2-0	5,000
Beitar Jerusalem win 3-1 on aggregate			

Preliminary Round Summary

P	HW	D	AW	HG	AG	TG
20	10	4	6	27	19	46

Ties won on aggregate:	8	
Ties won on away goals	1	
Ties won on penalty kicks	1	
Highest Aggregate game:	11-0	Croatia Zagreb v Tofta B68
Biggest Home win:	6-0	Croatia Zagreb v Tofta B68
Biggest Away win:	0-5	Croatia Zagreb v Tofta B68

leg to see Bent Skammelsrud's 70th minute strike end the Luxembourg champions' stubborn resistance.

In pan-European terms Iceland and Albania are at opposite ends of the spectrum and provided a match of curiosity, if nothing else, when IA Akranes were paired with Partizan Tirana. After a 0-0 draw in the first match in Tirana, IA – who had won their national title just a year after being promoted – experienced stubborn resistance from Partizan back on their own soil. Then, with 20 minutes of the game remaining and extra time looking a distinct possibility, Alexander Hognason struck. Four minutes later Thordur Gudjohnsson made victory certain before adding his second and IA's third nine minutes from time.

The tie between Skonto Riga and Olimpija Ljubljana proved to be the tightest in the round, requiring a prolonged penalty contest after both sides had recorded 1-0 away wins. Milinovic had given Olimpija their first-leg advantage and what looked to be a reasonably comfortable path into the first round. But with the return leg well into the second half and the game goalless, Proitski popped up to give the Latvians a vital advantage that they held through an extra half hour of play. The penalty shoot-out had all the closeness encountered across the two legs and with the drama well into the sudden death phase Skonto eventually pulled through with a 11-10 advantage.

If that was the tightest game of the round then the most one-sided came when the Croatian champions Croatia Zagreb were drawn against B68 from Tofta. The Faeroe Islands' first ever representatives in the competition were outclassed, losing 5-0 in their own back-yard. Croatia looked set to demolish B68 in the second leg, but stiff resistance and a general lack of motivation despite a 17th-minute goal by Zivkovic saw the home side happy to coast through. But the highlight of the two legs was still to come, when Goran Vlaovic's four goals inside four minutes completed his tally of five in the second leg and ensured an emphatic 11-0 aggregate win.

The final tie of the preliminary round pitted the champions of two countries new to European club competition. Beitar Jerusalem travelled to Moldova to meet Zimbru in the first leg and established a lead after just ten minutes of the tie when Israel international Ronan Harazi scored. Zimbru looked to be heading for a defeat, but with only seven minutes of the game remaining Revda popped up to equalise. In the second leg Harazi made his impact in double-quick time, scoring in just five minutes, and Greshnayev's 72nd-minute penalty secured a 3-1 aggregate victory for Beitar.

First Round

Almost as soon as the legal dust had settled on the Tbilisi bribery case, UEFA's premier event was rocked to its very core when Champions' Cup holders Marseille were sensationally expelled from the competition. In an unprecedented move taken on 6 September UEFA's executive committee announced their decision which was, in their words, 'provisional and preventative' and based on criminal investigations by the French authorities that had indicated there had been 'irregularities' in games involving the French champions. In the same announcement, UEFA's General Secretary Gerhard Aigner indicated that the French Football Federation had been given two days to nominate a replacement for Marseille, who had won the trophy for the first time by beating Milan 1-0 the previous May.

In a predictable reaction, the very next day Marseille – in the form of chairman Bernard Tapie – went straight to the courts in Paris and Bern in an attempt to overturn the ban. The latter approved an injunction instructing UEFA to reinstate Marseille in the Champions' Cup, just a day after the French Federation had nominated Marseille's local rivals Monaco as their replacements. Under pressure, in the face of acute embarrassment and with the distinct threat of a World Cup ban over them, the French Federation convinced Tapie and Marseille to drop their legal actions and accept the governing body's decision.

Nominating Marseille's replacements wasn't as straightforward as it first seemed. The logical choice was Paris Saint-Germain who had finished second in the league but it was Monaco, having finished third, who were eventually given the nod. The FFF offered the nomination to Paris Saint-Germain but they viewed that they were not the champions of France and this, along with a lucrative TV deal they had already signed covering their exploits in the Cup-Winners' Cup, motivated them to decline the nomination. Monaco had no such qualms in accepting the invitation and the potential millions that went with it.

In among all these shenanigans were AEK Athens – competing in the Champions' Cup for the second successive season and hoping to go further than the second round they reached the previous year before bowing out to PSV. Having prepared through the close and early season for a crack at the new European Champions they found all their plans and preparations thrown out of the window when their opponents were changed just five days before the first leg in France. A tight encounter, it proved to be a particularly unhappy game for AEK defender Mihalis Vlahos, who put through his own goal in quite amazing fashion nine minutes from time to give Monaco a slender advantage. Monaco substitute Christian Perez crossed the ball apparently aimlessly into the AEK penalty area and as Vlahos, under no great pressure, attempted to chest the ball back to his goalkeeper Atmatzidis he mistimed the action and it sailed into the net. The return leg proved equally tight even though Yuri Djorkaeff gave the French stand-ins an early lead. Encouraged by a 32,500 crowd the home side equalised on the night shortly after through Croatian Zoeran Sliskovic, but they were denied any further chances and Monaco moved into the second round.

Monaco weren't the only third-placed side to be taking to the

Steven Pressley (Rangers) and Daniel Borimirov (Levski Sofia).

field in the Champions' Cup first round. Lech Poznan had finished third in the Polish league the previous season but had been awarded the title after champions Legia Warsaw and runners-up LKS Lodz had been found guilty of match fixing on the very last day of the 1992–93 season. These allegations were upheld after the UEFA deadline for club entries but Europe's governing body confirmed the Polish FA's decision and accepted Lech in Legia's place. As it was, the side from Warsaw – in their fifth Champions' Cup campaign – were drawn to face Israeli opposition making their first appearance. Beitar Jerusalem travelled to Poznan having swept almost unchallenged to their national title in their first year after promotion, but they found themselves a goal down to Moskal inside the first six minutes and were all but out of the game when Podbrozny converted a penalty and Trzeciak added a third on the hour. In the return in the splendid new Malcha stadium Beitar looked for an early goal but it was Lech who obliged in the fourth minute through Wilkashik. Although Ohana equalised shortly afterwards to level the scores on the night, the Polish champions always looked in control and went on to win 4-2 and 7-2 on aggregate.

Scottish champions Rangers were strong favourites to progress through to the Champions' League stage, having been undefeated in the previous season's competition. Either through complacency or simply good old-fashioned giant-killing it was their opponents, Levski Sofia, who made it into the hat for the second round draw on the away goals rule following two highly-charged encounters. Rangers started their tie sporting a 10-game unbeaten run in the competition and looked to be easing themselves through. A goal right on the interval from defender Dave McPherson left the Ibrox crowd of 37,000 celebrating during the half-time break. The goal came when McPherson took advantage of a poor punch by Levski keeper Oleg Morgun following Ian Durrant's corner. Morgun was also largely responsible for Rangers' other two goals of the evening, both scored by Mark Hateley.

First he flapped at a long punt which allowed the ball to drop to McPherson, who set up Hateley after 56 minutes, and then he failed to stop the former England striker's near-post header 10 minutes from time. In between Hateley's double-whammy, however, Daniel Borimirov altered the course of the tie by taking advantage of slack marking to score in the 77th minute. Given the explosive nature of the match Rangers would probably have settled for taking a 3-1 lead to the Georgi Asparuchov Stadium in Sofia. However their task was made even more difficult when Nikolai Todorov reduced the deficit to 3-2 seven minutes from time.

Rangers' manager Walter Smith said after the game that the away goals could prove costly. 'If this game is anything to go by we have every chance of adding to our tally in Bulgaria – but if we defend like we did in this game so have they.' They were to prove prophetic words against a side whose four victories and one draw from their opening five matches had perched them at the top of their own domestic league.

Rangers' approached the second leg with a degree of trepidation and gambled by using McCall, the Scottish international midfield player who had not played for the previous six weeks following a groin operation. But when Nasko Sirakov scored on 36 minutes the tie was level on aggregate with Levski having the advantage of two away goals and the backing of a capacity crowd. The Levski captain's goal came at a time when Rangers had settled into a comfortable pattern of play. The striker – who had missed the first leg because of a leg injury – appeared to have nowhere to go when he received the ball surrounded by defenders and with his back to Maxwell's goal. A dip of the shoulder gave him the space he needed to turn and fire the ball into the Rangers net from about 15 yards.

Rangers had to score and did so a minute before the interval. Stevens took the ball down the right and crossed to Durrant who timed his run through the offside trap to head past Nikolov and put Rangers 4-3 ahead overall. Levski played the second half with more urgency and the Scottish champions needed Maxwell to make a series of good saves to keep them in what looked to be a match-winning position. But with the game already over the 90 minute mark Nikolai Todorov rifled a 30-yard drive past Maxwell to put the Bulgarian champions into the second round and send the 52,500 crowd wild with delight.

Manchester United, back in the Champions' Cup after an absence of 25 years, beat Kispest Honved more emphatically than the 5-3 aggregate score suggests. Their manager Alex Ferguson had promised his side would attack in the first leg in Hungary and his words translated into a high-scoring game and a 3-2 win that might have been more comprehensive had the Red Devils not missed a string of golden opportunities.

United took the lead in the Jozsef Bozsik stadium after just nine minutes. Roy Keane – a record £3.75m signing from Nottingham Forest – reacted quickly after Ryan Giggs' diagonal pass into the area was diverted into his path by sweeper Janos Banfi. His right-foot drive gave Brockhauser no chance. During the next 10 minutes United might have added another three to their count but Giggs shot wide twice with only the keeper to beat, and Sharpe and Ince were also less than convincing in front of goal when presented with glorious chances.

Honved, perhaps encouraged by United's slackness in front of their goal, equalised five minutes before the interval. Paul Parker looked to have Illes' centre under control only to play the ball straight to Joszef Szabados, who volleyed it gleefully past Schmeichel. United's response was even more vigorous and came

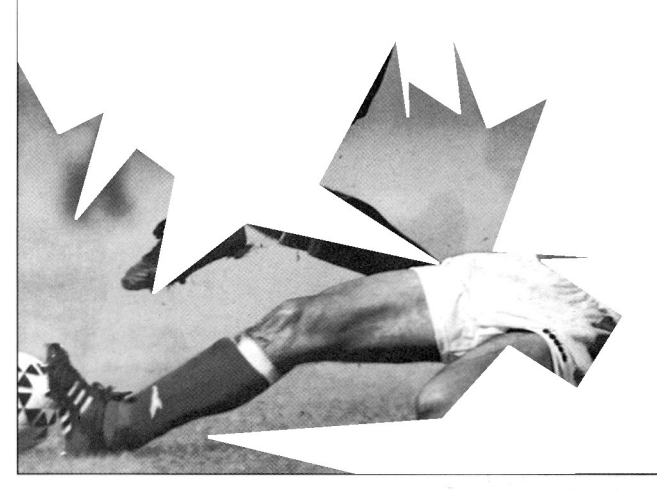

Eric Cantona of Manchester United (left) leaps past a Kispest Honved defender.

within two minutes, when Keane again produced a crisp finish after being set up by Sharpe. With most onlookers awaiting the half time whistle just seconds away Cantona made it 3-1. A typical piece of Giggs trickery took him past Csehi on the left before the Welshman put the ball into the path of the Frenchman.

In the second half United might have made it 4-1 but a cruel bounce of the ball resulted in Cantona ballooning his shot over from the edge of the six-yard box. That miss sparked the Hungarians, who reduced the deficit three minutes later with a sparkling counter attack. Stefanov broke clear down the right and steered the ball past Schmeichel from the corner of the area.

In the return leg at Old Trafford, United spent much of the first half searching for accuracy of pass and a modicum of determination. The Hungarians, needing to win showed little in the way of determination but they weren't helped by having to field seven players suffering with a viral infection. United – often rushing their attempts on goal in the first half absorbed their manager's advice during the interval and took their time in front of goal in the second period. It worked a treat as two set-piece headers from Steve Bruce put the result of the tie beyond any doubt; but for inspired goalkeeping by Brockhauser they would have had more.

Kubilay Turkyilmaz of Galatasaray (front) has the ball under close control as Cork City's Declan Daly looks on.

Bruce's first goal came on 55 minutes when he produced a looping header from Irwin's corner. The United defender claimed his second goal nine minutes later when Sharpe floated a free-kick to the far post and Bruce headed firmly down despite Brockhauser's attentions. With the game won and United clearly taking their foot off the pedal, Salloi claimed a curious consolation goal 12 minutes from time. Having collided with Schmeichel as they both went for a through-ball from Csabi, Salloi recovered the quicker of the two and it was a simple task for him to push the ball into an unguarded net.

FC Aarau's prize for disposing of Omonia Nicosia in the preliminary round was an encounter with the default number one seeds, Milan. Given the side's erratic form in the Swiss league a handsome two-leg victory looked to be very much on the cards for the Italian champions. Jean-Pierre Papin scored the only goal of the game in Switzerland as Milan completed their 80th Champions' Cup game. A 40,000 crowd was attracted to the Stadio Meazza for the return leg expecting to see a goal glut but they were frustrated as the game finished goalless and Milan went through despite the jeers of their fans at the final whistle.

One of the most intriguing ties of the round pitted the not inconsiderable talents of Barcelona and Dynamo Kiev. Barcelona travelled to Kiev with a win and a draw behind them in their opening two league encounters. 60,000 packed into the Republican Stadium for the first leg and they witnessed Ukrainian league leaders Kiev go ahead inside six minutes through Shkapenko. The first half saw another two goals, both coming from the penalty spot. A shot by Hristo Stoichkov appeared to be blocked by defender Mizin's chest only for referee Philip Don to rule that a hand had been used. Ronald Koeman levelled the match from the spot on 28 minutes after Mizin had been sent off for his troubles. Despite their man disadvantage Kiev battled every bit of the way and Leonenko restored Kiev's lead with a penalty with almost the last kick of the first half and then increased it 11 minutes into the second half to give Dynamo hope for the return leg.

With the tie so intriguingly balanced a near-capacity crowd turned out for the second leg in the Nou Camp and their vocal encouragement was given ample reward with a thrilling encounter. Michael Laudrup set the scene for Barca when he opened the scoring with a sweeping goal after just eight minutes. Another eight minutes had passed when Jose Maria Bakero scored to level the aggregate scores at three apiece but with the Catalans the beneficiaries of an away goal. The game swung back Kiev's way though as the half-hour mark approached when Rebrov hit a thunderous drive past Zubizarreta. Johan Cruyff's half-time team talk had his side all fired up for the second period and Bakero took only two minutes to level the tie at 4-4. With the game entering its final stages Barca were awarded a free-kick on the edge of the Kiev area and Ronald Koeman delivered it perfectly into the net to give the home side a 5-4 aggregate victory – but only after Zubizarreta's woodwork had come to the rescue.

Linfield looked well on their way into a historic place in the second round after an excellent 3-0 win over FC Copenhagen. Goals through Haylock and McConnell knocked the stuffing out of the Danes before Johnston added what looked to be a tie-winning third on the hour. After only two years in existence the Danish champions could be forgiven for being naive when it comes to European competition, but they set about putting the record straight in the right way as the second leg started, and Moller scored inside the first two minutes. Johansen made it 2-0 before the interval and set the stage for a nail-biting second half. And that's how it turned out. With the game already into the fifth minute of injury time and referee Roman Steindl consulting his watch, Lars Hojer scored a dramatic equaliser direct from a free-kick to send the game into extra time. The game erupted with the Linfield players protesting vehemently to the Austrian referee and the Irish League champions' assistant manager was ordered from the dug-out for his comments on the matter. The goal left the Irish deflated and when Kim Mikkelsen made it 4-0 on the night and 4-3 on aggregate six minutes into extra time there was no coming back.

Another close and delicately balanced tie involved Steaua Bucharest and the high scorers from the preliminary round,

First Round Results

AIK Stockholm Lidman (36)	**Sparta Prague**	1-0	5,854
Sparta Prague Siegl (15, 80)	**AIK Stockholm**	2-0	16,654

Sparta Prague win 2-1 on aggregate

Dynamo Kiev Shkapenko (6), Leonenko (45 pen, 56)	**Barcelona** Koeman (28 pen)	3-1	60,000
Barcelona Laudrup (8), Bakero (16, 47), Koeman (67)	**Dynamo Kiev** Rebrov (28)	4-1	88,600

Barcelona win 5-4 on aggregate

FC Aarau	**Milan** Papin (54)	0-1	12,000
Milan	**FC Aarau**	0-0	40,000

Milan win 1-0 on aggregate

FC Porto Kostadinov (8), Semedo (78)	**Floriana**	2-0	7,000
Floriana	**FC Porto**	0-0	5,000

FC Porto win 2-0 on aggregate

Galatasaray Turkyilmaz (31), Arif (51)	**Cork City** Barry (62)	2-1	17,000
Cork City	**Galatasaray** Turkyilmaz (76)	0-1	6,500

Galatasaray win 3-1 on aggregate

HJK Helsinki	**RSC Anderlecht** Bosman (59), Versavel (74), Boffin (80)	0-3	1,500
RSC Anderlecht Nilis (16, 21, 42)	**HJK Helsinki**	3-0	11,500

RSC Anderlecht win 6-0 on aggregate

Kispest Honved Szabados (40), Stefanov (70)	**Manchester United** Keane (9, 43), Cantona (44)	2-3	9,000
Manchester United Bruce (55, 64)	**Kispest Honved** Salloi (78)	2-1	35,781

Manchester United win 5-3 on aggregate

IA Akranes Thordarson (75)	**Feyenoord**	1-0	6,327
Feyenoord Refos (25), Obiku (65), Blinker (83)	**IA Akranes**	3-0	23,000

Feyenoord win 3-1 on aggregate

Linfield Haylock (38), McConnell (42), Johnston (60)	**FC Copenhagen**	3-0	7,000
FC Copenhagen Moller (2), Johansen (26), Hojer (90), Mikkelsen (96)	**Linfield**	4-0	4,890

FC Copenhagen win 4-3 on aggregate after extra time

Lech Poznan Moskal (6), Podbrozny (32 pen), Trzeciak (60)	**Beitar Jerusalem**	3-0	7,000
Beitar Jerusalem Ohana (11), Schwartz (72)	**Lech Poznan** Wilkashik (4), Scheczik (33), Brojana (31), Tapinski (70)	2-4	5,000

Lech Poznan win 7-2 on aggregate

AS Monaco Vlahos (Own goal 81)	**AEK Athens**	1-0	10,000
AEK Athens Sliskovic (12)	**AS Monaco** Djorkaeff (5)	1-1	32,500

AS Monaco win 2-1 on aggregate

Rangers McPherson (45), Hateley (56, 79)	**Levski Sofia** Borimirov (77), Todorov (83)	3-2	37,013
Levski Sofia Sirakov (36), Todorov (90)	**Rangers** Durrant (44)	2-1	52,500

Levski Sofia win on away goals. 4-4 on aggregate

Rosenborg BK Tangen (29 pen), Leonhardsen (35), Loeken (42)	**FK Austria** Zsak (33 pen)	3-1	9,619
FK Austria Nabekovas (12), Schmid (50), Zsak (74), Kogler (81)	**Rosenborg BK** Dahlum (32)	4-1	6,500

FK Austria win 5-4 on aggregate

Skonto Riga	**Spartak Moscow** Pogodin (2, 39), Rodionov (7, 41), Bestchastnykh (67)	0-5	2,900
Spartak Moscow Tsymbalar (4, 40), Pisarev (15), Onopko (87)	**Skonto Riga**	4-0	3,500

Spartak Moscow win 9-0 on aggregate

Steaua Bucharest Panduru (35)	**Croatia Zagreb** Cvitanovic (19), Jelicic (62)	1-2	12,000
Croatia Zagreb Vlaovic (7), Adziz (71)	**Steaua Bucharest** Panduru (14), Vladoiu (49, 61)	2-3	10,000

Steaua Bucharest win on away goals rule. 4-4 on aggregate

Werder Bremen Hobsch (26, 32, 60), Rufer (55, 90)	**Dinamo Minsk** Gerassimez (52), Velichko (77)	5-2	10,274
Dinamo Minsk Byelkevich (41)	**Werder Bremen** Rufer (80 pen)	1-1	7,500

Werder Bremen win 6-3 on aggregate

Croatia Zagreb. In Bucharest, Zagreb took the lead after just 19 minutes through Cvitanovic before Panduru's equaliser 10 minutes before half-time. Jelicic restored Zagreb's lead in the second half and the Croatian champions held on to take a goal advantage and two away goals back to their Maksimir Stadium. When Vlaovic scored seven minutes into the second leg the home side looked to be coasting at 3-1 ahead. However, just as he had in the first leg, Panduru equalised and two goals in 12 minutes from Vladoiu at the start of the second half first levelled and then gave Steaua the advantage, leaving Croatia needing two more goals without reply if they weren't going to be knocked out. Adziz scored the first with 19 minutes to go but, try as they

Leading Scorers after Preliminary and First Rounds

6	Vlaovic (Croatia Zagreb)
3	Hobsch (Werder Bremen), Nilis (RSC Anderlecht), Rufer (Werder Bremen)
2	Arveladze (Dynamo Tbilisi), Bakero (Barcelona), Bruce (Manchester United), Ford (Cwmbran Town), Gudjohnsson (IA Akranes), Hateley (Rangers), Harazi (Beitar Jerusalem), Keane (Manchester United), Koeman R. (Barcelona), Leonenko (Dynamo Kiev), Panduru (Steaua Bucharest), Pogoden (Spartak Moscow), Rodionov (Spartak Moscow), Shilikashvili (Omonia Nicosia), Siegl (Sparta Prague), Todorov (Levski Sofia), Tsymbalar (Spartak Moscow), Turkyilmaz (Galatasaray), Vladoiu (Steaua Bucharest), Zsak (FK Austria), Own Goals (Monaco)

First Round Summary

P	HW	D	AW	HG	AG	TG
32	20	4	8	64	35	99

Ties won on aggregate:	14
Ties won on away goals	2
Ties won on penalty kicks	0
Highest Aggregate game:	9
9-0	Spartak Moscow *v* Skonto Riga
5-4	FK Austria *v* Rosenborg BK
6-3	Werder Bremen *v* Dinamo Minsk
Biggest Home win:	
5-2	Werder Bremen *v* Dinamo Minsk
Biggest Away win:	
0-5	Skonto Riga *v* Spartak Moscow

Schmid pounced to make it 2-1. The game turned when Zsak made it 3-1 on the night and 4-4 on aggregate. With extra time looming Kogler swooped to score Vienna's winner just nine minutes from time.

Across the border in Sweden, but somewhat further south in Stockholm, AIK beat Sparta Prague by a single goal scored by Lidman after 36 minutes. Sparta reduced the deficit early in the second leg through Siegl, who also fired home the winner ten minutes from full time.

Dutch champions Feyenoord had the shock of their life when they suffered a humiliating 1-0 defeat in Akranes. IA's goal was scored by Thordarson 15 minutes from full-time. For the second leg in Rotterdam, IA held out for 25 minutes before Refos levelled the aggregate score and in the second half first Obiku and then Blinker put the tie beyond the Icelandic side.

German champions Werder Bremen had a more settled passage through to the second round. A hat-trick by Bernd Hobsch and a brace for Wynton Rufer gave them a three-goal advantage over Belarus champions Dinamo Minsk, who had got the score back to 2-4 at one point with goals from Gerassimez and Velichko. In the return leg Byelkevich opened the scoring late in the first half before Rufer converted a second-half penalty to kill off any thoughts the Minsk club might have had of glory, and give the Germans a 6-3 aggregate win.

Irish champions Cork produced a excellent performance to hold Galatasaray to 2-1 in Istanbul. Turkyilmaz and Arif scored the goals in each half to give the Turkish champions a comfortable lead, but Dave Barry pulled a goal back after 62 minutes to leave Cork a real chance of an upset over the number 12 seeds. In the second leg Cork dominated the play but were unable to turn their possessional superiority into goals. Barry – the hero of the first leg – was responsible for the ball that led to Galatasaray's goal against the run of play, when he tried an over-ambitious pass to Liam Murphy. Turgey intercepted and put Swiss international Turkyilmaz through for the decisive goal.

Former Champions' Cup semi-finalists Spartak Moscow gave Skonto Riga a real mauling, beating them 9-0 on aggregate. Having won 5-0 in Latvia only 3,500 turned up to witness the formality of the second leg. Equally emphatic, though not as high-scoring was RSC Anderlecht's 6-0 aggregate win over Finnish champions HJK of Helsinki. Highlight of the tie was Nilis' hat-trick in the second leg.

Having been involved in a disappointing goalless home draw with bottom of the table Famalicao, Porto's coach Tomislav Ivic would have been grateful for a relatively easy start in the Champions' Cup. As it was it needed goals at the start and end of their match with Floriana to give Porto a 2-0 lead to take to Malta, where they successfully defended to finish with the same aggregate score.

might, Croatia couldn't break through the Steaua defence and the side from Bucharest went through on the away goals rule.

Two penalties in the space of four minutes around the half-hour mark set the scene for an interesting match when FK Austria travelled north to the Arctic Circle to face Rosenborg in Trondheim. Tangen gave the Norwegian champions the lead with his spot kick which was cancelled out when Zsak converted his. However, the Norwegians had restored their lead two minutes later when Leonhardsen scored. Loeken made it 3-1 three minutes before half-time, which is the way it stayed. Around 6,500 turned up for the return leg in Vienna – more than twice the club's average home crowd, but only because the normal admission fee had been cut in half. They were treated to an exciting game after Nabekovas opened the scoring early on to breathe life into FK's attempts to turn the tie in their favour. However, Rosenborg went in at the interval on level terms after Dahlum had equalised. The Austrian champions again came out on the attack for the second half and they were rewarded five minutes into the period when

Second Round

With rewards of almost obscene proportions awaiting the winners in the UEFA Champions' League, the second round of the Champions' Cup offers more pressure than ever before for those who reach it. The line between success and failure, between winning and losing, and the pressure it can bring to bear was never illustrated more than in the pairing of Manchester United and Galatasaray. The Turkish champions showed their good and bad sides in a set of curious encounters in which they squeezed an over-confident and disappointing United out of the money.

The history books showed that honours in the Champions' Cup between sides for England and Turkey were even. Three encounters offered six games played, with two wins, draws and defeats each. England had slightly the better, though, as two of those three ties had seen the English club qualify for the next stage. Interestingly, the side to fail were United's deadliest rivals, Manchester City, who lost to Fenerbahce, 1-2 on aggregate in the first round of the 1968–69 competition.

United entered the first match having dropped just five points from their opening 11 league games, while the Turks sat in third place in their league having just won a nine-goal thriller at home to second-placed Kocaelispor by the skin of their teeth. At Old Trafford Galatasaray produced a sparkling display which combined inventiveness and daring as they played out a thrilling 3-3 encounter in one of the European cup games of the season. The match ended with United desperately seeking an equaliser as the Turkish champions looked to increase their lead even further by tearing United's back four apart with a series of razor-sharp raids. How different the game had looked early on as United, in irresistible form, stormed into a 2-0 lead inside the first 13 minutes.

The home supporters had witnessed the perfect start – a goal after just three minutes of play. Giggs took possession and, despite the attentions of three Gala defenders, cruised down the left flank before crossing deep. Keane and Hughes interchanged and as Cantona tried to return the ball to Hughes the Frenchman's pass took a deflection and Bryan Robson – in a rare appearance – reacted first to the diversion to bury the ball from ten yards before himself being buried under a torrent of team-mates. Ten minutes later United won a corner, Giggs swung it across and Hakan – the visitors' big forward who had come back to defend against the threat of Pallister and Bruce – himself became the threat and diverted the ball past his own keeper.

United were two goals to the good and apparently coasting. That mirage lasted just three minutes when a 25-yarder from Arif left Schmeichel rooted to the spot. The stimulus of a Galatasaray goal, which also brought their not inconsiderable following to life, transformed their play, with Hakan particularly looking the part. As the half-hour mark passed Galatasaray equalised. Tugay played the ball towards Turkyilmaz, and Lee Martin – a stand-in for flu victim Paul Parker – nudged the ball back and past his keeper. Turkyilmaz saved the United defender the embarrassment of an own goal by running on to thump the ball into the empty net before it crossed the line.

Turkyilmaz was to experience the joy of scoring in such

Wynton Rufer was on target for Werder Bremen in their 2-2 draw in Sofia.

simple fashion once again. Gala broke forward again for the umpteenth time and Arif's shot hit a post, with Turkyilmaz on hand to tap in the rebound. The players' celebrations were given added impetus by the appearance of two Kurdish demonstrators in their midst. Peter Schmeichel frog-marched one of them off the field of play which incensed the large TV audience in Turkey and set the foundation for a war of hate against the Manchester club that would boil over in the second leg.

Once the invaders were cleared from the pitch and the match restarted United had to set about undoing the damage. They did so nine minutes from time when Cantona was on hand to sweep in Giggs' long cross and take the applause of the much-relieved Stretford End who had witnessed the goal at close quarters. The match remained at 3-3 and Galatasaray's achievement meant that they joined Real Madrid as the only side to manage even a draw in a European cup tie at Old Trafford.

The second leg in Istanbul two weeks later proved to be as unpleasant and ill-tempered an affair as the first encounter was entertaining and enthralling. A war of words had been fought between the two games which let an unpleasant atmosphere develop. In the city where East meets West you could have forgotten that there was actually a football match about to be played. From the Ataturk airport to the banks of the Bosphorus

Manchester United's Paul Ince is beaten by Galatasaray's Yusuf during their explosive second leg encounter.

the scene was being set for a fanatical encounter which did nothing to enhance the reputation of the competition. The Turks as a people are often underestimated, possibly because of their position at the interface of Europe and Asia, but they are a sophisticated and proud nation. This is tempered by a fanatical love of 'their' game – so much so that the Ali Semi Yen stadium was full and the gates closed many hours before the scheduled kick-off, while an estimated TV audience of 30 million watched in their homes.

Prior to the first leg there was an air of over-optimism in those reporting the game in the British press. It went almost unnoticed that this was Galatasaray's 23rd season of European competition – seven more than United – and the Turks could point to a Champions' Cup semi-final place as recent as 1988–89, when they were beaten by Steaua Bucharest, and a quarter-final berth in the Cup-Winners' Cup in 1991–92, where they fell to the eventual winners, Werder Bremen.

United went into the game knowing that, barring an unlikely 4-4 or higher draw, they had to win the game, but had a morale booster having won 3-2 in a highly-charged local derby against Manchester City with a goal three minutes from time. Having to juggle his foreign stars, manager Alex Ferguson surprisingly left out Welsh striker Mark Hughes – so often their most effective player if not goalscorer – and went for an attack with greater pace, playing Eric Cantona in the middle and flanking him with Giggs and Sharpe. It was a formation that looked like it might work, especially in the first half an hour. In the first few minutes of the game Sharpe was put through one-on-one with the Galatasaray goalkeeper when Robson slid the ball through to him. The offside decision that stopped his advance was dealing in inches.

The Turks for their part began cautiously, electing for a safety-first approach. They packed their midfield and took advantage of the away goals already in the bank. However, as if a switch had been flicked off, United's resolve in the intimidating atmosphere seemed to diminish and suddenly the home side had three glorious opportunities inside the space of two minutes. Hakan's low angled shot went through Mike Phelan's legs only to be parried by Peter Schmeichel flinging himself to his left. But the block the United keeper made was even better as Hakan followed in for what most expected to be the kill. Then Turkyilmaz flicked the ball wide after beating Schmeichel to Tugay's chip over the top.

United, for all their need to score a goal, had only one attempt of note in the first half that might have been construed as dangerous, when shortly before the interval Robson put Giggs

Second Round Results

Barcelona Koeman (37 pen, 68), Quique Esterbaranz (89)	**FK Austria**	3-0	87,600
FK Austria Ogris (39)	**Barcelona** Stoichkov (6, 78)	1-2	22,500
Barcelona win 5-1 on aggregate			
FC Copenhagen	**Milan** Papin (1, 71), Simone (5, 14), B. Laudrup (43), Orlando (60)	0-6	34,285
Milan Papin (45)	**FC Copenhagen**	1-0	6,786
Milan win 7-0 on aggregate			
FC Porto Domingos Oliveira (90)	**Feyenoord**	1-0	40,000
Feyenoord	**FC Porto**	0-0	43,000
FC Porto win 1-0 on aggregate			
Lech Poznan Podbrozny (44)	**Spartak Moscow** Pisarev (8, 62), Karpin (10), Onopko (30, 53)	1-5	8,762
Spartak Moscow Karpin (6), Khlestov (81)	**Lech Poznan** Dembilski (28)	2-1	10,000
Spartak Moscow win 7-2 on aggregate			
Levski Sofia Yankov (75), Ginchev (90)	**Werder Bremen** Bode (50), Rufer (52)	2-2	46,500
Werder Bremen Basler (75)	**Levski Sofia**	1-0	28,000
Werder Bremen win 3-2 on aggregate			
Manchester United Robson (3), Own goal (Hakan 13), Cantona (81)	**Galatasaray** Arif (16), Turkyilmaz (31, 63)	3-3	39,396
Galatasaray	**Manchester United**	0-0	35,000
Galatasaray win on away goals rule. 3-3 on aggregate			
AS Monaco Ikpeba (50, 75), Klinsmann (52, 64)	**Steaua Bucharest** Dumitrescu (22 pen)	4-1	11,000
Steaua Bucharest Dumitrescu (84)	**AS Monaco**	1-0	21,000
AS Monaco win 4-2 on aggregate			
Sparta Prague	**RSC Anderlecht** Nilis (74)	0-1	25,621
RSC Anderlecht Bosman (2), Nilis (47, 71) Versavel (89)	**Sparta Prague** Dvirnik (18), Vonasek (60)	4-2	19,000
RSC Anderlecht win 5-2 on aggregate			

the game moved into the final 13 minutes, Hamza seemed to be feigning injury on the touch-line. The Frenchman dashed to the cinder track surrounding the pitch. He eventually wrestled the ball that was being held from him and the game from Galatasaray's physiotherapist but, sensing the arm of reserve goalkeeper Nezihi around his shoulders he felled the keeper with an elbow. Cantona could have had no complaints at that moment if referee Rothlisberger, a French teacher from Switzerland, had sent him off. As it was Rothlisberger's restraint was tested to the full and Cantona duly received his marching orders moments after the final whistle had signalled a 0-0 draw and a Champions' League place for the Turkish club.

When the whistle sounded Cantona punched the ball away and raced over to the referee and shook his hand. Rothlisberger understood Cantona's simultaneous abuse and gesticulations and without hesitation displayed the red card to set the scene on the events that were to continue as the two teams made their way down the tunnel and back into their dressing rooms. Both Cantona and Robson seemed to be the butt of the Turkish police's own revenge, with Robson taking the full force of a riot shield while Cantona was hit on the back.

When the hoo-hah had settled, United were out and Gala were through. Whether the Turks would use the footballing excellence to set the Champions' League alight or resort to brute force to pick up points and hard cash would remain to be seen. One suspected that they had already had their cup final.

The second round produced two other tight but thankfully more civilised ties. In Oporto, FC Porto entertained Feyenoord – the Dutch side travelled West following a traumatic 2-2 derby encounter with Ajax the previous weekend having let a two-goal lead slip against their deadliest rivals. Their cause wasn't helped any when they were reduced to 10 men following the expulsion of Bosz for a second bookable offence.

The home side secured a vital victory thanks to a goal in the dying seconds from Domingos Oliveira. It was heartbreak for the Dutch champions who had seen Jari Litmanen deny them a win in similar fashion just a few days before. That late, late goal proved to be decisive and enough to send Porto into the Champions' League after the two teams played out a goalless draw in Rotterdam, where the Portuguese champions produced a superb defensive display to celebrate their 100th birthday.

Werder Bremen became, surprisingly, the first German club to reach the Champions' League stage by beating Levski Sofia 3-2 on aggregate. Bremen – not having the best of fortunes in the Bundesliga in their attempts to retain their national title – did exceptionally well in the first leg played in Sofia. With no score in the first half Marco Bode gave the Germans the lead five minutes into the second half and the New Zealand international Wynton Rufer doubled it within two minutes of the match restarting. The game looked all up for Levski but they started to see the light at the end of the tunnel when Valeri Yankov pulled one back 15 minutes from time. Having seen a winner at the death in the previous round against Rangers, the home fans were given an equaliser in similar fashion when Gosho Ginchev popped up.

Werder won the second leg 1-0. Mario Basler scored the winner in the 75th minute by which time the visitors were down

through on the left but this centre flew aimlessly across the face of Hayrettin's goal.

The second half proved to be even more of a non-event in footballing terms and deteriorated into a shambles with Gala time-wasting at every opportunity. As the match deteriorated tempers began to fray. Particularly the temper of Cantona, who had a frustrating evening, having been marked so effectively by German Reinhard Stumpf. After several niggling incidents and as to 10 men following the dismissal of Ginchev. After the match Werder coach Otto Rehhagel admitted that his side was a little nervous as so much depended on the outcome. 'But now we're delighted at one of the biggest moments in the club's history,' he said.

On the French Riviera Monaco entertained Steaua Bucharest and were given a nasty shock when the Romanians took the lead, Ilie Dumitrescu converting a first-half penalty. The visitors' cause looked to be further aided when Monaco defender Lilian Thuram was sent off but two goals apiece in the second half from Nigerian Victor Ikpeba and German Jurgen Klinsmann gave the French stand-ins a remarkable 4-1 victory. Steaua's Prodan was also given his marching orders during the game.

It was going to be an uphill struggle in the return for the Romanian side, and despite their 1-0 win the French won on aggregate. The goal came after Klinsmann had missed two simple chances. A headed clearance flew straight into the back of another defender and Dumitrescu's looping shot caught keeper Jean Luc Ettori completely off guard.

RSC Anderlecht set themselves on course for a Champions' League berth with a first leg win in Prague. The goal that beat Sparta was scored by Belgian international Luc Nilis deep into the second half. A goal by John Bosman two minutes into the second leg looked to have killed off any chances Sparta might have had, but they were given hope when Ukrainian Viktor Dvirnik scored after 18 minutes. That's all it proved to be as Nilis added two more in the second half, and although Vonasek squeezed one in between, Bruno Versavel made it safe for the home side who won 4-2 on the night and 5-2 on aggregate.

Lech Poznan's chances of progress into the Champions' League all but disappeared in their home leg where Spartak Moscow were three up inside the first half hour of play. Nikolai Pisarev and Valery Karpin stunned the home crowd with goals inside the first ten minutes. Viktor Onopko added the third as the clock showed 30 minutes. Jerzy Podbrozny pulled a goal back seconds before the interval but Onopko restored the three-goal advantage shortly after the restart before Pisarev added his second of the night. At 5-1 the second leg was a mere formality which Spartak won 2-1.

Having been missed out on the Champions' League in their defence of the Champions' Cup the previous season, Barcelona were in no mood to let the same happen again, although their opponents in the second round this time around were less threatening than CSKA Moscow were a year before; and so it proved. Two goals from Ronald Koeman either side of the interval sent Barcelona on to a comprehensive win over FK Austria. Koeman's first came from the penalty spot after 37 minutes and there was immense relief in the Nou Camp when he fired in his and Barca's second on 68 minutes. The second leg was made even more of a formality when Quique Esterbaranz added a third in the final minute of play. Despite the 0-3 deficit a large crowd turned out in Vienna for the return. If they had come to see the Catalans' foreign stars in action they weren't disappointed, and Hristo Stoichkov opened the scoring shortly after the start. The Bulgarian found the net again 12 minutes from time, after the home supporters hadn't really been given a glimmer of hope all evening despite Andreas Ogris scoring an equaliser shortly before the interval.

If FK Austria's task in the second leg had been an uphill one then FC Copenhagen's was an impossibility against a virtually invincible Milan. Playing in front of a capacity crowd at their Parken Stadium, Copenhagen found themselves trailing a Papin goal inside the first minute. Simone made it 2-0 four minutes later and added a third before the game was a quarter of an hour old. Brian Laudrup, Orlando and Papin again found the score sheet to take a 6-0 advantage back to Milan. Not surprisingly fewer than 7,000 turned out to see the return leg, which Milan won by a single goal.

Leading Scorers – after Preliminary, First and Second Rounds

7	Vlaovic (Croatia Zagreb)
6	Nilis (RSC Anderlecht)
4	Koeman R. (Barcelona), Papin (Milan), Rufer (Werder Bremen)
3	Hobsch (Werder Bremen), Nilis (RSC Anderlecht), Onopko (Spartak Moscow), Pisarev (Spartak Moscow)

Second Round Summary

P	HW	D	AW	HG	AG	TG
16	8	4	4	24	23	47

Ties won on aggregate	7
Ties won on away goals	1
Ties won on penalty kicks	0

Highest aggregate game:
7-2   Spartak Moscow *v* Lech Poznan
Biggest home win:
4-1   Monaco *v* Steaua Bucharest
Biggest away win:
0-6   FC Copenhagen *v* Milan

UEFA Champions' League

Despite being shown live on TV around Europe the Grand Casino in Geneva was packed for the draw for the UEFA Champions' League. With the help of UEFA officials, players from the qualifying teams and Danish personality Line Baun Danielsen, the draw proceeded without drama. The ranking lists drawn up by UEFA on the basis of performances by clubs and their respective national associations led, not surprisingly, to the Italian and Spanish giants from Milan and Barcelona being the two seeded nations – this seeding was the first of two innovations announced by UEFA for its third Champions' League.

The second change was the introduction or re-introduction, depending on your point of view, of the semi-final stages. The top two teams in each group would qualify for single-leg semi-finals, with the winner of Group A playing the runner-up in Group B and the winner of Group B playing the runner-up of Group A. The semi-final games would be staged on the ground of the winner of the group. Apart from the obvious extra increase in revenue streams produced by these two, potentially dramatic, encounters, it would ensure that interest was maintained in the groups until the last round of games was completed and hopefully avoid some of the empty-looking stadia that had been evident on the final round of matches the season before.

Four clubs were making their second appearance in the Champions' League. Barcelona, who won the Champions' Cup at Wembley in 1991–92; RSC Anderlecht who finished third in Group A in the same year; Milan, who of course, lost the 1992–93 final to Marseille, and FC Porto, who had had a disappointing run of results. Out of the four veterans Milan's record in the League itself was by far the best, having won all six of their games to take a maximum 12 points, scoring 11 goals and conceding just one. Barcelona's results were slightly less emphatic, winning four of their six matches in 1991–92, drawing one and losing one (a 1-0 defeat to Sparta in Prague).

In terms of national representation the finalists continued to be dominated by Italy with Sampdoria and Milan (twice) ensuring a representative in each of the three years of competition. Werder Bremen were surprisingly the first Champions' League representatives from the home of the World Champions, Germany, while Galatasaray broke new ground for Turkish sides.

The draw itself went smoothly and placed Barcelona in Group A and Milan in Group B, and was completed with the following line-ups:

Group A	Barcelona	Spain
	Galatasaray	Turkey
	AS Monaco	France
	Spartak Moscow	Russia
Group B	FC Porto	Portugal
	Milan	Italy
	RSC Anderlecht	Belgium
	Werder Bremen	Germany

Try as he might the Barcelona player can't get to the ball as Monaco shield perfectly in the Nou Camp. Barca won 2-0.

FC Porto, who like the two seeded sides could point to winning success in the Champions' Cup, were probably not too thankful in being drawn in the same group as Milan. Apart from the Italian club's record in the competition, the Portuguese champions had been thrown in with the Milanese in the 1992–93 event and lost both encounters by a single goal. Coupled with RSC Anderlecht and Werder Bremen, Group B looked to be finely balanced in terms of who would contest the second qualification place, assuming that Milan would take one of them. Barcelona seemed to be in the weaker of the two groups with Galatasaray, Monaco and Spartak Moscow all making their debuts in the Champions' League, with the French side favourites to complete the semi-final line-ups. Time would tell.

The third UEFA Champions' League also saw an improvement in the financial rewards on offer. The bonus payment of 460,000 Swiss francs (£220,000) per point was maintained, but the fixed payment each club received for qualifying for this stage of the competition was increased from 2m Swiss francs to 2.7m Swiss francs (£1m to £1.3m).

Group A

Galatasaray had sent ripples through Europe with their explosive second leg encounter with Manchester United, and football eyes were centred on Istanbul for the first round of matches in Group A where the visitors were Barcelona. Galatasaray had only lost once in 10 years of European competition in their Ali Sami Yen stadium but they were hoping for more than the relatively dull 0-0 draw that was played out. In view of the importance of the game to both clubs they would have been happy that their domestic fixture list looked to be favourable to them with encounters against the bottom clubs.

Given their table-topping positions, wins and goals would have been perfect preparation. Gala duly obliged with a comfortable 2-0 win, but Barca lost in fortress Nou Camp to Lleida by a single goal which provoked coach Johan Cruyff to fine all his players and threaten to dismantle the squad at the end of the season. With the Catalans looking to restore a smidgen of pride and on an evening where a defeat had to be avoided at all costs as the axe hovered, the goalless encounter was rather predictable and the Spanish side went home more than happy with their first point.

In the other opening group game Monaco entertained Spartak. As fate would have it the 1992–93 Champions' League Group A also included a French and Russian side and curiously they both came within a few tens of miles of their predecessors. There Spartak hoped the similarities stopped, as Marseille had walloped CSKA 6-0 to record the biggest ever Champions' League victory. Nineteen years of European experience with semi-final appearances in both the Champions' Cup and Cup-Winners' Cup suggested that the Russians would provide stiff opposition. History has very little respect for such records, though, and on the night it was Monaco who made the biggest impact in the first group encounters, thumping Spartak by 4-1.

The result came as a big shock to the Moscow side, who had already captured their second successive Russian league title well in advance of their domestic season's end, which was fast approaching as the Siberian winds set in. The 16,000 packed into the compact Louis II stadium had only 17 minutes to wait before German Jurgen Klinsmann gave them the lead, and when Nigerian Victor Ikpeba made it 2-0 four minutes before the break the game looked over for Spartak. However, there was a brief respite for the visitors when Pisarev pulled a goal back within five minutes of the restart. But Monaco's two-goal advantage was restored from the penalty spot when Djorkaeff slotted the ball past Pomazuon after just over an hour of play and Thuram's last-minute goal completed the Russians' defeat.

Monaco's win in the first round of matches assured them of two points and their place at the top of Group A but it was to prove short-lived as they travelled south-west to face favourites Barcelona in the Nou Camp in the second round of matches and the last they would play before a three-month winter break.

> **Rules**
>
> The rules of engagement for the UEFA Champions' League are relatively straight-forward. Each club plays each other club on a home and away basis. Two points are awarded for a win, one for a draw and none for a defeat. In the event of two clubs being level on points the 'mutual result' rule is applied. The position of the two sides is decided by the result(s) between the two clubs. Thus if Club A beat Club B 2-0, and the two clubs later found themselves level on points, Club A would be placed above Club B. If there is no mutual result or the match was a draw then the clubs are separated by goal difference and then goals scored.
>
> This departure from the straight movement to goal difference is maintained to provide some link with the old aggregate score tradition employed in the earlier rounds. It is the rule that is probably least known and has led to a wide range of inaccurate Group tables being printed worldwide in the past few seasons!

UEFA Champions' League – All-Time Records 1991–92 to 1992–93

Psn	Team	Ctry	P	W	D	L	F	A	Pts
1	Milan	Ita	6	6	0	0	11	1	12
2	Barcelona	Spa	6	4	1	1	10	4	9
	Marseille	Fra	6	3	3	0	14	0	9
4	Rangers	Sco	6	2	4	0	7	5	8
	Sampdoria	Ita	6	3	2	1	10	5	8
6	IFK Gothenburg	Swe	6	3	0	3	7	8	6
	Red Star Belgrade	Yug	6	3	0	3	9	10	6
	RSC Anderlecht	Bel	6	2	2	2	8	9	6
	Sparta Prague	Cze	6	2	2	2	7	7	6
10	Benfica	Por	6	1	3	2	8	5	5
	Club Bruges	Bel	6	2	1	3	5	8	5
	FC Porto	Por	6	2	1	3	5	5	5
13	Dinamo Kiev	Ukr	6	2	0	4	3	12	4
	Panathinaikos	Gre	6	0	4	2	1	4	4
15	CSKA Moscow	Rus	6	0	2	4	2	11	2
16	PSV Eindhoven	Hol	6	0	1	5	4	13	1

Despite being doubtful due to injury, Sonor was able to play for the French club who were able to field the same side that faced Spartak. The Spanish giants for their part recalled Amor, Goikoetxea and Stoichkov but it was the striking power of Aitor Beguiristain that was the difference between the two sides. The Spanish international pounced twice inside the first half to allow the Catalans to effectively coast through the second half. Monaco coach Arsene Wenger looked to change things early in the second half, replacing Djorkaeff and Thuram with Amara Simba and Jerome Gnako, but it didn't have the desired result, and Cruyff, the Barcelona coach, even allowed himself the luxury of substituting his two-goal striker.

In Moscow, with the Russian season all but at an end, Spartak and Galatasaray quite literally fought out a goalless draw. In a match of frayed tempers three players were given their marching orders. Defender Ramiz Mamedov received his for a professional foul, while second yellow cards led to obligatory reds for Onopko and Gala's German Reinhard Stumpf. The cards were the only real statistic on a night without goals although Hayrettin could, like Zubizarreta, point to a shut-out in the Champions' League after the two rounds of games.

Barcelona's win over Monaco ensured that they went into the Christmas and New Year break at the head of Group A as the table started to take the shape many pundits had predicted.

The first week of March brought the fine spring weather to the south of Spain, but it was 15 degrees below zero as Barcelona took the field for their first encounter with Spartak in Moscow. However, the gloves and long shorts that many of their players wore to provide warmth to cold muscles were supplemented by a goal after just ll minutes when a quickly taken throw-in by Ivan found Stoichkov running into space on the left and with time to pick his shot past Lithuanian Stauche, now installed in the Spartak goal ahead of Pomazuon. The goal came just after Barca appeals for a penalty had been turned down by the Hungarian referee. Stoichkov was incensed when he had his heels clipped by Ivanov and referee Puhl waved play on, but the Bulgarian played a key role in Barca's second goal midway through the second half. A corner on the right was played short to him and he had plenty of time to pick out Romario with his cross and the Brazilian steered a perfect glancing header into the net for his 24th goal of the season and first in the Champions' League.

Barcelona looked to be in a comfortable position and well on the way to two more points but a mistake by Zubizarreta handed the Muscovites a life-line. There looked to be no real danger when a free-kick on the right was lifted into the area, but the Spanish goalkeeper missed his catch and Rodionov kept his shot low to beat the Barca defenders. He did and with 12 minutes remaining Spartak saw their semi-final hopes come alive again. The goal

Action in Istanbul as Galatasaray and Barcelona gain a point each in a goalless draw.

Group A Results 1993–94

Round One
Wednesday 24 November 1993
Galatasaray 0 **Barcelona** 0
Att: 30,000. *Ref:* Van den Wijngaert (Bel)
Galatasaray: Hayrettinn, Stumpf, Bulent, Yusuf Tepekule, Goetz (Yusuf 29), Tugay, Ugur, Arif (Arif 70), Hamza, Hakan, Suat, Turkyilmaz
Barcelona: Zubizarreta, Ferrer, Guardiola, R. Koeman, Nadal, Bakero, Juan Carlos (Amor 60), Eusebio (Quique Esterbaranz 77), M. Laudrup, Romario, Sergi
Yellow Cards: Turkyilmaz (Galatasaray), Nadal (Barcelona)

AS Monaco 4 **Spartak Moscow** 1
Klinsmann (17), Ikpeba (41), Pisarev (49)
Djorkaeff (62 pen), Thuram (89)
Att: 16,000. *Ref:* Baldas (Ita)
AS Monaco: Ettori, Valery, Petit, Dumas, Sonor, Puel, Thuram, Djorkaeff (Passi 85), Scifo, Ikpeba (Gnako 68), Klinsmann
Spartak Moscow: Pomazuon, Tsymbalar, Nikiforov, Mamedov, Ivanov, Khlestov, Ledyakhov, Onopko, Karpin, Beschastnykh, Pisarev
Yellow Cards: Sonor (AS Monaco), Ledyakhov and Ivanov (Spartak Moscow)

Round Two
Wednesday 8 December 1993
Spartak Moscow 0 **Galatasaray** 0
Att: 40,000. *Ref:* Blankenstein (Hol)
Spartak Moscow: Pomazuon, Khlestov (Ivanov 33), Mamedov, Tsymbalar, Pisarev, Nikiforov, Onopko, Karpin, Piatnitski, Ledyakhov, Beschastnykh (Ananko 58)
Galatasaray: Hayrettin, Stumpf, Bulent, Yusuf Tepekule, Mert (Erdal Keser 85), Tugay, Ugur, Hamza, Hakan, Suat, Arif.
Yellow Cards: Onopko (Spartak Moscow), Stumpf (Galatasaray)
Red Cards: Mamedov and Onopko (Spartak Moscow), Stumpf (Galatasaray)

Barcelona 2 **AS Monaco** 0
Beguiristain (16, 27)
Att: 89,000. *Ref:* Nielsen (Den)
Barcelona: Zubizarreta, Ferrer, Guardiola (Ivan 80), R. Koeman, Sergi, Bakero, Goikoetxea, Stoichkov, M. Laudrup, Amor, Beguiristain (Nadal 62)
AS Monaco: Ettori, Valery, Sonor, Petit, Dumas, Puel, Klinsmann, Djorkaeff (Simba 71), Thuram (Gnako 46), Scifo, Ikpeba
Yellow Cards: Dumas and Ikpeba (AS Monaco)

Round Three
Wednesday 2 March 1994
Spartak Moscow 2 **Barcelona** 2
Rodionov (78), Karpin (87) Stoichkov (11), Romario (67)
Att: 40,000. *Ref:* Puhl (Hun)
Spartak Moscow: Stauche, Khlestov, Nikiforov, Ternavski, Ivanov, Karpin, Tsymbalar, Pisarev (Rodionov 46), Ledyakhov, Piatnitski, Beschastnykh
Barcelona: Zubizarreta, Ferrer, R. Koeman, Nadal, Ivan, Amor, Bakero (Goikoetxea 73), Sergi, Beguiristain (Eusebio 81), Romario, Stoichkov

AS Monaco 3 **Galatasaray** 0
Scifo (36), Djorkaeff (40), Klinsmann (54)
Att: 18,000. *Ref:* Krug (Ger)
AS Monaco: Ettori, Blondeau, Thuram, Grimandfi, Petit (Valery 46), Puel, Viaud (Gnako 67), Djorkaeff, Scifo, Klinsmann, Ikpeba
Galatasaray: Hayrettin, Mert, Gotz, Bulent, Soner (Hamza 59), Yusuf, Tugay, Erdal, Ugur, Hakan, Arif (Okan 85)
Yellow Cards: Blondeau (AS Monaco), Erdal and Bulent (Galatasaray)

Round Four
Wednesday 16 March 1994
Barcelona 5 **Spartak Moscow** 1
Stoichkov (34), Amor (77), Karpin (3)
Koeman (77, 80), Romario (85 pen)
Att: 80,000. *Ref:* Muhmenthaler (Swi)
Barcelona: Zubizarreta, Ferrer, R. Koeman (Beguiristain 85), Nadal, Ivan, Guardiola, Bakero (Goikoetxea 66), Amor, Sergi, Romario, Stoichkov
Spartak Moscow: Stauche, Khlestov, Ivanov, Nikiforov, Ternavski, Onopko, Karpin, Ledyakhov (Rodionov 46), Tsymbalar, Piatnitski, Beschastnykh (Pisare 72)
Yellow Card: Nikiforov (Spartak Moscow)

Galatasaray 0 **AS Monaco** 2
Scifo (54), Gnako (90)
Att: 30,000. *Ref:* Sundell (Swe)
Galatasaray: Hayrettin, Yusuf, Mert, Gotz, Hamza, Ugur, Tugay (Mustafa 68), Bulent, Suat (Okan 80), Hakan, Arif
AS Monaco: Ettori, Valery, Thuram, Dumas, Blondeau, Puel, Viaud, Djorkaeff, Scifo (Grimandfi 79), Klinsmann, Ikpeba (Gnako 72)
Yellow Card: Viaud (AS Monaco)

Round Five
Wednesday 30 March 1994
Barcelona 3 **Galatasaray** 0
Amor (20), R. Koeman (70 pen), Eusebio (72)
Att: 85,000. *Ref:* Mottram (Sco)
Barcelona: Zubizarreta, Ferrer, R. Koeman, Nadal, Ivan, Sergi, Quique Esterbaranz (Goikoetxea 66), Amor, M. Laudrup, Romario, Beguiristain (Eusebio 57)
Galatasaray: Hayrettinn, Mert (Arif 50), Bulent, Goetz, K. Yusuf, Tugay, Ugur, Hamza, Hakan, Suat (Turkyilmaz 80), Erdal
Yellow Cards: Mert and Bulent (Galatasaray)

Spartak Moscow 0 **AS Monoco** 0
Att: 12,000. *Ref:* Ceccarini (Ita)
Spartak Moscow: Stauche, Mamedov, Ternavski (Khlestov 76), Tsymbalar, Rodionov (Pisarev 64), Nikiforov, Onopko, Karpin, Piatnitski, Ledyakhov, Beschastnykh
AS Monaco: Ettori, Blondeau, Petit, Dumas, Viaud, Puel, Thuram, Djorkaeff (Weah 70), Scifo (Perez 85), Klinsmann, Grimandi
Yellow Card: Rodinov (Spartak Moscow)

Round Six
Wednesday 13 April 1994
AS Monaco 0 **Barcelona** 1
Stoichkov (14)
Att: 18,500. *Ref:* Craciunescu (Rom)
AS Monaco: Ettori, Blondeau, Petit, Dumas, Gnako (Ikpeba 46), Puel (C. Perez 76), Thuram, Djorkaeff, Scifo, Klinsmann, Viaud.
Barcelona: Zubizarreta, Ferrer, R. Koeman, Nadal, Sergi, Guardiola, Bakero (Juan Carlos 59), Amor (Eusebio 73), Ivan, Romario, Stoichkov.
Yellow Cards: Thuram and Ikpeba (AS Monaco), Zubizarreta (Barcelona)

Galatasaray 1 **Spartak Moscow** 2
Cihat (86) Onopko (54), Karpin (82)
Att: 5,000. *Ref:* Grabher (Aus)
Galatasaray: Hayrettin, Cihat, K. Yusuf, Goetz, Mert, Tugay, Ugur, Hamza, Hakan, Suat, Turkyilmaz (Erdal 40 (Stumpf 46))
Spartak Moscow: Stauche, Mamedov, Ternavski, Tsymbalar (Ledyakhov 75), Pisarev, Nikiforov, Onopko, Karpin, Piatnitski, Massalitine (Alenichev 80), Beschastnykh
Yellow Cards: Ugur and Suat (Galatasaray)

Final Table	P	W	D	L	F	A	Pts
Barcelona	6	4	2	0	13	3	10
AS Monaco	6	3	1	2	9	4	7
Spartak Moscow	6	1	3	2	6	12	5
Galatasaray	6	0	2	4	1	10	2

Group A – Results

	AS Monaco	Barcelona	Galatasaray	Spartak
AS Monaco	—	0-1	3-0	4-1
Barcelona	2-0	—	3-0	5-1
Galatasaray	0-2	0-0	—	1-2
Spartak	0-0	2-2	0-0	—

inspired Spartak who started to play some neat football, and a well-worked move brought them an equaliser just three minutes from time. Karpin took a pass on his chest as he ran into the area and controlled it perfectly before drilling a shot past Zubizarreta.

Galatasaray started their game in Monte Carlo as the only Group A side to head their own national league but had arrived in the South of France with a variety of selection headaches for their German trainer, Rainer Hollmann. They would be without the suspended Stumpf and Suat while a hernia operation had ruled Turkyilmaz out for the rest of the season. There was also huge doubt over forward Hamza, who had damaged an ankle. He made up the numbers on the bench as Gala struggled to name a team worthy of the Champions' League.

As it was the Turks limited the French in the first half and created a good number of opportunities for themselves but fell behind moments after Laurent Viaud – in his first season with Monaco – had seen a great effort from 25 yards tipped over the bar. But from the ensuing corner Belgian Enzo Scifo headed home totally unchallenged as the Turks seemed more intent in dealing with any potential threat that Klinsmann and his dives might have to offer. The goal was the first conceded by Gala in the Champions' League but it wasn't the last on the night. Five minutes before half-time Monaco's pace going forward proved too much and a long cross in from the right fell perfectly to Djorkaeff, who prodded it home after Hayrettin had failed to gather the ball. Galatasaray's nervousness about the threat of Klinsmann proved founded when he nodded in the third at the far post nine minutes into the second half.

Monaco were well worth their three-goal advantage which would have been even more emphatic had the crossbar not come to the rescue of the Turks on no less than three occasions. The win kept them in second spot in the Group A table level on points with Barcelona but trailing by the mutual result rule – Monaco had lost in Nou Camp.

Barcelona came into the fourth round having won five games in a row but also aware that their normal miserly defence was shipping goals at an alarming rate. Spartak for their part had just started their new domestic season with a couple of wins and took to the field full of confidence. That particular state of mind was enhanced further when they took the lead with a move that went the entire length of the pitch. A loose ball by Ferrer was picked up deep in the Spartak half and when the ball was played to Ledyakhov, still in his own half, he slid a precision pass for

Barcelona's Romario keeps his pinkies warm with gloves as the temperatures drop in Moscow against Dynamo.

Karpin to race on to between defenders Nadal and Şergi. Zubizarreta was over-zealous in his attempts to come out and clear the ball and allowed Karpin the space he needed to steer the ball past him into the net from 25 yards, for his fourth goal of the season in Europe.

Spartak's alternating long–short passing game and quick running off the ball continued to create all sorts of problems for the home side, who were playing in a changed strip of all green. Barcelona slowly came into the game though as Spartak produced a blanket defence and endeavoured to use their pace on the break. Koeman was just over from a free-kick two yards outside the area and Stauche produced two excellent saves at Romario's feet to deny the Brazilian. Zubizarreta also needed to be at his best and required the use of his feet to thwart Karpin.

As the first half nudged towards its conclusion an equaliser for Barca looked more and more likely and it came thanks to a terrific first-time shot by Stoichkov after Sergi's penetrating run down the left had got him in behind the Spartak defence.

In the second period Barca continued to dominate. Johan Cruyff sent on Goikoetxea for Bakero and the change paid dividends with two goals inside a minute just 13 minutes from time. First Romario picked up a loose ball and slipped it around Ternavski before pulling a pass back for Amor to loft his shot into the net from ten yards. From the restart Barcelona regained possession and a foul on Ferrer five yards outside the area gave Ronald Koeman the chance to curl another classic free-kick around Spartak's four-man wall and high into the corner of the net.

At 3-1 Barca were coasting and the Spartak defenders failed to learn their lesson when they gave away another free-kick on the edge of the area a few minutes later. Once again Koeman drew admiring eyes as this time he fired the ball low into the other side of the net to make it 4-1. The Russians were clearly demoralised and it was no surprise when the packed Nou Camp was treated to a fifth via the penalty spot after Romario had been pulled down. The Brazilian took the kick himself to record the highest win in the Champions' League of the season so far.

Monaco's continued progression in the Champions' League was starting to draw comparisons to that of Denmark's European Championship win in 1992. One of the key reasons was Scifo's continued good form and he showed his intentions early on in the match in Istanbul with Galatasaray, when he rattled Hayrettin's bar with a shot from 25 yards. However, the Belgian international found his bearings early in the second half after Klinsmann's diagonal run had presented him with the ball and a chance to curl it inside the far post from the edge of the area.

The Turks had only one real chance of an equaliser, when Hakan's header from a corner came off a defender's shoulder and looped on to the bar. Monaco – whose coach said before the game that he would be delighted with a draw – made sure of the win in the dying seconds when Viaud got away down the right wing and swept the ball across into the path of the in-running Gnako, who couldn't miss the opening in front of him.

The wins for Barcelona and Monaco secured their positions at the head of the Group A table and virtually guaranteed their places in the semi-finals. Both Spartak and Galatasaray knew they would need massive wins in their final two games to stand any chance of catching them. Barca headed the table by virtue of the fact that they had beaten the French 2-0 in their game earlier in the rounds, and left both clubs with everything – in particular the home advantage offered to the semi-finalist topping the Group table – to play for.

As March drew to a conclusion Barcelona maintained the pressure at the top of the table with an emphatic 3-0 win over Galatasaray. Following the dour 0-0 draw in the first round of games Barca had a point to prove, which they duly did. Amor opened the scoring midway through the first half, but Gala – with players returning from suspension and injury – frustrated the home attack well into the second half. Then two goals in as many minutes changed the complexion of the game. A typical Koeman rocket from a free-kick outside the area made it 2-0, and substitute Eusebio added a third goal almost from the restart.

In Moscow only 12,000 turned up for the visit of Monaco as both sides shared a point and allowed the French to book their semi-final spot with the news that Barcelona had taken a point advantage over them at the top of Group A. The result meant that the final round of matches in which Monaco entertained Barcelona would decide who would gain home advantage in the semi-finals. Barcelona remained firm favourites, needing just a point to secure top spot, while Monaco needed to win to leapfrog over their Mediterranean rivals.

Both teams also came into the game laden down with yellow cards, each side sporting no less than eight players with the threat of suspension hanging over them. Barcelona's starting line-up was without the lively Beguiristain, who had scored the two goals that beat Monaco in their first Champions' League encounter.

Monaco had a great chance to take the lead early on when Scifo got clean away from Koeman and crossed from the left to present Klinsmann with a gilt edged chance. The German – a prolific but instinctive striker – had too much time on the ball and having switched it to his stronger foot curled it the wrong side of the post with Koeman, Zubizarreta and Guardiola relieved on-lookers. Monaco continued to look the more expansive side early on and Scifo wasted an opportunity, firing his shot straight into Zubizarreta's arms.

Barcelona were happy to hit on the break and in their first such move they scored what proved to be the decisive goal. A Monaco move on the right broke down and Guardiola took the ball on the rise to hit a perfect 50-yard pass into the home half for Stoichkov, timing his run to perfection, to run on to and fire first time across a stunned Ettori and into the net.

Monaco, now with nothing to lose, continued to go forward and Zubizarreta again came to his side's rescue when he turned Scifo's left-footed volley around the post. The Belgian international, who had teed himself up following an exchange

Cash Bonus

Barcelona and Milan as expected topped their two UEFA Champions' League groups and therefore also picked up large point bonuses to bring their UEFA earnings alone to over £3m. Barcelona's extra two points made them the biggest earners overall, while the four clubs who missed out on the semi-final stages can report payments totalling nearly £9m. The table gives the approximate amounts each club earned from their respective campaigns.

Club	Fixed	Bonus	Total	Gp/Psn
Barcelona	£1,300,000	£2,200,000	£3,500,000	Group A 1st
Milan	£1,300,000	£1,760,000	£3,060,000	Group B 1st
FC Porto	£1,300,000	£1,540,000	£2,840,000	Group B 2nd
AS Monaco	£1,300,000	£1,540,000	£2,840,000	Group A 2nd
Werder Bremen	£1,300,000	£1,100,000	£2,400,000	Group B 3rd
Spartak Moscow	£1,300,000	£1,100,000	£2,400,000	Group A 3rd
RSC Anderlecht	£1,300,000	£880,000	£2,180,000	Group B 4th
Galatasaray	£1,300,000	£440,000	£1,740,000	Group A 4th

Marco Bode (No. 9) of Werder Bremen produces a flying header that troubles the Milan defence in Bremen.

with Klinsmann, was desperately unlucky.

In the second half Barcelona – displaying a strange lack of interest in matters – continued to live dangerously at the back, but with Stoichkov the perfect outlet for long balls from defence they always looked like they might add to their tally. Djorkaeff proved to be the most dangerous of the Monaco forwards in the second half and only the excellence of the Spanish international goalkeeper kept him at bay.

Barcelona's win ensured them home advantage in the semi-finals and achieved without a booking – and perhaps a reason for their seeming uninterest. Not the same for Monaco, for whom Lilian Thuram and Victor Ikpeba succumbed with second yellow cards that would keep them out of their semi-final.

The final game of the group had little meaning other than the money involved for gaining points. However, there was another significant landmark for the Turkish champions. Cihat's goal for Gala just four minutes from time not only marked their first (and last for that matter) in the Champions' League for the season but also their 100th goal in all European competitions. The goal came after 653 minutes without one – Turkyilmaz's goal at Old Trafford in the 3-3 draw with Manchester United being the last they had scored until Cihat's strike. Spartak secured the two points with second-half goals from Onopko and Karpin, to finish in third place, two points behind Monaco.

Group B

With two qualification spots up for grabs RSC Anderlecht went into their first encounter with Group B favourites Milan having a single aim. Not to lose, and then to tag on to the Milanese shirt-tails so to speak by picking up points from the two other Group B

Milan substitute Simone fires a shot at Werder Bremen keeper Reck.

sides, in what was regarded as the more open of the two Champions' League groups. Like Milan the Belgian champions could call on the experience of a previous campaign. But whereas Milan had a 100 per cent record in their run to the 1992–93 final, Anderlecht had at least a consistent return, having won, drawn and lost two each of their six-game campaign in the inaugural Champions' League season. But this was a more resilient Anderlecht side who headed their national league by four points and had the encouragement of a 3-1 win at Ostend the previous weekend.

Milan had travelled to the snow-covered Constant Vanden Stock stadium following a tough goalless encounter with Parma with whom they also shared a three-way tie at the head of Serie A. With the wintry conditions setting in further as the night wore on both sides found it nigh-on impossible to develop any fluency in their play. Milan had more of the chances, even though the home side dominated the game and went closest to scoring when Johan Walem's shot thundered off Rossi's upright midway through the second half. The final whistle was greeted with a mixed reception by the home supporters. Anderlecht had achieved their initial aim and in doing so became the first club ever to take a point off Milan in the Champions' League.

The Portuguese champions, FC Porto, got their second consecutive Champions' League season off to the right start although their German opponents gave them a nasty fright in the final few minutes of an exciting finish. It was difficult to know what to expect from Werder, the World Cup-holders' first qualifiers at this stage. That in itself might have led to high expectations but an indifferent start to their defence of the Bundesliga title had cast doubts over their abilities to progress further.

Two first half goals by Domingos Oliveira and Rui Jorge put

Porto into a comfortable half-time lead and when Jose Carlos struck eight minutes from time to increase the margin to 3-0, the home side looked the comfortable recipients of their first two points. But two goals in as many minutes shortly afterwards, by Bernd Hobsch and Wynton Rufer, reduced the deficit to a single goal and painted a very different picture for the final five minutes. With the home supporters baying for referee Elleray to blow his final whistle, Porto held on as the visitors did their best in vain to complete a remarkable fight-back. Porto's win gave them pole position in the first Group A table with Milan and Anderlecht in joint second position.

Porto's next stop was Milan for the second round of matches. The game was played a week earlier than scheduled after the Portuguese had sportingly agreed to the new 1 December date, to allow Milan to make full preparations for their up and coming Toyota Cup World Club Championship match with Sao Paulo of Brazil in Tokyo.

Porto had lost the previous season's Champions' League encounter in the San Siro by a single goal and arrived looking to consolidate their position at the top of Group A. Milan had other ideas and produced a typically taunting display, tight at the back and elastic on the break, to win 3-0. Raducioiu – not included in the opening encounter with Anderlecht – opened the scoring after 16 minutes and full-back Panucci popped up to fire home shortly before the break. The revitalised Massaro sealed the win, not that it was ever in any doubt at that point, with a goal just after the hour.

The two points ensured Milan ownership of top spot in the Group table during the three-month winter recess unless Anderlecht could match or better their 3-0 win in Bremen the following week. Thirty-three minutes into that particular game they looked as though that was exactly what they were indeed going to do. Belgian international Philippe Albert opened the scoring for the visitors after 16 minutes and Danny Boffin made it 0-2 just two minutes later. Any disbelief the Werder supporters in the 32,000 crowd had was cemented solid when Boffin added a third after just over half an hour.

A remarkable result looked to be truly on the cards. And a remarkable result is exactly what the game produced but in the favour of Werder Bremen! Having nearly recovered a 0-3 deficit in Oporto two weeks earlier, the German side proceeded not just to recapture the game but to win it in what was one of the most remarkable come-backs of the season.

The impossible dream still looked some distance off when Rufer scored for the second successive Champions' League match just as the game moved into the second hour of play. It looked nothing more than a consolation goal, but when Bratseth made it 2-3 in the 72nd minute the crowd were lifted and there was real belief that a draw was within their grasp. But time looked to be against Werder as the game entered its final nine minutes. Then Hobsch netted to produce a roar that would have been heard in Portugal itself. All-tied at 3-3 the home supporters were still in full celebratory flight as Bode put Werder into the lead within 60 seconds of the restart. Then in the final minute, Rufer added his second of the night to complete the scoring and turn a 0-3 deficit into a 5-3 win of remarkable proportions.

Bernd Hobsch of Werder Bremen hands off the attentions of FC Porto's Aloisio.

The dramatic turn-round took its toll on Anderlecht, who had three players cautioned, and from being on the verge of topping Group B they were left firmly rooted to the bottom of it. Two defeats from the opening two games would have left Werder in a difficult position. This win kept them in touch and the manner in which it was achieved raised a few eyebrows around the other Group camps and teed things up nicely for their next encounter, in Milan.

As the Champions' League resumed its progress in early March, Milan went into their game with Werder a point ahead of them and having left out Papin in preference to Dejan Savicevic up front. His former team-mate at Marseille, French international Marcel Desailly, had transferred his allegiances as 1993 had drawn to a close, to further the causes of the team he helped beat in the 1992–93 final. Croat Zvonimir Boban made up the contingent of the three foreign players.

Group B Results 1993–94

Round One
Wednesday, 24 November 1993
RSC Anderlecht 0 **Milan** 0
Att: 28,000. *Ref:* Zhuk (Bls)
Anderlecht: De Wilde, Crasson, Rutjes, Albert, De Wolf, Walem, Zetterberg, Bosman, Haagdoren, Versavel, Boffin (Van Baekel 90)
Milan: Rossi, Panucci, Costacurta, Baresi, Maldini, B. Laudrup, Albertini, Donadoni, Orlando, Papin, Simone (Massaro 75)
Yellow Cards: Rossi, Albertini and Donadoni (Milan)

FC Porto 3 **Werder Bremen** 2
Domingos (7), Rui Jorge (34), Hobsch (85), Rufer (86)
Jose Carlos (82)
Att: 45,000. *Ref:* Elleray (Eng)
FC Porto: Vitor Baia, Joao Pinto, Rui Jorge, Aloisio, Jorge Costa, Jose Carlos, Secretario, Kostadinov (Jamie Magalhaes 75), Domingos, Semedo, Paulinho Santos (Rui Filipe 87)
Werder Bremen: Reck, Basler, Bode (Neubarth 65), Bratseth, Beiersdorfer (Wolter 46), Legat, Eilts, Votava, Hobsch, Herzog, Rufer
Yellow Cards: Kostadinov, Jorge Costa (FC Porto) and Votava (Werder Bremen)

Round Two
Wednesday, 1 December 1993
Milan 3 **FC Porto** 0
Raducioiu (16), Panucci (39),
Massaro (63)
Att: 35,000. *Ref:* Sundell (Swe)
Milan: Rossi, Panucci, Maldini, Albertini, Costacurta, Baresi, Massaro, Donadoni, Papin (Tassotti 64), Savicevic, Raducioiu
FC Porto: Vitor Baia, Joao Pinto, Paulo Pereira (Vinha 46), Aloisio, Fernando Couto, Jose Carlos, Secretario, Rui Jorge, Domingos, Semedo, Paulinho Santos (Rui Filipe 46)

Wednesday, 8 December 1993
Werder Bremen 5 **RSC Anderlecht** 3
Rufer (66, 89), Bratseth (72), Albert (16), Boffin (18, 33)
Hobsch (81), Bode (81)
Att: 32,000. *Ref:* Craciunescu (Rom)
Werder Bremen Reck, Basler (Wiedener 86), Bode, Bratseth, Beiersdorfer, Borowka, Eilts, Votava, Hobsch, Herzog (Wolter 46), Rufer
Anderlecht: De Wilde, Crasson, Rutjes, Albert, Emmers, Walem, Zetterberg (Kooiman 83), Bosman (Nilis 70), Haagdoren, Versavel, Boffin
Yellow Cards: Wiedener (Werder Bremen), Versavel, Bosman and Zetterberg (Anderlecht)

Round Three
Wednesday, 2 March 1994
Milan 2 **Werder Bremen** 1
Maldini (48), Savicevic (68) Basler (54)
Att: 40,000. *Ref:* Mottram (Sco)
Milan: Rossi, Tassotti, Costacurta, Baresi, Maldini, Eranio (Simone 46), Desailly, Donadoni, Boban, Massaro, Savicevic (Albertini 88)
Werder Bremen: Reck, Beiersdorfer, Neubarth, Votava, Wolter, Basler, Eilts, Bode (Hobsch 77), Legat, Herzog, Rufer
Yellow Cards: Baresi (Milan), Beiersdorfer, Wolter and Herzog (Werder Bremen)

RSC Anderlecht 1 **FC Porto** 0
Nilis (89)
Att: 15,000. *Ref:* Nikakis (Gre)
RSC Anderlecht: De Wilde, Surray (Crasson 46), N'Wanu, Albert, Versavel (Kooiman 89), Emmers, Walem, Degryse, Boffin, Bosman, Nilis
FC Porto: Vitor Baia, Bandeirinha, Aloisio, Fernando Couto, Rui Jorge, Costa, Secretario, Andre, Semedo (Rui Filipe), Kostadinov, Drulovic
Yellow Cards: N'Wanu (RSC Anderlecht), Rui Jorge, Kostadinov and Rui Filipe (FC Porto)

Round Four
Wednesday, 16 March 1994
Werder Bremen 1 **Milan** 1
Rufer (52 pen) Savicevic (75)
Att: 31,000. *Ref:* Nielsen (Den)
Werder Bremen: Reck, Beiersdorfer, Bratseth, Wiedener, Votava, Basler, Neubarth, Bode (Unger 88), Legat, Hobsch, Rufer
Milan: Rossi, Tassotti, Costacurta, Galli, Maldini, Eranio (Simone 56), Desailly, Donadoni, Boban, Massaro, Savicevic (Albertini 87)
Yellow Cards: Beiersdorfer (Werder Bremen), Eranio and Massaro (Milan)

FC Porto 2 **RSC Anderlecht** 0
Drulovic (10), Secretario (90)
Att: 30,000. *Ref:* Krondl (Aus)
FC Porto: Vitor Baia, Joao Pinto, Aloisio, Rui Jorge, Secretario, Semedo, Timofte (Folha 72), Andre, Domingos (Fernando Couto 87), Drulovic
RSC Anderlecht: DeWilde, Crasson, Rutjes, N'Wanu, Boffin, Suray, Emmers (Haagdoren 71), Walem, Versavel, (Bosman 46), Degryse, Nilis
Yellow Cards: Aloisio (FC Porto), Crasson and Suray (RSC Anderlecht)

Round Five
Wednesday, 30 March 1994
Werder Bremen 0 **FC Porto** 5
Rui Filipe (11), Kostadinov (34),
Secretario (70), Domingos (74),
Timofte (89 pen)
Att: 32,000. *Ref:* Diaz Vega (Spa)
Werder Bremen: Reck, Wiedener, Legat, Bratseth, Wolter, Basler, Bode, Votava, Harttgen (Neubarth 46), Herzog, Rufer (Bockenfeld 78)
FC Porto: Vitor Baia, Joao Pinto, Rui Jorge, Jorge Costa, Fernando Couto, Andre, Secretario, Kostadinov (Domingos 71), Timofte, Paulinho Santos (Rui Filipe 9), Drulovic
Yellow Cards: Wolter, Wiedener, Basler and Bode (Werder Bremen), Secretario and Kostadinov (FC Porto)
Red Card: Herzog (Werder Bremen)

Milan 0 **RSC Anderlecht** 0
Att: 40,000. *Ref:* Quiniou (Fra)
Milan: Rossi, Tassotti, Costacurta, Albertini, Maldini, Baresi, Desailly, Donadoni, B. Laudrup (Simone 51), Massaro, Raducioiu (Carbone 68)
RSC Anderlecht: De Wilde, Crasson, N'Wanu, Walem, Suray, Emmers, Degryse, Haagdoren, Bosman, Nilis, Boffin
Yellow Cards: Raducioiu, Maldini and Simone (Milan), Suray (RSC Anderlecht)

Round Six
Wednesday, 13 April 1994
FC Porto 0 **Milan** 0
Att: 60,000. *Ref:* Puhl (Hun)
FC Porto: Vitor Baia, Joao Pinto, Aloisio, Fernando Couto, Rui Jorge, Andre, Jorge Couto (Jamie Magalhaes 76), Rui Filipe, Timofte (Folha 68), Domingos, Drulovic
Milan: Rossi, Tassotti, Costacurta, Baresi, Maldini, Albertini, Desailly, Carbone, Boban, Savicevic (Panucci 84), Massaro
Yellow Cards: Domingos (FC Porto), Carbone and Maldini (Milan)

RSC Anderlecht 1 **Werder Bremen** 2
Bosman (44) Bode (33, 65)
Att: 15,000. *Ref:* Rothlisberger (Swi)
RSC Anderlecht: De Wilde, Crasson, Marchoul (M. De Wolf 46), N'Wanu, Boffin, Emmers (Peiremans 70), Walem, Versavel, Haagdoren, Bosman, Nilis
Werder Bremen: Reck, Borowka, Legat, Bratseth, Beiersdorfer, Basler, Bode, Votava, Schaaf, Neubarth, Rufer
Yellow Cards: Beiersdorfer and Schaaf (Werder Bremen)

Final Table	P	W	D	L	F	A	Pts
Milan	6	2	4	0	6	2	8
FC Porto	6	3	1	2	10	6	7
Werder Bremen	6	2	1	3	11	15	6
RSC Anderlecht	6	1	2	3	5	9	4

Group B – Results

	FC Porto	Milan	RSC Anderlecht	Werder Bremen
FC Porto	—	0-0	2-0	3-2
Milan	3-0	—	0-0	2-1
RSC Anderlecht	1-0	0-0	—	1-2
Werder Bremen	0-5	1-1	5-3	—

Savicevic's preference was a curious one given that he had not scored so far, but the move looked to be a good one early on as he forced Reck in the Werder goal to make a series of outstanding saves. Werder, who had taken massive support to the Stadio Giuseppe Meazza, were dangerous on the counter and it wasn't until late in the first half that Milan started to look like the home side.

They took their new role into the second half and within three minutes of it took the lead when slack marking allowed Maldini to ghost in unmarked to head home Donadoni's cross. But the German champions seemed to be at their most dangerous when behind and within six minutes had equalised through Basler – a shot going under the body of Rossi. A surprising spectacle given the fact that the Milan keeper had recently set a Serie A record of

Champion action as FC Porto entertain RSC Anderlecht.

929 minutes without conceding a goal.

What proved to be Milan's winner was nothing short of a gift and seemed to justify Capello's preference of Savicevic who will not get many easier chances in his career. A back pass to Rossi in the Milan goal was lofted into the Werder half where it was headed on by Massaro towards the large frame of Frank Neubarth. He looked to have the situation in control, but under no pressure totally missed his kick and Savicevic, alive to the situation, raced onto the ball, toe-ending it past the advancing Reck.

The win assured Milan of the two points and their position at the head of the Group B table regardless of what happened in Brussels, where Anderlecht entertained a slowly revitalising Porto side. Defeat for Anderlecht was unthinkable, while a win was essential if they were to stay on course for a semi-final spot. Porto arrived under new managership. Bobby Robson, who had been sacked as Sporting Lisbon's manager, found himself in his second stint of European football in the same season. His former club had been eliminated by the Austrians of Casino Salzburg in the third round of the UEFA Cup.

For large periods of the first half the Portuguese visitors outplayed their hosts, but they were limited to just one clear-cut chance when Kostadinov placed his free header right at the feet of the Anderlecht keeper De Wilde. Anderlecht also had their chances, the best falling to Versavel. Degryse was a constant threat to the Porto defenders and played a major role in setting up great scoring opportunities for Bosman and Nilis. Then, just as the game looked set to finish as a draw, Anderlecht scored a superb goal to revitalise their interest in the Champions' League. It was a move that swept the length of the pitch as De Wilde's long kick was eventually headed on by Degryse. Bosman accepted the ball and in one movement turned it inside and into the path of Nilis, who shot perfectly from just outside the area, low and hard into the right-hand corner of the net. The late, late win lifted the Belgians into second place, two points behind Milan and in contention for a semi-final berth. Porto dropped to third place ahead of Werder Bremen, having beaten them 3-2 in an earlier match.

Two weeks later, the fourth round of matches marked the returns from the last set of games. In Bremen a sell-out crowd came to witness what was billed by the German club as the biggest match they had ever staged. Having just qualified for their own domestic Cup final the hosts knew that they couldn't afford to lose if they were to keep on course for a semi-final spot. They were aided by the return of Bratseth after injury, but were missing their Austrian striker Herzog because of suspension. A second yellow card for Milan skipper Baresi in the match in Italy meant that he too was missing and his spot filled by Galli, with Tassotti captain for the night.

On an evening of driving rain and wind, Werder proceeded to dominate the match, playing six in midfield and just three across the back. However, the opening period might have been disastrous but for excellent saves by Reck from Massaro. Rossi in the Milan goal also had to be in top form and he produced a string of fine saves. Milan's half-time respite was short-lived as Werder were awarded a penalty after Galli was adjudged to have pulled down Hobsch. It was a harsh decision given by a referee some 40 yards away but was at least reward for the home side's constant attacking play. Rufer stepped up to chip the ball impudently past Rossi.

From the restart, Rufer might have made it 2-0 as Milan started to play with the urgency that had been lacking from their play to that point and Reck produced the save of the night from Savicevic's shot. As Milan continued to go forward Bratseth had to clear the ball off the line from substitute Simone and there was a clear lack of concentration in the home defence as the ball came back in for Boban to strike a low shot. The ball was intercepted by Savicevic, who had time to control, turn and fire past Reck from five yards for the equaliser.

In the other Group B game of the evening Bobby Robson's Porto side knew that they needed to beat Anderlecht to stand any realistic chance of qualifying for the semi-finals. The Belgians were pretty much in the same boat. Both sides were looking for a good start and it was the home team who got it when, after ten minutes, Drulovic raced onto a through ball and just beat Anderlecht keeper De Wilde to the ball to prod it past him and into the net. Porto failed to build on their lead in the first half and by the second Anderlecht had come back into the game superbly with a front line led by Nilis, the club's top scorer, forcing the Porto keeper into several fine saves.

The Belgians rode their luck though when Tomofte's free-kick from 30 yards cannoned off a post and somehow Secretario blasted the rebound over from eight yards. In the final minutes, with the visitors moving up more and more in search of a vital equaliser, their defence was caught square and Secretario couldn't miss from close range. The win lifted Porto into second place two points behind Milan but just one ahead of Werder Bremen and Anderlecht.

The fifth round of matches were the returns of the first round of games and Milan entertained Anderlecht needing just a point to secure their semi-final berth. Having drawn in Brussels, Milan were expected to win, but Anderlecht had shown a resurgence of form in their domestic league and took to the field with no fewer than seven Belgian internationals in their starting line-up. Milan, without over-exerting themselves, had the opportunities in the first half and were never really troubled at the back, where Baresi had been reinstalled.

Raducioiu should have put them into the lead after Albertini's mis-hit shot from the edge of the area fell at his feet. But De Wilde made a fine save from almost point-blank range to deny the forward. The Anderlecht keeper was a problem for the home side's offensive the whole evening, and produced good saves to deny Massaro and Desailly as Milan surged forward.

Anderlecht's chances were few and far between, though Baresi was lucky to escape without punishment after blatantly obstructing Degryse on his way to goal. In the second half things didn't improve, though both sides might have scored. Bosman, at full stretch, couldn't get the ball in at the far post from a right-wing cross and Albertini was unlucky to see his 30-yard free-kick cannon off the base of a post with De Wilde, for once, beaten. As with the first encounter the game ended goalless, which virtually finished Anderlecht's hopes.

Champions' League Appearance Details

Appearances in the Champions' League are listed by club and alphabetically by player. The number of starting appearances are given first and any appearances as substitutes are given after a '+' sign. Thus 2+1 indicates two starting appearances and one as a substitute.

AS Monaco – 19 Players
Blondeau 4, Djorkaeff 6, Dumas 5, Ettori 6, Gnako 1+5, Grimandi 2+1, Ikpeba 4+1, Klinsmann 6, Passi 0+1, Perez 0+2, Petit 5, Puel 6, Scifo 6, Simba 0+2, Sonor 1, Thuram 6, Valery 3+1, Viaud 4, Weah 0+1

Barcelona – 17 Players
Amor 5+1, Bakero 5, Beguiristain 3+1, Eusebio 1+3, Ferrer 6, Goikoetxea 1+3, Guardiola 4, Ivan 4+1, Juan Carlos 1+1, Koeman R. 6, Laudrup M. 3, Nadal 5+1, Quique Esterbaranz 1+1, Romario 5, Sergi 6, Stoichkov 4, Zubizarreta 6

FC Porto – 22 Players
Aloisio 5, Andre 4, Bandeirinha 1, Domingos 4+1, Drulovic 4, Fernando Couto 4+1, Folha 0+2, Jamie Magalhaes 0+2, Joao Pinto 5, Jorge Costa 4, Jorge Couto 1, Jose Carlos 2, Kostadinov 3, Paulinho Santos 3, Paulo Pereira 1, Rui Filipe 1+4, Rui Jorge 6, Secretario 5, Semedo 4, Timofte 3, Vinha 0+1

Galatasaray – 20 Players
Soner 1, Cihat 1, Mert 5, Bulent 5, Goetz 5, Mert 5, Suat 5, Hayrettin 6, K. Yusuf 6, Tugay 6, Ugur 6, Hakan 6, Mustafa 0+1, B. Yusuf 0+1, Okan 0+2, Stumpf 2+1, Turkyilmaz 2+1, Erdal 2+2, Arif 3+1, Hamza 5+1.

Milan – 20 Players
Albertini 4+2, B. Laudrup 2, Baresi 5, Boban 3, Carbone 1+2, Costacurta 6, Desailly 4, Donadoni 5, Eranio 2, Galli 1, Maldini 6, Massaro 5+1, Orlando 1, Panucci 2+1, Papin 2, Raduciozi 2, Rossi 6, Savicevic 4, Simone 1+3, Tassotti 4+1

RSC Anderlecht – 20 Players
Albert 3, Boffin 6, Bosman 5+1, Crasson 5+1, Degryse 3, De Wilde 6, De Wolf 1+1, Emmers 5, Haagdoren 4+1, Kooiman 0+2, Marchoul 1, N'Wanu 4, Nilis 4+1, Peiremans 0+1, Rutjes 3, Suray 3, Van Baekel 0+1, Versavel 5, Walem 6, Zetterberg 2

Spartak Moscow – 18 Players
Alenichev 0+1, Ananko 0+1, Beschastnykh 6, Ivanov 3+1, Karpin 6, Khlestov 4+1, Ledyakhov 5+1, Mamedov 4, Massalitine 1, Nikiforov 5, Onopko 5, Piatnitski 5+1, Pisarev 4+12, Pomazuon 2, Rodionov 1+3, Stauche 4, Ternavski 4, Tsymbalar 6

Werder Bremen – 19 Players
Basler 6, Beiersdorfer 5, Bode 6, Borowka 2, Bratseth 5, Brockenfield 0+1, Eilts 3, Harttgen 1, Herzog 4, Hobsch 3+1, Legat 5, Neubarth 3+2, Reck 6, Rufer 6, Schaaf 1, Unger 0+1, Votava 6, Wiedener 2+1, Wolter 2+2

Top Scorers – Both Groups

- 4 — Rufer (Werder Bremen)
- 3 — Bode (Werder Bremen), Karpin (Spartak Moscow), Koeman, R. (Barcelona), Stoichkov (Barcelona)
- 2 — Amor (Barcelona), Beguiristain (Barcelona), Boffin (RSC Anderlecht), Djorkaeff (Monaco), Domingos (FC Porto), Hobsch (Werder Bremen), Klinsmann (AS Monaco), Romario (Barcelona), Savicevic (Milan), Scifo (AS Monaco), Secretario (FC Porto)
- 1 — Albert (RSC Anderlecht), Basler (Werder Bremen), Bosman (RSC Anderlecht), Bratseth (Werder Bremen), Cihat (Galatasaray), Drulovic (FC Porto), Eusebio (Barcelona), Gnako (AS Monaco), Ikpeba (AS Monaco), Jose Carlos (FC Porto), Kostadinov (FC Porto), Maldini (Milan), Massaro (Milan), Nilis (RSC Anderlecht), Onopko (Spartak Moscow), Panucci (Milan), Pisarev (Spartak Moscow), Raducioiu (Milan), Rodionov (Spartak Moscow), Rui Filipe (FC Porto), Rui Jorge (FC Porto), Thuram (AS Monaco), Timofte (FC Porto)

Summary Both Groups

	P	HW	D	AW	GF	GA
Group A	12	5	4	3	29	29
Group B	12	6	4	2	32	32
Total	24	11	8	5	61	61

Champions' Cup – Top Scorers

- 8 — Rufer (Werder Bremen)
- 7 — Koeman R. (Barcelona), Nilis (RSC Anderlecht), Vlaovic (Croatia Zagreb)
- 5 — Hobsch (Werder Bremen), Karpin (Spartak Moscow), Stoichkov (Barcelona)
- 4 — Bode (Werder Bremen), Klinsmann (AS Monaco), Onopko (Spartak Moscow), Papin (Milan), Pisarev (Spartak Moscow)
- 3 — Bosman (RSC Anderlecht), Djorkaeff (AS Monaco), Domingos (FC Porto), Ikpeba (AS Monaco), Rodionov (Spartak Moscow)

In Bremen tensions were high as both sides needed to win to maintain their challenge. Porto, though, knew that victory for them would all but mathematically put them into the semi-finals and with eight wins from their last 10 games they were full of confidence against a Werder side with just two wins from 12 games and sliding alarmingly down the Bundesliga table. What unfolded in Bremen was one of the great European nights as Bobby Robson's side – weakened by injuries and suspensions – carved out a wonderful five-star and five-goal victory. It was to be the night of the substitutes. After nine minutes Rui Filipe went on for Paulinho, himself in for the injured Semedo, and with his first touch of the ball he beat Reck from 25 yards to stun the Germans.

With Couto in towering form at the heart of the Porto defence, Werder were always open to the counter-attack as they over-committed midfield players forward. And when Drulovic put Kostadinov clear he made no mistake. Two goals down, but

Werder at least knew they had what it takes to come from behind. It wasn't to be though and as the 36-year-old Andre, 10 years a Porto player, marshalled the midfield, Secretario jinked around Legat and drilled a low shot past Reck from a tight angle to make it 0-3. Some of the threat to Werder looked to have gone when Kostadinov limped off, but his replacement Domingos wasted no time in utilising his first touches of the ball to fire past Reck to make it 0-4. A last-minute penalty from Timofte sealed Werder's fate, which was augmented with the sending off of Herzog who had deliberately handled on the line. The result and points meant that Porto would have to lose by four goals in their final encounter at home to Milan to give Anderlecht any chance of pipping them at the post.

Anderlecht, then, faced their final match of the Champions' League looking for a hat-full against the worst defence in the two groups, but their chances took a blow early on when Bode was put away by a flick over the top of the Anderlecht defence and his shot from just inside the area took a deflection off a defender past De Wilde to put Werder into the lead. But faint hopes re-emerged as Anderlecht equalised on the half-time whistle, Bosman tucking away a relatively simple goal after a hopeful ball into the area had rebounded kindly for the striker. In the second half Werder looked the hungrier of the two sides and on 65 minutes won the game with a move that swept from one end of the pitch to the other and got the finish it deserved when Bode dived to head the ball home for his second goal of the night.

A capacity crowd filled Porto's ground to see if they could fulfil Bobby Robson's dream of securing the win over Milan, thus ensuring them a semi-final place and the advantage of hosting the one-off match itself. Milan, though, knew that a draw was all they needed to secure pole position in the group. On paper the game made an intriguing story. Porto, who were without two influential players in Secretario and Kostadinov, were the Champions' League's leading scorers, whereas Milan had the Champions' League's meanest defence. Kostadinov, who was serving a one-match suspension, missed the game entirely, choosing to travel with the Bulgarian national squad to Oman to prepare for the World Cup.

Perhaps predictably the game ended goalless but not for the want of trying by Porto, and Milan had their keeper to thank for their vital point. The game looked like it might swing Porto's way in the second half when Carbone was booked for the second time for exactly the same crime – a vicious tackle from behind on Jorge – and had his marching orders, leaving Milan to see out the final 25 minutes a man short. In the end it wasn't quite like the Alamo, but nevertheless Rossi was unbeatable and produced the save of the night in denying substitute Ljubinko Drulovic late on as both teams progressed to the semis.

Semi-Finals

UEFA's seeding system proved to be effective as both the Champions' League Group seeds topped their mini-leagues to earn home advantage in the one-leg semi-finals. Monaco (and one wonders how PSG were feeling about their rejection of a Champions' Cup place) made the relatively short journey to Milan, while a resurgent FC Porto crossed the Iberian peninsular to the Nou Camp where they faced Barcelona.

As expected both games went with home advantage and both by the same three-goal scoreline, although the outcomes were different in nature, Barcelona swamping Porto while Milan dismissed Monaco in somewhat dramatic circumstances to set up the heavyweight final that most neutral observers wished for.

In the San Siro, Milan went into the game, admittedly with home advantage but also with the pressure that expectant support brings, with no fewer than eight players on yellow cards. Monaco had six players a single caution away from a possible final suspension. Both sides had players of note missing as well. Milan defender Paolo Maldini – arguably the best left-back in the world – had been shown yellow cards in successive Champions' League games, while Monaco were without Lilian Thuram and Victor Ikpeba, also beaten by the yellow fever in their final Champions' League match, and Sonor, who was kept out with a broken leg.

Further flavour was added by Milan president and would-be Italian Premier Silvio Berlusconi publicly reminding his coach Fabio Capello on the day of the match that Milan had still to take Europe's biggest club prize under his reign. The notorious Milan pitch had had a facelift prior to the game, being relaid at a cost of £30,000, so there could be no excuses!

Monaco dominated the opening ten minutes of play with Scifo and Klinsmann looking lively and at home in the stadium where they had previously played for Milan's greatest rivals, Internazionale. However, it was Milan who should have taken the lead with their first real attack of the game. A quickly taken free-kick led to a long-range effort by Donadoni. The ball took a deflection and Savicevic looked set to score as he reacted first to lift the dropping ball over the advancing Ettori. The ball beat the French keeper but not the angle of the bar from which it rebounded into play – but Massaro couldn't find the inches to get above the ball and his follow-up header went over an open goal.

Emil Kostadinov dips to head towards goal as the Barcelona defenders Ronald Koeman (on floor) and Nadal look on.

> ### Semi-Final
>
> Wednesday, 27 April 1994
> **Milan**   **3**   **AS Monaco**   **0**
> Desailly (14), Albertini (48),
> Massaro (66)
> *Att:* 78,650.   *Ref:* Heynemann (Ger)
> *Milan:* Rossi, Panucci, Costacurta, Baresi, Tassotti, Albertini, Desailly, Donadoni, Boban, Savicevic (Simone 87), Massaro (Lentini 84)
> *AS Monaco:* Ettori, Blondeau (Weah 54), Grimandi, Dumas, Petit, Puel (Simba 67), Gnako, Viaud, Scifo, Djorkaeff, Klinsmann.
> *Yellow Cards:* Baresi, Costacurta (Milan), Puel (AS Monaco)
> *Red Card:* Costacurta (second yellow)
>
> **Barcelona**   **3**   **FC Porto**   **0**
> Stoichkov (10, 35), Koeman (72)
> *Att:* 98,000.   *Ref:* Zhuk (Bls)
> *Barcelona:* Zubizarreta, Ferrer, Koeman, Nadal, Sergi (Goiketxea 74), Guardiola, Bakero, Amor, Stoichkov, Romario, Beguiristain (Ivan 41)
> *FC Porto:* Vitor Baia, Joao Pinto, Jorge Costa, Aloisio, Fernando Couto, Secretario, Andre (Paulinho Santos 75), Folha (Semendo 65), Rui Filipe, Drulovic, Kostadinov
> *Yellow Cards:* Joao Pinto, Folha and Aloisio (FC Porto)
> *Red Card:* Joao Pinto (second yellow)

Alessandro Costacurta – received his marching orders in the semi-final with Monaco.

That near miss should have served as a warning for Monaco but it didn't and within a few minutes the home support were celebrating. There was no danger as Dumas looked to play the ball back to his keeper, but the defender slipped and had to beat off Savicevic to concede a corner. Boban delivered the ball into the area and Desailly rose above the small frame of Ettori to power his header into the corner of the net.

As the game approached half an hour of play Costacurta – an ever-present in Milan's 10 games in the Champions' Cup campaign – received a yellow card after he was adjudged to have fouled Klinsmann. The tackle was not malicious but it was from behind and Klinsmann produced his customary 'death throes'. Thankfully, or so it seemed, Costacurta was not one of the Milan players with a previous caution to his name. But worse was to follow. Shortly before half-time, in a mad minute, Milan's final aspirations suffered a serve jolt. First Baresi brought down Djorkaeff on the angle of the area and received a yellow card. It brought howls of derision from the Milanese, for it was his second of the competition and would keep him out of the final. However, within a minute Costacurta and Klinsmann were involved in another incident on the edge of the Milan area. Costacurta looked to have lifted his foot high and into Klinsmann's face as he went for a ball. Klinsmann fell to the ground and referee Heynemann produced a yellow card in Costacurta's direction for the second time in the game, so off he went. Television replays clearly showed that there was no contact and that the Monaco player had conned the referee.

Milan were down to 10 men for the second game in succession – and rearranged their formation with Desailly moving back alongside Baresi to fill the gap left by Costacurta's dismissal. Neither Milan nor Monaco changed their formations for the second half. Despite Milan leaving just Savicevic up front Monaco continued to play with four at the back, and three minutes into the half Milan's 10 doubled their lead. Once again there seemed no real danger when a long ball reached Savicevic. The Croat was fouled unnecessarily and from the subsequent free-kick Boban touched the ball a yard right to Albertini, who rifled a magnificent free-kick into the top of Ettori's goal from well outside the area.

Monaco, to their credit, continued to play with a belief that they could recover the deficit against 10 men but Klinsmann looked increasingly ineffectual against Desailly and was, not surprisingly, a fair target for the Milan crowd. The third, killing goal came in the 66th minute when a cross-field ball by Panucci found the roving Massaro. Petit looked to have had the cross covered but lost his footing at the vital moment to allow Massaro to fire a powerful angled right-foot volley past Ettori from 15 yards.

At the end of the evening the difference between the two sides was in the defences. Milan – even after Costacurta had gone – were superbly marshalled and organised while Monaco always looked suspect when put under pressure, even when faced with just a single forward for most of the game, and were severely punished for three defensive slips. Milan, with their players on £190,000 a man to win the competition, were well worth their place in the final.

Nou Camp was packed to capacity as Barcelona and Porto took to the field for the second semi-final. Injuries had deprived Porto of two players and they were well aware of the size of their task in a stadium where Barca had won all five of their Champions' Cup games, scoring 17 goals and conceding just two. However, the visitors nearly made the perfect start when Folha's corner picked out Pinto and his header coming in from the edge of the box was only just wide. As it was, that was to prove to be their best attempt of the evening for the Portuguese and Zubizarreta in the home goal didn't have a direct save to make.

Barcelona, almost inevitably, took the lead when Stoichkov was on hand to sidefoot home at the culmination of an excellent move, which started when Amor won the ball on the edge of his own area and finished with Sergi's cross. The Spaniards virtually secured their place in the final with a goal nine minutes from the break. Involving Romario, Sergi and Stoichkov it was a near replica of the opener, with Stoichkov this time finishing at the rear of the six-yard box.

The second half started badly for Porto when Joao Pinto was sent off following a second bookable offence, and 17 minutes from time Barca added a third goal courtesy of Ronald Koeman. With 19 goals in all competitions going into the game, Koeman had a prolific strike rate for a central defender, although they all had come from dead ball situations and penalty kicks. This time, however, when Guardiola played the ball infield Koeman found himself in space. The Dutchman powered through the centre circle and from nearly 40 yards hit a venomous curling shot which flew into the top right hand corner of the net. Baia did well to get a hand to the ball – there certainly cannot have been a harder hit shot all season, and it made Koeman joint top scorer in the Champions' Cup overall!

Marcel Desailly celebrates after scoring Milan's fourth goal.

Final: Milan's Campionato

The huge banner that unfurled over the edge of the upper tier of the Olympic Stadium in Athens in the final minutes of the game spelt out what the rest of the on-looking Europe were already only too aware: 'Milano Campionato Di Europa'. It might have included a few superlatives as well. Magnificent, superb, brilliant – take your pick. For Milan had not just completed an astonishing 4-0 victory over Barcelona but had humbled their opponents. If there is such a thing as perfection in football then this was it.

The Catalans had approached the game with the greater confidence, indeed the Spanish press had been proclaiming possibly one of the most one-sided finals for several years. How right and wrong they were. On a warm, humid evening Milan took to the field without five otherwise certain starters because of suspensions and injury. The absence of Franco Baresi and Alessandro Costacurta – the heart of even the national defence – through suspension was to be the telling factor, or so we were led to believe. Indeed it was, not negatively but positively, as the Serie A champions turned a tactical tune not to defend and hit on the counter but to attack and control. A tactical victory for Fabio Capello, the Milan coach. Milan were superior in every respect. Their control, passing, running on to and off the ball, even that most English of commodities – work rate – were matched with finishing of the highest class.

Barcelona for their part should not have been short of confidence. Their Champions' League record was far more impressive than Milan's. They had entered a free-scoring mode and were playing with a defence that even the rain in Spain would have had trouble penetrating. And, if a boost was needed above and beyond that, they had four days earlier captured their third successive league title in the last game of the season when all had looked lost. Six of the Barca line-up were part of the side that had beaten another Italian side – Sampdoria – to lift the trophy at Wembley two years earlier. Both finalists had no fewer than seven players who possessed winners' medals.

The early play set the trend as Milan denied Barcelona the ball, and more importantly their potentially match-winning attack of Stoichkov and Romario. With Donadoni, surprisingly playing wide on the left and posing Ferrer a constant stream of problems, Savicevic dropped deep and both Koeman and Nadal at the heart of the defence looked lost. Possession and domination gradually turned into goals and by the half-time interval the game had been decided thanks to two classic strikes by Daniele Massaro. It was fitting that the 33-year-old should claim the glory as it was he whose glaring misses in the previous season's defeat by Marseille had cost Milan so dear.

His first goal came in the 22nd minute when Savicevic waltzed around Nadal on the right and as Zubizarreta was drawn from his post the cross shot fell perfectly for the unmarked Massaro, whose left-foot shot did away with the previous season's nightmares. The Spaniards looked shell-shocked and with Desailly a rock in front of his back four, they were faced with an impenetrable barrier. Rather than shut up shop – after all nobody is better at defending a goal lead than Milan – they

Final

Olympic Stadium, Athens
Wednesday, 18 May 1994
Milan 4 Barcelona 0
Massaro (22, 45), Savicevic (47),
Desailly (58)
Att: 75,000. *Ref:* Don (Eng)
Milan: Rossi, Tassotti, Galli, Maldini (Nava 85), Panucci, Albertini, Desailly, Donadoni, Boban, Savicevic, Massaro
Barcelona: Zubizarreta, Ferrer, Nadal, Koeman R., Sergi (Enrique 71), Amor, Bakero, Guardiola, Beguiristain (Eusebio 53), Romario, Stoichkov
Yellow Cards: Tassotti, Albertini, Panucci (Milan) and Stoichkov, Nadal, Serai, Ferrer (Barcelona)

continued to move positively and Donadoni and Massaro both went close. Barcelona's first and only real attempt on goal came four minutes from half-time when Romario's run on to the ball and shot on the turn looked to be capable of beating Rossi, but was deflected off back-tracking Galli.

The only blot on the Milan copy-book was a feigned head injury by Rossi after Stoichkov looked like he was going to attempt to reach a rare ball through the Milanese back four. Significantly, it was during the time added on by referee Philip Don – who had an excellent game – that Massaro fired Milan into a soul-destroying 2-0 lead. Rossi collected the ball from a long and aimless Barcelona pass forward that had descended into his area. Fourteen passes and 50 seconds later, the ball nested in the back of the Zubizarreta's net. Those 14 passes spread the length and breath of the field, were a mixture of short and long, of dribbles and flicks. The last two created the finish. Boban found Donadoni on the left, he drifted past Ferrer and from the line, deep inside the Barca penalty area, cut the ball back for Massaro to score from 15 yards.

Against such a mean defence, Barcelona's task in the second half was more than difficult, and two minutes further on it became monumental when Savicevic won the ball on the right from the luckless Ferrer and, spotting Zubizarreta off his line, lobbed the Barcelona goalkeeper with a delicate and accurate left-foot shot. This superbly-taken goal incensed the Barcelona players, who had stopped expecting a free-kick. There is perhaps truth in their convictions that Savicevic showed his studs in the challenge with Ferrer and in normal Euro-parlance that would have been a foul. But not with an English referee in charge and the Milan player, unlike his opponents, played to the whistle. A fact that might have also escaped the Barcelona camp – though I doubt it – was that Don had refereed their only other defeat in that season's competition!

The heart went out of the Barcelona performance from that point and it was no surprise when Milan scored a fourth through Desailly, who collected a pass from Albertini and shot past Zubizarreta from the edge of the area. Milan played out the last half-hour with ease and Savicevic might have made it five near the end when he shot wide after Donadoni had made another raid down the wing, this time at the expense of Bakero.

The final whistle blew without Barcelona recording one shot of note on target and with Desailly collecting his second successive Champions' Cup medal but with different clubs. It

Milan celebrate with the Champions' Cup.

was Milan's third triumph in six years and will be remembered as one of the finest displays in the cup's 39-year history. Capello's team can now be ranked alongside the all-time greats of this wonderful competition.

After the game a despondent Barcelona coach, Johan Cruyff, said: 'We were never able to develop our usual game because Milan won all the tackles. They used the ball very well and we were unable to compete.' Simply and accurately put.

Champions' Cup Scorers 1993-94

- **8** Koeman R. (Barcelona), Rufer (Werder Bremen)
- **7** Nilis (RSC Anderlecht), Stoichkov (Barcelona), Vlaovic (Croatia Zagreb)
- **5** Hobsch (Werder Bremen), Karpin (Spartak Moscow)
- **4** Bode (Werder Bremen), Klinsmann (AS Monaco), Massaro (Milan), Onopko (Spartak Moscow), Papin (Milan), Pisarev (Spartak Moscow)
- **3** Boffin (Anderlecht), Bosman (RSC Anderlecht), Djorkaeff (AS Monaco), Domingos (FC Porto), Ikpeba (AS Monaco), Rodionov (Spartak Moscow)
- **2** Adziz (Croatia Zagreb), Amor (Barcelona), Arif (Galatasaray), Arveladze (Dynamo Tbilisi), Bakero (Barcelona), Basler (Werder Bremen), Beguiristain (Barcelona), Bruce (Manchester United), Cantona (Manchester United), Critanovic (Croatia Zagreb), Desailly (Milan), Dumitrescu (AS Monaco), Ford (Cwmbran Town), Gudjohnsson (IA Akranes), Hateley (Rangers), Haylock (Linfield), Hazari (Beitar Jerusalem), Johnston (Linfield), Keane (Manchester United), Kostadinov (FC Porto), Kubilay (Galatasaray), Leonenko (Dynamo Kiev), Loken (Rosenborg BK), Panduru (Steaua Bucharest), Podbrozny (Lech Poznan), Pogoden (Spartak Moscow), Romario (Barcelona), Savicevic (Milan), Scifo (AS Monaco), Secretario (FC Porto), Shilikashvili (Omonia Nicosia), Siegl (Sparta Prague), Simone (Milan), Todorov (Levski Sofia), Tsymbalar (Spartak Moscow), Turkyilmaz (Galatasaray), Versaval (RSC Anderlecht), Vladoiu (Steaua Bucharest), Zsak (FK Austria)
- **1** Albert (RSC Anderlecht), Albertini (Milan), Barry (Cork City), Bestchastnykh (Spartak Moscow), Blinker (Feyenoord), Borimirov (Levski Sofia), Borisov (Norma Tallinin), Bragstad (Rosenborg BK), Bratseth (Werder Bremen), Brojana (Lech Poznan), Buckley (Cork City), Buttigieg (Floriana), Byelkevich (Dynamo Minsk), Caulfield (Cork City), Cihat (Galatasaray), Dahlum (Rosenborg BK), Dembilski (Lech Poznan), Drulovic (FC Porto), Durrant (Rangers), Dvirnif (Sparta Prague), Eusebio (Barcelona), Gerassimez (Dinamo Minsk), Ginchev (Levski Sofia), Glynn (Cork City), Gnako (AS Monaco), Greshnayev (Beitar Jerusalem), Halilovic (Croatia Zagreb), Heinola (HJK Helsinki), Heldman (FC Aarau), Hognason (IA Akranes), Hojer (FC Copenhagen), Inalishvili (Dynamo Tbilisi), Jelicic (Croatia Zagreb), Johansen (FC Copenhagen), Jose Carlos (FC Porto), Khlestov (Spartak Moscow), King (Cwmbran Town), Kogler (FK Austria), Laudrup B. (Milan), Laudrup M. (Barcelona), Leonhardsen (Rosenborg BK), Leshak (Croatia Zagreb), Lidman (AIK Stockholm), Maldini (Milan), McConnell (Linfield), McNeil (Cwmbran Town), McPherson (Rangers), Mikkelsen (FC Copenhagen), Milinovic (Olimpija Ljubljana), Moller (FC Copenhagen), Morley (Cork City), Moskal (Lech Poznan), Nabekovas (FK Austria), Obiku (Feyenoord), Ogris (FK Austria), Ohana (Beitar Jerusalem), Orlando (Milan), Panucci (Milan), Proitski (Skonto Riga), Quique Esterbaranz (Barcelona), Raducioiu (Milan), Ratinho (FC Aarau), Rebrov (Dynamo Kiev), Refus (Feyenoord), Revda (Zimbru), Robson (Manchester United), Rui Filipe (FC Porto), Rui Jorge (FC Porto), Salloi (Kispest Honved), Savicevic (Milan), Scheczik (Lech Poznan), Schmid (FK Austria), Schwartz (Beitar Jerusalem), Semedo (FC Porto), Shkapenko (Dynamo Kiev), Sirakov (Levski Sofia), Skammelsrud (Rosenborg BK), Sliskovic (AEK Athens), Stefanov (Kispest Honved), Stiel (FC Aarau), Szabados (Kispest Honved), Tangen (Rosenborg BK), Tapinski (Lech Poznan), Thordarson (IA Akranes), Thuram (AS Monaco), Timofte (FC Porto), Trzeciak (Lech Poznan), Turkovic (Croatia Zagreb), Velichko (Dinamo Minsk), Vonasek (Sparta Prague), Wilkashik (Lech Poznan), Yankov (Levski Sofia), Zivkovic (Croatia Zagreb)

Own goals for: Manchester United, AS Monaco and HJK Helsinki

Cup-Winners' Cup

Preliminary Round

An increased entry meant that the 1993–94 Cup-Winners' Cup competition included eight preliminary round ties – twice as many as the previous season. Not surprisingly the draw featured many sides new to the competition, as the winners from the lesser nations sorted themselves out for a crack at the seeded teams in the first round proper.

Albania's Albpetrol had lost their national cup final by the only goal to Partizani Tirana but qualified for the competition because Partizani completed the Albanian 'double'. It was Albpetrol's first venture into Europe but they should have not been overawed by the task of visiting another European newcomer from Liechtenstein. No other club from the principality had ever managed a win in Europe but Balzers exceeded all expectations by winning their home leg by 3-1 in front of a small crowd. They took that particular achievement one step further by containing Albpetrol in the return leg to become the first Liechtenstein club ever to win a European tie. It should be remembered that there is no national league in Liechtenstein and therefore the Cup-Winners' Cup is the only route to the continent – chances to gain European experience are therefore somewhat limited.

While Balzers hosted the smallest crowd of the round, Karpaty Lvov's first-leg encounter with Shelbourne attracted the biggest, with some 25,000 at the Druzjba Stadium. The FAI Cup winners flew out to the Ukraine by sharing a plane chartered jointly with Linfield from Northern Ireland, who travelled to Tbilisi for their Champions' Cup tie with Dynamo. The plane dropped off the side from the Republic when it stopped off in Lvov *en route* to the Georgian capital.

Karpaty – whose only previous European experience was in the same competition during the 1970–71 season won the match with a goal from Yevtushok. In the return leg at Tolka Park, Shelbourne pulled back the deficit after nine minutes when Greg Costello popped up to score a rare goal. There were no more goals in the first half and the excitable crowd had to wait to midway through the second half to let their emotions run riot when Mooney swooped to make it 2-0.

With the Ukrainians searching for a goal that would level the tie and give them a match-winning away goal, Izzi made it 3-0 for the Irishmen. Dmitro Masur scored a consolation goal for the visitors two minutes from time but Shelbourne had pulled off a rousing victory in front of 5,000 ecstatic home supporters. The celebrations were readily understandable given the fact that this was only Shelbourne's second win in a European competition – and the first had been as far back as the 1964–65 season!

Greg Costello (white shorts) scored the first goal in Shelbourne's 3-1 win over Karpaty.

Preliminary Round Results

Bangor McEvoy (24)	**Apoel Nicosia** Sotiriou (45)	1-1	4,500
Apoel Nicosia Mihajlovic (15), Pounas (69)	**Bangor** Glendining (4)	2-1	15,000

Apoel Nicosia win 3-2 on aggregate

Balzers Nushohr (17) Mario Frick (47, 55)	**Albpetrol** Poci (37)	3-1	500
Albpetrol	**Balzers**	0-0	2,500

Balzers win 3-1 on aggregate

FC Lugano Anddrioli (37, 83), Subiat (59), Fink (68), Penzavali (87)	**Neman Grodno**	5-0	4,000
Neman Grodno Solodobvnikov (61)	**FC Lugano** Mazurchik (70), Subiat (29)	2-1	4,000

FC Lugano win 6-2 on aggregate

Karpaty Lvov Yevtushok	**Shelbourne**	1-0	25,000
Shelbourne Costello (9), Mooney (67), Izzi (76)	**Karpaty Lvov** Masur (88)	3-1	5,000

Shelbourne win 3-2 on aggregate

Maccabi Haifa Mizrahi (39)	**Dudelange**	1-0	1,363
Dudelange Olhauzen (89)	**Maccabi Haifa** Mizrahi (25, 51 pen), Kondoroav (32), Atar (56), Holtzmann (74), Harazi (77)	1-6	3,500

Maccabi Haifa win 7-1 on aggregate

Nikol Tallinn	**Lillestrom SK** Karlsson (4), Gulbrandsen (8), Schiller (37), Bjarmann (42)	0-4	7,500
Lillestrom SK Gulbrandsen (35), Bergdolmo (38), Mjelde (40), MacManus (71)	**Nikol Tallinn** Arendas (70)	4-1	1,120

Lillestrom SK win 8-1 on aggregate

Publikum Celje	**OB Odense** Nedergaard (82)	0-1	2,000
OB Odense	**Publikum Celje**	0-0	2,525

OB Odense win 1-0 on aggregate

RAF Jelgava Kozlov (79)	**Havnar HB**	1-0	1,000
Havnar HB	**RAF Jelgava**	3-0	

Tie awarded to Havnar HB (3-0) as RAF Jelgava failed to show for second leg

Sliema Wanderers Gregory (67)	**Degerfors IF** Octosson (6, 30), Froberg (52)	1-3	4,000
Degerfors IF Octosson (3), Froberg (15), Eriksson (63 pen)	**Sliema Wanderers**	3-0	4,019

Degerfors IF win 6-1 on aggregate

Valur Gregory (52, 59), Larusson (70)	**MyPa** Rajamaki (34)	3-1	2,000
MyPa	**Valur** Larusson (68)	0-1	3,000

Valur win 4-1 on aggregate

VSZ Kosice Danko (20), Podegayev (40)	**Zhalgiris Vilnius**	2-0	6,000
Zhalgiris Vilnius	**VSZ Kosice** Durisa (13)	0-1	3,000

VSZ Kosice win 3-0 on aggregate

Three times Israeli cup winners Maccabi Haifa and Luxembourg's Dudelange were both making their European debuts when they met in the first leg at Haifa's Kiriat Eliezer stadium. In a tight game it was new £125,000 signing Alon Mizrahi who headed the only goal after 39 minutes. This was a great European debut for Mizrahi, who had joined the Haifa club in the close season, having been the league's top scorer for Bnei Yehoudah in 1992-93.

Two years a first division club, Dudelange might have started the second leg with a degree of optimism. If they did it was short-lived, as the visitors moved into a 2-0 lead before the interval. Mirzahi did much of the damage on the evening, giving Haifa a 25th-minute lead and playing a part in Kondoroav's goal just after the half-hour. Mirzahi also converted a penalty early in the second half and Atar, Holtzmann and Harazi swooped to give the Israeli side a 6-0 lead. Olhauzen scored an 89th-minute consolation goal for Dudelange and Maccabi Haifa went into the first round 7-1 on aggregate.

Northern Ireland's Bangor were playing only their second tie in Europe, against more seasoned campaigners Apoel Nicosia, and gave a very good account of themselves over the two legs. It was Ricky McEvoy from south of the border who gave them a 24th-minute lead. Cypriot international Andros Sotiriou – no stranger to scoring vital goals, as he had scored the winner in the Cypriot cup final the previous season – equalised seconds before the interval for the visitors to earn them a 1-1 draw. Fifteen thousand turned out at the Makarion stadium for the second leg and were recipients of a fourth-minute shock when defender Mark Glendining gave the Irish a surprise lead. It lasted just 11 minutes before Yugoslav Vesko Mihajlovic – in his first season with Apoel – equalised. Bangor continued to hold out but on 69 minutes Apoel stalwart Christodoulos Pounas produced a winner to put the Cypriot side through 3-2 on aggregate.

The ramshackle Skalna Ket stadium was the venue for Publikum Celje's European debut as they entertained Denmark's OB Odense knowing that a money-spinning trip to Highbury was

Preliminary Round Summary

P	HW	D	AW	HG	AG	TG
22	13	3	6	33*	23	56

*Does not include UEFA's 3-0 awarded tie

Ties won on aggregate:	11
Ties won on away goals:	0
Ties won on penalty kicks:	0
Highest aggregate game:	8-1 Lillestrom SK v Nikol Tallinin
Biggest home win:	5-0 FC Lugano v Neman Grodno
Biggest away win:	1-6 Dudelange v Maccabi Haifa

awaiting the winners. Publikum Celje's qualification was as cup runners-up thanks to a Slovenian league and cup double by Olimpija Ljubljana. What proved to be the only goal of the game and tie was scored eight minutes from time by OB's Steen Nedergaard.

After an absence of some 20 years Swiss cup winners FC Lugano returned to European competition with a bang when they demolished first-time Belarus cup winners Neman Grodno 5-0. A first-half goal by Brazilian Paulo Anddrioli set the scene for four goals in the second period, with Anddrioli again getting on the score sheet along with Nestor Subiat, Martin Fink and long-time defender Daniele Penzavali. The second leg was little more than a formality that Neman won with goals from Sergei Solodobvnikov and Yuri Mazurchik, but only after Subiat had given Lugano a first-half lead.

Norwegian cup winners Lillestrom produced the largest aggregate win, defeating Nikol Tallinn 8-1 overall. The tie was pretty much over after just eight minutes of the first leg in Estonia. Goals by Karlsson and Gulbrandsen put Lillestrom in a control that was total by the end of the first 45 minutes as Schiller and Bjarmann added two more. The Norwegians took their foot off the accelerator in the second half, which remained goalless. In the second leg the team from Belarus did only marginally better, limiting the half-time deficit to three goals and scoring a debut goal through Arendas after 70 minutes. However, the glory of that goal was short-lived when MacManus made it 4-1 on the night right from the restart.

The most curious tie involved Latvia's RAF Jelgava and 11 times Faeroe Island cup winners Havnar Boltfelag. RAF won the first leg in Jelgava by a single goal scored by Kozlov 11 minutes from time. The result was not a real surprise given that RAF had finished as double runner-up the previous season. What was a big surprise though was the fact that they failed to turn up for the second leg in Torshavn. UEFA awarded the tie 3-0 to Havnar HB but did not take any further action against the Latvian club.

A 34th-minute goal by Marko Rajamaki gave Finland's debutants Myllkosken Pallo – more affectionately MyPa – the lead in Reykjavik over Valur. But a second-half revival aided by two goals in six minutes by Anthony Karl Gregory and a third by Larusson gave Valur their first win in the Cup-Winners' Cup at their 13th attempt – lucky for some, unlucky for MyPa.

Bangor's Ricky McEvoy (left) and Aristos Aristodeous (Apoel) tussle for the ball.

Larusson struck again in the second leg for the only goal of the game and Valur went forward to the first round 4-1 on aggregate.

The prospect of a money-spinning encounter with holders Parma awaited the winners of the Sliema Wanderers–Degerfors tie. The Swedish side, competing in Europe after winning their first domestic competition, made short work of the first leg in Malta, taking an early lead through Ulf Octosson, who was on the scoresheet again before the interval. Dan Froberg made it 3-0 to the visitors soon after the restart and although Martin Gregory pulled one back shortly afterwards the return leg looked a formality. So it proved with Octosson and Froberg once again adding to the Maltese woe, this time in the first 15 minutes, before Eriksson completed the rout from the penalty spot in the second half to provide comfortable passage.

Slovakia's Kosice entertained Lithuania's Zhalgiris Vilnius in the first leg of their encounter and established a winning lead inside the first half with goals from former Dukla Prague star Ondreji Danko and teenager Viktor Podegayev. A goal by Peter Durisa early in the second leg sealed the progress of Kosice 3-0 on aggregate.

First Round

No club had ever successfully retained the Cup-Winners' Cup as Parma began their defence of the trophy they won at Wembley with a stuttering start in Sweden against preliminary round qualifiers Degerfors. With 18 minutes of the first leg remaining Berger gave the Swedish side the lead that looked certain to turn into a famous victory in front of over 10,000 fans. But two goals in the final three minutes from Colombian Faustino Asprilla rescued the holders and set them up for the return leg in Parma. The new lights of Italian football needed just two minutes to increase their hold on the tie – that's how long it took defender David Balleri to open the scoring, and Tomas Brolin's effort against his Swedish countrymen midway through the second half saw passage for Parma.

Parma's national rivals and the competition's number two seeds, Torino, travelled to Norway for their 76th European encounter and established a two-goal advantage for the return with Lillestrom in Turin. Andrea Silenzi opened the scoring in the first half and midfield player Robert Jarni notched the second early in the second half. The six-foot frame of Silenzi gave Torino the lead on the stroke of half-time in the second leg, but the game turned immediately the second half started when Sinigaglia pulled a goal back. Ten minutes later Mons Ivar Mjelde had the Italians into a sweat when he scored Lillestrom's second on the night. A third goal for the Norwegians would have put them through on the away-goals rule but the Italians' defence held on to qualify 3-2 on aggregate.

The difficulties that were to afflict number three seeds Real Madrid in their domestic campaign were not evident when they entertained FC Lugano. More used to playing in the Champions' Cup down the years, Real were making their first appearance in the Cup-Winners' Cup for over 10 years. The Bernabeu Stadium was only half full to see them take a 3-0 lead. A goal just before the interval by £2.5m signing Peter Dubovsky knocked the stuffing out of the Swiss side before Michel converted a 66th-minute penalty. An own goal by Walter Fernandex completed the win. The goal was all the more embarrassing for Fernandex who, as his name suggests, is a Spanish national.

The second leg in Switzerland proved equally decisive. A goal late in the first half by Hierro moved Real into a 4-0 overall lead and despite a goal early in the second half by Subiat, two by Zamorano completed the rout for the Spanish club.

One of the most explosive ties of the round involved Standard Liege and Cardiff City. The Welsh club playing in the English second division had to reshuffle their side extensively because of foreign player stipulations and included 59-cap Kevin Ratcliffe in their line-up – nine years after he had previously lifted the Cup-Winners' Cup as captain of Everton. Roberto Bisconti put the 1982 finalists ahead in the 13th minute, but Welsh teenager

Joe Miller (left) opened the scoring against Valur at Pittodrie.

Anthony Bird robbed Brazilian sweeper Andre Cruz to level matters six minutes before the interval. Then he silenced the home supporters in the second half when he volleyed home a cross at the far post. His joy was short-lived though as the Belgians hit back with four quick goals through Marc Wilmots (two), Andre Cruz and Patrick Asselman. Any hopes of a famous fight-back in the second leg were dashed after 14 minutes when Marc Wilmots scored with a powerful far-post header. Stephen Williams, just 18 and making his debut in the Cardiff goal, did superbly well to stop Steve Baddeley's misdirected headed back-pass, only for Mohamet Lashaf to follow up and make it 2-0, which is how it remained until the second half.

When the players re-emerged for the second period the game was held up as the substitute Liege goalkeeper Munaron, who had replaced Bodart after 17 minutes, complained to Italian referee Cesari that the home supporters were throwing missiles at him. That didn't stop Roberto Bisconti from making it 3-0 for Liege just five minutes after the game was able to restart. Robbie James evoked memories of better days when he scored with a stunning volley ten minutes later.

Arsenal entered the competition having been beaten on penalties by Valencia in their only previous entry in the competition, in 1980. That run to the final – which was drawn 0-0 – had been done without incurring a defeat. The Gunners could therefore boast that they had an undefeated record in the Cup-Winners' Cup. However, that particular claim might have been blown to pieces inside the first four minutes of their game in Denmark against OB. Twice in that period the Danes overwhelmed Arsenal. An ill-timed tackle by Andy Linighan on Jess Thorup in the penalty area after only two minutes and 21 seconds was adjudged to be a deliberate foul by Turkish referee Kakar. Thorup got up and dusted himself down before firing the penalty against David Seaman's post and to the safety of a goal kick. Linighan – whose headed goal in the last minute of extra time in the FA Cup replay had won the trophy for the Gunners – was responsible again for a gross error when he totally under-hit a backpass to his keeper. The ball was picked up by the alert and advancing Allan Nielsen, who then shot wide with only Seaman to beat.

OB finally took a deserved lead after 18 minutes although the goal had an element of luck about it, when Brian Skaarup took the return ball from a short corner on the right and drilled a shot low into the Arsenal goalmouth, where it struck the luckless Keown and flew past Seaman into the net. Curiously, the goal seemed to calm the North London side's nerves and they slowly started to wrest control of the midfield. They equalised on 35 minutes when Ian Wright was on hand to tap in a rebound from Nigel Winterburn's free-kick. Wright's strike was significant because it was Arsenal's 100th goal in European competition. The winner came midway through the first half when Paul Merson beat two defenders before driving past Lars Hogh from 15 yards.

In the second leg at Highbury, Arsenal produced a lacklustre display which provided a constant source of frustration to the home crowd. OB, cheered on by a large contingent of travelling support, earned a creditable draw and might have snatched a winner and extra time at the very least had Allan Nielsen not missed a simple chance two minutes after the interval.

Arsenal's Paul Merson takes control in Odense.

Arsenal took the lead in the second half when Kevin Campbell headed in Paul Davis' free-kick. OB – one of three full-time professional clubs in Denmark – equalised four minutes from the end when Nielsen's initial shot was saved by Seaman, but he was first to react to follow up to bury the rebound into the back of the net from close range.

Two goals by Eoin Jess added to a ninth-minute lead by Duncan Shearer gave Aberdeen a 3-0 win in Rekjavik over Valur. The return leg in Aberdeen looked set to be nothing more than a shooting match but the Icelandic side put on a brave rearguard action that made the cakewalk a long time in coming. Joe Miller finally broke down the resistance in the 51st minute from close range after Kane's long cross had been fumbled to him by Sigurdsson. Jess accepted Stewart McKimmie's pass to drive Aberdeen's second goal, and nine minutes later completed his second double against Valur with a powerful drive. In between Jess's brace Brian Irvine headed a third from close range.

A goal for Besiktas by Sergen Yalcin two minutes into their match with Kosice gave the Turkish entrants the perfect start to their Cup-Winners' Cup campaign. With 20 minutes remaining things still looked grim for the Slovakian side, but then two penalty goals in nine minutes by Danko changed the tie's complexion and they held on for a 2-1 win. Besiktas needed an early goal in the second leg to turn the pressure from them to Kosice. The goal was not early, but was perfectly timed a minute before the interval, when Metin Tekin struck to level the aggregate scores. With the advantage of an away goal Besiktas could afford to keep things tight, and with the visitors more committed to attack Metin Tekin struck again to give Besiktas a 3-2 aggregate win.

Eighty-eight minutes was how long GKS Katowice held out in the Stadium of Light before Rui Aguas scored to give Benfica a slender win, which was whittled away on the stroke of half-time in the second leg when Kucz scored. Vitor Paneira equalised on the night for the Eagles to see them through to the second round, 2-1 on aggregate.

As Rui Aguas swooped for the Eagles, Borisov was doing the same for Torpedo in Moscow in their first leg encounter with

First Round Results

Apoel Nicosia	Paris Saint-Germain	0-1	13,000
	Sassus (78)		
Paris Saint-Germain	Apoel Nicosia	2-0	13,500
Le Guen (1), Gravelaine (32)			

Paris Saint-Germain win 3-0 on aggregate

Bayer Leverkusen	FC Boby Brno	2-0	6,100
Hapal (32), Thom (66)			
FC Boby Brno	Bayer Leverkusen	0-3	10,105
	Kirsten (16), Fischer (57), Worns (75)		

Bayer Leverkusen win 5-0 on aggregate

Benfica	GKS Katowice	1-0	30,000
Rui Aguas (88)			
GKS Katowice	Benfica	1-1	7,000
Kucz (45)	Vitor Paneira (70)		

Benfica win 2-1 on aggregate

CSKA Sofia	Balzers	8-0	35,000
Shishkov (12, 21, 57, 69), Andenov (41, 52), Nankov (67 pen, 80)			
Balzers	CSKA Sofia	1-3	1,200
Kuster (63)	Andenov (31), Tanev (54), Ciric (90)		

CSKA Sofia win 11-1 on aggregate

Degerfors IF	Parma	1-2	10,482
Berger (72)	Asprilla (87, 88)		
Parma	Degerfors IF	2-0	17,000
Balleri (2), Brolin (67)			

Parma win 4-1 on aggregate

FC Tirol-Innsbruck	Ferencvaros	3-0	7,500
Danek (48), Westerthaler (58), Carracedo (65)			
Ferencvaros	FC Tirol-Innsbruck	1-2	12,000
Detari (50)	Westerthaler (19, 90)		

FC Tirol-Innsbruck win 5-1 on aggregate

Hajduk Split	Ajax	1-0	10,000
Mornar (44)			

Match played in Ljubljana

Ajax	Hajduk Split	6-0	40,000
R. De Boer (11), Davids (36, 76), Litmanen (57), F. De Boer (61), Pettersson (71)			

Ajax win 6-1 on aggregate

Lillestrom SK	Torino	0-2	5,056
	Silenzi (26), Jarni (58)		
Torino	Lillestrom SK	1-2	25,000
Silenzi (45)	Sinigaglia (48), Mjelde (58)		

Torino win 3-2 on aggregate

OB Odense	Arsenal	1-2	9,850
Keown (own goal 18)	Wright (35), Merson (68)		
Arsenal	OB Odense	1-1	25,689
Campbell (52)	Nielsen (86)		

Arsenal win 3-2 on aggregate

Panathinaikos	Shelbourne	3-0	30,000
Donis (13), Saravakos (37), K. Warzycha (48)			
Shelbourne	Panathinaikos	1-2	2,000
Mooney (86)	Georgiadis (26), Saravakos (57)		

Panathinaikos win 5-1 on aggregate

Real Madrid	FC Lugano	3-0	37,600
Dubovsky (44), Michel (66 pen), Fernandez (Own goal 70)			
FC Lugano	Real Madrid	1-3	8,000
Subiat (62)	Hierro (40), Zamorano (78, 87)		

Real Madrid win 6-1 on aggregate

Standard Liege	Cardiff City	5-2	12,000
Bisconti (13), Wilmots (63, 84), Andre Cruz (71 pen), Asselman (76)	Bird (39, 62)		
Cardiff City	Standard Liege	1-3	6,096
James (59)	Wilmots (14), Lashaf (36), Bisconti (50)		

Standard Liege win 8-3 on aggregate

Torpedo Moscow	Maccabi Haifa	1-0	10,000
Borisov (88)			
Maccabi Haifa	Torpedo Moscow	3-1	13,000
Mizrahi (6), Petz (71), Holzmann (85)	Kalaychev (12)		

Maccabi Haifa win 3-2 on aggregate

Univ. Craiova	Havnar HB	4-0	9,000
Craioveanu (47), Gane (58,71), Calin (82)			
Havnar HB	Univ. Craiova	0-3	276
	Gane (27, 33), Vase (76)		

Universitatea Craiova win 7-0 on aggregate

Valur	Aberdeen	0-3	656
	D. Shearer (9), Jess (28, 58)		
Aberdeen	Valur	4-0	10,000
Miller (51), Jess (60, 69), Irvine (65)			

Aberdeen win 7-0 on aggregate

VSZ Kosice	Besiktas	2-1	6,000
Danko (70 pen, 79 pen)	Sergen Yalcin (2)		
Besiktas	VSZ Kosice	2-0	27,000
Metin Tekin (44, 72)			

Besiktas win 3-2 on aggregate

Maccabi Haifa. The second leg provided plenty of excitement for the capacity crowd, who saw Mizrahi continue his preliminary round scoring feats by squaring the aggregate scores after just six minutes. However, Kalaychev restored Torpedo's aggregate advantage six minutes later and despite Petz's 71st-minute goal it looked like Maccabi would be eliminated on the away goals rule. But in a dramatic finale Holzmann made it 3-1 and the Israeli side held on to claim their second European scalp and a place in the second round.

Paris Saint-Germain, who had turned down the chance to take part in the Champions' Cup following the exclusion of Marseille, were another team to score a winner late in their game, defender Jean-Lau Sassus netting with 12 minutes remaining against Apoel in Nicosia. Following the sequence of other late winners, the home side took little time to unhinge Apoel in the return, captain Paul Le Guen scoring inside the first 60 seconds. Xavier Gravelaine's strike just half an hour later sealed the tie for the French leaders.

Much of Bayer Leverkusen's experience in Europe has come in the past eight years or so and having won the German Cup for the first time ever in 1993 they found themselves in the Cup-Winners' Cup for the first time. Their opponents FC Boby Brno has made their Cup-Winners' Cup debut in the 1960–61 season under the name of Zbrojovaka Brno. Two goals either side of the interval gave Bayer a clear advantage in front of a surprisingly small crowd in the suburbs of Koln. Despite the two-goal deficit, Brno approached the return leg with a degree of confidence, but Kirsten's early strike for Bayer made the difficult impossible and Fischer and Worns in the second half simply reflected the Germans' dominance.

Having become the first club from Liechtenstein to win a match and then qualify for the next round, Balzers were happy at drawing of CSKA of Sofia in the first round. With some 120 European encounters behind them the Bulgarian cup winners were always firm favourites to progress further without too much trouble. Thirty-five thousand made it a night to remember for the visitors who were dealt with in a no-nonsense manner, Shishkov netting four of CSKA's eight goals. In the second leg the part-timers limited CSKA to two goals before they celebrated with a goal from Kuster. But it was more like Kuster's last stand as Ciric added a third for the visitors to complete a not surprising aggregate win by 11-1.

Ferencvaros were Hungary's representatives in the first Cup-Winners' Cup competition in the 1960–61 season, and for their 28th match in the tournament they went over the border to face FC Tirol-Innsbruck. With no score at the interval Ferencvaros fell apart in the opening 20 minutes of the second as Danek, Westerthaler and Carracedo gave the Austrians a three-goal advantage. Needing an early goal in the second leg FTC conceded one when Westerthaler scored, and although Detari levelled it on the night early in the second half Westerthaler snatched another goal at the death for the Austrian side, who raised a few eyebrows at their progression.

The acceptance of Croatia's cup winners Hajduk Split into the competition came at the eleventh hour, because of the troubles in the former Yugoslavia. As it was they had to agree to play their home ties in Ljubljana, but more than 10,000 turned out for their encounter with former holders Ajax. A goal a minute before half-time by Mornar gave the Croatians a morale-boosting if slender win to take to Amsterdam two weeks later. That aggregate lead lasted just 11 minutes of the second leg when Ronald De Boer shot home. A goal by Davids gave the Dutch club the advantage for the second half and four goals in a 19-minute spell gave Ajax a comfortable 6-0 win on the night.

Havnar Boltfelag's progression in the Cup-Winners' Cup continued, at least for the first 45 minutes, in the first round when they did marvellously well to keep Romanian's Universitatea Craiova at bay. That situation lasted only two minutes into the second period when 'U' took the lead through Craioveanu. Two goals by Gane and a late strike by Calin gave the scoreline an air of respectability for the home side. Gane's double was repeated in the second leg, this time midway through the first half and Vase added a third on the night in the later stages of the game, which was witnessed by just 276 spectators.

Having travelled and won in Georgia in the preliminary round, Shelbourne had an eastward journey for their first-round tie. Spiros Louis Stadium in Athens was the venue for their encounter with Panathinaikos, where the home side ran out comfortable 3-0 winners. The Greeks took a two-goal lead in the second leg and Mooney scored a consolation goal for the home side four minutes from time.

Top Scorers after Preliminary and First Rounds

4   Gane (Univ Craiova), Jess (Aberdeen), Mizrahi (Maccabi Haifa), Shishkov (CSKA Sofia)
3   Andenov (CSKA Sofia), Danko (VSZ Kosice), Octosson (Degerfors IF), Subiat (FC Lugano), Westerthaler (FC Tirol-Innsbruck), Wilmots (Standard Liege)
2   Anddrioli (FC Lugano), Asprilla (Parma), Bird (Cardiff City), Bisconti (Standard Liege), Davids (Ajax), Froberg (Degerfors IF), Gregory (Valur), Gulbrandsen (Lillestrom SK), Holtzmann (Maccabi Haifa), Larusson (Valur), Metin Tekin (Besiktas), Mjelde (Lillestrom SK), Mooney (Shelbourne), Nankov (CSKA Sofia), Saravakos (Panathinaikos), Silenzi (Torino), Zamorano (Real Madrid)

First Round Summary

P	HW	D	AW	HG	AG	TG
32	17	2	13	62	37	99

Ties won on aggregate: 16
Ties won on away goals: 0
Ties won on penalty kicks: 0

Highest aggregate game: 11-1   CSKA Sofia v Balzers
Biggest home win: 8-0   CSKA Sofia v Balzers
Biggest away win: 0-3   FC Boby Brno v Bayer Leverkusen
    Havnar HB v Univ Craiova
    Valur v Aberdeen

Second Round

The second round produced several surprising results in individual games and over two legs as a number of teams were given frights of differing degrees. Parma's defence of the trophy took them to Israel to face Maccabi Haifa and another far from convincing qualification. Another capacity crowd looked to have witnessed a goalless draw until Tomas Brolin stole up in the final seconds to snatch a victory for the Italians – so far so good. The fact that fewer than 10,000 turned up for the return leg in Parma showed the confidence that the home support felt about the progression of their side into the quarter-finals. But when Alon Mizrahi scored his fifth goal in the competition so far, six minutes into the second half, the game turned into a tense affair. There was no further score as the game entered and ended extra time. With the aggregate and away scores level the penalty shootout went Parma's way by 3-1 and the gallant Israelis were out, just.

If Parma had a fright in their tie then their fellow Italians had a near heart attack in their first leg with Aberdeen in Turin. Nine minutes had gone when Paatelainen put the Scottish side ahead and when Jess made it 2-0 for the visitors on 24 minutes the second seeds looked to be on the way out. But with half-time looming Raffaele Segio – generally regarded as a make-weight in the transfer deal that took Gregucci to Rome from Lazio in 1989 – popped up to add real weight to the attack and pull one back for Torino. Having gained a slight psychological advantage, the Italians came out fired up for a second half that saw them equalise through Daniele Fortunato early on and record a slender win thanks to a goal from Uruguayan Carlos Aguilera two minutes from time.

Even so, Aberdeen had two away goals in the bank and the knowledge that they had what it takes to dismantle a tough Italian defence hampered by the absence through injury and suspension of Croatian full-back Robert Jarni and Uruguayan striker Enzo Francescoli. Those thoughts looked well-founded when the former Blackburn and Watford player Lee Richardson put the Dons into the lead after just 12 minutes. The Serie A side's chances looked to have floundered further when Gregucci was carried off after 19 minutes suffering from concussion and a head wound that needed ten stitches. However, Italian Under-21 international Benito Carbone started to pull the strings for the visitors, scoring after 39 minutes and setting up a second half winner for Andrea Silenzi to give the Italian cup holders a 2-1 win on the night, 5-3 overall, and a fully deserved progression into the third round.

Mehmet Ozdilek's goal four minutes before the interval looked to have put the Turks of Besiktas in the driving seat in their tie with Ajax. But a typically powerful goal from Frank Rijkaard followed by Ronald De Boer's winner nine minutes from time gave the three-time European champions a slender lead to defend in the hostile atmosphere of the Inonu Stadium in Istanbul. Any heat in the game was taken out early on by the cool finishing of striker Jari Litmanen, who opened the scoring in the first half and added a further two in the second to notch his first European hat-trick. Pettersson completed the scoring on the night to give the Dutch a well deserved 6-1 aggregate triumph.

Carbone – scored a priceless equaliser against Aberdeen.

After their troubles in Wales, Standard Liege were rewarded with another trip to the British mainland for the second round. Arsenal, inspired by the mercurial Paul Merson, established a 3-0 lead with Merson scoring the second himself at the start of the second half with a magnificent free-kick, curled past Jacky Munaron from 25 yards. At 37 years of age Munaron – a former international who had been recalled to the Standard line-up after regular number one Gilbert Bodart had been ruled out the previous day with an ankle injury – needed the experience of his years to keep Arsenal at bay on other occasions but he had been helpless to prevent Ian Wright's stab past him from Martin Keown's cross. Keown's role of man-marking Marc Wilmots was so effective that the pacey winger hardy had a sight on goal not only at Highbury but in the return leg. Arsenal made the second leg a mere formality when Wright chipped Munaron just moments after the width of a post had prevented Paul Davis scoring a rare goal. The Gunners, though, were well worth their victory.

A booking for Wright in the first leg, was neutralised by the cushion of a three-goal advantage, so manager George Graham decided to leave the club's top-scorer out for the return in Liege. Most expected a typically resilient performance from the Gunners, but even without their most lethal weapon they recorded their biggest win in Europe since the 7-1 thrashing of Dinamo Bacu in the 1970 Fairs Cup winning season. A lucky omen perhaps?

Arsenal's 7-0 win on the night, 10-0 overall, gave the Belgian side's Dutch manager, Arie Haan, food for thought. After their encounter in the first round with Cardiff and following their pairing with Arsenal, Haan said, 'The English way is not my favourite. Cardiff City could not play football so they elbowed and kicked my players. I think all British clubs play the same way.'

Alan Smith put Arsenal ahead after two minutes, volleying home after a one-two between Merson and Ian Selley, and Selley's first senior goal was smartly taken after Munaron pushed out Merson's mis-hit shot. Munaron's failure to hold Campbell's header allowed Tony Adams to slam home from a corner. Three goals up, and with the dressing room beckoning for the home side, Campbell made it 4-0 after David Seaman's long goal-kick had been fluffed by defender Philippe Leonard leaving the Arsenal striker a free to run on goal.

If Standard had reorganised during the interval it didn't show in the second half as Merson piled on the agony, side-footing home Eddie McGoldrick's right-wing cross. Not surprisingly Arsenal took their foot off the pedal but even so Campbell added his second of the night from McGoldrick's pass before the Republic of Ireland winger set off on a run that took him half the length of the pitch before he blasted the ball past the bemused Standard keeper from the right side of the area for the goal of the night. Coach Haan couldn't manage any more twists of the tongue and was sacked by the club's board before the week was out.

If Arsenal had it easy then CSKA had a much more difficult task in the second round, having been paired with the Eagles of Lisbon. In the Stadium of Light, Benfica were presented with the lead when defender Boban Babunski put through his own goal midway through the first half. Rui Costa added a second before the interval but Ivailo Andonov looked to have altered the tie's complexion when he pulled a goal back for the Bulgarians on the hour. Benfica continued to search for a third goal and it came with the final whistle, Swede Stefan Schwarz doing the damage. So the result was 3-1 to Benfica and it was the same in the second leg, with Costa, Joao Pinto and Yuran adding to CSKA's woe, despite another Andonov goal.

Having disposed of one famous European name, FC Tirol, Innsbruck were rewarded with another in the form of Real Madrid. With the Spanish side troubled by financial and playing problems on the domestic scene, the Austrians must have fancied their chances at pocketing another famous scalp and a few more schillings. That dream lasted just 15 minutes, which was how

Frank Rijkaard scored the Ajax equaliser against Besiktas.

long it took for Alfonso to shoot his side into an away lead. The score stayed that way until midway through the second half when the home fans were given a goal to cheer, Streiter converting a penalty kick. At 1-1 Madrid wasted little time in the return in the Bernabeu, Michel firing Real into a sixth-minute lead. Goals early in the second half by the 'Vulture' Butragueno and Alfonso dismissed the Austrians and saw Madrid through to the quarter-finals.

In Athens, Panathinaikos entertained Bayer Leverkusen and two goals in two minutes just before the interval sent the teams in level. Paulo Sergio looked to have given the Germans a lead to take in at half-time but just as everyone was contemplating the whistle Kristof Warzycha equalised. Two goals in seven minutes by Thom and Kirsten after the restart put Bayer in control, which was made total when Hapal made it 4-1. The Greeks, needing to score at least four clear goals to stay in the competition, got off to a penalty start at the beginning of the second leg in Leverkusen, Saravakos converting. Georgiadis made it 2-0 in the second half but a brief rally by Bayer enabled Kirsten to score a tie-winning goal late on.

Second Round Summary

P	HW	D	AW	HG	AG	TG
16	6	1	9	23	31	54

Ties won on aggregate: 7
Ties won on away goals: 0
Ties won on penalty kicks: 1

Highest aggregate game: 10-0 Arsenal v Standard Liege
Biggest home win: 4-0 Paris Saint-Germain v Univ. Craiova
Biggest away win: 0-7 Standard Liege v Arsenal

Top Scorers – All Rounds

5 Andonov (CSKA Sofia), Jess (Aberdeen), Mizrahi (Maccabi Haifa)
4 Gane (Univ. Craiova), Litmanen (Ajax), Shishkov (CSKA Sofia)
3 Campbell (Arsenal), Danko (VSZ Kosice), Guerin (PSG), Kirsten (Bayer Leverkusen), Merson (Arsenal), Saravakos (Panathinaikos), Silenzi (Torino), Subiat (FC Lugano), Westerthaler (FC Tirol-Innsbruck), Wilmots (Standard Liege), Wright (Arsenal)

French league leaders Paris Saint-Germain continued to transfer their domestic form into Europe. They made short work of Universitatea Craiova with two goals in each half to take a substantial four-goal advantage to Romania, where Guerin added a further two to the one he scored in the first leg to give Paris Saint-Germain a 6-0 aggregate victory.

Second Round Results

Ajax   **Besiktas**   2-1   42,000
Rijkaard (60), R. De Boer (81)   Mehmet Ozdilek (41)
Besiktas   **Ajax**   0-4   27,000
Litmanen (19, 71, 74), Pettersson (77)
Ajax win 6-1 on aggregate

Arsenal   **Standard Liege**   3-0   25,258
Wright (39, 63), Merson (50)
Standard Liege   **Arsenal**   0-7   12,000
Smith (2), Selley (20), Adams (36), Campbell (41, 80), Merson (72), McGoldrick (82)
Arsenal win 10-0 on aggregate

Benfica   **CSKA Sofia**   3-1   40,000
Babunski (own goal 26), Rui Costa (37), Schwarz (90)   Andonov (60)
CSKA Sofia   **Benfica**   1-3   25,000
Andonov (56)   Costa (37), Joao Pinto (73), Yuran (89)
Benfica win 6-2 on aggregate

FC Tirol-Innsbruck   **Real Madrid**   1-1   10,000
Streiter (69 pen)   Alfonso (15)
Real Madrid   **FC Tirol-Innsbruck**   3-0   19,300
Michel (6), Butragueno (46), Alfonso (65)
Real Madrid win 4-1 on aggregate

Maccabi Haifa   **Parma**   0-1   13,000
Brolin (90)
Parma   **Maccabi Haifa**   0-1   9,312
Mizrahi (51)
Parma win 3-1 on penalties. 1-1 on aggregate

Panathinaikos   **Bayer Leverkusen**   1-4   60,000
K. Warzycha (44)   Paulo Sergio (42), Thom (52), Kirsten (59), Hapal (72)
Bayer Leverkusen   **Panathinaikos**   1-2   15,000
Kirsten (83)   Saravakos (6 pen), Georgiadis (66)
Bayer Leverkusen win 5-3 on aggregate

Paris Saint-Germain   **Univ. Craiova**   4-0   20,000
Guerin (12), Ginola (17 pen), Bita (own goal 58), Valdo (71)
Univ. Craiova   **Paris Saint-Germain**   0-2   20,000
Guerin (29, 48)
Paris Saint-Germain win 6-0 on aggregate

Torino   **Aberdeen**   3-2   25,000
Segio (45), Fortunato (51), Aguilera (88)   Paatelainen (9), Jess (24)
Aberdeen   **Torino**   1-2   21,655
Richardson (12)   Carbone (39), Silenzi (53)
Torino win 5-3 on aggregate

Quarter-Finals

The Cup-Winners' Cup has normally been regarded as the weaker of the three European competitions. This time, however, the quarter-final stage had one of the strongest line-ups ever. Ajax, Arsenal, Benfica, Bayer Leverkusen, Parma, Real Madrid, Torino and Paris Saint-Germain have their own places in European football folklore and at the time of the first leg encounters all eight teams were in the hunt for their respective league championships with the likes of Ajax, Benfica and PSG looking likely to take titles. The eight qualifiers were also among the top 11 seeds when the draw for the first round was made.

Due to the television coverage of the UEFA Champions' League most games were moved from their more normal Wednesday spots to the Tuesday or Thursday. In the first encounter 85,000 saw Benfica and Bayer Leverkusen play out an exciting game in Lisbon's Stadium of Light. After a first half that somehow remained goalless, despite several chances, the German side took the lead. The influential Becker won a corner on the left which was swung in to the near post, where Marcus Happe lost his marker Veloso to flick the ball off the top of his head and past a shocked Neno.

Roared on by a passionate crowd, Benfica set out in search of an equaliser which came with virtually the last kick of the game just as Bayer had thought it was won. Joao Pinto crossed from the right, Romanian Ionut Lupescu didn't get any real distance on his clearing header and the ball fell to Vitor Paneira, who had two attempts at goal. The second was more fortunate – taking a deflection that fell at the feet of substitute Isaias, who thrashed the ball home despite looking suspiciously offside. The Brazilian's goal was his 11th in European competition putting him in the top six of Benfica's all-time Euro scoring list, but still some way behind Eusebio's tally of 57!

Bayer returned to Leverkusen for the second leg optimistic that they had the firepower needed to dispose of the Portuguese, whom they regarded as lucky to earn the late first leg draw. And with just under an hour gone of the return matters seemed well in hand. A first-half goal from Ulf Kirsten provided breathing space and when Bernd Schuster slotted home Thom's precisely weighted pass on 58 minutes Bayer looked to be home and dry. But Schuster's goal marked the start of an amazing three-minute spell in which the visitors drew level. First a neat back-heel by Rui Costa provided Abel Xavier with the space he needed to drill the ball high into Heinen's net from 22 yards. Then poor marking at the near post gave Joao Pinto the space he required to twist and head home Rui Costa's corner. What had turned into a well-planned lead had rapidly metamorphosed into a nightmare, with the Portuguese now having the away goal advantage.

Accordingly Leverkusen upped the pace of their game and kept Neno in the Benfica goal occupied. But in over-committing themselves Bayer fell behind. Having won possession Rui Costa's pass inside found the Russian defender Vasily Kolkov breaking perfectly from deep and taking the ball in his stride to score from 15 yards. Bayer, having been two goals to the good, now needed two goals to level and get into a winning position and within five minutes of Kolkov's goal they had achieved just that in what was turning into a real topsy-turvy thriller. With the match clock showing 80 minutes played Kirsten stooped to glance his header, from substitute Paulo Sergio's cross, past Neno, and two minutes later Pavel Hapal headed home after Schuster's corner had been flicked on into his path.

Now, with just eight minutes remaining, it was Benfica's turned to lay siege to the Bayer goal and their pressure paid off when Joao Pinto rode several tackles to set up Kolkov again. His first time flick with the outside of his boot had enough pace to find the net to level the scores at 4-4 on the night and achieve a memorable away-goals win for Benfica.

Arsenal – the last surviving British club in European competition – travelled to Turin for a quarter-final against a Torino club riddled with debt and facing the spotlight not for just matters on the field but in the accountancy books, where a debt of

Emilio Butragueno – 'The Vulture' – swooped to score a shock goal for Real Madrid against Paris Saint-Germain in the Parc.

Quarter-Finals

Ajax	Parma	0-0

Att: 40,000 *Ref:* Don (Eng)
Ajax: Van der Sar, Silooy, Blind, Oulinda, F. de Boer, Rijkaard, Litmanen, Davids (Van Vossen 72), Petersen (Overmars 63), Pettersson, R. de Boer
Parma: Bucci, Maltagliati (Balleri 77), Pin, Apolloni, Matrecano, Brolin, Sensini, Zola, Crippa, Asprilla, Melli
Yellow Cards: R. de Boer and Blind (Ajax), Apolloni (Parma)

Parma	Ajax	2-0

Minotti (15), Brolin (49)
Att: 24,212. *Ref:* van den Wijngaert (Bel)
Parma: Bucci, Benarrivo, Minotti, Maltagliati, Di Chiara (Balleri 78), Brolin, Pin (Zoratto 78), Sensini, Zola, Crippa, Asprilla
Ajax: Van der Sar, Silooy, Blind, F. de Boer, Rijkaard (Petersen 56), Van den Brom (R. de Boer 56), Van Vossen, Davids, Seedorf, Pettersson, Overmars
Parma win 2-0 on aggregate

Benfica	Bayer Leverkusen	1-1

Isaias (89) Happe (64)
Att: 85,000. *Ref:* Pairetto (Ita)
Benfica: Neno, Abel Xavier, Mozer, Helder (Isaias 65), Veloso, Vitor Paneira, Rui Costa, Willam, Joao Pinto, Yuran, Ailton (Cesar Brito 73)
Bayer Leverkusen: Vollborn, Worns, Lupescu, Melzig, Happe, Becker (Fischer 78), Foda, Tolkmitt, Thom (Rydlewicz 88), Hapal, Paulo Sergio
Yellow Cards: Mozer (Benfica), Melzig and Foda (Bayer)

Bayer Leverkusen	Benfica	4-4

Kirsten (24, 80), Schuster (58), Abel Xavier (59), Joao Pinto (60), Hapal (82) Kolkov (77, 86)
Att: 21,000. *Ref:* McCluskey (Sco)
Bayer Leverkusen: Heinen, Lupescu, Worns, Happe, Becker (Fischer 66), Foda, Schuster, Hapal, Tolkmitt (Paulo Sergio 66), Kirsten, Thom
Benfica: Neno, Willam, Abel Xavier, Schwarz, Paneira, Helder, Kolkov, Rui Costa (Hernani 86), Isaias, Yuran, Joao Pinto.
Yellow Card: Lupescu (Bayer)
5-5 on aggregate. Benfica win on away goals rule

Real Madrid	Paris Saint-Germain	0-1

Weah (32)
Att: 62,000 *Ref:* Heynemann (Ger)
Real Madrid: Buyo, Chendo, Sanchis (Morales 57), Alkorta, Lasa (Prosinecki 82), Michel, Ramis, Milla, Dubovsky, Luis Enrique, Zamorano
Paris Saint-Germain: Lama, Sassus, Ricardo Gomes, Roche, Colleter, Fournier, Guerin, Llacer, Valdo, Weah (Bravo 84), Ginola (Gravelaine 88)

Paris Saint-Germain	Real Madrid	1-1

Ricardo (52) Butragueno (20)
Att: 45,000. *Ref:* Tsjoek (Bls)
Paris Saint-Germain: Lama, Sassus, Roche, Ricardo Gomes, Colleter, Fournier, Le Guen, Llacer, Valdo, Weah (Gravelaine 88), Ginola (Braco 77)
Real Madrid: Buyo, Velasco, Alkorta, Sanchis, Luis Enrique, Michel, Hierro, Prosinecki (Dubovsky 64), Martin Vazquez (Lasa 73), Butragueno, Zamorano
Yellow Card: Velasco (Real Madrid)
Paris Saint-Germain win 2-1 on aggregate

Torino	Arsenal	0-0

Att: 32,480. *Ref:* Quiniou (Fra)
Torino: Galli, Sottil (Sinigaglia (61), Jarni, Cois, Gregucci, Fusi, Mussi, Fortunato, Silenzi (Carbone 68), Francescoli, Venturin
Arsenal: Seaman, Dixon, Winterburn, Davis (Selley 83), Bould, Adams, Jensen, Campbell, Smith, Merson, Hillier

Arsenal	Torino	1-0

Adams (66)
Att: 34, 670. *Ref:* Blankenstein (Hol)
Arsenal: Seaman, Dixon, Winterburn, Davis, Bould, Adams, Jensen (Keown 87), Wright, Smith, Merson, Hillier (Selley 15)
Torino: Galli, Annoni, Fortunato, Fusi, Gregucci, Sinigaglia (Poggi 71), Cois, Mussi, Venturin (Jarni 26), Silenzi, Francescoli
Yellow Cards: Fortunato and Gregucci (Torino)
Red Card: Gregucci (Torino)
Arsenal win 1-0 on aggregate

Dates
1st Leg 1 March: Benfica-Bayer.
 2 March: Torino-Arsenal.
 3 March: Ajax-Parma, Real-Paris Sanit-Germain
2nd Leg 15 March: Bayer-Benfica, Arsenal-Torino, Paris Saint-Germain-Real Madrid.
 16 March: Parma-Ajax

£14m sat alongside allegations of corruption which had prompted an official UEFA enquiry. Turin was a happy hunting ground for the Gunners. It was there that they recorded a last-minute semi-final win over Juventus to gain passage to the 1980 Cup-Winners' Cup final. Torino for their part had only encountered English opposition once, when they lost to Leeds United in the 1965–66 Cup-Winners' Cup competition. The game itself was hardly a classic but will rank as one of the best results in Arsenal's history as they held steadfast for a 0-0 draw, limiting the Italians to very few chances. Manager George Graham played a perfect tactical game which might well have ended in a victory. The main talking point was the absence of top scorer Ian Wright from attack to accommodate the side's revised tactical formation.

Although chances were few and far between they were there. The first fell on the half hour to Arsenal. Paul Davis took a corner on the right, Kevin Campbell flicked on and skipper Tony Adams arrived at the far post but could only watch as the ball trickled outside. Just before the interval Daniele Fortunato headed wide from Roberto Jarni's left-wing centre and David Seaman needed a couple of attempts to hold a stinging shot from Jarni. In the dying seconds, a free-kick gave Francescoli the ball but he somehow fired over the bar.

As anticipated the second leg proved to be as tight as the first. Arsenal knew that they could ill-afford to lose a goal that would require them to score twice against the Italian outfit. Wright returned to the attack and the Gunners enjoyed the balance of play which lead to the vital breakthrough deep in the second half.

Arsenal were awarded a free-kick on the right after Angelo Gregucci had fouled Alan Smith. Paul Davis delivered the cross towards the far post and Tony Adams timed his run to perfection to nod the ball past Galli. It was to be a sad night for Gregucci, booked for an over-enthusiastic tackle on Wright in the first half, and sent off for a second bookable offence against the same player in the dying moments of the game. While Arsenal's chances were limited they dominated the play and the only time Seaman looked troubled when a poor back-pass by Steve Bould almost let Andrea Silenzi in.

Real Madrid's problems at home both on and off the field meant that Europe was probably their best chance of glory. Certainly it was generating much-needed revenue. But they were up against stiff opposition in Paris Saint-Germain. The draw was given further spice by the fact that it offered the Spaniards a chance of revenge. They had been knocked out at the same stage of the UEFA Cup the previous season by the French club.

Quarter-Final Summary

P	HW	D	AW	HG	AG	TG
16	6	1	9	23	31	54

Ties won on: aggregate 3   away goals: 1   penalty kicks: 0

Highest Aggregate game: 5-5   Benfica *v* Bayer Leverkusen
Biggest Home win: 2-0   Parma *v* Ajax
Biggest Away win: 0-1   Real Madrid *v* Paris Saint-Germain

Top Scorers – All Rounds

5 Andonov (CSKA Sofia), Jess (Aberdeen), Kirsten (Bayer Leverkusen), Mizrahi (Maccabi Haifa).
4 Gane (Univ Craiova), Litmanen (Ajax), Shishkov (CSKA Sofia).
3 Brolin (Parma), Campbell (Arsenal), Danko (VSZ Kosice), Gregory (Valur), Guerin (Paris Saint-Germain), Hapal (Bayer Leverkusen), Merson (Arsenal), Saravakos (Panathinaikos), Silenzi (Torino), Subiat (FC Lugano), Westerthaler (FC Tirol-Innsbruck), Wilmots (Standard Liege), Wright (Arsenal).

The tension between the two sides showed itself with a series of late tackles and free kicks in the opening period of the first leg in the Bernabeu. One such challenge on Michel inside the Paris Saint-Germain box looked worthy of a penalty but the claims of the Real players were waved away by the German referee. Real continued to apply pressure and Lama in the Paris goal was called upon to make several fine saves, none more so than from Luis Enrique's close-range effort.

Totally against the run of play Paris Saint-Germain took the lead. Ginola broke on the left, succeeded in getting around the back of the Real defence and cut the ball into the path of George Weah, who side footed home from eight yards. It was a classic counter goal and proved to be decisive although Real looked to have equalised when Chilean international Zamorano toe-ended Michel's corner goalward, but somehow the ball was cleared off the line with Lama stranded.

The second half was totally dominated by Real but they lacked the rub of the green. When Lama failed to connect with an attempted punched clearance the ball fell perfectly for Zamorano again, and he held his head in dismay as his goal-bound drive cannoned off a Paris Saint-Germain defender standing on the goal line. Madrid continued to launch wave after wave of attacks but the Paris Saint-Germain defence grouped well and held fast. Ginola had two great opportunities on the break to increase his side's lead but his control and a fine save by Buyo let him down.

Paris Saint-Germain were therefore clear favourites to progress into the semi-finals when Real arrived for the second leg in the Parc des Princes knowing that they had to score. And that they did after 20 minutes of play when Butragueno – who had missed the first leg – swept the ball home. The goal rocked the home side but they gradually recovered their composure and seven minutes into the second half Ricardo equalised. There was no further change and for the second successive season Paris Saint-Germain had succeeded in knocking Real Madrid out of the quarter-finals of a major European competition.

Holders Parma were drawn against the 1987 winners Ajax. For the first leg in Amsterdam the Italians were without their international full-back Benarrivo, who was suspended following his booking in the second leg of the European Super Cup encounter with Milan. For their part, Ajax suffered a blow in attack where they had to start the game without the pacy wing play of Marc Overmars – named as a substitute although suffering from flu.

In a first half in which honours were even the best chance fell to Ajax with a four-man move that was worthy of a goal. Danish international Dan Petersen found himself side-footing towards goal only to see Sensini clear. Parma's best chance came after a free-kick by Asprilla took a deflection but Melli's diving header went wide of Van der Sar's upright. Parma had another chance when Danny Blind's reckless tackle on Zola allowed the Italian to trouble the Ajax keeper with a curling free-kick. The second half was disappointing, not least for Jari Litmanen who would have scored on any other night after flicking the ball over Bucci, only to lose his balance under pressure from Apolloni.

After no goals in the first leg Ajax travelled to Parma knowing that they would be without one of their most prodigious talents. Litmanen – top scorer in Dutch football with 23 goals – had torn a muscle in training the previous Thursday. Ajax therefore included 17-year-old Clarence Seedorf in their side – the youngster had made his European debut at the age of 16 against Kaiserslautern in the UEFA Cup. Litmanen's absence was perhaps balanced by that of suspended Luigi Apolloni.

Parma controlled the early stages of the game by penning the Dutch side in their own half and Asprilla nearly produced the perfect start when the Ajax defence gave him too much space on the right side of the area. The Colombian turned a shot across the face of the goal and Edwin Van der Sar had to use a leg to deflect the ball away for a corner. Van der Sar continued to make a string of useful saves but he was at fault when Parma took the lead after almost 15 minutes of non-stop pressure.

Awarded a free-kick on the right and with Zola looking to swing the ball in, Minotti curled in a low left-footed effort that went past the three-man wall and across the line. Van der Sar had been drawn to the near post and was totally fooled by the shot. The goal occurred just as Ajax had started to produce a move or two of note, but lifted the home side and almost immediately. Tomas Brolin – who had been largely innocuous – side-footed the ball wide from six yards after arriving to meet Zola's cross.

Parma took a winning two-goal lead with a move that swept the length of the pitch. After a ponderous Ajax attack was broken down on the edge of the area the ball was fed from central midfield to Brolin, who made 40 yards before touching the ball wide to Zola on the left. Evading two tackles he drilled a shot goalward which Van der Sar could only parry to the incoming Brolin, having continued his run, and he couldn't miss from eight yards.

In a last-ditch effort to rescue the game Ajax made a double substitution, but it was Parma who continued to pose the attacking ideas and only a goal-line header by Silooy prevented Brolin from making it 3-0 ten minutes from time.

Semi-Finals

The semi-final draw produced two potentially fascinating encounters. Benfica and Parma were teams at contrasting ends of the European spectrum. The Eagles of Lisbon, twice Champions' Cup winners in the early sixties, had over 200 European ties behind them. Parma, after only three years in Serie A, won the Cup-Winners' Cup at their first attempt. Benfica had had many famous players in the past: the Italians were making present-day names.

Paris Saint-Germain and Arsenal were teams with excellent defensive records. Paris Saint-Germain had conceded only five goals at home in their domestic league and one in this particular European campaign. With the experience of being losing semi-finalists in the UEFA Cup the previous season they were looking to go one step better. Arsenal though came into the semi-finals still never having lost a game in the Cup-Winners' Cup and seemed to be saving their best performances for Europe. They were the competition's top scorers.

Parma travelled to Portugal for the first leg of their encounter with Benfica. It turned out to be a classic game producing some stunning football played out in front of 110,000 in the huge bowl of the Stadium of Light. The occasion and atmosphere affected a number of players early on, none more so that Faustino Asprilla, who was booked for a foul on Brazilian defender Carlos Mozer – a second yellow card that would keep him out of the return leg in Italy. How costly might that prove?

Lifted by their crowd The Eagles swept forward in the

Benfica's Vasili Kulkov tackles Gianfranco Zola of Parma.

Sensini stoops to score an amazing header, the tie-winning goal for Parma against Benfica.

opening period and went ahead after eight minutes with a goal of quality. Rui Costa received the ball in left midfield and produced a wonderful defence-splitting pass. Timing his run to perfection, Isaias took the ball in his stride and drilled it low past Bucci for the opener.

Parma responded wonderfully to the goal and set about restoring the status quo. Zola went down dramatically in the area looking for a penalty that never was and Asprilla's lofted shot had to be headed off the line. The eventual equaliser oozed the same quality of the Benfica opener, the ball being played short and swift in an arc across the face of the home goal. The final pass by Crippa to Zola on the left was as well executed as it was simple and the Italian shot past the Benfica keeper from 15 yards.

Rui Costa was the most productive of the Benfica players and his prompting was instrumental in the Portuguese side gradually getting back into the game. When he won a free-kick 25 yards out late in the half Bucci did well to pluck Mozer's goal-bound drive out of the air. As the tide continued to turn Benfica's way, Joao Pinto missed a relatively simple chance.

Bucci's handling in the Parma goal was excellent all evening and combined with a number of reflex saves there were occasions when he seemed to be keeping the home attack at bay on his own. Even when he failed to get the ball totally away he had the luck of the bar to his rescue. Eventually though the relentless pressure paid off after 60 minutes of play when Rui Costa turned to drive home after Vitor Paneira had touched Yuran's cross from the left to him.

Benfica had a real chance to put more pressure on Parma for the return when they were awarded a penalty after Yuran was flattened by Asprilla when making a powerful surge goalwards. The Colombian might have expected a red card but didn't even get shown a yellow, which would have also meant his dismissal given his booking at the start of the evening. Vitor Paneira's spot kick to Bucci's left was poor and the Italian keeper had a relatively simple save to make.

In the final stages of the game Parma looked to come forward and Minotti – playing with a broken nose – somehow failed to connect with Crippa's searching cross. Had he done so Parma would surely have had an equaliser.

Two weeks later Parma took to the field in the knowledge that a single goal would be enough to put them through to their second successive Cup-Winners' Cup final. Belgian international George Grun was back in the side for the first time since the first round, having recovered from injury.

With so much at stake the second leg proved to be a tense and untidy game – Benfica were content to defend and get forward when they could, Parma were left to play a chasing role. Apart from a disallowed goal by Brolin early on Parma lacked ideas in attack and the nearest they went to scoring was when Sensini's left-wing cross was nearly steered past Neno for an own goal by a Benfica defender. Significantly though, Brazilian defender Carlos Mozer was sent off after 35 minutes for a second bookable offence. Both yellow cards came as a result of reckless tackles, on Apolloni and Sensini.

Despite the missing man Benfica continued to play an effective spoiling game and early in the second half nearly took the lead when Schwarz stretched to volley goalbound only to see his effort come off Bucci's body. Moments later Zola showed immaculate control at the other end when he killed Brolin's crossfield pass with his left foot and curled a right-footed drive against Neno's upright.

Parma finally broke through with a goal that was as scrappy as the game itself. Zola lofted Parma's eighth corner of the game towards the far post. Neno left the ball and Kenedy Santos, presumably assuming that the ball was going to run out of play, ducked out of a clearing header. But Parma's Argentinean international Sensini stole in behind him to head the ball hard down on the pitch from almost on the goal line and somehow it squeezed in at the near post to cross the line.

The goal, not surprisingly, livened up Benfica's attacking ideas, and with three minutes of play remaining Vitor Paneira

Ricardo of Paris Saint-Germain and Arsenal's Ian Wright go for the ball in the first leg of their semi-final.

Semi-Finals

Benfica   **Parma**   2-1
Isaias (7), Rui Costa (60)   Zola (13)
Att: 110,000.   *Ref:* Heynemann (Ger)
Benfica: Neno, Abel Xavier, Mozer, Helder, Veloso (Kenedy Santos 44), Kulkov, Vitor Paneira, Joao Pinto, Yuran, Rui Costa, Isaias
Parma: Bucci, Benarrivo, Minotti, Di Chiara, Sensini, Pin, (Zoratto 85), Apolloni, Crippa, Zola, Brolin, Asprilla
Yellow Cards: Yuran, Abel Xavier, Helder (Benfica) and Minotti, Asprilla (Parma)

Parma   **Benfica**   1-0
Sensini (77)
Att: 25,000.   *Ref:* Van der Ende (Hol)
Parma: Bucci, Benarrivo (Balleri 30), Di Chiara, Pin, Apolloni, Grun (Colacone 63), Sensini, Zoratto, Crippa, Zola, Brolin
Benfica: Neno, Abel Xavier, Mozer, Andrade, Kenedy Santos, (Ceasar Brito 82), Kulkov, Vitor Paneira, Joao Pinto, Schwarz, Rui Costa, Isaias (Hernani 76)
Yellow Cards: Zoratto, Sensini, Colacone (Parma) and Joao Pinto, Mozer (Benfica)
Red Card: Mozer (Benfica 35 – second yellow card)
2-2 on aggregate. Parma win on away goals rule

Paris Saint-Germain   **Arsenal**   1-1
Ginola (50)   Wright (35)
Att: 46,000.   *Ref:* Sundell (Swe)
Paris Saint-Germain: Lama, Sassus, Ricardo, Colleter, Llacer (Bravo 46), Fournier, Le Guen, Valdo, Weah, Ginola
Arsenal: Seaman, Dixon, Bould, Adams, Winterburn, Davis (Keown 84), Jensen, Selley, Wright, Smith (Campbell 84), Merson
Yellow Cards: Adams, Merson (Arsenal)

Arsenal   **Paris Saint-Germain**   1-0
Campbell (6)
Att: 34,212.   *Ref:* Mikkelsen (Den)
Arsenal: Seaman, Dixon, Bould, Adams, Winterburn, Davis (Keown 88), Davis (Hillier 76), Jensen, Selley, Wright, Smith, Campbell
Paris Saint-Germain: Lama, Sassus (Llacer 79), Ricardo, Colleter, Roche, Fournier, Le Guen, Valdo, Guerin, Rai (Gravelaine 77), Ginola
Yellow Cards: Wright (Arsenal) and Colleter, Ricardo (PSG)
Arsenal win 2-1 on aggregate

Dates
1st Leg   29 March
2nd Leg   12 April: Arsenal v Paris Saint-Germain
           13 April: Parma v Benfica

thought he had equalised, but his goal was rightly disallowed for offside – though there wasn't much in it – and Parma had reached the final stage.

The Parc des Princes was a cauldron of noise as Paris Saint-Germain and Arsenal took to the field for their first leg. By the end of the evening it was the Gunners who were the happier of the two sides, having placed themselves in a position of strength with a superb display to earn a 1-1 draw. The pre-match talk was about the inclusion or otherwise of Wright in the Arsenal side. Manager Graham gave the England international the nod and he was repaid handsomely after 35 minutes when that player glanced home Davis free-kick to put his side into a deserved lead with his 32nd goal of the season.

Paris Saint-Germain – who preferred Brazilian Valdo to his World Cup skipper Rai in their starting line-up – equalised immediately after half-time when David Ginola headed home Valdo's corner at the near post.

Arsenal had dominated the early stages with John Jensen and Ian Selley in fine fettle. Only a magnificent save by Bernard Lama denied Jensen opening the scoring and his own goal account with the Gunners. Striker Alan Smith missed a golden opportunity to restore Arsenal's lead with just 17 minutes left to play when he turned on to Paul Merson's flick to find he had only Lama to beat but the former international mis-hit his shot straight at the keeper.

The second leg at Highbury was nearly a mirror image of the first. Paris Saint-Germain outplayed Arsenal for long periods, needing to go forward and look for a goal to level the tie. Having conceded one in Paris, Paris Saint-Germain had to score whatever happened and that fact didn't change any when Lee Dixon's short cross in from the right was glanced to perfection by Kevin Campbell, beating Lama at his near post to give Arsenal a sixth-minute lead. That did much to settle the team.

The pre-match talk had been of yellow plastic with no fewer than eight Arsenal players facing a possible final suspension. It said a lot for the team's determination that they came through the game almost unscathed in that respect. The only blot was Wright's 42nd-minute name-taking after he foolishly chased back and needlessly tackled Alain Roche from behind. The Arsenal striker was in tears when Danish referee Mikkelsen flourished his card.

Despite Paris Saint-Germain controlling the midfield they did little to trouble David Seaman in the home goal as a variety of shots went high and wide. Their best chance came early on and even before Campbell's header: Seaman threw the ball straight at Valdo who chickened out of shooting and elected to pass to his fellow countryman, Rai, whose effort was blocked by Tony Adams, an immovable object at the centre of the defence. David Ginola – who had been accused of theatricals in the first leg – missed the target from 12 yards after Ian Selley had a lapse in concentration.

Arsenal held on for a memorable victory on the night and progressed into their second Cup-Winners' Cup final in as many attempts and their first European final for 24 years.

Final

The absence of Ian Wright from the final in Copenhagen had received most of the media attention in the days after the two finalists were clarified. Parma had already been installed as firm favourites to win and thereby become the first club ever to retain the Cup-Winners' Cup. And as the 4 May final date drew closer their odds shortened as the Gunners lost more key players. Probably the biggest loss was that of John Jensen, a folk hero at Highbury, best remembered for his goal for Denmark in the European Championship final against Germany, who was in a superb vein of form for the North London side. Ironically, the injury that forced his premature end to the season came at the Parken Stadium, were the final was scheduled to take place two weeks later, during an international match against Hungary where he earned his 63rd cap. The injury was a blow for the Danes as much for Arsenal, who regard 'Faxes' as a favourite son.

As the days to the final fell from the calendar Jensen's replacement in midfield – David Hillier – failed to recover fully from an injury, and man-marker Martin Keown strained a hamstring. Goalkeeper David Seaman suffered badly bruised ribs that forced him to miss vital Premiership encounters and needed numerous painkilling injections in the hours leading up to the match. The Italians on the other hand had no such problems and domestically finished their fourth Serie A season in indifferent form but still high enough to ensure themselves the safety net of a UEFA Cup spot for the 1994–95 season should they fail to retain the trophy they held.

The game – the first in European competition between English and Italian sides since the Heysel disaster – was handled superbly by the Danish authorities. Despite some 20,000 supporters invading their capital for up to five days there was little trouble and the only sight of police was in and around the stadium. Both sets of supporters treated the match as the occasion it was and many Italians and English had swapped club colours even before the day.

While not rising to classic proportions the match was a fascinating tactical battle that was ultimately won by the London club. Parma dominated the opening spell attacking the massed banks of Arsenal supporters and as early as the first minute it needed every inch of Steve Bould's outstretched leg to take the ball off the marauding Asprilla, who sought Brolin's superbly weighted through-ball. Moments later Brolin's run from deep through the defence allowed him to meet Benarrivo's dangerous, deep cross from the right unchallenged with a header that dipped over Seaman and inches over the Arsenal bar.

Arsenal finally stopped the flood of Parma attacks forcing a couple of free-kicks and had Campbell been quicker turning on Davis' astute pass the Arsenal forward would surely have given them the lead. Almost immediately Parma showed their threat on the counter attack when Maradona's former striking partner at Napoli, Zola, delivered a diagonal pass that cut the Arsenal defence to shreds; Brolin's timed run from the right drew Seaman but somehow the Swede could only find the base of the far post and not the far corner of the net.

Alan Smith scores the goal that wins the Cup-Winners' Cup final for Arsenal. Parma's Argentine international Sensini cringes.

That thumping of the woodwork seemed to settle the Arsenal nerves and within five minutes they had taken the lead. A period of possession by the Gunners led to Lee Dixon crossing the ball in from the right and behind the Parma defence. With the ball arriving behind Lorenzo Minotti, the Parma captain, he was forced to attempt a scissors-kick clearance over his head. The ball dropped into the path of Alan Smith who in one move controlled perfectly on his chest, allowed the ball to bounce and from 20 yards hit a crisp, powerful left-footed drive that beat the diving Bucci and went in via his left upright. It was a magnificent strike by the Arsenal forward, later described by Graham as his man of the match.

For days prior to the final the streets of Copenhagen and the Tivoli Gardens had been ringing to the sound of the Pet Shop Boys' song 'Go West'. The lyrics were different "One Nil to the Arsenal" – but the singing became even more passionate within seconds of the goal as the simple song rose to a crescendo of noise and flag-waving. With the confidence of a goal and the knowledge that they were more than capable of defending it, Arsenal's players simply dug in with even more resilience.

Final

Parken Stadium, Copenhagen
4 May 1994
Arsenal   1   Parma   0
Smith (19)
Att: 33,765   *Ref:* Krondl (Cze)
Arsenal: Seaman, Dixon, Winterburn, Davis, Bould, Adams, Campbell, Morrow, Smith, Merson (McGoldrick 86), Selley
Subs not used: Linighan, Miller, Parlour, Dickov
Parma: Bucci, Benarrivo, Di Chiara, Minotti, Apolloni, Sensini, Brolin, Pin (Melli 70), Crippa, Zola, Asprilla
Subs not used: Maltagliati, Ballota, Balleri, Zoratto
Yellow cards: Adams (30), Campbell (47), Selley (53) all Arsenal. Crippa (42), Asprilla (45) both Parma.

Indeed, Parma had to wait nearly 20 minutes for another attempt on Seaman's goal. After Zola had taken two disputed free-kicks and blazed over from the edge of the box, the revitalised Italian international interchanged with Asprilla on the edge of the area before finding himself free inside it on the left and fired a powerful shot at goal. Seaman instinctively threw up an arm and produced the save of the night. The action did little for the keeper's bruised ribs, which needed more half-time attention.

Arsenal might have extended their lead before the interval when Davis' flag kick was meet by Campbell, whose glancing header was kicked off the line by Pin. In the second half Parma continued to dominate the possession but they had no answer to the stand-ins of Morrow and Selley in midfield, nor that of Arsenal captain Tony Adams. His personal performance was surpassed by that of Steve Bould who had probably his best game ever for Arsenal. Defender Nigel Winterburn went down late in the game after taking the full force of Asprilla's driven cross in his face and he, Seaman and several Arsenal officials were struck by a hail of missiles from the crowd.

There were a few final flutters for the Gunners not least created by the 11 minutes 31 seconds of stoppage time played by Vaclav Krondl. The ball ended up in the Arsenal net after Asprilla, Zola and Melli had interchanged but the linesman's flag was correctly up for offside long before the ball arrived. Alan Smith nearly made it 2-0 in the final seconds but as Bucci saved the whistle finally went and the strains of 'One Nil...' were heard again as the English supporters' signature tune gained even greater heights.

The result meant that English clubs had now won 24 of their 36 European finals in which they have appeared – not a bad record given the restraints of a five-year UEFA ban. Italian clubs however have won only 17 of the 37 finals they have reached. More remarkably Arsenal extended their record of never having lost a 'proper' game in two seasons of this competition. They drew the 1980 final 0-0 before Valencia won 5-4 on penalties, and few would bet against their becoming the first club to retain the trophy.

After the game both managers were ready to heap praise on their opponents. Parma coach Nevio Scala was magnanimous in defeat and said, 'Arsenal were the better side. They showed how to control our system of play and to me they are the least typical English team I have seen. In many ways they remind me of the early Real Madrid sides – it is strange they do not receive more praise.'

Ironically the Italians had found themselves out-Italianed by Arsenal and a restrained George Graham said, 'It was a very difficult because we had to put out an injury-hit side against one of the top teams in Europe.

'But the players showed tremendous character and once we went a goal in front we knew that we had a chance because our strength is keeping clean sheets. Every player deserves praise. We had a team of heroes, none more so that Alan Smith, who was absolutely outstanding.

'Parma looked much sharper. They have better technicians than we do in England and I thought we looked very tired because of the number of games we play. But it's nice for me to be able to make that point having won the game,' he added with a typical wry smile.

Smith said, 'That was a wonderful way to end the season. We've had a terrific run in Europe and it was lovely to score the goal that won the trophy. There is nothing quite like scoring a goal that wins a final, especially in Europe.'

George Graham poses with the Cup-Winners' Cup in the tunnel of the Parken Stadium after Arsenal's 1-0 victory over Parma.

Finals Scorers – All Rounds

5   Andenov (CSKA Sofia), Jess (Aberdeen), Kirsten (Bayer Leverkusen), Mizrahi (Maccabi Haifa).

4   Campbell (Arsenal), Gane (Univ. Craiova), Litmanen (Ajax), Shishkov (CSKA Sofia), Wright (Arsenal).

3   Brolin (Parma), Danko (VSZ Kosice), Gregory (Valur), Guerin (Paris Saint-Germain), Hapal (Bayer Leverkusen), Merson (Arsenal), Saravakos (Panathinaikos), Silenzi (Torino), Subiat (FC Lugano), Westerthaler (FC Tirol-Innsbruck), Wilmots (Standard Liege).

2   Adams (Arsenal), Alfonso (Real Madrid), Anddrioli (FC Lugano), Asprilla (Parma), Bird (Cardiff City), Bisconti (Standard Liege), Butragueno (Real Madrid), Davids (Ajax), De Boer, R. (Ajax), Frick, Mario (Balzers), Froberg (Degerfors IF), Georgiadis (Panathinaikos), Ginola (Paris Saint-Germain), Gulbrandsen (Lillestrom SK), Holtzmann (Maccabi Haifa), Isaias (Benfica), Joao Pinto (Benfica), Kolkov (Benfica), Larusson (Valur), Metin Tekin (Besiktas), Michel (Real Madrid), Mjelde (Lillestrom SK), Mooney (Shelbourne), Nankov (CSKA Sofia), Octosson (Degerfors IF), Pettersson (Ajax), Rui Costa (Benfica), Smith (Arsenal), Thom (Bayer Leverkusen), Warzycha K. (Panathinaikos), Zamorano (Real Madrid).

1   Abel Xavier (Benfica), Aguilera (Torino), Andre Cruz (Standard Liege), Arendas (Nikol Tallinn), Asselman (Standard Liege), Atar (Maccabi Haifa), Balleri (Parma), Bergdolmo (Lillestrom SK), Berger (Dugerfors IF), Bjarmann (Lillestrom SK), Borisov (Torpedo Moscow), Calin (Univ. Craiova), Carbone (Torino), Carracedo (FC Tirol-Innsbruck), Ciric (CSKA Sofia), Costa (Benfica), Costello (Shelbourne), Craioveanu (Univ Craiova), Danek (FC Tirol-Innsbruck), De Boer, F. (Ajax), Detari (Ferencvaros), Donis (Panathinaikos), Dubovsky (Real Madrid), Durisa (VSZ Kosice), Eriksson (Degerfors IF), Fink (FC Lugano), Fischer (Bayer Leverkusen), Fortunato (Torino), Glendining (Bangor), Gravelaine (Paris Saint-Germain), Happe (Bayer Leverkusen), Harazi (Maccabi Haifa), Hierro (Real Madrid), Irvine (Aberdeen), Izzi (Shelbourne), James (Cardiff City), Jarni (Torino), Kalaychev (Torpedo Moscow), Karlsson (Lillestrom SK), Kondoroav (Maccabi Haifa), Kozlov (RAF Jalgava), Kucz (GKS Katowice), Kuster (Belzers), Lashaf (Standard Liege), Le Guen (Paris Saint-Germain), MacManus (Lillestrom SK), Masur (Karpaty Lvov), Mazurchik (Neman Grodno), McEvoy (Bangor), McGoldrick (Arsenal), Mehmet Ozdilek (Besiktas), Mihajlovic (Apoel Nicosia), Miller (Aberdeen), Minotti (Parma), Mornar (Hajduk Split), Nedergaard (OB Odense), Nielsen (OB Odense), Nushohr (Balzers), Olhauzen (Dudelange), Ottosson (Degerfors IF), Paatelainen (Aberdeen), Paolo Sergio (Bayer Leverkusen), Penzavali (FC Lugano), Petz (Maccabi Haifa), Poci (Albpetrol), Podegayev (VSZ Kosice), Pounas (Apoel Nicosia), Rajamaki (MyPa), Ricardo (Paris Saint-Germain), Richardson (Aberdeen), Rijkaard (Ajax), Rui Aguas (Benfica), Sassus (Paris Saint-Germain), Schiller (Lillestrom SK), Schuster (Bayer Leverkusen), Schwarz (Benfica), Segio (Torino), Selley (Arsenal), Sensini (Parma), Sergen Yalcin (Besiktas), Shearer, D. (Aberdeen), Sinigaglia (Lillestrom SK), Solodobvnikov (Neman Grodno), Sotiriou (Apoel Nicosia), Streiter (Tirol Innsbruck), Tanev (CSKA Sofia), Valdo (Paris Saint-Germain), Vase (Univ Craiova), Vitor Paneira (Benfica), Weah (Paris Saint-Germain), Worns (Bayer Leverkusen), Yevtushok (Karpaty Lvov), Yuran (Benfica), Zola (Parma)

Own goals for: OB Odense, Real Madrid, Benfica and Paris Saint-Germain

UEFA Cup

First Round

One club who were not in the draw for the first round of the UEFA Cup found themselves pitted against the Spanish islanders from Tenerife. Auxerre, who had finished sixth in the French league, got their chance to join Nantes and Bordeaux in European competition after Monaco had been upgraded into the Champions' Cup following the expulsion of the holders, Marseille. For long periods of the first leg in the Heliodoro Rodriguez it looked as though the French club would be returning with a victory under their belts. Even though Pinilla's 19th-minute penalty equalised Vahirua's strike three minutes earlier, Saib's goal, within two minutes of the spot kick, silenced the home crowd of around 20,000. Victory though was denied Auxerre when Minambres produced another equaliser 20 minutes from the end. Even so, a creditable draw and two away goals would have been enough to give the previous season's semi-finalists ample optimism for the return. But with 68 minutes of the second leg gone Felipe swooped to snatch what proved to be the only goal of the game and put the Spaniards through to the second round 3-2 on aggregate.

It proved to be a doubly disappointing round for French clubs as Nantes also fell to Spanish opposition in the guise of the 1980 winners Valencia, but they needed extra time. A goal apiece in the first leg, both inside the first 15 minutes, made Valencia favourites for the return. However, when Pedros put Nantes ahead early in the second half, things looked to favour the French. But Penev's penalty in the 72nd minute rescued the game for the Spaniards and a goal in each period of the ensuing extra time sealed the fate of Nantes.

One French side did qualify for the second round, Bordeaux overcoming Bohemians. The Dubliners limited the French to a single goal in the first leg, scored by Dugarry, but five more in the second leg gave the French a comfortable passage. Playing their first ever UEFA Cup tie, Belfast side Crusaders held the more experienced Servette to a goalless draw at Seaview. In the second leg the game seemed to be going pretty much the same way, but then two goals inside a minute – the second an own goal by Dunlop – changed the course of the game and two more from Giallanza completed a 4-0 win for the Genevans.

Holders Juventus started their defence of the trophy against Lokomotiv Moscow, but as punishment for previous crowd misbehaviour Juve had to play their home leg in Bologna. Nevertheless a large number of supporters made the journey across country from Turin to see their side win 3-0, thanks to three second-half goals – two inevitably from Roberto Baggio, with the grey-haired Fabrizio Ravanelli getting in on the act in between. In Moscow a second-half goal by Giancarlo Marocchi completed the tie 4-0 on aggregate in Juve's favour.

Another Moscow side also bowed out of the competition with an emphatic defeat at the first hurdle. Dinamo entertained Eintracht Frankfurt, who scored three goals in each half to make the second leg a formality, and despite the Russians gaining a 2-1 win in Frankfurt, Eintracht progressed 7-2 on aggregate. Dinamo's Russian rivals Spartak Vladikavkaz, making their first appearance in Europe, did better against experienced German opposition. Having earned a fine goalless draw in Dortmund, Spartak would have fancied their chances in

Heimo Pfeifenberger (centre) of Casino Salzburg scored in both legs of the encounter with Slovenia's Dac Dunjaska Streda.

First Round Results

AaB Aalborg Thorst (66)	**Deportivo La Coruna**	1-0	8,100
Deportivo La Coruna Bebeto (18, 51, 71), Barragan (66, 86)	**AaB Aalborg**	5-0	20,000

Deportivo La Coruna win 5-1 on aggregate

Bohemians (Dublin)	**Bordeaux** Dugarry (16)	0-1	5,000
Bordeaux Zidane (22), Vercruysse (25, 72), Paille (60), Fofana (67)	**Bohemians (Dublin)**	5-0	18,000

Bordeaux win 6-0 on aggregate

Borussia Dortmund	**Spartak Vladikavkaz**	0-0	34,539
Spartak Vladikavkaz	**Borussia Dortmund** Chapuisat (62)	0-1	31,500

Borussia Dortmund win 1-0 on aggregate

Botev Plovdiv Balakov (15), Hvoinev (88)	**Olympiakos** Amanasidis (12), Tsiantakis (59), Batista (87)	2-3	25,000
Olympiakos Christensen (38, 78), Tsiantakis (73), Mitsibonas (77 pen), Batista (85)	**Botev Plovdiv** Dimitrov (67 pen)	5-1	19,000

Olympiakos win 8-3 on aggregate

Brondby Vilfort (20), Kristensen (46)	**Dundee United**	2-0	5,756
Dundee United McKinlay (67), Crabbe (79), Clarke (119)	**Brondby** Kristensen (91)	3-1	8,451

Brondby win on away goals. 3-3 on aggregate after extra time

Crusaders	**Servette**	0-0	5,000
Servette Anderson da Silva (57), Dunlop(own goal 58), Giallanza (60, 63)	**Crusaders**	4-0	5,000

Servette win 4-0 on aggregate

Dinamo Bucharest Moldovan (5, 30), Pana (87 pen)	**Cagliari** Prunea (own goal 13), Dely Valdes (38)	3-2	5,000
Cagliari Matteoli (6), Oliveira (63)	**Dinamo Bucharest**	2-0	37,500

Cagliari win 4-3 on aggregate

Dinamo Moscow	**Eintracht Frankfurt** Gaudino (9), Weber (25), Furtok (45), Bein (48), Okocha (81), Yeboah (89)	0-6	17,000
Eintracht Frankfurt Furtok (65)	**Dinamo Moscow** Simutenkov (22), Dobrovolski (54)	1-2	4,900

Eintracht Frankfurt win 7-2 on aggregate

Dnepr Dnepropetrovsk Maximov (77)	**Admira Wacker**	1-0	12,000
Admira Wacker Bacher (45), Ljung (90)	**Dnepr Dnepropetrovsk** Bezhanar (43), Pokhlebaev (50), Mikhaylenko (68)	2-3	7,300

Dnepr Dnepropetrovsk win 4-2 on aggregate

FC Nantes Oudec (12)	**Valencia** Mijatovic (15)	1-1	14,799
Valencia Penev (72 pen), Galvez (104), Gomez (112)	**FC Nantes** Pedros (50)	3-1	46,700

Valencia win 4-2 on aggregate after extra time

FC Twente Boerebach (64), Prince Polly (70), Vurens (75)	**Bayern Munich** Nerlinger (11), Ziege (27, 90), Scholl (65)	3-4	18,000
Bayern Munich Matthaus (18 pen), Karnebeek (own goal 45), Ziege (62)	**FC Twente**	3-0	24,000

Bayern Munich win 7-3 on aggregate

Gloria Bistrita	**Maribor Branik**	0-0	3,800
Maribor Branik Stanic (5, 80)	**Gloria Bistrita**	2-0	6,000

Maribor Branik win 2-0 on aggregate

Heart of Midlothian Robertson (70), Colquhoun (75)	**Atletico Madrid** Kosecki (77)	2-1	15,596
Atletico Madrid Pedro (34), Manolo (72), Luis Garcia (76)	**Heart of Midlothian**	3-0	40,000

Atletico Madrid win 4-2 on aggregate

IFK Norrkoping	**KV Mechelen** Czerniatynski (45)	0-1	5,557
KV Mechelen Eszenyi (113)	**IFK Norrkoping** Blohm (33)	1-1	6,500

KV Mechelen win 2-1 on aggregate after extra time

Internazionale Bergkamp (11 pen, 74, 78)	**Rapid Bucharest** Andrasi (52)	3-1	22,500
Rapid Bucharest	**Internazionale** Battistini (75), Jonk (83)	0-2	23,000

Internazionale win 5-1 on aggregate

***Juventus** R. Baggio (49, 87), Ravanelli (70)	**Lokomotiv Moscow**	3-0	27,500
Lokomotiv Moscow	**Juventus** Marocchi (54)	0-1	5,000

Juventus win 4-0 on aggregate

Karlsruhe SC Schmitt (20), Kiriakov (29)	**PSV** Popescu (35 pen)	2-1	25,000
PSV	**Karlsruhe SC**	0-0	24,000

Karlsruhe SC win 2-1 on aggregate

Kocaelispor Kulubu	**Sporting Lisbon**	0-0	15,000
Sporting Lisbon Cadete (6), A. Pacheco (57)	**Kocaelispor Kulubu**	2-0	45,000

Sporting Lisbon win 2-0 on aggregate

*Match played in Bologna

First Round Results continued

KR Reykjavik Ingimundarson (89)	**MTK-VM Budapest** Hamori (34), Zsivotzky (68)	1-2	600
MTK-VM Budapest	**KR Reykjavik**	0-0	1,000
MTK-VM Budapest win 2-1 on aggregate			
Kuusysi Lahti Annunen (17), Lius (19, 75), Lehtinen (25)	**KSV Waregem**	4-0	2,000
KSV Waregem De Kneef (54)	**Kuusysi Lahti** Annunen (84), Lius (88)	1-2	5,000
Kuusysi Lahti win 6-1 on aggregate			
Lazio Casiraghi (22), Cravero (55)	**Lokomotiv Plovdiv**	2-0	39,500
Lokomotiv Plovdiv	**Lazio** Luzardi (22), Cravero (66)	0-2	23,000
Lazio win 4-0 on aggregate			
Norwich City Ekoku (51), Goss (68), Polston (71)	**Vitesse**	3-0	16,818
Vitesse	**Norwich City**	0-0	9,133
Norwich City win 3-0 on aggregate			
Osters IF Persson (36)	**Kongsvinger IL** Engerback (33), Francis (57), Frigard (59)	1-3	1,956
Kongsvinger IL Frigard (36, 82, 89), Engerback (45)	**Osters IF** Landberg (41 pen)	4-1	3,759
Kongsvinger IL win 7-2 on aggregate			
Royal Antwerp Severyns (57), Bursac (90)	**Maritimo**	2-0	7,000
Maritimo Heitor Junio (66), Vado (77)	**Royal Antwerp** Severyns (57), Segers (62)	2-2	8,000
Royal Antwerp win 4-2 on aggregate			
Slavia Prague Berger (52)	**OFI Crete** Georgamlis (64)	1-1	4,106
OFI Crete Mahlas (42)	**Slavia Prague**	1-0	10,000
OFI Crete win 2-1 on aggregate			
Slovan Bratislava	**Aston Villa**	0-0	10,886
Aston Villa Atkinson (15), Townsend (22)	**Slovan Bratislava** Tittel (86)	2-1	24,461
Aston Villa win 2-1 on aggregate			
SV Casino Salzburg Amerhauser (40), Pfeinfenberger (85)	**Dac Dunjaska Streda**	2-0	6,500
Dac Dunjaska Streda	**SV Casino Salzburg** Stadler (19), Pfeifenberger (58)	0-2	8,000
SV Casino Salzburg win 4-0 on aggregate			
Tenerife Pinilla (19 pen), Minambres (70)	**Auxerre** Vahirua (16), Saib (21)	2-2	20,000
Auxerre	**Tenerife** Felipe (68)	0-1	14,000
Tenerife win 3-2 on aggregate			
Trabzonspor Ogun (28, 39), Hami (29)	**Valletta** Zarb (25)	3-1	20,000
Valletta Zarb (8)	**Trabzonspor** Hami (11), Ogun (43), Unal (66)	1-3	2,000
Trabzonspor win 6-2 on aggregate			
US Luxembourg	**Boavista FC** Casaca (40)	0-1	1,067
Boavista FC Oliveira (18, 26), Marlon Brandao (30 pen), Owubokiri (86)	**US Luxembourg**	4-0	4,000
Boavista FC win 5-0 on aggregate			
Vac FC Samsung Szedlacsek (43), Nyilas (78)	**Apollon Limassol**	2-0	4,000
Apollon Limassol Scepovic (40, 65), Spoliarec (111 pen), Kricmarevic (118)	**Vac FC Samsung**	4-0	8,000
Apollon Limassol win 4-2 on aggregate after extra time			
Young Boys Berne	**Celtic**	0-0	7,300
Celtic Baumann (own goal 106)	**Young Boys Berne**	1-0	21,500
Celtic win 1-0 on aggregate after extra time			

front of their own supporters. It was another tight and often tense game but a goal just after the hour by Swiss international striker Stephane Chapuisat gave Borussia Dortmund a narrow aggregate win.

Liam Brady's Celtic were involved in an even tighter game against Young Boys. Despite a 0-0 draw in the first leg in Berne, Celtic created enough chances to have sewn the tie up. Pat McGinlay in particular had two outstanding opportunities to give the Scots victory near the end, but both his efforts from within the penalty area failed to hit the target. Pat Bonner, Celtic's Republic of Ireland goalkeeper, had only one real save of note to make as the Swiss side's forwards showed a complete lack of imagination in attack. His opposite number, Peter Kobel, had a busier evening and denied Charlie Nicholas and Andy Payton goals.

Celtic faced the second leg in Glasgow with the news of an attempted £18m take-over by Canadian Fergus McCann and manager Liam Brady's future at Parkhead in doubt. Nevertheless the Glaswegians approached the return with confidence from their first-leg performance. The Swiss offered stubborn resistance and saw their crossbar struck on no less than four occasions in normal time. Packing the midfield, the visitors looked to be settling for a penalty shoot-out as the game went into extra time. Then Nicholas, a second-half substitute, steered a pass into the heart of the Young Boys' defence and watched incredulously as Alain Baumann diverted the ball into his own goal. It proved to be the only goal of the tie.

A lapse in concentration in the latter stages of their first leg with Atletico Madrid cost Heart of Midlothian dear. Despite having few opportunities Hearts found themselves two goals to the good with just 15 minutes remaining thanks to opportunist strikes by John Robertson and John Colquhoun. But two minutes after Hearts had established that lead Poland's Roman Kosecki raced through a static home defence to score a superb solo effort. Pedro's goal shortly before the interval put Atletico in control of the tie early on in the return leg in Madrid, and second-half efforts by Manolo and Luis Garcia earned the Spanish club a 4-2 aggregate win.

Brondby, in their 20th year of existence, had six European campaigns behind them as they faced their third appearance in the UEFA Cup against Dundee United. By the end of the first leg they looked to have established a useful lead with goals from Kim Vilfort and a decisive second right after the break from Jesper Kristensen. However, Dundee United had developed a history of great escapes at Tannadice and goals by Billy McKinlay and Scott Crabbe in a late 12-minute spell in the return match seemed to set the scene for another remarkable recovery. Up until Crabbe's low drive past Krogh, the Danes had looked impressive and worth their overall advantage. But with the game in the first minute of extra time a stunning 30-yard shot from Kristensen put them back into the driving seat. Kristensen had gone close to sealing United's fate in normal time with two stupendous drives from free-kicks, the latter saved brilliantly by Alan Main. With an away goal in the bank, United had to score twice and although Clarke made the aggregate scores level a minute from the final whistle it was the Danes who went through on the away-goals rule.

Having been beaten in the Cup-Winners' Cup final by Parma, Belgian side Royal Antwerp returned to European duty in the UEFA Cup having finished fifth in their previous season's domestic campaign. Portuguese opponents Maritimo also had finished fifth but were making their debut in Europe. The experience of the Antwerp side saw them through despite stubborn resistance from the Portuguese. Severyns' goal in the 57th minute was all Antwerp had to show for their efforts until Bursac popped up in the 90th minute to provide a reasonably comfortable lead for the second leg in the Barreiros stadium. Two goals in a manic five-minute spell early in the second half gave the Belgians an unassailable 4-0 aggregate lead despite a late revival in which Heitor Junio and Vado scored Maritimo's first European goals to level the scores on the night.

Alex Czerniatynski had been a big influence on Royal's run to that Cup-Winners' Cup final but the Belgian international started the season with a new club, KV Mechelen, and got their season's European campaign off to a great start by scoring the only goal of the game against IFK Norrkoping. KV held on to the lead for the return leg in Belgium. But it was the Swedes who surprised the home crowd by levelling the tie after 33 minutes of play through Per Blohm. Extra time was needed to separate the two sides and Hungarian Denes Eszenyi supplied the winner for KV just seven minutes away from a penalty shoot-out.

Third place in the Premiership would not have been enough to have provided Norwich with a UEFA Cup spot given that the second place awarded to English clubs went to the winners of the Coca-Cola Cup. However, when Arsenal won the FA Cup

First Round Summary

P	HW	D	AW	HG	AG	TG
64	32	14	18	107	58	165

Ties won on aggregate: 31
Ties won on away goals: 1
Ties won on penalty kicks: 0

Highest aggregate game: 11
8-3   Olympiakos *v* Botev Plovdiv
Biggest home win:
5-0   Deportivo La Coruna *v* AaB Aalborg
       Bordeaux *v* Bohemians (Dublin)
Biggest away win:
0-6   Dinamo Moscow *v* Eintracht Frankfurt

on top of their Coca-Cola Cup, they qualified for the Cup-Winners' Cup and the UEFA spot was available to City. Having suffered something of a goal drought in the league at Carrow Road, Norwich found their goal-scoring legs in their first European tie with three second-half strikes that pretty much decided the outcome of their tie with Vitesse, who were making what proved to be an unlucky 13th appearance in the competition.

The first 45 minutes told a different story as the seeded Dutch seemed to be giving the Canaries the bird. It took an explosive goal to ignite the tie and it came courtesy of a tremendous left-foot volley when Efan Ekoku latched onto Ian Crooks' perfect chip. The goal by the son of a Nigerian chief was only Norwich's second in over seven hours of home football, but proved to be the catalyst in what was eventually a swashbuckling performance. Jeremy Goss swept home a perfect back-heel from Gary Megson in the 68th minute and John Polston added the third inside the final 20 minutes. For the second leg in Arnhem, the Norwich manager, Mike Walker, reverted to the sweeper system he had abandoned for the first leg, and the ploy worked perfectly as the East Anglian side turned in a performance that frustrated the Dutch club. Bryan Gunn in the Norwich goal had only two saves of note to make. The match threatened to boil over on several occasions as tempers became frayed but City held on and moved into the second round of the competition.

Aston Villa were paired with Slovan Bratislava. The first leg ended goalless but Villa were denied the chance of an important away win when Italian referee Marcello Nicchi waved away what looked to be a legitimate penalty appeal. In Birmingham Villa dominated the second leg but went perilously close to losing their composure after a late goal by the Slovakians produced a nerve-wracking final five minutes. Playing an extra man up front, Villa profited within 15 minutes when Dalian Atkinson scored from close range after Andy Townsend had set him up with a header. A second goal six minutes later looked to have put Villa in a comfortable position, when Townsend drove the ball past Vencel. With four minutes remaining a speculative effort by sweeper Dusan Tittel whizzed past Spink and left the home side and their supporters hanging on for the final whistle.

Lazio's Roberto Cravero (right) is known for his tough tackling but he also found time to score important goals in both legs against Lokomotiv Plovdiv.

Cagliari were back in Europe for the first time in 21 years and the Sardinia-based club looked well on the way to a creditable draw against Dinamo Bucharest by twice equalising after the Romanians had taken the lead. Moldovan had twice put the home side in front but an own goal by Prunea and a second equaliser from Panamanian Dely Valdes sent the sides in all square at the interval. That's how it remained until the final three minutes of the match when Dinamo were awarded a hotly disputed penalty that Constantin Pana eventually converted. In the second leg an early goal by Gianfranco Matteoli levelled the aggregate scores, and Belgian Luis Oliveira netted midway through the second half to give Cagliari victory.

Lazio were another Italian club to make a return to the European stage after a long absence, against Bulgarians Lokomotiv Plovdiv. Lazio won both matches 2-0 with carbon-copy performances. In both encounters the Romans took the lead on 22 minutes through Casiraghi at home and Luzardi away, with Cravero scoring in the second half of both matches.

Dutch international and £6.4m signing Dennis Bergkamp got his European debut for Internazionale off with the sort of bang that was eluding him in Serie A by scoring a hat-trick against

Bebeto of Deportivo La Coruna scored a hat-trick against AaB Aalborg in the second leg of their 5-1 aggregate win.

Rapid Bucharest. Bergkamp's first came through an 11th-minute penalty. Then when Andrasi equalised early in the second half, Inter seemed to be transferring their rickety league form into the UEFA Cup. The two goals inside four minutes turned the game in its latter stages and eased the pressure for the second leg. In the Giulesti stadium, Inter turned in a typically disciplined performance, limiting Rapid to few chances, and Battistini's goal 15 minutes from time sealed the Romanians' fate. Wim Jonk, another of Inter's expensive close season signings from Holland, made his mark seven minutes from time to give his new club a comfortable-looking 5-1 aggregate win.

Only 1,600 spectators watched the two games involving KR Reykjavik and MTK-VM. Goals in each half gave the Budapest side a lead that was only reduced to a single goal in the final minute when Ingimundarson popped up to score. The return in Hungary had little to offer in terms of excitement and ended goalless.

The Finns from Lahti have made their small mark on Europe in recent years. Formed just 20 years ago following a sequence of mergers, Kuusysi have played in all three European competitions, and showed their potential with a four-goal thrashing of Belgian side KSV Waregem. Two late goals in the second leg gave them a 2-1 victory on Belgian soil and a comprehensive 6-1 aggregate win, against a club who reached the UEFA Cup semi-finals in 1985–86.

In an all-Scandinavian tie Osters fell behind at home when the Norwegians from Kongsvinger went ahead in what was their first competitive match in Europe. Persson equalised within three minutes for Osters but two second-half goals for the visitors enabled them to leave Sweden with a 3-1 advantage. In the second leg a hat-trick by Frigard helped the Norwegians on the way to a 4-1 win and overall 7-2 advantage. Another win to cause some surprise was achieved by OFI of Crete. Having drawn 1-1 in Prague, a goal three minutes from the interval by Mahlas gave them a 2-1 aggregate win over Slavia.

Denmark's European championship win has not been reflected by their club performances in the UEFA Cup. However Thorst's 66th-minute winner for AaB over Spanish league leaders Deportivo La Coruna – making their European debut – did raise one or two eyebrows. A Brazilian-style hat-trick by Bebeto and a couple from Barragan corrected matters in the second leg as Deportivo ran out 5-0 winners and 5-1 on aggregate.

Slovenia's Maribor Branik returned from Gloria Bistrita with a goalless draw in what was a rather uninspiring encounter. The Romanian newcomers fared little better in the second leg and two goals by Stanic at the start and end of the match gave Maribor the second-round spot.

Representing the Ukraine, Dnepr Dnepropetrovsk had gained considerable experience in the Champions' Cup as Soviet representatives in 1984–85 and 1989–90, reaching the quarter-finals stages on both occasions. A goal 13 minutes from time by Maximov provided a 1-0 margin win over Austrian opponents Admira Wacker. Bezhanar looked to have given the Ukrainians a firm hold on passage to the second round with his goal two minutes before the interval in the second leg, but Bacher's almost immediate equaliser gave both sides something to think about during the interval. Dnepr responded the more positively with a goal early on from Pokhlebaev, and Mikhaylenko sealed the Austrians' fate. They put a more respectable air on the scoreline with a goal in the final seconds from Ljung, but the Ukrainians went through 4-2 on aggregate.

Promotion as champions of the Turkish Second Division Group A in 1992 had been followed up with a third-place spot in 1992–93 to earn Kocaelispor Kulubu a spot in the UEFA Cup, where they found themselves paired with Bobby Robson's Sporting Lisbon. Fifteen thousand saw a goalless draw in the first leg at the Ispetpasa Stadium. Matters were rather different in Lisbon as Cadete shot Sporting into an early lead that was supplemented by Pacheco's goal early in the second half, to earn the Portuguese a 2-0 win overall.

Turkey did get a representative into the second round, though, as Trabzonspor produced home and away victories of 3-1 to see off the challenge of Valletta. The Maltese took the lead in both encounters through Zarb, only to see it erased within three minutes each time. Boavista had a comfortable win over US Luxembourg and Oliveira's second goal in the 4-0 win at home was the 50th scored by the Portuguese side in all European competitions. The Austrians SV Casino Salzburg achieved a very creditable 4-0 aggregate win over Slovakians Dac Dunjaska Streda, winning both encounters by two goals.

A goal three minutes from time in the Christa Botev stadium secured a 3-2 victory for visitors Olympiakos over Botev Plovdiv. The return in Piraeus was a one-sided affair as Olympiakos won 5-1 and Batista's goal five minutes from time was the club's 100th goal in 85 games of European cup competitions. Having beaten Apollon 2-0 in Vac, the Samsung club would have travelled to Limassol full of confidence. It turned out to be over-confidence as a goal either side of the interval by Scepovic levelled the tie. In the second period of extra time the home side were awarded a penalty which Spoliarec converted and as Vac went forward in search of what would have been a winning away goal, Kricmarevic broke to make it 4-0 on the night and 4-2 on aggregate to the Cypriots with just two minutes remaining.

The draw for the first round had pitted four of the stronger European sides against one another in two Germany *v* Netherlands encounters. Bayern Munich, playing their 50th game in the UEFA Cup, had established a two-goal lead by half-time in their match in Enschede against FC Twente. Two goals in a minute in the second half left the score at 1-3 but a period of concerted pressure by the Dutch side midway through the half saw goals by Prince Polly and Vurens level the scores at three each. The Germans, however, took a first-leg lead back to the Olympiastadion when Ziege scored his second goal of the night right on the full-time whistle. The game in the Bavarian capital was more decisive, with Bayern winning 3-0 helped by an own goal on the stroke of half-time by Karnebeek.

Karlsruhe looked to have the harder task against 13-times Dutch champions PSV. Two goals inside the first half-hour by Schmitt and Kiriakov put the Germans into a 2-0 lead, but Popescu pulled a goal back from the penalty spot shortly before the interval. That proved to be the last goal of the game and PSV looked set to finish the job in Eindhoven two weeks later. As it was Karlsruhe were more than up to the task of defending their slender lead, and PSV failed to break down the defence for the single score that would have put them through on the away-goals rule.

Second Round

The second round of the UEFA Cup continued to throw up surprises in line with those of the first. Top of them and the performance of the round belonged to Karlsruhe. The German club travelled to face a Valencia side who had just completed the month of October as league leaders following six wins and two draws from their opening nine games. The first leg bore out that point. The Spanish club's form was maintained as they took a three-goal lead, started by Mijatovic ten minutes before the interval and continued with a double by Penev in the second half. A late goal by Schmitt looked to have given KSC a fighting chance in the second leg in the Wildparkstadion.

As it was the events that unfolded were quite sensational as the Germans – embarking on only their fourth European match – demolished the Spanish with seven goals before an ecstatic full house of 25,000. It was without doubt the greatest night in the club's 99-year history. Karlsruhe's hero was striker Edgar Schmitt who scored four goals – two in each half. 'The greatest achievement in my sporting career', he said. Valencia returned home humiliated and the result was to have a profound effect on their domestic season.

Another Spanish side were to suffer an humiliating exit, this time through their status and not by the score. Luis Garcia scored a 58th-minute goal to give Atletico Madrid a home win over OFI Crete. Two weeks later in front of a near-capacity crowd OFI produced an unlikely 2-0 win on the night – 2-1 on aggregate – with second-half goals from Mahlas and Tsifoutis.

The second round wasn't a complete graveyard for the Spanish though and two clubs did enough to secure a third-round berth. In the second Spain *v* Greece encounter, Tenerife got the better of Olympiakos – just. A goal by Christensen gave Olympiakos an early lead in Tenerife, but goals either side of the break from Julio Llorente and Del Solar provided the home side a slender lead to take to Piraeus. Christensen was again an early starter for the Greeks and twice put the home side into the lead only to see it erased, first by Minambres and then from the penalty spot by Chano. Ioannides restored the home lead only for Amanatides to wipe it out with an own goal. With three away goals conceded, Olympiakos needed two more to avoid defeat. Six minutes from time Christensen completed his hat-trick but despite a volatile atmosphere, Tenerife held on to draw the tie 5-5, and go through on the away-goals rule.

Deportivo La Coruna looked to have blown their chances of progression into the third round. A 1-1 draw with Aston Villa was rescued only by a goal three minutes from time, and that after Australian international keeper Mark Bosnich had saved Bebeto's fourth-minute penalty awarded when Paul McGrath had brought the Brazilian down. Despite that early set-back, Deportivo continued to dominate the early stages, but Villa – with Daley a lone figure up front – were quick to turn defence into attack when the time arrived. Deportivo again spent much of the second half forcing Villa to the wall but with 11 minutes remaining a superbly-taken breakaway goal by Dean Saunders, set up by Dalian Atkinson's intelligent run, gave the visitors an unexpected lead. But with the seconds running out Riesco, a late substitute for

Manjarin, levelled the score to create a fascinating return leg.

Bosnich – the hero of the first leg for Villa – had his place in the return leg under threat. Having decided to play in the first leg of the World Cup eliminator for Australia against Argentina in Sydney, the highly-rated keeper flew back and put away the side effects of jet lag to get in the starting line-up ahead of Nigel Spink who, his club manager had threatened, might take his place. A crowd limit of 26,737 had been imposed on Villa Park by UEFA who had declared the match 'high risk', and the supporters had to watch a dismal performance by Villa against a thoroughly professional one from the Spanish side, who secured a deserved 1-0 win on the night to see them through to the third round. The goal came nine minutes from the break, when a graceful move from deep inside their own half gathered momentum with captain Fran's defence-splitting ball along the right flank into the path of the overlapping Nando, whose cross was perfect for Manjarin to nod home at the far post.

Another side continuing their first excursion into Europe produced a performance of the highest calibre to see off three-times Champions' Cup winners Bayern Munich. With much of Europe's press writing off Norwich City, the Canaries turned in an excellent display to go two goals ahead and stun the home supporters in the Olympiastadion. Both goals came from free-kicks – the first after Mark Robins had to be taken off following a foul that led to Rob Newman infiltrating behind the Brazilian international full-back Jorginho, and when his cross was headed out by Lothar Matthaus it fell perfectly for Jeremy Goss to volley back past an astonished Aumann.

The Bayern keeper was again helpless when Norwich scored their second. Crook flighted a free-kick from the right, and although Sutton was fouled for what should have been a penalty the ball carried on, bounced, and Mark Bowen scored with a header that was unchallenged. Just as Norwich had hoped to take their two-goal advantage to the safety of their dressing room, Bayern scored. Jorginho, who was guilty of ball-watching for both City's goals, atoned to some extent with a right-wing run and cross which picked out Christian Nerlinger eight yards out, and his header gave Gunn little chance. The second half produced a game of cat and mouse in which Adolfo Valencia had two excellent chances that produced saves of equal status by Bryan Gunn to earn City a victory and become the first British club to beat Bayern on their own soil.

Unsavoury after-match comments by Matthaus about the standard of the Norwich victory did little to calm what was likely to be a highly-charged encounter at Carrow Road, where Bayern arrived reportedly on £8,000 per man to win the tie. The Germans got off to the perfect start when the Colombian Valencia gave them a fourth-minute lead from close range following a corner.

Paul McGrath of Aston Villa beats Fran of Deportivo La Coruna to the ball.

Jeremy Goss scores the equalising goal for Norwich City against Bayern Munich at Carrow Road.

As the half progressed Gunn was forced to make a series of saves as City, without strikers Ekoku and Robins, found it difficult to muster attacks. Yet Norwich fought back to level the game and a packed Carrow Road rose as one when, early in the second half, Goss was on hand to side-foot home Sutton's flick from Bowen's left-wing centre. Bayern threatened once or twice but Norwich held on for a totally deserved aggregate victory.

In Glasgow, Celtic secured a one-goal win over Sporting Lisbon. However, the talk of the night wasn't the match but the news that Stoke City had given manager Lou Macari permission to talk to Celtic following the dismissal of Liam Brady. A first half of commitment and aggression was matched by fluent football and the boost of a ninth-minute goal scored by Creaney after Pexei tried to be too clever in cutting out a cross from Byrne. Paul McStay, dropped by Scotland the previous week for their match in Italy, was outstanding for the home side, who created and missed enough chances to have settled the tie on the night.

The return in Lisbon was a different matter, with Sporting asserting themselves early on and the triangular passing moves of Cadete and Chtcherbakov always threatening. Jorge Cadete, the Portuguese striker who had ended Scotland's World Cup ambitions, did the same to Celtic's European dreams. Sporting proved too skilful for a determined Celtic side who could do nothing to stop Cadete from scoring in the 18th and 60th minutes. With the defence looking for an offside that never came, Cadete skipped into the path of a through ball just inside the Celtic half and charged on to slide the ball past the advancing Pat Bonner. Celtic had opportunities but they went begging as Krasimir Balakov provided the ball for Cadete to place it wide of Bonner from close range and seal Celtic's fate.

Apollon – having knocked out Vac in the first round – gave Internazionale a large fright in what was turning into a disappointing domestic season for the Italians. Bergkamp continued to find his scoring legs in Europe, this time after six minutes of play in the San Siro. The expected goal glut never came and a disciplined display by the Cypriots limited Inter to that single goal. The second leg seemed to be flowing Inter's way as early goals by Shalimov and Bergkamp, again, swept them into a 2-0 lead on the night and 3-0 overall. But Inter's defence was not as strong as in recent years and Spolijiarec gave the home crowd something to celebrate when he scored. The celebrations turned to euphoria when Cepovic levelled the scores on the night at 2-2 just after the half-hour. But they were short-lived as Fontolan restored Inter's lead shortly before half-time. The score remained that way until five minutes from the end when

Second Round Results

Atletico Madrid Luis Garcia (58)	OFI Crete	1-0	11,600
OFI Crete Mahlas (51), Tsifoutis (64)	Atletico Madrid	2-0	13,000
OFI Crete win 2-1 on aggregate			
Bayern Munich Nerlinger (41)	Norwich City Goss (13), Bowen (30)	1-2	28,500
Norwich City Goss (50)	Bayern Munich Valencia (4)	1-1	20,829
Norwich City win 3-2 on aggregate			
Bordeaux Paille (35), Vercruysse (56)	Servette Anderson Da Silva (55)	2-1	15,000
Servette	Bordeaux Own goal (Schepul 66)	0-1	18,000
Bordeaux win 3-1 on aggregate			
Celtic Creaney (9)	Sporting Lisbon	1-0	31,321
Sporting Lisbon Cadete (18, 60)	Celtic	2-0	62,500
Sporting Lisbon win 2-1 on aggregate			
Deportivo La Coruna Riesco (87)	Aston Villa Saunders (80)	1-1	26,800
Aston Villa	Deportivo La Coruna Manjarin (36)	0-1	26,737
Deportivo La Coruna win 2-1 on aggregate			
Eintracht Frankfurt Furtok (65), Okocha (77)	Dnepr Dnepropetrovsk	2-0	6,900
Dnepr Dnepropetrovsk Chukhliba (43)	Eintracht Frankfurt	1-0	25,000
Eintracht Frankfurt win 2-1 on aggregate			
Internazionale Bergkamp (6)	Apollon Limassol	1-0	15,000
Apollon Limassol Spolijiarec (11), Cepovic (32), Iosephides (85)	Internazionale Shalimov (6), Bergkamp (8), Fontolan (38)	3-3	12,000
Internazionale win 4-3 on aggregate			
Kongsvinger IL Frigard (89)	Juventus Kohler (61)	1-1	10,213
Juventus Moller (27), Ravanelli (68)	Kongsvinger IL	2-0	14,000
Juventus win 3-1 on aggregate			
Kuusysi Lahti Ismo Lius (13)	Brondby Okechukwu (1), Vilfort (59), Strudal (64, 84)	1-4	5,000
Brondby Kristensen (39), Madsen (68), Hoegh (85 pen)	Kuusysi Lahti Annunen (6)	3-1	5,834
Brondby win 7-2 on aggregate			
KV Mechelen Eszenyi (44, 80, 83), De Boeck (59), Leen (72)	MTK Budapest	5-0	7,000
MTK Budapest Kovacs (59)	KV Mechelen Carlos Pereira (10)	1-1	1,500
KV Mechelen win 6-1 on aggregate			
Lazio Winter (74)	Boavista FC	1-0	40,000
Boavista FC Owubokiri (20, 52)	Lazio	2-0	10,000
Boavista win 2-1 on aggregate			
Maribor Branik	Borussia Dortmund	0-0	14,000
Borussia Dortmund Chapuisat (48, 52)	Maribor Branik Bozgo (21)	2-1	25,000
Borussia Dortmund win 2-1 on aggregate			
SV Casino Salzburg Jurcevic (67)	Royal Antwerp	1-0	11,000
Royal Antwerp	SV Casino Salzburg Feiersinger (84)	0-1	7,500
SV Casino Salzburg win 2-0 on aggregate			
Tenerife Julio Llorente (38), Del Solar (49)	Olympiakos Christensen (10)	2-1	20,000
Olympiakos Christensen (13, 34, 84), Ioannides (58)	Tenerife Minambres (23), Chano (49 pen), Amanatides (own goal 68)	4-3	28,000
Tenerife win on away goals rule. 5-5 on aggregate			
Trabzonspor Orhan Cikrikci (27)	Cagliari Dely Valdes (89)	1-1	21,500
Cagliari	Trabzonspor	0-0	30,000
Cagliari win on away goals rule. 1-1 on aggregate			
Valencia Mijatovic (35), Penev (47, 74)	Karlsruhe SC Schmitt (79)	3-1	42,900
Karlsruhe SC Schmitt (29, 34, 59, 63), Schutterle (37), Scmarov (46), Bilic (90)	Valencia	7-0	25,000
Karlsruhe win 8-3 on aggregate			

Iosephides produced a goal to secure a highly creditable 3-3 draw and an aggregate defeat for the side from Limassol by just a single goal – something the Italian press went to town about in the days after the tie.

Juventus became the second Italian side to qualify for the third round with a 3-1 aggregate win over Kongsvinger. Kohler's 61st-minute goal looked to have given Juve victory in Norway but a last-minute equaliser came from Frigard. A goal in each half by

Moller and Ravanelli proved to be too much in Turin as coach Trapattoni's side eased through.

Cagliari continued the progression of Italian sides by a slightly narrower margin over Trabzonspor. The Turks, with home advantage in the first leg, took the lead through Orhan Cikrikci and kept a hold on it until Dely Valdes netted in the final minute to give the Sardinians a draw and a vital away goal. Vital it proved, because the return leg ended goalless in front of a capacity crowd.

Two second-leg goals by Owubokiri gave Boavista a 2-1 aggregate win over Lazio to prevent all four Italians clubs from progressing to the third round. Dutchman Aron Winter had secured a 1-0 win in Rome for Lazio but it wasn't enough.

Royal Antwerp's fifth consecutive season in Europe came to an end at the feet of SV Casino Salzburg. Jurcevic's goal in the second half of the first leg gave the Austrians an advantage to take to the Belgian capital, and with the home side committing players forward in the dying minutes of the second leg, Feiersinger broke away to record another 1-0 win for the Austrians – 2-0 overall.

Maribor Branik held 1992–93 semi-finalists Borussia Dortmund to a goalless draw in Slovenia but with the return leg a supposed formality for the Germans, Bozgo gave Maribor a surprise lead midway through the first half. With the score remaining that way at the break the erratic Germans had to wait until Stephane Chapuisat levelled the scores three minutes into the second period. Four minutes later the Swiss international struck again to put Borussia ahead and through on aggregate.

Dnepr travelled to Frankfurt for the first leg of their second-round tie and annoyed the home crowd with a frustrating display. There was great relief when Furtok pounced 20 minutes into the second half. Okocha added a second shortly thereafter to give Eintracht a two-goal advantage to take to the Ukraine. It proved enough, despite Chukhliba's goal just before the interval, and the Germans held on for a 2-1 aggregate win.

Brondby had a relatively short journey for their second round, having been paired with Kuusysi Lahti. The Finns were put in their place as early as the first minute when Okechukwu scored and despite an equaliser 12 minutes later by Lius, three second-half goals gave the Swedes a comfortable 4-1 advantage to take home with them. It became slightly less comfortable when Annunen put Kuusysi ahead in the Brondby stadium. But Kristensen levelled the scores on the night before the break and Madsen and Hoegh made their mark in the second half to give Brondby a 7-2 aggregate victory.

In Bordeaux, Anderson Da Silva fired Servette a priceless away goal when he equalised Paille's opener for the French. Despite Vercruysse restoring Bordeaux's lead within a minute that still looked to be the key to the tie. The result was decided in favour of the French in the second leg, however, when Schepul put through his own goal midway through the second half.

KV Mechelen produced the second-highest score of the round with a 5-0 thumping of MTK. Eszenyi helped himself to a hat-trick against the Hungarians, who managed a 1-1 draw in the return in Budapest, watched by only 1,500 spectators.

Second Round Summary

P	HW	D	AW	HG	AG	TG
32	19	8	5	54	25	79

Ties won on aggregate:	30
Ties won on away goals:	2
Ties won on penalty kicks:	0
Highest aggregate game:	8-3 Karlsruhe v Valencia
Biggest home win:	7-0 Karlsruhe v Valencia
Biggest away win:	1-4 Kuusysi Lahti v Brondby

Top Scorers – All Rounds

6	Christensen (Olympiakos), Schmitt (Karlsruhe SC)
5	Bergkamp (Internazionale), Frigard (Kongsvinger IL)
4	Eszenyi (KV Mechelen)
3	Annunen (Kuusysi Lahti), Bebeto (Deportivo La Coruna), Cadete (Sporting Lisbon), Chapuisat (Borussia Dortmund), Furtok (Eintracht Frankfurt), Goss (Norwich City), Kristensen (Brondby), Lius (Kuusysi Lahti), Ogun (Trabzonspor), Owubokiri (Boavista FC), Penev (Valencia), Vercruysse (Bordeaux), Ziege (Bayern Munich)

Third Round

The draw for the third round threw together top clubs from Germany, Italy and Spain. The results, though, went pretty much to form without the real shocks of the second round – apart from one.

SV Casino Salzburg travelled to Lisbon knowing that they would need to produce perhaps their finest European performance if they were to have a chance of making the quarter-final stages. The task that faced them as they left Portugal would have looked even more daunting, trailing 2-0 to a goal in each half for Sporting, first from Sergi Cherbakov and then Cadete. The population of Salzburg seemed to think their task was perhaps too difficult and the Lehen stadium was only half full for the return leg. After a goalless first half the second period got off to a flying start for the home side who went ahead just two minutes into it when Austrian international Leo Lainer hit the back of the net. As the game neared full-time the Austrians swarmed around the Portuguese goal and Sporting's small band of travelling supporters – whistling frantically – were silenced as Hutter produced an aggregate equaliser with very nearly the last kick of the 90 minutes. The first period of extra time brought little goal mouth action but then midway through the second stretch of extra time Amerhauser hit a winner to send the crowd home knowing they had seen a great European encounter and eagerly looking forward to the quarter-final draw. Not so Sporting manager Bobby Robson, whose contract would be terminated shortly after.

Having whacked Valencia out of sight in the previous round, Karlsruhe travelled to Bordeaux needing fear no one. Zinedine Zidane's goal late in the second half gave the French side a lead to take to Germany but they must have been apprehensive when Schmitt – who scored four of that famous seven in the previous round – levelled the tie after 16 minutes. There was no further score until midway through the second half when the Russian international Sergei Kiriakov put Karlsruhe two goals ahead. Qualification for the quarter-finals was made secure when Schmitt notched his second of the evening and seventh European goal in four games.

One of the most intriguing ties of the third round involved the pairing of Eintracht Frankfurt and Deportivo La Coruna. The German club were dismayed at the low turnout for their game in the Waldstadion and as many of those were filtering out into the surrounding park having thought they had witnessed a goalless 'win' for the Spanish, defender Mirko Dickhaut, a product of the Eintracht juniors, popped up to score a last-minute winner that had the Spanish bench cursing but home trainer Klaus Toppmoller jumping for joy. A capacity crowd turned out for the return leg in La Coruna but they were quickly silenced as veteran Mauirizo Gaudino gave the Germans an early lead. Deportivo tried desperately to break through for a quick equalising goal but Uli Stein in the Eintracht goal – with some 450 first-class appearances behind him – was equal to the task and Deportivo's first excursion into European competition had ended after just six games.

In East Anglia, Dennis Bergkamp continued his single-handed demolition of English soccer when he gave Internazionale a 1-0 win over Norwich City. Having scored vital goals for Holland that effectively eliminated England from the World Cup finals, he converted an 80th-minute penalty to allow Internazionale to return to Milan with a 1-0 win. Bergkamp, who was having a generally miserable time in finding his Serie A scoring form, had no such trouble in Europe, but missed three excellent opportunities to make the second leg a formality. The City keeper Bryan Gunn produced two fine saves to deny the Dutchman and on the one occasion he was beaten, Ian Culverhouse was on hand to whip the ball off the line.

Frustration crept into the Norwich play and ended with their having collected 11 yellow cards from their five European encounters – although nobody would refer to them as a physical side. Norwich produced an effective passing game but other than a 25-yarder by Jeremy Goss that rattled Zenga's crossbar 14 minutes

Watch the ball! Davide Fontolan of Inter looks on with Rob Newman and John Polston of Norwich City.

Third Round Results

Bordeaux Zidane (77)	Karlsruhe SC	1-0	32,000		KV Mechelen Czerniatynski (38)	Cagliari Matteoli (33), Oliviera (82), Pusceddu (87)	1-3	7,000
Karlsruhe SC Schmitt (16, 75), Kiriakov (65)	Bordeaux	3-0	25,000		Cagliari Firicano (14), Allegri (79)	KV Mechelen	2-0	32,000
Karlsruhe SC win 3-1 on aggregate					*Cagliari win 5-1 on aggregate*			
Brondby Kristensen (19)	Borussia Dortmund Chapuisat (61)	1-1	16,817		Norwich City	Internazionale Bergkamp (81 pen)	0-1	20,805
Borussia Dortmund Zorc (29)	Brondby	1-0	35,000		Internazionale Bergkamp (88)	Norwich City	1-0	30,000
Borussia Dortmund win 2-1 on aggregate					*Internazionale win 2-0 on aggregate*			
Eintracht Frankfurt Dickhaut (89)	Deportivo La Coruna	1-0	12,000		OFI Crete Velic (89)	Boavista FC Artur Oliveira (4, 22, 54), Owubokiri (42)	1-4	10,000
Deportivo La Coruna	Eintracht Frankfurt Gaudino (15)	0-1	33,000		Boavista FC Nelson (24), Nogueira (77)	OFI Crete	2-0	7,000
Eintracht Frankfurt win 2-0 on aggregate					*Boavista win 6-1 on aggregate*			
Juventus Moller (3), R. Baggio (69 pen), Ravanelli (75)	Tenerife	3-0	10,000		Sporting Lisbon Cherbakov (24), Cadete (63)	SV Casino Salzburg	2-0	42,500
Tenerife Aguilera (37), Del Solar (86)	Juventus Moller (85)	2-1	21,000		SV Casino Salzburg Lainer (47), Hutter (90), Amerhauser (113)	Sporting Lisbon	3-0	10,500
Juventus win 4-2 on aggregate					*SV Casino Salzburg win 3-2 on aggregate*			

from time they did little to trouble the experienced keeper. But when Rob Newman fouled Ruben Sosa with ten minutes to go, the Swiss referee pointed to the spot and Bergkamp did not give Gunn any hope of saving his venomous kick.

Needing to win in the San Siro was always going to be a big task, but Norwich's away form had been far superior to that of home and had they not become the first British club to beat Bayern Munich in their own back yard? A tough job was made all the tougher, however, as Ian Butterworth, their skipper, playmaker Ian Crook and sweeper Ian Culverhouse were all missing having received their second bookings of the competition in the first leg.

Once again it was Bergkamp who did the damage, scoring the only goal of an entertaining game in its dying embers. He ghosted down the left with the ball and produced a perfect 'pass' into the back of the net, squeezing the ball between Gunn and the far post. Norwich had the better of the first half and both Sutton and stand-in Ullathorne had opportunities to open the scoring – the latter only eight yards away from a gaping goal. Ekoku produced the move of the night when he controlled the ball on a thigh and hooked it over the advancing Zenga, but also wide of the post. Inter looked more composed in the second half and Bergkamp dived in an effort to win a penalty before Norwich paid for not taking their chances.

Internazionale's win was just one of three by Italian clubs as they strengthened their hold on the competition. Holders Juventus got off to the perfect start against Tenerife in the Stadio Delle Alpi with a third-minute goal by Germany's Andreas Moller. A penalty converted by Roberto Baggio in the 69th minute helped ease the tension being generated by a small crowd before

Third Round Summary

P	HW	D	AW	HG	AG	TG
16	11	1	4	24	11	35

Ties won on aggregate: 8
Ties won on away goals: 0
Ties won on penalty kicks: 0

Highest aggregate game: 6-1 Boavista v OFI Crete
Biggest home win: 3-0 Karlsruhe v Bordeaux
  SV Casino Salzburg v Sporting Lisbon
Biggest away win: 1-4 OFI Crete v Boavista

Top Scorers – All Rounds

8	Schmitt (Karlsruhe SC)
7	Bergkamp (Internazionale
6	Christensen (Olympiakos)
5	Frigaard (Konigsvinger IL), Oliveira (Boavista FC)
4	Cadete (Sporting Lisbon), Chapuisat (Borussia Dortmund), Eszenyi (KV Mechelen), Kristensen (Brondby), Owubokiri (Boavista FC)
3	Annunen (Kuusysi Lahti), Baggio R. (Juventus), Bebeto (Deportivo La Coruna), Furtok (Eintracht Frankfurt), Goss (Norwich City), Lius (Kuusysi Lahti), Ogun (Trabzonspor), Penev (Valencia), Ravanelli (Juventus), Vercruysse (Bordeaux), Ziege (Bayern Munich)

Sergeij Kirjakow of Karlsruhe (white) and Marcio Santos of Bordeaux battle for possession of the ball during their third round UEFA Cup tie.

Ravenelli scored to effectively make the second leg a formality. Aguilera opened the scoring for the Spanish in the return but Moller's goal five minutes from time secured a quarter-final berth despite Del Solar's goal for Tenerife.

Sardinians Cagliari continued to make their mark in the competition, winning their first leg in Mechelen 3-1. Two goals in five minutes towards the end of the first half sent the sides in all-square at the break and that's the way it stayed until Oliveira and Pusceddu struck for the Italians in the final minutes for a decisive 3-1 win. MV had little to offer in the second leg, where the packed home support were soon celebrating a 2-0 win on the night, 5-1 overall.

OFI came unstuck in their attempt to progress in the competition, a hat-trick by Artur Oliveira helping Boavista to an impressive 4-1 win on Crete soil. The Portuguese had led 4-0 and it was only a last-minute consolation goal by Velic that gave the home side anything to celebrate. Boavista's passage was confirmed with a 2-0 win in Oporto two weeks later.

Jesper Kristensen gave Brondby an early lead at home to their German opposition from Dortmund. But Borussia went back to their Westfalenstadion with a draw thanks to Stephane Chapuisat's second-half equaliser. The second leg was as tight as the first in Denmark and Zorc's goal on the half-hour proved to be the decisive one as Borussia went through 2-1 on aggregate.

Quarter-Finals

Italian and German clubs dominated the quarter-final draw. Of the eight contestants there were three clubs from each country, with SV Casino Salzburg and Boavista making up the numbers. Not surprisingly the draw produced some very interesting confrontations. Holders Juventus were paired against Serie A rivals Cagliari, while Internazionale were to travel to the team Juve beat in the 1992–93 final, Borussia Dortmund. The Germans were spared national derby games, with Karlsruhe drawing Boavista and Eintracht Frankfurt travelling to Salzburg.

Sardinians Cagliari, experiencing their first venture into Europe for 21 years, might have felt somewhat disappointed at drawing Juventus. Some might say that it was better the devil you know, and the sides were in tenth and second positions in the league when they faced each other in the first leg of a highly entertaining tie in the Sant' Elia Stadium.

Juve – who had won the Serie A encounter 1-0 – went into the game missing a number of key players. Dino Baggio was serving a suspension balanced by the availability of their influential defender Andy Moller, who had been banned from three league matches following an outburst in which he accused an Italian referee of being part of the Mafioso.

The first half saw Juve making the more positive plays and Cagliari looking to develop their own attacks on the counter. Indeed Juve should have gone ahead early on in the game when Roberto Baggio and Fortunato combined to set Di Livio free. His header was cleared off the line and from the follow-up Ravenelli blasted over. Cagliari's response nearly brought a spectacular goal when Matteoli's bicycle kick was just wide following Herrera's penetrating cross.

Juve started the second half as they had the first – on the attack – but then in a blinding 10-minute spell Cagliari took the lead and might have easily have put the game beyond reach at the first time of asking. A move down the left culminated in Herrera playing a one-two with Dely Valdes on the edge of the area. Herrera tried to take the ball deeper but the attentions of four defenders limited his progress. The ball broke to Dely Valdes, whose first-time low drive from 10 yards went inside Peruzzi's right-hand post. Cagliari continued to look the more dangerous side and Peruzzi had to save brilliantly first from Moriero and then after Moller's outstretched leg had looked to have denied Dely Valdes a second chance.

For the return leg in Turin, Juventus were boosted by the return of Dino Baggio on what turned out to be an evening of inspired keeping by Cagliari's Valerio Fiori. In a frantic opening period he produced three excellent saves that probably would have brought Juve goals on other nights.

Juve's pressure had to tell, and in a glorious move they took the lead when Dino Baggio raced into the area to sidefoot the ball home, getting on the end of Di Livio's low cross and moving into the space created by Roberto Baggio's run across the face of the six-yard box.

But then, just as the Sardinians looked as though they might be swamped, they equalised. The referee awarded a dubious free-kick on the right that was hotly disputed by Conte, the supposed

Open mouthed as Karlsruhe's Dirk Schuster leans into a Boavista player.

perpetrator of the foul. Matteoli picked himself up to take the kick, dropped it into the centre of the penalty area, and Firicano got free of his marker, Kohler, to produce a firm downward header past Peruzzi.

Juventus were reduced to ten men when play-acting by Herrera resulted in Kohler getting his marching orders. After the interval, and despite being a man light, Juve continued to create chances. Ravenelli in particular went close with a header from a corner. Then, when Ravenelli broke into the area on to a through ball, he was adjudged to have been pulled down by Fiori and a penalty was awarded. Roberto Baggio stepped up and fired the ball wide to add further to an already over-passionate night.

Inspired by Baggio's miss, Cagliari gained new heart and moments after Dely Valdes's header was curiously disallowed for a supposed offside, Marco Sanna produced a superb 40-yard pass that set Oliveira away to drill the ball past Zenga – giving Cagliari a 2-1 win on the night and passage to the semi-finals 3-1 on aggregate.

Karlsruhe travelled to Porto boasting the best defence in the Bundesliga and showed why by dominating the Portuguese side, who were often reduce to producing cynical fouls. The Bolivian

Otto Konrad the SV Casino Salzburg goalkeeper is mobbed after scoring the penalty against Eintracht Frankfurt that put his side into the UEFA Cup semi-finals.

Sanchez was a particular culprit. Nevertheless the Germans kept their composure, with Nowotny playing as a sweeper to combat the pace of Boavista's Nigerian, Ricky Owubokiri.

Bobo nearly drew first blood for Boavista with a powerful shot from 25 yards following a free-kick. Oliver Kahn was equal to his effort. From that point it was the Germans who looked the more purposeful side, playing from the back and building patiently. A foul by Nogueira resulted in a free-kick that Manfred Bender drove from 40 yards. The ball looked certain to go into the top left hand corner of the net but Alfredo did well to palm it away for a corner. Bender had the ball in the net shortly after when he produced an excellent half-volley from 15 yards but the Austrian referee had blown for offside.

Having been under the cosh for a period, Boavista swept up field with Sanchez – showing his creative nature – delivering a dangerous pass into the area which took on an even more dangerous nature following a deflection. The ball dropped into the path of Paulo Sousa, whose first-time effort produced a brilliant reflex save from Kahn. The relief was short, for Boavista took the lead from the resultant corner.

The ball was delivered with pace to the near post and Sanchez held off the challenge of Nowotny to flick the ball on. Kahn – who had been caught in two minds – saw the ball sail past him and Owubokiri dipped his head to nod home from less than a yard. The goal came six minutes from the interval and was poor reward for Karlsruhe, who had dominated the play to that point.

Early in the second half Boavista missed a golden opportunity to double their lead when Artur intercepted a back pass and immediately fed it back square to Owubokiri, whose shot from the edge of the area thumped against the bar with Kahn well beaten.

From going within a whisker of being two goals up, Boavista immediately found themselves pulled back to 1-1 as Karlsruhe swept upfield from Kahn's goal-kick to record a deserved equaliser. Witter and Rolff combined well in the right of midfield and the long curling cross cannoned off Tavares just inside the 18 yard line. The ball fell perfectly for Witter, who shot into the net via a post. Bonan was unlucky not to steal a win for the visitors two minutes from time when his left-foot drive was only inches over the bar.

In the second leg Slaven Bilic proved to be Karlsruhe's most potent weapon and with a modicum of luck the Croatian defender might have had a hat-trick as headers from set-plays went within inches of finding the back of the net. What proved to be the only goal of the night came after half a minute of frantic pressure on the Boavista goal. Alfredo saved well to deny Kiriakov – who was a constant threat all evening – but his parry eventually fell to Rolff on the left of the area and his low shot at the keeperless goal was turned in by Nogueira in his attempt to whip the ball clear.

Needing to score, Boavista enjoyed more of the play in the second period and Kahn in the home goal had to be at his best to keep out three cleverly disguised corners by Nelo. There were few chances for the Germans to secure their lead other than in the last few minutes when Wolfgang Rolff almost set himself up with a neat flick through the defence, but Alfredo was alert to block his follow through. At the other end Owubokiri looked set to equalise but Kahn again did enough to foil him. In the dying minutes Paulo Sousa was sent off for a second bookable offence as the Germans held on to gain a place in the semi-final draw.

When SV Casino Salzburg were drawn against Eintracht Frankfurt they were only too aware that no Austrian club side had eliminated a German club from European competition in 18 attempts. But after a first leg best forgotten they were in with a shout of doing just that. UEFA had set a crowd limit of 8,500 for the game in Salzburg – the club upset many fans by moving the game 190 miles away to Vienna's Ernst Happel stadium. With 47,000 fans turning up for the match it seemed to be a popular switch in the end.

The game proved to be an often over-physical encounter best remembered for the sight of Anthony Yeboah's white cleats that earned him wolf-whistles the whole night. Hutter's goal on the half hour proved to be enough on the night, which ended with Salzburg trainer Otto Baric spitting at one of the German players. UEFA immediately imposed a five-match ban on the coach, who found himself having to sit in the stands for the rest of his side's campaign.

Quarter-Finals

SV Casino Salzburg   **Eintracht Frankfurt**   1-0
Hutter (30)
Att: 47,000   *Ref:* Tsjoesainov (Rus)
Salzburg: Konrad, Lainer, Weber, Winklhofer, Furstaller (Stadler 46), Aigner, Jurcevic, Pfeifenberger, Marquinho, Amerhausen, Hutter
Eintracht: Stein, Tschadadze, Weber, Dickhaut, Binz (Moller 89), Gaudino, Falkenmayer, Bommer, Yeboah, Komljenovic, Mihajlovic (Becker 74)
Yellow Cards: Pfeifenberger, Dickhaut, Furstaller and Weber (Salzburg) and Bommer (Eintracht)
Red Card: Dickhaut (Eintracht) – two yellow cards

Eintracht Frankfurt   **SV Casino Salzburg**   1-0
Gaudino (21)
Att: 26,000   *Ref:* Elleray (Eng)
Eintracht: Stein, Komljenovic, Tschadadze, Bommer (Bindwald 71), Moller (Reis 66), Gaudino, Binz, Bein, Weber, Furtok, Yeboah
Salzburg: Konrad, Lainer, Pfeifenberger, Garger, Winklhofer, Artner, Hutter, Feiersinger, Aigner, Jurcevic, Marquinho (Stadler 50 (Amerhausen 114))
Yellow Cards: Moller, Bommer, Weber (Eintracht) and Winklhofer, Artner, Marquinho, Hutter, Feiersinger, Jurcevic (Salzburg).
Red Card: Artner (Salzburg) – two yellow cards
1-1 on aggregate after extra time. Salzburg win 5-4 on penalties

Boavista   **Karlsruhe SC**   1-1
Owubokiri (39)   Witter (77)
Att: 10,000   *Ref:* Grabher (Aus)
Boavista: Alfredo, Paulo Sousa, Tavares, Rui Bento, Nogueira, Nelo, Bobo, Sanchez, Caetano (Bambo 80), Owubokiri, Artur (Jamie Alves 78)
Karlsruhe: Kahn, Metz, Witter, Bilic, Schutterle, Nowotny, Rolff, Bender, Bonan, E. Schmitt, Krieg (Carl 46)
Yellow Cards: Nogueira, Paulo Sousa (Boavista) and Bender (Karlsruhe)

Karlsruhe SC   **Boavista**   1-0
Own goal (Nogueira) 35
Att: 21,000   *Ref:* Craciunescu (Rom)
Karlsruhe: Kahn, Witter, Bilic, Schutterle (Metz 63), Nowotny, L. Schmitt, Rolff, Bonan, Schuster, E. Schmitt (Klinge 84), Kiriakov
Boavista: Alfredo, Barny, Rui Bento, Tavares, Jamie Alves (Caetano 39), Paulo Sousa, Bobo (Bambo 57), Sanchez, Nogueira, Nelo, Owubokiri
Yellow Cards: E. Schmitt, Rolff (Karlsruhe) and Barny, Bodo and Paulo Souso (Boavista)
Red Cards: Paulo Sousa (Boavista) – two yellow cards
Karlsruhe win 2-1 on aggregate

Borussia Dortmund   **Internazionale**   1-3
Schulz (82)   Jonk (33, 36), Shalimov (89)
Att: 36,000   *Ref:* Van der Ende (Hol)
Borussia: Klos, Kutowski, Sammer, Schulz, Reuter, Freund, Rodriguez, Zorc (Povlsen 46), Poschner (Ricken 76), Riedle, Chapuisat.
Inter: Zenga, A. Paganin, Bergomi, Ferri, M. Paganin, Orlando, Manicone, Jonk, Shalimov, Fontolan (Dell'Anno 71), Sosa.
Yellow Card: A. Paganin (Inter).

Internazionale   **Borussia Dortmund**   1-2
Manicone (81)   Zorc (40), Ricken (47)
Att: 35,000   *Ref:* Piraux (Bel)
Inter: Zenga, Battistini, Bergomi, Ferri, M. Paganin, Orlando, Manicone, Bergkamp, Shalimov (Berti 67), Fontolan, Sosa (Schillaci 82)
Borussia: Klos, Schmidt, Zelic, Schulz, Reuter, Sammer, Zorc, Ricken (Poschner 56), Reinhardt, Povlsen (Sippel 78), Chapuisat
Yellow Cards: Ferri, Bergkamp (Inter) and Zelic, Schulz (Borussia)
Internazionale win 4-3 on aggregate

Cagliari   **Juventus**   1-0
Dely Valdes (60)
Att: 29,426   *Ref:* Mikkelsen (Den)
Cagliari: Fiori, Villa, Firicano, Napoli, Matteoli, Sanna, Herrera, Pusceddu, Moriero, Dely Valdes, Oliveira
Juventus: Peruzzi, Porrini, Torricelli, Kohler, Fortunato, Galli, Di Livio, Conte, Moller, R. Baggio, Ravanelli (Ban 33)
Yellow Cards: Kohler, Torricelli, Ban (Juventus)

Juventus   **Cagliari**   1-2
D. Baggio (29)   Firicano (32), Oliveira (62)
Att: 45,000   *Ref:* Vojcik (Pol)
Juventus: Peruzzi, Porrini, Fortunato (Del Piero 68), D. Baggio, Kohler, Torricelli, Di Livio (Marocchi 77), Conte, Ravanelli, R. Baggio, Moller
Cagliari: Fiori, Villa, Pusceddu, Herrera, Napoli, Firicano, Moriero (Aloisi 86), Sanna, Dely Valdes, Matteoli, Oliveira (Criniti 71)
Yellow Cards: Moriero, Villa, Sanna (Cagliari)
Red Card: Kohler (Juventus)
Cagliari win 3-1 on aggregate

Match Dates
1st Leg   15 March: Eintracht-Salzburg, Juventus-Cagliari
2nd Leg   16 March: Karlsruhe-Boavista
              17 March: Inter-Borussia

The return leg was more entertaining although still lacking in real goalmouth action of note. Salzburg could have sewn the tie up on 15 minutes when Nikola Jurcevic found himself with a free run on goal. The forward flicked the ball over Uli Stein but held his head in despair as Gaudino cleared off the line. Salzburg continued to look dangerous and from a free-kick by Marquinho, Hemio Pfeifenberger rose unmarked for a point-blank header which was aimed straight at Stein.

Eintracht took the lead on 21 minutes and against the run of play. Ralf Weber poked the ball forward for Uwe Bein to flick it to Maurizio Gaudino, who curled the ball past Konrad from the right hand side of his goal area.

Chances continued to be few and far between after the goal and with two minutes of injury time played referee David Elleray created a stir when he sent off Peter Artner for a second bookable offence. Despite that disadvantage the Austrians continued to look the more likely side. Franz Aigner went close when he came forward to hit a stinging volley inches over Stein's bar. With the game in extra time Konrad made a final magnificent save to deny Bein and force a penalty shootout.

Conversions by Bein, Resi, Furtok and keeper Stein for Frankfurt and Lainer, Jurcevic, Hutter and Pfeifenberger for Salzburg left the penalty tally at 4-4 after Konrad had saved Gaudino's kick and Feiersinger had blazed over the bar. The shootout entered its sudden death phase and Salzburg keeper Otto Konrad – the reigning Footballer of the Year in Austria – became a national hero when he first saved Manny Binz's kick and then stepped up to fire the winner past Stein. Finally, an Austrian side had eliminated German rivals from a European club competition!

The final tie of the round saw Borussia Dortmund paired with Internazionale. The two teams had met before in European competition – in the semi-finals of the 1963-64 Champions' Cup. After a 2-2 draw in Dortmund the Milanese had won the return 2-0 in the San Siro to move into the final, where they lost to Real Madrid.

Any chances the Germans had of turning the tables on that particular memory were given a severe jolt in the first leg in Dortmund, when Dutchman Wim Jonk scored twice in a three-minute spell just before the interval. With the Italians in the driving seat, Borussia did their best to restore the balance and

Quarter-Final Summary						
P	HW	D	AW	HG	AG	TG
8	4	1	3	8	8	16

Ties won on aggregate: 3
Ties won on away goals: 0
Ties won on penalties: 1

Highest Aggregate game: 4-3 Internazionale v Borussia Dortmund
Biggest Home win: 1-0 (four)
Biggest Away win: 1-3 Borussia Dortmund v Internazionale

Top Scorers – All Rounds

- 8   E. Schmitt (Karlsruhe SC).
- 7   Bergkamp (Internazionale).
- 6   Christensen (Olympiakos).
- 5   Frigaard (Kongsvinger IL), Oliveira (Boavista FC), Owubokiri (Boavista FC).
- 4   Cadete (Sporting Lisbon), Chapuisat (Borussia Dortmund), Eszenyi (KV Mechelen), Kristensen (Brondby).
- 3   Annunen (Kuusysi Lahti), Baggio R. (Juventus), Bebeto (Deportivo La Coruna), Dely Valdes (Cagliari), Furtok (Eintracht Frankfurt), Gaudino (Eintracht Frankfurt), Goss (Norwich City), Jonk (Internazionale), Lius (Kuusysi Lahti), Ogun (Trabzonspor), Oliveira (Cagliari), Penev (Valencia), Ravanelli (Juventus), Vercruysse (Bordeaux), Ziege (Bayern Munich).

their prompting finally paid off eight minutes from time when defender Michael Schulz pulled a goal back. The Dortmund club searched for an important equaliser in the minutes that remained but Igor Shalimov restored the two-goal advantage with a goal on the break in the final minute of play.

Dortmund faced what seemed to be an impossible task – needing to win by three clear goals in the San Siro to be sure of making the final, but went within a whisker of doing it with a superb display for their hordes of fans who had made the journey south. Two perfectly timed goals either side of the half time break did little to soothe Inter's nerves. Under the cosh for much of the half, Inter would have been happy to make the dressing rooms on level terms. Michael Zorc put the kibosh on that with a goal five minutes from the interval. And when the two sides returned for the second half, Ricken whipped in the second goal. All square on aggregate, but the Italians still had the advantage of their away goals.

The Milanese looked jittery and twice Matthias Sammer – who had made 11 league appearances for Inter during a brief spell with the club the season before – went within a whisker of scoring that all-important third. With time running out, however, Manicone hit the Germans with a goal on the break. A third goal for the visitors would have forced extra time but the luck Borussia needed wasn't there and Internazionale held on to scrape through to the semi-finals.

Semi-Finals

The draw for the semi-finals ensured that there would be a side from Italy in the final for the sixth year running when Internazionale – winners of the trophy in 1991 – drew Cagliari. With the first leg being played in Sardinia, Inter made a confident start and were repaid for their positivity with a goal after just six minutes. Despite pressure from defenders, Dennis Bergkamp held on to a ball on the right of the Cagliari area before playing it out short to Orlando, whose cross found Davide Fontolan outjumping two defenders to drop the ball over Fiori.

Cagliari didn't allow their heads to drop and showed great character to equalise within five minutes. The ball was played to the feet of Luis Oliveira on the edge of the area and the Brazilian-born naturalised Belgian turned past Paganin before drilling the ball into the corner of the net. Oliveira and Panamanian Dely Valdes always looked dangerous running at the Inter defence and only Zenga's foot prevented Oliveira from scoring after the Belgian had turned Ferri.

Cagliari found themselves having to defend desperately at times but their goal remained intact. Even so Ruben Sosa's downward header was only just wide and his shot from 35 yards hit a post and rebounded off the keeper for a corner. Nevertheless Sosa finally scored his first European goal of the season when a ball from Antonio Manicone allowed him to scoop a right-foot shot on the turn past the keeper with the helping benefit of a deflection off an Inter defender on the way.

With time running out, Cagliari's coach Bruno Giorgi played his last cards and made two substitutions. They turned out to be trump cards. Only nine minutes remained when substitute Antonio Criniti equalised with a header from Sanna's long diagonal cross. Three minutes after the equaliser Giuseppe Pancaro went on for Bellucci and two minutes later he was celebrating the winner, scoring through a ruck of players.

For the return in Milan, Cagliari were pretty much at full strength. Inter though were without striker Sosa, who had suffered an injury, and Orlando and Paganin through suspensions. Early on Inter managed to produce some flowing football and Bergkamp headed over. Defender and captain Giuseppe Bergomi went close with two headers but then play started to deteriorate as both sides produced a series of late tackles that led to treatment and free-kicks, thereby disrupting the flow, which was probably to Cagliari's benefit at the time.

Inter took the lead and away-goals initiative late in the first half in controversial circumstances. Bergkamp's cross from the left-hand edge of the area hit Sanna on a hand and referee Philip Don pointed to the spot. There were howls of protest from the Sardinians at the decision which looked harsh – but then Sanna's arms were above his head. Bergkamp stepped up confidently to convert the kick for his ninth European goal of the season and his 18th in Europe overall.

Firicano nearly produced a sensational equaliser when he dived full-length to meet Matteoli's free-kick. He failed to make proper contact with the ball and both he and Zenga could only watch as it bounced wide of the far post.

Rainer Krieg, who scored the equaliser for Karlsruhe against SV Casino Salzburg.

Despite being ahead on away goals Inter continued to press forward in the second half and after Bergkamp and Fontolan combined on the right, Nicola Berti had a simple tap-in to increase his side's lead. Within ten minutes the tie was settled with a goal that was a real Dutch treat. Again Bergkamp played the role of play-maker, steering the ball into the path of Wim Jonk, who drove low and hard from the edge of the area.

Three-nil down and 5-2 on aggregate, Cagliari tried to salvage the game but apart from a late shot that rattled the woodwork, Inter weren't too troubled and they secured their spot in the final.

In the other tie, the outsiders from Salzburg continued to create upsets. Having become the first Austrian club to knock a German side out of European competition, they beat another one when they were paired with the competition's free-scorers from Karlsruhe.

The first leg in the Ernst Happel Stadium in Vienna was a tight affair with little goalmouth action. Salzburg made the running but Karlsruhe held on for a goalless draw in which five of their players received yellow cards. The return in Germany was equally tight although it did produce goals and the most important one of the evening came first, to the Austrians. On a quick advance Nikola Jurcevic darted into space on the right and swept the ball across, behind recovering defenders but well in front of keeper Oliver Kahn. Herman Stadler arrived on the left and his shot went in off the diving Kahn, with 11 minutes gone.

It was a vital away goal for the Salzburg side. Karlsruhe now needed to score twice against a team who were displaying a well-

Semi-Finals

Cagliari   **Internazionale**   **3-2**
Oliveira (11), Criniti (81),   Fontolan (6), Sosa (61)
Pancaro (86)
Att: 32,543   *Ref:* Lopez Nieto (Esp)
Cagliari: Fiori, Villa, Firicano, Bellucci (Pancaro 84), Pusceddu, Sanna, Napoli, Allegri (Criniti 64), Matteoli, Dely Valdes, Oliveira
Internazionale: Zenga, Paganin A, Bergomi, Ferri, Paganin M, Orlando, Jonk, Manicone, Fontolan, Bergkamp, Sosa (Bainchi 86)
Yellow Cards: Allegri (Cagliari) and A. Paganin, Orlando (Internazionale)

Internazionale   **Cagliari**   **3-0**
Bergkamp (38 pen), Berti (54),
Jonk (63)
Att: 58,848   *Ref:* Don (Eng)
Internazionale: Zenga, Bergomi, Shalimov, Jonk, Paganin M, Battistini, Bianchi, Manicone, Fontolan (Dell'Anno 89), Bergkamp, Berti
Cagliari: Fiori, Villa, Pusceddu, Herrera, Napoli, Firicano, Moriero, Sanna, Dely Valdes, Matteoli, Oliveira (Criniti 83)
Yellow Cards: Fontolan, Shalimov, Battistini, Bergomi (Internazionale) and Herrera, Oliveira (Cagliari)
Internazionale win 5-3 on aggregate

SV Casino Salzburg   **Karlsruhe**   **0-0**
Att: 48,000   *Ref:* Nikakis (Gre)
Salzburg: Konrad, Garger (Steiner 45), Weber, Furstaller, Aigner, Stadler (Reisinger 72), Marquinho, Hutter, Lainer, Pfeifenberger, Amerhauser
Karlsruhe: Kahn, Metz, Wittwer, Schuster, Schutterle, Nowotny, E. Schmitt, Simarov (Klinge 46), Bonan, Krieg, Kiriakov
Yellow Cards: Weber, Steiner (Salzburg) and Metz, Wittwer, Nowotny, Sjmarov, Klinge (Karlsruhe)

Karlsruhe   **SV Casino Salzburg**   **1-1**
Krieg (54)   Stadler (11)
Att: 23,000   *Ref:* Van den Wijngaert (Bel)
Karlsruhe: Kahn, Nowotny, Bilic, Schuster, Schutterle (Klinge 80), Reich (Krieg 46), Rolff, L. Schmitt, Bonan, E. Schmitt, Kiriakov
Salzburg: Konrad, Lainer, Furstaller, Winklhofer, Feiersinger, Stadler (Muzek 80), Marquinho (Amerhauser 60), Hutter, Aigner, Jurcevic, Pfeifenberger
Yellow Cards: Bonan (Karlsruhe) and Feiersinger, Hutter, Aigner, Jurcevic, Muzek (Salzburg)
1-1 on aggregate. SV Casino Salzburg win on away goals rule

Match Dates
1st Leg   29 March: SV Casino Salzburg *v* Karlsruhe
    30 March: Cagliari Internazionale
2nd Leg   12 April: Karlsruhe SV Casino Salzburg
    13 April: Internazionale Cagliari

organised and disciplined defence. Some light appeared at the end of the tunnel for the Germans nine minutes into the second half. A cross to the right was headed back into the area where Rainer Krieg – a half-time substitute – flicked the ball past Konrad with the outside of a boot. The scorer had looked suspiciously offside and the Salzburg players complained bitterly to the Belgian referee.

The Austrians defended well for the rest of the second half and were only threatened once, when Jens Nowotny produced an excellent 80-yard run that took him just inside the Salzburg area, but the tall defender ran out of steam and miscued his shot, sinking to his knees as the ball ran wide. The Austrians held on and became only the third side from that country to reach a European final.

Final

Internazionale's passage into the UEFA Cup final ensured that all three European club cup finals had an Italian representative and did something towards salvaging for Inter what had been a disastrous season at home. They were expected to win the two-legged tie without too much difficulty – the Austrians from Salzburg were already being branded as the worst side ever to reach a European final, even before a ball was kicked.

Casino faced an uphill task to wrestle the trophy from what had turned out to be an Italian vice-like grip on it, with five wins from the previous six finals. Napoli started the sequence of wins in 1989 followed by Juventus in 1990, Inter in 1991, and Juventus again in 1993. Only Torino had let the sequence lapse, losing the 1992 final to Ajax on the away goals rule.

Influential in the first leg in Sardinia, Ruben Sosa missed the return in the San Siro through injury.

UEFA Cup – Complete list of Scorers

8   Bergkamp (Internazionale), Schmitt (Karlsruhe SC)

6   Christensen (Olympiakos)

5   Frigaard (Kongsvinger IL), Jonk (Internazionale), Oliveira (Boavista FC), Owubokiri (Boavista FC)

4   Cadete (Sporting Lisbon), Chapuisat (Borussia Dortmund), Eszenyi (KV Mechelen), Kristensen (Brondby), Lius (Kuusysi Lahti), Oliveira (Cagliari)

3   Annunen (Kuusysi Lahti), Baggio R. (Juventus), Bebeto (Deportivo La Coruna), Dely Valdes (Cagliari), Furtok (Eintracht Frankfurt), Gaudino (Eintracht Frankfurt), Goss (Norwich City), Ogun (Trabzonspor), Penev (Valencia), Ravanelli (Juventus), Vercruysse (Bordeaux), Ziege (Bayern Munich)

2   Amerhauser (SV Casino Salzburg), Anderson da Silva (Servette), Barragan (Deportivo La Coruna), Batista (Olympiakos), Berti (Internazionale), Cravero (Lazio), Czerniatynski (KV Mechelen), Del Solar (Tenerife), Engerback (Kongsvinger IL), Firicano (Cagliari), Fontolan (Internazionale), Giallanza (Servette), Hami (Trabzonspor), Hutter (SV Casino Salzburg), Ioannides (Olympiakos), Kiriakov (Karlsruhe SC), Luis Garcia (Atletico Madrid), Mahlas (OFI Crete), Matteoli (Cagliari), Mijatovic (Valencia), Minambres (Tenerife), Moldovan (Dinamo Bucharest), Moller (Juventus), Nerlinger (Bayern Munich), Okocha (Eintracht Frankfurt), Paille (Bordeaux), Pfeinfenberger (SV Casino Salzburg), Scepovic (Apollon Limassol), Severyns (Royal Antwerp), Spoljaric (Apollon Limassol), Stadler (SV Casino Salzburg), Stanic (Maribor Branik), Strudal (Brondby), Tsiantakis (Olympiakos), Vilfort (Brondby), Zarb (Valletta), Zidane (Bordeaux), Zorc (Borussia Dortmund)

1   Aguilera (Tenerife), Allegri (Cagliari), Amanasidis (Olympiakos), Andrasi (Rapid Bucharest), Atkinson (Aston Villa), Bacher (Admira Wacker), Baggio D (Juventus), Balakov (Botev Plovdiv), Battistini (Internazionale), Bein (Eintracht Frankfurt), Berger (Slavia Prague), Bezhanar (Dnepr Dnepropetrovsk), Bilic (Karlsruhe SC), Blohm (IFK Norrkoping), Boerebach (FC Twente), Bowen (Norwich City), Bozgo (Maribor Branik), Bursac (Royal Antwerp), Carlos Pereira (KV Mechelen), Casaca (Boavista FC), Casiraghi (Lazio), Cepovic (Apollon Limassol), Chano (Tenerife), Cherbakov (Sporting Lisbon), Chukhliba (Dnepr Dnepropetrovsk), Clarke (Dundee United), Colquhoun (Heart of Midlothian), Crabbe (Dundee United), Creaney (Celtic), Critini (Cagliari), De Boeck (KV Mechelen), De Kneef (KSV Waregem), Dickhaut (Eintracht Frankfurt), Dimitrov (Botev Plovdiv), Dobrovolski (Dinamo Moscow), Dugarry (Bordeaux), Ekoku (Norwich City), Feiersinger (SV Casino Salzburg), Felipe (Tenerife), Fofana (Bordeaux), Francis (Kongsvinger IL), Galvez (Valencia), Georgamlis (OFI Crete), Gomez (Valencia), Hamori (MTK Budapest), Heitor Junio (Maritimo), Hoegh (Brondby), Hvoinev (Botev Plovdiv), Ingimundarson (KR Reykjavik), Julio Llorente (Tenerife), Jurcevic (SV Casino Salzburg), Kohler (Juventus), Kosecki (Atletico Madrid), Kovacs (MTK Budapest), Kricmarevic (Apollon Limassol), Krieg (Karlsruhe SC), Lainer (SV Casino Salzburg), Landberg (Osters IF), Leen (KV Mechelen), Lehtinen (Kuusysi Lahti), Ljung (Admira Wacker), Luzardi (Lazio), Madsen (Brondby), Manicone (Internazionale), Manjarin (Deportivo La Coruna), Manolo (Atletico Madrid), Marlon Brandao (Boavista FC), Marocchi (Juventus), Matthaus (Bayern Munich), Maximov (Dnepr Dnepropetrovsk), McKinlay (Dundee United), Mikhaylenko (Dnepr Dnepropetrovsk), Moller (Juventus), Mitsibonas (Olympiakos), Nelson (Boavista FC), Nogueira (Boavista FC), Nyilas (Vac FC Samsung), Okechukwu (Brondby), Orhan Cikrikci (Trabzonspor), Oudec (FC Nantes), Pacheco A. (Sporting Lisbon), Pana (Dinamo Bucharest), Pancaro (Cagliari), Pedro (Atletico Madrid), Pedros (FC Nantes), Persson (Osters IF), Pinilla (Tenerife), Pokhlebaev (Dnepr Dnepropetrovsk), Polston (Norwich City), Popescu (PSV Eindhoven), Prince Polly (FC Twente), Pusceddu (Cagliari), Ricken (Borussia Dortmund), Riesco (Deportivo La Coruna), Robertson (Heart of Midlothian), Saib (Auxerre), Saunders (Aston Villa), Scholl (Bayern Munich), Schultz (Borussia Dortmund), Schutterle (Karlsruhe SC), Scmarov (Karlsruhe SC), Segers (Royal Antwerp), Shalimov (Internazionale), Simutenkov (Dinamo Moscow), Shalimov (Internazionale), Sosa (Internazionale), Szedlacsek (Vac FC Samsung), Thorst (AaB Aalborg), Tittel (Slovan Bratislava), Townsend (Aston Villa), Tsifoutis (OFI Crete), Unal (Trabzonspor), Vado (Maritimo), Vahirua (Auxerre), Valencia (Bayern Munich), Velic (OFI Crete), Vurens (FC Twente), Weber (Eintracht Frankfurt), Winter (Lazio), Witter (Karlsruhe SC), Yeboah (Eintracht Frankfurt), Zsivotzky (MTK Budapest)

1   Own goal for: Bayern Munich, Servette, Karlsruhe SC, Cagliari, Celtic, Bordeaux, Tenerife.

    Inter's success in the UEFA Cup had been in direct contrast to their league displays and, at the time of the first leg, they were still threatened with the possibility of relegation to Serie B. If they needed a confidence-booster then it was provided by the fact that Salzburg were missing three of their regular players, including the Austrian league's top scorer, Jurcevic, through suspension. And, at the start of the match in Vienna, all but one of the Austrian starting line-up had one caution to their name and were just a yellow card away from missing the second leg a fortnight later.

    Salzburg started the game the more lively of the two sides and gave the Inter defence a number of problems to deal with in the first ten minutes, teenager Amerhauser missing an excellent chance when side-footing the ball over from 10 yards after a good move down the left had left the Inter rearguard floundering. Shortly afterwards Bianchi was only inches away from conceding a penalty and Pfeifenberger should have done better with a header, before he then hooked the ball over Zenga's bar from close range. In between Pfeifenberger's efforts, Inter's Sosa missed a gilt-edged chance. He volleyed the ball wide when clear in front of goal and with time to control before shooting.

    Inter took the lead against the run of play, when Berti was first to react to Sosa's quickly taken free-kick on the left. He did exceptionally well to hold off two defenders before firing home from an acute angle. Sosa might have added to that score close on half-time when he took Jonk's pass and showed a great turn of pace before rattling the crossbar with a 25-yarder.

    The second half started in controversial fashion when Inter's Bianchi was sent off for a second yellow card offence following an earlier foul on Aigner. The foul amounted to nothing more

LEFT: *Dennis Bergkamp skips past Salzburg's Leo Lainer.*

BELOW LEFT: *Walter Zenga celebrating with a replica of the UEFA Cup after helping Internazionale beat SV Casino Salzburg.*

than a tug of the shirt as the two players raced along the touchline, but the Danish referee showed yellow and then red. A one-goal lead away from home is just about enough excuse for an Italian side to defend en masse. Given a deficiency in the number of players it became a full-blown necessity, and for the majority of the second half Inter shut up shop and Casino had very few chances to worry Zenga. The one that did come on the hour was not taken, when a loose ball carried to Stadler on the left and with the far side of the goal to aim at he dragged his shot wide. In the final minutes Jonk raced forward, Bergkamp laid the perfect pass into his path, and the shot shaved Konrad's far post.

Salzburg travelled to the San Siro for the second leg with nothing to lose. Trailing by a goal, they had to attack and try to recapture the goal they had hardly deserved to lose by in the first leg. Bianchi was missing from the Italian line-up, and the Austrians had Jurcevic back after suspension along with Hutter and Feiersinger.

For the first 40 minutes Inter were not overly troubled by the Salzburg attack; indeed it was they who had the best chances without ever over-committing themselves. Konrad did well to stop a stinging shot from Sosa early on and had Bergkamp had the run of the ball then his half-hit shot in front of Konrad would surely have bobbled inside the post rather than outside it. But then with five minutes of the half left Hutter hit a first-time drive from 40 yards that caught Zenga by surprise. The goalkeeper did well to react and get to the ball, but it left him fuming at the players in front of him and provided the Austrians with a bit of inspiration that they were lacking.

The opening 20 minutes of the second half had the Austrians playing their best football of the season. And in one ten-minute spell that pulverised the Italian defence, only the brilliance of Zenga – who made four world-class saves – and the woodwork prevented the visitors not only levelling the score but taking a match-winning lead. Twice the 34-year-old Zenga had to dive full length to deny Feiersinger and then be alert to pluck Aigner's header from under the bar.

Then on 55 minutes, the Brazilian Marquinho turned and fired a shot from 25 yards. The ball beat Zenga and rebounded from a post, across the face of the Italian goal, back off the other post and eventually rolled to safety. It was an amazing sight and at that point the match was lost and won.

Seven minutes later Inter broke; Sosa slipped the ball to Jonk on his left and the Dutch midfielder controlled it before flicking the most delightful of chips over the diving Konrad and into the net. It was a killer blow for the Austrians and one that they didn't deserve. Inter played out the formality of the remaining time to lift the trophy that was their only passport back into Europe. The players of SV Casino Salzburg at least proved that they were certainly not the worst side ever to reach a European cup final, and could argue that they were possibly the unluckiest to lose one.

Final

1st Leg – 26 April
SV Casino Salzburg   **Internazionale**   **0-1**
Berti (35)

Att: 47,500   *Ref:* K. Milton Nielsen (Den)
Salzburg: Konrad, Lainer, Weber, Winklhofer (Steiner 61), Furstaller, Aigner, Amerhauser (Muzek 46), Artner, Marquinho, Pfeifenberger, Stadler
Internazionale: Zenga, A.Paganin, Orlando, Jonk, Bergomi, Battistini, Bianchi, Manicone, Berti, Bergkamp (Dell'Anno 89), Sosa (Ferri 74)
Yellow Cards: Pfeifenberger, Stadler (Salzburg); Bianchi, Jonk (Inter)
Red Cards: Bianchi (Inter)

2nd Leg – 11 May
Internazionale   **SV Casino Salzburg**   **1-0**
Jonk (63)

Att: 80,326   *Ref:* McCluskey (Sco)
Internazionale: Zenga, A. Paganin, Fontolan (R. Ferri 67), Jonk, Bergomi, Battistini, Orlando, Manicone, Berti, Bergkamp (M. Paganin 89), Sosa
Salzburg: Konrad, Winklhofer (Amerhauser 67), Lainer, Weber, Furstaller, Aigner, Jurcevic, Artner (Steiner 75), Hutter, Marquinho, Feiersinger
Yellow Cards: Orlando, Fontolan (Inter); Feiersinger, Steiner (Salzburg)

World Club Championship 1993

Milan dominant in defeat

Milan – three times World Club Champions – returned to Tokyo in December looking for a third win in five years. Their opponents were the reigning World Club Champions, Sao Paulo of Brazil, who had won the title by beating Barcelona 2-1 12 months earlier, and duly retained it. Having twice come from behind, Milan were finally defeated by a goal four minutes from time following a misunderstanding between goalkeeper Sebastiano Rossi and captain Franco Baresi.

Toninho Cerezo's pass beyond Baresi seemed to carry no real danger. But with Baresi covering the ball before deciding to let Rossi take charge, the giant keeper hesitated as Muller came into the picture and the ball slipped from his grasp and into the net via the

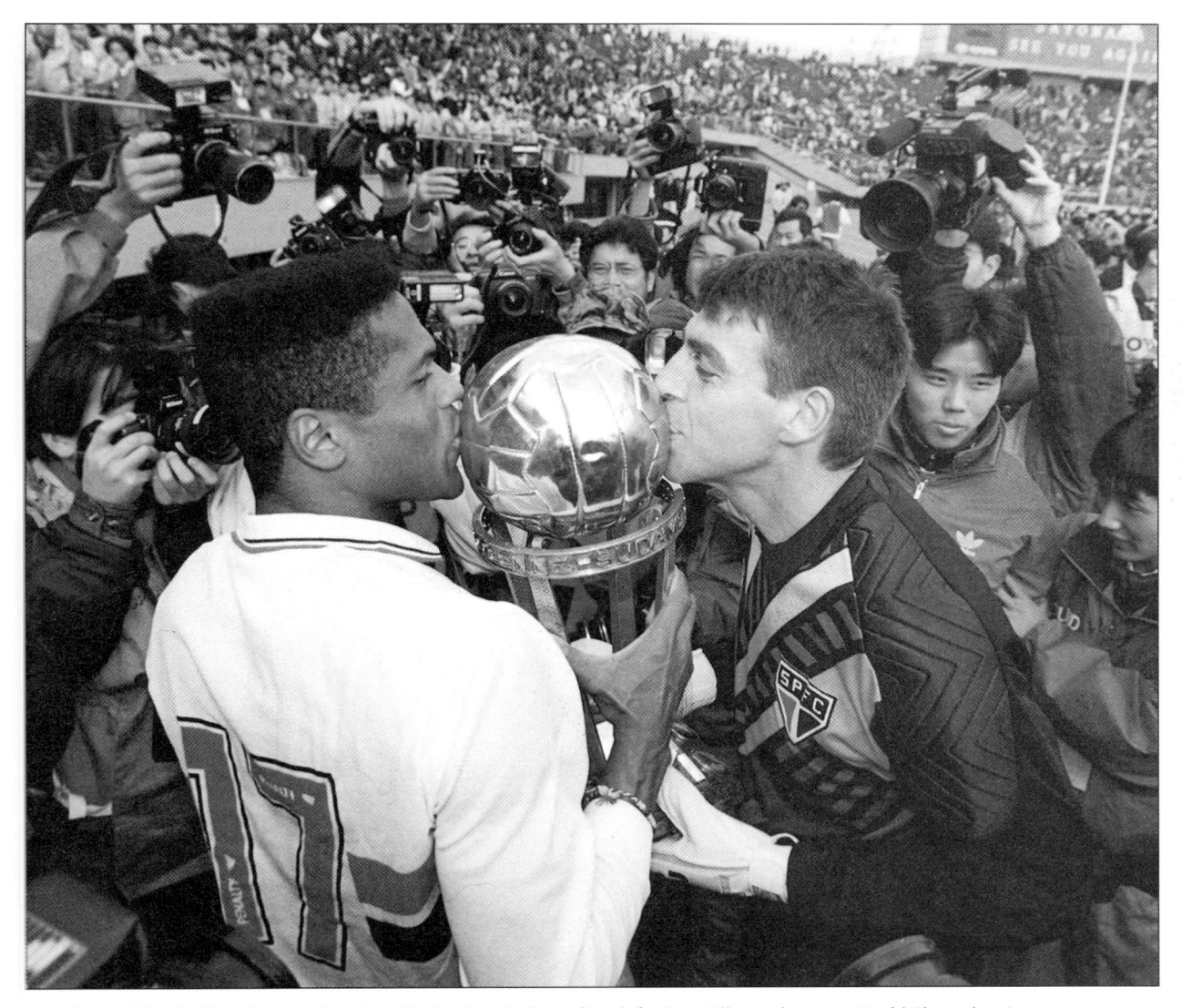

Ronaldo and Zetti of Sao Paulo celebrate with the Toyota Cup after defeating Milan to become World Champions!

12 December 1993, Tokyo

Milan	Sao Paulo	2-3
Massaro (48), Papin (82)	Palhinha (20), Cerezo (59), Muller (86)	

Att: 33,765 *Ref:* Krondl (Cze)
Milan: Rossi, Panucci, Costacurta, Baresi, Maldini, Donadoni, Desailly, Albertini (Tassotti 79), Massaro, Raducioiu (Orlando 79), Papin
Sao Paulo: Zetti, Cafu, Valber, Ronaldo, Andre, Cerezo, Doriva, Leonardo, Dinho, Palhinha (Juninho 64), Muller

Brazilian forward's boot. Such was the nature of the goal that it took even Muller a while to realise that he had indeed scored what was undoubtedly the winner before setting off in typical Brazilian-style celebrations heralding the recapture of the Toyota Cup.

The result in the December sunshine of Tokyo's national football stadium was a travesty in a game in which Milan peppered Zetti's goal with efforts, only to see Sao Paulo score three goals from five shots on target. Coach Fabio Capello laid the blame for the defeat on his goalkeeper: 'It was Rossi's mistake that cost us the game,' he said after the match. 'I'm sure we would have won in extra time.'

Milan had started the game depleted of many of their players. UEFA – having approved their role as stand-ins for the dethroned Marseille – dithered as to whether the Montenegrin Dejan Savicevic was suspended from the event, after having been dismissed in the 1991 final when he helped Red Star Belgrade to a 3-0 win over Colo Colo. UEFA decided he was eligible at the 11th hour but Capello had already formulated his tactical plans without him. The crocks list had also grown. Already without long-term casualties Marco Van Basten and Gigi Lentini, he was further deprived of Brian Laudrup, Zvonimir Boban, Stefano Eranio and Marco Simone.

If Rossi's error cost Milan the game it was Zetti at the other end who almost played an unwitting part in giving Milan an early lead when Daniele Massaro hit a 25-yard volley against the underside of the bar. It rebounded, hit Zetti on the back of his head and moved goalward. Milan's luck stopped there as the Sao Paulo keeper managed to recover the ball into his grasp before it rolled over the line.

The Brazilians, without Rai, now making his mark with Paris Saint-Germain, took nearly 20 minutes to mount their first attack of real note and it produced the opening goal of the game. Andre's long ball found Cafu on the right and the full-back delivered a cross which Palhinha had little difficulty in stabbing home.

Milan continued to control the game and after a number of chances went begging the equaliser came three minutes into the second half when Massaro slipped the ball between Zetti's legs after running onto Desailly's high pass into the area. However, shoddy defending by Europe's most miserly rearguard allowed Sao Paulo to regain the lead 11 minutes later. Leonardo's cross was totally missed by three defenders as it flew across the face of Rossi's goal and Cerezo – later to be named Man of the Match – was on hand at the far post to score.

With ten minutes remaining Capello made a double substitution. On paper it looked a curious move, introducing two defenders for attackers. Within a minute, however, Milan had drawn level when Papin headed home Massaro's back-header from Donadoni's cross. For the next few minutes it looked as though Milan were set to run riot, but then came Rossi's error which let in Muller, who ensured a second successive Toyota Cup for Sao Paulo.

European Super Cup

Parma make ham of Milan

Parma completed a remarkable two-leg win over Milan to add the European Super Cup to the Cup-Winners' Cup they won at Wembley the previous year. Having lost the first leg Parma did what they do best – winning in Milan – this time by two clear goals to record yet another remarkable chapter in the club's history. It was Parma who had ended Milan's 58-match unbeaten run the previous season in their mighty San Siro. Indeed that defeat was the only one in a total of 90 games as the teams arrived at the decisive second leg.

For Milan this defeat also marked the third final they had lost inside 10 months. In May they had lost the Champions' Cup final to Marseille, in December the World Club Championship to Sao Paulo and now this. Perhaps justice was done however, certainly in this event, given the fact that Milan were only appearing in the final by default. Parma had at least won the competition that gained them entry.

The first leg in Parma proved to be a dour affair played on a pitch heavy from rain that made anything other than basic football impossible. However, Frenchman Jean Pierre Papin looked to have given Milan a firm grip on the silverware with a goal two minutes from the interval. The goal itself was one of the few real offerings of class in a game that was at best pedestrian in its progress. It came against what run of play there was, when Eranio exchanged a neat one-two with Savicevic to find himself free on the right-hand side of the area with time and space to drop the ball on to Papin's head. The Frenchman made no mistake, from eight yards, heading down and beyond Ballotta unchallenged and with the entire home defence seemingly happy to watch the events unfold around them!

Milan were facing a Parma side who started the match having lost their previous two home games and playing like it. Both sides were able to field players who otherwise would have been ineligible for European competition. Parma's Argentine Nestor Sensini (from Udinese) and Milan's Marcel Desailly (from, ironically, Marseille) were both signed in November and required special dispensation from Europe's governing body to play. UEFA – presumably because it was agreeable by both clubs and

Parma celebrate with the European Super Cup after beating Italian rivals Milan.

1st Leg – 12 January 1994
Parma **Milan** **0-1**
Papin (43)
Att: 8,083 *Ref:* Manuel Diaz Vega (Spa)
Parma: Ballotta, Balleri, Benarrivo (Di Chiara 76), Minotti, Apolloni, Sensini, Brolin, Pin, Crippa, Zola, Asprilla
Milan: Rossi, Tassotti, Maldini, Albertini (Massaro 67), Costacurta, Baresi, Eranio, Desailly, Papin, Savicevic (Panucci 86), Donadoni

2nd Leg – 2 February 1994
Milan **Parma** **0-2**
Sensini (67), Crippa (95)
Att: 24,000 *Ref:* Rothlisberger (Swi)
Milan: Rossi, Panucci, Maldini, Albertini (Lentini 67), Costacurta, Baresi, B. Laudrup (Carbone 76), Desailly, Papin, Donadoni, Massaro
Parma: Ballotta, Balleri, Benarrivo (Di Chiara 76), Minotti, Matrecano, Sensini, Brolin, Pin, Crippa, Zola (Zoratto 104), Asprilla

Parma win 2-1 on aggregate after extra time

involved both clubs – agreed. So much for registration rules and qualification dates.

The visitors' goal did little to awaken the Parma side apart from forcing Rossi to tip the ball over the bar from Minotti's headed effort off a corner almost from the restart. Indeed it took ten minutes of the game for the first effort of note to be delivered on goal when a hopeful ball in from the Parma right was met by Zola, who directed his header just wide. Milan had little more to offer, taking 25 minutes to make their first attempt at Ballotta's goal, when Eranio had a golden opportunity but scuffed his shot well wide of the post. Brolin went close for Parma just prior to Papin's clincher, when he was first to react to a loose ball some 35 yards out, controlling masterfully with his thigh before forcing Rossi into a diving save with a crisply-struck volley.

Little changed in the second period, with Colombian Asprilla being forced to track deeper and deeper in search of the ball. Papin might have made the second leg a mere formality on 73 minutes but his effort lacked the control one has come to anticipate, and the ball cleared the bar to Ballotta's relief. Milan no doubt left the pitch confident that the main thrust of their work had been done for the two legs. How wrong they were.

Three weeks later a small crowd turned out to witness what was supposed to be a formality for Milan. Unlike the first leg the second match was played with great style, which perhaps made a statement for the return to one-off encounters. Parma, playing simple neat football, took the game to Milan at every opportunity and Asprilla's sudden change of pace left the home defence in a quandary. Milan, though, were not content to sit on their lead and looked to play an effective counter-attack game.

Parma started positively – they had no option – but it still took nearly half an hour for them to force Rossi into his first real save of the evening when Asprilla bounced up from an injury to drill a 25-yarder at the Milan goal. Shortly afterwards Asprilla somehow missed what appeared to be an open goal from six yards when his effort was blocked by recovering Milan defenders, after Zola had turned Panucci on the right to get in a great cross.

Ballotta needed all his wits about him to keep concentrating as Milan hit on the counter attack with some force, and he produced an outstanding save from Massaro's point-blank shot. Apart from an effort by Brian Laudrup early in the second half that was parried by Ballotta, Milan were less effective and in the 63rd minute Albertini was replaced by Lentini, who was sent on for his first appearance since suffering injuries in a car crash in the previous August.

The swap had little effect though and just five minutes later Parma deservedly took the lead to level the aggregate scores. Awarded a free-kick some 30 yards out after Brolin had been fouled, Zola lined up to take the kick and his curling shot cannoned off the upright and bar and back into play, where Benarrivo was first to react to head the bouncing ball back across the goal into the six-yard area. Sensini arrived to volley the ball home with his left foot.

Parma's teamwork continued to be far superior and Pin and Crippa both had outstanding games, particularly in the second half, but they couldn't add to the score in normal time. But only five minutes of extra time were needed for Parma to make the decisive breakthrough when Crippa scored with a drive from 14 yards after Asprilla had created mayhem down the right-hand side of the Milan defence, drawing no fewer than four players to him.

Parma had won the tactical battle once again with Milan. Playing three centre defenders and two wing-backs they effectively cut off any threat Laudrup might have posed, made Lentini totally ineffective, and limited Papin to just one chance in the full 120 minutes.

Around the Leagues

Albania	194
Austria	196
Belgium	199
Bulgaria	203
Croatia	206
Cyprus	208
Czech Republic	210
Denmark	212
England	216
Estonia	224
Faeroe Islands	226
Finland	227
France	230
Germany	237
Greece	244
Holland	247
Hungary	254
Iceland	256
Israel	258
Italy	261
Latvia	270
Lithuania	272
Luxembourg	274
Malta	276
Moldova	278
Northern Ireland	280
Norway	283
Poland	286
Portugal	288
Republic of Ireland	292
Romania	295
Russia	299
Scotland	301
Slovakia	307
Slovenia	309
Spain	311
Sweden	317
Switzerland	321
Turkey	325
Ukraine	328
Wales	330
Minor Countries	
Armenia	332
Azerbaijan	332
Belarus	333
FYR Macedonia	334
Georgia	334
Liechtenstein	335
San Marino	336
Yugoslavia	337

ROTHMANS PUBLICATIONS

Albania

Back in the fold

After time in the European wilderness the 1993–94 season marked the return of Albanian clubs to European club competition. Having been excluded for the previous two seasons due to the archaic nature of the country's infrastructure, Partizani Tirana found themselves drawn against Iceland's IA in the Champions' Cup while Albpetrol made their debut in the Cup-Winners' Cup against Balzers of Liechtenstein. Neither side made an impression and both fell at the first hurdle, but at least there was the carrot of European competition for the teams contesting the championship for the 1993–94 season, plus an extra UEFA Cup place to chase.

After the first 16 rounds of games Flamurtari – who had narrowly avoided relegation the previous season – led the table but only seven points separated the top 10 clubs. Elbasani and SK Teuta occupied the second and third positions respectively. Reigning champions Partizani were having an indifferent season and rode up and down through the middle rank of clubs. They fared better in the Cup, having made the semi-final stage where they were joined by Dinamo, SK Tirana and SK Teuta. Teuta had started to create the surprises and turn heads, and despite having not won any domestic honours in their 70-year history they found themselves growing in confidence and in a good position to start a new chapter.

The club from the town of Durresi started to apply the pressure on those above them as the season entered its closing stage and an impressive 2-0 home win over leaders Flamurtari in front of 15,000 – the largest crowd of the season by far – pushed them into second spot as SK Tirana dropped a point at lowly Sopoti. And when Flamurtari fell by the only goal at Albpetrol, Teuta's 2-0 win over Partizani was enough to give them pole position on goal difference with five weeks of the season remaining. Two wins and a draw built a four-point advantage at the top and virtually assured them of the title on goal difference alone. SK Tirana made ground into second place, mainly thanks to a last-minute goal by Indrit Fortuzi against Flamurtari.

Federata Shqiptare E Futbollit

Founded:	1930
Address:	Rruga Dervish Hima Nr31, Tirana
Phone:	+355 42 27877
Fax:	+355 42 27877
UEFA Affiliation:	1954
FIFA Affiliation:	1932
National Stadium:	Qemal Stafa
Capacity:	24,000
Season:	August to May
Colours:	Red, Red, Red
Change:	White, White, White

Final League Table 1993–94

	P	W	D	L	F	A	Pts
SK Teuta	26	14	9	3	37	10	37
SK Tirana	26	13	7	6	36	16	33
Flamurtari Vlore	26	11	8	7	26	21	30
Vllaznia Shkoder	26	11	6	9	33	28	28
Partizani Tirana	26	6	13	7	27	25	25
Dinamo Tirana	26	5	15	6	25	27	25
Apolonia	26	8	9	9	25	28	25
Elbasani	26	9	7	10	26	30	24
Albpetrol	26	8	8	10	31	31	24
Beselidhja Leshne	26	9	6	11	27	33	24
Besa Kavaje	26	8	8	10	24	37	24
Laci	26	8	7	11	32	36	23
Lushnja	26	7	9	10	20	25	23
Sopoti	26	6	6	14	19	42	18

Top Scorers
14 Edi MARTINI (Vllaznia Shkoder)
11 Gert HAXIHU (Flamurtari Vlore)

Promotions and Relegations
Promoted: Shqiponia Girokaster (previously Luftetari), Iliria Fush Kruja.
Relegated: Lushnja, Sopoti

Five-Year Records League 1-2-3 and Cup Winners

League Results

	1st	Pts	2nd	Pts	3rd	Pts
1990	Dinamo Tirana	50	Partizani Tirana	49	Flamurtari Vlore	39
1991	Flamurtari Vlore	54	Partizani Tirana	48	Vllaznia Shkoder	45
1992	Vllaznia Shkoder	44	Partizani Tirana	38	SK Teuta	33
1993	Partizani Tirana	43	SK Teuta	38	Besa Kavaje	37
1994	SK Teuta	37	SK Tirana	33	Flamurtari Vlore	30

Cup Final Results

1990	Dinamo Tirana	1-1	Flamurtari Vlore	4-2 on pens
1991	Partizani Tirana	1-1	Flamurtari Vlore	5-3 on pens
1992	Elbasani	2-1	Besa Kavaje	
1993	Partizani Tirana	1-0	Albpetrol	
1994	SK Tirana	1-0	SK Teuta	after 0-0 draw

SK Teuta were officially crowned champions for the first time on the penultimate weekend of the season – a 1-0 home win over fourth-placed Vllaznia was enough. SK Tirana had to wait another week to make sure of the runners-up spot.

Flamurtari didn't finish the season without reward. SK Tirana's win in the Cup final meant that Flamurtari were the country's nomination for the UEFA Cup, where they will join

International Results 1993–94

Date	Opponents	Result	Venue	Comp.	Scorers
8/9/93	Denmark	0-1	Tirana	WCQ3	
22/9/93	Spain	1-5	Tirana	WCQ3	Kushta (40)

National Record	P	W	D	L	F	A
European Championships	33	3	4	26	14	77
World Cup Finals	Never qualified					
World Cup Qualifiers	44	4	5	35	24	97

Albanian Championship Results 1993–94

	Albpetrol	Apolonia	Besa Kavaje	Beselidhja Leshne	Dinamo Tirana	Elbasani	Flamurtari Vlore	Laci	Lushnja	Partizani Tirana	SK Teuta	SK Tirana	Sopoti	Vllaznia Shkoder
Albpetrol	—	1-1	2-2	3-0	0-0	2-1	1-0	2-2	3-0	2-1	1-1	2-1	4-0	2-1
Apolonia	4-0	—	0-0	2-0	1-1	4-0	0-2	3-0	1-0	0-0	0-2	0-2	1-0	1-0
Besa Kavaje	2-1	0-0	—	2-0	1-1	1-0	0-0	2-0	0-2	1-1	0-3	1-0	2-0	1-0
Beselidhja Leshne	1-0	2-0	5-1	—	1-1	2-0	1-3	1-0	2-1	0-0	0-0	2-1	2-0	2-1
Dinamo Tirana	1-1	1-0	1-2		—	0-0	2-2	1-0	1-0	2-0	0-0	0-3	1-1	0-0
Elbasani	3-0	0-0	2-2	2-0	1-0	—	0-0	1-1	0-0	1-1	1-0	2-1	2-0	2-1
Flamurtari Vlore	1-1	0-0	2-1	1-0	2-1	2-0	—	2-0	3-0	1-1	0-0	1-0	3-0	1-0
Laci	2-1	1-0	4-0	2-2	2-2	2-1	5-0	—	2-0	3-1	0-0	0-0	3-1	0-2
Lushnja	2-1	1-1	2-1	4-0	2-3	0-0	1-0	1-0	—	0-0	0-1	0-0	3-0	1-1
Partizani Tirana	0-0	2-2	2-0	1-1	0-0	3-1	3-1	4-0	0-0	—	0-3	1-0	3-0	1-1
SK Teuta	1-0	4-0	1-0	1-0	1-3	0-1	2-0	4-0	2-1	2-0	—	2-2	4-0	1-0
SK Tirana	1-0	3-0	2-0	2-0	1-0	3-1	1-0	1-1	0-0	1-0	1-1	—	2-0	5-0
Sopoti	1-0	3-4	4-1	1-0	2-1	1-0	0-0	2-0	0-0	1-1	0-0	0-0	—	0-2
Vllaznia Shkoder	3-1	3-0	1-1	2-0	2-2	3-2	0-0	1-0	3-0	2-1	0-0	2-3	2-1	—

champions SK Teuta. Teuta's championship was fitting reward and built on three seasons of hard work. Third in 1991–92, second in 1992–93, the club completed their rise to the top as many had expected. Without doubt the player of their campaign was goalkeeper Xhevair Kapplani, who conceded just 10 goals in all and during one period managed to keep a clean sheet for 762 minutes. Striker Alvaro Zalla, midfield player Anesti Qendro and defender Ardian Abazi were also key players.

While 1994–95 sees SK Teuta make their European debut, SK Tirana can point to experience in the Cup-Winners' Cup when they were known as 17 Nentori. They were knocked out in the first round in the 1983–84 season, but reached the second round in 1986–87.

Besa Kavaje finished fourth from bottom and are looking to old hands for the 1994–95 season to re-charge their batteries, having appointed 68-year-old Zihni Gjinali as coach. Gjinali knows the club well, having been at the reins 15 years earlier.

True to form, or rather lack of it, the national team finished bottom of World Cup Qualifying Group Three. Two home ties and two defeats, 0-1 to Denmark and 1-5 to Spain, although Kushta's goal five minutes before the interval gave the 8,000 Tiranaian crowd something to cheer. Lack of funds made it difficult for the side to travel for more internationals and preparation will be limited before Albania open their 1996 European Championship campaign in Wales in September as a member of Group Seven. Pitted with Germany, Moldova, Bulgaria and Georgia they look likely to take the wooden spoon once again, although victories over Moldova may prove possible.

There are players of quality coming through the ranks though, none more so than Gert Haxihu, who ended the season as Flamurtari's top scorer and looks set for an international career. If he does make it into the national side he'll be following in father's footsteps. Mexhit Haxihu played for the national side in the 1960s and made his mark in the national management area during 1993 by taking the Under-16 side through to the European Championships in Ireland.

SK Tirana's Indrit Fortuzi – having moved across town from Dinamo at the start of the season – continued his progress on the international scene. Having made his debut while still 18, Fortuzi, now 21, missed the match with Denmark but did well in the defeat by Spain and looks set to add to his tally of nine caps during the coming years.

Austria

Casino gamble pays off

SV Casino Salzburg finally got rid of their tag of the nearly men by capturing the championship title after finishing second twice in a row and having a magnificent run to the UEFA Cup final for good measure. Their success – their first major honour – was made even more sweeter by virtue of the fact that they pipped arch-rivals and reigning champions FK Austria to lift it.

The league season had started in August with a remodelled first division consisting of ten clubs each playing one another home and away twice. Relegation was a certainty for the club finishing last while the club in ninth place could earn a reprieve by beating the second division runner-up in a two-leg play-off.

After the first five rounds of games the league table had a distinctly lop-sided look to it with newly-promoted VfB Modling and Sturm Graz at the top, Modling raising more than a few eyebrows by winning 2-1 in Salzburg. But after the early excitement, the table started to develop a more familiar feel as Admira Wacker set the pace with eight straight wins.

A shuffling of personnel might have had something to do with the mixed results in the first part of the season. Salzburg had the coup of securing the services of Peter Artner from Wacker, where he had served for six years, while the Admira club had also needed time to adjust, having lost Olaf Marschall to Dynamo

Veteran Tony Polster became a big hit with the Koln fans during the season.

Osterreichischer Fussball-Bund

Founded:	1904
Address:	Meierestrasse, Praterstadion, Sektor A/F, A-1020 Vienna
Phone:	+43 1 727 18 0
Fax:	+43 1 728 16 32
UEFA Affiliation:	1954
FIFA Affiliation:	1905
Season:	August to June
National Staduim:	Ernst Happel Stadion
Capacity:	47,500
Colours:	White, Black, Black
Change:	Red, White, Red

National League Final League Table 1993–94

	P	W	D	L	F	A	Pts
SV Casino Salzburg	36	21	9	6	56	18	51
FK Austria	36	22	5	9	63	39	49
Admira Wacker	36	18	8	10	51	35	44
FC Tirol Innsbruck	36	14	11	11	48	33	39
Rapid Vienna	36	12	11	13	38	42	35
VfB Modling	36	12	11	13	32	49	35
Sturm Graz	36	12	9	15	37	42	33
Vorwarts Steyr	36	8	10	18	43	54	26
St Pollen	36	9	8	19	37	57	26
Sportsclub	36	5	12	19	21	57	22

Top Scorers
- 14 Nikola JURCEVIC (SV Casino Salzburg)
-     Hemio PFEIFENBERGER (SV Casino Salzburg)
- 12 Vaclac DANEK (FC Tirol Innsbruck)
- 11 Ralph HASENHUTTL (FK Austria)
- 10 Christoph WESTERTHALER (FC Tirol Innsbruck)

Promotions and Relegations
Promoted: FC Linz, Linz Ask (LASK)
Relegated: Sportsclub, St Pollen

International Results 1993–94

Date	Opponents	Result	Venue	Comp.	Scorers
25/8/93	Finland	3-0	Vienna	WCQ6	Kuhbauer (28), Pfeifenberger (41), Herzog (89 pen)
13/10/93	Bulgaria	1-4	Sofia	WCQ6	Herzog (51)
27/10/93	Israel	1-1	Tel Aviv	WCQ6	Reinmayr (15)
10/11/93	Sweden	1-1	Vienna	WCQ6	Herzog (69)
23/3/94	Hungary	1-1	Linz	Friendly	Pfeifenberger (30)
20/4/94	Scotland	1-2	Vienna	Friendly	Hutter (13)
17/5/94	Poland	4-3	Katowice	Friendly	Stoeger (5, 26, 65), Hochmaier (69)
2/6/94	Germany	1-5	Vienna	Friendly	Polster (77 pen)

National Record	P	W	D	L	F	A
European Championship	54	21	11	22	88	77
World Cup Finals	26	12	2	12	40	43
World Cup Qualifiers	63	30	14	19	122	69

Five-Year Records League 1-2-3 and Cup Winners

League Results

	1st	Pts	2nd	Pts	3rd	Pts
1990	FC Wacker Innsbruck	38	FK Austria	31	Admira Wacker	29
1991	FK Austria	36	FC Wacker Innsbruck	35	Sturm Graz	32
1992	FK Austria	33	SV Austria Salzburg	33	FC Wacker Innsbruck	33
1993	FK Austria	36	SV Austria Salzburg	36	Admira Wacker	28
1994	SV Casino Salzburg	51	FK Austria	49	Admira Wacker	44

Cup Final Results

1990	FK Austria	3-1	Rapid Vienna
1991	SV Stockerau	2-1	Rapid Vienna
1992	FK Austria	1-0	Admira Wacker
1993	FC Wacker Innsbruck	3-1	Rapid Vienna
1994	FK Austria	4-0	FC Linz

Name changes: SV Casino Salzburg (SV Austria Salzburg)
FC Tirol Innsbruck (FC Wacker Innsbruck)

OFB Cup

OFB Cup

Fourth Round

SW Bregenz v FC Tirol Innsbruck	0-2
Grazer AK v Vorwarts Steyr	1-0
Admira Wacker v Rapid Vienna	1-0
FK Austria v SV Casino Salzburg	2-1
FC Puch v FC Linz	1-2
SV Sefra Oberwart v Sportsclub	0-1†
Kottingbrunn* v Neustadter	0-0†
Klagenfurt * v First Vienna	0-0†

Quarter-Finals

Kottingbrunn v FC Linz	1-4
Klagenfurt v Admira Wacker	0-2
Grazer AK v FC Tirol Innsbruck	2-1†
FK Austria v Sportsclub	3-1†

Semi-Finals

FC Linz v Grazer AK	3-1
Admira Wacker v FK Austria	0-5

Final

FK Austria	4
Zsak (40), Prosenik (74), Narbekouas (80), Stoeger (90)	
FC Linz	0

† aet * win on penalties

Dresden along with coach Siggi Held. However, under new manager Dietmar Constantini they started to achieve the winning habit and for much of the season looked as though they might win the title for the first time since 1966.

As the halfway stage of the season approached Casino Salzburg flirted briefly with the leadership. A two-goal win at FK Austria was their first success there in 11 years of trying, but FK had restored their advantage by the time of the winter break.

In European club competitions only Salzburg survived, in the UEFA Cup. FK Austria had seen off Rosenborg in the first round of the Champions' Cup before Barcelona proved too much of an obstacle in the second round. In the Cup-Winners' Cup, Innsbruck created a surprise in their emphatic elimination of Ferencvaros but again a Spanish obstacle, this time Real Madrid, proved immovable.

But in the UEFA Cup things were moving. Although Admira Wacker fell to Dnepr at the first hurdle, the Salzburger had wins over Dac Dunjaska Streda and Royal Antwerp to sweep them into a quarter-final with Eintracht Frankfurt. A penalty shoot-out – the winner scored by keeper Otto Konrad – meant they became the first side to knock a German club out of European competition, this at the 19th time of asking. There was controversy though for manager Otto Barrick, who was found guilty of spitting at a German player and was subsequently banned for five games by UEFA.

As the end of the year approached SV Casino Salzburg were in joint top spot having won 3-0 at Rapid. The Viennese were in deep shock, having been put under threat of bankruptcy from the bank that owns the majority of their shares. With debts amounting to £1.2m the club had been guaranteed the use of the stadium in Hutteldorf until only the end of the season and would be looking to raise monies to clear their obligations, or face closure.

When the season restarted in March the fixture list had ensured an intriguing opening day, as second-placed Salzburg travelled to Vienna to face FK Austria. Four second-half goals by Nikola Jurcevic gave the Salzburgers a sensational second win on the Vienna ground and secured top spot on goal difference. The lead lasted just two weeks; having been held 0-0 at struggling St Pollen, FK Austria went a point clear with a win at third-placed Wacker. FK Austria got some form of revenge for those defeats by beating Salzburg 2-1 in the fourth round of the OFB Cup.

Meanwhile the draw for the UEFA Cup pitted Salzburg against German opposition – Karlsruhe – and again another narrow victory was achieved, this time on the away goals rule. So a major European final had been reached for only the third time in the country's history.

With seven rounds of the season to go Salzburg had the ideal opportunity to recapture the lead when they entertained FK. The 15,000 who packed into their stadium witnessed a championship performance they could scarcely believe as the home side ripped the reigning champions apart to win 6-0, with three goals in each half.

The win set Salzburg up for the UEFA Cup final that was ultimately lost to Internazionale, but generated a lot of support from within their own national boundaries despite their being ridiculed externally as being 'possibly the worst side to reach a European final'. Back in the league Salzburg maintained their lead and at the penultimate weekend secured the championship with a 0-0 draw at Rapid Vienna, while FK Austria made certain of the runners-up spot. Admira Wacker's season was rewarded with third place and another crack at success in the UEFA Cup. There was some consolation for the former champions, who took the OFB Cup with an emphatic 4-0 win over second division FC Linz.

At the bottom Vienna Sportsclub's demise was finally confirmed, their place going to Linz ASK (LASK) while St Pollen lost the play-off with the division two runners-ups and beaten cup finalists FC Linz, having finished just behind Vorwarts Steyr on goal difference.

Internationally, Austria had a quiet season in which they were overshadowed by neighbours Switzerland. As the season got under way there was virtually no chance of World Cup glory for Herbert Prohaska's side and a 3-0 win over Finland was quickly put into perspective with a 4-1 defeat by Bulgaria in Sofia. Draws against Israel and Sweden were well earned, but the season ended disastrously with a 5-1 drubbing by arch-rivals Germany.

Austrian players continued to do well abroad, none more so than Tony Polster. The veteran proved an instant success at Koln, where he quickly became a cult hero, while Andreas Herzog helped Werder Bremen back into Europe with a cup winner's medal.

The 1994–95 season gives cash-starved clubs something to build on. With a profit of more than £4m in the bank, plus a lucrative sponsorship deal, SV Casino Salzburg have a basis to secure their position at the pinnacle of Austrian football. Their raised profile, and in particular their performance in the second leg of the UEFA Cup final, should send more scouts into the Alps looking for players on the cheap. Even so, that might be a little too late for Rapid Vienna, who need a money-bags godfather soon or they might not have the opportunity to add to their 29 domestic titles.

Austrian Championship Results 1993–94

	Admira Wacker	FK Austria	Rapid Vienna	Sportsclub	St Pollen	Sturm Graz	SV Casino Salzburg	FC Tirol Innsbruck	VfB Modling	Vorwarts Steyr
Admira Wacker	—	0-3 / 4-2	2-0 / 0-0	3-0 / 2-0	4-3 / 3-1	2-2 / 1-1	1-0 / 0-3	0-0 / 2-0	2-0 / 0-1	2-0 / 4-0
FK Austria	2-0 / 3-1	—	2-1 / 2-0	3-1 / 1-1	3-0 / 0-1	3-0 / 0-0	1-2 / 0-4	2-1 / 1-0	1-0 / 3-0	4-1 / 1-0
Rapid Vienna	1-2 / 0-3	0-3 / 1-1	—	3-1 / 0-0	4-0 / 5-3	2-1 / 2-4	0-3 / 0-0	2-0 / 2-0	0-0 / 0-2	1-1 / 3-0
Sportsclub	0-2 / 1-1	0-1 / 0-3	0-1 / 0-1	—	1-1 / 3-1	0-0 / 1-0	0-0 / 0-1	1-1 / 1-2	1-1 / 0-2	2-1 / 1-1
St Pollen	0-1 / 1-0	3-2 / 2-3	1-1 / 1-1	0-1 / 0-0	—	2-1 / 2-1	1-0 / 0-0	0-0 / 0-0	1-0 / 2-1	3-1 / 3-1
Sturm Graz	1-2 / 1-0	2-4 / 0-0	1-0 / 1-2	3-1 / 3-1	1-0 / 2-0	—	0-2 / 0-1	1-0 / 0-0	1-0 / 2-1	1-1 / 3-1
SV Casino Salzburg	0-0 / 2-0	2-0 / 6-0	1-0 / 2-1	3-1 / 0-1	2-0 / 4-1	2-0 / 0-0	—	1-0 / 0-0	1-2 / 0-0	2-0 / 3-1
FC Tirol Innsbruck	2-1 / 0-1	3-1 / 0-1	1-1 / 0-1	2-0 / 6-0	2-1 / 2-1	4-2 / 2-1	2-0 / 1-1	—	4-2 / 4-0	3-0 / 4-2
VfB Modling	1-1 / 0-3	0-2 / 0-4	1-1 / 0-0	1-0 / 0-0	1-0 / 4-1	1-0 / 2-0	1-1 / 3-2	1-1 / 0-0	—	2-1 / 0-5
Vorwarts Steyr	4-1 / 0-0	2-0 / 1-1	3-0 / 0-1	6-0 / 1-1	2-0 / 1-1	0-1 / 0-0	0-2 / 1-3	1-1 / 2-0	1-1 / 1-2	—

Belgium

Royal again Anderlecht

The Belgian league maintained its usual cosmopolitan appearance for 1993–94 as the summer sales brought Swedish, Hungarian, Slovenian, Zairean, Romanian, Dutch, Bosnian, Croatian, Polish, Nigerian and Moroccan players into the country. Reigning champions RSC Anderlecht made only moderate investments, perhaps feeling that their squad was good enough to carry them to further success. Their only signings of note were Swedish midfielder Par Zetterberg and Olivier Suray, from Charleroi, and Filip Haagdoren from Lommel. Injury-prone Dutch striker Peter Van Vossen was sold to Ajax for £3m, useful revenue to help cover the cost of further development of the ultra-modern Vanden Stock Stadium.

The league season began in early August with Anderlecht recording a 2-0 home win over European finalists Royal Antwerp, Zetterberg scoring the opening goal on his debut. The winning ways continued for the champions and they ended the month with five wins from five games, 20 goals for, five against, maximum points and a three-point lead from Lommel in second place. Lommel, having just survived relegation the previous season, were the big surprises.

Little changed as September came, with Anderlecht getting the better of seven goals at Molenbeek in the Brussels derby. Promoted Seraing scored three times in seven second-half minutes as they beat Waregem 5-2 to stay in mid-table. Then, at the end of September, there was a huge shock when Club Bruges won 3-0 at Anderlecht. International midfielder Staelens scored all the goals as the visitors narrowed the gap at the top to just a point after nine games. Anderlecht's defeat could be attributed to over-confidence, their biggest enemy according to club president Constant Vanden Stock. In Europe though, Anderlecht – along with Standard, Antwerp and Mechelen – safely negotiated the opening rounds.

The big problems were in Liege, where Standard were having

Josip Weber of Cercle Bruges was the top scorer in Belgium for the third successive season. He also scored five goals on his international debut!

real difficulties and already floundering in mid-table. Arie Haan's team were torn apart by internal strife which resulted in striker Marc Wilmots being suspended after being sent off, Dutch playmaker Frans Van Rooy fined and banned for failing to show up for extra training, and out-of-favour defender Stephane Demol considering a move to Dundee United. A 2-0 defeat at promoted Oostende didn't help matters, but on the coast the seasiders celebrated and remained unbeaten after nine games in third place.

National coach Paul Van Himst – voted Belgium's Best Dressed Man – was allowed maximum time with his squad prior to the World Cup qualifying game against Romania with the postponement of league games. Things didn't go according to plan though as Romania won 2-1 to leave Belgium needing a point from their final game, at home to the RCS, to be sure of qualifying. Anderlecht, meanwhile, used the spare time to good effect, signing Maciej Terlecki, the 16-year-old son of former Poland international Stanislaw Terlecki.

Anderlecht compounded Standard's problems with a 3-0 win in Liege with a hat-trick by Luc Nilis. It was the start of a terrible fortnight for Standard, who were beaten 7-0 on their own soil by

Union Royal Belge des Societes de Football-Association	
Founded:	1895
Address:	Avenue Houba de Strooper 145, B-1020 Brussels
Phone:	+32 2 477 12 11
Fax:	+32 2 478 23 91
UEFA Affiliation:	1954
FIFA Affiliation:	1904
National Stadium:	Constant Vanden Stock
Capacity:	36,000
Season:	August to May
Colours:	Red, Red, Red
Change:	White, White, White

High fly, touch the sky! Jean Claude Mukanya (left) of Lommel and Nigerian World Cup star Daniel Amokachi of Club Bruges (now Everton).

Arsenal to complete a humiliating 10-0 aggregate defeat in the Cup-Winners' Cup that led to Haan being replaced by former international Rene Vandereycken. Anderlecht though made it through to the UEFA Champions' League with a 5-2 aggregate win over Sparta Prague, while Mechelen thrashed MTK Budapest 6-2 on aggregate in the UEFA Cup. Antwerp went out to SV Casino Salzburg, beaten 1-0 in both legs.

October ended as Anderlecht continued to consolidate their position at the top of the table, this time with a 1-0 over Lierse. Other notable cup results included Sporting Charleroi's 4-2 win at Charleroi, Club Bruges' victory over Mechelen and holders Standard's 3-2 defeat of Liege in a tense derby.

Van Himst named his squad for the crucial World Cup qualifier against the RCS, without skipper Georges Grun, sweeper Marc Emmers and striker Marc Degryse, who were all injured. Anderlecht defender Michel De Wolf, who had retired from international football in 1991, agreed to return one more time to cover for Emmers. The league programme was again postponed in advance of the World Cup qualifier, which ended in a 0-0 draw – too close for comfort, especially as Albert was dismissed after 50 minutes – but good enough for qualification.

Cercle's Josip Weber ended the month on a high with all four goals in a 4-2 win over Lierse. Indeed, Croat Weber made such an impression in his adopted country — in five and a half seasons he scored 119 goals — that he applied for Belgian citizenship to enable him to play in the World Cup.

Anderlecht opened their Champions' League campaign with a hard-fought 0-0 draw at home to Milan, but slumped 5-3 away to Werder Bremen in their next game, having led 3-0 at one stage.

Final League Tables 1993–94

	P	W	D	L	F	A	Pts
RSC Anderlecht	34	24	7	3	79	31	55
Club Bruges	34	20	13	1	54	19	53
Seraing	34	15	13	6	50	27	43
Charleroi	34	18	5	11	61	49	41
Royal Antwerp	34	14	13	7	44	38	41
Standard Liege	34	13	12	9	43	22	38
KV Oostende	34	10	16	8	45	41	36
KV Mechelen	34	11	11	12	42	40	35
SK Beveren	34	11	10	13	49	47	33
Germinal Ekeren	34	11	10	13	49	47	32
SK Lommel	34	10	10	14	41	50	30
Cercle Bruges	34	9	11	14	52	63	29
RFC Liege	34	9	11	14	40	59	29
Lierse	34	7	14	13	30	42	28
Gent	34	7	13	14	43	57	27
RWD Molenbeek	34	7	11	16	32	49	25
SV Waregem	34	6	7	21	32	62	19
RC Genk	34	4	10	20	38	79	18

Top Scorers
- 31 Josip WEBER (Cercle Bruges)
- 25 Luc NILIS (RSC Anderlecht)
- 20 Johnny BOSMAN (RSC Anderlecht)
- 19 Saso UDOVIC (Beveren)
- 18 Nebosja MALBASA (Charleroi)
- 15 Paulo da Silva EDMILSON (Seraing)
- Jacques MISSE MISSE (Charleroi)

Promotions and Relegations
Promoted: Eendracht Aalst, St Truiden
Relegated: RC Genk, SV Waregem

Five-Year Records League 1-2-3 and Cup Winners

League Results

	1st	Pts	2nd	Pts	3rd	Pts
1990	Club Bruges	57	RSC Anderlecht	53	KV Mechelen	50
1991	RSC Anderlecht	53	KV Mechelen	50	Club Bruges	47
1992	Club Bruges	53	RSC Anderlecht	49	Standard Liege	46
1993	RSC Anderlecht	58	Standard Liege	45	KV Mechelen	42
1994	RSC Anderlecht	55	Club Bruges	53	Seraing	43

Cup Final Results

1990	RFC Liege	2-1	Ekeren	
1991	Club Bruges	3-1	KV Mechelen	
1992	Royal Antwerp	2-2	KV Mechelen	5-4 on pens
1993	Standard Liege	2-0	Charleroi	
1994	RSC Anderlecht	2-0	Club Bruges	

International Results 1993–94

Date	Opponents	Result	Venue	Comp.	Scorers
13/9/93	Gabon	2-1	Brussels	Friendly	Wilmots (44, 87)
13/10/93	Romania	1-2	Bucharest	WCQ4	Scifo (88)
17/11/93	RCS	0-0	Brussels	WCQ4	
16/2/94	Malta	0-1	Valletta	Friendly	
2/6/94	Zambia	9-0	Brussels	Friendly	Weber (9, 14, 57, 59, 88), Degryse (28, 38, 65), Nilis (55)
5/6/94	Hungary	3-1	Brussels	Friendly	Weber (5), Degryse (36), Nilis (65)
19/6/94	Morocco	1-0	Orlando	WCFF	Degryse (11)
25/6/94	Holland	1-0	Orlando	WCFF	Albert (65)
29/6/94	Saudi Arabia	0-1	Washington	WCFF	
2/7/94	Germany	2-3	Chicago	WCF2	Grun (7), Albert (90)

National Record	P	W	D	L	F	A
European Championships	61	27	16	18	91	69
World Cup Finals	29	9	4	16	37	53
World Cup Qualifiers	72	40	15	18	137	81

Mechelen also ran into trouble, crashing out of the UEFA Cup to Cagliari, 5-1 on aggregate.

Standard, starting to put their problems on the field behind them, continued their revival with a useful 1-1 draw at Antwerp and a 2-0 home win over Waregem. The club then took Romanian World Cup goalkeeper Bogdan Stelea on loan from Spain's Mallorca. Anderlecht and Club Bruges continued their head-to-head struggle at the top of the table right through December, with both clubs managing a win and two draws apiece. Anderlecht, however, lost defender Michel De Wolf with a serious injury and were forced to buy a replacement. They turned to Beveren's Nigerian Chidi Nwanu, and signed him for £700,000. On the final weekend of 1993 Malbasa hit a hat-trick for Charleroi as they won 4-0 at bottom club Genk.

The fifth round of the Belgian Cup were the last games played in 1993 and the most notable result was a 3-2 win for Club Bruges over an improving Standard Liege. There were easy wins for Anderlecht, Ekeren, Antwerp and Charleroi.

The New Year started with a double high for the defending champions. Johnny Bosman scored a hat-trick in Anderlecht's crushing 6-1 win over Waregem and their Swedish midfielder, Par Zetterberg, was voted Footballer of the Year — only the third foreigner to win the accolade in Belgium. Club Bruges continued to keep the pressure up and at the end of January they reduced the gap to a single point when Anderlecht suffered a shock 0-2 defeat at home to Seraing. At the other end of the table, Genk coach Luka Peruzovic resigned after just 10 games in charge, with assistant Pierre Denier and former player Norbert Beuls taking over. Standard, struggling to keep pace, decided not to keep goalkeeper Stelea, and after he had returned to Spain learned that Luxembourg international Guy Hellers would miss up to three months with a knee injury.

Cercle's Josip Weber was in the news in February, after his formal naturalisation as a Belgian citizen was rushed through in time for him to play for Belgium in the World Cup finals, with 67 per cent in favour of his joining the national squad, according to one newspaper poll. Anderlecht wobbled slightly when they lost 1-0 at old rivals Mechelen, allowing Club Bruges to draw level at the top, but recovered with a 3-2 win over Beveren and beat Beerschot 3-1 in the Cup quarter-finals, to claim a semi-final place alongside Ekeren, Molenbeek and Bruges.

The opening week in March brought Anderlecht an important 1-0 win over FC Porto in the Champions' League, reviving hopes of success, and restored confidence for the top-of-the-table clash against Club Bruges. The match finished 0-0, and was more noteworthy because it was the first time professional stewards had been used in Belgium. The game was costly in that Anderlecht defender Philippe Albert's torn knee ligaments ruled him out for the rest of the domestic season. In his absence, Anderlecht lost 2-0 to FC Porto and drew 0-0 with Milan in the Champions' League, ending their hopes of reaching the semi-finals with a

Cup Results

Quarter-Finals
Germinal Ekeren v Charleroi	2-0
Royal Antwerp v Club Bruges	0-3
Beerschot v RSC Anderlecht	1-3†
RWD Molenbeek v Lommel	2-0

Semi-Finals
RSC Anderlecht v RWD Molenbeek	0-0; 2-2
Club Bruges v Germinal Ekeren	4-0; 3-1

Final

RSC Anderlecht 2
Versavel (36), Nilis (74)
Club Bruges 0
Att: 20,000   Ref: Schelings
RSC Anderlecht: De Wilde, Boffin (Crasson 35), Rutjes, P. Albert, M. De Wolf, Emmers, Walem, Versavel, Haagdoren, Nilis, J. Bosman (Zetterberg 85)
Club Bruges: Verlinden, Renier, Medved (Vermant 72), Okon, Borkelmans, Plovie, Staelens, F. Van der Elst, Verheyen, Amokachi, Eykelkamp
†aet

Belgian Championship Results 1993–94

	AA Gent	Cercle Bruges	Charleroi	Club Bruges	Club Liege	Germinal Ekeren	KV Mechelen	KV Oostende	Lierse SK	RC Genk	Royal Antwerp	RSC Anderlecht	RWD Molenbeek	Seraing	SK Beveren	SK Lommel	Standard Liege	SV Waregem
AA Gent	—	2-0	0-0	0-4	4-1	1-1	3-1	1-2	0-0	2-3	1-2	1-2	1-1	0-0	2-3	1-0	0-0	2-2
Cercle Bruges	2-2	—	0-1	2-4	3-3	1-1	0-1	2-0	4-2	1-1	2-4	0-0	1-0	1-1	1-0	3-0	1-1	2-1
Charleroi	4-2	5-3	—	0-1	6-4	0-0	1-0	2-1	1-0	2-1	3-2	1-5	3-2	3-1	2-1	3-0	1-0	2-1
Club Bruges	1-2	2-0	2-1	—	3-0	0-0	2-1	1-0	1-0	2-1	0-0	0-0	5-1	0-0	2-1	4-1	1-0	3-1
Club Liege	0-0	2-1	2-1	0-0	—	0-0	3-2	1-2	3-0	4-0	0-0	1-2	1-0	0-0	0-2	1-1	0-2	1-0
Germinal Ekeren	2-0	4-1	1-0	0-1	4-1	—	0-2	1-2	2-0	1-1	1-3	2-4	4-1	1-2	0-0	4-1	1-1	1-0
KV Mechelen	4-1	0-4	1-3	1-1	2-2	3-1	—	2-0	0-0	2-2	1-1	0-0	3-1	2-1	1-0	1-1	1-1	1-1
KV Oostende	2-2	1-1	1-0	2-2	2-0	2-2	0-0	—	2-2	4-0	2-4	1-3	1-1	0-0	1-1	1-1	2-0	1-1
Lierse SK	1-2	3-2	2-2	1-1	0-1	3-2	0-0	0-1	—	3-1	1-1	1-4	1-1	1-1	1-0	1-1	1-0	1-2
RC Genk	3-3	2-2	0-4	2-4	2-2	1-3	2-0	2-2	0-3	—	0-2	0-2	1-4	0-0	2-0	1-3	0-2	2-1
Royal Antwerp	1-1	0-3	2-1	0-1	1-1	1-1	0-0	0-4	0-0	3-1	—	0-0	1-0	2-1	2-0	4-0	1-1	2-0
RSC Anderlecht	2-1	2-0	3-1	0-3	6-0	5-2	1-1	2-0	1-0	6-2	2-0	—	0-0	0-2	3-2	1-0	0-0	6-1
RWD Molenbeek	2-0	1-3	2-4	0-0	2-2	1-3	0-2	2-1	0-0	1-1	0-1	3-4	—	0-1	0-1	0-0	1-0	1-0
Seraing	3-0	1-1	2-2	1-1	2-0	1-0	1-0	3-0	2-0	3-1	4-2	1-2	0-0	—	3-0	1-0	2-2	5-2
SK Beveren	3-1	4-2	1-1	1-1	3-0	3-1	1-1	3-3	1-1	3-1	0-0	0-2	0-0	1-1	—	2-1	0-2	3-0
SK Lommel	1-3	5-1	2-0	0-0	1-2	3-1	3-0	1-2	0-0	1-1	5-0	1-1	3-1	0-3	2-0	—	1-0	3-0
Standard Liege	2-0	4-0	2-0	0-0	3-1	3-0	2-2	0-0	3-0	2-0	0-0	0-3	0-1	1-0	0-0	7-0	—	2-0
SV Waregem	2-2	2-3	2-1	0-1	2-1	0-2	1-1	0-0	0-1	2-1	1-2	2-4	1-2	2-1	0-0	0-0	2-0	—

match still to play. Despite this big setback, they rounded off March with two consecutive 5-1 thrashings, of Ekeren and Charleroi respectively, with Luc Nilis scoring three in the first game and four in the second! In the Cup semi-finals, they narrowly defeated Molenbeek in the Brussels derby, while Club Bruges beat Ekeren 7-1 on aggregate.

There was depressing news in Liege though, where FC were rumoured to be on the brink of folding with debts of £2.5m and coach Eric Gerets announced he would be quitting at the end of the season to move to Holland.

April marked the beginning of a managerial merry-go-round. Standard coach Rene Vandereycken was told that he would not have his contract renewed in the summer and that Robert Waseige – in charge at Charleroi – would take over for the new season. Vendereycken though was immediately recruited by Molenbeek, in succession to Freddy Smets. Charleroi, meanwhile, announced that they would replace Waseige with Georges Leekens. And Gent completed the musical hot-seats by announcing that former international defender Leo Clijsters would take over from Walter Meeuws for the 1994–95 season. Clijsters had served his apprenticeship with third division Patro Eisden, and guided them to the second division.

All of this action off the field did little to halt the march of Anderlecht, who strode to the title with a draw at home to Standard and consecutive wins against Lierse, Lommel, Oostende, Gent and Cercle. Club Bruges struggled to keep pace, and when they could only draw at home to Seraing, Anderlecht clinched the title with a match to spare after a 2-1 win at Gent. As if to celebrate and announcing their intentions to remain at the top, they agreed to buy veteran defender Georges Grun from Parma, and opened negotiations with Cercle for Weber's signature, which was duly captured.

Then, to cap a memorable season for Jan Boskamp's side, they beat Bruges 2-0 in the Cup Final, despite being without suspended Degryse. The match also marked the return, after a long injury lay-off, of Zetterberg. Success in Europe had eluded them, but Anderlecht were the undisputed best team in Belgium. Bruges, who fought so hard, had to settle for a place in the Cup-Winners' Cup, with surprise team Seraing along with Royal Antwerp and Charleroi qualifying for the UEFA Cup. At the bottom of the table, Genk, as expected, and Waregem were relegated, with Eendracht Aalst and St Truiden coming up to replace them.

With the domestic season over, attention turned to the national side and the introduction of newly naturalised Weber in the starting line-up to face Zambia in Brussels. The new man wasted little time in making his mark, scoring after nine minutes. That turned out to be the first of five on the night (some debut!) as the Belgians whacked the Zambians out of sight by 9-0. Almost unnoticed Degryse notched a hat-trick and Nilis scored his first international goal. A few days later Weber made it six goals in two games by scoring the first in a 3-1 win over Hungary, as Belgium completed their World Cup preparations.

Bulgaria

Levski Sofia were once again the dominant team in Bulgarian club football. Having won the championship for the first time in five years the previous season, they used 1993–94 to go one better by completing a comfortable league and cup double. The league was won by a margin of 17 points from CSKA, while the cup final against Pirin proved a little tighter, needing a goal two minutes from time by Ilian Iliev, in front of 25,000, for Levski to take the trophy.

Levski started the season at a flying pace and quickly established their superiority. They dropped just three points from their opening seven games, which included a 3-1 home win over Yantra Gobrovo. That in itself was not a major talking point at the time but then an enquiry found Yantra guilty of trying to buy the points in a match against Beroe Stara Zagora a few weeks earlier. Given the tough line adopted by UEFA with regard to the Marseille affair and the Polish attitude in dealing with a similar scandal involving Legia Warsaw and LKS Lodz at the end of the 1992–93 season, the Bulgarian Football Union (BFU) wasted no time in taking action. This involved expelling Yantra from the league and all competitions and banning the parties implicated in the action for life, including the defender Stefan Bachev, who was alleged to have made the offer of inducement of some £2,000.

The net effect of this was that Yantra's results were expunged and Levski lost the points they had acquired by virtue of their win, which in turn meant that CSKA took over at the top of the table. It was a brief flirtation for the former army side as the following weekend Levski won 3-1 at newly promoted Shumen to regain the lead as CSKA crashed by the only goal at home to Lokomotiv GO. The leader position didn't change hands again all season.

By the arrival of the winter break Levski were five points clear of CSKA and when the league resumed business in March they were strengthened further by the arrival of midfielder Magdi Tolba, an Egyptian signed from the Greek club PAOK. With four rounds of games still to be played Levski secured the championship by virtue of a 2-0 win at Spartak Varna, for whom defeat meant relegation. Spartak were one of a trio of clubs from the Black Sea who were faced with the drop – the others being Chernomorets and Cherno More, the latter after only one year in the top division. Despite the relegation of Chernomorets, the city of Bourgas will not be without a top side, because Neftohimik gained promotion from the second division. The surprise side of the league campaign, though, were Shumen, who finished fourth in their first season and were beaten only once at home, by the champions.

In the Bulgarian Cup Final, Levski faced Pirin from Blagoevgrad, who were trying to record their first domestic honour. They went close but ultimately fell to that late, late goal. It was the second time in three years that Pirin had lost to Levski in the final and given their circumstances they had done well to reach it. The club had been left in turmoil following the sacking of coach Milan Goranov, and it had been left to the players to pick the team and sort out match tactics. The problems didn't end there, because the ground was closed for several games following a bottle-throwing incident.

Final League Table 1993–94

	P	W	D	L	F	A	Pts
Levski Sofia	28	22	5	1	78	17	71
CSKA Sofia	28	17	3	8	58	27	54
Botev Plovdiv	28	15	5	8	50	29	50
Shumen	28	14	6	8	49	34	48
Etar	28	10	10	8	42	33	40
Lokomotiv Plovdiv	28	12	4	12	38	43	40
Beroe Stara Zagora	28	11	5	12	33	38	38
Lokomotiv GO	28	11	5	12	25	39	38
Slavia Sofia	28	9	9	10	30	37	36
Pirin	28	10	6	12	33	35	36
Lokomotiv Sofia	28	10	4	14	37	40	34
Dobrudja	28	8	10	10	37	42	34
Chernomorets Bourgas	28	8	6	14	30	36	30
Cherno More	28	5	6	17	24	68	21
Spartak Varna	28	4	4	20	18	65	16
Yantra	0	0	0	0	0	0	0

Top Scorers
30 Nasko SIRAKOV (Levski Sofia)
25 Ivajlo ANDONOV (CSKA Sofia)
18 Plamen GUETOV (Shumen)
15 Daniel BORIMIROV (Levski Sofia)

Promotions and Relegations
Promoted: Lovtch Lex, Neftohimik Bourgas, Spartak Plovdiv, Spartak Plevenou Montana.
Relegated: Yantra (expelled for corruption), Chernomorets Bourgas, Cherno More, Spartak Varna.

Bulgarski Futbolen Soius

Founded:	1923
Address:	Karnigradska 19, Boite postale 559, BG-1000 Sofia
Phone:	+359 2 87 74 90
Fax:	+359 2 80 32 37
UEFA Affiliation:	1954
FIFA Affiliation:	1924
National Stadium:	Stadion Vasilij Levski
Capacity:	55,000
Season:	August to May
Colours:	White, Green, Red
Change:	Red, Green, White

International Results 1993–94

Date	Opponents	Result	Venue	Comp.	Scorers
8/8/93	Sweden	1-1	Sofia	WCQ6	Stoichkov (21 pen)
13/10/93	Austria	4-1	Sofia	WCQ6	Penev (6, 75), Stoichkov (32 pen), Lechkov (89)
17/11/93	France	2-1	Paris	WCQ6	Kostadinov (36, 90)
19/1/94	Mexico	1-1	San Diego	Friendly	Balakov (78)
15/4/94	Oman	1-1	Muscat	Friendly	Yankov (83)
28/4/94	Kuwait	2-2	Kuwait	Friendly	Yankov (25), Own Goal (31)
21/6/94	Nigeria	0-3	Dallas	WCFD	
26/6/94	Greece	4-0	Chicago	WCFD	Stoichkov (5 pen, 56 pen), Lechkov (56), Borimirov (90)
30/6/94	Argentina	2-0	Dallas	WCFD	Stoichkov (61), Sirakov (90)
5/6/94	Mexico	1-1	New Jersey	WCF2	Stoichkov (7)
10/7/94	Germany	2-1	New Jersey	WCFQ	Stoichkov (72), Lechkov (78)
13/7/94	Italy	1-2	New Jersey	WCFS	Stoichkov (44 pen)
16/7/94	Sweden	0-4	Pasadena	WCF3/4	

National Record	P	W	D	L	F	A
European Championship	57	24	13	20	84	66
World Cup Finals	23	3	7	13	21	46
World Cup Qualifiers	71	35	12	24	115	94

Five-Year Records League 1-2-3 and Cup Winners

League Results

	1st	Pts	2nd	Pts	3rd	Pts
1990	CSKA Sofia	47	Levski Spartak	36	Slavia Sofia	36
1991	Etar	44	Slavia Sofia	37	CSKA Sofia	37
1992	CSKA Sofia	47	Levski Sofia	45	Botev Plovdiv	37
1993	Levski Sofia	50	CSKA Sofia	42	Botev Plovdiv	38
1994	Levski Sofia	71	CSKA Sofia	54	Botev Plovdiv	50

Cup Final Results

1990	Sliven	2-0	CSKA Sofia
1991	Levski Sofia	2-1	Botev Plovdiv
1992	Levski Sofia	5-0	Pirin
1993	CSKA Sofia	1-0	Botev Plovdiv
1994	Levski Sofia	1-0	Pirin

Cup Results

Quarter-Finals

Chernomorets v Levski Sofia	1-4; 1-4
Lokomotiv GO v Spartak Plovdiv	0-2; 0-4
Pirin v Dorostol	3-0; 1-2
Tchirpan v Doupnista	1-0; 0-2

Semi-Finals

Levski Sofia v Doupnista	7-0; 3-0
Pirin v Spartak Plovdiv	1-0; 0-0

Final

Levski Sofia v Pirin	1-0

The two clubs from Plovdiv had indifferent seasons despite pushing the Bulgarian maximum of five foreign players per club to its limit. Lokomotiv added four Serbs to their ranks along with Slavia's Marinov and Lokomotiv Sofia's Vasev. Across town Botev had signed Donlov (Levski), Draganov (CSKA) and Lokomotiv Sofia's Donev and Stoyanov, but other than being the only side to beat Levski in the league the large change in personnel hindered rather than helped. Competition for support in the city will be even greater from the 1994–95 season with the promotion of Spartak Plovdiv from the second division.

Levski's dominating form at home spread short term into their Champions' Cup progression, where they thwarted the not inconsiderable resources of Scottish champions Rangers. Although twice falling two goals behind at Ibrox, Levski battled to 2-3 with goals by Borimirov and Todorov. In a superb atmosphere in the Georgi Asparuchov stadium, Sirakov scored after 36 minutes but Rangers equalised and looked to be going through until Todorov rifled a 30-yard drive into the net well inside injury time. The result was even more remarkable given the fact that it was the club's first win over two legs for seven years! The excitement was short-lived, though as German efficiency saw Werder Bremen through in the second round and Levski missing the UEFA Champions' League.

CSKA didn't fare any better, losing to Benfica in the the Cup-Winners' Cup after Luxembourg side Balzers had been thrashed out of sight by 11-1. Both the clubs from Plovdiv, Botev and Lokomotiv, found themselves in and out of the UEFA Cup at the first hurdle, to Olympiakos and Lazio respectively. A one-year UEFA ban means that Botev's third place in 1993–94 fails to set them back in the competition for 1994–95 – their place going to Shumen, along with CSKA and Levski Sofia.

Bulgarian Championship Results 1993–94

	Beroe Stara Zagora	Botev Plovdiv	Cherno More	Chernomorets Bourgas	CSKA Sofia	Dobrudja	Etar	Levski Sofia	Lokomotiv Sofia	Lokomotiv GO (Gorna)	Lokomotiv Plovdiv	Pirin	Shumen	Slavia Sofia	Spartak Varna
Beroe Stara Zagora	—	1-0	3-3	1-0	0-2	4-1	1-1	1-2	2-1	2-0	2-0	1-1	0-2	0-2	1-0
Botev Plovdiv	0-2	—	4-0	1-0	2-1	2-2	2-0	1-0	3-2	1-1	1-2	1-0	4-2	6-0	6-1
Cherno More	1-3	0-3	—	0-0	0-3	1-0	1-1	0-5	0-2	1-0	2-1	2-0	0-0	0-0	1-2
Chernomorets Bourgas	1-1	2-2	3-0	—	2-2	1-1	0-1	2-1	3-0	3-0	1-0	3-3	1-0	1-0
CSKA Sofia	3-0	2-1	6-1	4-1	—	3-0	2-1	1-4	1-0	0-1	6-0	4-1	2-1	3-1	7-0
Dobrudja	3-1	0-0	3-0	3-0	1-1	—	4-1	2-2	4-3	3-2	2-0	1-1	1-2	0-0	2-0
Etar	5-2	3-0	0-2	3-2	2-0	1-1	—	2-2	0-0	5-2	1-1	3-0	2-0	1-1	3-1
Levski Sofia	2-0	2-0	5-1	1-0	2-1	5-0	1-0	—	6-0	6-0	2-0	4-3	1-1	4-1	5-0
Lokomotiv Sofia	1-0	0-1	5-0	1-0	0-1	3-1	1-3	0-4	—	2-0	1-0	1-3	3-1	0-0	7-0
Lokomotiv GO (Gorna)	0-1	0-0	3-1	1-0	1-0	2-0	0-0	0-0	2-0	—	1-0	2-0	1-0	2-0	1-0
Lokomotiv Plovdiv	2-1	1-3	4-2	4-2	0-0	2-1	2-1	1-1	1-0	1-0	—	2-1	4-0	1-2	3-0
Pirin	1-1	2-0	2-0	1-0	3-0	2-0	2-0	0-3	1-1	3-0	1-2	—	2-2	2-1	3-0
Shumen	2-0	2-0	4-1	1-0	2-1	3-1	1-1	1-3	3-0	4-0	3-1	2-0	—	1-1	3-0
Slavia Sofia	2-1	1-3	4-2	2-0	0-1	0-0	1-1	1-3	0-0	3-0	2-2	2-0	1-0	—	2-0
Spartak Varna	0-1	0-3	2-2	2-1	0-1	0-0	0-1	0-2	1-2	3-3	2-1	0-0	1-3	3-1	—

Levski could finish only 27th in the UEFA ranking list – behind clubs from Luxembourg, Denmark and Norway – and therefore missed out on the Champions' competition. But their co-efficient will no doubt increase in the coming seasons given the surge to form of the national side, who qualified for the final stages of the World Cup in dramatic fashion with a last-minute win over France in the Parc des Princes. Even getting to that point had not been easy, as squabbles within the leading clubs seemed likely to tear the heart out of the national side. Andrej Jeliaskov, the Levski manager, had threaten to pull his players out of the game in Paris given the BFU's unwillingness to postpone important league matches to allow players time to prepare for international and European games. The Levski players backed their manager to the hilt, with letters of confirmation by them to president Valentin Mihov. Ultimately a meeting between all parties sorted the differences out. Bulgaria got their chance in the World Cup Finals – and had an impact bigger than anyone could have believed possible.

Krassimir Balakov of Bulgaria wins header against Andreas Moller of Germany.

Croatia

Waiting in the wings

Hajduk Split – a famous name from the recent past of Yugoslavian football – won their second Croatian title in three years, on the final day of the season.

With three rounds of matches to play four points separated the top three sides, Hajduk leading the two clubs from the capital – NK and Croatia. The Zagreb pair could only keep on winning and hope that the club from Split slipped up in their final matches against Radnicki, former Yugoslav league rivals Rijeka, and Durava. Both Radnicki and Durava were looking certain for relegation and the former played like it in Split, where Hajduk thumped ten goals past them to record the biggest win in the short history of the Croatian League. Croatia were also involved in a ten-goal bonanza, slaying Dubrovnik by 8-2 while NK were held to a 1-1 draw at mid-table NK Zadar. That point dropped by NK proved to be costly as in the penultimate round of games Hajduk travelled to Rijeka and were beaten 2-1 in a tense affair. NZ Zagreb produced a 2-1 home win over Istra Pola and moved to within a point of the leaders. Croatia, still in with a mathematical chance of retaining the title that they had won the previous year, once again treated their supporters to a ten-goal encounter, this time beating Pazinka Pazin 6-4.

As the final day of the season arrived, Hajduk knew that a win would guarantee them the championship no matter what those around them did. Croatia continued their run with a 7-1 win to bring their tally to 21 goals in their final three matches, leaving them just two short of a ton for the season. NK did all they could by winning with the only goal of the game at Cibalia, but Hajduk had a comfortable 4-0 win over Durava, the other relegated club, to retake the title.

With no UEFA Cup place available for Croatian teams for another year, the remaining route to Europe was through the Croatian Cup. Croatia Zagreb grabbed the Cup-Winners' Cup spot by beating Rijeka in the two-leg final. It was hard luck for Rijeka, who had dismissed Hajduk in the semi-finals, while Croatia won an exciting Zagreb derby to beat NK on aggregate.

Croatian Football Association

Founded:	1991 (1912)
Address:	Illica 31, 41000 Zagreb
Phone:	+38 41 42 46 47
Fax:	+38 41 42 46 39
UEFA Affiliation:	1992
FIFA Affiliation:	1992
Season:	to July
National Staduim:	Maksimir, Zagreb
Capacity:	60,000
Colours:	Red, White, Blue

Final League Table 1993–94

	P	W	D	L	F	A	Pts
Hajduk Split	34	22	6	6	84	36	50
NK Zagreb	34	20	9	5	58	30	49
Croatia Zagreb	34	20	8	6	98	34	48
Inker Zapresic	34	17	8	9	48	34	42
Varteks	34	16	9	9	51	30	41
Rijeka	34	11	17	6	40	27	39
Cibalia Vinkovci	34	11	13	10	37	27	35
Osijek	34	12	11	11	56	58	35
Segesta Sisak	34	12	10	12	48	44	34
Istra Pola	34	13	8	13	40	36	34
Zadar	34	8	17	9	24	36	33
Belisce	34	12	8	14	55	51	32
Sibenik	34	12	8	14	36	42	32
Primorac Stobrec	34	11	7	16	42	54	29
Pazinka Pazin	34	8	9	17	51	67	25
HNK Dubrovnik	34	7	9	18	26	60	23
Durava Zagreb	34	7	9	18	28	63	23
Radnicki VG	34	3	2	29	17	109	8

Top Scorers
28 Goran VLAOVIC (Croatia Zagreb)
27 Igor CVITANOVIC (Croatia Zagreb)
26 VIDA (Belisce)

Promotions and Relegations
Promoted: Nerevta Metkovic, Marsonia Slavonskibrod,
Relegated: Pazinka Pazin, HNK Dubrovnik, Durava Zagreb, Radnicki VG

(League reduced to 16 teams for 1994–95)

For the 1993–94 season the Croatian first division consisted of 18 clubs, five of whom had been major influences on the former Yugoslav first division – Hajduk, NK Zagreb, Rijeka, Osijek and Croatia. Croatia Zagreb established a more famous past as Dinamo Zagreb before changing their name to HASK-Gradjanski and then the political move to Croatia during the course of the 1992–93 season. The remaining clubs have little tradition among them other than a smattering of lower order and regional titles. Nevertheless the current bunch of top sides can point to a degree of tradition which could enable the country's clubs to re-establish themselves among the elite when the upheavals around them subside.

As Dinamo, Croatia Zagreb became the first Yugoslav side to lift a major European club cup, winning the Fairs Cup in 1967 by beating an outstanding Leeds United side with two goals by Cercek in front of a 40,000 full house. During the campaign they had needed a toss of a coin to see them past Spartak Brno, but countered that with a sparkling 5-1 aggregate win over Juventus in the quarter-final. Times had been leaner, with only one of their four Yugoslav championships coming in the eighties. It was

International Results 1993–94

Date	Opponents	Result	Venue	Comp.	Scorers
23/3/94	Spain	2-0	Valencia	Friendly	Prosinecki (6), Suker (52)
20/4/94	Slovakia	1-4	Bratislava	Friendly	Popovic (67)
18/5/94	Hungary	2-2	Gyor	Friendly	Mladenovic (52, 63)
4/6/94	Argentina	0-0	Zagreb	Friendly	

Croatian Championship Results 1993–94

	Belisce	Cibalia Vinkovci	Croatia Zagreb	Durava Zagreb	HNK Dubrovnik	Hajduk Split	Inker Zapresic	Istra Pola	Osijek	Pazinka Pazin	Primorac Stobrec	Radnicki VG	Rijeka	Segesta Sisak	Sibenik	Varteks	Zadar	NK Zagreb
Belisce	—	1-1	0-6	3-0	2-1	2-0	1-1	1-2	3-3	2-0	1-1	7-1	1-1	3-0	3-0	3-0	1-0	2-4
Cibalia Vinkovci	3-2	—	1-2	2-0	3-0	1-0	2-0	0-0	1-1	3-0	3-0	3-0	0-0	3-1	2-0	0-0	0-0	0-1
Croatia Zagreb	1-2	0-0	—	5-3	8-2	4-0	2-3	3-2	7-1	10-1	1-0	5-0	2-0	2-0	4-0	1-1	3-0	1-1
Durava Zagreb	2-1	1-2	1-0	—	0-0	3-4	0-0	0-0	1-0	3-2	3-0	0-1	0-0	1-1	3-1	1-0	2-2	0-2
HNK Dubrovnik	0-0	1-0	0-1	0-0	—	1-1	0-1	0-1	0-0	2-0	3-2	1-0	0-0	0-1	1-2	1-1	1-2	1-0
Hajduk Split	4-2	3-2	4-2	4-0	6-0	—	2-1	4-1	3-1	5-1	4-1	10-0	0-2	1-1	2-0	2-0	3-0	4-0
Inker Zapresic	2-1	0-0	1-1	2-0	3-0	1-1	—	2-0	3-1	4-0	4-0	3-1	2-1	1-2	1-1	1-0	2-0	1-0
Istra Pola	4-2	1-0	0-0	0-0	2-1	0-1	2-3	—	2-0	1-0	0-1	5-1	1-0	0-0	2-1	1-0	2-0	2-3
Osijek	0-2	1-1	2-2	4-2	3-0	1-4	1-0	2-1	—	1-1	4-2	3-1	2-0	2-1	2-1	1-1	2-0	1-3
Pazinka Pazin	4-1	2-0	4-6	4-0	3-1	1-2	2-3	0-0	4-1	—	4-0	6-1	0-0	1-1	2-3	0-0	0-0	2-4
Primorac Stobrec	1-0	2-1	0-4	7-0	4-2	0-2	1-1	3-1	2-1	1-3	—	4-0	1-1	2-0	1-0	0-1	0-1	1-1
Radnicki VG	1-2	1-1	0-5	0-1	2-0	1-3	0-2	0-4	0-7	2-1	0-3	—	0-3	0-1	0-1	0-3	2-4	0-1
Rijeka	2-0	0-0	0-3	2-1	2-2	2-1	2-1	2-0	1-1	3-1	0-0	6-0	—	0-0	1-1	3-0	0-0	2-2
Segesta Sisak	1-3	1-1	2-6	5-1	4-0	1-1	2-0	1-1	4-2	1-1	3-0	4-0	2-0	—	3-1	1-2	3-1	0-1
Sibenik	2-1	2-0	0-0	2-0	2-2	0-0	4-1	1-0	0-0	0-0	0-0	2-0	1-1	2-1	—	3-1	3-0	0-1
Varteks	1-0	2-0	1-0	5-0	0-1	3-1	3-0	2-0	4-2	4-0	3-1	3-0	1-1	3-0	2-0	—	1-1	0-2
Zadar	0-0	1-0	1-0	1-0	1-2	1-1	0-0	0-0	1-1	0-0	1-1	1-1	0-0	0-0	2-1	1-1	—	1-1
NK Zagreb	1-1	1-1	1-1	2-0	3-0	0-1	2-0	2-1	1-1	2-1	1-0	4-1	1-2	2-0	1-0	2-2	3-0	—

perhaps fitting that in the Champions' Cup they were drawn against another side representing their country for the first time, but there the similarities ended. B68 from the Faeroe Islands were demolished 11-0 on aggregate in the preliminary round, with Goran Vlaovic scoring four of his five goals in the second leg inside a four-minute period. Thoughts of a prolonged run in the competition were still there after a 1-1 draw against Steaua in Bucharest, but despite an excellent attempt in their own Maksimir Stadium, Croatia eventually went out on the away goals rule. Hajduk stuttered at the first attempt in the Cup-Winners' Cup, having beaten Ajax by a single goal in Ljubljana. The Dutch side cruised to a 6-0 win in the second leg.

Croatian football's biggest problem, given their existing political situation, will continue to be their inability to keep their best players at home. The top men are already earning top money in places such as Spain, where eight locally-based players were in the Croatia team who beat Spain 2-0 in Valencia with goals from Robert Prosinecki and Davor Suker. Nearer home, more stable economies such as Bulgaria and Romania beckon now that borders are fully open. But national teams are now willing to look at travelling to the state for matches, the biggest coup for the Croatian FA being the agreement of the Argentinian national side to play a friendly in a packed Zagreb stadium.

Three-Year Records League 1-2-3 and Cup Winners

	1st	Pts	2nd	Pts	3rd	Pts
1992	Hajduk Split	36	NK Zagreb	33	NK Osijek	27
1993	Croatia Zagreb	49	Hajduk Split	42	NK Zagreb	40
1994	Hajduk Split	50	NK Zagreb	49	Croatia Zagreb	48

Cup Final Results

1992	Inter Zapresic	1-1, 1-0	HASK-Gradjanski	2-1 on agg
1993	Hajduk Split	4-1, 1-2	Croatia Zagreb	5-3 on agg
1994	Croatia Zagreb	0-1, 2-0	NK Rijeka	2-1 on agg

Cyprus

Limassol-based Apollon won only their second Cypriot league championship but did so under a cloud of bribery accusations. The allegations – which will sound like sour grapes – came from arch-rivals Anorthosis, the team who finished as runners-up for the third time in four years and who are still looking for their first championship sucess since 1963.

Anorthosis were the early pacesetters in the league and by the tenth round of matches a 4-1 win over Apollon placed them four points ahead of the Limassol club, with Ethnikos as an unlikely running mate. But, with three points for a win and one for a draw, the club from Famagusta maintained their unbeaten run but let points slip in draws. Apollon on the other hand suffered two further defeats, by 0-1 at home to Olympiakos and 0-3 at Paralimni, both sides who finished in the lower half of the table, but maintained the pace with three draws compared to their rival's seven. So by the time the penultimate weekend of the season had arrived Anorthosis had seen a seven-point gap whittled back to one as they travelled to Limassol for what was likely to be the championship decider. A win for Anorthosis would clinch the title, a win for Apollon would put them in the driving seat with a game each to play. It went Apollon's way by 2-0, ensured the race went to the final round of games, and sparked the bribery protests by Anorthosis officials.

There was the real possibility that the championship could produce one final twist. Apollon had to travel to Olympiakos, the only side to beat them all season, and there was also the memory of the previous season's finale when Apollon had been in a similar situation only to be pipped by Omonia Nicosia. Anorthosis maintained the pressure with a 8-1 thrashing of luckless Apep, but Apollon kept their heads in Nicosia to secure the three points and their second triumph in four years.

The scramble to keep out of the relegation zone was less fraught than usual with Apep, another Limassol club, struggling all season and dropping back into the second division a year after being promoted, accumulating just three points after having four deducted. Three clubs were again relegated at the end of the 1993–94 season but only one was promoted, from the second division as the first division is reduced to 12 clubs and played in three rounds – this being part of a plan to shrink its size even further to ten 'premier' clubs. The new league will also start earlier, in September, so that teams competing in the early stages of European club competitions will have had more match practice.

That lack of match fitness was clearly evident in Omonia's Champions' Cup preliminary round encounter with Swiss side FC Aarau. Playing in their 37th Champions' Cup match, goals by

Cyprus Football Association

Founded:	1934
Address:	Stasinos Street 1, Engomi 152, PO Box 5071, CY-Nicosia
Phone:	+357 2 44 53 41
Fax:	+357 2 47 25 44
UEFA Affiliation:	1954
FIFA Affiliation:	1948
National Stadium:	Makarion Athletic Centre
Capacity:	20,000
Season:	October to June
Colours:	Blue, White, Blue
Change:	White, Blue, White

Final League Table 1993–94

	P	W	D	L	F	A	Pts
Apollon	26	20	3	3	67	23	63
Anorthosis	26	18	7	1	67	16	61
Apoel	26	17	5	4	64	25	56
Omonia	26	16	4	6	77	33	52
Ethnikos	26	15	2	9	45	40	47
AEL	26	12	4	10	43	47	40
ENP	26	9	7	10	34	34	34
Pezoporikos	26	10	4	12	34	37	34
NEA Salamina	26	8	8	10	32	31	32
Aradippu	26	8	5	13	29	49	29
Olympiakos	26	8	3	15	36	51	27
EPA †	26	7	2	17	30	53	23
Evagoras	26	2	5	19	15	65	11
Apep*	26	2	1	23	2	89	3

*=4pts deducted. † Relegation playoff

Promotions and Relegations
Promoted: Aris
Relegated: Evagoras, Apep, EPA
League reduced to 12 teams from 1994–95 season.

Five-Year Records League 1-2-3 and Cup Winners

League Results

	1st	Pts	2nd	Pts	3rd	Pts
1990	Apoel	41	Omonia Nicosia	35	Pezoporikos	31
1991	Apollon	44	Anorthosis	41	Apoel	35
1992	Apoel	60	Anorthosis	58	Apollon	53
1993	Omonia Nicosia	59	Apollon	57	Salamina	48
1994	Apollon	63	Anorthosis	61	Apoel	56

Cup Final Results

1990	Salamina	3-2	Omonia Nicosia
1991	Omonia Nicosia	1-0	Olympiakos
1992	Apollon	1-0	Omonia Nicosia
1993	Apoel	4-1	Apollon
1994	Omonia Nicosia	1-0	Anorthosis

International Results 1993–94

Date	Opponents	Result	Venue	Comp.	Scorers
6/10/93	Israel	2-2	Limassol	Friendly	Pitas (24), Iksioropas (71)
13/10/93	Wales	0-2	Cardiff	WCQ4	
27/10/93	RCS	0-3	Kosice	WCQ4	

National Record	P	W	D	L	F	A
European Championships	48	1	4	43	16	148
World Cup Finals	Never qualified					
World Cup Qualifiers	56	3	1	50	29	184

Cyprus Championship Results 1993–94

	AEL	Apollon	Apoel	Anorthosis	Apep	Ethinikos	ENP	Evagoras	EPA	NEA Salamina	Olympiakos	Omonia Nicosia	Omonia Aradippu	Pezoporikos
AEL	—	0-2	1-3	1-4	3-1	0-0	1-1	2-0	1-0	1-1	3-1	3-2	4-1	1-0
Apollon	1-3	—	2-0	1-4	7-1	6-1	4-0	6-1	4-0	2-0	2-0	2-1	1-0	1-0
Apoel	3-1	1-1	—	0-2	7-0	4-0	0-0	2-0	5-2	2-1	4-1	3-2	3-0	4-0
Anorthosis	4-1	0-2	1-1	—	8-1	1-0	3-1	1-0	5-0	3-0	1-0	1-1	5-0	1-1
Apep	1-6	2-4	1-3	2-5	—	1-3	1-1	0-1	1-4	1-2	2-1	0-5	0-1	1-2
Ethinikos	0-1	1-2	1-1	0-4	3-1	—	3-0	1-0	1-0	2-1	2-1	4-3	5-2	2-1
ENP	6-3	3-0	1-2	0-0	2-1	0-3	—	3-0	0-1	0-1	0-2	3-1	1-1	1-0
Evagoras	1-2	0-2	0-5	1-5	1-0	0-3	1-2	—	1-1	1-1	1-1	0-1	0-0	1-2
EPA	0-1	0-2	0-2	1-3	1-0	1-3	2-1	6-2	—	0-0	2-3	0-5	3-1	2-0
NEA Salamina	3-2	1-1	0-1	0-0	3-0	2-0	1-1	4-0	2-1	—	3-1	0-3	0-1	1-3
Olympiakos	3-2	1-0	1-4	0-2	6-0	2-4	2-0	5-1	1-0	1-1	—	1-3	0-1	1-0
Omonia Nicosia	3-0	1-1	3-1	1-1	7-0	1-2	2-1	6-0	6-2	2-2	7-2	—	3-1	4-2
Omonia Aradippu	1-1	2-5	1-1	0-2	3-1	0-3	3-0	3-1	1-0	0-3	1-1	1-3	—	3-0
Pezoporikos	4-0	2-3	3-2	1-1	0-1	2-1	1-1	1-1	2-1	1-0	3-0	0-1	3-1	—

Shilikashvili a quarter of an hour into each half looked to have secured a firm base for the return in Aarau. But a goal against tiring opponents gave the Swiss ample encouragement for the return, which they took 2-0, and the tie 3-2 on aggregate.

Apoel did somewhat better in the Cup-Winners' Cup, when drawn against Northern Ireland's Bangor. A goal by Cypriot international Andros Sotiriou earned a 1-1 draw in the away leg, and 15,000 turned out at the Makarion stadium for the second, to see goals by Yugoslav Vesko Mihajlovic – in his first season with Apoel – and stalwart Christodoulos Pounas produce a 3-2 aggregate win. The Nicosian side were drawn against highflying Paris Saint-Germain in the first round and only a goal late in the first leg prevented them from treating their home supporters to a famous draw before the tie was lost 3-0 overall.

But it was Apollon's performances in the UEFA Cup that were the most creditable. Having lost 2-0 in Hungary to Vac, a goal either side of the interval by Scepovic levelled the tie. In the second period of extra time the home side were awarded a penalty which Spoliarec converted and as Vac went forward in search of what would be a winning away goal, Kricmarevic broke to make it 4-0 on the night and 4-2 on aggregate to the Cypriots with just two minutes remaining. The reward was a mouth-watering, money-spinning tie with Internazionale. The expected goal-glut never came in the San Siro and at the end of 90 minutes only a single goal separated the sides, which created a great stir and banner headlines in the Cypriot press. Early goals gave the Italians a 2-0 lead in Limassol but first Spolijiarec and then Cepovic scored. The Italians restored their lead but five minutes from time Iosephides produced another equaliser for the home crowd to talk about. Back at home Omonia Nicosia won the Cypriot Cup Final with Xaourouppas scoring the winning goal against Anorthosis late in extra time.

Internationally, Cyprus were out of contention in Group 4 of the World Cup qualifying rounds long before the season arrived and two defeats in Cardiff and Kosice consigned them to the World Cup wilderness for another two years. There was a worthy 2-2 draw with Israel in Limassol in October, and the prospect of a European Championship group containing Denmark, Spain, Belgium, FYR Macedonia and Armenia.

Czech Republic

Czech out

It was ultimately a case of 'same again' in the first Czech league since the split with Slovakia, as Sparta Prague led virtually all season to reinforce their position as the republic's leading club. The achievement was made more notable because, like so many leading Eastern European clubs since 1989, they are regularly faced with having to sell their best players to wealthier clubs in the West. The pre 1993–94 season proved no exception, with Vrabec and Nemec going to Germany, and Harald Cerny succumbing to the lure of the yen in Hiroshima.

The incoming Sparta coach, Karol Dobias, a scorer in Czechoslovakia's European Championship victory of 1976, had inherited a young side brimming with talent but short on experience. However, marshalled by ex-national skipper Joszef Chovanec, they never looked in danger of relinquishing the lead, finishing six points ahead of city rivals Slavia.

At the onset of the new league many thought that it would be largely business as usual. Bar Slovan and DAC, the Slovak clubs had been largely overshadowed by the Czech clubs in recent years, and so the new league would follow a familiar pattern. To the surprise of many however, all six 'promoted' clubs acquitted themselves well, each holding a place in the top five at some point.

Sparta's early challengers were the previously unsung Ceske Budejovice, a town known principally for its beer (Budweiser) rather than football. Built around an uncompromising defence, Ceske chased Sparta for most of the autumn, inflicting Sparta's first defeat shortly before the winter break. Ultimately they faded, allowing the big guns of Slavia and Ostrava to come through to take the UEFA Cup places. Slavia lost Kuka to Kaiserslautern midway through the season, and suffered for it, goals being hard to come by thereafter. Sparta were able to clinch the title with a home draw with Ostrava with four games left to play. Siegl's 20 goals was far and away the highest tally, earning him with it the Czech Player of the Year award, with Frydek's influential midfield displays making him a regular in the new national side.

The one black spot in Sparta's season came in the Cup Final,

Peter Dubovsky – seen here in RCS uniform – made a big money move to Spain.

Football Association of Czech Republic

Founded:	1990
Address:	Kozi ulice 7, 11000 Prague 1
Phone:	+42 2 231 70 26
Fax:	+42 2 232 51 38
UEFA Affiliation:	1993
FIFA Affiliation:	1993
Season:	to June
National Stadium:	Evenza Rosickeho
Capacity:	36,000
Colours:	Red, White, Blue
Change:	White, White, White

Final League Table 1993–94

	P	W	D	L	F	A	Pts
Sparta Prague	30	18	9	3	62	21	45
Slavia Prague	30	16	7	7	55	28	39
Banik Ostrava	30	14	8	8	52	25	36
Union Cheb	30	13	10	7	31	29	36
Viktoria Plzen	30	12	11	7	35	23	35
Ceske Budejovice	30	11	13	6	33	31	35
Sigma Olomouc	30	14	6	10	44	29	34
Viktoria Zizkov	30	12	9	9	40	28	33
Slovan Liberec	30	11	10	9	36	32	32
Petra Drnovice	30	13	6	11	38	36	32
Svit Zlin	30	10	7	13	37	48	27
Boby Brno	30	10	6	14	38	46	26
Hradec Kralove	30	9	6	15	29	40	24
Bohemians Prague	30	8	7	15	29	54	23
SSK Vitkovice	30	3	7	20	22	64	13
Dukla Prague	30	1	8	21	21	68	10

Top Scorers
20 Horst SIEGL (Sparta Prague)
12 Rene WAGNER (Boby Brno)
11 Josef OBJDIN (Slovan Liberec)

Promotions and Relegations
Promoted: EK Jablonec, Svarc Benesov
Relegated: SSK Vitkovice, Dukla Prague

Cup Final
1994 Viktoria Zizkov 2-2 Sparta Prague 6-5 on penalties

International Results 1993–94

Date	Opponents	Result	Venue	Comp.	Scorers
8/9/93	Wales	2-2	Cardiff	WCQ4	Kuka (16), Dubovsky (67)
27/10/93	Cyprus	3-0	Kosice	WCQ4	Dubovsky (10), Hapal (22), Skuhravy (76)
17/11/93	Belgium	0-0	Brussels	WCQ4	
23/2/94	Turkey	4-1	Istanbul	Friendly	Novotny (12), Latal (18), Siegl (59, 63)
20/4/94	Switzerland	0-3	Zurich	Friendly	
25/5/94	Lithuania	5-3	Prague	Friendly	Kuka (20, 51), Frydek (23), Kubik (27), Postulka (81)
5/6/94	Republic of Ireland	3-1	Dublin	Friendly	Kuka (25 pen; 53), Suchoparek (84)

National Record (Czechoslovakia and RCS)

	P	W	D	L	F	A
European Championships	64	34	16	14	119	58
World Cup Finals	30	11	5	14	44	45
World Cup Qualifiers	71	40	15	16	146	63

NB: World Cup games played as RCS

Czech Republic Results Championship 1993–94

	Banik Ostrava	Boby Brno	Bohemians Prague	Ceske Budejovice	Dukla Prague	Hradec Kralove	Petra Drnovice	Sigma Olomouc	Slavia Prague	Slovan Liberec	Sparta Prague	SSK Vitkovice	Svit Zlin	Union Cheb	Viktoria Plzen	Viktoria Zizkov
Banik Ostrava	—	4-1	1-1	4-2	4-1	3-0	0-1	1-1	1-2	2-0	1-3	5-0	0-0	5-0	2-1	1-0
Boby Brno	0-1	—	3-0	1-1	2-2	2-1	1-2	0-1	2-1	1-0	0-2	1-0	3-0	0-0	0-1	1-1
Bohemians Prague	0-2	2-3	—	1-1	3-1	2-2	0-1	2-1	0-1	2-0	1-1	1-1	1-0	1-2	0-0	2-1
Ceske Budejovice	0-0	3-2	2-0	—	1-1	2-1	2-1	2-1	1-1	2-1	1-2	1-0	1-0	0-0	0-0	1-0
Dukla Prague	0-3	1-1	1-2	1-2	—	1-1	0-2	1-1	2-3	0-1	2-6	1-2	1-1	1-2	0-0	0-2
Hradec Kralove	1-0	1-0	0-0	1-0	0-1	—	3-1	1-0	1-0	1-1	0-2	2-2	3-0	1-3	1-2	3-2
Petra Drnovice	2-1	2-1	4-1	4-0	4-0	1-0	—	0-1	2-2	1-0	1-1	2-0	1-3	2-1	3-0	0-2
Sigma Olomouc	1-1	0-3	5-0	0-0	1-0	2-0	3-0	—	0-1	1-2	1-0	3-1	3-0	1-1	1-0	0-1
Slavia Prague	1-0	6-0	2-3	1-1	3-0	4-2	0-0	0-2	—	0-2	1-1	6-0	5-0	4-0	0-0	1-0
Slovan Liberec	0-0	2-1	4-0	3-3	1-1	1-2	4-2	3-2	0-0	—	2-1	2-0	1-1	0-2	0-0	0-0
Sparta Prague	1-1	5-1	5-0	0-1	4-0	2-0	0-0	2-1	4-1	2-0	—	4-0	3-2	3-0	1-0	0-0
SSK Vitkovice	1-3	0-2	0-1	1-1	1-0	1-1	1-1	1-4	1-2	1-1	1-2	—	3-2	0-2	1-1	0-1
Svit Zlin	1-4	3-2	4-1	1-0	3-0	1-0	1-1	2-4	0-1	1-0	1-1	4-1	—	0-1	1-0	1-0
Union Cheb	2-2	1-1	2-0	0-0	2-1	1-0	2-0	0-1	2-0	0-1	0-0	2-1	1-1	—	0-0	1-1
Viktoria Plzen	1-0	1-2	3-2	2-2	3-1	2-0	1-0	2-0	0-2	0-0	2-4	2-0	4-1	2-0	—	1-1
Viktoria Zizkov	1-0	2-1	1-0	1-0	7-0	1-0	2-0	2-2	1-4	3-4	0-0	4-1	2-2	0-1	1-1	—

which was shrouded in controversy. Viktoria Zizkov, a famous club of the pre-war era with a rich benefactor have, some say, earned their place in the first division under suspicious circumstances, and some dubious refereeing decisions in the final got them a 2-2 draw and a 6-5 penalty shoot-out victory.

Dukla Prague, the old army club, now bereft of supporters – home crowds of under 1,000 – and money, finished bottom with just one win all season, and were relegated along with SSK Vitkovice, champions eight years ago.

European competition itself brought little joy, with Slavia and Boby Brno surrendering meekly in round one of the UEFA Cup and Cup-Winners' Cup respectively, Slavia losing out 2-1 on aggregate to Greek club OFI Crete, and Brno 5-0 to Bayer Leverkusen. Sparta managed to earn a pay-day against Anderlecht by eliminating AIK Stockholm thanks to two goals by Siegl, but the Belgians as expected proved to be too strong over two games, despite Dvirnik and Vonasek twice equalising in Brussels.

The last international match played as the RCS saw a frustrating goalless draw in Brussels against the Belgians. A win would have ensured at least three more games for Vaclac Jezek's team.

This meant that the new Czech Republic side could start in earnest. However, Dusan Uhrin's team made a disastrous start, beaten heavily in Switzerland, but nine goals in two games against Lithuania and Turkey followed by a magnificent attacking display against the Republic of Ireland in Dublin to record a 3-1 win.

Denmark

Silkeborg's finale!

For the second successive year, the Danish season produced an exciting finale and a new name on the Superliga trophy, with Silkeborg the surprise champions. Founded in 1917, Silkeborg had never previously won a major honour. They have played in the top division for only seven seasons, but since 1988 have made steady progress. Although they were largely discounted as genuine title contenders by most experts, their success is a tribute to all at the club who have worked long and hard to reach the top.

That progress started to gather momentum in the early stages of the Grundspil, when Silkeborg comprehensively beat Brondby 4-2. It was their first game since the departure of their talented defender, Jakob Kjeldbjerg, to Chelsea, but anyone who thought that Kjeldbjerg's absence would affect Silkeborg's challenge was mistaken, for while the big two from Copenhagen – FC and Brondby – were struggling through transition, the side from Central Jutland kept going. The reigning champions, FC Copenhagen, were lacking consistency, despite the addition of Peter Moller from AaB to their ranks. Moller, who had topped the Superliga's goalscoring list for the previous two years, had not hit his best form since his arrival in the capital. Meanwhile, Brondby, whose financial problems had made more headlines than their on-pitch successes in the past two years, were also rebuilding.

Both clubs, along with OB and AaB, were involved in interesting European ties. FC Copenhagen overcame a three-goal deficit against Linfield of Northern Ireland in the Champions' Cup, before being humbled by six goals at home by Milan. To the credit of Benny Johansen's side, they held Milan to a single goal in the second leg. Brondby looked to be off on one of their fine European runs after their defeat of Dundee United in the UEFA Cup. They then impressively disposed of Finnish side Kuusysi Lahti, before losing to Borussia Dortmund. In the Cup-Winners' Cup, OB

Dansk Boldspil Union	
Founded:	1889
Address:	Ved Amagerbanen 15, DK- 2300 Copenhagen S
Phone:	+45 31 95 05 11
Fax:	+45 31 95 05 88
UEFA Affiliation:	1954
FIFA Affiliation:	1904
National Stadium:	Parken, Copenhagen
Capacity:	48,000
Season:	First phase (Grundspil): August to November
	Second phase (Slutspil): March to June
Colours:	Red, White, Red
Change:	White, White, Red

Final League Table 1993-94

Grundspil 1993

		P	W	D	L	F	A	Pts
Silkeborg	(13)	18	9	7	2	34	20	25
OB	(12)	18	9	6	3	27	16	24
FC Copenhagen	(11)	18	10	2	6	32	22	22
Brondby	(10)	18	7	6	5	32	24	20
Lyngby	(10)	18	5	10	3	19	23	20
AaB	(9)	18	4	9	5	28	25	17
Ikast	(9)	18	5	7	6	31	29	17
AGF	(8)	18	5	5	18	30	31	15
Naestved		18	3	4	11	28	46	10
Viborg		18	3	4	11	25	50	10

Top eight teams qualify for championship phase taking half their points total with them into final stage. Bottom two sides play in promotion/relegation league with top six sides from division one, again taking half their points totals with them. Points totals – rounded up to nearest whole point – given in brackets.

Slutspil 1994

	P	W	D	L	F	A	Pts
Silkeborg	14	8	2	4	23	15	31
FC Copenhagen	14	8	2	4	27	19	29
Brondby	14	6	5	3	21	14	27
OB	14	5	5	4	17	16	27
AaB	14	4	6	4	18	19	23
Lyngby	14	5	1	8	17	21	21
Ikast	14	3	5	6	16	23	20
AGF	14	3	2	9	11	23	16

Top Scorers

18 Soren FREDERIKSEN (Silkeborg/Viborg)
16 Kent HASEN (Ikast)
13 Mark STRUDAL (Brondby)
12 Hojer NIELSEN (FC Copenhagen)
   Erik Bo ANDERSEN (AaB)
   Heine FERNANDEZ (Silkeborg)

Kvalifikationsliga Forfar 1994

	P	W	D	L	F	A	Pts
Naestved	14	8	3	3	32	10	19
Fremad Amager	14	7	5	2	30	17	19
Herfolge	14	7	4	4	24	17	18
Viborg	14	7	3	4	23	16	15
Olstykke	14	4	5	5	17	26	13
Vejle BK	14	3	4	7	20	26	12
Horsens	14	2	4	8	14	30	8
Bronshoj	14	3	2	9	19	37	8

Promotions and Relegations

Promoted: Naetved, Fremad Amager BK
Relegated: Viborg

FC Copenhagen's Peter Moller acknowledges the crowd in the Parken. Moller was top scorer in the Superliga.

narrowly lost to Arsenal, while AaB were soundly beaten by a Bebeto-inspired Deportivo La Coruna in the UEFA Cup.

Silkeborg, meanwhile, moved to the top of the league after seven games, and for the next 11 weeks, only OB could match their consistency. The Odense club's sheer persistence meant that at the end of the 18-match *Grundspil* season, only one point separated Silkeborg from their nearest challengers. During the winter break Silkeborg quickly moved to add more bite to their attack, signing leading scorer Soren Frederiksen from relegated Viborg FC, and Copenhagen also added a major signing to their squad when they obtained the services of OB midfielder Allan Nielsen.

There were ominous signs, however, that the current format of Danish football was not appealing to the public. The attendances for the *Grundspil* stage showed a decrease of over 16 per cent, reflecting the public's selective attitude. With a season consisting of two halves, and the over-familiarity caused by meeting most sides four times, this apparent decline prompted much discussion over the future composition of the Danish Football League. The national team's exit from the World Cup in November also cast a shadow over a season that was, nevertheless, becoming most intriguing.

The winter break also marked the decline of two big-name clubs – Frem and B1909. Both had played in the 1992–93 Superliga, but had suffered from massive financial problems and under the Danish League's constitution were automatically relegated to the Danish equivalent of non-league football.

When play resumed in March with the Danish Cup semi-finals, it looked as though Brondby had found new vigour during the recess. The manner in which they disposed of AGF by six clear goals suggested that their young team were coming good at the right time. Silkeborg, chasing the double, also figured in the last four, but they crashed out to Naestved, who had just been relegated from the *Grundspil*. They soon bounced back from their Cup exit, however, when they produced arguably the most stunning result of the entire season in thrashing FC Copenhagen 5-0, and proved once and for all that their claims to the title were genuine.

But a week later OB took advantage of a ten-man Silkeborg, suffering from the sending-off of their impressive sweeper, Michael Larsen, and in the last 13 minutes of a pulsating game three goals rattled into the league leader's net. OB had drawn level on points, but trailed on goal difference. That signalled the halfway stage of the *Slutspil*, and with FC Copenhagen two points behind, and AaB and Brondby just behind them, it was rapidly building up into a very close-run finale.

FC Copenhagen soon replaced OB as the real challengers, and with four games to go they drew level on points after Lyngby had beaten Silkeborg 4-1. Silkeborg were now suffering from an attack of nerves as they entered the home straight. Lyngby, champions in 1992, had assumed the role of spoilers after beating Brondby, OB and Silkeborg. Brondby, who were now almost out of the title race, consoled themselves with Cup Final victory, albeit on penalties, against Naestved. A crowd of 27,069 watched a game that was dominated by Naestved, and Brondby, by their own admission, were extremely fortunate to go away with the Giro Cup.

Silkeborg were equally lucky to beat Brondby a few days later, thanks to a last-gasp goal from their out-of-form signing, Soren Frederiksen, who was only recalled to the side as a replacement for the injured Heine Fernandez.

FC Copenhagen kept up their challenge with a three-goal victory over Lyngby, thus maintaining parity at the top. The gap

International Results 1993–94

Date	Opponents	Result	Venue	Comp.	Scorers
25/8/93	Lithuania	4-0	Copenhagen	WCQ3	L.Olsen (13), Pingel (44), B.Laudrup (64), own goal (71)
8/9/93	Albania	1-0	Tirana	WCQ3	Pingel (63)
13/10/93	N. Ireland	1-0	Copenhagen	WCQ3	B.Laudrup (81)
17/10/93	Spain	0-1	Sevilla	WCQ3	
2/2/94	Norway	3-3	Kuala Lumpur	Dunhill	Tengbjerg (78), Pedersen (80), Falch (85)
5/2/94	Malaysia	5-1	Kuala Lumpur	Dunhill	Povlsen (19. 23), Pedersen (28, 44), Sommer (72)
6/2/94	Japan	6-1	Kuala Lumpur	Dunhill	U. Pederson (6, 18), D. Poulsen (16), J. Tengbjerg (48, 88), M. Bisgaard (70)
10/2/94	United States	0-0	Hong Kong	Carlsberg	(Denmark won 4-2 on pens)
13/2/94	Hong Kong Lge	2-0	Hong Kong	Carlsberg	F. Kristensen (20), Fernandez (38)
9/3/94	England	0-1	Wembley	Friendly	
20/4/94	Hungary	3-1	Copenhagen	Friendly	M. Laudrup (pen 21, 43), Povlsen (60)
25/5/94	Sweden	0-0	Copenhagen	Friendly	
1/6/94	Norway	1-2	Oslo	Friendly	Povlsen (41)

National Record	P	W	D	L	F	A
European Championship	71	26	14	31	103	108
World Cup Finals	4	3	0	1	10	6
World Cup Qualifiers	60	24	10	26	93	92

opened up again a week later, as Silkeborg beat OB, thus ending that side's challenge, while Brondby were damaging the chances of FC Copenhagen with a one-goal victory. The penultimate fixture could not have been more dramatic – FC Copenhagen played host to Silkeborg! A record crowd of 26,679 attended the game at the Parken and witnessed the reigning Champions' destruction of the Champions-elect. Silkeborg were crushed by four goals to one, and for the first time since the early stages of the season they were removed from the top of the table. Two goals from the flame-haired Michael Johansen, one of Denmark's most exciting talents, contributed to a result which looked to have deprived Silkeborg of their first Championship. And so it all came down to the final day of the season. FC Copenhagen travelled to Odense while Silkeborg entertained AaB, and the two sides were once again level on points.

At half-time, the Champions led OB, while in Jutland the derby game was goalless. As it stood at the interval, FC Copenhagen would win their second consecutive title. The 55th minute in both games was the turning point. OB equalised, while Fernandez opened the scoring for Silkeborg. Fernandez added a second goal ten minutes later, but the fate of the Superliga was finally settled in the last minutes in Odense when OB clinched victory. Silkeborg won by those two Fernandez goals, and clinched the title by two clear points. The scenes of jubilation were unprecedented at Silkeborg Stadium, but Bo Johanssen's workmanlike side fully deserved the plaudits.

After the lukewarm public response for the qualifying league stage, the exciting run-in had clearly captured the imagination of the Danish football fan. The *Slutspil* stage of the season showed a very healthy eight per cent increase in attendances on 1992–93's figures.

Away from the Superliga, there was promotion for Cup Finalists Naestved and surprise package Fremad Amager, while it was reassuring to see three names from the past – B93, Hvidovre and AB – all making a comeback in the lower divisions.

Five-Year Records League 1-2-3 and Cup Winners

League Results

	1st	Pts	2nd	Pts	3rd	Pts
1990	Brondby	42	B1903	31	Ikast BK	30
1991	Brondby	26	Lyngby BK	24	Frem	19
1992	Lyngby BK	32	Apollon	29	Frem	26
1993	FC Copenhagen	32	OB	31	Brondby	30
1994	Silkeborg	31	FC Copenhagen	29	Brondby	27

Cup Final Results

1990	Lyngby BK	6-1	AGF Aarhus	after 0-0 draw
1991	OB	0-0	AaB Aalborg	after 0-0 draw 4-3 on pens
1992	AGF Aarhus	3-0	B1903	
1993	OB	2-0	AaB Aalborg	
1994	Brondby	0-0	Naestved	3-1 on pens

Giro Cup

First Round

Aabenraa v Aalborg Freja	3-1
Ammitsbol/Jerlev v Skive IK	0-2
Bramming v Skovbakken	5-1
CIK v Taarbaek	2-5
Dollefjelde Musse v Prespa	4-7
Dragor v B 1921	3-0
Esbjerg IF92 v Lemvig	2-1
GVI v Tuse	5-0
Herlufsholm v Holbaek	4-3
Herning KFUM v Egebjerg	6-5
Koge v Tarup	5-4
Kolding B v Allested	3-0
Kolding IF v Struer	0-2
Marienlyst v Asaa	1-3
Noddebo v Albertslund	1-6
Roskilde KFUM v Humlebaek	3-4
Ryvang v Valby	1-3
Skt Klemens Fangel v Lindholm	7-4
Slagelse v Birkerod	1-3
Sundby v Maribo	4-0
Taars/Uglit v Dalum	3-2
Viking Ronne v Avedore	0-1
Vivild v Aarup	3-2
Vorup v Aarhus KFUM	4-1
Esbjerg fB v Esbjerg IF 92	1-0
Fr Amager v Olstykke	3-1
Frederikshavn v Svendborg	3-5
Haderslev v B 1913	6-5
Helsingor v Skovshoved	2-1
Herfolge v Vanlose	5-0
Herlev v Hvidovre	2-0
HIK v Skive	0-1
Holstebro v Vejle	2-1
Koge v Bronshoj	2-5
Norresundby v Randers Freja	1-0
Nr Aaby v Horsens fS	2-1
Struer v Taars/Uglit	5-0
Sundby v AB	8-9

Second Round

Albertslund v Kastrup	2-5
Asaa v Randers Freja	1-2
Avarta v Herlufsholm	5-2
FC Frederica v Haderslev FK	1-3
Frederikshavn v Aabenraa	3-0
GVI v Hvidovre	1-2
Herlev v Taarbaek	5-1
Herning Fremad v Holstebro	0-1
Herning KFUM v Esbjerg IF92	1-4
HIK v Avedore	4-1
Humlebaek v AB	0-3
Koge v Dragor	9-4
Nr Aaby v Kolding B	5-3
Roskilde BK06 v Birkerod	1-3
Skive IK v Bramming	5-0
Struer v Skt Klemens Fangel	1-0
Sundby v Prespa	2-1
Taars/Uglit v Vorup	1-0
Valby v Skovshoved	1-3
Vivild v Svendborg	0-5

Third Round

B 93 v Kastrup	4-1
Birkerod v Avarta	0-1
AB v Svendborg	1-0
AGF v Haderslev	10-1
B 1909 v Herlev	2-1
B 93 v Skive	1-4
Bronshoj v Struer	1-3
Helsingor v Esbjerg fB	0-6
Herfolge v Viborg	5-2
Holstebro v Avarta	5-2
Ikast v Fr Amager	0-2
Norresundby v Naestved	1-4
Nr Aaby v Lyngby	2-4
Silkeborg v Frem	3-1

Fifth Round

Aab v AB	2-1
AGF v Herfolge	6-2
B 1909 v FC Copenhagen	3-0
Brondby v OB	2-1
Fr Amager v Skive	5-3
Lyngby v Esbjerg fB	5-3
Naestved v Struer	6-0
Silkeborg v Holstebro	8-1

Quarter-Finals

Brondby v AaB	3-0
Silkeborg v B1909	4-0
Naestved v Fremad Amager	3-1
Lyngby v AGF	4-7

Semi-Finals

Brondby v AGF	6-0
Naestved v Silkeborg	2-0

Final

Brondby v Naestved	0-0
(3-1 pens)	

First Round

	AaB	AGF	Brondby	FC Copenhagen	Ikast	Lyngby	Naestved	OB	Silkeborg	Viborg
AaB	—	4-1	2-2	0-1	2-2	3-0	2-0	1-1	2-2	2-2
AGF	2-1	—	3-1	1-2	2-2	0-0	4-0	2-2	1-2	6-0
Brondby	1-1	2-0	—	0-1	1-1	1-1	5-0	4-2	3-0	3-1
FC Copenhagen	2-0	2-0	3-1	—	0-3	0-1	0-0	0-1	1-2	4-1
Ikast	2-1	2-2	0-1	2-3	—	1-1	5-2	1-0	2-2	3-0
Lyngby	1-0	3-1	0-0	1-1	2-0	—	2-2	0-0	2-2	2-0
Naestved	2-3	3-2	1-2	2-4	3-2	8-2	—	0-2	1-1	1-2
OB	0-0	3-0	2-1	1-0	1-1	0-0	3-1	—	2-0	4-0
Silkeborg	2-2	0-0	4-2	4-1	3-1	3-0	0-0	3-0	—	1-0
Viborg	2-2	2-3	2-2	2-7	3-1	1-1	5-2	2-3	0-3	—

Championship Round

	AaB	AGF	Brondby	FC Copenhagen	Ikast	Lyngby	OB	Silkeborg
AaB	—	0-0	1-3	0-3	1-0	2-0	2-2	1-1
AGF	1-1	—	0-2	0-1	2-4	0-1	2-1	0-3
Brondby	1-1	2-1	—	1-0	1-1	2-1	0-0	2-2
FC Copenhagen	3-3	1-3	2-1	—	2-1	3-0	1-1	4-1
Ikast	1-4	0-1	1-1	0-2	—	2-2	0-0	0-3
Lyngby	0-1	4-0	2-1	0-3	1-2	—	2-0	4-1
OB	2-1	2-0	0-3	1-0	2-2	1-0	—	3-0
Silkeborg	2-0	1-0	1-0	5-0	0-1	2-0	1-0	—

Promotion/Relegation Round

	Bronshoj	Fr. Amanger	Herfolge	Horsens	Naestved	Olstykke	Vejle	Viborg
Bronshoj	—	3-6	0-3	3-1	2-1	3-0	1-3	0-4
Fremad Amanger	3-1	—	2-1	1-2	0-1	1-1	1-1	1-1
Herfolge	0-0	0-3	—	4-1	1-0	3-1	4-1	2-1
Horsens	2-2	2-4	2-2	—	0-6	1-1	0-1	2-0
Naestved	7-1	1-1	3-0	2-0	—	4-0	2-0	1-1
Olstykke	2-1	0-3	1-1	1-0	0-0	—	4-2	3-0
Vejle	2-1	2-2	1-2	1-1	2-4	2-2	—	0-2
Viborg	3-1	1-2	1-1	2-0	2-0	5-1	2-0	—

England

United's double take

The close season in England brought more progression off the pitch or more literally around the pitch, as the improvements and renovations instigated as part of the Taylor Report continued to move stadia forward and into the 21st century. All Premiership and first division grounds had just one season left to become all-seater. Many games during the course of the season were be played in eerie atmospheres as clubs demolished old stands for new.

Pre and early season transfers included a number of high-value moves. Top of those was the £3.75m signing by Manchester United of Roy Keane from relegated Nottingham Forest, who also disposed of Nigel Clough to Liverpool for £2.275m. £2.7m was paid by Sheffield Wednesday for QPR's Andy Sinton where he joined Des Walker, newly arrived from Sampdoria. Leeds United bought Brian Deane from Sheffield United for a similar amount, Sheffield replaced him with Jostein Flo from Norwegian club Sogndal, Jason Dozzell moved from Ipswich to Tottenham for £1.8m and in a surprise move Newcastle United welcomed back Peter Beardsley from Everton.

The season kicked off with Manchester United still celebrating their first championship title in 26 years and already installed as favourites to retain the title. They faced double cup-winners Arsenal in the traditional curtain raiser – the FA Charity Shield – at Wembley and after an exciting 1-1 draw captured the trophy in a penalty shoot-out.

The Premiership got under way with the three newcomers – Newcastle United, West Ham United and Swindon Town – all suffering defeats. England international Carlton Palmer became the first player to be sent off, only 13 minutes into the new

The Football Association

Founded:	1863
Address:	16 Lancaster Gate, London, W2 3LW
Phone:	+44 71 262 4542
Fax:	+44 71 402 0486
UEFA Affiliation:	1954
FIFA Affiliation:	1905-1920, 1924-1928, 1946
National Stadium:	Empire Stadium, Wembley
Capacity:	80,000 (all seated)
Season:	August to May
Colours:	White, Blue, White
Change:	Red, White, Red

The photo that's only been taken four times this century! Manchester United with the FA Premier League Trophy and the FA Cup.

Chris Waddle of Sheffield Wednesday blasts the ball at the Liverpool wall.

campaign, as Sheffield Wednesday went down 2-0 at Anfield. In London, Arsenal – opening their new all-seater North Bank stand – were on the end of the shock of the day, losing 3-0 at home to Coventry, for whom Mick Quinn notched the season's first hat-trick. Manchester United meanwhile recorded a 2-0 win at Norwich City, who started the season contemplating European competition for the first time in their history. As ever, Wimbledon were not far from the headlines, with club chairman Sam Hammam reported to the FA for scribbling obscenities on the dressing room wall at West Ham, where his team had won 2-0. All in all it was a typical day in English league soccer and it mirrored perfectly the events to come during the following nine months of rough and sometimes a bit too much tumble.

Peter Swales, the controversial Manchester City chairman, handed over the day-to-day running of the club to newly-appointed general manager John Maddock, who in turn sacked player-manager Peter Reid, four games into the new season. City's poor start – one point from those four games – was cited as the cause. Reid was the eleventh manager at Maine Road since Swales took over in 1973. Brian Horton, ex-manager of Oxford United, was announced as Reid's successor.

Across the Pennines at Elland Road there were calls for Howard Wilkinson's resignation after Leeds were defeated by two goals at Liverpool. There was slightly better news for Swindon Town as the end of the month arrived, gaining their first Premiership point in a 0-0 draw at Norwich City. It was their fifth game. Likewise there was call for celebrations in the Sheffield Wednesday camp when they scored their first goal of the season – after 371 minutes – in a 1-1 draw at Chelsea.

September saw the national side beat Poland 3-0 at Wembley in a World Cup qualifying encounter. England played their hearts out and ran Poland off the pitch with a display full of skill, understanding and application. Stuart Pearce had returned from injury, took back the captain's arm-band and scored into the bargain.

Manchester United continued to set the pace, increasing their lead at the top, but suffered their first defeat of the season and their first league defeat in six months, losing 1-0 at Chelsea. On the other side of the city the fans didn't know whether to boo or

Footballer of the Year – Alan Shearer of Blackburn Rovers shields the ball from Aston Villa's Paul McGrath.

cheer. Manchester City won 3-0 over QPR but there was a protest after the game by 10,000 fans calling for the resignation of Swales. Former player and multi-millionaire Francis Lee was the favourite to take over. Leeds gained their first away win since they won the championship two seasons before – 2-0 at Southampton.

The first round of European competition brought a clean bill of health for all English clubs. Manchester United saw off Honved; Arsenal recovered from an own goal to beat OB Odense in the Cup-Winners' Cup and in the UEFA Cup Aston Villa disposed of Slovan Bratislava while Norwich City eased past Vitesse. Norwich City's Euro form finally rubbed off in the league as Efan Ekoku scored four goals – a record for the Premiership – in their 5-1 win at Goodison Park. Across Stanley Park Liverpool completed a month with no league goals and no league points, and speculation started about the future of manager Graeme Souness.

In October the Premiership sides entered the second round of the Coca-Cola (League) Cup and with a few exceptions came through unscathed. The exceptions were Sheffield United, deposed by second division Blackpool, Leeds, who were beaten by first division Sunderland, and Southampton, humiliated by third division Shrewsbury.

Internationally, England's brief revival faltered, leaving qualification for USA94 only a slim possibility. A 2-0 defeat in Rotterdam was surrounded in controversy, not least because of Ronald Koeman's manhandling of David Platt when he was clear through on goal.

There were also mixed results in the second round of European competitions. Manchester United threw away a 2-0 lead before scraping a 3-3 home draw with Galatasaray. Arsenal fared better with a 3-0 win over Standard Liege while, in only their third European game, Norwich City managed what no other English team had accomplished – victory in Germany against three times European champions, Bayern Munich. Norwich's victory overshadowed Aston Villa's success in holding in-form Spanish side Deportivo La Coruna to a 1-1 draw away, after Mark Bosnich had saved an early penalty.

As the month drew to a close Bobby Gould resigned as manager of Coventry City after watching his side lose 5-1 to in-form QPR. In the third round of the Coca-Cola Cup, first division Nottingham Forest knocked out struggling Eastenders West Ham, but they were the only lower division side to succeed over higher opposition. Meanwhile Manchester United extended their lead to 11 points as the chasing pack dropped points in a series of draws.

While it was good news in the league it was bad news in the Champions' Cup for Manchester United as November dawned. A disappointing 0-0 draw in Istanbul which ended controversially meant that they missed the lucrative Champions' League stage. It was also bad news in Birmingham, where Aston Villa lost 1-0 to a formidable Deportivo La Coruna side to go out of the UEFA Cup. Better news came from East Anglia though as Norwich completed their mini demolition of Bayern Munich in Norfolk's biggest night in football. In the Cup-Winners' Cup, Arsenal, without a goal in their previous four league games, dropped top scorer Ian Wright and travelled to Liege to defend a 3-0 lead. They won 7-0!

Blackburn Rovers continued their sweeping up of top players by breaking the British record for a goalkeeper, spending £2.4m on Southampton's Tim Flowers. Arsenal's scoring glut looked to have rubbed off from Europe when they scored their first league goal in seven hours and 33 minutes, but they conceded two to lose at home to Aston Villa.

There was uproar when Sepp Blatter, FIFA General Secretary, accused British football of being 30 years behind the times. In response the FA unveiled a range of plans aimed at helping youth soccer in this country. It didn't help the national side, as Holland won in Poland and England failed to do the business against San Marino, suffering the humiliation of going behind to the amateurs after only nine seconds of play. As if to amplify Blatter's thoughts, a major shake-up of the British game from the way it is coached, played and administered was called for from all quarters. Many remain sceptical and as expected England manager Graham Taylor resigned and Terry Venables was installed as favourite to take over the FA's hot seat. Things also looked bleak for Norwich City in the UEFA Cup, as they lost at home to Internazionale through a goal from Dennis Bergkamp.

After four weeks as caretaker manager, Phil Neal was confirmed as Coventry City's new boss. There was further controversy for Wimbledon as Tottenham's Gary Mabbutt was carried off with a fractured skull after a collision with John

Final League Tables 1993–94

FA Carling Premiership 1993–94

	P	W	D	L	F	A	Pts
Manchester United	42	27	11	4	80	38	92
Blackburn Rovers	42	25	9	8	63	36	84
Newcastle United	42	23	8	11	82	41	77
Arsenal	42	18	17	7	53	28	71
Leeds United	42	18	16	8	65	39	70
Wimbledon	42	18	11	13	56	53	65
Sheffield Wednesday	42	16	16	10	76	54	64
Liverpool	42	17	9	16	59	55	60
QPR	42	16	12	14	62	61	60
Aston Villa	42	15	12	15	46	50	57
Coventry City	42	14	14	14	43	45	56
Norwich City	42	12	17	13	65	61	53
West Ham United	42	13	13	16	47	58	52
Chelsea	42	13	12	17	49	53	51
Tottenham Hotspur	42	11	12	19	54	59	45
Manchester City	42	9	18	15	38	49	45
Everton	42	12	8	22	42	63	44
Southampton	42	12	7	23	49	66	43
Ipswich Town	42	9	16	17	35	58	43
Sheffield United	42	8	18	16	42	60	42
Oldham Athletic	42	9	13	20	42	68	40
Swindon Town	42	5	15	22	47	100	30

Top Scorers

- 34 Andy COLE (Newcastle United)
- 31 Alan SHEARER (Blackburn Rovers)
- 25 Chris SUTTON (Norwich City)
- Matt LE TISSIER (Southampton)
- 23 Ian WRIGHT (Arsenal)
- 21 Peter BEARDSLEY (Newcastle United)
- 19 Mark BRIGHT (Sheffield Wednesday)
- 18 Eric CANTONA (Manchester United)
- 17 Les FERDINAND (QPR)
- Dean HOLDSWORTH (Wimbledon)
- Rod WALLACE (Leeds United)
- 16 Tony COTTEE (Everton)
- 14 Kevin CAMPBELL (Arsenal)
- Ian RUSH (Liverpool)
- 13 Ryan GIGGS (Manchester United)
- Trevor MORLEY (West Ham United)
- Teddy SHERINGHAM (Tottenham Hotspur)
- Mark STEIN (Chelsea)
- 12 Efan EKOKU (Norwich City)
- Jan FJORTOFT (Swindon Town)
- Robbie FOWLER (Liverpool)
- Mark HUGHES (Manchester United)
- Gordon WATSON (Sheffield Wednesday)

Promotions and Relegations

Promoted: Crystal Palace, Nottingham Forest, Leicester City

Relegated: Oldham Athletic, Sheffield United, Swindon Town

Fashanu's elbow. The subsequent FA inquiry cleared Fashanu of intent. Bottom-placed Swindon's 16th Premiership match was their first victory in the top flight – 1-0 over QPR – while Manchester United stretched their lead at to 14 points and City's Peter Swales resigned and was replaced by Francis Lee.

In the fourth round of the Coca-Cola Cup, holders Arsenal lost their first cup tie in 25 games, 1-0 at home to Aston Villa. First division Tranmere Rovers toppled Oldham 3-0 and Manchester United marched on with a 2-0 win at Everton.

December started with another resignation. After Everton beat Southampton 1-0 in front of their smallest Premiership crowd, manager Howard Kendall announced his decision. As expected Norwich bowed out of the UEFA Cup with their pride intact and their reputation enhanced. As the fourth round of the Coca-Cola Cup progressed, Wimbledon beat Liverpool on penalties after a 2-2 draw and Manchester City lost their replay 2-1 at home to Nottingham Forest.

The FA Carling Premiership reached its halfway stage and showed Manchester United as leaders, having taken 52 from a possible 63 points. In the first games after the Christmas festivities only a last-minute equaliser rescued United from a first home defeat of the season at the hands of chasers Blackburn Rovers.

The New Year began with more new faces in new jobs. Troubled Everton poached a disillusioned Mike Walker from Norwich City, for whom John Deehan stepped up. Ian Branfoot left Southampton and the fans' choice, Alan Ball, took over. And Terry Venables was finally announced as England coach after months of FA dithering. Graeme Souness stepped down as Liverpool boss after his team's first defeat in 13 games – a 1-0 shocker at Anfield to Bristol City which put the Reds out of the FA Cup. Promotion from within put long-time boot-room 'boy' Roy Evans in charge.

Manchester United cleared the often difficult Christmas hurdle without losing, although a few too many draws left Blackburn in contention, albeit at a distance. One of United's draws was a 3-3 thriller at Anfield, where they surrendered a 3-0 lead built in just 25 minutes. United also marched on in the third round of the FA Cup, succeeding where they failed the previous season – 1-0 at Sheffield United. Queens Park Rangers fell to second division Stockport County, Everton stumbled at home to Bolton of the first, and non-League Kidderminster captured the headlines by winning at troubled Birmingham City.

A replay win at Portsmouth put Manchester United through to the semi-finals of the Coca-Cola Cup, where they were joined by Sheffield Wednesday, Villa and Tranmere Rovers. As the month drew to a close the FA Cup fourth round saw Manchester City bow out to second division strugglers Cardiff City but most other games followed form apart from that at Kidderminster, where Harriers made the last 16 by beating Preston North End. The nation was saddened by the news of Sir Matt Busby's death at the age of 84, shortly before the European Championship draw was held in Manchester.

As the dust settled on the hectic cup month of January the talk was of Manchester United's possibilities of winning an unprecedented 'Treble'. Odds of 4-1 were aided by the performances of possible contenders in the FA Cup, where

International Results 1993–94

Date	Opponents	Result	Venue	Comp.	Scorers
8/9/93	Poland	3-0	Wembley	WCQ2	Ferdinand (5), Gascoigne (49), Pearce (53)
13/10/93	Holland	0-2	Rotterdam	WCQ2	
17/10/93	San Marino	7-1	Bologna	WCQ2	Ince (21, 73), Wright (32, 46, 78, 90), Ferdinand (43)
9/3/94	Denmark	1-0	Wembley	Friendly	Platt (17)
17/5/94	Greece	5-0	Wembley	Friendly	Anderton (24), Beardsley (37), Platt (45, 55), Shearer (66)
22/5/94	Norway	0-0	Wembley	Friendly	

National Record	P	W	D	L	F	A
European Championship	62	35	16	11	123	43
World Cup Finals	41	18	12	11	55	38
World Cup Qualifiers	55	33	15	7	141	41

Five-Year Records League 1-2-3 and Cup Winners

League Results

	1st	Pts	2nd	Pts	3rd	Pts
1990	Liverpool	79	Aston Villa	70	Tottenham H	63
1991	Arsenal	83	Liverpool	76	Crystal Palace	69
1992	Leeds United	82	Manchester Utd	78	Sheffield Wed	75
1993	Manchester Utd	84	Aston Villa	74	Norwich	72
1994	Manchester Utd	92	Blackburn Rvrs	84	Newcastle Utd	77

Cup Final Results

1990	Manchester Utd	1-0	Crystal Palace	after 3-3 draw
1991	Tottenham Hot.	2-1	Nottingham Forest	
1992	Liverpool	2-0	Sunderland	
1993	Arsenal	2-1†	Sheffield Wed	after 1-1 draw
1994	Manchester Utd	4-0	Chelsea	

†after extra time

holders Arsenal tumbled to first division Bolton Wanderers in extra time of a replay at Highbury. Other clubs to fall included Newcastle United, Leeds United, Blackburn Rovers and Aston Villa. In the Coca-Cola Cup semi-finals Aston Villa inched out Tranmere Rovers on penalties to clinch a place at Wembley and Manchester United saw off Sheffield Wednesday.

In the league only Blackburn remained as a possible threat to Manchester United's lead as the chasing pack shed points. Tottenham Hotspur set an unwanted club record as they slumped to seven consecutive league defeats, leaving manager Osvaldo Ardiles under a cloud of mounting pressure spiced with news of FA investigations into the club's financial dealings.

As March dawned Chelsea remained the only team to have beaten Manchester United in the league and they made it a double with a win at Old Trafford, with Peacock again grabbing the only goal. At the same time Tottenham scraped a 1-1 home draw with Villa to earn their first league point of the year. John Deehan was finally appointed manager at Norwich and he immediately recorded a 3-0 win over previous manager Mike Walker's Everton side.

New England coach Terry Venables picked his first international squads to play Denmark. He chose 18 'elite' players, most of whom the media had been citing for inclusion in previous World Cup squads. Matthew Le Tissier, Graeme Le Saux, Darren Anderton, Peter Beardsley and Alan Shearer were among them. England won 1-0, playing with considerable panache. Not surprisingly Venables was accorded an ovation by the Wembley crowd and the talk was of what might have been…

Back in the real world the Premiership teams asserted themselves in the FA Cup. United disposed of Charlton 3-1, despite the dismissal of keeper Peter Schmeichel, and Oldham overcame the first division's Cup heroes, Bolton. Chelsea had no difficulty beating Wolves 1-0 and it was left to Luton Town to fly the minnows' flag. They held West Ham to a goalless draw at Upton Park and took the replay 3-2 thanks to a hat-trick from Scott Oakes.

Eric Cantona started to make the back page headlines for all the wrong reasons. He was sent off at Swindon and followed that up with a dismissal at Highbury, where United were fortunate to gain a point in a 2-2 draw. Cantona had some good news, though, as he was voted the Professional Footballers' Player of the Year. The Football Writers' Association award went to Alan Shearer.

Dreams of Trebles were finally dashed as, without suspended Schmeichel, United lost a thrilling Coca-Cola Cup final at Wembley, 1-3 to Aston Villa. United's woe was completed by the sending off of Andrei Kanchelskis at the very end of play for deliberate handball – the club's fourth dismissal in five games.

The penultimate month of the league season saw Blackburn Rovers draw level on points with United at the top of the Premiership as the Manchester club faltered. They lost 2-0 at Ewood Park, with Shearer bagging both goals in spectacular fashion.

In the FA Cup semi-finals, controversially held at Wembley, Chelsea put paid to the first division dreams by disposing of Luton Town. The following day Oldham and Manchester United needed extra time before a goal materialised. But United forced a replay inside the last minute thanks to a superb Mark Hughes goal. In the replay there was only one team in it, and United showed the style of football which won them so many plaudits during the season. Arsenal continued to fly the flag in Europe and got through to the final of the Cup-Winners' Cup, proving too

FA Cup Results

3rd Round

Barnet v Chelsea	0-0, 0-4
Birmingham City v Kidderminster Hrs	1-2
Blackburn Rvs v Portsmouth	3-3, 3-1
Bolton Wanderers v Everton	1-1, 3-2†
Bristol City v Liverpool	1-1, 1-0
Bromsgrove Rvs v Barnsley	1-2
Cardiff City v Middlesbrough	2-2, 2-1
Charlton Ath v Burnley	3-0
Exeter City v Aston Villa	0-1
Grimsby Town v Wigan Ath	1-0
Leeds Utd v Crewe Alexandra	3-1
Luton Town v Southend Utd	1-0
Manchester City v Leicester City	4-1
Millwall v Arsenal	0-1
Newcastle Utd v Coventry City	2-0
Notts County v Sutton Utd	3-2
Oldham Ath v Derby County	2-1
Oxford Utd v Tranmere Rvs	2-0
Peterborough Utd v Tottenham Hotspur	1-1, 1-1†, 4-5 aps
Plymouth Argyle v Chester City	1-0
Preston NE v Bournemouth	2-1
Sheffield Utd v Manchester Utd	0-1
Sheffield Wednesday v Nottingham Forest	1-1, 2-0
Southampton v Port Vale	1-1, 0-1
Stockport County v Queens Park Rangers	2-1
Stoke City v Bath City	0-0, 4-1
Sunderland v Carlisle Utd	1-1, 1-0
Swindon Town v Ipswich Town	1-1, 1-2
West Ham Utd v Watford	2-1
Wimbledon v Scunthorpe	3-0
Wolverhampton Wanderers v Crystal Palace	1-0
Wycombe Wanderers v Norwich City	0-2

4th Round

Bolton Wanderers v Arsenal	2-2, 3-1
Cardiff City v Manchester City	1-0
Charlton Ath v Blackburn Rvs	0-0, 1-0
Chelsea v Sheffield Wednesday	1-1, 3-1
Grimsby v Aston Villa	1-2
Ipswich Town v Tottenham Hotspur	3-0
Kidderminster Hrs v Preston NE	1-0
Newcastle Utd v Luton Town	1-1, 0-2
Norwich City v Manchester Utd	0-2
Notts County v West Ham Utd	1-1, 0-1
Oldham Ath v Stoke City	0-0, 1-0
Oxford Utd v Leeds Utd	2-2, 3-2
Plymouth Argyle v Barnsley	2-2, 0-1
Port Vale v Wolverhampton Wdrs	0-2
Stockport County v Bristol City	0-4
Wimbledon v Sunderland	2-1

5th Round

Bolton Wanderers v Aston Villa	1-0
Bristol City v Charlton Ath	1-1, 0-2
Cardiff City v Luton Town	1-2
Kidderminster Harriers v West Ham Utd	0-1
Oldham Ath v Barnsley	1-0
Oxford Utd v Chelsea	1-2
Wimbledon v Manchester Utd	0-3
Wolverhampton Wdrs v Ipswich Town	1-1, 2-1

6th Round

Bolton Wanderers v Oldham Athletic	0-1
Chelsea v Wolverhampton Wdrs	1-0
Manchester United v Charlton	3-1
West Ham United v Luton Town	0-0, 2-3

Semi-Finals

Chelsea v Luton Town	2-0
Manchester United v Oldham Athletic	1-1†, 4-1

Final

Manchester United 4
Cantona (60 pen, 66 pen); Hughes (68); McClair (90)
Chelsea 0
Att: 79,634. Ref: Elleray

Manchester United: Schmeichel, Parker, Irwin (Sharpe 84), Bruce, Pallister, Cantona, Ince, Keane, Kanchelskis (McClair 84), Hughes, Giggs
Chelsea: Kharin, Clarke, Johnsen E, Kjeldbjerg, Sinclair, Burley (Hoddle 68), Newton, Spencer, Peacock, Stein (Cascarino 78), Wise

---

strong over two legs for Paris Saint-Germain.

Swindon achieved their first away win of the season, at QPR, but were still relegated back to the first division. In the first Crystal Palace were crowned as champions with Nottingham Forest claiming the second automatic promotion place.

In early May Coventry City's defeat of Blackburn Rovers at Highfield Road meant that the Premiership title went to Manchester United for the second year running. It was the first successful title defence since the 1986–87 season. Blackburn were assured of their UEFA Cup place for next season, having made sure of the runners-up spot. Newcastle United took third place and were later granted a UEFA Cup spot. Arsenal produced another magnificent European performance to lift the Cup-Winners' Cup, without four key players. Alan Smith rifled in the only goal of the game against the holders, Parma, in Copenhagen.

The final Saturday of the season saw any two from Oldham, Everton, Ipswich Town, Sheffield United and Southampton facing relegation alongside Swindon. Oldham failed to make the cut, drawing 1-1 at Norwich. Everton looked set to say farewell to 40 years of football in the top flight as they fell 2-0 behind at home to Wimbledon, but recovered strongly to win 3-2 and saved their skins. Ipswich and Southampton did just enough, drawing 0-0 at Blackburn and 3-3 at West Ham respectively. That left Sheffield United. They were 2-1 up with a quarter of an hour left to play at Cup finalists Chelsea, when they conceded another goal to make the game 2-2. That still would have been just enough but a Chelsea goal in the 90th minute condemned them to the first division.

Coca-Cola (League) Cup

3rd Round

Arsenal v Norwich City	1-1, 3-0
Blackpool v Peterborough United	2-2, 1-2
Blackburn Rovers v Shrewsbury Town	0-0, 4-3
Derby County v Tottenham Hotspur	0-1
Everton v Crystal Palace	2-2, 4-1
Liverpool v Ipswich	3-2
Manchester City v Chelsea	1-0
Manchester United v Leicester City	5-1
Middlesbrough v Sheffield Wednesday	1-1, 1-2
Nottingham Forest v West Ham United	2-1
Oldham Athletic v Coventry City	2-0
QPR v Millwall	3-0
Sunderland v Aston Villa	1-4
Swindon Town v Portsmouth	2-0
Wimbledon v Newcastle United	2-1

4th Round

Arsenal v Aston Villa	0-1
Everton v Manchester United	0-2
Liverpool v Wimbledon	1-1, 2-2†, 3-4 aps
Nottingham Forest v Manchester City	0-0, 2-1
Peterborough United v Portsmouth	0-0, 0-1†
Queens Park Rangers v Shef. Wednesday	1-2
Tottenham Hotspur v Blackburn Rovers	1-0
Tranmere Rovers v Oldham Athletic	3-0

Quarter-Finals

Manchester United v Portsmouth	2-2, 1-0
Nottingham Forest v Tranmere Rovers	1-1, 0-2
Tottenham Hotspur v Aston Villa	1-2
Wimbledon v Sheffield Wednesday	1-2

Semi-Finals – Two legs

Tranmere Rovers v Aston Villa	3-1, 1-3, 4-5 aps
Manchester Utd v Sheffield Wednesday	1-0, 4-1

Final

Aston Villa v Manchester United	3-1

† aet

Down but not out – a year to forget for Tottenham's Teddy Sheringham and his club – seen here with Tony Gale of West Ham United.

FA Cup Final day arrived with the usual fanfare and Chelsea went to Wembley knowing that they would be playing in the next season's Cup-Winners' Cup whatever the result, thanks to Manchester United's Champions' Cup commitments. Fortune favoured the Reds. Despite dominating the first two-thirds of the game and rattling the United crossbar, Chelsea were beaten 4-0. The first two United goals were penalties, leaving rueful Chelsea player-manager Glenn Hoddle to reflect after the game that United's first clear chance was their third goal.

The result crowned a wonderful season for Manchester United. They became only the fourth team this century to complete the double of league championship and FA Cup and joined an exclusive list of the greatest English league teams: Tottenham Hotspur (1961), Arsenal (1971) and Liverpool (1986).

National optimism continued as England thrashed World Cup qualifiers Greece 5-0 at Wembley, but arch-rivals Norway spoiled the final party of the season by keeping England at bay in a goalless draw. A nervous summer was in prospect for Tottenham Hotspur, who were certain to be investigated on multiple charges of financial irregularities with the possibility of relegation from the Premiership. The FA took the unprecedented step of announcing that Sheffield United would remain in the Premiership should Tottenham be demoted.

On the field, the play-offs continued and were third time lucky for Leicester City, who beat Derby County with a last-minute goal to clinch the final promotion place. That match took place at Wembley and in early June Tottenham went to the same venue to learn their fate. Having found them guilty of financial

FA Carling Premiership Results 1993–94

	Arsenal	Aston Villa	Blackburn Rovers	Chelsea	Coventry City	Everton	Ipswich Town	Leeds United	Liverpool	Manchester City	Manchester United	Newcastle United	Norwich City	Oldham Athletic	QPR	Sheffield United	Sheffield Wednesday	Southampton	Swindon Town	Tottenham Hotspur	West Ham United	Wimbledon
Arsenal	—	1-2	1-0	1-0	0-3	2-0	4-0	2-1	1-0	0-0	0-0	2-1	0-0	1-1	0-0	3-0	1-0	1-0	1-1	1-1	0-2	1-1
Aston Villa	1-2	—	0-1	1-0	0-0	0-0	0-1	1-0	2-1	0-0	1-2	0-2	0-0	1-2	4-1	1-0	2-2	0-2	5-0	1-0	3-1	0-1
Blackburn Rovers	1-1	1-0	—	2-0	2-1	2-0	0-0	2-1	2-0	2-0	2-0	1-0	2-3	1-0	1-1	0-0	1-1	2-0	3-1	1-0	0-2	3-0
Chelsea	0-2	1-1	1-2	—	1-2	4-2	1-1	1-1	1-0	0-0	1-0	1-0	1-2	0-1	2-0	3-2	1-1	2-0	2-0	4-3	2-0	2-0
Coventry City	1-0	0-1	2-1	1-1	—	2-1	1-0	0-2	1-0	4-0	0-1	2-1	1-1	0-1	0-0	1-1	1-1	1-0	1-1	1-0	1-1	1-2
Everton	1-1	0-1	0-3	4-2	0-0	—	0-0	1-1	2-0	1-0	0-1	0-2	1-5	2-1	0-3	4-2	0-2	1-0	6-2	0-1	0-1	3-2
Ipswich Town	1-5	1-2	1-0	1-0	0-2	0-2	—	0-0	1-2	2-2	1-2	1-1	2-1	0-0	1-3	3-2	1-4	1-0	1-1	2-2	1-1	0-0
Leeds United	2-1	2-0	3-3	4-1	1-0	3-0	0-0	—	2-0	3-2	0-2	1-1	0-4	1-0	1-1	2-1	2-1	0-0	3-0	2-0	1-0	4-0
Liverpool	0-0	2-1	0-1	2-1	1-0	2-1	1-0	2-0	—	2-1	3-3	0-2	0-1	2-1	3-2	1-2	2-0	4-2	2-2	1-2	2-0	1-1
Manchester City	0-0	3-0	0-2	2-2	1-1	1-0	2-1	1-1	1-1	—	2-3	2-1	1-1	1-1	3-0	0-0	1-3	1-1	2-1	0-2	0-0	0-1
Manchester United	1-0	3-1	1-1	0-1	0-0	1-0	0-0	0-0	1-0	2-0	—	1-1	2-2	3-2	2-1	3-0	5-0	2-0	4-2	2-1	3-0	3-1
Newcastle United	2-0	5-1	1-1	0-0	4-0	1-0	2-0	1-1	3-0	2-0	1-1	—	3-0	3-2	1-2	4-0	4-2	1-2	7-1	0-1	2-0	4-0
Norwich City	1-1	1-2	2-2	1-1	1-0	3-0	1-0	2-1	2-2	1-1	0-2	1-2	—	1-1	3-4	0-1	1-1	4-5	0-0	1-2	0-0	0-1
Oldham Athletic	0-0	1-1	1-2	2-1	3-3	0-1	0-3	1-1	0-3	0-0	2-5	1-3	2-1	—	4-1	1-1	0-0	2-1	2-1	0-2	1-2	1-1
QPR	1-1	2-2	1-0	1-1	5-1	2-1	3-0	0-4	1-3	1-2	2-3	1-2	2-2	2-0	—	2-1	1-2	1-3	1-1	1-1	0-0	1-0
Sheffield United	1-1	1-2	1-2	1-0	0-0	0-0	1-1	2-2	0-0	0-1	0-3	2-0	1-2	2-1	1-1	—	1-1	0-0	3-1	2-2	3-2	2-1
Sheffield Wednesday	0-1	0-0	1-2	3-1	0-0	5-1	5-0	3-3	3-1	1-1	2-3	0-1	3-3	0-3	3-1	3-1	—	2-0	3-3	1-0	5-0	2-2
Southampton	0-4	4-1	3-1	3-1	1-0	0-2	0-1	0-2	4-2	0-1	1-3	2-1	0-1	1-3	0-1	3-3	1-1	—	5-1	1-0	0-2	1-0
Swindon Town	0-4	1-2	1-3	1-3	3-1	1-1	2-2	0-5	0-5	1-3	2-2	2-2	3-3	0-1	1-0	0-0	0-1	2-1	—	2-1	1-1	2-4
Tottenham Hotspur	0-1	1-1	0-2	1-1	1-2	3-2	1-1	1-1	3-3	1-0	0-1	1-2	1-3	5-0	1-2	2-2	1-3	3-0	1-1	—	1-4	1-1
West Ham United	0-0	0-0	1-2	1-0	3-2	0-1	2-1	0-1	1-2	2-2	2-4	3-3	2-0	0-4	0-0	2-0	3-3	0-0	1-3	1-3	—	0-2
Wimbledon	0-3	2-2	4-1	1-1	1-2	1-1	0-2	1-0	1-1	1-0	1-0	4-2	3-1	3-0	1-1	2-0	2-1	1-0	3-0	2-1	1-2	—

irregularities, the FA handed out record punishment. A fine of £600,000, banishment from the FA Cup for season 1994–95, a deduction of 12 points for season 1994–95 and payment of all costs of the hearing. Chairman Alan Sugar immediately accused the FA of a vendetta against him and announced that his club would fight the punishment all the way. His subsequent appeal had mixed results – with the points deduction being halved to six, but the fine doubled to £1.2m.

Graham Fenton of Aston Villa and Lee Sharpe of Manchester United.

Estonia

Flora take the mantle

It was the tightest of championships and one of the most bizarre. Flora Tallinn denied Norma Tallinn a hat-trick of championship wins by winning a play-off match, as the season ended in turmoil with Kalev Sillamae unable to complete their season because of cash problems and Tevalte Tallinn – nee Vigri Tallinn – being relegated to the second division on grounds of corruption in the penultimate weekend of the season, as they stood on the verge of a three-way championship play-off!

The season had started in a more orderly fashion and after the first six rounds of games Norma Tallinn remained the only side with a 100 per cent record, as Tevalte Tallinn suffered a 1-2 defeat at Nikol Tallinn. Flora were three points off the pace, having lost in the third week to Tevalte. By week eight the top of the league table was being dominated by the 'big' four clubs from Tallinn, with Norma consolidating their position by a single-goal victory over Tevalte. Flora used the opportunity to move into joint second place as only five points separated the four clubs.

By the winter break the gang of four remained but Nikol had won their game in hand to move into second place ahead of Flora and Tevalte. At the bottom things didn't look too good for Kalev Sillamae, who were still seeking for their first point having conceded 28 goals in their eight games to date, scoring just five in reply. The winter respite did some good as Kalev immediately earned a goalless draw to secure their first point, but it was to prove a false dawn. Tevalte recorded a 10-1 win over strugglers Merkuur Tartu, as Norma and Flora drew 1-1. So Norma remained four points ahead of Flora, who were still in fourth position. Tevalte's score was bettered the following week, when poor old Kalev lost 11-0 to mid-table Trans Narva.

If that thrashing wasn't enough to be endured, weeks 17 and 18 were decisive in the history of Kalev. An 8-0 defeat at home by Norma was followed a 24-0 slaughter against Tevalte – the biggest scoreline in Estonian league history – with the club in financial difficulties and unable to field a competitive side. Drastic action was required and Kalev were withdrawn from the league, with the Estonian authorities awarding their remaining four games to their opponents rather than expunging existing results. As teams level on points are positioned according to the results between them, in preference to goal difference, this didn't cause the uproar that might have been expected within other European countries.

Matters at the top of the table were coming to a head and with three weeks of the season left Norma missed an opportunity to move three points ahead of their city rivals, when Flora won 1-0 in the tiny Norma Stadium. This result left Tevalte and Norma at the top with two games to play. Flora were one point behind them, with a game in hand on the same number of points as fourth-placed Nikol. Flora could only draw that game in hand, with Trans Narva, which left the top three sides level on 32 points with two games to play.

In the penultimate round of fixtures Flora won 4-0 at Dunamo and Norma bettered that with a six-goal salvo at the relegated Merkuur. But the fireworks were flying at the Kalev stadium, where Tevalte beat Tervis Parnu 3-0. After the game charges of corruption were brought to bear, and subsequently upheld. So what had started as a season of promise for Tevalte ended in enforced relegation.

In the final weekend both sides needed the other to slip if a play-off was to be avoided. Flora looked to have the most difficult task, entertaining Nikol, but produced a nail-biting victory with the only goal of the game. Norma duly beat the relegated Dunamo with two goals and so a play-off was ordered by the Estonian FA, which Flora won 5-2 to capture their first Estonian title. There was some consolation for Norma, though,

Final League Table 1993–94

	P	W	D	L	F	A	Pts
Flora Tallinn	22	15	6	1	61	9	36
Norma Tallinn	22	17	2	3	69	11	36
Tevalte Tallinn †	22	15	4	3	70	9	34
Nikol Tallinn	22	15	3	4	49	19	33
Trans Narva	22	12	6	4	50	16	30
Sadam Tallinn	22	11	3	8	38	26	25
EP Johvi	22	9	6	7	39	16	24
Esdag Tartu	22	6	2	14	22	59	14
Tervis Parnu	22	5	2	15	18	47	12
Dunamo Tallinn	22	5	2	15	25	54	12
Merkuur Tartu	22	2	1	19	12	101	6
Kalev Sillamae	22	1	1	20	11	97	3

† Previously Vigri Tallinn.

Promotions and Relegations
Promoted: JK Kalev
Relegated: Kalev Sillamae, Merkuur Tartu, Dunamo Tallinn, Tervis Parnu, Telvalle Tallinn

Estonian Football Association

Founded:	1989 (Original: 1921)
Address:	Regati Pst 1, Tallinn EE0103
Phone:	+372 2 23 82 53
Fax:	+372 2 23 83 87
UEFA Affiliation:	1992
FIFA Affiliation:	1992 (Original: 1923)
Season:	September to June
National Stadium:	Kalev
Capacity:	12,000
Colours:	Blue, Black, White

International Results 1993–94

Date	Opponents	Result	Venue	Comp.	Scorers
5/9/93	Portugal	0-2	Tallinn	WCQ1	
22/9/93	Italy	0-3	Tallinn	WCQ1	
26/10/93	Liechtenstein	2-0	Balzers	Friendly	Bragin (54), Rajala (89)
10/11/93	Portugal	0-3	Lisbon	WCQ1	
17/11/93	Switzerland	0-4	Zurich	WCQ1	
7/5/94	USA	0-4	California	Friendly	
23/5/94	Wales	1-2	Tallinn	Friendly	Reim (85 pen)
1/6/94	FYR Macedonia	0-2	Skopje	Friendly	
29/7/94	Lithuania	0-3	Vilnius	Baltic Cup	
30/7/94	Latvia	0-2	Vilnius	Baltic Cup	

National Record	P	W	D	L	F	A	
European Championship	Never participated						
World Cup Finals	Never qualified						
World Cup Qualifiers	4	1	0	3	6	17	(pre-war)
World Cup Qualifiers	10	0	1	9	1	27	(post-war)

Five-Year Records League 1-2-3 and Cup Winners

League Results

	1st	Pts	2nd	Pts	3rd	Pts
1990	VMV Tallinn					
1991	VMV Tallinn					
1992	Norma Tallinn					
1993	Norma Tallinn	42	Flora Tallinn	34	Nikol Tallinn	33
1994	Flora Tallinn	36	Norma Tallinn	36	Tevalte Tallinn	35

Cup Final Results

1990	KP Parnu			
1991	VMV Tallinn			
1992	VMV Tallinn *(now Nikol Tallinn)*			
1993	Nikol Tallinn	0-0	Norma Tallinn	4-2 on pens, aet
1994	Norma Tallinn	4-1	Trans Narva	

Estonian Championship Results 1993–94

	Dunamo Tallinn	EP Johvi	Esdag Tartu	Flora Tallinn	Kalev Sillamae	Merkuur Tartu	Nikol Tallinn	Norma Tallinn	Sadam Tallinn	Tevalte Tallinn	Tervis Parnu	Trans Narva
Dunamo Tallinn	—	1-1	2-4	0-4	3-2	0-0	0-4	1-3	1-2	0-6	2-1	1-6
EP Johvi	1-0	—	1-0	0-2	1-0	9-0	0-1	1-2	0-0	1-2	4-0	0-2
Esdag Tartu	1-3	0-5	—	1-4	3-1	2-1	0-3	0-3	0-6	0-1	1-0	2-2
Flora Tallinn	5-1	0-0	5-1	—	6-0	4-0	1-0	1-1	3-0	1-2	2-0	1-1
Kalev Sillamae	2-1	1-5	1-2	0-3	—	0-1	1-5	0-8	0-6	1-2	0-0	0-1
Merkuur Tartu	1-5	0-3	1-2	0-6	4-1	—	0-5	0-6	1-5	0-6	1-2	0-5
Nikol Tallinn	0-2	1-0	4-1	1-1	4-1	8-1	—	1-3	0-0	2-1	4-2	2-1
Norma Tallinn	2-0	1-1	4-0	0-1	7-0	7-1	3-0	—	7-0	1-0	4-0	0-1
Sadam Tallinn	4-1	0-0	3-0	0-4	3-0	3-0	0-1	0-2	—	0-3	2-0	0-0
Tevalte Tallinn	2-1	0-0	2-0	0-0	24-0	10-1	0-0	3-1	1-0	—	3-0	0-0
Tervis Parnu	2-0	2-5	4-0	0-6	1-0	3-0	0-2	0-2	0-2	—	—	2-2
Trans Narva	1-0	1-0	1-1	1-1	11-0	0-0	0-1	0-3	2-1	0-0	3-0	—

when they beat Trans Narva 4-1 to lift the Estonian Cup for the first time and grab their European spot in the Cup-Winners' Cup.

At the bottom, with Kalev and Tevalte already relegated, Merkuur and Dunamo filled the other automatic relegation spots, leaving Tervis to face Parnu rivals JK Kalev in a promotion-relegation play-off during the close season, to leave a league of just eight teams for the 1994–95 season.

Estonia's representatives in European competition failed to show any improvement on the previous year, although Norma had wretched luck in their Champions' Cup tie with HJK Helsinki. Having fallen behind in Finland they equalised within a minute thorough Borisov to earn an encouraging 1-1 draw. In the second leg, Norma looked to be going through on the away goals rule until a disastrous own goal by Belokhovostov nine minutes from time turned the tie in HJK's favour. Nikol's demise in the Cup-Winners' Cup was more emphatic. They lost 0-4 to Lillestrom in the first leg and did little better in the second, to bow out none too gracefully 1-8 on aggregate.

The national side already were out of the reckoning for the World Cup finals when both Portugal and Italy visited Tallinn in search of vital qualification points. In many respects the Estonians did well to limit the score to 0-2 and 0-3 respectively, and secured a first win of the season 2-0 in Luxembourg, with second-half goals by Bragin and Rajala. Another 0-3 defeat in Portugal was followed by a 0-4 mauling by the Swiss in Zurich as the year came to an end. A goal was finally scored by Martin Reim in a 1-2 defeat by Wales but two successive defeats against Baltic neighbours Lithuania and Latvia ended the season on a low note. Whether they can do any better in the curious Group 4 of the European Championship, where they face Italy, Ukraine, Croatia, Lithuania and Slovenia, remains to be seen.

Faeroe Islands

Fotboltssambund Foroya

Founded:	1979
Address:	PO Box 1028, Gundadular, FR-110 Torshavn
Phone:	+298 16707
Fax:	+298 19079
UEFA Affiliation:	1988
FIFA Affiliation:	1988
National Stadium:	Gundadulur
Capacity:	8,000
Colours:	White, Blue, White

Gotu Itrottarfelag – GI – won the championship of the Faeroe Islands for only the third time in their 74-year history and for the first time since 1986. GI carried on the surge of form they had shown towards the end of the previous season that took them to second place. They finished three points ahead of HB, and took their first steps into Europe in the UEFA Cup. They will hope to fare better than B68, thrashed by Croatia Zagreb 11-0 on aggregate in the preliminary round. HB did better in the Cup-Winners' Cup, when they were awarded their tie with RAF Jelgava 3-0 after the Latvians failed to show for the second leg in Torshavn. Any further progress was halted by Universitatea Craiova in the first round, who won 7-0 on aggregate.

A 7-0 mauling by Norway in Toftir was followed by a 4-0 defeat at the hands of the Romanians in the final Group 4 World Cup qualifying game. After the Norway result coach Pall Gudlaugsson resigned. The pastings handed out by even some of Europe's lesser nations have been noted by the powers that be, wishing to build on the famous 1-0 win over Austria in the 1990 European Championship qualifying rounds, and they appointed Allan Simonsen as the new coach for the all-amateur team. Simonsen, a former Danish international with 56 caps and 21 goals during the period from 1972 to 1986, made his name as a player on mainland Europe, where he played for Borussia Monchengladbach and Barcelona before having a brief spell in England with Manchester United and Charlton Athletic.

The post is a part-time one and Simonsen has a 21-month contract to run alongside his position as chief coach with Danish first division side Vejle. His first job will be to add some of the abrasiveness of the North Sea weather to his defence before European Championship matches with Russia, Greece, Scotland, Finland, France and perhaps the opponents the Faeroes await most of all – San Marino.

Final League Table 1993

	P	W	D	L	F	A	Pts
GI	18	11	6	1	32	14	28
HB	18	9	7	2	41	20	25
KI	18	9	5	4	24	15	23
B71	18	10	3	5	30	26	23
B36	18	6	6	6	21	17	18
B68	18	5	6	7	30	28	16
TB	18	5	3	10	24	30	14
IF	18	5	3	10	27	41	13
LIF	18	3	6	9	25	46	12
VB	18	3	2	13	18	35	8

Promotions and Relegations
Promoted: NSI Runavik, EB Streymur
Relegated: LIF, VB

International Results 1993–94

Date	Opponents	Result	Venue	Comp.	Scorers
11/8/93	Norway	0-7	Toftir	Friendly	
8/9/93	Romania	0-4	Toftir	WCQ4	

National Record

	P	W	D	L	F	A
European Championship	8	1	1	6	3	26
World Cup Finals	*Never qualified*					
World Cup Qualifiers	10	0	0	10	1	38

Five-Year Records League 1-2-3 and Cup Winners

One, Two, Three Records

	1st	Pts	2nd	Pts	3rd	Pts
1990	HB	24	B36	20	MB	19
1991	KI	24	B36	24	GI	23
1992	B68	27	GI	25	KI	23
1993	GI	28	HB	25	KI	23

Cup Final Results

1989	HB	1-1, 2-0	B71	3-1 on agg
1990	KL	6-1	GI	
1991	B36	1-0	HB	
1992	HB	1-0	KI	
1993	B71	2-0	HB	

Finland

Jazz's festival season

A decade of domination by HJK Helsinki and Kuusysi Lahti was broken by FC Jazz when they won the 1993 championship title. Not since 1983, when Ilves won it, has the big two's domination been broken – that it should be broken by a club in only their third season in the top division, without any current internationals in their side and recording their first-ever honour, made it all the more remarkable. Perhaps it is no coincidence that the Jazz coach, Jussi Ristimaki, was the coach of Ilves in their championship year!

Porin Pallo Toverit – PPT – won the second division championship in 1990 and during their first season in the first division decided to opt for a more familiar name. They plumped for FC Jazz, on the basis of the annual jazz and blues festivals held in Pori each year. Finland is not the place you would look for Brazilians but FC Jazz signed four for the start of the 1993 campaign, and Rodrigo, Luis Antonio, Dionisio and Piracaia all did well. This was Luis Antonio's second season at the club and he has been a major source of goals, although Antti Sumiala topped the pile with 20, not bad for a 20-year old who has already gained experience with Anderlecht in Belgium and Ikast in Denmark.

After the first phase of 22 games FC Jazz led the table, two points ahead of MyPa and HJK. The top eight clubs advanced to the final round of games, with MP Mikkeli, Haka, Jaro and Ilves going into the promotion-relegation phase with clubs from the second division. After the first round in the championship phase HJK had drawn level as Jazz were held at home to TPV – after being 2-0 up with ten minutes to play – and the three points for HJK's win at Turku allowed them to close the two-point gap. The following week's fixtures saw Jazz's championship credentials given the toughest scrutiny as they travelled to Helsinki to face HJK, and won 2-0 to re-establish their lead and extend it by a point to three.

In the final few weeks MyPa renewed their challenge and when in the penultimate round of games Jazz were involved in a scoreless draw in Lahti, MyPa moved to within a point with a two-goal home win over bottom club TPS. Those results set up a

Final League Table 1993

	P	W	D	L	F	A	Pts
FC Jazz	22	12	5	5	50	28	41
MyPa	22	11	6	5	31	20	39
HJK Helsinki	22	12	3	7	27	17	39
FinnPa	22	11	5	6	34	23	38
TPV Tampere	22	10	6	6	34	29	36
Kuusysi Lahti	22	11	3	8	30	34	36
TPS Turku	22	8	4	10	25	26	28
RoPs Rovenemi	22	8	3	11	22	25	27
MP	22	7	5	10	32	32	26
Haka	22	7	4	11	27	36	25
Jaro	22	5	6	11	17	26	21
Ilves	22	3	5	15	22	55	13

Championship Play-off 1993

	P	W	D	L	F	A	Pts
FC Jazz	29	17	7	5	67	33	58
MyPa	29	16	6	7	47	33	54
HJK Helsinki	29	15	4	10	34	26	49
Kuusysi Lahti	29	14	5	10	41	44	47
FinnPa	29	13	7	9	45	35	46
TPV Tampere	29	10	8	11	38	39	38
RoPs Rovenemi	29	11	5	13	32	35	38
TPS Turku	29	9	5	15	31	39	32

Relegation Play-off 1993

	P	W	D	L	F	A	Pts
MP	7	4	3	0	19	7	15
Jaro	7	4	2	1	9	5	14
KuPS	7	3	2	2	15	10	11
Haka	7	3	1	3	13	11	10
FC Oulu	7	3	1	3	10	10	10
Ilves	7	2	3	2	5	7	9
KajHa	7	2	1	4	7	12	7
KontU	7	0	1	6	4	20	1

Top Scorers
- 20 Antti SUMIALA (FC Jazz)
- 13 Tommi PAAVOLA (HJK)
- 12 Jari RANTANEN (HJK)
- 11 Ismo LIUS (Kuusysi Lahti)
-     Jukka TURUNEN (MyPa)
- 10 Marko RAJAMAKI (MyPa)

Promotions and Relegations
Promoted: FC Oulu, KuPS
Relegated: None

Suomen Palloliito Finlands

Founded:	1907
Address:	Football Association of Finland, PO Box 179, Lantinen Brahenkatu 2, 00511 Helsinki
Phone:	+358 0 701 01 01
Fax:	+358 0 701 01 099/098
UEFA Affiliation:	1954
FIFA Affiliation:	1908
Season:	April to October
National Stadium:	Olympiastadion
Capacity:	50,000
Colours:	White, Blue, White
Change:	Blue, White, Blue

International Results 1993-94

Date	Opponents	Result	Venue	Comp.	Scorers
25/8/93	Austria	0-3	Vienna	WCQ6	
8/9/93	France	0-2	Tampere	WCQ6	
13/10/93	Sweden	2-3	Stockholm	WCQ6	Suominen (14), Litmanen (60)
10/11/93	Israel	3-1	Tel Aviv	WCQ6	Hiekkinen (54), Hjelm (74, 85)
24/2/94	Morocco	0-0	Casablanca	Friendly	
27/5/94	Italy	0-2	Parma	Friendly	
2/6/94	Spain	1-2	Tampere	Friendly	Jarvinen (17)

National Record	P	W	D	L	F	A
European Championship	44	4	12	28	31	88
World Cup Finals	Never qualified					
World Cup Qualifiers	73	12	8	53	61	213

Suomen Cup 1993

7th Round
TPS v AIFK	11-0
ToPS v FC 1991	4-0
Kuusysi Lahti v KajHa	2-0
KuPS v MyPa	0-1 †
HJK Helsinki v FC Oulu	4-1
Reipas v Haka	1-5
HyPS v FinnPa	0-8
TP55 v KePS	0-1

Quarter-Finals
FC Haka v FinnPa	5-2
RoPS v TPS	3-2
Kuusysi Lahti v KePS	5-0
MyPa v HJK Helsinki	0-1

Semi-Finals
HJK Helsinki v Kuusysi Lahti	2-0
FC Haka v RoPS	1-2

Final
HJK Helsinki v RoPS	2-0

† aet

remarkable finale: in the final game Jazz played hosts to MyPa. Not surprisingly this drew the season's biggest crowd – 11,193 – and a thrilling finish to an excellent season, with nine goals and Jazz winning 6-3. MyPa, who needed to win in the Porin Stadium to steal the title, came back from two down to draw level. But then elementary errors in defence cost them dear and goals from Luis Antonio (2), Miika Juntunen (2), Piracaia and Antti Sumiala ensured that the band played on.

With the first division extended to 14 clubs for the 1994 season, things were less tense in the relegation pool than normal. The four clubs who missed out on the championship play-off group all won back their places, being joined by FC Oulu and KuPS. KajHa and KontU were unsuccessful in their attempts and find themselves back in the second division, which has also been expanded to 14 clubs from 1994. The 1993 championship play-offs were the last of their kind, as with the reorganisation of Finnish league football two teams will be relegated from the first division and replaced by the top two in the second.

HJK won the Suomen (FA) Cup, beating RoPS 2-0 in the final, having had to face MyPa, Kuusysi Lahti, FC Oulu and TPV en route. FC Jazz were never in with a shout, going out at the first time of asking at home to TPS.

The season in Finland runs through the summer months like those in the neighbouring Baltic states. This means that clubs qualify for European club competitions long in advance and also has them at a disadvantage in playing games during part of the close season. There could be no excuses when HJK were drawn to face Estonian opposition in the preliminary round of the Champions' Cup. A goal by Antti Heinola gave the Helsinki club a perfect start against Norma Tallinn but an equaliser shortly after levelled the first leg in Finland. With ten minutes of the second leg remaining an own goal rescued HJK, who were looking likely to fall on the away goals rule. The prize was a first-round encounter with RSC Anderlecht, but the Belgians proved much too strong and ran out 3-0 winners in each leg.

In the Cup-Winners' Cup, MyPa fell disappointingly at the first hurdle to Valur, 4-1 on aggregate despite taking an early lead in the first leg through Marko Rajamaki. In the UEFA Cup, Kuusysi produced an excellent performance to beat Belgian side KSV Waregem 6-1 on aggregate. The fans in Lahti could hardly believe their eyes as they stormed to a 4-0 lead, and then went on to win 2-1 in Belgium. Juha Annunen scored important goals in both legs and Ismo Lius supplied three overall. The euphoria lasted only a round, though, as Brondby produced a 7-2 aggregate dismissal.

World Cup Final qualification was never a serious prospect in a group with France, Sweden and Bulgaria, but a narrow defeat in Stockholm by the odd goal in five lifted morale and contributed to

Five-Year Records League 1-2-3 and Cup Winners

League Results

	1st	Pts	2nd	Pts	3rd	Pts
1990	Kuusysi Lahti	41	TPS Tuku	39	RoPS	34
1991	Play off: HJK Helsinki v Kuusysi Lahti 2-1 on agg (1-1, 1-0)					
1992	Kuusysi Lahti	59	MP Mikkeli	58	Haka	54
1993	HJK Helsinki	66	Kuusysi Lahti	63	FC Jazz	63
1994	FC Jazz	58	MyPa	54	HJK Helsinki	49

Cup Final Results

1990	Ilves Tampere	2-1	HJK Helsinki	
1991	TPS Turku	0-0	Kuusysi Lahti	5-3 on pens
1992	MyPa	2-0	Jaro	
1993	HJK Helsinki	2-0	ROPS	
1994	TPS Turku	2-1	HJK Helsinki	

First Phase

	FC Jazz	FinnPa	Haka	HJK Helsinki	Ilves	Jaro	Kuusysi Lahti	MP Mikkeli	MyPa	RoPS	TPS Turku	TPV Tampere
FC Jazz	—	3-1	5-1	0-2	4-0	0-0	7-1	5-3	2-2	3-2	1-0	1-1
FinnPa	2-0	—	1-1	1-0	0-2	3-0	1-1	2-0	3-0	5-2	2-1	1-2
Haka	0-2	0-0	—	1-3	6-0	2-0	0-2	1-0	2-1	2-0	2-0	1-3
HJK Helsinki	1-0	0-2	2-1	—	4-0	0-0	0-0	1-0	0-2	2-1	3-2	0-2
Ilves	2-4	2-0	1-1	1-3	—	0-3	2-4	0-1	1-2	1-1	1-1	2-4
Jaro	0-1	1-0	0-1	0-1	1-1	—	3-1	1-1	0-1	1-0	2-3	0-0
Kuusysi Lahti	2-1	1-3	2-1	1-0	2-1	3-1	—	2-3	2-0	2-1	1-0	0-1
MP Mikkeli	2-5	0-0	6-0	0-0	5-1	1-1	5-0	—	1-1	1-0	0-1	3-1
MyPa	1-3	2-0	3-1	1-0	4-0	1-0	1-1	3-0	—	0-1	3-1	0-0
RoPS	2-0	1-2	1-0	0-1	1-0	0-2	1-0	3-0	1-1	—	1-0	2-0
TPS Turku	1-1	3-3	1-0	2-0	1-2	2-1	1-0	0-1	0-0	—		0-1
TPV Tampere	2-2	1-2	3-3	0-4	3-2	3-1	0-1	3-0	1-1	2-1	1-2	—

Championship Round

	FC Jazz	FinnPa	HJK Helsinki	Kuusysi Lahti	MyPa	RoPS	TPS Turku	TPV Tampere
FC Jazz	—	4-1			6-3		2-0	1-1
FinnPa		—		0-3	6-1		0-2	2-0
HJK Helsinki	0-2	0-0	—			0-2		1-0
Kuusysi Lahti	0-0		1-2	—		2-2		
MyPa			2-0	3-0	—	3-0	2-0	
RoPS	0-2	2-2				—		1-0
TPS Turku			2-4	1-2		1-3	—	
TPV Tampere				2-3	1-2		0-0	—

Marko Myyry – who plays his club football in Belgium (with Lokeren) marshalls the Fins defence against Scotland.

a good performance in the final game, a 3-1 win over Israel in Tel Aviv thanks to goals from TPS defender Ari Hiekkinen and a brace from Ari Hjelm. Hjelm is just one of an increasing number of Finns earning their living playing in continental Europe. Ajax's Jari Litmanen is probably the most famous, finishing as the top scorer in Holland with 26 goals and being voted Dutch Footballer of the Year, a fact that was sure to send the scouts scurrying back to Finland during the summer months.

The out-of-kilter season is already well under way and the first qualifiers for the 1995–96 European competitions are known, with TPS of Turku reaching the Cup-Winners' Cup following a 2-1 victory over former holders HJK. Briton Stuart Beards gave TPS the lead after 13 minutes when national goalkeeper Antii Niemi dropped a cross. Mika Nurmela, playing his last game on loan from Malmo, made it 2-0 on 73 minutes with a powerful shot. HJK scored what proved to be a consolation goal seven minutes from time through another on-loan striker, Alexei Yeremenko from Jaro.

France

The good, the bad, the ugly

For France, the 1993–94 season was the one they will want to forget as soon as possible. At the start they were in possession of their first European trophy, thanks to Marseille's Champions' Cup victory over Milan, and the national side were well on course for the World Cup finals. By the end of it Marseille had been stripped of their title, banned from Europe and forcibly relegated to the second division; hooliganism had become a national issue, and Les Bleus had crashed out of the World Cup thanks to last-minute sucker punches from Israel and Bulgaria.

As the pre-season went through its traditional paces, everything seemed quite normal – the calm before the storm perhaps. Marseille led the way in transfers, selling six players and buying seven. Manuel Amoros, Igor Dobrovolski, Pascal Olmeta, Francois Omam-Biyik, Abedi Pele and Franck Sauzee were allowed to leave, while Daniel Dutuel, Pascal Fugier, Paulo Futre, Gilles Rousset, Rui Barros, Fabrice Henry and William Prunier moved to the Stade Velodrome.

Paris Saint-Germain, desperate to prevent Marseille winning a sixth consecutive title, strengthened their already-impressive squad by signing Brazilian midfielder Rai from World champions Sao Paulo, and the promising young international Xavier Gravelaine from Caen. Monaco, not to be outdone by their two main rivals, bought Belgian midfielder Enzo Scifo from Torino and Nigerian striker Victor Ikpeba from FC Liege. Bordeaux were active in the market too, aquiring Dutch international Richard Witschge from Barcelona, Ivorian forward Youssouf Fofana from Monaco and French internationals Stephane Paille and Philippe Vercruysse from Caen and Nimes respectively.

Other pre-season moves of note included Israeli international Tal Banin's move to promoted Cannes, St Etienne brought Laurent Blanc back to France from Napoli, and Lille ended Kennet Andersson's torment at Mechelen, where the Swedish striker had been serving time in the reserves.

David Ginola of Paris Saint-Germain was voted Footballer of the Year in France.

Féderation Française de Football	
Founded:	1918
Address:	60 bis, Avenue d'Iena, F-75783 Paris Cedex 16,
Phone:	+33 1 44 31 73 00
Fax:	+33 1 47 20 82 96
UEFA Affiliation:	1954
FIFA Affiliation:	1904
National Stadium:	Parc des Princes
Capacity:	49,000
Season:	August to May
Colours:	Blue, White, Red
Change:	White, Blue, Red

The League season opened on 24 June with the investigations into the Marseille–Valenciennes bribery scandal still hanging over the country. Marseille, for their part, put their troubles behind them and opened with a 1-0 win against Lens through a goal by Basile Boli, the hero of Munich. Paris Saint-Germain went down 1-0 at old rivals Bordeaux while Monaco lost by the same score at Nantes. Nantes followed that up with wins over St Etienne and Toulouse to establish themselves as the early-season leaders, with Sochaux, Bordeaux and Cannes tucked in behind.

Indeed, Cannes were the big surprise in the opening month of the season. Coach Luis Fernandez's newly-promoted team brought that Riviera touch to the league, chalking up a fine 2-1 victory at St Etienne, an even better 2-1 win at home to Marseille, a 0-0 draw away to Bordeaux, a 2-1 win over Lille, a 2-2 draw at Strasbourg and a 1-1 draw with Sochaux in their opening six games, to go top.

Challengers Bordeaux and Nantes met on the fourth weekend of the season, with Bordeaux winning 2-0, while one of the

French Cup Final action: Christophe Cocard of Auxerre and Serge Blanc of Montpellier.

season's biggest matches produced a 1-0 win for Marseille at home to Paris Saint-Germain. There was trouble at the Parisians' next match when fighting broke out between home fans and visiting Caen supporters at the Parc des Princes. Ten policemen were injured trying to quell the violence, and the ugly scenes prompted the Interior Ministry to appoint a football security officer and the police to call for a government-level inquiry into football hooliganism.

Then, in September, the bombshell. UEFA's executive committee met and decided to bar Marseille from defending their Champions' Cup title in the wake of the allegations that the club had bribed three Valenciennes players in a league game back in May. Uproar followed and, despite club president Bernard Tapie's preliminary legal actions, Marseille, under pressure from the French Football Federation, accepted their punishment.

The FFF proposed Monaco as Marseille's replacements in the Champions' Cup, with Auxerre moving up to take Monaco's berth in the UEFA Cup, and, under threat of international suspension from FIFA, stripped Marseille of their league title and banned midfielder Jean-Jacques Eydelie and general manager Pierre Bernes *sine die*.

The off-field traumas took their toll on Marseille's players, as they could only draw 0-0 at bottom club Toulouse in their next league game, and on their fans, who invaded the pitch three minutes before the end of the home game with Metz. Marseille lost the game 3-0 and finished with just nine players after Boli and goalkeeper Fabien Barthez had been sent off.

Worse was to come for Marseille and by the end of the month they had also been barred from taking their place in the World Club Cup final against Sao Paulo and had their ground shut for one game, as punishment for the crowd trouble at the end of the game against Metz. Faced with losing millions through their banishment from the Champions' Cup, the club began selling players to help balance the books. Midfielder Jean-Marc Ferreri was the first to go, sold to Mediterranean neighbours Martigues after just one season back at the Velodrome. Without a doubt September 1993 was the blackest month in the Club's 95-year history.

Paulo Futre wore the colours of Marseille but had to be sold to ease the club's cash crisis.

Away from the machinations in Marseille, Cannes continued their fine run with wins over Angers and Lyon, but a 2-1 home defeat by an average Montpellier was a sign of things to come for Fernandez's side. Paris Saint-Germain took over from Cannes at the top with a 4-0 home win over Auxerre.

Internationally, the French side beat Finland 2-0 in a World Cup qualifier to stay on course for the finals while the European campaigns opened with a mixed bag of results. Monaco, Paris Saint-Germain and Bordeaux went through but Auxerre and Nantes were knocked out of the UEFA Cup by Tenerife and Valencia respectively.

October opened with a 2-1 win for Marseille at Lille, but Tapie was forced to reveal that Alen Boksic and Paolo Futre would have to be sold to ease the severe cash-flow problems. Paris Saint-Germain stayed on top with three consecutive one-goal wins over Lens, Metz and Cannes repectively, the latter slipping to sixth place as the pressure started to mount. Monaco also made strides up the table, rounding off the month with a 7-0 thrashing of Martigues as Youri Djorkaeff scored four goals. But,

to add to the sense of gloom hanging over the country, the national side went down to a shock, last-minute 3-2 defeat at home to Israel in the World Cup qualifiers when only a point was required to guarantee qualification for the USA finals. Monaco carried the flag in Europe though to the UEFA Champions' League stage with a fine 4-2 aggregate win over Steaua Bucharest. Paris Saint-Germain also progressed into the quarter-finals of the Cup-Winners' Cup with a 6-0 whitewash of Romania's Universitatea Craiova. Bordeaux kept French interests alive in the UEFA Cup by overcoming Switzerland's Servette.

November started with a 1-1 draw between Monaco and Paris Saint-Germain, allowing Bordeaux to move into second place following a 2-0 win over Lyon as Marseille slumped to defeats against Lyon and Auxerre. Monaco opened their Champions' League account in fine style with a 4-1 demolition of Spartak Moscow, but then went down 2-0 in Barcelona. French interest in the UEFA Cup ended when Bordeaux lost 3-0 in Karlsruhe.

Then, to compound all the problems at Marseille, the national team self-destructed in their final World Cup qualifier. Needing just a point at home to Bulgaria to qualify, the French took a 1-0 lead through émigré Eric Cantona before allowing Emil Kostadinov to equalise. That would have been enough but, with the last kick of the game, Kostadinov grabbed a second to send France – hosts of the 1998 tournament – tumbling down their group table and missing out on the finals. Manager Gerard Houllier resigned shortly afterwards, and was replaced by Aime Jacquet.

A bad month closed with Marseille regaining some momentum with a 3-0 win at Martigues, where new Brazilian striker Anderson 'Sonny' Da Silva, signed from the Zurich-based Grasshopper Club, scored on his debut. But Paris Saint-Germain still led the way with a 1-0 win over St. Etienne.

Paris Saint-Germain continued where they left off in December, wins over Lille and Strasbourg taking them six points clear of Bordeaux at the top. Da Silva's arrival sparked Marseille into life and the champions closed their year of disaster with wins over Cannes, Le Havre and Nantes to draw level with Bordeaux in second place. The Girondins club maintained their position with an important 1-0 win over Monaco, while little Auxerre moved into fourth place with a 2-2 draw at Angers.

As the curtain came to fall on a traumatic year, two unusual transfers were completed. Strasbourg sold Czech midfielder Ivan Hasek to Japan's Sanfrecce Hiroshima and Metz, crippled by an injury crisis, re-signed Yugoslav midfielder Dragoljub Brnovic, who had been without a club since Metz released him in 1992!

League action began again in the second week of January and provided *Le Crunch* between Paris Saint-Germain and Marseille at the Parc des Princes. Guerin put the Parisians into an 11th-minute lead, but an equaliser by Voller three minutes later gave Marseille a share of the points, and put a temporary brake on Paris Saint-Germain's title charge. Bordeaux, in third place, slumped to a 4-1 defeat at rising Nantes, while Auxerre stayed in contention with a 2-0 win against Metz.

But most of January's headlines were hogged, inevitably, by Marseille. A few days after the draw in Paris, the French Federation asked the Swiss FA for more information regarding

FRANCE

International Results 1993–94

Date	Opponents	Result	Venue	Comp.	Scorers
22/8/93	Sweden	1-1	Stockholm	WCQ6	Sauzee (77)
8/9/93	Finland	2-0	Tampere	WCQ6	Blanc (47), Papin (55 pen)
13/10/93	Israel	2-3	Paris	WCQ6	Sauzee (29), Ginola (39)
17/11/93	Bulgaria	1-2	Paris	WCQ6	Cantona (31)
16/2/94	Italy	1-0	Naples	Friendly	Djorkaeff (44)
22/3/94	Chile	3-1	Lyon	Friendly	Papin (7), Djorkaeff (35), Martins (50)
26/5/94	Australia	1-0	Kobe	Kirin Cup	Cantona (42)
29/5/94	Japan	4-1	Tokyo	Kirin Cup	Djorkaeff (16), Papin (18), Ginola (53, 55)

National Record	P	W	D	L	F	A
European Championship	62	31	15	16	118	76
World Cup Finals	34	15	5	14	71	56
World Cup Qualifiers	69	41	9	19	146	62

Final League Table 1993–94

	P	W	D	L	F	A	Pts
Paris Saint-Germain	38	24	11	3	54	22	59
Marseille	38	19	13	6	56	33	51
AJ Auxerre	38	18	10	10	54	29	46
Bordeaux	38	19	8	11	54	37	46
FC Nantes	38	17	11	10	47	32	45
AS Cannes	38	16	12	10	50	43	44
Montpellier	38	15	13	10	41	37	43
Lyon	38	17	8	13	38	40	42
AS Monaco	38	14	13	11	52	36	41
Lens	38	13	13	12	49	40	39
St. Etienne	38	12	13	13	38	36	37
Metz	38	12	13	13	36	35	37
Strasbourg	38	10	14	14	43	47	34
Sochaux	38	10	13	15	39	48	33
Lille	38	8	16	14	41	52	32
Caen	38	12	7	19	29	54	31
Le Havre	38	7	15	16	29	48	29
Martigues	38	5	17	16	37	58	27
Toulouse	38	4	15	19	26	60	23
Angers	38	4	13	21	37	63	21

Leading Scorers
- 20 Roger BOLI (Lens)
-    Youri DJORKAEFF (AS Monaco)
-    Nicolas OUEDEC (FC Nantes)
- 18 Franck PRIOU (Cannes)
- 16 ANDERSON da SILVA (Marseille)

Promotions and Relegations
Promoted: Nice, Stade Rennes, SC Bastia
Relegated: Marseille, Toulouse, Angers

Five-Year Records League 1-2-3 and Cup Winners

League Results

	1st	Pts	2nd	Pts	3rd	Pts
1990	Marseille	53	Bordeaux	51	Monaco	46
1991	Marseille	55	Monaco	51	Auxerre	48
1992	Marseille	58	Monaco	52	Paris Saint-Germain	47
1993	Marseille	55	Paris Saint-Germain	51	Monaco	51
1994	Paris Saint-Germain	59	Marseille	51	Auxerre	46

Cup Final Results

1990	Montpellier	2-1	Racing Club Paris
1991	Monaco	1-0	Marseille
1992	*Competition cancelled after stand collapsed at Bastia.*		
1993	Paris Saint-Germain	3-0	Nantes
1994	Auxerre	3-0	Montpellier

Brazilian striker Anderson Da Silva's move from Servette. French media reports suggested that Servette had agreed to continue paying part of Da Silva's wages, which is strictly forbidden. The scandal was followed by a very narrow escape in the French Cup, where Marseille were expected to deal with third division Brive easily. They couldn't force a breakthrough, and had to be content with a 4-2 victory on penalty kicks. Penalties also figured in Bordeaux's victory against Strasbourg, Montpellier's win against Saint Malo, and in St. Etienne's defeat at Pau.

The main cup headlines, though, were made by non-league side Cote Chaude Sportif. The amateurs attracted a 35,000 crowd to St. Etienne's Stadium to see Paris Saint-Germain knock 10 goals past them. However, it all ended in tears as seven of the Sportif side quit following an argument over the distribution of profit from the cup run. The seven demanded bonuses in cash while the rest wanted the money pooled to go on a group holiday!

With penalties on and off the field out of the way, Marseille won the south coast derby game with Monaco 2-1 at the Velodrome, but had defender Angloma sent off — for the second week running — in a bad-tempered match. Angloma, for his sins, was suspended by the FFF for four games. Relegation-threatened Lille also suffered the wrath of the Federation and were hit with a £500 fine after being found guilty of not being in control of their crowd – after a fan had thrown a bag of chips at a visiting player back in December!

Coupe De France

Coupe De France

32nd Finals

Ales v Perpignan	2-1
Bourges v Chatellerault	0-0 † 5-6 on pens
Brive v Marseille	0-0 † 2-4 on pens
Chateauroux v Anges	1-0
Corquefou v Lorient	0-1
Cote-Chaude v Paris Saint-Germain	0-10
CS Avion v Lons-le-Saunier	1-1 † 3-1 on pens
Epinal v Sochaux	1-2 †
Evry v Charleville	0-1
Fecamp v Valenciennes	1-1 † 3-4 on pens
Forbach v Sedan	0-1
Guingamp v AS Cannes	3-2 †
Laval v Rouen	2-0
Le Harve v Beauvais	2-3
Lille v Rennes	1-2 †
Lorient-Pontivy v AJ Auxerre	0-2
Lyon v Nimes	2-0
Lyon-La-Duchere v Rodez	1-0
Martigues v Bastia	0-2
Murat v AS Monaco	0-1
Pau v Saint Etienne	1-1 † 4-3 on pens
Racing 92 v Paris FC	2-1
Saint-Gratien/Saint-Leu v Metz	0-1
Saint-Malo v Montpellier	0-0 † 2-4 on pens
Sens v Le Mans	0-4
Sete v Caen	1-0
Strasbourg v Bordeaux	1-1 † 2-3 on pens
Trelaze v Lens	0-5
Vaulx-en-Velin v FC Nantes	0-2
Viry-Chatillon v Libourne	0-1
Vitrolles v Red Star	0-4

16th Finals

Ales v Lyon-Duchere	3-0
Auxerre v Sedan	4-2
Avions v Paris Saint-Germain	1-4 †
Beauvais v Montpellier	0-3
Chateauroux v Racing 92	1-1 † 1-4 on pens
Chatellerault v Metz	3-1 †
Guingamp v Red Star	2-1
Laval v Lyon	1-1 † 3-1 on pens
Le Mans v Bordeaux	0-0 † 7-8 on pens
Lens v Bastia	3-0
Lorient v FC Nantes	0-2 †
Pau v Charleville	1-1 † 6-7 on pens
Rennes v Valenciennes	1-1 † 3-4 on pens
Sete v Libourne	1-0
Sochaux v Marseille	0-1
Toulouse v AS Monaco	0-2

8th Finals

Chatellerault v Racing 92	0-1
Guingamp v Paris Saint-Germain	0-1
Laval v Montpellier	1-2
Lens v Charleville	3-1 †
AS Monaco v Marseille	0-0 † 3-4 on pens
FC Nantes v Bordeaux	1-0
Sete v AJ Auxerre	1-4
Valenciennes v Ales	2-1

Quarter-Finals

Marseille v Montpellier	0-0 † 3-4 on pens
FC Nantes v Valenciennes	3-1
Paris Saint-Germain v Lens	1-2
Racing 92 v AJ Auxerre	1-2

Semi-Finals

AJ Auxerre v FC Nantes	1-0
Lens v Montpellier	0-2

Final

AJ Auxerre 3 Montpellier 0

Saib (17), Baticle (48), Martins (86)

Att: 45,189   *Ref:* Batta

AJ Auxerre: Charbonnier, Goma, Silvestre, Verlaat, Mahe, Guerreiro, Saib, Martins, Cocard (Laslandes 87), Baticle, Vahirua (Rabarivony 86).

Montpellier: Barrabe, Reuzeau (Alicarte 57), Der Zakarian, Laurey, Blanc, Perilleux (Divert 57), Bonnissel, Carotti, Rizetto, Sanchez, Lefevre.

Marseille made some ground on Paris Saint-Germain in the league after the leaders had dropped a point in a goalless draw with Montpellier in February, but apart from that the table remained largely unchanged. Attention turned to the national side who regained some much-needed pride after the Bulgarian debacle with a fine 1-0 win against Italy in Naples. Djorkaeff scored the only goal of the game and Cantona took the captain's armband for the first time.

March began with European appointments for Monaco at home to Galatasaray, whom they comprehensively beat 3-0 to go top of the UEFA Champions' League Group A ahead of Barcelona, and for Paris Saint-Germain, who recorded a splendid 1-0 win away to Real Madrid in the quarter-final, first leg, of the Cup-Winners' Cup. In the league, Da Silva scored two more for Marseille, in a 3-2 win over Lille, while Paris Saint-Germain – drained by their efforts in Madrid – were held to a 2-2 draw at home by lowly Martigues. They bounced back, though, with a 2-1 win against Lens, while Marseille's challenge slipped further with a 1-1 draw at Strasbourg. Then, in the European returns, Paris Saint-Germain held on for a 1-1 draw to beat Real 2-1 on aggregate, as Monaco completed a double over Galatasaray in the Champions' League, winning 2-0 in Istanbul to retain first place. A busy month continued with the third round of the French Cup, and wins for Racing Nantes, Lens, Montpellier, Valenciennes, Auxerre and Paris Saint-Germain. But the tie of the round was Monaco v Marseille, which Marseille won on penalties after a goalless draw.

Bad news followed for Bordeaux, when former president Claude Bez was found guilty of fraud and sentenced to two years

Sylvain Deplace of Lyon.

in prison, with one year suspended. He was also fined £200,000 for embezzling £1m from a contract to build a new club training centre. The Girondins still won 3-0 at home to Caen to keep the pressure on the leaders. Paris Saint-Germain, rising to the challenge, won 1-0 against Metz while Marseille, fading down the home stretch, drew 1-1 with Montpellier.

The national side, rebuilding after the World Cup failure, beat Chile 3-1 in Lyon with the opening goal coming from Papin in his 50th appearance. March concluded with a 0-0 draw for Monaco against Moscow Spartak, guaranteeing them second place in their Champions' League group and safe passage into the semi-finals, but Paris Saint-Germain were held to a 1-1 draw at home to Arsenal in the first leg of their Cup-Winners' Cup semi-final.

Paris Saint-Germain began April with a 2-1 win against Cannes, extending their unbeaten run to 27 matches, a record for the French league. Their last league defeat had been at Marseille on 15 August, and the record bettered their previous best of 26 in a row back in 1986 the year they won their first and only previous French title. The record was celebrated with a seven-point lead at the top as Marseille lost ground and with only six games remaining the title was beckoning. Surprisingly, the following Tuesday, Paris Saint-Germain lost 3-0 at Nantes, who were mounting a serious challenge of their own for a place in Europe. Marseille and Bordeaux kept up the pressure as best they could, both winning at home against sides in relegation trouble.

Monaco and Paris Saint-Germain were excused league duty the following weekend to concentrate on their European campaigns. Monaco lost 1-0 at home to Barcelona in a meaningless match — both were already through — but Paris Saint-Germain could find no way past a solid Arsenal defence, and went down to an early goal and out of the Cup-Winners' Cup. Fortunately for them, neither of their nearest rivals could take advantage, Marseille losing 1-0 at Caen, Bordeaux going down 4-2 at Lyon.

Paris Saint-Germain then extended their lead over Marseille to six points with a 1-1 draw at home against Monaco and, six days later, were virtually assured of the title when the French Federation announced their judgement on the Marseille-Valenciennes bribery scandal.

Marseille were found guilty, and as punishment would be forcibly relegated to division two at the end of the season. President Tapie and former secretary Bernes were banned for life,

French Championship Results 1993–94

	Angers	AJ Auxerre	Bordeaux	Caen	AS Cannes	Le Harve	Lens	Lille	Lyon	Marseille	Martigues	Metz	AS Monaco	Montpellier	FC Nantes	Paris-Saint Germain	St. Etienne	Sochaux	Strasbourg	Toulouse
Angers	—	2-2	1-3	2-0	1-1	0-0	1-2	1-2	3-1	0-1	1-3	1-2	1-1	2-3	0-0	1-1	1-1	1-2	1-3	0-0
AJ Auxerre	0-0	—	0-1	1-0	0-0	3-0	1-0	5-0	3-2	2-2	3-0	2-0	4-0	3-1	3-1	0-0	3-0	1-0	2-1	5-1
Bordeaux	1-0	3-0	—	3-0	0-0	2-1	4-2	2-1	2-0	1-0	1-1	2-0	1-0	1-1	2-0	1-0	1-2	4-1	2-0	2-0
Caen	2-3	1-0	1-0	—	1-1	1-1	1-0	2-3	1-0	1-0	4-1	1-1	0-1	0-0	0-0	0-2	1-0	2-1	3-1	1-0
AS Cannes	4-3	2-1	2-1	3-0	—	1-0	3-1	2-1	1-0	2-1	2-1	2-0	0-2	2-0	4-0	0-1	1-0	1-1	1-1	2-1
Le Harve	2-1	1-0	0-3	1-2	3-1	—	1-1	1-0	0-1	1-3	2-0	0-1	1-0	0-0	0-0	0-2	0-0	0-0	0-1	1-1
Lens	0-1	1-1	1-0	2-0	2-1	5-1	—	1-1	2-0	2-3	1-1	2-0	3-3	2-1	1-1	1-2	3-1	2-0	0-0	4-0
Lille	1-1	1-1	1-1	3-1	1-0	2-2	0-0	—	2-1	1-2	1-1	0-4	1-1	0-0	0-0	0-2	0-2	3-1	1-1	3-0
Lyon	1-1	1-0	4-2	2-0	2-2	1-1	1-2	0-0	—	1-0	0-0	2-0	1-0	3-2	2-1	1-3	1-0	1-0	2-1	1-0
Marseille	2-1	0-3	3-1	2-0	3-1	1-1	1-0	3-2	3-0	—	0-0	0-3	2-1	1-1	3-1	1-0	3-1	1-1	2-1	5-1
Martigues	0-0	0-1	0-0	4-1	4-0	3-0	1-2	2-2	0-1	0-3	—	1-1	1-3	1-1	1-2	1-1	2-1	1-1	0-3	1-1
Metz	2-0	0-0	1-0	2-1	0-0	2-0	2-1	1-1	0-1	0-0	0-0	—	1-1	1-1	2-0	0-1	0-1	1-1	2-1	1-0
AS Monaco	3-0	0-1	3-2	3-0	2-0	1-1	0-0	1-0	1-1	0-0	7-0	1-1	—	1-2	1-0	1-1	1-1	2-0	2-1	3-0
Montpellier	2-1	1-0	0-0	0-0	2-1	2-1	0-0	1-3	1-1	0-0	1-0	3-2	0-3	—	1-0	0-0	3-0	1-0	4-0	3-1
FC Nantes	2-1	1-2	4-1	1-0	0-0	3-1	1-2	2-0	1-0	0-0	2-1	2-0	1-0	0-0	—	3-0	1-0	2-0	2-2	4-0
Paris Saint-Germain	3-0	4-0	4-1	2-0	2-1	0-0	1-0	2-1	0-0	1-1	2-2	1-0	1-1	1-0	1-0	—	1-0	1-0	2-0	1-0
St. Etienne	2-0	2-0	0-0	5-0	1-2	0-0	0-0	2-1	3-0	0-0	1-1	1-0	2-0	2-0	1-1	1-2	—	0-0	0-0	2-2
Sochaux	4-1	1-0	2-2	0-0	1-1	4-2	1-1	1-0	0-1	1-1	1-0	2-1	2-0	2-1	1-1	1-2	3-2	—	1-3	0-0
Strasbourg	2-2	1-1	0-2	3-0	2-2	0-3	2-0	1-1	0-1	1-1	3-0	0-0	1-1	0-1	0-3	2-2	2-0	2-0	—	1-0
Toulouse	2-1	0-0	0-0	0-1	1-2	0-0	1-1	1-1	2-0	0-0	2-2	2-2	2-1	0-0	0-3	1-2	1-2	3-2	0-0	—

and the three players involved, Robert, Burruchaga and Eydelie, were suspended for two years each. But, seemingly as a sweetener, the FFF declared that Marseille would be eligible to play in Europe in the 1994–95 season if they finished in a qualifying position. That move did little to appease the outraged Marseille fans — who felt their team had suffered enough — and the forthcoming Cup tie against Montpellier was postponed for fear of crowd trouble.

The other Cup quarter-finals went ahead as planned, with Auxerre and Nantes going through, along with Lens — surprise 2-1 victors at Paris Saint-Germain. In the league, the Parisians marched on. A 2-0 win at Le Havre put them in sight of the winning post in spite of a stubborn 3-0 win for Marseille against Lyon. In the Champions' League, Monaco's challenge ended in the semi-finals with a comprehensive 3-0 defeat by Milan. As late replacements for Marseille, however, Monaco had given a good account of themselves in the competition.

Then, on the last Saturday in April, Paris Saint-Germain made sure of the title, with two games to spare, thanks to a 1-0 home win over relegation-bound Toulouse. The title was theirs for only the second time in their history, rubbishing the doubters who said they were boring and would lose out to Marseille.

For Marseille, a turbulent season was doomed to end trophyless when they lost their rearranged Cup quarter-final to Montpellier, on penalties. They did at least gain some consolation by finishing as runners-up in the league, giving them a place in the UEFA Cup, despite their relegation. They were joined in that competition by Bordeaux, who finished third, and Nantes, who finished fifth. The destination of the remaining UEFA Cup place would have to wait until after the Cup Final, which Montpellier reached by beating Lens 2-0 in the semis. They were joined by little Auxerre, 1-0 winners over Nantes, who had two men sent off, leaving Cannes sweating on an Auxerre victory for them to take the last UEFA Cup place.

Auxerre did not fail them. Guy Roux's team won 3-0 to give him his first trophy after a glorious career at the little club. For Cannes, the outcome gave them a first European appearance, and there was more drama to come for coach Luis Fernandez on the last day of the season. Paris Saint-Germain, celebrating their title in a party atmosphere at home to Bordeaux, romped to a 4-1 win, and then announced that coach Jorge was sacked! Fernandez, a former Paris Saint-Germain stalwart, was then revealed as the coach for the new season, a fine reward for his efforts with Cannes.

At the bottom, Angers and Toulouse joined Marseille in the second division, with Rennes, Nice and Bastia winning promotion. One final twist in an incredible French season: Marseille's enforced relegation meant that their local rivals, Martigues, stayed up despite finishing third from bottom, which would usually mean the drop, and a French court ruled that Tapie could return to Marseille as president. Many eyes will be on the second division during the 1994–95 season, that's for sure!

Germany

Bayern come good

German football started the season celebrating 30 years of existence of the first national league, the Bundesliga. Up until 1963 the championship had been organised on a regional basis – at the conclusion of the programme in the geographically divided groups the winners and runners-up played off in two sections of four teams each against the other contestants home and away. The two group winners then disputed the grand all-German final for the title.

The creation of a national First Division, and the introduction of full-time professional football at the same time, have been instrumental in turning Germany into one of the world's leading soccer powers. The national side now had the best record in football: three times world champions and three times runners-up, twice European champions and twice runners-up.

The 1993–94 season raised expectations of another dramatic finish just as in the previous three years. In the 1992–93 campaign record champions Bayern Munich, having led for 32 out of the 34 rounds, were pipped at the post by Werder Bremen. But the northerners were not generally rated strong enough to successfully defend their crown and were the only club among the top outfits not to sign any noteworthy newcomers.

Many pundits were tipping Borussia Dortmund following their acquisition of the international striker Karlheinz Riedle from Italy's Lazio for the German record fee of nearly £4.5m. He linked up with international midfielder Matthias Sammer, who had returned from Internazionale six months earlier and at £3.4m became the second most expensive Bundesliga player. But since Borussia made a record £10m profit from the UEFA Cup alone the previous year, they could afford to splash out.

Main interest centred as usual on Bayern Munich, who engaged the Colombian international striker Adolfo Valencia from Independiente Santa Fe for £2.5m and Marcel Witeczek

Andreas Thom of Bayer Leverkusen.

from Kaiserslautern for £2.3m. Another fancied contender for the title, Eintracht Frankfurt, hired the highly regarded Italian-born midfielder Maurizio Gaudino (ex VfB Stuttgart) and the Polish international forward Jan Furtok from Hamburg SV.

Two oldies whose return enriched the Bundesliga were the World Cup hero Andy Brehme (33) who after a successful spell with Internazionale and later with Spain's Zaragoza returned home to finish his career with one of his former clubs, Kaiserslautern, and Bernd Schuster, also 33, the great enigma of German football. After 13 years in Spain with the Big Three, Real Madrid, Barcelona and Atletico Madrid, he decided to try one last fling in the Bundesliga.

For the first time many clubs were able to compete with top Italian and Spanish clubs in being able to afford top-class players and the wages they demanded. The 1993–94 season was starting with the Bundesliga showing a turnover of over £130m – a far cry from the inaugural £7m – satellite television in particular providing the main portion of the jam, with every one of the 18 Bundesliga clubs collecting £1.6m even before the first ball was kicked. No wonder that the players no longer look over the Alps to the 'promised' land of Italy, but elect to stay home. Not one

Deutscher Fussball-Bund	
Founded:	1900 (1948 for East German DFB)
Address:	Otto-Fleck-Schneise 6, Postfach 710265, D-60528, Frankfurt am Main
Phone:	+49 69 678 80
Fax:	+49 69 678 82 66
UEFA Affiliation:	1954
FIFA Affiliation:	1904–1946, 1950 (1952–90 for the East German DFB)
National Stadium:	Olympiastadion, Munich
Capacity:	73,000
Season:	August to May
Colours:	White, Black, White
Change:	Green, White, White

Thomas Helmer, Bayern Munich, scores the 'goal that wasn't' against Nuremberg.

current international had joined an Italian club by the start of the season.

The season on the pitch got under away in August and the early rounds were dominated by Eintracht Frankfurt who, under new team manager Klaus Toppmoller, were holding off champions Werder Bremen and cup holders Bayer Leverkusen on goal difference. Two rounds of the DFB Cup were also played. The first round comprised just 12 pairings, while 52 teams received a bye into the next stage. It was then that the sparks began to fly. The biggest sensation was Borussia Dortmund's 1-0 home defeat by second division Carl Zeiss Jena.

September set the alarm bells ringing with the disclosure that a record 25 players had been sent off in the first 63 Bundesliga matches. The most contentious factor proved to be the two-tone yellow and red cards introduced in 1991. A player who has been booked but commits another, perhaps merely technical, offence is shown the double-coloured card and sent off. He is automatically banned for the next game and no further disciplinary proceedings are taken against him. If, however, he is shown the red card, then he must appear before a commission and usually a lengthy suspension follows.

In the championship Eintracht continued to set the pace, pursued by Werder. The champions remarkably had no current German internationals in their ranks, all their key men being foreigners: Andy Herzog (Austrian) as schemer, Rune Bratseth (Norwegian) as libero and Wynton Rufer (Swiss-New Zealander) as striker. Bayern found themselves faltering after two defeats, while a highly publicised row between superstar Lothar Matthaus and general manager Uli Hoeness was still simmering.

In the cup Eintracht crashed out to newly promoted Freiburg after extra time. The amateur section of Bayern created huge embarrassment in Koln with a win, while Werder Bremen needed a penalty shoot-out to beat the amateurs of Kickers Offenbach. The month ended with a bad knee injury to Frankfurt's Ghanaian striker Anthony Yeboah, who was then the league's top scorer.

Eintracht, who had made their best start to the season in 31 years, soon felt Yeboah's absence when they slumped to their first defeat, at the hands of MSV Duisburg. Promoted for the second time in three seasons, the unfashionable side without stars remained unbeaten after 10 matches. They caused the first big sensation by winning 5-1 away at champions Werder Bremen. The biggest disappointment, though, were Borussia Dortmund, whose team manager Ottmar Hitzfeld lamented: 'The pressure is too great. Our midfield lacks ideas and when we concede a goal some players lose their heads.'

German club football earned praise when for the first time in 13 years all six contestants survived the opening round of the three European competitions. Andreas Kopke of FC Nuremberg won the Footballer of the Year award and became the national team's goalkeeper. Kopke polled a massive 194 votes from sports journalists while Austrian midfielder Andy Herzog (Werder) finished as runner-up, collecting 73 votes. Yeboah got 64.

In the domestic cup fourth round Duisburg were knocked out by Rot-Weiss Essen from the second division, while Bayer Leverkusen scraped through against the amateurs of FC Augsburg on penalties.

The third week of November marked the halfway stage of the season with 17 matches gone. Top of the table Eintracht became the 'autumn champions' – this is regarded as a lucky omen for so far 20 out of the 30 half-time Bundesliga leaders had gone on to win the title.

By contrast Bayern Munich looked back on a bleak November having suffered three hammer blows. Within eight days they were dumped out of the UEFA Cup by an effervescent Norwich City, whom they totally underestimated. Next they lost the Bavarian derby to struggling Nuremberg by 2-0. And finally this expensive collection of stars stumbled out the DFB Cup to another unfancied opponent, Dynamo Dresden, by 2-1.

While Munich was plunged into mourning, euphoria enveloped Karlsruhe. The European debutants surprised themselves and the whole country by their triumph over Valencia in the UEFA Cup. After losing the away leg by 3-1, KSC demolished the then Spanish league leaders by 7-0 before an ecstatic full house of 25,000. It was the greatest night in the club's 99-year history. Karlsruhe's hero was striker Edgar Schmitt, who scored four goals. 'The greatest achievement in my sporting career,' he said.

The first half of the season produced an average gate of 27,761, the best since 1977–78 when it reached 28,414. More goals had been scored – 466 as against 459 at the corresponding stage last year. Although there were 18 red/yellow cards (last season 15) and 20 red (19), there was a significant drop in bookings from 627 to 527.

German clubs covered themselves with glory in the European tournaments, the remaining five having reached the later stages. Werder Bremen became the first German outfit to reach the prestigious and highly lucrative Champions' League and they figured in the most astonishing comeback in the competition thus far. Trailing by 3-0 at home at half-time, they hit five goals in 24 minutes to win in sensational fashion 5-3, against Belgian champions RSC Anderlecht. The club were revelling in a financial bonanza and paying their players in the Champions' League

Lothar Matthaus, Bayern Munich, celebrates with the Budesliga trophy.

£2,000 per point – small fry compared with the £220,000 per point the club received from the UEFA Champions' League pool!

Bayer Leverkusen rewarded their men with a record bonus of £20,000 each for reaching the last eight in the Cup-Winners' Cup. However, Leverkusen's demise at Dynamo Dresden on penalties in the DFB Cup quarter-finals was a big surprise for the holders.

The national side looked back on a highly satisfactory first half of the season. After drawing 1-1 with Tunisia the Germans beat Uruguay 5-0 and Brazil 2-1. In this match captain Matthaus overtook Franz Beckenbauer's German record of 103 caps, while Brehme celebrated his comeback into the national colours, his 75th.

In the Bundesliga three further rounds were played before the winter break began. Leverkusen were then ahead of Frankfurt on goal difference. The break was scheduled between 11 December and 12 February, during which the national side embarked on a trip to America where they lost to Argentina 2-1, beat the USA 3-0 and drew with Mexico 0-0. The media described the trip largely as an 'irrelevance', but team manager Berti Vogts was

International Results 1993–94

Date	Opponents	Result	Venue	Comp.	Scorers
22/9/93	Tunisia	1-1	Tunis	Friendly	Moller (55)
13/10/93	Uruguay	5-0	Karlsruhe	Friendly	Buchwald (8), Moller (11, 88), Riedle (13), Kirsten (70)
17/11/93	Brazil	2-1	Koln	Friendly	Buchwald (37), Moller (40)
15/12/93	Argentina	1-2	Miami	Friendly	Moller (8)
18/12/93	United States	3-0	Palo Alto	Friendly	Moller (15), Kuntz (79), Thom (89)
22/12/93	Mexico	0-0	Mexico City	Friendly	
23/3/94	Italy	2-1	Stuttgart	Friendly	Klinsmann (45,47)
27/4/94	United Arab Emirates	2-0	Abu Dhabi	Friendly	Kirsten (66), Gaudino (90)
29/5/94	Republic of Ireland	0-2	Hanover	Friendly	
2/6/94	Austria	5-1	Vienna	Friendly	Sammer (22), Moller (50, 66), Klinsmann (62), Basler (90)
8/6/94	Canada	2-0	Montreal	Friendly	Sammer (31), Voller (90)
17/6/94	Bolivia	1-0	Chicago	WCFC	Klinsmann (60)
21/6/94	Spain	1-1	Chicago	WCFC	Klinsmann (47)
27/6/94	South Korea	3-2	Dallas	WCFC	Klinsmann (12, 36), Riedle (20)
2/7/94	Belgium	3-2	Chicago	WCF2	Voller (5, 39), Klinsmann (10)
10/7/94	Bulgaria	1-2	New Jersey	WCFQ	Matthaus (48 pen)

pleased to have had the opportunity to assemble his World Cup candidates together and foster team spirit. The clubs allowed their players just a few weeks off over the Christmas and New Year holidays before all reported back for training in the first week in January. Throughout that month all Bundesliga teams took part in a series of indoor tournaments; most of them also organised training camps in warmer climates.

The biggest story was the managerial change at Bayern Munich, where team boss Erich Ribbeck was relieved of his duties and vice-president Beckenbauer took over until the end of the season. Germany's most famous footballer intended to bring some order to the disjointed team, confused by Ribbeck's constant tactical switches and personnel changes. Beckenbauer – the only man to win the World Cup both as captain and manager – worked his charges hard in training, but started with a 3-1 defeat by struggling VfB Stuttgart. Still, the largest and most expensive squad in the Bundesliga staged a recovery to remain in contention for the title. Main challengers Eintracht Frankfurt borrowed former international midfielder Thomas Doll from Italy's Lazio, while Yeboah, having recovered from torn ligaments, began scoring goals again.

The restart in February brought another sensation: MSV Duisburg took over at the top for the first time in 20 years. They became the only leaders in the Bundesliga's 30-year existence with a negative goal tally, 29-30! But their next match was against Bayern Munich, who outclassed them to win by 4-0. Bayern continued to set the pace, taking advantage of the temporary loss of form of their main pursuers, Frankfurt and Bayer Leverkusen. Failure in European tournaments badly affected morale of both these clubs.

March was a bad month for the German Euro contenders. Leverkusen (Cup-Winners' Cup) failed against Portugal's Benfica on the away goals rule. Frankfurt (UEFA Cup) were eliminated by outsiders SV Austria Salzburg in a penalty shoot-out, the first time after 18 attempts that a German team had been put out by Austrian opposition. And Borussia Dortmund lost at home to Internazionale by 3-1, so that even the unexpected 2-1 win in Italy was not enough. Karlsruhe SC did reach the semi-finals but also went out against Salzburg, on away goals. The sorry exodus was completed by Werder Bremen, playing in the UEFA Champions' League, who failed to advance into the semi-finals following a catastrophic 5-0 home thrashing by Porto. Their superb fight back against Anderlecht was soon forgotten. Consolation for the 'Werderaner' came in the DFB Cup in which they reached the final, thanks to a 2-0 away victory over Dresden Dynamo. The other finalists were Rot Weiss Essen, who beat another second division outfit, Tennis Borussia Berlin.

Frankfurt created a stir when they sacked their controversial goalkeeper and captain, Uli Stein. The former international, at nearly 40 the oldest player in the league, had alienated two national team managers, while his rows with team-mates repeatedly upset the atmosphere in the dressing room. Team chief Klaus Toppmoller sided with Stein, and he too was dismissed. Stein was promptly snapped up by Hamburg after seven years at Frankfurt.

The national team continued their World Cup preparations with an impressive 2-1 win against Italy in Stuttgart. Vogts sprang a surprise by recalling the much-maligned defender, Thomas Berthold. He was last picked nearly three years before in a European Championship qualifying tie against Wales in Cardiff and was sent off. He then had problems at Bayern and eventually was transferred to VfB Stuttgart during the summer of 1993. There he became a key man in defence.

The preparations were seriously disrupted by the cancellation of the international against England. This was scheduled for Berlin on 20 April, coinciding unfortunately with Adolf Hitler's birthday. Manager Vogts was upset over this turn of events, but anxious to

GERMANY

Final League Table 1993–94

	P	W	D	L	F	A	Pts
Bayern Munich	34	17	10	7	68	37	44
Kaiserslautern	34	18	7	9	64	36	43
Bayer Leverkusen	34	14	11	9	60	47	39
Borussia Dortmund	34	15	9	10	49	45	39
Eintracht Frankfurt	34	15	8	11	57	41	38
Karlsruhe SC	34	14	10	10	46	43	38
VfB Stuttgart	34	13	11	10	51	43	37
Werder Bremen	34	13	10	11	51	44	36
MSV Duisberg	34	14	8	12	41	52	36
Borussia M'gladbach	34	14	7	13	65	59	35
FC Koln	34	14	6	14	49	51	34
Hamburg SV	34	13	8	13	48	52	34
Dynamo Dresden	34	10	10	14	33	44	30
Schalke 04	34	10	9	15	38	50	29
SC Freiburg	34	10	8	16	54	57	28
FC Nuremberg	34	10	8	16	41	55	28
Wattenscheid	34	6	11	17	48	70	23
VfB Leipzig	34	3	11	20	32	69	17

Top Scorers

- 18 Stefan KUNTZ (Kaiserslautern)
   Anthony YEBOAH (Eintracht Frankfurt)
- 17 Stephane CHAPUISAT (Borussia Dortmund)
   Tony POLSTER (Koln)
- 16 PAULO SERGIO (Bayer Leverkusen)
- 15 Thomas VON HEESEN (Hamburg SV)
   Marek LESNIAK (Wattenscheid)
- 13 Souleyman SANE (Wattenscheid)
   Sergio Fabian ZARATE (FC Nuremberg)
   Ulf KIRSTEN (Bayer Leverkusen)

Promotions and Relegations

Promoted: VfL Bochum, Bayer Uerdingen, 1860 Munich.
Relegated: FC Nuremberg, Wattenscheid, VfB Leipzig.

National Record

	P	W	D	L	F	A
Pre-war record						
World Cup Finals	6	3	1	2	14	13
World Cup Qualifiers	4	4	0	0	20	2
East Germany – Complete record	P	W	D	L	F	A
European Championship	46	20	12	14	76	57
World Cup Finals	6	2	2	2	5	5
World Cup Qualifiers	47	22	8	17	87	65
West Germany – Complete record	P	W	D	L	F	A
European Championship	50	30	15	5	99	31
World Cup Finals	62	36	14	12	131	77
World Cup Qualifiers	40	31	8	1	122	28
Germany – Post-reunification	P	W	D	L	F	A
European Championship	10	6	1	3	17	10
World Cup Finals	5	3	1	1	9	7
World Cup Qualifiers	0	0	0	0	0	0

(Germany qualify for 1994 World Cup Finals as holders)

Five-Year Records League 1-2-3 and Cup Winners

League Results

	1st	Pts	2nd	Pts	3rd	Pts
1990	Bayern Munich	49	FC Koln	43	Eint. Frankfurt	43
1991	Kaiserslautern	48	Bayern Munich	45	Werder Bremen	42
1992	VfB Stuttgart	52	Bor. Dortmund	52	Eint. Frankfurt	50
1993	Werder Bremen	48	Bayern Munich	47	Eint. Frankfurt	42
1994	Bayern Munich	44	Kaiserslautern	43	Bayer Leverkusen	39

Cup Final Results

1990	Kaiserslautern	3-2	Werder Bremen	
1991	Werder Bremen	1-1	FC Koln	4-3 on pen
1992	Hanover 96	0-0	B. Monchengladbach	4-3 on pen
1993	Bayer Leverkusen	1-0	Hertha Berlin	
1994	Werder Bremen	3-1	Rot Weiss Essen	

---

fill the gap in his planning he organised a match against the United Arab Emirates in Abu Dhabi. This was overshadowed by an unseemly row between him and his predecessor, Beckenbauer, sparked by Bayern being forced to replay their league match against Nuremberg. When the international Thomas Helmer, standing three yards from goal, back-heeled the ball past a post, a linesman inexplicably signalled a goal, which the referee acknowledged despite furious protests by the Nuremberg players. Bayern won 2-1, but after studying filmed evidence the DFB ordered the game to be staged again. The hapless linesman, Jorg Jablonski, was suspended from officiating at Bundesliga, regional and amateur matches forthwith.

Vogts had promised Beckenbauer that in the event of a replay he would immediately release the Bayern players, captain Lothar Matthaus and defender Helmer. But having lost five candidates through injury and a club call, he kept the two stars, though using them for only 45 minutes each. The Germans won 2-0 but it was a tame performance, the opposition being unable to extend the world champions. Bayern won the replay against Nuremberg by 5-0. They also succeeded in their final match, beating Schalke 2-0, and thus became champions for a record-breaking 13th time. Kaiserslautern – who put in a late spurt – captured the runners-up position.

Nuremberg, Wattenscheid and VfB Leipzig were relegated to Liga 2, where an exciting climax to the season ended with VfL Bochum, Bayer Uerdingen and former Cup-Winners' Cup finalists 1860 Munich promoted to the top flight.

Bayern continued to make the headlines when they engaged the Italian Giovanni Trapattoni as team manager for the 1994–95

Germany's World Cup team.

season. The management tried to persuade Beckenbauer to continue as coach, but he could not break his various contractual commitments around the world. Bayern had earlier approached four managers active in the Bundesliga, but apparently all insisted on fulfilling their contracts. The signing of Trapattoni stretched the German FA's rules to the limit because he does not meet the criteria demanded of a Bundesliga team manager. He does not hold a German coaching licence, is not a national manager with a proven record of success and doesn't speak German. But he won 16 national and international club trophies with Juventus and Internazionale, so he was deemed acceptable to manage in the Bundesliga. Vice-president Karl-Heinz Rummenigge and Matthaus, formerly with Italian clubs, will act as interpreters.

Meanwhile Bayern have embarked on strengthening the team for next season, when they will be automatically qualified for the Champions' League. They signed the French striker and former European Footballer of the Year Jean-Pierre Papin for £2.2m from Milan, the country's current best goalkeeper Oliver Kahn (Karlsruhe) and striker Karsten Baron, while Matthaus extended his contract for another three years.

Gates in the Bundesliga rose for the fifth year in a row from an average of 19,765 (1989–90) to 26,486 per match. Yeboah deserves special commendation. Despite being out of the game for five months he still finished the Bundesliga's top scorer with 18 goals. He shares the 'golden cannon' with Stefan Kuntz of runners-up Kaiserslautern.

The Cup was won by Werder Bremen for the third time; they beat Rot Weiss Essen by 3-1 before a capacity crowd of 76,391 in Berlin's Olympic stadium. This was the second division Essener's last match as a professional outfit. Because of financial machinations the club were refused an extension to their professional licence and demoted to the amateur ranks, while the

DFB Cup

Quarter-Finals

TB Berlin v SC Freiburg	1-0
Dynamo Dresden v Bayer Leverkusen	1-1 (4-5 pens)
Rot Weiss Essen v Carl Zeiss Jena	0-0 (6-5 pens)
Werder Bremen v Kaiserslautern	1-1 (4-3 pens)

Semi-Finals

Rot Weiss Essen v TB Berlin	2-0
Dynamo Dresden v Werder Bremen	0-2

Final Berlin

Werder Bremen	**3**	**Rot Weiss Essen**	**1**
Beiersdorfer (17), Herzog (38), Rufer (88 pen)		Bangoura (50)	

Att: 76,000 *Ref:* Amerell

Werder Bremen: Reck, Bratseth, Beiersdorfer, Wolter, Basler (Wiedener 75), Votava, Herzog (Borowka 84), Elits, Bode, Hobsch, Rufer
Rot Weiss Essen: Kurth, Jack, Kugler, Picenacker (Geschlecht 39), Margret, Lipinski, Bangoura, Spyrka, Zedi, Reichert (Grein 49), Dondera

Bundesliga Results 1993–94

	Bayer Leverkusen	Bayern Munich	Borussia Dortmund	Borussia Monchengladbach	Dynamo Dresden	Eintracht Frankfurt	Freiburg SC	Hamburg SV	Kaiserslautern	Karlsruhe SC	FC Koln	MSV Duisberg	FC Nurenberg	Schalke 04	VfB Leipzig	VfB Stuttgart	Wattenscheid	Werder Bremen
Bayer Leverkusen	—	2-1	2-1	0-1	1-1	2-2	2-1	1-2	3-2	3-1	2-1	2-1	4-0	5-1	3-1	1-1	1-1	2-2
Bayern Munich	1-1	—	0-0	3-1	2-1	2-1	3-1	4-0	4-0	1-0	1-0	4-0	5-0	2-0	3-0	1-3	3-3	2-0
Borussia Dortmund	1-0	1-1	—	3-0	4-0	2-0	3-2	2-1	2-1	2-1	2-1	2-1	4-1	1-1	0-1	1-2	2-0	3-2
Borussia Monchengladbach	2-2	2-0	0-0	—	2-1	0-4	1-1	2-2	3-1	1-2	4-1	4-1	2-0	3-2	6-1	0-2	3-3	3-2
Dynamo Dresden	1-1	1-1	3-0	2-1	—	0-4	1-2	1-1	3-1	1-1	1-1	0-1	1-1	1-0	1-0	1-0	1-1	1-0
Eintracht Frankfurt	2-0	2-2	2-0	0-3	3-2	—	3-0	1-1	1-0	3-1	0-3	1-2	1-1	1-3	2-1	0-0	5-1	2-2
Freiburg SC	1-0	3-1	4-1	3-3	0-1	1-3	—	0-1	2-3	3-3	2-4	1-2	0-0	2-3	1-0	2-1	4-1	0-0
Hamburg SV	2-1	1-2	0-0	1-3	1-1	3-0	1-1	—	1-3	1-1	2-4	0-1	5-2	4-1	3-0	3-2	2-1	1-1
Kaiserslautern	3-2	4-0	2-0	4-2	0-0	1-1	1-0	3-0	—	0-0	3-0	2-0	3-1	0-0	1-0	5-0	4-1	2-3
Karlsruhe SC	2-0	1-1	3-3	1-0	1-0	1-0	2-1	2-0	1-1	—	2-0	5-0	3-2	0-0	3-2	0-0	2-0	0-3
FC Koln	1-1	0-4	2-0	0-4	0-1	2-3	2-0	3-0	0-2	2-1	—	1-0	0-1	1-1	3-1	3-1	3-2	2-0
MSV Duisberg	2-2	2-2	2-2	2-0	1-1	1-0	0-2	0-1	1-7	1-2	0-0	—	1-0	1-0	2-1	2-2	2-1	1-0
FC Nurenberg	2-3	2-0	0-0	2-4	3-0	1-5	2-2	0-1	0-2	1-1	1-0	0-0	—	1-0	5-0	1-0	4-1	0-1
Schalke 04	1-1	1-1	1-0	2-1	0-0	1-3	1-3	1-0	2-0	2-0	1-2	1-3	1-2	—	3-1	0-1	4-1	1-1
VfB Leipzig	2-3	1-3	2-3	1-1	3-3	1-0	2-2	1-4	0-0	1-0	2-3	1-1	0-2	2-2	—	0-0	0-0	1-1
VfB Stuttgart	1-4	2-2	2-2	3-0	3-0	0-2	0-4	4-0	1-1	3-0	1-1	4-0	1-0	3-0	0-0	—	3-0	0-0
Wattenscheid	1-2	1-3	1-2	3-1	1-1	0-0	3-1	3-1	5-1	5-1	2-2	0-2	2-1	3-0	2-2	2-4	—	2-2
Werder Bremen	2-1	1-0	4-0	4-2	0-1	1-0	3-2	0-2	2-0	0-2	3-1	1-5	2-2	0-1	3-1	5-1	0-0	—

professional contracts of their players were declared null and void. In Germany all league clubs are required to submit to the DFB detailed accounts every year before their licence is renewed. Those clubs who are heavily in debt and have no means of repaying the money are not allowed to continue in professional football. Now wouldn't the introduction of that rule create a heart flutter or two in England!

Jean-Pierre Papin – Bayern Munich's £2.2m signing.

Greece

Three in a row for AEK

AEK made it a hat-trick of league championships but failed to complete the double in the Cup Final when city rivals Panathinaikos beat them 4-2 on penalty kicks after an exciting 3-3 draw. It was the 11th title for AEK, who are still some way off Olympiakos' record of 25 triumphs. But the story that grabbed the country during the spring months was of the national side's qualification for the World Cup Finals for the first time. It was a welcome boost to the game in a land where standards have dropped and poor matches, coupled with an increase in live television led to a drop in attendances by over one-third. Some games in the first division attracted fewer than 1,000 paying spectators.

Matters are not helped by the dire financial plight that the country's most popular club, Olympiakos, find themselves in, with a loss of around £2.5m being predicted for the 1993-94 season. Refinancing plans hoped to get this to under £1m by the end of 1994-95 season. The problems relate to indiscretions by past regimes which have left the club owing huge sums, believed to be running into millions of pounds, in back taxes. Ironically, Olympiakos managed to spend more than any other club during the close season, with nearly £6m going out in new signings, including Denmark's Brent Kristensen from Schalke 04 and Albanian Foto Strakosha from Ethnikos. Chilean striker Fabian Estay of Universidad was later added for £750,000 against the wishes of coach Lubomir Petrovic, who was promptly fired!

Hopes that a close title race might spark the season into life never materialised and although never more than six points separated the top three or four clubs in the first half of the season, once AEK got their noses in front there was no dislodging them. By the end of January a 2-0 win over second-placed Panathinaikos in the Athens derby game had established them with a nine-point lead. The headliner that day was 25-year-old international Alexis Alexandris, scoring for the sixth successive game. The glut of goals helped the midfielder to top the scoring charts in Greece alongside Kristof Warzycha of Panathinaikos, much to his surprise. Alexandris' goals came at the right time as team-mate Vasilis Dimitriadis – top scorer in AEK's two previous championships – had struck out and had been relegated to the reserves by coach Dusan Bayevic for parts of the season.

AEK's hopes for a lucrative run in the Champions' Cup were dashed at the first hurdle, though they had every right to feel somewhat aggrieved. Having prepared to face Marseille in the first round, they found all their plans and preparations thrown out of the window when their opponents were changed only five days before the first leg in France. Marseille were banned and Monaco substituted, but nevertheless things were going well until the final ten minutes when Vlahos put through his own goal trying to chest

Federation Hellenique de Football

Founded:	1926
Address:	Singrou Avenue 137, GR- 17121 Athens
Phone:	+30 1 933 88 50
Fax:	+30 1 935 96 66
UEFA Affiliation:	1954
FIFA Affiliation:	1927
Season:	September to June
National Stadium:	Olympic
Capacity:	74,000
Colours:	White, Blue, White
Change:	Blue, White, Blue

Final League Table 1993-94

	P	W	D	L	F	A	Pts
AEK Athens	34	25	4	5	63	28	79
Panathinaikos	34	22	6	6	82	32	72
Olympiakos	34	18	14	2	63	27	68
Aris Salonika	34	18	9	7	55	34	63
PAOK	34	14	9	11	45	38	51
Iraklis	34	13	10	11	59	45	49
OFI Crete	34	13	8	13	55	42	47
Xanthi	34	12	9	13	62	63	45
Panionios	34	12	7	15	49	58	43
Levakiakos	34	11	9	14	38	45	42
Larissa	34	11	9	14	45	53	42
Athinaikos	34	11	7	16	34	50	40
Apollon	34	9	13	12	30	41	40
Edessaikos	34	11	6	17	41	56	39
Doxa	34	11	5	18	37	64	38
Panachaiki	34	9	10	15	36	56	37
Kalamaria	34	8	8	18	42	66	32
Naussa	34	5	3	26	28	76	18

Top Scorers
- 24 Alexis ALEXANDRIS (AEK Athens)
-     Kristof WARZYCHA (Panathinaikos)
- 20 Theofanis TOUNTZARIS (Iraklis)
- 15 Milan LUHOVY (PAOK)
- 15 Dimitris SARAVAKOS (Panathinaikos)
- 13 Zoran LONCAR (Aris Salonika)
- 12 Ljubisa MILOJEVIC (Aris Salonika)
-     Sasa SKARA (Edessaikos)
- 11 Vasilis DIMITRIADIS (AEK Athens)
-     Yiotis TSALOUHIDIS (Olympiakos)

Promotions and Relegations
Promoted: Ionikos, Ethnikos, Kavala
Relegated: Naussa, Kalamaria, Panachaiki

International Results 1993–94

Date	Opponents	Result	Venue	Comp.	Scorers
12/10/93	Luxembourg	3-1	Luxembourg	WCQ5	Maglas (31), Apostolakis (63), Saravakos (72)
17/10/93	Russia	1-0	Athens	WCQ5	Machlas (68)
23/3/94	Poland	0-0	Salonika	Friendly	
27/4/94	Saudi Arabia	5-1	Athens	Friendly	Mahlas (10), Alexudis (47), Kostis (74), Tuntziaris (90)
9/5/94	Cameroon	0-3	Athens	Friendly	
13/5/94	Bolivia	0-0	Athens	Friendly	
17/5/94	England	0-5	Wembley	Friendly	
28/5/94	USA	1-1	New Haven	Friendly	Chatzidid (49)
5/6/94	Colombia	0-2	East Rutherford	Friendly	
21/6/94	Argentina	0-4	Boston	WCFD	
26/7/94	Bulgaria	0-4	Chicago	WCFD	
30/6/94	Nigeria	0-2	Boston	WCFD	

National Record	P	W	D	L	F	A
European Championship	53	18	14	21	70	77
World Cup Finals	3	0	0	3	0	10
World Cup Qualifiers	64	21	13	30	71	115

a cross back to his goalkeeper, Atmatzidis. A goal by Croatian Sliskovic forced a 1-1 draw in the second leg but Monaco moved on.

Panathinaikos went one round better in the Cup-Winners' Cup, falling 5-2 to Bayer Leverkusen despite having taken a two-goal advantage in the second leg, after Shelbourne were disposed of in the first round. Olympiakos were looking for some attractive ties to attract fans and cash, but after an 8-3 aggregate win over Botev Plovdiv they fell foul of Tenerife on the away goals rule. Ironically it was another own goal that did the damage, with Amanatides putting into his own net to leave the score 4-3 on the night but 5-5 on aggregate.

Batista's goal five minutes from time in the 5-1 home win over Botev was Olympiakos' 100th goal in 85 games of European cup competitions and marked the Portuguese-born player's naturalisation as a Greek. So Batista with the Ruud Gullit dreadlocks, may well become the first black player to appear for the Greek national side. Crete side OFI produced the best surge of form in Europe, disposing of both Slavia Prague and Atletico Madrid 2-1 on aggregate before falling emphatically 6-1 to Boavista.

As November dawned the national side faced two final World Cup games. With qualification already assured thanks to a 1-0 win in Moscow earlier in the year, a 3-1 win in Luxembourg set up a top-of-the-table clash with the Russians in Athens. A goal by Machlas midway through the second half secured the two points against a ten-man Russian side and ensured that the Greeks finished top of Group Five.

Without the distraction of European competition, attention turned back to the league action and the final run-in of games, with UEFA Cup spots were still very much up for grabs. With two games remaining AEK retained their championship with a 2-1 win at Kalamaria – a defeat which sent the Apollon club from Salonika down to the second division. Scoring draws for Panathinaikos at Athinaikos and Olympiakos at home to Apollon ensured UEFA Cup spots for both clubs, while Panathinaikos made sure of runner-up medals by winning their last league match of the season. Squeezed in between this was a 3-0 aggregate win over Iraklis to secure a place in the Greek Cup final. An Athens derby final was set up when AEK qualified by beating Aris Salonika 2-1 on aggregate – a result that had a snowball effect. As AEK were league champions Panathinaikos were assured a place in the Cup-Winners' Cup whatever the outcome of the final, which meant that their place in the UEFA Cup went to the fourth team, Aris Salonika.

Up until midway through the second half of the final Panathinaikos were well in control, taking a two-goal lead through Warzycha and an own goal by Manolas. Then two goals in five minutes from perpetual danger-men Alexandris and Dimitriadis levelled the scores and sent the match into extra time. Alexandris put AEK into the lead but Marcos made it 3-3 in the second period. In the penalty shoot-out Panathinaikos succeeded to make up for two league defeats at the hands of their deadliest rivals.

Last season's second division champions, Naussa, made a quick return to the lower league, finishing some way off the other relegated side, Kalamaria. Xanthi announced the appointment of Howard Kendall as manager while Olympiakos were quick to get back on the player merry-go-round by signing the Nigerian and African Footballer of the Year, Rashidi Yekini from Vitoria Setubal.

The season ended with national preparations for the World Cup Finals. What had started as a season full of optimism for the country was gradually descending into one of wishful thinking. A goalless draw with Poland was followed by a 5-1 win over the Saudis in Athens, but the next five warm-up matches went

Greece Results 1993–94

	AEK Athens	Apollon	Aris Salonika	Athinaikos	Doxa Dramas	Edessaikos	Naussa	Iraklis	Kalamaria	Larissa	Levakiakos	OFI Crete	Olympiakos	Panathinaikos	Panchaiki	Panionios	PAOK	Xanthi
AEK Athens	—	4-0	3-0	3-2	3-1	4-1	4-2	2-1	3-0	1-0	2-1	2-1	1-2	2-0	2-0	1-0	2-0	2-2
Apollon	1-3	—	1-2	1-1	3-1	1-1	0-0	2-0	2-0	0-0	1-0	0-0	0-0	0-1	1-0	3-1	3-1	
Aris Salonika	2-0	0-0	—	2-0	1-2	3-1	2-1	1-1	3-0	1-0	3-0	2-0	1-1	1-2	2-0	3-1	1-0	3-1
Athinaikos	1-0	3-1	0-0	—	1-0	3-0	1-3	1-0	3-1	1-1	0-0	2-0	0-1	1-1	0-0	0-1	4-0	2-1
Doxa Dramas	1-3	0-0	1-0	1-0	—	0-1	3-2	1-2	2-1	1-2	2-1	0-0	0-1	1-2	3-2	3-1	1-1	1-0
Edessaikos	0-1	1-1	2-2	5-1	1-2	—	3-1	1-0	3-1	1-0	1-2	2-2	0-2	2-0	0-0	3-1	1-0	2-0
Iraklis	0-1	3-1	3-3	2-0	5-0	1-0	4-2	—	3-1	3-1	5-1	0-0	1-2	2-3	2-0	2-1	1-1	5-3
Kalamaria	1-2	1-2	1-2	1-3	4-0	2-2	1-0	1-1	—	5-2	1-0	2-1	0-0	0-1	1-0	1-1	1-1	0-0
Larissa	0-0	0-0	3-1	3-0	2-0	2-0	1-1	0-1	3-1	—	1-1	3-1	2-2	4-4	1-0	5-0	1-1	1-1
Levakiakos	0-1	0-0	1-1	3-0	3-0	2-1	3-1	4-3	2-1	0-1	—	1-0	0-0	1-2	5-0	1-1	1-0	1-1
Naussa	1-3	1-0	1-4	2-0	2-3	0-1	—	3-3	0-1	2-3	2-1	0-0	0-5	0-3	0-1	0-1	0-1	0-1
OFI Crete	1-2	5-1	2-0	4-0	3-2	3-0	4-0	3-3	3-1	2-1	4-0	—	2-0	0-0	2-0	3-0	1-0	2-2
Olympiakos	3-0	1-1	1-1	2-0	3-0	3-0	2-1	1-1	6-0	4-1	2-2	2-0	—	0-0	3-2	1-1	1-0	1-1
Panathinaikos	1-2	3-0	1-1	5-1	8-0	3-1	2-1	2-0	5-1	5-0	3-0	4-1	1-2	—	1-0	3-1	2-0	5-0
Panchaiki	0-2	0-0	0-2	0-2	2-2	2-0	5-4	1-1	5-5	1-0	1-0	3-3	2-1	0-4	—	1-1	1-1	2-1
Panionios	2-2	3-2	0-1	2-0	4-3	2-1	3-0	1-0	2-1	5-1	0-1	0-3	1-1	2-4	0-2	—	1-1	4-1
PAOK	0-0	1-0	1-2	3-0	1-0	6-1	1-0	2-0	1-1	2-0	2-0	2-1	1-1	3-1	4-1	3-2	—	2-1
Xanthi	1-0	4-1	3-2	1-1	1-1	3-2	3-4	1-0	2-3	3-0	3-2	2-1	4-6	2-1	1-1	6-2	5-2	—

Five-Year Records League 1-2-3 and Cup Winners

League Results

	1st	Pts	2nd	Pts	3rd	Pts
1990	Panathinaikos	53	AEK Athens	50	PAOK	46
1991	Panathinaikos	54	Olympiakos	46	AEK Athens	42
1992	AEK Athens	54	Olympiakos	51	Panathinaikos	48
1993	AEK Athens	78	Panathinaikos	77	Olympiakos	68
1994	AEK Athens	79	Panathinaikos	72	Olympiakos	68

Cup Final Results

1990	Olympiakos	4-2	OFI Crete	
1991	Panathinaikos	3-0, 2-1	Athinaikos	5-1 on agg
1992	Olympiakos	1-1, 2-0	PAOK	3-1 on agg
1993	Panathinaikos	1-0	Olympiakos	
1994	Panathinaikos	3-3	AEK Athens	4-2 pens

disastrously wrong, three defeats and two draws, only one goal scored and nine conceded, including a 5-0 thrashing at Wembley. The omens bore themselves out in the Finals, where Greece finished with the worst record in the first round league phase after defeats by Argentina (0-4), Bulgaria (0-4) and Nigeria (0-2).

Cup Results

Quarter-Finals

Olympiakos v Iraklis	2-2	0-1
Larissa v AEK Athens	0-1	1-1
Panathinaikos v Ionikos	2-2	2-0
Ioannina v Aris Salonika	2-1	0-2

Semi-Finals

Aris Salonika v AEK Athens	0-0	1-2
Panathinaikos v Iraklis	0-0	3-0

Final

Panathinaikos 3   **AEK Athens** 3
Warzycha (31), Own goal (54), Alexandris (71, 95),
Marcos (105)   Dimitriadis (77)
Att: 58,000   *Ref:* Spatas
Panathinaikos win 4-2 on penalties

Panathinaikos: Wandzik, Apostolakis, Ourzounidis, Christodoulou, Kalitzakis, Nioplias, Borelli (Maraguos 67), Kolitsidakis, Warzycha (Donis 65), Georgiadis, Marcos.

AEK Athens: Atmatzidis, Kopitsis, Karayannis, Manolas, Vlahos (Tsartas 46), Sabanadzovic (Dimitriadis 46), Alexandris, Savevski, Kassapis, Stamatis, Sliskovic.

Holland

Ajax clean up!

Pre-season in Holland is usually a time for the 'big three' – Ajax, Feyenoord and PSV – to cover their season's wage bills by selling Dutch internationals to Italy and Spain. Last summer, however, Ajax reversed the trend by bringing home three Dutch internationals from overseas.

The most important move of the three was Frank Rijkaard's return to Amsterdam. Rijkaard had become surplus to requirements at Milan, and Ajax, his first club, were more than happy to welcome him home, especially as Milan accepted a bargain fee of only £510,000 as a mark of thanks to 31-year-old Rijkaard for his outstanding service to Silvio Berlusconi's club. Ajax then bought striker Peter Van Vossen from Belgian champions RSC Anderlecht for a colossal £3m and completed their hat-trick of returning sons by re-acquiring the services of Wilbert Suvrijn from Montpellier of France. Ajax also signed international squad forward John Van Den Brom from Vitesse and teenage prodigy Finidi George from Sharkes Calabar of Nigeria.

Inevitably, though, players had to fund this exercise. Dennis Bergkamp and Wim Jonk were sold to Internazionale, for a combined fee of £11m, while Marciano Vink went to Genoa and, in a move of smaller proportions, Alphonse Groenendijk moved to Manchester City to join forces with fellow countryman Michel Vonk.

Feyenoord, after their successful 1992–93 campaign, remained fairly quiet in the transfer market, the signing of Rob Maas from RKC Waalwijk being their only major acquisition. PSV Eindhoven, struggling to come to terms with the disasters of the previous season, lost Brazilian striker Romario to Barcelona and out-of-form midfielder Gerald Vanenburg to Japan's Yamaha. Apart from a few minor deals, their only major imports were Erik Meijer, from MVV Maastricht, Swedish midfielder Klas Ingesson, from Mechelen of Belgium, and Ghanaian Nii Lamptey, on loan from RSC Anderlecht. Perhaps the most significant move though was the 'relegation' of coach Hans Westerhof to youth team coach, with Aad de Mos brought in as the man to resurrect the Philips-backed giants. Another Dutch international returning home was Hans Gillhaus. He walked out on Aberdeen and joined the ambitious Arnhem club, Vitesse, about to enter European competition for only the third time in their history.

In the pre-season tournaments, Feyenoord beat Barcelona 4-2 in a friendly in Rotterdam, while Ajax beat Lazio 2-0 for third place in the annual Makita Trophy in London. The real business though began on 15 August and Rijkaard, fittingly, opened the scoring in the new season after 2 minutes 35 seconds of Ajax's 3-0 home win over RKC. Defending champions Feyenoord opened with a 1-0 home win over Cambuur, while PSV won 2-1 at Groningen. Most opening-day plaudits went to Vitesse, as they won 4-1 at Go Ahead Eagles with Gillhaus scoring a hat-trick on his league debut for the club.

Ajax continued their winning streak through August with victories over Utrecht, Sparta Rotterdam and Vitesse to lead the table with maximum points after four matches. Roda JC Kerkrade kept pace with them following four wins out of four, with PSV a point behind in third place.

Ajax dropped their first point of the season in their first game in September, a 1-1 draw at MVV, and then hosted PSV in the first 'classic' of the season. The Amsterdammers emerged victorious with goals by George and Finnish on-loan striker Jari Litmanen in a 2-0 win. But Feyenoord came through as the new leaders, taking maximum points during September from victories over RKC, NAC Breda, Volendam, Groningen and Go Ahead Eagles to maintain their 100 per cent record. Curiously, though, they suffered a bad attack of the jitters in their opening Champions' Cup tie, and were beaten 1-0 by IA Akranes in Iceland before recovering to win 3-1 on aggregate. Ajax experienced problems of a different kind when their Cup-Winners' Cup tie with Hajduk Split had to be moved to Ljubljana in Slovenia because of continued fighting in Croatia. The disruption proved to be only a minor distraction, and Ajax won 6-1 on aggregate. Disaster, though, in the UEFA Cup where all three Dutch entrants – PSV, Vitesse and FC Twente – fell in the first round, to Karlsruhe, Norwich City and Bayern Munich respectively.

Gillhaus kept Vitesse moving in the right direction in the league, with goals in consecutive matches against MVV, Sparta, RKC and Heerenveen as they moved up to third position behind Ajax. His rich vein of scoring form earned him a recall to the national squad for the World Cup qualifier against San Marino, as coach Dick Advocaat reshaped his attack in anticipation of a goal-chase in Bologna. The plan worked splendidly as the Dutch won 7-0, with the help of a Johnny Bosman hat-trick, to heap pressure on group rivals England.

Feyenoord continued their hot streak into the cool October weather with a 3-1 win away to Heerenveen and a 2-0 home win over Willem II. But their run ended when Ajax held them to a 2-2 draw in Amsterdam thanks to two goals by Litmanen, who led the

Koninklijke Nederlandsche Voetbalbond	
Founded:	1889
Address:	Woudenbergseweg 56, Postbus 515, NL-3700 Am Zeist
Phone:	+31 3439 92 11
Fax:	+31 3439 13 97
UEFA Affiliation:	1954
FIFA Afffiliation:	1904
National Stadium:	Olympisch Stadion Amsterdam
Capacity:	59,000
Season:	August to May
Colours:	Orange, White, Orange
Change:	White, White, White

scoring charts with 10 – prompting Ajax's fans to question the worth of new signing Van Den Brom, the man seen as the direct replacement for Bergkamp. The Ajax faithful also had a new star on their hands – Finidi George. His equaliser for Nigeria, in a 1-1 draw with Algeria, secured the point which took the 'Super Eagles' to the World Cup finals for the first time.

While Ajax breezed through to the quarter-finals of the Cup-Winners' Cup with a 6-1 aggregate demolition of Turkey's Besiktas, Feyenoord crashed out of the Champions' Cup, beaten 1-0 on aggregate by FC Porto, and lost a potential £3m from the Champions' League.

Roda clung on to third place with a useful 2-1 win over Vitesse – Gillhaus got their goal – while PSV crept up to fourth on the strength of victories against Utrecht and Roda. Coach De Mos, despite being awash with cash from Romario's sale, resisted the temptation to splash out on new players, preferring instead to work with what he already had before making any decisions. With PSV moving nicely up the table and with money to spend, the signs looked bleak for the rest of the field as the winter drew in.

Newly promoted Breda club NAC chalked up the biggest win of the season so far when they trounced fellow new-boys Heerenveen 6-0, with John Lammers scoring three. But the main talking point of the month came in Rotterdam, where the national side beat England 2-0 in a World Cup qualifier amid much controversy. The English complained, with some justification, that Ronald Koeman should have been sent off for a foul on David Platt inside the penalty box. German referee Karl-Josef Assenmacher awarded neither and, to twist the knife, Koeman then scored the opening goal with a twice-taken free-kick. The victory left Holland on the brink of qualification with only a slim mathematical chance of the English catching them.

As the season moved into November, so Ajax moved into top gear. NAC were thumped 5-0 on their own patch, Volendam left Amsterdam on the wrong end of a 3-1 scoreline and Groningen were outclassed in a 4-0 away win for Louis Van Gaal's side. Feyenoord, though, still stubbornly clung on to top spot, despite a disappointing draw with VVV Venlo and a hard-earned point at home to Vitesse, who proved their worth with a 1-0 victory over PSV, Gillhaus inevitably scoring, as they leapfrogged over PSV back into third place. Poor Cambuur were still waiting for their first league win of the season after 13 unsuccessful attempts. With only seven goals scored and 30 conceded at that stage, it looked like being a long season for the bottom club.

The national side, as expected, qualified for USA94 with a 3-1 win in Poland. The outcome became academic when news came through that England had failed to beat San Marino by the required seven clear goals.

The year ended badly for Feyenoord as they lost their general manager, Wim Jansen, and their lead at the top. Jansen had made it plain that he wanted to return to coaching and, when he got a call from fellow Dutchman Leo Beenhakker, then in charge of Saudi Arabia's national side, the bait was too good to refuse. December had started well enough for the Rotterdammers with a fine 3-1 win away to PSV. But a home draw with Utrecht, a 1-0 defeat at Roda and a postponed game against Cambuur allowed Ajax to wrest the lead from them. Ajax had two games postponed as winter took its usual toll, but they also managed to beat Go Ahead Eagles and Willem II to close the year on top with 30 points from 17 games.

De Mos decided the time was right to spend some of the Romario money and he wasted no time in persuading Jan Wouters to end his exile with Bayern Munich. Wouters, a mainstay of the national side even at 37, helped PSV consolidate their position in fourth place, level on points with Vitesse, who showed no signs of weakening. If anything, they were getting better as Gillhaus continued to score consistently, three against Groningen and two against Go Ahead Eagles in a 5-0 win.

The first weekend of the New Year saw all four leading clubs registering impressive victories to maintain the position at the top. Feyenoord led the goal spree, beating VVV 5-0 in Rotterdam, PSV

OPPOSITE: *Ajax's Frank de Boer (left) and Jari Litmanen. The spearhead of the Dutch league champions' attack.*

John De Wolf – led Feyenoord to victory in the Dutch Cup Final.

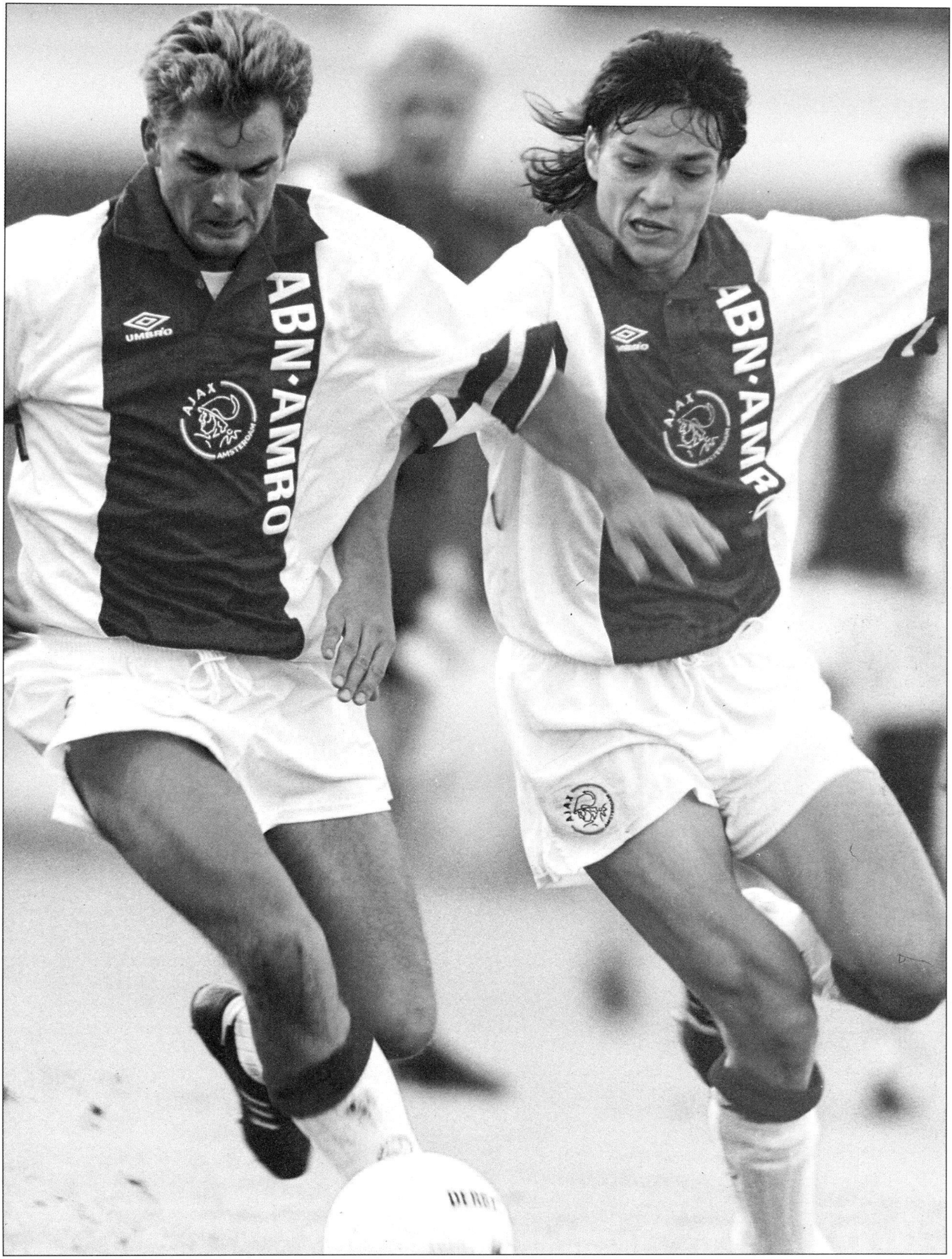
ABN·AMRO
UMBRO
AJAX
AMSTERDAM
ABN·AMRO
AJAX

Feyenoord celebrate with the Dutch Cup after beating NEC in the final.

won 4-0 at Go Ahead Eagles, Ajax hammered MVV 4-1 and Vitesse won 4-0 at Heerenveen, though Gillhaus for once failed to score.

PSV, seeking to re-establish themselves among Europe's leading clubs, underwent an internal reorganisation. Former Denmark international Frank Arnesen was appointed technical manager, with veteran defender Johnny Metgod becoming a full-time youth coach. As if to emphasise the point, PSV also made an audacious bid for 17-year-old Brazilian wonder-kid Ze Elias Moendin, of Sao Paulo's Corinthians. The moves did little to help PSV on the pitch, however, and they were held to a 1-1 draw at home by Heerenveen in their next game. The top three were inactive because of postponements.

The following week, Ajax scored an important psychological victory, beating Vitesse 3-1 in Amsterdam with two goals by Litmanen, while PSV and Feyenoord could only draw. Feyenoord, meanwhile, were resisting overtures from Newcastle United for their lightning-quick international defender Ulrich Van Gobbel. United offered £700,000, Feyenoord told them it was double or nothing!

Ajax then won 3-0 at RKC in a rearranged midweek game, before crashing to a 4-1 defeat at PSV, for whom on-loan Lamptey scored twice. The defeat did little to weaken Ajax's position, though, because Vitesse went down 3-1 at home to MVV and Feyenoord could only draw at home with NAC. Then came the Dutch Cup quarter-finals, and goals galore. Ajax thrashed second division Helmond Sport 7-1, with no fewer than six players scoring, NEC Nijmegen beat Den Haag 3-1, Feyenoord won 4-2 at RKC and, in a huge upset, NAC Breda beat PSV 1-0 with an extra-time goal by Van Hooijdonck.

In among all this the national side drew the first of a series of internationals designed to prepare them for the World Cup finals. Goals in each half by Frank Rijkaard and Ronald Koeman helped them to a 2-2 draw against Tunisia in the heat of Tunis.

The annual Dutch football awards produced few surprises, Litmanen was voted Footballer of the Year, Feyenoord's Ed de Goey was Goalkeeper of the Year, Ajax's Clarence Seedorf was Young Player of the Year and NAC Club of the Year, in recognition of their fine performances having been promoted last summer. Good news, too, for the Dutch national team. An allocation of 14,000 World Cup finals tickets proved to be far too few, as 55,000 requests for tickets were received, and when coaches Beenhakker and Jansen were sacked by the Saudis, they returned with a full dossier on one of Holland's first-round opponents!

The following weekend proved a good one for Ajax. They won 3-0 against Utrecht while Feyenoord, PSV and Vitesse all lost. Bad weather wiped out most of the following week's programme, so Vitesse took advantage by flying to Saudi Arabia for a lucrative friendly with the Saudis. The trip was a happy one as they won 4-3

HOLLAND

International Results 1993–94

Date	Opponents	Result	Venue	Comp.	Scorers
22/9/93	San Marino	7-0	Bologna	WCQ2	Bosman (1, 66, 76), Jonk (21, 43), R. De Boer (51), R. Koeman (79 pen)
13/10/93	England	2-0	Rotterdam	WCQ2	R. Koeman (61), Bergkamp (67)
17/11/93	Poland	3-1	Poznan	WCQ2	Bergkamp (10, 56), R. De Boer (88)
19/1/94	Tunisia	2-2	Tunis	Friendly	Rijkaard (31), R. Koeman (55)
23/3/94	Scotland	1-0	Glasgow	Friendly	Roy (22)
20/4/94	Republic of Ireland	0-1	Tilburg	Friendly	
25/5/94	Scotland	3-1	Utrecht	Friendly	Roy (17), Van Vosien (61), own goal (72)
1/6/94	Hungary	7-1	Eindhoven	Friendly	Bergkamp (12, 90), Roy (17), R. Koeman (23 pen), Taument (46), Rijkaard (58, 78)
12/6/94	Canada	3-0	Montreal	Friendly	Bergkamp (7), Overmars (12), Rijkaard (36)
20/6/94	Saudi Arabia	2-1	Washington	WCFF	Jonk (50), Taument (86)
25/6/94	Belgium	0-1	Orlando	WCFF	
29/6/94	Morocco	2-1	Orlando	WCFF	Bergkamp (43), Roy (77)
4/7/94	Republic of Ireland	2-0	Orlando	WCF2	Bergkamp (11), Jonk (41)
9/7/94	Brazil	2-3	Dallas	WCFQ	Bergkamp (62), Winter (76)

National Record	P	W	D	L	F	A
European Championship	70	44	12	14	152	61
World Cup Finals	25	10	8	7	45	29
World Cup Qualifiers	67	37	17	13	141	58

Final League Table 1993–94

	P	W	D	L	F	A	Pts
Ajax	34	26	2	6	86	26	54
Feyenoord	34	19	13	2	61	27	51
PSV	34	17	10	7	60	36	44
Vitesse	34	17	6	11	63	37	40
FC Twente	34	15	9	10	57	43	39
Roda JC	34	15	8	11	55	40	38
NAC	34	14	10	10	61	52	38
Willem II	34	15	7	12	48	42	37
Sparta	34	12	8	14	58	57	32
MVV	34	11	10	13	49	58	32
FC Volendam	34	13	4	17	46	55	30
Go Ahead Eagles	34	10	8	16	44	57	28
SC Heerenveen	34	9	10	15	35	61	28
FC Groningen	34	9	8	17	42	65	26
FC Utrecht	34	9	8	17	40	63	26
RKC	34	8	9	17	38	56	25
VVV	34	7	11	16	30	62	25
Cambuur Leeuwarden	34	6	7	21	28	64	19

Top Scorers
- 26 Jari LITMANEN (Ajax)
- 25 Pierre VAN HOOYDONK (NAC)
- 22 Hans GILLHAUS (Vitesse)
- 19 John LAMMERS (NAC)
- 16 Richard ROELOFSEN (MVV)
- Peter HOFSTEDE (Roda JC)

Promotions and Relegations
Promoted: Dordrecht '90, NEC
Relegated: VVV, Cambuur Leewarden

Five-Year Records League 1-2-3 and Cup Winners

League Results

	1st	Pts	2nd	Pts	3rd	Pts
1990	Ajax	49	PSV	48	FC Twente	42
1991	PSV	53	Ajax	53	FC Groningen	46
1992	PSV	58	Ajax	55	Feyenoord	49
1993	Feyenoord	53	PSV	51	Ajax	49
1994	Ajax	54	Feyenoord	51	PSV	44

Cup Final Results

1990	PSV	1-0	Vitesse
1991	Feyenoord	1-0	Den Bosch
1992	Feyenoord	3-0	Roda JC
1993	Ajax	6-2	SC Heerenveen
1994	Feyenoord	2-1	NEC

in Jeddah. Two more wins in March, against Cambuur and VVV, kept Ajax top, and with the clubs below them struggling for consistency they were three points clear of Feyenoord at the beginning of April, with PSV and Vitesse fading. Roda JC had moved up into fourth place with two wins out of three during March.

Hooliganism, a constant problem in Holland in recent years, came under discussion when the KNVB (Dutch FA) proposed that all clubs should transport fans by bus, not train, for the 1994–95 season to cut down the number of travelling supporters and the opportunity for trouble. They went further, by suggesting that a reduction in the number of professional clubs would reduce the amount of hooliganism still further.

The semi-finals of the Dutch Cup produced an easy 3-0 win for

Dutch Cup Results

First Round
ADO '20 v Huizen	3-4
Be Quick Groningen v Halsteren	1-3
BVV v TONEGIDO	1-5
Excelsior M v IJsselmeervogels	1-2
FC Lisse v Appingedam	7-1
Panningen v Achilles '29	2-4
Quick Boys v ACV	1-3
SC Genemuiden v AFC	0-5
SDVB v WHC	6-2
SV Meerssen v De Treffers	1-2

Second Round
ADO den Haag v ACV	5-2
AZ v Huizen	2-1
Cambur L v Sparta	0-1
De Treffers v Vitesse 2	2-1
Eindhoven v De Graafschap	1-2
Emmen v FC Zwolle	2-0
Excelsior v Kozakken Boys	6-0
FC Den Bosch v TONEGIDO	3-0
Haarlem v Telstar	1-2
Halsteren v Dordrecht '90	0-2
Helmond Sport v Achilles '29	3-1
Holland v TOP Oss	3-3
IJsselmeervogels v GA Eagles	1-2
Katwijk v Fortuna Sittard	2-5
NAC v AFC	5-2
NEC v FC Lisse	2-1
RBC v FC Groningen	1-0
SC Heracles v Quick '20	2-0
SDVB v SC Heerenveen	1-5
Veendam v Lunteren	2-3
VVV v Geldrop	5-3

Third Round
Ajax v SC Heerenveen	8-3
AZ v Fortuna Sittard	2-0
De Graafschap v Vitesse	2-1
De Treffers v NEC	1-3
Dordrecht '90 v Emmen	6-2
Excelsior v Feyenoord	2-3
FC Utrecht v FC Den Bosch	2-3
GA Eagles v ADO Den Haag	2-3
Helmond Sport v Roda JC	1-0
Holland v FC Twente	1-7
MVV v Lunteren	5-3
NAC v VVV	3-2
RKC v RBC	4-0
SC Heracles v Willem II	0-0
Sparta v PSV	2-2
Telstar v FC Volendam	2-1

Fourth Round
ADO Den Haag v MVV	5-1
Ajax v FC Twente	4-1
Dordrecht '90 v Feyenoord	0-2
Helmond Sport v FC Den Bosch	1-0
NAC v AZ	3-2
NEC v De Graafschap	2-0
PSV v Willem II	2-1
RKC v Telstar	2-1

Quarter-Finals
Ajax v Helmond Sport	7-1
ADO Den Haag v NEC	3-1
RKC v Feyenoord	0-2
NAC v PSV	1-0

Semi-Finals
Ajax v NEC	1-2
NAC v Feyenoord	0-3

Final
Feyenoord 2 NEC 1
Heus (7 pen), Van Loen (80) Dekker (90)

Feyenoord: De Goey, Van Gobbel, De Wolf, Fraser, Heus, Scholten, Bosz (Maas 46), Witschge, Taument, Larsson (Van Loen 71), Blinker.
NEC: Brookhuis, Van der Weerden, Van der Linden, Aalbers, Stock, Cruden, Van Wonderen, Kooistra, Van Wanrooy (De Jong 74), Lok, Dekker.

Feyenoord against NAC, and a shock 2-1 defeat for Ajax against NEC. It was the first of three demoralising losses for the Amsterdammers in the space of just 10 days. They were also eliminated from the Cup-Winners' Cup, beaten 2-0 on aggregate by defending holders Parma, and there was more bad news when Litmanen was ruled out for a month with a thigh injury. Then came a 2-1 defeat to Feyenoord in Rotterdam, which suggested that maybe Ajax could still be caught, though they remained on top of the table.

Feyenoord, though, had their own problems to deal with. Striker Van Loen was banned for three games and fined £10,000 for elbowing an opponent, and the club found out that they would have to find around £37m to redevelop their De Kuip stadium. Still, at least coach Jansen signed a new contract, which will keep him at the club for life.

Problems, too, at PSV where new director Bill Maeyer, unhappy with the team's form, transfer-listed several established stars, including Jan Heintze, Erwin Koeman, Adri Van Tiggelen, Berry Van Aerle, Wim Kieft, Jerry De Jong, Jules Ellerman and Kalusha Bwalya. With goalkeeper Hans Van Breukelen due to retire at the end of the season, it means PSV have an awful lot of rebuilding work to do for the start of the 1994-95 season. Another ex-PSV employee, coach Hans Westerhof, was also in the news, joining Groningen as coach.

March, April and May brought two wins and a home defeat for the Dutch. A first-half goal by Roy ensured a win in Glasgow over the Scots, who were beaten again 3-1 in Utrecht eight weeks later. Roy started the scoring in that game as well. But sandwiched in between this was a jolting 1-0 defeat by the Republic of Ireland in

Dutch Championship Results 1993-94

	Ajax	Cambuur Leeuwarden	Feyenoord	Go Ahead Eagles	FC Groningen	SC Heerenveen	MVV	NAC	PSV	RKC	Roda JC	Sparta	FC Twente	FC Utrecht	Vitesse	FC Volendam	VVV	Willem II
Ajax	—	3-2	2-2	4-0	0-2	2-1	4-1	5-0	2-0	3-0	2-0	3-0	6-0	3-0	3-1	3-1	2-0	3-1
Cambuur Leeuwarden	0-3	—	0-0	1-0	0-2	1-2	2-1	1-3	1-3	1-1	0-1	1-1	1-1	2-1	1-3	3-1	2-1	0-1
Feyenoord	2-1	1-0	—	1-0	2-2	0-0	4-0	1-1	2-1	1-1	2-1	5-1	1-0	1-1	1-1	2-0	5-0	2-0
Go Ahead Eagles	0-3	3-0	1-1	—	3-0	2-3	2-2	0-0	0-4	2-0	3-1	1-5	3-3	4-0	1-4	0-1	2-0	3-0
FC Groningen	0-4	2-2	0-4	3-1	—	2-2	3-2	0-0	1-2	1-2	3-5	1-4	1-1	4-1	0-0	0-0	0-3	4-1
SC Heerenveen	1-4	1-2	1-3	1-4	2-0	—	3-1	1-3	0-0	0-3	0-0	1-0	2-2	1-0	0-4	3-1	1-0	1-2
MVV	1-1	0-0	1-1	2-2	2-0	3-1	—	2-1	2-1	1-1	1-0	0-0	0-2	2-1	0-2	1-1	0-0	1-0
NAC	0-5	2-0	1-2	2-2	2-1	6-0	1-4	—	2-2	3-0	2-3	4-3	2-1	2-2	2-2	3-1	4-1	1-1
PSV	4-1	2-0	1-3	3-0	1-1	1-1	4-2	3-1	—	1-1	2-0	2-1	3-2	1-0	0-1	3-0	3-2	2-1
RKC	0-3	3-0	1-2	1-2	2-3	1-1	0-2	1-0	1-1	—	1-1	3-1	1-3	3-0	0-0	1-3	1-2	1-0
Roda JC	1-2	1-1	1-0	2-1	2-0	1-1	4-1	1-2	4-0	2-0	—	4-0	1-4	4-0	2-1	2-0	0-0	1-1
Sparta	0-1	4-0	3-4	1-0	3-0	3-0	2-2	0-0	0-0	1-1	2-0	—	2-5	3-2	4-1	4-1	2-2	1-0
FC Twente	2-1	4-1	1-1	1-1	0-1	2-1	4-2	0-1	0-0	2-1	2-1	0-0	—	1-0	0-1	2-0	3-0	4-0
FC Utrecht	1-4	2-0	0-0	2-0	2-0	0-1	3-0	0-5	0-4	3-1	1-1	3-1	1-0	—	2-1	3-1	2-3	1-1
Vitesse	0-1	2-1	1-2	5-0	4-1	3-0	1-3	3-1	0-0	4-1	1-3	2-0	3-0	2-2	—	2-1	4-0	0-1
FC Volendam	1-0	4-1	0-1	0-1	1-0	3-0	5-0	1-3	3-2	3-1	2-0	2-1	2-5	2-2	2-0	—	1-1	0-3
VVV	0-1	1-0	1-1	1-0	1-3	1-1	1-7	1-1	0-3	0-2	2-2	1-4	0-0	1-1	2-1	2-0	—	0-0
Willem II	2-1	4-1	2-1	0-0	4-1	1-1	1-0	2-0	1-1	4-1	0-3	5-1	2-0	4-1	0-3	0-2	3-0	—

Tilburg that at least had the desired effect of getting rid of any over-confidence in the *Oranje* camp.

April turned out to be a strange month for Ajax. They had three games postponed, but managed to win the other three, 5-0 against NAC, 6-0 against FC Twente, with Litmanen scoring in his comeback match despite Blind's second-half dismissal, and 3-0 against Go Ahead Eagles. Two more wins in the first week of May, against Roda and Heerenveen, guaranteed Ajax the title, even though they lost their final match of the season, 2-0 at home to Groningen. Feyenoord finished as runners-up, with PSV, Vitesse and FC Twente taking the three UEFA Cup places. Feyenoord's path into Europe lay in the Dutch Cup, where they beat Second Division NEC 2-1 in the Final, to win the trophy for the third time in four years. What proved to be the winning goal was scored by Van Iven shortly after coming on as a substitute.

With the season over the national side were able to prepare in earnest for the World Cup and with Cruyff spurning the chance to manage the national side at the finals, Dick Advocaat was able to concentrate fully on his preparation, which included a massive 7-1 win over Hungary. But on the day before the official squad was announced the simmering battle between Advocaat and Gullit came to a head when Gullit announced that he would not be going to the Finals with the national squad – 'For reasons I will state after the World Cup,' he said!

Marc Overmars with the Republic's Terry Phelan.

Hungary

Capital power moves

After several near misses in recent years, Vac finally won their first Hungarian championship, and in doing so became the first club from outside Budapest to take the title since Raba ETO from Gyor 11 years ago. As far as the title race was concerned it was the 'year of the provincials'. Newly-promoted Debrecen set the early pace, dropping just one point from their first seven games, which included a 2-1 defeat of the reigning champions Kispest Honved inspired by teenage starlet Tamas Sandor. Ferencvaros maintained a surge of form to take advantage as Debrecen dropped points, to gain top spot, but as the winter break approached 'Fradi' were surprisingly beaten by Videoton and as Honved lost at home to Bekescsaba, Vac recorded their sixth consecutive win to take over the leadership.

The break over, Bekescsaba became the fourth side to head the table when they recorded a crucial 2-1 win in Vac, to take a two-point lead. Honved were falling off the pace in sixth position and a five-goal thrashing in Goyr put intolerable pressure on their Finnish manager, Marttii Kuusela, who was not helped by a flu bug that incapacitated many of his players. It was only a matter of time until Kuusela was replaced by the Serbian Dimitri Davidovics.

Josef Pasztor's young Bekescsaba side continued to maintain their position at the top, and were briefly buoyed by the naming of uncapped midfielder Janos Argyelan as Player of the Year for 1993, but eventually the pressure on the club from near the Romanian border started to tell. Defeat to Ujpesti in April, the first loss since October, hinted that there was a wobble in form that eventually manifested itself in the final weeks.

With three rounds of games to play Bekescsaba and Vac were tied on 41 points, but then a 4-2 win by Ferencvaros over Bekescsaba allowed them to renew their UEFA Cup hopes and Vac to take a two-point advantage at the top with a win at Sopron.

Magyar Labdarugo Szovetseg

Founded:	1901
Address:	Nepstadion, Toronyepulet, Istvanmezei Ut 3-5, H-1146 Budapest
Phone:	+36 1 252 92 96
Fax:	+36 1 252 99 86
UEFA Affiliation:	1954
FIFA Affiliation:	1906
Season:	September to June
National Stadium:	Nepstadion, Budapest
Capacity:	72,000
Colours:	Red, White, Green
Change:	White, White, White

Final League Table 1993–94

	P	W	D	L	F	A	Pts
VAC FC-Samsung	30	19	8	3	58	29	46
Kispest Honved	30	18	7	5	66	33	43
Bekescsaba	30	19	3	8	68	29	41
Ferencvaros	30	16	5	9	50	32	37
ETO FC Gyor	30	15	7	8	51	37	37
Ujpesti TE	30	13	8	9	44	35	34
Debreceni VSC	30	12	9	9	40	33	33
Csepel-Kordax	30	12	8	10	36	44	32
Parmalat FC (Videoton Waltham)	30	8	9	13	33	46	25
Vasas-Ilzer	30	8	8	14	36	43	24
PMSC-Fordan (Pecs)	30	7	10	13	23	39	24
BVSC-Dreher	30	7	10	13	32	52	24
Siofok	30	6	10	14	33	49	22
Sopron	30	8	6	16	31	52	22
Haladas VSE	30	5	9	16	31	52	22
MTK	30	4	9	17	30	58	17

Top Scorers

- 17 Bela ILLES (Kispest Honved)
- 16 Janos SZARVAS (Bekescsaba)
- 15 Antal FULE (VAC FC Samsung)
- 14 Tamas SANDOR (Debreceni)
  Laszlo WUKOVICS (Ferencaros)

Promotions and Relegations

Promoted: Nagykanizsa, FC Stadler, Zalaegerszeg
Relegated: MTK, Haladas USE, Siofok

Five-Year Records League 1-2-3 and Cup Winners

League Results

	1st	Pts	2nd	Pts	3rd	Pts
1990	Ujpest Dozsa	58	MTK-VM	58	Ferencvaros	48
1991	Honved	45	Ferencvaros	40	Pecsi MSC	37
1992	Ferencvaros	46	Vac	45	Kispest Honved	40
1993	Kispest Honved	43	Vac FC Samsung	42	Ferencvaros	41
1994	Vac FC Samsung	46	Kispest Honved	43	Bekescsaba	41

Cup Final Results

1990	Pecsi MSC	2-0	Kispest Honved
1991	Ferencvaros	1-0	Vaci Izzo
1992	Ujpest TE	1-0	Vaci Izzo
1993	Ferencvaros	1-1	Haladas USE after 1-1 draw 5-3 on pens
1994	Ferencvaros	2-1, 3-0	Kispest Honved 5-1 on agg.

Name changes: Vac FC Samsung (Vaci Izzo)
Ujpest TE (Ujpest Dozsa)
Parmalat FC (Videoton Waltham)

International Results 1993–94

Date	Opponents	Result	Venue	Comp.	Scorers
8/9/93	Russia	1-3	Budapest	WCQ5	Own Goal (Nikiforov 20)
27/10/93	Luxembourg	1-0	Budapest	WCQ5	Detari (20)
3/9/93	Switzerland	1-2	Budapest	Friendly	Eszenyi (75)
23/3/94	Austria	1-1	Linz	Friendly	Illes (20)
20/4/94	Denmark	1-3	Copenhagen	Friendly	Vincze (2)
4/5/94	Poland	2-3	Krakow	Friendly	Vincze (10), Klausz (50)
9/5/94	Croatia	2-2	Gyor	Friendly	Keresturi (51, 57)
1/6/94	Holland	1-7	Eindhoven	Friendly	Illes (9pen)
5/6/94	Belgium	1-3	Brussels	Friendly	Jagodics (54)

National Record	P	W	D	L	F	A
European Championship	64	29	13	22	119	89
World Cup Finals	32	15	3	14	87	57
World Cup Qualifiers	64	35	15	14	133	76

At the bottom a 1-4 home defeat by Honved meant that MTK suffered the indignity of relegation. Honved produced another win in the penultimate game at Bekescsaba and a 2-2 draw for Vac at home to Vasas was enough to clinch the championship at last after two successive seasons as runners-up. Poor Bekescsaba lost their third game in succession, and another win by Honved allowed the outgoing champions to snatch the runners-up spot as a consequence.

Vac's tittle owed much to the talents of their highly-respected manager, Janos Csank, whose mid-season purchase of ex-Ferencvaros striker Joszef Dzurjak helped push the title north. Honved's young side missed the midfield talents of broken leg victim Istvan Pisont, and although new manager Davidovics inspired a late revival, it wasn't enough to retain the championship. Videoton Waltham had a much-needed windfall during the season when they secured a sponsorship deal that meant they took on the name of their dairy giant benefactors – Parmalat FC.

In the basement Budapest club MTK were joined on the long slide down by Haladas and Siofok, who were thrashed 6-0 by Zalaegerszeg in the play-offs. Soproni survived by winning their play-off encounter with Hatvan. Fradi – by far the best supported team in Hungary – won through to the Cup Final with a semi-final victory over Vasas, where they met Honved, who came from behind to beat Siofokl. A Detari-inspired Ferencvaros proved too much for Honved in the two-legged final, despite a home leg victory.

The international fortunes of Hungarian football have taken a severe dip in recent years, and the 1993–94 season produced no sign of the trend abating. Only relegation-bound MTK made it to the second round of European competition, scraping past KR of Reykjavik only to fall to Mechelen and goals from Hungarian Denes Eszenyi in the UEFA Cup. Honved were perhaps unlucky to draw Manchester United in the Champions' Cup, and their defensive naivety was exposed, especially in the home leg. Fradi slipped out of the Cup-Winners' Cup, losing both legs to FC Tirol-Innsbruck, while Vac were ignominiously ousted in extra time by Cypriots Apollon in Limassol, after letting slip a two-goal first-leg lead.

The World Cup qualifying campaign fared no better, and the national sides' 1-0 win over Luxembourg was hardly an optimistic note on which to finish. It had been hoped that new manager Jozef Verebes could turn things around, but his reluctance to select nationals playing abroad, such as Feyenoord's Kiprich and Kovacs of Valenciennes, clearly back-fired. His first game in charge was a 3-1 home defeat by Russia which consigned the Magyars to fourth place in a group many felt they should have qualified from, given the bonus of Yugoslavia's enforced absence. The subsequent poor performances of both Russia and Greece in the Finals simply added insult to injury for many Hungarian football supporters.

The knives were already waiting for the 53-year-old Verebes, who continued in a dual capacity, as national coach as well as being in charge of Raba ETO. Calls for MTK coach Imre Gellei were made from some quarters as the one-year contract between Verebes and the Federation approached its end. Late-season friendlies held little promise, and included a 7-1 thrashing by the Dutch in Eindhoven. Perhaps the young lions of Honved and Bekescsaba can rescue Hungary from what at present is the bargain bin of European football.

But there are things more important than football and the World Cup match with Russia in September was tinged with sadness. Gabor Zsiboras, the 35-year-old MTK goalkeeper, had been recalled to the national squad by Verebes after a six-year absence. A week before the game he was taken ill during training. He slipped into a deep coma from which he never recovered, dying on the day before the game and leaving a widow and triplet daughters.

Iceland

Akranes continue in style

Knattspyrnufelag Ithrottabandalags Akranes – thankfully more simply known as IA – won a league and cup double to complete, or maybe just continue, a remarkable turnaround in the club's fortunes. Having suffered the indignation of relegation, IA won promotion back to the first division in 1991 as champions at the first attempt. They followed that by winning the first division title in their first season back in the top flight – the first side ever to do so in Iceland – and the 1993 double was their 14th championship. Curiously the last time they won the title before relegation was in 1984, when they also did the double.

Manager Gudjon Thordarson has constructed a formidable side based around the Siggi Jonsson. The former Arsenal and Sheffield Wednesday midfielder who was forced out of the English game with a back injury, has been able to cope with the less demanding needs of Icelandic football to good effect, aided by Serbian newcomer Mihajlo Bibercic and Bosnian-born captain Lukas Kostic. With the talented Gunnlaugsson twins sold to Feyenoord, IA relied on Thordur Gudjohnson for goals – 19 of the 63 scored in 18 matches. Not surprisingly Gudjohnson caught the attention of the national manager and made his debut at the age of 20 before securing a lucrative move to German club Bochum. Bibercic's 13 goals were another a major contribution towards IA's success.

IA dropped just five points all season winning 16 games. Reykjavik club Fram were the stumbling block to a perfect season beating them 4-2 and drawing 3-3 in the Akranesvollur. However IA's bogey team could not build on their triumphs and had to settle for fourth position. With IA winning the championship with three rounds to go, FH finished in a comfortable second spot to gain a UEFA Cup place, but felt the full force of IA's determination to retain the title and lost both their crunch matches by 5-0.

IBK gave a good account of themselves back in the top flight. The club from Keflavik, who won the last of their three championships in 1973, finished third with the aid of 15 goals from Oli Thor Magnusson. IBK also reached the Icelandic Cup final, where they lost 1-2 to IA, but Akranes' championship win means a return to European football for IBK in the Cup-Winners' Cup. A goal in each half from Gudjohnson and Bibercic secured

Final League Table 1993

	P	W	D	L	F	A	Pts
IA Akranes	18	16	1	1	62	16	49
FH	18	12	4	2	39	21	40
IBK	18	8	3	7	31	31	27
Fram	18	8	1	9	38	37	25
KR	18	7	3	8	37	34	24
Valur	18	6	4	8	25	24	22
Thor	18	5	5	8	20	30	20
IBV	18	5	4	9	26	41	19
Fyikir	18	6	1	11	22	35	19
Vikingur	18	3	2	13	23	54	11

Top Scorers
- 19 Thordur GUDJOHNSON (IA Akranes)
- 15 Oli Thor MAGNUSSON (IBK)
- 14 Helgi SIGURDSSON (Fram)
- Haraldur INGOLFSSON (IA Akranes)
- 13 Hordur MAGNUSSON (FH)
- Mihajlo BIBERCIC (IA Akranes)
- 12 Tryggvi GUDMUNDSSON (KR)
- 9 Anthony Karl GREGORY (Valur)
- Kristinn TOMASSON (Fyikir)

Promotions and Relegations
Promoted: UBK, Stjarnau
Relegated: Vikingur, Fyikir

Five-Year Records League 1-2-3 and Cup Winners

League Records

	1st	Pts	2nd	Pts	3rd	Pts
1989	KA	34	FH	32	Fram	32
1990	Fram	38	KR	38	IBV	37
1991	Vikingur	37	Fram	37	KR	28
1992	IA Akranes	40	KR	37	Thor	37
1993	IA Akranes	49	FH	40	IBK	27

Cup Final Results

1989	Valur	0-0	KR after 1-1 draw, 5-4 on pens
1990	Valur	2-1	FH
1991	Valur	1-0	FH after 1-1 draw
1992	Valur	5-2	KA
1993	IA Akranes	2-1	IBK

Knattspyrnusamband Islands

Founded:	1947
Address:	Laugardal, 104 Reykjavik
Phone:	+345 1 81 44 44
Fax:	+354 1 68 97 93
UEFA Affiliation:	1954
FIFA Affiliation:	1929
National Stadium:	Laugardalsvollur, Reykjavik
Capacity:	14,000
Season:	May to September
Colours:	Blue, White, Blue
Change:	White, Blue, White

International Results 1993–94

Date	Opponents	Result	Venue	Comp.	Scorers
31/8/93	United States	0-1	Reykjavik	Friendly	
8/9/93	Luxembourg	1-0	Reykjavik	WCQ5	Ingolfsson (61)
17/10/93	Tunisia	1-3	Tunis	Friendly	Brousson (28)
21/3/94	Japan	2-1	Utsunomiya	Friendly	
20/4/94	Saudi Arabia	0-2	Toulon	Friendly	
24/4/94	USA	2-1	California	Friendly	Sigurdsson (20), B. Gunnlaugsson (86)
4/5/94	Brazil	0-3	Florianopolis	Friendly	
19/5/94	Bolivia	1-0	Reykjavik	Friendly	T. Orlygsson (54)

National Record	P	W	D	L	F	A
European Championship	40	6	6	28	22	71
World Cup Finals	*Never qualified*					
World Cup Qualifiers	46	8	8	30	39	115

Mjolkurbikarinn Results

1/8th Finals
- Fram v KR 0-1
- Fylkir v FH 2-0
- Vioir v Vikingur 1-2
- Hottur v Leiftur 0-1
- HK v IA Akranes 0-3
- IBV v KA 4-0
- Valur v UBK 1-0
- IBK v Thor 1-0

Quarter-Finals
- Fylkir v Valur 1-2
- IA Akranes v Vikingur 4-1
- IBK v Leiftur 4-2
- KR v IBV 3-1

Semi-Finals
- Valur v IBK 1-2
- KR v IA Akranes 0-1

Final
- IA Akranes v IBK 2-1

Icelandic Championship Results 1993

	FH	Fram	Fyikir	IA	IBK	IBV	KR	Thor	Valur	Vikingur
FH	—	3-1	4-0	0-5	5-1	3-1	2-0	4-1	1-1	4-2
Fram	0-4	—	5-0	4-2	2-1	5-1	2-4	1-2	3-2	4-1
Fyikir	0-2	3-0	—	1-3	2-2	1-2	2-1	1-0	2-1	1-2
IA	5-0	3-3	4-1	—	2-0	3-1	1-0	6-0	1-0	10-1
IBK	0-1	2-1	2-1	1-2	—	4-0	1-4	5-2	1-3	3-2
IBV	2-2	1-2	1-0	2-5	1-2	—	2-4	1-1	0-2	3-2
KR	1-2	1-4	1-3	1-4	2-2	2-2	—	2-0	2-0	7-2
Thor	0-0	1-0	1-0	0-1	1-1	1-1	1-2	—	1-1	5-1
Valur	1-2	4-1	4-2	0-2	0-2	0-1	1-1	2-1	—	3-1
Vikingur	0-0	2-0	0-2	1-3	0-1	2-9	3-2	1-2	0-0	—

the trophy for IA, although Marko Tanasic fired in an equaliser in front of nearly 6,000 spectators.

Vikingur – champions in 1991 – slide into the second division after finishing bottom in a disastrous season, and are joined there by another side from Reykjavik, Fyikir, who won promotion the previous season but lost out to IBV on goal difference.

IA took their form into the Champions' Cup and after disposing of the Albanians of Partizan Tirana 3-0 on aggregate, with three late goals on home soil, they created one of the shocks of the competition by beating Feyenoord 1-0 in Iceland. Over 6,000 saw Thordarson hit the winner with quarter of an hour remaining. Although Refos equalised the aggregate score for the Dutch midway through the first half of the second leg, it wasn't until late in the second half that Feyenoord secured their aggregate win with two more goals.

In the Cup-Winners' Cup, Valur beat Finnish side MyPa with two wins but couldn't handle Scottish representatives Aberdeen, who won 7-0 on aggregate. In the UEFA Cup, KR held the Hungarians of MTK to a goalless draw in Budapest, but a 1-2 home defeat ended their participation at the first round.

The national side completed a satisfactory World Cup qualifying campaign with eight points, to finish third above Hungary and Luxembourg. A goal by Haraldur Ingolfsson just after the hour ensured a win in the final Group Five game over Luxembourg in Reykjavik, and the international season finished with two wins in the last three games. Those final three games were all against World Cup finalists and the 0-3 defeat by Brazil was hardly a disgrace

The Icelandic close season brought a number of shock moves – the most notable of them being the 'transfer' of IA manager Gudjon Thordarson to KR to make him the highest-paid manager in the league. Thordarson's was followed by IA's international goalkeeper, Kristjan Finnbogason – who was returning to the club were he spent his youth. To complete his re-building plans, Thordarson also signed IBV's top scorer Tryffvi Gudmundsson and Salih Porca from Eylkir. Siggi Jonsson's move home from North London and his subsequent success was noted by Tottenham Hotspur player Gudni Bergsson, the Icelandic national team skipper, who signed for Valur.

Israel

Maccabi domination continues

Israeli football continued to make positive moves during the 1993–94 season both at club and international level. The highlight of the season was undoubtedly the national team's historic victory in Paris, coming from behind with two goals in the final seven minutes. Even though that win affected France's qualification hopes, the Israeli players and staff were brought back to earth with a bump when defeat at home to Finland consigned them to the wooden spoon of the group, and led to renewed calls for the sacking of coach Shlomo Scharf. The protests fell on deaf ears, and he was given an extension to his contract to cover the 1996 European Championships, despite having been widely criticised. In some ways it's not hard to see why – he consistently left out Israel's finest young player, Alon Mizrahi of Maccabi Haifa, and was notoriously inconsistent with tactics. Wins over Georgia and Ukraine (twice) show that potential remains but a 3-0 home defeat by Argentina prior to the World Cup illustrates that there is still some way to go.

Israeli club performances in Europe were a good barometer of progression in the international arena, and there was cause for optimism with an excellent performance by Maccabi Haifa in the Cup-Winners' Cup. Having sailed past Dudelange 7-1 in the preliminary round, they then accounted for seasoned campaigners Torpedo Moscow, 3-2 on aggregate, the winning goal coming from Holzmann just five minutes from time. So they became the first Israeli side to reach the second round of a European competition, and the reward was considerable – a draw against the holders, star-studded Italians Parma.

Brolin's last-minute winner in Haifa looked to have made the second leg a formality for the holders, but they reckoned without Mizrahi, who fired a second-half goal to level the aggregate score and force extra time, after having hit a post late in the game. Haifa lost their nerve in the penalty shoot-out, scoring just once as Parma squeezed through. Beitar, Israel's representative in the Champions' Cup, lost to Lech Poznan in the first round after comfortably beating the Moldovians of Zimbru in the preliminary round.

The relative success of the national and club sides in European competitions was reflected by a marvellous league season, dominated by two clubs – Maccabi Tel Aviv and Maccabi Haifa. Maccabi Tel Aviv started the season at blistering pace, winning their first 11 games, scoring 33 goals and conceding just four in reply, yet still led Maccabi Haifa by only four points. The two sides then faced each other for the first time and the match began in controversial circumstances, as Haifa's Mizrahi was sent off after only one minute. Despite the man disadvantage they earned a point in a 1-1 draw to break that run of victories.

Three weeks later Tel Aviv lost to local rivals Bnei Yehoudah; Nir Shitrit and Ukrainian Nikolai Kodritsky scored the goals in the 2-0 win, and Bnei became not only the first side to beat the leaders but also the first to keep a clean sheet against them.

Final League Table 1993–94

National Division 1993–94

	P	W	D	L	F	A	Pts
Maccabi Haifa	39	28	11	0	97	27	95
Maccabi Tel Aviv	39	27	7	5	80	36	88
Hapoel Beersheva	39	18	11	10	53	37	65
Beitar Jerusalem	39	19	7	13	75	66	64
Hapoel Tel Aviv	39	16	6	17	61	59	54
Maccabi Natanya	39	13	10	16	64	71	49
Hapoel Petach Tikva	39	12	12	15	53	56	48
Maccabi Petach Tikva	39	11	14	14	37	46	47
Bnei Yehoudah	39	13	8	18	55	67	47
Hapoel Zafririm Holon	39	11	12	16	42	67	45
Maccabi Herzlia	39	10	11	18	41	53	41
Maccabi Ironi Ashdod	39	9	11	19	53	57	38
Hapoel Haifa	39	7	13	19	39	80	34
Hapoel Kfar Saba	39	7	11	21	36	64	32

League has a third phase: Each club plays the others home and away and then there is a final round where each club plays each other once again – the top seven clubs at the end of 26 matches have the advantage of playing seven fixtures at home and six away. The bottom seven clubs play home six times and away seven times.

Top Scorers
- 28 Alon MIZRAHI (Maccabi Haifa)
- 22 Itzhak ZOHAR (Maccabi Tel Aviv)
- 21 Mordechai KAKOON (Hapoel Petch Tikva)
- 20 Nikolai KUDRICKI (Bnei Yehoudah)
- 19 Vladimir GRESCHNAIV (Beitar Jerusalem)

Promotion/Relegation
Promoted: Hapoel Rishon Le Zion, Hapoel Beit Shean, Beitar Tel Aviv
Relegated: Hapoel Kfar Saba

Israel Football Association

Founded:	1928
Address:	299 Aba Hilell Street, Ramat Gan 52594
Phone:	+972 3 570 9059
Fax:	+972 3 570 2044
FIFA Affiliation:	1929
UEFA Affiliation:	1992
Season:	August to June
National Stadium:	Ramat Gan, Tel Aviv
Capacity:	55,000
Colours:	White, Blue, White
Change:	Blue, White, White

International Results 1993–94

Date	Opponents	Result	Venue	Comp.	Scorers
22/9/93	Romania	0-1	Bucharest	Friendly	
6/10/93	Cyprus	2-2	Limassol	Friendly	Harazi (36, 56)
13/10/93	France	3-2	Paris	WCQ6	Harazi (21), Berkovich (83), Atar (90)
27/10/93	Austria	1-1	Tel Aviv	WCQ6	Rosenthal (3)
10/11/93	Finland	1-3	Tel Aviv	WCQ6	Harazi (89)
23/2/94	Georgia	2-0	Tel Aviv	Friendly	Ohana (27, 89)
15/3/94	Ukraine	1-0	Haifa	Friendly	Banin (40 pen)
20/4/94	Lithuania	1-1	Vilnius	Friendly	R. Harazi (7)
31/5/94	Argentina	0-3	Tel Aviv	Friendly	

National Record	P	W	D	L	F	A
European Championship	Never participated					
World Cup Finals	3	0	2	1	1	3
World Cup Qualifiers	66	17	16	33	82	98

Three-Year Records League 1-2-3 and Cup Winners

League Results

	1st	Pts	2nd	Pts	3rd	Pts
1992	Maccabi Tel Aviv	75	Bnei Yehoudah	62	Maccabi Haifa	48
1993	Beitar Jerusalem	71	Maccabi Tel Aviv	62	Bnei Yehoudah	56
1994	Maccabi Haifa	95	Maccabi Tel Aviv	88	Hapoel Beersheba	65

Cup Final Winners

1992	Hapoel Petach Tikva	3-1	Maccabi Tel Aviv
1993	Maccabi Haifa	1-0	Maccabi Tel Aviv
1994	Maccabi Tel Aviv	2-0	Hapoel Tel Aviv

Israel FA Cup

1/8th Finals

Bnei Yehoudah v Hapoel Kfar Saba	5-1
Hapoel Haifa v Maccabi Nathanya	2-0
Hapoel Petach Tikva v Hapoel Ashkelon	3-1
Hapoel Tel Aviv v Hapoel Taibe	2-1
Hapoel Zafririm Holon v Maccabi Herzlia	2-1
Maccabi Ironi Ashdod v Maccabi Yavne	5-1
Maccabi Petach Tikva v Beitar Jerusalem	5-3
Maccabi Tel Aviv v Maccabi Haifa	2-1

Quarter-Finals

Hapoel Tel Aviv v Hapoel Haifa	4-1
Hapoel Zafririm Holon v Maccabi Ironi Ashdod	1-0
Maccabi Petach Tikva v Hapoel Petach Tikva	2-0
Maccabi Tel Aviv v Bnei Yehoudah	2-0

Semi-Finals

Maccabi Tel Aviv v Hapoel Zafririm Holon	3-3 5-4 on pens
Hapoel Tel Aviv v Maccabi Petach Tikva	1-1 3-1 on pens

Final

Maccabi Tel Aviv v Hapoel Tel Aviv	2-0

Kodritsky's goal was his 14th of the season, but the last he would ever score; he was killed in a car accident the following week. With Maccabi Haifa winning, Tel Aviv's lead was cut to a single point and it was Haifa who took over the leadership when Tel Aviv suffered another defeat, this time 2-3 at home to Beitar who were a long way off the pace in fifth place. Maccabi Haifa's 4-0 home win over local rivals Hapoel Haifa was therefore made doubly sweet.

The leadership swapped back and forth although Maccabi Haifa held on to it for six weeks from the end of January until Maccabi Tel Aviv won it back, but only briefly. With the first stage of the season coming to a close, Maccabi Haifa thrashed Maccabi Tel Aviv by 5-0 to open up a three-point lead and remain the only unbeaten side in the league. The match marked the end of the first phase of games home and away, and meant that Haifa would have the right to stage the third league encounter two weeks later.

The result was not welcomed by cross-town rivals Hapoel Haifa who, despite a goalless draw with Maccabi Petach Tikva, were rooted to the bottom of the table and looking increasingly certain for relegation. Things didn't change the following weekend when they travelled for the Haifa derby and lost 1-6. When the top two meet again, Tel Aviv coach Avraham Grant had prepared his side much better and forced a 1-1 draw. Their hard-line approach brought a good deal of criticism from his opposite number, Gloria Speigel, after he had seen his Ukrainian defender Roman Petz carried off with a broken leg.

The 5-0 win proved to be the turning point for Maccabi Haifa, who continued their unbeaten run through to the end of the season, and secured the title with two games to go when Maccabi Tel Aviv dropped points in a 2-2 draw to Bnei Yehuodah; Haifa's late equaliser at Petach Tikvah was enough.

Maccabi Tel Aviv didn't finish the season empty-handed. A quarter-final win over Maccabi Haifa was some revenge and left the way clear for them to win the cup by beating Hapoel Tel Aviv 2-0 in the final. The last European position went to Hapoel Beersheba, who finished third to win Israel's first-ever UEFA Cup spot. For Maccabi Tel Aviv the season was completed with a coup when they signed Alon Mizrahi from Maccabi Haifa. His scoring talents will give Tel Aviv a big boost for the 1994–95 championship.

Israel Championship Results 1993-94

	Maccabi Haifa	Maccabi Tel Aviv	Maccabi Nathanya	Maccabi Herzelia	Maccabi Petach Tikva	Maccabi Ironi Ashdod	Hapoel Beersheva	Hapoel Zafririm Holon	Hapoel Tel Aviv	Hapoel Petach Tikva	Hapoel Kfar Saba	Hapoel Haifa	Beitar Jerusalem	Bnei Yehuda
Maccabi Haifa	—	1-1	2-4	0-1	0-4	1-3	1-2	0-3	0-1	1-3	1-1	0-0	2-3	0-3
	—	0-5	2-2	0-2	0-1	1-2	0-2	0-0	1-2	1-2	1-4	0-4	0-4	0-1
	—	1-1	1-1	1-3	1-1	1-1	2-2	0-1	2-3	0-6	0-0	1-6	1-5	1-5
Maccabi Tel Aviv	1-1	—	0-1	0-1	0-4	0-1	0-2	0-6	1-2	1-2	1-2	0-7	0-1	1-5
	5-0	—	1-3	1-1	1-1	0-2	0-3	0-0	0-1	1-2	1-2	0-3	3-2	2-0
	1-1	—	1-2	1-2	1-1	2-5	0-1	3-2	0-0	2-1	0-2	2-3	1-2	2-2
Maccabi Nathanya	4-2	1-0	—	2-1	1-2	5-1	2-1	1-2	3-1	2-2	0-3	1-7	5-1	1-1
	2-2	3-1	—	3-4	1-4	2-3	1-1	2-0	3-1	4-2	1-0	0-0	1-1	0-2
	1-1	2-1	—	0-2	1-1	4-1	0-0	0-2	2-3	3-0	1-3	1-1	1-2	4-2
Maccabi Herzelia	1-0	1-0	1-2	—	0-1	0-0	3-2	1-0	3-1	0-2	2-2	1-1	2-2	1-2
	2-0	2-1	4-3	—	0-0	0-3	1-1	1-5	1-1	3-0	0-1	0-1	2-0	0-1
	3-1	2-1	2-0	—	3-0	0-0	2-2	2-0	1-0	0-0	2-0	1-3	1-0	2-2
Maccabi Petach Tikva	4-0	4-0	2-1	1-0	—	1-0	3-0	1-1	2-1	1-0	0-4	0-0	3-1	1-1
	1-0	1-1	4-1	0-0	—	0-1	0-1	0-1	0-3	1-1	0-0	0-0	0-1	0-1
	1-1	1-1	1-1	0-3	—	5-0	0-0	0-4	2-1	0-0	1-1	1-2	1-2	3-1
Maccabi Ironi Ashdod	3-1	1-0	1-5	0-0	0-1	—	1-0	2-0	2-1	1-1	2-0	0-7	2-0	0-2
	2-1	2-0	3-2	3-0	1-0	—	0-0	1-1	2-2	3-1	2-0	1-1	2-0	0-6
	1-1	5-2	1-4	0-0	0-5	—	3-1	0-0	5-2	0-2	0-0	1-2	3-1	3-1
Hapoel Beersheva	2-1	2-0	1-2	2-3	0-3	0-1	—	0-0	1-3	0-1	0-1	1-3	0-2	1-0
	2-0	3-0	1-1	1-1	1-0	0-0	—	1-1	1-3	1-2	0-2	1-2	3-2	0-4
	2-2	1-0	0-0	2-2	0-0	1-3	—	0-0	0-1	1-3	2-0	0-0	3-1	0-3
Hapoel Zafririm Holon	5-0	6-0	2-1	0-1	1-1	0-2	0-0	—	1-1	1-3	1-2	3-1	4-2	1-1
	0-0	0-0	0-2	5-1	1-0	1-1	1-1	—	2-3	0-0	1-4	0-0	1-5	1-0
	1-0	2-3	2-0	0-2	4-0	0-0	0-0	—	4-0	4-1	1-2	2-0	6-1	3-1
Hapoel Tel Aviv	1-0	2-1	1-3	1-3	1-2	1-2	3-1	1-1	—	3-1	0-3	2-0	4-0	4-0
	2-1	1-0	1-3	1-1	3-0	2-2	3-1	3-2	—	0-2	0-3	4-1	1-1	0-2
	3-2	0-0	3-2	0-1	1-2	2-5	1-0	0-4	—	0-0	1-4	2-3	1-0	0-2
Hapoel Petach Tikva	3-1	2-1	2-2	2-0	0-1	1-1	1-0	3-1	1-3	—	1-1	1-1	1-1	0-1
	2-1	2-1	2-4	0-3	1-1	1-3	2-1	0-0	2-0	—	1-2	0-4	3-0	2-1
	6-0	1-2	0-3	0-0	0-0	2-0	3-1	1-4	0-0	—	1-1	2-1	3-3	1-3
Hapoel Kfar Saba	1-1	2-1	3-0	2-2	4-0	0-2	1-0	2-1	3-0	1-1	—	0-2	3-2	3-1
	4-1	2-1	0-1	1-0	0-0	0-0	2-0	4-1	3-0	2-1	—	0-2	1-1	0-1
	0-0	2-0	3-1	0-2	1-1	0-0	0-2	2-1	4-1	1-1	—	4-3	1-0	2-2
Hapoel Haifa	0-0	7-0	7-1	1-1	0-0	7-0	3-1	1-3	0-2	1-1	2-0	—	1-1	3-1
	4-0	3-0	0-0	1-0	0-0	1-1	2-1	0-0	1-4	4-0	2-0	—	3-1	0-0
	6-1	3-2	1-1	3-1	2-1	2-1	0-0	0-2	3-2	1-2	3-4	—	1-3	1-1
Beitar Jerusalem	3-2	1-0	1-5	2-2	1-3	0-2	2-0	2-4	0-4	1-1	2-3	1-1	—	3-1
	4-0	2-3	1-1	0-2	1-0	0-2	2-3	5-1	1-1	0-3	1-1	1-3	—	8-2
	5-1	2-1	2-1	0-1	2-1	1-3	1-3	1-6	0-1	3-3	0-1	3-1	—	1-2
Bnei Yehuda	3-0	5-1	1-1	2-1	1-1	2-0	0-1	1-1	0-4	1-0	1-3	1-3	1-3	—
	1-0	0-2	2-0	1-0	1-0	6-0	4-0	0-1	2-0	1-2	1-0	0-0	2-8	—
	5-1	2-2	2-4	2-2	1-3	1-3	3-0	1-3	2-0	3-1	2-2	1-1	2-1	—

At the bottom, a late revival by Hapoel Haifa allowed them to move ahead of Hapoel Hfar Saba, who dropped back into the State League a year after promotion. Hapoel Haifa's escape was by virtue of the fact that for the 1994-95 season the four Israeli leagues are being expanded to 16 teams and reverting to the traditional home and away format. Hapoel Rishon Le Zion easily won the State League to gain promotion to the National League, along with Hapoel Beit Shean and Beitar Tel Aviv – the latter winning their place back a season after being relegated.

Italy

Milan grind out another Scudetto

The pre-season provided Italian clubs with the chance to boost their squads and trim their rosters where necessary, but austerity was the watchword as most clubs cut back and made only modest investments by their extraordinary standards. Evidence of this was shown by the number of foreign players the *stranieri* imported during the close season – just seven, compared to 34 at the start of 1992-93.

Sampdoria caused a stir by signing England midfielder David Platt from Juventus for £5.2m, making Platt the most expensive footballer in the world at a combined total cost of £17.4m. Platt was joined at the Stade Luigi Ferraris by Ruud Gullit, the Dutch striker who had become surplus to requirements at import-laden Milan, but England defender Des Walker was sold to Sheffield Wednesday for £2.7m after one disappointing season in Serie A. Lazio also broke a record ... their £6.5m signing of Torino's Luca Marchegiani made him the world's most expensive goalkeeper. The Rome club also unloaded striker Karlheinz Riedle back to Germany, where Borussia Dortmund paid a Bundesliga-record £4.5m for his services.

Other notable moves in Italy during the pre-season included Cagliari's signing of Julio Dely Valdes, the first Panamanian to play in Serie A; Internazionale's combined fee of £11m for Ajax Amsterdam's international duo Dennis Bergkamp and Wim Jonk; Milan took demoted and financially plagued Fiorentina's Danish striker Brian Laudrup and Brescia's Romanian striker Florin Raducioiu on loan for the season while selling Dutch midfielder Frank Rijkaard back to his former club Ajax; Atalanta signed French midfielder Franck Sauzee from Marseille, AS Roma bought Argentinian striker Abel Balbo from Udinese as a replacement for his suspended compatriot Claudio Caniggia; Napoli ditched Frenchman Laurent Blanc, sold to St Etienne, and Brazilian Careca, sold to Kashiwa Reysol in Japan; Torino sold

Francesco Turrini of Piacenza (left) shields the ball from Giovanni Stroppa of Foggia during their Serie A encounter.

Belgian midfielder Enzo Scifo to Monaco and Brazilian striker Casagrande to Flamengo. Only newly promoted Piacenza – in Serie A for the first time – could boast an all-Italian squad. They were also referred too, perhaps unkindly, as the most environmentally friendly side in Serie A, due to their large contingent of 'recycled' players!

In pre-season friendlies, Lazio finished last in both the Makita Tournament in London and the Trofeo Teresa Herrera in La Coruna, Milan lost 3-0 to Barcelona in the Ciudad de Oviedo, Platt scored for Sampdoria in a 1-1 draw with Udinese, Inter beat

Federazione Italiana Giuoco Calcio	
Founded:	1898
Address:	Via Gregorio Allegri 14, CP 2450, 1-00198 Rome
Phone:	+39 6 849 11 11
Fax:	+39 6 849 91 22 39
UEFA Affiliation:	1954
FIFA Affiliation:	1905
National Stadium:	Stadio Olimpico, Rome
Capacity:	80,000
Season:	August to May
Colours:	Blue, White, Blue
Change:	White, Blue, Blue

David Platt of Italian Cup winners Sampdoria.

Real Madrid 10-9 on penalties after a 2-2 draw in the Santiago Bernabeu Trophy, and Milan beat Real Madrid in a TV-funded prestige friendly at San Siro. Milan then travelled to Washington DC for the Italian Supercup match against Torino, another TV-inspired spectacle which Milan won 1-0.

The season kicked off on 29 August with a muted 1-0 win for champions Milan against Lecce, thanks to a goal by Croat Zvonimir Boban. Platt and Gullit were on target as Sampdoria won 2-1 away to Napoli, and Cagliari coach Gigi Radice was dismissed just 24 hours into the new season following his side's 5-2 defeat at Atalanta. Experienced Bruno Giorgi was drafted in as his replacement.

The second Sunday of the season was a disaster for Juventus as they went down 2-1 at AS Roma. Roberto Baggio and Gianluca Vialli both missed penalties and Vialli, in doing so, stumbled and broke a bone in a foot, which ruled him out of action for two months. There was similar bad news for Inter when their midfielder Nicola Berti damaged a knee ligament in the midweek 2-1 win over Cremonese and was also out, for six months.

After the first month of the season Torino and Milan led the way with seven points apiece from four games. Torino then slipped badly at Parma, where a hat-trick by Faustino Asprilla gave the home side a 3-0 win, while Milan made top spot all their own with a 2-0 win over Roma.

Azeglio Vicini, manager of Italy's 1990 World Cup team, became the second coach sacked of the new season – Udinese pushed the eject button on him, after three consecutive defeats which left them third from bottom after six matches, and replaced him with Adriano Fedele. In Europe, all seven Italian clubs safely negotiated the first round, although Milan only just managed a 1-0 aggregate win over Switzerland's FC Aarau in the Champions' Cup and Torino only scraped through 3-2 on aggregate after losing 2-1 at home to Lillestrom of Norway. September closed with two more World Cup points for the Azzurri, thanks to a 3-0 win in Estonia.

October opened with Sampdoria closing the gap on leaders Milan to one point after a 4-1 success against Atalanta, while Milan were being held to a goalless draw at home by Lazio. It was a mixed month for Paul Gascoigne's club, who crashed 2-0 at home to third division Avellino in the first leg of an Italian Cup tie, prompting an angry demonstration by fans at the club's training ground, and then paid £8m to Marseille for Croat striker Alen Boksic. The national side continued their progress in the World Cup qualifiers with a 3-1 home win over Scotland, which took them to the top of Group One with one match to play.

The month closed on a high note for Sampdoria when they beat Milan 3-2 at home. Gullit gained some measure of revenge on his old club with the winning goal as Samp fought back from two goals down in an exciting encounter. The win pushed Sampdoria into a three-way tie at the top with new leaders Parma, and Milan on 19 points after 13 games. Serie A casualties in the second round of the Italian Cup included Cagliari (beaten by Cesena), Juventus (Venezia), Cremonese (Brescia), Napoli (Ancona), Lazio (Avellino), Lecce (Udinese) and Reggiana (Fiorentina).

November began with a win for Milan in the derby against Internazionale, but at a cost – midfielder Zvonimir Boban injured a knee and was ruled out for two months. Parma kept the pressure up with a 2-0 home win over Juventus and then strengthened their hand by buying Argentinian midfielder Nestor Sensini from Udinese. Lazio were the only failures in the second round of European competition, losing 2-1 on aggregate to Portugal's Boavista in the UEFA Cup. Parma were given a severe fright by Israel's Maccabi Haifa in their defence of the Cup-Winners' Cup, needing penalties to progress after a 1-1 aggregate draw. Inter also struggled through against Cypriots Apollon Limassol in the UEFA Cup. Milan won their first leg tie in the Champions' Cup 6-0 away to FC Copenhagen, and took the unusual step of allowing school children free entry to the 'academic' return at San Siro, which they also won, 1-0, to take their predicted place in the UEFA Champions' League.

Lecce, bottom of the table and in deep trouble, sacked coach Nedo Sonetti following a 2-1 defeat at Cremonese. Rino Marchese was the new man in the hot seat, but he could do little as Lecce then lost 2-0 at home to Roma in his first game in charge to stay rooted to the bottom. Milan were held 1-1 at home by Piacenza in a third-round Cup game, but the good news was the return, as a substitute, of Lentini after his terrible car crash during the close season.

Struggling Reggiana were overjoyed when new Portuguese

winger Paulo Futre, signed from cash-strapped Marseille, scored on his debut in a welcome 2-0 win over Cremonese. The joy was short-lived though, as Futre tore knee ligaments and was ruled out for three months. Highlight of the month was the national side's 1-0 win over Portugal in Milan, a Dino Baggio goal securing the points and a place in the World Cup finals during the summer. The month closed with a 0-0 draw in the top-of-the-table clash between Parma and Milan.

Napoli hit the headlines in December for all the wrong reasons. The club owed £3m in back taxes and had to sell Gianfranco Zola and Massimo Crippa (both to Parma) to help balance the books. Even so, the government still had to give them extra time to pay the outstanding balance.

In Europe, Milan took control of their group in the Champions' League with a draw against Anderlecht and a 3-0 home win over FC Porto. In the UEFA Cup Cagliari scored a fine 5-1 win over Belgium's Mechelen, Juventus knocked out Tenerife and Internazionale disposed of Norwich City.

Milan clung on to top spot with a 1-0 win over Torino before flying to Tokyo for the World Club Championship match against Sao Paulo. As late replacements for disgraced Marseille it was perhaps understandable when the 'Rosso Nero' went down 3-2 to the powerful Brazilians, despite dominating the game.

Parma took advantage of Milan's absence by beating Cagliari 4-0 away to go top on goal difference. But Milan returned to League action with a 2-1 win over Cagliari while Parma were surprisingly beaten 3-1 at home by Napoli. Sampdoria and Juventus kept up their pursuit with home wins over Reggiana and

Never far from the headlines was Lazio's Paul Gascoigne (centre). It was another season of injury and incident for the England player seen here during the Rome derby.

International Results 1993–94

Date	Opponents	Result	Venue	Comp.	Scorers
22/9/93	Estonia	3-0	Tallinn	WCQ1	R. Baggio (20 pen, 73), Mancini (59)
13/10/93	Scotland	3-1	Rome	WCQ1	Donadoni (3), Casiraghi (16), Eranio (80)
17/11/93	Portugal	1-0	Milan	WCQ1	D. Baggio (83)
16/2/94	France	0-1	Naples	Friendly	
23/3/94	Germany	1-2	Stuttgart	Friendly	D. Baggio (44)
27/5/94	Finland	2-0	Parma	Friendly	Signori (24), Casiraghi (66)
3/6/94	Switzerland	1-0	Rome	Friendly	Signori (25)
11/6/94	Costa Rica	1-0	New Haven	Friendly	Signori (70)
18/6/94	Rep. Ireland	0-1	New York	WCFE	
23/6/94	Norway	1-0	New York	WCFE	D. Baggio (68)
28/6/94	Mexico	1-1	Washington	WCFE	Massaro (48)
5/7/94	Nigeria †	2-1	Boston	WCF2	R. Baggio (89, 102 pen)
9/7/94	Spain	2-1	Boston	WCFQ	D. Baggio (26), R. Baggio (87)
13/7/94	Bulgaria	2-1	New Jersey	WCFS	R. Baggio (21, 26)
17/7/94	Brazil †	0-0	Pasadena	WCFF	

Brazil won 3-2 on penalties

† *after extra time*

National Record	P	W	D	L	F	A
European Championships	61	28	22	11	88	44
World Cup Finals	61	35	14	12	97	59
World Cup Qualifiers	53	36	10	7	122	37

Piacenza respectively. It was a good month for Juventus as Roberto Baggio won FIFA's World Footballer of the Year trophy to add to his European award.

The year closed with a huge shock in the third round of the Italian Cup when Milan were knocked out by struggling Piacenza. No problems though for Torino, Parma, Inter and Sampdoria who all went through, although Samp needed penalties to get past Roma. There was embarrassment, too, for Lazio when it was revealed that Paul Gascoigne's rare appearances were costing the club a whopping £400 per minute!

Ring out the old, ring in the new – but there was nothing new in Milan as the champions continued to grind out old familiar results with a victory at Reggiana, where French midfielder Marcel Desailly scored the only goal of the game, and his compatriot, Jean-Pierre Papin, was sent off. Juventus, too, were in good form, winning 3-0 at Udinese, but Sampdoria lost ground after they were held to a 1-1 draw at Lazio. And so 1994 got under way, but scoreless draws by Milan against relegation-threatened Udinese and rock-bottom Lecce allowed the chasing pack a rare chance to gain ground. But, with Parma losing and Juventus drawing at Cremonese, only Sampdoria took the opportunity, beating Napoli 4-1 with two goals for Roberto Mancini taking him past the Serie A 100 goal mark – this after David Platt had missed a penalty!

Milan and Parma took time out from League action to contest the first leg of an all-Italian European Super Cup, with Milan – replacements for the barred Marseille – sneaking a 1-0 'Papin' win in Georgio Armani's home town. But Milan still seemed vulnerable in the league, and played out another score-less draw with struggling opposition in Genoa. But again, neither Juve nor Parma could use the opportunity to close the gap. The San Siro blues were in abundance as Parma produced a sparkling 2-0 win to reverse the European Super Cup first leg and take their second European trophy in only three years of active competition.

Struggling sides continued to make the headlines, this time in the encounter between Reggiana and Atalanta, when goalkeeper Fabrizio Ferron had to have heart massage on the pitch following a clash with Reggiana's Michele Padovano. Ferron was kept in hospital overnight, and woke to discover that Atalanta had gone down 3-0 to one of their main relegation rivals. While those at the bottom were hogging the limelight, Milan chalked up a 2-0 win over lowly Piacenza as Sampdoria and Parma drew 1-1 in Genoa. In the Italian Cup, Parma, Ancona, Torino and Sampdoria battled their way through to the semi-finals, with Parma the most impressive in thrashing Foggia 9-1 on aggregate, Tomas Brolin scoring twice.

In the league, however, Milan simply never let up. A 2-0 win at Roma kept them four points clear of their three remaining challengers, and, by mid-February, they had opened up a six-point lead over Juventus. All attention at this stage had switched to the San Siro's other residents, Internazionale. A 2-1 home defeat by Lazio — on top of a Cup exit against Sampdoria and a 3-3 home draw with Cagliari — proved too much to take and coach Osvaldo Bagnoli was sacked. What had started as a season of great promise for Inter had degenerated into a shambles, with only the UEFA Cup offering any hope of success. Giampiero Marini, the club's youth coach, took over but had great difficulty motivating a demoralised side with too many veterans and too

Final Serie A Table 1993–94

	P	W	D	L	F	A	Pts
Milan	34	19	12	3	36	15	50
Juventus	34	17	13	4	58	25	47
Sampdoria	34	18	8	8	64	39	44
Lazio	34	17	10	7	55	40	44
Parma	34	17	7	10	50	35	41
Napoli	34	12	12	10	41	35	36
Roma	34	10	15	9	35	30	35
Torino	34	11	12	11	39	37	34
Foggia	34	10	13	11	46	46	33
Cremonese	34	9	14	11	41	41	32
Genoa	34	8	16	10	32	40	32
Cagliari	34	10	12	12	39	48	32
Internazionale	34	11	9	14	46	45	31
Reggiana	34	10	11	13	29	37	31
Piacenza	34	8	14	12	32	43	30
Udinese	34	7	14	13	35	48	28
Atalanta	34	5	11	18	35	65	21
Lecce	34	3	5	26	28	72	11

Top Scorers
- 26 Giuseppe SIGNORI (Lazio)
- 18 Gianfranco ZOLA (Parma)
- 17 Roberto BAGGIO (Juventus)
  Andrea SILENZI (Torino)
- 16 Ruben SOSA (Internazionale)
- 15 Daniel FONSECA (Napoli)
  Rudd GULLIT (Sampdoria)
- 14 Marco BRANCA (Udinese)
- 13 Julio DELY VALDES (Cagliari)
- 12 Luis Airton OLIVEIRA (Cagliari)
  Bryan ROY (Foggia)
  Roberto MANCINI (Sampdoria)
- 11 Andrea TENTONI (Cremonese)
  Daniele MASSARO (Milan)
  Abel BALBO (Roma)
- 10 Faustino ASPRILLA (Parma)
  Michele PADOVANO (Reggiana)

Promotions and Relegations
Promoted: Fiorentina, Bari, Brescia, Padova
Relegated: Piacenza, Udinese, Atalanta, Lecce

The Foreigners

When the first ball was kicked in Serie A at the start of the 1993–94 season there were no fewer than 58 *stranieri* in place. With the exception of Piacenza all clubs had at least two players with origins outside of Italy. Although eight players originated from the Netherlands, South America had a big influence with no fewer than 20 players provided by Argentina, Brazil and Uruguay.

Atalanta:	Sauzee (Fra), Alemao (Bra), Montero (Uru), Rodriguez (Arg)
Cagliari:	Valdes (Pan), Oliveira (Bra), Herrera (Uru)
Cremonese:	Dezotti (Arg), Floriancic (Slo)
Foggia:	Chamot (Arg), Roy (Hol), Kolyanov (Rus)
Genoa:	Vink (Hol), Petrescu (Rom), Van't Schip (Hol), Skuhravy (Cze)
Internazionale:	Bergkamp (Hol), Jonk (Hol), Sosa (Uru), Shalimov (Rus), Pancev (Mac)
Juventus:	Ban (Cro), Kohler (Ger), Moller (Ger), Cesar (Bra)
Lazio:	Winter (Hol), Gascoigne (Eng), Doll (Ger)
Lecce:	Gerson (Bra), Gaucho (Bra)
Milan:	B. Laudrup (Den), Raducioiu (Rom), Van Basten (Hol), Papin (Fra), Savicevic (Yug), Boban (Cro)
Napoli:	Fonseca (Uru), Thern (Swe)
Parma:	Asprilla (Col), Brolin (Swe), Grun (Bel), Beti (Arg)
Piacenza:	–
Reggiana:	Ekstrom (Swe), Taffarel (Bra)
Roma:	Balbo (Arg), Hassler (Ger), Mihajlovic (Yug), Aldair (Bra), Caniggia (Arg)
Sampdoria:	Gullit (Hol), Platt (Eng), Jugovic (Yug), Katanec (Slo)
Torino:	Jarni (Cro), Francescoli (Uru), Aguilera (Uru)
Udinese:	Senseni (Arg), Koziminski (Pol)

many new faces. Marini's first game in charge was a 2-1 defeat at Piacenza, and signalled the start of an ungracious slide down the table that stopped just short of relegation.

In the Cup semi-finals, Sampdoria accounted for Parma with a 2-1 aggregate win, while second division promotion contenders Ancona held out against holders Torino 1-0 on aggregate. Milan, meanwhile, continued to churn out victories in the league, and their goalkeeper, Sebastiano Rossi, set a record by going unbeaten for 929 minutes. Foggia's Igor Kolyvanov finally got the ball past him but Milan already had made sure of two more points on that occasion.

In Europe's all-Italian encounter Cagliari beat Juventus 3-1 on aggregate in the UEFA Cup quarter-finals. After the 1-0 first leg win in Sardinia the home club had to appeal for the return of the UEFA flag, stolen from the Sant'Elia stadium. The No. 9 shirt worn by Cagliari's Panamanian striker Julio Dely Valdes was offered in part exchange! Inter, out of sorts in the league, found their form in their UEFA Cup clash with Borussia Dortmund, winning 4-3 on aggregate. Parma progressed to the semi-finals beating Ajax, but Torino – under pressure from mounting debts and an official UEFA inquiry relating to bribes – fell under the spell of Arsenal. Milan stayed on course in the UEFA Champions' League

Giuseppe Signori was top scorer in Serie A for the second successive season, but despite scoring for Italy consistently in friendly internationals he was out of luck in the World Cup Finals.

and, after a 2-1 win over Werder, secured a semi-final spot with a 1-1 draw in Bremen.

Squeezed in between all this action was a fortnight in which Milan virtually confirmed that they would retain their Serie A *scudetto* with wins over their closest rivals. A goal by Eranio on the hour was enough to take the points against Juventus, and a 1-0 win over Sampdoria the following week extended their lead to eight points, leaving the chasing clubs with a massive and improbable task.

Milan ended March with a 2-1 win over Inter, thanks to a goal a minute from time by Massaro, the man who took on the role of goalscorer in Van Basten's absence, and an uncharacteristic 1-0 defeat at Napoli. Coach Capello blasted his players for their relaxed attitude, and confounded everyone when he then confirmed that Milan were negotiating with Sampdoria for Gullit's return. Across the city, Internazionale were making news of their own with the announcement that Ottavio Bianchi,

Five-Year Records League 1-2-3 and Cup Winners

League Results

	1st	Pts	2nd	Pts	3rd	Pts
1990	Napoli	51	Milan	49	Internazionale	44
1991	Sampdoria	51	Milan	46	Internazionale	46
1992	Milan	56	Juventus	48	Torino	43
1993	Milan	50	Internazionale	46	Parma	41
1994	Milan	50	Juventus	47	Sampdoria	44

Cup Final Results

1990	Juventus	0-0	1-0	Milan	1-0 on aggregate
1991	Roma	3-1	1-1	Sampdoria	4-2 on aggregate
1992	Parma	0-1	2-0	Juventus	2-1 on aggregate
1993	Torino	3-0	2-5	Roma	5-5 on aggregate
	Torino win on away goals rule				
1994	Sampdoria	0-0	6-1	Ancona	6-1 on aggregate

Italian Cup

Third Round	1st Leg	2nd Leg	Agg
Ancona v Avellino	1-0	2-2	3-2
Atalanta v Torino	0-3	0-0	0-3
Fiorentina v Venezia	1-2	0-0	1-2
Foggia v Cesena	1-1	2-0	3-1
Milan v Piacenza	1-1	0-1	1-2
Parma v Brescia	1-1	3-2	4-3
Sampdoria v Roma	2-1	1-2	3-3
5-4 on pens			
Udinese v Internazionale	0-0	1-2	1-2
Quarter-Finals			
Foggia v Parma	0-3	1-6	1-9
Venice v Ancona	0-0	0-2	0-2
Piacenza v Torino	2-2	1-2	3-4
Sampdoria v Internazionale	1-0	1-1	2-1
Semi-Finals			
Sampdoria v Parma	2-1	1-0	3-1
Ancona v Torino	1-0	0-0	1-0

Final 1st Leg
Ancona 0 Sampdoria 0
Att: 16,871 *Ref:* Trentalange
Ancona: Armellini, Sogliano, Centofanti, Pecoraro, Mazzarano, Glonek, Lupo, Bruniera (Caccia 49), M. Agostini, De Angelis, Vecchiola.
Sampdoria: Pagliuca, Dall'Igna, M. Serena, Gullit, Vierchowod, S. Sacchetti, Lombardo, Jugovic (Invernizzi 70), Platt, R. Mancini, Evani.

Final 2nd Leg
Sampdoria 6 Ancona 1
Vecchiola own goal (50), Lupo (71)
Lombardo (57, 75),
Vierchowod (66), Bertarelli (80 pen),
Evani (85 pen)
Att: 40,000 *Ref:* Luci
Sampdoria: Pagliuca, Invernizzi, M. Serena, Vierchowod, S. Sacchetti (M. Mannini 87), Jugovic, Gullit, Lombardo, Platt, Bertarelli (Salsano 87), Evani.
Ancona: Nista, Fontana, Sogliano, Glonek, Mazzarano, Pecoraro, Lupo, Gadda (Caccia 59), De Angelis (Bruniera 68), M. Agostini, Vecchiola.
Sampdoria win 6-1 on aggregate.

Anglo-Italians! Paul Gascoigne of Lazio and David Platt of Sampdoria.

formerly with Napoli, would be their coach for the 1994–95 season, and that Toto Schillaci – the star of the 1990 World Cup in Italy – was moving to Jubilo Iwata of Japan.

April opened with an important meeting in Milan between AC and Parma, and a 1-1 draw of more advantage to the home side than the visitors. Lazio also had bad news when Paul Gascoigne broke a leg in a training game, ruling him out for anything up to a year. But their improved league form had pushed them steadily up the table, and confirmed them as certain UEFA Cup candidates. At the other end of the table Internazionale, still facing the serious threat of relegation, eased their worries with a 4-1 win against Lecce, who were in dire trouble. Sampdoria, having given up the pursuit of Milan in the League, switched their attention to the Italian Cup Final, securing a 0-0 draw in the away leg at Ancona to put them in command for the return.

A 0-0 draw at Torino moved Milan to within a point of their third consecutive *scudetto*, a feat last achieved by Torino in the 1940s. They then made more transfer headlines, announcing the end-of-season sale of Jean-Pierre Papin to Bayern Munich for £2.1m, before clinching a 1-1 draw with Udinese to make sure of the title with two games to spare. For Juventus, a 6-1 thrashing of Lazio — with Vialli scoring a hat-trick — was scant consolation, and they were rocked further when coach Giovanni Trapattoni announced that he was also moving to Bayern Munich for the new season, thus becoming the first Italian coach in the Bundesliga.

There was further success on all fronts in Europe, with Italian clubs winning through to all three finals. Milan made no mistake against Monaco despite the dismissal of Costacurta; away goals squeezed Parma past a stubborn Benfica, and Internazionale saw off the spirited challenge of Cagliari. These victories meant that Milan

Serie A Championship Results 1993–94

	Atalanta	Cagliari	Cremonese	Foggia	Genoa	Internazionale	Juventus	Lazio	Lecce	Milan	Napoli	Parma	Piacenza	Reggiana	Roma	Sampdoria	Torino	Udinese
Atalanta	—	5-2	0-0	1-1	2-1	2-1	1-3	1-1	3-4	0-1	1-1	0-2	0-0	2-1	1-1	1-4	2-2	1-1
Cagliari	1-1	—	0-0	1-1	0-0	1-0	0-1	4-1	2-1	0-0	1-2	0-4	2-0	3-0	1-1	0-0	2-1	1-2
Cremonese	2-0	3-1	—	2-0	1-1	1-4	1-1	1-0	2-1	0-2	2-0	0-0	4-0	1-1	1-1	0-0	1-1	1-1
Foggia	1-1	0-1	1-1	—	3-0	1-1	1-1	4-1	5-0	1-1	0-1	3-2	1-0	1-0	1-1	1-2	1-0	2-2
Genoa	2-1	1-1	1-0	1-4	—	1-0	1-1	1-1	2-0	0-0	0-0	0-4	0-1	0-0	2-0	1-1	1-1	3-0
Internazionale	1-2	3-3	2-1	3-1	1-3	—	2-2	1-2	4-1	1-2	0-0	3-2	2-0	2-1	2-2	3-0	0-0	1-0
Juventus	2-1	1-1	1-0	2-0	4-0	1-0	—	6-1	5-1	0-1	1-0	4-0	2-0	4-0	0-0	3-1	3-2	1-0
Lazio	3-1	4-0	4-2	0-0	4-0	0-0	3-1	—	3-0	0-1	3-0	2-1	1-0	2-0	1-0	1-1	1-2	2-1
Lecce	5-1	0-1	2-4	0-2	0-0	1-3	1-1	1-2	—	0-1	0-1	1-1	2-0	2-4	0-2	0-3	1-2	1-0
Milan	2-0	2-1	1-0	2-1	1-0	2-1	1-1	0-0	0-0	—	2-1	1-1	2-0	0-1	2-0	1-0	1-0	2-2
Napoli	4-0	1-2	2-1	1-1	1-1	0-0	0-0	1-2	3-1	1-0	—	2-0	0-0	5-0	1-1	1-2	0-0	2-1
Parma	2-1	3-1	2-1	3-0	2-1	4-1	2-0	2-0	1-0	0-0	1-3	—	0-0	1-0	0-2	2-1	3-0	0-1
Piacenza	4-0	1-1	1-1	5-4	1-1	2-1	0-0	1-2	2-1	0-0	1-1	1-1	—	3-2	1-0	2-1	0-3	0-0
Reggiana	3-0	3-1	2-0	0-0	1-1	1-0	0-0	0-0	1-0	0-1	1-0	2-0	1-1	—	0-0	1-1	1-0	1-1
Roma	2-1	2-0	1-2	0-0	1-1	1-1	2-1	1-1	3-0	0-2	2-3	2-0	3-1	0-0	—	0-1	2-0	0-2
Sampdoria	3-1	1-2	3-1	6-0	1-1	3-1	1-1	3-4	2-1	3-2	4-1	1-1	2-1	1-0	0-1	—	1-0	6-2
Torino	2-1	2-1	1-1	1-4	2-0	2-0	1-1	1-1	3-0	0-0	1-1	1-2	1-0	2-0	1-1	2-3	—	1-0
Udinese	0-0	1-1	3-3	3-0	0-4	0-1	0-3	2-2	2-1	0-0	3-1	0-1	2-2	2-1	0-0	0-2	1-1	—

On the ball for Parma – Gianfranco Zola after his big-money transfer from Napoli.

The Italian side that started the World Cup match against Norway.

became the first city to provide the winners of two UEFA trophies in the same season. Only Parma failed to make it a clean sweep. Milan's 4-0 demolition of Barcelona ranked along the all-time great performances and their closest rivals and co-residents Internazionale secured the UEFA Cup with 1-0 wins in both legs against SV Casino Salzburg. Parma, though, could find no way through a resilient Arsenal side, who won by the only goal of the game. That defeat was bad news for AS Roma, who had been hoping to secure the extra UEFA Cup spot that would be freed if Parma gained re-entry into the Cup-Winners' Cup.

At home Sampdoria secured a place in the Cup-Winners' Cup with the 6-1 second-leg dismantling of Ancona. The Serie B side had kept the game scoreless at half-time but fell apart in the second 45 minutes.

The final round of games in Serie A ended with a 1-0 defeat for Milan – resting many of their top players – at home to Reggiana, who thus managed to avoid relegation. Lecce, Atalanta, Udinese and Piacenza were not so fortunate: all four went down, to be replaced by Fiorentina, Bari, Brescia and Padova. Fiorentina, promoted at the first attempt, played their final match in total silence as their fans protested at their earlier relegation. A banner at one end of the stadium read: "We have nothing to celebrate, promotion was the least we could expect!"

Cagliari, who narrowly avoided relegation despite their fine run in the UEFA Cup, announced that they had signed former Uruguay coach Oscar Washington Tabarez as coach for next season, but the end of the 1993–94 Italian season belonged to Milan… as the rest of it had.

Gullit was duly confirmed as a Milan player for 1994–95, Giovanni Stroppa was signed up from Foggia, Brazilian striker Elber, who had been on loan at Servette, was sold to VfB Stuttgart, and Van Basten announced that he would be fit for the start of next season, but would start his training with Ajax.

How will it all pan out in the coming season? That is open to question, but Milan will certainly be among the front-runners once more, when Italian teams will compete for three points per win for the first time.

Internationally the Azzurri reached the World Cup Finals, Dino Baggio's goal against the Portuguese seven minutes from time clinching qualification from Group One, a point ahead of Switzerland. Results in the build-up to USA94 were mixed and included defeats by the French and Germans. The national Under-21 side won the European title, thanks to a 1-0 win over Portugal in Montpellier.

The draw for the European Championships was greeted with mixed views, with several potentially punishing trips breaking new ground in Croatia, Ukraine, Lithuania, Estonia and Slovenia. Nevertheless qualification for England 1996 should not provide too many problems and 1994–95 seems as though it will be another season in which the Italian club sides will dominate the international arena.

Latvia

The 1993–94 season saw Latvian football develop a more professional approach to the rest of Europe. Following the break-up of the Soviet Union the Baltic state found themselves near to chaos because of a lack of two fundamental commodities – money and communications. Thankfully, the country and the clubs have now started to take those first tentative steps into the World football arena, albeit with the odd hiccough on the way.

Internationally, having been accepted by FIFA for participation in the 1994 World Cup qualifying tournament, the Latvian national side did well to win five points and avoided the qualifying group wooden spoon through the coaching of Yanis Gilis. During 1993–94 they completed their first campaign with a two-goal defeat in Belfast at the hands of Northern Ireland. Defender Vaslery Ivanov, who started the season at RAF Jelgava and finished it in Sweden with HIF, now reigns as his country's most-capped player with 19 appearances and 1682 minutes of international football behind him. Another Swedish-based player, top scorer Ainars Linards, found appearances harder to come by, otherwise he could have been leading the caps chart.

Skonto Riga achieved their third successive championship, finishing eight points ahead of cross-town rivals Olimpia. The foundation for their hat-trick was an impregnable record at home, where nine wins and 35 goals were the bedrock of success. Indeed only three visiting clubs managed to score a goal in Skonto's stadium.

Skonto set the pace from the start of the 18-round championship and ended the first half of their series with a 4-1 win at Gauja Valmiera to put them three points clear of Vidus. Although the retention of the title was never really in doubt, Skonto had to wait until week 16 to make sure with a 4-0 win over Vairogs Rezekne. Curiously, the last round of matches brought together top and bottom – Skonto and Gauja Valmiera. It produced the biggest win anywhere in the league during the season, the champions confirming their status with a resounding 11-0 victory.

Olimpia Riga secured second spot from RAF by virtue of two 1-0 victories. In the Virsliga, if teams are level on points, positions are decided by the number of wins, then results between the two sides and then goal difference. At the bottom of the table, the play-off position was never really in doubt, with Gauja Valmiera collecting just one point in a dismal season – in a 1-1 draw with Vairogs Rezekne.

In the second division, Gemma Riga piped Baltnet Daugavpils

Final League Table 1993

Virsliga 1993	P	W	D	L	F	A	Pts
Skonto Riga	18	17	0	1	63	7	34
Olimpia Riga	18	12	2	4	31	17	26
RAF Jelgava	18	12	2	4	34	11	26
Pardaugava Riga	18	10	4	4	29	13	24
Auseklis Daugavpils	18	7	5	6	22	17	19
Vidus Riga	18	6	7	5	19	13	19
Olimpia Liepaya	18	3	6	9	24	46	12
FC DAG Riga	18	3	4	11	15	29	10
Vairogs Rezekne	18	3	3	12	12	36	9
Gauja Valmiera	18	0	1	18	14	74	1

Top Scorers

- 20 Alexandr YELISEYEV (Skonto Riga)
- 10 Vyacheslav ZHEVNEROVICH (Auseklis Daugavpils)
- 8 Andrey SHTOLCERS (Olimpia Riga)
- 7 Rihards BUTKUS (Pardaugava Riga)
- 6 Mickhail ZEMLINSKY (Skonto Riga), Alexey SHARANDO (Olimpia Riga), Aivars POZNYAK (RAF Jelgava)

Promotions and Relegation

Promoted: Gemma Riga, Baltnet Daugavpils, Inter Skonto (formerly Skonto-II Riga)

Relegated: Gauja Valmiera

Latvijas Futbola Federacija

Founded:	1921
Address:	Augsiela 1, Riga, LV-1009, Latvia
Phone:	+371-2 292998
Fax:	+371 8828331
UEFA Affiliation:	1992
FIFA Affiliation:	1922
National Stadium:	Daugava, Riga
Capacity:	15,700
Season:	April to November
Colours:	Carmine Red, White, Carmine Red
Change:	White, Carmine Red, White

Five-Year Records League 1-2-3 and Cup Winners

League Results

	1st	pts	2nd	pts	3rd	pts
1942	ASK Riga	9	Olimpia Liepaya	6	RFK Roga	4
1943	ASK Riga	11	Olimpia Liepaya	10	RFK Riga	8
1991	Skonto Riga	32	Pardaugava Riga	26	Olimpia Liepaya	25
1992	Skonto Riga	38	RAF Jelgava	38	VEF Riga	33
1993	Skonto Riga	34	Olimpia Riga	26	RAF Jelgava	26

Cup Final Results

1991	Stroitel Daugavpils	0-0	Skonto Riga	4-1 on pens
1992	Skonto Riga	1-0	Kompar/Daugava Riga aet	
1993	RAF Jelgava	1-0	Pardaugava Riga	
1994	Olimpia Riga	2-0	FC Dag Riga	

International Results 1993–94

Date	Opponents	Result	Venue	Comp.
8/9/93	N. Ireland	0-2	Belfast	WCQ3
3/6/94	Malta	2-0	Riga	Friendly
30/7/94	Estonia	2-0	Vilnius	Baltic Cup
31/7/94	Lithuania	0-1	Vilnius	Baltic Cup

National Record

	P	W	D	L	F	A
European Championship	Never participated					
World Cup Finals	Never qualified					
World Cup Qualifiers	3	2	0	1	10	5
World Cup Qualifiers†	12	0	5	7	4	21

† Post-war

Championship Results 1993

	Auseklis Daugavpils	Gauja Valmeria	Olimpia Liepaia	Olimpia Riga	Pardaugava Riga	RAF Jelgava	FC Dag Riga	Skonto Riga	Vairogs Rezekne	Vidus Riga
Auseklis Daugavpils	—	4-0	3-0	0-1	0-2	0-1	1-0	1-0	0-0	0-0
Gauja Valmeria	1-5	—	1-3	1-2	1-4	1-6	1-4	1-5	1-2	0-3
Olimpia Liepaia	2-2	7-3	—	0-3	0-0	1-1	1-1	1-6	1-3	0-0
Olimpia Riga	1-1	3-0	4-3	—	1-2	1-0	4-1	0-2	4-1	1-0
Pardaugava Riga	3-0	3-1	6-0	2-1	—	0-1	2-0	0-3	1-0	0-0
RAF Jelgava	3-0	3-0	5-1	0-1	2-1	—	4-1	1-3	4-0	1-0
FC Dag Riga	0-1	4-1	3-3	0-1	0-0	0-1	—	0-3	0-0	1-0
Skonto Riga	2-1	11-0	6-1	4-0	1-0	1-0	3-0	—	4-0	3-1
Vairogs Rezekne	1-3	1-1	0-1	1-5	0-1	0-1	2-0	1-6	—	0-2
Vidus Riga	0-0	4-0	3-0	0-0	2-2	0-0	1-0	0-4	3-1	—

to the championship by a single point. The third-place, play-off spot went to Skonto Riga's reserve side. With the first division expanding from ten to 12 clubs Gauja Valmiera and Skonto-II faced a two-leg play-off for the final extra place. Skonto-II were much too powerful, beating Gauja 5-2 on aggregate to take the final promotion spot, and will go into the Virsliga under the name 'Inter Skonto'.

Skonto Riga also took their second step into the Champions' Cup and for the second season they progressed from the preliminary round into the first. Unlike the previous season's comfortable win at the first hurdle, Skonto required a prolonged penalty shoot-out. Having lost by a single goal at home, full-back Proitski popped up five minutes from time to give the Rigans a 1-0 win over Olimpija Llubljana. With no further score in extra time, penalties were needed and the Latvians finally won 11-10. In the first round, Skonto faced the might of Spartak Moscow, and the Russians proved a mite too much with an emphatic 9-0 aggregate win.

But, the chaos factor that had affected the Latvian scene two years earlier was in effect again in the preliminary round of the Cup-Winners' Cup, where RAF faced HB from the Faeroe Islands. Having won at home through Kozlov's goal 11 minutes from time, RAF were in a good position to make progress into the first round where the Romanians of Universitatea Craiova waited. But RAF failed to turn up for the second leg, and UEFA awarded the overall tie to HB by an aggregate score of 3-0.

Latvia FA Cup

Second Round
BJSS Jelgava v FK Liepaya	2-0
FK Aizkraukle v Starts Brotseni	2-5
FK Livani v Khimikis Daugavpils	1-2
FK Tukums v Inter Skonto Riga	0-3
FK Valmeira v Vidus Riga	0-3
Kvadrats Riga v Auseklis Daugavpils	0-1
Latgale Daugavpils v Lokomotiv Daugavpils	2-1
Venta Ventspils v FC DAG Riga	0-5
Yuras akademya Riga v Vairogs Rezekne	0-1
Yurnieks Riga v FK Riga	1-2

Third Round
Auseklis Daugavpils v FC DAG	0-1
FK Riga v Skonto Riga	0-1
Inter Skonto Riga v Vairogs Rezekne	0-4
Khimikis Daugavpils v BJSS Yelgava	3-1
Latgale Daugavpils v RAF Jelgava	2-1
Sardzes Pulks Riga v Olympia Riga	0-2
Starts Brotseni v Pardaugava Riga	0-2
Vidus Riga v Gemma Riga	1-1 aet

4-3 on pens

Quarter-Finals
FC DAG v Pardaugava Riga	1-1
Khimikis Daugavpils v Olympia Riga	0-1
Vairogs Rezekne v Latgale Daugavpils	1-0
Vidus Riga v Skonto Riga	0-0 aet

3-2 on pens

Semi-Finals
Olympia Riga v Vairogs Rezekne	1-0 aet
Vidus Riga v FC DAG Riga	0-1

Final
Olympia Riga v FC DAG Riga	2-0

Alexeyenko (64), Shtolcers (78)

Lithuania

The unknowns of ROMAR from Mazeikiai pinched the Lithuania championship from under the noses of the bigger clubs from Vilnius to record their first-ever honour. Almost unknown outside the bounds of their own country, ROMAR finished sixth in the 1992–93 championship season and now find themselves playing in European club competitions for the first time, although it will be in the UEFA Cup not the Champions' League. In addition to a new name on the championship trophy there are a couple of new names in the ranks if not a new team, as Lietuvos Makabi changed their playing name to Neris Vilnius, and Elektronas Taurage became Tauras-Karsuva Taurage.

ROMAR set and maintained the pace for virtually all the season, winning 17 of their 22 games and losing only once. Having set their stall out with five straight wins in which they scored 19 goals, that one and only defeat came in week six at reigning champions Ekranas Panevezys. Despite that setback ROMAR's lead was sufficient to ensure they maintained their lead by a couple of points. The pre-season name change seemed not to have suited Neris, who occupied bottom place at this point of the season.

By the halfway stage ROMAR's lead had been whittled down to goal difference as Zhalgiris Vilnius moved level on points having played a game more, but this was extended when ROMAR caught up on their outstanding game. With four rounds of game to play ROMAR led by a point from Zhalgiris Vilnius and maintained that with a tricky 2-1 win over Ekranas. Zhalgiris had a similar win over Banga and so set the stage for the second game of the season between the top two sides – the first having been won 1-0 by the league leaders. With so much at stake a 0-0 draw wasn't such a surprising result, although up until that stage both sides had been scoring goals with relative ease, totalling around 20 more than those below them.

With two games to play Zhalgiris needed to get maximum points and hope that ROMAR slipped up. Neither side did, with Zhalgiris thrashing GV Vilnius 7-1 as ROMAR had a title-winning win by the only goal over Sirius in Klaipeda. Zalgris had the consolation of finishing in second spot and gaining entry into Europe via the Cup-Winners' Cup.

Nationally qualification for the World Cup finals was long gone before the start of the 1993–94 season, and defeats by Denmark in Copenhagen and the Republic of Ireland in Dublin meant fifth position in the final Group Three table. A respectable tally of seven points in what was their first World Cup campaign since before the Second World War meant that Lithuania finished ahead of neighbours Latvia and Albania. The position might have been improved had Lithuania been able to call on players earning their living abroad. But insurance demands by clubs couldn't be met by a hard-up Lithuania FA, and games had to be played without them.

In European club competition, Lithuania doubled their entrant list on the previous season with representatives in the Champions' Cup and Cup-Winners' Cup. Both sides fell at the preliminary stage, showing that the standards within still have a long way to progress. In the Champions' Cup Ekranas lost both legs to Malta's Floriana by single goals, while Kosice got the better of Zhalgris Vilnius in the Cup-Winners' Cup by 3-0 on aggregate. Lithuania finished the international season on a high note with victories over Estonia and Latvia to capture the Baltic Cup.

Final League Table 1993–94

	P	W	D	L	F	A	Pts
ROMAR	22	17	4	1	53	10	38
Zhalgiris Vilnius	22	17	3	2	57	13	37
Ekranas Panevezys	22	13	5	4	48	12	31
Panerys Vilnius	22	12	5	5	35	17	29
Banga Kaunas	22	12	4	6	31	18	28
Aras Klaipeda	22	7	8	7	31	27	22
Sirius Klaipeda	22	7	5	10	25	31	19
Inkaras Kaunas	22	4	7	11	22	34	15
Sakalas Siauliai	22	6	3	13	22	50	15
GV Vilnius	22	3	7	12	14	50	13
Neris Vilnius	22	1	7	14	12	46	9
Tauras-Karsuva	22	2	4	16	13	55	8

Top Scorers
- 16 V. STEKYS (Ekranas Panevezys)
- R. ZALYS (Banga Kaunas)
- 12 V. DONTCHENKA (ROMAR)
- 10 A. BANEVICIUS (Ekranas Panevezys)
- R. BUBLIAUSKAS (Sirius Klaipeda)
- R. POCIUS (ROMAR)

Five-Year Records League 1-2-3 and Cup Winners

League Results

	1st	Pts	2nd	Pts	3rd	Pts
1993	Ekranas Panevezys	46	Zhalgiris Vilnius	43	Panerys Vilnius	36
1994	ROMAR	38	Zhalgiris Vilnius	37	Ekranas Panevezys	31

Cup Final Results

1993 Zhalgiris Vilnius 1-0 Sirius Klaipeda

Football Association of Lithuania

Founded:	1922
Address:	3/11 Rinktines Str, LIT-2051 Vilnius
Phone:	+370 2 35 36 54
Fax:	+370 2 35 36 51
UEFA Affiliation:	1992
FIFA Affiliation:	1992
National Stadium:	Zhalgiris, Vilnius
Capacity:	15,000

International Results 1993–94

Date	Opponents	Result	Venue	Comp.	Scorers
25/8/93	Denmark	0-4	Copenhagen	WCQ3	
8/9/93	Rep. Ireland	0-2	Dublin	WCQ3	
20/4/94	Israel	1-1	Vilnius	Friendly	Baltsunikas (40)
27/5/94	Czech Republic	3-5	Prague	Friendly	Narbekovas (52), own goal (76), Strumbrys (85)
29/7/94	Estonia	3-0	Vilnius	Baltic Cup	Ivanauskas (10, 23), Mikalajunas (60)
31/7/94	Latvia	1-0	Vilnius	Baltic Cup	Terechkinas (68 pen)

National Record	P	W	D	L	F	A
European Championship	*Never participated*					
World Cup Finals	*Never qualified*					
World Cup Qualifiers	3	0	0	3	3	11
World Cup Qualifiers†	12	2	3	7	8	21

† *Post-war*

Luxembourg

Avenir at the double

Avenir Beggen completed a double double, by taking the championship and cup for the second successive season. It was their sixth league championship and the third year in succession they had won the cup to make them one of the Duchy's all-time top sides, under the guidance of coach Michel Clement.

At the end of the first round of 18 games Avenir Beggen and Grevenmacher occupied the top two positions and took 13.5 and 13 points into the championship phase with them, ahead of Jeunesse's 12 points and Union's 11. They were joined by Dudelange and Aris, whose 9.5 and 7.5 points effectively ruled them out of championship contention – but there was still a UEFA Cup place to play for. Petange, Fola Esch, Spora and Red Boys Differdange were left to fight it out in the two promotion/relegation pools. CS Grevenmacher immediately made ground as Avenir Beggen were held to a 1-1 draw at Jeunesse, and a 2-0 victory over Aris moved them half a point ahead at the top. A defeat the following week at Dudelange made matters worse for Avenir Beggen, as Grevenmacher scored an important win at Jeunesse to open up a 2.5 point lead with Dudelange now only a point behind Avenir Beggen in third place.

In the third round of games Avenir Beggen travelled to Grevenmacher and, against form, secured a 4-1 win to reduce the deficit to 1.5 points. This was turned back into a 3.5 point advantage as Grevenmacher lost to Union and Aris in successive weeks while Avenir Beggen won at Aris and gained revenge on Jeunesse. The eighth round of games had Grevenmacher travelling to Avenir needing to avoid defeat – they didn't, and the 4-0 win for Avenir Beggen gave them the title with two games to spare. Player of the Year Luc Holtz was the star, scoring twice. Below them, Union's 2-0 win at Jeunesse took them into second place a point ahead of Grevenmacher. In the following week Grevenmacher were able to retake second spot as Union couldn't contain an Avenir Beggen side happy to celebrate their championship win in

Federation Luxembourgeoise de Football

Founded:	1908
Address:	50 Rue de Strasbourg, L-2560 Luxembourg
Phone:	+352 48 86 65
Fax:	+352 40 02 01
UEFA Affiliation:	1954
FIFA Affiliation:	1910
Season:	September to June
National Stadium:	Stade Municipal
Capacity:	10,000
Colours:	Red, White, Blue
Change:	Blue, White, Blue

Final League Tables 1993–94

First Round

	P	W	D	L	F	A	Pts
Avenir Beggen	18	12	3	3	48	20	27
Grevenmacher	18	11	4	4	34	15	26
Jeunesse	18	8	8	2	21	9	24
Union	18	10	2	6	27	22	22
Dudelange	18	7	5	6	34	28	19
Aris	18	4	7	7	19	25	15
Petange	18	4	6	8	32	37	14
Fola Esch	18	3	7	8	20	33	13
Spora	18	5	2	11	20	38	12
Red Boys	18	2	4	12	24	52	8

Final Round Table 1993–94

	P	W	D	L	F	A	Pts
Avenir Beggen	10	7	1	2	28	12	28.5
Grevenmacher	10	5	1	4	12	13	24
Union	10	5	2	3	12	12	23
Jeunesse	10	2	2	6	13	15	18
Aris	10	4	1	5	12	17	16.5
Dudelange	10	3	1	6	14	22	16.5

Promotions and Relegations

Promotion: Wiltz 71, Hesperange
Relegated: Red Boys, Fola Esch

Five-Year Records League 1-2-3 and Cup Winners

League Results

	1st	Pts	2nd	Pts	3rd	Pts
1990	Union	29.5	Avenir Beggen	27.5	Jeunesse	26.5
1991	Union	28	Jeunesse	25	Spora	22.5
1992	Union	26	Avenir Beggen	26	Jeunesse	23
1993	Avenir Beggen	28.5	Union	27.5	Jeunesse	23
1994	Avenir Beggen	28.5	Grevenmacher	24	Union	23

Cup Final Results

1990	Swift Hesperange	7-1	Differdange	after 3-3 draw
1991	Union	3-0	Jeunesse	
1992	Avenir Beggen	1-0	Petange	
1993	Avenir Beggen	5-2	Dudelange	
1994	Avenir Beggen	3-1	Dudelange	

style with a 4-1 victory, which meant that second place would be decided by the final fixture, pairing the two contenders. It ended in a 1-1 draw, which was good enough for Grevenmacher to maintain their advantage.

Avenir Beggen's ability to soak up the best players in Luxembourg should ensure that they maintain their position at the top for several years to come. Their campaign for 1993–94 was helped by the signing of Michail Zaritski from Borussia Monchen-

International Results 1993-94

Date	Opponents	Result	Venue	Comp.	Scorers
8/9/93	Iceland	0-1	Reykjavik	WCQ5	
12/10/93	Greece	1-3	Luxembourg	WCQ5	Fanelli (82)
27/10/93	Hungary	0-1	Budapest	WCQ5	
23/3/94	Morocco	1-2	Luxembourg	Friendly	Wolf (72)

National Record	P	W	D	L	F	A
European Championship	51	1	7	43	28	167
World Cup Finals	Never qualified					
World Cup Qualifiers	74	2	2	70	39	258

First Round

	Aris	Avenir Beggen	Dudelange	Fola Esch	Grevenmacher	Jeunesse	Petange	Red Boys Dif.	Spora	Union
Aris	—	0-4	1-1	0-0	0-0	0-0	2-0	4-1	4-2	0-3
Avenir Beggen	4-0	—	2-1	3-1	2-0	1-1	3-1	6-0	0-0	3-0
Dudelange	2-2	2-3	—	3-2	3-0	0-0	4-2	3-2	1-2	2-1
Fola Esch	1-0	0-0	1-5	—	0-4	0-1	2-2	4-2	2-1	1-1
Grevenmacher	1-1	1-2	1-0	3-0	—	2-1	2-2	3-1	3-1	2-0
Jeunesse	1-0	2-0	0-0	0-0	0-0	—	1-0	4-1	2-1	0-1
Petange	3-0	4-3	1-1	2-2	0-4	1-1	—	1-1	7-0	0-3
Red Boys Dif.	1-1	2-4	1-2	4-4	1-2	1-5	2-1	—	1-3	3-2
Spora	1-0	2-6	0-4	1-0	0-2	0-0	2-3	3-0	—	1-2
Union	0-4	3-2	3-0	1-0	1-2	4-2	0-0	1-0	—	

Final Round

	Aris	Avenir Beggen	Dudelange	Grevenmacher	Jeunesse	Union
Aris	—	0-1	2-5	1-0	0-4	0-2
Avenir Beggen	1-3	—	3-1	4-0	1-1	4-0
Dudelange	1-4	3-2	—	0-2	1-1	0-2
Grevenmacher	2-0	1-4	3-1	—	2-1	1-1
Jeunesse	0-1	2-4	3-1	0-1	—	0-2
Union	1-1	1-4	0-1	1-0	2-1	—

Coup De Luxembourg

Fifth Round

AS Schifflange v Jeunesse	0-4
Ettelbruck v Union	0-1
Hesperange v Hollerich	1-3
Junglinster v Dudelange	1-3
Mondercange v Petange	0-1
Red Boys v Aris	0-2
Rodange v Spora	2-4 †on pens
Rumelange v Avenir Beggen	1-5

Quarter-Finals

Dudelange v Hollerich	6-2
Jeunesse v Spora	1-0 †
Petange v Aris	3-1
Union v Avenir Beggen	1-2

Semi-Finals

Avenir Beggen v Jeunesse	1-0
Dudelange v Aris	3-0

Final

Avenir Beggen v Dudelange	3-1

† aet

gladbach. While Zaritski didn't make a Bundesliga appearance during the previous season the experience he gained in training with some of Europe's leading players will no doubt prove invaluable to his new side.

The two promotion and relegation groups had mixed results for the clubs trying to maintain their national division status. In Group A Spora and Pentage both came good to win their places back, along with Wiltz 71. In Group B Fola Esch missed out by a point, but Red Boys Differdange scraped through to join Hesperange and Wormeldange. With six clubs 'promoted' and only two relegated the national division will consist of 12 clubs for the 1994–95 season.

In the cup, Avenir Beggen beat Dudelange in the final for the second year in succession. The tournament had a good deal of giant killing, Ettelbruck's 1-0 fourth round win over Grevenmacher being of particular note.

In European competition Avenir Beggen gave a good account of themselves but couldn't stop Rosenborg, who won 3-0 on aggregate. Dudelange returned from Haifa with only a 0-1 defeat by Maccabi in the Cup-Winners' Cup but crashed out 1-6 at home. Union fared only slightly better in the UEFA Cup, losing 5-0 on aggregate to Portuguese side Boavista.

The national side finished bottom of Group Five in the World Cup qualifiers, having lost to Iceland, Greece and Hungary. Stephano Fanelli's goal in the 1-3 defeat in Luxembourg was only the second in the eight games played. Nevertheless manager Paul Phillip remains ever the optimist.

Malta

Hibs return

Hibernians, managed by the former England international Brian Talbot, won their first championship title for 12 years. Despite suffering only one defeat all season the margin of the victory was just three points and that was achieved by beating Floriana in a barnstorming finale. At the halfway stage Hibs had already announced their intentions by installing themselves at the top of the table and the championship developed into a three-horse race between them, reigning champions Floriana and Hamrun, with just two points separating the sides. The omens were good for Hibernians at that point. This was their first time in the top berth since their 1981–82 championship season.

Pole position had been gained with a 3-1 win over Floriana. The equalising goal for Hibs in that game, scored by Charles Scerri, was notable because it was the first time Floriana's international goalkeeper, David Cluett, had been beaten in 572 minutes; it also smashed Floriana's unbeaten league run which had lasted nearly nine months.

Hibs maintained their slender advantage and set up the championship decider in the last-but-one round of games when the two sides met. Floriana needed a win to take the race to the last game, while Hibernians could clinch the silverware by taking all three points. The game lived up to its billing with Talbot's side winning 4-3 after being 2-0 down and then 3-2 down, before two goals in three minutes secured the win. Floriana managed to stay in front of Valletta on the final day's games and clinched their place in the UEFA Cup.

While it was a revival season for Hibernians it was another disappointing one for Sliema Wanderers, who won the last of their record 22 championship titles back in 1989. Despite new signings in strikers John Muir and Dean Edwards (ex-Torquay United) they still struggled to find the old form and flair that made them one of the more glamorous Maltese sides. But perhaps the fact that the club gave trials to some 20 foreigners pre-season is indicative of the problems they are having on and off the field.

Sliema rejected George Lawrence, the former Southampton and Millwall player, at the start of the season. He signed for Hibs instead and his goals turned out to be instrumental in their run to the title, although the Dane Carl Zacchau topped the scoring charts alongside Valletta's Joe Zarb, with 17 goals apiece.

Other points of note in the league season were that Zacchau and Hamrun's Stefan Sultana both managed to score five goals in a match, thus equalling a record set back in the 1974–75 season by Ray Xuereb of Floriana. Only eight players managed to be ever present and not substituted and no team managed to score in every

Final League Table 1993–94

Premier League

	P	W	D	L	F	A	Pts
Hibernians	18	14	3	1	48	15	31
Floriana	18	12	4	2	29	7	28
Valletta	18	12	3	3	42	17	27
Hamrun Spartans	18	8	9	1	35	10	25
Sliema Wanderers	18	7	5	6	23	14	19
Zurrieq	18	5	4	9	18	29	14
St Andrews	18	5	3	10	18	29	13
Birkirkara	18	6	0	12	19	36	12
Rabat Ajax	18	2	6	10	16	38	10
Mqabba	18	0	1	17	3	55	1

Top Scorers

- 17 Carl ZACCHAU (Hibernians)
- Joe ZARB (Valletta)
- 13 Stefan SULTANA (Hamrun Spartans)
- 11 Gilbert AGIUS (Valletta)
- 10 George LAWRENCE (Hibernians)

Promotions and Relegations

Promoted: Naxxar Lions, Pieta Hotspur
Relegated: Mqabba, Rabat Ajax

Five-Year Records League 1-2-3 and Cup Winners

League Results

	1st	Pts	2nd	Pts	3rd	Pts
1990	Valletta	28	Sliema Wand's	24	Hamrun Spartans	23
1991	Hamrun Spartans	24	Valletta	19	Floriana	18
1992	Valletta	33	Floriana	24	Hamrun Spartans	23
1993	Floriana	29	Hamrun Spartans	24	Valletta	24
1994	Hibernians	31	Floriana	28	Valletta	27

Cup Final Results

1990	Sliema Wanderers	1-0	Birkirkara	
1991	Valletta	2-1	Sliema Wanderers	
1992	Hamrun Spartans	3-3	Valletta	2-1 on pens
1993	Floriana	5-0	Sliema Wanderers	
1994	Floriana	2-1	Valletta	

Malta Football Association

Founded:	1900
Address:	280 St Paul Street, M-La Valletta
Phone:	+356 22 26 97
Fax:	+356 24 51 36
UEFA Affiliation:	1960
FIFA Affiliation:	1959
Season:	October to May
National Stadium:	Ta'Qali Stadium
Capacity:	18,000
Colours:	Red, White, Red
Change:	White, White, Red

International Results 1993–94

Date	Opponents	Result	Venue	Comp.	Scorers
5/11/93	Egypt	0-3	Tunis	Friendly	
7/11/93	Gabon	2-1	Tunis	Friendly	Brincat (11), Busuttil (37)
17/11/93	Scotland	0-2	Valletta	WCQ1	
8/2/94	Tunisia	1-1	Valletta	Malta Tmt	S. Vella
10/2/94	Georgia	0-1	Valletta	Malta Tmt.	
12/2/94	Slovenia	0-1	Valletta	Malta Tmt.	
16/2/94	Belgium	1-0	Valletta	Friendly	Busuttil (34)
30/3/94	Slovakia	1-2	Valletta	Friendly	Laferla (45)
	Azerbaijan	5-0	Valletta	Friendly	

National Record	P	W	D	L	F	A
European Championship	43	2	5	36	18	146
World Cup Finals	Never qualified					
World Cup Qualifiers	42	1	4	37	15	128

Rothmans FA Trophy 1994

Quarter-Finals
Sliema Wanderers v St Andrews	1-0	
Zurrieq v Rabat Ajax	2-0	
Floriana v Birkirkara	3-1	
Valletta v Hibernians	1-1	6-5 on pens

Semi-Finals
Valletta v Sliema Wanderers	1-1, 1-0
Floriana v Rabat Ajax	3-1

Final
Floriana v Valletta	2-1

Maltese Championship Results 1993-94

	Birkirkara	Floriana	Hamrun Spartans	Hibernians	Mqabba	Rabat Ajax	Sliema Wanderers	St. Andrews	Valletta	Zurrieq
Birkirkara	—	0-2	0-1	0-2	3-0	3-0	0-1	1-2	1-4	0-2
Floriana	1-0	—	0-0	1-3	2-0	3-0	0-0	4-1	3-0	2-0
Hamrun Spartans	3-0	0-0	—	0-0	2-0	1-1	1-1	1-1	1-2	4-1
Hibernians	6-2	3-1	0-3	—	2-0	6-0	1-0	2-0	1-0	3-0
Mqabba	0-2		0-8	0-5	—	2-4	0-4	0-1	0-4	1-5
Rabat Ajax	1-2	0-3	2-2	1-1	0-0	—	0-2	0-0	1-3	1-0
Sliema Wanderers	2-0	0-3	0-3	0-2	6-0	1-1	—	0-1	1-2	3-0
St. Andrews	0-1	0-1	0-3	2-5	3-0	1-1	0-2	—	0-2	0-0
Valletta	8-0	0-0	0-0	3-4	2-0		0-0	4-2	—	3-2
Zurrieq	1-4	0-2	1-1	2-2	1-0	2-1	0-0	1-0	0-2	—

league match, although Hibernians went closest, scoring in 16 games. One unwanted new record was the increase in dismissals, with 26 players being shown the red card. Three of them had the dubious honour of being expelled twice.

In the Rothmans FA Trophy a late own goal allowed Floriana to take the silverware for a record 18th time. In front of nearly 8,000 only three minutes remained when a quickly taken throw by Richard Buhagiar fell to Dennis Cauchi, whose first time shot was deflected by Gilbert Agius. It was hard luck for the youngster, who had earlier produced a magnificent 30-yarder to equalise an early Albert Busuttil goal.

The Maltese clubs have not taken favourably to the re-organisation of the Champions' Cup, which means that they are unlikely to see one of their kind in this competition again, but Floriana at least achieved their first qualification in the competition by beating the Lithuanians Ekranas Panevezys 2-0 on aggregate in the preliminary round. A goal by John Buttigieg in each leg was enough, but FC Porto produced the knock-out in the first round. Sliema Wanderers couldn't match that performance in the Cup-Winners' Cup, losing to Degerfors in the preliminary round. In the UEFA Cup, Valletta took a shock lead against Trabzonspor through Zarb, but the Turks produced three goals in both legs to win through.

Internationally, Malta started the season with a new manager, Pietro Ghedin, the under-21 coach, who stepped up to take over from Pippo Psaila. His first competitive match as team manager was a 2-0 home defeat by Scotland in their final World Cup Group One match, and Malta finished last but one in the group with three points, two ahead of Estonia. This had followed a 2-1 win in a friendly with Gabon, the 20th victory for the national side.

That form produced high hopes for the seventh Rothmans International Tournament staged in Valletta, where there were hopes of retaining the title won the previous year. Those hopes soon faded as a 1-1 draw with Tunisia was followed by single-goal defeats by Georgia and Slovenia. But the season finished on a couple of highs: a 1-0 win over Belgium which had the home crowd ecstatic, especially as the goal was scored by Carmel Busuttil, who plays his football in Belgium, with Genk. The match marked the retirement of veteran midfielder Ray Vella on his 66th appearance. The 'Viva Malta' chants continued as the season ended with a 5-0 win over Azerbaijan – Malta's biggest win in 37 years of international soccer.

Moldova

Zimbru's third success

For the third year running Zimbru and Tiligul contested the championship, although in the early part of the season it looked like there might be a new challenger in the Codru club from Calarasi, who led the table. In the end, though, Zimbru took their third successive title, although it was a near-run thing. Tiligul looked more likely winners in the final weeks.

The two clubs offered a distinct contrast, Zimbru having gone for youth, capturing many of the players who formed the national and Olympic squads, and Tiligul relying on experienced, mature personnel. This perhaps cost them their first title when the younger legs of Zimbru came through. Zimbru have also been able to keep their squad together and in Alexandru Spridon have an outstanding leader. In addition to skippering the side to success and rattling in 13 goals, Spridon is also the club coach and well respected by those around him. Other key players included 14-goal Serghi Clescenko, Alexandru Cuetianu, Radu Rebja, Serghei Nani, Ion Testemitanu and Iurie Mitrev. This nucleus should ensure more honours in the coming seasons.

The Tiraspol club Tiligul had to settle for second place once again and coach Evghenii Sincarenco will be looking to add new blood to help wrestle the top position in Moldovian football away from his counterpart. The two rivals were drawn to face one another in the semi-finals of the Moldovan Cup, with Tiligul winning 3-1 on aggregate before going on to beat Nistru in the final to hold the trophy they had captured for the first time the previous season.

Zimbru took their first steps into Europe where they were drawn against Beitar Jerusalem in the preliminary round. The Kishinev club gave a good account of themselves in front of over 10,000 supporters in their Republican stadium. Despite going behind to an early goal, Zimbru earned a credible draw thanks to a goal by Revda seven minutes from time. The second leg was lost 2-0 in Israel but that first experience will help Zimbru in this year's UEFA Cup, where they take their place as a low-ranked champion club. They will not be alone in Europe, as Tiligul are able to compete in the Cup-Winners' Cup preliminary round.

The national side were limited to two friendly internationals against the USA in California as part of the American build-up to the World Cup Finals. One was drawn and one lost, but there are

Federatia Moldoveneasca De Fotbal

Founded:	1990
Address:	Bd Stefan cel Mare 73, 277001 Chisnau
Phone:	+373 2 22 44 98
Fax:	+373 2 22 22 44
UEFA Affiliation:	1994
FIFA Affiliation:	1994
Season:	July to May
National Stadium:	Republican
Capacity:	23,000
Colours:	Blue, Red, Yellow
Change:	Yellow, Blue, Red

Final League Table 1993–94

	P	W	D	L	F	A	Pts
Zimbru	30	25	2	3	86	22	52
Tiligul	30	23	3	4	94	32	49
Codru	30	15	10	5	47	22	40
Nistru Octaci	30	14	10	6	44	21	38
Olimpia	30	13	8	9	35	41	34
Bugeac	30	14	5	11	42	36	33
Torentul	30	10	9	11	34	30	29
FC Agro	30	10	6	14	40	53	26
Sportul	30	9	8	13	30	40	26
Cristalul	30	9	8	13	29	40	26
Tighina	30	9	8	13	43	55	26
Nistru Ciuburciu	30	8	8	14	36	47	24
Vilia	30	9	5	16	27	52	23
Sinteza	30	7	9	14	22	51	23
Moldova	30	5	7	18	18	49	17
Speranta	30	5	4	21	27	63	14

Top Scorers

- 24 KOSSE (Tiligul)
- 16 CIUDIAC (FC Agro)
- 14 CLESENCO (Zimbru)
  DOJOVCHI (Olimpia)
- 13 DOVGJII (Nistru Ciuburciu)
  SPIRIDON (Zimbru)
  CUCIUC (Bugeac)

Promotion and Relegations
Promoted: MHM-93
Relegated: Sinteza, Moldova, Speranta

Three-Year Records League 1-2-3 and Cup Winners

League Results

	1st	Pts	2nd	Pts	3rd	Pts
1992	Zimbru	35	Tiligul	35	Bugeac	33
1993	Zimbru	50	Tiligul	47	Moldova	41
1994	Zimbru	52	Tiligul	49	Codru	40

Cup Final Results

1992	Bugeac (Comrat)	5-0	Tiligul
1993	Tiligu	1-0	Dinamo (Chrisinta)
1994	Tiligul	1-0	Nistru Octaci

International Results 1993–94

Date	Opponents	Result	Venue	Comp.
16/3/94	USA	1-1	California	Friendly
20/3/94	USA	0-3	California	Friendly

National Record   P   W   D   L   F   A
European Championship   Never participated
World Cup Finals   Never qualified
World Cup Qualifiers   Never participated

Moldova Cup

	1st	2nd	Agg
1/8th Finals			
Bucuria v Nistru Octaci	1-4	0-5	1-9
Torentul v Olimpia	1-0	0-2	1-2
Zimbru v Tighina	3-1	0-0	3-1
FC Agro v MHM 93	0-3	0-2	0-5
Sinteza v Nistru Ciuburciu	2-1	0-3	2-4
Sportul v FC Constructorul	0-0	0-2	0-2
Vilia v Bugeac	1-2	0-2	1-4
Tiligul v Izvoras	4-0	5-2	9-2
Quarter-Finals			
Olimpia v Nistru Octaci	0-1	0-1	0-2
Sportul v Bugeac	1-0	1-2	2-2
Zimbru v MHM 93	2-0	2-0	4-0
Nistru Ciuburciu v Tiligul	0-4	0-8	0-12
Semi-Finals			
Zimbru v Tiligul	1-1	0-2	1-3
Sportul v Nistru Octaci	2-1	0-1	2-2
Final			
Tiligul v Nistru Octaci	1-0		

optimistic hopes for local encounters with Bulgaria, Georgia and Albania in the European Championships, in a group that also contains Wales and the Germans. Nevertheless the Moldovans remain confident that they can surprise a few people.

The 1994–95 season sees a small restructuring of the league set-up. With three clubs being relegated from the national division and only one being promoted the league will consist of 14 clubs while Division A will contain 18 and Division B 42, divided into three regional leagues – North, Centre and South.

Moldova Championship Results 1993–94

	Bugeac	Codru	Cristalul	FC Agro	Moldova	Nistru Octaci	Nistru Ciuburciu	Olimpia	Sinteza	Speranta	Sportul	Tighina	Tiligul	Torentul	Vilia	Zimbru
Bugeac	—	0-1	2-0	0-2	*	1-0	2-0	0-0	3-0	2-0	3-1	2-1	1-1	0-2	1-0	1-0
Codru	3-1	—	0-0	2-0	0-0	0-0	1-0	3-0	5-1	3-0	1-1	5-0	1-2	2-1	5-0	1-4
Cristalul	2-1	1-1	—	0-2	3-1	1-1	3-1	1-2	0-0	1-0	3-0	7-0	0-5	2-0	1-0	1-3
FC Agro	1-3	1-1	1-1	—	0-1	0-2	2-1	5-0	3-2	1-0	2-2	0-0	0-3	1-5	3-1	3-4
Moldova	0-4	1-2	1-0	1-1	—	0-0	1-1	0-1	2-3	5-2	0-0	0-0	0-3	0-1	2-1	1-3
Nistru Octaci	1-0	0-1	4-0	1-0	2-0	—	1-0	2-0	0-0	2-4	2-0	3-0	1-1	0-0	7-0	1-3
Nistru Ciuburciu	1-1	1-1	2-0	3-2	3-0	0-2	—	4-0	0-0	5-1	0-2	1-1	0-3	0-0	0-1	1-4
Olimpia	4-4	1-1	0-0	2-1	1-0	0-1	2-2	—	1-2	1-0	0-0	2-1	3-1	1-0	1-0	0-3
Sinteza	2-1	0-0	0-1	1-3	3-0	3-0	1-0	1-3	—	1-0	0-2	0-0	1-4	0-0	2-1	0-1
Speranta	0-2	1-2	2-0	0-2	0-2	3-3	2-3	1-1	3-0	—	0-2	0-0	1-2	1-0	0-1	1-1
Sportul	2-0	2-2	4-0	1-1	0-0	0-0	0-1	0-2	3-0	0-2	—	0-3	0-2	1-0	0-3	1-2
Tighina	2-0	2-1	1-1	1-0	3-0	2-6	2-3	0-1	4-2	5-1	2-1	—	1-3	1-2	0-0	1-3
Tiligul	4-2	0-0	3-0	10-0	6-0	4-1	3-0	3-2	3-0	7-1	3-1	6-7	—	2-1	3-0	0-3
Torentul	4-4	2-0	0-0	2-2	1-0	0-1	2-1	3-0	1-0	4-0	0-1	0-0	0-2	—	2-0	0-3
Vilia	0-1	0-1	1-0	2-1	1-0	0-0	1-1	0-2	0-0	2-1	1-3	2-1	5-4	2-2	—	1-2
Zimbru	2-0	0-2	2-0	2-0	4-0	1-0	6-1	2-2	8-0	3-0	5-0	3-2	0-1	3-0	6-1	—

* Moldova failed to turn up for game – points awarded to Bugeac

Northern Ireland

Linfield snatch dramatic treble

While there may have been many dramatic title finishes around the European leagues, there could not have been any more exciting than the one that ensured Linfield retained their title and won a record 42nd championship. It ended an incredible fortnight for the Belfast side, who completed a remarkable treble by lifting the FA and League Cups.

The season had begun with the announcement that the format of the 103-year-old league was to change with the introduction of promotion and relegation for the 1995–96 season. This is to be done by taking the total of the points won by clubs during 1993–94 and 1994–95 to form a ranking list from which the top eight clubs go into the new premier division and the bottom eight into the first division. With each club playing each other four times there will be just one promotion and relegation place. The pressure was therefore on the clubs to ensure that they got into the right half of the cut.

Linfield started the season by signing Gary Haylock from Shelbourne and Gary Peebles from Partick Thistle to help bolster an already impressive squad, and took a share of the Charity Shield in a 1-1 draw with Bangor. They followed that by getting the league season off to a perfect start with a 3-0 win at Ards, while the other title favourites, Portadown, beat Distillery. Linfield's win was the first of seven on the trot but Portadown and Glenavon were still only two points behind when Crusaders produced a surprise 1-0 win at Windsor Park to halt their march. Glenavon and Portadown leap-frogged into the top two places with wins over Larne and Newry Town respectively. Linfield slipped to fourth place the following weekend when they went down 3-2 at Glenavon, but Portadown's 6-1 win at Carrick allowed them to take over the leadership, having scored 24 goals and conceded just four in nine games.

By the end of the year Glenavon led the table from Portadown and Linfield, and created a club record when they won 12 successive league matches before losing to Cliftonville and Portadown. In January they suffered another defeat, at Bangor, that allowed Portadown and Linfield to move in front with Linfield ahead on goal difference at the end of February, when Portadown dropped vital points.

With two weeks of the championship remaining nothing was clear cut, but the match of the day was at Portadown, where

Final League Table 1993–94

	P	W	D	L	F	A	Pts
Linfield	30	13	2	14	49	55	41
Distillery	30	11	8	11	41	40	41
Cliftonville	30	11	10	9	40	32	*40
Glentoran	30	10	7	13	46	42	37
Coleraine	30	10	7	13	41	50	37
Ballymena United	30	9	6	15	36	55	33
Ballyclare Comrades	30	9	6	15	35	57	33
Carrick Rangers	30	6	7	17	42	81	25
Newry Town	30	5	9	16	26	52	24
Omagh Town	30	6	5	19	32	58	23
Larne	30	5	7	18	30	62	22

Cliftonville three points deducted.

Top Scorers
- 21 Gary HAYLOCK (Linfield)
-    Stephen McBRIDE (Glenavon)
-    Darren ERSKINE (Ards)
- 19 SMITH (Portadown)
- 15 Brian ROBSON (Carrick Rangers)

The Irish Football Association

Founded:	1880
Address:	20 Windsor Avenue, Belfast BT9 6EG
Phone:	+44 232 669 458
Fax:	+44 232 667 620
UEFA Affiliation:	1954
FIFA Affiliation:	1911-20, 1924-28, 1946
Season:	August to May
National Stadium:	Windsor Park
Capacity:	28,000
Colours:	Green, White, Green
Change:	White, Green, Green

Five-Year Records League 1-2-3 and Cup Winners

League Results

	1st	Pts	2nd	Pts	3rd	Pts
1990	Portadown	55	Glenavon	54	Glentoran	44
1991	Portadown	71	Bangor	61	Glentoran	60
1992	Glentoran	77	Portadown	65	Linfield	60
1993	Linfield	66	Crusaders	66	Bangor	64
1994	Linfield	70	Portadown	68	Glenavon	68

Cup Final Results

1990	Glentoran	3-0	Portadown
1991	Portadown	2-1	Glenavon
1992	Glenavon	2-1	Linfield
1993	Bangor	1-0	Ards
1994	Linfield	2-0	Bangor

NORTHERN IRELAND

International Results 1993–94

Date	Opponents	Result	Venue	Comp.	Scorers
8/9/93	Latvia	2-0	Belfast	WCQ3	J. Quinn (35), Gray (80)
13/10/93	Denmark	0-1	Copenhagen	WCQ3	
17/11/93	Rep. Ireland	1-1	Belfast	WCQ3	J. Quinn (73)
23/3/94	Romania	2-0	Belfast	Friendly	Morrow (42), Gray (49)
20/4/94	Liechtenstein	4-1	Belfast	ECQ6	J. Quinn (5, 33), Lomas (23), Dowie (48)
4/6/94	Colombia	0-2	Boston	Friendly	
11/6/94	Mexico	0-3	Miami	Friendly	

National Record	P	W	D	L	F	A
European Championship	53	21	10	22	58	61
World Cup Finals	13	3	5	5	13	23
World Cup Qualifiers	72	26	18	28	83	87

Irish Cup Results 1993-94

Quarter Finals
Distillery v Glenavon	2-4
Linfield v Cliftonville	0-0, 1-0
Glentoran v Bangor	0-2
Omagh Town v Portadown	0-2

Semi Finals
Glenavon v Linfield	0-3
Bangor v Portadown	2-0

Final
Linfield v Bangor	2-0

Scorers: Peebles (44), Fenlon (89)

Linfield were the visitors. The Belfast side won 2-0 to inflict on Portadown their first home defeat for more than two years, and with Glenavon winning at Cliftonville all three clubs went into their final fixtures on 67 points. To add spice to the final day the top two, Glenavon and Portadown, were in opposition, while Linfield played local rivals Glentoran. At half-time Glenavon looked certain to lift their first title in 34 years; they led 2-0 while Linfield were drawing 0-0 at Windsor Park. But with six minutes of the season remaining, Portadown scored an equaliser and Linfield produced two second-half goals to beat Glentoran and thereby retain the title.

In between the excitement of the final league games, Linfield beat Coleraine 2-0 to lift the League Cup and Bangor by the same score to lift the Irish Cup for the first time since 1982. The scorers included Pat Fenlon, a mid-season £23,000 buy from Dublin side Bohemians. The semi-finals of the Irish Cup had been a contest between the top three. Linfield had beaten Glenavon 3-0 while Bangor had produced an upset in beating Portadown 2-0. Portadown's defeat meant that they had to avoid defeat in that final match, with Glenavon, to finish second and secure a place in Europe. They did, on goal difference.

Not surprisingly Linfield's manager Trevor Anderson was named Manager of the Year after his side went their last 32 games without defeat. Haylock proved to be a valuable signing, finishing as the league's top scorer. Three sets of brothers also helped create what must be a unique record in Linfield's 1-0 win over Bangor,

Iain Dowie scored against Liechtenstein for Northern Ireland in the European Championship.

when Lee Doherty, Jeff Spiers and Alan Dorman all lined up against their brothers, Dean Doherty, Eddie Spiers and Reg Dorman!

Linfield became the first club side to progress in a European Cup tie when they made it past Dinamo Tbilisi, but not until they had lost the tie 3-2 on aggregate. The referee's report to UEFA included details of a bribery attempt by the Georgian club, which ultimately led to their expulsion and Linfield's reinstatement. They looked to be well on their way to a historic place in the second round after an

Northern Ireland Championship Results 1993–94

	Ards	Ballyclare Comrades	Ballymena United	Bangor	Carrick Rangers	Cliftonville	Coleraine	Crusaders	Distillery	Glenavon	Glentoran	Larne	Linfield	Newry Town	Omagh Town	Portadown
Ards	—	2-0	1-2	5-3	3-3	1-2	3-2	2-4	1-0	4-1	1-0	4-0	0-3	9-0	3-3	1-2
Ballyclare Comrades	1-0	—	1-1	3-0	0-3	0-0	0-1	0-0	2-2	1-1	2-1	1-0	1-2	1-2	4-1	2-0
Ballymena United	0-3	2-3	—	1-2	0-2	2-1	1-0	0-0	1-1	1-3	3-2	2-0	0-1	0-0	1-3	1-1
Bangor	0-2	4-2	1-0	—	5-1	2-1	2-0	2-1	1-2	1-0	0-3	2-1	0-1	3-1	4-2	1-1
Carrick Rangers	1-2	2-4	2-5	3-2	—	1-0	1-1	3-2	2-2	1-5	1-2	2-1	1-2	0-0	0-0	1-6
Cliftonville	6-2	0-2	0-2	1-0	3-1	—	1-2	2-1	2-1	0-1	1-1	0-1	2-2	1-1	1-1	1-1
Coleraine	4-0	3-2	5-2	3-1	3-2	0-0	—	0-2	0-2	0-2	1-1	2-1	2-2	1-1	2-0	0-1
Crusaders	3-1	4-0	1-0	4-0	3-0	1-1	2-0	—	2-2	2-4	3-2	3-1	1-1	2-1	3-0	1-1
Distillery	3-2	4-0	4-1	1-2	2-0	1-1	1-2	1-2	—	1-1	0-2	0-1	2-2	1-0	1-1	1-6
Glenavon	1-0	5-2	3-2	3-1	8-0	0-1	2-1	2-0	1-0	—	2-1	6-1	3-2	5-0	1-0	2-2
Glentoran	2-0	3-0	1-1	2-2	3-1	1-4	5-3	0-1	0-2	0-1	—	0-0	0-2	4-0	3-1	1-3
Larne	4-1	1-1	5-1	1-1	1-1	0-3	3-3	1-1	1-2	0-2	2-2	—	0-2	0-3	4-2	0-5
Linfield	2-1	5-0	2-1	1-0	2-1	3-1	5-0	0-1	3-0	0-0	2-0	3-0	—	1-0	4-1	2-2
Newry Town	1-3	2-0	1-2	1-2	2-2	0-3	0-0	0-2	0-1	1-1	1-1	2-0	1-1	—	1-2	0-2
Omagh Town	1-2	2-0	1-2	0-1	3-3	0-1	1-0	0-1	0-1	1-2	2-3	1-0	1-3	1-0	—	1-2
Portadown	1-0	4-0	5-0	2-0	6-1	1-1	4-0	3-0	1-0	3-1	1-0	4-0	0-2	1-1	5-0	—

excellent 3-0 first leg win over FC Copenhagen. But in the return leg the Danes pulled back two goals, then scored a dramatic equaliser in the fifth minute of injury time and a overall winner in extra time.

In the Cup-Winners' Cup, Bangor were unlucky to lose in the preliminary round to Cypriot side Apoel. A goal in the home leg cost them dear, as they went out 3-2 on aggregate. Crusaders held Servette 0-0 in the first leg of their UEFA Cup tie but four goals in the second half of the return meant a first-round exit for the Belfast side.

Internationally there was an emotional farewell to Billy Bingham as Irish team manager. In charge since 1980, Bingham was the longest-serving manager at national level and bowed out as the Irish held the Republic to a 1-1 draw at a packed Windsor Park. It was his 117th game in charge – he also had been national manager from 1967 to 1971 – in which his sides had won 40, drawn 33, lost 44, scored 114 and conceded 128. Former international Bryan Hamilton took over as Bingham's successor and started with two wins. A 2-0 defeat of the Bulgarians was followed by a 4-1 thrashing of Liechtenstein in the first European Championship qualifying match.

The 1994–95 season will be as much about premier division qualification as whether Linfield can make it a championship hat-trick. But the champions, along with Portadown, Glenavon, Crusaders, and Bangor, are all in good positions, while the likes of Larne, Omagh Town, Newry and Carrick Rangers look to be destined for the first division. The real battle seems set to be between Ards, Distillery, Cliftonville, Glentoran, Coleraine, Ballymena and Ballyclare for who goes up or down. With a lot more than a simple championship at stake, this season looks set to be as exciting as the one just gone!

Norway

In from the cold

It was in the international arena that Norway made their mark and signalled the culmination of the three-year reign of national manager Egil Olsen. Without doubt Norge completed their best-ever season by reaching the World Cup Finals for only the second time in their history, and they did so by gaining top spot in a six-nation qualification group. In truth the hard work had already been done as the 1993–94 season opened but a Jostein Flo goal against an unlucky Polish side on a heady night in Oslo late in September all but assured their place in the USA. Goalkeeper Erik Thorstvedt will remember the game for different reasons, receiving his marching orders for a professional foul, but the Tottenham player could record a more memorable achievement in the coming season when he should pass Thorbjorn Svenssen's record of 104 appearances for Norway. Frode Grodas took over from the suspended Thorstvedt for the return game in Poznan three weeks later, and a 3-0 win merely confirmed Norway's position at the head of Group Two, which they retained despite a 2-1 reversal in Istanbul a month later. At the conclusion of their qualifying campaign Olsen's record in charge made particularly impressive reading: played 33 with 18 wins, 9 draws and 6 defeats. Goal difference 70-23.

International success has meant international recognition for many of the Norwegian stars who have become household names from the Skagerrak to the Barents Sea, and an exodus of players, especially to England. Nevertheless, domestically, football has taken a front seat with the single national network showing live games and the national cup final becoming a sell-out event.

In the Tippeligaen (Top League) Rosenborg retained their title with a two-point advantage over surprise runners-up Bodo/Glimt, who had looked odds-on with a one-point lead and three matches to go. The fixture list had deemed that their next visitors would be Rosenborg, who went away with a 2-1 win and leap-frogged over Bodo, two points clear, two games to play and both of those at home in Trondheim. In the penultimate round of games Bodo travelled to Lillestrom and lost 5-3, which meant that Rosenborg's 2-1 victory over strugglers Start was enough to ensure them their third title in five years.

Bodo/Glimt did exceptionally well in taking the runners-up spot and in doing so silenced the knockers who had been quick to rubbish their promotion to the Tippeligaen in 1992, when they played their home games indoors and on an artificial surface. For the 1993 season they had to return to the outdoor world of the far north and played at the city's Aspmyra Stadion.

Lillestrom finished third – apparently not good enough for their board, who sacked manager Ivan Hoff, appointing Teitur Thordarsson in his place for the start of the new campaign. In Mons Ivar Mjelde they had the Tippeligaen's top scorer with 19 goals, but six defeats to middle-of-the-table teams cost them dear.

VIF Fotball (Oslo) and Sogndal won the two automatic promotion places into the Tippeligaen, replacing Lyn and Fyllingen. In the play-off for the third place Stromgodset of Drammen won through to emphatically overcome Bryne and the now-relegated Molde. Tromso had looked certain to occupy the third-from-bottom play-off place but a 1-0 win at Molde on the final day of the season ensured their stay in the top flight for another season.

Goran Sorloth leads the Rosenborg BK attack during a league encounter.

Norges Fotballforbund	
Founded:	1902
Address:	PO Box 3823, Ullevaal Hageby, 0805 Oslo, Norway
Phone:	+47 22 95 10 00
Fax:	+47 22 95 10 10
UEFA Affiliation:	1954
FIFA Affiliation:	1908
National Stadium:	Ullevaal Stadion
Capacity:	22,500 (all seated)
Season:	April to November
Colours:	Red, White, Blue
Change:	Blue, White, Blue

International Results 1993-94

Date	Opponents	Result	Venue	Comp.	Scorers
11/08/93	Faeroe Islands	7-0	Toftir	Frdly	Bohinen (6 pen), Leonhardsen (9), Mjelde (27, 39), Ostenstad (74, 87), JO Pedersen (76)
08/09/93	USA	1-0	Oslo	Friendly	Bjorneby (13)
22/09/93	Poland	1-0	Oslo	WCQ2	Flo (55)
13/10/93	Poland	3-0	Poznan	WCQ2	Flo (61), Fjortoft (63), Johnsen (89)
10/1/931	Turkey	1-2	Istandbul	WCQ2	Bohinen (49)
15/01/94	USA	1-2	Phoenix	Friendly	Strandli (44)
19/01/94	Coasta Rica	0-0	San Diego	Friendly	
2/2/94	Denmark	3-3	Kuala Lumpur	Dunhill	Petter (11, 49), Undheim (54)
5/2/94	Japan	3-2	Kuala Lumpur	Dunhill	Stakkeland (9), T.Larsen (64), Flo (73)
09/03/94	Wales	3-1	Cardiff	Friendly	Flo (6), Mykland (49), Jakobsen (51)
20/04/94	Portugal	0-0	Oslo	Friendly	
22/5/94	England	0-0	Wembley	Friendly	
01/06/94	Denmark	2-1	Oslo	Friendly	Jakobsen (35), O. Berg (44)
05/06/94	Sweden	0-2	Stockholm	Friendly	
19/06/94	Mexico	1-0	Washington	WCFE	Rekdal (82)
22/06/94	Italy	0-1	New Jersey	WCFE	
28/06/94	Rep. Ireland	0-0	New Jersey	WCFE	

National Record	P	W	D	L	F	A
European Championships	52	7	11	34	48	101
World Cup Finals	4	1	1	2	2	3
World Cup Qualifiers	68	22	13	33	89	117

Tippeligaen 1993-94

	P	W	D	L	F	A	Pts
Rosenborg	22	14	5	3	47	30	47
Bodo/Glimt	22	14	3	5	51	24	45
Lillestrom	22	13	3	6	47	26	42
Viking	22	13	2	7	38	27	41
Ham-Kam	22	10	3	9	42	39	33
Tromso	22	6	8	8	25	25	26
Brann	22	7	5	10	31	28	36
Kongsvinger	22	7	4	11	33	41	25
Start	22	6	5	11	26	29	23
Molde	22	5	7	10	23	36	22
Lyn	22	6	4	12	39	53	22
Fyllingen	22	4	3	13	21	55	17

Tippeligaen Topscorers
- 19 Mons Ivar MJELDE (Lillestrom)
- 16 Petter BELSVIK (Ham-Kam)
  Trond Egil SOLTVEDT (Brann)
- 13 Kjell Roar KAASA (Lyn)
- 12 Geir FRIGARD (Kongsvinger)

Promotions and Relegations
Relegated: Fyllingen, Lyn, Molde
Promoted: VIF Fotball, Sogndal, Stromgodset

Bodo/Glimt didn't finish the season empty handed – they won the Norgesmesterskapene for only the second time, beating Stromgodset 2-0 in the Final at the Ullevaal Stadium. Bodo, from inside the Arctic Circle, had a relatively easy path to the final, only encountering top league opposition in the quarter and semi-finals. Stromgodset overcame relegated Fyllingen in the semi, having put paid to the team who cost them the first division A title – VIF – in the quarters. As such the citizens of Bergen were denied the final they sought, Fyllingen v Brann, when the latter lost to Bodo.

Fyllingen produced perhaps the result of the competition when disposing of Lillestrom 3-1 in the last 16. Champions Rosenborg had fallen to Lillestrom in the previous round but can boast the top score of the competition, having put 15 without reply past the regional division three side, Vuku.

In Europe all three Norwegian representatives survived their first two-leg encounters and in the Cup-Winners' Cup and UEFA Cup only the might of Italian giants overcame their stubbornness.

In the Champions' Cup Rosenborg beat Luxembourg opposition in the form of Avenir Beggen in the preliminary round but succumbed in the first round to FK Austria. Having won the first leg at home 3-1 they lost 4-1 in Vienna, the final goal coming nine minutes from time after the sides had been 1-1 at the interval. Lillestrom lost the first leg at home by 0-2 to Torino, then put on a magnificent display in the second leg in Turin, winning 2-1 after falling behind to a goal immediately after the interval. Having overcome Oesters in the first round of the UEFA Cup, Kongsvinger drew Juventus in the second round and bowed out 3-1 on aggregate

Five-Year Records League 1-2-3 and Cup Winners

League Results

	1st	Pts	2nd	Pts	3rd	Pts
1989	Lillestrom	52	Rosenborg	44	Tromso	37
1990	Rosenborg	44	Tromso	42	Molde	40
1991	Viking	41	Rosenborg	36	Start	34
1992	Rosenborg	45	Kongsvinger	40	Start	39
1993	Rosenborg	47	Bodo/Glimt	45	Lillestrom	42

Cup Final Results

Year	Winner	Score	Runner-up	Notes
1989	Viking	2-1	Molde	after 2-2 draw
1990	Rosenborg	5-1	Fyllingen	
1991	Stromgodset	3-2	Rosenborg	
1992	Rosenborg	3-2	Lillestrom	
1993	Bodo/Glimt	2-0	Stromgodset	

NM Cup 1993

16th Finals
Aalesund v VIF	1-4
Brann v Andalsnes	2-0
Drobak/Frogn v Hodd	2-1
Elk v Asane	5-4
Fana v Start	2-1
Ham-Kam v Fram	1-0
Hana v Viking	0-2
Jevnaker v Fyllingen	2-4
Lillestrom v Ski	3-0
Molde v Strindheim	1-0
Odd v Sogndal	1-3
Oyestad v Stromgodset	0-5
Rosenborg v Tromsdalen	6-0
Sandefjord v Kongsvinger	1-0
Stordals Blink v Bodo/Glimt	1-2
Tromso v Mjolner	5-1

8th Finals
Bodo/Glimt v Drobak/Frogn	2-1
Brann v Viking	1-0
(after 2-2 draw)	
Elk v Ham-Kam	0-2
Fana v Molde	0-6
Lillestrom v Rosenborg	3-1
Sogndal v Fyllingen	3-4
Tromso v Sandefjord	2-1
VIF v Stromgodset	1-3

Quarter-Fnals
Bodo/Glimt v Tromso	3-0
Brann v Molde	2-0
Fyllingen v Lillestrom	1-0
Stromgodset v Ham-Kam	2-1

Semi-Finals
Brann v Bodo/Glimt	2-4
Stromgodset v Fyllingen	2-1

Final
Bodo/Glimt v Stromgodset 2-0
Scorers: Johnsen (64), Staurvik (82)

Erik Thorstvedt looks to net a record appearance for Norway.

after a creditable 1-1 draw at the Gjemselund Stadion.

The season began as it had started for the Norwegians in the international spotlight of the World Cup, and that particular saga is recounted elsewhere.

Norway Championship Results 1993–94

	Brann	Bodo/Glimt	Fyllingen	Ham-Kam	Kongsvinger	Lillestrom	Lynn	Molde	Rosenborg	Start	Tromso	Viking
Brann	—	1-3	3-2	2-1	0-0	2-1	3-7	1-1	0-2	2-1	1-1	0-2
Bodo/Glimt	2-1	—	5-1	3-0	4-1	1-2	8-0	3-0	1-2	2-1	1-0	4-1
Fyllingen	1-6	0-0	—	0-1	5-3	1-2	0-0	2-1	0-4	3-0	0-0	2-1
Ham-Kam	3-0	2-1	6-0	—	1-2	4-3	3-1	1-1	2-4	1-0	2-0	3-3
Kongsvinger	0-2	0-1	6-0	1-2	—	0-2	2-1	2-2	3-0	3-0	2-4	1-0
Lillestrom	2-1	5-3	3-1	2-0	3-0	—	2-0	3-0	2-3	1-2	3-2	3-0
Lynn	5-1	1-2	3-0	0-6	1-1	1-1	—	5-3	0-1	1-3	2-0	2-3
Molde	2-0	0-2	1-1	0-0	1-1	0-0	6-3	—	0-2	1-0	0-1	3-2
Rosenborg	0-4	2-2	5-1	3-2	3-2	1-1	4-2	2-0	—	2-1	4-2	1-1
Start	0-0	0-1	4-1	2-0	3-0	1-5	2-2	4-0	2-2	—	0-0	0-1
Tromso	1-1	1-1	0-0	4-1	4-0	2-1	0-2	0-1	0-0	0-0	—	2-1
Viking	1-0	3-1	1-0	7-1	2-3	1-0	2-0	1-0	2-0	1-0	2-1	—

Poland

Legia's double

Legia Warsaw took their fifth Polish championship title and their first since 1970 despite the handicap of starting the season with a three-point deduction. They achieved their win on goal difference from GKS Katowice, who still wait to claim their first championship triumph. It was sweet revenge for Legia, who had been stripped of their championship win at the end of the 1992–93 season when they were found guilty, with LKS Lodz, of match fixing. Along with that went a ban from European club competition and having to start the 1993–94 season with that deficit of three points. As if to emphasise the bad feelings both clubs had about their punishment, they reached the Polish Cup Final, which Legia won 2-0 to claim a double.

The season had started with the Legia players asking their colleagues at the other league clubs to boycott the season because of the punishment enforced on them by the Polish authorities. Not surprisingly the players' union declined.

Gornik did the best deals, on the transfer front, signing Jerzy Brzeczek and Aleksander Klak, who teamed up with international colleagues Tomasz Waldoch and Ryzyard Staniek. The club immediately reaped the benefits by maintaining a position at the top of the table for most of the season before faltering at the final run-in to finish third. The first half of the championship proved to be very tight, and as the winter break approached only seven points separated 16 of the 18 clubs.

Gornik led the table at the break with a 2-1 win over Legia, and when the season restarted in March little changed, with a handful of points separating around half a dozen sides still in with a realistic chance of taking the title. Legia started to make ground on Gornik, a vital win over LKS Lodz taking them into second place three points behind. But with the season entering its final stretch Gornik dropped a vital point at Zaglebie Lubin and then followed with a surprise defeat at home to Hutnik Krakow, which allowed Legia and LKS to move up into first and second place respectively.

With three games to play Legia consolidated their lead with two

Federation Polonaise de Football

Founded:	1919
Address:	Al. Ujazdowskie 22, PL-00478 Warsaw
Phone:	+48 22 29 24 89
Fax:	+48 22 21 91 75
UEFA Affiliation:	1954
FIFA Affiliation:	1923
Season:	September to May
National Stadium:	Stadion Slaski, Chorzow
Capacity:	70,000
Colours:	White, Red, White
Change:	Red, White, Red

Final League Table 1993–94

	P	W	D	L	F	A	Pts
Legia Warsaw †	34	19	13	2	72	24	48
GKS Katowice	34	18	12	4	52	28	48
Gornik Zagreb	34	17	12	5	56	32	46
LKS Lodz †	34	17	11	6	49	24	42
Pogon Szcezecin	34	11	19	4	39	24	41
Hutnik Krakow	34	12	15	7	34	28	38
Widzew	34	11	15	8	43	34	38
Ruch Chorzow	34	13	10	11	48	41	36
Lech Poznan	34	12	11	11	39	32	35
TM Pniewy	34	11	11	12	41	40	33
Stal Mielec	34	11	10	13	32	45	31
Stal Staowa Wola	34	8	15	11	25	37	31
Zaglebie Lubin	34	9	12	13	40	47	30
Warta Poznan	34	11	8	15	32	45	30
Wisla Krakow	34	6	13	15	30	46	22
Polina Warsaw	34	4	11	19	28	61	19
Siarka	34	4	10	20	25	57	18
Zawisza Bydgoszch	34	3	10	21	30	70	16

† deducted three points.

Top Scorers

21 BURZAWA (TM Pniewy)
14 Maurian JANSOZKA (GKS Katowice)
   Jerzy PODBROZNY (Legia Warsaw)

Promotions and Relegations

Promoted: Olimpia Poznan, Stomil Olsztyn, Petrochemia Plock, Rakow Czestochowa
Relegated: Polina Warsaw, Siarka, Wisla Krakow, Zawisza Bydogoszch

Five-Year Records League 1-2-3 and Cup Winners

League Results

	1st	Pts	2nd	Pts	3rd	Pts
1990	Lech Poznan	42	Zaglebie Lubin	40	GKS Katowice	40
1991	Zaglebie Lubin	44	Gornik Zabrze	40	Wisla Krakow	40
1992	Lech Poznan	49	GKS Katowice	44	Widzew Lodz	43
1993	Lech Poznan	47	Legia Warsaw	49	LKS Lodz	49
1994	Legia Warsaw	48	GKS Katowice	48	Gornik Zagreb	46

Cup Final Results

1990	Legia Warsaw	2-0	GKS Katowice	
1991	GKS Katowice	1-0	Legia Warsaw	
1992	Miedz Legnica	1-1	Gornik Zabrze	4-3 on pens
1993	GKS Katowice	1-1	Ruch	5-4 on pens
1994	Legia Warsaw	2-0	LKS Lodz	

International Results 1993–94

Date	Opponents	Result	Venue	Comp.	Scorers
8/9/93	England	0-3	Wembley	WCQ2	
22/9/93	Norway	0-1	Oslo	WCQ2	
13/10/93	Norway	0-3	Poznan	WCQ2	
27/10/93	Turkey	1-2	Istanbul	WCQ2	Kowalczyk (17)
17/11/93	Holland	1-3	Poznan	WCQ2	Lesniak (12)
9/2/94	Spain	1-1	Tenerife	Friendly	Kosecki (37)
23/3/94	Greece	0-0	Salonika	Friendly	
13/4/94	Saudi Arabia	1-0	Cannes	Friendly	Wieszcycki (74)
4/5/94	Hungary	3-2	Krakow	Friendly	Jalocha (48), Baluszinski (80), Fedoruk (85)
17/5/94	Austria	3-4	Katowice	Friendly	Juskowiak (22 pen), Brzeczek (47), Moskal (89)

National Record	P	W	D	L	F	A
European Championship	50	19	14	17	70	61
World Cup Finals	25	13	5	7	39	29
World Cup Qualifiers	58	29	10	19	105	29

Polish Cup

	1st Leg	2nd Leg	Agg
Quarter-Finals			
Gornik Zagreb v Gornik Pszow	8-0	1-1	9-1
GKS Katowice v Ruch Chorzow	3-0	0-1	3-1
Szombierki v LKS Lodz	2-2	1-5	3-7
Legia Warsaw v Hetman Zamosc	3-0	1-1	4-1
Semi-Finals			
Legia Warsaw v Gornik Zagreb	5-2		
GKS Katowice v LKS Lodz	0-0		
Final			
Legia Warsaw v LKS Lodz	2-0		

wins, to leave only second-placed GKS Katowice capable of catching them as the final round of games arrived, although such was Legia's goal difference that most accepted that the title was already theirs. Legia need just a point from their final game, which was ironically achieved against Gornik, who were resigned to third place after leading the title charge for most of the season. Legia won the championship as top scorers, which was all the more remarkable given the fact that they had sold their top scorer, Macief Silwowski, to Rapid Vienna at the start of the season.

Relegated Siarka were saved from extinction during the early part of 1994 when their German manager, Heinz Gruerel, agreed to 'buy' one of his own players, Cezary Kucharski, before eventually recouping the money by loaning him out to Swiss side FC Aarau, where he scored on his debut. Marek Lesniak, who plays for Wattenscheid in Germany, was voted Footballer of the Year, having returned to play for the national side after a four-year break at the age of 30.

The cup final was played in front of 20,000 and two goals in the final 14 minutes settled the contest in favour of Legia. Kowalczyk put the Warsaw club into the lead, and with LKS looking for an equaliser Podbrozny made it safe with three minutes of play remaining. LKS have the consolation of a Cup-Winners' Cup place, while Gornik Zabrze and GKS Katowice represent Poland in the UEFA Cup.

Nationally Poland failed to qualify for the World Cup finals for the second time in succession and had three managers during the course of the season. Following a comprehensive defeat at Wembley by England and an unlucky single-goal reversal in Norway, Andrzej Strejlau resigned, quoting ill health. He was replaced by his assistant, Leslaw Cikiewicz, whose first game in charge was against the Norwegians, 3-0 winners in Poznan. At that point Cikiewicz decided to resign but was talked into staying on. Then a 1-3 defeat by Holland reaffirmed Cikiewicz's resolve to leave. He was eventually replaced by 53-year-old Henryk Apostel. Apostel's first match was in Spain and a 1-1 draw, a fine result given five successive defeats, was achieved by a team comprised totally of home-based players. This was followed by a goalless draw with Greece and wins over Saudi Arabia and Hungary. The Saudi game was in Cannes in front of just 200 'fans' despite there being no admission charge! Defeat by the odd goal in seven by Austria in Katowice meant that the season finished a little disappointingly.

The Polish authorities also find themselves being put under pressure by FIFA, who have warned them about the lack of stadia that meet the required international standards. The Polish FA need to upgrade the stadiums in Warsaw, Lodz, Poznan and Chorzow if they are to stage their European Championship qualifying matches on home soil. With no funds they have asked the Polish government for help but so far there has been no positive response.

Poland had no representatives in the UEFA Cup due to the ban on Legia and LKS, but Lech Poznan and GKS Katowice flew the flag in the other competitions. Lech made it as far as the second round in the Champions' Cup, beating Beitar Jerusalem 7-2 on aggregate in the first before falling to Spartak Moscow by the same scoreline. GKS travelled to Lisbon to face Benfica in the Cup-Winners' Cup and were beaten by the only goal two minutes from time. Kucz equalised that on aggregate right on the interval in the return in Katowice, but another late goal secured a 1-1 draw for the Portuguese and an overall 2-1 win.

Portugal

No shift in power base

No matter where you live in Portugal, even if you support the local side, you will also follow either Benfica or Sporting. Such is the attraction of the two Lisbon clubs you will probably be a member of the supporters club and carry the card alongside that of your local team. That Benfica should regain the championship from FC Porto was a cause for great rejoicing throughout the club, and the fact that they should virtually ensure success by beating arch-rivals Sporting in a wonderfully entertaining 6-3 encounter to virtually seal it was another. This in a year when the Eagles stand on the verge of bankruptcy.

For FC Porto, who like Benfica have not finished outside of the top two for six years, there was some consolation in winning the Portuguese Cup in a replay 2-1. The manager was Englishman Bobby Robson, and it was a victory made sweet by the fact that the team defeated in the final were Sporting Lisbon – the side he had started the season with, only to have his contract terminated in the approach to Christmas. The smile was a broad one for Robson, who must have set some sort of record by having managed two sides in different European competitions, from the same country in the same year!

Sporting had to look back on another year of failure, finishing third for the fifth successive season and not having had either a domestic cup or league triumph since 1982. The pressure will again be on the new incumbent, national manager Carlos Queiroz, to produce the goods. This after the Sporting aficionados had seen Robson's managerial magic motivate his new side to overhaul them in the league and take them into the semi-finals of the Champions' Cup. But then Robson was always going to prove a point.

Things had started much more brightly for Sporting under Robson. They topped the table with 15 points from their first eight matches, with a very young side – average under 23 – and including a number of the players who had won the World Youth Championship for Portugal just two years earlier. The side had been strengthened with the arrival of Pacheco and Paulo Sousa from Benfica and Bulgarian Balakov, who would prove to be an able goal-getter. Benfica and FC Porto sat in third and fourth place behind the other club from Oporto, Boavista, while another famous name from recent years, Vitoria Setubal, were bottom with just three points, after having won back their place in the top division.

By the following weekend Benfica had taken over top position on goal difference, winning their game in hand at Pacos Ferreira thanks to a last-minute goal by Joao Pinto and then comprehensively disposing of mid-table Salgueiros. Sporting had not travelled well to second-placed Boavista, who maintained their challenge with goals by Nelo and Paulo Torres, leaving Benfica, Boavista and Sporting – in that order – equal on 15 points but separated on goal difference. Porto were in fourth position two points behind the pack, thanks to Kostadinov's winning goal on the stroke of half-time at home to a stubborn Estrela Amadora side.

By this time most clubs had made their mark in European club competition. Porto had secured their place in the UEFA Champions' League with a none-too-inspiring victory over Maltese side Floriana in the first round, before showing great resolve to beat Dutch champions Feyenoord with a last-minute goal from Domingos Oliveira. Benfica had two trips to Eastern Europe in the Cup-Winners' Cup, late goals in both legs inching them past GKS Katowice 2-1 on aggregate before an emphatic 6-2 aggregate demolition of CSKA Sofia.

In the UEFA Cup, European debutants Maritimo fell to Royal Antwerp at the first hurdle, but Union Sportive from Luxembourg hardly troubled Boavista. They were joined in the second round by Sporting, for whom two second-leg goals proved enough to ease them past Turkish side Kocaelispor. Both Sporting and Boavista then made it through to the third round with carbon copy performances. Having lost the first legs by single goals to Celtic and Lazio respectively, second leg wins by 2-0 produced 2-1 aggregate qualifications.

At this point, the national side had failed to qualify for the World Cup Finals despite three wins, over Estonia (twice) and long-time Group leaders Switzerland. Portugal went to Italy in their last game knowing that they needed to win, while a draw would see the Italians through on the assumption that the Swiss would beat Estonia. A late, highly disputed goal gave the Italians a victory and consigned Portugal to missing out on the World Cup for the second successive tournament.

The period around the end of November and start of December proved to be a turning point for Sporting. First, in the UEFA Cup, they established a 2-0 lead against SV Casino Salzburg, with goals in each half by Cherbakov and Cadete. This expected win was followed by a 3-0 home defeat from FC Porto. Progress in the Portuguese Cup was made very difficult by Lecea, who were ousted only by the odd goal in nine. At the end of this came the return against Salzburg, who scored two minutes after the interval and then stunned Sporting with an equaliser with virtually the last

Federacao Portuguesa de Futebol

Founded:	1914
Address:	Praca de Alegria 25, CP 21100, P-1128 Lisbon Codex
Phone:	+351 1 347 59 32
Fax:	+351 1 346 72 31
UEFA Affiliation:	1954
FIFA Affiliation:	1926
National Stadium:	Estadio Nacional
Capacity:	60,000
Season:	August to June
Colours:	Red, Green, Red
Change:	White, Red, White

Final League Table 1993–94

	P	W	D	L	F	A	Pts
Benfica	34	23	8	3	73	25	54
FC Porto	34	21	10	3	56	15	52
Sporting Lisbon	34	23	5	6	71	29	51
Boavista	34	16	6	12	46	31	38
Maritimo	34	13	12	9	45	40	38
Vitoria Setubal	34	14	6	14	56	42	34
Farense	34	13	7	14	44	46	33
Estrela Amadora	34	9	15	10	39	36	33
Guimaraes	34	11	11	12	30	31	33
Uniao Madeira	34	11	9	14	36	42	31
Gil Vicente	34	10	11	13	27	47	31
Salgueiros	34	14	3	17	48	56	31
Belenenses	34	12	6	16	39	51	30
Beira-Mar	34	9	11	14	28	38	29
Sporting Braga	34	9	10	15	33	43	28
Pacos Ferreira	34	7	12	15	31	49	26
Famalicao	34	7	8	19	26	72	22
Estoril	34	5	8	21	22	57	18

Top Scorers
- 21 Rashidi YEKINI (Vitoria Setubal)
- 17 Ljubinko DRULOVIC (FC Porto/Gil Vincente)
- 16 Emil KOSTADINOV (FC Porto)
- Nadar HASSAN (Farense)
- 15 Krasimir BALAKOV (Sporting Lisbon)
- Chiquinho CONDE (Vitoria Setubal)

Promotion and Relegation
Promoted: GD Chaves, Tirsense, Uniao Leiria
Relegated: Estoril, Famalicao, Pacos Ferreira.

Five-Year Records League 1-2-3 and Cup Winners

League Results

	1st	Pts	2nd	Pts	3rd	Pts
1990	FC Porto	59	Benfica	55	Sporting Lisbon	46
1991	Benfica	69	FC Porto	67	Sporting Lisbon	56
1992	FC Porto	56	Benfica	46	Sporting Lisbon	44
1993	FC Porto	54	Benfica	52	Sporting Lisbon	45
1994	Benfica	54	FC Porto	52	Sporting Lisbon	51

Cup Final Results

1990	Estrela Amadora	2-0	Farense	
1991	FC Porto	3-1	Beira Mar	
1992	Boavista	2-1	FC Porto	
1993	Benfica	5-2	Boavista	
1994	FC Porto	2-1	Sporting Lisbon	after 0-0 draw

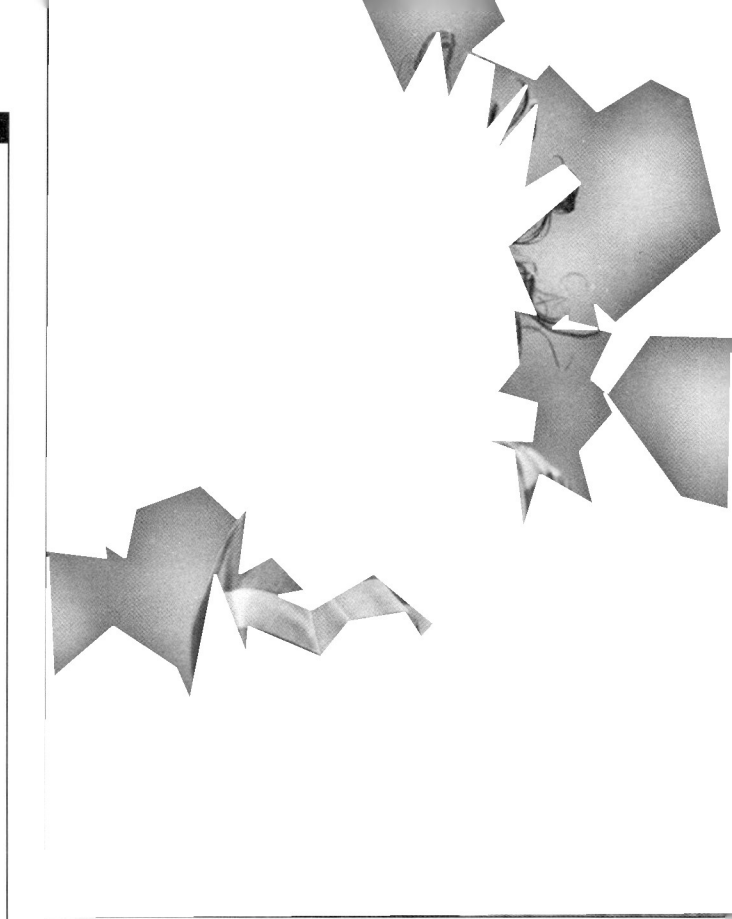

Unmistakeable! FC Porto's Fernando Couto – seen here in action for Portugal.

kick of the first 90 minutes. Amerhauser scored during the second period of extra time to put the Austrians through.

This sequence of events proved to much for President Jose Sousa Cintra, who sacked Robson and replaced him with Queiroz, although he had never managed a club side to that point and was not overly popular, given the national side's World Cup failure. The problems didn't stop there. A road traffic accident left the Russian player Cherbakov crippled, and Benfica won the Lisbon derby 2-1, Isaias scoring the winner five minutes from time. All these events overshadowed another good European performance by Boavista, who whipped OFI Crete to reach the quarter-finals of the UEFA Cup.

Benfica supporters were of course lapping all this up, and although they had won the Lisbon derby by only the odd goal they had produced an outstanding display of football that totally humiliated their rivals. But the Eagles had financial problems which meant that wages hadn't been paid and ultimately led to an election among the fee-paying members of the club – the *socios* – who settled for a new board and a new president, Manuel Damasio, who polled 87 per cent of the vote.

As the halfway point in the league was reached in January, Benfica were three points ahead of Sporting, who led FC Porto by a point. Robson had now been appointed Porto's coach, after Tomislav Ivic had joined the FIFA coaching staff. The challenge of Boavista looked to be fading, four points adrift of the leading pack. In the relegation zone, Estoril were slipping away at the bottom, while Vitoria Setubal had moved just outside the danger area but only a point clear of it.

For FC Porto, Robson had turned what looked to be elimination

Bobby Robson started the 1993–94 season as coach of Sporting Lisbon and finished it by coaching FC Porto to Portuguese Cup success over his former club.

squeezed past Bayer Leverkusen on away goals but only after the situation had been rescued in both legs with late, late goals. Boavista weren't so lucky in their UEFA Cup match with Germans Karlsruhe winning 2-1 on aggregate.

With eight rounds to play in the league Sporting suddenly found themselves on level terms with Benfica when the Eagles suffered a shock defeat by Salgueiros, the only goal being scored in the 85th minute by Sa Pinto. Sporting's 3-1 win over Boavista took them level and left FC Porto four points behind.

In Europe, FC Porto had secured a semi-final match at the Nou Camp, but Barcelona proved too difficult an obstacle and had little trouble in winning 3-0. Benfica encountered a similar barrier in the Cup-Winners' Cup, losing on the away goals rule to holders Parma. Qualification for the final should have been a formality after a sparkling display in Lisbon, but a goal conceded and a missed penalty proved expensive in the final analysis.

With thoughts of European glory gone, attention turned back to the league and Sporting lost a crunch match in Porto, in a game of three red cards and eight yellow, leaving them to play the last 25 minutes of the game with eight players. Drulovic and Vinha scored the goals for FC Porto and set up a virtual championship decider in the up-and-coming Lisbon derby match. Estoril became the first side to be relegated when they were beaten at Gil Vicente, with the other two relegation positions still threatening no fewer than seven clubs.

In Round 30 an amazing Lisbon derby took place in front of a rain-soaked capacity crowd in the Alvalade Stadium. The game had started with Benfica a point ahead of Sporting, but with Joao Pinto

from the Champions' Cup into a position of strength from which the semi-finals were a real possibility. A narrow win over Werder Bremen and a heavy defeat in Milan had made the situation precarious at the end of the year, not helped by defeat by RSC Anderlecht, but a 2-0 victory in the return game with the Belgians showed qualification was still a possibility given the right results in their final two fixtures. In the Cup-Winners' Cup, Benfica

Portugal Championship Results 1993–94

	Beira Mar	Belenenses	Benfica	Boavista	Estoril	Estrela Amadora	Famalicao	Farense	FC Porto	Gil Vicente	Maritimo	Pacos Ferreira	Salgueiros	Sporting Braga	Sporting Lisbon	Uniao Madeira	Vitoria Guimaraes	Vitoria Setubal
Beira Mar	—	1-1	1-1	1-1	0-0	0-1	1-0	3-0	0-2	1-0	3-1	0-1	2-1	0-0	0-4	0-0	1-0	2-1
Belenenses	2-0	—	0-2	2-1	1-0	2-1	4-0	4-2	0-2	1-0	2-1	1-1	2-3	0-0	0-3	2-1	0-0	1-2
Benfica	1-0	3-0	—	3-1	1-1	1-1	8-0	4-1	2-0	0-0	2-0	2-1	4-1	2-0	2-1	1-0	0-0	2-0
Boavista	2-1	3-0	1-0	—	3-0	1-1	3-0	0-1	1-1	1-2	3-2	2-0	3-1	1-0	2-1	3-0	1-1	1-0
Estoril	1-0	1-0	0-3	0-2	—	3-3	1-1	0-1	0-1	1-1	0-1	2-1	2-3	1-1	2-0	0-2	2-1	0-2
Estrela Amadora	2-2	2-2	0-1	1-1	3-0	—	2-0	1-2	0-0	3-0	1-1	3-1	3-1	1-1	0-4	2-0	0-1	0-0
Famalicao	2-1	2-3	1-5	0-3	1-0	0-2	—	2-1	0-5	3-0	0-2	4-1	1-0	1-0	1-1	0-0	1-1	1-1
Farense	2-2	1-0	0-0	1-0	1-2	1-0	5-0	—	1-0	4-2	0-0	3-0	4-1	0-0	0-1	1-3	0-1	2-1
FC Porto	0-0	1-0	3-3	1-0	3-0	2-1	0-0	1-0	—	3-0	2-0	0-0	1-0	5-0	2-0	4-1	1-1	2-0
Gil Vicente	1-1	0-3	0-3	0-0	2-0	1-0	1-0	0-0	1-1	—	1-0	1-1	2-0	1-1	0-0	0-0	2-1	2-1
Maritimo	0-2	1-2	1-1	1-0	1-1	0-0	3-2	5-2	1-0	0-0	—	3-3	2-1	4-0	2-1	3-2	2-0	0-0
Pacos Ferreira	1-1	1-1	1-2	1-0	0-0	1-0	2-0	1-0	0-2	3-1	2-2	—	0-2	1-0	1-2	1-1	2-2	1-1
Salgueiros	2-0	1-0	1-0	2-0	4-1	1-1	2-2	3-2	0-3	2-1	1-1	2-1	—	5-1	0-1	1-0	1-0	1-2
Sporting Braga	2-0	4-2	0-2	0-1	2-1	0-1	2-0	4-0	0-2	4-0	0-1	0-0	4-3	—	1-1	3-0	0-0	2-1
Sporting Lisbon	1-0	3-1	3-6	3-1	3-1	3-0	3-0	3-1	0-1	6-0	1-1	3-1	2-1	2-0	—	1-0	3-0	2-1
Uniao Madeira	2-0	2-0	0-2	2-1	3-0	2-2	0-0	0-0	0-2	1-2	1-1	2-0	3-1	3-1	0-0	—	2-0	2-1
Vitoria Guimaraes	1-2	3-0	1-2	1-0	2-0	0-0	3-0	2-2	0-0	2-1	0-1	1-0	1-0	0-0	1-4	2-0	—	1-0
Vitoria Setubal	2-0	3-0	5-2	1-3	2-1	1-1	6-1	2-0	3-3	0-2	4-1	3-0	4-0	1-0	2-3	2-3	1-0	—

International Results 1993–94

Date	Opponents	Result	Venue	Comp.	Scorers
5/9/93	Estonia	2-0	Tallinn	WCQ1	Rui Costa (60), Folha (76)
13/10/93	Switzerland	1-0	Oporto	WCQ1	Joao Vieira Pinto (8)
10/11/93	Estonia	3-0	Lisbon	WCQ1	Futre (2), Oceano (37 pen), Rui Aguas (86)
17/11/93	Italy	0-1	Milan	WCQ1	
19/1/94	Spain	2-2	Vigo	Friendly	Own Goal (73), Oceano (83 pen)
20/4/94	Norway	0-0	Oslo	Friendly	

National Record	P	W	D	L	F	A
European Championship	59	28	14	17	75	65
World Cup Finals	9	6	0	3	19	12
World Cup Qualifiers	73	31	16	26	107	103

playing what he later described as 'the game of his life', scoring a hat-trick and making a couple more, they had the trump card. Sporting twice took the lead but shortly after the interval fell behind. They never recovered as Benfica stormed 6-2 ahead before a Balakov penalty made it 6-3 near the end. Sporting lost 2-1 at Maritimo the following week, when Benfica beat Uniao Madeira and FC Porto won again to move into second place.

A win over Gil Vicente set the stage for Benfica to take the title on their own ground, against Guimaraes. Over 120,000 turned up to celebrate and despite the lack of goals the Eagles were crowned champions for the 30th time. FC Porto subsequently secured the runners-up spot ahead of Sporting, while at the other end of the table Famalicao and Pacos Ferreira were relegated. Vitoria Setubal, who had had such a wretched start, finished in a commendable eighth position but not high enough for one of the UEFA Cup places, which went to the same three who had done well the previous season – Sporting, Boavista and Maritimo.

The Cup Final brought together FC Porto and Sporting for what was regarded as a grudge affair. The first match ended goalless, but FC Porto and Bobby Robson had the last laugh as his side won the replay 2-1 – thanks to an extra time penalty by Aloisio.

Portuguese Cup 1993–94

Quarter-Finals
FC Porto v Aves	6-0
Courosa v Belenenses	2-0
Rio Ave v Amadora	0-3
Sporting Lisbon v Trofense	3-1

Semi-Finals
Amadora v FC Porto	1-2
Sporting Lisbon v Courosa	6-0

Final

FC Porto	0	Sporting Lisbon	0

Final Replay

FC Porto	0	Sporting Lisbon	1

Rui Jorge (35), Aloisio (92 pen)   Vujacic (55)
After extra time
Att: 60,000   *Ref:* Fortunato Azevedo
FC Porto: Victor Baia, Joao DS Pinto, Rui Jorge, Aloisio, Fernando Couto, Andre (Vinha 83), Secretario, Paulinho Santos, Timofte (Rui Filipe 68), Folha, Drulovic.
Sporting Lisbon: Iemajic, Nelson, Paulo Torres (Marinho 65), Vujacic (Carlos Jorge 69), Peixe, Paulo Sousa, Figo, Capucho, Poejo, Pacheco, Cadete.

Republic of Ireland

Cash boost for league

Football in the Republic of Ireland continues to be dominated by the exploits of the national side, who have maintained their status as one of the top European nations by virtue of their performance in the World Cup qualifying rounds and Finals. Paradoxically the League of Ireland clubs have failed to make any real progress within the realms of the European club competitions, all falling at the first round stage, although qualification through the preliminary round stages of the two major competitions did take place at the expense of inexperienced opposition. The problem of course lies in the fact that the best international players continue to move abroad, most notably to England, to realise their ambitions, and the national side are based almost exclusively on players earning a living outside their native borders.

In their Champions' Cup preliminary round encounter with Cwmbran Town, Cork came from three down to score two vital away goals in Wales. Two late goals at their Bishoptown ground ensured Cork qualified for the first round on the away goals rule. Waiting for them there were the Turkish champions Galatasaray, and a late goal by Dave Barry in Istanbul meant that at 1-2 there was a fighting chance for the second leg. However, a goal by Swiss international Turkyilmaz saw the Turks through 3-1 on aggregate.

Shelbourne had only once won in European competition prior to their encounter with Karpaty in the Cup-Winners' Cup, and that had been as far back as the 1964–65 season, but a one-goal deficit was turned around at Tolka Park with goals from Costello, Mooney and Izzi, and they went through 3-2 on aggregate. Panathinaikos waited in the first round and the Greek side proved much too strong, winning 5-1 over the two legs. In the UEFA Cup Bohemians couldn't find away through the Bordeaux defence and bowed out 6-0 on aggregate.

Domestically, Shamrock Rovers won their 15th League of Ireland title with room to spare to record what was their first championship success since 1987. Rovers fans will hope that manager Ray Treacy will be able to keep his successful side together and recapture the glory years in which they did the Irish double three seasons on the trot, the last in 1987. The title triumph was particularly sweet for Treacy who insisted on persisting with his total football approach despite only just avoiding relegation at the end of the 1992–93 season.

Rovers completed the first round of 22 games seven points ahead of Cork City – a margin they had maintained at the end of the championship phase. After the 12 first division sides had played

The Football Association of Ireland

Founded:	1921
Address:	80 Merrion Square, South Dublin 2
Phone:	+353 1 676 68 64
Fax:	+353 1 661 09 31
UEFA Affiliation:	1954
FIFA Affiliation:	1923
Season:	August to May
National Stadium:	Lansdowne Road
Capacity:	48,000
Colours:	Green, White, Green
Change:	White, Green, White

Final League Table 1993–94

First Round	P	W	D	L	F	A	Pts
Shamrock Rovers	22	15	3	4	43	16	48
Cork City	22	12	5	5	43	24	41
Shelbourne	22	10	6	6	33	27	36
Galway United	22	9	7	6	30	26	34
Bohemians	22	8	7	7	23	17	31
Derry City	22	8	7	7	21	21	31
Monaghan United	22	9	3	10	27	27	30
Dundalk	22	7	7	7	25	20	29
St Patrick's Athletic	22	6	9	7	24	24	27
Cobh Ramblers	22	5	4	13	20	34	19
Limerick	22	3	8	11	15	40	17
Drogheda United	22	4	5	13	16	44	17

Championship	P	W	D	L	F	A	Pts
Shamrock Rovers	32	21	3	8	62	30	66
Cork City	32	17	8	7	60	36	59
Galway United	32	14	8	10	47	42	50
Derry City	32	12	10	10	37	35	46
Shelbourne	32	11	10	11	42	42	43
Bohemians	32	11	8	13	34	35	41

Relegation/Promotion	P	W	D	L	F	A	Pts
Monaghan United	32	13	8	11	41	38	47
Dundalk	32	10	13	9	37	27	43
St Patrick's Athletic	32	9	12	11	32	38	39
Cobh Ramblers	32	8	8	16	31	41	32
Limerick	32	6	11	15	23	50	29
Drogheda United	32	7	7	18	26	58	28

Top Scorers
- 23 GEOGHEGAN (Shamrock Rovers)
- 15 MORLEY (Cork City)
- 14 BRENNAN (Galway United)
- 13 O'CONNOR (Shelbourne)
- SARRAGUER (Galway United)

Promotions and Relegations
Promoted: Sligo Rovers, Athlone Town
Relegated: Drogheda United, Limerick

REPUBLIC OF IRELAND

International Results 1993–94

Date	Opponents	Result	Venue	Comp.	Scorers
8/9/93	Lithuania	2-0	Dublin	WCQ3	Aldridge (4), Kernaghan (24)
13/10/93	Spain	1-3	Dublin	WCQ3	Sheridan (71)
17/10/93	N. Ireland	1-1	Belfast	WCQ3	McLoughlin (78)
23/3/94	Russia	0-0	Dublin	Friendly	
20/4/94	Holland	1-0	Tilburg	Friendly	Coyne (55)
24/5/94	Bolivia	1-0	Dublin	Friendly	Sheridan (35)
29/5/94	Germany	2-0	Hannover	Friendly	Cascarino (31), G.Kelly (68)
5/6/94	Czech Republic	1-3	Dublin	Friendly	
18/6/94	Italy	1-0	New Jersey	WCFE	Houghton (11)
24/6/94	Mexico	1-2	Orlando	WCFE	Aldridge (84)
28/6/94	Norway	0-0	New Jersey	WCFE	
4/7/94	Holland	0-2	Orlando	WCF2	

National Record	P	W	D	L	F	A
European Championship	59	21	17	21	84	77
World Cup Finals	9	1	5	3	4	7
World Cup Qualifiers	73	26	17	30	95	109

Five-Year Records League 1-2-3 and Cup Winners

League Results

	1st	Pts	2nd	Pts	3rd	Pts
1990	St Patrick's Ath.	52	Derry City	49	Dundalk	42
1991	Dundalk	52	Cork City	50	St Patrick's Ath.	44
1992	Shelbourne	49	Derry City	44	Cork City	43
1993	Cork City won play-offs					
1994	Shamrock Rovers	66	Cork City	59	Galway United	50

Cup Final Results

1990	Bray Wanderers	3-0	St Francis
1991	Galway United	1-0	Shamrock Rovers
1992	Bohemians	1-0	Cork City
1993	Shelbourne	1-0	Dundalk
1994	Sligo Rovers	1-0	Derry City

FAI Cup Results

Quarter-Finals
Sligo Rovers v Cobh Ramblers	1-0
Home Farm v Bohemians	1-1
Limerick v Monaghan United	2-1
Derry City v St Patrick's Athletic	1-0

Semi-Finals
Bohemians v Derry City	0-1
Sligo Rovers v Limerick	1-0

Final
Sligo Rovers v Derry City	1-0

Republic of Ireland First Round Results

	Bohemians	Cobh Ramblers	Cork City	Derry City	Drogheda United	Dundalk	Galway United	Limerick City	Monaghan United	Shamrock Rovers	Shelbourne	St Patrick's Ath
Bohemians	—	2-0	3-4	2-0	0-1	1-0	3-0	1-0	0-0	2-0	1-0	0-0
Cobh Ramblers	0-0	—	2-1	1-3	1-2	0-2	0-2	0-0	2-0	1-3	1-1	0-1
Cork City	2-0	2-0	—	1-0	1-1	0-1	1-2	3-0	1-0	2-2	3-1	1-1
Derry City	3-0	2-0	0-1	—	1-1	1-4	0-0	0-0	1-0	0-0	1-4	2-0
Drogheda United	1-4	1-3	0-5	0-1	—	0-3	1-4	0-2	1-4	2-1	1-1	1-1
Dundalk	1-1	0-2	2-2	2-2	0-1	—	0-0	0-0	1-3	1-2	5-1	0-2
Galway United	1-1	4-0	0-0	2-1	2-0	0-0	—	1-2	1-0	0-5	1-1	1-2
Limerick City	0-0	1-5	1-7	0-1	1-1	0-1	0-3	—	2-3	0-2	0-0	2-1
Monaghan United	1-0	2-1	2-1	1-1	1-0	1-0	3-1	0-0	—	0-1	4-5	1-2
Shamrock Rovers	2-1	3-0	3-0	0-1	2-0	0-0	3-1	7-3	2-1	—	2-0	2-0
Shelbourne	2-1	1-0	0-1	2-0	1-0	1-2	1-1	3-0	3-0	1-0	—	1-0
St Patrick's Ath.	0-0	1-1	3-4	0-0	4-1	0-0	2-3	1-1	1-0	0-1	2-2	—

each other home and away, the top six sides regrouped to form the championship group and the bottom six the relegation group, both sets of teams playing each other home and away once again.

With all teams taking their full sets of points with them, Shamrock were assured of a comfortable buffer when they went into their first game of the second phase at Derry City. The comfort factor took a knock as they lost 1-0, but the damage wasn't as great as it might have been given that Cork could only draw at Shelbourne. But the alarm bells were starting to sound as home defeats by Galway (2-5) and Bohemians (1-2) allowed Cork to narrow the gap to three points. In the relegation group, division one was looking a near certainty for Drogheda and Limerick as both sides could only gain three points from their first three games. Cobh Ramblers were also losing touch with the top three but were relatively safe in the play-off zone.

In week four of the championship round Shamrock visited Cork and needed to produce a resolute display to ensure that their

Championship Round Results

	Bohemians	Cork City	Derry City	Galway United	Shamrock Rovers	Shelbourne
Bohemians	—	1-1	1-3	0-1	1-2	2-0
Cork City	3-1	—	4-2	2-0	2-1	3-1
Derry City	4-0	3-2	—	1-1	1-0	0-0
Galway United	3-1	0-1	2-1	—	2-3	2-5
Shamrock Rovers	1-2	2-0	3-0	2-5	—	2-1
Shelbourne	0-2	1-1	1-1	0-1	0-3	—

Relegation Round Results

	Cobh Ramblers	Drogheda United	Dundalk	Limerick City	Monaghan United	St Patrick's Ath
Cobh Ramblers	—	1-0	1-1	1-0	1-2	0-1
Drogheda United	2-1	—	0-2	0-0	1-1	2-0
Dundalk	0-0	4-0	—	2-0	1-1	0-2
Limerick City	0-0	1-0	2-1	—	2-1	2-2
Monaghan United	1-1	3-2	1-1	2-1	—	0-0
St Patrick's Ath.	0-5	1-3	0-0	1-0	1-2	—

lead didn't evaporate totally. They failed and Cork inflicted Rovers' fourth successive defeat – as many as they had experienced in the whole of the first round – to take over at the top of the table on goal difference with a game in hand. Shamrock at last arrested their ominous slide with a 2-1 win at bottom-placed Bohemians but Cork beat Galway and picked up a draw in their game in hand to move a point clear at the top. In the relegation group the bottom three of Drogheda, Cobh and Limerick had totally lost touch and were now involved in a dog-fight to avoid the two automatic relegation places.

By week eight Shamrock had re-established a two-point lead at the top by beating Derry 3-0 as Shelbourne grabbed a point at Cork in a 1-1 draw. Week nine – the penultimate weekend – saw both championship contenders win again which, barring a total collapse by Rovers in their last game, gave them the title. That last game was at home to Cork and Shamrock won 2-0. What had started off with a disastrous run of four defeats had been turned around with six straight victories. Cork's reward as the second-placed team was a UEFA Cup place alongside Shamrock Rovers, whose co-efficient wasn't high enough to get them into the Champions' League preliminary round. As a strange quirk of fate, Shamrock will therefore be the Republic's first representatives in the UEFA Cup as champions, just as they were their first representatives as champions in the Champions' Cup back in 1957. They will have to make their assault on the competition without the services of top striker Stephen Geoghegan, who has joined Shelbourne. Geoghegan, who topped the scoring charts with 23 goals, was voted both the PFAI Player of the Year and The Soccer Writers' Personality of the Year, and will be joined at Shelbourne by his team-mate, Alan Byrne. Those arrivals went some way towards the loss of goalscorer Gary Haylock who went north to Linfield at the start of the season.

In the relegation group, the inevitable had long since happened with Limerick and Drogheda being relegated to division one, from where Sligo Rovers and Athlone Town had won promotion. The final place in the premier division was decided by a two-legged play-off between Cobh Ramblers and the third team in division one, Finn Harps. The tie was won by Cobh; the club from Cork had shown excellent form in the final two weeks of the season, winning twice and scoring six times without reply to earn the right to play-off.

There was an upset in the FAI Cup, when Sligo Rovers beat neighbours Derry City in the final, and took the trophy for only the second time in their history, thanks to a 63rd-minute goal by Gerry Carr. Derry did manage cup success, winning the League Cup for the fourth time in six years by beating Shelbourne.

Internationally the Republic's lack of striking power cost them dear in America, two goals in four games producing just one win. Qualification had been done the hard way, with the team having been perhaps over-confident going into the match with Spain. A late John Sheridan strike added a little bit of gloss to what had been a comprehensive 1-3 defeat. Facing the North in the final match of the group and needing a win to ensure qualification, Alan McLoughlin popped up to score an equaliser, and results elsewhere were kind enough to allow the Republic to qualify, not on goal difference, but on goals scored. A milestone for manager Jack Charlton was reached when John Aldridge scored in the fourth minute against Lithuania – it was the 100th goal scored by the Republic under Charlton's reign, coming in his 71st match in charge since 1986.

With a series of excellent results prior to travelling out to New York, confidence was high but tempered by a 1-3 home defeat by the Czech Republic, in which goalkeeper Pat Bonner broke Liam Brady's cap record when he made his 73rd appearance.

The World Cup provided a huge financial boost for the FAI, who from the start of the 1994–95 season have taken over the management of the league and scrapped the two-group play-off system, reverting to a three-round championship, just two years after it was started. With most clubs now having floodlights installed and the national stadium at Lansdowne Road also undergoing changes, things could start to take a turn for the better for club football in the Republic. But the real need is to keep a number of their better players at home or to play out their later years on their native soil.

Romania

In many respects the Romanian championship was really all about second place for most of the season. From the opening weekend Steaua Bucharest got their noses in front and never looked threatened as they went about establishing a lead that they were never likely to surrender on their way to a 16th title triumph. Over 50,000 attended the opening day derby game between Steaua and cross-town rivals Dinamo, where two goals by Vladoiu and one by Dumitrescu set the tone in a comprehensive 3-0 win.

Steaua didn't totally hog top spot in the league. A dropped point at home to Farul Constanta combined with Universitatea Craiova's 3-0 win over the other University side, Cluj, allowed 'U' to take over at the top in week three. Week five saw Farul in top position by virtue of having played a game more than the sides below them, but two weeks later Steaua had nudged themselves back into the number one place on goal difference, despite having played a game fewer than the sides nearest them. 'U' remained close in third position while the other Bucharest sides, Dinamo and Rapid, were already six points off the pace and struggling in the lower half of the table. Dinamo were hampered further after a 1-1 draw at Progresul was overturned by the Romanian FA and awarded 3-0 to the home side after the visitors' coaching staff had been involved in unruly behaviour! Dinamo were also ordered to play their next two home games at neutral venues.

As November approached Steaua continued to sit pretty, but then a goalless draw at home to Rapid was followed by a 3-1 defeat in Craiova and allowed 'U' to move a point in front – but only for a week, as their defeat by Brasov let Steaua regain the lead with another win. A surprise defeat at Otelul Galati allowed Steaua to open up a three-point gap ahead of 'U', who then suffered a second successive defeat, at home to Ploiesti. This might have been Steaua's opportunity to increase their margin, but an improving UT Arad secured a surprise 1-0 win over the leaders and moved into second position, having been promoted from the second division only the previous season.

That proved to be Arad's peak. Steaua edged five points ahead of Ploiesti and 'U' in the coming weeks, while Dinamo hit a surge of form that took them up the table into fourth place. With the winter break looming, Steaua increased their lead to seven points by virtue of winning their game in hand, and looked to have slapped down Dinamo's rise up the table by beating them by a single goal on the penultimate weekend of the year. Nevertheless results went in Dinamo's favour elsewhere and a 6-1 win over Brasov pushed them into second place as Cluj beat 'U' 3-1. Steaua, though, remained seven points clear and looked in a very strong position.

Campionatlui National de Fotbal 1993–94

	P	W	D	L	F	A	Pts
Steaua Bucharest	34	22	9	3	63	10	53
Universitatea Craiova	34	16	8	10	64	46	40
Dinamo Bucharest	34	16	7	11	65	40	39
Rapid Bucharest	34	16	6	12	43	32	38
Petrolul Ploiesti	34	14	10	10	34	30	38
Farul Constanta	34	15	7	12	42	38	37
Gloria Bistrita	34	16	3	15	47	43	35
Inter Sibiu	34	13	8	13	40	41	34
Progresul	34	14	4	16	44	42	32
Ceahlaul Piatra Neamt	34	11	10	13	47	40	32
UT Arad	34	12	8	14	35	49	32
Universitatea Cluj	34	11	9	14	39	42	31
Brasov	34	13	5	16	38	52	31
Electroputere Craiova	34	10	10	14	25	34	30
Otelul Galati	34	12	5	17	38	47	29
Sportul Studentesc	34	11	7	16	30	45	29
Politehnica Timisoara	34	11	6	17	39	53	28
Dacia Unirea Braila	34	9	6	19	33	53	24

Top Scorers
- 21 Gheorghe CRAIOVEANU (Universitatea Craiova)
- 17 Ilie LAZAR (Gloria Bistrita)
     Ilie DUMITRESCU (Steaua Bucharest)
- 16 Marian IVAN (Brasov)
- 15 Ioan UNGUR (UT Arad)
- 13 Marius PREDATU (Universitatea Cluj)
     Constantin VARGA (Politehnica Timisoara)
- 12 Cristian SAVU (Dinamo Bucharest)
     Iulian CHIRITA (Rapid Bucharest)
     Gheorghe CEAUSILA (Sportul Studentesc)
     Ovidiu STINGA (Universitatea Craiova)
- 11 Gheorghe BUTOIU (Farul Constanta)
- 10 Rodin VOINEA (Rapid Bucharest)
     Marin DUNA (Progresul)

Promotions and Relegations
Promoted: Arges Dacia, FC Maramures
Relegated: Politehnica Timisoara, Dacia Unirea Braila

Federatia Romania De Fotbal

Founded:	1908
Address:	Bucureati, Str. Poligrafiei nr. 3 Sector 1
Phone:	+40 1 617 33 43
Fax:	+40 1 312 83 24
UEFA Affiliation:	1954
FIFA Affiliation:	1930
Season:	August to April
National Stadium:	Stadionul 23 August, Bucharest
Capacity:	65,000
Colours:	Yellow, Blue, Red
Change:	Blue, Yellow, Red

International Results 1993–94

Date	Opponents	Result	Venue	Comp.	Scorers
8/9/93	Faeroe Islands	4-0	Toftir	WCQ4	Raducioiu (23, 58, 60, 76)
22/9/93	Israel	1-0	Bucharest	Friendly	Panduru (49)
13/10/93	Belgium	2-1	Bucharest	WCQ4	Raducioiu (67 pen), Dumitrescu (85)
17/11/93	Wales	2-1	Cardiff	WCQ4	Hagi (32), Raducioiu (83)
10/2/94	Hong Kong	1-1	Hong Kong	Carlsberg	Dumitrescu (63)
					Hong Kong won 5-4 on penalties
13/2/94	United States	2-1	Hong Kong	Carlsberg	Dumitrescu (6, 72 pen)
16/2/94	South Korea	2-1	Seoul	Friendly	Dumitrescu (43, 73)
23/3/94	N. Ireland	0-2	Belfast	Friendly	
20/4/94	Bolivia	3-0	Bucharest	Friendly	Dumitrescu (22, 49), Niculescu (64)
25/5/94	Nigeria	2-0	Bucharest	Friendly	Dumitrescu (22), Petrescu (49)
1/6/94	Slovenia	0-0	Bucharest	Friendly	
12/6/94	Sweden	1-1	Mission Viejo	Friendly	Hagi (74)
18/6/94	Colombia	3-1	Pasadena	WCFA	Raducioiu (16, 89), Hagi (34)
22/6/94	Switzerland	1-4	Detroit	WCFA	Hagi (35)
26/6/94	United States	1-0	Pasadena	WCFA	Petrescu (17)
3/7/94	Argentina	3-2	Pasadena	WCF2	Dumitrescu (17, 18), Hagi (56)
10/7/94	Sweden	2-2	San Francisco	WCFQ	Raducioiu (88, 100)

Sweden won 5-4 on penalties after extra time

National Record	P	W	D	L	F	A
European Championship	58	25	16	17	96	66
World Cup Finals	17	6	4	7	26	29
World Cup Qualifiers	64	33	14	17	111	66

Five-Year Records League 1-2-3 and Cup Winners

League Results

	1st	Pts	2nd	Pts	3rd	Pts
1990	Dinamo Bucharest	57	Steaua Bucharest	56	Univ. Craiova	44
1991	Univ. Craiova	50	Steaua Bucharest	50	Dinamo Bucharest	43
1992	Dinamo Bucharest	55	Steaua Bucharest	48	Electro. Craiova	39
1993	Steaua Bucharest	48	Dinamo Bucharest	47	Univ. Craiova	37
1994	Steaua Bucharest	53	Univ. Craiova	40	Dinamo Bucharest	39

Cup Final Results

1990	Dinamo Bucharest	6-4	Steaua Bucharest	
1991	Univ. Craiova	2-1	Bacau	
1992	Steaua Bucharest	1-1	Timisoara	4-3 on pens
1993	Univ. Craiova	2-0	Braila	
1994	Gloria Bistrita	1-0	Univ. Craiova	

Ilie Dumitrescu in Steaua Bucharest colours before his big money move to Tottenham Hotspur.

By the end of the year Romanian interest in European club competition had been exhausted, although the same was not true of the national side, who had clinched a place in the World Cup finals with a win over the Welsh. A 2-1 win over the Belgians in Bucharest, with goals from Raducioiu and a late winner by Dumitrescu, had placed Anghel Iordanescu's side in a strong

Romanian FA Cup

First Round

Arges Pitesti v UTA Arad	2-0
Aro Campu Lung Muscel v Rapid Bucharest	0-0, 5-3 on pens
Ceahlaul Piatra Neamt v Dinamo Bucharest	1-2
Cetatea Targu Neamt v Inter Sibiu	0-3
Energia Iernut v Universitatea Craiova	0-1
Gloria Resita v Gloria Bistrita	1-3
Jiul Petrosani v Farul Constanta	0-1
Metalurgistul Cugir v Progresul	0-2
Petrolul Berca v Sportul	
Poiana Campina v Petrolul Ploiesti	2-1
Politehnica Timisoara v Dacia Unirea Braila	0-1
Rapid Miercurea Ciuc v Electroputere Craiova	2-1
Selena Bacau v Otelul Galati	3-1
Severnav Tr. Severin v Brasov	0-1
Sportul Calarasi v Universitatea Cluj	0-0, 3-5 on pens
Vrancart Adjud v Steaua Bucharest	0-0, 2-3 on pens

Second Round

Arges Pitesti v Steaua Bucharest	0-0, 4-3 on pens
Dinamo Bucharest v Progresul	2-0
Gloria Bistrita v Petrolul Berca	5-0
Inter Sibiu v Brasov	3-1
Poiana Campina v Rapid Miercurea Ciuc	1-1, 5-4 on pens
Selena Bacau v Dacia Unirea Braila	3-0
Universitatea Cluj v Aro Campu Lung Muscel	2-1
Universitatea Craiova v Farul Constanta	5-0

Quarter-Finals

Arges Pitesti v Dinamo Bucharest	1-0
Gloria Bistrita v Poiana Campina	3-0
Universitatea Cluj v Brasov	0-0, 6-5 on pens
Universitatea Craiova v Selena Bacau	2-0

Semi-Finals

Gloria Bistrita v Universitatea Cluj	4-1
Universitatea Craiova v Arges Pitesti	1-0

Final

Gloria Bistrita v Universitatea Craiova	1-0

(games from second round played on neutral ground)

Romanian Championship Results 1993–94

	Braila	Brasov	Ceahlaul Piatra Neamt	Dinamo Bucharest	Electroputere Craiova	Farul	Gloria Bistrita	Inter Sibiu	Otelul Galati	Petrolul Ploiesti	Politehnica Timisoara	Progresul	Rapid Bucharest	Sportul	Steaua Bucharest	Universitatea Cluj	Universitatea Craiova	UT Arad
Braila	—	0-0	0-0	1-0	3-0	1-0	2-4	2-0	1-0	2-1	0-3	4-0	0-0	2-1	2-5	0-0	1-1	2-0
Brasov	2-0	—	2-0	0-0	1-0	0-1	1-0	3-1	4-0	1-1	1-3	2-1	0-2	1-0	0-1	2-1	2-0	3-0
Ceahlaul Piatra Neamt	4-2	2-1	—	2-1	0-0	1-0	1-0	0-0	1-0	0-0	2-0	0-2	2-0	1-1	1-1	1-1	1-7	2-0
Dinamo Bucharest	2-0	6-1	4-0	—	4-2	2-1	2-0	4-1	3-1	3-1	4-0	2-0	3-1	0-0	0-3	4-1	2-3	5-2
Electroputere Craiova	1-0	0-1	0-0	2-2	—	0-1	2-1	1-0	5-1	0-0	0-0	1-0	1-0	1-0	0-0	2-0	2-2	1-1
Farul	2-1	0-1	2-0	2-1	3-1	—	1-0	2-3	0-3	0-0	3-1	3-0	2-1	4-0	1-1	3-0	1-1	1-1
Gloria Bistrita	3-0	2-1	2-0	1-1	1-0	3-1	—	2-0	1-0	2-1	4-0	1-0	1-2	5-0	0-1	1-0	3-2	3-1
Inter Sibiu	2-0	4-1	3-1	1-0	2-0	0-0	2-0	—	1-0	1-1	2-1	2-0	2-0	1-2	0-2	3-2	2-2	3-1
Otelul Galati	4-3	1-0	0-1	2-0	1-0	2-0	1-1	1-1	—	4-0	6-3	1-0	1-1	3-1	0-1	1-1	3-1	0-0
Petrolul	1-0	3-0	3-0	0-1	1-0	2-0	2-0	0-0	2-0	—	1-0	2-0	1-0	1-1	1-0	1-2	1-0	1-0
Politehnica Timisoara	2-1	0-0	2-0	2-2	2-0	1-1	2-0	2-1	4-0	1-1	—	0-3	0-2	0-0	2-2	1-0	1-2	1-0
Progresul	2-1	1-1	0-0	3-0*	3-0	2-3	6-0	2-0	3-0	1-0	1-0	—	1-5	2-0	0-3	0-0	5-2	1-0
Rapid Bucharest	0-0	2-1	0-1	0-0	0-1	3-0	1-2	2-0	1-0	3-0	1-0	2-2	—	1-0	2-1	2-1	3-1	3-1
Sportul	2-1	3-2	2-1	0-4	0-1	1-0	2-0	1-0	0-1	1-1	4-0	0-2	0-1	—	0-0	2-0	0-1	2-1
Steaua Bucharest	2-0	2-0	2-0	1-0	2-0	0-0	2-1	4-1	2-1	4-0	2-0	3-0	0-0	3-1	—	2-0	1-1	6-0
Universitatea Cluj	2-1	5-1	2-1	1-1	0-0	1-1	3-2	1-0	2-0	1-0	5-1	1-0	2-0	1-1	1-2	—	3-1	1-2
Universitatea Craiova	5-0	6-2	3-0	3-2	0-0	1-2	2-0	0-0	1-0	0-1	1-0	2-1	3-1	1-2	3-1	3-0	—	7-1
UT Arad	2-0	4-0	1-1	1-0	2-1	0-1	1-1	1-1	2-0	1-0	1-0	2-1	2-0	1-0	0-0	1-1	—	

* Match awarded to Progesul after 1-1 draw

position in the Group Four table. A similar scoreline in Cardiff, where the Romanians included nine overseas players in their starting line-up, put Romania top on goal difference from Belgium. Hagi and Raducioiu hit the vital goals.

In the Champions' Cup, Steaua needed the benefit of the away goals rule to get past Croatia Zagreb. Having lost the first leg 1-2 at home, two goals by Vladoiu in the second allowed them a 3-2 win in Zagreb, but a 1-4 defeat in Monaco in the first leg of the second round made Champions' League qualification difficult. Steaua had taken the lead through Dumitrescu but the French hit

The Romanian side that reached the quarter-finals of the World Cup. Pictured here before their 1-4 defeat by Switzerland.

back despite being down to ten men for most of the game after defender Thuram had been sent off. Steaua's Prodan was also given his marching orders during the game but the result was already beyond the league leaders, and although a late goal by Dumitrescu gave Steaua win on the night in the return game, Monaco went through 4-2 on aggregate.

In the Cup-Winners' Cup 'U' Craiova made mincemeat of HB, beating the Faeroe Islanders 7-0 on aggregate in the first round, only to find themselves on the chopping block in the second as Paris Saint-Germain produced a 6-0 overall win. Matters were worse in the UEFA Cup, where all three Romanian representatives fell at the first hurdle. A late penalty gave Dinamo Bucharest a 3-2 home win over Cagliari in their first leg but the Italians had a reasonably easy passage with a 2-0 win in Sardinia. Rapid fell to a Dennis Bergkamp hat-trick in Milan, and Internazionale won 2-0 in Bucharest to go through 5-1 on aggregate. Gloria Bistrita couldn't make a breakthrough in the home leg against Maribor Branik, and two goals in the second leg saw the Slovenians through to the second round.

Rapid Bucharest still continued to struggle in the lower reaches of the table and featured in a take-over bid at the start of the New Year when Ana Electronic, a subsidiary of Samsung, brought a 51% stake in the club. With so many stars abroad it was no surprise when Gheorghe Hagi, playing for Brescia in Italy's Serie B, was named as the Romanian Footballer of the Year.

With ten rounds of matches to play the league table had started to take on a more consistent shape without the turmoil of movement that had been evident in the first half of the season. Steaua remained seven points in front of Dinamo, who were in turn one in front of 'U'. Progresul, Ploiesti and Inter Sibiu were in the following pack of clubs chasing UEFA Cup places. While a Bucharest side led the table one also had been propping it up for most of the season – Sportul looked certain for the drop – and the students of Politehnica and the other side from Craiova, Electroputere, looked likely to be battling it out to avoid the other relegation position.

In the quarter-finals of the cup, Dinamo's demise at the hands of second division club Arges Pitesti meant that there was no Bucharest side in the semi-finals. The draw kept the two university sides apart, and 'U' Craiova beat Dinamo's conquerors to earn a place in the final, where they would face Gloria Bistrita, who demolished Cluj in the other semi.

In the league programme a 3-1 win by 'U' in Bucharest over Dinamo allowed them to leap-frog into second spot. Steaua maintained their margin at the top despite a 3-1 defeat at Rapid, for whom the win virtually ensured their position in the first division. A 1-1 draw between Steaua and 'U' let Dinamo to regain their second position, while at the bottom Sportul and Politehnica were undergoing mini revivals that had dragged Dacia into the mire.

With three weeks to play Steaua gained revenge for the early defeat by UT Arad, hammering them by 6-0 to clinch the championship. A 1-0 defeat of Dinamo by bottom club Dacia allowed 'U' to move back into second place and ensured them a UEFA Cup place. 'U' stayed second despite losing their final two fixtures, as Dinamo stuttered but maintained their grip on third spot to take a European position. At the bottom, Sportul completed their escape act and Dacia and Politehnica were relegated. Gloria Bistrita beat Universitatea Craiova by a single goal – scored by Ileas after 25 minutes – to lift the cup and capture a place in the Cup-Winners' Cup, which was bad news for Rapid. Their surge up the table had enabled them to finish in fourth place, but they missed what would have been a UEFA Cup place had 'U' lifted the cup.

For the 1994–95 season the league will be awarding three points for a win. Whether that will stop Steaua from making it a hat-trick of championships remains to be seen, although if Dinamo and Rapid can manage better starts it will make for a very interesting domestic campaign, to follow on from a quite remarkable World Cup.

Russia

Reds at sea

It was a year of turmoil for the Russian national side as a row between players and officials led to several of them boycotting the World Cup Finals. Domestically, the lack of government backing meant that many clubs were struggling to keep afloat and those who secured sponsorship deals were often having their team selection and tactics dictated to them by their sponsors. But amidst all this, Russia qualified for the finals and only just missed out on the second phase, Spartak Moscow retained their domestic title and, despite having to play home games away due to the harsh Muscovite winter, qualified for the UEFA Champions' League.

The Russian delight at having qualified for the World Cup Finals turned sour when, after a 1-0 defeat in their last game in Greece, coach Pavel Sadyrin criticised the performances of his foreign-based stars such as Shalimov, Yuran, Kanchelskis, Salenko and Kiryakov. The players took exception to this and in return criticised the coach's style and the methods he employed and called on the Russian Federation to reinstall their former manager, the popular Ukrainian Anatoli Byshovets. With disputes over financial rewards coming to a boil, the Russian Federation insisted that all players intending to take part in USA94 had to sign contracts or else. A 'call my bluff' situation prevailed and ultimately both sides lost out as some relented and some reneged.

With the threat of World Cup replacement hanging over Russia, the Russian Football authorities finally presented a united front, but defeats by Brazil and Sweden in the opening games showed a distinct lack of team spirit. Some pride was restored against a demoralised Cameroon side as Oleg Salenko set a scoring record with five goals in a 6-1 win. The so-called 'players' revolt' arguably destroyed what could have been a real chance of progress on the international stage, by the slimmest of margins.

Domestically, little could stop Spartak from retaining their title. The surprise early leaders were the previously insignificant provincial club Rotor Volgograd. Ably led by Oleg Veretennikov, they maintained second spot for most of the season while never quite applying pressure on the reigning champions, and qualified for Europe for the first time. Dinamo and CSKA ensured further Moscow representation in Europe, the former by clinching third spot, the latter by compensating for a disappointing league season, most of it spent hauling themselves out of relegation trouble, by reaching the Cup Final. Early goals from Spartak's Ledyahkov and Karpin suggested a rout was on the cards, but just

Russian Football Union

Founded:	1912
Address:	Luzhnetskaja Naberzhnaja 8, Moscow 119270
Phone:	+7 095 201 08 34
Fax:	+7 095 201 13 03
UEFA Affiliation:	1954
FIFA Affiliation:	1946
Season:	March to November
National Stadium:	Lenin Central
Capacity:	102,000
Colours:	White, Blue, White

Final League Table 1993

	P	W	D	L	F	A	Pts
Spartak Moscow	34	21	11	2	81	18	53
Rotor Volgograd	34	17	8	9	56	35	42
Dinamo Moscow	34	16	10	8	65	38	42
Tekstilchik	34	14	11	9	45	34	39
Lokomotiv Moscow	34	14	11	9	45	29	39
Spartak Vladikavkaz	34	16	6	12	49	45	38
Torpedo Moscow	34	15	8	11	35	40	38
Uralmash	34	16	4	14	51	52	36
CSKA Moscow	34	12	6	16	43	45	30
Kamaz Nag. Tch	34	12	6	16	45	53	30
LN Novgorod	34	12	6	16	34	49	30
Dynamo Stavropol	34	11	8	16	39	49	30
Zhemchizhina	34	10	10	14	52	62	30
Krylija Sovekov	34	9	12	13	37	47	30
Luch Vladivostok	34	11	7	16	29	56	29
Okean Nakhodka	34	10	8	16	28	40	28
Rostelmash	34	8	12	14	35	52	28
Asmaral Moscow	34	7	6	21	28	53	20

Promotions and Relegations
Promoted: Dinamo Gazovik Tyumen, Lada Toljatti
Relegated: Luch Vladivostok, Okean Nakhodka, Rostselmash, Asmaral Moscow

Five-Year Records and Cup Winners

League Results

	1st	Pts	2nd	Pts	3rd	Pts
1989	Spartak Moscow	44	Dnepr Dnep'sk	42	Dynamo Kiev	38
1990	Dynamo Kiev	34	CSKA Moscow	31	Dynamo Moscow	31
1991	CSKA Moscow	43	Spartak Moscow	41	Torpedo Moscow	36
1992	Spartak Moscow	24	Vladikavkaz	17	Dynamo Moscow	16
1993	Spartak Moscow	53	Rotor Volograd	42	Dynamo Moscow	42

Cup Final Results

1989	Dynamo Kiev	6-1	Lokomotiv Moscow	
1990	CSKA Moscow	3-2	Torpedo Moscow	
1991	Spartak Moscow	2-0	CSKA Moscow	
1992	Torpedo Moscow	1-1	CSKA Moscow	5-4 on pens
1993	Spartak Moscow	2-2	CSKA Moscow	4-2 on pens

International Results 1993–94

Date	Opponents	Result	Venue	Comp.	Scorers
8/9/93	Hungary	3-1	Budapest	WCQ5	Piatnitski (14), Kiriakov (53), Borodyuk (89)
6/10/93	Saudi Arabia	2-4	Riyadh	Friendly	Mostovoi (9, 72)
17/11/93	Greece	0-1	Athens	WCQ5	
29/1/94	United States	1-1	Seattle	Friendly	Radchenko (52)
2/2/94	Mexico	4-1	Oakland, Ca.	Friendly	Borodyuk (4, 45, 55), Radchenko (37)
23/3/94	Rep. Ireland	0-0	Dublin	Friendly	
20/4/94	Turkey	1-0	Bursa	Friendly	Radchenko (9)
29/5/94	Slovakia	2-1	Moscow	Friendly	Piatnitski (49), Tsimbalar (60)
20/6/94	Brazil	0-2	San Francisco	WCFB	
24/6/94	Sweden	1-3	Detroit	WCFB	Salenko (4 pen)
28/6/94	Cameroon	6-1	San Francisco	WCFB	Salenko (14, 41, 45pen, 72, 75), Radchenko (81)

National Record

(Including record as CIS)	P	W	D	L	F	A
European Championships	74	41	20	13	121	57
World Cup Finals	34	16	6	12	60	41
World Cup Qualifiers	60	40	11	9	115	36

before half-time Vladislav Radimov pulled a goal back, and on the hour CSKA equalised through Dmitri Bytrov. With no more goals, a penalty shoot-out enabled Spartak to clinch the double 4-2. The final UEFA Cup place went to another provincial side, Tekstilchik, who really did come from nowhere, brushing aside the fading challenge of Spartak Vladikavkaz and Torpedo.

League football continued to be ignored by the majority of hard-up Russians, and the apathy that prevailed was typified by the fact that only 15,000 turned up for the Moscow derby between Spartak and Dinamo, first and second places at the time.

The game between Zhemchizhina and newcomers Kamaz on the last day of the season ended in controversy and howls of 'fix'. Zhemchizhina needed a win to be sure of avoiding relegation; they produced one in high-scoring fashion, 5-4. Kamaz's striker Victor Panchenko needed three goals from the game to ensure he won the top scorer award, which he duly did. Kamaz, from the city of Naberezhnyz Chelney, are one of several clubs fortunate to have substantial backing that has allowed them to recruit a number of former Ukrainian players as they strive to break the stranglehold of Spartak Moscow and take domestic titles to Grenada Park.

For the 1994 season the Russian league reduces in size from 18 clubs to 16, with the bottom four having been relegated and only two sides promoted. The majority of Russian clubs will not be sorry that Siberia's two clubs were among the four relegated. Both Okean Nakhodka and Luch Vladivostok are situated in Russia's Far East, which necessitates what are probably the longest and most expensive away trips in the world! Surprisingly, perhaps, Asmaral of Moscow also went down, another sign of the growing shift of the balance of power in Russian's domestic football.

But there was no shift in power in Europe from Moscow as Spartak, after easily disposing of Skonto Riga in the first round, made qualification for the league stage a formality by putting five goals past Lech Poznan, two from Viktor Onopko helping to seal his winter transfer to Werder Bremen. Once in the Champions' League, however, Spartak faced the same problem as their predecessors Dynamo Kiev and CSKA, that of having to play during their close season and often on neutral grounds to combat extremes of weather in the harsh Muscovite winter. Spartak didn't qualify for the semi-final stage but a creditable 2-2 draw with Barcelona and a win over Galatasaray in Istanbul, a feat no other team achieved in 1993–94, gave some indication as to what might be achieved if teams were faced on level terms.

Russia's other European challengers bowed out in the first round. Vladikavkaz were perhaps the unluckiest, losing to a late goal after a goalless draw in Dortmund in the UEFA Cup. Lokomotiv were unlucky to draw holders Juventus and were defeated without ceremony, while Dinamo suffered their heaviest defeat ever in European competition, hammered 6-0 at home by Eintracht Frankfurt. Torpedo faired no better in the Cup-Winners' Cup, going down disappointingly to Maccabi Haifa.

As expected, the likes of Karpin, Onopko and Beschastnykh joined the inevitable exodus to the wealthier, western clubs – Spartak already having lost Radchenko and Popov to Racing Santander of Spain. Fortunately, Nikolai Pisarev and his spectacular goals should still be in Moscow to lead the forthcoming UEFA Champions' League campaign and Spartak's assault on a hat-trick of championships.

Scotland

Rangers six pack

The pre-season in Scotland was dominated by the 'Old Firm' of Rangers and Celtic as they each prepared for the new battles ahead. Rangers were looking to launch their bid for a sixth consecutive title while arch rivals Celtic were clearly intent on stopping them.

Rangers, for years the leaders in the transfer market, again led the way with a record-breaking move. Dundee United striker Duncan Ferguson had been manager Walter Smith's main target for several months, but United's chairman, Jim McLean, was determined to continue the policy of refusing to sell players to other Scottish clubs which he had always implemented as manager. Ferguson was linked with a move South to Leeds United, but the intervention of Rangers chairman David Murray proved decisive. He backed Smith's £4m bid, which United simply had to accept. After all, every player has his price. Ferguson had become the most expensive player in British football at the ripe old age of 21.

It was the champions' only major move of the close season, but it served as a warning to the rest that Rangers intended to maintain their position as Scotland's finest. Several squad players were released too, most notably winger Dale Gordon, sold to West Ham, and striker Gary McSwegan, to Notts County.

Celtic, unable to spend such vast amounts on players, sought another route to success. They brought in former Hearts manager Joe Jordan as number two to Liam Brady, hoping that the old saying 'Two heads are better than one' would inspire the Bhoys, who last won a trophy in 1989. Despite being £4m in debt, the club managed to find the cash to buy Hibernian midfielder Pat McGinlay and, at less expense, Northern Irish forward Paul Byrne from Bangor. But reserve striker Joe Miller had to be sold, to Aberdeen, to fund the deals.

Dundee United were under new management after McLean's decision to quit as manager and move upstairs to a permanent place in the boardroom. Their surprise choice as his replacement was Serbian import Ivan Golac, a former Yugoslav international full-back who enjoyed a successful spell with Southampton in the early 1980s. Across the street, Dundee signed Polish centre-back Dariusz Adamczuk from Germany's Eintracht Frankfurt.

Hibernian also caused a stir by recruiting 35-year-old former international goalkeeper Jim Leighton from Dundee, despite having two top keepers already. Midfielder Kevin McAllister was signed for £245,000 from Falkirk to replace McGinlay, and manager Alex Miller also strengthened his backroom staff by appointing Hearts midfielder Eamonn Bannon as coach. Edinburgh rivals Hearts signed controversial striker Justin Fashanu from Airdrie, and former Tynecastle favourite John Colquhoun returned to the fold from his English exile with Sunderland. But the best news of all for Hearts came on the day of the draw for the three European competitions. Two Polish

Old Firm action as Richard Gough of Rangers (right) outjumps Celtic's Charlie Nicholas (No. 10).

The Scottish Football Association	
Founded:	1873
Address:	6 Park Gardens, Glasgow, G3 7YF
Phone:	+44 41 332 6372
Fax:	+44 41 332 7559
UEFA Affiliation:	1954
FIFA Affiliation:	1910-20, 1924-28, 1946
National Stadium:	Hampden Park, Glasgow
Capacity:	38,335
Season:	August to May
Colours:	Blue, White, Red
Change:	White, Blue, Red

Jerron Nixon of Dundee United tussles with Aberdeen's Duncan Shearer.

Final League Table 1993–94

Premier Division

	P	W	D	L	F	A	Pts
Rangers	44	22	14	8	74	41	58
Aberdeen	44	17	21	6	58	36	55
Motherwell	44	20	14	10	58	43	54
Celtic	44	15	20	9	51	38	50
Hibernian	44	16	15	13	53	48	47
Dundee United	44	11	20	13	47	48	42
Heart of Midlothian	44	11	20	13	37	43	42
Kilmarnock	44	12	16	16	36	45	40
Partick Thistle	44	12	16	16	46	57	40
St Johnstone	44	10	20	14	35	47	40
Raith Rovers	44	6	19	19	46	80	31
Dundee	44	8	13	23	42	57	29

Top Scorers

- 22 Mark HATELEY (Rangers)
- 17 Duncan SHEARER (Aberdeen)
- 16 Keith WRIGHT (Hibernian)
  Craig BREWSTER (Dundee United)
- 15 Albert CRAIG (Partick Thistle)
  Roddy GRANT (Partick Thistle)
- 12 Gordon DURIE (Rangers)
- 11 Tommy COYNE (Motherwell)
- 10 John McGINLAY (Celtic)

Promotions and Relegations

Promoted: Falkirk
Relegated: St Johnstone, Raith Rovers, Dundee.
Premier League reduced to 10 clubs for 1994–95 season.

Five-Year Records League 1-2-3 and Cup Winners

League Results

	1st	Pts	2nd	Pts	3rd	Pts
1990	Rangers	51	Aberdeen	44	Heart of Midlothian	44
1991	Rangers	55	Aberdeen	53	Celtic	41
1992	Rangers	72	Heart of Midlothian	63	Celtic	62
1993	Rangers	73	Aberdeen	64	Celtic	60
1994	Rangers	58	Aberdeen	55	Motherwell	54

Cup Final Results

1990	Aberdeen	0-0	Celtic	9-8 on pens
1991	Motherwell	4-3	Dundee United	
1992	Rangers	2-1	Airdrieonians	
1993	Rangers	2-1	Aberdeen	
1994	Dundee United	1-0	Rangers	

representatives were barred because of a match-fixing scandal, and Hearts were one of the beneficiaries with a surprise place in the UEFA Cup and a plum draw against Atletico Madrid in the first round.

Unlike recent seasons, which ended with many 'dead' matches because the title and relegation positions already had been decided, the 1993–94 season offered each club something to aim at because of the restructuring for the start of the 1994–95 season. The 38 senior clubs, plus two from the Highland league, will be reorganised into four divisions of 10. The complicated formula for producing the end result of four even divisions meant that all teams had something to play for.

August saw a testimonial match against Newcastle United for Rangers striker Ally McCoist. The match raised £500,000 for the injured striker, out with a broken leg, although Kevin Keegan's side were winners on the day, 2-1. The league began on 8 August in familiar fashion. Rangers won 2-1 at home to Hearts, with goals by young striker David Hagen and old warrior Mark Hateley. The fact that the Gers had £20m worth of talent on the sidelines through injury seemed to make little difference.

Celtic, meanwhile, opened with a 2-2 draw at Motherwell while Dundee United and Aberdeen drew 1-1 at Tannadice.

The third weekend brought the first Old Firm derby of the season, a dull 0-0 draw at Parkhead, while Motherwell, fresh from

International Results 1993–94

Date	Opponents	Result	Venue	Comp.	Scorers
8/9/93	Switzerland	1-1	Aberdeen	WCQ1	Collins (50)
13/10/93	Italy	1-3	Rome	WCQ1	Gallacher (18)
17/11/93	Malta	2-0	Valletta	WCQ1	McKinlay (15), Hendry (74)
23/3/94	Holland	0-1	Glasgow	Friendly	
20/4/94	Austria	2-1	Vienna	Friendly	McGinlay (35), McKinlay (60)
27/5/94	Holland	1-3	Utrecht	Friendly	D. Shearer (81)

National Record	P	W	D	L	F	A
European Championship	48	19	14	15	66	56
World Cup Finals	23	5	6	12	26	38
World Cup Qualifiers	69	37	13	19	125	85

a 2-1 win at Dundee the week before, won 1-0 at Kilmarnock to establish themselves as the early pace-setters. They confirmed their position the following week with a 4-1 win over Raith while Rangers, amazingly, were beaten 2-1 at home by Kilmarnock. Tommy McLean's Motherwell could even afford to sell Dutch defender Luc Nijholt to newly promoted Swindon Town.

The fifth week brought a 1-0 win for Aberdeen at Celtic and a 2-1 win for Hearts at home to Partick. Rangers could only draw 1-1 at Dundee to leave Motherwell, Aberdeen and Hearts level at the top after five matches.

The national side battled to a 1-1 draw at home to Switzerland in their World Cup group. But, with qualification virtually beyond them, coach Andy Roxburgh resigned, with his assistant Craig Brown taking over as caretaker. Roxburgh had been in charge of the national side for seven years and his regard in the game was clear when he was later appointed as UEFA Technical Director. No small accolade.

Motherwell asserted their superiority the following weekend with a 2-0 home win over Hearts. Aberdeen went down 2-1 at Hibernian and Celtic fans at last had something to cheer as old favourite Charlie Nicholas scored twice in a 4-1 win at Raith. Rangers were held to a 1-1 draw by Partick at Ibrox and, when the team lost 2-0 at Aberdeen the following week, the aura of invincibility which had surrounded the club for half a decade suddenly seemed to have disappeared.

Rangers did, however, summon up enough strength to beat Celtic 1-0 in the League Cup semi-final, Hateley again proving to be the club's saviour. Hibernian won the other semi-final with a 10th-minute Darren Jackson goal against Dundee United. September ended with a rehearsal of the League Cup final at Ibrox, which Rangers won 2-1, while Motherwell forced a 0-0 draw at Dundee United. Motherwell then strengthened their hand by signing highly-regarded Paul Lambert, from St Mirren, to add to a battle-hardened squad containing former Rangers and Scotland winger Davie Cooper, Under-21 star Phil O'Donnell and tough striker Paul McGrillen.

In Europe, though, the first round proved a disaster for the Scottish clubs. Rangers crashed out of the Champions' Cup to a last-second goal by Levski Sofia, while Hearts and Dundee United were knocked out of the UEFA Cup, leaving Celtic and Aberdeen to fly the flag following wins over Young Boys of Berne and Valur.

Hibernian's excellent form took them to the top in October, with wins over Dundee United, Raith and, in a top-of-the-table clash, Motherwell. But the big news of the month came from Parkhead. A 2-1 defeat at St Johnstone forced manager Liam Brady to 'resign'. His assistant, Joe Jordan, took over as caretaker manager, but he lasted just a day, leaving the club in a desperate position. The national side carried on regardless in the World Cup qualifiers, going down to a 3-1 defeat in Italy.

The month ended with yet another trophy at Ibrox. Star striker Ally McCoist returned from a five-month absence to score the winner in the 2-1 League Cup final win over brave Hibernian. Suddenly, the Ibrox machine seemed to be running smoothly once more. But, as if to prove that football still is a funny old game, Parkhead emerged to spoil the party on the last day of October.

Tommy Burns, a legend at Celtic and currently working minor miracles with promoted Kilmarnock, was widely expected to get the vacant Parkhead job but the unpredictable board opted instead for Stoke City boss Lou Macari, another former Celtic great. He got off to a brilliant start with a 2-1 win over Rangers at Ibrox, thanks to a last-minute goal by Brian O'Neil, but could do little to prevent Celtic's elimination from the UEFA Cup, knocked out 2-1 on aggregate by Bobby Robson's Sporting Lisbon. Aberdeen also went out in the second round of the Cup-Winners' Cup, losing both legs to Torino – that after leading 2-0 in Turin in the first leg – to complete a miserable, short season in Europe for Scotland.

But Rangers soon returned to winning ways to increase the pressure on Motherwell at the top, while Aberdeen moved above Hibs into second place. The pressure at the bottom proved even stronger and struggling St Johnstone parted company with boss John McClelland. He was replaced by former Dundee United skipper Paul Sturrock, and he got off to a good start with a crucial 1-0 win at bottom club Dundee, who could not turn down an £800,000 offer from Italy's Udinese for Adamczuk.

Macari began his reconstruction work at Celtic by swapping striker Andy Payton to Barnsley for Wayne Biggins, while midfielder Stuart Slater returned south in a £750,000 deal, to Ipswich, after a disappointing time in Scotland. Golac also

Scottish FA Cup

First Round		
Albion Rovers v Huntly	0-0, 3-5	
Cowdenbeath v Queen's Park	1-1, 3-2	
East Fife v Rothes	5-0	
Forfar Athletic v Queen of the South	8-3	
Ross County v St Cuthbert Wanderers	11-0	
Stranraer v Whitehill Welfare	3-3, 4-0	
Second Round		
Alloa v Gala Fairydean	4-0	
Berwick Rangers v East Fife	1-0	
Cowdenbeath v Stenhousemuir	1-0	
East Stirlingshire v Cove Rangers	4-1	
Forfar Athletic v Ross County	0-4	
Huntly v Stranraer	0-2	
Meadowbank Thistle v Montrose	1-2	
Selkirk v Arbroath	3-0	
Third Round		
Airdrieonians v Dunfermline Athletic	1-1, 3-1	
Alloa v Ross County	2-0	
Arbroath v Dundee United	2-3	
Clydebank v Dundee	1-1, 1-2	
East Stirlingshire v Aberdeen	1-3	
Greenock Morton v Cowdenbeath	2-2, 2-1	
Hibernian v Clyde	2-1	
Kilmarnock v Ayr	2-1	
Motherwell v Celtic	1-0	
Partick Thistle v Heart of Midlothian	0-1	
Raith Rovers v Brechin City	2-0	
Rangers v Dumbarton	4-1	
St Johnstone v Hamilton Academical	2-0	
St Mirren v Montrose	2-0	
Stirling Albion v Berwick Rangers	1-0	
Stranraer v Falkirk	2-1	
Fourth Round		
Aberdeen v Raith	1-0	
Airdrieonians v Stranraer	1-0	
Dundee v St Mirren	3-1	
Dundee United v Motherwell	2-2, 1-0	
Greenock Morton v Kilmarnock	0-1	
Hibernian v Heart of Midlothian	1-2	
Rangers v Alloa	6-0	
St Johnstone v Stirling Albion	3-3, 2-0	
Quarter-Finals		
Airdrieonians v Dundee United	0-0, 0-2	
Kilmarnock v Dundee	1-0	
Rangers v Heart of Midlothian	2-0	
St Johnstone v Aberdeen	1-1, 0-2	
Semi-Finals		
Aberdeen v Dundee United	1-1, 0-1	
Rangers v Kilmarnock	0-0, 2-1	
Final		
Dundee United v Rangers	1-0	

entered the market, paying Partizan Belgrade £500,000 for highly rated centre-back Gordan Petric to help shore up a suspect defence which relinquished two-goal leads two weeks running at the end of November. The national side completed their disappointing World Cup qualifying programme with a 2-0 win in Malta to mark the start of the Craig Brown era.

Celtic's Macari-inspired revival continued in December with wins over Motherwell, St Johnstone and Hibernian taking them up to fourth. Aberdeen took over the leadership when they thrashed declining Hibernian 4-0, but a 2-0 defeat at Rangers pegged them back. Motherwell experienced a see-saw month with wins over Partick, Hearts and Dundee countered by defeats to Celtic, Rangers and Hibernian. Good news for the Fir Park team, though, in the form of striker Tommy Coyne. He had been out of football since his wife's sad death forced him to leave Tranmere and return to his native Glasgow. Several clubs tried to sign him, but a deal was eventually agreed with Motherwell and he repaid them with five goals in his first four games back.

But the result of the month – possibly even the season – was Dundee United's epic 3-0 win at Rangers. The Tangerines scored their goals in the first 20 minutes to remind the whole league that Rangers are only human and can be beaten. The game was a disaster for Rangers, who also had midfielder Iain Ferguson sent off for spitting at the commanding Petric. The year ended with Aberdeen top of the pile, followed by an improving Rangers, a steady Motherwell and a resurgent Celtic.

The New Year began with another Old Firm derby, at Parkhead. But Celtic's recent revival was shot to pieces by rampant Rangers, who won 4-2 with goals by Hateley and the Ukrainians Mikhailichenko (two) and Kuznetsov. The defeat led to the most public show yet of discontent among Celtic's fans, who fought among themselves and hurled missiles into the directors' box. Macari, acting as mediator, set up a meeting between fans and directors to clear the air, but when only one director bothered to turn up, Macari was left embarrassed, the fans bemused.

With Aberdeen's game at Dundee postponed because of bad weather, Rangers pulled level with the Dons at the top of the table … an ominous sign. In the only other game played on New Year's Day, Motherwell battled for a 0-0 draw at Kilmarnock.

Celtic's mauling by Rangers seemed to drain confidence, and Macari's side embarked on a barren run. Defeats at Partick and Motherwell followed, and the home game against Aberdeen was abandoned after an hour with the score at 0-0. Rangers, however, continued to find results when they mattered. Kilmarnock were brushed aside, 3-0 at Ibrox, and a week later a goal by Durie a minute from time earned the Gers a 1-1 draw at Dundee. Aberdeen, too, were battling through the worst of the winter weather, drawing with St Johnstone, beating Dundee away and then gaining a point at Parkhead, when the re-arranged game with Celtic finished 2-2.

Then came the top-of-the-table clash between Aberdeen and

Dundee United celebrating with the cup after beating Rangers.

Rangers at Pittodrie. Not surprisingly, this produced a blank scoreline, which probably suited Rangers more than Aberdeen, now back in the familiar position of chasing the Glasgow giants at the top of the table.

January ended with the third round of the Scottish Cup. To complete a miserable month for Celtic, they were beaten 1-0 at Motherwell thanks to a goal by Coyne, a former Celtic player. The disastrous run of seven games without victory prompted Macari to delve into the transfer market once more. But, with limited funds available, he was able only to make modest purchases. Goalkeeper Carl Muggleton was bought from Macari's previous club, Stoke, reserve defender Lee Martin arrived from Manchester United, and Willie Falconer moved back north of the border, from Sheffield United.

The barren run ended with a 2-0 win at Hearts in mid-February. But it was an old hero who scored both goals — Charlie Nicholas. Two other players returned to Scotland in transfer deals: Ray McKinnon moved from Nottingham Forest to Aberdeen, and Kilmarnock ended Alan McInally's German exile by signing him on a free transfer from Bayern Munich.

Rangers, meanwhile, steamrollered Dumbarton 4-1 in the Cup, and there were wins also for Dundee United, Hibs, Kilmarnock, Hearts, Raith, St Johnstone, Dundee and Aberdeen. The only Premier Division casualties apart from Celtic were Partick, who lost 1-0 at home to Hearts. League action resumed with a 4-0 win for Aberdeen over Raith, a 2-1 victory for Motherwell at Dundee United, and an important 2-0 win for Rangers against Hibs at Ibrox. The match was also significant because it marked the return of Andy Goram, the Rangers goalkeeper who had been dogged by injury. Thus, after 30 games, Rangers were top with 40 points, two ahead of Aberdeen and Motherwell, with Hibs three points further adrift in fourth place. At the bottom, things were looking grim for Dundee, five points adrift of Raith and clearly headed for relegation. In an attempt to reverse the inevitable, Dundee made an unusual move in the transfer market, signing French goalkeeper Michel Pageau from Valenciennes for a modest fee.

In the fourth round of the Scottish Cup, Rangers destroyed Alloa 6-0, with McCoist scoring a hat-trick. Hearts won the all-Edinburgh clash, beating Hibs 2-1 at Easter Road, Aberdeen narrowly squeezed past Raith, and Dundee United and Motherwell fought out a 2-2 draw. February ended with another clutch of postponements, with only Rangers and Dundee United able to play, both winning away.

March started with a replay victory for Dundee United over Motherwell in the Cup, and a 1-0 win for Celtic in the league, against Kilmarnock. The following weekend's league programme must have been enjoyed by all at Ibrox as they came from behind to beat Motherwell 2-1, while Aberdeen were losing 1-0 at home to struggling Hearts. Ominously, it was beginning to look like Rangers all the way again. That view was reinforced the following week when Motherwell and Aberdeen — the only realistic challengers left — shared a 1-1 draw, followed by a 0-0 draw for Motherwell at home to Hibernian, who had improved steadily since the turn of the year. With none of their rivals able to string together a run of victories, it became only a matter of time for Rangers, at least in the league.

The Gers were also making good progress in the Scottish Cup.

Scottish Championship Results 1993-94

	Aberdeen	Celtic	Dundee	Dundee United	Hearts	Hibernian	Kilmarnock	Motherwell	Partick Thistle	Raith Rovers	Rangers	St Johnstone
Aberdeen	—	1-1	1-0	2-0	0-0	4-0	1-0	1-1	2-1	4-1	2-0	0-0
	—	1-1	1-1	1-0	0-1	2-3	3-1	0-0	2-0	4-0	0-0	1-1
Celtic	0-1	—	2-1	1-1	0-0	1-1	0-0	2-0	3-0	2-0	0-0	1-0
	2-2	—	1-1	0-0	2-2	1-0	1-0	0-1	1-1	2-1	2-4	1-1
Dundee	1-1	1-1	—	1-2	2-0	3-2	1-0	1-2	2-2	0-1	1-1	0-1
	0-1	0-2	—	1-1	0-2	4-0	3-0	1-3	1-0	2-2	1-1	0-1
Dundee United	1-1	1-3	1-0*	—	0-0	2-2	0-0	0-0	2-2	2-2	1-3	2-0
	0-1	1-3	1-1	—	3-0	3-0	1-3	1-2	2-2	2-3	0-0	0-0
Hearts	1-1	1-0	1-2	1-1	—	1-0	0-1	2-3	2-1	1-0	2-2	1-1
	1-1	0-2	0-2	2-0	—	1-1	1-1	0-0	1-0	0-1	1-2	2-2
Hibernian	2-1	1-1	2-0	2-0	0-2	—	2-1	3-2	0-0	3-2	0-1	0-0
	3-1	0-0	2-0	0-1	0-0	—	0-0	0-2	5-1	3-0	1-0	0-0
Kilmarnock	1-1	2-2	1-0	1-1	0-0	1-1	—	0-1	3-1	1-0	0-2	0-0
	2-3	2-0	1-0	1-1	0-1	0-3	—	0-0	1-2	0-0	1-0	0-0
Motherwell	0-0	2-2	1-0	2-0	2-0	0-2	2-2	—	1-0	4-0	0-2	1-0
	1-1	2-1	3-1	1-2	1-1	0-0	1-0	—	2-2	3-1	2-1	0-1
Partick Thistle	3-2	0-1	3-2	1-2	0-0	0-0	0-1	1-0	—	1-1	1-1	4-1
	1-1	1-0	1-0	1-0	0-1	1-0	1-0	0-0	—	2-2	1-2	0-0
Raith Rovers	1-1	1-4	2-1	1-1	1-0	2-2	2-0	2-0	3-2	—	1-1	1-1
	0-2	0-0	1-1	0-2	2-2	1-1	3-2	3-3	0-1	—	1-2	1-1
Rangers	2-0	1-2	3-1	0-3	2-1	2-1	1-2	1-2	1-1	2-2	—	2-0
	1-1	1-1	0-0	2-1	2-2	2-0	3-0	2-1	5-1	4-0	—	4-0
St Johnstone	1-1	2-1	2-1	1-1	2-0	1-3	0-1	3-0	1-3	1-1	1-2	—
	0-1	0-1	1-1	1-1	0-0	2-2	0-1	2-1	1-0	2-0	0-4	—

Hearts were the visitors to Ibrox for the quarter-final, but could not contain Rangers in the second half, and lost 2-0. Kilmarnock also went through, beating Dundee 1-0, but the two other ties ended in draws. The replays went with form, Aberdeen beating St Johnstone 2-0, Dundee United beating Airdrie 2-0.

The top three all won their next league encounters, while Celtic had to be content with a 0-0 draw at Hibs. There was better news for Celtic, though, when Scots-Canadian businessman Fergus McCann finally obtained a controlling interest in the club after months of problems in the boardroom. McCann pledged an injection of funds, vital if Celtic are ever to gain ground on arch-rivals Rangers.

All thoughts then turned to the national side, and a prestige home friendly against Holland. The game was all the more significant because it marked the re-opening of the refurbished, all-seat Hampden Park. A capacity crowd of 35,000 turned out on a miserable, wet Glasgow night, and were disappointed by a limp Scotland side, beaten 1-0 by an under-strength Dutch team clearly playing well within themselves.

The top three all won, again, in the league, but when Aberdeen lost 3-2 at home to Hibs the following week, it was left to Motherwell to challenge Rangers. Tommy McLean's modest side had more than held their own during the season, and now emerged as the main, if unexpected, challengers to the Ibrox machine. A 0-0 draw at Hearts kept them in contention, but with Rangers winning at Partick, the gap was still widening.

Aberdeen gave the whole league hope the following weekend, with a 1-1 draw at Ibrox. But Motherwell could not capitalise, held to a 2-2 draw at home by Partick in the other Glasgow derby. In midweek, all four matches played ended in draws, with Rangers, Aberdeen, Celtic and Hearts each picking up a point. Then came the Scottish Cup semi-finals, which both produced draws. In the replays, a week later, Dundee United beat Aberdeen 1-0 and Rangers won 2-1 against Kilmarnock, thanks to two goals from Hateley, the leading scorer in the country.

But, the following weekend, Rangers were in the headlines for all the wrong reasons. Duncan Ferguson's long-awaited first goal duly arrived in a 4-0 win over Raith, but the game was overshadowed by a butting incident involving Ferguson and Raith's John McStay. Ferguson was left facing a court action, and was banned for a record 12 games by the SFA, the latest in a long line of problems which have bedevilled this tempestuous striker. With Aberdeen and Motherwell cancelling each other out in a 0-0 draw, Rangers were well on course to retain the title. April ended with a 2-1 win for Rangers against Dundee United, leaving the Gers unbeaten between January and May, a run which helped shake off the chasing pack and establish their position at the top of Scottish football once more.

Rangers duly went on to win the title for the sixth year running, but in unusual fashion. They failed to win any of their last five league games, but were still assured of the title, despite being beaten by Motherwell. Indeed, Motherwell were pipped for the runners-up spot by Aberdeen, though both clubs qualified for the UEFA Cup. At the bottom, Dundee and Raith were relegated along with St Johnstone. Falkirk won the First Division championship, to claim the only promotion place available because of the league restructuring.

The final piece of the season was the Scottish Cup Final, between Rangers and Dundee United. In one of the biggest Cup Final shocks ever, the Tangerines won 1-0 with a goal from Craig Brewster just after half-time. United had denied Rangers yet another treble, and had booked their place in Europe in the process, a marvellous first season for Golac and Co.

But that was not the end of the drama. As soon as the season ended, Tommy McLean quit as Motherwell boss after 10 years in charge at Fir Park, citing contract problems as the root of his decision. He was not out of work long. Chris Robinson gained control of Hearts in a £2m takeover, and promptly sacked boss Sandy Clark, bringing in McLean as the new manager. Then Celtic sacked Macari, claiming that he was not giving his full attention to the club or the job. Macari denied this, but to no avail. Celtic now face next season under new management, playing all home games at Hampden Park while Parkhead undergoes a £25m refurbishment to bring it in line with the Taylor Report.

Finally, and perhaps most importantly of all, the SFA also announced that, as from the 1994–95 season, Scottish clubs would be playing for three points per win in their new four-division Scottish league.

Slovakia

Bratislava rule the roost

Slovan Bratislava won the first official Slovak championship by a margin of ten points from their city rivals Inter and made it a first-time double by beating Tatran Pesov in the cup final. It was Slovan's second title triumph in three years, having won the last full Czechoslovakian championship in 1991–92 and finished third in the 1992–93 RSC championship. They did it without the services of top scorer Peter Dubovsky, who was sold at the start of the season to Real Madrid for £2.5m.

At the end of the first 'qualifying' round Slovan had established a seven-point lead over Inter with an exceptionally mean defence ensuring that leads, once established, were never surrendered. Indeed Slovan dropped just seven points in the first phase of 22 games. At that point the 12-team league was divided into two pools of six. The top six sides formed the championship group and played each other again on a round robin basis to determine final placements and European qualification. The bottom six did the same but here the interest was in avoiding relegation.

After the first three rounds of games in the championship phase, Slovan hadn't managed a single win, drawing their matches with Dac, Tatran and SK Zilina. Inter used this to their advantage to claw back two points with a couple of wins and a draw. The chasing pack of SK Zilina, Dac, Tatran and FC Kosice had little to play for other than pride even though they all still stood a mathematical chance of making the UEFA Cup by finishing second. In all reality, though, only SK Zilina and Dac were still in with a shout. A 3-0 win over FC Kosice got Slovan back on winning ways and established confidence for the next match at Inter, who had won by the only goal of the game at SK Zilina.

A 3-2 win for Slovan meant that another two points from their final five games would clinch the championship. A 4-3 win over Dac in front of over 10,000 provided that requirement with still four games to play. Dac remained in contention for the runner-up spot despite the Slovan defeat because Tatran had taken the points in a 2-0 win over Inter. However Inter's defeat of FC Kosice coupled with Dac's dropped point at SK Zilina made the matter academic, as Inter were assured of second place and a UEFA Cup position. Having won what were the two most important games of the championship phase, Slovan failed to win another, which included a 1-1 draw with Inter in the last match of the season.

One game they did manage to win, though, was the Slovakian Cup Final, beating Tatran Pesov 2-1. They had to come from behind to do so, with Timko equalising Matta's early opening goal. The winner came seven minutes into the second half and was scored by Fakkor.

Slovan manager Dusan Galis was never far from the headlines. Having decided not to talk to the press he broke his silence and his feud with national team boss Jozsef Venglos continued to simmer. The availability of Slovan players and the co-operation of Galis remain a talking point. Venglos wanted players for Slovakia's first international matches in United Arab Emirates as part of the Sharjah Tournament, while Slovan wanted

Slovak Football Association

Founded:	1990
Address:	Junacka 6, 83280 Bratislava
Phone:	+42 7 279 0151
Fax:	+43 7 279 0554
UEFA Affiliation:	1993
FIFA Affiliation:	1993
Season:	August to June
National Stadium:	Tehelne-Pole, Bratislava
Capacity:	32,000
Colours:	Blue, Blue, Blue

Final League Table 1993–94

First Round

	P	W	D	L	F	A	Pts
Slovan Bratislava	22	17	3	2	45	15	37
Inter Bratislava	22	14	2	6	49	28	30
Dac Dunajska Sreda	22	11	4	7	38	26	26
SK Zilina	22	9	6	7	32	22	24
FC Kosice	22	7	8	7	25	31	22
Tatran Pesov	22	6	9	7	24	28	21
Bystrica	22	8	5	9	23	29	21
Spartak Trnava	22	5	8	9	19	26	18
Chemlon Humenne	22	5	7	10	22	34	17
Lokomotive Kosice	22	4	9	9	21	40	17
FC Nitra	22	7	2	13	24	30	16
Prievidza	22	5	5	12	21	34	15

Final Round

	P	W	D	L	F	A	Pts
Slovan Bratislava	32	20	10	2	63	28	50
Inter Bratislava	32	18	4	10	65	45	40
Dac Dunajska Sreda	32	13	10	9	62	47	36
Tatran Pesov	32	10	14	8	47	43	34
SK Zilina	32	11	11	10	50	42	33
FC Kosice	32	8	11	13	35	54	27

Promotions and Relegations
Promoted: BSC Bardejov
Relegated: FC Nitra

Cup Final Results
1993 Kosice 0-0 Dunajska Sreda 5-4 on pens
1994 Slovan Bratislava 2-1 Tatran Pesov

International Results 1993–94

Date	Opponents	Result	Venue	Comp.	Scorers
2/2/94	UAE	1-0	Sharjah, UAE	Sharjah	Weiss (47)
4/2/94	Egypt	0-1	Sharjah, UAE	Sharjah	
6/2/94	Morocco	1-2	Sharjah, UAE	Sharjah	Faktor (27)
30/3/94	Malta	2-1	Friendly	Valletta	Timko (13), Hyravy (69)
20/4/94	Croatia	4-1	Friendly	Bratislava	Dubovsky (24 pen, 61), Kinder (68), Moravcik (83)
29/5/94	Russia	1-2	Friendly	Moscow	Tittel (35)

National Record
European Championship — Never participated
World Cup Finals — Never participated
World Cup Qualifiers — Never participated

Slovak Championship First Round Results

	Bystrica	Chemlon Humenne	Dac Dunajska Sreda	FC Kosice	FC Nitra	Inter Bratislava	Lokomotive Kosice	Prievidza	SK Zilina	Slovan Bratislava	Spartak Trnava	Tatran Pesov
Bystrica	—	1-0	4-1	0-1	1-0	1-3	0-0	4-0	0-2	1-2	0-0	1-0
Chemlon Humenne	1-1	—	2-0	1-0	4-2	3-1	1-1	1-0	3-3	0-2	0-0	0-0
Dac Dunajska Sreda	4-0	1-0	—	0-0	1-0	2-2	4-0	4-1	2-0	4-3	1-0	2-0
FC Kosice	0-0	4-2	2-1	—	2-1	2-0	0-1	3-1	0-0	1-1	1-1	2-2
FC Nitra	0-2	0-0	1-3	2-0	—	2-4	1-0	0-1	1-0	0-1	2-1	4-1
Inter Bratislava	4-0	3-2	2-1	5-0	2-1	—	7-1	2-1	1-2	1-0	0-2	4-0
Lokomotive Kosice	1-1	3-0	2-1	2-2	1-4	1-2	—	1-1	1-0	0-1	1-1	1-1
Prievidza	1-2	0-0	3-1	1-1	1-0	1-3	3-1	—	0-0	0-1	3-0	2-3
SK Zilina	3-0	6-1	0-3	1-3	0-2	3-0	3-0	1-0	—	2-2	3-0	0-0
Slovan Bratislava	3-0	1-0	2-0	6-1	0-0	1-0	5-1	4-1	2-1	—	3-1	2-0
Spartak Trnava	0-4	2-0	0-0	2-0	2-0	2-3	1-1	0-0	1-2	0-1	—	2-0
Tatran Pesov	3-0	3-1	2-2	1-0	3-1	0-0	1-1	2-0	0-0	1-2	1-1	—

Slovak Championship Round

	Dac Dunajska Sreda	FC Kosice	Inter Bratislava	SK Zilina	Slovan Bratislava	Tatran Pesov
Dac Dunajska Sreda	—	4-1	4-1	2-2	1-1	1-1
FC Kosice	2-2	—	1-1	3-0	1-1	1-3
Inter Bratislava	3-1	3-1	—	2-4	2-3	2-0
SK Zilina	2-2	4-0	0-1	—	1-1	2-2
Slovan Bratislava	4-2	3-0	1-1	1-1	—	2-2
Tatran Pesov	4-4	2-0	2-0	5-1	1-1	—

them for a South American winter tour which was eventually cancelled.

A goal by Weiss in the first game against the UAE ensured a win in Slovakia's debut in world football but it was a far from convincing performance. The three points gained were the only ones of the tournament, and defeats against Egypt and Morocco didn't provide much for Venglos to cheer about. A partial excuse was that he was without skipper Moravcik (Saint Etienne) and Slovak Footballer of the Year Dubovsky (Real Madrid) due to club commitments.

The first official international match on home soil took place in April when Croatia were the visitors. A crowd of 6,511 in Bratislava saw two goals from Dubovsky and others from Kinder and Moravcik beat the visitors by 4-1.

Action by Slovak clubs in Europe was limited to the first rounds as Slovan, Dac and FC Kosice all made early exits. FC Kosice came through their Cup-Winners' Cup preliminary round tie against Zhalgiris Vilnius with relative ease, winning 3-0 on aggregate, but never recovered from conceding an early goal in the home leg which cost them dear against Turkish side Besiktas. In the UEFA Cup, a 2-1 win for Aston Villa in the second leg was good enough to dispose of Slovan, Tittel's goal coming just too late too leave them any chance of drawing level. Dac were beaten 2-0 in each leg by eventual finalists SV Casino Salzburg.

Slovenia

Olimpija home alone

The continual fragmentation of Europe has ensured that some new states have clubs who are likely to dominate the national scene for years to come. One such side is Olimpija Ljubljana, who won their third successive Slovenian championship, doing it with relative ease once again. Maribor Branik, who had been runners-up the previous two seasons, had to be content with third place, being ousted from the second place by Mura Murska Sobota.

Olimpija had set their stall out once again and headed the table by the arrival of the long winter break, without being able to create a comfortable gap between themselves and Mura, who trailed just two points behind. With two-thirds of matches played Olimpija had edged another point away as Mura couldn't get through a resolute Cosmos defence in one of the many capital derby games. While they were playing out a goalless draw, Olimpija were scoring five at Optimizem in the other big match in Ljubljana. Draws were starting to cost Mura dear, and with Olimpija winning game after game the small gap started to develop more.

Having won eight games on the trot after the winter recess, Olimpija's march was halted by a 1-1 draw with Cosmos in the ZDS stadium, but with Mura also playing out a 1-1 draw with third-placed Maribor Branik the chasing sides failed to make any dent on the leaders. Olimpija's slight stutter steeled them for the visit of Slovan Mavrica, who felt the full force of their wrath in a humiliating 11-0 thrashing that put them and Studio DNM into the second division.

Olimpija's lead became almost unassailable with four weeks to play when Mura, needing to beat the leaders, lost 2-1, which meant that the defeat of Publikum the following week ensured the championship was retained, leaving Mura and Maribor to fight it out for the runners-up spot and a place in the UEFA Cup. The knock-out punch was landed by Mura, despite a 5-1 defeat in their final game of the season. They held on mainly because Maribor also lost vital points in the last two games. There was

Final League Table 1993–94

	P	W	D	L	F	A	Pts
Olimpija Ljubljana	30	23	5	2	95	20	51
Mura Murska Sobota	30	19	7	4	59	23	45
Maribor Branik	30	16	10	4	55	24	42
Publikum Celje	30	14	10	6	50	34	38
Gorica	30	12	11	7	40	38	35
Potrosnik	30	13	6	11	57	40	32
Koper	30	11	10	9	43	38	32
Zivila Naklo	30	11	7	12	32	40	29
Rudar	30	10	7	13	37	49	27
Isola	30	9	8	13	45	51	26
Cosmos	30	8	9	13	29	44	25
Primorje	30	8	8	14	46	55	24
Optimizem	30	9	5	16	31	59	23
Istragas	30	7	7	16	25	50	21
Slovan Mavrica	30	5	8	17	35	70	18
Studio DNM	30	2	8	20	14	58	12

Nogometna Zveza Slovenije

Address:	Dunajska 47-V, PP90 61109 Ljubljana
Phone:	+38 61 31 18 88
Fax:	+38 61 30 23 37
Founded:	1920
UEFA Affiliation:	1993
FIFA Affiliation:	1992
Season:	August to May
National Staduim:	Bezigrad, Llubljana
Capacity:	22,000
Colours:	Black/Blue, Blue, Red

consolation for Maribor, though, when they defeated Mura in the Cup Final, 3-2 on aggregate, to take their place in the Cup-Winners' Cup.

Olimpija's strength undoubtedly lies on their own soil, and they are virtually invincible in their Bezigrad stadium. With the exception of a 1-1 draw with Maribor Branik they won all their home matches and many of them in emphatic fashion, including that 11-0 thrashing of Slovan Mavrica and others by 9-1, 7-1, 6-0 and 5-0. Only two matches were lost all season, one of those being a surprise 3-0 defeat at Publikum.

But Olimpija's dominance at home couldn't be turned into European success and their failure to get past Latvia's Skonto Riga in the preliminary round of the Champions' Cup is perhaps a damning indication of the current level of football in Slovenia. Having won the first leg in Riga with an early goal by Zeljko Milinovic, Olimpija looked to have a reasonably comfortable path into the first round. But with the return leg well into the second half and the game goalless, Proitski popped up to give the Latvians a vital advantage that they held through an extra half hour of play. The penalty shoot-out had all the closeness encountered across the two legs and with the drama well into the sudden death phase, Skonto pulled through with a 12-11 advantage.

Publikum couldn't do much better at the same stage of the Cup-Winners' Cup although in Denmark's OB they had somewhat tougher and more experienced opposition. But the knowledge that a lucrative tie with Arsenal lay in wait in the first round was a spur for both sides.

The ramshackle Skalna Ket stadium in Celje was the venue for the first leg and what proved to be the only goal of the game and

International Results 1993–94

Date	Opponents	Result	Venue	Comp.	Scorers
13/10/93	Yugoslavia/Macedonia	1-4	Kranj	Frdly	Pate (40)
8/2/94	Georgia	1-0	Valletta	Malta Tmt	Chelia
10/2/94	Tunisia	2-2	Valletta	Malta Tmt	Jarmanic, Binkovsic
12/2/94	Malta	1-0	Valletta	Malta Tmt	Gilha
23/3/94	FYR Macedonia	0-2	Skopje	Friendly	
1/6/94	Romania	0-0	Bucharest	Friendly	

National Record
European Championship — *Never participated*
World Cup Finals — *Never participated*
World Cup Qualifiers — *Never participated*

tie was scored eight minutes from time by OB's Steen Nedergaard. Publikum's brief flirtation with European football was over.

The international side did rather better, with two victories over Georgia and Malta combined with a 2-2 draw against Tunisia winning them the Malta International Tournament, played out in Valletta during February. Defeats by a combined Yugoslav/Macedonian side and then Macedonia were balanced by a highly commendable draw in Bucharest with Romania on which to end the season.

Three-Year Records League 1-2-3 and Cup Winners

League Results

	1st	Pts	2nd	Pts	3rd	Pts
1992	Olimpija Ljubljana	66	Maribor Branik	59	Belvedur Izola	56
1993	Olimpija Ljubljana	52	Maribor Branik	48	Mura Murska Sobota	46
1994	Olimpija Ljubljana	51	Mura Murska Sobota	45	Maribor Branik	42

Cup Final Results

1992	Maribor Branik	0-0	Olimpija Ljubljana	4-3 on pens
1993	Olimpija Ljubljana	2-1	Publikum	
1994	Maribor Branik	0-1, 3-1	Mura Murska Sobota	3-2 on agg

Spain

Barca's reign in Spain is far from plain

The pre-season began in August with the traditional Spanish appetite for soccer totally whetted by the nation's TV channels screening an amazing 128 matches in seven weeks prior to the start of the league kick-off. These included Real Sociedad's 2-2 draw with Real Madrid which inaugurated Sociedad's brand-new 29,000-capacity stadium at Anoeta, their new home after 80 years of football at the Atocha ground.

The transfer market was not as buoyant as in recent years but the early flurry of activity left Barcelona manager Johan Cruyff insisting that the fee of £2m plus the proceeds from six friendlies made Brazilian striker Romario a better buy than Slovak striker Peter Dubovsky, signed by Real Madrid for £2.5m. Valencia fans, after watching Pedrag Mijatovic hit 13 pre-season goals, argued that the £2m paid to Partizan Belgrade (despite the UN trade embargo on Serbia!) was the snip of the summer. Elsewhere belts were tightened and only Atletico Madrid made mass signings, hoping that Kiko and Quevode (Cadiz), Caminero (Valladolid), Pirri (Oviedo), Brazilian midfielder Moacir and Polish striker Kosecki could help new manager Jair Pereira win the league.

The Liga got under way in earnest in September and a Romario hat-trick enabled Barcelona to beat John Toshack's Real Sociedad. Real Madrid had beaten Osasuna 4-1 in Pamplona on the previous evening and nobody suspected that it would be their only league win of the month. After losing 3-1 at home to Valladolid, they were trounced 4-0 by Deportivo La Coruna, and a 1-0 defeat by Oviedo in the Bernabeu Stadium left them in 18th place, five points behind joint leaders Valencia and Athletic Bilbao. While Real president Ramon Mendoza admitted that modernising the Bernabeu had created "certain cash-flow problems", Barcelona still unveiled plans to convert the Nou Camp into an all-seater stadium. However, reducing the capacity from 120,000 to 105,000 caused a great deal of unrest among the season ticket holders and the building plans were later revised to allow the higher capacity to be maintained by lowering the pitch three metres!

Romario of Barcelona shows great control during a pre-season friendly with Ajax.

In European competitions all six entrants survived the first round even though debutants Tenerife and Deportivo were not among the UEFA seeded sides. At international level the rift that had been developing between national team manager Javier Clemente and Cruyff deepened when no fewer than eight Barcelona players were called up for the 2-0 win over Chile in Alicante, with Bilbao's new star, Julen Guerrero, scoring both goals. Six Barcelona players then took part in the 5-1 World Cup win over Albania in Tirana, in which Julio Salinas, unable to hold a first-team place at his club, scored a hat-trick. The match was surrounded by controversy following revelations by a Federation official that the 'chance' to rig the result had been offered for between £30,000 and £40,000. The Spanish team's charter company, Air Europa, later issued a communiqué explaining that food and clothing given to Albanians had been acquired via private donations from the airline's employees and not from any funny money laundered to cover up the allegations.

The war of words aimed at Clemente from the Spanish media continued into October when he was slammed for selecting nine defence-minded players for the vital World Cup qualifying game in Dublin against the Republic of Ireland. Spain won 3-1, with goals from Julio Salinas (two) and Jose Luis Caminero, and prompted Clemente to dedicate the result to "all the hooligans who wanted us to lose". On a more positive note the match marked goalkeeper Andoni Zubizarreta's 82nd cap, making him Spain's most capped player of all time.

Real Federacion Espaniola de Futbol	
Founded:	1913
Address:	Alberto Bosch 13, Apartado Postal 347, E-28014 Madrid
Phone:	+34 1 420 13 62
Fax:	+34 1 420 20 94
UEFA Affiliation:	1954
FIFA Affiliation:	1904
Season:	August to May
Colours:	Red, Blue, Black
Change:	Blue, Blue, Black

International Results 1993–94

Date	Opponents	Result	Venue	Comp.	Scorers
8/9/93	Chile	2-0	Alicante	Friendly	Guerrero (61, 89)
22/8/93	Albania	5-1	Tirana	WCQ3	Salinas (4, 30, 58), Toni (18), Caminero (67)
13/10/93	Rep. Ireland	3-1	Dublin	WCQ3	Caminero (11), Salinas (14, 26)
17/11/93	Denmark	1-0	Copenhagen	WCQ3	Hierro (63)
19/1/94	Portugal	2-2	Vigo	Friendly	Salinas (43), Juanele (77)
9/2/94	Poland	1-1	Tenerife	Friendly	Sergi (19)
23/3/94	Croatia	0-2	Valencia	Friendly	
2/6/94	Finland	2-1	Tampere	Friendly	Felipe (11), Salinas (15)
10/6/94	Canada	2-0	Montreal	Friendly	Salinas (9), Juanele (84)
17/6/94	South Korea	2-2	Dallas	WCFC	Salinas (51), Goikoetxea (56)
21/6/94	Germany	1-1	Chicago	WCFC	Goikoetxea (14)
27/6/94	Bolivia	3-1	Chicago	WCFC	Guardiola (19 pen), Caminero (65, 71)
2/7/94	Switzerland	3-0	Washington	WCF2	Hierro (15), Enrique (74), Beguiristain (87 pen)
9/7/94	Italy	1-2	Boston	WCFQ	Caminero (59)

National Record	P	W	D	L	F	A
Euro Championships	70	37	15	18	136	71
World Cup Finals	37	15	9	13	53	43
World Cup Qualifiers	66	41	9	16	126	60

Nationally, Barcelona were beaten twice. A goal by Bebeto was enough to sink them in La Coruna and they ended the month with an amazing defeat in Madrid. A Romario hat-trick gave Barca a 3-0 half-time lead over Atletico in a match where ten players were booked and home mid-fielder Pirri was sent off. Kosecki (two) and Pedro scored in the second half and an 88th-minute goal from Caminero secured a 4-3 win for Atletico. Madrid's so-called 'second' team were being coached temporarily by 'Cacho' Heredia, Jair Pereira having been sacked after seven league and three UEFA Cup games.

Valencia ended the month as league leaders with six wins and two draws from nine games. Two wins and two draws allowed Real Madrid to crawl up the table while they took the national headlines because of their shaky financial situation. A stormy AGM approved, by 398 votes to 301, accounts recording a loss of £825,000 on the year. However an audit put the losses at over £8.2m. President Mendoza blamed the £32m spent on the stadium for debts totalling nearly £29m, though increasing opposition within the club claimed that the real figure was nearer £40m.

November brought mixed blessings in Europe. Atletico Madrid were beaten 2-1 on aggregate by OFI Crete and Valencia were on the end of a 7-0 UEFA Cup drubbing in Karlsruhe. After losing 0-3 at home to Real Madrid in the league they sacked their Dutch manager, Guus Hiddink, replacing him with Francisco Real. Danish signing Soren Andersen helped newly promoted Lleida to beat Real Sociedad 1-3 in Anoeta – their first win of the season – and two weeks later they ruined millions of pools coupons by beating Barcelona 0-1 in the Nou Camp.

Internationally things looked much brighter as Spain secured a place in the World Cup finals with a 1-0 win over Denmark in Sevilla, despite having keeper Zubizarreta sent off, and by the middle of November Barcelona, Valencia, Sevilla, Deportivo, Real Madrid and Bilbao all shared the lead – the first six-way tie ever registered. Back in the Bernabeu, Mendoza called an emergency general meeting to approve urgent financial measures aimed at rescuing the club from the precipice situation. Looking to take the club into liquidation, his opponents actively canvassed 'no' votes but could only secure 28.9 per cent instead of the 33 per cent needed. The EGM however did approve plans for the club to request a £17.5m loan from bankers Banesto.

December brought rare smiles at Real Madrid after a 4-2 aggregate Super Cup win over Barcelona allowed them to perform a mischievous lap of honour with the Super Cup in the Nou Camp. Their joy was short lived as they ended the year with a 2-0 defeat at Real Sociedad and with the shock news that the Spanish government had taken control of Banesto, thus condemning the club to look elsewhere for the life-saving loan. Cruyff fined his Barca players £750 after their 2-2 home draw with Logrones. However, things improved in Europe. After a goalless draw with Turkish champions Galatasaray, Barcelona went top of their Champions' League group by beating Monaco.

Deportivo ended the year two points clear of Barcelona at the top, keeper Francisco Liano having conceded just five goals in 17 games. On the south coast, Valencia's president Melchor Hoyos, sacked Francisco Real after five games had produced one win, and named Uruguayan coach Hector Nunezas his successor. Other coaches found themselves looking for a job as New Year approached – 'Pep' More replaced Felipe Mesones at Valladolid and former player Enrique Martin took over at Osasuna when Pedro Maria Zabalza resigned after eight years in charge.

Real Madrid supporters were hoping that the dawn of the New Year would bring a change in fortunes both on and off the pitch – but there would have been mixed feelings about having to start it with a trip to the Nou Camp. A win would restore pride; a defeat... It was the Catalans who spent the following weeks celebrating after they handed out a 5-0 thrashing to record their best home result against Real since 1945 and the first 5-0 since Cruyff the player led the side to an identical scoreline 20 years previously. But panic stations were gradually transformed into battle stations at Real where, after drawing 2-2 at home to Atletico in the first leg, they were faced with cup elimination four days after the Barcelona debacle. In the event, Butragueno, Luis Enrique and Lasa gave them a 3-2 win. League leaders Deportivo fared less well, beaten 3-2 on aggregate by Oviedo.

Emilio Cruz resigned as Atletico coach immediately following a 2-1 defeat by Rayo in the Madrid derby, and was replaced by backroom boy Jose Luis Romero.

As January progressed there was uproar when the league received two bills for Valencia's £900,000 share of TV rights – one from the club and the other from a finance company claiming that club secretary Vicente Pons had taken the cash in advance and signed the TV money over to them. An investigation found that the documents had been forged and Pons resigned. Romario also found himself in hot water when Barcelona played Sevilla. The Brazilian flattened Argentine midfielder Diego Simeone with an uppercut that led to a four-match ban.

After a hectic start to the New Year on and off the field, Real Madrid began February on a better foot, beating leaders Deportivo 2-0. With Barcelona losing 2-3 to Bilbao, the title race was starting to liven up. But both clubs crashed out of the Copa del Rey, Real humiliated 3-0 at home by Tenerife and a solitary goal by Juanito allowing second division Betis to beat Barcelona in the Nou Camp. Zaragoza then hammered Cruyff's team 6-3 in the league (the first time they had conceded six since November 1962) and Cruyff announced that it was 'the end of an era' and that a dressing room clear-out would take place at the end of the season. The metaphorical kick up the backside worked and Barca beat Osasuna 8-1 in their next game.

Valencia's unhappy season took another blow when they were told that they would be without Bulgarian striker Lubo Penev for the rest of the season because he would need surgery and chemotherapy for a cancer of the left testicle. The growth was discovered by accident after he had been hit by a medicine ball in training. Back on the field 20-year-old Jose Luis Morales scored the only goal in Real's 1-0 win over Atletico in the Madrid derby. Atletico were then beaten 2-4 by Sevilla and new coach Jose Luis Romero was sacked and replaced by Iselin Santos Ovejero. Barcelona kept their championship aspirations alive by beating Deportivo 3-0, reducing the Galician club's lead to four points.

March brought the restart in Europe with Barcelona surrendering a 0-2 lead in the last 13 minutes of the Champions' League match against Spartak in Moscow. Real lost 0-1 at home to Paris Saint-Germain, their *bete noire* of the previous season, and their crisis continued when they were then beaten 2-1 by tail-enders Lleida. This combination of results finally brought an end

Andoni Zubizarreta (Barcelona and Spain).

to the speculation and Floro was sacked, with second-team coach Vicente Del Bosque accepting the first-team noose. Across town, Atletico sacked Santos Ovejero after a 0-4 defeat by Zaragoza and appointed Jorge D'Alessandro their sixth coach of the season, who started securing Atletico's first away win of the season, 0-1 against Osasuna in Pamplona.

For the first time since 1948, none of the Big Four was in the line-up for the Copa del Rey semi-finals. Celta beat Tenerife 3-0 and 2-2 while Zaragoza, having beaten Betis by a single goal in the away leg, needed extra time to win 3-1 at home. Another side to secure a semi-final spot, Barcelona, did so in Europe after a 3-0 win over Galatasaray. Barca continued to get stronger in the league with the foreign factor playing a big role. Four of them accounted for 22 of the side's 27 goals in February and March, during which Romario scored his fifth hat-trick of the season!

Internationally Spain suffered their first home defeat since October 1991, losing 0-2 to a Croatian side which included no fewer than six Spanish-based players! John Toshack announced that he had resigned as national team manager to Wales after just one game and was returning to full-time duty with Real Sociedad.

After four games without a win, leaders Deportivo thrashed Athletic Bilbao 4-1 to end the month two points clear of Barcelona. Valencia, after sacking Hector Nunez and naming Jose Manuel Rielo as caretaker manager, persuaded Guus Hiddink to return for the last nine matches of the season while new president

Copa Su Majestad Del Ray

Third Round	1st Leg	2nd Leg	Agg
Alcoyano v Toledo	2-2	1-6	3-8
Arosa v Villarreal	0-1	0-0	0-1
Atletico Gramanet v Celta Vigo	1-0	0-2	1-2
Atletico Tomelloso v Cadiz	0-0	0-1	0-1
Cacereno v Sevilla	0-3	2-1	2-4
Caravaca v Espanol	0-3	0-3	0-6
Cordoba v Hercules	1-2	2-3	3-5
Corralejo v Rayo Vallncano	3-3	0-4	3-7
Dep Alaves v Real Murcia	0-2	0-3	0-5
Ecija Balompie v Castellon	1-1	1-3	2-4
Elche CF v Real Burgos	2-1	2-3	4-4
Elche won on penalties			
Ejido v Leganes	2-1	2-1	4-2
Endesa Andorra v Logrones	0-3	1-3	1-6
Escobedo v Lleida	0-0	0-3	0-3
Ferrol v Yeclano	0-1	1-2	1-3
Figueres v Real Sociedad	1-1	0-4	1-5
Getafe v Real Aviles Ind	2-1	2-0	4-1
Gimnastica v Eibar	1-4	0-1	1-5
Huelva v Real Oviedo	1-2	0-4	1-6
Izarra v Real Zaragoza	2-1	0-7	2-8
UP Langreo v Palamos	2-2	1-1	3-3
Las Palmas v Athletic Club	2-2	1-3	3-5
Lemona v Almeria CF	1-0	0-3	1-3
Leonesa v Sporting Gijon	3-2	1-5	4-7
Levante v Vallodolid	0-0	1-2	1-2
Lugo v Compostela	1-0	0-2	1-2
Marmol Macael v Real Racing Club	2-2	1-4	3-6
Mensajero v Betis	0-0	2-3	2-3
Ponferradina v Osasuna	1-2	0-4	1-6
Rubi v Merida	0-2	0-3	0-5
Salamanca v Mallorca	3-1	1-0	4-1
Santa Eulalia v Badajoz	0-3	0-7	0-10
Talavera v Atletico Marbella	3-1	2-1	5-2
Fourth Round			
Almeira v Espanol	0-2	1-5	1-7
Athletic Club v Real Zaragoza	0-2	1-1	1-3
Cadiz v Real Oviedo	0-2	0-4	0-6
Castellon v Sevilla	2-0	0-3	2-3
Celta Vigo v Albacete	4-0	1-4	5-4
Compostela v Lleida	1-2	1-4	2-6
Elche v Betis	2-1	0-5	2-7
Getafe v Logrones	0-1	1-2	1-3
Hercules v Real Sociedad	1-1	0-0	1-1
Real Sociedad won on penalties			
Merida v Rayo Vallecano	1-0	1-1	2-1
Palamos v Toledo	0-0	0-1	0-1
Polid Ejido v Salalmanca	3-0	4-1	7-1
Real Murcia v Real Valladolid	0-3	1-3	1-6
Talavera v Real Racing Club	2-0	2-3	4-3
Fifth Round			
Espanol v Villarreal	2-0	1-2	3-2
Logrones v Lleida	3-1	0-0	3-1
Merida v Eibar	0-0	1-0	1-0
Polid Ejido v Betis	1-3	1-2	2-5
Real Sociedad v Sevilla	3-3	0-1	3-4
Sporting Gijon v Real Valladolid	3-1	0-1	3-2
Real Zaragoza v Osasuna	1-0	1-1	2-1
Talavera v Celta Vigo	1-2	0-0	1-2
Toledo v Real Oviedo	1-1	1-2	1-3
Yelcano v Badajoz	1-0	0-2	1-2
Sixth Round			
Badajoz v Real Zaragoza	1-0	0-3	1-3
Deportivo La Coruna v Real Ovideo	1-3	1-0	2-3
Espanol v Sevilla	0-1	2-2	2-3
Logrones v Celta Vigo	1-0	0-1	1-1
Celta Vigo won on penalties			
Betis v Merida	3-1	1-1	4-2
Real Madrid v Atletico Madrid	2-2	3-2	5-4
Sporting Gijon v Barcelona	0-3	1-1	1-4
Tenerife v Valencia	3-1	2-3	5-4
Quarter-Finals			
Betis v Barcelona	0-0	1-0	1-0
Real Oviedo v Celta Vigo	1-0	0-5	1-5
Real Zaragoza v Sevilla	2-1	1-1	3-2
Tenerife v Real Madrid	2-1	3-0	5-1
Semi-Final			
Betis v Real Zaragoza	0-1	1-3	1-4
Celta Vigo v Tenerife	3-0	2-2	5-2

Final

Real Zaragoza 0 **Celta Vigo** 0

Att: 65,000 *Ref:* Lopez Nieto

Real Zaragoza: Cedrun, Belsue, Solana, Caceres, Aguado, Gay, Aragon, Nayim, Poyet (Garcia San Juan 72), Pardeza (Dario Franco 90), Higuera.

Celta Vigo: Canizares, Alejo, Otejo, Salinas, Dadie, Vincente, Ratkovic (Gil 58), Engonga, Salva (Losada 95), Andrijasevic, Gudelj.

Real Zaragoza won 5-4 on penalties after extra time

Francisco Roig sorted out a new coach (or several) for the 1994–95 season.

April started with a goal spree for Bilbao, who thrashed Gijon 7-0, with Julen Guerrero strengthening his World Cup claims by scoring four of them. Real Madrid, having produced a burst of good football in their opening games under Vicente Del Bosque, were put back in their place by Celta, who beat them 3-2 in Vigo, and then by Gijon who, recovering from the trauma in Bilbao, held them 2-2 in Madrid after which Jorge Valdano was named as Real's new manager for 1994–95. Atletico Madrid dropped into the relegation mire after a 3-0 home defeat by Oviedo, but a hat-trick by Mexican striker Luis Garcia helped them make amends with a 4-2 win over Bilbao.

With the league building up to a thrilling climax, the final of the Copa del Rey was 'buried' in midweek. Zaragoza – the favourites – and Celta took about 30,000 fans apiece to the

Final League Table 1993–94

Primera Division

	P	W	D	L	F	A	Pts
Barcelona	38	25	6	7	91	42	56
Deportivo La Coruna	38	22	12	4	54	18	56
Real Zaragoza	38	19	8	11	71	47	46
Real Madrid	38	19	7	12	61	50	45
Athletic Bilbao	38	16	11	11	61	47	43
Sevilla	38	15	12	11	56	42	42
Valencia	38	14	12	12	55	50	40
Racing Santander	38	15	8	15	44	42	38
Real Oviedo	38	12	13	13	43	49	37
Tenerife	38	15	6	17	50	57	36
Real Sociedad	38	12	12	14	39	47	36
Atletico Madrid	38	13	9	16	54	54	35
Albacete	38	10	15	13	49	58	35
Sporting Gijon	38	15	5	18	42	57	35
Celta Vigo	38	11	11	16	41	51	33
Logrones	38	9	15	14	47	58	33
Rayo Vallecano	38	9	13	16	40	58	31
Real Valladolid	38	8	14	16	28	51	30
Lleida	38	7	13	18	29	48	27
Osasuna	38	8	10	20	34	63	26

Top Scorers
- 30 ROMARIO Da Souza (Barcelona)
- 24 Davor SUKER (Sevilla)
- 23 Meho KODRO (Real Sociedad)
- 20 CARLOS Munoz (Real Oviedo)
- 18 Julien GUERRERO (Athletic Bilbao)
- Jose Angel CIGANDA (Athletic Bilbao)
- 16 BEBETO (Deportivo La Coruna)
- Hugo SANCHEZ (Real Valladolid)
- Pedrag MIJATOVIC (Valencia)
- Oleg SALENKO (Logrones)
- Hristo STOICHKOV (Barcelona)

Promotions and Relegations
Promoted: Espanol, Betis, Compostela
Relegated: Osasuna, Lleida, Rayo Vallecano

Five-Year Records League 1-2-3 and Cup Winners

League Results

	1st	Pts	2nd	Pts	3rd	Pts
1990	Real Madrid	62	Valencia	53	Barcelona	51
1991	Barcelona	57	Atletico Madrid	47	Real Madrid	46
1992	Barcelona	55	Real Madrid	54	Atletico Madrid	53
1993	Barcelona	58	Real Madrid	57	Deportivo La Coruna	54
1994	Barcelona	56	Deportivo La Coruna	56	Real Zaragoza	46

Cup Final Results

1990	Barcelona	2-0	Real Madrid	
1991	Atletico Madrid	1-0	Mallorca	
1992	Atletico Madrid	2-0	Real Madrid	
1993	Real Madrid	2-0	Real Zaragoza	
1994	Real Zaragoza	0-0	Celta Vigo	5-4 pens

Manzanares stadium in Madrid but the players didn't respond to the great atmosphere. Zaragoza were technically superior but physically second-best and the final stayed goalless at the end of extra time. Defender Alejo miskicked Celta's last spot kick in the first round of penalties and when Higuera stroked his shot home, Victor Fernandez's Zaragoza had won the Cup. Three days later the title race took another twist with Barcelona's 0-4 win in Vigo while Deportivo could only draw in Lleida. A week later, Deportivo were also held to a goalless draw by Rayo Vallecano and Barcelona thrashed Gijon 4-0.

Barcelona's merry month of May continued as they beat Bobby Robson's FC Porto 3-0 in the Nou Camp to reach the final of the Champions' Cup. The final against Milan was billed as the match of the century, with Cruyff claiming his side were the favourites; announcing that he didn't like Milan's football; and proclaiming that Barcelona had to win 'for the good of football in general'. Three days later 110,000 fans packed into the Bernabeu stadium to see if Real could get revenge for January's 5-0 drubbing by Barcelona with the added satisfaction of handing the title on a plate to Deportivo if they won. They didn't. Although they played better in the second half, a late goal from Guillermo Amor gave the visitors a 0-1 win. Deportivo, 2-0 winners in Logrono, now needed only to beat Valencia at home to clinch the title. Lleida's 0-1 home defeat by Atletico Madrid made them favourites to go down, along with Osasuna, relegated after 14 seasons in the top flight.

The championship was decided in comic-book fashion not just on the last day of the season but also in its last minutes. Deportivo needed to win their home encounter with Valencia to be sure of the title, whilst a draw would have been enough if Barcelona failed to beat Sevilla in the Nou Camp. At half-time events favoured Deportivo who were scoreless; Barca were surprisingly losing 2-1. In a rampant second half Barcelona took control of their game and went on to win 5-2. With Deportivo unable to break through the Valencia defence the title looked to be staying in Catalan. However, in the dying embers of the game in La Coruna, Deportivo were awarded a penalty. With the championship at stake Bebeto, the normal penalty taker, declined the responsibility, which was entrusted to sweeper Miroslav Djukic. The Serbian shot tamely and Valencia keeper Gonzalez had an easy save. Despair in La Coruna but jubilation in Barcelona, who had won the title on the last day of the season for the third successive year! The consolation for Deportivo was a UEFA Cup spot with Bilbao along with Real Madrid, who rounded off a dismal season with a 4-1 drubbing in Zaragoza to finish fourth.

Barcelona's jubilation was short lived as, just four days later, they were played off the park in Athens as Milan scored four times to win the Champions' Cup. In the aftermath of Barcelona's awesome humiliation, Michael Laudrup announced his departure 'because I can't put up with Cruyff any longer.' Cruyff kept his threat of a clear-out as goalkeeper Andoni Zubizarreta, Spain's most-capped player of all time, and five other members of the

Claudio Barragan of Deportivo (right) challenges Albacete's Menendez for the ball during a league encounter.

World Cup squad were transfer listed. Cruyff's clear-out provoked another war of words with national team manager Clemente. The list of managerial departures continues with Jupp Heynckes (Bilbao), Victor Esparrago (Albacete), Chechu Rojo (Celta) and Carlos Almar (Logrones) to add to Valdano's move from Tenerife to Real Madrid. Barcelona midfielder Guillermo Amor, who ended the season on a very high note, was the only surprise exclusion from the World Cup squad which reported to the training camp near Santander.

Lleida and Osasina were relegated, being replaced by Barcelona's other club Espanol and Betis. However the June sun shone brightly for Valladolid, who retained their first division status by beating Toledo 4-1 in the play-offs, but Rayo Vallecano were less fortunate. They were held 1-1 at home by Compostela and held on for a 0-0 draw in the return match in Santiago. The decider, played on neutral ground in Oviedo, gave 'Compos' promotion to the top division for the first time. Nigerian inside-forward Christopher Ohen, scorer of their goal in the first match, added the first two in Oviedo. Rayo's Mexican World Cup striker, Hugo Sanchez, was sent off as Compostela won 3-1.

The close season merry-go-round started to get into full swing before the national side departed for the World Cup Finals. Real Madrid snapped up Michael Laudrup from Barcelona and Argentine Fernando Redondo from coach Valdano's former club, Tenerife. Jose Maria Arrate won the presidential elections at Athletic Bilbao and announced that Racing Santander boss Javier Irureta would be the new coach.

One doubts if the 1994–95 season will be any quieter!

Spanish Championship Results 1993–94

	Albacete	Athletic Bilbao	Atletico Madrid	Barcelona	Celta Vigo	Deportivo La Coruna	Lleida	Logrones	Osasuna	Racing Santander	Rayo Vallecano	Real Madrid	Real Oviedo	Real Sociedad	Real Valladolid	Real Zaragoza	Sevilla	Sporting Gijon	Tenerife	Valencia
Albacete	—	1-0	2-2	0-0	0-4	0-0	2-1	2-2	2-1	3-0	1-1	1-4	5-0	1-1	1-1	2-1	2-2	3-1	2-3	3-1
Athletic Bilbao	4-1	—	3-2	0-0	2-1	3-1	4-0	0-0	1-2	1-2	0-0	2-1	1-1	0-0	3-0	2-1	1-1	7-0	3-2	2-1
Atletico Madrid	0-0	4-2	—	4-3	3-2	0-1	0-0	1-0	3-0	4-0	2-0	0-0	0-3	1-2	2-0	0-4	2-4	2-0	2-0	2-0
Barcelona	2-1	2-3	5-3	—	1-0	3-0	0-1	2-2	8-1	2-1	1-0	5-0	1-0	3-0	3-0	4-1	5-2	4-0	2-1	3-1
Celta Vigo	1-4	1-1	3-2	0-4	—	0-0	1-0	2-0	4-0	0-0	0-0	3-2	1-1	3-2	1-2	1-0	2-1	0-2	1-0	1-2
Deportivo La Coruna	5-1	4-1	2-1	1-0	0-0	—	2-0	3-0	3-1	1-0	0-0	4-0	4-0	0-1	0-0	1-1	2-0	2-1	2-0	0-0
Lleida	0-1	1-2	0-1	1-2	0-0	0-0	—	1-1	1-2	0-0	0-1	2-1	1-1	1-0	1-0	0-1	0-3	1-1	1-1	1-1
Logrones	2-2	4-2	1-0	0-0	1-1	0-2	2-1	—	3-2	0-1	1-1	3-4	2-2	2-0	0-0	2-2	1-1	1-2	1-2	2-0
Osasuna	3-1	0-0	0-1	2-3	0-1	0-0	1-0	1-3	—	0-0	1-1	1-4	2-0	0-2	2-0	0-0	0-0	3-0	1-0	3-3
Racing Santander	1-1	2-2	2-0	1-1	2-1	0-1	2-1	0-0	3-1	—	1-0	1-3	1-2	4-1	5-1	2-0	1-0	2-0	1-0	0-1
Rayo Vallecano	0-0	1-2	2-1	2-4	1-1	0-0	1-2	3-1	1-0	1-1	—	0-2	0-0	4-1	0-1	1-2	2-1	2-1	4-3	1-1
Real Madrid	2-0	2-1	1-0	0-1	2-1	2-0	5-0	2-1	0-0	2-1	5-2	—	0-1	0-2	1-3	3-2	0-0	2-2	1-1	3-2
Real Oviedo	1-1	3-0	1-1	1-3	1-0	2-5	0-0	1-2	1-0	3-0	5-0	0-1	—	2-1	1-0	2-1	0-2	0-1	1-0	0-3
Real Sociedad	1-1	0-0	2-1	2-1	2-1	0-1	1-3	2-2	1-0	2-0	1-1	2-0	2-2	—	1-0	2-2	0-0	0-1	2-1	0-0
Real Valladolid	1-0	1-1	1-1	1-3	0-0	0-0	0-2	2-0	2-1	0-3	1-3	0-0	0-0	0-0	—	0-0	2-2	0-1	2-0	1-1
Real Zaragoza	1-1	1-0	2-1	6-3	4-1	0-1	1-1	1-1	2-1	2-0	4-1	4-1	2-1	3-0	2-0	—	1-2	3-0	6-2	1-0
Sevilla	2-0	1-3	2-1	0-0	4-1	0-0	2-1	4-1	1-1	2-1	3-1	0-1	2-0	1-0	3-3	0-1	—	1-2	4-0	0-1
Sporting Gijon	1-0	0-1	1-1	2-0	2-1	0-2	1-1	1-2	7-1	0-2	2-0	2-1	0-0	3-2	2-0	0-3	0-1	—	1-2	2-0
Tenerife	2-1	2-1	1-1	2-3	0-0	0-1	1-0	2-0	1-0	1-0	3-1	0-0	2-2	2-1	0-2	5-3	2-1	3-0	—	1-0
Valencia	4-0	1-0	2-2	0-4	3-0	1-3	3-3	3-1	0-0	2-1	3-1	0-3	2-2	0-0	5-1	3-0	1-1	1-0	3-2	—

Sweden

Norrkoping miss out again!

IFK Gothenburg won the Allsvenskan but the sympathy vote in Sweden went with IFK Norrkoping, who finished in the runners-up position for the fourth year in succession. Although Norrkoping have won the title 12 times they have taken it only once since 1963, that success coming in 1989. However, there can be no doubting Gothenburg's pedigree as champions. They lost just three games in the new-format league and conceded far fewer goals than anyone else. Part of the reason for that was the form of their international and record-capped goalkeeper, Thomas Ravelli, who managed to keep clean sheets in no fewer than half of the 26 league games, and this despite the loss of defenders Ola Svensson and Joachim Bjorklund with long-term injuries.

It was the 14th championship for the Gothenburg club, the seventh in just over ten years, and the third in four years under the coaching of Roger Gustafsson – only the previous season's surprise success by AIK Stockholm interrupting what otherwise would have been total domination. Despite those injuries, and that to forward Magnus Erlingmark, Gustafsson was able to unearth new talent to sustain the pace, including Jesper Blomqvist, a 19-year-old midfield player signed from provincial side Umea, who was in the squad for the World Cup Finals. Gothenburg's midfield ace Stefan Rehn was perhaps the mainstay behind their sustained drive at the top of the table.

By the halfway stage of the season the table had taken a familiar look. Gothenburg led but were closely followed by Norrkoping and AIK. Malmo were some 15 points off the pace and still struggling with the indifferent form that had plagued them during the 1992 season. In an effort to arrest that and get back to the form that had last brought a championship in 1988, Danish coach Viggo Jensen had been sacked – which caused something of a stir. He was replaced by Rolf Zettterlund, a much-respected figure. The change hadn't produced the desired results and Malmo looked to be out of the title race but still in with a shout for the cup.

Svenska Fotboll Forbundet	
Founded:	1904
Address:	Box 1216, S-17123 Stockholm
Phone:	+46 8 735 09 00
Fax:	+46 8 27 51 47
UEFA Affiliation:	1954
FIFA Affiliation:	1904
Season:	April to October
National Stadium:	Rasunda Stadion
Capacity:	41,000
Colours:	Yellow, Blue, Yellow
Change:	Blue, Blue, Blue

Mats Lilenberg of Trelleborgs celebrates yet another goal.

The big match at that stage was won by Gothenburg, who trounced reigning champions AIK 5-1 on their own ground, after they had taken an early lead, to open up an eight-point gap across the top three clubs. That defeat effectively ended AIK's brief flirtation with the championship. Gothenburg and Norrkoping gradually opened up a sizeable gap, with never more than three points, and more often just one, separating them. With five games to play, AIK's defeat at bottom club Brage confirmed their title

International Results 1993–94

Date	Opponents	Result	Venue	Comp.	Scorers
11/8/93	Switzerland	1-2	Boras	Friendly	Dahlin (17)
22/8/93	France	1-1	Stockholm	WCQ6	Dahlin (89)
8/9/93	Bulgaria	1-1	Sofia	WCQ6	Dahlin (26)
13/10/93	Finland	3-2	Stockholm	WCQ6	Dahlin (27, 44), Larsen (40)
10/11/93	Austria	1-1	Vienna	WCQ6	Mild (68)
18/2/94	Colombia	0-0	Miami	RC 1R	
20/2/94	United States	3-1	Miami	RC 1R	Larsson (30), K. Andersson (34), Lillenberg (56)
24/2/94	Mexico	1-2	Fresno	Friendly	Mild (81)
20/4/94	Wales	2-0	Wrexham	Friendly	
5/5/94	Nigeria	3-1	Stockholm	Friendly	Schwarz (3), Larsson (42), Ingesson (78)
26/5/94	Denmark	0-0	Copenhagen	Friendly	
5/6/94	Norway	2-0	Stockholm	Friendly	Brolin (56, 61 pen)
19/6/94	Cameroon	2-2	Pasadena	WCFB	Ljung (9), Dahlin (75)
24/6/94	Russia	3-1	Detroit	WCFB	Brolin (39 pen), Dahlin (80, 82)
28/6/94	Brazil	1-1	Detroit	WCFB	K. Andersson (24)
3/7/94	Saudi Arabia	3-1	Dallas	WCF2	Dahlin (6), K. Andersson (51, 88)
10/7/94	Romania	2-2 †	San Francisco	WCFQ	Brolin (78), K. Andersson (114)
	Won 5-4 on pens				
13/7/94	Brazil	0-1	Pasadena	WCFS	
16/7/94	Bulgaria	4-0	Pasadena	WC3/4	Brolin (8), Mild (30), H. Larsson (37), K. Andersson (39)

RC=Robbie Cup. † aet

National Record	P	W	D	L	F	A
European Championships	50	21	12	17	69	61
World Cup Finals	37	13	9	15	62	60
World Cup Qualifiers	67	39	12	16	140	70

surrender as wins pushed the two pace-setters still further ahead still. Norrkoping captured the lead just once by having played a game more. That was soon recovered and when Norrkoping lost 3-2 at Vasta after having trailed 3-0, Gothenburg took advantage to pull ahead with a comprehensive 5-1 win over a still indifferent Malmo.

On the last but one weekend, Gothenburg travelled to Norrkoping for a potential title decider. A win for the visitors would ensure them the title, three points for the hosts would put them in pole position, and a draw would leave Norrkoping dependent on Gothenburg faltering at the post. The game, watched by 19,160, ended goalless and with Gothenburg maintaining their two-point advantage. The final weekend had both sides facing difficult away ties at relegation-threatened clubs, and anything was possible. Gothenburg won 2-0 at Osters with a goal in each half from Nilsson and Eriksson, but Norrkoping lost to a 77th-minute goal at Degerfors and their final hope had gone. The win was of vital importance for Degerfors, as it moved them out of the second automatic relegation position and into the play-off zone. With Brage already relegated, Orgryte slipped into the void left by Degerfors.

The deposed champions, AIK, finished third to win a UEFA Cup spot, but still replaced coach Tommy Soderberg with Osters' Hans Backe, who quickly dipped into the transfer market. Malmo were 10th – just two points off the relegation play-off zone – and their last game, a 4-5 defeat at home to Vastra, illustrated their problems. They recovered from being 0-4 at the interval to draw level with just four minutes to play, only to lose to a goal right at the final whistle.

In the Skandia Cupen, Gothenburg fell foul of giant-killing in the fourth round, losing 3-4 at the regional Division II side Veberods. Holders Degerfors went in the fifth round to a Malmo side reserving their best performances for the cup, but not quite able to make it to the final. The lower sides continued to create upsets but by the time the semi-finals were reached only one – Lulea from Division I – remained, and they failed in their bid to reach the final. Norrkoping duly beat Helsingborgs in sudden death during extra time after a 3-3 90-minute score.

In Europe it was a pretty dismal season from Swedish clubs, all four representatives being eliminated in their first-round matches. AIK beat Sparta Prague in the first leg of the Champions' Cup but couldn't stop the Czech side from reversing the result in the return. Degerfors were given a dream draw

Allsvenskan Final Table 1993

	P	W	D	L	F	A	Pts
IFK Gothenburg	26	18	5	3	48	17	59
IFK Norrkoping	26	17	3	6	56	23	54
AIK Stockholm	26	14	4	8	49	43	46
Trelleborgs	26	12	6	8	46	39	42
Halmstad	26	11	5	10	50	41	38
Hacken BK	26	11	4	11	44	49	37
Vastra Frolunda	26	11	4	11	38	45	37
Osters	26	10	6	10	43	34	36
Helsingborgs	26	10	6	10	43	46	36
Malmo FF	26	10	5	11	43	38	35
Orebro	26	10	3	13	35	38	33
Degerfors	26	6	5	15	32	54	23
Orgryte	26	5	6	15	26	44	21
Brage	26	4	4	18	26	68	16

Top Scorers
- 18 Henrik BERYILSSON (Halmstad)
- Mats LILENBERG (Trelleborgs)
- 16 Dick LIDMAN (AIK Stockholm)
- Henrik LARSSON (Helsingborgs)
- Hans EKLUND (Osters)
- 13 Issa MANGLIND (Trelleborgs)
- Miroslaw KUBISZTAL (Orebro)
- 12 Milenko VUKCEVIC (Degerfors)
- 11 Kim BERGSTRAND (AIK Stockholm)
- Jan-Ake ENSTROM (Hacken BK)
- 10 Patrik ANDERSSON (IFK Norrkoping)

Promotions and Relegations
Promoted: Hammarby IF, Landskrona Bois
Relegated: Brage, Orgryte

Five-Year Records League 1-2-3 and Cup Winners

League Results
1989 Play-off: IFK Norrkoping v Malmo FF 0-2, 1-0
   One win each therefore Replay: 0-0
   IFK Norrkoping win 4-3 on pens
1990 Play-off: IFK Gothenburg v IFK Norrkoping 3-0, 0-0

	1st	Pts	2nd	Pts	3rd	Pts
1991	IFK Gothenburg	36	IFK Norrkoping	31	Orebro SK	28
1992	AIK Stockholm	34	IFK Norrkoping	32	Osters	30
1993	IFK Gothenburg	59	IFK Norrkoping	54	AIK Stockholm	46

Cup Final Results
1990	Djurgardens IF	2-0	Hacken BK
1991	IFK Norrkoping	4-1	Osters
1992	IFK Gothenburg	3-2	AIK Stockholm
1993	Degerfors	3-0	Landskrona
1994	IFK Norrkoping	4-3*	Helsingborgs

(* after sudden death)

Skandia Cupen

Last 32
Gefle IF v Halmstads BK	2-2, 2-3
Hammerby IF v Orgryte IS	0-0, 0-0, 2-4
IF Algarna v Osters IF	2-9
IF Elfsborg v AIK Stockholm	1-1, 1-1, 6-5
IF Vesta v IFK Norrkoping	0-6
IFK Lulea v Spanga IS	1-1, 2-1
IFK Umea v GIF Sundsvall	1-3
Kalmar FF v Hacken BK	1-1, 1-2
Kiruna FF v Degerfors IF	2-4
Landskrona Bois v IK Oddevold	1-1, 2-1
Ope IF v Helsingborg IF	0-4
Saters IF v Kvarnsvedens IK	2-3
Skelleftea AIK v Vastra Froulnda	0-3
Sparvagens FF v Malmo FF	1-2
Valbo IF v Djurgardens IF	2-7
Veberods AIF v IFK Gothenburg	4-3

Last 16
Djurgardens IF v Vastra Froulnda	2-0
GIF Sundsvall v Helsingborgs	2-2, 2-3
IFK Lulea v Halmstads BK	3-2
Kvarnsvedens IK v IFK Norrkoping	1-1, 1-2
Landskrona Bois v Hacken BK	1-0
Malmo FF v Degerfors IF	3-1
Osters v Orgryte IS	2-2, 2-2, 6-4
Veberods AIF v IF Elfsborg	1-1, 2-1

Quarter-Finals
Helsingborg v IF Elfsborg	6-1
IFK Lulea v Djurgardens IF	3-2
IFK Norrkoping v Osters IF	5-1
Landskrona Bois v Malmo FF	0-2

Semi-Finals
IFK Lulea v IFK Norrkoping	1-3
Malmo FF v Helsingborgs	2-4

Final
IFK Norrkoping v Helsingborgs	4-3†

† *after sudden death extra time*

against holders Parma for their European debut, but two goals in the final three minutes by Asprilla denied them victory in the home leg, and Brolin sealed his countrymen's exit in the return. In the UEFA Cup, Norrkoping went out after extra time to KV Mechelen, and Kongsvinger made easy work of Osters.

Thankfully things went much better for the national side, who qualified for the World Cup Finals with a game to spare. But manager Tommy Svensson was given a tough time by some of his 'stars' who dropped out for an important game with Finland, notably Brolin and Ekstrom. Injuries and suspensions denied him the services of at least four other squad regulars and Finland took a shock lead before two goals by Martin Dahlin – the Swedish Player of the Year – and one by debutant Henrik Larsson ensured a 3-2 win. Two weeks after that, a goal by Mild ensured a point in Austria and tickets to USA94, where the side produced some

Sweden Championship Results 1993–94

	AIK Stockholm	Brage	Degerfors	Halmstads	Helsingborgs	Hacken BKIFK	Gothenburg	Malmo FF	IFK Norrkoping	Trelleborgs	Vastra Frolunda	Orebro	Orgryte	Osters
AIK Stockholm	—	9-3	3-0	2-3	2-1	2-0	1-5	0-4	1-0	2-1	1-0	3-1	1-2	3-2
Brage	2-1	—	1-1	0-0	2-3	0-2	0-1	1-3	2-3	0-4	1-2	1-3	2-0	1-3
Degerfors	1-2	2-4	—	1-1	4-2	1-2	2-4	1-0	1-0	4-0	3-0	1-1	2-3	2-5
Halmstads	3-3	3-2	6-1	—	3-0	4-2	2-1	0-1	1-3	2-0	2-3	3-1	4-2	1-2
Helsingborgs	2-3	4-1	2-1	2-2	—	3-2	1-2	0-2	0-2	0-0	1-1	2-1	3-0	2-0
Hacken BK	5-2	3-0	3-0	2-1	2-2	—	0-2	4-2	3-2	3-3	2-1	1-3	0-0	1-1
IFK Gothenburg	1-1	0-0	1-0	2-0	2-0	3-0	—	5-1	2-1	2-1	0-1	2-0	1-1	1-1
Malmo FF	2-0	7-0	0-1	0-0	3-3	3-0	0-1	—	1-3	1-4	4-5	1-1	2-0	0-2
IFK Norrkoping	2-0	8-1	2-0	1-0	1-1	3-0	0-0	2-2	—	3-0	5-1	2-0	2-0	3-2
Trelleborgs	1-1	1-1	1-0	2-1	5-4	6-2	3-1	1-0	2-1	—	2-1	1-1	3-1	1-1
Vastra Frolunda	0-2	1-0	1-1	3-1	1-2	1-0	1-5	1-2	3-2	2-1	—	4-1	1-1	1-2
Orebro	0-1	1-0	4-1	1-4	4-0	2-1	0-1	0-1	0-1	1-0	1-2	—	4-1	2-1
Orgryte	1-2	0-1	1-1	2-0	0-2	0-1	0-1	3-1	0-2	2-3	1-1	1-2	—	2-0
Osters	1-1	3-0	5-0	2-3	0-1	2-3	0-2	0-0	0-2	2-0	2-0	2-0	2-2	—

excellent displays to reach the semi-finals and eventually take third place.

The close season wasn't without controversy; Norrkoping fullback, the former Red Star Belgrade player Slobodan Marovic, quit the club after being refused a pay rise. The transfer market was also starting to bubble with Henrik Larsson's money-spinning move to Dutch Cup winners Feyenoord, following his 16 goals for Helsingborgs after their promotion from the Second Division South. While the cash will help and Larsson's move was almost inevitable, Helsingborgs faced a double blow when their other striker, Matts Magnusson, announced his retirement.

Sweden's Martin Dahlin falls under the tackling spell of Romania's Daniel Prodan during the World Cup quarter-finals.

Switzerland

As far as Swiss football was concerned, for most people there was only one talking point as the 1993–94 season drew to a remarkable close – the national side's qualification for the World Cup Finals for the first time in 28 years. A 4-0 win over Estonia in Zurich clinched a place in USA94, after a single-goal defeat by Portugal in Oporto and a 1-1 draw with Scotland had left Switzerland needing to win their final match to be sure. With neighbours Italy winning their last game against Portugal with a late goal, the Swiss had to be satisfied with second place in the group, having led the table for much of the qualifying period. Chapuisat's second goal against Estonia made him the Group's top scorer with six.

Roy Hodgson's side produced an impressive sequence of wins right up to their opening match in Detroit against the USA, beating fellow qualifiers Mexico 5-1 in California, before seeing off Hungary, the Czech Republic and not surprisingly Liechtenstein, with Sutter and ageing Bregy the stars of the show.

If the Swiss qualification was a surprise for most outside the country's borders then Servette's first championship since 1985 took most pundits by surprise inside them. After the first round of 22 games the Grasshopper Club and Sion had established themselves as the main contenders for the championship phase, taking 16 of their 31 points with them into the final round of 14 games. Young Boys lay third ahead of Servette whose 25 points were halved and rounded up to 13. The surprise 1993–94 champions, Aarau, only just made the cut into the championship round, finishing a point ahead of FC Zurich in eighth place.

Grasshopper, under the managership of 'bald eagle' Christian Gross, were the first team to qualify. Gross, whose only previous managerial experience had been in taking a minor provincial side all the way from the fourth to the first division, was better known as a player who had gained much of his experience abroad. Having lost talented players such as Sforza, Sutter and Kozle before the start of the season, Gross did well to build and gel together a well-organised unit at the Hardturm, opting for a blend of experience and youth from both home-grown and foreign talent. Much of that foreign talent came in the form of the Brazilian Elber, who having been sold to Milan returned on loan and scored vital goals.

At the other end of the table, FC Zurich, Neuchatel Xamax, Yverdon-Sports and Kriens dropped into the relegation group. Neuchatel Xamax's slump into the bottom four wasn't aided by the departure of manager Stielike at a crucial stage of the season after losing internationals Rothenbuler to Servette and Bovin to Sion. Stielike, Hodgson's predecessor as national team manager, was replaced by the former Republic of Ireland player Don Givens.

Grasshopper, looking for their 23rd championship, didn't make the best start to the final round of games, losing 1-2 at home to FC Aarau and allowing Sion to take over at the top after a 2-2 draw with Lucerne. Sion's lead lasted but a week, as they were held by Lugano, so Grasshopper's 3-2 win at Lausanne put them ahead on goal difference. Servette remained three points behind after a 1-1 result in Aarau but made up ground the following week, drawing to within a point of Sion by beating them 4-3 in Zurich having led 4-0. A second-minute goal by Sion's Brazilian, Marcio, defeated Grasshopper the following week and Servette's 3-0 win in Lausanne meant that now just one point separated the top three. Servette hit the top for the first time when another Brazilian, Sinval, secured points from Lugano, while Sion were held at home by Aarau and Grasshopper lost at Lucerne.

By this time the cup had reached the quarter-final stages, with Grasshopper and FC Zurich producing away wins to reach the semis, where they would face giant-killers Basel and Schaffhausen. Grasshopper's win gave them renewed confidence for their top-of-the-table clash with Servette, which was won 4-2 with the aid of a hat-trick by Elber. A late equaliser by Comisetti meant that Sion dropped a point at Lausanne, so Grasshopper regained the leadership and celebrated by beating Zurich in the semi-finals of the Swiss Cup. National League A side Schaffhausen beat Basel 6-5 on penalties after a goalless draw to set up a repeat of the 1988 Cup Final.

Matches between the top three continued to produced new leaders almost weekly but with two rounds of games to play Grasshopper missed the chance to make a decisive move ahead as Sion and Servette played out a 0-0 draw. Elber and the rest could find no way through a tough Young Boys defence. Sion's challenge fell away in the penultimate week when they lost at Lugano and Grasshopper, taking advantage of another Elber hat-trick to dispose of Lausanne, looked to be moving out in front – until a goal four minutes from time by Neuville gave Servette a priceless win over FC Aarau.

As the final games started Servette led Grasshopper on goal difference 12 to 11, with Grasshopper playing in Aarau and Servette playing Young Boys in Berne. Neuville was again the Servette hero, scoring three in their 4-1 win, and although Grasshopper came from behind they could only draw 1-1, so the championship was Servette's. There was some joy for

Association Suisse de Football

Founded:	1895
Address:	Worbstrasse 48, CH-3074 Muri
Phone:	+41 31 950 81 11
Fax:	+41 31 950 81 81
UEFA Affiliation:	1954
FIFA Affiliation:	1904
National Stadium:	Wankdorf, Bern
Capacity:	58,000
Season:	First round: July to December
	Championship round: February to May
Colours:	Red, White, Red
Change:	White, White, Red

International Results 1993–94

Date	Opponents	Result	Venue	Comp.	Scorers
11/8/93	Sweden	2-1	Boras	Friendly	Knup (18), Herr (73)
8/9/93	Scotland	1-1	Aberdeen	WCQ1	Bregy (69)
13/10/93	Portugal	0-1	Oporto	WCQ1	
17/11/93	Estonia	4-0	Zurich	WCQ1	Knup (32), Bregy (34), Ohrel (45), Chapuisat (61)
22/1/94	United States	1-1	Fullerton	Friendly	Fournier (64)
26/1/94	Mexico	5-1	Oakland, Ca.	Friendly	Subiat (7, 53), Grassi (65, 87), Bonvin (25)
9/3/94	Hungary	2-1	Budapest	Friendly	Sforza (10), Subiat (30)
20/4/94	Czech Republic	3-0	Zurich	Friendly	Chapuisat (12, 37), Bregy (28 pen)
27/5/94	Liechtenstein	2-0	Basel	Friendly	Herr (30), Hottiger (65)
11/6/94	Bolivia	0-0		Friendly	
18/6/94	United States	1-1	Detroit	WCFA	Bregy (39)
22/6/94	Romania	4-1	Detroit	WCFA	Sutter (16), Chapuisat (52), Knup (65, 72)
28/6/94	Colombia	0-2	Pasadena	WCFA	
2/7/94	Spain	0-3	Washington	WCF2	

National Record	P	W	D	L	F	A
European Championships	50	16	13	21	78	75
World Cup Finals	22	6	3	13	33	51
World Cup Qualifiers	70	28	18	24	95	92

Five-Year Records League 1-2-3 and Cup Winners

League Results

	1st	Pts	2nd	Pts	3rd	Pts
1990	Grasshopper Club	31	Lausanne	31	Neuchatel Xamax	30
1991	Grasshopper Club	33	Sion	29	Neuchatel Xamax	29
1992	Sion	33	Neuchatel. Xamax	31	Grasshopper Club	30
1993	FC Aarau	34	Young Boys	28	Lugano	27
1994	Servette	34	Grasshopper Club	33	Sion	31

One, Two, Three Records

1990	Grasshopper Club	2-1	Neuchatel Xamax
1991	Sion	3-2	Young Boys
1992	Lucerne	3-1	Lugano
1993	Lugano	4-1	Grasshopper Club
1994	Grasshopper Club	4-0	Schaffhausen

Grasshopper the following week, when they won the Swiss Cup by beating Schaffhausen 4-0, with goals from Bickel, Vega and two from Magnin. Sion finished third and Grasshopper's cup win meant that fourth-placed FC Aarau won a UEFA Cup spot alongside Sion.

In the relegation play-offs, Neuchatel Xamax and FC Zurich maintained their national division status and were joined by Basel and St Gallen at the expense of Kriens and Yverdon-Sports. Basel remained one of the best-supported sides, drawing over 42,000 for their match with Zurich. Most sides in the championship round struggled to reach 10,000 for even top clashes, and 5,000 was considered good.

FC Aarau needed little incentive to beat Omonia Nicosia in the preliminary round of the Champions' Cup knowing that Milan

Georges Bregy – Young Boys and Switzerland.

National Liga 1993–94

First Round

	P	W	D	L	F	A	Pts
Grasshopper Club	22	12	7	3	37	15	31
Sion	22	11	9	2	34	14	31
Young Boys	22	9	7	6	37	25	25
Servette	22	9	7	6	38	37	25
Lausanne	22	9	6	7	28	27	24
Lugano	22	7	8	7	23	27	22
Lucerne	22	8	5	9	26	32	21
FC Aarau	22	8	5	9	24	31	21
FC Zurich	22	6	8	8	25	22	20
Neuchatel Xamax	22	4	9	9	24	31	17
Yverdon-Sports	22	3	8	11	19	33	14
Kriens	22	3	7	12	17	38	13

Top eight clubs take half their points (rounded up) into the final championship round. Bottom four teams into play-off round, no points carried forward.

Championship Round

	P	W	D	L	F	A	Pts
Servette	14	8	5	1	29	14	34
Grasshopper Club	14	6	5	3	28	17	33
Sion	14	5	5	4	21	15	31
FC Aarau	14	7	4	3	23	16	29
Lugano	14	5	5	4	21	19	26
Young Boys	14	2	6	6	13	23	23
Lausanne	14	4	1	9	14	28	21
Lucerne	14	2	3	9	15	32	18

If teams level on points – position determined on First Round placing.

Promotion and Relegation Round

	P	W	D	L	F	A	Pts
Basel	14	7	6	1	22	7	20
St Gallen	14	8	4	2	28	14	20
Neuchatel Xamax	14	7	4	3	24	15	18
FC Zurich	14	7	4	3	24	15	18
Kriens	14	4	4	6	21	20	12
Etoile Carouge	14	3	5	6	14	24	11
Schaffhausen	14	2	3	9	14	31	7
Yverdon-Sports	14	1	2	11	8	29	4

Top Scorers

- 21 ELBER (Grasshopper Club)
- 17 Nestor SUBIAT (Lugano)
- 16 Oliver NEUVILLE (Servette)
- 15 Alexandre REY (Sion)
- 13 Adrian KUNZ (Young Boys)
- 12 SOGLIE (Lausanne)
- 11 ANDERSON Da Silva (Servette)

Promotions and Relegations

Promoted to NLA: Basel, St. Gallen, Neuchatel Xamax, FC Zurich
Relegated to NLB: Kriens, Etoile Carouge, Schaffhausen, Yverdon

Schweizercup Results

4th Round

Altstetten ZH v Chiasso	1-5
Baden v Locarno	3-1
Basel v Laussane	2-0
Bellinzona v Neuchatel Xamax	0-1
Chenois v Sion	7-5 on pens
Gossau v Grasshopper Club	0-1
Martigny Sports v Muensingen	5-2
SC Buempliz 78 v Old Boys	0-3
Solothurn v Lugano	1-3
SR Delemont v Monthey	3-0
St Gallen v FC Zurich	4-5 on pens
Stade Nyonnais v Grenchen	6-5 on pens
Suhr v Scaffhausen	0-2
Winterthur v Lucerne	0-1
Wyler v Servette	1-6
Yverdon Sports v Young Boys	2-1

5th Round

Basel v Neuchatel Xamax	1-0
Chenois v FC Zurich	1-3
Chissao v Servette	2-1
Lugano v Grasshopper Club	1-2
Martigny Sports v Old Boys	0-1
Scaffhausen v SR Delemont	5-4 on pens
Stade Nyonnais v Baden	10-11 on pens
Yverdon Sports v Lucerne	3-1

Quarter-Finals

Baden v Grasshopper Club	1-5
Basle v Yverdon Sports	1-0 †
Chissao v FC Zurich	0-1
Schaffhausen v Old Boys	3-1

Semi-Finals

Basle v Schaffhausen	0-0 (5-6 pens)
FC Zurich v Grasshopper Club	1-2

Final

Grasshopper Club v Schaffhausen 4-0
Bickel (5), Vega (35), Magnin (70, 75)

First Round

	Aarau	Grasshopper	Kriens	Lausanne Sports	Lucern	Lugano	Neuchatel Xamax	Servette	Sion	Young Boys	Yverdon-Sports	Zurich
Aarau	—	2-1	2-0	0-0	1-2	0-2	4-0	1-1	0-2	1-0	3-1	1-0
Grasshopper	1-1	—	1-1	4-1	2-0	2-0	5-1	1-0	1-1	3-3	3-1	2-0
Kriens	0-1	0-2	—	1-3	1-0	0-3	1-1	2-2	1-1	2-4	2-0	0-2
Lausanne Sports	2-0	2-1	2-1	—	0-2	1-2	2-0	2-3	1-1	2-1	0-0	0-0
Lucern	5-2	0-1	2-1	3-1	—	2-2	1-0	0-4	1-1	0-0	2-0	0-1
Lugano	1-3	0-3	0-0	0-0	1-0	—	2-2	1-1	2-0	0-2	2-1	2-2
Neuchatel Xamax	3-0	0-0	0-0	0-2	1-2	0-0	—	4-1	0-0	2-2	5-0	0-0
Servette	1-1	1-3	3-2	3-2	1-1	1-0	1-0	—	3-4	1-1	2-0	4-2
Sion	4-0	1-0	0-0	0-0	3-0	2-0	2-0	1-1	—	1-0	4-1	3-1
Young Boys	2-0	0-0	6-0	1-4	3-1	3-0	2-3	4-2	0-2	—	1-0	0-0
Yverdon-Sports	0-0	0-0	3-1	0-1	2-2	1-2	2-0	5-1	1-1	0-0	—	1-1
Zurich	3-1	0-1	0-1	4-0	4-0	1-1	2-2	0-1	1-0	1-2	0-0	—

Championship Round

	Aarau	Servette	Grasshopper	Lausanne Sports	Lucern	Lugano	Sion	Young Boys
Aarau	—	1-1	1-1	0-1	3-0	4-3	2-1	2-2
Grasshopper	1-2	4-2	—	3-0	3-0	3-3	3-1	4-0
Lausanne Sports	1-0	0-3	2-3	—	1-3	0-2	1-1	1-2
Lucern	1-3	2-4	3-1	2-1	—	1-3	2-2	0-0
Lugano	1-2	1-1	1-1	2-1	4-1	—	1-0	0-4
Servette	1-0	—	1-1	3-0	3-0	1-0	4-3	1-1
Sion	1-1	0-0	1-0	5-0	2-0	0-0	—	1-0
Young Boys	1-2	1-4	0-0	0-4	1-1	0-0	1-3	—

Promotion/Relegation Round

	Basel	Etoile Carouge	Kriens	Neuchatel Xamax	Schaffhausen	St Gallen	Yverdon-Sports	Zurich
Basel	—	0-0	1-0	3-1	3-0	3-0	1-1	1-1
Etoile Carouge	1-1	—	2-2	0-2	2-2	3-0	2-0	0-0
Kriens	0-1	3-0	—	0-0	5-0	1-1	2-0	1-2
Neuchatel Xamax	1-0	2-1	2-0	—	1-0	1-1	3-1	1-0
Schaffhausen	1-4	1-2	2-2	1-3	—	0-1	2-0	0-1
St Gallen	0-0	5-1	3-0	3-1	4-1	—	3-1	3-0
Yverdon-Sports	0-3	1-0	1-4	0-2	1-2	1-1	—	1-2
Zurich	1-1	5-0	5-1	2-1	2-2	1-3	2-0	—

awaited the winners in the first round. A late goal by Ratinho in the first leg in Cyprus gave them a vital away goal in a 2-1 defeat that was pulled around in the home leg for them to win through 3-2 on aggregate. If Milan had been expecting an easy ride, their trip across the Alps was a most uneasy one. Papin scored the only goal in Aarau early in the second half. That was the aggregate score, as the Swiss constantly frustrated Milan in the San Siro to earn a moral win, 0-0.

Lugano found themselves in a similar position in the Cup-Winners' Cup, knowing that Real Madrid awaited them if they could dispose of Belarus side Neman Grodno. A 6-2 aggregate win did that, three goals in each leg for Real put paid to any hopes of 'doing an Aarau,' and the Spanish side won 6-1 on aggregate.

Young Boys and Servette flew the flag in the UEFA Cup and having played out most of extra time in Glasgow, Young Boys looked to be heading to a penalty shoot-out until Baumann diverted the ball into his own goal to give Celtic a win. Servette had an easier time making light work of Crusaders, 4-0 on aggregate, before losing 3-1 to Bordeaux in the second round.

Thankfully for Swiss football Servette will be taking part in the UEFA Champions' League preliminary round. Swiss football's recent renaissance at national level helped move them up the ranking list to 22nd. That fact hopefully will help bring the fans back through the turnstiles and generate much-needed sponsorship monies. The game continues to be run on a shoestring.

Turkey

Home gala, European disaster

Three wins in their final three games ensured that Galatasaray retained their slender advantage over Fenerbahce at the top of the table to retain the championship title, but they were denied a second successive double as arch-rivals Besiktas twice came from behind to win the Turkish Cup. But it was a draining Champions' Cup, where the headlines were made, as Galatasaray qualified for the league stage after an ugly brawl with Manchester United, that showed the bitter-sweet side of Turkish football.

The season started with Galatasaray as double champions for the first time in five years having beaten Besiktas on goal difference and by the odd goal in a two-legged cup final – a victory that was greeted passionately by the club's faithful fans, who had seen the balance of power shift to the other side of town in a barren spell. Interest as ever at the start of the season was on the traditional influx of foreign players, and none drew more attention than Gala's signing of the Swiss international striker Kubilay Turkyilmaz from Bologna for a record fee. Fenerbahce were also in the news for recruiting German Holger Osiek as their new coach. He wasted no time in signing defender Andreas Wagenhaus from Dynamo Dresden. Sepp Piontek, the former national manager, signed Scandinavians Frank Pingel and Goran Sorloth for Bursaspor to boost the large contingent of foreigners in the Turkish league. Indeed as the season got under way only newly promoted Karabukspor could boast an all Turkish line-up.

Kocaelispor were the early leaders, taking 18 points from their first seven games. They lost by the odd goal in a nine-goal thriller at Galatasaray. This ironically handed the lead to Fenerbahce, who had inflicted Gala's first defeat of the season two weeks earlier. But with a third of the season gone Galatasaray moved to the top on goal difference with a game in hand by defeating Besiktas by a single goal while the other two pace-setters, Fenerbahce and Kocaelispor, played out a goalless draw.

This all followed on from events in Istanbul that made the

Turkiye Futbol Federasyonu

Founded:	1923
Address:	Konur Sokak 10, Kizilay, TR-Ankara
Phone:	+90 4 425 91 82
Fax:	+90 4 417 10 90
UEFA Affiliation:	1962
FIFA Affiliation:	1923
Season:	August to May
National Stadium:	Inonu Stadi, Ankara
Capacity:	30,000
Colours:	White and Red, White, Red and White
Change:	Red, White, Red and White

Final League Table 1993–94

	P	W	D	L	F	A	Pts
Galatasaray	30	22	4	4	67	28	70
Fenerbahce	30	21	6	3	69	26	69
Trabzonspor	30	17	8	5	67	28	59
Besiktas	30	16	6	8	58	30	54
Samsunspor	30	15	5	10	53	47	50
Kocaelispor	30	13	7	10	44	47	46
Genclerbirligi	30	13	5	12	51	51	44
Gaziantepspor	30	10	5	15	49	54	35
Bursaspor	30	9	8	13	26	39	35
Altay	30	8	8	14	33	45	32
Ankaragucu	30	8	8	14	39	52	32
Kayserispor	30	8	7	15	31	49	31
Zeytinburnuspor	30	8	6	16	33	51	30
Karabukspor	30	7	7	16	35	62	28
Karsiyaka	30	7	6	17	19	43	27
Sariyer	30	6	8	16	28	50	26

Top Scorers
22 BULENT (Fenerbahce)
20 SAFFET (Kocaelispor)
19 KONA (Genclerbirligi)
17 ERTUGRUL (Samsunspor)
16 HAKAN (Galatasaray)

Promotions and Relegations
Promoted: Adanademirspor, Antalyaspor, Petrolofisi, Vanspor, Denizlispor
Relegated: Karabukspor, Karsiyaka, Sariyer

news off the pitch. Goals by new-boy Turkyilmaz in both legs helped secure a 3-1 aggregate win over Cork City which was rewarded by a second-round draw against Manchester United. In the first leg United took a quick two-goal lead that was pulled back through Arif and Turkyilmaz. Another goal by Turkyilmaz put Gala into a sensational lead, and only a late goal by Cantona saved United from a home defeat. A war of words followed the match and the second leg took on an unsavoury air. It finished 0-0 and in ugly scenes as Gala qualified for the UEFA Champions' League.

In the Cup-Winners' Cup Besiktas finally won a European tie for only the second time in eight seasons, beating VSK Kosice 3-2 on aggregate, but only after their English manager, Gordon Milne, had resigned. Milne, having delivered the championship four times and the Cup twice, did not satisfy everyone and it was ironically his lack of success in Europe that was his downfall. The belated Euro success was short lived, though, for having taken the lead in Amsterdam against Ajax, Besiktas returned 1-2 down and lost 0-4 on the own soil to crash out again. A bad start for new

International Results 1993–94

Date	Opponents	Result	Venue	Comp.	Scorers
27/10/93	Poland	2-1	Istanbul	WCQ2	Sukur (53), Bulent (67)
10/11/93	Norway	2-1	Istanbul	WCQ2	Ertugrul (5, 26)
23/2/94	Czech Republic	1-4	Istanbul	Friendly	Ertugrul (5)
20/4/94	Russia	0-1	Bursa	Friendly	

National Record	P	W	D	L	F	A
European Championships	48	12	9	27	31	92
World Cup Finals	3	1	0	2	10	11
World Cup Qualifiers	64	15	7	42	61	125

manager Christoph Daum. Kocaelispor couldn't get past Sporting Lisbon in the first round of the UEFA Cup but Trabzonspor had little difficulty in disposing of Valletta 6-2. Then they were unlucky to lose out to Cagliari in the second round – a last-minute strike putting the Italians through on the away goals rule.

Injuries looked like playing a major role in Gala's attempts to retain the championship and make a worthwhile attempt on the Champions' League. Okan Buruk, a midfielder with great potential, lasted only ten minutes of a comeback match having supposedly recovered from a fractured leg. Turkyilmaz – a main source of goals – was ruled out for two months with a torn muscle, and Hakan was continually plagued with a shoulder injury. Despite this Gala still led the table by three points with two-thirds of the season gone, followed by Fenerbahce, for whom Bulent was finding the net with increased regularity. The Black Sea derby between Samsunspor and Trabzonspor had to be abandoned after home fans had attacked the referee. Trabzon were credited with a win after a Turkish FA investigation and Samsun had their ground closed for one game as punishment.

In the Champions' League Gala made a steady start with goalless draws at home to Barcelona and in Moscow to Spartak. After that, however, Gala failed to pick up another point, losing twice to Monaco and once to Barcelona before completing their sixth match with a 1-2 home defeat by Spartak. Cihat, goal four minutes from time was their first in the league stage of the competition.

With players looking tired, Gala lost 0-2 at home to Trabzonspor with eight games remaining. But the damage was limited as second-placed Fenerbahce had lost to Gala 1-2 the previous week, so a three-point gap was maintained. Gala reached the Cup final with a 3-2 aggregate win over Kocaelispor, who had slipped to fifth place in the league, and Besiktas triumphed 4-2 over Trabzonspor.

With three games to play Galatasaray's lead at the top was cut to a point when they surprisingly lost at Genclerbirligi, whose manager, Augusto Palacios, had resigned early in the season after

Turkish Championship Results 1993–94

	Altay	Ankaragucu	Besiktas	Bursaspor	Fenerbahce	Galatasaray	Gaziantepspor	Genclerbirligi	Karabukspor	Karsiyaka	Kayserispor	Kocaelispor	Samsunspor	Sariyer	Trabzonspor	Zeytinburnuspor
Altay	—	0-0	3-2	0-0	1-2	0-2	3-1	1-0	3-2	1-1	3-1	2-2	2-3	2-1	2-2	1-0
Ankaragucu	0-0	—	1-3	3-1	1-2	2-4	2-1	0-3	1-1	2-0	3-0	1-2	0-1	1-0	2-0	0-3
Besiktas	3-0	4-1	—	0-0	1-2	1-1	1-0	3-0	4-1	2-0	1-0	4-0	3-1	2-0	7-1	2-2
Bursaspor	0-1	3-2	0-0	—	0-0	2-1	1-0	4-3	0-4	0-0	2-0	2-3	0-0	1-2	0-0	2-0
Fenerbahce	3-2	4-3	2-1	2-0	—	2-0	4-2	5-0	4-1	1-0	0-0	0-0	8-1	3-1	1-1	4-0
Galatasaray	3-1	3-0	1-0	2-0	2-1	—	3-1	4-1	0-0	2-0	3-1	5-4	6-1	2-0	0-2	3-0
Gaziantepspor	1-0	1-3	2-1	3-0	0-2	3-4	—	3-1	2-2	1-2	4-0	2-4	1-1	3-1	1-1	1-0
Genclerbirligi	3-1	1-1	0-1	2-0	1-1	2-1	3-1	—	6-1	0-0	4-0	1-2	2-1	3-1	0-2	3-0
Karabukspor	2-1	2-2	2-1	1-2	2-3	0-0	2-2	1-2	—	1-0	0-1	2-1	0-3	3-1	0-2	1-2
Karsiyaka	1-0	1-2	0-1	1-2	0-4	0-3	4-1	0-1	0-0	—	1-0	0-0	0-2	1-2	1-0	1-4
Kayserispor	1-0	2-1	3-1	2-1	1-1	1-2	1-4	1-3	0-1	0-0	—	4-0	1-0	2-2	1-1	4-1
Kocaelispor	1-1	2-0	1-1	1-0	1-0	1-3	3-1	3-0	2-1	1-0	2-1	—	3-2	2-1	1-2	1-0
Samsunspor	2-0	3-1	0-0	4-0	2-0	1-1	1-2	2-2	5-1	1-2	5-2	3-2	—	0-0	0-3	2-0
Sariyer	1-0	1-1	0-3	1-1	2-5	0-2	1-1	2-1	3-1	2-0	0-0	0-0	1-3	—	0-1	1-0
Trabzonspor	4-1	1-1	4-2	1-1	0-1	1-2	3-1	6-0	6-0	5-0	3-1	2-0	4-0	4-2	—	5-0
Zeytinburnuspor	1-1	3-1	2-3	1-0	0-2	0-2	3-1	3-3	3-0	2-3	0-0	2-1	0-2	1-1	0-0	—

TURKEY

Five-Year Records League 1-2-3 and Cup Winners

League Results

	1st	Pts	2nd	Pts	3rd	Pts
1990	Besiktas	75	Fenerbahce	70	Trabzonspor	68
1991	Besiktas	69	Galatasaray	64	Trabzonspor	51
1992	Besiktas	76	Fenerbahce	71	Galatasaray	60
1993	Galatasaray	68	Besiktas	64	Kocaelispor	62
1994	Galatasaray	70	Fenerbahce	69	Trabzonspor	59

Cup Final Results

1990	Besiktas	2-0		Trabzonspor	
1991	Galatasaray	3-1		MKE Ankaragucu	
1992	Trabzonspor	0-3 5-1	Bursaspor		5-4 on agg
1993	Galatasaray	1-0 2-2	Besiktas		3-2 on agg
1994	Besiktas	0-0 3-2	Galatasaray		3-2 on agg

Turkish Cup Results

Quarter-Finals
Besiktas v Fenerbache	0-2
Kayserispor v Galatasaray	2-3
Kocaelispor v Samsunspor	4-3
Trabzonspor v Sariyer	7-0

Semi-Finals

	1st leg	2nd leg	Agg
Kocaelispor v Galatasaray	2-1	0-2	2-3
Besiktas v Trabzonspor	3-1	1-1	4-2

Final 1st Leg
Galatasaray 0 Besiktas 0
Att: 12,869

Final 2nd leg
Besiktas 3 Galatasaray 2
B. Metin (16), Madida (24) Hakan (12), Bulent (79)
Alpay (32)
Att: 23,400
Besiktas win 3-2 on aggregate

---

his first three games in charge had produced three defeats. Fenerbahce won their final three games, as did Gala, and goals from Hakan and mid-season Swedish import Roger Ljung enabled them to beat Bursaspor 2-0 on the final day of the season to take the championship.

Gala's win followed on from a derby defeat by Besiktas in the Turkish Cup final, which gave Daum a trophy after only half a season in charge. The club's fans, however, had to settle for what would be regarded as a disappointing fourth place in the league. Fenerbahce kept the runners-up spot, had the league's top scorer in Bulent, with 22 goals, and joined third-placed Trabzonspor in the UEFA Cup for 1994–95. Gala supporters ended the season wondering whether they would retain the services of German coach Rainer Holmann, who was not a popular person among the club's officials despite his achievement in his first full season in charge. Moves were afoot to tempt former coach Karl-Heinz Feldkamp back to Istanbul, but as the season went into hibernation Feldkamp remained adamant that the health reasons he cited for retiring remained prevalent.

With World Cup qualification hopes long gone, the final two Group Two fixtures were more about pride and blooding new players. Both produced 2-1 wins as Poland and Norway fell in Istanbul late in 1993 but home defeats against the Czech Republic and Russia in the early part of the year left Turkish international football in turmoil again.

Ukraine

Twenty-three wins and only one defeat from 34 games pretty much speak for themselves as Dynamo Kiev chalked up their second successive Ukrainian championship title to add to the 13 they won in the Supreme Soviet League. However, the season finished under a cloud for the famous old club, who face the threat of bankruptcy with heavy debts and lack the means to pay them off.

Internationally it was a disaster off the field – with no World Cup Finals position to play for the Ukraine found themselves losing many of their best players to the Russian national side, Kanchelskis, Onopko and Yuran the most notable. It was ironic that arguments in the Russian camp meant that many defecting players missed the Finals after all. Nevertheless national coach Oleg Basilevich has stated his intentions to look towards a mixture of home and foreign-based players to fuel Ukraine's European Championship efforts in a group that features Italy, Croatia, Lithuania, Estonia and Slovenia. Oleg Protasov (Olympiakos) and Alexander Zavarov (Nancy) have both expressed a willingness to play for their national side, while Genady Litovchenko's return from Austrian club side Admira Wacker to Kiev means that Basilevich has an excellent playmaker. Another Kiev player, Viktor Leonenko, popped up with two goals in as many minutes to ensure a winning start to the national season with a 2-1 win over the USA. Defeats by Mexico and Israel left room for thought but a 3-1 win over Belarus in Kiev ended the season on a more positive note.

Dynamo Kiev faced a daunting task in the first round of the Champions' Cup, where they played Barcelona. The 60,000 packed into the Republican Stadium for the first leg saw Ukrainian league leaders Kiev go ahead inside six minutes through Shkapenko. The first half brought another two goals – one for each side and both from the penalty spot – to leave the match 2-1 at the interval, with Kiev reduced to ten men after Mizin had been sent off. Even so, Leonenko made it 3-1 early in the second half to put Dynamo in a position of strength. A near capacity crowd turned out for the return in the Nou Camp and they witnessed a thrilling encounter. Barcelona went 2-0 up before Rebrov hit a thunderous drive past Zubizarreta to make it 2-1 on the night, but two second-half goals saw Barcelona through 5-4 on aggregate.

The generally low standard throughout the middle and lower reaches of the Ukraine league was never emphasised more than by Karpaty Lvov, who found Irish side Shelbourne too tough a nut to crack in the preliminary round of the Cup-Winners' Cup. Having won the first leg by the only goal of the game in Lvov, the

Final League Table 1993–94

	P	W	D	L	F	A	Pts
Dynamo Kiev	34	23	10	1	61	21	56
Shakhtyor Donetsk	34	20	9	5	64	32	49
Chernomorets Odessa	34	20	8	6	52	23	48
Dnepr Dnepropetrovsk	34	16	9	9	53	38	41
Karpaty Lvov	34	16	8	10	37	30	40
Krivbass	34	14	8	12	26	26	36
Niva Ternopol	34	13	10	11	44	26	36
Tavria Simferopol	34	13	10	11	43	35	36
Temp Sepetovca	34	12	8	14	39	38	32
Niva Vinita	34	12	8	14	37	45	32
Veres Rovno	34	10	12	12	32	36	32
Volyn Lutc	34	9	12	13	28	32	30
Torpedo Zaporozhje	34	9	10	15	27	39	28
Zarya Lugansk	34	10	6	18	24	46	26
Kremen Kremenchuk	34	9	8	17	26	39	26
Metallug Zaporozhje	34	9	6	19	26	49	24
Bucovina Cernovtsy	34	7	6	21	25	51	20
Metallist Kharkov	34	6	8	20	22	63	20

Top Scorers
18 Temerlain GUSEINOV (Chernomorets Odessa)
17 Oleg MATVEEV (Shakhtyor Donetsk)
15 Viktor LEONENKO (Dynamo Kiev)

Promotions and Relegations
Promoted: Evis Nikolaiev, Prikarpattia
Relegated: Bucovina Cernoutsy, Mettalist Kharkov

Football Federation of Ukraine

Founded:	1991
Address:	42 Kuybysheva Street, 252023 Kiev
Phone:	+7 044 220 13 44
Fax:	+7 044 220 12 94
UEFA Affiliation:	1993
FIFA Affiliation:	1992
National Stadium:	Republican
Capacity:	100,000
Colours:	Yellow, Blue, Yellow

Five–Year Records League 1-2-3 and Cup Winners

League Results

	1st	Pts	2nd	Pts	3rd	Pts
1993	Dynamo Kiev	44	Dnepr Dnepropetrovsk	44	Chernomorets Odessa	38
1994	Dynamo Kiev	56	Shakhtyor Donetsk	49	Chernomorets Odessa	48

Cup Final Results
1993 Dynamo Kiev   2-1   Karpaty Lvov
1994 Chernomorets Odessa 5-3   Tavria Simferopol after 0-0 draw

International Results 1993–94

Date	Opponents	Result	Venue	Comp.	Scorers
16/10/93	United States	2-1	N. Carolina	Friendly	Leonenko (41, 43)
20/10/93	Mexico	1-2	San Diego	Friendly	Litovtchenko (33)
23/10/93	United States	1-0	Pasadena	Friendly	Popov (36)
15/3/94	Israel	0-1	Haifa	Friendly	
25/5/94	Belarus	3-1	Kiev	Friendly	Leonenko (62), Bezhenar (65pen), Mikhailenko (82)
3/6/94	Bulgaria	1-1	Sofia	Friendly	Sak (55)

Ukrainian Cup

Semi-Finals	1st leg	2nd leg	Agg
Chernomorets Odessa v Karpaty Lvov	2-1	0-0	2-1
Veres Rovno v Tavria Simferopol	0-0	0-2	0-2

Final
Chernomorets Odessa v Tavria Simferopol 0-0 aet
5-3 on pens

Irish side stormed into a 3-0 lead in the return and a late goal by Masur made little difference to the outcome as Shelbourne went through 3-2 on aggregate. In the UEFA Cup, Dnepr won both legs to dispose of Admira Wacker 4-2 on aggregate but came unstuck against Eintracht Frankfurt in the second round. Dnepr trailed by 0-2 after the first leg and although a late goal by Yury Maximov ensured a 1-0 victory in Dnepropetrovsk, it wasn't enough to force extra time and the German side went through.

Domestically, Dynamo Kiev led the table when the winter break arrived, remaining unbeaten in their first 17 games. But the club had a shock as the season restarted, when coach Mikhail Fomenko resigned citing health reasons. Surprise elimination Rovno from the Ukraine Cup by second division side Veres Rovno might have been just a little too humiliating for the coach, who had seen his side lose only three times since he took over at the end of November 1992. The vacant position was given to Jozef Szabo, at least to the end of the season, as Dynamo continued to move onward. Their title was eventually secured with a comfortable seven-point margin from Shakhtyor, with Chernomorets taking third place.

Results from some of the provincial clubs were encouraging, showing that given the chance and the rub of the green that so often favours the bigger city clubs they can mix it with the best. A prime example of this was Veres, who finished bottom in the 1992–93 season and only retained their top division status as the league was being enlarged from 16 to 18 clubs. Although finishing just below the halfway point they had done well enough before the break to maintain a relatively high position along with the likes of Krivbas and Temp Sepetovca. Indeed it proved to be a season in which some of the former Soviet league sides struggled right through to the end, most notably Metallurg and Metallist, who won the Soviet cup in 1988.

The Ukraine Cup went to the shores of the Black Sea, with Chernomorets winning 5-2 on penalties after they had played out a goalless draw with Tavria Simferopol.

Wales

Reasons to remember

The Welsh season will be remembered for a variety of reasons – a missed penalty that probably would have secured a World Cup Finals place; a stray firework that lead to the death of a fan in the national stadium; and the managerial reign of John Toshack – the shortest in Welsh history. Added to this was the second season of the national League of Wales, which still lacks the top sides to make it truly national, and the considerable upset of Barry Town, winning the Welsh Cup to secure a place in Europe from outside the league.

The prognosis for the Welsh national side at the start of the 1993–94 season had been good. Qualification for the World Cup Finals for the first time since 1958 was a very real possibility, with games against two of the main contenders to be played in Cardiff. First up were the RCS, one of three other sides challenging for the two places, and a 2-2 draw favoured neither side. That didn't close the door but made two points from Cyprus in the next match imperative. Late goals by Saunders and Rush overcame the resolute Cypriot side, whose strong-arm tactics had them reduced to nine men before the end of the game.

When Romania arrived in Cardiff in November the Welsh knew that they needed to win by two clear goals; this later developed into a straight win as results elsewhere started to unfold. The omens were mixed. This was manager Terry Yorath's 100th match as player and manager, but the absence of Hughes through suspension was not helpful. After the Romanians had taken the lead, Saunders equalised and shortly afterwards the Welsh were awarded a penalty. Normal taker Rush declined the task of conversion and Bodin fired the ball against the bar. Welsh heads dropped and Raducioiu stole a late winning goal.

After the disappointment the national manager's post became the subject of debate, and Yorath's reign ended on 31 December. This was followed by the appointment of Toshack in a curious arrangement whereby he would take charge on a match-by-match basis while remaining as full-time manager of Spanish club side Real Sociedad, with former manager Mike Smith acting as his full-time assistant.

Toshack's first, and what turned out to be last, game in charge was against the Norwegians, who took advantage of a tactically confused Welsh team to win 3-1. The crowd vented their disappointment and shortly afterwards Toshack announced that he

The Football Association of Wales

Founded:	1876
Address:	Plymouth Chambers, 3 Westgate Street, Cardiff CF1 1DD
Phone:	+44 222 372 325
Fax:	+44 222 343 961
UEFA Affiliation:	1954
FIFA Affiliation:	1910-20, 1924-28, 1946
Season:	August to May
National Stadium:	Cardiff Arms Park
Capacity:	58,000
Colours:	Red, Red, Red
Change:	Yellow Yellow, Yellow

Final League Table 1993–94

	P	W	D	L	F	A	Pts
Bangor City	38	26	5	7	82	26	83
Inter Cardiff	38	26	3	9	97	44	81
Ton Pentre	38	21	8	9	62	37	71
Flint Town United	38	20	5	12	70	47	66
Holywell Town	38	18	10	10	74	57	64
Newtown	38	18	9	11	52	48	63
Connah's Quay	38	16	11	11	59	47	59
Cwmbran Town	38	16	9	13	51	46	57
Ebbw Vale	38	16	9	13	68	66	57
Aberystwyth	38	15	10	13	57	56	55
Porthmadog	38	14	7	17	90	71	49
Llanelli	38	14	4	20	76	100	46
Conwy United	38	13	6	19	55	70	45
Mold Alexandra	38	12	7	19	59	75	43
Haverfordwest	38	10	10	18	40	81	40
Afan Lido	38	8	15	15	52	66	39
Caersws	38	9	12	17	39	56	39
Llansantffraid	38	9	7	22	46	77	34
Maesteg Park	38	8	9	21	43	71	33
Briton Ferry Athletic	38	8	9	21	33	84	33

Top Scorers
42 Dave TAYLOR (Porthmadog)
23 Paul EVANS (Inter Cardiff)
22 Marc LLOYD-WILLIAMS (Porthmadog)
20 Neil DAVIES (Holywell Town)

Five-Year Records League 1-2-3 and Cup Winners

League Results

	1st	Pts	2nd	Pts	3rd	Pts
1993	Cwmbran Town	87	Inter Cardiff	83	Aberystwyth	78
1994	Bangor City	83	Inter Cardiff	81	Ton Pentre	71

Cup Final Results

1990	Hereford United	2-1	Wrexham
1991	Swansea City	2-0	Wrexham
1992	Cardiff City	1-0	Hednesford Town
1993	Cardiff City	5-0	Rhyl
1994	Barry Town	2-1	Cardiff City

Welsh FA Cup 1993–94

Quarter-Finals	1st Leg	2nd Leg	Agg
Bangor City v Inter Cardiff	1-1,	0-1	
Barry Town v Flint Town United	1-0		
Ebbw Vale v Cardiff City	1-1,	0-3	
Swansea City v Hereford United	1-0		
Semi-Finals (over 2 legs)			
Bangor City v Barry Town	1-1,	0-1	1-2
Swansea City v Cardiff City	2-1,	1-4	3-5
Final			
Barry Town v Cardiff City	2-1		

Barry Town celebrate with the Welsh Cup and look forward to European football!

would not be continuing in the post for reasons that have never really become clear. The job was eventually handed over to Mike Smith for his second spell in charge. He now prepares for the European Championships and games against Germany, Bulgaria, Georgia, Albania, and Moldova. As the finals are being staged in England there has never been a greater incentive to qualify, although the Germans and revitalised Bulgarians will prove difficult obstacles to surmount. Neville Southall became the most-capped Welsh footballer of all time, overtaking Peter Nicholas, as he won his 74th cap in Estonia.

The second League of Wales championship was won by Bangor Town on the very last day of the season and in somewhat controversial fashion from Inter Cardiff. As the penultimate weekend arrived Bangor led the table by two points but Inter had a superior goal difference. Bangor's nine-goal thrashing of Haverfordwest County kept the points margin and cancelled out Inter's goal advantage. The scoreline was no doubt influenced by County fielding a weakened side – a fact that led to threats by Inter to withdraw from the league. The hoo-ha was made irrelevant in the end, as Bangor won 2-0 at Porthmadog on the last day to maintain their lead. Inter Cardiff held second place to line up alongside Bangor in the UEFA Cup draw.

Wales' first and last representatives in the Champions' Cup for the foreseeable future were Cwmbran Town, who were drawn against Cork in the preliminary round. A capacity crowd of 8,000 saw them storm into a 3-0 lead inside the first half hour, with two goals from Ford after a penalty by King had given them a great start to their campaign. A late revival enabled Cork to pull the game back to 3-2, but Cwmbran travelled to Ireland vowing to restore their advantage. They did so when 36-year-old McNeil gave them the lead after just seven minutes, only for Cork to come back, score twice more and go through on away goals.

In the Cup-Winners' Cup, Cardiff City were involved in one of the most explosive ties of the first round. Paired with Standard Liege, Cardiff went 2-1 ahead in Belgium but eventually lost 5-2 on the night. An early goal in the second leg by the Belgians pretty much killed off any chances City thought they might have, and Liege won 3-1 on the night and 8-3 on aggregate.

Any hopes Cardiff might have had of restoring pride in the 1994–95 Cup-Winners' Cup were dashed when Barry Town beat them 2-1 in the final to lift the cup for the first time since 1955. The amateurs' 2-1 win over the professionals from the English second division was thoroughly deserved. Ex-Swansea players D'Auria and Hough got the goals.

International Results 1993–94

Date	Opponents	Result	Venue	Comp.	Scorers
8/9/93	RCS	2-2	Cardiff	WCQ4	Giggs (21), Rush (35)
13/10/93	Cyprus	2-0	Cardiff	WCQ4	Saunders (70), Rush (86)
17/11/93	Romania	1-2	Cardiff	WCQ4	Saunders (61)
9/3/94	Norway	1-3	Cardiff	Friendly	Coleman (89)
20/4/94	Sweden	0-2	Wrexham	Friendly	
23/5/94	Estonia	2-1	Tallinn	Friendly	Rush (77), Phillips (83)

National Record	P	W	D	L	F	A
European Championship	46	19	11	16	61	54
World Cup Finals	5	1	3	1	4	4
World Cup Qualifiers	62	21	11	30	80	84

Armenia

Football Federation of Armenia

Founded: 1992
Address: 9 Abovian Str, 375001 Erevan
Phone: +7 885 252 7014
Fax: +7 885 252 5616
UEFA Affiliation: 1992
FIFA Affiliation: 1992
National Staduim: Razdan Stadium, Erevan
Capacity: 70,000
Colours: Orange, Blue, Red

International Results 1993–94

Date	Opponents	Result	Venue	Comp.
15/5/94	USA	0-1	California	Friendly

National Record
European Championship — *Never participated*
World Cup Finals — *Never qualified*
World Cup Qualifiers — *Never participated*

Final League Table 1993

	P	W	D	L	F	A	Pts
Ararat Erevan	28	23	5	0	92	9	51
Chirak Gumri	28	24	1	3	101	20	49
Banants Abovian	28	23	2	3	111	21	48
Homenetmen	28	21	3	4	80	29	45
Van Erevan	28	15	2	11	71	49	32
Tsement Ararad	28	12	6	10	56	50	30
Homenmen Fima	28	12	2	14	54	43	26
Yerazank Erevan	28	11	3	14	44	55	25
Nayrit Erevan	28	8	4	16	29	61	20
Kanaz Erevan	28	8	4	16	37	75	20
Kotaik Abovian	28	9	1	18	57	76	19
Impouls Dilidjan	28	8	2	18	42	89	18
Zvarnots Etchm	28	6	4	18	42	79	16
Kassakh Achtarak	28	5	2	21	15	116	12
Malatia Cilicie	28	2	5	21	25	92	9

Top Scorers
26 HOUSEPAIN (Banants Abovian)
   HOUHANISIAN (Homenetmen)

Azerbaijan

The third domestic championship ended with the Turan club, from the small town of Tauz, clinching the national title, and Kapaz Ganja winning the Azerbaijan Cup. Ganja is the country's second largest city and the team are likely to provide a good number of players for the national side.

The Football Association of Azerbaijan – AFFA – were founded on 26 March 1992 and admitted as a full member of UEFA in 1994. The country will make their international debut in the Euro 96 qualifying competition, meeting France, Romania, Poland, Israel and Slovakia.

AFFA Azerbaijan

Founded: 1992
Address: St. H. Hadijev 42, Baku 3700009
Phone: +9 942 940542
Fax: +9 942 989393
UEFA Affiliation: 1994
FIFA Affiliation: 1994
Season: May to November
National Staduim: The Republic Stadium
Capacity: 37,000
Colours: Blue, Red, Green

National Playing Record

European Championship — *Never participated*
World Cup Finals — *Never qualified*
World Cup Qualifiers — *Never participated*

Belarus

The Football Association of the Republic of Belarus

Founded:	1946
Address:	8-2 Kyrov Str. 220600 Minsk
Phone:	+7-0172 27 23 25
Fax:	+7-0172 27 29 20
UEFA Affiliation:	1993
FIFA Affiliation:	1992
National Stadium:	Dinamo
Capacity:	51,000
Colours:	White and Red, White or Red, White or Red

International Results 1993–94

Date	Opponents	Result	Venue	Comp	Scorers
25/5/94	Ukraine	1-3	Kiev	Friendly	Belkevich (44)

National Record

European Championship	Never participated
World Cup Finals	Never qualified
World Cup Qualifiers	Never participated

Dinamo Minsk again proved that they were by far the best side in Belarus – not only winning their third successive championship title but completing the double with a 3-1 win over Fandok in the cup final. They won 24 out of their 30 games in the enlarged Belarussian League and suffered only two defeats on the way to their title. Second place went to Dinamo-93 who, having played under the name of Belarus Minsk the previous season, finished second by virtue of a 2-1 win over KIM in Vitebsk on the last day of the season.

With virtually no international activity to date, Belarus find themselves in Group Five of the European Championship Qualifying Groups and were due to visit Norway in early September. Wins over Malta and Luxembourg should not be too difficult but in a group also containing Holland, Norway and the Czech Republic the national side, who undoubtedly will be based around Dinamo Minsk players, will do well to stay in touch after the first round of games.

Belarussian sides made their debut in two of the three European club competitions during the season. Dinamo Minsk had of course represented the Soviet Union in Europe and reached the quarter-final stages of all three cups. Perhaps the lack of strong domestic opposition has weakened their resolve, and there was only going to be one winner when they were drawn to face German champions Werder Bremen in the first round of the Champions' Cup. A hat-trick by Bernd Hobsch and a brace for Wynton Rufer gave Werder a three-goal advantage over Dinamo Minsk, who had got the score back to 2-4 at one point with goals from Gerassimez and Velichko. In the return leg in Minsk, Byelkevich opened the scoring late in the first half before Rufer converted a second-half penalty to kill off any lingering thoughts Dinamo might have had of glory and give the Germans a 6-3 aggregate win.

Cup winners Neman Grodno fared no better in their European debut in the preliminary round of the Cup-Winners' Cup. They faced Swiss side FC Lugano, making their European return after an absence of some 20 years, and a goal by Brazilian Paulo Anddrioli set the scene for four in the second period, with Anddrioli again getting on the score sheet along with Nestor Subiat, Martin Fink and long-time club defender Daniele Penzavali. The second leg was little more than a formality that Neman won with goals from Sergei Solodobvnikov and Yuri Mazurchik, after Subiat had given Lugano a first-half lead.

Dinamo Minsk and Fandok are the country's 1994–95 representatives, with Dinamo playing their champion's role in the UEFA Cup.

Final League Table 1993–94

	P	W	D	L	F	A	Pts
Dinamo Minsk	30	24	4	2	76	20	52
Dinamo-93	30	18	7	5	46	16	43
KIM	30	17	9	4	32	14	43
Dnepr Moghiliov	30	17	6	7	45	22	40
Fandok	30	13	7	10	32	25	33
Torpedo Minsk	30	9	15	6	18	18	33
Sinnik	30	15	1	14	41	41	31
Molodecino Molodecino	30	10	11	9	35	31	31
Dinamo Brest	30	11	9	10	30	29	31
Lokomotiv Vitebsk	30	8	9	13	25	39	25
Neman Grodno	30	8	8	14	29	41	24
Sahtior	30	5	11	14	21	39	21
Vedrici	30	7	7	16	20	41	21
Torpedo Moghiliov	30	5	10	15	20	43	20
Gomselmas	30	7	5	18	36	47	19
Stroiteli	30	3	7	20	13	53	13

Top Scorer:
Piotr KACIURO (Dinamo-93 and Dinamo Minsk)

Three-Year Records League 1-2-3 and Cup Winners

League Results

	1st	Pts	2nd	Pts	3rd	Pts
1992	Dinamo Minsk					
1993	Dinamo Minsk	57	Kim Vitebsk	47	Belarus Minsk	46
1994	Dinamo Minsk	52	Dinamo-93	43	KIM	43

Cup Final Results

1993	Neman Grodno	2-1	Vedrich Rechista
1994	Dinamo Minsk	3-1	Fandok

Name changes: Dinamo-93 (Belarus Minsk)

FYR Macedonia

Former Yugoslav Republic of Macedonia

Phone:	+389 91 236434
Fax:	+389 91 235448
Founded:	1992
UEFA Affiliation:	1994
FIFA Affiliation:	1994

International Results 1993–94

Date	Opponents	Result	Venue	Comp.	Scorers
23/3/94	Slovenia	2-0	Skopje	Friendly	Micevski, Boskovski

National Record

European Championships	Never participated
World Cup Finals	Never qualified
World Cup Qualifiers	Never participated

Final League Table 1993

	P	W	D	L	F	A	Pts
Vardar Skopje	34	27	7	0	119	16	61
Sileks	34	17	6	11	73	50	40
Balkan	34	15	10	9	36	21	40
Pelister	34	14	8	12	47	36	36
Sasa	24	14	8	12	41	44	36
Sloga	34	13	8	13	46	37	34
Tikves	34	12	10	12	52	51	34
Osogovo	34	13	8	13	39	41	34
Rudar	34	15	4	15	33	47	34
Belasica	34	12	10	12	41	44	34
Pobeda	34	14	5	15	51	48	33
Borec	34	12	8	14	42	43	32
ECU	34	13	6	15	37	53	32
Macedonia	34	10	12	12	31	51	32
Metalurg	34	12	7	15	37	42	31
Bregalnica	34	11	8	15	38	45	30
Teteks	34	12	6	16	35	56	30
Vardarski	34	2	5	27	16	100	9

Cup Final
Vardar Skopje 1-0 Pelister

The first ever Macedonian league season didn't provide too many surprises. The league included two former Yugoslav national league sides along with a number from lower divisions. Vardar Skopje finished sixth in the 1991–92 Yugoslav season and in keeping with that status romped away with the Macedonian title. Unbeaten at home, they scored an amazing 119 goals en route. As the season drew to a close they completed the double, beating Pelister Bitolija in the final. It was Vardar's first cup success since they lifted the Yugoslav Cup in 1961. Pelister could finish only fourth despite being competitive in the Yugoslav national league, 15th in the 1991–92 season.

In their only international of the season Macedonia beat Slovenia by 2-0 in front of a 10,000 crowd in the Gradski stadium.

Georgia

Football Federation of Georgia

Address:	Shota Iamanidze Str 5, Tbilisi 380012
Phone:	+7 8832 96 08 20
Fax:	+49-5151 86 33
Founded:	1992
UEFA Affiliation:	1993
FIFA Affiliation:	1992
National Stadium:	Dinamo Stadium
Capacity:	75,000
Colours:	White, Black, Grey

International Results 1993–94

Date	Opponents	Result	Venue	Comp.	Scorers
8/2/94	Slovenia	0-1	Valetta	Malta Int.	
10/2/94	Malta	1-0	Valetta	Malta Int.	Ketsbaia
12/2/94	Tunisia	2-0	Valetta	Malta Int.	Kizilashvili, Kudunov
23/2/94	Israel	0-2	Tel Aviv	Friendly	
11/6/94	Nigeria	1-5		Friendly	Kezu (2)

National Record

European Championships	Never participated
World Cup Finals	Never qualified
World Cup Qualifiers	Never participated

Liechtenstein

Liechtensteiner Fussballverbund

Founded:	1933
Address:	Postfach 165, FL-9490 Vaduz
Phone:	+41 75 233 24 28
Fax:	+41 75 233 24 30
Formed:	1933
UEFA Affiliation:	1976
FIFA Affiliation:	1974
Colours:	Blue, Red, Blue
Change:	Yellow, Red, Yellow

International Results 1993–94

Date	Opponents	Result	Venue	Comp.	Scorers
26/10/93	Estonia	0-2	Balzers	Friendly	
21/04/94	N. Ireland	1-4	Belfast	ECQ6	Hasler (84)
27/05/94	Switzerland	0-2	Basel	Friendly	

National Record

	P	W	D	L	F	A
European Championships	1	0	0	1	1	4
World Cup Finals	*Never qualified*					
World Cup Qualifiers	*Never participated*					

The 1993–94 season marked the end of the first phase of the redevelopment of football in Liechtenstein as they made their competitive international debut in the European Championships. Although they were totally overwhelmed in Belfast by Northern Ireland, they managed to keep the score to a respectable level and celebrated a late consolation goal which clearly delighted the whole entourage of players, officials and supporters at Windsor Park. 'We don't have a chance of winning any of the games,' said national president Ernst Nigg. 'That's not a smokescreen – just a true assessment. Our national team haven't played many matches and we haven't won any of them.'

A two-goal defeat at home to Estonia in late October was the only other notice the European community had of the principality's efforts to gain a more regular say in footballing events. With a population of under 30,000 there are just 20 football pitches in 160 sq kms for the seven clubs, who support 1350 players. But Liechtenstein are currently moving ahead with a major redevelopment programme with funding from their own government, sponsorship and UEFA. All players in Liechtenstein are amateur and the clubs participate in the Swiss regional leagues, although some players – notably midfielder Roland Moser (FC Vaduz) and striker Mario Frick (FC Balzers) – are arousing interest from some of the leading German clubs.

Liechtenstein, the 142nd member of FIFA, were admitted to UEFA in 1976 but until recently little progress had been made either on or off the pitch. However, two years ago German-born Dietrich Weise, formerly with Eintracht Frankfurt and Kaiserslautern, was appointed coach and gradually things are changing. That appearance in the European Championship draw is just one step along the road in that process.

Things seem to be moving in European club competition as well. Liechtenstein's only representation comes through entry into the Cup-Winners' Cup and FC Balzers became the country's first club ever to progress through the opening round. That was achieved with a 3-1 home win over Albania's Albpetrol and a battling goalless draw in the return. Their reward was a trip to CSKA in Sofia, where they were thumped 8-0, but enjoyed the experience of playing in front of 35,000 – no mean achievement for a side who are used to playing crowds counted in tens and hundreds. The return was less emphatic, with a goal by Kuster for the home side in a 1-3 defeat. The 1994–95 season sees a European debut for FC Schaan in the Cup-Winners' Cup. Effectively a village side, FC Schaan beat favourites FC Balzers 3-0 in the final.

Regular training and team meetings help to produce the organisation that is certainly needed and for the international squad this is now held every Monday with players from the clubs of Valduz, FC Balzers, USV Eschen-Mauren, FC Triesenberg, FC Gams and FC Schaan. The man likely to be most active in the coming few years is goalkeeper Martin Oehry, who is with the Austrian side SV Frastanz.

Liechtenstein know that they are likely to be the whipping boys in a European Championship group that also contains Austria and Portugal, but every game is an experience and according to coach Weise: 'We have learned a lot'. And as the Faeroe Islands showed, even whipping boys can create the odd upset. Just ask Austria.

San Marino

Federazione Sanmarinese Gioco Calcio

Founded:	1931
Address:	Viale Campo dei Giudei 14, 47031 Rep. San Marino
Phone:	+39 549 90 05 15
Fax:	+39 549 90 23 48
UEFA Affiliation:	1988
FIFA Affiliation:	1988
Season:	October to June
National Stadium:	Olimpico, Seravalle
Capacity:	5,000
Colours:	Sky Blue, Sky Blue, Sky Blue

Final League Table 1993–94

Serie A1 Final Table 1993–94

	P	W	D	L	F	A	Pts
Tre Fiori	18	11	5	2	44	17	27
Faetano	18	9	6	3	19	15	24
Domagnano	18	8	6	4	25	12	22
Murata	18	7	6	5	23	23	20
Juvenes	18	7	4	7	21	17	18
Libertas	18	5	6	7	25	26	16
Cosmos	18	6	4	8	26	42	16
Cailungo	18	4	6	8	19	30	14
Folgore	18	3	6	9	14	24	12
Montevito	18	1	9	8	17	28	11

Serie A2 Final Table 1993–94

	P	W	D	L	F	A	Pts
La Fiorita	15	9	5	1	23	14	23
Virtus	15	9	3	3	30	14	21
San Giovanni	15	9	0	6	33	22	18
Tre Penne	15	5	1	9	21	22	11
Pennarossa	15	2	6	7	15	32	10
Dogana	15	2	3	10	18	36	7

Promotions and Relegations
Promoted: La Fiorita, Virtus
Relegated: Folgore, Montevito

San Marino Serie A1 Results

	Cailungo	Cosmos	Domagnano	Faetano	Folgore	Juvenes	Liberatas	Montevito	Murata	Tre Fiori
Cailungo	—	1-1	1-2	0-1	1-0	1-2	2-0	3-1	2-3	0-1
Cosmos	2-3	—	1-4	1-2	3-0	1-0	5-2	1-0	5-2	0-6
Domagnano	0-0	7-0	—	1-2	2-0	0-2	0-0	1-1	0-0	1-0
Faetano	1-0	3-2	1-0	—	0-2	0-0	0-0	2-1	0-0	2-1
Folgore	0-0	1-1	0-0	1-1	—	0-1	2-0	1-1	2-3	1-5
Juvenes	1-1	0-1	0-1	1-0	2-1	—	0-0	2-2	1-2	1-2
Liberatas	6-0	4-0	0-3	0-0	1-2	3-2	—	1-1	0-0	1-3
Montevito	1-1	1-1	1-1	1-2	2-1	0-3	1-3	—	2-3	1-1
Murata	1-1	1-1	0-1	2-0	1-0	1-3	1-2	1-0	—	1-2
Tre Fiori	7-3	5-0	3-1	1-1	0-0	1-0	4-2	0-0	1-1	—

International Results 1993–94

Date	Opponents	Result	Venue	Comp.	Scorers
22/9/93	Holland	0-7	Bologna	WCQ2	
17/11/93	England	1-7	Bologna	WCQ2	Gualtieri (9 seconds)

National Record

	P	W	D	L	F	A
European Championship	8	0	0	8	1	33
World Cup Finals	Never qualified					
World Cup Qualifiers	10	0	1	9	2	46

The 1993–94 season ended up being a carbon copy of the previous one as both the champions and cup holders retained the trophies that had won the year before. Tre Fiore, having won the Serie A1 by three points from Faetano, automatically qualified for the championship play-off semi-final. Faetano, Domagnano and Murata went into the play-off round where they were joined by Serie A2 winners La Fiorita.

The four qualifiers played on a semi-knock-out basis whereby a team were eliminated after they had lost two games. In the end, both Serie winners reached the championship final, which Tre Fiori won 2-0. Promotion and relegation take place on a two-up, two-down basis with the bottom two sides in Serie A1 swapping divisions with the top two in Serie A2.

In the Titano Cup, Tre Fiori, having qualified through the group phase, surprisingly lost their first two final round matches to be eliminated. In the end Faetano and Folgore reached the final and Faetano produced a 3-1 victory to retain the trophy and record what was also their second domestic cup win overall.

The international side's first exploits in the World Cup qualifying competition panned out as predicted, with six defeats from six games. There was however an upset in the match with England, as Davide Gualtieri etched his name in history by scoring the quickest goal ever recorded in international football. It came after just nine seconds of play against England in Bologna, a lead that they held for a further 20 minutes before Paul Ince produced the first of England's seven goals.

Titano Cup

Group A
Qualifiers: Libertas, Folgore
Group B
Qualifiers: Tre Fiori, Tre Penne
Group C
Qualifiers: Virtus, Faetano
Group D
Qualifiers: Cailungo, San Giovanni
Final Round
(Team eliminated after second defeat)

Cailungo v Virtus	4-2	
Tre Fiori v Libertas	1-2	
Faetano v San Giovanni	2-1	
Folgore v Tre Penne	1-4	
Virtus v Tre Fiori *	3-0	
Cailungo v Libertas	0-0	6-7 on pens
San Giovanni * v Folgore	1-2	
Faetano v Tre Penne	3-0	
Virtus v Tre Penne *	2-1	
Folgore v Cailungo	1-1	
Libertas v Faetano	0-0	1-4 on pens
Folgore v Virtus *	2-0	
Folgore v Virtus *	2-0	

Final
Faetano v Folgore   3-1

Championship Play-offs

Championship Play-offs

La Fiorita v Faetano	3-3 †	8-7 on pens
Domagnano v Murata	3-1	
Faetano v Murata *	3-1	
La Fiorita v Domagnano	1-2	
La Fiorita v Faetano *	2-1	
Domagnano v Tre Fiori	1-1 †	4-6 on pens
La Fiorita v Domagnano *	0-0 †	4-2 on pens

Championship Final
Tre Fiori v La Fiorita   2-0

† *after extra time*
* *eliminated team*

Yugoslavia

Yugoslav Football Association

Founded:	1919
Address:	PO Box 263, Terazije 35, 11000 Belgrade
Phone:	+38 11 33 42 53
Fax:	+38 11 33 34 33
UEFA Affiliation:	1954
FIFA Affiliation:	1919
Colours:	Blue, White, Red

Final League Table 1993–94

	P	W	D	L	F	A	Pts
Partizan Belgrade	18	13	3	2	47	10	42
Red Star Belgrade	18	12	2	4	40	18	37
Vojvodina	18	8	5	5	29	19	31
Spartak Subotica	18	6	5	7	22	26	24
OFK Belgrade	18	7	3	8	21	29	24
Zemun	18	6	3	9	19	25	23
Buducnost	18	7	2	9	21	33	23
Radnicki Belgrade	18	5	5	8	15	28	19
Proleter	18	4	3	11	8	28	18
Becej	18	1	11	2	22	81	7

Top Scorer
21   MILOSEVIC (Partizan Belgrade)

Cup Final   *agg*
Partizan Belgrade v Spartak Subotica   3-2   6-1   9-3

European Internationals and Finals 1993-94

Full Internationals 1993–94	340
World Cup Finals 1930–94	351
European Championship Finals 1960–92	353
Champions' Cup Finals 1956–94	354
Cup-Winners' Cup Finals 1961–94	357
Fairs Cup/UEFA Cup Finals 1958–94	360
World Club Championship 1960–93	365
European Super Cup Finals 1973–93	369

ROTHMANS PUBLICATIONS

Full Internationals 1993–94

The following pages contain details of international matches played by European nations during the 1993–94 season, with the exception of those in the World Cup qualifying rounds, the World Cup Finals and the European Championship. Full details of these games can be found in the respective sections of this annual.

August 1993

11 August Friendly Toftir Att: 850
FAEROE ISLANDS 0
NORWAY 7 (Bohinen 6 pen; Leonhardsen 9; Mjelde 27, 39; Ostenstad 74, 87; J. O. Pedersen 76)
Faeroes: Johannsen (Knudsen 46), J. Jakobsen, Oli Johannesen (Justinussen 33), K. Morkore, Dam, Jon Johannesen (Pall a Reynatugvu 23; Olsen 31), A. Hansen, Reyheim, Mohr (Rasmussen 53), A. Morkore, Arhge (Suni Fridi Johannesen 64)
Norway: Rossbach, Martinsen, T. Pedersen, Eggen, Brendesaetner, J. O. Pedersen, Leonhardsen, Mykland (Staurvik 48), Bohinen, Flo, Mjelde (Ostenstad 72)
Ref: Gerner (Den)

11 August Friendly Boras Att: 14,712
SWEDEN 1 (Dahlin 17)
SWITZERLAND 2 (Knup 18; Herr 73)
Sweden: Ravelli (L. Eriksson 46), R. Nilsson, Eriksson, P. Andersson, Ljung, Limpar, Rehn (Schwarz 73), Ingesson, Landberg, Zetterberg (Bertilsson 81), Dahlin
Switzerland: Pascolo, Ohrel, Herr, Geiger, Rothenbuhler, Sylvestre (Hottiger 77), Bregy, Sforza, Turkyilmaz (Grassi 70), Knup (Quentin 86), Chapuisat
Ref: Amendolia (Ita)

13 August Friendly Reykjavik Att: 3,700
ICELAND 0
UNITED STATES 1 (Stewart 87)
Iceland: B. Kristinsson, Birgisson, A. Marteinsson, Jonsson (P. Marteinsson 57), Dervir, Stefansson (Kristinsson 62), R. Kristinsson, Gretarsson, Bjarsson (Kolbeinsson 82), Dadason (Gudjohnsen (Sigurdsson 57)
United States: Friedel, Lalas, Armstrong, Lapper, Agoos, Dooley, Sorber, H. Perez (Chung 46), Henderson (Moore 87), C. Jones, Stewart
Ref: M. Elleray (Eng)

September 1993

8 September Friendly Oslo Att: 16,348
NORWAY 1 (Bjornebye 13)
UNITED STATES 0
Norway: Thorstvedt, Halle, Berg, T. Pedersen, Bjornebye, Flo, Leonhardsen, Rekdal, Bohinen, J. O. Pedersen (J. I. Jakobsen 46), Sorlorth (Fjortoft 46)
United States: Friedel, Armstrong, Lalas, Lapper, Agoos, Wynalda (Moore 71), Sorber, Dooley, Perez (Chung 65), Jones, Wegerle
Ref: Zen Ruffinen (Swi)

8 September Friendly Alicante Att: 28,000
SPAIN 2 (Guerrero 61, 89)
CHILE 0
Spain: Zubizarreta, Goikoetxea, Alkorta (Caminero 46), Hierro, Solozabal (Otero 46), Toni, Guardiola (Camarasa 46), Guerrero, Nadal, Claudio (Kiko 46), Salinas (Estebaranz 46)
Chile: Ramirez, Mendoza, J. Gonzalez, H. Gonzalez*, Richard Gonzalez (Ruiz 70), Salas, Lepe, Tupper, Guevara (Sierra 46), Estay, Carreno
**H. Gonzalez sent off 89 min*
Ref: Melo Pereira (Pol)

22 September Friendly Tunis Att: 43,000
TUNISIA 1 (F. Rouissi 61)
GERMANY 1 (Moller 55)
Tunisia: El Quaer, Thabet, Okbi, Taoufik, Nouira, Maaloul, Chihi (Trabelesi 87), L. Rouissi, Mahjoubi (Ordi 87), F. Rouissi, Sellimi
Germany: Illgner, Matthaus, Schulz, Kohler, Effenberg, Buchwald (Hobsch 80), Guardino, Bein, Ziege, Moller, Riedle (Kirsten 66)
Ref: Madjiba (Alg)

22 September Friendly Bucharest Att: 4,000
ROMANIA 1 (Panduru 49)
ISRAEL 0
Romania: Prunea, Cadar (Cristescu 71), Dobos, Pirvu (Bratianu 86), Panduru (C. Pana 77), Gilca, Stiunga, Dumitrescu, Moldovan (Popa 61), Adrian, Llie (Craioveanu 61)
Israel: Cohen (Ginzburg 46), A. Harazi, Klinger, Shelah, Glamm, Hazan (Elimeleh 88), Ravivo (Atar 64), Nimny, Levy (Schwartz 69), R. Harazi, Mizrahi (Berkovich 61)

October 1993

6 October Friendly Ryad Att: 15,000
SAUDI ARABIA 4 (Messad 23, 60; Idris 65; Mhallel)
RUSSIA 2 (Mostovoi 9, 72)

6 October Friendly Limassol Att: 500
CYPRUS 2 (Pitas 24; Iksioropas 71)
ISRAEL 2 (R. Harazi 36, 56)
Cyprus: Petrodis (Anossiporou 46), Ceralambos, Constantinou (Panaei 46), Costa, Jangidakis (Andreou 46), Fassoulitis (Cileia 46), Larco, Pitas, Selodios, Iksioropas (Rouagilopas 46), Sotiriou
Israel: Ginzburg (R. Cohen 46), A. Harazi, Klinger, Shelah, Halfon, Attar, Berkowitz (Glamm 46), Hazan, Nimny (Elimeleh 59), Rosenthal, R. Harazi
Ref: M. Louissos (Cyp)

13 October Friendly Brussels Att: 6,000
BELGIUM 2 (Wilmots 44, 87)
GABON 1 (Makaya 38)
Belgium: Preud'homme (De Wilde 49), Medved, De Boeck, Albert, Smidts (Genaux 46), Borkelmans (Van der Heyden 46), Van Meir, Boffin, Staelens, Czerniatynski, Wilmots
Gabon: Mendome, Nkouma (Koumba 35), Kassa-Ngoma, Ndong-nze, Amegasse, Ondo, Ndong, Aubame, Ogandaga (Mboungha Nze 64), Makaya (Ngoma 82), Nzamba
Ref: Kaupe (Aus)

13 October Friendly Karlsruhe Att: 29,000
GERMANY 5 (Buchwald 8; Moller*11, 88; Riedle 13; Kirsten 70)
URUGUAY 0
Germany: Kopke, Effenberg (Ritter 87), Ziege, Kohler, Helmer (Zonc 71), Buchwald, Moller, Hassler, Riedle (Kirsten 61), Matthaus, Klinsmann

Uruguay: Ferro, Jose Gonzalez (Bitancourt 46), Montero, Kanapkis, Romero, Ostolaza, Dos Santos (Albino 57), Poyet, Cabrera (Canobbio 62), Ferreri, Rodriguez
Germany's second goal was originally credited to Klinsmann but officially amended to Moller after the match
Ref: M. Grabber (Aus)

13 October Friendly   *Kranj*   *Att: 3,000*
SLOVENIA   **1**   (Pate 40)
YUGOSLAVIA/MACEDONIA   **4**   (Boskovski 4; Pancev 37 pen; Jenevski 48 pen; Kanatlarovski 55)
Slovenia: Simeunovic (Zupan), Zidan (Jarmanic), Novak, Milanic, Blatnik, Poljaak (Englaro), Ceh, Zulic (Pate), Zahovic, Udovic (Gliha), Florjancic
Yugoslavia/Macedonia: Miskovski, Grozdanov (Madjimedov), Jovanovski, Najdoski, Kanatlarovski, Janevski, Boskovski, Markovski, Babunski (Milosevski), Pancev, Mincevski
Ref: Poljak (Cro)

16 October Friendly   *High Point, N. Carolina*   *Att: 4,298*
UNITED STATES   **1**   (Perez 26)
UKRAINE   **2**   (Leonenko 41, 43)
United States: Meola, Armstrong, Lapper, Caligiuri, Clavijo, Dooley, Quinn, Michallik, Kinnear (Washington 62), Perez (Chung 46), Vermes
Ukraine: Koutepov (Bolkei 75), Homin, Vasilichuk, Leyentsev, Popov, Sak, Shkapenko, Yabchendo, Litovchenko (Prudius 46), Khusainov (Rebrov 46), Leonenko

17 October Friendly   *Tunis*   *Att: 15,000*
TUNISIA   **3**   (El Okbi 7, 60; Ben Tahar 86)
ICELAND   **1**   (Brousson 28)
Tunisia: El Quaer, Thabet, Nouira, Mahjoubi, Okbi, Gharbi (Sdri 85), Boukadida, Chihi (Medjoub 65), Maalaoui, Hamrouni (Ben Tahar 65), A. Sellimi
Iceland: Fridriksson (Finn Bogas 57), Martinsson, Gislasson (Kristiansson 59), Bergsson, Dervir, Gretarsson, Jonsson, Petersson, Kristinsson (Danielsson 87), Gollsson (Gudlaugsson 46), Gretarsson (Sigurvinsson 87)
Ref: Sendid (Alg)

20 October Friendly   *San Diego, California*   *Att: 58,892*
MEXICO   **2**   (Salvador 14; Galindo 35)
UKRAINE   **1**   (Litovchenko 33)
Mexico: Campos, Bernal, Ambriz (Guitierrez 69), Castaneda, Espinoza, Galindo (Garcia Aspe 46), Rodriguez, Ayala, Del Olmo (Patino 81), Alves Zague (Guzman 65), Salvador
Ukraine: Koutepov, Sak (Toptchiev 78), Kohmine (Proudious 69), Lejentev, Popov, Jabtchenko (Boukel 63), Leonenko, Litovchenko, Vassilichouk

23 October Friendly   *Bethlehem, Pennsylvania*   *Att: 7,896*
UNITED STATES   **0**
UKRAINE   **1**   (Popov 36)
United States: Friedel, Armstrong, Lapper, Agoos, Lalas, Dooley, Santel (Washington 46), Sorber, Moore, Perez (Chung 74), Jones
Ukraine: Kutepov, Sak, Khomin, Leyentseu (Bukel 46), Popov, Prudius (Yabchenko 46), Shkapenko, Topchiev, Rebrov (Prizetko 70), Leonenko, Litovchenko (Vasilicholk 88)
Ref: D'Aquila (US)

26 October Friendly   *Balzers*   *Att: 1,200*
LIECHTENSTEIN   **0**
ESTONIA   **2**
Liechtenstein: Oegry, Moser, Telser, C. Frick, Stocker, Quaderer (Klaunzer 66), Ospelt, Ritter, Hefti, M. Frick, Zech (Beck 21; Hasler 66)
Estonia: Poom, Kaljend, Lemsalu (Bragin 46), Prins, R. Kalleste, Borrisow, Olumets (Ratnikov 74), T. Kalleste, Klavan (Zamorski 46), Reim, Rajala
Ref: Grabher (Aus)

November 1993

5 November Friendly   *Tunis*
EGYPT   **3**   (H. Hassan 21; Abdeljelil 71; Kashaba 90)
MALTA   **0**

7 November Friendly   *Tunis*   *Att: 1,000*
MALTA   **2**   (Brincat 11; Busuttil 37)
GABON   **1**   (Ndong Nze 84)
Malta: Cluett, Vella, Buhagiar (Agius), Galea, Brincat, Buttigieg, Busuttil, Spiteri, Suda (S. Aliba), Laferla, Gregory
Gabon: Deckoussoud, Ndong, Amegasse, Koumba, Kassa Ngoma, Kassa, Ndong Nze, Ondo, Manon, Ogandaga, Makaya

17 November Friendly   *Koln*   *Att: 51,000*
GERMANY   **2**   (Buchwald 37; Moller 40)
BRAZIL   **1**   (Evair 39)
Germany: Illgner, Effenberg, Brehme, Kohler, Helmer, Buchwald, Moller, Hassler, Riedle (Kristen 32), Matthaus, Klinsmann (Gaudino 86)
Brazil: Ronaldo, Jorginho, Marcio Santos (Mozer 46), Ricardo Gomes, Dunga, Branco, Edmundo, Zinho, Envair (Edilson 66), Rai (Valber 66), Paulo Sergio
Ref: Damgaard (Den)

December 1993

15 December Friendly   *Miami*   *Att: 33,000*
ARGENTINA   **2**   (Hernan Diaz 5; Balbo 64)
GERMANY   **1**   (Moller 8)
Argentina: Goycochea, Vazquez (Jorge Borelli 86), MacAllister, Ruggeri, Hernan Diaz, Mancuso, Perez, Cagna, Rodriguez (Monserrat 88), Medina Bello (Ortega 90), Balbo
Germany: Kopke, Brehme, Kohler, Helmer, Buchwald, Matthaus, Moller (Sammer 70), Hassler, Effenberg, Klinsmann (Thom 68), Kirsten
Ref: Don (Eng)

18 December Friendly   *Palo Alto*   *Att: 52,397*
UNITED STATES   **0**
GERMANY   **3**   (Moller 16; Kuntz 79; Thom 89)
United States: Friedel, Armstrong, Lapper, Lalas, Agoos (Bliss 60), Sorber, Dooley, Moore (Kinnear 71), Jones, Perez (Deering 46), Stewart
Germany: Illgner, Matthaus, Kohler, Sammer 46, Eilts, Effenberg, Hassler (Strunz 75), Buchwald, Brehme (Ziege 46), Moller, Klinsmann (Thom 63), Kuntz
Ref: Pedersen (Nor)

22 December Friendly   *Mexico City*   *Att: 114,000*
MEXICO   **0**
GERMANY   **0**
Mexico: Campos, Rodriguez, Ramirez Perales, Ambriz, Ramon Ramirez (Castaneda 79), Bernal, Garcia Aspe (Herrera 46), Del Olmo, Luis Garcia, Zague Alves, Patino (Galindo 46)
Germany: Illgner, Kohler, Matthaus, Schulz, Effenberg (Eilts 78), Guadino (Hassler 53), Sammer, Strunz, Ziege (Kuntz 64), Klinsmann (Kirsten 70), Moller
Ref: Sawtell (Can)

January 1994

15 January Friendly   *Arizona*   *Att: 15,386*
UNITED STATES   **2**   (Balboa 55; Jones 89)
NORWAY   **1**   (Strandli 44)
United States: Meola, Armstrong (Balboa 37), Lapper, Agoos (Burns 72), Lalas, Sorber, (Clavijo 81), Dooley, Henderson (Brose 46), Jones, Kinnear (Reyna 61), Moore
Norway: Grodas, H. Berg, R. Johnsen, T. Pedersen, Nilsen, Flo (J. O. Pedersen 58), Mykland (Bohinen 67), Leonhardsen, Rekdal (Runar Berg 84), Frigard, Strandli
Ref: Salas (Mex)

19 January Friendly San Diego Att: 56,222
COSTA RICA **0**
NORWAY **0**
Costa Rica: Cubillo (Barrantes 71), Chaves, Joseph, Marchena, Gomez (Jaikel 35), Jara, Obando, Solis, Astua (Soto 74), Chavarria (Rothe 86), Gutrie (Castro 50)
Norway: Thorstvedt, Haaland, R. Nilsen, T. Pedersen, Bohinen, Brandesaeper (R. Johnsen 23), Mykland, Rekdal (Runar Berg 27), Frigard, Starvik, J. O. Pedersen
Ref: Angeles (USA)

19 January Friendly Vigo Att: 32,000
SPAIN **2** (Salinas 43; Juanele Castano 77)
PORTUGAL **2** (Juan Lopez own goal 73; Oceano 83 pen)
Spain: Zubizarreta, Otero, Alkorta, Voro (Lopez 46), Larrainza, Felipe, Nadal (Hierro 46), Guerrero, Camarasa, Fran (Juanele 46), Salinas (Luis Enrique 46)
Portugal: Vitor Baia (Neno 46), Joao D. S. Pinto (Veloso 46), Fernando Couto, Paulo Sousa (Paulinho Santos 46), Vitor Paneira, Oceano, Rui Costa, Semedo (Figo 54), Nogueira, Rui Barros, Joao M.V. Pinto (Domingos 54)
Ref: Baldas (Ita)

19 January Friendly Tunis Att: 40,000
TUNISIA **2** (Fawzi Rouissi 11; Ayadi Hamrouni 50)
HOLLAND **2** (Rijkaard 31; R. Koeman 55)
Tunisia: El Ouaer, Thabet, Hichri, Okbi, Samir Sellimi, Gharbi (Souayeh 74), Maaloul, Ali Mahjoubi, Bouzaiane, Adel Sellimi (Hamrouni 46), Rouissi (Liman 68)
Holland: De Goey, Blind (Winter 32), R. Koeman, F. De Boer, Rijkaard, Wouters (Jonk 46), Bergkamp (E. Koeman 82), Numan, Overmars (Gillhaus 59), R. De Boer, Blinker
Ref: Hadaki (Mor)

22 January Friendly California Att: 10,173
UNITED STATES **1** (Egli own goal 88)
SWITZERLAND **1** (Fournier 64)
United States: Friedel, Armstrong, Lapper (Balboa 46), Lalas, Caligiuri, Sorber (Burns 46), Dooley, Michallik (Brose 55), Jones, Perez (Reyna 46), Moore (Vermes 77)
Switzerland: Lehmann, Rueda (Geiger 84), Egli, Studer, Quentin, Sylvestre (Hottiger 67), Bickel, Wyss, Fournier (Bonvin 72), Grassi (Subiat 4), B. Sutter
Ref: Badilla (Costa Rica)

26 January Friendly California Att: 23,000
MEXICO **1** (Duran 31)
SWITZERLAND **5** (Subiat 7, 53; Grassi 65, 87; Bonvin 25)
Mexico: Chavez, Espana, Suarez, Dios Ramirez, Patino (Herrera 71), Marcelino, Ambriz, Rodriguez, Ramon Ramirez (Del Olmo 57), Hermosillo, Duran (Garcia Aspe 46)
Switzerland: Pascolo, Hottiger, Herr (Vega 80), Geiger, Quentin (Studer 83), Ohrel (Sylvestre 85), Bregy (Wyss 66), Bickel, Bonvin (Fournier 75), Subiat, Grassi
Ref: Baharmast (US)

29 January Friendly Seattle, USA Att: 43,651
UNITED STATES **1** (Lalas 85)
RUSSIA **1** (Radchenko 52)
United States: Meola, Armstrong, Lapper, Lalas, Agoos, Burns, Dooley (Quinn 70), Henderson, Jones (Chung 83), Kinnear, Moore (Reyna 60)
Russia: Khapov, Gorlukovich, Galiamin, Popov, D. Kuznetsov (Chernishev 74), Tetradze, Tatarchuk (Tadeyev 57), Korneyev (Rashimov), Salenko, Borodiuk, Radchenko
Ref: Sawtell (Canada)

February 1994

2 February De Charjah Tournament Sharjah, UAE Att: 5,000
UNITED ARAB EMIRATES **0**
SLOVAKIA **1** (Weiss 47)
United Arab Emirates: Mousaba, Sallah, Ismail, Al-Hadid, Mir, Naser, Abdelkhalek (Bakhit 46), Hamdun (Matar 64), Galum (Jaher 85), Al-Taliani, Atik (Azoz 46)
Slovakia: Vencel, Stupala, Moravec, Hipp, Kinder, O. Danko, Tomaschek, Hyravy, Weiss, Timko, Faktor (Zvara 75)

2 February Friendly Oakland, USA
RUSSIA **4** (Borodjuk 4, 45, 55; Radtchenko 37)
MEXICO **1** (Garcia Aspe 25 pen)
Russia: Khapov, Gorlukovich, Galjamine, Tetradze, D. Popov (Podpaly), D. Kuznetsov, Korneyev, Tadeyev (Cheryshev), Boroduk, Salenko, Radchenko (Tatarchuk)
Mexico: Campos, Suarez, Ramiez Perates, Ambriz, Ramon Ramirez (Espana), Bernal, Rodriguez (Patino), Garcia Aspe (Herrera), Salvador, Del Olmo, Duran

2 February Dunhill Cup Kuala Lumpur
NORWAY **3** (Petter 11, 49; Undheim 54)
DENMARK **3** (Tengbjerg 78; Pedersen 80; Falch 85)

4 February De Charjah Tournament Sharjah, UAE
EGYPT **1** (Hossam Hassan 75)
SLOVAKIA **0**
Egypt: Shoubeir, Mansour, Ramzy, Hamza, Youssef (Ashrav 46), Ibrahim Hassan, Abdel Galil, El Shour, El Bechir (Rayan 60), El Kas (Chadour 77), Hossam Hassan
Slovakia: L. Molnar, Stupala, Moravec, Hipp, Kinder, Hyravy, Tomaschek, Malatinski (Obaitnik 61), Solar, Timko, Zvara (Dina 61)

4 February Dunhill Cup Kuala Lumpur
NORWAY **3** (Stakkeland 9; T. Larsen 64; Flo 73)
JAPAN **2** (Matsubara 48; Takade 90)

4 February Dunhill Cup Kuala Lumpur
MALAYSIA **1** (Chong 26)
DENMARK **5** (D. Povlsen 19, 23; Pedersen 28, 44; Sommer 72)

6 February Dunhill Cup Kuala Lumpur
DENMARK **6** (Urik Pederson 6, 18; D. Poulsen 16; J. Tengbjerg 48, 88; M. Bisgaard 70)
JAPAN **1** (Matsubara 24)

6 February Dunhill Cup Kuala Lumpur
NORWAY **2** (T. Larsen 17; Rune Stakkeland 21)
MALAYSIA **0**

6 February De Charjah Tournament Sharjah, UAE Att: 8,000
MOROCCO **2** (Fertout 23; El-Hadrioui 87)
SLOVAKIA **1** (Faktor 27)
Morocco: Amzi, Mouidi, El Graoui, Nekroaz, Abdallah (El Hadrioui 46), Lakhlaj (Fradin 73), Azzouzi, Daoudi, El Ouali (Boublal 60), Boyyboud, Fertout
Slovakia: Vencel, Stupala, Vidumsky, Hipp, Solar, Kinder 85), Weiss, Tomaschek, Obaitnik, O. Danko, Faktor (Timko 75), Dina (Malatinsky 65)
(Final Placing: 1. Egypt 5pts; 2. Morocco 4pts; 3. Slovakia 3pts; 4. UAE 2pts.)

8 February Malta International Tournament A Ta'Qali
SLOVENIA **1** (Chelia)
GEORGIA **0**

8 February Malta International Tournament A Ta'Qali
MALTA **1** (S. Vella)
TUNISIA **1** (Suujah)

9 February Friendly Tenerife Att: 23,600
SPAIN **1** (Sergi 19)
POLAND **1** (Kosecki 37)
Spain: Zubizarreta, Sergi, Alkorta, Abelardo, Otero, Hierro (Camarasa 46), Chano, Nadal (Guardiola 46), Salinas (Juanele 46), Fran (Beguiristain 46), Felipe
Poland: Wozniak, Grembocki, Lapinski, Bak (Staniek 46), Jebor, Lewandowski (Czerwiec 76), Brzeczek, J. Jalocha (Jaskulski 71), Kuskowiak (Ballusynski 62), Kosecki, Kowalczyk
Ref: Bodenham (Eng)

FULL INTERNATIONALS 1993–94

10 February Carlsberg Cup, Semi-Final Hong Kong Att: 8,600
DENMARK 0 *Denmark won 4-2 on pens*
UNITED STATES 0
Denmark: Brodersen, Bruun, Dethlefsen, Ekelund, Fernandez (Moller 88), Hogh, B. Jensen, J. Kristensen, Krogh, Rieper, Thomsen
United States: Friedel, Lapper, Burns, Dooley (Perez 46), Moore (Quinn 46), Jones (Reyna 86), Lalas, Henderson, Kinnear, Armstrong
Ref: Cheung Kai-ming (HK)

10 February Carlsberg Cup, Semi-Final Hong Kong Att: 8,600
HONG KONG 1 (Tempest 77)
 Hong Kong won 5-4 on pens
ROMANIA 1 (Dumitrescu 63)
Hong Kong: McKnight, Manley, Ku Kam-fai, Berry, Harvey, Tempest, Cheung Chi-tak, Nang Cheun-chung, Fairweather (Matthews 67), Bajkusa, Crabo (Clarkson 75)
Romania: Prunea, Kadar (Zontica 46), Tanase, Mihali, Prodan, Galca, Grozavu, Panduru, Dumitrescu, Niculescu (Craioveanu 75), I. Stan
Ref: Nang Yimkim (HK)

10 February Malta International Tournament A Ta'Qali
MALTA 0
GEORGIA 1 (Ketsbaia)
Malta: Cluett, Buhagiar (Saliba 33), Cauchi (Galea 46), Brincat, Camilleri, Buttigieg, Gregory, S. Vella, Laferla, Scerri, Spiteri (Cardona 18)
Georgia: Zoiuze, Revichvilli, Tskhadadze, Koudinov (Sidamonidze 56), Chelia (Beradze 75), Kazelachvili, Nemsadze, Jamazauli, Kinkladze, Ketsbaia, Kizilachvilli
Ref: Darko (Slo)

10 February Malta International Tournament A Ta'Qali
SLOVENIA 2 (Jarmanic, Binkovsic)
TUNISIA 2 (Hamrouni, Soussi)
Slovenia: Boskovic, Galic, Cifer, Englaro, Polsjak, Katanec, Jermanis (Binkovski 46), Pate (Zulic 54), Zahovic (Rudonja 69), Florjancic, Gliha
Tunisia: El Quaer, Thabet, Mahjoubi, Souissi, Boukadida, Mizouri, Chihi, Hamrouni, S. Sellimi (Majdoub 74), A. Sellimi, Souyah (Limam 44)
Ref: Milallef (Mal)

12 February Malta International Tournament A Ta'Qali
GEORGIA 2 (Kizilashvili, Kudunov)
TUNISIA 0

12 February Malta International Tournament A Ta'Qali
MALTA 0
SLOVENIA 1 (Gliha 54)
Malta: Cluett, S. Vella, Galea, Brincat (Spiteri 46), Camilleri, Buttigieg (Agius 66), Gregory, Saliba, Suda, Scerri, Laferla
Slovenia: Simeunovic, Galic, Krizan, Cifer, Polsjak, Katanec (Zulic 46), Binkovski, Zidan, Zahovic, Rudonja, V. Molosevic (Gliha 46)
Ref: Bellaghia (Tunisia)
(Final Placings: 1. Slovenia 5pts; 2. Georgia 4pts; 3. Tunisia 2pts; 4. Malta 1pt.)

13 February Carlsberg Cup, 3rd place play-off Hong Kong Att: 9,000
ROMANIA 2 (Dumitrescu 6, 72 pen)
UNITED STATES 1 (Balboa 14)
Romania: Prunea, Kadar, Mihali, Gilca, Grozavu, Zotinca (Stan 89), Dumitrescu (Craioveanu 84), Panduru, Prodan, Papura, Niculescu
United States: Meola, Balboa, Lapper, Armstrong, Lalas, Dooley (Quinn 66), Burns, Henderson, Jones, Perez, Moore (Michallik 51)
Ref: Pang Cham Kai (HK)

13 February Carlsberg Cup, Final Hong Kong Att: 9,000
HONG KONG 0
DENMARK 2 (J. Kristensen, H. Fernandez)
Hong Kong: McKnight, Manley, Ku Kam-fai, Berry, Harvey (McPaland 70), Tempest, Clarkson, Cheung Chi-tak, Nang Cheun-chung, Bajkusa (Matthews 39), Crabo (Fairweather 54)

Denmark: Krogh, Hogh, Rieper, Brunn, Dethlesfen, Ekelund, Jensen, J. Kristensen (Nielsen 76), Thomsen, H. Hernandez, Frederiksen (Johansen 83)
Ref: Cheung Kai-ming (HK)

16 February Friendly Naples Att: 17,241
ITALY 0
FRANCE 1 (Djorkaeff 44)
Italy: Pagliuca, Benarrivo, Maldini, Eranio, Costacurta, Baresi (Minotti 65), Evani, Albertini, Casiraghi (Silenzi 46), R. Baggio, Stroppa (Cappioli 65)
France: Lama, Karembeu (Cyprien 73), Di Meco, Roche, Desailly (Martins 89), Le Guen, Cantona, Gnako (Guerin 53), Ginola, Djorkaeff, Deschamps
Ref: Merk (Ger)

16 February Friendly Ta'Qali Att: 7,000
MALTA 1 (Busuttil 34)
BELGIUM 0
Malta: Cluett, S. Vella, Galea, Buttigieg, Brincat, Buhagiar (Delia 88), Gregory, R. Vella (Suda 460) (Carabott 76), Laferla, Busuttil, Saliba (Spiteri 75)
Belgium: Preud'homme, Medved, Emmers, Albert (Van Meir 46), Smidts, Staelens, Degryse, Boffin, Oliviera (Van der Heyden 46), Nilis, Czerniatynski
Ref: Amendolia (Ita)

16 February Friendly Seoul Att: 12,000
SOUTH KOREA 1 (Ko Jeong-woon 19)
ROMANIA 2 (Dumitrescu 43,73)
Romania: Prunea, Zegrean, Mihali, Tanase (Galca 46), Prodan, Grozavu, Zotinca (Calin 46), Panduru, Dumitrescu, Papura (I. Stan 46), Niculescu (A. Ungur 46)

18 February Robbie Cup, 1st round Miami Att: 15,676
SWEDEN 0
COLOMBIA 0
Sweden: Ravelli, Kamark, Erlingmark, Bjorklund*, M. Nilsson, Limpar, Rehn, Jan Jansson (Alexandersson 65), Landberg (Blomqvist 71), Larsson (Lillenberg 75), Andersson (Kindvall 80)
*Bjorklund sent off, 45 min
Colombia: Cordoba, Andres Escobar, Mendoza, Herrera, Perez, J. G. Gomez, Valderrama*, Alvarez, Aristizabal (Serna 46), Trellez, Valenciano (Alexander Escobar 46)
*Valderrama sent off, 45 min
Ref: Helder Dias (US)

20 February Robbie Cup, 2nd round Miami Att: 20,171
UNITED STATES 1 (Perez 4)
SWEDEN 3 (Larsson 30; K. Andersson 34; Lillenberg 56)
United States: Friedel, Balboa (Caligiuri 46), Lapper (Reyna 63), Lalas, Armstrong, Burns, Dooley, Michallik (Quinn 63), Jones, Perez, Moore (Klopas 46)
Sweden: L. Eriksson, Kamark, Erlingmark, M. Nilsson, Rehn, Jesper Jansson, Alexandersson (Landberg 73), Blomqvist (Limpar 59), Larsson, K. Andersson (Kindvall 77), Lillenberg
Ref: Marrufo Mendoza (Mex)
(Final Placings: 1. Sweden; 2. Colombia; 3. Bolivia; 4. USA.)

23 February Friendly Istanbul Att: 4,000
TURKEY 1 (Ertegrul 4)
CZECH REPUBLIC 4 (Novotny 12; Latal 18; Siegl 59, 63)
Turkey: Hayrettin, Ali, Tugay (Yusuf 46), Bulent, Recep, Suat (Hami 63), Oguz, K. Bulent, Abdullah, Ertegrul (Orhan 46), Hakan
Czech Republic: Stejskal, Latal (Samec 85), Suchoparek, Kadiec, Novotny, Poborsky (Repka 80), Nemecek, Nemec, Frydek (Smejkal 75), Siegl (Vonacek 85), Kuka
Ref: Dellwing (Ger)

23 February Friendly   Tel Aviv   Att: 1,500
ISRAEL   **2**   (Ohana 27, 89)
GEORGIA   **0**
Israel: R. Cohen (Ginzburg 46), A. Harazi (Keissy 46), Klinger, Shelah, Biton, R. Levi, Hazan (Ben Shimon 69), Nimny (Attar 46, Torgemar 80), Berkovitz (Zohar 46), R. Harazi (Tykvah 46), Ohana
Georgia: Dobze, Fredze, Tskhadadze, Lobonikze, Zishkarianu, Djamrauli, Romoshvili, Nemsadje (Oloshvili 46), S. Arbeladze (Gourouli 46), Tougoushi (Kabalashvili 46), A. Arbeladze
Ref: Likovitch (Isr)

24 February Friendly   Casablanca   Att: 12,000
MOROCCO   **0**
FINLAND   **0**
Morocco: Deghay, Nacer, Triki, Lagraoui, Naybet, Mjid, El Haddaoui (El Ouali), Azzouzi (El Khalej, Hajri), Daoudi, Hadji, Chaouch (Nader)
Finland: Jakonnen, Petaja, Keikinen, Kamarua, Lindberg, Suominen, Kinnunen, Altonen, Sumiala, Nurmela, Paavola
Ref: Belleftouh (Mor)

25 February Friendly   Fresno   Att: 27,172
MEXICO   **2**   (Hernandez 33; Rodriguez 58)
SWEDEN   **1**   (Mild 81)
Mexico: Campos, Hernandez (Del Olmo 71), Suarez, Ramirez Perales, Ramirez, Ambriz, Rodriguez, A. Garcia Aspe (Gallaga 46), Galindo, Duana (Guzman 46), Hermosilio*
*Hermosilio sent off, 44 min
Sweden: Ravelli (Eriksson 46), Kamark, Erlingmark, Bjorklund, M. Nilsson, Limpar, Rehn, Jansson, Mild, Kindvall (Blomqvist 78), Eklund (Andersson 67)
Ref: Briandhold (US)

March 1994
9 March Friendly   Wembley   Att: 71,970
ENGLAND   **1**   (Platt 17)
DENMARK   **0**
England: Seaman, Parker, Adams, Pallister, Le Saux, Platt, Gascoigne (Le Tissier 66), Ince (Batty 66), Beardsley, Anderton, Shearer
Denmark: Schmeichel, Kjeldbjerg, Rieper, L. Olsen, Dethlefsen, Jensen, Vilfort (J. Hogh 71), M. Laudrup, Larsen, B. Christensen (Frederiksen 71), B. Laudrup
Ref: Uilenberg (Hol)

9 March Friendly   Cardiff   Att: 10,000
WALES   **1**   (Coleman 89)
NORWAY   **3**   (Flo 6; Mykland 49; J. I. Jacobsen 51)
Wales: Southall, Phillips, Young, Melville, Coleman, Perry, Horne, Blake (Pembridge 59), Speed (Saunders 59), Rush, M. Hughes (C. Hughes 46)
Norway: Grodas, Loken, T. Pedersen, Berg, Bjornebye, Flo, Mykland, Bohinen, Fjortoft (Frigard 79), Rekdal (Solbakken 68), J. I. Jacobsen
Ref: Ferry (NI)

9 March Friendly   Budapest   Att: 5,000
HUNGARY   **1**   (Eszenyi 77)
SWITZERLAND   **2**   (Sforza 10; Subiat 33)
Hungary: Vegh, F. Urban (Lipscei 46), Bamfi (Marton 46), Keresztfuri, Mracsko, Balog (Hilies 68), Hamar (Eszenyi 46), Pisont, Detari (Halmai 46), Klauz, Vincze
Switzerland: Pascolo, Hottiger, Herr, Geiger, Quentin, Ohrel, Bregy, Sforza (T. Wyss 46), A. Sutter (S. Fournier 75), Subiat
Ref: Gadosi (Slovakia)

15 March Friendly   Haifa   Att: 5,000
ISRAEL   **1**   (Banin 40 pen)
UKRAINE   **0**
Israel: Ginzburg (R. Cohen 46), A. Harazi, Klinger, Shelan, Glam (Bittom 60), Hazan, R. Levi (Ben Shimon 46), Berkowitz (Turdjman 59), Banin, Attar (R. Harazi 59), Ohana
Ukraine: Tiapouchkine, Loujni, Bezenar, Diravka, Khomine (Boukel 79), Polounine, Poklebaiev (Jabtchenko 82), Popov, Mikailenko (Youtchenko 60), Leonenko, Konovalov (Touraimski 68)
Ref: Suhil (Isr)

21 March Friendly   Utsunomiya   Att: 10,000
JAPAN   **1**
ICELAND   **2**

22 March Friendly   Lyon   Att: 15,000
FRANCE   **3**   (Papin 7; Djorkaeff 35; Martins 50)
CHILE   **1**   (Zamorano 11)
France: Lama, Angloma, Roche (Le Guen 78), Desailly (Karembeu 72), Lizarazu, Deschamps, Djorkaeff (Martins 46), Ferri, Cocard, Papin, Ginola (Vahirua 46)
Chile: Tapia, R. Fuentes, Lopez, C. Fuentes, Jaque, Tupper (Alvarez 60), Parraguez, Estay (Tudor 83), Lepe, Zamorano, Gonzalez (Rojas 73)
Ref: Arceo (Esp)

23 March Friendly   Stuttgart   Att: 45,000
GERMANY   **2**   (Klinsmann 45, 47)
ITALY   **1**   (D. Baggio 44)
Germany: Illgner, Strunz, Brehme, Kohler (Berthold 72), Effenberg, Buchwald, Moller, Hassler (Basler 78), Klinsmann, Matthaus, Sammer
Italy: Pagliuca, Benarrivo, Maldini, D. Baggio (Stroppa 71), Costacurta, Baresi, Donadoni, Albertini (Evani 46), Casiraghi (Massaro 64), Mancini (Zola 46), Signori
Ref: McCluskey (Sco)

23 March Friendly   Belfast   Att: 5,500
NORTHERN IRELAND **2**   (Morrow 42; Gray 49)
ROMANIA   **0**
Northern Ireland: Wright, Fleming, Taggart, Donaghy, C. Wilson, Magilton, Morrow, Lomas, M. Hughes (Black 46), J. Quinn (Dowie 76), Gray
Romania: Prunea (Stelea 73), Belodedici, Prodan, Popescu (Gilca 76), Petrescu (Moldovan 70), Sabau (Mihali 70), Lupescu, Hagi*, Munteanu, Raducioiu, Dumitrescu
*Hagi sent off
Ref: Burge (Wal)

23 March Friendly   Skopje   Att: 10,000
MACEDONIA   **2**   (Micevski, Boskovski)
SLOVENIA   **0**
Macedonia: Tracjev, Jovanovski (Grozdanoc, Stankovski), Stojkovski, Kanatlarovski, Djurovski, Markovski, Cerafimovski (Tomovbski), Georgijevski, Boskovski, Nemed, Micevski
Slovenia: Simunovic (Zupan), Milanic, Poljsak, Tifer, Binkovski (Kosic), Jermanis, Novak, Zidan, Oblak (Pavlin), Udovic, Siljak (Skaper)

23 March Friendly   Linz   Att: 19,000
AUSTRIA   **1**   (Pfeifenberger 30)
HUNGARY   **1**   (Illes 20)
Austria: Wohlfahrt (Konrad 46), Schottel, Kogler, Pfeffer*, Winklhofer (Hutter 46), Reinmayr (Prosenik 46), Stoger (Streiter 54), Herzog, Feiersinger, Pfeifenberger, Polster (Cerny 46)
*Pfeffer sent off 54 min
Hungary: Vegh, Telek, Meszoly, Lipcsei, Mracsko (Keller 46), Halmai, Gy Bognar Ivanic**, Illes, Kereszturi*, Csertoi (Orosz 52), Klaus
*Kereszturi sent off 67 min; **Ivanic sent off 73 min
Ref: Cinciripini (Ita)

23 March Friendly   Luxembourg   Att: 5,000
LUXEMBOURG   **1**   (Wolf 72)
MOROCCO   **2**   (Harabi 5; El Hadrioui 89)
Luxembourg: Koch, Ferron, Strasser, Holtz, Wolf, Cardoni (Thome 68), Birsens, Weiss, Fanelli (Morocutti 60), Langers (Marchione 83), Groff
Morocco: D'Ghay (Azmi 46), Abdellah, Triki, Abrami, Lagroumi, Daoudi (El Hadrioui 77), M'Tid, Kachloul (Fertout 40), Ben Mahoud, Hababi, Hadji
Ref: Pauchard (Fra)

23 March Friendly   *Glasgow*   *Att: 35,000*
SCOTLAND   **0**
HOLLAND   **1**   (Roy)
Scotland: Goram, McKimmie, Robertson (Collins 65), McLaren, Hendry, Levein (Jess 66), McCall, McStay (McKinlay 46), Durie, McAllister, Nevin (Boyd 46)
Holland: De Goey, Van Gobbel, F. De Boer, Blind, Rob Witschge, Jonk, Taument (Overmars 78), Rijkaard, Bosman (Winter 46), Bergkamp (Gillhaus 46), Roy

23 March Friendly   *Salonika*   *Att: 20,000*
GREECE   **0**
POLAND   **0**
Greece: Minou (Atmatsidis 46), Apolstolakis (Karataidis 46), Ioannou 88), Kolitsidakis, Kalitzakis, Manolas (Alexiou 46), Tsaluhidis, Saravakos (Tuntziaris 46), Nioplias (Kofidis 46), Hantzidis (Machlas 39), Mitropoulos, Tsiantakis
Poland: Wozniak, Grembocki (Czerwec 82), Waldoch, Jegor, Lapinski (Mokal 53), Szewczyk, Jalocha, Fedoruk (Szubert 82), Gesior, Kosecki, Kowalczyk (Cebula 46)
Ref: Angelov (Bul)

23 March Friendly   *Dublin*   *Att: 34,550*
REPUBLIC OF IRELAND   **0**
RUSSIA   **0**
Republic of Ireland: Bonner (A. Kelly 46), G. Kelly, McGoldrick, Babb, Carey, Whelan, McAteer, O'Brien, Cascarino, D. Kelly (Coyne 46), McLoughlin
Russia: Kharin, Kuznetsov, Gorlukovich, Rakhimov, Kovtun, Tetradze, Korneyev (Chernishev 60), Popov, Salenko, Borodiuk, Radchenko (Kosolapov 88)
Ref: Fallstrom (Swe)

23 March Friendly   *Valencia*   *Att: 45,000*
SPAIN   **0**
CROATIA   **2**   (Prosinecki 6; Suker 52)
Spain: Zubizarreta (Lopetegui 65), Ferrer, Alkorta, Abelardo, Voro, Otero, Hierro (Guardiola 46), Goikoetxea (Beguristain 46), Nadal (Camarasa 46), J. Salinas (Juanele 46), Higuera
Croatia: Ladic, Stimac (Pavlicic 78), Andrijasevic (Vlaovic 88), Bilic, Jarni, Jerkan, Jankovic (Mornar 46, Mise 84), Prosinecki, Asanovic, Boksic, Suker
Ref: Veissiere (Fra)

30 March Friendly   *Valetta*
MALTA   **1**   (Laferla 45)
SLOVAKIA   **2**   (Timko 13; Hyravy 69)
Malta: Cluett, S. Vella, Buttigieg (Cauchi 87), Galea, Brincat, Buhagiar, Gregory, Camilleri, Scerri (Aguis 79), Suda (Zarb 54), Laferla
Slovakia: L. Molnar, Stupala, Glonek, Tittel, Kinder, Weiss (Danko 58), Tomaschek, Hyravy, Morarvcik, Timko, Dubovski
Ref: Stafoggia (Ita)

April 1994
13 April Friendly   *Cannes*   *Att: 2,000*
POLAND   **1**   (Wieszczycki 74)
SAUDI ARABIA   **0**
Poland: Wozniak, Jegor, Lapinski, Szewczyk, Jalocha, Wieszczycki, Rudy, Kosecki, Lesniak, Fedoruk, Ponan
Saudi Arabia: Muhyammad Al Daeaya, Ahmad Jameel, Muhammad Al Khilawe, Muhammad Al Qarni, Sulaiman Rashoodhi, Fouad Auwar, Khalid Al Musaed, Luai Subaei, Saced Al Owairan, Fahd Al Gheyshyan, Fahd Al Hamdan
Ref: Veissiere (Fra)

15 April Friendly   *Muscat*   *Att: 2,000*
OMAN   **1**   (Nabil Mubarak 69)
BULGARIA   **1**   (Yankov 83)
Bulgaria: Mikhailov (Popov 46), Kremenliev (Anghelov 70), Ivanov, Tsvetanov (Urukov 70), G. Georgiev (Rakov 70), Yankov, Guentchev, Sirakov, Vidolov (Andonov 70), Kostadinov, Mikhtarski (Borimirov 46)

16 April Friendly   *Jacksonville*   *Att: 6,103*
UNITED STATES   **1**   (Sorber 47)
MOLDOVA   **1**   (Kosse 85 pen)
United States: Friedel, Balboa, Lalas, Caligiuri, Clavijo, Dooley (Burns 76), Sorber, Henderson (Michallik 46), Jones, Perez, Kinnear (Reyna 46)
Moldova: Koshelev, Pogorelov, Karas (Chebotar 73), Guzun (Secu 89), Gaidamaschuk, Stoenco, Oprea (Belous 73), Kurtean, Kosse, Spiridon, Kleschenko (Nemechkalo 76)
Ref: Boulos (USA)

20 April Friendly   *Oslo*   *Att: 17,509*
NORWAY   **0**
PORTUGAL   **0**
Norway: Grodas, Loken, Berg, Bratseth, Bjornebye (Nilsen 68), Strandli, Mykland, Bohinen (Leonhardsen 46), Mjelde (Flo 83), Rekdal, J. I. Jakobsen (Fjortoft 72)
Portugal: Adelino Neno (Alfredo 46), Paulo Madeira, Helder, Oceano, Rui Jorge, Paulo Bento (Helio 87), Vitor Paneira (Jorge Couto 64), Rui Barros (Folha 15), Nogueira, Tavares, Cadete (Pedro 80)
Ref: Waddell (Sco)

20 April Friendly   *Vilnius*   *Att: 4,200*
LITHUANIA   **1**   (Baltusnikas 40)
ISRAEL   **1**   (R. Harazi 7)
Lithuania: Stauce, Zuikas, Mazeikis, Baltusnikas, Sukristovas, Tereskinas, Skarbalius, Olsanskis, Stumbrys (Aparavicius 60), Vaneikis, Stekys (Tarincevas 75)
Israel: Ginzburg (R. Cohen 46), A. Harazi, Shelach, Klinger, Glam, A. Hazan, R. Levi, Nimny, Attar (Turdjman 77), J. Schwartz (Bitom 46), R. Harazi
Ref: Zhuk (Bls)

20 April Friendly   *Bursa*   *Att: 10,000*
TURKEY   **0**
RUSSIA   **1**   (Radchenko 9)
Turkey: Engin, Recep, B. Bulent (Feti 84), Gokhan, Ali, Ogun (H. Ibrahim 69), Osman (Bulent 61), Ergun, Ertugrul, Abdullah (Hasan 80), Orhan
Russia: Kharin, Galiamin, Gorlukovich, Nikiforov (Tatarchuk 81), Ternavski, D. Kuznetsov, D. Popov, Borodiuk (Beschastnikh 60), Tsimbalar, Yuran (Onopko 46), Radchenko (Lediakhov 85)
Ref: Porombolu (Rom)

20 April Friendly   *Bucharest*   *Att: 13,000*
ROMANIA   **3**   (Dumitrescu 22, 49; Niculescu 64)
BOLIVIA   **0**
Romania: Stelea, D. Petrescu, G. Popescu, Prodan, Selimesi (Niculescu 46), Lupescu, Munteanu (Papura 72), Chirita, Panduru, Paducioiu, Dumitrescu
Bolivia: Trucco (Rojas 75), Chavez, O. Sanchez, Rimba, Sandy, Cristaldo, E. Sanchez, Soria (Pioneda 78), Baldivieso (Pena 73), Moreno (Melgar 61), Ramallo (Soruco 46)
Ref: Craciunescu (Rom)

20 April Friendly   *Bratislava*   *Att: 6,511*
SLOVAKIA   **4**   (Dubovsky 24 pen, 61; Kinder 68; Moravcik 83)
CROATIA   **1**   (Popovic 67)
Slovakia: Vencel, Stupala, Moravec, Hipp, Kinder, Weiss (Obaitnik 78), Tomaschek, Dubovsky (Zvara 78), Moravcik, S. Rusnak, Gostic
Croatia: Ladic, Topiak, Istvanic, Brajkovic, Pavlicevic, Mose, Kosniku (Mumlek 46), Racunica (Popovic 46), Vukic (Rapajic 46), Mladenovic, Cvitanovic
Ref: Puhl (Hun)

20 April Friendly   *Zurich*   *Att: 16,200*
SWITZERLAND   **3**   (Chapuisat 12, 37; Bregy 28 pen)
CZECH REPUBLIC   **0**
Switzerland: Pascolo, Hottiger, Geiger (Rueda 80), Herr (Egli 80), Quentin, Ohrel (Studer 77), Sforza (Bickel 46), Bregy (Wyss 70), A. Sutter, Knup (S. Fournier 70), Chapuisat (Subiat 59)
Czech Republic: Kouba, Kadlec (Kubik 46), J. Novotny, Suchoparek, Latal, Pborsky, Nemecek, Frydek (Smejkal 66), Nemec, Kuka (Samec 46), Siegl
Ref: Sandra (Bel)

20 April Friendly		Vienna	Att: 35,000
AUSTRIA	1	(Hutter 13)	
SCOTLAND	2	(McGinlay 35, McKinlay 60)	

Austria: Wohlfahrt (Konsel 46), Schottel, W. Kogler, Hochmaier, Prosenik, P. Toger (Kuhbauer 46), Baur, A. Herzog, A. Hutter, Cerny, Polster (Wessenberger 62)
Scotland: Leighton, McKimmie, Hendry, McLaren, Irvine, McKinlay, McAllister, Collins (McCall 85), Boyd (Ferguson 46), McGinlay (D. Shearer 76), Jess (Nevin 84)
Ref: Albrecht (Ger)

20 April Friendly		Tilburg	Att: 14,000
HOLLAND	0		
REPUBLIC OF IRELAND	1	(Coyne 55)	

Holland: De Goey, Valckx, R. Koeman (De Wolf 46), F. De Boer, Rijkaard, Jonk (Winter 46), Davids, Overmars, Bergkamp (Taument 46), R. De Boer, Roy
Rep. Ireland: Bonner, G. Kelly, Moran, Babb, T. Phelan, (McLoughlin 84), McGoldrick (McAteer 71), Sheridan, R. Whelan, Townsend, Staunton, Coyne (Coyle 86)
Ref: Strampe (Ger)

20 April Friendly		Wrexham	Att: 4,694
WALES	0		
SWEDEN	2	(Larsson 83, Brolin 90)	

Wales: Southall, Bowen (Blackmore 60), Neilson, Melville, Bodin, Horne, Phillips, Goss (C. Hughes 81), Speed, Rush, I. Roberts (Blake 81)
Sweden: Ravelli, R. Nilsson (M. Nilsson 72), P. Andersson, Bjorklund, Ljung, Schwarz, Limpar (Blomqvist 70), Ingesson, K. Andersson (Kinsvall 81), Larsson, Brolin
Ref: Shorte (Rlr)

20 April Friendly		Copenhagen	Att: 12,512
DENMARK	3	(M. Laudrup 21, pen 43; Povlsen 60)	
HUNGARY	1	(Vincze 2)	

Denmark: Krogh, Hogh, L. Olsen, Rieper, J. Jensen (Helveg 15), Vilfort, N. Bielsen, H. Larsen (Kristensen 70), M. Laudrup, B. Laudrup (Christensen 70), Pingel (Povlsen 58)
Hungary: Vegh, Lipcsei, Marton, G. Meszoly, Simon (Csabi 46), Halmai (Puglits 70), Sandor (Pisont 42), Illes, Keller, Klausz (Cseroi 63), Vincze (Jagodics 89)
Ref: Oskarsson (Fin)

20 April Friendly		Toulon	Att: 500
SAUDI ARABIA	2	(Oweiran 16, Al-Mohalal 25)	
ICELAND	0		

Saudi Arabia: Aldeaya, Saleh (Souleiman 76), Abdul Jawad, Alkhelwi, Jamil, Anwar, Hamzah Saleh, Aldawood, Oweiran, Al-Mohalal (Rushudi 70), Ghosheiyan (Abas 60)
Iceland: Kristiansson, Marteinsson (Gislasson 61), Jonsson, Dervic, B. Gunnlaugsson (Ingolfsson 61), Kristinsson, Thordarsson, Orlygsson, Stefansson, A. Gunnlaugsson (Sogurdsson 87), Gudjohnsen
Ref: Leduc (Fra)

20 April Friendly		N. Carolina	Att: 4,790
UNITED STATES	3	(Klopas 3, Lapper 40, Reyna 59)	
MOLDOVA	0		

United States: Meola, Balboa (Dooley 46), Armstrong, Lapper, Agoos, Quinn, Burns (Sorber 70), Michallik (Henderson 74), C. Jones, Reyna (Kinnear 70), Klopas (Vermes 46)
Moldova: Koshelev, Pogorelov, E. Karas (B. Cibotaru 36), Guzun (Secu 68), Gaidamaschuk (Belous 42), S. Stroenco, Oprea, Kurtean (Nemechkalo 74), Kosse, Spiridon, Kieschenko
Ref: Zimmermann (USA)

24 April Friendly		Chuta Vista, California	Att: 3,017
UNITED STATES	1	(Klopas 47)	
ICELAND	2	(Sigurdsson 20, B. Gunnlaugsson 86)	

United States: Friedel, Balboa (Kinnear 46), Lalas, Agoos (Caligiuri 46), Clavijo, Dooley, Quinn, Reyna, Jones, Perez, Klopas
Iceland: B. Kristinsson (Finnbogasson 74), O. Kristjansson (Adolfsson 56), A. Gretarsson (Egilsson 78), S. Jonsson, Dervic, R. Kristinsson, Sigurdsson (Marteinsson 71), Gislasson, A. Gunnlaugsson (B. Gunnlaugsson 71), Thordarsson, Ongolfsson
Ref: Patlak (USA)

27 April Friendly		Athens	
GREECE	5	(Nikos Mahlas 10, 44; Alexis Alexudis 47; Kristos Kostis 74; Vasilis Tuntziaris 90)	
SAUDIA ARABIA	1	(Sami Al-Jaber 60 pen)	

27 April Friendly		Abu Dhabi	Att: 12,000
UNITED ARAB EMIRATES	0		
GERMANY	2	(Kirsten 66; Gaudino 90)	

United Arab Emirates: Mohsin Masbahfarraj, Saleh Joma, Abdul Rahman al Haddad, Khamis, Mohammad Obaid Hilal, Ismail Rashed, Bakheet Saad (Abdel Thaliq 58), Khalid Ismail Mubarak, Ahmed Ibrahim (Hussein Ghuloom 63), Abdulrazaq Ibrahim (Sultan 77), Adnan al-Taliani (Abdul Aziz Mohammad Ali 78)
Germany: Kopke, Matthaus (Sammer 46), Berthold, Kohler, Basler, Strunz, Buchwald, Brehme (Helmer 46), Moller (Guadino 82), Thom (Hassler 65), Kirsten

28 April Friendly		Kuwait	Att: 5,000
KUWAIT	2	(Mohammed Edeilem 15; Walleed Nassar 36)	
BULGARIA	2	(Zlatko Yankov 25; og Mohammed Edeilem 31)	

May 1994

4 May Friendly		Krakow	Att: 8,000
POLAND	3	(Jalocha 48; Baluszinski 80; Fedoruk 85)	
HUNGARY	2	(Vincze 10; Klausz 50)	

4 May Friendly		Florianopolis	
BRAZIL	3	(Ronaldo 31; Zinho 42 pen; Viola 84)	
ICELAND	0		

Brazil: Zetti, Jorginho, Marcio Santos, Aldair, Branco, Dunga, Mazinho, Paulo Sergio, Zinho, Viola, Ronaldo
Iceland: Birkir, Runar, Gislasson, Egillsson, Arnor, Kristian Jonsson, Bjarki, Jonsson, Sverrisson, Thordarsson, Arnar

5 May Friendly		Stockholm	Att: 19,000
SWEDEN	3	(Schwarz 3; Larsson 42; Ingesson 78)	
NIGERIA	1	(Odegbami 75)	

Sweden: L. Eriksson, R. Nilsson, P. Andersson (J. Eriksson 46), Bjorklund, M. Nilsson, Larsson (Blomqvist 66), Thern, Schwarz, Ingesson, Dahlin (Erlingmark 79), K. Andersson (Kindvall 56)
Nigeria: Agu, Okafor, Eguavon (Semitoje 46), Iroha (West 61), Keshi, Edema, Kanu, Oliha (Odegbami 46), Ugbade, George (Emma Okocha 46), Daniels (Ojigwe 68)
Ref: Kelly (Rlr)

7 May Friendly		California	Att: 2,158
UNITED STATES	4	(Klopas 36; Reyna 41; Balboa 76; Moore 87)	
ESTONIA	0		

United States: Friedel, Balboa, Lalas (Lapper 46), Agoos, Armstrong, Burns, Reyna, Henderson (Kinnear 65), Jones (Michallik 83), Perez, Klopas (Moore 46)
Estonia: Poom, Prins, Kallaste, Kaljend, Klavan, Lemsalu (Zelinski 70), Kristal, Linnumae, Kirs, Reim, Krom
Ref: Patlak (USA)

9 May Friendly		Athens	Att: 8,000
GREECE	0		
CAMEROON	3	(Embe 26; Tataw 45; Loga 72)	

Greece: Minou (Karkamis 46), Manolas, Karataidis, Ioannides, Hadjidis, Karapialis (Kofides 48), Machlas (Vrizas 50), Tsalouhidis, Nioplias (Tsartas 60), Tsiantakis (Marangos 48), Mitropoulos*
*Mitropoulos sent off 36 min
Cameroon: Songo'o, Tataw, Agbo, Mbouh, Mfede, Loga, Kalla (Milla 72), Ebongue, Kana Biyik (Foe 57), Misse Misse (Moyeme 46), Embe (Tchami 46)

13 May Friendly   *Athens*   *Att: 20,000*
GREECE   **0**
BOLIVIA   **0**
Greece: Minou (Karkamis 46), Machlas (Dimitriadis 46), Nioplias (Tsartas 46), Hadjidis, Karayannis, Alexiou, Kolitsidakis, Marangos (Tsalouhides 67), Alexandris (Kostis 46), Alexoudis, Tsiantakis (Kofides 46)
Bolivia: Rojas, Rimba, Sandy, Cristaldo, Melgar, Baldivieso (Pinedo 60), Moreno (Borja 82), J. M. Pena, Ramos (Castillo 68), A. Pena, D. Rojas
Ref: Wieser (Aus)

15 May Friendly   *California*   *Att: 9,753*
UNITED STATES   **1**   (Klopas 64)
ARMENIA   **0**
United States: Meola, Balboa, Lalas, Caligiuri, Burns, Dooley (Sorber 83), Reyna, Kinnear (Henderson 87), Jones (Moore 74), Perez, Klopas
Armenia: Armen Petrosian, Gspeyan, Tonoyan, S. Hovsepian, Vardanian, Sukiason, Avetisian, Grigorian, A. Hovsepian (H. Petrosian 75), Mikhitarian, Shakhgeldian (Arthur Petrosian 71)
Ref: Hall (USA)

17 May Friendly   *Wembley*   *Att: 23,659*
ENGLAND   **5**   (Anderton 24; Beardsley 37; Platt 44 pen, 55; Shearer 65)
GREECE   **0**
England: Flowers, R. Jones (Pearce 82), Bould, Adams, Le Saux, Richardson, Platt, Merson, Anderton (Le Tissier 62), Shearer, Beardsley (I. Wright 69)
Greece: Karkamanis, Apostolakis, Karayannis, Kolitsidakis, Kalitsakis, Tsalouhides, Hantzidis (Saravakos 46), Nioplias, Tsiantakis, Kofidis (Kostis 69), Machlas (Mitropoulos 46)
Ref: McCluskey (Sco)

17 May Friendly   *Katowice*   *Att: 5,000*
POLAND   **3**   (Juskowiak 22 pen; Brzeczek 47; Moskal 89)
AUSTRIA   **4**   (Stoeger 5, 26, 65; Hochmaier 69)
Poland: Jojko (Wozniak 46), Bak, Lapinski, Jegor, Grembocki (Gesior 65), Jalocha, Rudy, Brzeczek, Lesniak (Szubert 16, Kubik 35), Juskowiak, Kowalczyk (Moskal 46)
Austria: Wohlfahrt, Hochmaier, Streiter (Schoettel 79), Pfeffer, Feiersinger, Hutter, Stoger, Artner, Aigner, Polster, Pfeifenberger
Ref: Rothlisberger (Swi)

18 May Friendly   *Gyor*   *Att: 3,000*
HUNGARY   **2**   (Kereszturi 51, 75)
CROATIA   **2**   (Mladenovic 52, 63)
Hungary: Vegh, Lipcsei, Marton, G. Meszoly, Puglits (Kuttor 69), Halmai, G. Bognar (Jagodics 64), Kereszturi, Keller, J. Kovacs (Hertzeg 46), Vincze
Croatia: Ladic, Jerkan, Stimac (Pavlicic 46), Bilic, Jarni, Jankovic, Andrijasevic (Soldo 77), Prosinecki (Turkovic 46), Asanovic, Boksic, Civitanovic (Mladenovic 46)
Ref: Pucek (Cze).

19 May Friendly   *Reykjavík*   *Att: 2,000*
ICELAND   **1**   (T. Orlygsson 54)
BOLIVIA   **0**

22 May Friendly   *Wembley*   *Att: 64,327*
ENGLAND   **0**
NORWAY   **0**
England: Seaman, R. Jones, Bould, Adams, Le Saux, Platt, Ince (I. Wright 76), Wise, Anderton (Le Tissier 76), Beardsley, Shearer

Norway: Thorstvedt (By Rise 86), H. Berg (Haaland 46), Johnsen, Bratseth, R. Nielsen, O. Berg (Ingebrigtsen 67), Rekdal, J. I. Jakobsen, Flo, Bohinen, Fjortoft (Sorloth 46)
Ref: M. Nielsen (Den)

23 May Friendly   *Tallinn*   *Att: 2,000*
ESTONIA   **1**   (Reim 86 pen)
WALES   **2**   (Rush 56, Phillips 83)
Estonia: Poom, R. Kallaste, Lemsalu, Prins, Kaljend, Klavan, Olumets (Pari 78), Linnumae, Kristal, Reim, Lindmaa
Wales: Southall, A. Williams, Coleman, Melville (Bodin 73), Neilson, Phillips, Horne, J. Bowen, Rush, Jones, C. Hughes
Ref: Lajuks (Lat)

24 May Friendly   *Dublin*   *Att: 32,500*
REPUBLIC OF IRELAND   **1**   (Sheridan 35)
BOLIVIA   **0**
Republic of Ireland: Bonner, Irwin (Kernaghan), K. Moran (G. Kelly), Babb, Phelan, Keane, Townsend, R. Houghton (McAteer 60), Sheridan, Staunton, Coyne (Cascarino 83)
Bolivia: Trucco, Sandy, Soruco, Angel, Quinteros, Ramos, Pinedo, Melgar, Baldivieso, Cristaldo, A. Pena
Ref: Howells (Wal)

25 May Friendly   *Prague*   *Att: 8,407*
CZECH REPUBLIC   **5**   (Kuka 20, 51; Frydek 23; Kubik 27; Postulka 81)
LITHUANIA   **3**   (Narbekovas 52; og Nemecek 76; Sturmbrys 85)
Czech Republic: Kouba (Stejskal 46), Repka, Kubik, Novotny, Latal (Poborsky 8), Nemecek, Nemec, Frydek (Suchopanek 60), Smejkal, Skuhravy (Siegl 53), Kuka (Postulka 66)
Lithuania: Skrupskis, Ziukas, Baltusnikas, Mazeikis, Tereskinas, Sukristovas, Skarbalius (Vainoras 80), Narbekovas, Sturmbrys, Slekys (Zalys 56), Olsanskis (Apanavicius 46)
Ref: Kowalczyk (Pol)

25 May Friendly   *Bucharest*   *Att: 11,500*
ROMANIA   **2**   (Dumitrescu 22; Petrescu 49)
NIGERIA   **0**
Romania: Stelea (Prunea 75), Petrescu, Belodedici, Mihali (Prodan 72), Galca, Lupescu (Stanga 27), Popescu, Panduru, Niculescu (Chirita 60), Ivan (Moldovan 52), Dumitrescu (Papura 80)
Nigeria: Rufai, Eguavon (Agu 86), Keshi, Okafor, Iroha, Oliseh, Okocha (Adepoju 52), Siasia, Amunike, Ikpeba (Oliha 60), Babangida (George 53)
Ref: Nikakis (Gre)

25 May Friendly   *Kiev*   *Att: 20,000*
UKRAINE   **3**   (Leonenko 62; Bezhenar 65 pen; Mikhailenko 82)
BELARUS   **1**   (Belkevich 44)

26 May Friendly   *Copenhagen*   *Att: 28,689*
DENMARK   **0**
SWEDEN   **0**
Denmark: Schmeichel, Helveg, Olsen, Rieper, Kjeldbjerg, Friis-Hansen (B. Jensen 46), Vilfort, Steen Nielsen, M Laudrup, Povlsen (Pingel 77, B Laudrup
Sweden: Ravelli, Kamark (M. Nilsson 33), P. Andersson, Bjorklund (J. Eriksson 46), Ljung (Erlingmark 69), H. Larsson (Limpar 46), Rehn, Thern (Blomqvist 62), Mild, Dahlin, Brolin

26 May Kirin Cup   *Kobe*   *Att: 16,743*
AUSTRALIA   **0**
FRANCE   **1**   (Cantona 42)
Australia: Kalac, Tony Vidmar (Polak 71), Tobin, Ivanovic, Durakovic, Wade (Markowski 82), Slater, Zelic, Veart, Aurelio Vidmar, Van Blerk
France: Barthez, Angloma, Blanc, Di Meco, Karembeu, Petit, Ferri, Cantona, Dugarry (Martins 73), Ginola (Pedros 73), Papin

27 May Friendly *Parma* Att: 28,000
ITALY 2 (Signori 24; Casiraghi 66)
FINLAND 0
Italy: Marchegiani, Benarrivo (Tassotti 46), Costacurta, Baresi (Minotti 46), Apolloni, Conte (Donadoni 72), Evani, D. Baggio, Berti (Casiraghi 46), R. Baggio (Zola 46), Signori
Finland: Jakonen, Kinnunen, Heikkinen, Petaja, Kanerva (Hyrylainen 68), Suominen, Litmanen, Lindberg (Paavola 71), Hjelm, Aaltonen (Rami Rantanen 88), Jarvinen
Ref: Vagner (Hun)

27 May Friendly *Basel* Att: 10,000
SWITZERLAND 2 (Herr 30; Hottiger 65)
LIECHTENSTEIN 0
Switzerland: Lehmann, Hottiger, Herr, Geiger, Quentin, Ohrel, Bregy, Sforza, A. Sutter, Subiat, Chapuisat
Liechtenstein: Heeb, Moser, C. Frick, J. Ospelt (Hanselmann 46), Ritter, Telser (Matt 78), Zech, Klaunzer, Hasler (Marxer 88), W. Ospelt, M. Frick
Ref: Hamer (Lux)

27 May Friendly *Utrecht* Att: 15,000
HOLLAND 3 (Roy 17; Van Vossen 61; og Irvine 72)
SCOTLAND 0
Holland: De Goey, Valckx, F. De Boer, R. De Boer (Numan 46), Jonk, Witschge, Wouters, Winter, Overmars, Gullit (Van Vossen 46), Roy (Taument 71)
Scotland: Leighton (Gunn 46), Clarke, McKimmie, McCall, Hendry, Irvine, Durie (Jess 46), McKinlay (Nevin 81), McGinlay (Shearer 75), McAllister, Collins (Ferguson 61)
Ref: Ansuategui Roca (Esp)

28 May Friendly *New Haven* Att: 21,317
UNITED STATES 1 (Klopas 45)
GREECE 1 (Chatzidis 49)
United States: Friedel, Balboa*, Lalas, Caligiuri, Burns, Sorber, Dooley, Reyna (Wegerle 78), Ramos, Perez (Wynalda 46), Klopas (Stewart 47)
* Balboa sent off 71 min
Greece: Atmatzidis, Manolas, Kolitzidakis, Apostolakis (Chatzidis 46), Kalitzakis, Tsalouhides, Mitropoulos (Maragos 46), Tsiantakis (Vaios Karagianis 63), Nioplias, Saravakos (Alexoudis 78), Machlas
Ref: Benito Archundia (Mex)

29 May Friendly *Hannover* Att: 50,000
GERMANY 0
REPUBLIC OF IRELAND 2 (Cascarino 31; G. Kelly 68)
Germany: Illgner, Strunz, Kohler (Effenberg 46), Matthaus, Buchwald (Berthold 36), Moller (Hassler 46), Wagner, Sammer, Basler, Klinsmann, Riedle (Voller 68)
Republic of Ireland: A. Kelly, Irwin (G. Kelly 46), Phelan, McGrath, Babb, Keane, Townsend, McAteer, Sheridan (Whelan 46), Staunton, Cascarino (Houghton 86)
Ref: Aranba (Esp)

29 May Kirin Cup *Tokyo* Att: 60,000
JAPAN 1 (Ogura 78)
FRANCE 4 (Djorkaeff 16; Papin 18; Ginola 53, 55)
Japan: Maekawa, Kondo, Iwamoto (Endo 70), Natsuka, Ihara, Hashiratani, Asano (Moriyasu 65), Sawanobori, Miura, Hasegawa (Ogura 78), Kurosaka
France: Lama, Angloma, Blanc, Di Meco (Lizarazu 72), Desailly, Deschamp, Le Guen, Djorkaeff (Ouedec 72), Cantona, Ginola, Papin

29 May Friendly *Moscow* Att: 15,000
RUSSIA 2 (Piatnitski 49; Tsimbalar 60)
SLOVAKIA 1 (Tittel 35)
Russia: Kharin, Galiamin, Onopko, Nikoforov, Dmitry Kuznetsov, Ternavski, Piatnitski, Tsimbalar, Salenko, Mostovoi, Radchenko
Slovakia: Molnar, Stupala (Obsitnik 46), Vrto, Glonek, Kinder, Tittel, Veiss, Moravec (Moravcik 52), Faktor, Zvara, Rusnak

31 May Friendly *Tel Aviv* Att: 30,000
ISRAEL 0
ARGENTINA 3 (Batistuta 26, 50; Caniggia 52)
Israel: Ginzburg, Hazan, Klinger, A. Harazi, Glam, Levi (Nimni 46), Banin, Berkovitz, Attar (Revivo 46), Rosenthal (Ohana 46), R. Harazi
Argentina: Islas, Sensini, Vazquez, Ruggeri, Chamot, Simeone, Redondo, Balbo, Maradona (Franco 76), Batistuta, Caniggia (Ortega 85)
Ref: Luisou (Cyp)

June 1994

1 June Friendly *Skopje* Att: 10,000
FYR MACEDONIA 2 (Boskovski 12; Kanatirovski 36)
ESTONIA 0
Macedonia: Trajcev (Z. Micevski 86), Grozdanov (Stankovski 73), Jovanovski, Kanatlarovski (V. Micevski 82), Mitko Stojkovski, Marovski, Serafimovski, Memet (Marjan Stojkovski 63), T. Micenski (Borov 38), Pancev, Boskovski
Estonia: Poom, R. Kallaste, T. Kallaste, Lemsalu, Olsek, Linnumae, Olumets (Pari 60), Klavan, Reim, Lindmaa, Kristal
Ref: Momirov (Bul)

1 June Friendly *Eindhoven* Att: 27,450
HOLLAND 7 (Bergkamp 12, 90; Roy 17; R. Koeman 23 pen; Taument 46; Rijkaard 58, 78)
HUNGARY 1 (Illes 9 pen)
Holland: De Goey, Rijkaard, R. Koeman, F. De Boer (Valckx 46), Winter (Van Gobbel 46), Jonk (De Wolf 84), Witschge, Overmars (Taument 46), Bergkamp, R. De Boer (Van Vossen 62), Roy
Hungary: Vegh, Puglits, Meszoly, Lipcsei (Albert 46), Marton, Keller, Halmai, Illes, Kereszturi (T. Balog 32), Klausz (Czertoi 46), Vincze (Dombi 46)

1 June Friendly *Oslo* Att: 22,000
NORWAY 2 (J. I. Jakobsen 35; O. Berg 44)
DENMARK 1 (Povlsen 41)
Norway: Thorstvedt, Haaland, Johnsen, Bratseth, H. Berg, J. I. Jakobsen (Halle 63), Bohinen, Mykland, Leonhardsen, Flo, Fjortoft (Sorloth 81)
Denmark: Schmeichel, Olsen (Kjeldbjerg 46), Vilfort, Rieper, J. Hoegh, Helveg, M. Laudrup, Larsen, B. Jensen (Steen Nielsen 70), B. Laudrup, Povlsen

1 June Friendly *Bucharest* Att: 15,000
ROMANIA 0
SLOVENIA 0
Romania: Prunea (Preda 76), Petrescu, Prodan (Mihali 75), Belodedici, Munteanu (Moldovan 64), Popescu (Chirita 64), Panduru (Gilca 46), Lupescu, Dumitrescu, Raducioiu (Ivan 43), Niculescu (Stinga 46)
Slovenia: Boskovic, Galic, Krizan, Milanic, Jermanis (Brinkovski 46), Ceh, Novak, Zidan, Zahavic (Kosic 86), Belek (Englaro 82), Gliha (Cvikl 60)
Ref: Werner (Pol)

2 June Friendly *Tampere* Att: 10,251
FINLAND 1 (Jarvinen 17)
SPAIN 2 (Felipe 11; Salinas 15)
Finland: Niemi, Kinnunen, Hyrylainen, Petaja, Makela, Paavola (Suominen 59), M. Altonen, R. Rantanen (Lindberg 59), Jarvinen, Litmanen, Hjelm
Spain: Zubizarreta (Canizares 46), Ferrer, Abelardo, Alkorta, Camarasa, Goikoetxea (Beguiristain 58), Hierro, Guardiola, Felipe, Guerrero (Voro 46), Salinas (Juanele 58)
Ref: Fallstrom (Swe)

2 June Friendly *Vienna* Att: 35,000
AUSTRIA 1 (Polster 77 pen)
GERMANY 5 (Sammer 22; Moller 50, 66; Klinsmann 62; Basler 90)
Austria: Wohlfahrt, Feiersinger, Streiter (Kogler 75), Pfeffer, Hochmaier (Schoettel 75), Aigner (Kuhbauer 65), Polster, Stoger, Hutter (Cerny 65)
Germany: Illgner, Strunz, Brehme, Kohler, Moller (Kuntz 77), Hassler, Matthaus (Basler 85), Berthold, Sammer (Helmer 72), Klinsmann (Riedle 63), Effenberg

FULL INTERNATIONALS 1993–94

3 June Friendly   *Riga*   Att: 2,500
LATVIA   **2**   (Droupas 41; Astafiev 47)
MALTA   **0**
Latvia: Karavaiev (Laizans 70), Troytski, Sevliakov, Sprogis, Mongak (Gniedouis 64), Emelianov, Astafiev, Staucers (Eliseiev 46), Ivanov, Babitchev (Erglis 73), Droupas
Malta: Sullivan, Vella, Buttigieg, Galea, Brincat, Buhagiar, Gregory, Spiteri (Suda 23), Saliba, Busuttil, Laferla
Ref: Timofeiev (Est)

3 June Friendly   *Sofia*   Att: 15,000
BULGARIA   **1**   (Sirakov 18)
UKRAINE   **1**   (Sak 55)
Bulgaria: P. Nikolov, Kremenliev (Kirakov 44), T. Ivanov, Houbtchev (N. Ilev 46), Tzevtanov, Z. Yankov (Gueorguiev 46), Balakov (I. Yordanov 46; Andonov 76), Letchkov (B. Guentchev 46), Sirakov (Alexandrov 46), Borimirov (Mihtakarski 46), Stoitchkov (Iotov 66)
Ukraine: Tiapouchine, Loujni, Bezenar, Diriavka, Popoc (Sak 46), Kovalets (Maximov 80), Chmatovalenko, Mikhailichenko, Schapenko, Leonenko, Skatchenk

3 June Friendly   *Rome*   Att: 40,000
ITALY   **1**   (Signori 25)
SWITZERLAND   **0**
Italy: Pagliuca, Tassotti (Mussi 46), Costacurta, Baresi, Maldini (Benarrivo 46), Albertini (Evani 46), D. Baggio, Donadoni, Berti, R. Baggio, Signori (Massaro 46)
Switzerland: Lehmann, Hottiger, Herr (A. Egli 46), Geiger, Quentin, Ohrel (Subiat 78), Bregy, Sforza, Bickel (Grassi 78), A. Sutter, Chapuisat (Sylvestre 78)
Ref: Brito (Esp)

4 June Friendly   *Brussels*   Att: 5,000
BELGIUM   **9**   (Weber 9, 14, 57, 59, 88; Degryse 28, 38, 62; Nilis 55)
ZAMBIA   **0**
Belgium: Preud'homme, Grun (Renier), De Wolf, Albert (Smits), Staelens (Emmers), Van der Elst, Scifo, Boffin, Nillis, Degryse (Wilmots), Weber
Zambia: Piri, Latina, Choongo*, Ghiyangi, Langu, Skala, J. Bwalya, Malavsa, Saleti, Shilumba, Nyavenda
* *Choongo sent off 35 min*

4 June Friendly   *Boston*   Att: 4,000
COLOMBIA   **2**   (Perez 30, Valencia 44)
NORTHERN IRELAND   **0**
Colombia: Cordoba, A. Escobar, Herrera, Gomez, Valderrama, Valencia (De Avila 61), Alvarez, Perea, Rincon, Perez, Asprilla (Aristizabal 62)
Northern Ireland: Wright, Fleming, Worthington, Taggart, Donaghy, Magilton (Dennison 76), Wilson (Lomas 59), Morrow, Quinn (O'Boyle 59), Dowie (Paterson 46), Hughes

4 June Friendly   *Zagreb*   Att: 40,000
CROATIA   **0**
ARGENTINA   **0**
Croatia: Ladic, Turkovic, Jami, Stimac, Jerkan, Bilic, Asanovic (Andrijasevic 46), Prosinecki (Mladenovic 82), Suker (Cvitanovic 75), Boban, Jurcevic (Mornar 46)
Argentina: Goycoechea, Vasquez (Caceres 89), Chamot, Sensini, Redondo, Ruggeri, Caniggia (Ortega 82), Simeone, Balbo (Mancuso 70), Maradona, Batistuta
Ref: Grabher (Aus)

5 June Friendly   Att: 16,000
BELGIUM   **3**   (Weber 5; Degryse 36; Nilis 65)
HUNGARY   **1**   (Jagodics 54)
Belgium: Preud'homme, M. De Wolf, Grun, Albert (Smidts 46), Boffin (Borkelmans 46), Staelens, Van der Elst, Scifo, Degryse, Nilis (Emmers 80), Weber (Wilmots 74)
Hungary: Vegh (Koszta 78), Puglits, G. Meszoly, Lipcsei, Marton, Keller, Halmai, Illes, Balogh, Klausz, Jagodics
Ref: Przesmycki (Pol)

5 June Friendly   *Stockholm*   Att: 29,600
SWEDEN   **2**   (Brolin 56, 61 pen)
NORWAY   **0**
Sweden: Ravelli, R. Nilsson (Kamark 68), P. Andersson, Bjorklund, J. Eriksson, Ingesson, Schwarz, Thern, Blomqvist (Limpar 89), Dahlin (K. Andersson 80), Brolin
Norway: Thorstvedt, H. Berg, Eggen, Bratseth, Bjornebye, Flo (Halle 36), Bohinen, Rekdal, Mykland (Fjortoft 65), J. I. Jakobsen, S. Rushfeldt (Strand 65)
Ref: Milton Nielsen (Den)

5 June Friendly   *Dublin*   Att: 43,465
REPUBLIC OF IRELAND   **1**   (Townsend 43)
CZECH REPUBLIC   **3**   (Kuka 25 pen, 53; Suchoparek 84)
Republic of Ireland: Bonner, G. Kelly, McGrath (Babb 77), Kernaghan, Phelan, McGoldrick (Keane 53), Sheridan, Townsend, Staunton, Cascarino (Coyne 64), Aldridge (McAteer 53)
Czech Republic: Kouba, Kubik, Kotulek, Repka, Suchoparek, Poborsky, Nemec (Medved 86), Frydek, Samec 89), Novotny, Smejkal, Kuka
Ref: Sundell (Swe)

5 June Friendly   *East Rutherford*   Att: 73,511
COLOMBIA   **2**   (Gaviria 48; Rincon 68)
GREECE   **0**
Colombia: Cordoba, Mendoza, Perea (A. Escobar 46), Alvarez, Gaviria, Valderrama, Ortiz (Serna 73), De Avila (Valencia 46), Lozano (Rincon 16), Aristizabal (F. Asprilla 46)
Greece: Atmatzides, Apostolakis, Kolitsidakis, Manolas, Kalintzakis, Tsalouhidis (Mitropoulos 81), Nioplias, Marangos (Alexandris 72), Handzitis (Dimitriadis 55), Machlas (Saravakos 55), Kofidis

5 June Friendly   Att: 16,000
BELGIUM   **3**   (Weber 5; Degryse 36; Nilis 65)
HUNGARY   **1**   (Jagodics 54)
Belgium: Preud'homme, M. De Wolf, Grun, Albert (Smidts 46), Boffin (Borkelmans 46), Staelens, Van der Elst, Scifo, Degryse, Nilis (Emmers 80), Weber (Wilmots 74)
Ref: Przesmycki (Pol)

8 June Friendly   *Toronto*   Att: 22,000
CANADA   **0**
GERMANY   **2**   (Sammer 31; Voller 90)
Canada: Forrest, Yallop, Samuel, Watson (Doliscat 46), Fraser (Carter 54), Miller, Hooper (Limniatis 73), Aunger (Norman 65), Dasovic, Berdusco (Catliff 46), Corrazin (Mobilio 60)
Germany: Illgner, Berthold, Matthaus, Kohler (Helmer 46), Strunz (Gaudino 69), Basler (Kuntz 81), Hassler (Wagner 66), Sammer, Brehme, Klinsmann (Riedle 46), Voller
Ref: Lodge (Eng)

10 June Friendly   *Montreal*
CANADA   **0**
SPAIN   **2**   (Salinas 9; Juanele 84)
Canada: Dolan, McDonald, Yallop, Doliscat, Fraser, Dasovic, Aunger, Miller, Hooper, Catliff, Corrazin
Spain: Canizares, Ferrer (Otero 57), Alcorta, Abelardo, Sergi (Camarasa 74), Goikoetxea (Guardiola 57), Guerrero, Nadal, Caminero, Luis Enrique (Beguiristain 57), Salinas (Juanele 58)
Ref: Reed (Eng)

11 June Friendly   *New Haven*   Att: 23,547
ITALY   **1**   (Signori)
COSTA RICA   **0**
Italy: Pagliuca, Tassotti, Costacurta, Baresi, Benarrivo, D. Baggio (Donadoni 46), Albertini, Evani, Berti (Massaro 46), R. Baggio, Signori
Costa Rica: A. Rojas, Montero, Rodriguez (Solano 83), Solis, Parx, Delgardo, Smith (Arnaez 74), Gutrie, Medford, Gomez, Meyer (Fonseca 72)
Ref: Baharmast (USA)

11 June Friendly   *Att: 5,500*
BOLIVIA   **0**
SWITZERLAND   **0**
Bolivia: Trucco, Borja (Sorucco 69), Rimba, Quinteros, Sandy, Cristaldo, Melgar, E. Sanchez (Ramos 82), Soria, Baldivieso, Ramallo (Moreno 77)
Switzerland: Pascolo (Lehmann 46), Hottiger, Herr, Geiger, Quinten, Ohrel, Bregy, Sforza, Sutter, Knupp (Subiat 72), Chapuisat

11 June Friendly
NIGERIA   **5**   (Yekini 11, 43; Siasia 58, 60; Adepoju 70)
GEORGIA   **1**   (Kezu 2)

11 June Friendly   *Miami*
MEXICO   **3**   (Garcia 18 pen, 30; Hermosillo 77)
N. IRELAND   **0**
Mexico: Campos, Ambriz, Guitierrez, Ramirez Perales, Ramierz, Saurez, Bernal, Del Olmo, Zague, Luis Garcia (Galindo 47), Sanchez (Hermosillo 69)
N. Ireland: Fettis (Wright 46), Fleming (Morrow 74), Worthington, Taggart, Donaghy, Magilton (Patterson 46), Hughes, K. Wilson (Lennon 46), J. Quinn (Dowie 46), O'Boyle, Lomas

12 June Friendly   *Montreal*   *Att: 20,184*
CANADA   **0**
HOLLAND   **3**   (Bergkamp 7; Overmars 12; Rijkaard 36)
Canada: Forrest, Fraser, Samuel, Yallop, Carter, Dasovic, Hooper (Morman 46), Aunger, Berdusco (Liminitias 78), Miller (Fenwick 65), Corrazin (Catliff 46)
Holland: De Goey, F. De Boer, Rijkaard (Van Gobbel 67), R. Koeman, Valkx (Witschge 46), Jonk, Overmars, Wouters, R. De Boer (Van Vossen 46), Bergkamp, Roy (Bosman 77)
Ref: Reed (Eng)

12 June Friendly   *Mission Viejo*
SWEDEN   **1**   (Ingesson 57)
ROMANIA   **1**   (Hagi 74)
Sweden: Ravelli (Eriksson 46), R. Nilsson (Karmark 78), Bjorklund, Eriksson, Jung, Ingesson, Thern, Rehn (Mild 46), Limpar (Blomqvist 46), Brolin, Dahlin (Andersson 46), Svensson
Romania: Stelea (Prunea 69), Petrescu, Prodan, Mihali (Gilca 77), Belodedeci, Munteanu (Selymesi 87), Popescu (Vladiou 61), Lupescu, Dumitrescu (Stinga 79), Hagi (Papura 86), Raducioiu (Ivan 61)
Ref: Patlak (USA)

July 1994

29 July Baltic Cup   *Vilnius*   *Att: 1000*
LITHUANIA   **3**   (Ivanauskas 10, 23; Mikalajunas 60)
ESTONIA   **0**
Lithuania: Stauce, Ziukas (Pankratievas 70), Baltusnikas (Stonkus 57), Gudaitis, Terechkinas, Skarbailus, Korsakovas, Strumbrys (Zalys 63), Apanavitchus (Mikalajunas 55), Vaineikis (Zuta 52), Ivanauskas
Estonia: Poom, R. Kallaste, Linnumae*, G. Olesk, T. Kallaste, Saks (O'Konnel 56), Klavans (Lemsalu 69), Lindmae, Paris (Ratnikov 46), Kristal (Lelov 69), Reim
*Linnumae sent off 44 min
Ref: Lajkus (Lat)

30 July Baltic Cup   *Vilnius*   *Att: 200*
LATVIA   **2**   Astafiev 31; Boulders 37)
ESTONIA   **0**
Latvia: Karavaiev (Laizans 62), Troisky, Astafiev, Erglis, Zemlicky, Popkov (Monjak 62), Emelianov (Fedotov 46), Mikutsky, Zeiberlinch (Blagonadiezdine 46), Charanda (Rither 56), Boulders
Estonia: Poom, Lemsalu, R. Kallaste, G. Olesk, T. Kallaste, Lindmae, Paris (Ratnikov 53), Klavans, O'Konnel (Saks 28), Reim, Kristal
Ref: Dubinskas (Lit)

31 July Baltic Cup   *Vilnius*   *Att: 500*
LITHUANIA   **1**   (Terechnikas 68 pen)
LATVIA   **0**
Lithuania: Stauce, Ziukas, Stonkus, Gudaitis, Terechkinas, Skarbailus, Korsakovas (Vainoras 58), Strumbrys (Zuta 55), Mikalajunas (Apanavitchus 46), Vaineiki, Zalys (Darincevas 85)
Latvia: Karavaiev, Troisky, Astafiev (Rither), Erglis, Zemlinsky, Jeliseiev (Popkov 46), Emelianov, Mikoutsky, Zeiberlinch (Blagonadiezdine 46), Charanda, Boulders
Ref: Timofeev (Est)
Final Placings: 1st: Lithuania (2 wins 4-0)
                        2nd: Latvia (1 win 2-1)
                        3rd: Estonia (0 win 0-5)

World Cup Finals 1930–94

1930
30 July 1930   *Centenario, Montevideo*   93,000
Uruguay **4** **Argentina** **2**
Dorado (12), Cea (58), Peucelle (20), Stabile (37)
Iriarte (68), Castro (89)
Uruguay: Ballesteros, Nasazzi, Mascheroni, Andrade J., Fernandez, Gestido, Dorado, Scarone, Castro, Cea, Iriarte
Argentina: Botasso, Della Torre, Paternoster, Evaristo J., Monti, Suarez, Peucelle, Varallo, Stabile, Ferreira, Evaristo M.

1934
10 June 1934   *PNF, Rome*   55,000
Italy **2** **Czechoslovakia** **1**
Orsi (81), Schiavio (95) Puc (71)
Italy: Combi, Monzeglio, Allemandi, Ferraris IV, Monti, Bertolini, Guaita, Meazza, Schiavio, Ferrari, Orsi
Czechoslovakia: Planicka, Zenisek, Ctyroky, Kostalek, Cambal, Krcil, Junek, Svoboda, Sobotka, Nejedly, Puc

1938
19 June 1938   *Colombes, Paris*   55,000
Italy **4** **Hungary** **2**
Colaussi (5, 35), Piola (16, 82) Titkos (7), Sarosi (70)
Italy: Olivieri, Foni, Rava, Serantoni, Andreolo, Locatelli, Biavati, Meazza, Piola, Ferrari, Colaussi
Hungary: Szabo, Polgar, Biro, Szalay, Szucs, Lazar, Sas, Vincze, Sarosi, Szengeller, Titkos

1950
16 July 1950   *Maracana, Rio*   199,000
Uruguay **2** **Brazil** **1**
Schiaffino (66), Ghiggia (79) Friaca (48)
Uruguay: Maspoli, Gonzales, Tejera, Gambetta, Varela O., Andrade V., Ghiggia, Perez, Miguez, Schiaffino, Moran
Brazil: Barbosa, Augusto, Juvenal, Bauer, Danilo, Bigode, Friaca, Zizinho, Ademir, Jair R Pinto, Chico

1954
4 July 1954   *Wankdorf, Berne*   60,000
West Germany **3** **Hungary** **2**
Morlock (11), Rahn (16, 83) Puskas (6), Czibor (8)
West Germany: Turek, Posipal, Liebrich, Kohlmeyer, Eckel, Mai, Rahn, Morlock, Walter O., Walter F., Schafer
Hungary: Grosics, Buzanszky, Lorant, Lantos, Bozsik, Zakarias, Czibor, Kocsis, Hidegkuti, Puskas, Toth

1958
29 June 1958   *Rasunda, Stockholm*   49,000
Brazil **5** **Sweden** **2**
Vava (10, 32), Pele (56, 89), Liedholm (4), Simonsson (80)
Zagalo (68)
Brazil: Gilmar, Djalma Santos, Bellini, Orlando Pecanha, Nilton Santos, Zito, Didi, Garrincha, Vava, Pele, Zagalo
Sweden: Svensson, Bergmark, Gustavsson, Axbom, Borjesson, Parling, Hamrin, Gren G., Simonsson, Liedholm, Skoglund

1962
17 June 1962   *Estadio Nacional, Santiago*   68,000
Brazil **3** **Czechoslovakia** **1**
Amarildo (18), Zito (69), Masopust (16)
Vava (77)
Brazil: Gilmar, Djalma Santos, Mauro R. Oliveira, Zozimo, Nilton Santos, Zito, Didi, Garrincha, Vava, Amarildo, Zagalo
Czechoslovakia: Schrojf, Tichy, Pluskal, Popluhar, Novak, Kvasnak, Masopust, Pospichal, Scherer, Kadraba, Jelinek

1966
30 July 1966   *Wembley, London*   96,000
England **4** **West Germany** **2**
Hurst (19, 100, 119), Peters (77) Haller (13), Weber (89)
England: Banks, Cohen, Charlton J, Moore, Wilson, Stiles, Charlton B, Ball, Hunt, Hurst, Peters
West Germany: Tilkowski, Hottges, Schulz, Weber, Schnellinger, Haller, Beckenbauer, Seeler, Held, Overath, Emmerich

1970
21 June 1970   *Azteca, Mexico City*   107,000
Brazil **4** **Italy** **1**
Pele (18), Gerson (66), Boninsegna (37)
Jairzinho (71), Carlos Alberto (86)
Brazil: Felix, Carlos Alberto, Brito, Piazza, Everaldo, Clodoaldo, Gerson, Jairzinho, Tostao, Pele, Rivelino
Italy: Albertosi, Burgnich, Cera, Rosato, Facchetti, Bertini (Juliano), Mazzola, De Sisti, Domenghini, Boninsegna (Rivera), Riva

1974
7 July 1974   *Olymiastadion, Munich*   77,000
West Germany **2** **Holland** **1**
Breitner (25), Muller (43) Neeskens (1)
West Germany: Maier, Vogts, Schwarzenbeck, Beckenbauer, Breitner, Bonhof, Hoeness, Overath, Grabowski, Muller, Holzenbein
Holland: Jongbloed, Suurbier, Rijsbergen (De Jong), Haan, Krol, Jansen, Neeskens, Van Hanegem, Rep, Cruyff, Rensenbrink (Van de Kerkhof)

1978
25 June 1978   *Monumental, Buenos Aires*   77,000
Argentina **3** **Holland** **1**
Kempes (37, 104), Bertoni (114) Nanninga (81)
Argentina: Fillol, Olguin, Galvan, Passarella, Tarantini, Ardiles (Larrosa), Gallego, Kempes, Bertoni, Luque, Ortiz (Houseman)
Holland: Jongbloed, Krol, Poortvliet, Brandts, Jansen (Suurbier), Van de Kerkhof W., Neeskens, Haan, Rep (Nanninga), Rensenbrink, Van de Kerkhof R.

1982
11 July 1982   *Bernabeu, Madrid*   90,000
Italy **3** **West Germany** **1**
Rossi (56), Tardelli (69), Breitner (82)
Altobelli (80)
Italy: Zoff, Cabrini, Scirea, Gentile, Collavati, Oriali, Bergomi, Tardelli, Conti, Rossi, Graziani (Altobelli) (Causio)
West Germany: Schumacher, Kaltz, Stielike, Forster K-H, Forster B, Breitner, Briegel, Dremmler (Hrubesch), Rummenigge (Muller), Littbarski, Fischer

1986
29 July 1986 *Azteca, Mexico City* *114,000*
Argentina 3 **West Germany** 2
Brown (22), Valdano (56), Rummenigge (73), Voller (82)
Burruchaga (84)
Argentina: Pumpido, Cuciuffo, Brown, Ruggeri, Olarticoechea, Batista, Giusti, Enrique, Burruchaga (Trobbiani), Maradona, Valdano
West Germany: Schumacher, Jakobs, Forster K-H, Briegel, Brehme, Eder, Berthold, Matthaus, Magath (Hoeness), Rummenigge, Allofs (Voller)

1990
8 July 1990 *Olimpic, Rome* *73,000*
West Germany 1 **Argentina** 0
Brehme (85)
West Germany: Illgner, Berthold, Kohler, Augenthaler, Buchwald, Brehme, Hassler, Matthaus, Littbarski, Voller, Klinsmann
Argentina: Goycochea, Ruggeri, Simon, Serrizuela, Sensini, Basualdo, Burruchaga, Trogilo, Lorenzo, Maradona, Dezotti

1994
17 July *Rose Bowl, Pasadena* *94,194*
Brazil 0 **Italy** 0
Brazil win 3-2 on penalties after extra time
Brazil: Taffarel, Jorginho (Cafu 21), Aldair, Marcio Santos, Branco, Mauro Silva, Dunga, Zinho (Cafu 109), Mazinho, Bebeto, Romario.
Italy: Pagliuca, Benarrivo, Baresi, Maldini, Mussi (Apolloni 34), D. Baggio (Evani 101), Albertini, Berti, Donadoni, R.Baggio, Massaro

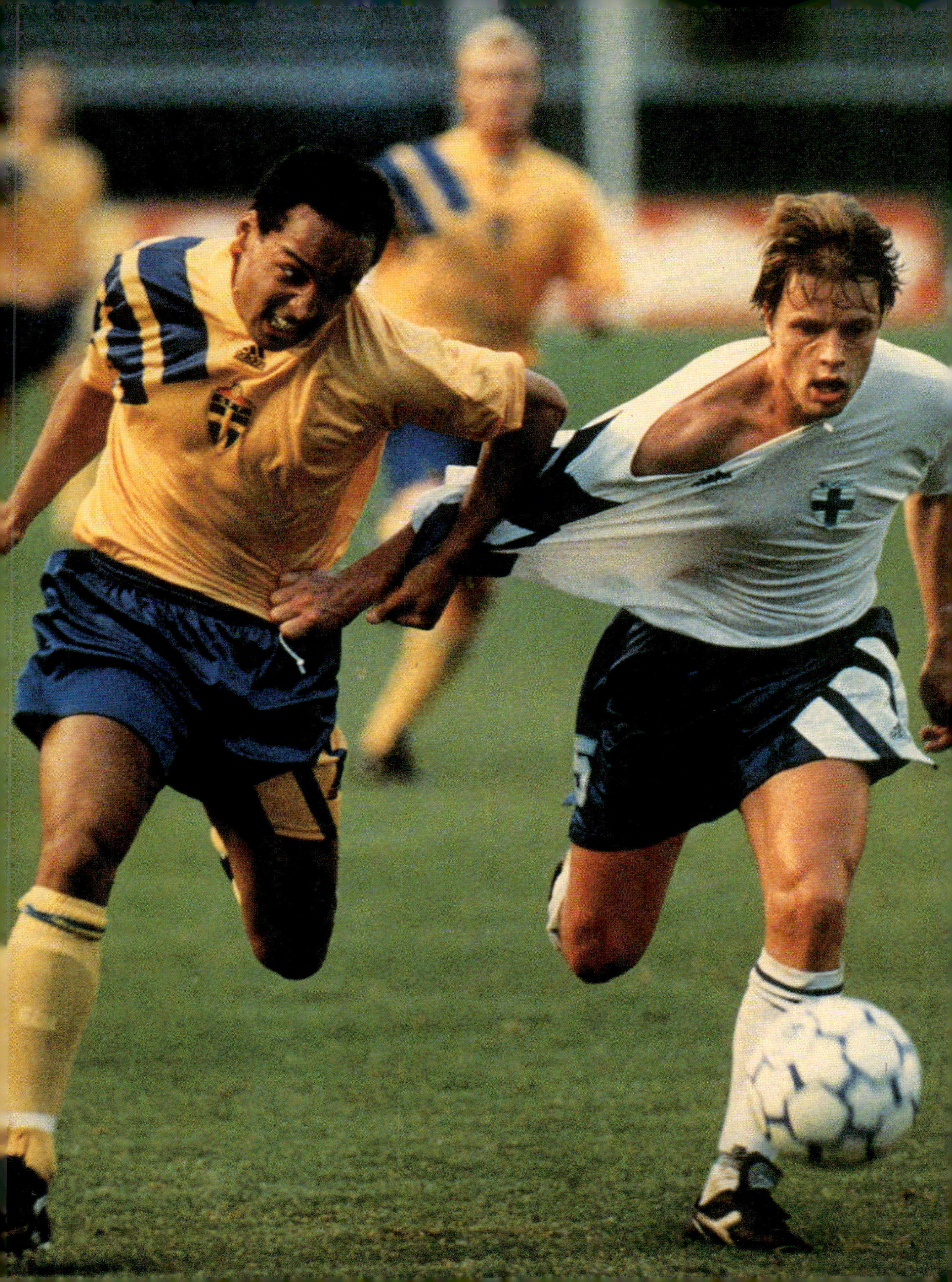

PREVIOUS PAGE: *Sweden's Martin Dahlin gets shirty with Finland's midfield during their Group Six encounter in Stockholm.*

World Cup Qualifying Rounds

ABOVE: *Paul Ince of England gets a close-up of the studs of San Marino's Bonini during the 7-1 win in Group Two.*

RIGHT: *Luboslav Penev of Bulgaria takes Alain Roche of France for a ride in a Group Six encounter.*

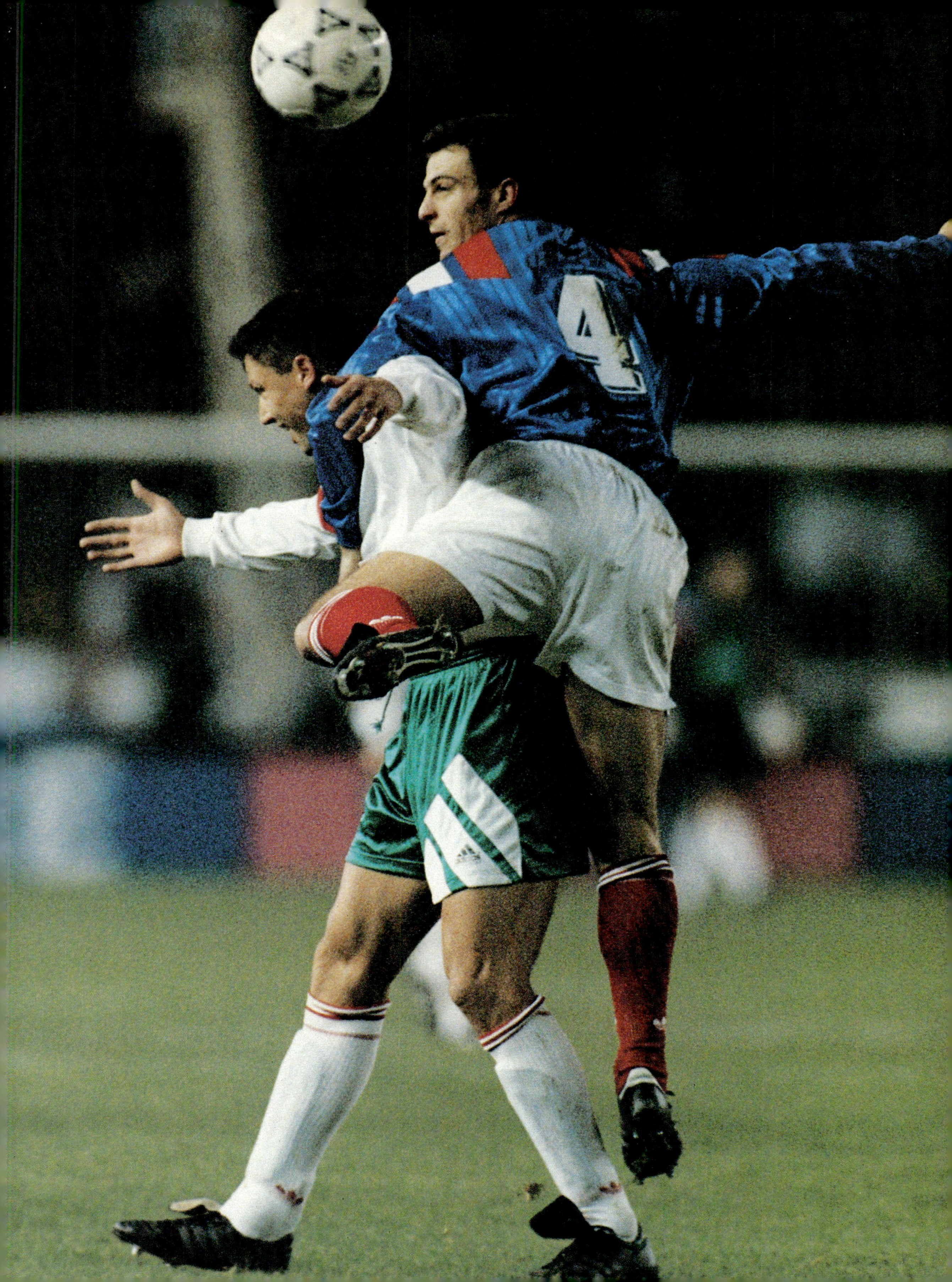

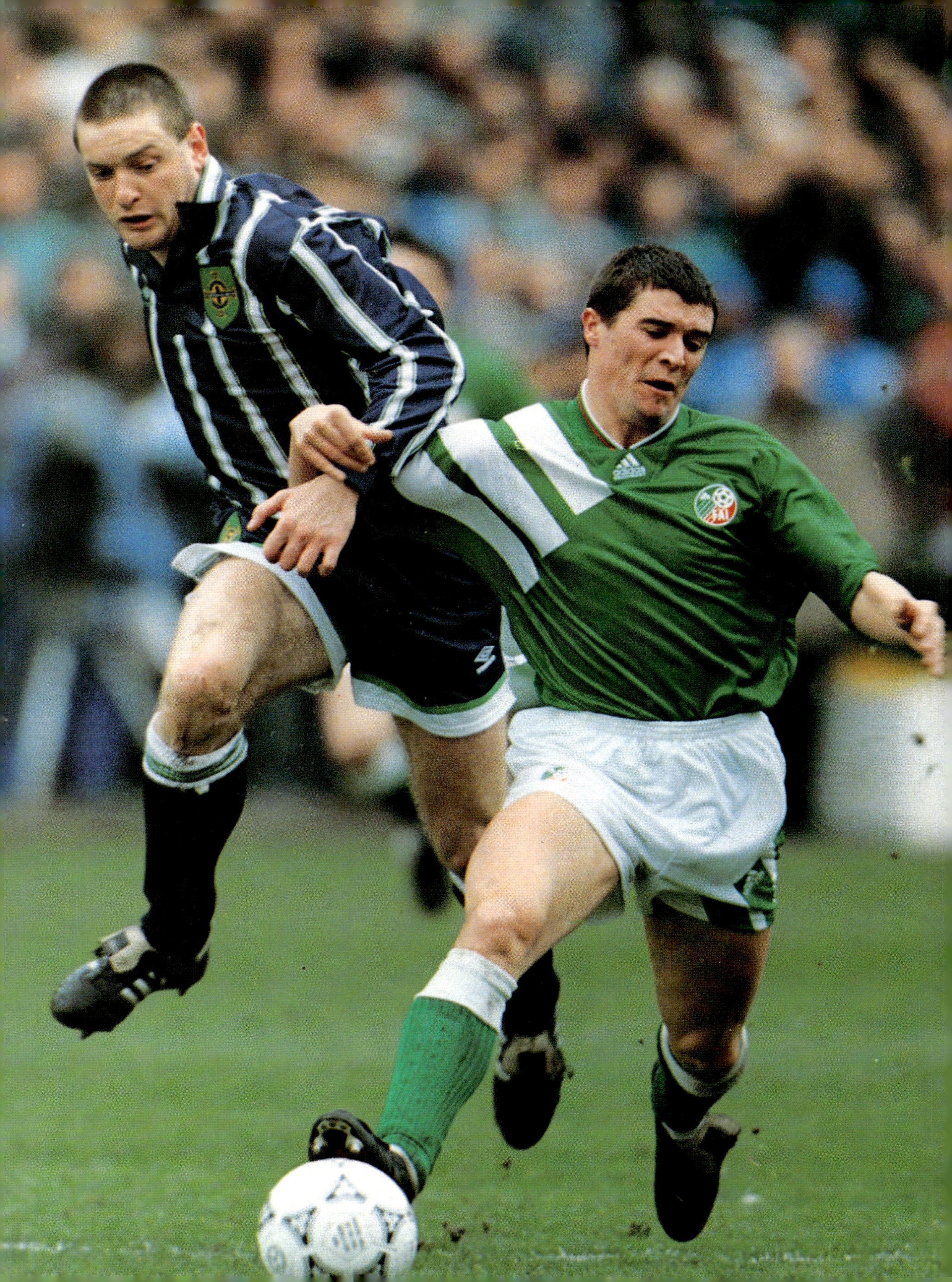
adidas

LEFT: *Ged Taggart of Northern Ireland tussles with the Republic of Ireland's Roy Keane (green).*

RIGHT: *Graham Taylor sings the National Anthem for the last time as England manager before the game against San Marino.*

BELOW: *Jean-Pierre Papin in action for France against Israel.*

Champions' Cup

LEFT: *Eric Cantona of Manchester United is escorted off the field after the explosive 0-0 draw with Galatasaray in Istanbul, in the second round of the Champions' Cup.*

RIGHT: *Barcelona's Miquel Nadal (right) and FC Porto's Kostadinov during the Champions' Cup semi-final in the Nou Camp.*

BELOW: *Manchester United's rising star Ryan Giggs outjumps the Galatasaray defence.*

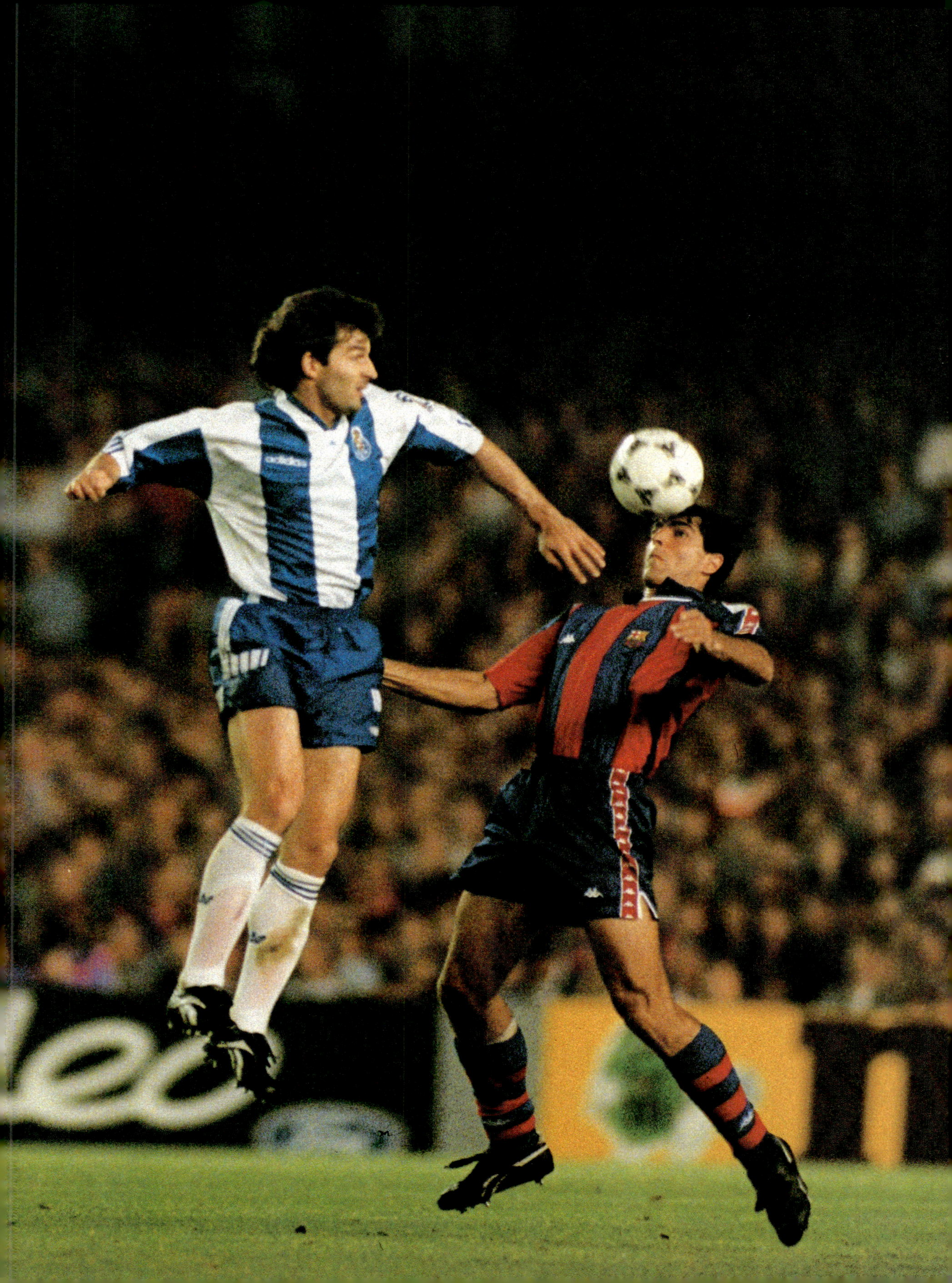

LEFT: *Action as Anderlecht stretch out against FC Porto in the UEFA Champions' League.*

BELOW: *Champions' Cup first round action between Rangers and Levski Sofia. (L/R) Ian Durrant and Alexander Markov.*

LEFT: *Mauro Tassotti – captain for the night of his life – lifts the Champions' Cup for Milan.*

BELOW: *Milan's Roberto Donadoni on the ball against Barcelona during the Champions' Cup final in Athens.*

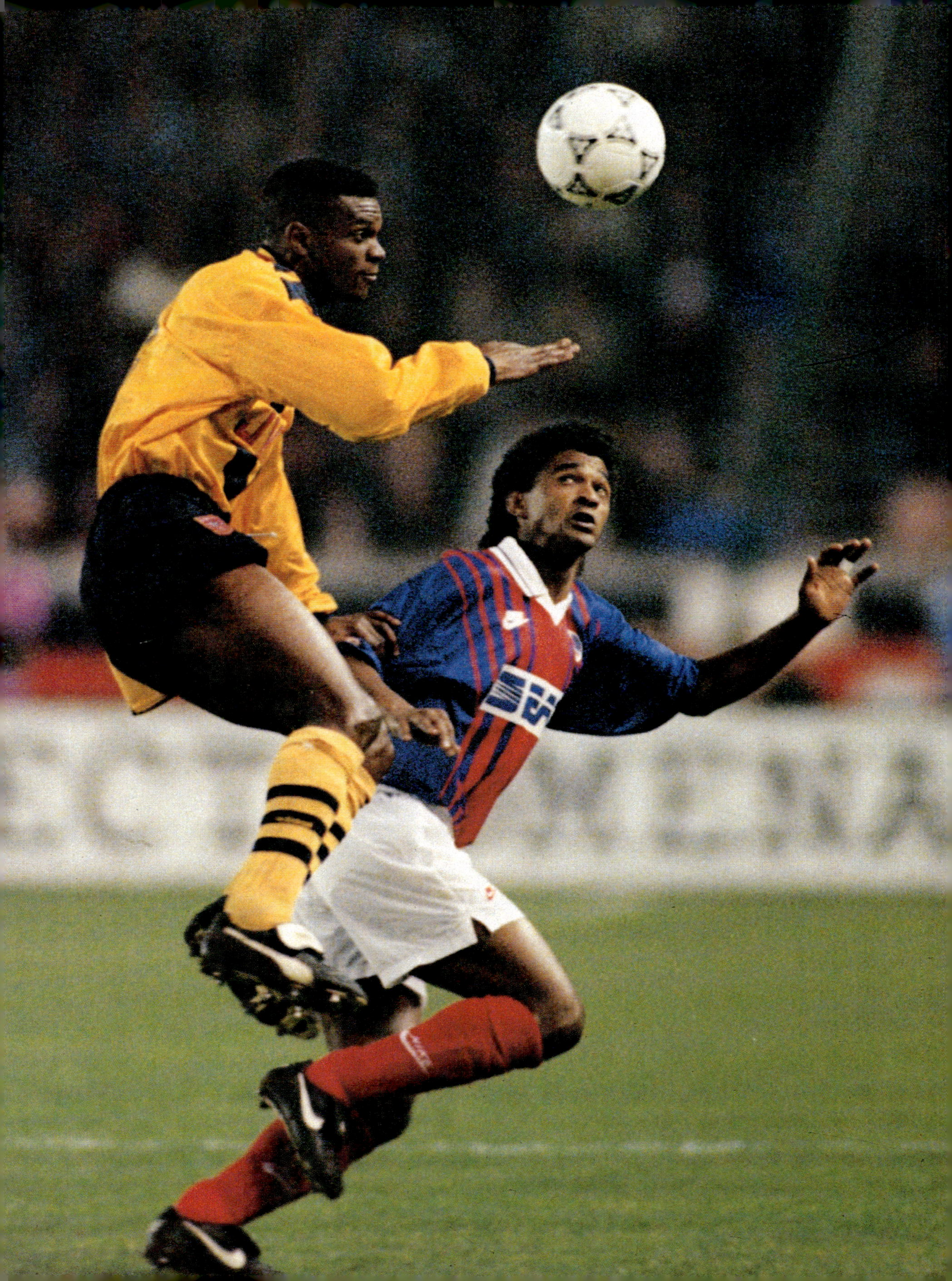

Cup-Winners' Cup action

ABOVE: *Arsenal celebrate after beating Parma to capture the Cup-Winners' Cup.*

RIGHT: *The agony – Massimo Crippa of Parma is tackled by Benfica's Vitor Aravio.*

LEFT: *Up, up and away to a 1-1 draw as Arsenal's Paul Davis takes off watched by Paris Saint-Germain's Ricardo during the Cup-Winners' Cup semi-final 1st leg.*

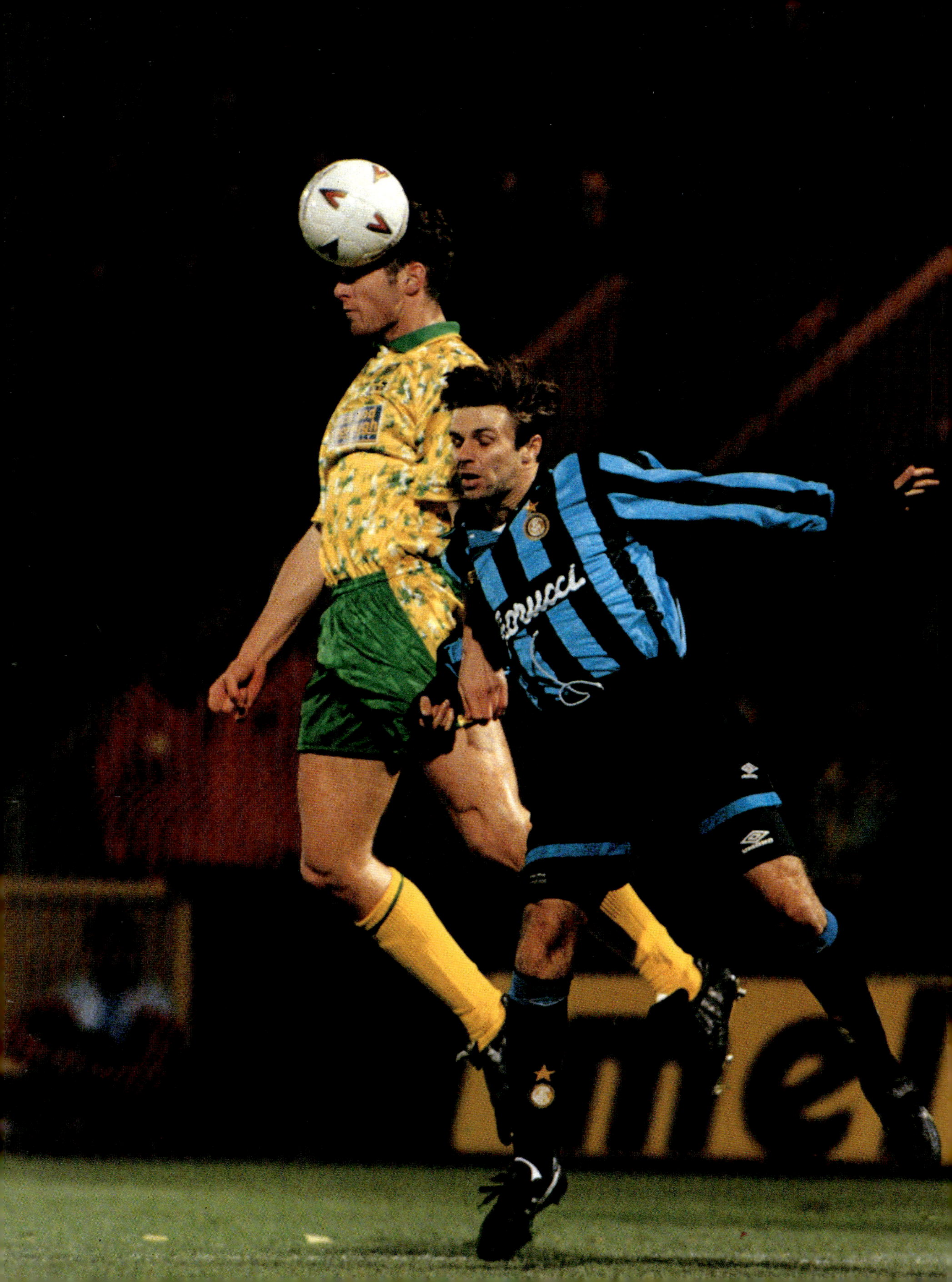

UEFA Cup action

LEFT: *Chris Sutton gets ahead of Internazionale's Davide Fontolan during their third round tie.*

RIGHT: *Dennis Bergkamp of Internazionale celebrates with the UEFA Cup.*

BELOW: *Near post action between Karlsruhe and Boavista.*

LEFT: *A dejected Romario leaves the pitch after losing to Milan.*

BELOW: *AC Milan Japanese style prior to the Toyota Cup final in Tokyo.*

RIGHT: *Watch the ball! Gerson of Lecce and David Platt of Sampdoria.*

LEFT: *The ecstasy – Tomas Brolin with the European Super Cup.*

OVERLEAF: *Top Man – Newcastle United's Andy Cole was the FA Premiership's top scorer.*

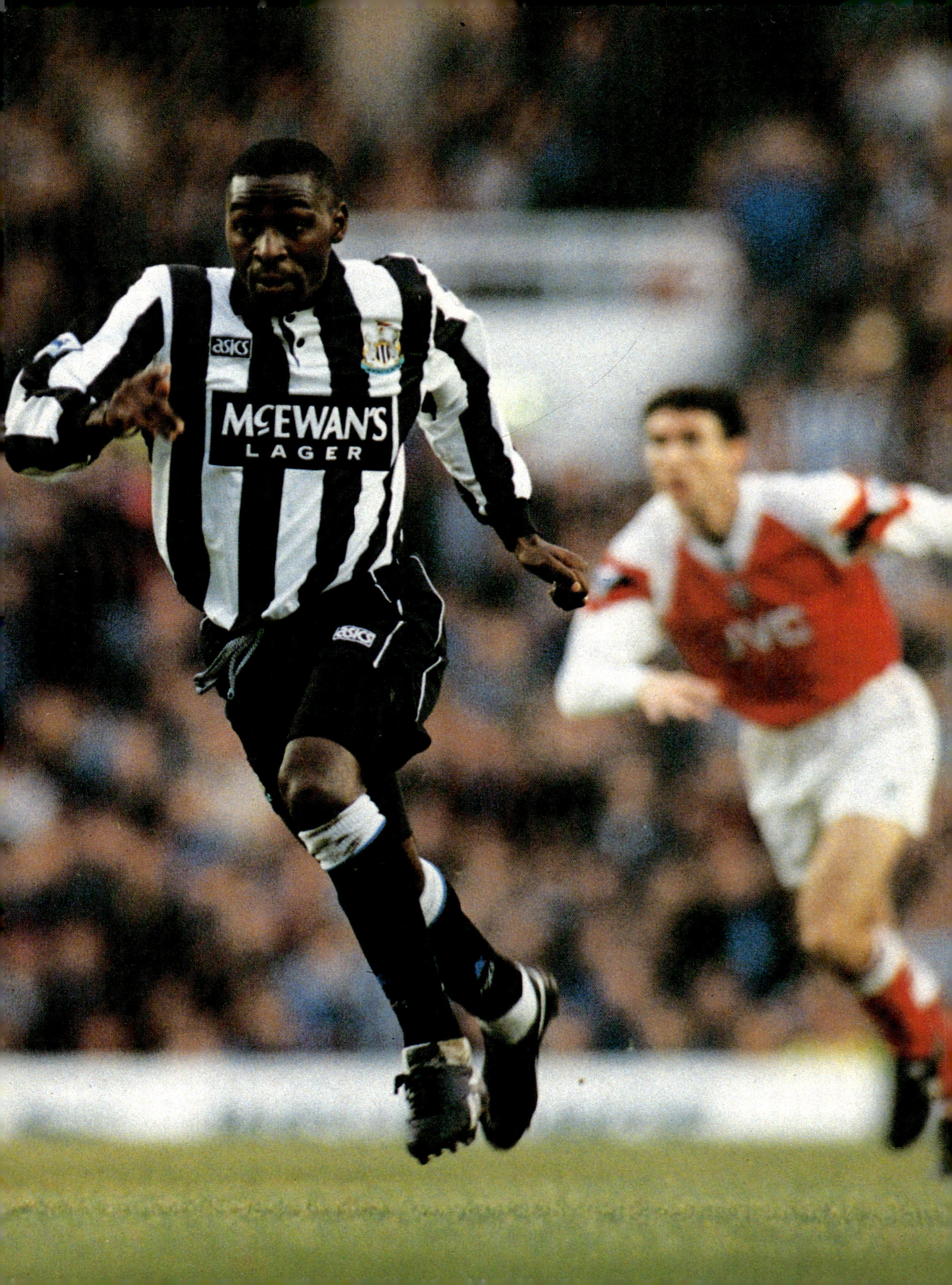
asics
McEWAN'S
LAGER
asics

European Championship Finals 1960–92

1960
10 July 1960   *Parc des Princes, Paris*   18,000
Soviet Union   **2**   **Yugoslavia**   **1**
Metreveli (49), Ponedelnik (113)   Galic (41)
After extra time
Soviet Union: Yashin, Tchekeli, Maslenkin, Droutikov, Voinov, Netto, Metreveli, Ivanov V., Ponedelnik, Bubukin, Meshki
Yugoslavia: Vidinic, Durkovic, Miladinovic, Jusufi, Zanetic, Perusic, Sekularac, Jerkovic, Galic, Matus, Kostic

1964
21 June 1964   *Bernabeu, Madrid*   105,000
Spain   **2**   **Soviet Union**   **1**
Pereda (6), Marcelino (83)   Khusainov (8)
Spain: Iribar, Rivilla, Olivella, Calleja, Zoco, Fuste, Amancio, Pereda, Marcelino, Suarez, Lapetra
Soviet Union: Yashin, Chustikov, Shesterniev, Anitchkin, Mudrik, Voronin, Korniev, Chislenko, Ivanov V., Ponedelnik, Khusainov

1968
8 June 1968   *Stadio Olimpico, Rome*   85,000
Italy   **1**   **Yugoslavia**   **1**
Domenghini (80)   Dzajic (39)
Italy: Zoff, Burgnich, Guarneri, Facchetti, Ferrini, Castano, Domenghini, Juliano, Anastasi, Lodetti, Prati
Yugoslavia: Pantelic, Fazlagic, Paunovic, Holcer, Damjanovic, Pavlovic, Trivic, Petkovic, Musemic, Acimovic, Dzajic

Replay
10 June 1968   *Stadio Olimpico, Rome*   50,000
Italy   **2**   **Yugoslavia**   **0**
Riva (11), Anastasi (32)
Italy: Zoff, Burgnich, Guarneri, Facchetti, Rosato, Salvadore, Domenghini, Mazzola, Anastasi, De Sisti, Riva
Yugoslavia: Pantelic, Fazlagic, Paunovic, Holcer, Damjanovic, Pavlovic, Trivic, Acimovic, Musemic, Hosic, Dzajic

1972
18 June 1972   *Heysel, Brussels*   65,000
West Germany   **3**   **Soviet Union**   **0**
Muller (27, 58), Wimmer (52)
West Germany: Maier, Hottges, Schwarzenbeck, Beckenbauer, Breitner, Wimmer, Hoeness, Netzer, Heynckes, Muller G., Kremmers
Soviet Union: Rudakov, Dzodzuashvili, Khurtsilava, Kaplichny, Istomin, Kolotov, Troshkin, Konkov (Dolmatov), Baidachni, Banishevski (Kozinkievits), Onishenko

1976
20 June 1976   *Red Star, Belgrade*   45,000
Czechoslovakia   **2**   **West Germany**   **2**
Svehlik (8), Dobias (25)   Muller D (28), Holzenbein (89)
Czechoslovakia won 5-4 on penalties
Czechoslovakia: Viktor, Pivarnik, Ondrus, Capkovic, Gogh, Dobias (Vesely F.), Moder, Panenka, Masney, Svehlik (Jurkemik), Nehoda
West Germany: Maier, Vogts, Schwarzenbeck, Beckenbauer, Dietz, Wimmer (Flohe), Beer (Bongartz), Bonhof, Hoeness, Muller D., Holzenbein

1980
22 June 1980   *Stadio Olimpico, Rome*   48,000
West Germany   **2**   **Belgium**   **1**
Hrubesch (10, 88)   Vandereycken (72)
West Germany: Schumacher, Kaltz, Forster K.-H., Stielike, Dietz, Briegel (Cullmann), Schuster, Muller H., Rummenigge, Hrubesch, Allofs
Belgium: Pfaff, Gerets, Millecamps, Meeuws, Renquin, Cools, Vandereycken, Van Moer, Mommens, Van der Elst, Ceulemans

1984
27 June 1984   *Parc des Princes, Paris*
France   **2**   **Spain**   **0**
Platini (57), Bellone (90)
France: Bats, Battiston (Amoros), Le Roux, Bossis, Domergue, Giresse, Tigana, Fernandez, Platini, Lacombe (Genghini), Bellone
Spain: Arconada, Urquiaga, Salva (Roberto), Gallego, Senor, Francisco, Victor, Camacho, Julio Alberto (Sarabia), Santillana, Carrasco

1988
25 June 1988   *Olympiastadion, Munich*   72,000
Holland   **2**   **Soviet Union**   **0**
Gullit (32), Van Basten (53)
Holland: Van Breukelen, Van Aerle, Rijkaard, Koeman R., Van Tiggelen, Vanenburg, Wouters, Muhren, Koeman E., Gullit, Van Basten
Soviet Union: Dasayev, Demianenko, Aleinikov, Khidiatulin, Rats, Litovchenko, Zavarov, Mikhailichenko, Gotsmanov (Baltacha), Protasov (Pasulko), Belanov

1992
26 June 1992   *Nya Ullevi, Gothenburg*   28,000
Denmark   **2**   **Germany**   **0**
Jensen J (18), Vilfort (78)
Denmark: Schmeichel, Sivebaek (Christiansen), Nielsen K., Olsen L., Piechnik, Christofte, Jensen J., Vilfort, Larsen H., Povlsen, Laudrup B.
Germany: Illgner, Helmer, Reuter, Kohler, Buchwald, Brehme, Hassler, Sammer (Doll), Effenberg (Thon), Riedle, Klinsmann

Champions' Cup Finals 1956–94

1956
13 June *Parc des Princes, Paris* *38,000*
Real Madrid 4 **Stade de Reims** 3
Di Stefano (14), Rial (30, 79), Leblond (6), Templin (10),
Marquitos (67) Hidalgo (62)
Real Madrid: Alonso, Atienza, Marquitos, Lesmes, Munoz, Zarraga, Joseito, Marchal, Di Stefano, Rial, Gento. *Tr:* Villalonga
Stade de Reims: Jacquet, Zimny, Jonquet, Giraudo, Leblond, Siatka, Hidalgo, Glovacki, Kopa, Bliard, Templin. *Tr:* Batteaux

1957
30 May *Bernabeu, Madrid* *124,000*
Real Madrid 2 **Fiorentina** 0
Di Stefano (70), Gento (76)
Real Madrid: Alonso, Torres, Marquitos, Lesmes, Munoz, Zarraga, Kopa, Mateos, Di Stefano, Rial, Gento. *Tr:* Villalonga
Fiorentina: Sarti, Magnini, Orzan, Cervato, Scaramucci, Segato, Julinho, Gratton, Virgili, Montuori, Bizzarri. *Tr:* Bernardini.

1958
28 June *Heysel, Brussels* *67,000*
Real Madrid 3 **Milan** 2 aet
Di Stefano (74), Rial (79), Schiaffino (69), Grillo (78)
Gento (107)
Real Madrid: Alonso, Atienza, Santamaria, Lesmes, Santisteban, Zarraga, Kopa, Joseito, Di Stefano, Rial, Gento. *Tr:* Carniglia
Milan: Soldan, Fontana, Maldini, Beraldo, Bergamaschi, Radice, Danova, Liedholm, Schiaffino, Grillo, Cucchiaroni. *Tr:* Viani

1959
3 June *Neckarstadion, Stuttgart* *80,000*
Real Madrid 2 **Stade de Reims** 0
Mateos (2), Di Stefano (47)
Real Madrid: Dominguez, Marquitos, Santamaria, Zarraga, Santisteban, Ruiz, Kopa, Mateos, Di Stefano, Rial, Gento. *Tr:* Carniglia
Stade de Reims: Colonna, Rodzik, Jonquet, Giraudo, Penverne, Leblond, Lamartine, Berard, Fontaine, Piantoni, Vincent. *Tr:* Batteux

1960
18 May *Hampden Park, Glasgow* *135,000*
Real Madrid 7 **Eintracht Frankfurt** 3
Di Stefano (27, 30, 77), Kress (10), Stein (64, 72)
Puskas (45, 56, 60, 71)
Real Madrid: Dominguez, Marquitos, Santamaria, Pachin, Vidal, Zarraga, Canario, Del Sol, Di Stefano, Puskas, Gento. *Tr:* Munoz
Eintracht Frankfurt: Loy, Lutz, Eigenbrodt, Hofer, Weilbacher, Stinka, Kress, Lindner, Stein, Pfaff, N. Meier. *Tr:* Oswald

1961
31 May *Wankdorf, Berne* *27,000*
Benfica 3 **Barcelona** 2
Aguas (30) Own Goal (32), Kocsis (20), Czibor (75)
Coluna (55)
Benfica: Costa Pereira, Joao, Germano, Angelo, Neto, Cruz, Augusto, Santana, Aguas, Coluna, Cavem. *Tr:* Guttmann
Barcelona: Ramallets, Foncho, Gensana, Gracia, Verges, Garay, Kubala, Kocsis, Evaristo, Suarez, Czibor. *Tr:* Orizaola

1962
2 May *Olympisch Stadion, Amsterdam* *65,000*
Benfica 5 **Real Madrid** 3
Aguas (25), Cavem (34), Puskas (17, 23, 38)
Coluna (51), Eusebio (65, 68)
Benfica: Costa Pereira, Joao, Germano, Angelo, Cavem, Cruz, Augusto, Eusebio, Aguas, Coluna, Simoes. *Tr:* Guttmann
Real Madrid: Araquistain, Casado, Santamaria, Miera, Felo, Pachin, Tejada, Del Sol, Di Stefano, Puskas, Gento. *Tr:* Munoz

1963
22 May *Wembley, London* *45,000*
Milan 2 **Benfica** 1
Altafini (58, 70) Eusebio (19)
Milan: Ghezzi, David, Maldini, Trebbi, Benitez, Trapattoni, Pivatelli, Sani, Altafini, Rivera, Mora. *Tr:* Rocco
Benfica: Costa Pereira, Cavem, Cruz, Humberto, Raul, Coluna, Santana, Augusto, Torres, Eusebio, Simoes. *Tr:* Riera

1964
27 May *Prater, Vienna* *72,000*
Internazionale 3 **Real Madrid** 1
Mazzola (43, 76), Milani (61) Felo (70)
Internazionale: Sarti, Burgnich, Guarneri, Facchetti, Tagnin, Picchi, Jair, Mazzola, Milani, Suarez, Corso. *Tr:* Herrera
Real Madrid: Vicente, Isidro, Santamaria, Pachin, Zoco, Muller, Amancio, Felo, Di Stefano, Puskas, Gento. *Tr:* Munoz

1965
27 May *San Siro, Milan* *85,000*
Internazionale 1 **Benfica** 0
Jair (42)
Internazionale: Sarti, Burgnich, Guarneri, Facchetti, Bedin, Picchi, Jair, Mazzola, Peiro, Suarez, Corso. *Tr:* Herrera
Benfica: Costa Pereira, Cavem, Cruz, Germano, Raul, Neto, Coluna, Augusto, Eusebio, Torres, Simoes. *Tr:* Schwartz

1966
11 May *Heysel, Brussels* *55,000*
Real Madrid 2 **Partizan Belgrade** 1
Amancio (70), Serena (75) Vasovic (55)
Real Madrid: Araquistain, Pachin, De Felipe, Zoco, Sanchis, Pirri, Velazquez, Serena, Amancio, Grosso, Gento. *Tr:* Munoz
Partizan Belgrade: Soskic, Jusufi, Rasovic, Vasovic, Milhailovic, Kovacevic, Becejac, Bajic, Hasanagic, Galic, Pirmajer. *Tr:* Gegic

1967
25 May *Estadio Nacional, Lisbon* *54,000*
Celtic 2 **Internazionale** 1
Gemmell (63), Chalmers (85) Mazzola (8)

Celtic: Simpson, Craig, McNeill, Gemmell, Murdoch, Clark, Johnstone, Wallace, Chalmers, Auld, Lennox. *Tr:* Stein
Internazionale: Sarti, Burgnich, Guarneri, Facchetti, Bedin, Picchi, Domenghini, Mazzola, Cappellini, Bicicli, Corso. *Tr:* Herrera

1968
29 May   *Wembley Stadium, London*   100,000
Manchester United   4   **Benfica**   1 aet
Charlton (53, 99), Best (93),   Graca (75)
Kidd (94)
Manchester United: Stepney, Brennan, Stiles, Foulkes, Dunne, Crerand, Charlton, Sadler, Best, Kidd, Aston. *Tr:* Busby
Benfica: Henrique, Adolfo, Humberto, Jacinto, Cruz, Graca, Coluna, Augusto, Eusebio, Torres, Simoes. *Tr:* Gloria

1969
28 May   *Bernabeu, Madrid*   31,000
Milan   4   **Ajax**   1
Prati (7, 40, 75), Sormani (67)   Vasovic (60)
Milan: Cudicini, Malatrasi, Anquilletti, Schnellinger, Rosato, Trapattoni, Lodetti, Rivera, Hamrin, Sormani, Prati. *Tr:* Rocco
Ajax: Bals, Suurbier (Muller), Hulshoff, Vasovic, Van Duivenbode, Pronk, Groot (Nanninga), Swart, Cruyff, Danielsson, Keizer. *Tr:* Michels

1970
6 May   *San Siro, Milan*   53,000
Feyenoord   2   **Celtic**   1 aet
Israel (31), Kindvall (117)   Gemmell (29)
Feyenoord: Pieters Graafland, Romeijn (Haak), Laseroms, Israel, Van Duivenbode, Hasil, Jansen, Van Hanegem, Wery, Kindvall, Moulijn. *Tr:* Happel
Celtic: Williams, Hay, Grogan, McNeill, Gemmell, Murdoch, Auld (Connelly), Johnstone, Lennox, Wallace, Hughes. *Tr:* Stein

1971
2 June   *Wembley, London*   83,000
Ajax   2   **Panathinaikos**   0
Van Dijk (5) Own Goal (87)
Ajax: Stuy, Neeskens, Hulshoff, Vasovic, Suurbier, Rijnders (Blankenburg), Muhren G., Swart (Haan), Cruyff, Van Dijk, Keizer. *Tr:* Michels
Panathinaikos: Oeconomopoulos, Tomaras, Kapsis, Sourpis, Viahos, Kamaras, Ileferakia, Gammos, Antoniadis, Domazos, Filakouris. *Tr:* Puskas

1972
31 May   *Feyenoord, Rotterdam*   61,000
Ajax   2   **Internazionale**   0
Cruyff (47, 78)
Ajax: Stuy, Suurbier, Blankenburg, Hulshoff, Krol, Neeskens, Haan, Muhren G., Swart, Cruyff, Keizer. *Tr:* Kovacs
Internazionale: Bordon, Burgnich, Facchetti, Bellugi, Oriali, Giubertoni (Bertini), Bedin, Frustalupi, Jair (Pellizarro), Mazzola, Boninsegna. *Tr:* Invernizzi

1973
30 May   *Red Star, Belgrade*   89,000
Ajax   1   **Juventus**   0
Rep (4)
Ajax: Stuy, Suurbier, Hulshoff, Blankenburg, Krol, Neeskens, Muhren G., Haan, Rep, Cruyff, Keizer. *Tr:* Kovacs
Juventus: Zoff, Salvadore, Marchetti, Morini, Longobucco, Causio (Cuccureddu), Furino, Capello, Altafini, Anastasi, Bettega (Haller). *Tr:* Vycpalek

1974
15 May   *Heysel, Brussels*   49,000
Bayern Munich   1   **Atletico Madrid**   1 aet
Schwarzenbeck (119)   Luis (114)
Bayern Munich: Maier, Hansen, Breitner, Schwarzenbeck, Beckenbauer, Roth, Zobel, Hoeness, Torstensson (Durnberger), Muller, Kapellmann. *Tr:* Lattek
Atletico Madrid: Reina, Melo, Capon, Adelardo, Heredia, Luis, Eusebio, Irureta, Ufarte (Becerra), Garate, Salcedo (Alberto). *Tr:* Lorenzo

Replay – 17 May   *Heysel, Brussels*   23,000
Bayern Munich   4   **Atletico Madrid**   0
Hoeness (28, 83), Muller (58, 71)
Bayern Munich: Maier, Hansen, Breitner, Schwarzenbeck, Beckenbauer, Roth, Zobel, Hoeness, Torstensson, Muller, Kapellmann. *Tr:* Lattek
Atletico Madrid: Reina, Melo, Capon, Adelardo (Benegas), Heredia, Luis, Eusebio, Alberto (Ufarte), Garate, Salcedo, Becerra. *Tr:* Lorenzo

1975
28 May   *Parc des Princes, Paris*   48,000
Bayern Munich   2   **Leeds United**   0
Roth (71), Muller (81)
Bayern Munich: Maier, Beckenbauer, Schwarzenbeck, Durnberger, Andersson (Weiss), Zobel, Roth, Kapellmann, Hoeness (Wunder), Muller, Torstensson. *Tr:* Cramer
Leeds United: Stewart, Reaney, Gray F., Madeley, Hunter, Bremner, Giles, Yorath (Gray E.), Lorimer, Clarke, Jordan. *Tr:* Armfield

1976
12 May   *Hampden Park, Glasgow*   63,000
Bayern Munich   1   **Saint-Etienne**   0
Roth (57)
Bayern Munich: Maier, Hansen, Schwarzenbeck, Beckenbauer, Horsmann, Roth, Durnberger, Kapellmann, Rummenigge, Muller, Hoeness. *Tr:* Cramer
Saint-Etienne: Curkovic, Repellini, Piazza, Lopez, Janvion, Bathenay, Santini, Larque, Revelli P., Revelli H., Sarramagna (Rocheteau). *Tr:* Herbin

1977
25 May   *Stadio Olimpico, Rome*   52,000
Liverpool   3   **Bor. Monchengladbach**   1
McDermott (29), Smith (67),   Simonsen (50)
Neal (85)
Liverpool: Clemence, Neal, Jones, Smith, Hughes, Case, Kennedy R., Callaghan, McDermott, Keegan, Heighway. *Tr:* Paisley
Bor. Monchengladbach: Kneib, Vogts, Klinkhammer, Wittkamp, Schaffer, Wohlers (Hannes), Wimmer (Kulik), Stielike, Bonhof, Simonsen, Heynckes. *Tr:* Lattek

1978
10 May   *Wembley, London*   92,000
Liverpool   1   **Club Bruges**   0
Dalglish (64)
Liverpool: Clemence, Neal, Thompson, Hansen, Hughes, McDermott, Kennedy R., Souness, Case (Heighway), Fairclough, Dalglish. *Tr:* Paisley
Club Bruges: Jensen, Bastijns, Krieger, Leekens, Maes (Volders), Cools, Decubber, Vandereycken, Ku (Sanders), Simoen, Sorensen. *Tr:* Happel

1979
30 May   *Olympiastadion, Munich*   57,000
Nottingham Forest   1   **Malmo**   0
Francis (45)
Nottingham Forest: Shilton, Anderson, Lloyd, Burns, Clark, Francis, McGovern, Bowyer, Robertson, Woodcock, Birtles. *Tr:* Clough
Malmo: Moller, Andersson R., Jonsson, Andersson M., Erlandsson, Tapper (Malmber), Ljungberg, Prytz, Kindvall, Hansson (Andersson T.), Cervin. *Tr:* Houghton

1980
28 May   *Bernabeu, Madrid*   50,000
Nottingham Forest   1   **SV Hamburg**   0
Robertson (21)
Nottingham Forest: Shilton, Anderson, Gray (Gunn), Lloyd, Burns, O'Neill, McGovern, Bowyer, Mills (O'Hare), Robertson, Birtles. *Tr:* Clough
SV Hamburg: Kargus, Kaltz, Nogly, Buljan, Jakobs, Hieronymus (Hrubesch), Magath, Memering, Keegan, Reimann, Milewski. *Tr:* Zebec

1981
27 May *Parc des Princes, Paris* 48,000
Liverpool 1 Real Madrid 0
Kennedy A (82)
Liverpool: Clemence, Neal, Thompson, Hansen, Kennedy A., Lee, McDermott, Souness, Kennedy R., Dalglish (Case), Johnson. *Tr:* Paisley
Real Madrid: Agustin, Cortes (Pineda), Navajas, Sabido, Del Bosque, Angel, Camacho, Stielike, Juanito, Santillana, Cunningham. *Tr:* Boskov

1982
26 May *Feyenoord, Rotterdam* 46,000
Aston Villa 1 Bayern Munich 0
Withe (67)
Aston Villa: Rimmer (Spink), Swain, Evans, McNaught, Williams, Bremner, Cowans, Mortimer, Shaw, Withe, Morley. *Tr:* Barton
Bayern Munich: Muller, Dremmler, Weiner, Augenthaler, Horsmann, Mathy (Guttler), Breitner, Kraus (Niedermayer), Durnberger, Rummenigge, Hoeness. *Tr:* Csernai

1983
25 May *Olympiako Stadio, Athens* 75,000
SV Hamburg 1 Juventus 0
Magath (7)
Hamburg: Stein, Kaltz, Hieronymus, Jakobs, Wehmeyer, Groh, Folff, Magath, Milewski, Bastrup (Von Heesen), Hrubesch. *Tr:* Happel
Juventus: Zoff, Gentile, Brio, Scirea, Cabrini, Bonini, Tardelli, Bettega, Platini, Rossi (Marocchino), Boniek. *Tr:* Trapattoni

1984
30 May *Stadio Olimpico, Rome* 69,000
Liverpool 1 Roma 1
Neal (13) Pruzzo (42)
Liverpool: Grobbelaar, Neal, Lawrenson, Hansen, Kennedy A., Johnston (Nicol), Lee, Souness, Whelan, Dalglish (Robinson), Rush. *Tr:* Fagan
Roma: Tancredi, Nappi, Bonetti, Righetti, Nela, Di Bartolomei, Falcao, Cerezo (Strukelj), Conti, Pruzzo (Chierico), Graziani. *Tr:* Liedholm
After extra time. Liverpool won 4-2 on penalties

1985
29 May *Heysel, Brussels* 58,000
Juventus 1 Liverpool 0
Platini (56)
Juventus: Tacconi, Favero, Cabrini, Brio, Scirea, Bonini, Platini, Tardelli, Briaschi (Prandelli), Rossi (Vignola), Boniek. *Tr:* Trapattoni
Liverpool: Grobbelaar, Neal, Beglin, Lawrenson (Gillespie), Hansen, Nicol, Dalglish, Whelan, Wark, Rush, Walsh (Johnston). *Tr:* Fagan

1986
7 May *Sanchez Pizjuan, Seville* 70,000
Steaua Bucharest 0 Barcelona 0
Steaua Bucharest: Ducadam, Iovan, Belodedici, Bumbescu, Barbulescu, Balint, Balan (Iordanescu), Boloni, Majaru, Lacatus, Piturca (Radu). *Tr:* Jenei
Barcelona: Urruti, Gerardo, Migueli, Alexanco, Julio Alberto, Victor, Marcos, Schuster (Moratalla), Pedraza, Archibald (Pichi Alonso), Carrasco. *Tr:* Venables
After extra time. Steaua won 2-0 on penalties

1987
27 May *Prater, Vienna* 56,000
FC Porto 2 Bayern Munich 1
Madjer (77), Juary (79) Kogi (24)
Porto: Mlynaraczyk, Joao Pinto, Eduardo Luis, Celso, Inacio (Frasco), Quim (Juary), Magalhaes, Madjer, Sousa, Andre, Futre. *Tr:* Jorge
Bayern Munich: Pfaff, Winklhofer, Nachtweih, Eder, Pfluger, Flick, Brehme, Matthaus, Rummenigge, Hoeness, Kogi. *Tr:* Lattek

1988
25 May *Neckarstadion, Stuttgart* 55,000
PSV Eindhoven 0 Benfica 0
PSV Eindhoven: Van Breukelen, Gerets, Van Aerle, Koeman R., Nielsen, Heintze, Vanenburg, Linskens, Lerby, Kieft, Gillhaus (Janssen). *Tr:* Hiddink
Benfica: Silvino, Veloso, Dito, Mozer, Alvaro, Elzo, Sheu, Chiquinho, Pacheco, Rui Aguas (Vando), Magnusson (Hajiri). *Tr:* Toni
After extra time. PSV Eindhoven won 6-5 on penalties

1989
24 May *Nou Camp, Barcelona* 97,000
Milan 4 Steaua Bucharest 0
Gullit (17, 38), Van Basten (26, 46)
Milan: Galli G., Tassotti, Costacurta (Galli F.), Baresi, Maldini, Colombo, Rijkaard, Ancelotti, Donadoni, Gullit, Van Basten. *Tr:* Sacchi
Steaua Bucharest: Lung, Iovan, Petrescu, Bumbescu, Ungureanu, Hagi, Stoica, Minea, Rotariu (Balaci), Lacatus, Piturca. *Tr:* Iordanescu

1990
23 May *Prater, Vienna* 57,000
Milan 1 Benfica 0
Rijkaard (68)
Milan: Galli G., Tassotti, Costacurta, Baresi, Maldini, Colombo (Galli F.), Rijkaard, Ancelotti (Massaro), Evani, Gullit, Van Basten. *Tr:* Sacchi
Benfica: Silvino, Jose Carlos, Aldair, Ricardo, Samuel, Vitor Paneira, Valdo, Thern, Hernani, Magnusson, Pacheco. *Tr:* Eriksson

1991
29 May *San Nicola, Bari* 50,000
Red Star Belgrade 0 Marseille 0
Red Star Belgrade: Stajanovic, Belodedici, Najdoski, Sabanadzovic, Jugovic, Marovic, Mihajlovic, Binic, Savicevic (Stosic), Prosinecki, Pancev. *Tr:* Petrovic
Marseille: Olmeta, Amoros, Boli, Mozer, Di Meco (Stojkovic), Fournier (Vercruysse), Germain, Casoni, Pele, Papin, Waddle. *Tr:* Goethals
After extra time. Red Star Belgrade won 5-3 on penalties

1992
20 May *Wembley, London* 71,000
Barcelona 1 Sampdoria 0 aet
Koeman R (112)
Barcelona: Zubizarreta, Eusebio, Ferrer, Koeman R., Munoz, Juan Carlos, Bakero, Guardiola (Alexanco), Laudrup M., Salinas, Stoichkov. *Tr:* Cruyff
Sampdoria: Pagliuca, Mannini, Lanna, Vierchowod, Katanec, Lombardo, Cerezo, Pari, Bonetti (Invernizzi), Vialli (Buso), Mancini. *Tr:* Boskov

1993
26 May *Olympiastadion, Munich* 64,444
Milan 0 Marseille 1
Boli (43)
AC Milan: Rossi, Tassotti, Costacurta, Baresi, Maldini, Donadoni (Papin), Rijkaard, Albertini, Lentini, Van Basten (Eranio), Massaro. *Tr:* Capello
Marseille: Barthez, Angloma (Durand), Boli, Desailly, Di Meco, Pele, Sauzee, Deschamps, Eydelie, Boksic, Voller (Thomas). *Tr:* Goethals

* Marseille subsequently stripped of cup by UEFA. Cup not awarded.

1994
18 May *Olympic Stadium, Athens* 75,000
Milan 4 Barcelona 0
Massaro (22, 45),
Savicevic (47), Desailly (58)
Milan: Rossi, Tassotti, Galli, Maldini (Nava 85), Panucci, Albertini, Desailly, Donadoni, Boban, Savicevic, Massaro
Barcelona: Zubizarreta, Ferrer, Nadal, Koeman R., Sergi (Enrique 71), Amor, Bakero, Guardiola, Beguiristain (Eusebio 53), Romario, Stoichkov
Yellow Cards: Tassotti, Albertini, Panucci (Milan) and Stoichkov, Nadal, Serai, Ferrer (Barcelona)

Cup-Winners' Cup Finals 1961–94

1961
1st Leg – 17 May   *Ibrox, Glasgow*   80,000
Rangers   **0**   **Fiorentina**   **2**
Milani (12, 88)
Rangers: Ritchie, Shearer, Caldow, Davis, Paterson, Baxter, Wilson, McMillan, Scott, Brand, Hume
Fiorentina: Albertosi, Robotti, Castelletti, Gonfiantini, Orzan, Rimbaldo, Hamrin, Micheli, Da Costa, Milani, Petris

2nd Leg – 27 May   *Communale, Florence*   50,000
Fiorentina   **2**   **Rangers**   **1**
Milani (12), Hamrin (86)   Scott (60)
Fiorentina: Albertosi, Robotti, Castelletti, Gonfiantini, Orzan, Rimbaldo, Hamrin, Micheli, Da Costa, Milani, Petris
Rangers: Ritchie, Shearer, Caldow, Davis, Paterson, Baxter, Scott, McMillan, Millar, Brand, Wilson
Fiorentina win 4-1 on aggregate

1962
10 May   *Hampden Park, Glasgow*   27,000
Atletico Madrid   **1**   **Fiorentina**   **1**
Peiro (11)   Hamrin (27)
Atletico Madrid: Madinabeytia, Rivilla, Calleja, Ramirez, Griffa, Glaria, Jones, Adelardo, Mendonca, Peiro, Collar
Fiorentina: Albertosi, Robotti, Castelletti, Malatrasi, Orzan, Marchesi, Hamrin, Ferretti, Milani, Dell-Angelo, Petris

Replay – 5 September   *Neckarstadion, Stuttgart*   38,000
Atletico Madrid   **3**   **Fiorentina**   **0**
Jones (8), Mendonca (27), Peiro (59)
Atletico Madrid: Madinabeytia, Rivilla, Calleja, Ramirez, Griffa, Glaria, Jones, Adelardo, Mendonca, Peiro, Collar
Fiorentina: Albertosi, Robotti, Castelletti, Malatrasi, Orzan, Marchesi, Hamrin, Ferretti, Milani, Dell-Angelo, Petris

1963
15 May   *Feyenoord Stadion, Rotterdam*   49,000
Tottenham Hotspur   **5**   **Atletico Madrid**   **1**
Greaves (16, 80), White (35),   Collar (47)
Dyson (67, 85)
Tottenham Hotspur: Brown, Baker, Norman, Henry, Blanchflower, Marchi, Jones, White, Smith, Greaves, Dyson
Atletico Madrid: Madinabeytia, Rivilla, Griffa, Rodriguez, Ramiro, Glaria, Jones, Adelardo, Chuzo, Mendonca, Collar

1964
13 May   *Heysel, Brussels*   3,000
Sporting Lisbon   **3**   **MTK Budapest**   **3**
Mascaranhas (40), Figueiredo (45, 80)   Sandor (19, 75), Kuti (73)
Sporting Lisbon: Carvalho, Gomez, Perdis, Battista, Carlos, Geo, Mendes, Oswaldo, Mascaranhas, Figueiredo, Morais
MTK Budapest: Kovalik, Keszei, Dansky, Jenei, Nagy, Kovacs, Sandor, Vasas, Kuti, Bodor, Halapi

Replay – 15 May   *Bosuil, Antwerp*   19,000
Sporting Lisbon   **1**   **MTK Budapest**   **0**
Morais (19)
Sporting Lisbon: Carvalho, Gomez, Perdis, Battista, Carlos, Geo, Mendes, Oswaldo, Mascaranhas, Figueiredo, Morais
MTK Budapest: Kovalik, Keszei, Dansky, Jenei, Nagy, Kovacs, Sandor, Vasas, Kuti, Bodor, Halapi

1965
19 May   *Wembley, London*   100,000
West Ham United   **2**   **1860 Munich**   **0**
Sealey (70, 72)
West Ham United: Standen, Kirkup, Burkett, Moore, Peters, Brown, Sealey, Boyce, Hurst, Dear, Sissons
1860 Munich: Radenkovic, Wagner, Kohlars, Reich, Bena, Luttrop, Heiss, Kuppers, Brunnenmeier, Grosser, Rebele

1966
5 May   *Hampden Park, Glasgow*   41,000
Borussia Dortmund   **2**   **Liverpool**   **1 aet**
Held (62), Libuda (109)   Hunt (68)
Borussia Dortmund: Tilkowski, Cyliax, Paul, Redder, Kurrat, Assauer, Libuda, Schmidt, Held, Sturm, Emmerich
Liverpool: Lawrence, Lawler, Yeats, Byrne, Milne, Stevenson, Callaghan, Hunt, Smith, St John, Thompson

1967
31 May   *Frankenstadion, Nuremberg*   69,000
Bayern Munich   **1**   **Rangers**   **0 aet**
Roth (108)
Bayern Munich: Maier, Nowak, Kupferschmidt, Beckenbauer, Olk, Roth, Koulmann, Nafziger, Ohlhauser, Muller, Brenninger
Rangers: Martin, Johansen, Provan, McKinnon, Greig, Jardine, Smith D., Henderson, Hynd, Smith A., Johnston

1968
23 May   *Feyenoord Stadion, Rotterdam*   53,000
Milan   **2**   **Hamburg**   **0**
Hamrin (3, 19)
Milan: Cudicini, Anquilletti, Schnellinger, Rosato, Scala, Trapattoni, Lodetti, Hamrin, Sormani, Rivera, Prati
Hamburg: Ozcan, Sandmann, Schulz, Horst, Kurbjuhn, Dieckmann, Dramer, Dorfel B., Seeler, Honig, Dorfel G.

1969
21 May   *St Jakob, Basle*   19,000
Slovan Bratislava   **3**   **Barcelona**   **2**
Cvetler (2), Hrivnak (30),   Zaldua (16), Rexach (52)
Jan Capkovic (42)
Slovan Bratislava: Vencel, Filo, Horvath, Hrivnak, Zlocha, Hrdlicka, Josef Capkovic, Cvetler, Moder (Hatar), Jokl, Jan Capkovic
Barcelona: Sadurni, Franch (Pereda), Eladio, Rife, Olivella, Zabalza, Pellicer, Castro (Mendoza), Zaldua, Fuste, Rexach

1970
29 April *Prater, Vienna* *8,000*
Manchester City   **2**   **Gornik Zabrze**   **1**
Young (11), Lee (43)   Oslizlo (70)
Manchester City: Corrigan, Book, Booth, Heslop, Pardoe, Doyle (Bowyer), Towers, Oakes, Bell, Lee, Young
Gornik Zabrze: Kostka, Oslizlo, Florenski (Deja), Gorgon, Olek, Latocha, Szoltysik, Wilczek (Skowronek), Szarynski, Banas, Lubanski

1971
19 May *Karaiskaki, Piraeus* *42,000*
Chelsea   **1**   **Real Madrid**   **1 aet.**
Osgood (55)   Zoco (90)
Chelsea: Bonetti, Boyle, Dempsey, Webb, Harris, Cooke, Hudson, Weller, Hollins, Osgood, Houseman
Real Madrid: Borja, Jose Luis, Benito, Zoco, Zunzunegui, Pirri, Grosso, Velazquez, Perez, Amancio, Gento

Replay – 21 May *Karaiskaki, Piraeus* *35,000*
Chelsea   **2**   **Real Madrid**   **1**
Dempsey (32), Osgood (38)   Fleitas (74)
Chelsea: Bonetti, Boyle, Dempsey, Webb, Harris, Cooke, Hudson, Weller, Baldwin, Osgood (Smethurst), Houseman
Real Madrid: Borja, Jose Luis, Benito, Zoco, Zunzunegui, Pirri, Grosso, Velazquez (Gento), Fleitas, Amancio, Bueno (Grande)

1972
24 May *Nou Camp, Barcelona* *24,000*
Rangers   **3**   **Dinamo Moscow**   **2**
Stein (23), Johnstone (40, 49)   Estrekov (60), Makovikov (87)
Rangers: McCloy, Jardine, Johnstone, Smith, Mathieson, Greig, Conn, MacDonald, McLean, Stein, Johnston
Dinamo Moscow: Pilgui, Basalev, Dolmatov, Zikov, Dobonosov (Gerschkovitch), Zhukov, Yakubik (Estrekov), Sabo, Baidatchini, Makovikov, Evriuschkin

1973
16 May *Harilaou, Salonicia* *45,000*
Milan   **1**   **Leeds United**   **0**
Chiarugi (5)
Milan: Vecchi, Sabadini, Zignoli, Anquilletti, Turone, Rosato (Dolci), Rivera, Benetti, Sogliano, Bigon, Chiarugi
Leeds United: Harvey, Reaney, Cherry, Bates, Madeley, Hunter, Gray E., Yorath (McQueen), Lorimer, Jordan, Jones

1974
8 May *Feyenoord Stadion, Rotterdam* *4,000*
Magdeburg   **2**   **Milan**   **0**
(Own goal 43), Seguin (74)
Magdeburg: Schulze, Enge, Zapf, Tyll, Abraham, Seguin, Pommerenke, Gaube, Raugust, Sparwasser, Hoffmann
Milan: Pizzaballa, Sabadini, Anquilletti, Lanzi, Schnellinger, Benetti, Maldera, Rivera, Tresoldi, Bigon, Bergamaschi (Turin)

1975
14 May *St Jakobs, Basle* *10,000*
Dinamo Kiev   **3**   **Ferencvaros**   **0**
Onischenko (18, 39), Blokhin (67)
Dinamo Kiev: Rudakov, Troshkin, Matvienko, Reshko, Fomenko, Muntjan, Konkov, Burjak, Kolotov, Onischenko, Blokhin
Ferencvaros: Geczi, Martos, Megyesi, Pataki, Rab, Nyilasi (Onhaus), Juhasz, Mucha, Szabo, Mate, Magyar

1976
5 May *Heysel, Brussels* *58,000*
RSC Anderlecht   **4**   **West Ham United**   **2**
Rensenbrink (42, 73),   Holland (28), Robson (68)
Van der Elst (48, 87)
RSC Anderlecht: Ruiter, Lomm, Van Binst, Thissen, Broos, Dockx, Coeck (Vercauteren), Haan, Van der Elst, Ressel, Rensenbrink
West Ham United: Day, Coleman, Lampard (Taylor A.), Taylor T., McDowell, Bonds, Brooking, Paddon, Holland, Jennings, Robson

1977
11 May *Olympicschstadion, Amsterdam* *66,000*
SV Hamburg   **2**   **RSC Anderlecht**   **0**
Volkert (78), Magath (88)
SV Hamburg: Kargus, Kaltz, Ripp, Nogly, Hidien, Memering, Magath, Keller, Steffenhagen, Reimann, Volkert
RSC Anderlecht: Ruiter, Van Binst, Van den Daele, Thissen, Broos, Dockx (Van Poucke), Coeck, Haan, Van der Elst, Ressel, Rensenbrink

1978
3 May *Parc des Princes, Paris* *48,000*
RSC Anderlecht   **4**   **Austria Vienna**   **0**
Rensenbrink (13, 41), Van Binst (45, 80)
RSC Anderlecht: De Bree, Van Binst, Thissen, Dusbaba, Broos, Van der Elst, Haan, Nielsen, Coeck, Vercauteren (Dockx), Rensenbrink
Austria Vienna: Baumgartner, Sara R., Sara J., Obermayer, Baumeister, Prohaska, Daxbacher (Martinez), Gasselich, Morels (Drazen), Pirkner, Parits

1979
16 May *St Jakobs, Basle* *58,000*
Barcelona   **4**   **Fortuna Dusseldorf**   **3 aet**
Sanchez (5), Asensi (34),   Allofs K. (8), Seel (41, 114)
Rexach (104), Krankl (111)
Barcelona: Artola, Zuviria, Migueli, Costas (Martinez), Albaladejo (Del la Cruz), Sanchez, Neeskens, Asensi, Rexach, Krankl, Carrasco
Fortuna Dusseldorf: Daniel, Baltes, Zewe, Zimmermann (Lund), Brei (Weik), Kohnen, Schmitz, Bommer, Allofs T., Allofs K., Seel

1980
15 May *Heysel, Brussels* *36,000*
Valencia   **0**   **Arsenal**   **0 aet**
Valencia: Pereira, Carrette, Botubot, Arias, Tendollo, Solsona, Saura, Bonhof, Subirats (Castellanos), Kempes, Pablo
Arsenal: Jennings, Rice, Nelson, O'Leary, Young, Rix, Talbot, Price (Hollins), Brady, Sunderland, Stapleton
After extra time. Valencia won 5-4 on penalties

1981
13 May *Rheinstadion, Dusseldorf* *9,000*
Dinamo Tbilisi   **2**   **Carl Zeiss Jena**   **1**
Gutsayev (67), Daraselia (86),   Hoppe (63)
Dinamo Tbilisi: Gabelia, Kostave, Chivadze, Khisanishvili, Tavadze, Svanadze (Kakilashvili), Sulakvelidze, Daraselia, Gutsayev, Kipiani, Shengelia
Carl Zeiss Jena: Grapenthin, Brauer, Kurbjuweit, Schnuphase, Schilling, Hoppe (Overmann), Krause, Lindemann, Bielau (Topfer), Raab, Vogel

1982
12 May *Nou Camp, Barcelona* *100,000*
Barcelona   **2**   **Standard Liege**   **1**
Simonsen (44), Quini (63)   Vandermissen (7)
Barcelona: Urruti, Gerardo, Migueli, Alexanco, Manolo, Sanchez, Moratalla, Esteban, Simonsen, Quini, Carrasco
Standard Liege: Preud'homme, Gerets, Poel, Meeuws, Plessers, Vandermissen, Daerden, Haan, Botteron, Tahamata, Wendt

1983
11 May *Nya Ullevi, Gothenburg* *17,000*
Aberdeen   **2**   **Real Madrid**   **1 aet**
Black (4), Hewitt (112)   Juanito (15)
Aberdeen: Leighton, Rougvie, McLeish, Miller, McMaster, Cooper, Strachan, Simpson, McGhee, Black (Hewitt), Weir
Real Madrid: Agustin, Juan Jose, Metgod, Bonet, Camacho (San Jose), Angel, Gallego, Stielike, Isidro (Salguero), Juanito, Santillana

1984
16 May *St Jakobs, Basle* *60,000*
Juventus 2 **FC Porto** 1
Vignola (12), Boniek (41) Sousa (29)
Juventus: Tacconi, Gentile, Brio, Scirea, Cabrini, Tardelli, Bonini, Vignola (Aricola), Platini, Rossi, Boniek
FC Porto: Ze Beto, Joao Pinto, Lima Pereira, Enrico, Eduardo Luis (Costa), Magalhaes (Walsh), Frasco, Pacheco, Sousa, Gomes, Vermelinho

1985
15 May *Feyenoord Stadion, Rotterdam* *50,000*
Everton 3 **Rapid Vienna** 1
Gray (57), Steven (72), Krankl (83)
Sheedy (85)
Everton: Southall, Stevens, Van den Hauwe, Ratcliffe, Mountfield, Reid, Steven, Bracewell, Sheedy, Gray, Sharp
Rapid Vienna: Konsel, Lainer, Weber, Garger, Brauneder, Hrstic, Kranjcar, Kienast, Weinhofer (Panenka), Pacult (Gross), Krankl

1986
2 May *Stade de Gerland, Lyon* *39,000*
Dinamo Kiev 3 **Atletico Madrid** 0
Zavarov (5), Blokhin (85), Yevtushenko (88)
Dinamo Kiev: Chanov, Baltacha (Bal), Bessonov, Kuznetsov, Demianenko, Rats, Yakovenko, Yaremchuk, Zavarov (Yevtushenko), Belanov, Blokhin
Atletico Madrid: Fillol, Tomas, Arteche, Ruiz, Villaverde, Prieto, Ramos, Marina, Landaburu (Setien), Cabrera, Da Silva

1987
13 May *Olympiao Stadio, Athens* *35,000*
Ajax 1 **Lokomotive Leipzig** 0
Van Basten (21)
Ajax: Menzo, Silooy, Rijkaard, Verlaat, Boeve, Wouters, Winter, Muhren (Scholten), Van't Schip, Van Basten, Witschge (Bergkamp)
Lokomotive Leipzig: Muller, Kreer, Baum, Lindner, Zotzsche, Scholz, Liebers (Kuhn), Bredow, Marschal, Richter, Edmond (Leitzke)

1988
11 May *Strasbourg* *40,000*
KV Mechelen 1 **Ajax** 0
Den Boer (53)
KV Mechelen: Preud'homme, Clijsters, Sanders, Rutjes, Deferm, Hofkens (Theunis), Emmers, Koeman, De Wilde (Demesmeker), Den Boer, Ohana
Ajax: Menzo, Blind, Wouters, Larsson, Verlaat (Meijer), Van't Schip (Bergkamp), Winter, Muhren, Scholten, Bosman, Witschge

1989
10 May *Wankdorf, Berne* *45,000*
Barcelona 2 **Sampdoria** 0
Salinas (4), Recarte (79)
Barcelona: Zubizarreta, Alosio, Alexanco, Urbano, Milla (Soler), Amor, Eusebio, Roberto, Lineker, Salinas, Beguiristain (Recarte)
Sampdoria: Pagliuca, Pellegrini L. (Bonomi), Mannini (Pellegrini), Lanna, Salsano, Pari, Victor, Cerezo, Dossena, Vialli, Mancini

1990
9 May *Nya Ullevi, Gothenburg* *20,000*
Sampdoria 2 **RSC Anderlecht** 0 aet
Vialli (105, 107)
Sampdoria: Pagliuca, Pellegrini L., Mannini, Vierchowod, Carboni, Pari, Katanec (Salsano), Invernizzi (Lombardo), Dossena, Vialli, Mancini
RSC Anderlecht: De Wilde, Grun, Marchoul, Keshi, Kooiman, Veroort, Musonda, Gudjohnson, Jankovic (Oliveira), Degryse (Nilis), Van der Linden

1991
15 May *Feyenoord Stadium, Rotterdam* *42,000*
Manchester United 2 **Barcelona** 1
Bruce (67), Hughes (74) Koeman (79)
Manchester United: Sealey, Irwin, Bruce, Pallister, Blackmore, Phelan, Robson, Ince, Sharpe, Hughes, McClair
Barcelona: Busquets, Alexanco (Pinilla), Nando, Koeman R., Ferrer, Goikoetxea, Eusebio, Baquero, Beguiristain, Salinas, Laudrup

1992
6 May *Estadio da Luz, Lisbon* *15,000*
Werder Bremen 2 **Monaco** 0
Allofs (41), Rufer (54)
Werder Bremen: Rollmann, Wolter (Schaaf), Borowka, Bratseth, Bode, Bockenfeld, Eilts, Votova, Neubarth (Kohn), Rufer, Allofs
Monaco: Ettori, Valery (Djorkaeff), Petit, Mendy, Sonor, Dib, Gnako, Passi, Barros, Weah, Fofana (Clement)

1993
12 May *Wembley, London* *37,393*
Parma 3 **Royal Antwerp** 1
Minotti (9), Melli (30), Cuoghi (83) Severeyns (12)
Parma: Ballotta, Benarrivo, Di Chiara, Minotti, Apolloni, Grun, Melli, Zoratto (Pin), Osio (Pizzi), Cuoghi, Brolin
Royal Antwerp: Stojanovic, Kiekens, Broeckaert, Taeymans, Smidts, Jakovljevic (Van Veirdeghem), Van Rethy, Segers (Moukrim), Severeyns, Lehnhoff, Czerniatynski

1994
4 May *Parken Stadium, Copenhagen* *33,765*
Arsenal 1 **Parma** 0
Smith (19)
Arsenal: Seaman, Dixon, Winterburn, Davis, Bould, Adams, Campbell, Morrow, Smith, Merson (McGoldrick 86), Selley
Subs not used: Linighan, Miller, Parlour, Dickov
Parma: Bucci, Benarrivo, Di Chiara, Minotti, Apolloni, Sensini, Brolin, Pin (Melli 70), Crippa, Zola, Asprilla
Subs not used: Maltagliati, Ballota, Balleri, Zoratto
Yellow cards: Adams (30), Campbell (47), Selley (53) all Arsenal. Crippa (42), Asprilla (45) both Parma.

Fairs Cup/UEFA Cup Finals 1958-93

1958
1st Leg – 5 March   Stamford Bridge, London   45,000
London Select XI   **2**   **Barcelona**   **2**
Greaves (5), Langley (83)   Tejada (4), Martinez (43)
London Select XI: Kelsey, Sillett, Langley, Blanchflower, Norman, Coote, Groves, Greaves, Smith, Haynes, Robb
Barcelona: Estrems, Olivella, Segarra, Gracia, Gensana, Ribelles, Basora, Evaristo, Martinez, Villaverde, Tejada

2nd Leg – 1 May   Nou Camp, Barcelona   62,000
Barcelona   **6**   **London Select XI**   **0**
Suarez (2 goals), Evaristo (2 goals), Martinez, Verges
Barcelona: Ramallets, Olivella, G Segarra, Verges, Brugue, Gensana, Tejada, Evaristo, Martinez, Suarez, Basora
London: Kelsey, Wright, Cantwell, Blanchflower, Brown, Bowen, Medwin, Groves, Smith, Bloomfield, Lewis
Barcelona win 8-2 on aggregate

1960
1st Leg – 29 March   St. Andrews, Birmingham   40,000
Birmingham City   **0**   **Barcelona**   **0**
Birmingham City: Schofield, Farmer, Allen, Watts, Smith, Neal, Astall, Gordon, Weston, Orritt, Hooper
Barcelona: Ramallets, Olivella, Gracia, Segarra, Rodri, Gensana, Coll, Kocsis, Martinez, Ribelles, Villaverde

2nd Leg – 4 March   Nou Camp, Barcelona   70,000
Barcelona   **4**   **Birmingham City**   **1**
Martinez (3), Czibor (6, 48), Coll (78)   Hooper (82)
Barcelona: Ramallets, Olivella, Gracia, Verges, Rodri, Segarra, Coll, Ribelles, Martinez, Kubala, Czibor
Birmingham City: Schofield, Farmer, Allen, Watts, Smith, Neal, Astall, Gordon, Weston, Murphy, Hooper
Barcelona win 4-1 on aggregate

1961
1st Leg – 27 September   St Andrews, Birmingham   21,000
Birmingham City   **2**   **Roma**   **2**
Hellawell (78), Orritt (85)   Manfredini (30, 56)
Birmingham City: Schofield, Farmer, Sissons, Hennessey, Foster, Beard, Hellawell, Bloomfield, Harris, Orritt, Auld
Roma: Cudicini, Fontana, Corsini, Guiliano, Losi, Carpanesi, Orlando, Da Costa, Manfredini, Angelillo, Menichelli

2nd Leg – 11 October   Stadio Olimpico, Rome   60,000
Roma   **2**   **Birmingham City**   **0**
Own Goal (56), Pestrin (90)
Roma: Cudicini, Fontana, Corsini, Carpanesi, Losi, Pestrin, Orlando, Angelillo, Manfredini, Lojacono, Menichelli
Birmingham City: Schofield, Farmer, Sissons, Hennessey, Smith, Beard, Hellawell, Bloomfield, Harris, Singer, Orritt
Roma win 4-2 on aggregate

1962
1st Leg – 8 September   Luis Casanova, Valencia   56,000
Valencia   **6**   **Barcelona**   **2**
Yosu (14, 42),   Kocsis (4, 20)
Guillot (35, 54, 67), Nunez (74)
Valencia: Zamora, Piquer, Mestre, Sastre, Quincoces, Chicao, Nunez, Ribelles, Waldo, Guillot, Yosu
Barcelona: Pesudo, Benitez, Rodri, Olivella, Verges, Gracia, Cubilla, Kocsis, Re, Villaverde, Camps

2nd Leg – 12 September   Nou Camp, Barcelona   60,000
Barcelona   **1**   **Valencia**   **1**
Kocsis (46)   Guillot (87)
Barcelona: Pesudo, Benitez, Garay, Fuste, Verges, Gracia, Cubilla, Kocsis, Goyvaerts, Villaverde, Camps
Valencia: Zamora, Piquer, Mestre, Sastre, Quincoces, Chicao, Nunez, Urtiaga, Waldo, Guillot, Yosu
Valencia win 7-3 on aggregate

1963
1st Leg – 12 June   Dinamo Stadion, Zagreb   40,000
Dinamo Zagreb   **1**   **Valencia**   **2**
Zambata (13)   Waldo (64), Urtiaga (67)
Dinamo Zagreb: Skoric, Belin, Braun, Biscam, Markovic, Perusic, Kobesnac, Zambata, Knez, Matus, Lamza
Valencia: Zamora, Piquer, Chicao, Paquito, Quincoces, Sastre, Manio, Sanchez-Lage, Waldo, Ribelles, Urtiaga

2nd Leg – 26 June   Luis Casanova, Valencia   55,000
Valencia   **2**   **Dinamo Zagreb**   **0**
Manio (68), Nunez (78)
Valencia: Zamora, Piquer, Chicao, Paquito, Quincoces, Sastre, Manio, Sanchez-Lage, Waldo, Ribelles, Nunez
Dinamo Zagreb: Skoric, Belin, Braun, Matus, Markovic, Perusic, Kobesnac, Lamza, Raus, Zambata, Knez
Valencia win 4-1 on aggregate

1964
25 June   Nou Camp, Barcelona   50,000
Real Zaragoza   **2**   **Valencia**   **1**
Villa (40), Marcelino (83),   Urtiaga (42)
Real Zaragoza: Yarza, Cortizo, Santamaria, Reija, Isasi, Pais, Canario, Duca, Marcelino, Villa, Lapetra
Valencia: Zamora, Arnal, Villegani, Paquito, Quincoces, Roberto, Suco, Guillot, Waldo, Urtiaga, Ficha
One match only – Real Zaragoza win 2-1

1965
23 June   Communale, Turin   25,000
Ferencvaros   **1**   **Juventus**   **0**
Fenyvesi (74)
Ferencvaros: Geczi, Novak, Horvath, Juhasz, Matrai, Orosz, Karaba, Varga, Albert, Rakosi, Fenyvesi
Juventus: Anzolin, Gori, Sartri, Bercellino, Castano, Leoncini, Stachini, Del Sol, Combin, Mazzia, Menichelli
One match only – Ferencvaros win 1-0

1966
1st Leg – 14 September Nou Camp, Barcelona 70,000
Barcelona   0   **Real Zaragoza**   1
                                 Canario (30)
Barcelona: Sadurni, Benitez, Eladio, Montesinos, Gallego, Torres, Zaballa, Muller, Zaldua, Fuste, Vidal
Real Zaragoza: Yarza, Irusquieta, Reija, Pais, Santamaria, Violeta, Canario, Santos, Marcelino, Villa, Lapetra

2nd Leg – 21 September La Romareda, Zaragoza 35,000
Real Zaragoza   2   **Barcelona**   4
Marcelino (24, 87)   Pujol (3, 86, 120), Zaballa (89)
Real Zaragoza: Yarza, Irusquieta, Reija, Pais, Santamaria, Violeta, Canario, Santos, Marcelino, Villa, Lapetra
Barcelona: Sadurni, Foncho, Eladio, Montesinos, Gallego, Torres, Zaballa, Mas, Zaldua, Fuste, Pujol
Barcelona win 4-3 on aggregate

1967
1st Leg – 30 August Dinamo Stadion, Zagreb 40,000
Dinamo Zagreb   2   **Leeds United**   0
Cercek (39, 59)
Dinamo Zagreb: Skoric, Gracanin, Brncic, Belin, Ramljak, Blaskovic, Cercek, Piric, Zambata, Gucmirtl, Rora
Leeds United: Sprake, Reaney, Cooper, Bremner, Charlton, Hunter, Bates, Lorimer, Belfitt, Gray E., O'Grady

2nd Leg – 6 September Elland Road, Leeds 35,000
Leeds United   0   **Dinamo Zagreb**   0
Leeds United: Sprake, Bell, Cooper, Bremner, Charlton, Hunter, Reaney, Belfitt, Greenhoff, Giles, O'Grady
Dinamo Zagreb: Skoric, Gracanin, Brncic, Belin, Ramljak, Blaskovic, Cercek, Piric, Zambata, Gucmirtl, Rora
Dinamo Zagreb win 2-0 on aggregate

1968
1st Leg – 7 September Elland Road, Leeds 76,000
Leeds United   1   **Ferencvaros**   0
Jones (41)
Leeds United: Sprake, Reaney, Cooper, Bremner, Charlton, Hunter, Lorimer, Madeley, Jones (Belfitt), Giles (Greenhoff), Gray, E.
Ferencvaros: Geczi, Novak, Pancsics, Havasi, Juhasz, Szucs, Szoke, Varga, Albert, Rakosi, Fenyvesi (Balint)

2nd Leg – 11 September Nepstadion, Budapest 76,000
Ferencvaros   0   **Leeds United**   0
Ferencvaros: Geczi, Novak, Pancsics, Havasi, Juhasz, Szucs, Rakosi, Szoke (Karaba), Varga, Albert, Katona
Leeds United: Sprake, Reaney, Cooper, Bremner, Charlton, Hunter, O'Grady, Lorimer, Jones, Madeley, Hibbitt (Bates)
Leeds United win 1-0 on aggregate

1969
1st Leg – 29 May St James' Park, Newcastle 60,000
Newcastle United   3   **Ujpest Dozsa**   0
Moncur (63, 72), Scott (83)
Newcastle United: McFaul, Craig, Clark, Gibb, Burton, Moncur, Scott, Robson, Davies, Arentoft, Sinclair (Foggon)
Ujpest Dozsa: Szentmilhalyi, Kaposzta, Solymosi, Bankuti, Nosko, Dunai E., Fazekas, Gorocs, Bene, Dunai A., Zambo

2nd Leg – 11 June Dozsa, Budapest 37,000
Ujpest Dozsa   2   **Newcastle United**   3
Bene (31), Gorocs (44)   Moncur (46), Arentoft (50), Foggon (74)
Ujpest Dozsa: Szentmilhalyi, Kaposzta, Solymosi, Bankuti, Nosko, Dunai E., Fazekas, Gorocs, Bene, Dunai A., Zambo
Newcastle United: McFaul, Craig, Clark, Gibb, Burton, Moncur, Scott (Foggon), Arentoft, Robson, Davies, Sinclair
Newcastle United 6-2 on aggregate

1970
1st Leg – 22 May Parc Astrid, Brussels 37,000
RSC Anderlecht   3   **Arsenal**   1
Devrindt (25), Mulder (30, 74)   Kennedy (82)
RSC Anderlecht: Trappeniers, Heylens, Velkeneers, Kialunda, Cornelis (Peeters), Nordahl, Desanghere, Puis, Devrindt, Van Himst, Mulder
Arsenal: Wilson, Storey, McNab, Kelly, McLintock, Simpson, Armstrong, Sammels, Radford, George (Kennedy), Graham

2nd Leg – 28 April Highbury, London 51,000
Arsenal   3   **RSC Anderlecht**   0
Kelly (25), Radford (75), Sammels (76)
Arsenal: Wilson, Storey, McNab, Kelly, McLintock, Simpson, Armstrong, Sammels, Radford, George, Graham
RSC Anderlecht: Trappeniers, Heylens, Velkeneers, Kialunda, Martens, Nordahl, Desanghere, Puis, Devrindt, Mulder, Van Himst
Arsenal win 4-3 on aggregate

1971
1st Leg – 28 May Communale, Turin 65,000
Juventus   2   **Leeds United**   2
Bettega (27), Capello (55)   Madeley (48), Bates (77)
Juventus: Piloni, Spinosi, Salvadore, Mardhetti, Furino, Morini, Haller, Capello, Causio, Anastasi (Novellini), Bettega
Leeds United: Sprake, Reaney, Cooper, Bremner, Charlton, Hunter, Lorimer, Clarke, Jones (Bates), Giles, Madeley

2nd Leg – 3 June Elland Road, Leeds 42,000
Leeds United   1   **Juventus**   1
Clarke (12)   Anastasi (20)
Leeds United: Sprake, Reaney, Cooper, Bremner, Charlton, Hunter, Lorimer, Clarke, Jones, Giles, Madeley (Bates)
Juventus: Tancredi, Spinosi, Salvadore, Mardhetti, Furino, Morini, Haller, Capello, Causio, Anastasi, Bettega
Leeds United win on away goals rule. 3-3 on aggregate

1972
1st Leg – 3 May Molineux, Wolverhampton 38,000
Wolverhampton Wanderers 1   **Tottenham Hotspur**   2
McCalliog (72)   Chivers (57, 87)
Wolverhampton Wanderers: Parkes, Shaw, Taylor, Hegan, Munro, McAlle, McCalliog, Hibbitt, Richards, Dougan, Wagstaffe
Tottenham Hotspur: Jennings, Kinnear, Knowles, Mullery, England, Beal, Gilzean, Perryman, Chivers, Peters, Coates (Pratt)

2nd Leg – 17 May White Hart Lane, London 54,000
Tottenham Hotspur   1   **Wolverhampton Wanderers** 1
Mullery (30)   Wagstaffe (41)
Tottenham Hotspur: Jennings, Kinnear, Knowles, Mullery, England, Beal, Gilzean, Perryman, Chivers, Peters, Coates
Wolverhampton Wanderers: Parkes, Shaw, Taylor, Hegan, Munro, McAlle, McCalliog, Hibbitt (Bailey), Richards, Dougan (Curran), Wagstaffe
Tottenham win 3-2 on aggregate

1973
1st Leg – 10 June Anfield, Liverpool 41,000
Liverpool   3   **Bor. Monchengladbach** 0
Keegan (21, 32), Lloyd (61)
Liverpool: Clemence, Lawler, Lindsay, Smith, Lloyd, Hughes, Keegan, Cormack, Toshack, Heighway (Hall), Callaghan
Bor Monchengladbach: Kleff, Michallik, Netzer, Bonhof, Vogts, Wimmer, Danner, Kulik, Jensen, Rupp (Simonsen), Heynckes

2nd Leg – 23 June   Bokelbergstadion, Monchen   35,000
Bor. Monchengladbach   2   Liverpool   0
Heynckes (29, 40)
Bor. Monchengladbach: Kleff, Surau, Netzer, Bonhof, Vogts, Wimmer, Danner, Kulik, Jensen, Rupp, Heynckes
Liverpool: Clemence, Lawler, Lindsay, Smith, Lloyd, Hughes, Keegan, Cormack, Heighway (Boersma), Toshack, Callaghan
Liverpool win 3-2 on aggregate

1974
1st Leg – 21 June   White Hart Lane, London   46,000
Tottenham Hotspur   2   Feyenoord   2
England (39) Own Goal (64)   Van Hanegem (43), de Jong (85)
Tottenham Hotspur: Jennings, Evans, Naylor, Pratt, England, Beal, McGrath, Perryman, Peters, Chivers, Coates
Feyenoord: Treytel, Rijsbergen, Van Daele, Israel, Vos, de Jong, Jansen, Van Hanegem, Ressel, Schoemaker, Kristensen

2nd Leg – 29 May   Feyenoord, Rotterdam   59,000
Feyenoord   2   Tottenham Hotspur   0
Rijsbergen (43), Ressel (84)
Feyenoord: Treytel, Rijsbergen, Van Daele, Israel, Vos, Ramljak, Jansen, de Jong, Ressel, Schoemaker, Kristensen (Boskamp) (Wery)
Tottenham Hotspur: Jennings, Evans, Naylor, Pratt (Holder), England, Beal, McGrath, Perryman Peters, Chivers, Coates
Feyenoord win 4-2 on aggregate

1975
1st Leg – 7 May   Rheinstadion, Dusseldorf   42,000
Bor. Monchengladbach   0   FC Twente   0
Bor. Monchengladbach: Kleff, Wittkamp, Stielike, Vogts, Surau, Bonhof, Wimmer, Danner (Del'Haye), Kulik (Schaffer), Simonsen, Jensen
FC Twente: Gross, Drost, Van Iessel, Overweg, Oranen, Thijssen, Pahlplatz, Van der Vall, Bos, Jeuring (Achterberg), Zuidema

2nd Leg – 21 May   Diekman, Enschede   21,000
FC Twente   1   Bor. Monchengladbach   5
Drost (76)   Simonsen (2, 86), Heynckes (9, 50, 60)
FC Twente: Gross, Drost, Van Iessel, Overweg, Oranen, Bos (Muhren), Thijssen, Pahlplatz (Achterberg), Van der Vall, Jeuring, Zuidema
Bor. Monchengladbach: Kleff, Wittkamp, Vogts, Surau (Schaffer), Klinkhammer, Bonhof, Wimmer (Koppel), Danner, Simonsen, Jensen, Heynckes
Bor. Monchengladbach win 5-1 on aggregate

1976
1st Leg – 28 April   Anfield, Liverpool   49,000
Liverpool   3   Club Bruges   2
Kennedy (59), Case (61), Keegan (65)   Lambert (5), Cools (15)
Liverpool: Clemence, Smith, Neal, Thompson, Hughes, Keegan, Kennedy, Callaghan, Fairclough, Heighway, Toshack (Case)
Club Bruges: Jensen, Bastijns, Krieger, Leekens, Volders, Cools, Vandereycken, Decubber, Van Gool, Lambert, Lefevre

2nd Leg – 19 May   Olympiastadion, Bruges   32,000
Club Bruges   1   Liverpool   1
Lambert (11)   Keegan (15)
Club Bruges: Jensen, Bastijns, Krieger, Leekens, Volders, Cools, Vandereycken, Decubber (Hinderyckx), Van Gool, Lambert (Sanders), Lefevre
Liverpool: Clemence, Smith, Neal, Thompson, Hughes, Keegan, Kennedy, Callaghan, Case, Heighway, Toshack (Fairclough)
Liverpool win 4-3 on aggregate

1977
1st Leg – 4 May   Communale, Turin   75,000
Juventus   1   Athletic Bilbao   0
Tardelli (15)
Juventus: Zoff, Cuccureddu, Gentile, Scirea, Morini, Tardelli, Furino, Benetti, Causio, Boninsegna (Gori), Bettega
Athletic Bilbao: Iribar, Quaderra, Escalza, Goicoechea, Guisasola, Villar, Irureta, Rojo M., Churruca, Dani, Rojo J.

2nd Leg – 18 May   San Mames, Bilbao   43,000
Athletic Bilbao   2   Juventus   1
Churruca (11), Carlos (78)   Bettega (7)
Athletic Bilbao: Iribar, Lasa (Carlos), Guisasola, Alexanco, Escalza, Villar, Churruca, Irureta, Amarrortu, Dani, Rojo J.
Juventus: Zoff, Cuccureddu, Morini, Scirea, Gentile, Causio, Tardelli, Furino, Benetti, Boninsegna (Spinosi), Bettega
Juventus win on away goals rule. 2-2 on aggregate

1978
1st Leg – 26 April   Furiani, Bastia   15,000
SEC Bastia   0   PSV Eindhoven   0
SEC Bastia: Hiard, Burkhard, Guesdon, Orlanducci, Cazes, Papi, Lacuesta (Felix), Larios, Rep, Krimau, Mariot
PSV Eindhoven: Van Beveren, Van Draay, Drijgh, Stevens, Breandts, Poortvliet, Van der Duijlen, Van de Kerkhof W., Deijkers, Van de Kerkhof R., Lubse

2nd Leg – 9 May   Philips Stadion, Eindhoven   27,000
PSV Eindhoven   3   SEC Bastia   0
W. Van der Kerkhof (24), Deijkers (67) Van der Kuijlen (69)
PSV Eindhoven: Van Beveren, Krijgh, Stevens, Van Draay (Deacy), Brandts, Van de Kerkhof W., Poortvliet, Van der Duijlen, Lubse, Deijkers, Van de Kerkhof R.
SEC Bastia: Hiard (Weller), Marchioni, Orlanducci, Guesdon, Cazes, Lacuesta, Larios, Papi, Rep, Krimau, Mariot (De Zerbi)
PSV Eindhoven win 3-0 on aggregate

1979
1st Leg – 9 May   Crevna Zvezda, Belgrade   87,000
Red Star Belgrade   1   Bor. Monchengladbach   1
Sestic (21)   Own Goal (60)
Red Star Belgrade: Stojanovic, Jovanovic, Miletovic, Jurisic, Jovin, Muslin (Krmpotic), Petrovic, Blagojevic, Milosavljevic (Milovanovic), Savic, Sestic
Bor. Monchengladbach: Kneib, Vogts, Hannes, Schaffer, Ringels, Schafer, Kulik, Nielsen (Danner), Wohlers (Gores), Simonsen, Lienen

2nd Leg – 23 May   Rheinstadion, Dusseldorf   45,000
Bor. Monchengladach   1   Red Star Belgrade   0
Simonsen (15)
Bor. Monchengladbach: Kneib, Vogts, Hannes, Schaffer, Ringels, Schafer, Kulik (Koppel), Gores, Wohlers, Simonsen, Lienen
Red Star Belgrade: Stojanovic, Jovanovic, Miletovic, Jurisic, Jovin Muslin, Petrovic, Blagojevic, Milovanovic (Sestic), Savic, Milosavljevic
Bor. Monchengladbach win 2-1 on aggregate

1980
1st Leg – 7 May
Bor. Monchengladbach   3   Eintracht Frankfurt   2
Kulik (44, 88), Matthaus (76)   Karger (37), Holzbein (71)
Bor. Monchengladbach: Kneib, Bodeker, Hannes, Schafer, Ringels, Matthaus, Kulik, Nielsen (Thychosen), Del'Haye (Bodeker), Nickel, Lienen
Eintracht Frankfurt: Pahl, Pezzey, Neuberger, Korbel, Ehrmanntraut, Lorant, Holzbein (Nachtweih), Borchers, Nickel, Tscha, Karger (Trapp)

2nd Leg – 21 May
Eintracht Frankfurt   1   Bor. Monchengladbach   0
Schaub (81)

Eintracht Frankfurt: Pahl, Pezzey, Neuberger, Korbel, Ehrmanntraut, Lorant, Holzenbein, Borchers, Nickel, Tscha, Nachtweih (Schaub)
Bor. Monchengladbach: Kneib, Bodeker, Hannes, Schafer, Ringels, Matthaus (Thychosen), Fleer, Kulik, Nielsen (Del'Haye), Nickel, Lienen
Eintracht Frankfurt win on away goals rule. 3-3 on aggregate

1981

1st Leg – 6 May	*Portman Road, Ipswich*		*27,000*
Ipswich Town	**3**	**AZ 67 Alkmaar**	**0**

Wark (28), Thijssen (46), Mariner (56)
Ipswich Town: Cooper, Mills, Osman, Butcher, McCall, Thijssen, Wark, Muhren, Mariner, Brazil, Gates
AZ 67 Alkmaar: Treytel, Van de Meer, Spelbos, Metgod, Hovenkamp, Peters, Jonker, Arntz, Nygaard (Welzl), Kist, Tol

2nd Leg – 20 May	*Olympisch Stadion, Amsterdam*		*28,000*
AZ 67 Alkmaar	**4**	**Ipswich Town**	**2**

Welzl (7), Metgod (25), Tol (40), Thijssen (4), Wark (32)
Jonker (80)
AZ 67 Alkmaar: Treytel, Reijnders, Spelbos, Metgod, Hovenkamp, Peters, Arntz, Jonker, Nygaard, Tol (Van den Dungen) (Kist)
Ipswich Town: Cooper, Mills, Osman, Butcher, McCall, Thijssen, Wark, Muhren, Mariner, Brazil, Gates
Ipswich Town win 5-4 on aggregate

1982

1st Leg – 5 May	*Nya Ullevi, Gothenburg*		*42,000*
IFK Gothenburg	**1**	**SV Hamburg**	**0**

Tord Holmgren (87)
IFK Gothenburg: Wernersson, Svensson, Hysen, Karlsson C., Fredriksson, Tord Holmgren, Karlsson J., Stromberg, Corneliusson, Nilsson (Sandberg), Tommy Holmgren (Schiller)
SV Hamburg: Stein, Kaltz, Jakobs, Hieronymus, Groh, Hartwig, Wehmeyer, Magath, Von Heesen (Memering), Bastrup, Hrubesch

2nd Leg – 19 May	*Volksparkstadin, Hamburg*		*60,000*
SV Hamburg	**0**	**IFK Gothenburg**	**3**

Corneliusson (26), Nilsson (61), Fredriksson (63)
SV Hamburg: Stein, Kaltz (Hidien), Hieronymus, Groh, Wehmeyer, Hartwig, Memering, Magath, Von Heesen, Hrubesch, Bastrup
IFK Gothenburg: Wernersson, Svensson, Hysen (Schiller), Karlsson C., Fredriksson, Tord Holmgren, Stromberg, Karlsson J., Corneliusson (Sandberg), Nilsson, Tommy Holmgren
IFK Gothenburg win 4-0 on aggregate

1983

1st Leg – 4 May	*Heysel, Brussels*		*55,000*
RSC Anderlecht	**1**	**Benfica**	**0**

Brylle (29)
Anderlecht: Munaron, Hofkens, Peruzovic, Olsen, De Groote, Frimann, Coeck, Vercauteren, Lozano, Vandenbergh (Czerniatynski), Brylle
Benfica: Bento, Pietra, Alvaro, Humberto Coelho, Jose Luis, Sheu (Bastos Lopes), Frederico, Carlos Manuel, Chalana (Nene), Diamantino, Filipovic

2nd Leg – 18 May	*Estadio da Luz, Lisbon*		*80,000*
Benfica	**1**	**RSC Anderlecht**	**1**

Sheu (36) Lozano (38)
Benfica: Bento, Pietra, Humberto Coelho, Bastos Lopes, Veloso (Alves), Carlos Manuel, Stromberg, Sheu (Filipovic), Chalana, Nene, Diamantino
RSC Anderlecht: Munaron, Peruzovic, De Greef, Broos, Olsen, De Groot, Frimann, Lozano, Coeck, Vercauteren, Vandenbergh (Brylle)
RSC Anderlecht win 2-1 on aggregate

1984

1st Leg – 9 April	*Parc Astrid, Brussels*		*35,000*
RSC Anderlecht	**1**	**Tottenham Hotspur**	**1**

Olsen (85) Miller (57)

RSC Anderlecht: Munaron, Grun, De Greef, Olsen, De Groot, Hofkens, Vandereycken, Scifo, Brylle, Vandenbergh (Arnesen), Czerniatynski (Vercauteren)
Tottenham Hotspur: Parks, Thomas, Roberts, Hughton, Perryman, Miller, Stevens (Mabbutt), Hazard, Galvin, Archibald, Falco

2nd Leg – 23 May	*White Hart Lane, London*		*46,000*
Tottenham Hotspur	**1**	**RSC Anderlecht**	**1**

Roberts (84) Czerniatynski (60)
Tottenham Hotspur: Parks, Thomas, Hughton, Roberts, Miller (Ardiles), Mabbutt (Dick), Hazard, Stevens, Galvin, Archibald, Falco
RSC Anderlecht: Munaron, Hofkens, Grun, De Greef, Olsen, De Groot, Arnesen (Gudjohnsen), Vercauteren, Scifo, Czerniatynski (Brylle), Vandereycken
Tottenham Hotspur won 4-3 on penalties – 2-2 on aggregate

1985

1st Leg – 8 May	*Sostoi, Szedesfehervar*		*30,000*
Videoton SC	**0**	**Real Madrid**	**3**

Michel (31), Santillana (77), Valdano (89)
Videoton SC: Disztl P., Borsanyi, Disztl L., Csuhay, Horvath, Palkovics, Vegh, Wittman, Vadasz, Novath (Gyenti), Burcsa
Real Madrid: Miguel Angel, Chendo, Sanchis, Stielike, Camacho, San Jose, Michel, Gallego, Butragueno (Juanito), Santillana (Salguero), Valdano

2nd Leg – 22 May	*Bernabeu, Madrid*		*90,000*
Real Madrid	**0**	**Videoton SC**	**1**

Majer (86)
Real Madrid: Miguel Angel, Chendo, Sanchis, Stielike, Camacho, San Jose, Michel, Gallego, Butragueno, Santillana, Valdano (Juanito)
Videoton SC: Disztl P., Csuhay, Disztl L., Vegh, Horvath, Burcsa, Csongradi (Wittman), Vadasz, Szabo, Majer, Novath (Palkovics)
Real Madrid win 3-1 on aggregate

1986

1st Leg – 30 April	*Bernabeu, Madrid*		*85,000*
Real Madrid	**5**	**Cologne**	**1**

Sanchez (38), Gordillo (42), Allofs (29)
Valdano (51 84), Santillana (89)
Real Madrid: Agustin, Salguero, Solana, Camacho, Martin Vazquez (Santillana), Michel, Juanito, Gordillo, Butragueno, Sanchez, Valdano
Cologne: Schumacher, Geilis, Gielchen, Steiner, Prestin, Geilenkirchen, Honerbach, Bein (Hassler), Janssen, Littbarski (Dickel), Allofs

2nd Leg – 6 May	*Olympiastadion, Berlin*		*15,000*
Cologne	**2**	**Real Madrid**	**0**

Bein (22), Geilenkirchen (72)
Cologne: Schumacher, Prestin, Gielchen, Geilis (Schmitz), Geilenkirchen, Steiner, Bein, Honerbach, Janssen (Pisanti), Littbarski, Allofs
Real Madrid: Agustin, Chendo, Maceda, Solana, Camacho, Michel, Gallego, Valdano, Gordillo, Butragueno (Juanito), Sanchez (Santillana)
Real Madrid win 5-3 on aggregate

1987

1st Leg – 6 May	*Nya Ullevi, Gothenburg*		*50,000*
IFK Gothenburg	**1**	**Dundee United**	**0**

Pettersson (38)
IFK Gothenburg: Wernersson, Carlsson, Hysen, Larsson, Fredriksson, Johansson (Nilsson R.), Tord Holmgren (Zetterlund), Andersson, Tommy Holmgren, Pettersson, Nilsson L.
Dundee United: Thompson, Malpas, Narey, Hegarty (Clark), Holt, McInally, Kirkwood, Bowman, Bannon, Sturrock (Beaumont), Redford

2nd Leg – 20 May	*Tannadice Park, Dundee*		*21,000*
Dundee United	**1**	**IFK Gothenburg**	**1**

Clark (60) Nilsson L (22)

Dundee United: Thompson, Malpas, Clark, Narey, Holt (Hegarty), McInally, Ferguson, Kirkwood, Sturrock, Redford (Bannon), Gallacher
IFK Gothenburg: Wernersson, Carlsson, Hysen, Larsson, Fredriksson, Nilsson R. (Johansson), Tord Holmgren (Mordt), Andersson, Tommy Holmgren, Pettersson, Nilsson L.
IFK win 2-1 on aggregate

1988

1st Leg – 4 May   Sarria, Barcelona   42,000
Espanol   3   Bayer Leverkusen   0
Losada (45, 56), Soler (49)
Espanol: N'Kono, Job, Miguel Angel, Gallart, Soler, Orejuela (Golobart), Urquiaga, Inaki, Valverde, Pichi Alonso (Lauridsen), Losada
Bayer Leverkusen: Volborn, Rolff, De Dayser, Reinhardt A., Hinterberger, Cha-Bum-Kun (Gotz), Tita, Buncol, Falkenmayer (Reinhardt K.), Waas, Tauber

2nd Leg – 18 May   Haberlandstadion, Leverkusen   22,000
Bayer Leverkusen   3   Espanol   0
Tita (57), Gotz (63), Cha-Bum-Kun (81)
Bayer Leverkusen: Volborn, Rolff, Seckler, Reinhardt A., Reinhardt K., Schreier (Waas), Buncol, Falkenmayer, Cha-Bum-Kun, Gotz, Tita (Tauber)
Espanol: N'Kono, Miguel Angel, Golobart (Ziniga), Gallart, Urquiaga, Job, Orejuela (Zubillaga), Inaki, Soler, Pichi Alonso, Losada
Bayer Leverkusen won 3-2 on penalties. 3-3 on aggregate

1989

1st Leg – 3 May   San Paola, Naples   83,000
Napoli   2   VfB Stuttgart   1
Maradona (68), Careca (87)   Gaudino (17)
Napoli: Giuliani, Renica, Ferrera, Francini, Corradini (Crippa), Alemao, Fusi, De Napoli, Careca, Maradona, Carnevale
VfB Stuttgart: Immel, Allgower, Schmaler N., Hartmann, Buchwald, Schafer, Katanec, Sigurvinnson, Schroder, Walter (Zietsch), Gaudino

2nd Leg – 17 May   Neckarstadion, Stuttgart   67,000
VfB Stuttgart   3   Napoli   3
Klinsmann (27), Own Goal (70),   Alemao (18), Ferrera (39),
Schmaler (89)   Careca (62)
VfB Stuttgart: Immel, Allgower, Schmaler N., Hartmann, Schafer, Katanec, Sigurvinnson, Schroder, Walter (Schmalero), Klinsmann, Gaudino
Napoli: Giuliani, Renica, Ferrera, Francini, Corradini, Alemao (Carranante), Fusi, De Napoli, Careca, Maradona, Carnevale
Napoli win 5-4 on aggregate

1990

1st Leg – 2 May   Communale, Turin   45,000
Juventus   3   Fiorentina   1
Galia (3), Casiraghi (59),   Buso (10)
De Agostini (73)
Juventus: Tacconi, Napoli, De Agostini, Galia, Bruno (Alessio), Bonetti, Aleinikov, Barros, Marocchi, Casiraghi, Schillaci
Fiorentina: Landucci, Dell'Oglio, Volpecina, Pin, Battistini, Dunga, Nappi, Kubik (Malusci), Baggio R., Buso, Di Chiara

2nd Leg – 16 May   Stadio Partenio, Avellino   32,000
Fiorentina   0   Juventus   0
Fiorentina: Landucci, Dell'Oglio, Volpecina, Pin, Battistini, Dunga, Nappi (Zironelli), Kubik, Baggio R., Buso, Di Chiara
Juventus: Tacconi, Napoi, De Agostini, Galia, Bruno, Alessio, Aleinikov, Barros (Avallone), Marocchi, Casiraghi (Rosa), Schillaci
Juventus win 3-1 on aggregate

1991

1st Leg – 8 May   Giuseppe Meazza, Milan   75,000
Internazionale   2   Roma   0
Matthaus (55), Berti (67)
Internazionale: Zenga, Bergomi, Brehme, Battistini, Ferri, Paganin (Baresi), Bianchi, Berti, Matthaus, Klinsmann, Serena (Pizzi)
Roma: Cervone, Tempestilli, Nela, Berthold, Aldair (Carboni), Comi (Muzzi), Gerolin, Di Mauro, Giannini, Voller, Rizzitelli

2nd Leg – 22 May   Stadio Olimpico, Rome   71,000
Roma   1   Internazionale   0
Rizzitelli (81)
Roma: Cervone, Tempestilli (Salsano), Gerolin, Berthold, Aldair, Nela, Desideri (Muzzi), Di Mauro, Giannini, Voller, Rizzitelli
Internazionale: Zenga, Bergomi, Brehme, Battistini, Ferri, Paganin, Bianchi, Berti, Matthaus, Klinsmann, Pizzi (Mandorlini)
Internazionale win 2-1 on aggregate

1992

1st Leg – 29 April   Delle Alpi, Turin   65,000
Torino   2   Ajax   2
Casagrande (65, 82)   Jonk (17), Pettersson (73)
Torino: Marchegiani, Bruno, Annoni, Cravero (Bresciani), Mussi (Sordo), Benedetti, Scifo, Vasquez M., Venturi, Lentini, Casagrande
Ajax: Menzo, Silooy, Blind, Jonk, De Boer, Winter, Kreek, Bergkamp, Van't Schip, Pettersson, Roy (Gronendijk)

2nd Leg – 13 May   Olympisch Stadion, Amsterdam   42,000
Ajax   0   Torino   0
Ajax: Menzo, Silooy, Blind, Jonk, De Boer, Winter, Kreek (Vink), Alflen, Van't Schip, Pettersson, Roy (Van Loen)
Torino: Marchegiani, Mussi, Cravero (Sordo), Benedetti, Fusi, Policano, Vasquez M., Scifo (Bresciani), Venturi, Casagrande, Lentini
Ajax win on away goals rule. 2-2 on aggregate

1993

1st Leg – 5 May   Westfalenstadion, Dortmund   37,000
Borussia Dortmund   1   Juventus   3
M. Rummenigge (2)   D. Baggio (27), R. Baggio (31, 74)
Borussia Dortmund: Kios, Grauer, Reuter, Schmidt, Lusch, Franck (Mill), Zorc (Karl), Rummenigge M., Poschner, Reinhardt, Chapuisat
Juventus: Peruzzi, Julio Cesar, Carrera, Kohler, De Marchi, Conte, Baggio D., Baggio R., (Di Canio), Marocchi, Vialli, Moller (Galia)

2nd Leg – 19 May   Delle Alpi, Turin   60,000
Juventus   3   Borussia Dortmund   0
D. Baggio (5, 40), Moller (65)
Juventus: Peruzzi, Carrera, Torricelli (Di Canio), De Marchi, Kohler, Julio Cesar, Moller, Baggio D., Vialli (Ravenelli), Baggio R., Marocchi
Borussia Dortmund: Kios, Reinhardt, Schmidt, Schulz, Zelic, Poschner, Reuter (Lusch), Karl, Mill, Rummenigge M. (Franck), Sippel
Juventus win 6-1 on aggregate

1994

1st Leg – 26 April   47,500
SV Casino Salzburg   Internazionale   0-1
    Berti (35)
Salzburg: Konrad, Lainer, Weber, Winklhofer (Steiner 61), Furstaller, Aigner, Amerhauser (Muzek 46), Artner, Marquinho, Pfeifenberger, Stadler
Internazionale: Zenga, A.Paganin, Orlando, Jonk, Bergomi, Battistini, Bianchi, Manicone, Berti, Bergkamp (Dell'Anno 89), Sosa (Ferri 74)
Yellow Cards: Pfeifenberger, Stadler (Salzburg); Bianchi, Jonk (Inter)
Red Cards: Bianchi (Inter)

2nd Leg – 11 May   80,326
Internazionale   1   SV Casino Salzburg   0
Jonk (63)
Internazionale: Zenga, A. Paganin, Fontolan (R. Ferri 67), Jonk, Bergomi, Battistini, Orlando, Manicone, Berti, Bergkamp (M. Paganin 89), Sosa
Salzburg: Konrad, Winklhofer (Amerhauser 67), Lainer, Weber, Furstaller, Aigner, Jurcevic, Artner (Steiner 75), Hutter, Marquinho, Feiersinger
Yellow Cards: Orlando, Fontolan (Inter); Feiersinger, Steiner (Salzburg)

World Club Championship 1960–93

1960

1st Leg – 3 July Centenario, Montevideo 75,000
Penarol 0 **Real Madrid** 0
Penarol: Maidana, Martinez, Augerre, Pino, Salvador, Goncalves, Cubilla, Linazza, Hohberg, Spencer, Borges
Real Madrid: Dominguez, Marquitos, Santamaria, Pachin, Vidal, Zarraga, Canario, Del Sol, Di Stefano, Puskas, Bueno

2nd Leg – 4 September Bernabeu, Madrid 125,000
Real Madrid 5 **Penarol** 1
Puskas (3, 9), Di Stefano (4), Borges (69)
Herrera (44), Gento (54)
Real Madrid: Dominguez, Marquitos, Santamaria, Pachin, Vidal, Zarraga, Herrera, Del Sol, Di Stefano, Puskas, Gento. *Tr:* Munoz
Penarol: Maidana, Pino, Mayewski, Martinez, Augerre, Salvador, Cubilla, Linazza, Hohberg, Spencer, Borges. *Tr:* Scarone

1961

1st Leg – 4 September Estadio da Luz, Lisbon 50,000
Benfica 1 **Penarol** 0
Coluna (60)
Benfica: Costa Pereira, Angelo, Saraiva, Joao, Neto, Cruz, Augusto, Santana, Aguas, Coluna, Cavem
Penarol: Maidana, Gonzales, Martinez, Cano, Augerre, Goncalvez, Ledesma, Cubilla, Spencer, Cabrera, Sasia

2nd Leg – 17 September Centenario, Montevideo 56,000
Penarol 5 **Benfica** 0
Sasia (10), Joya (18,28), Spencer (42, 60)
Penarol: Maidana, Gonzales, Martinez, Augerre, Cano, Goncalvez, Ledesma, Cubilla, Sasia, Spencer, Joya
Benfica: Costa Pereira, Angelo, Saraiva, Joao, Neto, Cruz, Augusto, Santana, Mendes, Coluna, Cavem

Play-off – 19 September Centenario, Montevideo 62,000
Penarol 2 **Benfica** 1
Sasia (6, 41) (Eusebio 35)
Penarol: Maidana, Gonzales, Martinez, Augerre, Cano, Goncalvez, Cabrera, Cubilla, Ledesma, Sasia, Spencer. *Tr:* Scarone
Benfica: Costa Pereira, Angelo, Humberto, Cruz, Neto, Coluna, Augusto, Eusebio, Aguas, Cavem, Simoes. *Tr:* Guttmann

1962

1st Leg – 19 September Maracana, Rio de Janeiro 90,000
Santos 3 **Benfica** 2
Pele (31, 86), Coutinho (64) Santana (58, 87)
Santos: Gilmar, Lima, Mauro, Calvet, Dalmo, Zito, Mengalvio, Dorval, Coutinho, Pele, Pepe
Benfica: Costa Pereira, Jacinto, Raul, Humberto, Cruz, Cavem, Coluna, Augusto, Santana, Eusebio, Simoes

2nd Leg – 11 October Estadio da Luz, Lisbon 75,000
Benfica 2 **Santos** 5
Eusebio (87), Santana (89) Pele (17, 28, 64), Coutinho (49), Pepe (77)
Benfica: Costa Pereira, Jacinto, Raul, Humberto, Cruz, Cavem, Coluna, Augusto, Santana, Eusebio, Simoes. *Tr:* Reira
Santos: Gilmar, Olavo, Mauro, Calvet, Dalmo, Lima, Zito, Dorval, Coutinho, Pele, Pepe. *Tr:* Lula

1963

1st Leg – 16 October San Siro, Milan 80,000
Milan 4 **Santos** 2
Trapattoni (4), Amarildo (15, 65), Pele (59, 87)
Mora (80)
Milan: Ghezzi, David, Maldini, Trapattoni, Trebbi, Pelagalli, Lodetti, Rivera, Mora, Altafini, Amarildo
Santos: Gilmar, Lima, Haroldo, Calvet, Geraldino, Zito, Mengalvio, Dorval, Coutinho, Pele, Pepe

2nd Leg – 14 November Maracana, Rio de Janeiro 150,000
Santos 4 **Milan** 2
Pepe (50, 67), Almir (60), Altafini (12), Mora (17)
Lima (63)
Santos: Gilmar, Ismael, Dalmo, Mauro, Haroldo, Lima, Mengalvio, Dorval, Coutinho, Pele, Pepe
Milan: Ghezzi, David, Maldini, Trapattoni, Trebbi, Pelagalli, Lodetti, Rivera, Mora, Altafini, Amarildo

Play-off – 16 November Maracana, Rio de Janeiro 121,000
Santos 1 **Milan** 0
Dalmo (26)
Santos: Gilmar, Ismael, Dalmo, Mauro, Haroldo, Lima, Mengalvio, Dorval, Coutinho, Almir, Pepe. *Tr:* Lula
Milan: Balzarini (Barluzzi), Pelagalli, Maldini, Trebbi, Benitez, Lodetti, Trapattoni, Mora, Altafini, Amarildo, Fortunato. *Tr:* Carnigilia

1964

1st Leg – 9 September Cordero, Avellaneda 70,000
Independiente 1 **Internazionale** 0
Rodriguez (60)
Independiente: Santoro, Ferreiro, Guzman, Maldonado, Rolan, Acevedo, Mura, Bernao, Prospitti, Rodriguez, Savoy
Internazionale: Sarti, Burgnich, Guarneri, Picchi, Facchetti, Tagnin, Suarez, Corso, Jair, Mazzola, Peiro

2nd Leg – 23 September San Siro, Milan 70,000
Internazionale 1 **Independiente** 0
Corso (120)
Internazionale: Sarti, Malatrasi, Guarneri, Picchi, Facchetti, Tagnin, Suarez, Corso, Domenghini, Peiro, Milani. *Tr:* Herrera
Independiente: Santoro, Guzman, Paflik, Decaria, Maldonado, Acevedo, Prospitti, Suarez, Bernao, Rodriguez, Savoy. *Tr:* Guidice

Play-off – 26 September Bernabeu Madrid 45,000
Internazionale 2 **Independiente** 0
Mazzola (8), Corso (39)
Internazionale: Sarti, Burgnich, Guarneri, Picchi, Facchetti, Malatrasi, Suarez, Corso, Jair, Mazzola, Milani
Independiente: Santoro, Ferreiro, Paflik, Maldonado, Decaria, Acevedo, Prospitti, Suarez, Mura, Rodriguez, Savoy

1965

1st Leg – 8 September   San Siro, Milan   70,000
Internazionale   **3**   **Independiente**   **0**
Peiro (3), Mazzola (23, 61)
Internazionale: Sarti, Burgnich, Guarneri, Picchi, Facchetti, Bedin, Suarez, Corso, Jair, Mazzola, Peiro. *Tr:* Herrera
Independiente: Santoro, Pavoni, Guzman, Navarro, Ferreiro, Acevedo, De La Mata, Avalay, Bernao, Rodriguez, Savoy. *Tr:* Guidice

2nd Leg – 15 September   Cordero, Avellaneda   70,000
Independiente   **0**   **Internazionale**   **0**
Independiente: Santoro, Navarro, Avalay, Pavoni, Guzman, Ferreiro, Rolan, Mori, Bernao, Mura, Avalay, Savoy. *Tr:* Guidice
Internazionale: Sarti, Burgnich, Guarneri, Picchi, Facchetti, Bedin, Suarez, Corso, Jair, Mazzola, Peiro. *Tr:* Herrera

1966

1st Leg – 12 October   Centenario, Montevideo   70,000
Penarol   **2**   **Real Madrid**   **0**
Spencer (39, 82)
Penarol: Mazurkiewicz, Forlan, Lezcano, Varela, Gonzalez, Goncalvez, Cortes, Rocha, Abbedie, Spencer, Joya
Real Madrid: Betancort, Pachin, De Felipe, Zoco, Sanchis, Ruiz, Pirri, Velasquez, Serena, Amancio, Bueno

2nd Leg – 26 October   Bernabeu, Madrid   70,000
Real Madrid   **0**   **Penarol**   **2**
                              Rocha (28), Spencer (37)
Real Madrid: Betancort, Calpe, De Felipe, Zoco, Sanchis, Pirri, Grosso, Velasquez, Serena, Amancio, Gento. *Tr:* Munzo
Penarol: Mazurkiewicz, Gonzalez, Lezcano, Varela, Caetano, Rocha, Goncalvez, Cotes, Abbadie, Spencer, Joya. *Tr:* Mazpoli

1967

1st Leg – 18 October   Hampden Park, Glasgow   103,000
Celtic   **1**   **Racing Club**   **0**
McNeil (67)
Celtic: Simpson, Craig, McNeil, Gemmell, Murdoch, Clark, Johnstone, Lennox, Wallace, Auld, Hughes
Racing Club: Cejas, Martin, Perfumo, Basile, Diaz, Rulli, Mori, Maschio, Cardenas, Rodriguez, Raffo

2nd Leg – 1 November   Mozart y Cuyo, Avellaneda   80,000
Racing Club   **2**   **Celtic**   **1**
Raffo (32), Cardenas (48)   Gemmell (20)
Racing Club: Cejas, Perfumo, Chabay, Basile, Martin, Rulli, Maschio, Raffo, Cardoso, Cardenas, Rodriguez
Celtic: Fallon, Craig, Clark, McNeil, Gemmell, Murdoch, O'Neill, Johnstone, Wallace, Chalmers, Lennox

Play-off – 4 November   Centenario, Montevideo   65,000
Racing Club   **1**   **Celtic**   **0**
Cardenas (55)
Racing Club: Cejas, Perfumo, Chabay, Martin, Basile, Rulli, Maschio, Raffo, Cardoso, Cardenas, Rodriguez. *Tr:* Pizzuti
Celtic: Fallon, Craig, Clark, McNeil, Gemmell, Murdoch, Auld, Johnstone, Lennox, Wallace, Hughes. *Tr:* Stein

1968

1st Leg – 25 September   Banbonera, Buenos Aires   65,000
Estudiantes LP   **1**   **Manchester United**   **0**
Conigliaro (28)
Estudiantes LP: Poletti, Malbernat, Aguirre-Suarez, Medina, Pachame, Madero, Ribaudo, Bilardo, Togneri, Conigliaro, Veron
Manchester United: Stepney, Dunne, Sadler, Faulkes, Burns, Stiles, Crerand, Charlton, Morgan, Law, Best

2nd Leg – 16 October   Old Trafford, Manchester   60,000
Manchester United   **1**   **Estudiantes LP**   **1**
Morgan (8)   Veron (5)
Manchester United: Stepney, Dunne, Sadler, Foulkes, Brennan, Crerand, Charlton, Morgan, Kidd, Law (Sartori), Best. *Tr:* Busby
Estudiantes LP: Poletti, Malbernat, Aguirre-Suarez, Medina, Bilardo, Pachame, Madero, Togneri, Ribaudo, Conigliaro, Veron (Echecopar). *Tr:* Zubeldia

1969

1st Leg – 8 October   San Siro, Milan   80,000
Milan   **3**   **Estudiantes LP**   **0**
Sormani (8, 73), Combin (44)
Milan: Cudicini, Malatrasi, Anquilletti, Rosato, Schnellinger, Lodetti, Rivera, Fogli, Sormani, Combin (Rognoni), Prati
Estudiantes LP: Poletti, Aguirre-Suarez, Manera, Madero, Malbernat, Bilardo, Togneri, Echecopar (Ribaudo), Flores, Conigliaro, Veron

2nd Leg – 22 October   Bonbonera, Buenos Aires   65,000
Estudiantes LP   **2**   **Milan**   **1**
Conigliaro (43),   Rivera (30)
Aguirre-Suarez (44)
Estudiantes LP: Poletti, Manera, Aguirre-Suarez, Madero, Malbernat, Bilardo (Echecopar), Romero, Togneri, Conigliaro, Taverna, Veron. *Tr:* Zubeldia
Milan: Cudicini, Malatrasi (Maldera), Anquilletti, Rosato, Schnellinger, Foglio, Lodetti, Rivera, Sormani, Combin, Prati, (Rognoni). *Tr:* Rocco

1970

1st Leg – 26 August   Bonbonera, Buenos Aires   65,000
Estudiantes LP   **2**   **Feyenoord**   **2**
Echecopar (6), Veron (10)   Kindvall (21), Van Hanegem (65)
Estudiantes LP: Errea, Pagnanini, Spadaro, Togneri, Malbernat, Bilardo (Solari), Pachame, Echecopar (Rudzki), Conigliaro, Flores, Veron
Feyenoord: Treytel, Romeyn, Israel, Laseroms, Van Duivenbode, Hasil, Jansen, Van Hanegem (Boskamp), Wery, Kindvall, Moulijn

2nd Leg – 9 September   Feyenoord Stadion, Rotterdam   70,000
Feyenoord   **1**   **Estudiantes LP**   **0**
Van Deale (65)
Feyenoord: Treytel, Romyen, Israel, Laseroms, Van Duivenbode, Hasil (Boskamp), Van Hanegem, Jansen, Wery, Kindvall, Moulijn (Van Deale). *Tr:* Happel
Estudiantes LP: Pezzano, Malbernat, Spadaro, Togneri, Medina (Pagnanini), Bilardo, Pachame, Romero, Conigliaro (Rudzki), Flores, Veron. *Tr:* Zubeldia

1971

Panathinaikos took the place of Ajax who declined to play
1st Leg – 15 December   Athens   60,000
Panathinaikos   **1**   **Nacional Montevideo**   **1**
Filakouris (48)   Artime (50)

2nd leg – 29 December   Cetenario, Montevideo   70,000
Nacional Montevideo   **2**   **Panathinaikos**   **1**
Artime (34, 75)   Filakouris (89)

1972

1st Leg – 6 September   Mozart y Cuya, Avellaneda   65,000
Independiente   **1**   **Ajax**   **1**
Sa (82)   Cruyff (6)
Independiente: Santoro, Commisso, Lopez, Sa, Pavoni, Pastoriza, Semenewicz, Raimundo (Bulla), Balbuena, Maglioni, Mircoli
Ajax: Stuy, Suurbier, Hulshoff, Blankenburg, Krol, Haan, Neeskens, Muhren G., Swart, Cruyff (Muhren A.), Keizer

2nd Leg – 28 September   Olympisch Stadion, Amsterdam   60,000
Ajax   **3**   **Independiente**   **0**
Neeskens (12), Rep (16, 78)

Ajax: Stuy, Suurbier, Hulshoff, Blankenburg, Krol, Haan, Neeskens, Muhren G., Swart (Rep), Cruyff, Keizer. *Tr:* Kovacs
Independiente: Santoro, Commisso, Sa, Lopez, Pavoni, Pastoriza, Garisto (Magan), Semenewicz, Balbuena, Maglioni, Mircoli (Bulla)

1973
Juventus took the place of Ajax who declined to play
28 November   Stadio Olimpico, Rome   35,000
Independiente   **1**   **Juventus**   **0**
Bochini (40)

1974
Atletico Madrid took the place of Bayern Munich who declined to play
1st Leg – 12 March   Mozart y Cuyo, Buenos Aires   60,000
Independiente   **1**   **Atletico Madrid**   **0**
Balbuena (33)

2nd Leg – 10 April   Vicente Calderon, Madrid   45,000
Atletico Madrid   **2**   **Independiente**   **0**
Irureta (21), Ayala (86)

1975
No competition as Independiente and Bayern Munich could not agree on dates for fixtures

1976
1st Leg – 23 November   Olympiastadion, Munich   22,000
Bayern Munchen   **2**   **Cruzeiro**   **0**
Muller (80), Kapellmann (83)
Bayern Munich: Maier, Andersson, Beckenbauer, Schwarzenbeck, Horsmann, Durnberger, Kapellmann, Torstensson, Hoeness, Muller, Rummenigge
Cruzeiro: Raul, Nelinho, Moraes, Osiris, Vanderlay, Ze Carlos, Piazza, Eduardo, Jairzinho, Palinha, Joaozinho

2nd Leg – 21 December
     Magalhaes Pinto, Mineirao, Belo Horizonte   114,000
Cruzeiro   **0**   **Bayern Munchen**   **0**
Cruzeiro: Raul, Moraes, Osiris, Piazza (Eduardo), Nelinho, Vanderlay, Dirceu (Forlan), Ze Carlos, Jairzinho, Palinha, Joaozinho. *Tr:* ?
Bayern Munchen: Maier, Andersson, Beckenbauer, Schwarzenbeck, Horsmann, Weiss, Hoeness, Kapellman, Torstensson, Muller, Rummenigge. *Tr:* Lattek

1977
Borussia Monchengladbach took the place of Liverpool who declined to play
1st Leg – 22 March   Bonbonera, Buenos Aires   50,000
Boca Juniors   **2**   **Bor. Monchengladbach**   **2**
Mastrangelo (16), Ribolzi (51)   Hannes (24), Bonhof (29)

2nd Leg – 26 July   Wildpark Stadion, Karlsruhe   21,000
Bor. Monchengladbach   **0**   **Boca Juniors**   **3**
     Zanabria (2), Mastrangelo (33), Salinas (35)

1978
No competition as Boca Juniors and Liverpool declined to play each other

1979
Malmo FF took the place of Nottingham Forest who declined to play
1st Leg – 18 November   Malmo Stadion, Malmo   4,000
Malmo FF   **0**   **Olimpia**   **1**
     Isas (41)

2nd Leg – 3 March   Manuel Ferreira, Asuncion   35,000
Olimpia   **2**   **Malmo FF**   **1**
Solalinde (40), Michelagnoli (71)   Earlandsson (48)

1980
11 February   National Stadium, Tokyo   62,000
Nacional Montevideo   **1**   **Nottingham Forest**   **0**
Victorino (10)
Nacional Montevideo: Rodriguez, Moreira, Blanco, Enriquez, Gonzalez, Milar, Esparrago, Luzardo, Morales, Bica, Victorino. *Tr:* Mujica
Nottingham Forest: Shilton, Anderson, Lloyd, Burns, Gray F., Ponte (Ward), O'Neil, Gray, Robertson, Francis, Wallace. *Tr:* Clough

1981
13 December   National Stadium, Tokyo   62,000
Flamengo   **3**   **Liverpool**   **0**
Nunes (13, 41), Adilio (34)
Flamengo: Raul, Leandro, Junior, Mozer, Marinho, Adilio, Tita, Andrade, Zico, Lico, Nunes. *Tr:* Paolo Cesar
Liverpool: Grobbelar, Neal, Lawrenson, Hansen, Thompson, Kennedy R., Lee, McDermott (Johnson), Souness, Dalglish, Johnston. *Tr:* Paisley

1982
12 December   National Stadium, Tokyo   62,000
Penarol   **2**   **Aston Villa**   **0**
Jair (27), Charrua (69)
Penarol: Fernandez, Diogo, Oliveira, Morales, Gutierrez, Saralegui, Bossio, Jair, Ramos (Charrua), Morena, Silva. *Tr:* Bagnolo
Aston Villa: Rimmer, Jones, Evans, McNaught, Williams, Bremner, Mortimer, Cowans, Shaw, Withe, Morley. *Tr:* Barton

1983
11 December   National Stadium, Tokyo   62,000
Gremio   **2**   **SV Hamburg**   **1**
Renato (37, 93)   Schroder (85)
Gremio: Mazzaropi, Paulo, Roberto, Baidek, De Leon, Magallanes, Sergio, Paulo, Cesar (Caio), Osvaldo (Bonamigo), China, Renato, Tarciso, G. *Tr:* Espinosa
SV Hamburg: Stein, Wehmeyer, Jacobs, Hieronymus, Schroder, Hartwig, Groh, Rolff, Magath, Wuttke, Hansen. *Tr:* Happel

1984
9 December   National Stadium, Tokyo   62,000
Independiente   **1**   **Liverpool**   **0**
Percudani (6)
Independiente: Goyen, Villaverde (Monzon), Enriquo, Clausen, Trossoro, Marangoni, Burruchaga, Giusti, Bochini, Percudani, Barbcron. *Tr:* Pastoriza
Liverpool: Grobbelar, Neal, Kennedy A., Gillespie, Hanson, Nicol, Dalglish, Molby, Wark (Whelan), Rush, Johnston. *Tr:* Fagan

1985
8 December   National Stadium, Tokyo   62,000
Juventus   **2**   **Argentinos Juniors**   **2**
Platini (63), Laudrup (82)   Ereros (55), Castro (75)
Juventus: Tacconi, Favero, Brio, Scirea (Pioli), Cabrini, Bonini, Manfredonia, Platini, Mauro (Briaschi), Serena, Laudrup. *Tr:* Trapattoni
Argentinos Juniors: Vidalle, Villalba, Pavoni, Olguin, Domenech, Videla, Batista, Commisso (Corsi), Castro, Borghi, Ereros (Lopez). *Tr:* Yudica
Juventus won 4-2 on penalties

1986
14 December   National Stadium, Tokyo   62,000
River Plate   **1**   **Steaua Bucharest**   **0**
Alzamendi (28)
River Plate: Pumpido, Gordillo, Gutierrez, Montenegro, Ruggeri, Alfaro (Sperandio), Alonso, Enrique, Gallego, Alzamendi, Funes. *Tr:* Viera
Steaua Bucharest: Stimgaciu, Iovan, Bumbescu, Belodedici, Barbulescu (Majaru), Weisenbacher, Stoica, Balint, Balan, Lacatus, Piturca. *Tr:* Iordanescu

1987
13 December *National Stadium, Tokyo* 45,000
FC Porto 2 **Penarol** 1
Gomes (41), Madjer (108) Viera 80
FC Porto: Mlynarczyk, Joao Pinto, Geraldao, Lima Periera, Inacio, Rui Barros (Quim), Magalhaes, Andre, Sousa, Gomes, Madjer. *Tr:* Ivic
Penarol: Periera, Herrera (Goncalves), Rotti, Trasante, Dominguez, Perdomo, Viera, Aguirro, Cabrera (Matosas), Vidal, Da Silva. *Tr:* Tabarez

1988
11 December *National Stadium, Tokyo* 62,000
Nacional Montevideo 2 **PSV Eindhoven** 2
Ostolaza (7, 119) Romario (75), Koeman (109)
Nacional Montivideo: Sere, Gomez, De Leon, Revelez, Saldana, Ostolaza, Vargas (Moran), Lemos, De Lima, Cardaccio (Carreno), Castro. *Tr:* Fleitas
PSV Eindhoven: Van Breukelen, Gerets, Koot, Koeman, Heintze (Valckx), Lerby, Van Aerle, Vanenburg (Gillhaus) Romario, Kieft, Ellerman. *Tr:* Hiddink
Nacional won 7-6 on penalties

1989
17 December *National Stadium, Tokyo* 62,000
Milan 1 **Nacional Medellin** 0
Evani (118)
Milan: Galli, Baresi, Tassotti, Maldini, Fuser (Evani), Costacurta, Donadoni, Rijkaard, Ancolotti, Van Basten, Massaro (Simone). *Tr:* Sacchi
Nacional Medellin: Higuita, Escobar, Gomez, Herrera, Cassiani, Perez, Arango (Restrepo), Alvarez, Arboleda (Uzurriaga), Garcia, Trellez. *Tr:* Maturana

1990
9 December *National Stadium, Tokyo* 60,000
Milan 3 **Olimpia** 0
Rijkaald (43, 65), Stroppa (62)
Milan: Pazzagli, Baresi, Tassotti, Costacurta, Maldini (Galli), Carbone, Donadoni (Guerreiri), Rijkaard, Stroppa, Gullit, Van Basten. *Tr:* Sacchi
Olimpia: Almeida Fernandez, Caceres, Guasch, Ramirez (Chamac), Suarez, Hoyn (Cubilla), Balbuena, Monzon, Amarilla, Samaniego. *Tr:* Cubilla

1991
8 December *National Stadium, Tokyo* 60,000
Red Star Belgrade 3 **Colo Colo** 0
Jugovic (19, 58), Pancev (72)
Red Star Belgrade: Milojevic, Radinovic, Vasilijevic, Belodedic, Najdoski, Jugovic, Stosic, Ratkovic, Savicevic, Mikhailovic, Pancev. *Tr:* Popovic
Colo Colo: Moron, Garrido, Margas, Ramirez M., Salvatierra (Dabrowski), Mendoza, Vilches, Barticciotto, Pizarro, Yanez, Martinez (Rubio). *Tr:* Josic

1992
12 December *National Stadium, Tokyo* 80,000
Sao Paulo 2 **Barcelona** 1
Rai (26, 79) Stoichkov (13)
Sao Paulo: Zetti, Victor, Adilson, Ronaldo, Pintado, Ronaldo Luiz, Muller, Toninho Cerezo (Dinho), Palinha, Rai, Cafu. *Tr:* Santana
Barcelona: Zubizarreta, Ferrer, Guardiola, Koeman, Eusebio, Bakero (Goicoechea), Amor, Stoichkov, Laudrup, Witschge, Berguiristain (Nadal). *Tr:* Cruyff

1993
33,765
Milan 2 **Sao Paulo** 3
Massaro (48), Papin (82) Palhinha (20), Cerezo (59), Muller (86)
Milan: Rossi, Panucci, Costacurta, Baresi, Maldini, Donadoni, Desailly, Albertini (Tassotti 79), Massaro, Raducioiu (Orlando 79), Papin
Sao Paulo: Zetti, Cafu, Valber, Ronaldo, Andre, Cerezo, Doriva, Leonardo, Dinho, Palhinha (Juninho 64), Muller

European Super Cup Finals 1973–93

The European Super Cup is staged between the holders of the Champions' Cup and the Cup-Winners' Cup. The event was originally the brainchild of the Dutch newspaper *De Telegraaf* who wanted to see how their European champions, Ajax, would fare against the Cup-Winners' Cup holders, Glagow Rangers. Since then it has been a near-annual event and in recent years has received recognition from UEFA, who now sanction the contest.

1972

1st Leg – 16 January 1973 *Ibrox, Glasgow*
Glasgow Rangers 1 **Ajax** 3
MacDonald (39) Rep (31), Cruyff (43), Haan (44)
Glasgow Rangers: McCloy, Jardine, Johnstone, Mathieson, Greig, Forsyth, Parlane, Conn, McDonald, Smith, Young
Ajax: Stuy, Suurbier, Krol, Haan, Hulshoff, Blanckenburg, Rep, G. Muhren, Cruyff, A. Muhren, Keizer
Ref: MacKenzie (Sco)

2nd Leg – 23 January 1973 *Amsterdam*
Ajax 3 **Glasgow Rangers** 2
Haan (9), Muhren (39), Cruyff (43) McDonald (7, 26)
Ajax: Stuy, Suurbier, Krol, Haan, Hulshoff, Blanckenburg, Neeskens, Swart, G. Muhren, Cruyff, Kelzer
Glasgow Rangers: McCloy, Jardine, Johnstone, Mathieson, Greig, Forsyth, Parlane, Smith, McDonald, McLean, Young
Ref: MacKenzie (Sco)
Ajax win 6-3 on aggregate

1973

1st Leg – 9 January 1974 *San Siro, Milan*
Milan 1 **Ajax** 0
Chiarugi (77)
Milan: Vecchi, Sabadini, Anquiletti, Maldera, Turone, Schnellinger, Turini (Bergamaschi 46), Benetti, Chiarugi, Rivera, Biasolo
Ajax: Stuy, Suurbier, Krol, Haan, Hulshoff, Blanckenburg, Rep, Neeskens, Mulder, G. Muhren, Keizer
Ref: Scheurer (Swi)

2nd Leg – 16 January 1974 *Amsterdam*
Ajax 6 **Milan** 0
Mulder (26), Keizer (35), Neeskens (71), Rep (81), Muhren (84), Haan (87)
Ajax: Stuy, Suurbier, Krol, Haan, Hulshoff, Blackenburg, Rep, Neeskens, Mulder, G. Muhren, Keizer
Milan: Vecchi, Anquiletti, Maldera, Dolci, Turone, Schnellinger, Sabadini, Benetti, Chiarugi, Rivera, Biasolo (Tresoldi 71)
Ref: Gloekner (E Ger)
Ajax win 6-1 on aggregate

1974
No Competition

1975

1st Leg – 9 September 1975 *Munich*
Bayern Munich 0 **Dynamo Kiev** 1
Blokhin (66)
Bayern Munich: Maier, Horsmann, Duernburger (Roth 46), Beckenbauer, Schwarzenbeck, Zobel, Rummenigge, Weiss, Muller, Kappelmann, Wunder
Dynamo Kiev: Rudakov, Konkov, Reshko, Zuev, Fomenko, Damin, Troshkin, Slobodjan, Burjak, Kolotov, Blokhin
Ref: Gonella (Ita)

2nd Leg – 6 October 1975 *Kiev*
Dynamo Kiev 2 **Bayern Munich** 0
Blokhin (40, 53)
Dynamo Kiev: Rudakov, Konkov, Reshko, Zuev, Fomenko, Troshkin, Muntlaa, Veremeev, Buriak, Onishenko, Blokhin
Bayern Munich: Maier, Horsmann, Duernburger (Hansen 70), Schwarzenbeck, Beckenbauer, Roth, Weiss, Schuster (Torstensson 78), Rummenigge, Kappelmann, Wunder
Ref: Babacan (Tur)
Dynamo Kiev win 3-0 on aggregate

1976

1st Leg – 17 August 1976 *Munich*
Bayern Munich 2 **RSC Anderlecht** 1
Muller (58, 88) Haan (16)
Bayern Munich: Maier, Schwarzenbeck, Horsmann, Duernburger, Beckenbauer, Torstensson, Hoeness, Kunkel, Muller, Kappelmann, Rummenigge
RSC Anderlecht: Ruiter, Van Bist, Dockx (De Groot 64), Broos, Van den Daele, Vercauteren, Van der Elst, Coek, Ressel, Haan, Rensenbrink
Ref: Burns (Eng)

2nd Leg – 30 August 1976 *Brussels*
RSC Anderlecht 4 **Bayern Munich** 1
Rensenbrink (20, 28), Van der Elst (25), Haan (59) Muller (63)
RSC Anderlecht: Ruiter, F. Van der Elst, Dockx, Broos, Van den Daele, Vercauteren, Haan, Coek, McKenzie, Ressel, Rensenbrink
Bayern Munich: Maier, Andersson, Horsmann, Schwarzenbeck, Beckenbauer, Duernburger, Hoeness (Kunkel 85), Torstensson, G. Muller, Kappellmann, Rummenigge
Ref: Schiller (Aus)
RSC Anderlecht win 5-3 on aggregate

1977

1st Leg – 22 November 1977 *Hamburg*
Hamburg SV 1 **Liverpool** 1
Keller (29) Fairclough (65)
Hamburg SV: Stars, Ripp, Kaltz, Buljan (Karow 67), Eigl, Zaczuk, Memering, Keegan, Keller, Magath (Bertl 64), Steffenhagen
Liverpool: Clemence, Neal, Hughes, Jones (Smith 34), Thompson, R. Kennedy, Dalglish, Case (Johnson 58), Heighway, Callaghan, Fairclough
Ref: Da Silva Garrido (Por)

2nd Leg – 6 December 1977 *Liverpool*
Liverpool 6 Hamburg SV 0
Thompson (21),
McDermott (40, 56, 57),
Fairclough (84), Dalglish (88)
Liverpool: Clemence, Neal, Hughes, Smith, Thompson, R. Kennedy, Dalglish, Case, Heighway (Johnson 75), McDermott, Fairclough
Hamburg SV: Kargus, Ripp, Hidien, Kaltz, Nogly, Zaczyk (Eigl 69), Volkert, Keegan, Keller (Steffenhagen 69), Magath, Bertl
Ref: Erikkson (Swe)
Liverpool win 7-1 on aggregate

1978

1st Leg – 4 December 1978 *Brussels*
RSC Anderlecht 3 Liverpool 1
Vercauteren (17), Case (27)
Van der Elst (38), Rensenbrink (87)
RSC Anderlecht: De Bree, Van der Elst, Thissen, Broos, Dusbaba, Nielsen, Haan, Coek, Geels, Vercauteren, Rensenbrink
Liverpool: Clemence, Neal, A. Kennedy, Hansen, Hughes, McDermott, Case, Souness, Johnson (Heighway 54), R. Kennedy, Dalglish
Ref: Rainea (Rom).

2nd Leg – 9 December 1978 *Liverpool*
Liverpool 2 RSC Anderlecht 1
Hughes (13), Fairclough (85) Van der Elst (71)
Liverpool: Ogrizovic, Neal, Hughes, Thompson, Hansen, McDermott, Dalglish, Case, Fairclough, Souness, R. Kennedy
RSC Anderlecht: Munaron, Van Bist, Thissen, Van Toorn, Dusbaba, Van der Elst, Haan, Coek, Geels (Marteens 46), Vercauteren, Rensenbrink
Ref: Rainea (Rom)
RSC Anderlecht win 4-3 on aggregate

1979

1st Leg – 30 January 1980 *Nottingham*
Nottingham Forest 1 Barcelona 0
George (9)
Nottingham Forest: Shilton, Anderson, Gray, Burns, Lloyd, Bowles, Birtles, Gray, Francis, George, Robertson
Barcelona: Artola, Zuviria, Serrat, Olmo, Migueli, Costas, Simonsen (Canito 88), Landaburu, Carlos Roberto (Carrasco 88), Asensi, Rubio
Ref: Prokop (E. Ger)

2nd Leg – 5 February 1980 *Barcelona*
Barcelona 1 Nottingham Forest 1
Roberto (25) Burns (42)
Barcelona: Artola, Estella, Serrat (Vigo 75), Olmo, Migueli, Sanchez, Simonsen, Rubio, Carlos Roberto, Asensi, Carrasco
Nottingham Forest: Shilton, Anderson, Gray, Lloyd, Burns, McGovern, Birtles, Bowles, Francis (O'Neill 69), George, Robertson
Ref: Eschweiler (E. Ger)
Nottingham Forest win 2-1 on aggregate

1980

1st Leg – 25 November 1980 *Nottingham*
Nottingham Forest 2 Valencia 1
Bowyer (57, 81) Felman (47)
Nottingham Forest: Shilton, Anderson, Gray, McGovern, Lloyd, Burns, Ward (Ponte 76), Bowyer, Wallace, Mills, Robertson
Valencia: Pereira, Carrete, Cervero, Castellanos, Botubot, Arias, Saura, Solsona, Morena, Subirats, Felman (Jimenez 86)
Ref: Ponnet (Bel)

2nd Leg – 17 December 1980 *Valencia*
Valencia 1 Nottingham Forest 0
Morena (51)
Valencia: Sempere, Carrete, Tendillo, Castellanos, Botubot, Arias, Saura, Solsona, Morena, Subirats, Kempes
Nottingham Forest: Shilton, Anderson, Gunn, McGovern, Lloyd, Burns, O'Neill, Ponte, Francis, Ward, Wallace
Ref: Woehrer (Aus)
2-2 on aggregate; Valencia win on away goals

1981

No Competition.

1982

1st Leg – 19 January 1983 *Barcelona*
Barcelona 1 Aston Villa 0
Marcos (52)
Barcelona: Urruti, Sanchez, Julio Alberto, M. Alonso (Urbano 75), Migueli, Alexanco, Marcos, Schuster, Quini (A. Alonso 70), Victor, Carrasco
Aston Villa: Spink, Jones (Gibson 37), Williams, Mortimer, Evans, McNaught, Bremner, Shaw, Withe, Cowans, Morley
Ref: Galler (Swi)

2nd Leg – 26 January 1983 *Birmingham*
Aston Villa 3 Barcelona 0
Shaw (80), Cowans (pen 99),
McNaught (104)
Aston Villa: Spink, Williams (Birch 115), Gibson, Blair, Evans, McNaught, Bremner, Shaw, Withe, Cowans, Morley (Walters 75)
Barcelona: Urruti, Sanchez, J. Alberto, M. Alonso, Migueli, Alexanco, Marcos, Schuster, Urbano, Victor, Carrasco (Quini 33), Manolo 60
Ref: Ponnet (Bel)
Aston Villa win 3-1 on aggregate after extra time

1983

1st Leg – 22 November 1983 *Hamburg*
Hamburg SV 0 Aberdeen 0
Hamburg SV: Stein, Wehmeyer, Schroeder, Groh, Hieronymus, Jakobs, Hartwig (Wuttke 46), Rolff, Schatzschneider, Magath, Von Heesen
Aberdeen: Leighton, Cooper, McLeish, Rougvie, Simpson, Miller, Strachan, Hewitt, McGhee, Weir, Bell
Ref: Christov (Cze)

2nd Leg – 20 December 1983 *Aberdeen*
Aberdeen 2 Hamburg SV 0
Simpson (47) McGhee (65)
Aberdeen: Leighton, McKimmie, McLeish, McMaster, Simpson, Miller, Strachan, Hewitt (Black 65), McGhee, Weir, Bell
Hamburg: Stein, Kaltz (Hansen 68), Wehmeyer, Hieronymus, Jakobs, Groh, Hartwig, Rolff, Schatzschneider (Wuttke 41) Magath, Schroder
Ref: Brummeier (Aus)
Aberdeen win 2-0 on aggregate

1984

16 January 1985 *Turin*
Juventus 2 Liverpool 0
Boniek (39, 79)
Juventus: Bodini, Favero, Cabrini, Bonini, Brio, Scirea, Briaschi, Tardelli, Rossi, Platini, Boniek
Liverpool: Grobbelaar, Neal, A. Kennedy, Lawrenson (Gillespie 46), Hansen, Nicol, Whelan, MacDonald, Rush, Wark, Walsh
Ref: Pauly (E. Ger)

1985

No Competition

EUROPEAN SUPER CUP FINALS 1973–93

1986

24 February 1987   *Monte Carlo*
Steaua Bucarest   **1**   **Dynamo Kiev**   **0**
Hagi (44)
Steaua Bucarest: Stingaciu, Iovan, Barbulescu, Bumbescu, Stoica, Belodedici, Lacatus (Mejarul 89), Balan, Boloni, Hagi (Balint 84), Piturca
Dynamo Kiev: Chanov, Bal, Demainenko, Baltacha, Kutznetsov, Rats, Evtushenko, Zavarov (Morozov 77), Blokhin, Yakovenko, Belanov (Mikhailichenko 50)
Ref: Agnolin (Ita)

1987

1st Leg – 24 November 1987   *Amsterdam*
Ajax   **0**   **FC Porto**   **1**
                            Rui Barros (5)
Ajax: Menzo, Blind, Verlaat, R. Witschge, Wouters (De Boer 68), Winter, Van't Schip, Dick, Bosman, Muhren (B.Witschge 46), Bergkamp
FC Porto: Mlynarczyk, Joao Pinto, Geraldao, Lima Pereira, Inacio, Andre, Magalhaes, Frasco (Quim 84), Sousa, Rui Barros, Gomes
Ref: Valentine (Sco)

2nd Leg – 13 January 1988   *Oporto*
FC Porto   **1**   **Ajax**   **0**
Sousa (70)
FC Porto: Mlynarczyk, Joao Pinto, Inacio, Geraldao, Lima Pereira, Banderinha (Semedo 83), Magalhaes, Rui Barros, Gomes (Jorge Placido 68), Sousa, Andre
Ajax: Menzo, Blind, Hesp, Larsson, Wouters, Winter, Van't Schip, Bergkamp (Meijer 81), Bosman, Muhren, B. Witschge (Roy 63)
Ref: Schmidhuber (E. Ger)
FC Porto win 2-0 on aggregate

1988

1st Leg – 1 February 1989   *Mechelen*
KV Mechelen   **3**   **PSV Eindhoven**   **0**
Bosman (16, 50), Valcx (17og)
KV Mechelen: Preud'homme, Sanders, Emmers, Rutjes, Versavel, Hofkens, E. Koeman (Deferm 57), De Wilde, Bosman (Wilmots 89), Demesmaeker, Den Boer.
PSV Eindhoven: Lodewijks, Gerets, Valcx, R. Koeman, Valdman, Lerby, Van Aerle, Vanenburg, Romario, Gillhaus, Janssen (Ellerman 72)
Ref: Kirschen (E. Ger)

2nd Leg – 8 February 1989   *Eindhoven*
PSV Eindhoven   **1**   **KV Mechelen**   **0**
Gillhaus (78)
PSV Eindhoven: Lodewijks, Gerets, Heintze, R. Koeman, Chovanec, Van Aerle, Linskens (Valcx 66), Vanenburg, Romario, Gillhaus, Ellerman
KV Mechelen: Preud'homme, Sanders, Deferm, Emmers (E. Koeman 39), Rutijes, Hofkens, De Wilde, Versavel, Bosman, Demensmaeker, Den Boer
Ref: Fredriksson (Swe)
KV Mechelen win 3-1 on aggregate

1989

1st Leg – 23 February 1989   *Barcelona*
Barcelona   **1**   **Milan**   **1**
Amor (67)   Van Basten (pen 44)
Barcelona: Zubizarreta, Aloisio, Serna, Koeman, Milla, Bakero, J. Salinas (Roberto 65), Eusebio, Laudrup, Amor (Onesimo 76), Beguiristain
Milan: G. Galli, Salvadori, Maldini, Fuser, Tassotti, Costacurta, Donadoni (Stroppa 82), Rijkaard, Van Basten, Evani, Massaro (Simone 88)
Ref: Quiniou (Fra)

2nd Leg – 7 December 1989   *Milan*
Milan   **1**   **Barcelona**   **0**
Evani (55)
Milan: G. Galli, Carobbi, Maldini, Fuser, Tassotti, Costacurta, Donadoni, Rijkaard, Van Basten, Evani, Massaro (Simone 65)
Barcelona: Zubizarreta, Rekarte (Onesimo 70), Alexanco, Milla, Serna, Bakero, Roura (Soler 11), Eusebio, J. Salinas, Roberto, Beguiristain
Ref: Kohl (Aus)
Milan win 2-1 on aggregate

1990

1st Leg – 10 October 1990   *Genoa*
Sampdoria   **1**   **Milan**   **1**
Mikhailichenko (31)   Evani (40)
Sampdoria: Pagliuca, Mannini, Invernizzi, Lanna, Pellegrini, Mikhailichenko, Lombardo, Branca, Mancini, Dossena
Milan: Pazzagli, Tassotti, Costacurta, Gaudenzi, Galli, Baresi, Donadoni (Rijkaard 59), Ancelotti, Massaro, Gullit, Evani (Stroppa 70)
Ref: Rosa dos Santos (Por)

2nd Leg – 29 November 1990   *Milan*
Milan   **2**   **Sampdoria**   **0**
Gullit (44), Rijkaard (77)
Milan: Pazzagli, Tassotti, Maldini, Carbone, Costacurta (F Galli 79), Baresi, Ancelotti, Rijkaard, Agostini, Gullit, Evani (Stroppa 70)
Sampdoria: Pagliuca, Lanna, Bonetti, Pari, Vierchowod, Pellegrini, Mikhailichenko (Dossena 68), Katanec (Branca 84), Vialli, Mancini, Lombardo
Ref: Petrovic (Yug)

1991

29 November 1991   *Manchester*
Manchester United   **1**   **Red Star Belgrade**   **0**
McClair (69)
Manchester United: Schmeichel, Martin (Giggs 73), Irwin, Bruce, Webb, Pallister, Kanchelskis, Ince, McClair, Hughes, Blackmore.
Red Star Belgrade: Milojevic, Radinovic, Vasiljevic, Taniga, Belodedic, Najdoski, Slosic, Jugovic, Pancev, Savicevic (Ivic 83), Mihaijlovic
Ref: Van der Ende (Hol).

1992

1st Leg – 10 February 1993   *Bremen*
Werder Bremen   **1**   **Barcelona**   **1**
Salinas (37)   Allofs (87)
Werder Bremen: Reck, Bockenfeld, Legat, Bratseth, Bode (Kohn 68), Borowka, Eilts, Votava, Hobsch (Allofs 76), Herzog, Neubarth
Barcelona: Zubizarreta, Ferrer, Koeman, Goicoechea, Eusebio, Amor, Baquero (Beguiristain 65), Nadal, Witschge, Julio Salinas (Christiansen 80), Stoichkov
Ref: Nielsen (Den)

2nd Leg – 10 March 1993   *Barcelona*
Barcelona   **2**   **Werder Bremen**   **1**
Stoichkov (32), Goicoechea (48)   Rufer (41 pen)
Barcelona: Zubizarreta, Ferrer, Guardiola (Julio Salinas 80), Koeman, Nadal, Baquero (Beguiristain 48), Goicoechea, Stoichkov, Laudrup, Amor, Eusebio
Werder Bremen: Reck, Schaaf (Gundelach 31), Legat (Allofs 78), Bratseth, Bode, Borowka, Eilts, Wolter, Hobsch, Herzog, Rufer
Ref: Karlsson (Swe)
Barcleona win 3-2 on aggregate

1993

1st Leg – 12 January 1994   8,083
Parma   **0**   **Milan**   **1**
                            Papin (43)
Parma: Ballotta, Balleri, Benarrivo (Di Chiara 76), Minotti, Apolloni, Sensini, Brolin, Pin, Crippa, Zola, Asprilla
Milan: Rossi, Tassotti, Maldini, Albertini (Massaro 67), Costacurta, Baresi, Eranio, Desailly, Papin, Savicevic (Panucci 86), Donadoni
Ref: Manuel Diaz Vega (Spa)

2nd Leg – 2 February 1994
Milan   **0**   **Parma**   **2**
                            Sensini (67), Crippa (95)
Milan: Rossi, Panucci, Maldini, Albertini (Lentini 67), Costacurta, Baresi, B. Laudrup (Carbone 76), Desailly, Papin, Donadoni, Massaro
Parma: Ballotta, Balleri, Benarrivo (Di Chiara 76), Minotti, Matrecano, Sensini, Brolin, Pin, Crippa, Zola (Zoratto 104), Asprilla
Ref: Rothlisberger (Swi)
Parma win 2-1 on aggregate after extra time

Clubs in Europe 1994–95

UEFA CHAMPIONS' CUP
A – Z 375

CUP-WINNERS' CUP
A – Z 381

UEFA CUP
A – Z 390

This section contains details of all the clubs competing in the three European club competitions. Clubs are grouped by the three cups and then listed alphabetically – most of the information should be easy to follow. After a brief history and club details a PWDLFA summary is given for each competition which is summarised at the bottom:

> CC   Champions' Cup including Champions' League
> CWC   Cup-Winners' Cup
> UEFA   UEFA Cup

Below this are listed the years in which the club has competed in each competition and these are followed, in brackets, by the round they reached. Key:

> P   Preliminary round
> 1   First round
> 2   Second round
> 3   Third round
> CL   Champions' League
> Q   Quarter-finals
> S   Semi-finals
> F   Finalists
> W   Winners

Wherever possible I have used the common form of club name. This has posed a few problems – for example aficionados of European football now commonly use Milan and Internazionale while others persist with AC Milan and Inter Milan. If you are having trouble finding a club then refer to the qualifiers list on page 43 where entrant clubs are listed by country. Many clubs also have FC at the start of the name, ie FC Porto, FC Nantes. In such cases the club are listed by city name not the FC, thus FC Porto will be listed under P.

There have also been a large number of club name-changes in recent years, not least due to the restructuring of Eastern Europe and the former Soviet states. As an example, Dynamo Tbilisi is a very famous name – however the club is now called Iberya Tbilisi. Hungarian and Austrian clubs can also pose a problem as they now tend to include sponsors' names in their club names. For example, the Hungarian club side Videoton Waltham are now FC Parmalat and SV Salzburg are now SV Casino Salzburg. Again, refer to the country qualifiers list if in doubt.

UEFA Champions' League

AEK Athens — Greece

Founded by Greek refugees from Turkey, AEK, in Greek, means Athletic Union of Constantinople. Joined the domestic league in 1930, and were founder members of the unified national league in 1959–60 when they were runners-up. Ten times league champions and eight times cup winners. Reached the UEFA Cup semi-finals in 1976–77.

Full Name:	AEK FC Athens
Founded:	1924
Address:	Tritis Septemvriou 144, GR-11251 Athens, Greece
Phone:	1-8215645
Stadium:	Neas Filadelfias
Capacity:	33,494

Euro Record

	P	W	D	L	F	A
CC:	26	7	7	12	38	50
CWC:	4	2	0	2	5	7
UEFA:	38	14	5	19	41	58
TOTAL:	68	23	12	33	84	115

CC: (8)   63-64 (1), 68-69 (Q), 71-72 (1), 78-79 (2), 79-80 (1), 89-90 (2), 92-93 (2), 93-94 (1)
CWC: (3)   66-67(1), 64-65 (1), 83-84 (1)
UEFA: (10)   70-71 (1), 72-73 (2), 76-77 (S), 77-78 (2), 82-83 (1), 85-86 (1), 86-87 (1), 88-89 (1), 91-92 (3), 75-76 (2)

Ajax — Holland

Founded in March 1913 and named after the hero of Ancient Greece. Won the domestic cup in 1917 and joined the league for the following season winning it at the first attempt. Founder members of the championship in its professional form in 1954, and have now won the domestic competition a record 24 times. The Dutch cup has been won 11 times, also a record. Ajax were the first Dutch club to play in the Cup-Winners' Cup, 1961–62, a competition won in 1987. Champions' Cup winners three consecutive times 1971–73, having been losing finalists in 1969. Won the UEFA Cup in 1992. Winners of the first two European Super Cups, 1972 and 1973, and World Club champions in 1972.

Full Name:	Ajax
Founded:	1913
Address:	Middenweg 401, Postbus 41885, 1098 AV Amsterdam
Phone:	2-6654440/6946515
Stadium:	De Meer
Capacity:	19,500
Colours:	White/Red, White, White/Red

Euro Record

	P	W	D	L	F	A
CC:	79	44	15	20	151	84
CWC:	28	18	2	8	53	22
UEFA:	61	36	6	19	21	69
TOTAL:	168	98	23	47	225	175

CC: (15)   57-58 (Q), 60-61 (1), 66-67 (Q), 67-68 (1), 68-69 (F), 70-71 (W), 71-72 (W), 72-73 (W), 73-74 (2), 77-78 (Q), 79-80 (S), 80-81 (2), 82-83 (1), 83-84 (1), 85-86 (1)
CWC: (5)   61-62 (2), 81-82 (1), 86-87 (W), 87-88 (F), 93-94 (Q)
UEFA: (10)   69-70 (S), 74-75 (3), 75-76 (3), 76-77 (1), 78-79 (3), 84-85 (2), 88-89 (1), 89-90 (1), 91-92 (2), 91-92 (W), 92-93 (Q)

Avenir Beggen — Luxembourg

Based in the suburbs of the capital city. Avenir have won the championship six times, the cup five times. Domestic league champions in 1992 and 1994, they were runners-up in 1993. Their European debut came in the 1969–70 Champions' Cup.

Full Name:	FC Avenir Beggen
Founded:	1915
Address:	BP 382, 2013 Luxembourg
Phone:	78253
Stadium:	Beggen
Capacity:	4,800
Colours:	Yellow/Black, Black, Yellow

Euro Record

	P	W	D	L	F	A
CC:	10	0	0	10	0	47
CWC:	12	1	2	9	7	2
UEFA:	6	1	0	5	2	22
TOTAL:	28	2	2	24	9	71

CC: (5)   69-70 (1), 82-83 (1), 84-85 (1), 86-87 (1), 93-94 (P)
CWC: (5)   74-75(2), 86-87(1), 87-88 (1), 88-89 (1), 92-93 (1)
UEFA: (3)   75-76 (1), 85-86 (1), 90-91 (1)

RSC Anderlecht — Belgium

Founded as Sporting Club Anderlecht in 1908, the Brussels club reached the first division for the first time in 1921. Became Royal Sporting Club Anderlecht in 1933. They have won the domestic championship a record 23 times, all in the post-war period, and the domestic cup eight times, also a record. Took part in the first Champions' Cup competition, 1955–56. Both winners and runners-up in the Cup-Winners' Cup twice, they have won the UEFA Cup once, and been runners-up twice. Twice winners of the European Super Cup but did not compete for the World Club championship.

Full Name:	Royal Sporting Club Anderlecht
Founded:	1908
Address:	Avenue Theo Verbeek 2, 1070 Brussels
Phone:	2-5229400
Stadium:	Constant Vanden Stock
Capacity:	36,000
Colours:	White, White, White

Euro Record

	P	W	D	L	F	A
CC:	90	40	15	34	141	136
CWC:	44	29	3	12	86	34
UEFA:	58	21	9	28	72	95
TOTAL:	192	90	27	74	299	265

CC: (17)	55-56 (1), 56-57 (1), 59-60(1), 62-63 (Q), 64-65 (2), 65-66 (Q), 66-67 (2), 67-68 (2), 68-69 (2), 72-73 (2), 74-75 (Q), 81-82 (S), 85-86 (S), 86-87 (Q), 87-88 (Q), 91-92 (CL), 93-94 (CL	
CWC: (7)	73-74 (1), 75-76 (W), 76-77 (F), 77-78 (W), 78-79 (2), 88-89 (2), 89-90 (F)	
UEFA: (10)	69-70 (F), 70-71 (3), 71-72 (1), 79-80 (1), 80-81 (1), 82-83 (W), 83-84 (F), 84-85 (3), 90-91 (Q), 92-93 (3)	

Barcelona — Spain

Founded by a Swiss emigrant. Founder members and first champions of the Spanish league in 1929, having been winners of the first domestic cup competition in 1902. Now have 14 league titles and 22 cup wins to their credit. Were Spain's first representative in the Fairs Cup, participating in and winning the inaugural competition, 1956–58, and subsequently winning twice more and being runners-up once. Champions' Cup winners in 1992 and losing finalists three times. They have also won the Cup-Winners' Cup (three times) and been runners-up (twice). European Super Cup winners in 1993.

Full Name:	Futbol Club Barcelona
Founded:	1899
Address:	Aristides Maillol s/n, 08028 Barcelona
Phone:	3-330-9411
Stadium:	Nou Camp
Capacity:	115,000
Colours:	Blue/Dark and Red stripes, Blue/Dark and Red, Blue/Dark Red

Euro Record

	P	W	D	L	F	A
CC:	62	35	13	14	115	61
CWC:	76	45	14	17	164	82
UEFA:	120	59	25	36	228	144
TOTAL:	258	139	52	67	507	287

CC: (8)	59-60 (S), 60-61 (F), 74-75 (S), 85-86 (F), 91-92 (2), 91-92 (W), 92-93 (2), 93-94 (F)
CWC: (11)	63-64 (2), 71-72 (2), 78-79 (W), 79-80 (Q), 81-82 (W), 82-83 (Q), 83-84 (Q), 84-85 (1), 88-89 (W), 89-90 (2), 90-91 (9)
UEFA: (19)	57-58 (W), 59-60 (W), 60-61 (Q), 61-62 (F), 62-63 (2), 64-65 (3), 65-66 (W), 66-67 (2), 67-68 (1), 69-70 (3), 70-71 (2), 72-73 (1), 73-74 (1), 75-76 (S), 76-77 (Q), 77-78 (S), 80-81 (2), 86-87 (Q), 87-88 (Q)

Bayern Munich — Germany

Bayern achieved one German domestic championship (1932) and a West German cup win before joining the Bundesliga in 1965 two years after its formation. Subsequently they have won the league championship a record 13 times and the domestic cup seven times, also a record. Runners-up in the second German championship following reunification, and champions in 1994. Champions' Cup winners three consecutive times 1974–76, and twice runners-up in the 1980s. Cup-Winners' Cup winners in 1967 and World Club champions in 1976.

Full Name:	FC Bayern Munich
Founded:	1900
Address:	Sabener Strasse 51, 8000 Munich, 90, Germany
Phone:	89-69931-2
Stadium:	Olympiastadion
Capacity:	73,132
Colours:	Red, Red, Red

Euro Record

	P	W	D	L	F	A
CC:	94	58	18	18	210	87
CWC:	39	19	14	6	67	36
UEFA:	54	29	9	16	113	65
TOTAL:	187	106	41	40	390	188

CC: (13)	69-70 (1), 72-73 (Q), 73-74 (W), 74-75 (W), 75-76 (W), 76-77 (Q), 80-81 (S), 81-82 (F), 85-86 (Q), 86-87 (F), 87-88 (Q), 89-90 (S), 90-91 (S)
CWC: (5)	66-67 (W), 67-68 (S), 71-72 (S), 82-83 (Q), 84-85 (S)
UEFA: (8)	62-63 (Q), 70-71 (Q), 77-78 (3), 79-80 (S), 83-84 (3), 88-89 (S), 91-92 (2), 93-94 (2)

Benfica — Portugal

Founded in February 1904 as Grupo Sport Lisboa by a fan who had learnt the game from Englishmen, and in 1908 merged with the sports club Sport Clube e Benfica under the present title. League founder members in 1935, finishing third of eight. A record 30 times domestic champions not out of the top two since 1985, and 25 times domestic cup winners, also a record. Portugal's first European winners, claiming the Champions' Cup in 1961 and 1962. Five times Champions' Cup runners-up, UEFA Cup runners-up once.

Full Name:	Sport Lisboa e Benfica
Founded:	1904
Address:	Avenida General Norton de Matos, 1500 Lisbon, Portugal
Phone:	1-7622129
Stadium:	Sport Lisboa e Benfica
Capacity:	120,000
Colours:	Red, White, Red

Euro Record

	P	W	D	L	F	A
CC:	133	67	29	37	266	141
CWC:	35	17	11	7	57	28
UEFA:	36	18	10	8	58	33
TOTAL:	204	102	50	52	381	202

CC: (22)	57-58 (1), 60-61 (W), 61-62 (W), 62-63 (F), 63-64 (2), 64-65 (F), 65-66 (Q), 67-68 (F), 68-69 (Q), 69-70 (2), 71-72 (S), 72-73 (Q), X73-74 (2), 75-76 (Q), 76-77 (1), 77-78 (Q), 81-82 (2), 83-84 (Q), 84-85 (2), 87-88 (F), 89-90 (F), 91-92 (CL)
CWC: (6)	70-71 (2), 74-75 (Q), 80-81 (S), 85-86 (Q), 86-87 (2), 93-94 (S)
UEFA: (7)	66-67 (3), 78-79 (2), 79-80 (1), 82-83 (F), 88-89 (2), 90-91 (1), 92-93 (Q)

Dynamo Kiev — Ukraine

The capital city club have in the past been USSR representatives in Europe. 13 times Soviet champions and nine times cup winners. Cup-Winners' Cup winners in 1975 and 1986 and Super Cup winners in 1976. Fifth in the last Soviet Super League when they also won the Championship play-off, then runners-up in the Ukrainian League in 1992 and champions in 1993 and 1994.

Full Name:	Dynamo Kiev
Founded:	1927
Address:	Ul. Kirova 3, Kiev, Ukraine
Phone:	299520
Stadium:	Republican
Capacity:	100,169
Colours:	White, White, White

Euro Record

	P	W	D	L	F	A
CC:	64	34	12	18	84	60
CWC:	30	20	6	4	72	27
UEFA:	28	12	8	8	34	25
TOTAL:	122	66	26	30	190	112

CC: (12) 67-68 (2), 69-70 (2), 72-73 (Q), 75-76 (Q), 76-77 (S), 78-79 (2), 81-82 (Q), 82-83 (Q), 86-87 (S), 87-88 (1), 91-92 (CL), 93-94 (1)
CWC: (4) 65-66 (Q), 74-75 (W), 85-86 (W), 90-91 (Q)
UEFA: (7) 73-74 (3), 77-78 (1), 79-80 (3), 80-81 (1), 83-84 (1), 89-90 (3), 92-93 (2)

Galatasaray — Turkey

League founder members and first runners-up, 1959, and ten times winners since then. Cup winners nine times, including the first four competitions, 1963 to 1966. First Turkish participants in the Champions' Cup, 1956–57. Champions' Cup semi-finalists 1968–69 and played in the UEFA Champions' League in 1994.

Full Name:	Galatasaray Spor Kulubu
Founded:	1905
Address:	Hasnun Galip Sokak 7-11, Beyoglu, Istanbul, Turkey
Phone:	1-1511707
Stadium:	Ali Sami Yen
Capacity:	34,000

Euro Record	P	W	D	L	F	A
CC:	44	15	11	18	52	66
CWC:	27	9	6	12	33	49
UEFA:	18	5	2	9	18	30
TOTAL:	89	29	19	39	103	145

CC: (10) 56-57 (1), 62-63 (Q), 63-64 (2), 69-70 (Q), 71-72 (1), 72-73 (1), 73-74 (1), 87-88 (1), 88-89 (S), 93-94 (CL)
CWC: (7) 64-65 (2), 65-66 (1), 66-67 (1), 76-77 (2), 82-83 (2), 85-86 (2), 91-92 (Q)
UEFA: (6) 75-76 (2), 78-79 (1), 79-80 (1), 86-87 (1), 89-90 (1), 92-93 (3)

Hajduk Split — Croatia

Nine times Yugoslavian league champions, the last time in 1979, and nine times Cup winners. First Croatian league champions in the experimental 1992 season, and again in 1994.

Full Name:	NK Hajduk
Founded:	1911
Address:	Stadion Poljud, P. Box 218, 58000 Split
Phone:	58-41755
Stadium:	Poljud
Capacity:	50,000

Euro Record	P	W	D	L	F	A
CC:	18	12	2	4	41	18
CWC:	30	10	3	17	31	46
UEFA:	42	23	5	14	74	46
TOTAL:	90	45	10	35	146	110

CC: (4) 71-72 (1), 74-75 (2), 5-76 (Q), 79-80 (Q)
CWC: (8) 67-68 (1), 68-69 (S), 76-77 (2), 77-78 (Q), 84-85 (1), 87-88 (2), 91-92 (Q), 93-94 (1)
UEFA: (7) 70-71 (2), 78-79 (2), 81-82 (3), 82-83 (2), 83-84 (S), 85-86 (Q), 86-87 (3)

Legia Warsaw — Poland

Domestic league founder members in 1921. Won league and cup double in 1955 and 1956, their first victories in the competitions. Now have five titles, with a 24-year gap between their fourth and fifth, and a two-point deduction costing them the 1993 championship. Were Poland's first Fairs Cup entrant, 1968–69. They were Champions' Cup semi-finalists in 1970 and have reached the Cup-Winners' Cup quarter-finals twice.

Full Name:	Centralny Wojskowy Klub Sportowy Legia Warsaw
Founded:	1916
Address:	ul. Lazienkowska 3, 00-950 Warsaw
Phone:	+22 210896
Stadium:	Wojska Polskiego
Capacity:	21,940

Euro Record	P	W	D	L	F	A
CC:	18	11	2	5	29	16
CWC:	33	13	10	10	47	35
UEFA:	24	9	7	8	34	30
TOTAL:	75	33	19	23	110	81

CC: (4) 56-57 (1), 60-61 (1), 69-70 (S), 70-71 (Q)
CWC: (8) 64-65 (Q), 66-67 (1), 72-73 (2), 73-74 (1), 80-81 (1), 81-82 (Q), 89-90 (1), 90-91 (S)
UEFA: (6) 68-69 (3), 71-72 (2), 74-75 (1), 85-86 (3), 86-87 (2), 88-89 (1)

IFK Gothenberg — Sweden

Share with Malmo FF the record number of domestic league championships, 14. Founder members and runnners-up in the first formal league championship in 1925. They were, however, relegated from the top flight in 1982. Won the UEFA Cup in 1982 and 1987. Cup-Winners' Cup quarter-finalists in 1980 and Champions' Cup League participants in 1993.

Full Name:	Idrottsforeningen Kamraterna Goteborg
Founded:	1904
Address:	Alfreds Gardesvag, 416 55 Gothenberg
Phone:	+31 408600
Stadium:	Ullevi
Capacity:	37,800

Euro Record	P	W	D	L	F	A
CC:	46	23	4	19	89	72
CWC:	8	2	3	3	7	11
UEFA:	30	18	9	3	53	25
TOTAL:	84	43	16	25	149	108

CC: (10) 58-59 (2), 59-60 (2), 61-62 (1), 70-71 (1), 83-84 (1), 84-85 (Q), 85-86 (S), 88-89 (Q), 91-92 (2), 92-93 (CL)
CWC: (2) 79-80 (Q), 82-83 (1)
UEFA: (5) 80-81 (1), 81-82 (W), 86-87 (W), 87-88 (1), 89-90 (1)

Maccabi Haifa — Israel

One of the oldest club sides in Israel, but all their major honours have come inside the past ten seasons. Five times league champions and three times domestic cup winners, doing the domestic double in 1991. Made their European debut in the 1993–94 Cup-Winners' Cup, losing to then holders Parma on penalty kicks.

Full Name:	Maccabi Haifa
Founded:	1919
Address:	Hinrich Haina St 14, Hafia.
Phone:	972 4 38 66 20
Stadium:	Kiriat Eliezer
Capacity:	18,000

Euro Record	P	W	D	L	F	A
CC:	0	0	0	0	0	0
CWC:	6	4	0	2	11	4
UEFA:	0	0	0	0	0	0
TOTAL:	6	4	0	2	11	4

CC: (0)
CWC: (1) 93-94 (2)
UEFA: (0)

Manchester United — England

Formed by railway workers as Newton Heath and turned professional in 1885. Joined the Football League in 1892. Manchester United formed on the bankruptcy of Newton Heath in 1902 and became league champions six seasons later. Moved to present ground in 1910. Seven league championships all told before being founder members and first winners of the FA Premier League in 1993, a title retained in 1994, when the league and cup double was achieved. Eight times domestic cup winners, equalling Tottenham's record. First English club to compete in the Champions' Cup (1956–57) and winners in 1968, the first English club to take the major European prize. Subsequently winners of the Cup-Winners' Cup (1991). Super Cup winners in 1991.

Full Name:	Manchester United FC
Founded:	1887
Address:	Old Trafford, Manchester, M16 ORA
Phone:	+61-8721661
Stadium:	Old Trafford
Capacity:	44,750
Colours:	Red, White, Black

Euro Record

	P	W	D	L	F	A
CC:	45	28	9	8	108	51
CWC:	31	16	9	6	55	35
UEFA:	29	12	11	6	46	24
TOTAL:	105	56	29	20	209	110

CC: (6) 56-57 (S), 57-58 (S), 65-66 (S), 67-68 (W), 68-69 (S), 93-94 (2)
CWC: (5) 63-64 (Q), 77-78 (2), 83-84 (S), 90-91 (W), 91-92 (2)
UEFA: (6) 64-65 (S), 76-77 (2), 80-81 (1), 82-83 (1), 84-85 (Q), 92-93 (1)

Milan — Italy

Founded as Milan Cricket and Football Club under English and Swiss influence. Became Milan Associazione Sportiva in 1930 and Milan Associazione Calcio in 1939. Won league honours in the early years of the century, but it was the 1950s before they again became a leading side. Now 14 times league champions and four times domestic cup winners. They took part in the first Champions' Cup in 1955–56, and have now won the competition on five occasions, the first at Wembley in 1963. Twice Cup-Winners' Cup winners, twice Super Cup winners, and three times World Club Champions.

Full Name:	Milan Associazione Calcio
Founded:	1899
Address:	Via Turati 3, 20121 Milan, Italy
Phone:	+2-6559016
Stadium:	Giuseppe Meazza
Capacity:	75,510
Colours:	Red/Black, White, White

Euro Record

	P	W	D	L	F	A
CC:	91	55	18	18	194	74
CWC:	30	17	10	3	47	20
UEFA:	51	22	10	19	71	57
TOTAL:	172	94	38	40	312	151

CC: (13) 55-56 (S), 57-58 (F), 59-60 (2), 62-63 (W), 63-64 (Q), 68-69 (W), 69-70 (2), 79-80 (1), 88-89 (W), 89-90 (W), 90-91 (Q), 92-93 (F), 93-94 (W)
CWC: (4) 67-68 (W), 72-73 (W), 73-74 (F), 77-78 (1)
UEFA: (9) 61-62 (1), 64-65 (1), 65-66 (3), 71-72 (S), 75-76 (Q), 76-77 (3), 78-79 (3), 85-86 (3), 87-88 (2)

Paris Saint-Germain — France

Paris FC were founded in 1970 as an attempt to bring top football back to the capital and were joined by local amateurs Saint Germain in the second division. The venture failed and the two split, Paris Saint-Germain starting as a division three side in 1973. Promoted in successive seasons, they have never been relegated. League champions twice and three times cup winners.

Full Name:	Paris Saint-Germain
Founded:	1973
Address:	30 Avenue du Parc des Princes, 75016 Paris
Phone:	+40 719191
Stadium:	Parc des Princes
Capacity:	48,725

Euro Record

	P	W	D	L	F	A
CC:	2	0	1	1	1	3
CWC:	18	11	5	2	28	11
UEFA:	18	6	5	7	24	20
TOTAL:	38	17	11	10	53	34

CC: (1) 86-87(1)
CWC: (3) 82-83 (Q), 83-84 (2), 93-94 (S)
UEFA: (3) 84-85 (2), 89-90 (2), 92-93 (S)

Rangers — Scotland

Founded by a family and their brothers from Gairloch. Early members of the English FA and cup semi-finalists in the 1880s. Founder members and joint champions of the Scottish league 1890–91. A record 42 times champions – they have never been relegated – and 25 times cup winners. First club from Scotland to play in the Cup-Winners' Cup, in 1960–61, when they were runners-up, this being repeated in 1967 before the trophy was secured in 1972. Played in the UEFA Champions' League in 1992–93.

Full Name:	Rangers FC
Founded:	1873
Address:	Ibrox Stadium, Edminston Drive, Glasgow, G51 2XD
Phone:	+41-427 8500
Stadium:	Ibrox Stadium
Capacity:	45,407
Colours:	Royal Blue, White, Royal Blue

Euro Record

	P	W	D	L	F	A
CC:	69	32	12	25	112	103
CWC:	58	28	11	19	107	74
UEFA:	50	23	9	18	82	69
TOTAL:	177	83	32	62	301	246

CC: (15) 56-57 (2), 57-58 (2), 59-60 (S), 61-62 (Q), 63-64 (1), 64-65 (Q), 75-76 (2), 76-77 (1), 78-79 (Q), 87-88 (2), 89-90 (1), 90-91 (2), 91-92 (1), 92-93 (CL), 93-94 (1)
CWC: (10) 60-61 (F), 66-67 (F), 69-70 (2), 71-72 (W), 73-74 (2), 77-78 (1), 79-80 (2), 81-82 (1), 83-84 (2)
UEFA: (8) 67-68 (Q), 68-69 (S), 70-71 (1), 82-83 (2), 84-85 (2), 85-86 (1), 86-87 (3), 88-89 (2)

Servette — Switzerland

Servette is a district of Geneva. The club played mostly rugby before joining the Swiss FA in 1900. First champions of the national league, 1934, and winners 16 times all told. Took part in first Champions' Cup, 1955–56. Cup-Winners' Cup quarter-finalists twice. They survived the league relegation play-offs in 1990.

Full Name:	Servette FC
Founded:	1890
Address:	Case Postale 12, 1219 Chatelaine, Geneva
Phone:	22-7890922
Stadium:	Charmiles
Capacity:	30,000

Euro Record	P	W	D	L	F	A
CC:	17	6	4	7	27	30
CWC:	24	11	4	9	36	25
UEFA	30	9	7	14	39	51
TOTAL	71	26	15	30	102	106

CC: (5)   55-56 (1), 61-62 (2), 62-63 (1), 79-80 (2), 85-86 (2)
CWC: (6) 66-67 (Q), 71-72 (1), 76-77 (P), 78-79 (Q), 83-84 (2), 84-85 (2)
UEFA: (10) 63-64 (1), 64-65 (1), 65-66 (3), 67-68 (1), 74-75 (1), 77-78 (1), 80-81 (1), 82-83 (3), 88-89 (2), 93-94 (2)

Silkeborg   Denmark

No domestic honours until winning the championship in 1994. A second division side until 1987 when they finished first to gain promotion. They entered the Superliga for the start of the 1991 season, finishing 9th, 5th and 5th before last year's surprise title triumph. This is their first appearance in European competition.

Full Name:	Silkeborg Idraets Forening
Founded:	1917
Address:	Ansvej 110, 8600 Silkeborg
Phone:	+86 804477
Stadium:	Silkeborg Stadion
Capacity:	11,000

Euro Record	P	W	D	L	F	A
CC:	0	0	0	0	0	0
CWC:	0	0	0	0	0	0
UEFA:	0	0	0	0	0	0
TOTAL:	0	0	0	0	0	0

Sparta Prague   Czech Republic

Founded as Athletic Club Vinohrady when Prague was in Bohemia. The next year they became AC Sparta and, after 1948, played under several names before taking on the current one in 1965. Czechoslovakian league founder members and first runners up, 1925. League champions 19 times, including the last championship, 1993, and eight times national cup winners. Mitropa Cup winners in 1927 and 1935. First winners of the new Czech Republic league championship in 1994. They reached the Cup-Winners' Cup semi-finals in 1972–73.

Full Name:	AC Sparta Prague
Founded:	1893
Address:	Trida Obrancu miru 98, 170 82 Prague 7
Phone:	(02) 372119/382441
Stadium:	Letna
Capacity:	36,000
Colours:	Dark Red, White, Black

Euro Record	P	W	D	L	F	A
CC:	46	20	9	17	70	67
CWC:	24	13	2	9	53	25
UEFA:	22	8	4	10	31	37
TOTAL:	92	41	15	36	154	129

CC: (10)   65-66 (Q), 67-68 (Q), 84-85 (Q), 85-86 (1), 87-88 (2), 88-89 (1), 89-90 (2), 90-91 (1), 91-92 (CL), 93-94 (2)
CWC: (5)   64-65 (2), 72-73 (S), 76-77 (1), 80-81 (2), 92-93 (Q)
UEFA: (6) 66-67 (2), 69-70 (1), 70-71 (3), 81-82 (1), 83-84 (Q), 86-87 (1)

Spartak Moscow   Russia

Founded as Moskovskij Klub Sporta and run by the Trade Union of Co-operative Producers. MKS played under several different names before becoming Spartak in 1935. Twelve times Soviet champions, including the first title in 1937, and a record ten times Soviet Cup winners. Russian league champions twice. Were the first Soviet club to take part in the UEFA Cup, 1971–72. Reached the Champions' Cup semis in 1990 and played in the Champions' Cup League last season. Cup-Winners' Cup semi-finalists in 1993.

Full Name:	Spartak Moscow
Founded:	1922
Address:	Ul. Verhniaia Krasnoselskaia 38/19, Moscow
Phone:	95-2088736
Stadium:	Lenin
Capacity:	100,360
Colours:	Red, White, White

Euro Record	P	W	D	L	F	A
CC:	30	14	8	8	54	31
CWC:	18	10	4	4	31	17
UEFA:	60	34	11	15	97	65
TOTAL:	108	58	23	27	182	113

CC: (5)   70-71 (1), 80-81 (Q), 88-89 (2), 90-91 (S), 93-94 (CL)
CWC: (3)   66-67 (2), 72-73 (Q), 92-93 (S)
UEFA: (12) 71-72 (2), 74-75 (1), 75-76 (3), 81-82 (2), 82-83 (3), 83-84 (Q), 84-85 (3), 85-86 (3), 86-87 (3), 87-88 (2), 89-90 (2), 91-92 (2)

Steaua Bucharest   Romania

Founded 1947 as Armata, the army team. Changed to CSCA in 1948 and to CCA in 1950. Became Steaua in 1961. League champions 16 times and 18 times cup winners. Won the Champions' Cup in 1986 and were runners-up in 1989. Super Cup winners 1986.

Full Name:	Steaua Bucharest
Founded:	1947
Address:	35 Boul. Ghencia, Bucharest
Phone:	0-497727
Stadium:	Steaua
Capacity:	30,000
Colours:	Red, Red, Red/Blue

Euro Record	P	W	D	L	F	A
CC:	46	22	8	16	72	62
CWC:	36	13	12	11	48	48
UEFA:	10	1	3	6	10	19
TOTAL:	92	36	23	33	130	129

CC: (11) 57-58 (2), 61-62 (1), 68-69 (1), 76-77 (1), 78-79 (P), 85-86 (W), 86-87 (2), 87-88 (S), 88-89 (F), 9-90 (2), 93-94 (2)
CWC: (11) 67-68 (2), 62-63 (1), 64-65 (2), 66-67 (1), 69-70 (1), 70-71 (1), 71-72 (Q), 79-80 (2), 84-85 (1), 0-91 (2), 92-93 (Q)
UEFA: (3) 77-78 (1), 80-81 (1), 91-92 (3)

SV Casino Salzburg   Austria

Known as Casino to reflect their sponsorship, but previously called SV Austria Salzburg. Founded 1933 by amalgamation of Hertha and Rapid Salzburg. Promoted to the top division for the first time in 1953, but relegated immediately only to return in 1961. Relegated a further four times before promotion in 1989. League runners-up in 1971 and 1992. Three times cup runners-up, but until 1994 won no major domestic honours. They did, however, get to the 1994 UEFA Cup final.

Full Name:	SV Casino Salzburg
Founded:	1933
Address:	Schumacherstrasse 14, 5020 Salzburg
Phone:	662-33332
Stadium:	Lehen
Capacity:	20,000

Euro Record	P	W	D	L	F	A
CC:	0	0	0	0	0	0
CWC:	2	0	0	2	0	8
UEFA:	20	9	2	9	23	21
TOTAL:	22	9	2	11	23	29

CC: (0)
CWC: (1) 80-81 (1)
UEFA: (4) 71-72 (1), 76-77(2), 92-93 (1), 93-94 (F)

Vac FC Samsung   **Hungary**

Founded in the town to the north of the capital as Vaci VSE. Went through several name changes and known as Vaci Izzo MTE from 1969 until 1992, amalgamating with Budapest Vasas Izzo in 1987 when promoted to the first division for the first time. League champions, league runners-up and twice Cup winners, all in the 1990s, achievements not previously recorded.

Full Name: Vac FC Samsung
Founded: 1889
Address: Stadion Utca 2, 2600 Vac
Phone: 27-10324
Stadium: Varosi
Capacity: 12,000

Euro Record	P	W	D	L	F	A
CC:	0	0	0	0	0	0
CWC:	0	0	0	0	0	0
UEFA:	8	3	1	4	7	14
TOTAL:	8	3	1	4	7	14

CC: (0)
CWC: (0)
UEFA: (3) 91-92 (1), 92-93 (2), 93-94 (1)

Cup-Winners' Cup

AJ Auxerre — France

Although nearly 90 years old, the club only emerged from regional competition in 1970, reaching the national second division in 1974. They were division 2B champions in 1980 and since then have been ever present in the first, their best finishing position, third, being achieved in 1984, 1991 and 1994. A domestic cup win in 1994 was their first major honour, although they had been runners-up once.

Full Name:	Association De La Jeunesse Auxerroise
Founded:	1905
Address:	Route de Vaux, 89000 Auxerre
Phone:	86 522471
Stadium:	Abbe-Deschamps
Capacity:	22,000

Euro Record	P	W	D	L	F	A
CC:	0	0	0	0	0	0
CWC:	0	0	0	0	0	0
UEFA:	30	15	6	9	61	33
TOTAL:	30	15	6	9	61	33

CC: (0)
CWC: (0)
UEFA: (7) 84-85 (1), 85-86 (1), 87-88 (1), 89-90 (Q), 91-92 (2), 92-93 (S), 93-94 (1)

Arsenal — England

Founded by workers at Royal Arsenal in south east London and soon known as Woolwich Arsenal. Joined the Football League in 1892. Took present title in 1913 when they moved to North London and were voted into the top division, where they have stayed ever since. Founder members of the Premier League in 1992. Ten times domestic league champions and six time cup winners, they achieved the 'Double' in 1971. Have played in all three European competitions and have won the Fairs Cup (1970) and been both winners (1994) and runners-up (1980) in the Cup-Winners' Cup.

Full Name:	Arsenal FC
Founded:	1886
Address:	Highbury, London, N5 1BU
Phone:	071 226 0304
Stadium:	Arsenal Stadium
Capacity:	39,500
Colours:	Red & White, White, Red & White

Euro Record	P	W	D	L	F	A
CC:	10	5	1	4	21	10
CWC:	18	9	9	0	29	8
UEFA:	36	19	6	11	66	33
TOTAL:	64	33	16	15	116	51

CC: (2) 71-72 (Q), 91-92 (2)
CWC: (2) 79-80 (F), 93-94 (W)
UEFA: (6) 63-64 (2), 69-70 (W), 70-71 (Q), 78-79 (3), 81-82 (2), 82-83 (1)

B71 Sandoyar — Faeroe Islands

Founded 1970 and domestic league champions once, 1989, when they were also cup runners-up, losing in a replay in their debut appearance. This is their first appearance in the European club competitions.

Full Name:	Sandoyar Itrottarefelag
Founded:	1970
Address:	210 Sandur
Phone:	61592
Stadium:	Sandur
Capacity:	2,000

Euro Record	P	W	D	L	F	A
CC:	0	0	0	0	0	0
CWC:	0	0	0	0	0	0
UEFA:	0	0	0	0	0	0
TOTAL:	0	0	0	0	0	0

Bangor — Northern Ireland

Cup runners-up in 1938-39. League runners-up 1990-91, this bringing them their European debut in the UEFA Cup 1991-92. Domestic cup winners for the first time in 1993, and runners-up in 1994.

Full Name:	Bangor FC
Founded:	1918
Address:	Clandeboye Road, Bangor, Co. Down, BT20 3JT
Phone:	0247 457712
Stadium:	Clandeboye Park
Capacity:	5,000

Euro Record	P	W	D	L	F	A
CC:	0	0	0	0	0	0
CWC:	2	0	1	1	2	3
UEFA:	2	0	0	2	0	6
TOTAL:	4	0	1	3	2	9

CC: (0)
CWC: (1) 93-94 (P)
UEFA: (1) 91-92 (1)

Barry Town — Wales

Spent most of the time playing in English non-league football as members of the Southern League. Missed election to the Football League a couple of times before falling on hard times and barely surviving. Known for a while as Barri, playing in exile outside Wales, but now back in Barry and winners of the Welsh league division one championship in 1993–94. Beat Football League second division side Cardiff City to win the Welsh Cup.

Full Name:	Barry Town
Founded:	1923
Address:	Jenner Park, Barry, South Glamorgan CG6 7BG
Phone:	
Stadium:	Jenner Park
Capacity:	1,000

Euro Record	P	W	D	L	F	A
CC:	0	0	0	0	0	0
CWC:	0	0	0	0	0	0
UEFA:	0	0	0	0	0	0
TOTAL:	0	0	0	0	0	0

Besiktas — Turkey

Based in Istanbul, they have won the league eight times – three in a row from 1990 – and the Cup four times. They have won the local Istanbul league 13 times. Their European debut came in the 1958–59 Champions' Cup.

Full Name:	Besiktas SK					
Founded:	1903					
Address:	Spor Cad. 92, Akaretler, Istanbul					
Phone:	1-1615804					
Stadium:	Inonu					
Capacity:	38,000					
Colours:	White/Black, White, White/Black					

Euro Record	P	W	D	L	F	A
CC:	20	4	4	12	15	35
CWC:	12	2	1	9	9	27
UEFA:	8	2	1	5	5	13
TOTAL:	40	8	6	26	29	75

CC: (9) 58-59 (2), 60-61 (1), 66-67 (1), 67-68 (1), 82-83 (1), 86-87 (Q), 90-91 (1), 91-92 (1), 92-93 (1), 79-80 (1), 84-85 (2)
CWC: (5) 75-76 (1), 77-78 (1), 84-85 (1), 89-90 (1), 93-94 (2)
UEFA: (4) 74-75 (1), 85-86 (1), 87-88 (1), 88-89 (1)

Bodo/Glimt — Norway

Based in Bodo well inside the Arctic Circle. Finished second in the league having been promoted from the second division only at the end of the 1992 season. Won the domestic cup twice, the first time in 1975 and then again in 1993. Beaten finalists in 1978.

Full Name:	FK Bodo/Glimt
Founded:	1916
Address:	Boks 179, 8001 Bodo
Phone:	081 22277
Stadium:	Aspmyra
Capacity:	10,000

Euro Record	P	W	D	L	F	A
CC:	0	0	0	0	0	0
CWC:	6	1	0	5	5	12
UEFA:	0	0	0	0	0	0
TOTAL:	6	1	0	5	5	12

CC: (0)
CWC: (2) 76-77 (1), 78-79 (2)
UEFA: (0)

Brondby IF — Denmark

Five domestic league titles and two cup wins, all achieved since 1985. They reached the UEFA Cup semi-finals in 1990–91, the furthest any Danish club has ever been in European competition. Have a habit of turning out international stars in the past few years, notably Peter Schmeichel, Kim Vilfort, John Jensen and Tomas Brolin.

Full Name:	Brondbyernes Idraets Forening
Founded:	1964
Address:	Gildhoj 6, 2605 Brondby, Denmark
Phone:	42-630810/459394
Stadium:	Brondby
Capacity:	14,000
Colours:	Yellow, Blue, Blue

Euro Record	P	W	D	L	F	A
CC:	14	4	5	5	18	17
CWC:	0	0	0	0	0	0
UEFA:	20	10	4	6	31	18
TOTAL:	34	14	9	11	49	35

CC: (4) 86-87 (Q), 88-89 (1), 89-90 (1), 91-92 (2)
CWC: (0)
UEFA: (2) 93-94 (3), 87-88 (2), 90-91 (S)

Chelsea — England

Founded as a club to use the Stamford Bridge Athletic Ground and joined the Football League in 1906. Spent seven separate periods in division two, yet promoted as champions only twice. League champions once, 1954–55, and domestic cup winners once, 1970. Were the first English club invited into European competition, but did not take part until a 1965 League Cup win gave them a Fairs Cup place. Cup-Winners' Cup winners in 1971, beating Real Madrid in a replay.

Full Name:	Chelsea FC
Founded:	1905
Address:	Fulham Road, London, SW6 1HS
Phone:	071 385 5545
Stadium:	Stamford Bridge
Capacity:	37,500
Colours:	Blue, Blue, Blue

Euro Record	P	W	D	L	F	A
CC:	0	0	0	0	0	0
CWC:	14	9	4	1	39	7
UEFA:	18	10	4	4	33	25
TOTAL:	32	19	8	5	72	32

CC: (0)
CWC: (2) 70-71 (W), 71-72 (2)
UEFA: (2) 65-66 (S), 68-69 (2)

Chernomorets Odessa — Ukraine

Odessa is located on the Black Sea coast. Reached the Soviet top division for the first time in 1965 when they finished 14th. Relegated in 1970 and again in 1984. They were fourth in the Soviet table in 1991. Represented the Soviet Union in the UEFA Cup and were the first Ukrainian club in the Cup-Winners' Cup, 1993.

Full Name:	Chernomorets Odessa
Founded:	1958
Address:	270 014 Odessa
Phone:	(0482) 250411/259250
Stadium:	Central
Capacity:	43,000

Euro Record	P	W	D	L	F	A
CC:	0	0	0	0	0	0
CWC:	4	3	0	1	13	4
UEFA:	10	3	2	5	10	13
TOTAL:	14	6	2	6	23	17

CC: (0)
CWC: (1) 92-93 (1)
UEFA: (3) 75-76 (1), 85-86 (2), 90-91 (2)

Club Bruges — Belgium

Nine times domestic league champions, the first in 1920, but the second not until 1973. Five times domestic cup winners, the first in 1968. Have been runners-up in both the Champions' Cup (1978) and the UEFA Cup (1976), losing both to Liverpool. Played in the UEFA Champions' League in 1993, but missed a European place last season when they finished sixth in the Belgian league.

Full Name:	Club Brugge KV
Founded:	1891
Address:	Olympialaan 74, 8200 Brugge
Phone:	(050) 387155
Stadium:	Olympiastadion
Capacity:	27,000

CUP-WINNERS' CUP 383

Euro Record	P	W	D	L	F	A
CC:	41	19	6	16	62	51
CWC:	10	4	1	5	18	19
UEFA:	48	20	6	22	83	7
TOTAL:	99	43	13	43	163	77

CC: (8) 73-74 (2), 76-77 (Q), 77-78 (F), 78-79 (1), 80-81 (1), 88-89 (2), 90-91 (2), 92-93 (CL)
CWC: (4) 68-69 (1), 70-71 (Q), 86-87 (1), 91-92 (S)
UEFA: (10) 67-68 (1), 69-70 (2), 71-72 (1), 72-73 (2), 75-76 (F), 81-82 (1), 84-85 (2), 85-86 (2), 87-88 (S), 89-90 (2)

Croatia Zagreb — Croatia

Founded as Dinamo Zagreb in 1945 as successors to Gradjanska, first league champions in 1923, who had closed down during the war. Dinamo won four Yugoslavian league championships and won the Yugoslavian cup eight times. They were Yugoslavia's representative in the first Cup-Winners' Cup, 1960-61, when they reached the semi-final. Won the Fairs Cup in 1967, having been runners-up in 1963. Played in the experimental 1992 Croatian championship and started the next season as HASK-Gradjanski, changing to their present title mid-way through the year.

Full Name: Croatia Zagreb
Founded: 1945
Address: Maksimirska 128, YU-41000, Zagreb
Phone: 41-223-234
Colours: Blue, Blue, Blue

Euro Record	P	W	D	L	F	A
CC:	8	4	1	3	19	11
CWC:	28	10	5	13	28	34
UEFA:	63	24	18	21	101	76
TOTAL:	99	38	24	37	148	121

CC: (3) 58-59 (1), 82-83 (1), 93-94 (1)
CWC: (8) 60-61 (S), 63-64 (2), 64-65 (Q), 65-66 (1), 69-70 (Q), 73-74 (1), 80-81 (1), 83-84 (1)
UEFA: (14) 59-60 (Q), 61-62 (2), 62-63 (F), 66-67 (W), 67-68 (2), 68-69 (1), 70-71 (3), 71-72 (2), 76-77 (2), 77-78 (2), 79-80 (1), 88-89 (2), 90-91 (1)

CSKA Moscow — Russia

The initials mean the Central House of the Soviet Army. Originally OLLS Moscow and later CDKA Moscow. Founder members of the Soviet league in spring 1936, they were champions seven times and cup winners five times. Suffered relegation from the top flight, however, in 1984 and 1987. Soviet representatives in Europe and, as Russia's top club, played in the Champions' League in 1993.

Full Name: CSKA Moskva
Founded: 1923
Address: Leningradski prospekt 39, 125 167 Moskva
Phone: (095) 2131898/2132809
Stadium: Lenin Central
Capacity: 102,000

Euro Record	P	W	D	L	F	A
CC:	14	5	4	5	17	16
CWC:	2	1	0	1	2	2
UEFA:	2	1	0	1	2	2
TOTAL:	18	7	4	7	21	20

CC: (2) 71-72 (2), 92-93 (CL)
CWC: (1) 91-92 (1)
UEFA: (1) 81-82 (1)

Dundee United — Scotland

Founded as Dundee Hibernian. Joined the league in 1910–11 but led a precarious existence until adopting current name (though nearly becoming Dundee City) in 1923. Members of the top division since 1960. One league championship, 1983. Six times cup runners-up, all since 1974, before finally winning it in 1994. Reached the Champions' Cup semi-finals in 1983–84 and the UEFA Cup final in 1986–87.

Full Name: Dundee United FC
Founded: 1909
Address: Tannadice Park, Dundee DD3 7JW
Phone: 0382-833166
Stadium: Tannadice Park
Capacity: 20,862
Colours: Tangerine/Black, Black/Tangerine/White, Tangerine/Black

Euro Record	P	W	D	L	F	A
CC:	8	5	1	2	15	4
CWC:	8	2	3	3	5	5
UEFA:	86	39	22	24	131	88
TOTAL:	102	46	26	29	151	97

CC: (1) 83-84 (S)
CWC: (2) 74-75 (2), 88-89 (2)
UEFA: (18) 66-67 (3), 67-68 (S), 69-70 (1), 70-71 (2), 75-76 (2), 77-78 (1), 78-79 (1), 79-80 (2), 80-81 (2), 81-82 (Q), 82-83 (Q), 84-85 (3), 85-86 (3), 86-87 (F), 87-88 (2), 89-90 (2), 90-91 (2), 93-94 (1)

F91 Dudelange — Luxembourg

Founded 1991 in the town on the French border. Promoted from the second division as runners-up in the play-offs in 1992. Domestic cup runners-up in 1993.

Full Name: F91 Dudelange
Founded: 1991
Address: 146 Rue RPJ Thiel, 3572 Dudelange, Luxembourg
Phone: 518468
Stadium: Jos Nosbaum
Capacity: 4,000

Euro Record	P	W	D	L	F	A
CC:	0	0	0	0	0	0
CWC:	2	0	0	2	1	7
UEFA:	0	0	0	0	0	0
TOTAL:	2	0	0	2	1	7

CC: (0)
CWC: (0) 93-94 (P)
UEFA: (0)

Fandok — Belarus

Fifth in domestic league in 1994 having been fifth in 1993, this hitherto minor club had no significant Soviet soccer experience. Formed in 1984, they were once known as Traktor Bobruisk.

Full Name: Fandok Bobruisk
Founded: 1984
Address: ul. Octoberskaya 117, 213800 Bobruisk
Phone: (02251) 26175/20962
Stadium: Spartak
Capacity: 3,500

Euro Record	P	W	D	L	F	A
CC:	0	0	0	0	0	0
CWC:	0	0	0	0	0	0
UEFA:	0	0	0	0	0	0
TOTAL:	0	0	0	0	0	0

Ferencvaros — Hungary

Founded as FTC Budapest, becoming Ferencvaros, a district of the capital named after Emperor Franz Joseph, in 1926. Generally known as FTC – Ferencvaros Torna (ie, gymnastics) Club – until the early 1950s. They played as Kinizsi (the name of a national hero) for a handful of seasons before emerging under their familiar name. League founder members 1901, when they finished third. A record 24 times champions and 15 times cup winners. Were Hungary's representative in the first Cup-Winners' Cup, 1960–61. Between-the-wars winners of the Mitropa Cup twice. Were Cup-Winners' Cup runners-up in 1975. Won the Fairs Cup in 1965 and were beaten finalists three years later.

Full Name:	Ferencvaros Torna Club
Founded:	1899
Address:	Ulloi ut 129, 1091 Budapest IX
Phone:	1-1136025
Stadium:	Ulloi
Capacity:	20,000
Colours:	Green, Green, Green

Euro Record	P	W	D	L	F	A
CC:	0	0	0	0	0	0
CWC:	39	12	6	11	50	10
UEFA:	68	32	11	25	109	79
TOTAL:	107	44	17	36	159	89

CC: (6) 63-64 (1), 65-66 (Q), 69-70 (2), 76-77 (2), 81-82 (1), 92-93 (1)
CWC: (7) 60-61 (1), 72-73 (2), 74-75 (F), 78-79 (2), 89-90 (2), 91-92 (2), 93-94 (1)
UEFA: (12) 62-63 (S), 64-65 (W), 66-67 (3), 67-68 (F), 70-71 (1), 71-72 (S), 73-74 (1), 77-78 (1), 79-80 (1), 82-83 (2), 83-84 (1), 90-91 (2)

Feyenoord — Holland

Founded by the head of a mining company and known as Stadionklub Rotterdam. 12 times league champions and nine times cup winners. Won the Champions' Cup and World Club Championship in 1970 and the UEFA Cup in 1974.

Full Name:	Feyenoord
Founded:	1908
Address:	Olympiaweg 50, 3077 AL Rotterdam, Netherlands
Phone:	4929400
Stadium:	Feyenoord
Capacity:	55,000

Euro Record	P	W	D	L	F	A
CC:	43	21	11	11	93	43
CWC:	18	9	3	6	26	18
UEFA:	58	31	9	18	112	69
TOTAL:	119	61	23	35	231	130

CC: (9) 61-62 (2), 62-63 (S), 65-66 (1), 69-70 (W), 70-71 (1), 71-72 (Q), 74-75 (2), 84-85 (1), 93-94 (2)
CWC: (3) 80-81 (S), 92-93 (Q), 91-92 (S)
UEFA: (12) 68-69 (1), 72-73 (2), 73-74 (W), 75-76 (1), 76-77 (Q), 79-80 (3), 81-82 (3), 83-84 (2), 85-86 (1), 86-87 (2), 87-88 (3), 89-90 (1)

FK Austria — Austria

Founded as Amateure (league champions 1924 and 1926) until 1926. Twice Mitropa Cup winners in the 1930s. Joined with Wiener Athletik Club in 1972. League champions 21 times and 22 times cup winners. Represented Austria in the first Cup-Winners' Cup, 1960–61 and won that competition in 1978.

Full Name:	FK Austria-Memphis
Founded:	1911
Address:	Ernst Happel Stadion, Meiereistrasse, Sektor D, 1020 Vienna
Phone:	(0222) 2186491
Stadium:	Horr
Capacity:	10,500

Euro Record	P	W	D	L	F	A
CC:	59	22	11	26	89	92
CWC:	35	9	12	14	36	52
UEFA:	20	8	5	7	38	34
TOTAL:	114	39	28	47	163	178

CC: (14) 61-62 (2), 62-63 (2), 63-64 (1), 69-70 (1), 70-71 (1), 76-77 (1), 78-79 (S), 79-80 (1), 80-81 (1), 81-82 (2), 84-85 (Q), 85-86 (2), 86-87 (2), 93-94 (2)
CWC: (7) 60-61 (Q), 67-68 (1), 71-72 (2), 74-75 (2), 77-78 (F), 82-83 (S), 90-91 (2)
UEFA: (5) 72-73 (1), 83-84 (Q), 87-88 (1), 88-89 (2), 89-90 (2)

Floriana — Malta

Founder members of the league and first champions, 1910. First cup runners-up, 1935. A record 25 league titles, and they have 17 cup wins. First Maltese club to play in Cup-Winners' Cup, 1961–62.

Full Name:	Floriana FC
Founded:	1900
Address:	28 St. Anne Street, Floriana
Phone:	238864/220559
Stadium:	National, Ta'Qali
Capacity:	35,000

Euro Record	P	W	D	L	F	A
CC:	16	2	3	11	5	51
CWC:	18	1	2	15	11	71
UEFA:	6	1	1	4	3	16
TOTAL:	40	4	6	30	19	138

CC: (7) 62-63 (1), 68-69 (1), 70-71 (1), 73-74 (1), 75-76 (1), 77-78 (1), 93-94 (1)
CWC: (9) 61-62 (1), 65-66 (1), 66-67 (1), 67-68 (1), 72-73 (1), 76-77 (1), 78-79 (1), 81-82 (1), 88-89 (1)
UEFA: (3) 69-70 (1), 91-92 (1), 92-93 (1)

Gloria Bistrita — Romania

Losing domestic cup semi-finalists in 1993, they went one stage further in 1994 by winning their first domestic honour. Made their debut in European club competition in the UEFA Cup in 1993–94.

Full Name:	Gloria Bistrita
Founded:	1926
Address:	Str. Parcului nr. 3, 4400 Bistrita
Phone:	90-12998
Stadium:	Gloria
Capacity:	10,000

Euro Record	P	W	D	L	F	A
CC:	0	0	0	0	0	0
CWC:	0	0	0	0	0	0
UEFA:	2	0	1	1	0	2
TOTAL:	2	0	1	1	0	2

CC: (0)
CWC: (0)
UEFA: (1) 93-94 (1)

Grasshopper Club — Switzerland

Founded by students, many English, in 1886, and Swiss FA founder members in 1895. Played in the first championship in 1899 and won it in 1900. Runners-up in the first national league championship in 1934. Domestic league champions a record 22 times and cup winners 18 times. They were UEFA Cup semi-finalists in 1978 and Cup-Winners' Cup quarter-finalists in 1990.

Full Name: Grasshopper Club Zurich
Founded: 1886
Address: Fussball-Sektion, Postfach 217, 8037 Zurich
Phone: (01) 2723388
Stadium: Hardturm
Capacity: 30,000

Euro Record	P	W	D	L	F	A
CC:	24	11	5	8	46	40
CWC:	8	2	2	4	9	9
UEFA:	54	21	6	27	77	99
TOTAL:	86	34	13	39	132	148

CC: (7)   56-57 (Q), 1-72 (2), 78-79 (Q), 82-83 (1), 83-84 (1), 84-85 (2), 90-91 (1)
CWC: (2) 88-89 (1), 89-90 (Q)
UEFA: (13) 68-69 (1), 70-71 (1), 72-73 (2), 73-74 (1), 74-75 (2), 75-76 (1), 76-77 (1), 77-78 (S), 79-80 (3), 80-81 (Q), 81-82 (2), 87-88 (1), 92-93 (2)

HJK Helsinki — Finland

Founded as Helsingin Jalkapallo Klubi Helsinki. Record 18 domestic league titles, the first in 1911 when they won the championship match, their first when the champions were determined on a league basis coming in 1936. Four domestic cup wins, the first in 1966.

Full Name: Helsingin Jalkapallo Klubi
Founded: 1907
Address: Stadion, 00250 Helsinki, Finland
Phone: 90-448693
Stadium: Olympiastadion
Capacity: 50,000

Euro Record	P	W	D	L	F	A
CC:	20	5	0	15	17	55
CWC:	6	3	0	3	9	18
UEFA:	6	0	0	6	2	20
TOTAL:	32	8	0	24	28	93

CC: (8)   65-66 (1), 74-75 (2), 79-80 (1), 82-83 (2), 86-87 (1), 88-89 (1), 89-90 (1), 93-94 (1)
CWC: (2) 67-68 (1), 85-86 (2)
UEFA: (4) 71-72 (1), 75-76 (1), 83-84 (1), 84-85 (1)

IBK — Iceland

The club from Keflavik, west of the capital, have three league titles to their credit, having been runners-up twice. Relegated from the first division in 1989, they were promoted again as second division runners-up in 1992. Have won the domestic cup once. Reached the second round of the UEFA Cup in 1980.

Full Name: IBK Keflavik
Founded: 1946
Address: 230 Keflavik
Phone: (2) 15088/14137
Stadium: Keflavikurvollur
Capacity: 2,000

Euro Record	P	W	D	L	F	A
CC:	8	0	0	8	5	35
CWC:	2	0	1	1	1	4
UEFA:	10	1	1	8	6	31
TOTAL:	20	1	2	17	12	70

CC: (4)   65-66 (1), 70-71 (1), 72-73 (1), 74-75 (1)
CWC: (1) 76-77 (1)
UEFA: (4) 71-72 (1), 73-74 (1), 75-76 (1), 79-80 (2)

IFK Norrkoping — Sweden

Norrkoping is 100 miles south west of the capital. League champions 12 times, the 11th in 1963, the 12th in 1989. Six times league winners. League runners-up in each of the last four seasons. First Swedish club to participate in the Cup-Winners' Cup, 1968–69.

Full Name: Idrottsforeningen Kamraterna Norrkoping
Founded: 1897
Address: Box 12067, 600 12 Norrkoping, Sweden
Phone: 11-132225
Stadium: Norrkopings Idrottsparken
Capacity: 18,000
Colours: White, Blue, White

Euro Record	P	W	D	L	F	A
CC:	12	2	5	5	14	20
CWC:	14	6	2	6	23	17
UEFA:	16	4	6	6	14	19
TOTAL:	42	12	13	17	51	56

CC: (4)   56-57 (2), 57-58 (2), 62-63 (2), 63-64 (2)
CWC: (4) 68-69 (2), 69-70 (2), 88-89 (1), 91-92 (2)
UEFA: (6) 72-73 (2), 78-79 (1), 82-83 (2), 90-91 (1), 92-93 (1), 93-94 (1)

LKS Lodz — Poland

Known as Wlokniarz between 1948 and 1954. Lodz is 60 miles south west of the capital. Domestic cup winners in 1957 and league champions the following season. Losing finalists in the 1994 cup final. Having finished second in the league in 1992–93 they had three points deducted due to match-fixing charges and were banned from the UEFA Cup for the following season.

Full Name: Lodzki Klub Sportowy
Founded: 1908
Address: Al. Unii 2, 94-020 Lodz
Phone: (042) 860236/863778/863745
Stadium: LKS
Capacity: 35,000

Euro Record	P	W	D	L	F	A
CC:	2	1	0	1	2	6
CWC:	0	0	0	0	0	0
UEFA:	0	0	0	0	0	0
TOTAL:	2	1	0	1	2	6

CC: (1)   59-60 (1)
CWC: (0)
UEFA: (0)

Maccabi Tel Aviv — Israel

League champions 15 times, the first in 1937, and 18 times cup winners, the first in 1929, both record numbers. Twice winners of the short-lived Asian Champions' Cup in the 1960s.

Full Name:	Maccabi Tel Aviv
Founded:	1906
Address:	Maccabi St 4, Tel-Aviv 63293
Phone:	(03) 293283
Stadium:	Ramat-Gan
Capacity:	55,000

Euro Record	P	W	D	L	F	A
CC:	4	2	0	2	3	4
CWC:	0	0	0	0	0	0
UEFA:	0	0	0	0	0	0
TOTAL:	4	2	0	2	3	4

CC: (1) 92-93 (1)
CWC: (0)
UEFA: (0)

Maribor Branik — Slovenia

No Yugoslavian league honours before 1991, finishing seventh in Division Three (North) in their final season, although a very successful regional side. Slovenian league members and runners up, 1992 and 1993. Cup winners in 1992, winning a penalty shoot-out. This gave them their European debut in the 1992–93 Cup-Winners' Cup as the first Slovenian representative in that competition.

Full Name:	NK Maribor Branik
Founded:	1958
Address:	Mladinska 29, 62000 Maribor
Phone:	(062) 28534
Stadium:	Ljudski vrt
Capacity:	15,000

Euro Record	P	W	D	L	F	A
CC:	0	0	0	0	0	0
CWC:	4	1	0	3	6	11
UEFA:	4	0	2	2	3	1
TOTAL:	8	1	2	5	9	12

CC: (0)
CWC: (1) 92-93 (1)
UEFA: (1) 93-94 (2)

Norma Tallinn — Estonia

Having won the Estonian league championship in 1991–92 and 1992–93 they finished joint first in 1993–94, losing the title in a play-off decider. Won the domestic cup for the first time in 1993–94.

Full Name:	Norma Tallinn
Founded:	1959
Address:	14 Loki Street, Tallinn EE 0100
Phone:	(2) 538206/471960
Stadium:	Norma
Capacity:	1,000

Euro Record	P	W	D	L	F	A
CC:	4	0	1	3	1	7
CWC:	0	0	0	0	0	0
UEFA:	0	0	0	0	0	0
TOTAL:	4	0	1	3	1	7

CC: (2) 92-93 (P), 93-94 (P)
CWC: (0)
UEFA: (0)

Olimpija Riga — Latvia

Won the domestic cup in 1993–94 to record their first honour. Making their European debut.

Full Name:	Olimpija
Address:	Ezermalas Str. 10, Riga, LV1010
Phone:	371-54 20 449

Euro Record	P	W	D	L	F	A
CC:	0	0	0	0	0	0
CWC:	0	0	0	0	0	0
UEFA:	0	0	0	0	0	0
TOTAL:	0	0	0	0	0	0

Omonia Nicosia — Cyprus

League champions 17 times including 1993, ten times cup winners. In the Champions' Cup they have reached the second round four times, 1988 being the last occasion. They made their European debut in the 1965–66 Cup-Winners' Cup.

Full Name:	Omonia FC
Founded:	1948
Address:	PO Box 617, Nicosia
Phone:	2-444544
Stadium:	Makarion
Capacity:	20,000
Colours:	White, White, White

Euro Record	P	W	D	L	F	A
CC:	38	12	2	24	46	90
CWC:	8	0	1	7	2	16
UEFA:	6	1	2	3	7	10
TOTAL:	52	13	5	34	55	116

CC: (15) 66-67 (1), 72-73 (2), 75-76 (1), 76-77 (1), 77-78 (1), 78-79 (1), 79-80 (2), 1-82 (1), 82-83 (1), 83-84 (1), 84-85 (1), 85-86 (2), 87-88 (2), 89-90 (1), 93-94 (P)
CWC: (4) 65-66 (1), 80-81 (1), 88-89 (1), 91-92 (1)
UEFA: (2) 86-87 (1), 90-91 (2)

Panathinaikos — Greece

Founded as Panhellenic by Englishmen and known until 1980 as PAO (Panathinaikos Athletikos Omilos). Joined the domestic league in 1929, and were founder members of the unified national league in 1959-60 when they were champions and cup winners. League champions 16 times and 13 times cup winners. They were Champions' Cup runners-up to Ajax in 1971.

Full Name:	FC Panathinaikos
Founded:	1908
Address:	Armatolon & Klefton 47, Ampelokipi, 11471 Athens
Phone:	1-6445322
Stadium:	OAKA Spiros Louis
Capacity:	74,433
Colours:	Green, Green, Green

Euro Record	P	W	D	L	F	A
CC:	53	13	19	21	60	71
CWC:	18	7	2	9	21	34
UEFA:	28	9	4	15	40	41
TOTAL:	99	29	25	45	121	146

CC: (13) 60-61 (2), 61-62 (1), 62-63 (1), 64-65 (2), 65-66 (2), 69-70 (1), 70-71 (F), 72-73 (1), 77-78 (2), 84-85 (S), 86-87 (1), 90-91 (1), 91-92 (CL)

CWC: (6)   67-68 (1), 75-76 (1), 82-83 (1), 88-89 (2), 89-90 (2), 93-94 (2)
UEFA: (9) 68-69 (2), 73-74 (1), 74-75 (1), 78-79 (1), 80-81 (1), 81-82 (1), 85-86 (1), 87-88 (Q), 92-93 (2)

Pirin — Bulgaria

Known at various times as Botev, Macedonia, Torpedo, and Strojtel. Blagoevgrad is 50 miles south of the capital in the far west of the country. Third in the domestic league, their highest finishing place, in 1985, two points adrift of the top two, gave them UEFA Cup experience in 1985–86. Army Cup runners-up in 1981 and Cup of the Republic runnners-up in 1992 and 1994.

Full Name: FC Pirin
Founded: 1934
Address: Stadion Christo Botev, 2700 Blagoevgrad
Phone: 073 23332/20791
Stadium: Christo Botev
Capacity: 20,000

Euro Record	P	W	D	L	F	A
CC:	0	0	0	0	0	0
CWC:	0	0	0	0	0	0
UEFA:	2	0	0	2	1	7
TOTAL	2	0	0	2	1	7

CC: (0)
CWC: (0)
UEFA: (1)   85-86 (1)

FC Porto — Portugal

First cup winners, in 1922, and founder members and first champions of the Portuguese league, in 1935. Now 13 times league champions, including six times in the last decade, and 12 times cup winners. Cup-Winners' Cup runners-up in 1984. In 1987 were Champions' Cup and European Super Cup winners as well as World Club champions.

Full Name: Futebol Clube do Porto
Founded: 1906
Address: Estadio das Antas, Avenida Fernao de Magalhaes, 4300 Porto
Phone: 2-481738
Stadium: Das Antas
Capacity: 72,500
Colours: Blue/White, Blue, White

Euro Record	P	W	D	L	F	A
CC:	58	29	10	19	102	58
CWC:	35	17	7	11	48	41
UEFA:	50	23	8	9	70	61
TOTAL:	143	69	25	39	220	160

CC: (10)   56-57 (1), 59-60 (1), 78-79 (1), 79-80 (2), 85-86 (2), 86-87 (W), 87-88 (2), 88-89 (2), 90-91 (Q), 92-93 (CL)
CWC: (8)   64-65 (2), 68-69 (2), 77-78 (Q), 81-82 (Q), 83-84 (F), 84-85 (1), 91-92 (2)
UEFA: (14) 62-63 (1), 63-64 (1), 65-66 (2), 66-67 (1), 67-68 (1), 69-70 (2), 71-72 (1), 72-73 (3), 74-75 (2), 75-76 (3), 76-77 (1), 80-81 (2), 82-83 (2), 89-90 (3)

Real Zaragoza — Spain

Domestic league runners-up in 1975 and third three times. Domestic cup winners four times and were runners-up three times. Won the Fairs Cup in 1964 and runners-up two seasons later.

Full Name: Real Zaragoza Club Deportivo
Founded: 1932
Address: Luis Bermejo 3, Estadio La Romareda, 50009 Zaragoza
Phone: 976 567777
Stadium: La Romareda
Capacity: 43,349

Euro Record	P	W	D	L	F	A
CC:	0	0	0	0	0	0
CWC:	0	0	0	0	0	0
UEFA:	54	29	6	19	106	80
TOTAL:	54	29	6	19	106	80

CC: (0)
CWC: (0)
UEFA: (9) 62-63 (2), 63-64 (W), 65-66 (F), 67-68 (2), 68-69 (3), 74-75 (3), 75-76 (1), 89-90 (2), 92-93 (3)

Sampdoria — Italy

The Genoa club were founded in 1946, but had their roots in Andrea Doria, started in the 1890s by Italians to counter the rise of clubs founded by other Europeans, and Sampierdarense, named after an area of the city. These had joined forces in 1927 as Dominante, then became Liguria, a name they returned to after a period as Sampierdarense. Twice relegated from Serie A, they returned after a break of five seasons in 1982. Subsequently they won the domestic cup three times, the last giving them a Cup-Winners' Cup place which ended with their only European honour, winning the 1990 competition. Their only league championship to date followed the next season.

Full Name: Sampdoria Unione Calcio
Founded: 1946
Address: Via XX Settembre 33, 16121 Genova
Phone: (010) 585343
Stadium: Luigi Ferraris
Capacity: 41,918

Euro Record	P	W	D	L	F	A
CC:	11	6	2	3	21	10
CWC:	28	15	7	6	39	21
UEFA:	4	3	0	1	4	6
TOTAL:	43	24	9	10	64	37

CC: (1)   91-92 (F)
CWC: (4)   85-86 (2), 88-89 (F), 89-90 (W), 90-91 (Q)
UEFA: (1) 62-63 (2)

FC Schaan — Liechtenstein

Won the Liechtenstein Cup for the first time in 1994. No previous European club competition experience.

Full Name: FC Schaan

Euro Record	P	W	D	L	F	A
CC:	0	0	0	0	0	0
CWC:	0	0	0	0	0	0
UEFA:	0	0	0	0	0	0
TOTAL:	0	0	0	0	0	0

Sligo Rovers — Republic of Ireland

League of Ireland champions in 1937 and 1977, and cup winners twice, 1983 and 1994, having been runners-up five times. Relegated from the top division in 1993 but won promotion back in 1994.

Full Name: Sligo Rovers FC
Founded: 1928
Address: The Showgrounds, Sligo
Phone: (071) 42141
Stadium: The Showgrounds
Capacity: 10,000

Euro Record	P	W	D	L	F	A
CC:	2	0	0	2	0	6
CWC:	2	0	0	2	0	4
UEFA:	0	0	0	0	0	0
TOTAL:	4	0	0	4	0	10

CC: (1) 77-78 (1)
CWC: (1) 83-84 (1)
UEFA: (0)

SK Tirana — Albania

Founded in 1920 as Agmi and played under several names, including 17 Nentori during the period 1958–91, 17 November being the date of the modern country's independence. Won play-off to take the first national championship in 1930 and league champions 14 times overall. Seven times Cup winners, the first in 1963.

Full Name: Klubi Sportiv Tirane
Founded: 1920
Address: Rruga Konferenca e Pezes, nr. 71 Trirane
Phone: (42) 27006
Stadium: Qemol Stafa
Capacity: 20,000

Euro Record	P	W	D	L	F	A
CC:	16	3	3	10	14	24
CWC:	6	3	1	2	5	9
UEFA:	0	0	0	0	0	0
TOTAL:	22	6	4	12	19	33

CC: (6) 65-66 (1), 69-70 (1), 70-71 (1), 82-83 (2), 88-89 (2), 89-90 (2)
CWC: (2) 83-84 (1), 86-87 (2)
UEFA: (0)

Tatran Presov — Slovakia

Played under several names just after the Second World War, including PTS Presov, Sparta Presov, Sparta Dukla Presov and CSSZ, settling on the present name in 1953. Promoted to the Czechoslovakian league top division in 1949, relegation subsequently overtook them several times, with promotion usually following after a couple of seasons. Czechoslovakian cup runners-up in 1992.

Full Name: FC Tatran Presov
Founded: 1931
Address: Capajevova 47, 080 01 Presov
Phone: (091) 32566/33553/41464
Stadium: FC Tatran
Capacity: 16,000

Euro Record	P	W	D	L	F	A
CC:	0	0	0	0	0	0
CWC:	2	0	1	1	3	4
UEFA:	4	1	1	2	9	11
TOTAL:	6	1	2	3	12	15

CC: (0)
CWC: (1) 66-67 (1)
UEFA: (1) 73-74 (2)

Tiligul — Moldova

Second Division runners-up in the Russian championship of 1991–92 which still included clubs from outside Russia. They then moved to the Moldavian League. Play at Minisipal stadium but will stage European ties at the national Republican stadium.

Full Name: FC Tiligul
Founded: 1990
Address: Sverdlov Street, 46 ap I, Tiraspol
Stadium: Minisipal
Capacity: 12,000
Colours: Red, Red, Red

Euro Record	P	W	D	L	F	A
CC:	0	0	0	0	0	0
CWC:	0	0	0	0	0	0
UEFA:	0	0	0	0	0	0
TOTAL:	0	0	0	0	0	0

Viktoria Zizkov — Czech Republic

The Prague side were formed by technical college students. Known as Sokol Viktoria Zizkov in 1950 and as Sokol CSAD in 1951. Czechoslovakian league founder members and third in the first season, 1925. League champions for the only time in 1928. Four times winners of the national cup competition before the Second World War. Gained a place in the new Czech Republic league by being champions of the Czech section of the second division in 1993.

Full Name: FK Viktoria Zizkov
Founded: 1903
Address: Seifertova ul., 130 00 Prague 3-Zizkov
Phone: (02) 273398
Stadium: FK Viktoria
Capacity: 8,500

Euro Record	P	W	D	L	F	A
CC:	0	0	0	0	0	0
CWC:	0	0	0	0	0	0
UEFA:	0	0	0	0	0	0
TOTAL:	0	0	0	0	0	0

Werder Bremen — Germany

From the northern port of Bremen, were founder members of the Bundesliga in 1963 and finished 10th that season. Relegated in 1980, they were promoted the following season as Division II North champions. Twice West German league champions and West German cup winners once. They were German champions in 1993 and cup winners in 1994. Won the Cup-Winners' Cup in 1992 and took part in the UEFA Champions' League in 1994.

Full Name: SV Werder Bremen
Founded: 1899
Address: Weserstadion, 2800 Bremen 1
Phone: 421-498106
Stadium: Weserstadion
Capacity: 40,640

Euro Record	P	W	D	L	F	A
CC:	20	9	5	6	37	27
CWC:	17	10	2	5	34	17
UEFA:	36	17	8	11	65	42
TOTAL:	73	36	15	22	136	86

CC: (3) 65-66 (2), 88-89 (Q), 93-94 (CL)
CWC: (3) 61-62 (Q), 91-92 (W), 92-93 (2)
UEFA: (7) 82-83 (3), 83-84 (2), 84-85 (1), 85-86 (1), 86-87 (1), 87-88 (S), 89-90 (S)

Zhalgiris Vilnius — Lithuania

Founded as Dinamo, and were known from 1948 until 1962 as Sparkak. They spent a handful of early post-war seasons in the top division and third place in the Soviet league in 1987 brought them their European debut in the UEFA Cup 1988-89 competition. Withdrawn from the 1990 Soviet league, they were champions of the Baltic league and then the Spring 1991 Lithuania league, the latter bringing them a Champions' Cup place as the country's first such representative. Won the domestic cup in 1993.

Full Name:	FC Zhalgiris Vilnius
Founded:	1947
Address:	Zolyno str. 29, Vilnius
Phone:	741494/742360
Stadium:	Zhalgiris
Capacity:	15,000
Colours:	Green and White stripes, White, White

Euro Record

	P	W	D	L	F	A
CC:	2	0	0	2	0	8
CWC:	2	0	0	2	0	3
UEFA:	6	2	0	4	7	11
TOTAL:	10	2	0	8	7	22

CC: (1) 92-93 (1)
CWC: (1) 93-94 (P)
UEFA: (2) 88-89 (1), 89-90 (2)

UEFA Cup

Note: The use of † by a club's name indicates a champion club qualification.

FC Aarau — Switzerland

Twice national champions before the First World War when regional champions took part in a mini-league, but not again until 1993. Promoted to the top division for the first time in 1935, then relegated immediately. Frequently fighting further relegation in the fifties, they reverted to amateur status for a short period before gaining promotion again in 1981. Cup winners once, in 1985. In 1990 they survived the relegation play-offs.

Full Name:	FC Aarau
Founded:	1902
Address:	Postfach 2738, 5001 Aarau, Switzerland
Phone:	64-247561
Stadium:	Brugglifield
Capacity:	14,000

Euro Record

	P	W	D	L	F	A
CC:	4	1	1	2	3	3
CWC:	2	0	1	1	2	4
UEFA:	2	0	0	2	0	7
TOTAL:	8	1	2	5	5	14

CC: (1) 93-94 (1)
CWC: (1) 85-86 (1)
UEFA: (1) 88-89 (1)

Aberdeen — Scotland

Founded by members of Victoria United and Orion. Joined the Scottish league in 1906 and have never been relegated. Four times league champions and seven times cup winners. Won the Cup-Winners' Cup in 1983.

Full Name:	Aberdeen FC
Founded:	1903
Address:	Pittodrie Park, Aberdeen, AB2 1QH
Phone:	(0224) 632328
Stadium:	Pittodrie Park
Capacity:	21,779
Colours:	Red, Red, Red

Euro Record

	P	W	D	L	F	A
CC:	12	5	4	3	14	12
CWC:	39	22	5	12	79	37
UEFA:	34	12	9	13	42	45
TOTAL:	85	39	18	28	135	94

CC: (3) 80-81 (2), 84-85 (1), 85-86 (Q)
CWC: (8) 67-68 (2), 70-71 (1), 78-79 (2), 82-83 (W), 83-84 (S), 86-87 (1), 90-91 (2), 93-94 (2)
UEFA: (11) 68-69 (2), 71-72 (2), 72-73 (1), 73-74 (2), 77-78 (1), 79-80 (1), 81-82 (3), 87-88 (2), 88-89 (1), 89-90 (1), 91-92 (1)

Admira Wacker — Austria

Founded as Admira Vienna and in 1959 became WSC Admira-Energie when under commercial sponsorship. Joined with Wacker Vienna (founded 1908) in 1971. Nine domestic league championships and six times cup winners, but since 1971 have only been runners-up once.

Full Name:	FC Baumit Admira Wacker
Founded:	1905
Address:	Johann-Steinbock-Strasse 1, 2344 Maria Enzersdorf
Phone:	2236-23479
Stadium:	Bundesstadion
Capacity:	18,600
Colours:	White, White, White

Euro Record

	P	W	D	L	F	A
CC:	2	0	1	1	0	1
CWC:	12	5	2	5	16	16
UEFA:	18	7	1	10	18	27
TOTAL:	32	12	4	16	34	44

CC: (1) 66-67 (1)
CWC: (3) 64-65 (1), 89-90 (Q), 92-93 (2)
UEFA: (5) 73-74 (2), 82-83 (1), 87-88 (1), 90-91 (3), 92-93 (1), 93-94 (1)

AIK Stockholm — Sweden

AIK means General Sports Club. In 1900 they were the first club from the capital to win the league championship when it was dominated by clubs from Gothenburg. Domestic league champions nine times and cup winners four times. Founder members of the formal league in 1924–25, but relegated three times.

Full Name:	Allmanna Idrotts Klubben
Founded:	1891
Address:	Box 1408, S-171 27 Stockholm
Phone:	8-735 80 80
Stadium:	Rasunda Stadion
Capacity:	27,500

Euro Record

	P	W	D	L	F	A
CC:	2	1	0	1	1	2
CWC:	8	2	4	2	16	10
UEFA:	16	5	5	6	20	26
TOTAL:	26	8	9	9	37	38

CC: (1) 93-94 (1)
CWC: (3) 76-77 (1), 85-86 (2), 92-93 (1)
UEFA: (6) 65-66 (2), 68-69 (2), 73-74 (1), 75-76 (1), 84-85 (1), 87-88 (1)

Anorthosis — Cyprus

Six times league champions in the period 1950–63, the last occasion enabling them to become the first Cypriot Champions' Cup entrant, 1963–64. League runners-up six times including 1991, 1992 and 1994. Domestic cup winners four times and three times runners-up. Based in Larnaca on the island's south coast because their former home in Famagusta is now under Turkish administration.

Full Name:	Anorthosis FC of Famagusta
Founded:	1911
Address:	PO Box 756, Larnaca
Phone:	(04) 635833/4
Stadium:	Antonis Papadopoulos
Capacity:	8,000

Euro Record		P	W	D	L	F	A
	CC:	2	0	0	2	1	6
	CWC:	6	0	1	5	3	4
	UEFA:	6	0	1	5	4	25
	TOTAL:	14	0	2	12	8	35

CC: (1)   63-64 (1)
CWC: (2)   71-72 (1), 75-76 (1)
UEFA: (2)   83-84 (1), 91-92 (1)

Apollon †   Cyprus

League champions twice, in 1991 and 1994, being runners-up three times including 1993. Domestic cup winners four times. Reached the second round of the the Champions' Cup 1991–92, their European debut having been in the 1966–67 Cup-Winners' Cup.

Full Name: Apollon FC
Founded: 1954
Address: 1 Mesolongiou Str., PO Box 3206, Limassol
Phone: (05) 363702/379082/356952
Stadium: Tsirion
Capacity: 22,000

Euro Record		P	W	D	L	F	A
	CC:	4	1	0	3	4	7
	CWC:	8	0	1	7	2	14
	UEFA:	8	2	2	4	11	18
	TOTAL:	20	3	3	14	17	39

CC: (1)   91-92 (2)
CWC: (5)   66-67 (1), 67-68 (1), 82-83 (1), 86-87 (1), 92-93 (1)
UEFA: (3)   84-85 (1), 89-90 (1), 93-94 (2)

Ararat Erevan †   Armenia

Known as Dynamo until 1954 and then Spartak until 1962. Promoted to the top Soviet division for the first time in 1949. Relegated after two seasons, they returned in 1960, and were relegated again three seasons later only to return in 1966. They stayed in the top flight until the break-up of the USSR, finishing seventh in 1991–92. Soviet champions in 1973 and cup winners twice, and have been Soviet representatives in European competition, reaching the Champions' Cup quarter-finals in 1975.

Full Name: FC Ararat
Founded: 1937
Address: Tigran Mets Ave 4, 375010 Erevan
Phone: 7 8852 52 20 52

Euro Record		P	W	D	L	F	A
	CC:	6	5	0	1	14	5
	CWC:	4	1	2	1	12	5
	UEFA:	6	5	0	1	11	5
	TOTAL:	16	11	2	3	37	15

CC: (1)   74-75 (Q)
CWC: (1)   75-76 (2)
UEFA: (1)   72-73 (3)

Aris Salonika   Greece

Named after the ancient Roman God of War, Mars. Joined the domestic league in 1922, and were founder members of the unified national league in 1959–60 when they finished eighth. Three times league champions, three times runners-up, and domestic cup winners once.

Full Name: Aris
Founded: 1914
Address: Yonni Angelouv 146, 54250 Thessalonika
Phone: (031) 307123/313700
Stadium: Hariloou
Capacity: 27,000

Euro Record		P	W	D	L	F	A
	CC:	0	0	0	0	0	0
	CWC:	2	0	1	1	2	6
	UEFA:	26	9	5	12	37	55
	TOTAL:	28	9	6	13	39	61

CC: (0)
CWC: (1)   70-71 (1)
UEFA: (9)   64-65 (1), 65-66 (2), 66-67 (1), 68-69 (2), 69-70 (1), 74-75 (1), 79-80 (3), 80-81 (1), 81-82 (2)

AS Cannes   France

Founder members of the French league when they were runners-up, a position never bettered. Relegated from the first division in 1992, then promoted back after play-off success the following season. Domestic cup winners in 1932.

Full Name: Association Sportive de Cannes
Founded: 1902
Address: Stade Pierre de Coubertin, Avenue Pierre Poesi, 06150 Cannes-La Bocca
Phone: (93) 902420
Stadium: Pierre de Coubertin
Capacity: 20,000

Euro Record		P	W	D	L	F	A
	CC:	0	0	0	0	0	0
	CWC:	0	0	0	0	0	0
	UEFA:	4	1	1	2	2	3
	TOTAL:	4	1	1	2	2	3

CC: (0)
CWC: (0)
UEFA: (1)   91-92 (2)

Aston Villa   England

Founded by local cricketers, they were founder members of the Football League in 1888. Moved to their present ground in 1897, although it was not known as Villa Park until later. League and cup double achieved in 1897, the championship being won six times by 1910. Seven times FA Cup winners. Their seventh league championship was won in 1981 and in their debut in the Champions' Cup they won the competition, beating Bayern Munich 1-0 in Rotterdam. Went on to win the European Super Cup. Founder members and first runners-up of the FA Premier League in 1992–93. League Cup winners for the fourth time in 1994.

Full Name: Aston Villa FC
Founded: 1874
Address: Villa Park, Trinity Road, Birmingham, B6 6HE
Phone: 021-3272299
Stadium: Villa Park
Capacity: 40,000
Colours: Claret/Blue, White, Blue

Euro Record		P	W	D	L	F	A
	CC:	15	9	3	3	24	10
	CWC:	0	0	0	0	0	0
	UEFA:	22	9	6	7	34	24
	TOTAL:	37	18	9	10	58	34

CC: (2) 81-82 (W), 82-83 (Q)
CWC: (0)
UEFA: (5) 75-76 (1), 77-78 (Q), 83-84 (2), 90-91 (2), 93-94 (2)

Athletic Bilbao   Spain

League founder members in 1929 when they finished third. Domestic league champions eight times and runners-up six times. Domestic cup winners on 23 occasions, the first in 1903. Runners-up in the UEFA Cup in 1977.

Full Name:	Athletic Club de Bilbao
Founded:	1898
Address:	Avenido Alameda Mazarredo 23, 48009 Bilbao
Phone:	(94) 4240877/8
Stadium:	San Mames
Capacity:	47,000

Euro Record	P	W	D	L	F	A
CC:	12	5	3	4	22	20
CWC:	0	0	0	0	0	0
UEFA:	68	33	11	24	93	82
TOTAL:	80	38	14	28	115	102

CC: (3) 56-57 (Q), 83-84 (2), 84-85 (1)
CWC: (2) 69-70 (1), 73-74 (2)
UEFA: (13) 64-65 (Q), 66-67 (1), 67-68 (Q), 68-69 (Q), 70-71 (1), 71-72 (2), 76-77 (F), 77-78 (3), 78-79 (1), 82-83 (1), 85-86 (3), 86-87 (2), 88-89 (2)

Bangor City †   Wales

Founded 1875 and domestic cup winners twice in the 1890s. Played in many league competitions based in North Wales and the North West of England, being founder members of both the Northern Premier League (1968) and the Alliance Premier League (now the Vauxhall Conference, 1979). League of Wales founder members in 1992 and fifth in the first season. After winning the domestic cup for the third time in 1962, played in the Cup-Winners' Cup and, extraordinarily for a non-league club, took Napoli to a third, deciding match in the preliminary round. FA Trophy runners-up in 1984, but no major honours between 1962 and their 1994 championship.

Full Name:	Bangor City FC
Founded:	1875
Address:	12 Lon y Bryn, Menai Bridge, Ynys Mon LL57 5NM
Phone:	(0248) 712820
Stadium:	Farrar Road
Capacity:	10,000

Euro Record	P	W	D	L	F	A
CC:	0	0	0	0	0	0
CWC:	7	1	2	4	5	9
UEFA:	0	0	0	0	0	0
TOTAL:	7	1	2	4	5	9

CC: (0)
CWC: (2) 62-63 (1), 85-86 (2)
UEFA: (0)

Bayer Leverkusen   Germany

Promoted to West Germany's Division II North as a regional third division champion in 1975 and to the Bundesliga in 1979 as the division's champions. No major domestic honours before winning the cup in 1993, but won the UEFA Cup on their European debut. Founder members of the German league in 1992.

Full Name:	TSV Bayer 04 Leverkusen
Founded:	1904
Address:	Postfach 120 140, 5090 Leverkusen
Phone:	214-46030
Stadium:	Ulrich Haberland Stadion
Capacity:	25,350
Colours:	White, White, White

Euro Record	P	W	D	L	F	A
CC:	0	0	0	0	0	0
CWC:	6	3	2	1	15	8
UEFA:	24	11	9	4	30	16
TOTAL:	30	14	11	5	45	24

CC: (0)
CWC: (1) 93-94(Q)
UEFA: (4) 86-87 (2), 87-88 (W), 88-89 (1), 90-91 (3)

Bekescsaba   Hungary

Founded in 1912, becoming Bekescsaba Elore Spartacus in 1970. Promoted to the first division for the first time in 1974, avoiding relegation by one point in their first season. Beat Honved to win the domestic cup for the only time in 1988.

Full Name:	Bekescsaba Elore Spartacus FC
Founded:	1912
Address:	Korhaz u. 6, 5601 Bekescsaba
Phone:	(66) 323656
Stadium:	Elore
Capacity:	18,000

Euro Record	P	W	D	L	F	A
CC:	0	0	0	0	0	0
CWC:	4	2	0	2	5	4
UEFA:	0	0	0	0	0	0
TOTAL:	4	2	0	2	5	4

CC: (0)
CWC: (1) 88-89 (1)
UEFA: (0)

Blackburn Rovers   England

Founded by local school-leavers. Founder members of the Football League in 1888. Moved to their present ground in 1890. Great deal of early success winning the league championship twice and the FA Cup five times before the First World War. Won the cup again in 1928, but following relegation from the top division in 1966 spent many years in the doldrums, including two periods in division three. After 12 seasons in division two, won promotion to be founder members of the FA Premier League in 1992 as winners of the play-offs for the third promotion place, having finished sixth.

Full Name:	Blackburn Rovers FC
Founded:	1875
Address:	Ewood Park, Blackburn BB2 4JF
Phone:	(0254) 55432
Stadium:	Ewood Park
Capacity:	30,000

Euro Record	P	W	D	L	F	A
CC:	0	0	0	0	0	0
CWC:	0	0	0	0	0	0
UEFA:	0	0	0	0	0	0
TOTAL:	0	0	0	0	0	0

Boavista — Portugal

Based in Oporto and were league runners-up in 1975–76, their highest position. They also recorded a third place, 1991–92. Four times cup winners (all since 1975), the first bringing them their European debut in the 1975–76 Cup-Winners' Cup.

Full Name:	Boavista Futebol Clube
Founded:	1903
Address:	No Estadio do Bessa, Rua O Primeiro de Janeiro, 4100 Porto
Phone:	2-698159/668506
Stadium:	Bessa
Capacity:	23,421

Euro Record	P	W	D	L	F	A
CC:	0	0	0	0	0	0
CWC:	16	6	6	4	25	13
UEFA:	30	8	5	17	25	46
TOTAL:	46	14	11	21	50	59

CC: (0)
CWC: (4) 75-76 (2), 76-77 (2), 79-80 (2), 92-93 (2)
UEFA: (8) 77-78 (1), 80-81 (2), 81-82 (2), 85-86 (1), 86-87 (2), 89-90 (1), 91-92 (2), 93-94 (Q)

Bordeaux — France

League champions four times and three times cup winners. Relegated from division one in 1956 and 1960, and again in 1991, this time because of financial irregularities. Division 2B champions and promoted again in 1992. They reached the semi-final of the Champions' Cup in 1985 and the same stage of the Cup-Winners' Cup in 1987.

Full Name:	Girondins de Bordeaux
Founded:	1881
Address:	Rue Joliot-Curie, 33186 Le Haillan
Phone:	56-086363
Stadium:	Parc Lescure
Capacity:	50,000
Colours:	Navy Blue, Navy Blue, Navy Blue

Euro Record	P	W	D	L	F	A
CC:	16	6	8	2	17	12
CWC:	10	6	1	3	11	10
UEFA:	44	22	4	18	62	63
TOTAL:	70	34	13	23	90	85

CC: (3) 84-85 (S), 85-86 (1), 87-88 (Q)
CWC: (2) 68-69 (1), 86-87 (S)
UEFA: (11) 64-65 (1), 65-66 (1), 66-67 (2), 67-68 (2), 69-70 (1), 81-82 (2), 82-83 (3), 83-84 (1), 88-89 (3), 90-91 (3), 93-94 (3)

Borussia Dortmund — Germany

Three pre-Bundesliga West German championships including the last one in 1963 before becoming Bundesliga founder members, when they finished fourth. Relegated in 1972, but were promoted following play-offs in 1976. Twice Bundesliga runners-up and twice West German cup winners. Cup-Winners' Cup winners in 1966 and runners-up in the UEFA Cup in 1993.

Full Name:	BV Borussia Dortmund
Founded:	1909
Address:	Westfalenstadion, Strobelallee, Postfach 10059, 4600 Dortmund 1
Phone:	231-22083/4
Stadium:	Westfalenstadion
Capacity:	53,870
Colours:	Yellow, Black, Yellow

Euro Record	P	W	D	L	F	A
CC:	18	8	3	7	44	30
CWC:	15	9	3	3	22	15
UEFA:	38	20	4	14	52	47
TOTAL:	71	37	10	24	118	92

CC: (3) 56-57 (2), 57-58 (Q), 63-64 (S)
CWC: (3) 65-66 (W), 66-67 (2), 89-90 (2)
UEFA: (6) 64-65 (2), 82-83 (1), 87-88 (3), 90-91 (3), 92-93 (F), 93-94 (Q)

Charleroi — Belgium

Belgian league runners-up in 1969, the highest finishing position ever attained, they were later relegated, only to be accelerated back into the top division in 1974 when they had finished 14th in the second division. Domestic cup runners-up in 1978, the only time they have ever got to the final. They were relegated again in 1980 and promoted back in 1985.

Full Name:	Royal Charleroi Sporting Club
Founded:	1904
Address:	Boulevard Zoe Drion 19
Phone:	(071) 328734
Stadium:	Mambour
Capacity:	23,000

Euro Record	P	W	D	L	F	A
CC:	0	0	0	0	0	0
CWC:	0	0	0	0	0	0
UEFA:	4	3	0	1	8	5
TOTAL:	4	3	0	1	8	5

CC: (0)
CWC: (0)
UEFA: (1) 69-70 (2)

FC Copenhagen — Denmark

Formed on the amalgamation of KB and B1903, founded in 1876 and 1903 respectively, and with over 20 league titles between them together with many European campaigns. Took B1903's UEFA Cup place for 1992–93 as league runners-up. Won the domestic championship under their own name for the first and only time in 1992–93.

Full Name:	FC Copenhagen
Founded:	1992
Address:	Baunegardsvej 7L, 2820 Gentofte, Copenhagen
Phone:	31-656055
Stadium:	Gentofte Stadion
Capacity:	18,000

Euro Record	P	W	D	L	F	A
CC:	4	1	0	3	4	10
CWC:	0	0	0	0	0	0
UEFA:	4	2	0	2	10	8
TOTAL:	8	3	0	5	14	18

CC: (1) 93-94 (2)
CWC: (0)
UEFA: (1) 92-93 (3)

Cork City — Republic of Ireland

League runners-up in 1990–91 and champions in 1992–93. Twice cup runners-up, the first bringing them their European debut, in the 1989–90 Cup-Winners' Cup.

Full Name:	Cork City FC
Founded:	1984
Address:	Turner's Cross, Cork
Phone:	(021) 885694
Stadium:	Turner's Cross
Capacity:	20,000

Euro Record	P	W	D	L	F	A
CC:	4	1	0	3	5	7
CWC:	2	0	0	2	0	4
UEFA:	2	0	1	1	1	3
TOTAL:	8	1	1	6	6	14

CC: (1) 93-94 (1)
CWC: (1) 89-90 (1)
UEFA: (1) 91-92 (1)

CS Grevenmacher — Luxembourg

Promoted to the top division in 1985 and have been there ever since. Third in the league in 1960 but until 1994 never higher. Four times cup runners-up.

Full Name:	Club Sportif Grevenmacher
Founded:	1909
Address:	BP 60, 6701 Grevenmacher
Phone:	478211
Stadium:	Op Flohr
Capacity:	3,500

Euro Record	P	W	D	L	F	A
CC:	0	0	0	0	0	0
CWC:	0	0	0	0	0	0
UEFA:	0	0	0	0	0	0
TOTAL:	0	0	0	0	0	0

CSKA Sofia — Bulgaria

The Army club played under various names, including CDNA Sofia between 1949 and 1966, as other clubs were absorbed. Following disbanding in 1985, reformed as Stredets in 1985, became CFKA Stredets in 1987, and CSKA Sofia in 1989. 27 times league champions, six times cup winners. Bulgaria's first entrant in the Champions' Cup, 1956–57. Champions' Cup semi-finalists twice and Cup-Winners' Cup semi-finalists once.

Full Name:	FC CSKA
Founded:	1948
Address:	Bul Dragan Zankov 3, Sofia
Phone:	2-662036
Stadium:	Stadion Narodna Anna
Capacity:	35,000
Colours:	Red, Red, Red

Euro Record	P	W	D	L	F	A
CC:	88	36	15	37	128	130
CWC:	22	12	0	10	49	29
UEFA:	16	3	5	8	16	29
TOTAL:	126	51	20	55	193	188

CC: (22) 56-57 (Q), 57-58 (1), 58-59 (2), 59-60 (1), 60-61 (2), 61-62 (1), 62-63 (2), 66-67 (S), 69-70 (1), 71-72 (2), 72-73 (2), 73-74 (2), 75-76 (1), 76-77 (1), 0-81 (Q), 81-82 (S), 82-83 (2), 83-84 (2), 87-88 (1), 89-90 (Q), 90-91 (2), 92-93 (1)
CWC: (5) 65-66 (2), 70-71 (2), 74-75 (1), 88-89 (S), 93-94 (2)
UEFA: (7) 77-78 (1), 78-79 (1), 79-80 (1), 84-85 (2), 86-87 (1), 91-92 (1), 91-92 (2)

Deportivo La Coruna — Spain

Highest league position, runnners-up, achieved in 1949–50 and 1993–94, missing out on goal difference on the latter occasion. Promoted as division two runners-up in 1990–91, they survived the relegation play-offs in 1991–92.

Full Name:	Real Club Deportivo La Coruna
Founded:	1904
Address:	Plaza de Pontevedra 19-1, 15003 Coruna
Phone:	981-259500
Stadium:	Riazor
Capacity:	28,956

Euro Record	P	W	D	L	F	A
CC:	0	0	0	0	0	0
CWC:	0	0	0	0	0	0
UEFA:	6	2	1	3	7	4
TOTAL:	6	2	1	3	7	4

CC: (0)
CWC: (0)
UEFA: (1) 93-94 (3)

Dynamo Bucharest — Romania

Founded on the merger of Ciocanul and Unirea Tricolour, the 1941 league champions and themselves a 1926 amalgamation of Unirea and Tricolour. 14 subsequent league championships and seven cup wins. They were Romania's first representative in Europe, taking part in the 1956–57 Champions' Cup. They reached the Cup-Winners' Cup semi-finals in 1989–90.

Full Name:	FC Dinamo Bucharest
Founded:	1948
Address:	Stefan cel Mare 9, Bucharest
Phone:	990-105700
Stadium:	Dinamo
Capacity:	18,000
Colours:	Red, Red, Red

Euro Record	P	W	D	L	F	A
CC:	52	21	7	24	81	81
CWC:	20	8	4	8	25	18
UEFA:	32	12	7	16	54	41
TOTAL:	104	41	18	48	160	140

CC: (14) 90-91 (2), 56-57 (2), 62-63 (1), 63-64 (2), 64-65 (2), 65-66 (2), 71-72 (2), 73-74 (2), 75-76 (1), 77-78 (1), 82-83 (2), 83-84 (S), 84-85 (2), 92-93 (2)
CWC: (5) 68-69 (2), 86-87 (1), 87-88 (1), 88-89 (Q), 89-90 (S)
UEFA: (9) 66-67 (3), 70-71 (2), 74-75 (2), 76-77 (1), 79-80 (2), 81-82 (3), 85-86 (1), 91-92 (2), 93-94 (1)

Dinamo Minsk † — Belarus

Known as Dynamo, Spartak and, until 1962, as Belarus. Soviet champions once, in 1982, which gave them their European debut as Soviet representatives. Reached the quarter-final of all three European tournaments during the 1980s. In the last three seasons of the Soviet league finished 9th, 12th and 8th, and have since been Belarus league champions three times in succession.

Full Name:	Dinamo Minsk
Founded:	1928
Address:	ul. Kirov 8, 220600 Minsk
Phone:	(1072) 270990/272321
Stadium:	Dinamo
Capacity:	50,050

Euro Record		P	W	D	L	F	A
	CC:	8	3	3	2	16	14
	CWC:	6	2	2	2	6	4
	UEFA:	14	7	2	5	22	13
	TOTAL:	28	12	7	9	44	31

CC: (2)   83-84 (Q), 93-94 (1)
CWC: (1)   87-88 (Q)
UEFA: (3)   84-85 (Q), 86-87 (1), 88-89 (2)

Dynamo Moscow — Russia

Founded 1923, but their origins were in the 1880s when formed by British cotton mill owners. The Orekhovo Klub Sport became Morozovstia, a prominent Moscow league club, later being adopted by the Soviet Electrical Trade Union. Eleven times Soviet champions and six times cup winners. Sixth in the last season of the Soviet league in 1991. Their European debut came in the 1971–72 Cup-Winners' Cup, in which they were losing finalists.

Full Name:	Dynamo Moscow
Founded:	1923
Address:	Lenningradski Pr. 36, 125190 Moscow
Phone:	2145463
Stadium:	Dinamo
Capacity:	50,475

Euro Record		P	W	D	L	F	A
	CC:	0	0	0	0	0	0
	CWC:	29	15	8	6	46	25
	UEFA:	24	8	6	10	26	32
	TOTAL:	53	23	14	16	72	57

CC: (0)
CWC: (5)   71-72 (F), 77-78 (2), 77-78 (S), 79-80 (Q), 84-85 (S)
UEFA: (7)   74-75 (2), 76-77 (1), 80-81 (1), 82-83 (1), 87-88 (2), 91-92 (3), 92-93 (3), 93-94 (1)

Dynamo Tbilisi † — Georgia

Joined the Soviet league for its second campaign in the autumn of 1936. Left that league in 1990 when the Georgian FA resigned from the Soviet FA never having been relegated and having been champions twice. Also Soviet cup winners twice and Soviet representatives in Europe, winning the Cup-Winners' Cup in 1981. As Georgia representatives won their first Champions' Cup preliminary round tie, 1993-94, but were later disqualified due to bribery charges.

Full Name:	Iberya Tblisi
Founded:	1925
Address:	Digomski Massiv, III Kvartal, 380009 Tbilisi
Phone:	7 8832 98 40 17
Stadium:	Dynamo
Capacity:	50,000

Euro Record		P	W	D	L	F	A
	CC:	6	2	1	3	10	10
	CWC:	21	11	3	7	30	17
	UEFA:	26	13	5	8	39	32
	TOTAL:	53	26	9	18	76	57

CC: (2)   79-80 (2), 93-94 (P)
CWC: (6)   76-77 (2), 80-81 (W), 81-82 (S), 71-72 (1), 82-83 (1), 89-90 (1)
UEFA: (6)   72-73 (1), 73-74 (3), 77-78 (3), 78-79 (2), 82-83 (1), 87-88 (3)

Eintracht Frankfurt — Germany

West German champions just once, in 1959. Bundesliga founder members in 1963 but have never finished higher than third. Four times West German cup winners. Took part in the first Fairs Cup competition, 1956–58, and in 1960 they were Champions' Cup runners-up. Won the UEFA Cup in 1979–80.

Full Name:	SH Eintracht Frankfurt
Founded:	1899
Address:	Am Erlenburch 25, 6000 Frankfurt am Main 60
Phone:	69-4209700
Stadium:	Waldstadion
Capacity:	61,146
Colours:	Red/Black, Black, Black

Euro Record		P	W	D	L	F	A
	CC:	7	4	2	1	23	15
	CWC:	24	14	3	7	41	23
	UEFA:	66	33	11	22	130	74
	TOTAL:	97	51	16	30	194	112

CC: (1)   59-60 (F)
CWC: (4)   74-75 (2), 75-76(S), 81-82 (Q), 88-89 (Q)
UEFA: (13)   56-58 (1), 64-65 (1), 66-67 (S), 67-68 (1), 68-69 (3), 72-73 (1), 77-78 (Q), 79-80 (W), 80-81 (3), 90-91 (1), 91-92 (2), 92-93 (2), 93-94 (Q)

Fenerbahce — Turkey

One of the clubs from the country's capital, whose league they won nine times. They have been domestic league champions a record 12 times, and four times cup winners. First Turkish participants in the Cup-Winners' Cup 1963–64 when they were quarter-finalists, progress never bettered.

Full Name:	Fenerbahce Spor Kulubu
Founded:	1907
Address:	Fenerbahce Burnu, Kadikoy, Istanbul
Phone:	(1) 3306643/3450940
Stadium:	Fenerbahce
Capacity:	40,000

Euro Record		P	W	D	L	F	A
	CC:	33	9	4	20	30	70
	CWC:	8	3	1	4	11	11
	UEFA:	24	8	3	13	28	47
	TOTAL:	65	20	8	37	69	128

CC: (12)   59-60 (2), 61-62 (2), 64-65 (1), 65-66 (1), 68-69 (2), 70-71 (1), 74-75 (2), 75-76 (1), 78-79 (1), 83-84 (1), 85-86 (2), 89-90 (1)
CWC: (2)   63-64 (Q), 79-80 (1)
UEFA: (9)   71-72 (1), 72-73 (1), 73-74 (2), 76-77 (1), 77-78 (1), 80-81 (1), 84-85 (1), 90-91 (2), 92-93 (2)

Flora Tallinn † — Estonia

Won their first major honour in 1993-94 securing the Estonian league title. After finishing level on points they beat Norma Tallinn in a play-off. No previous European experience.

Full Name:	FC Flora Tallinn
Address:	A. Kopi 9-10, Tallinn EE 0031
Phone:	(2) 451706
Stadium:	Kadriog
Capacity:	6,000

Euro Record	P	W	D	L	F	A
CC:	0	0	0	0	0	0
CWC:	0	0	0	0	0	0
UEFA:	0	0	0	0	0	0
TOTAL:	0	0	0	0	0	0

GI Gotu † — Faeroe Islands

Domestic league champions four times (1983, 1986, 1987 and 1993) and cup winners twice (1983 and 1985). No previous European experience.

Full Name: Gotu Itrottarfelag (GI)
Founded: 1926
Address: 510 Gotu
Phone: 41022
Stadium: Gotu
Capacity: 3,000

Euro Record	P	W	D	L	F	A
CC:	0	0	0	0	0	0
CWC:	0	0	0	0	0	0
UEFA:	0	0	0	0	0	0
TOTAL:	0	0	0	0	0	0

GKS Katowice — Poland

The Gorniczy Klub Katowice were founded 1964. Katowice is 170 miles south west of the capital near the Czech border. Three times domestic league runners-up, the first in 1988, and twice cup winners.

Full Name: Gorniczy Klub Sportowy Katowice
Founded: 1964
Address: Al. Korfantego 117a, 40-157 Katowice
Phone: (832) 597570/583025/581275
Stadium: GKS
Capacity: 14,000

Euro Record	P	W	D	L	F	A
CC:	0	0	0	0	0	0
CWC:	10	3	2	5	10	14
UEFA:	12	1	2	9	8	22
TOTAL:	22	4	4	14	18	36

CC: (0)
CWC: (3) 86-87 (2), 91-92 (2), 93-94 (1)
UEFA: (5) 70-71 (1), 87-88 (1), 88-89 (1), 90-91 (2), 92-93 (1)

Gornik Zabrze — Poland

Founded in Katowice, Silesia, in 1948. Now have the record number of championship wins, 14, including five in a row during 1963–67. Domestic cup winners six times. Champions' Cup quarter-finalists in 1968, Cup-Winners' Cup runners-up in 1970.

Full Name: Klub Sportowy Gornik Zabrze
Founded: 1948
Address: ul. Roosevelta 81, 41-800 Zabrze
Phone: (832) 714926/712942
Stadium: Gornik
Capacity: 22,500

Euro Record	P	W	D	L	F	A
CC:	42	22	5	15	70	64
CWC:	16	9	3	4	38	20
UEFA:	8	1	3	4	10	16
TOTAL:	66	32	11	23	118	100

CC: (12) ,61-62 (1), 63-64 (2), 64-65 (1), 65-66 (2), 66-67 (2), 67-68 (Q), 71-72 (1), 72-73 (2), 85-86 (1), 86-87 (1), 87-88 (2), 88-89 (2)
CWC: (2) 69-70 (F), 70-71 (Q)
UEFA: (4) 74-75 (1), 77-78 (2), 89-90 (1), 91-92 (1)

Hafnarfjordur — Iceland

Founded in 1929, but have attained no domestic honours. Known as IBH Hafnarfjordur until 1961. League runners-up in 1989 and 1993 and twice cup runners-up.

Full Name: Fimlekafelag Hafnarfjordur (FH)
Founded: 1929
Address: Knattspyrnudeild, Kaplakrika, 22 Hafnarfjordur
Phone: (1) 652534/650711/53834
Stadium: Kaplakrika
Capacity: 3,000

Euro Record	P	W	D	L	F	A
CC:	0	0	0	0	0	0
CWC:	0	0	0	0	0	0
UEFA:	2	0	1	1	3	5
TOTAL:	2	0	1	1	3	5

CC: (0)
CWC: (0)
UEFA: (1) 90-91 (1)

Hapoel Beersheba — Israel

Founded in 1949 and domestic league champions in 1975 and 1976. Finished third in 1993–94. No previous European experience.

Full Name: Hapoel Beersheba
Founded: 1949
Address: Derech H'nesiem St., Moetzet Hapoalim, Beer Sheva 84105
Phone: (057) 463011
Stadium: Municipal
Capacity: 17,000

Euro Record	P	W	D	L	F	A
CC:	0	0	0	0	0	0
CWC:	0	0	0	0	0	0
UEFA:	0	0	0	0	0	0
TOTAL:	0	0	0	0	0	0

HB — Faeroe Islands

Fourteen times league champions, the first in 1955. One of the clubs from the capital and have won the cup more than any other – 11 times.

Full Name: Havnar Boltfelag (HB)
Founded: 1904
Address: Postrum 1333, 110 Torshavn
Phone: 14046/17898
Stadium: Gundadalur
Capacity: 8,000

Euro Record	P	W	D	L	F	A
CC:	0	0	0	0	0	0
CWC:	4	1	0	3	3	8
UEFA:	0	0	0	0	0	0
TOTAL:	4	1	0	3	3	8

CC: (0)
CWC: (0) 93-94 (1)
UEFA: (0)

Hibernians — Malta

Seven times league champions, nine times runners-up. Cup winners five times and runners-up nine times, securing their first double in 1982. Based in Paola to the south-east of the capital, they were Malta's first Cup-Winners' Cup entrants, 1961–62. Reached the second round of that competition the following season, a feat not subsequently beaten by a team from the island.

Full Name: Hibernians FC
Founded: 1931
Address: Hibernians Football Ground, Corradino
Phone: 802544
Stadium: National, Ta' Qali
Capacity: 18,000

Euro Record	P	W	D	L	F	A
CC:	12	1	2	9	8	36
CWC:	10	2	2	6	4	17
UEFA:	10	1	0	9	3	45
TOTAL:	32	4	4	24	15	98

CC: (6) 61-62 (1), 67-68 (1), 69-70 (1), 79-80 (1), 81-82 (1), 82-83 (1)
CWC: (4) 62-63 (2), 70-71 (1), 71-72 (1), 80-81 (1)
UEFA: (6) 68-69, 74-75, 76-77, 78-79, 86-87, 90-91

IA Akranes † — Iceland

First club from outside the capital to win the league, and they now have 14 titles and have been runners-up 11 times. They have won the cup five times. Relegated in 1990, but promoted as champions at first attempt. Reached the second round of the Champions' Cup 1975-76.

Full Name: Knattspyrnufelag Ithrottiabanidalags Akranes
Founded: 1946
Address: Postholf 30, 300 Akranes
Phone: (3) 13311/11163
Stadium: Akranesvollur
Capacity: 3,000

Euro Record	P	W	D	L	F	A
CC:	18	3	4	11	18	34
CWC:	0	0	0	0	0	0
UEFA:	10	0	1	9	2	48
TOTAL:	28	3	5	20	20	82

CC: (7) 71-72 (1), 75-76 (2), 76-77 (1), 78-79 (1), 84-85 (1), 85-86 (1), 93-94 (1)
CWC: (4) 77-78 (1), 79-80 (1), 83-84 (1), 87-88 (1)
UEFA: (5) 70-71 (1), 80-81 (1), 86-87 (1), 88-89 (1), 89-90 (1)

Inter Bratislava — Slovakia

Formed in 1942 and known early on as Red Star, they became Slonaft in 1962 and Internatacional in 1965. Amalgamated with ZTS Petrzalka in 1986 to become ZTS, and adopted current name in 1990. Czechoslovakian league runners-up in 1975 and 1977 and cup runners-up three times in the 1980s.

Full Name: ASK Inter Slovnaft Bratislava
Founded: 1942
Address: Vajnorska 100, 832 84 Bratislava
Phone: (07) 68887
Stadium: Pasienky
Capacity: 25,000

Euro Record	P	W	D	L	F	A
CC:	4	3	1	0	8	6
CWC:	6	1	1	4	4	13
UEFA:	18	11	0	7	43	23
TOTAL:	28	15	2	11	55	42

CC: (1) 59-60 (2)
CWC: (2) 84-85 (2), 88-89 (1)
UEFA: (4) 75-76 (3), 77-78 (2), 83-84 (2), 90-91 (2)

Inter Cardiff — Wales

Formed as successors to an amateur side playing in South Wales local football. No major honours and missed out on the 1994 League of Wales championship on the last day of the inaugural season.

Full Name: Inter Cardiff FC
Founded: 1990
Address: 7 Lloyd Avenue, Barry, South Glamorgan CF6 6BT
Phone: (0446) 734389
Stadium: Ninian Park
Capacity: 24,000

Euro Record	P	W	D	L	F	A
CC:	0	0	0	0	0	0
CWC:	0	0	0	0	0	0
UEFA:	0	0	0	0	0	0
TOTAL:	0	0	0	0	0	0

Internazionale — Italy

Founded as an offshoot of neighbours Milan, they won the Italian championship within two seasons. Outside influences brought a change in name to Ambrosiana during the 1930s and much of the 1940s, but they continued to periodically win league honours. Eclipsed by their neighbour's achievements in the late 1950s, they came back to win three championships and twice win the Champions' Cup and World Club Cup in the early 1960s. Subsequently three more titles brought their total to 13. They have won the domestic cup three times and won the UEFA Cup in 1991 and 1994.

Full Name: FC Internazionale Milano SpA
Founded: 1908
Address: Piazza Eleonora Duse 1, 20122 Milan, Italy
Phone: 2-782531
Stadium: Giuseppe Meazza
Capacity: 75,510
Colours: Blue/ Black, Black, Black/Blue

Euro Record	P	W	D	L	F	A
CC:	51	27	14	10	74	38
CWC:	12	6	2	4	22	9
UEFA:	129	63	27	39	210	127
TOTAL:	192	96	43	53	306	174

CC: (7) 63-64 (W), 64-65 (W), 65-66 (S), 66-67 (F), 71-72 (F), 80-81 (S), 89-90 (1)
CWC: (2) 78-79 (Q), 82-83 (Q)
UEFA: (21) 57-58 (1), 59-60 (Q), 60-61 (S), 61-62 (Q), 69-70 (S), 70-71 (1), 72-73 (3), 73-74 (1), 74-75 (2), 76-77 (1), 77-78 (1), 79-80 (2), 81-82 (2), 83-84 (3), 84-85 (S), 85-86 (S), 86-87, (Q), 87-88 (3), 88-89 (3), 90-91 (W), 91-92 (1), 93-94 (W)

FC Jazz † — Finland

Based in Pori, the venue of the annual jazz festival, on the Baltic coast on the far west of the country. Relegated from the top division in 1988, they were promoted again in 1990 and changed their name from Porin Pallo-Torerit for the 1992 season. Third in the league in 1992, then their best ever, the 1993 championship.

Full Name: FC Jazz
Founded: 1934
Address: Isolinnankatu 2, 28 100 Pori
Phone: (939) 331999
Stadium: Porin
Capacity: 10,000

Euro Record	P	W	D	L	F	A
CC:	0	0	0	0	0	0
CWC:	0	0	0	0	0	0
UEFA:	0	0	0	0	0	0
TOTAL:	0	0	0	0	0	0

Juventus — Italy

The Turin club founded by students under English and Swiss influences as Sport Club Juventusin 1897, adopted their celebrated black and white stripes in 1903. During World War One adopted by the owners of car makers Fiat. Founders of the league when first arranged on the current format in 1928–29, finishing third. Never relegated, they have won the championship 22 times, the last in 1986, and the domestic cup a record eight times. Won the Champions' Cup in 1985 and the Cup-Winners' Cup in 1984, and they have also won the UEFA Cup (three times), the Super Cup and the World Club Cup.

Full Name:	Juventus FC SpA
Founded:	1897
Address:	Piazza Crimea 7, 10147 Torino
Phone:	11-6509706
Stadium:	Delle Alpi
Capacity:	70,012
Colours:	White/Black, White, White/Black

Euro Record	P	W	D	L	F	A
CC:	77	41	15	21	124	70
CWC:	27	17	5	5	53	19
UEFA:	123	78	17	28	232	101
TOTAL:	227	136	37	54	409	190

CC: (14) 58-59 (1), 60-61 (1), 61-62 (Q), 67-68 (S), 72-73 (F), 73-74 (1), 75-76 (2), 77-78 (S), 78-79 (1), 81-82 (2), 82-83 (F), 84-85 (W), 85-86 (W), 86-87 (2)
CWC: (4) 65-66 (1), 79-80 (S), 83-84 (W), 90-91 (S)
UEFA: (15) 63-64 (Q), 64-65 (F), 66-67 (Q), 68-69 (2), 69-70 (2), 70-71 (F), 71-72 (Q), 74-75 (S), 76-77 (W), 80-81 (2), 87-88 (2), 88-89 (Q), 89-90 (W), 92-93 (W), 93-94 (Q)

Kaiserslautern — Germany

West German champions twice and runners-up three times. Bundesliga founder members in 1963 when they finished 12th. Champions in 1991, having won the West German cup for the first time the previous season. Reached the UEFA Cup semi-final in 1982.

Full Name:	FC Kaiserslautern
Founded:	1900
Address:	Postfach 2427, 67653 Kaiserslautern
Phone:	(0631) 12008
Stadium:	Fritz Walter Stadion
Capacity:	38,500

Euro Record	P	W	D	L	F	A
CC:	0	0	0	0	0	0
CWC:	2	1	0	1	1	2
UEFA:	50	27	4	19	105	65
TOTAL:	52	28	4	20	106	67

CC: (0)
CWC: (1) 90-91 (1)
UEFA: (8) 72-73 (Q), 76-77 (2), 79-80 (Q), 80-81 (2), 81-82 (S), 82-83 (Q), 83-84 (1), 92-93 (3)

Kispest Honved — Hungary

Budapest Kispest, named after a district of the country's capital, had one Cup win and a league runners-up spot before the war, having finished 11th out of 12 in their first domestic league season, 1916–17. Became Kispesti AC on turning professional in 1926. Absorbed into the new Ministry of Sports team Honved in 1949. Mitropa Cup winners in 1959. Took present name in 1991. All told 13 times league champions and four times cup winners.

Full Name:	Kispest-Honved Futball Club
Founded:	1909
Address:	Ujtemeto utca 1, 1194 Budapest
Phone:	1-2671602/2671614
Stadium:	Jozsef Bozsik
Capacity:	15,000

Euro Record	P	W	D	L	F	A
CC:	28	12	3	13	44	50
CWC:	12	5	1	6	25	17
UEFA:	36	15	5	16	62	59
TOTAL:	76	32	9	35	131	126

CC: (9) 56-57 (2), 80-81 (2), 84-85 (1), 85-86 (2), 86-87 (1), 88-89 (1), 89-90 (2), 91-92 (2), 93-94 (1)
CWC: (3) 64-65 (1), 65-66 (Q), 70-71 (2)
UEFA: (7) 72-73 (2), 73-74 (3), 75-76 (2), 76-77 (2), 78-79 (Q), 83-84 (2), 87-88 (3)

Lazio — Italy

The Rome-based club reached the league championship final in the days before a single league format, only to lose on each occasion. It was 1958 before they won a major honour, the Italian cup, but they were relegated to Serie B for the first time in 1961. Two seasons after promotion, 1973–74, they won their only championship title but were unable to take up a Champions' Cup place because of disciplinary action following crowd trouble. After a further period in Serie B, they returned again to the top flight in 1988 when Serie A was increased in size.

Full Name:	Societa Sportiva Lazio SpA
Founded:	1900
Address:	Via Margutta 54, 00187 Roma
Phone:	6-6781843
Stadium:	Olimpico
Capacity:	82,656
Colours:	Sky Blue, Sky Blue, Sky Blue

Euro Record	P	W	D	L	F	A
CC:	0	0	0	0	0	0
CWC:	0	0	0	0	0	0
UEFA:	18	8	1	9	25	30
TOTAL:	18	8	1	9	25	30

CC: (0)
CWC: (0)
UEFA: (5) 70-71 (1), 73-74 (2), 75-76 (2), 77-78 (2), 93-94 (2)

Levski Sofia † — Bulgaria

Founded by teenagers as Levski and subsequently drew players from Government ministries. Amalgamated with Spartak Sofia in 1969 and became Levski-Spartak. Following disbanding in 1985, reformed as Vitosha (the name of a nearby mountain), but became Levski Sofia in 1989. League champions 19 times and six times winners of the Bulgarian Cup. UEFA Cup quarter-finalists 1975–76.

Full Name:	FC Levski 1914
Founded:	1914
Address:	ul. Todorini Kukli 47, Sofia 1515
Phone:	(02) 457013/476064/453071
Stadium:	Georgi Asparuchov
Capacity:	60,000

Euro Record	P	W	D	L	F	A
CC:	24	5	5	14	36	47
CWC:	28	12	3	13	57	43
UEFA:	30	10	7	13	44	57
TOTAL:	82	27	15	40	137	147

CC: (8)	65-66 (2), 70-71 (P), 74-75 (1), 77-78 (2), 79-80 (1), 84-85 (2), 88-89 (1), 93-94 (2)
CWC: (8)	67-68 (1), 69-70 (Q), 71-72 (1), 76-77 (Q), 86-87 (Q), 87-88 (1), 91-92 (1), 92-93 (1)
UEFA: (8)	72-73 (2), 75-76 (Q), 78-79 (2), 80-81 (2), 81-82 (1), 82-83 (1), 83-84 (2), 89-90 (1)

Lillestrom SK — Norway

Five times league champions and four times cup winners, all since 1959. Reached the second round of the Champions' Cup in 1978–79.

Full Name:	Lillestrom Sportsklubb
Founded:	1917
Address:	Postboks 196, 2001 Lillestrom
Phone:	6-812341
Stadium:	Arasen
Capacity:	12,000
Colours:	Yellow, Black, Yellow

Euro Record	P	W	D	L	F	A
CC:	10	3	4	3	9	12
CWC:	10	3	0	7	11	18
UEFA:	2	0	0	2	1	5
TOTAL:	22	6	4	12	21	35

CC: (4)	90-91 (1), 78-79 (2), 87-88 (2), 77-78 (1)
CWC: (4)	79-80 (P), 82-83 (1), 86-87 (1), 93-94 (1)
UEFA: (2)	84-85 (1), 89-90 (1)

Linfield † — Northern Ireland

Founded by workers from the Linfield Spinning Mills in Belfast. A record 42 times winners of the all-Ireland and Northern Ireland championship and 32 times winners of the All-Ireland and Northern Ireland Cup. In 1994 they won their 14th double. Founder members and first champions of the All-Ireland League, 1891 and first winners of the Northern Ireland Cup, 1922. Reached the Champions' Cup quarter-final stage 1966–67.

Full Name:	Linfield FC
Founded:	1886
Address:	Windsor Park, Donegal Avenue, Belfast BT12 6LW
Phone:	(0232) 244198
Stadium:	Windsor Park
Capacity:	28,500

Euro Record	P	W	D	L	F	A
CC:	44	6	13	25	41	86
CWC:	4	2	0	2	5	6
UEFA:	8	1	2	5	4	20
TOTAL:	56	9	15	32	50	112

CC: (18)	59-60 (1), 61-62 (1), 62-63 (1), 66-67 (Q), 69-70 (1), 71-72 (1), 75-76 (1), 78-79 (1), 79-80 (P), 80-81 (1), 82-83 (1), 83-84 (1), 84-85 (2), 85-86 (1), 6-87 (1), 87-88 (1), 89-90 (1), 93-94 (1)
CWC: (2)	63-64 (2), 70-71 (1)
UEFA: (4)	67-68 (1), 68-69 (1), 81-82 (1), 88-89 (1)

Maritimo — Portugal

A very successful Madeira regional side, they were promoted to the first division for the first time in 1977. Relegated in 1981, but returned after one season only to be relegated immediately. Promoted again in 1985. One pre-war cup win to their name, in 1926, but otherwise no major domestic honours.

Full Name:	Clube Sport Maritimo
Founded:	1910
Address:	Rua D. Carlos l 17, 9000 Funchal
Phone:	91-23679/33063
Stadium:	Barreiros
Capacity:	13,000

Euro Record	P	W	D	L	F	A
CC:	0	0	0	0	0	0
CWC:	0	0	0	0	0	0
UEFA:	2	0	1	1	2	4
TOTAL:	2	0	1	1	2	4

CC: (0)
CWC: (0)
UEFA: (1)   93-94 (1)

Marseille — France

Nine times league champions, including five consecutive titles 1989–1993, Relegated from the top section in 1959, 1964 and 1980, they were promoted again from Division 2(A) as champions 1984. Ten times cup winners. Were runners-up in the Champions' Cup in 1991 and won the final in 1993 but did not keep the trophy and were relegated to division two again for the 1994–95 season following a bribery investigation, but were allowed to compete in the UEFA Cup for 1994–95 season.

Full Name:	Olympique de Marseille
Founded:	1898
Address:	441 Avenue du Prado, BP 124, 13257 Marseille Cedex 08
Phone:	91-765609
Stadium:	Velodrome
Capacity:	46,000
Colours:	White, White, White

Euro Record	P	W	D	L	F	A
CC:	38	22	10	6	68	42
CWC:	14	8	2	4	19	13
UEFA:	12	3	0	3	21	19
TOTAL:	64	33	12	13	108	74

CC: (6)	71-72 (2), 72-73 (1), 89-90 (S), 90-91 (F), 91-92 (2), 92-93 (W†)
CWC: (3)	69-70 (2), 76-77 (1), 87-88 (S)
UEFA: (5)	62-63 (1), 68-69 (1), 70-71 (1), 73-74 (2), 75-76 (1)

†Title stripped due to bribery scandal.

Motherwell — Scotland

Founded as Wee Alpha in 1885, becoming Motherwell the following year. Scottish league division two founder members in 1893, they joined the first division for the first time in 1903. League champions in 1932 and runners-up four times: Cup winners twice and runners-up four times.

Full Name:	Motherwell FC
Founded:	1886
Address:	Fir Park, Motherwell ML1 2QN
Phone:	(0698) 261437/8/9
Stadium:	Fir Park
Capacity:	15,500

Euro Record	P	W	D	L	F	A
CC:	0	0	0	0	0	0
CWC:	2	1	0	1	3	3
UEFA:	0	0	0	0	0	0
TOTAL:	2	1	0	1	3	3

CC: (0)
CWC: (1)   91-92 (1)
UEFA: (0)

Mura Murska — Slovenia

Founded 1946 and regional champions in 1970. Did not attain any national Yugoslav honours. Finished as runner-up in the Slovenian league in 1993–94.

Full Name:	Mura Murska Sobota
Founded:	1946
Address:	Miklosiceva 89, 69000 Murska Sobota
Phone:	(069) 21411
Stadium:	Fazanerija
Capacity:	5,000

Euro Record	P	W	D	L	F	A
CC:	0	0	0	0	0	0
CWC:	0	0	0	0	0	0
UEFA:	0	0	0	0	0	0
TOTAL:	0	0	0	0	0	0

MyPa — Finland

Promoted as champions of the first division in 1991 and finished as runners-up in 1993. Cup winners in 1992.

Full Name:	Myllykosken Pallo-47
Founded:	1947
Address:	Myllykoski Oy c/o Oksanen, 46800 Anjalankoski
Phone:	951-50352
Stadium:	Saviniemi
Capacity:	10,000

Euro Record	P	W	D	L	F	A
CC:	0	0	0	0	0	0
CWC:	2	0	0	2	1	4
UEFA:	0	0	0	0	0	0
TOTAL:	2	0	0	2	1	4

CC: (0)
CWC: (1) 93-94 (P)
UEFA: (0)

FC Nantes — France

Founded on the merger of four local sides. Became Stade de Nantes in 1945. Reached the first division for the first time in 1964 and have stayed there ever since, winning the championship six times. Domestic cup winners once and runners-up four times. They reached the Cup-Winners' Cup semi-finals in 1980.

Full Name:	Football Club de Nantes
Founded:	1943
Address:	Centre Sportif Jose-Arribas, Route de la Chapelle, 44240 La Chapelle-sur-Erdre
Phone:	40-291559
Stadium:	La Beaujoire
Capacity:	38,000

Euro Record	P	W	D	L	F	A
CC:	18	5	6	7	25	28
CWC:	16	8	1	7	35	27
UEFA:	24	4	10	10	20	38
TOTAL:	58	17	17	24	80	93

CC: (6) 65-66 (1), 66-67 (2), 73-74 (1), 77-78 (2), 80-81 (2), 83-84 (1)
CWC: (3) 70-71 (2), 78-79 (2), 79-80 (S)
UEFA: (7) 71-72 (2), 74-75 (2), 78-79 (1), 81-82 (1), 85-86 (Q), 86-87 (1), 93-94 (1)

Napoli — Italy

Formed originally in 1922 by the amalgamation of Naples (formed by foreigners in 1904) and Internazionale Napoli. The present Napoli club came into being in 1926. Founder members of the national league competition in 1929. Relegated for the first time in 1942, they spent several periods in Serie B until promoted 1965. Twice domestic league champions and three times cup winners. Won the UEFA Cup in 1989.

Full Name:	Societa Sportiva Calcio Napoli
Founded:	1926
Address:	Via Vicinale Paradisa 70, 80126 Napoli
Phone:	(081) 7661701
Stadium:	San Paola
Capacity:	72,810

Euro Record	P	W	D	L	F	A
CC:	6	2	3	1	6	3
CWC:	17	9	4	4	23	16
UEFA:	66	27	20	19	79	73
TOTAL:	89	38	27	24	108	92

CC: (2) 87-88 (1), 90-91 (2)
CWC: (2) 62-63 (Q), 76-77 (S)
UEFA: (15) 66-67 (3), 67-68 (2), 68-69 (2), 69-70 (3), 71-72 (1), 74-75 (3), 75-76 (1), 78-79 (1), 79-80 (2), 81-82 (1), 82-83 (2), 86-87 (1), 88-89 (W), 89-90 (3), 92-93 (2)

Newcastle United — England

Formed in 1882 as Newcastle East End. Moved to the other side of the city in 1892 to the home of Newcastle West End, the club's present ground, and became Newcastle United the same year. Joined the Football League in 1893. League champions four times, three in the 1900s, and six times domestic cup winners, including three times in five years in the 1950s. Spent several periods in division two and were relegated there again in 1989. Champions of the division, restyled as 'division one' in 1993, and promoted to the FA Premier Division. Fairs Cup winners in 1969 on their European debut, beating Ujpest Dozsa in both legs.

Full Name:	Newcastle United FC
Founded:	1882
Address:	St. James' Park, Newcastle-upon-Tyne NE1 4ST
Phone:	(091) 2328361
Stadium:	St. James' Park
Capacity:	37,000

Euro Record	P	W	D	L	F	A
CC:	0	0	0	0	0	0
CWC:	0	0	0	0	0	0
UEFA:	28	14	7	7	43	26
TOTAL:	28	14	7	7	43	26

CC: (0)
CWC: (0)
UEFA: (4) 68-69 (W), 69-70 (Q), 70-71 (2), 77-78 (2)

OB — Denmark

Three league championships and two cup wins to their credit, all since 1977, the last championship and cup wins coming in 1989 and 1993 respectively. Survived the relegation play-offs in 1991.

Full Name:	Odense Boldklub
Founded:	1887
Address:	Sdr. Boulevard172, 5000 Odense C, Denmark
Phone:	66-121703
Stadium:	Odense Stadion
Capacity:	24,362
Colours:	Blue/White, Blue, White

Euro Record	P	W	D	L	F	A
CC:	6	0	1	5	4	20
CWC:	14	3	4	7	18	32
UEFA:	4	0	0	4	4	11
TOTAL:	24	3	5	16	26	63

CC: (3)   78-79 (1), 83-84 (1), 90-91 (1)
CWC: (2) 91-92 (1), 93-94 (1)
UEFA: (2) 68-69 (1), 84-85 (1)

Olimpija Ljubljana †   Slovenia

Merged with Erotnost and Odred in 1962. Yugoslavian cup runners-up 1970, but no league honours before formation of Slovenian league in 1991, which they have won each time. They were the first club to represent Slovenia in Europe in the Champions' Cup, 1992–93. Domestic cup winners 1993. Their European debut for Yugoslavia came in the 1966–67 Cup-Winners' Cup

Full Name:	NK SCT Olimpija
Founded:	1945
Address:	Vodovodna 20, 61000 Ljubljana
Phone:	(061) 348397
Stadium:	Bezigrad
Capacity:	22,000

Euro Record	P	W	D	L	F	A
CC:	6	3	0	3	6	8
CWC:	2	0	1	1	2	9
UEFA:	4	0	1	3	4	11
TOTAL:	12	3	2	7	12	28

CC: (2)   92-93 (1), 93-94 (P)
CWC: (1) 70-71 (1)
UEFA: (2) 66-67 (1), 68-69 (1)

Olympiakos   Greece

Founded in 1925 out of Union Piraeus, founded 1920. Joined the domestic league in 1929, and were founder members of the unified national league in 1959–60 when they finished third. A record 25 times league champions and 19 times cup winners. First Greek entrant in the Cup-Winners' Cup, 1961–62.

Full Name:	Olympiakos
Founded:	1925
Address:	Vassileos Yeoryiou & Kountouriotou 138, 18532 Piraeus
Phone:	1-4128323
Stadium:	Karaiskakis
Capacity:	34,023
Colours:	Red/White, White, White

Euro Record	P	W	D	L	F	A
CC:	34	13	7	14	65	43
CWC:	34	14	6	14	54	45
UEFA:	28	14	5	9	52	37
TOTAL:	96	41	18	37	171	125

CC: (11) 59-60 (1), 66-67 (1), 67-68 (1), 73-74 (1), 74-75 (2), 75-76 (1), 80-81 (1), 81-82 (1), 82-83 (2), 83-84 (2), 87-88 (1)
CWC: (9) 61-62 (2), 63-64 (2), 65-66 (2), 68-69 (2), 69-70 (1), 71-72 (1), 86-87 (2), 90-91 (2), 92-93 (Q)
UEFA: (8) 72-73 (2), 76-77 (1), 77-78 (1), 78-79 (1), 79-80 (1), 84-85 (2), 89-90 (3), 93-94 (2)

Parma   Italy

Founded by locals in 1913 under the name of composer Verdi, but soon took on the name of the city, Parma Foot Ball Club, joining the Italian League in 1922. Founder members of Serie B in 1928, they were promoted but soon relegated during which time they became Parma Associazione Sportiva. They spent long periods in the doldrums and merged with newly formed Parmense, playing under that name for a short period before becoming, in 1970, Associazione Calcio Parma. In the 1980s the owner of dairy company Parmalat took an interest in the club and in 1990 promotion to Serie A was secured for the first time. Won the domestic cup in 1992, the Cup-Winners' Cup at the first attempt in 1993, and reached the final again in 1994.

Full Name:	Parma Associazione Calcio
Founded:	1913
Address:	Via Furlotti 8, 43100 Parma
Phone:	521-240019/240007
Stadium:	Ennio Tardini
Capacity:	20,480
Colours:	White, White, White

Euro Record	P	W	D	L	F	A
CC:	0	0	0	0	0	0
CWC:	18	10	4	4	20	9
UEFA:	2	0	2	0	1	1
TOTAL:	20	10	6	4	21	10

CC: (0)
CWC: (2) 92-93 (W), 93-94 (F)
UEFA: (1) 91-92 (1)

Portadown   Northern Ireland

Northern Ireland league runners-up five times before winning their first championship in 1990. Won the domestic cup for the first time in 1991 and, by retaining the championship, secured their first double. Reached the second round of the UEFA Cup in 1975, progress not bettered by any other club from Northern Ireland.

Full Name:	Portadown FC
Founded:	1924
Address:	Brownstown Road, Portadown
Phone:	(0762)
Stadium:	Shamrock Park
Capacity:	15,000

Euro Record	P	W	D	L	F	A
CC:	4	0	0	4	1	21
CWC:	2	1	0	1	4	7
UEFA:	6	1	3	2	3	12
TOTAL:	12	2	3	7	8	40

CC: (2)   90-91 (1), 91-92 (1)
CWC: (1) 62-63 (2)
UEFA: (2) 74-75 (2), 92-93 (1)

PSV   Holland

Philips Sport Vereniging (PSV) have been league champions 13 times and cup winners six times. Took part in first Champions' Cup, 1955–56, winning it for the first and only time so far in 1987–88. Played in the 1992–93 Champions' League. Won the UEFA Cup in 1977–78 and have twice reached the semi-finals of the Cup-Winners' Cup.

Full Name:	Philips Sport Vereniging
Founded:	1913
Address:	Frederiklaan 10 A, 5616 NH Eindhoven
Phone:	40-511917
Stadium:	Philips Stadion
Capacity:	29,700
Colours:	Red/ White, White, White

Euro Record	P	W	D	L	F	A
CC:	59	23	15	21	97	61
CWC:	22	13	3	6	45	17
UEFA:	44	21	7	16	74	50
TOTAL:	125	57	25	43	216	128

CC: (11) 55-56 (1), 63-64 (Q), 75-76 (S), 76-77 (2), 78-79 (2), 86-87 (1), 87-88 (W), 88-89 (Q), 89-90 (Q), 91-92 (2), 92-93 (CL)
CWC: (4) 69-70 (2), 70-71 (S), 74-75 (S), 90-91 (1)
UEFA: (10) 71-72 (3), 77-78 (W), 79-80 (2), 80-81 (2), 81-82 (2), 82-83 (1), 83-84 (2), 84-85 (2), 85-86 (2), 93-94 (1)

Rapid Bucharest — Romania

Founded as Casa Ferovarilul Rapid. In 1936 became Rapid, but changed back in 1946. Reached Mitropa Cup semi-finals in 1938. In 1950 became Locomotiva, then Rapid again in 1958. League champions for the only time in 1967, though have been runners-up since. Nine times Cup winners, their European debut came in the 1967–68 Champions' Cup.

Full Name:	Rapid Bucharest
Founded:	1923
Address:	Calea Giulesti 18, Bucharest, Romania
Phone:	0-170301
Stadium:	Giulesti
Capacity:	18,000

Euro Record	P	W	D	L	F	A
CC:	0	0	0	0	0	0
CWC:	8	3	1	4	9	13
UEFA:	12	3	0	9	13	27
TOTAL:	20	6	1	13	22	40

CC: (1) 67-68 (2)
CWC: (2) 72-73 (Q), 75-76 (1)
UEFA: (4) 68-69 (1), 69-70 (1), 71-72 (3), 93-94 (1)

Real Madrid — Spain

One of the world's best-known club sides. Formed by students in the late 1890s, and formalised as Madrid FC in 1902. In 1920 King Alfonso XIII allowed the club to add Real (Royal) to the title. Founder members of the Spanish league and first runners-up, 1929. Now have 25 league titles and 17 cup wins. Were Spain's first representative in Europe by taking part in the first Champions' Cup, 1955–56. Champions' Cup winners 1956, 1957, 1958, 1959, 1960 and 1966 and runners-up 1962, 1964 and 1981. Cup-Winners' Cup runners-up 1971 and 1983 and UEFA cup winners 1985 and 1986. World Club champions 1960.

Full Name:	Real Madrid Club de Futbol
Founded:	1902
Address:	Avda. Concha Espina 1, 28038 Madrid
Phone:	1-2500600
Stadium:	Santiago Bernabeu
Capacity:	90,200
Colours:	White, White, White

Euro Record	P	W	D	L	F	A
CC:	173	102	25	46	407	195
CWC:	31	16	9	6	57	24
UEFA:	58	30	9	19	100	62
TOTAL:	262	148	43	71	564	281

CC: (27) 55-56 (W), 56-57 (W), 57-58 (W), 58-59 (W), 59-60 (W), 60-61 (2), 61-62 (F), X62-63 (1), 63-64 (F), 64-65 (1), 64-65 (Q), 65-66 (W), 66-67 (Q), 67-68 (S), 68-69 (2), 70-70 (2), 72-73 (S), 75-76 (S), 76-77 (2), 78-79 (2), 79-80 (W), 80-81 (F), 86-87 (S), 87-88 (S), 88-89 (S), 89-90 (2), 90-91 (Q)
CWC: (4) 70-71 (F), 74-75 (Q), 82-83 (F), 93-94 (Q)
UEFA: (8) 71-72 (2), 73-74 (1), 81-82 (Q), 83-84 (1), 84-85 (W), 85-86 (W), 91-92 (S), 92-93 (1)

Rosenborg † — Norway

The Trondheim-based club have won the league championship eight times, all since 1967. They have won the cup five times, the first time in 1960, the year they reached the top division for the first time. Reached the second round of the UEFA Cup in 1971–72 and of the Champions' Cup in 1986–87.

Full Name:	Rosenborg Ballklub
Founded:	1917
Address:	Boks 4126, 7002 Trondheim
Phone:	(07) 939300/940240
Stadium:	Lerkendal
Capacity:	28,455

Euro Record	P	W	D	L	F	A
CC:	18	4	3	11	17	43
CWC:	4	2	0	2	7	8
UEFA:	12	6	0	6	18	27
TOTAL:	34	12	3	19	42	78

CC: (7) 68-69 (1), 70-71 (1), 72-73 (1), 86-87 (2), 89-90 (1), 91-92 (1), 93-94 (1)
CWC: (1) 65-66 (2)
UEFA: (5) 69-70 (1), 71-72 (2), 74-75 (1), 90-91 (1), 92-93 (1)

Rotor Volograd — Russia

Founded as Traktor Stalingrad. Known as Torpedo Stalingrad between 1948 and 1957. The city's name was changed in 1970. Reached the Soviet top division for the first time in 1938, and although relegated were promoted again.

Full Name:	Rotor Volgograd
Founded:	1933
Address:	prospekt Lenina 76, 400 005 Volgograd
Phone:	(8442) 348371
Stadium:	Central
Capacity:	40,000

Euro Record	P	W	D	L	F	A
CC:	0	0	0	0	0	0
CWC:	0	0	0	0	0	0
UEFA:	0	0	0	0	0	0
TOTAL:	0	0	0	0	0	0

FC ROMAR † — Lithuania

No Russian Supreme League experience before participating in the second Lithuanian championship, 1992–93, when they finished sixth. Surprise league champions in 1993–94 – their first honour.

Full Name:	FC ROMAR Mazeikei
Address:	Vaizganto Street 10-22
Phone:	370 93 66 822

Euro Record	P	W	D	L	F	A
CC:	0	0	0	0	0	0
CWC:	0	0	0	0	0	0
UEFA:	0	0	0	0	0	0
TOTAL:	0	0	0	0	0	0

Royal Antwerp — Belgium

Founded by English dock workers. Belgian league founder members and first runners-up, 1896. Four times national champions, the last in 1957 which gave them their first European experience. Domestic cup winners in 1955 and 1992 when they won a penalty shoot-out 9-8. Were runners-up in the Cup-Winners' Cup on their only appearance in the competition, in 1993.

Full Name:	Royal Antwerp FC
Founded:	1880
Address:	Oude Basuilbaan 54/a, 2100 Deurne, Antwerp, Belgium
Phone:	3-3246270
Stadium:	Bosuil
Capacity:	35,000
Colours:	Red/White, Red, Red

Euro Record	P	W	D	L	F	A
CC:	2	0	0	2	1	8
CWC:	9	2	4	3	14	14
UEFA:	42	15	9	18	57	59
TOTAL:	53	17	13	23	72	81

CC: (1)   57-58 (2)
CWC: (1)   92-93 (F)
UEFA: (11)   64-65 (2), 65-66 (2), 66-67 (2), 67-68 (1), 74-75 (2), 75-76 (2), 83-84 (2), 88-89 (1), 89-90 (Q), 90-91 (1), 93-94 (2)

FC Shumen   Bulgaria

Won promotion to the first division in 1992–93 finishing fourth but qualifying for Europe for the first time due to ban on third-placed club Botev.

Full Name: FC Shumen
Founded: 1919
Address: Dobri Voinkov 179, Schumen
Phone: 054 69894
Stadium: Panaiot Volov
Capacity: 30,000

Euro Record	P	W	D	L	F	A
CC:	0	0	0	0	0	0
CWC:	0	0	0	0	0	0
UEFA:	0	0	0	0	0	0
TOTAL:	0	0	0	0	0	0

Seraing   Belgium

Seraing is a town five miles south west of Liege city centre to the east of the country. Second division champions and promoted to the top division in 1993. Third in the second division, they had missed out in the play-offs in 1992 having been promoted to the second division in 1992 following play-off success. Had five seasons in the top flight after their first promotion in 1982.

Full Name: RFC Seraing
Founded: 1900
Address: Rue de la Boverie 253, 4100 Seraing
Phone: 32 41 372825
Stadium: Stade Communal
Capacity: 15,000

Euro Record	P	W	D	L	F	A
CC:	0	0	0	0	0	0
CWC:	0	0	0	0	0	0
UEFA:	0	0	0	0	0	0
TOTAL:	0	0	0	0	0	0

Shamrock Rovers †   Republic of Ireland

A record 15 times League of Ireland champions and 24 times cup winners. Were the first club from the Republic to play in the Champions' Cup, while they have reached the second round of both the other European competitions (Cup-Winners' Cup three times and the Fairs/UEFA Cup twice), neither feat bettered by any other Republic team.

Full Name: Shamrock Rovers FC
Founded: 1899
Address: 11-12 York Road, Ringsend, Dublin 4
Phone: (01) 6685433
Stadium: Royal Dublin Society Showgrounds
Capacity: 22,000

Euro Record	P	W	D	L	F	A
CC:	14	0	4	10	7	28
CWC:	16	5	2	9	19	27
UEFA:	8	2	2	4	11	11
TOTAL:	38	7	8	23	37	66

CC: (7)   57-58 (1), 59-60 (1), 64-65 (1), 84-85 (1), 85-86 (1), 86-87 (1), 87-88 (1)
CWC: (6)   62-63 (2), 66-67 (2), 67-68 (1), 68-69 (1), 69-70 (1), 78-79 (2)
UEFA: (3)   63-64 (1), 65-66 (2), 82-83 (2)

Shakhtyor Donetsk   Ukraine

Founded in 1936 as Shakhyorr Stalino and run by the miners' union. Took present title when the city's name was changed. Reached the Soviet top division for the first time in 1938 when they finished 11th. Relegated in 1940, 1952 and 1971 when they returned after one season and were subsequently twice runners-up. They were 12th in the Soviet table in 1991. Soviet cup winners four times. They represented the Soviet Union in both the Cup-Winners' and UEFA Cups.

Full Name: Shakhtyor Donetsk
Founded: 1936
Address: ul. Artema 86a, 340 045 Donetsk
Phone: (0622) 904126/911675/660552
Stadium: Lokomotiv
Capacity: 40,485

Euro Record	P	W	D	L	F	A
CC:	0	0	0	0	0	0
CWC:	8	4	2	2	16	12
UEFA:	10	6	1	3	14	12
TOTAL:	18	10	3	5	30	24

CC: (0)
CWC: (2)   78-79 (1), 83-84 (Q)
UEFA: (3)   76-77 (3), 79-80 (1), 80-81 (1)

FC Sion   Switzerland

Reached the national league for the first time for the 1962–63 season but were relegated in 1970. They were promoted again after just one season and have stayed in the top flight ever since. League champions once, 1992, having been runners-up the previous season. Won the domestic cup six times, the first in 1965. Reached the Cup-Winners' Cup quarter-finals in 1987.

Full Name: FC Sion
Founded: 1909
Address: Case Postale 401, 1951 Sion
Phone: (027) 224251
Stadium: Tourbillon
Capacity: 19,400

Euro Record	P	W	D	L	F	A
CC:	4	2	1	1	9	8
CWC:	20	5	7	8	23	35
UEFA:	12	6	1	5	17	20
TOTAL:	36	13	9	14	49	63

CC: (1)   92-93 (2)
CWC: (6)   65-66 (2), 74-75 (1), 80-81 (1), 82-83 (P), 86-87 (Q), 91-92 (2)
UEFA: (4)   73-74 (1), 84-85 (2), 87-88 (1), 89-90 (2)

SK Teuta † — Albania

Formed in 1925 as Teuta in the coastal town of Durres 20 miles west of the country's capital. The 1994 championship was their first honour, although they were league runners-up in 1931 and third for the next two seasons. Third again in 1993 and runners-up for the second time in 1993. Losing cup finalist in 1994. Known as Yllikug 1945–49, Puna 1950–57 and Lokomotiva until 1991.

Full Name:	Klubi Sportiv Teuta
Founded:	1925
Address:	Rruga Mujo Ulginoka, nr. 19, Durres
Phone:	2215
Stadium:	Teuta
Capacity:	10,000

Euro Record	P	W	D	L	F	A
CC:	0	0	0	0	0	0
CWC:	0	0	0	0	0	0
UEFA:	0	0	0	0	0	0
TOTAL:	0	0	0	0	0	0

Skonto Riga † — Estonia

Latvian champions in 1991 and, following a play-off, in 1992. Won the title again in 1993 and 1994. They took part in the 1992–93 Champions' Cup as Latvia's first representative.

Full Name:	Skonto Ltd
Address:	Elizabetes Str 75, Riga LV 1010.
Phone:	371 2 21 79 99
Stadium:	Tallinn

Euro Record	P	W	D	L	F	A
CC:	8	3	1	4	7	13
CWC:	0	0	0	0	0	0
UEFA:	0	0	0	0	0	0
TOTAL:	8	3	1	4	7	13

CC: (2) 92-93 (1), 93-94 (1)
CWC: (0)
UEFA: (0)

Slavia Prague — Czech Republic

Founded when Prague was in Bohemia, from part of a sports club, ACOS Prague, already ten years old. Czechoslovakian league founder members and first champions, 1925. League champions nine times, but not since 1947. Mitropa Cup winners in 1938. Known as Sokol Slavia, Dynamo Slavia and Dynamo in the seasons just after the Second World War, settling on the present name in 1977.

Full Name:	SK Slavia Praha Ips
Founded:	1893
Address:	Stadion dr. V. Vacka, 100 05 Prague 10
Phone:	2-743725/746519
Stadium:	Dr. Vacka
Capacity:	35,000

Euro Record	P	W	D	L	F	A
CC:	0	0	0	0	0	0
CWC:	2	1	0	1	1	1
UEFA:	16	6	2	8	21	25
TOTAL:	18	7	2	9	22	26

CC: (0)
CWC: (1) 74-75 (1)
UEFA: (7) 67-68 (1), 68-69 (2), 76-77 (1), 77-78 (1), 85-86 (1), 92-93 (1), 93-94 (1)

Slovan Bratislava † — Slovakia

Founded 1919 and became SK Bratislava in 1939 and Sokol Bratislava in 1953. Amalgamated with Dimitrov Bratislava in 1961 and adopted the current name. For many years were backed by the city's chemical works. Eight times Czechoslovakian league champions and five times cup winners, all in the post-war period. First Czechoslovakian entrant in the Champions' Cup, 1956–57. Cup-Winners' Cup winners in 1969.

Full Name:	Slovan SK Bratislava
Founded:	1919
Address:	Junacka 2, 832 15 Bratislava
Stadium:	Tehelne Poli
Capacity:	48,000

Euro Record	P	W	D	L	F	A
CC:	16	7	2	7	21	25
UEFA:	12	4	4	4	18	17
CWC:	25	14	3	8	40	28
TOTAL:	53	25	9	19	79	70

CC: (5) 56-57 (2), 70-71 (2), 74-75 (1), 75-76 (1), 92-93 (2)
CWC: (6) 62-63 (Q), 63-64 (Q), 68-69 (W), 69-70 (1), 82-83 (1), 89-90 (1)
UEFA: (4) 72-73 (2), 76-77 (2), 91-92 (1), 93-94 (1)

Sporting Lisbon — Portugal

League founder members 1935 and first runners-up. Had also been first runners-up in the cup competition, 1922. Now have 16 league titles and 15 cup wins. Were Portugal's first representative in European football when they took part in 1955–56 Champions' Cup. Won the Cup-Winners' Cup in 1964.

Full Name:	Sporting Clube de Portugal
Founded:	1906
Address:	Estadio Jose de Alvalade, Apartado 4120, 1503 Lisbon Codex
Phone:	1-7589021
Stadium:	Jose Alvalade
Capacity:	70,000
Colours:	Green/White, Black, Green/White

Euro Record	P	W	D	L	F	A
CC:	28	9	5	14	41	48
CWC:	36	16	8	12	76	44
UEFA:	81	37	20	24	136	87
TOTAL:	145	62	33	50	253	179

CC: (9) 55-56 (1), 58-59 (2), 61-62 (1), 62-63 (2), 66-67 (1), 70-71 (2), 74-75 (1), 80-81 (1), 82-83 (Q)
CWC: (7) 63-64 (W), 64-65 (2), 71-72 (2), 72-73 (1), 73-74 (S), 78-79 (1), 87-88 (Q)
UEFA: (17) 65-66 (2), 67-68 (3), 68-69 (2), 69-70 (2), 75-76 (2), 77-78 (1), 79-80 (1), 81-82 (3), 83-84 (2), 84-85 (2), 85-86 (Q), 86-87 (2), 88-89 (2), 89-90 (1), 90-91 (S), 91-92 (1), 92-93 (1), 93-94 (3)

Tekstilchik — Russia

No Soviet national league experience, but 11th in Division Two of the CIS League in 1991–92. Survived the relegation play-off group in 1992 to remain in the top flight of the Russian league last season.

Full Name:	Tekstilchik Kamyshin
Founded:	1958
Address:	ul. Titova 1, 403 850 Kamyshin
Phone:	(84457) 38018
Stadium:	Tekstilschik
Capacity:	7,200

Euro Record	P	W	D	L	F	A
CC:	0	0	0	0	0	0
CWC:	0	0	0	0	0	0
UEFA:	0	0	0	0	0	0
TOTAL:	0	0	0	0	0	0

FC Tirol Innsbruck — Austria

Current club founded on the amalgamation of SC Wacker (founded 1913) and WSGS Wattens (founded 1923) but changed to Swarovski-Wacker. Separated again in 1978 and in 1986 SC Wacker became Tirol Innsbruck. Reached the top division for the first time in 1964. Relegated in 1979 but returned in 1981. Seven times league champions and seven times cup winners. They reached the semi-finals of the UEFA Cup in 1987.

Full Name:	FC Innsbruck Capillaris Tirol
Founded:	1913
Address:	Resselstrasse 18/11, A6020 Innsbruck
Phone:	43 512 47 880
Stadium:	Tivoli
Capacity:	17,500

Euro Record	P	W	D	L	F	A
CC:	22	7	3	12	34	46
CWC:	18	8	3	7	27	28
UEFA:	30	11	4	15	35	47
TOTAL:	70	26	10	34	96	121

CC: (7) 71-72 (1), 72-73 (1), 73-74 (1), 75-76 (1), 77-78 (Q), 89-90 (2), 90-91 (2)
CWC: (6) 70-71 (2), 78-79 (2), 79-80 (1), 83-84 (1), 87-88 (1), 93-94 (2)
UEFA: (7) 68-69 (1), 74-75 (1), 76-77 (2), 84-85 (1), 85-86 (1), 86-87 (S), 91-92 (3)

Trabzonspor — Turkey

Trabzon is on the Black Sea coast far to the east of the country. Six times league champions and four times cup winners, with a double in 1977. Their European debut came in the 1976–77 Champions' Cup.

Full Name:	Trabzonspor Kulubu
Founded:	1967
Address:	PK 27 Havaalani alti, Trabzon
Phone:	31-50967
Stadium:	Avni Aker
Capacity:	27,500
Colours:	Claret Red/Blue, Blue, Claret Red

Euro Record	P	W	D	L	F	A
CC:	14	6	1	7	12	19
CWC:	8	3	3	2	10	12
UEFA:	14	6	4	4	21	20
TOTAL:	36	15	8	13	43	51

CC: (6) 76-77 (2), 77-78 (1), 79-80 (1), 80-81 (1), 81-82 (1), 84-85 (1)
CWC: (2) 90-91 (1), 92-93 (1)
UEFA: (4) 82-83 (1), 83-84 (1), 91-92 (3), 93-94 (2)

Trelleborgs — Sweden

Founded in 1926 but have no domestic honours. Trelleborg is a coastal town on the southern tip of Sweden.

Full Name:	Trelleborgs Fotbollforening
Founded:	1926
Address:	Hejderidaregatan 2, 231 44 Trelleborg
Phone:	(0410) 13190
Stadium:	Trelleborgs Idrottsplats
Capacity:	9,000

Euro Record	P	W	D	L	F	A
CC:	0	0	0	0	0	0
CWC:	0	0	0	0	0	0
UEFA:	0	0	0	0	0	0
TOTAL:	0	0	0	0	0	0

Turan Tauz † — Azerbaijan

Winners of the 1993–94 league in Azerbaijan. No other honours and first season in European club competition.

Full Name:	Turan FC
Address:	Bozangahli Str, Settlement, Tauz.

Euro Record	P	W	D	L	F	A
CC:	0	0	0	0	0	0
CWC:	0	0	0	0	0	0
UEFA:	0	0	0	0	0	0
TOTAL:	0	0	0	0	0	0

FC Twente — Holland

Founded 1965 on the amalgamation of Enschede (founded 1910 and national champions once, having been founder members of the National League in 1957 when they finished third) and Enschede Boys. Present club have one domestic honour, 1977 cup winners. Spent some of the 1980s in the second division. Were UEFA Cup runners-up in 1975.

Full Name:	FC Twente
Founded:	1965
Address:	JJ Van Deinselaan 30, 7541 PE Enschede
Phone:	53-310080
Stadium:	Het Diekman
Capacity:	18,000
Colours:	White/Red, Red, Red

Euro Record	P	W	D	L	F	A
CC:	0	0	0	0	0	0
CWC:	10	6	1	3	17	9
UEFA:	50	20	11	19	89	67
TOTAL:	60	26	12	22	106	76

CC: (0)
CWC: (2)   77-78 (S), 79-80 (1)
UEFA: (10) 69-70 (1), 70-71 (Q), 72-73 (S), 73-74 (3), 74-75 (F), 78-79 (1), 80-81 (2), 89-90 (1), 90-91 (1), 93-94 (1)

Universitatea Craiova — Romania

Known as Stiinta between 1950 and 1966. Reached the first division in 1964 and since 1974 have won the league championship four times and the cup five times. Reached the UEFA Cup semi-finals in 1982–83.

Full Name:	Universitatea Craiova
Founded:	1948
Address:	Str. Libertrati 9, 1100 Craiova
Phone:	41-324804
Stadium:	Central
Capacity:	40,000
Colours:	White, Blue, White

Euro Record	P	W	D	L	F	A
CC:	12	4	2	6	14	17
CWC:	10	4	2	4	19	15
UEFA:	40	20	6	14	42	39
TOTAL:	62	28	10	24	75	71

CC: (4) 74-75 (1), 80-81 (1), 81-82 (Q), 91-92 (1)
CWC: (3) 78-79 (1), 85-86 (2), 93-94 (2)
UEFA: (11) 70-71 (1), 73-74 (2), 75-76 (1), 79-80 (3), 82-83 (S), 83-84 (1), 84-85 (3), 86-87 (2), 87-88 (1), 90-91 (2), 92-93 (1)

Vardar Skopje †   FYR Macedonia

Founded 1947 as successors to the earlier club known as Gradjanski between 1922 and 1939 and Pobeda 1939 to 1947. Won first Macedonia championship by 21 points. Won Yugoslavian cup in 1961 and were sixth in the last Yugoslav national league, 1991–92.

Full Name: FK Vardar Skopje
Founded: 1947
Address: 13 Novembri, Kula 1, 9100 Skopje
Stadium: Gradski
Capacity: 28,000

Euro Record	P	W	D	L	F	A
CC:	2	0	0	2	0	6
CWC:	2	1	0	1	2	5
UEFA:	4	1	1	2	3	5
TOTAL:	8	2	1	5	5	16

CC: (1)   87-88 (1)
CWC: (1)   61-62 (2)
UEFA: (1) 85-86 (2)

Valletta   Malta

Founded 1904 as Valletta United, their name until 1939. Have gained 14 league titles and six cup wins. European debut in the 1963–64 Champions' Cup.

Full Name: Valletta FC
Founded: 1904
Address: 126 St. Lucia Street, Valletta
Phone: 224939
Stadium: National, Ta'Qali
Capacity: 35,000
Colours: White, White, White

Euro Record	P	W	D	L	F	A
CC:	14	1	0	13	6	57
CWC:	10	0	1	9	2	45
UEFA:	10	0	0	10	4	34
TOTAL:	34	1	1	32	12	136

CC: (7)   92-93 (P), 63-64 (1), 74-75 (1), 78-79 (1), 80-81 (P), 84-85 (1), 90-91 (1)
CWC: (5)   91-92 (1), 64-65 (1), 75-76 (1), 77-78 (1), 83-84 (1)
UEFA: (5) 72-73 (1), 79-80 (1), 87-88 (1), 89-90 (1), 93-94 (1)

Vitesse   Holland

Founded 1892. Runners-up in first the league championship in 1898 and four times more before the First War, though not since. Three times cup runners-up.

Full Name: Vitesse
Founded: 1892
Address: Postbus 366, 6800 AJ Arnhem
Phone: 85-425402
Stadium: Monnikenhuize
Capacity: 13,000
Colours: Yellow/Black, White, White

Euro Record	P	W	D	L	F	A
CC:	0	0	0	0	0	0
CWC:	0	0	0	0	0	0
UEFA:	14	6	2	6	14	10
TOTAL:	14	6	2	6	14	10

CC: (0)
CWC: (0)
UEFA: (3) 90-91 (3), 92-93 (3), 93-94 (1)

Zimbru †   Moldova

Have won the Moldovian national championship in its first three seasons. Previously in the Soviet Supreme League second division where they finished 19th in their last season of participation – 1992. Have played under various names, including Dinamo, Burevestnik, Moldova, Avantul and Nistru. Made their debut in Europe last season when they were eliminated in the preliminary round of the Champions' Cup.

Full Name: Zimbru
Founded: 1947
Address: 1 Butucului Street, Chisinau.
Stadium: Republican
Capacity: 23,000

Euro Record	P	W	D	L	F	A
CC:	2	0	1	1	1	3
CWC:	0	0	0	0	0	0
UEFA:	0	0	0	0	0	0
TOTAL:	2	0	1	1	1	3

CC: (1)   93-94 (P)
CWC: (0)
UEFA: (0)

Fixtures 1994–95

Belgium	408
Cyprus	408
England	409
Finland	409
France	410
Germany	410
Holland	411
Italy	411
Northern Ireland	412
Portugal	412
Republic of Ireland	413
Scotland	413
Spain	414
Diary of Events 1994–95	415

ROTHMANS PUBLICATIONS

Belgium 1994-95

	AA Gent	Cercle Bruges	Charleroi	Club Bruges	Club Liege	Endr Aalst	Germinal Ekeren	KV Mechelen	KV Oostende	Lierse SK	Royal Antwerp	RSC Anderlecht	RWD Molenbeek	Seraing	SK Beveren	SK Lommel	St Truiden	Standard Liege
AA Gent	—	19/11	1/10	31/8	1/4	21/12	15/4	17/9	18/3	6/5	4/2	21/5	22/10	21/1	20/8	3/12	18/2	4/3
Cercle Bruges	8/4	—	5/3	5/2	15/4	21/5	4/12	19/2	9/11	21/12	17/9	20/8	18/3	31/8	22/1	6/5	1/10	22/10
Charleroi	25/2	15/10	—	21/12	28/1	19/11	11/3	20/8	24/9	1/4	21/5	15/4	11/2	6/5	3/12	29/10	21/1	10/9
Club Bruges	29/1	11/9	14/5	—	20/11	16/10	12/2	30/4	28/8	26/2	27/11	12/3	15/1	2/4	30/10	25/9	10/12	8/1
Club Liege	9/11	26/11	31/8	8/4	—	4/2	10/12	21/12	22/10	21/1	29/4	18/2	1/10	18/3	4/3	21/5	20/8	17/9
Endr Aalst	14/5	8/1	9/4	5/3	11/9	—	15/1	19/3	10/12	29/1	23/10	18/9	30/4	2/10	19/2	28/8	9/11	27/11
Germinal Ekeren	27/11	30/4	23/10	18/9	7/5	21/8	—	2/10	9/4	21/5	19/2	22/1	9/11	5/2	31/8	21/12	5/3	19/3
KV Mechelen	11/2	24/9	14/1	3/12	14/5	29/10	26/2	—	10/9	11/3	6/5	1/4	28/1	15/4	19/11	15/10	7/1	27/8
KV Oostende	30/10	2/4	19/2	22/1	12/3	7/5	20/11	5/2	—	4/12	31/8	21/12	5/3	21/8	21/5	16/4	18/9	2/10
Lierse SK	10/12	14/5	9/11	1/10	27/8	31/8	7/1	22/10	29/4	—	4/3	4/2	26/11	18/2	17/9	14/1	18/3	8/4
Royal Antwerp	10/9	11/2	7/1	16/4	3/12	11/3	24/9	10/12	28/1	15/10	—	30/10	27/8	19/11	1/4	25/2	14/5	15/1
RSC Anderlecht	7/1	14/1	26/11	22/10	24/9	11/2	27/8	9/11	14/5	10/9	18/3	—	10/12	4/3	1/10	28/1	8/4	29/4
RWD Molenbeek	11/3	29/10	17/9	20/8	26/2	3/12	1/4	31/8	15/10	15/4	21/1	6/5	—	21/5	21/12	19/11	4/2	18/2
Seraing	28/8	29/1	10/12	9/11	30/10	26/2	11/9	27/11	15/1	25/9	9/4	16/10	8/1	—	12/3	12/2	30/4	14/5
SK Beveren	14/1	27/8	29/4	18/3	15/10	24/9	28/1	8/4	7/1	11/2	9/11	25/2	14/5	22/10	—	10/9	26/11	10/12
SK Lommel	29/4	10/12	18/3	18/2	7/1	21/1	14/5	4/3	26/11	20/8	1/10	31/8	8/4	17/9	4/2	—	22/10	9/11
St Truiden	24/9	25/2	27/8	6/5	14/1	1/4	15/10	21/5	11/2	29/10	21/12	19/11	10/9	3/12	15/4	11/3	—	28/1
Standard Liege	15/10	11/3	4/2	21/5	11/2	15/4	29/10	21/1	25/2	19/11	20/8	3/12	24/9	21/12	6/5	1/4	31/8	—

Cyprus 1994-95

	AEL	Anorthosis	Apoel	Apollon	Aris	ENP	Ethnikos	Nea Salamina	Olympiakos Nicosia	Omonia Aradippou	Omonia Nicosia	Pezoporikos
AEL	—	2/10	18/2	10/12	28/1	1/9	22/10	14/1	17/9	9/11	5/1	27/11
Anorthosis	28/12	—	8/1	19/2	19/11	29/10	4/12	24/9	10/11	16/10	11/9	28/1
Apoel	28/8	22/10	—	4/1	11/9	17/9	6/11	12/2	1/10	19/11	14/1	10/12
Apollon	24/9	28/8	15/10	—	10/11	7/1	11/9	3/12	29/1	28/12	20/11	29/10
Aris	5/11	31/8	26/11	11/2	—	11/12	1/10	23/10	15/1	19/2	18/9	4/1
ENP	20/11	14/1	3/12	22/10	24/9	—	11/2	27/8	4/1	11/9	5/1	1/10
Ethnikos	7/1	17/9	28/1	26/11	28/12	9/11	—	15/10	31/8	29/10	10/12	18/2
Nea Salamina	30/10	10/12	9/11	18/9	7/1	18/2	5/1	—	27/11	29/1	1/10	31/8
Olympiakos Nicosia	3/12	11/2	29/12	5/11	30/10	15/10	20/11	10/9	—	25/9	28/8	7/1
Omonia Aradippou	11/2	4/1	1/9	2/10	27/8	26/11	15/1	6/11	11/12	—	22/10	17/9
Omonia Nicosia	16/10	26/11	29/10	31/8	4/12	28/1	24/9	28/12	18/2	8/1	—	9/11
Pezoporikos	10/9	5/11	25/9	14/1	15/10	29/12	28/8	20/11	23/10	3/12	12/2	—

First two rounds of fixtures only.

England 1994–95

	Arsenal	Aston Villa	Blackburn Rovers	Chelsea	Coventry City	Crystal Palace	Everton	Ipswich Town	Leeds United	Leicester City	Liverpool	Manchester City	Manchester United	Newcastle United	Norwich City	Nottingham Forest	QPR	Sheffield Wednesday	Southampton	Tottenham Hotspur	West Ham United	Wimbledon
Arsenal	—	26/12	30/8	15/10	22/10	1/10	14/1	15/4	17/12	11/2	11/3	20/8	26/11	17/9	1/4	21/2	31/12	5/11	24/1	29/4	4/3	6/5
Aston Villa	17/4	—	4/3	27/12	8/2	27/8	10/12	10/9	2/1	22/2	6/5	8/4	5/11	1/10	15/10	22/10	14/1	26/11	24/8	25/1	18/3	11/2
Blackburn Rovers	7/3	24/9	—	18/3	27/8	8/4	10/9	24/1	27/12	23/8	15/10	17/4	22/10	6/5	25/2	14/1	26/11	11/2	10/12	5/11	2/1	21/2
Chelsea	13/5	15/4	18/9	—	5/11	4/3	26/11	22/10	11/3	8/10	17/12	31/8	26/12	1/4	20/8	25/1	29/4	14/1	22/2	11/2	1/10	31/12
Coventry City	21/1	29/8	11/3	4/2	—	2/11	13/5	8/10	17/9	25/2	3/12	29/10	29/4	17/12	19/11	26/12	1/4	15/4	24/9	31/12	18/2	20/8
Crystal Palace	25/2	11/3	31/12	24/9	11/2	—	22/10	5/11	30/8	14/1	20/8	1/4	24/1	15/10	17/12	29/4	26/12	21/2	26/11	15/4	6/5	17/9
Everton	29/10	20/8	1/4	18/2	15/10	21/1	—	31/12	3/12	24/9	19/11	11/3	25/2	15/4	4/2	30/8	17/9	26/12	6/5	17/12	1/11	29/4
Ipswich Town	27/12	1/4	19/11	21/1	6/5	4/2	8/4	—	1/11	2/1	29/10	3/12	24/9	18/2	17/9	20/8	11/3	15/10	25/2	30/8	17/4	17/12
Leeds United	23/8	29/4	15/4	27/8	18/3	7/3	21/2	11/2	—	22/10	31/12	1/10	11/10	26/12	6/5	26/11	24/1	4/3	14/1	15/10	10/12	5/11
Leicester City	2/11	3/12	17/12	6/4	1/10	29/10	4/3	29/4	21/1	—	26/12	19/11	15/4	21/8	18/2	11/3	31/8	31/12	15/10	17/9	4/2	1/4
Liverpool	28/8	8/10	13/5	24/8	22/2	10/12	25/1	14/1	8/4	17/4	—	27/12	18/3	4/3	2/1	5/11	11/2	1/10	8/3	26/11	10/9	22/10
Manchester City	10/12	31/12	26/12	8/3	14/1	10/9	27/8	22/2	25/2	25/1	15/4	—	11/3	29/4	24/9	8/10	13/5	18/3	5/11	22/10	24/8	26/11
Manchester United	18/2	4/2	21/1	17/4	2/1	19/11	1/10	4/3	1/4	27/12	17/9	9/11	—	29/10	3/12	17/12	20/8	6/5	8/4	11/3	15/10	31/8
Newcastle United	18/3	25/2	9/10	10/9	24/8	13/5	27/12	26/11	17/4	10/12	24/9	2/1	14/1	—	8/4	11/2	5/11	22/10	27/8	22/2	8/3	25/1
Norwich City	10/9	13/5	1/10	10/12	25/1	24/8	5/11	18/3	8/10	26/11	29/4	4/3	22/2	31/12	—	15/4	22/10	8/3	11/2	26/12	27/8	14/1
Nottingham Forest	3/12	21/1	29/10	19/11	17/4	2/1	8/3	10/12	18/2	27/8	4/2	6/5	22/8	2/11	27/12	—	2/10	10/9	18/3	4/3	8/4	15/10
QPR	8/4	29/10	18/2	2/1	10/9	17/4	18/3	27/8	19/11	8/3	2/11	15/10	10/12	4/2	21/1	25/2	—	24/8	27/12	6/5	3/12	24/9
Sheffield Wednesday	4/2	18/2	2/11	29/10	27/12	3/12	17/4	13/5	26/9	8/4	25/2	17/9	8/10	21/1	31/8	1/4	17/12	—	2/1	20/8	19/11	11/3
Southampton	19/11	17/12	20/8	3/12	4/3	18/2	8/10	1/10	29/10	13/5	31/8	4/2	31/12	11/3	2/11	17/9	15/4	29/4	—	1/4	21/1	26/12
Tottenham Hotspur	2/1	2/1	4/2	2/1	8/4	27/12	24/8	8/3	13/5	18/3	18/2	21/1	27/8	3/12	17/4	24/9	8/10	10/12	12/9	—	29/10	25/2
West Ham United	25/9	17/9	29/4	25/2	26/11	10/10	11/2	26/12	20/8	5/11	1/4	17/12	13/5	31/8	11/3	31/12	22/2	25/1	22/10	14/1	—	15/4
Wimbledon	8/10	1/11	3/12	8/4	10/12	18/3	2/1	23/8	4/2	10/9	21/1	18/2	7/3	19/11	29/10	13/5	4/3	27/8	17/4	1/10	27/12	—

Finland 1994–95

	FC Haka	FC Ilves	FC Jazz	FC Kuus	FC Oulu	FinnPa	HJK	Jaro	KuPS	MP	MyPa	RoPS	TPS	TPV
FC Haka	—	19/6	31/7	25/9	19/5	1/5	27/8	14/7	4/8	8/5	12/6	8/10	3/7	21/8
FC Ilves	18/9	—	12/6	8/5	30/6	8/10	15/5	21/8	28/8	1/5	7/8	24/7	16/6	22/5
FC Jazz	22/5	14/8	—	1/5	2/10	11/9	24/4	12/5	3/7	18/9	24/7	16/6	4/8	15/5
FC Kuus	15/6	11/9	21/8	—	24/4	12/5	24/7	7/8	12/6	15/5	22/5	18/9	2/10	29/5
FC Oulu	24/7	4/8	1/5	8/10	—	3/7	21/8	12/6	8/5	28/8	15/5	22/5	18/9	15/6
FinnPa	2/10	24/4	8/5	28/8	7/8	—	22/5	30/6	21/8	24/7	16/6	12/6	15/5	18/9
HJK	12/5	14/7	8/10	19/5	5/6	31/7	—	25/9	19/6	3/7	11/9	4/8	14/8	1/5
Jaro	15/5	5/6	28/8	3/7	14/8	4/8	16/6	—	1/5	22/5	8/5	24/7	8/7	17/12
KuPS	30/6	12/5	7/8	14/8	11/9	5/6	18/9	2/10	—	16/6	24/4	15/5	22/5	24/7
MP	11/9	2/10	19/6	14/7	12/5	19/5	7/8	31/7	25/9	—	30/6	21/8	24/4	12/6
MyPa	14/8	3/7	19/5	31/7	14/7	25/9	8/5	19/6	8/10	4/8	—	1/5	5/6	28/8
RoPS	24/4	19/5	25/9	19/6	31/7	14/8	30/6	11/9	14/7	5/6	2/10	—	12/5	7/8
TPS	7/8	25/9	30/6	1/5	19/6	14/7	12/6	19/5	31/7	8/10	21/8	28/8	—	8/5
TPV	5/6	31/7	17/7	4/8	25/9	19/6	2/10	24/4	19/5	14/8	12/5	3/7	11/9	—

France 1994–95

	Auxerre	Bastia	Bordeaux	Caen	Cannes	Le Havre	Lens	Lille	Lyon	Martigues	Metz	Monaco	Montpellier	Nantes	Nice	Paris Saint-Germain	Rennes	Sochaux	St. Etienne	Strasbourg
Auxerre	—	13/8	29/4	11/2	8/2	9/11	20/5	17/10	27/8	14/10	21/1	17/12	8/4	2/8	28/10	4/3	22/3	26/11	1/10	31/5
Bastia	7/1	—	14/10	20/8	31/5	8/4	28/10	28/1	5/8	4/3	2/12	26/11	17/10	20/5	11/2	31/8	1/10	29/4	22/3	9/11
Bordeaux	5/11	1/4	—	6/5	27/8	8/2	10/9	19/11	15/4	5/8	22/10	11/10	2/12	10/3	29/7	27/5	7/1	24/2	20/8	23/9
Caen	10/9	21/1	9/11	—	2/8	20/5	26/11	4/3	8/2	8/4	27/8	13/8	14/10	17/12	22/3	1/10	28/10	31/5	29/4	24/2
Cannes	31/8	29/7	28/1	2/12	—	28/10	4/3	1/10	20/8	17/10	5/8	20/5	9/11	26/11	7/1	8/4	11/2	22/3	8/4	29/4
Le Havre	6/5	22/10	31/8	19/11	15/4	—	24/2	27/5	5/11	7/1	1/4	10/9	20/8	11/10	5/8	29/7	2/12	23/9	28/1	10/3
Lens	19/11	15/4	11/2	27/5	23/9	17/10	—	29/7	22/10	20/8	6/5	5/11	7/1	1/4	28/1	2/12	5/8	10/3	31/8	11/10
Lille	24/2	27/8	20/5	23/9	10/3	26/11	31/5	—	10/9	2/12	8/2	21/1	29/4	13/8	14/10	22/3	8/4	17/12	9/11	2/8
Lyon	28/1	17/12	28/10	31/8	21/1	29/4	8/4	11/2	—	26/11	13/8	2/8	22/3	31/5	1/10	17/10	14/10	9/11	4/3	20/5
Martigues	1/4	23/9	17/12	22/10	24/2	13/8	21/1	15/4	27/5	—	11/10	10/3	31/5	10/9	6/5	5/11	19/11	27/8	2/8	8/2
Metz	20/8	2/8	8/4	28/1	17/12	14/10	9/11	31/8	7/1	22/3	—	31/5	1/10	29/4	17/10	11/2	4/3	20/5	28/10	26/11
Monaco	5/8	27/5	22/3	7/1	19/11	11/2	29/4	20/8	2/12	1/10	29/7	—	4/3	9/11	31/8	28/1	17/10	28/10	17/12	8/4
Montpellier	22/10	24/2	2/8	1/4	6/5	3/11	11/10	29/7	10/3	23/9	—	27/8	—	19/11	15/4	27/5	8/2	17/12	10/9	
Nantes	2/12	19/11	1/10	5/8	22/5	14/10	7/1	29/7	11/2	5/11	6/5	28/1	—	4/3	20/8	31/8	8/4	17/10	28/10	
Nice	15/4	10/9	31/5	11/10	13/8	17/12	27/8	1/4	10/3	9/11	24/2	8/2	20/5	23/9	—	22/10	29/4	2/8	26/11	21/1
Paris Saint-Germain	23/9	8/2	26/11	10/3	1/4	31/5	2/8	11/10	24/2	29/4	10/9	27/8	28/10	21/1	8/4	—	9/11	13/8	20/5	17/12
Rennes	11/10	10/3	13/8	15/4	10/9	2/8	17/12	22/10	1/4	20/5	23/9	24/2	26/11	8/2	5/11	6/5	—	21/1	31/5	27/8
Sochaux	27/5	5/11	17/10	29/7	11/10	4/3	1/10	5/8	6/5	28/1	19/11	15/4	31/8	22/10	2/12	7/1	20/8	—	11/2	1/4
St. Etienne	10/3	11/10	21/1	5/11	22/10	27/8	8/2	6/5	23/9	2/12	15/4	1/4	5/8	24/2	27/5	19/11	29/7	10/9	—	13/8
Strasbourg	29/7	6/5	4/3	17/10	5/11	1/10	22/3	2/12	19/11	31/8	27/5	22/10	11/2	15/4	20/8	5/8	28/1	14/10	7/1	—

Germany 1994–95

	Bayer Leverkusen	Bayern Munich	Bayer Uerdingen	Bochum	Borussia Dortmund	Borussia Monchengladbach	Dynamo Dresden	Eintracht Frankfurt	Freiburg SC	Hamburg SV	Kaiserslautern	Karlsruhe SC	Koln	MSV Duisberg	Schalke 04	TSV 1860	VfB Stuttgart	Werder Bremen
Bayer Leverkusen	—	27/5	15/10	11/3	17/9	8/4	17/6	28/8	25/3	6/5	19/8	12/11	3/12	22/4	29/10	20/5	1/10	25/2
Bayern Munich	26/11	—	5/6	20/8	22/4	27/8	3/12	15/10	25/2	17/9	8/4	20/6	1/10	11/3	12/11	25/3	29/10	17/6
Bayer Uerdingen	15/4	5/11	—	27/5	1/10	17/6	13/5	25/3	3/12	25/2	17/9	29/4	11/3	20/8	22/10	27/8	8/4	19/11
Bochum	3/9	18/2	25/11	—	11/11	25/3	23/8	6/5	16/9	8/4	28/10	29/11	22/4	30/9	10/6	14/10	20/5	4/3
Borussia Dortmund	18/3	22/10	1/4	13/5	—	27/5	29/4	11/3	19/11	17/6	26/8	15/4	25/2	2/12	8/10	20/8	24/9	6/11
Borussia Monchengladbach	7/10	4/3	29/11	24/9	26/11	—	2/9	20/5	1/4	22/4	11/11	24/8	6/5	15/10	18/2	29/10	10/6	18/3
Dynamo Dresden	10/12	10/6	12/11	25/2	29/10	11/3	—	22/4	26/8	25/3	15/10	26/11	8/4	17/9	20/5	30/9	6/5	20/8
Eintracht Frankfurt	4/3	15/4	23/9	5/11	3/9	19/11	22/10	—	13/5	3/12	25/2	7/10	20/8	27/5	1/4	17/6	18/3	29/4
Freiburg SC	24/9	23/8	10/6	18/3	20/5	2/10	4/3	12/11	—	14/10	6/5	18/2	29/10	8/4	9/12	22/4	26/11	2/9
Hamburg SV	5/11	18/3	24/8	9/10	10/12	21/10	24/9	10/6	15/4	—	26/11	3/9	20/5	29/4	4/3	13/11	18/2	1/4
Kaiserslautern	18/2	5/10	18/3	29/4	4/3	13/5	4/9	23/8	5/11	27/5	—	1/4	17/6	19/11	24/9	2/12	3/9	23/10
Karlsruhe SC	13/5	19/11	28/10	17/6	15/10	25/2	27/5	8/4	20/8	11/3	1/10	—	25/3	27/8	6/5	16/9	22/4	3/12
Koln	10/6	1/4	3/9	21/10	23/8	5/11	8/10	18/2	29/4	18/11	29/11	24/9	—	13/5	18/3	26/11	4/3	15/4
MSV Duisberg	22/10	2/9	18/2	1/4	10/6	15/4	18/3	27/11	8/10	30/10	20/6	4/3	12/11	—	24/8	6/5	10/12	23/9
Schalke 04	29/4	13/5	22/4	4/12	8/4	20/8	18/11	1/10	6/5	25/3	4/11	17/9	25/2	—		11/3	15/10	22/5
TSV 1860	19/11	21/9	4/3	15/4	18/2	29/4	1/4	10/12	2/10	13/5	10/6	18/3	27/6	5/11	3/9	—	23/8	9/10
VfB Stuttgart	1/4	29/4	8/10	19/11	25/3	3/12	4/11	17/9	27/5	19/8	11/3	22/10	27/8	17/6	15/4	25/2	—	13/5
Werder Bremen	24/8	10/12	20/5	27/8	6/5	18/9	18/2	29/10	11/3	6/10	22/4	10/6	15/10	25/3	25/11	8/4	12/11	—

Holland 1994-95

	Ajax	Dordrecht '90	Feyenoord	Go Ahead Eagles	FC Groningen	SC Heerenveen	MVV	NAC	NEC	PSV	RKC	Roda JC	Sparta Rotterdam	FC Twente	FC Utrecht	Vitesse	FC Volendam	Willem II
Ajax	—	24/9	18/12	16/10	9/11	26/10	27/11	5/2	19/3	22/1	28/8	15/2	5/3	28/5	30/4	11/9	14/5	9/4
Dordrecht '90	18/2	—	27/8	29/10	26/11	9/11	17/12	11/3	8/4	4/2	10/9	1/10	18/3	21/1	13/5	21/9	28/5	29/4
Feyenoord	21/5	15/1	—	29/1	5/3	15/2	19/3	6/11	18/9	7/5	20/11	8/1	31/8	17/4	16/10	4/12	30/10	25/9
Go Ahead Eagles	11/3	1/4	10/9	—	17/12	26/11	8/10	15/4	29/4	18/2	21/9	26/10	5/11	4/2	28/5	1/10	21/1	'13/5
FC Groningen	17/4	7/5	2/10	21/5	—	15/1	21/9	11/9	8/1	2/4	26/10	20/11	4/12	12/3	5/2	6/11	19/2	31/8
SC Heerenveen	1/4	15/4	21/9	6/5	27/8	—	10/9	17/12	3/12	11/3	1/10	5/11	19/11	18/2	21/1	22/10	4/2	28/5
MVV	6/5	21/5	26/10	14/1	15/2	28/1	—	1/10	31/8	14/4	5/11	3/12	7/1	1/4	24/9	19/11	11/3	17/9
NAC	17/9	15/10	8/4	9/11	28/1	21/5	4/3	—	26/11	7/1	13/5	24/9	22/10	29/4	15/2	31/8	18/3	14/1
NEC	30/10	6/11	5/2	20/11	28/5	14/5	22/1	7/5	—	2/10	19/2	2/4	17/4	21/9	28/8	12/3	11/9	18/12
PSV	23/10	17/9	26/11	31/8	29/10	15/10	9/11	28/5	4/3	—	17/12	28/1	15/2	13/5	8/4	14/1	29/4	18/3
RKC	15/1	29/1	30/4	15/2	19/3	5/3	9/4	4/12	25/9	21/5	—	31/8	18/9	27/11	30/10	8/1	9/11	16/10
Roda JC	21/9	4/3	28/5	18/3	29/4	8/4	13/5	18/2	22/10	10/9	21/1	—	15/10	27/8	26/11	4/2	17/12	9/11
Sparta Rotterdam	2/10	26/10	22/1	9/4	14/5	30/4	28/5	2/4	9/11	21/9	5/2	12/3	—	11/9	18/12	19/2	9/10	27/11
FC Twente	8/1	31/8	23/10	18/9	16/10	25/9	30/10	20/11	15/2	4/12	7/5	15/1	29/1	—	19/3	21/5	9/4	5/3
FC Utrecht	20/11	4/12	12/3	8/1	18/9	31/8	19/2	9/10	15/1	6/11	2/4	7/5	21/5	13/11	—	17/4	2/10	29/1
Vitesse	29/1	15/2	14/5	5/3	9/4	19/3	30/4	22/1	16/10	28/8	28/5	18/9	25/9	18/12	9/11	—	27/11	30/10
FC Volendam	4/12	8/1	2/4	28/8	25/9	18/9	16/10	26/10	29/1	20/11	17/4	21/5	15/1	6/11	5/3	7/5	—	15/2
Willem II	5/11	19/11	18/2	3/12	21/1	7/1	4/2	27/8	21/5	26/10	11/3	15/4	'6/5	1/10	10/9	1/4	21/9	—

Italy 1994-95

	Bari	Brescia	Cagliari	Cremonese	Fiorentina	Foggia	Genoa	Internazionale	Juventus	Lazio	Milan	Napoli	Padova	Parma	Reggiana	Roma	Sampdoria	Torino
Bari	—	15/4	2/10	20/11	2/4	4/12	30/10	5/3	5/2	4/9	15/1	12/3	19/2	18/12	18/9	14/5	28/5	30/4
Brescia	27/11	—	19/2	21/5	30/10	5/2	16/10	18/9	4/9	22/1	26/2	7/5	2/4	23/4	8/1	20/11	11/12	23/10
Cagliari	26/2	25/9	—	16/10	29/1	2/4	20/11	8/1	22/1	4/12	11/9	21/5	30/4	12/2	15/4	12/3	7/5	30/10
Cremonese	9/4	15/1	5/3	—	12/2	2/10	15/4	4/12	23/10	19/3	25/9	11/9	14/5	29/1	30/4	28/5	6/11	18/12
Fiorentina	6/11	19/3	4/9	18/9	—	18/12	5/2	19/2	23/4	2/10	28/5	9/4	23/10	15/1	5/3	11/12	27/11	14/5
Foggia	23/4	11/9	6/11	26/2	7/5	—	8/1	23/10	16/10	21/5	11/12	27/11	19/3	9/4	22/1	29/1	12/2	25/9
Genoa	19/3	5/3	9/4	27/11	11/9	14/5	—	6/11	7/5	23/10	29/1	25/9	15/1	11/12	2/10	12/2	23/4	28/5
Internazionale	16/10	12/2	14/5	23/4	25/9	12/3	2/4	—	26/2	18/12	9/4	11/12	28/5	27/11	30/10	11/9	15/1	29/1
Juventus	11/9	29/1	28/5	12/3	4/12	5/3	18/12	2/10	—	30/4	30/10	12/2	15/4	14/5	20/11	15/1	25/9	2/4
Lazio	29/1	28/5	23/4	30/10	26/2	15/1	12/3	7/5	11/12	—	12/2	16/10	20/11	25/9	2/4	27/11	11/9	11/9
Milan	21/5	2/10	9/2	19/2	22/1	30/4	4/9	20/11	19/3	18/9	—	8/1	5/3	6/11	4/12	7/5	23/10	15/4
Napoli	23/10	18/12	15/1	5/2	20/11	15/4	19/2	30/4	18/9	5/3	14/5	—	2/10	28/5	4/9	2/4	19/3	4/12
Padova	25/9	6/11	11/12	8/1	12/3	30/10	21/5	22/1	27/11	9/4	16/10	26/2	—	11/9	7/5	23/4	29/1	12/2
Parma	7/5	4/12	18/9	4/9	21/5	20/11	30/4	15/4	8/1	19/2	2/4	22/1	5/2	—	23/10	30/10	5/3	2/10
Reggiana	12/2	14/5	27/11	11/12	16/10	28/5	26/2	19/3	9/4	6/11	23/4	29/1	18/12	12/3	—	25/9	11/9	15/1
Roma	8/1	9/4	23/10	22/1	30/4	4/9	18/9	5/2	21/5	15/4	18/12	6/11	4/12	19/3	19/2	—	2/10	5/3
Sampdoria	22/1	30/4	18/12	2/4	15/4	18/9	4/12	21/5	19/2	8/1	12/3	30/10	4/9	16/10	5/2	26/2	—	20/11
Torino	11/12	23/10	19/3	7/5	8/1	19/2	22/1	4/9	6/11	5/2	27/11	23/4	18/9	26/2	21/5	16/10	9/4	—

Northern Ireland 1994–95

	Ards	Ballyclare Comrades	Ballymena United	Bangor	Carrick Rangers	Cliftonville	Coleraine	Crusaders	Distillery	Glenavon	Glentoran	Larne	Linfield	Newry Town	Omagh	Portadown
Ards	—	25/3	7/1	29/4	4/3	26/11	29/10	15/4	22/10	24/9	12/11	17/12	31/12	17/4	8/10	28/1
Ballyclare Comrades	19/11	—	24/9	17/12	11/2	5/11	18/3	31/12	14/1	10/12	15/10	26/11	7/1	25/2	29/4	17/4
Ballymena United	1/10	2/1	—	17/4	17/9	18/3	26/12	1/4	19/11	28/1	14/1	29/10	22/10	22/4	4/3	10/12
Bangor	26/12	22/4	3/12	—	15/4	17/9	19/11	22/10	5/11	8/10	2/1	28/1	25/2	18/3	1/4	1/10
Carrick Rangers	5/11	22/10	31/12	10/12	—	15/10	14/1	24/9	7/1	25/2	17/4	29/4	1/4	19/11	17/12	18/3
Cliftonville	1/4	4/3	12/11	31/12	28/1	—	3/12	29/4	24/9	17/12	29/10	7/1	19/11	22/10	15/4	8/10
Coleraine	25/2	12/11	29/4	25/3	8/10	17/4	—	7/1	17/12	22/10	4/3	24/9	10/12	28/1	31/12	26/11
Crusaders	10/12	17/9	26/11	11/2	2/1	26/12	1/10	—	15/10	17/4	22/4	25/3	5/11	14/1	18/3	29/10
Distillery	11/2	8/10	25/3	4/3	1/10	2/1	22/4	28/1	—	26/11	10/12	12/11	17/4	26/12	29/10	17/9
Glenavon	2/1	15/4	15/10	14/1	29/10	22/4	11/2	3/12	1/4	—	1/10	4/3	18/3	17/9	19/11	26/12
Glentoran	18/3	28/1	8/10	24/9	3/12	25/2	5/11	17/12	15/4	7/1	—	31/12	29/4	1/4	22/10	19/11
Larne	22/4	1/4	25/2	15/10	26/12	1/10	2/1	19/11	18/3	5/11	17/9	—	14/1	10/12	3/12	11/2
Linfield	17/9	1/10	11/2	29/10	26/11	25/3	15/4	4/3	3/12	12/11	26/12	8/10	—	2/1	28/1	22/4
Newry Town	3/12	29/10	17/12	12/11	25/3	11/2	15/10	8/10	29/4	31/12	26/11	15/4	24/9	—	7/1	4/3
Omagh Town	14/1	26/12	5/11	26/11	22/4	10/12	17/9	12/11	25/2	25/3	11/2	17/4	15/10	1/10	—	2/1
Portadown	15/10	3/12	15/4	7/1	12/11	14/1	1/4	25/2	31/12	29/4	25/3	22/10	17/12	5/11	24/9	—

Portugal 1994–95

	Beira-Mar	Belenenses	Benfica	Boavista	Estrela Amadora	Farense	FC Porto	GD Chaves	Gil Vicente	Guimaraes	Maritimo	Salgueiros	Sporting Braga	Sporting Lisbon	Tirsense	Uniao Leiria	Uniao Madeira	Vitoria Setubal
Beira-Mar	—	12/3	21/1	6/11	23/10	27/9	28/8	18/9	12/2	25/2	11/12	9/4	30/4	26/3	27/11	15/1	31/12	21/5
Belenenses	16/10	—	20/11	11/9	21/8	21/5	15/4	7/5	1/2	31/12	15/1	19/2	5/3	5/2	27/9	2/4	19/3	30/10
Benfica	21/3	9/4	—	11/12	27/11	6/11	1/10	23/10	12/3	26/3	25/2	14/5	18/5	30/4	8/1	19/2	5/2	11/9
Boavista	2/4	12/2	7/5	—	18/9	28/8	31/12	15/1	21/5	21/1	1/10	16/10	30/10	25/3	19/3	1/12	20/11	15/4
Estrela Amadora	19/3	21/1	15/4	19/2	—	15/1	1/12	31/12	7/5	21/5	28/8	27/9	16/10	11/9	5/3	20/11	30/10	2/4
Farense	5/3	8/1	2/4	5/2	28/5	—	20/11	1/12	15/4	7/5	14/5	11/9	27/9	21/8	19/2	30/10	16/10	19/3
FC Porto	5/2	27/11	5/3	14/5	30/4	9/4	—	26/3	23/10	6/11	12/3	8/1	21/8	11/12	28/5	27/9	11/9	19/2
GD Chaves	19/2	11/12	19/3	28/5	14/5	30/4	30/10	—	2/4	27/11	9/4	21/8	11/9	8/1	5/2	16/10	27/9	5/3
Gil Vicente	11/9	30/4	16/10	8/1	11/12	27/11	19/3	6/11	—	9/4	26/3	28/5	5/2	14/5	21/8	5/3	19/2	27/9
Guimaraes	27/9	14/5	30/10	21/8	8/1	11/12	2/4	15/4	20/11	—	30/4	5/2	19/2	28/5	11/9	19/3	5/3	16/10
Maritimo	7/5	28/5	27/9	5/3	15/2	31/12	16/10	20/11	30/10	1/12	—	19/3	15/4	19/2	2/4	11/9	8/1	21/8
Salgueiros	20/11	18/9	31/12	12/3	25/2	12/2	21/5	21/1	15/1	28/8	23/10	—	2/4	1/10	30/10	15/4	1/12
Sporting Braga	1/12	1/10	15/1	26/3	12/3	25/2	21/1	12/2	28/8	18/9	27/11	6/11	—	23/10	9/4	21/5	7/5	31/12
Sporting Lisbon	30/10	28/8	1/12	27/9	12/2	21/1	7/5	21/5	31/12	15/1	18/9	5/3	19/3	—	16/10	15/4	2/4	20/11
Tirsense	15/4	25/2	21/5	23/10	1/10	18/9	15/1	28/8	21/1	12/2	6/11	26/3	20/11	12/3	—	31/12	1/12	7/5
Uniao Leiria	28/5	6/11	13/9	20/4	9/4	26/3	25/2	12/3	1/10	23/10	12/2	11/12	8/1	27/11	14/5	—	21/8	5/2
Uniao Madeira	14/5	23/10	28/8	9/4	26/3	12/3	12/2	25/2	18/9	1/10	21/6	27/11	11/12	6/11	3/4	21/1	—	15/1
Vitoria Setubal	8/1	26/3	12/2	27/11	6/11	23/10	18/9	1/10	25/2	12/3	21/1	30/4	14/5	9/4	11/12	28/8	28/5	—

Republic of Ireland 1994-95

	Athlone Town	Bohemians	Cobh Ramblers	Cork City	Derry City	Dundalk	Galway United	Monaghan United	St Patrick's Athletic	Shamrock Rovers	Shelbourne	Sligo Rovers
Athlone Town	—	18/12	16/10 9/4	2/10 19/3	30/10 23/4	15/1	20/11	4/9 12/2	1/1	18/9 5/3	4/12	28/8 22/1
Bohemians	25/9 17/3	—	9/10 26/3	20/11	26/12	28/8 22/1	4/9 12/2	4/12	11/12	6/11	23/10 16/4	8/1
Cobh Ramblers	8/1	1/1	—	4/9 12/2	23/10 16/4	4/12	18/12	18/9 5/3	2/10 19/3	28/8 22/1	20/11	6/11
Cork City	26/12	31/8 5/2	27/11	—	11/9 26/2	16/10 9/4	15/1	30/10 23/4	13/11	9/10 26/3	11/12	25/9 17/3
Derry City	6/11	2/10 19/3	15/1	4/12	—	18/12	18/9 5/3	1/1	16/10 9/4	4/9 12/2	28/8 22/1	20/11
Dundalk	23/10 16/4	13/11	11/9 26/2	8/1	25/9 17/3	—	30/10 23/4	31/8 5/2	27/11	26/12	9/10 26/3	11/12
Galway United	31/8 5/2	27/11	25/9 17/3	23/10 16/4	11/12	6/11	—	13/11	11/9 26/2	8/1	26/12	9/10 26/3
Monaghan United	27/11	11/9 26/2	11/12	6/11	9/10 26/3	20/11	28/8 22/1	—	25/9 17/3	23/10 16/4	8/1	26/12
St Patrick's Athletic	9/10 26/3	18/9 5/3	26/12	28/8 22/1	8/1	4/9 12/2	4/12	18/12	—	20/11	6/11	23/10 16/4
Shamrock Rovers	11/12	30/10 23/4	13/11	1/1	27/11	2/10 19/3	16/10 9/4	15/1	31/8 5/2	—	25/9 17/3	11/9 26/2
Shelbourne	11/9 26/2	15/1	31/8 5/2	18/9 5/3	13/11	1/1	2/10 19/3	16/10 9/4	30/10 23/4	18/12	—	27/11
Sligo Rovers	13/11	16/10 9/4	30/10 23/4	18/12	31/8 5/2	18/9 5/3	1/1	2/10 19/3	15/1	4/12	4/9 12/2	—

Scotland 1994-95

	Aberdeen	Celtic	Dundee United	Falkirk	Heart of Midlothian	Hibernian	Kilmarnock	Motherwell	Partick Thistle	Rangers
Aberdeen	—	26/12 15/4	29/10 6/5	20/8 7/1	13/8 31/12	9/11 18/3	3/12 1/4	15/10 25/2	17/9 14/1	24/9 11/2
Celtic	8/10 4/3	—	20/8 7/1	22/10 31/12	10/12 19/4	24/9 11/2	17/9 14/1	3/12 1/4	9/11 18/3	29/10 6/5
Dundee United	27/8 2/1	5/11 13/5	—	24/9 11/2	19/11 21/3	22/10 29/4	26/12 15/4	10/9 31/1	15/10 25/2	3/12 1/4
Falkirk	5/11 13/5	13/8 29/4	26/11 8/4	—	1/10 4/2	15/10 15/2	8/11 18/3	26/12 15/4	27/8 2/1	17/9 14/1
Heart of Midlothian	22/10 29/4	15/10 25/2	17/9 14/1	3/12 1/4	—	27/8 2/1	24/9 11/2	5/11 13/5	26/12 15/4	9/11 18/3
Hibernian	10/9 31/1	26/11 8/4	13/8 31/12	10/12 18/4	29/10 6/5	—	20/8 7/1	19/11 21/3	1/10 4/2	8/10 4/3
Kilmarnock	1/10 4/2	19/11 21/3	8/10 4/3	10/9 31/1	26/11 8/4	5/11 13/5	—	27/8 2/1	22/10 29/4	10/12 18/4
Motherwell	10/12 18/4	1/10 4/2	8/11 18/3	8/10 4/3	20/8 7/1	17/9 14/1	29/10 6/5	—	26/11 8/4	22/10 31/12
Partick Thistle	19/11 22/3	10/9 31/1	10/12 18/4	29/10 6/5	8/10 4/3	3/12 1/4	13/8 31/12	24/9 11/2	—	20/8 7/1
Rangers	26/11 8/4	27/8 2/1	1/10 4/2	19/11 21/3	10/9 21/1	26/12 15/4	15/10 25/2	13/8 29/4	5/11 13/5	—

Spain 1994–95

	Albacete	Athletic Bilbao	Atletico Madrid	Barcelona	Betis Seville	Celta Vigo	Compostella	Deportivo La Coruna	Espanol	Logrones	Racing Santander	Real Madrid	Real Oviedo	Real Sociedad	Real Valladolid	Real Zaragoza	Seville	Sporting Gijon	Tenerife	Valencia
Albacete	—	9/10	27/11	22/1	12/2	4/9	6/11	18/6	9/4	26/2	23/10	18/9	8/1	21/5	4/6	23/4	5/3	19/3	11/12	7/5
Athletic Bilbao	12/3	—	7/5	18/6	18/9	12/2	23/4	4/9	6/11	2/10	9/4	26/2	4/6	8/1	22/1	27/11	19/3	23/10	21/5	11/12
Atletico Madrid	30/4	4/12	—	12/3	30/10	2/4	15/1	16/10	28/5	20/11	21/12	16/4	26/2	18/9	2/10	11/6	29/1	14/5	12/2	4/9
Barcelona	11/6	29/1	9/10	—	21/12	14/5	25/9	4/12	19/2	15/1	11/9	28/5	6/11	9/4	23/4	5/3	27/11	5/2	23/10	19/3
Betis Seville	11/9	19/2	9/4	21/5	—	4/6	19/3	8/1	9/10	5/2	5/3	29/1	7/5	27/11	11/12	23/10	11/6	25/9	23/4	6/11
Celta Vigo	5/2	11/9	23/10	11/12	15/1	—	9/10	21/5	5/3	29/1	25/9	11/6	27/11	23/4	7/5	19/3	8/1	19/2	6/11	9/4
Compostella	16/4	20/11	4/6	26/2	16/10	12/3	—	2/10	14/5	30/10	4/12	2/4	12/2	4/9	18/2	3/1	21/5	30/4	18/6	22/1
Deportivo La Coruna	29/1	5/2	19/3	7/5	28/5	21/12	5/3	—	25/9	11/6	19/2	15/1	23/4	6/11	27/11	9/10	11/12	11/9	9/4	23/10
Espanol	30/10	16/4	8/1	18/9	12/3	2/10	11/12	26/2	—	2/4	30/4	16/10	4/9	18/6	12/2	21/5	7/5	30/11	22/1	4/6
Logrones	25/9	5/3	23/4	4/6	4/9	18/6	9/4	22/1	23/10	—	19/3	12/2	21/5	11/12	8/1	6/11	19/2	9/10	7/5	27/11
Racing Santander	2/4	30/10	21/5	12/2	2/10	26/2	7/5	18/9	27/11	16/10	—	12/3	13/6	22/1	4/9	11/12	23/4	16/4	4/6	8/1
Real Madrid	19/2	25/9	6/11	8/1	18/6	22/1	23/10	4/6	19/3	11/9	9/10	—	11/12	7/5	21/5	9/4	5/2	5/3	27/11	23/4
Real Oviedo	28/5	15/1	25/9	16/4	4/12	30/4	11/9	20/11	5/2	21/12	29/1	14/5	—	19/3	30/10	19/2	23/10	11/6	9/10	2/10
Real Sociedad	21/12	28/5	19/2	30/10	30/4	20/11	5/2	16/4	29/1	14/5	11/6	4/12	16/10	—	2/4	11/9	9/10	15/1	5/3	25/9
Real Valladolid	15/1	11/6	5/3	20/11	14/5	4/12	19/2	30/4	11/9	28/5	5/2	21/12	9/4	23/10	—	25/9	6/11	29/1	19/3	9/10
Real Zaragoza	20/11	30/4	22/1	2/10	2/4	16/10	28/5	12/3	21/12	16/4	14/5	30/10	18/9	12/2	26/2	—	4/6	4/12	4/9	18/6
Seville	2/10	16/10	18/6	30/4	22/1	28/6	21/12	14/5	4/12	18/9	20/11	4/9	2/4	12/3	16/4	15/1	—	30/10	26/2	12/2
Sporting Gijon	16/10	2/4	11/12	4/9	26/2	18/9	27/11	12/2	23/4	12/3	6/11	2/10	22/1	4/6	18/6	7/5	9/4	—	8/1	21/5
Tenerife	14/5	21/12	11/9	26/3	20/11	16/4	29/1	30/10	11/6	4/12	15/1	30/4	12/3	2/10	16/10	5/2	25/9	28/5	—	19/2
Valencia	4/12	14/5	5/2	16/10	16/4	30/10	11/6	2/4	15/1	30/4	28/5	20/11	2/10	26/2	12/3	29/1	11/9	21/12	18/9	—

Diary of Events 1994-95

European club competitions: Tuesdays are designated days for UEFA Cup matches and Thursdays designated days for Cup-Winners' Cup matches. However, teams may switch these days by mutual consent for security reasons. UEFA Champions' League games are played on Wednesday. International weeks are designated weeks in which European Championship games or general international matches must be played. The 'week' will normally cover a five-day period running from Saturday to Wednesday.

9	August	UEFA Cup Preliminary Round 1st leg
10	August	Cup-Winners' Cup Preliminary Round 1st leg
23	August	UEFA Cup Preliminary Round 2nd leg
24	August	Cup-Winners' Cup Preliminary Round 2nd leg
26	August	Draw 1st Round: Cup-Winners's Cup, UEFA Cup
4-7	September	International week
13	September	UEFA Cup 1st Round 1st leg
14	September	UEFA Champions' League
15	September	Cup-Winners' Cup 1st Round 1st leg
27	September	UEFA Cup 1st Round 2nd leg
28	September	UEFA Champions' League
29	September	Cup-Winners' Cup 1st Round 2nd leg
30	September	Draw 2nd Round: Cup-Winners' Cup, UEFA Cup
8-12	October	International week
18	October	UEFA Cup 2nd Round 1st leg
18	October	UEFA Champions' League
20	October	Cup-Winners' Cup 2nd Round 1st leg
1	November	UEFA Cup 2nd Round 2nd leg
2	November	UEFA Champions' League
3	November	Cup-Winners' Cup 2nd Round 2nd leg
4	November	Draw 3rd Round: UEFA Cup
		Draw Quarter-Finals: Cup-Winners' Cup
12-16	November	International week
22	November	UEFA Cup 3rd Round 1st leg
23	November	UEFA Champions' League
6	December	UEFA Cup 3rd Round 2nd leg
7	December	UEFA Champions' League
14	December	Draw Quarter-Finals: UEFA Cup
14-18	December	International week

1995

28	February	UEFA Cup Quarter-Final 1st leg
1	March	Champions' Cup Quarter-Final 1st leg
2	March	Cup-Winners' Cup Quarter-Final 1st leg
14	March	UEFA Cup Quarter-Final 2nd leg
15	March	Champions' Cup Quarter-Final 2nd leg
16	March	Cup-Winners' Cup Quarter-Final 2nd leg
17	March	Draw Semi-Finals: Cup-Winners' Cup, UEFA Cup
25-29	March	International week
4	April	UEFA Cup Semi-Final 1st leg
5	April	Champions' Cup Semi-Final 1st leg
6	April	Cup-Winners' Cup Semi-Final 1st leg
18	April	UEFA Cup Semi-Final 2nd leg
19	April	Champions' Cup Semi-Final 2nd leg
20	April	Cup-Winners' Cup Semi-Final 2nd leg
25-26	April	International week
2	May	UEFA Cup Final 1st leg
10	May	Cup-Winners' Cup Final
17	May	UEFA Cup Final 2nd leg
24	May	Champions' Cup Final
7-11	June	International week
12	July	Draw Preliminary Round 1995–96: UEFA Champions' League, Cup-Winners' Cup, UEFA Cup